*Long Island's*

*Prominent Families*

*in the Town of Hempstead:*

*Their Estates and Their Country Homes*

Raymond E. and Judith A. Spinzia

VirtualBookworm

College Station, Texas

2023

"Long Island's Prominent Families in the Town of Hempstead: Their Estates and Their Country Homes" by Raymond E. and Judith A. Spinzia ISBN 978-1-63868-107-6.

Published 2010; 2023 (revised) by Virtualbookworm.com Publishing Inc., P.O. Box 9949, College Station, TX 77842, US.

© 2023, Raymond E. and Judith A. Spinzia. All rights reserved. No part of this publication may be reproduced, stored in a retrieval system, or transmitted in any form or by any means, electronic, mechanical, recording or otherwise, without the prior written permission of Raymond E. and Judith A. Spinzia.

*Also by* Raymond E. and Judith A. Spinzia

*Long Island: A Guide to New York's Suffolk and Nassau Counties*
(*with* Kathryn Spinzia Rayne)

*Long Island's Prominent North Shore Families:*
*Their Estates and Their Country Homes, Volumes I and II*

*Long Island's Prominent South Shore Families:*
*Their Estates and Their Country Homes*
*in the Towns of Babylon and Islip*

*Long Island's Prominent Families*
*in the Town of Southampton:*
*Their Estates and Their Country Homes*

*Long Island's Prominent Families*
*in the Town of East Hampton:*
*Their Estates and Their Country Homes*

*offered as tribute to our Island*
*which grows and is nurtured by its people*

# Table of Contents

Acknowledgments . . . . . . . . *vi*

Factors Applicable to Usage . . . . . . . *vii*

Introduction . . . . . . . . . *ix*

Maps of Long Island Estate Areas . . . . . . . *xviii*

Surname Entries A – Z . . . . . . . . 1

*Appendices*:

    Architects . . . . . . . . 533

    Civic Activism . . . . . . . . 539

    Estate Names . . . . . . . . 549

    Golf Courses on Former Town of Hempstead Estates . . . 555

    Landscape Architects . . . . . . . 557

    Maiden Names . . . . . . . . 561

    Occupations . . . . . . . . 591

    Rehabilitative Secondary Uses of Surviving Estate Houses . . . 613

    Statesmen and Diplomats Who Resided in the Town of Hempstead . . 615

    Village Locations of Estates . . . . . . . 619

    America's First Age of Fortune: A Selected Bibliography . . . 629

    Selected Bibliographic References to Individual
    Town of Hempstead Estate Owners . . . . . . 639

Biographical Sources Consulted . . . . . . . 647

Maps Consulted for Estate Locations . . . . . . 649

Illustration Credits . . . . . . . . 651

*The authors are sincerely indebted to the following for their assistance:*

Victoria Aspinwall, Long Island Studies Institute, Hofstra University, Hempstead, NY

George William Fisher, Photographic Project Manager, Nassau County Department of Parks, Recreation, and Museums, Old Bethpage Village Restoration, Old Bethpage, NY

Brick Howe, Trustee, Village of Garden City, Garden City, NY

John Ellis Kordes, Village of Garden City Historian, Garden City, NY

Susan Kovarik, Librarian, Westbury Memorial Public Library, Westbury, NY

Thomas A. Kuehhas, Director, Oyster Bay Historical Society, Oyster Bay, NY

Dr. Natalie A. Naylor, Director Emerita, Long Island Studies Institute, Hofstra University, Hempstead, NY

Kristen J. Nyitray, Director, Department of Special Collections and University Archives, Stony Brook University, Stony Brook, NY

Millicent Vollono, Librarian, Hewlett–Woodmere Public Library, Hewlett, NY

Debra Willett, Associate Director, Long Island Studies Institute, Hofstra University, Hempstead, NY

*We would especially like to thank:*

Philip Cottone, John Vanderveer Gibson, Ann Marmon Mallouk, Thomas E. Mallouk, Timothy Breese Miller, and Dr. Joseph Arnold Spinzia for reviewing entries pertaining to their families and for providing invaluable genealogical information.

*Raymond E. and Judith A. Spinzia*

Even though an individual may not have used Sr., Jr., I, II, etc., they have been added to the surnames in an attempt to designate relationships and alleviate confusion. In some instances, birth dates have been calculated using the age at the time of death as given in *The New York Times* obituary. In addition, years of birth may not be totally accurate as some people became progressively younger in subsequent census records.

The exact street address of some houses could not be determined due to the diminution of the estates by subdivision. In these cases, the road on which a major portion of the estate bordered has been recorded as the address. It should also be noted that some of the subsequent owners may not have lived in the estate's main house but rather in a service building that had been converted into a residence. To aid in tracing the estate properties, these owners have been included in the hope that this will prove useful to future researchers.

*The Spinzias*

*farm fields, early 1940s*

*same area after the construction of Levittown*

*Introduction*

The Town of Hempstead, for the most part, is located on the only plain east of the Appalachian Mountains. The boundaries of the approximately sixty thousand-acre Hempstead Plains roughly corresponds in the North to the present-day villages of New Hyde Park, Garden City, Garden City Park, Mineola, Carle Place, Westbury, and New Cassel; Sunrise Highway to the South; and from eastern Queens County in New York City to just east of the Nassau/Suffolk County border.[1] When early settlers first viewed the Plains in its pristine state, they saw a level topography, generously interspersed with small streams. Virtually treeless, it was instead covered by five- to six-foot-high grasses and a profusion of wildflowers.

As early as the 1600s the Plains had been designated as a commons to be used by all primarily for haying and as grazing land for cattle. It was not until 1784, when the Town of North Hempstead separated from the Town of Hempstead, that land was assigned to individual farmers and the cultivation of the Plains began in earnest. The scattered farms interspersed among the equally scattered villages gradually developed into thriving communities. Suburbanization, industrialization, and ultimately urbanization have created that which we see today.[2]

Flat and, for the most part, unobstructed by trees, the Hempstead Plains was conducive to the early introduction of sporting events. In 1665 Governor Richard Nicolls established the New Market Race Course, the country's first formal race track, in the northwestern section of the Town of Hempstead. Continued interest in horseracing led to the establishment of Belmont Park Racetrack in 1905 and Roosevelt Raceway in 1940.[3]

Hunting was formalized as a sport when in 1877 Robert Center, William C. Peet, August Belmont Purdy, and Frank Gray Griswold rented a farm from the heirs of Alexander Turney Stewart and established the Queens County Drag Hounds Club just east of Garden City on land that would later become Mitchel Field. In 1880 the club moved to Westchester County for two years after which it returned to the Island following its merger with the Rockaway Hunting Club.

In 1880 the Meadow Brook Hunt Club was organized on the future Mitchel Field site thus enabling the Rockaway Hunting Club, which had been established in 1878 in Far Rockaway by J. D. Ceever, Louis Neilson, George Work, Ernest C. La Montagne, Rene La Montagne, Edward Nicoll Dickerson, and William Voss, to lay claim to being the oldest country club in the United States in continuous use.[4]

The problems encountered by the two clubs were legendary. The rapid development of Far Rockaway and the lack of adequate numbers of foxes in the area, which had plagued the Rockaway from its inception, induced the club

*Rockaway Hunting Club*

to relocate to its present site in Lawrence in 1884.[5] The dramatic increase in both residential and commercial development was a constant concern to both clubs resulting in the secession of hunting at the Rockaway by 1920.[6]

The Meadow Brook chose to relocate their hunting activities to the Jericho area. However, even here they would face similar difficulties when Robert Moses proposed to construct the Northern State Parkway through their hunting grounds. A bitter dispute developed between the club's members and Moses. New York State Governor Alfred E. Smith's highly unusual and impractical solution was to create a tunnel under the parkway so that the foxes could reach the other side of the parkway. Presumably the terrified foxes, which were being chased by hounds and huntsmen, would have the common sense to use the underpass rather than chance crossing the roadway.[7]

*Meadow Brook Hunt Club at Foxhall Parker Keene's Old Westbury Estate, Rosemary Hall, 1906*

The intense rivalry between the two hunting clubs gradually shifted to polo. Introduced into New York City in 1876 by James Gordon Bennett, it quickly became the rage among the Island's socially elite. In 1881 members of the Meadow Brook Hunt Club formally incorporated the Meadow Brook [original spelling] Polo Club. Its roster of players was a veritable who's who of the Island's social register.[8] The club's "Big Four," Harry Payne Whitney, Devereaux Milburn, Sr., and Larry and Monty Waterbury, dominated international polo winning the Westchester Cup from Great Britain in 1909 and successfully defending it in 1911 and 1913. With the retirement of Whitney in 1914, the cup was lost and would not be regained until 1921 when Devereaux Milburn, Sr., Louis Ezekiel Stoddard, Sr., James Watson Webb, Sr., and Thomas Hitchcock, Jr. defeated the British team.[9]

The game reached its zenith in the 1920s and 1930s with polo players becoming the era's celebrities. The Meadow Brook, known as the "Heart of American Polo," with its eight fields each larger than seven football fields and its forty thousand-spectator International Field, became the site of the internationally prestigious United States Polo Open and Westchester Cup matches.[10] On days that matches were held, the Island's roads were clogged with traffic as fans attempted to reach the polo fields while other fans were accommodated by special trains scheduled by the Long Island Rail Road. Indeed, polo had become so popular that when the DuPont Company was approached to sponsor a radio program to be aired at 3 o'clock on Sundays, the company rejected the proposal stating, "Everyone is playing polo."[11] World War II would take a significant toll on the popularity of polo on the Island as the country's priorities addressed the war effort. Its diminished popularity continued after the war culminating in 1953 when the U.S. Polo Open moved from the Meadow Brook, where it had been held since 1923, to the Oak Brook Polo Club in Hinsdale, Illinois, as the hub of polo activities migrated westward.[12] A year later the Meadow Brook Polo Club's site was sold to the federal government and became a runway for jet airplanes at Mitchel Field. The club's activities were relocated to Jericho and in 1968 that site was sold for a housing development. No longer commanding the popularity of its heyday, the Meadow Brook Polo Club currently holds matches at Bethpage State Park and at the club's field on Whitney Lane in Old Westbury while the Rockaway Hunting Club has shifted its emphasis to golf and tennis.

*Meadow Brook Polo Club's International Field*

With the advent of World War I, the airplane was no longer viewed as a phenomenon; it was evolving into an important industry and Long Island was in the forefront. Estates that had been established by polo and hunting club members as well as others of the Island's socially elite in the communities of Hempstead, Uniondale, Salisbury, and East Meadow gradually gave way to the development of the aviation industry. The large estates of William Sake Hofstra, *The Netherlands*, Sidney Dillon Ripley Sr., *The Crossways*, Elliot Roosevelt, Sr., *Half Way Nirvana*, Adolph Ladenburg, *Heathcote*, Jacques Lebaudy, *Phoenix Lodge*, and Oliver Hazard Perry Belmont, *Brookholt,* disappeared as the focus of the Plains changed.

While most people will recognize Roosevelt Field as the site of Charles Lindbergh's 1927 transatlantic flight, few will be aware of or recognize the significance of Washington Avenue Field, Nassau Boulevard Field, Hempstead Plains Airfield, Camp Mills, Hazelhurst Field, Aviation Field #2, Curtiss Field, and Curtiss Airport in the creation and development of the aviation industry.[13] Six years after the Wright Brothers' 1903 flight at Kitty Hawk, Washington Avenue Field (sometimes referred to as Mineola Field) was established by the New York Aeronautic Society on land leased from the Garden City Company. Located adjacent to the present-day site of the Mineola Court House complex in Garden City, the field extended southward from Old Country Road and was bounded on the west by Garden City's Washington Avenue.[14] The very year the field was established, Glenn Curtiss would win the Scientific American Trophy and $10,000 when he flew a fifteen-and-a-half-mile circuit over Mineola and Westbury in a historic fifty-eight-minute flight which originated and ended at Washington Avenue Field.[15]

The Hempstead Plains again came to the forefront of aviation history when in 1910 the First American International Aerial Tournament was held at the Belmont Park Racetrack. The week-long event attracted some forty contestants and more than seventy-five thousand spectators to watch the competitions between aviators from Europe and the United States. The event was somewhat marred when one of the highlights of the tournament, a race from Belmont Park Racetrack to the Statue of Liberty, a hotly contested event with national pride and international standing at stake, was won by the American entry John Moisant over the Englishman Claude Graham White in an extremely close and disputed finish.[16]

Garden City's Nassau Boulevard Field was established in 1910 because of the inadequacies at the Washington Avenue Field. The three hundred and fifty-acre field was located in the northwestern section of Garden City, roughly corresponding to the area between the village's present-day Nassau Boulevard and Merillon Avenue railroad stations. Much more extensive than the Washington Avenue Field, it consisted of thirty-one hangers, five grandstands, repair shops, a refreshment stand, an administrative building, and Giuseppe Bellanca's flying school. Just one year after the establishment of the field it hosted the Island's Second International Aerial Tournament. It was during this meet that Earl Lewis Ovington, the country's first airmail pilot, made the United States' first airmail delivery flying five and a half miles from the Nassau Boulevard Field to Mineola where at five hundred feet he tossed the mail pouch over the side near the Mineola post office.

The meet also saw the first demonstration of aerial reconnaissance by the military when Lieutenants Henry Harley "Hap" Arnold and Thomas DeWitt Milling successfully demonstrated how concealed enemy soldiers could be located from the air.[17]

By 1912 the constant complaints of excessive noise by the area's residents caused the Washington Avenue and Nassau Boulevard Fields to be relocated to the nine hundred-acre Hempstead Plains Airfield, which had been established in 1911 east of Garden City's Clinton Road. For its time, it was a truly impressive facility with thirty-five hangers, Glenn Curtiss' flying school, and four grandstands that could accommodate sixteen hundred spectators.[18]

Five years after the establishment of the Hempstead Plains Airfield, Camp Mills was established near the airfield as a training facility and a principal embarkation center for World War I soldiers. Named for Brigadier General Albert L. Mills, it quickly evolved from a tent encampment to an 838-building compound. Facilities sufficient to support fifty thousand troops included 9 administrative buildings, 398 enlisted men's barracks, 36 officers' quarters, 108 lavatories, 105 mess halls, 69 quarantine huts, 2 delousing stations, and a 2,500-bed hospital. The site had its own water and sewer pump stations and an electrical sub-station. A Liberty Theatre, a library, and seven post exchanges were available to the troops; three stables and two haysheds were provided for the horses of the mounted troops.[19] In 1918 Camp Mills was merged with the adjacent Aviation Field #2 to become Mitchel Field, a training facility for Army pilots. With the ending of hostilities, Mitchel Field became the only army post in the northeastern United States, the defense point for the metropolitan area, and a

*Camp Mills*

center for aviation experimentation.[20] With the outbreak of World War II Mitchel Field became the headquarters of the army's First Air Force and continued its role as the primary defense for the New York metropolitan area. By 1945 the field had become the headquarters of the Air Defense Command for the entire United States.

Mitchel Field would also become a victim of the area's population density when in 1949 all tactical aircraft were moved off the Island to other air bases. It finally closed in 1961 with most of its property being conveyed to Nassau County. Mitchel Field was the last airfield used for military operations in Nassau County. Today it is the site of Hofstra University's northern campus, Nassau Veterans' Memorial Coliseum, the Long Island Children's Museum, the Nassau County Firefighters Museum, and the Cradle of Aviation Museum together with hotels, restaurants, and a host of office buildings.

Hazelhurst Field had been established in 1917 on the site of the former Hempstead Plains Airfield as a World War I army pilot training center, on property previously used by the New York National Guard. The naming of the field honored Second Lieutenant Leighton Wilson Hazelhurst, Jr., who was killed in an airplane accident on June 11, 1912, at College Park, Maryland.[21] In 1918 Hazelhurst was renamed Roosevelt Field in honor of President Theodore Roosevelt's son Quentin, who had trained at Hazelhurst and who was killed in 1918 during aerial combat over France.[22]

Abandoned by the military after World War I, Roosevelt Field became a civilian commercial airport. By the mid-1930s it had become the country's largest and busiest private airport. In the period between the two world wars Roosevelt Field became the center of aeronautical experimentation, daredevil air shows, and record-breaking cross-country and transatlantic flights. Its decline was precipitated by a massive increase in the area's population, its lack of proximity to Manhattan, and the development of LaGuardia Airport which began operation in 1939. The real estate development company of Webb and Knapp purchased two hundred and fifty acres of the field as well as one hundred and ten acres of the adjacent Westbury Golf Club in 1951 for the construction of Roosevelt Field Shopping Mall thus ending another chapter in aviation history on the Plains.[23]

In 1920 the western half of Roosevelt Field was sold to the Curtiss Aeroplane and Motor Corporation and renamed Curtiss Field. In 1929 Curtiss Field was reincorporated into Roosevelt Field when the company built Curtiss Airport in Valley Stream. From 1930 to 1933 the Valley Stream facility was the largest commercial airport on Long Island but was forced to close in 1933 due to financial pressures caused by the Depression.[24]

The Aviation Country Club was established on the Hempstead Plains in 1929 in what was a more unusual use of the aviation facilities as the post-Lindbergh mania for flying became a leisure activity for the Island's socially elite. Seventy-six of the club's one hundred and seventy-five members owned their own planes while most of the remaining membership were licensed pilots. The club which, sold and rented planes, had a landing field, hangar, mechanics, fuel, and a flight instructor. The four-bedroom clubhouse had an adjacent swimming pool and tennis courts. In 1948 the club, which never had an accident in its almost twenty-year history, was sold to William Jaird Levitt, Sr. and became part of Levittown.[25] For a while a few of the club's members entertained the idea of relocating the club to a small private airport in Commack but abandoned the idea due to lack of interest by the general membership. In 1950 the Aviation Country Club formally dissolved. The only reminder of the club's existence in the area is a street named Pilots Lane in Levittown.

Without question, the existence of the Island's approximately eighty airfields contributed to the continuing development of Long Island's aviation industry. In 1917 Glenn Curtiss built a plant in Garden City for the Curtiss Engineering Corporation. Devoted to aeronautical research and development, it was a separate company from his Curtiss Aeroplane and Motor Corporation, based in Hammondsport, New York.[26] The Garden City facility became a training ground for aeronautical engineers who were able to test their designs in the company's ten-foot-diameter wind-tunnel, which at the time was the largest in the country. In 1920 Curtiss decided to close his Hammondsport factory and move the headquarters of the Curtiss Aeroplane and Motor Corporation, as well as most of its airplane production, to Garden City where his company manufactured three-quarters of the nation's planes.[27] In 1929 the Curtiss Aeroplane and Motor Corporation merged with Wright Aeronautical Corporation to form the Curtiss–Wright Corporation. Two years later the firm relocated its manufacturing facilities to Buffalo, New York.

*Curtiss Garden City factory, aerial view*

Beginning with the Curtiss Engineering Corporation, the Island's aviation industry mushroomed into such industry leaders as Grumman (Bethpage and Calverton), Republic (Bethpage), Sperry Gyroscope (Garden City, Lake Success, and Bethpage), and Fairchild Camera and Instrument (Farmingdale), which, in turn, gave impetus to the Island's numerous aviation sub-contractors.

With the end of the Cold War and the resulting reduction in the military complex, aviation companies gradually began to merge and relocate off the Island. Today the industry, which employed about five thousand workers by the end of the 1930s and which had reached its peak of some ninety to one hundred thousand employees during World War II, accounts for only about twenty-five to thirty thousand of the Island's jobs.

In an odd twist of fate, the military bases and the aeronautical industry they spawned on the Hempstead Plains, once the powerhouse of the Island's economy, became victims of the post-war boom in residential and industrial development which they were instrumental in creating. The original flora of the Plains has been diminished as well by suburbanization to a fraction of its original sixty thousand acres. Seventy-nine acres, the Hempstead Plain Preserve just south of Charles Lindbergh Boulevard and nineteen additional acres located on the campus of Nassau Community College, are all that remain.[28] The estate homes in the Five Towns area, that have survived, have, in many instances, had their architectural integrity compromised by subsequent owners. What remains virtually untouched is what Garden City residents refer to as the original estate area located in the central section of their village. The estate areas in the villages of Hempstead, East Meadow, Uniondale, and Salisbury are, however, forever gone.

## Endnotes

1. The area south of Sunrise Highway for the most part was a swampy area into which the streams from the Plains to its north drained. Henry Hicks, with foreword by Judith A. Spinzia and afterwards by Natalie A. Naylor, "The Hempstead Plains and It's Flora, 1871," *Nassau County Historical Society Journal* 58 (2003), pp. 30-40.

2. The population of the Village of Hempstead has risen from 2,316 in 1870 to an estimated 53,896 in 2008 while that of Nassau County has increased from 31,134 to an estimated 1,351,625 during the same period.

3. Historians generally agree that the New Market Race Track was located in the northwestern section of the Town of Hempstead but there is a lack of consensus as to its exact location. They have placed the site of the tract in the present day villages of New Hyde Park, Garden City, and Garden City Park prior to its relocation in the early 1800s to a site three miles west of Jamaica in Queens County when it became the Union Race Track.

The Belmont Park Racetrack is situated on the grounds of de Forest Manice's estate *Oatlands*. The track's original Turf and Field Clubhouse was the estate's main residence. *See* Manice entry in this volume.

Roosevelt Raceway was the site of an ill-fated automobile racetrack created to host the dormant Vanderbilt Cup races, a project that was abandoned after only two races. It became the site of Roosevelt Raceway in 1940. Harness racing ceased at Roosevelt Raceway in 1988.

*Vanderbilt Cup Race*

4. Charles S. Pelham–Clinton, "Fox Hunting Near the Metropolis" *The Cosmopolitan* 7 (May 1889), pp. 82-83, 87, and "Country Clubs and Hunt Clubs" *Scribners Magazine* July – Dec. 1895, p. 308.

5. Mrs. John King Van Rensselaer and Frederic Van De Water, *The Social Ladder* (New York: Henry Holt & Company, 1924), p. 288.

6. George de Forest Lord, *Now or Then* (Bloomington, IN: AuthorHouse, 2007), p. 13.

7. Cleveland Amory, *Who Killed Society?* (New York: Harper & Brothers, Publishers, 1960), p. 87.

8. For prominent Long Island polo players George Herbert Bostwick, Sr., Winston Frederick Churchill Guest, William Averell Harriman, Thomas Hitchcock, Jr. and Sr., David Stewart Iglehart, Foxhall Parker Keene, and Devereaux Milburn, Sr. *see* entries in Spinzia, *Long Island's Prominent North Shore Families: Their Estates and Their Country Homes*, vol. *I* (College Station, TX: VirtualBookworm, 2006); Charles Cary Rumsey, Sr., James Watson Webb, Sr., and Harry Payne Whitney in Spinzia, *Long Island's Prominent North Shore Families: Their Estates and Their Country Homes*, vol. *II* (College Station, TX: VirtualBookworm, 2006); August Belmont II, Oliver William Bird, Jr., and Elliot Roosevelt, Sr. in this volume.

9. Thomas Hitchcock, Jr. was awarded a ten-goal rating (the highest) in eighteen of nineteen seasons from 1922 through 1940 and is considered by many to be the greatest player in the history of polo. He was a member of the United States Polo Open teams in 1923, 1927, 1935, and 1936; a member of the Westchester Cup teams of 1921, 1924, 1927, 1930, and 1939; and captain of the United States Olympic Polo team of 1924.

10. Edward J. Smits, *Nassau Suburbia, USA: The First Seventy-five Years of Nassau County, New York 1899-1974* (Garden City: Doubleday & Company, Inc., 1974), p. 127.

*Thomas Hitchcock, Jr.*

11. Amory, *Who Killed Society?* p. 87

Polo made several contributions to the fashion world by introducing the camel hair polo coat, the polo shirt, and the button-down collar dress shirt, which was developed by Brooks Brothers in 1913.

12. The U.S. Polo Open ended a forty-one-year hiatus when in 1994 it returned to the Meadow Brook for two consecutive years.

13. The Hempstead Plains Airfield, Camp Mills, Hazelhurst Field, Aviation Field #2, and Curtiss Field were located slightly to the east of Garden City's Clinton Road; Curtiss Airport was in Valley Stream; and the Washington Avenue and Nassau Boulevard Fields were in Garden City.

14. Mildred Smith, *History of Garden City* (Garden City: Garden City Historical Society, 1980), p. 85.

15. *See* Curtiss entry in this volume for Glenn Curtiss' Garden City residence.

16. Bernie Bookbinder, *Long Island: People and Places Past and Present* (New York: Harry N. Abrams, Inc., 1983), p. 165.

17. Henry Harley "Hap" Arnold would become a five-star general in the Army and, later, in the Air Force. He is the only officer to hold a five-star grade in two different branches of the military. Thomas DeWitt Milling would end his military career as a brigadier general.

18. Smith, *History of Garden City*, pp. 70 and 86.

19. Smith, *History of Garden City*, p. 100.

Douglas MacArthur trained the Rainbow Division at Camp Mills prior to its embarkation for France during World War I.

*Rainbow Division on parade at Camp Mills, 1917*

20. James Harold "Jimmy" Doolittle, who during World War II was awarded the Medal of Honor for planning and leading the 1942 B-25 bomber raid on Japan from the aircraft carrier USS *Hornet*, was a member of Mitchel Field's Naval Testing Board, a high-speed airplane racer, a test pilot, and an aeronautical engineer, who took an active role in the development of instrument flying. In 1929, while stationed at Mitchel Field, he successfully tested Sperry's horizon and directional gyroscopes to take off, fly, and land a plane solely by the use of instruments thereby becoming the first pilot to ever "fly blind."

21. Also known as Aviation Field #2, Hazelhurst was later incorporated into Mitchel Field.

22. By 1918 Hazelhurst and Mitchel Field had become the two largest airfields in the United States.

23. Smits, *Nassau Suburbia, USA*, p. 108.

24. In 1956 the northern portion of Curtiss Airport would become Valley Stream's Green Acres Mall.

A plaque, originally installed at the Green Acres Mall but now on display at the American Airpower Museum in East Farmingdale, honors the Ninety-Nines, an international organization of licensed women fliers, organized in 1929 at Curtiss Airport. In 1931 the ninety-nine charter members elected Amelia Earhart the organization's first president.

25. For a description of William Jaird Levitt, Sr.'s Mill Neck estate *La Colline*, see Spinzia, *Long Island's Prominent North Shore Families*, vol. I.

26. The Curtiss Aeroplane and Motor Corporation owned fifty-one percent of the Garden City-based Curtiss Engineering Corporation.

27. C. R. Roseberry, *Glenn Curtiss: Pioneer of Flight* (Syracuse, NY: Syracuse University Press, 1991), p. 429.

28. The nineteen-acre preserve at Nassau Community College is managed by The Nature Conservancy. The Hempstead Plains Preserve is supervised by Nassau County Department of Parks, Recreation, and Museums.

*Harold Jacobi, Sr. residence,
bedroom*

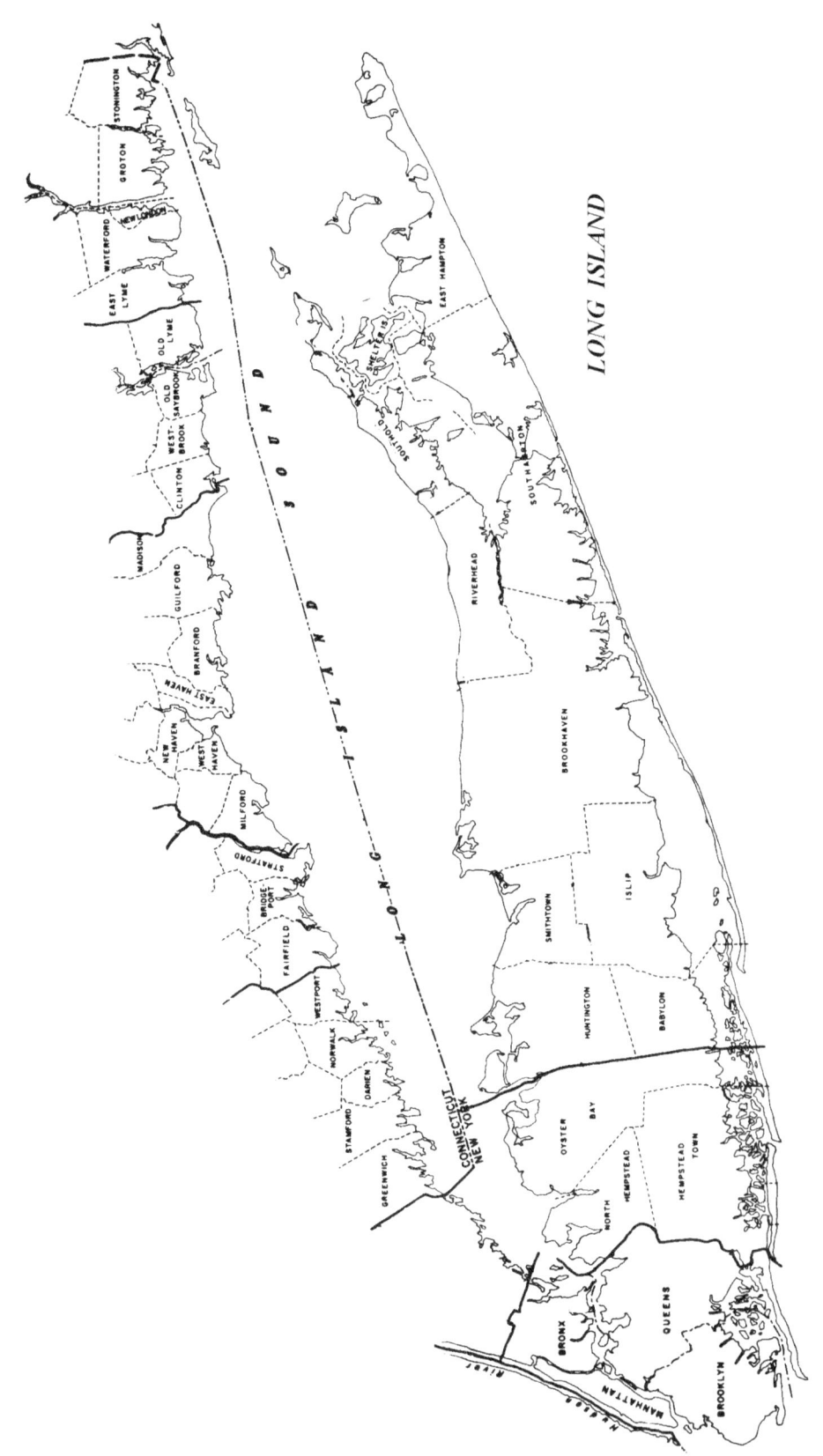

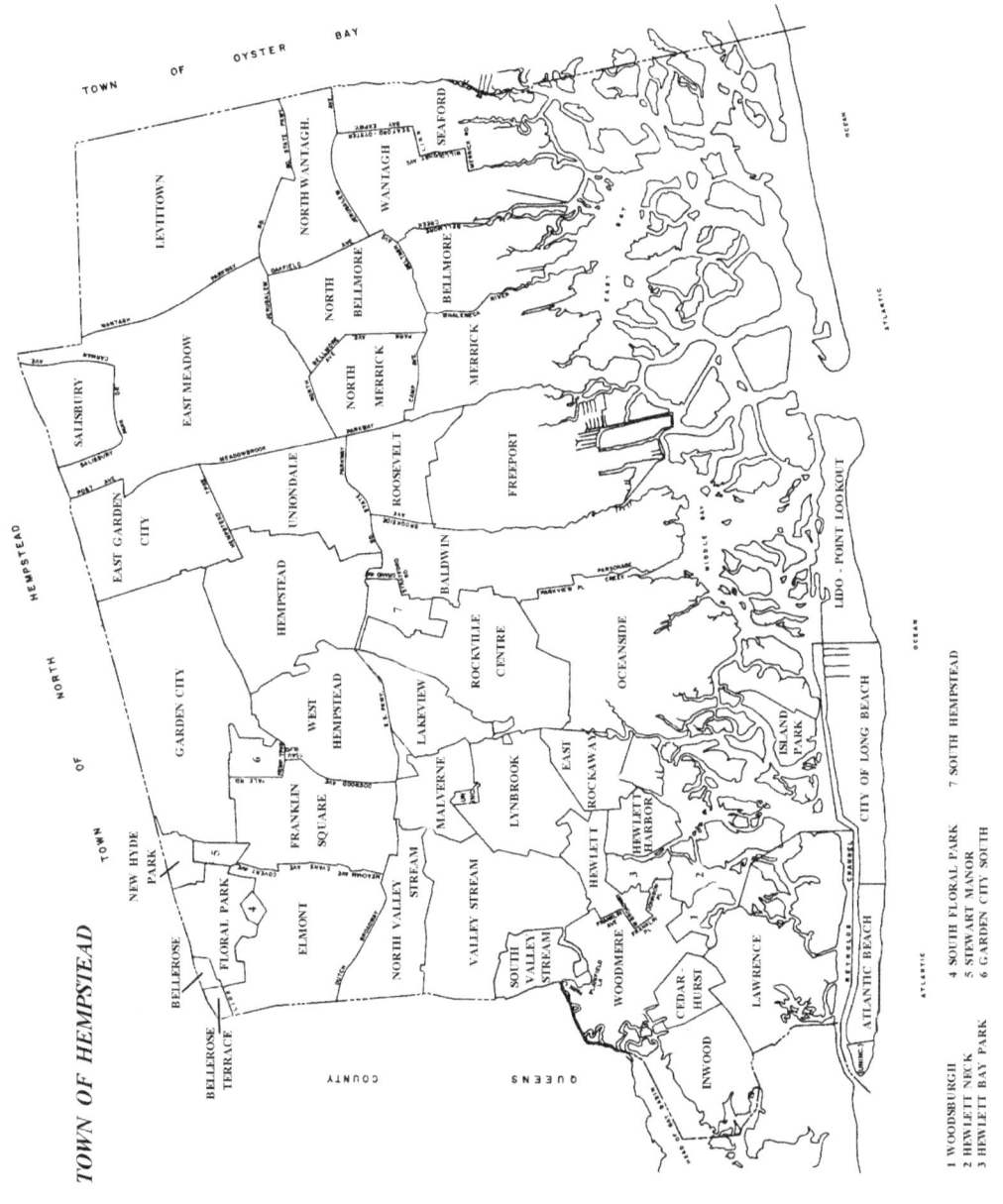

**Talbot Jones Taylor, Jr. residence, *Talbot House*, 1906**

### Ackerman, Raymond Pryor, Sr. (1887-1976)

| | |
|---|---|
| Occupation(s): | financier - member, George H. Burr and Co. (bond brokerage firm); member, Shields and Co. (stock brokerage firm); member, Nicholas J. Del Re (stock brokerage firm); member, Pogue, Willard, and Co. (stock brokerage firm); office manager, Orvis Brothers and Co. (stock brokerage firm) |
| Marriage(s): | 1913-1930 – Mildred Chadbourn Irish (1892-1930) |
| Address: | 23 Hilton Avenue, Garden City |
| Name of estate: | |
| Year of construction: | 1924 |
| Style of architecture: | Colonial Revival |
| Architect(s): | |
| Landscape architect(s): | |
| House extant: yes | |
| Historical notes: | |

*front facade, 2000*

The *Long Island Society Register, 1929* lists Raymond Pryor and Mildred Chadbourn Irish Ackerman [Sr.] as residing on Hilton Avenue, Garden City.

He was the son of T. C. and Ella R. Ackerman of Brooklyn.

Mildred Chadbourn Irish Ackerman was the daughter of Clarence C. Irish of Park Slope, Brooklyn.

Raymond Pryor and Mildred Chadbourn Irish Ackerman, Sr.'s son John married Doris Adel Fick, the daughter of George Henry Fick of Brooklyn. Their son Raymond Pryor Ackerman, Jr. married Seeley Hiltz, the daughter of Harry Blyth Hiltz of Beech Street, Garden City, and, later, Elizabeth De Tienne, the daughter of Dr. John Antoine and Mrs. Maude Olive Waterman De Tienne of Garden City.

In 1993 the house was remodeled.


### Adams, Charles Closson, Sr. (1858-1938)

| | |
|---|---|
| Occupation(s): | financier - a founder, president, and chairman of board, Peninsula National Bank, Cedarhurst |
| | capitalist - manager, Pittsburgh, PA, office, Mutual Union Telegraph Co.; manager, Philadelphia, PA, office, Postal Telegraph Co., 1884; vice-president, Postal Telegraph Co.; vice-president, Brooklyn District Telegraph Co. |
| Civic Activism: | president, Village of Lawrence |
| Marriage(s): | M/1 – Netta Alice Herrington (1861-1902) |
| | M/2 – 1896-1938 – Elizabeth K. Spillin (b. 1872) |
| Address: | Ocean Avenue, Lawrence |
| Name of estate: | *Oak Lodge* |
| Year of construction: | |
| Style of architecture: | |
| Architect(s): | |
| Landscape architect(s): | |
| House extant: unconfirmed | |
| Historical notes: | |

The *Long Island Society Register, 1929* lists Charles C. and Elizabeth K. Spillin Adams [Sr.] as residing at *Oak Lodge* on Ocean Avenue, Cedarhurst [Lawrence].

He was the son of Alexander Ainsworth and Isabella Thompson Adams.

Their daughter Katherine married William Malcolm Bunn, the son of Benton S. Bunn of Paris, France. Their son Charles Closson Adams, Jr. married Willie–James Credille, the daughter of John McBride Credille of Manhattan.

### Adams, John Trevor, Sr. (1891-1962)

| | |
|---|---|
| Occupation(s): | entertainers and associated professions - <br>     member, Wolfsohn Musical Bureau, NYC (later, Radio Program Bureau); <br>     general manager, WMCA, 1934-1938 (New York City radio station); <br>     director, Irwin & Wasey, NYC (theatrical agency)*; <br>     director, Atwater Hour (radio program); <br>     president, Jack Adams, Inc. (theatrical agency) <br> capitalist - a founder, with Elliot Roosevelt, and president, Transcontinental Broadcasting Co., 1940** |
| Civic Activism: | member, bishop's committee, St. Thomas' Episcopal Church, NYC; <br> member, bishop's committee, St. Giles' Episcopal Church, Jefferson, ME |
| Marriage(s): | M/1 – 1916-div. 1926 – Helen Dunham Haynes (1896-1974) <br> M/2 – 1929-1962 – Alice Randolph |
| Address: | Seventh Street, Garden City |
| Name of estate: | |
| Year of construction: | |
| Style of architecture: | |
| Architect(s): | |
| Landscape architect(s): | |
| House extant: | unconfirmed |

Historical notes:

   The *Long Island Society Register, 1929* lists Mr. and Mrs. John Trevor Adams as residing on Seventh Street, Garden City.

   He was the son of Avon Franklin and Margaret Gordon Hall Adams of Manhattan.

   Helen Dunham Haynes Adams was the daughter of David Oliphant and Helen Dunham Williams Haynes, Sr. of Garden City.

   John Trevor and Helen Dunham Haynes Adams, Sr.'s son John Trevor Adams, Jr. married Ruth Higgins with whom he resided in Larchmont, NY. Their son Robert married Lena O'Brien and resided at *The Moorings* in Southampton. [*See* Spinzia, *Long Island's Prominent Families in the Town of Southampton* – Adams entry.] Their daughter Patricia married Henry Collery and, later, Henry B. Lent, Jr. with whom she resided in Pomfret, VT.

   Alice Randolph Adams was the daughter of Richard Randolph of Richmond, VA. She had previously been married to Carlos T. Ritter.

   *Irwin & Wasey represented radio and television personality Arthur Godfrey.

   **Elliot Roosevelt was the son of President Franklin Delano Roosevelt.

### Adams, William, Jr. (1870-1956)

| | |
|---|---|
| Occupation(s): | architect - partner, Adams and Warren <br>     *[See Architects appendix for selected list of commissions in the Town of Hempstead.]* |
| Civic Activism: | governor, Rockaway Hunting Club, Lawrence, 1911 |
| Marriage(s): | 1894-1956 – Alice Cameron Greenleaf (1875-1955) <br>     - Civic Activism: corresponding secretary, Lawrence Garden Club, 1938 |
| Address: | 80 Causeway, Lawrence |
| Name of estate: | |
| Year of construction: | |
| Style of architecture: | Dutch Colonial with Georgian elements |
| Architect(s): | William Adams, Jr. designed his own residence |
| Landscape architect(s): | |
| House extant: | no |

*front / side facade, 1918*

Historical notes:

   The house was built by William Adams, Jr.

   The *Long Island Society, 1929* lists William and Alice C. Greenleaf Adams [Jr.] as residing in Lawrence.

   He was the son of William and Helen Coolidge Adams, Sr.

   Alice Cameron Greenleaf Adams was the daughter of Dr. Richard Cranch and Mrs. Adeline Emma Stone Greenleaf, Sr. of Lenox, MA.

   William and Alice Cameron Greenleaf Adams, Sr.'s son John married Elinor S. Bright. Their son Lewis Greenleaf Adams was a noted architect. Their son William Adams III married Grace Sinclair Raymond and resided at *Landfall* in Lawrence. *[See following entry.]*

### Adams, William, III (b. 1895)

| | |
|---|---|
| Occupation(s): | capitalist - builder |
| Marriage(s): | 1925 – Grace Sinclair Raymond (1901-1988) |
| Address: | 70 Causeway, Lawrence |
| Name of estate: | *Landfall* |
| Year of construction: | 1897 |
| Style of architecture: | Eclectic |
| Architect(s): | William Adams, Jr. designed the house (for A. O. Norris) |
| Landscape architect(s): | |
| House extant: yes | |
| Historical notes: | |

The house was built by Alfred Oliphant Norris. It was later owned by William Adams III who called in *Landfall*. The *Social Register Summer, 1947* lists William and Grace S. Raymond Adams [III] as residing at 70 Causeway, Lawrence.

He was the son of William and Alice Cameron Greenleaf Adams, Jr. of Lawrence. *[See previous entry.]*

Grace Sinclair Raymond Adams was the daughter of Irving Edward and Maud Sloan Sinclair Raymond of *The Cedars* in Shippan Point, CT.

William and Grace Sinclair Raymond Adams III's son Peter married Mary Louise Evans, the daughter of Robert A. Evans of Providence, RI.

In 1951 Adams sold the house to Stephen Baker Finch, Sr. [*The New York Times* October 24, 1951, p. 53.]

In 2006 the house was remodeled.

*front facade, 2006*

### Adams, William Herbert (d. 1957)

| | |
|---|---|
| Occupation(s): | attorney |
| | entertainers and associated professions - theatrical producer |
| Marriage(s): | M/1 – 1911 – Gertrude Slocum |
| | M/2 – Mary Miner |
| Address: | Burton Lane, Lawrence |
| Name of estate: | |
| Year of construction: | |
| Style of architecture: | |
| Architect(s): | |
| Landscape architect(s): | |
| House extant: unconfirmed | |
| Historical notes: | |

The *Long Island Society Register, 1929* lists W. Herbert and Mary Miner Adams as residing in Cedarhurst [Lawrence]. The *Social Register New York, 1951* lists William H. and Mary Miner Adams as residing on Burton Lane, Lawrence.

He was the son of Samuel and Anna Burns Adams.

Gertrude Slocum Adams was the daughter of Henry Warner and Grace Edsall Slocum, Jr. of Cedarhurst.

William Herbert and Gertrude Slocum Adams' daughter Gay married Richard Charles Potter Coogan, the son of W. Gordon Coogan, Sr. of Madison, NJ, and the grandson of Edward Clarkson and Emily Blanche Havemeyer Potter, Sr. of Glen Cove. [*See* Spinzia, *Long Island's Prominent North Shore Families, vol. II* – Potter entry.]

### Addison, Charles Lambert (1869-1929)

| | |
|---|---|
| Occupation(s): | capitalist - director, Long Island Traction Co.; |
| | general superintendent, Long Island Rail Road; |
| | director, Huntington Railroad; |
| | director, Consolidated Electrical Co.; |
| | director, Montauk Water Co.; |
| | director, Northport Traction Co.; |
| | director, Ocean Electric, R'y Island Railroad |
| | shipping - director, Montauk Steamboat Co. |
| Civic Activism: | member, Atlantic Avenue Board of Improvements, Brooklyn |
| Marriage(s): | 1895-1929 – Katharine Onderdonk Weller (b. 1876) |
| Address: | 224 Fulton Avenue, Hempstead |
| Name of estate: | |
| Year of construction: | |
| Style of architecture: | |
| Architect(s): | |
| Landscape architect(s): | |
| House extant: no | |
| Historical notes: | |

The *Long Island Society Register, 1929* lists Charles Lambert and Katharine Onderdonk Weller Addison as residing on Fulton Avenue, Hempstead.

Katharine Onderdonk Weller Addison was the daughter of Queens County Surrogate Judge Augustus Nobel Weller and Mrs. Katharine Onderdonk Weller of Hempstead.


### Addison, James, Jr. (1873-1941)

| | |
|---|---|
| Occupation(s): | capitalist - general auditor, Board of Transportation, Brooklyn; |
| | controller, Brooklyn and Manhattan Transit Co. |
| | financier - controller, National City Bank; |
| | treasurer, Williamsburgh Bank, Brooklyn; |
| | vice-president, Garden City Bank and Trust Co. |
| Civic Activism: | first treasurer after incorporation, Village of Garden City, 1919-1920; |
| | trustee, Village of Garden City, 1920-1923; |
| | president, Village of Garden City, 1922-1923; |
| | member, advisory board, Pace Institute, Reading, PA |
| Marriage(s): | Mima Petrie (1877-1952) |
| Address: | 148 Hampton Road, Garden City |
| Name of estate: | |
| Year of construction: | 1928 |
| Style of architecture: | Colonial Revival |
| Architect(s): | |
| Landscape architect(s): | |
| House extant: yes | |
| Historical notes: | |

*front facade, 2009*

The house was built by James Addison, Jr.

The *Long Island Society Register, 1929* lists Mr. and Mrs. James Addison [Jr.] as residing at 10 Nassau Boulevard, Garden City. They relocated to 148 Hampton Road, Garden City.

He was the son of James and Janet Ines Smith Addison, Sr. of Lent, Scotland.

James and Mima Petrie Addison, Jr.'s son James Addison III married Helen Peck and resided in Garden City. Their daughter Janet married Stevens Manning, the son of Dr. Van H. and Mrs. Emily Stevens Manning, Sr. of Forest Hills.

### Akin, Albert John, II (1882-1942)

| | |
|---|---|
| Occupation(s): | industrialist - director, secretary, and treasurer, Cuban American Sugar Co.; official, Panel Corp. (railroad equipment manufacturing firm) |
| Civic Activism: | official, American Red Cross during World War I |
| Marriage(s): | M/1 – 1907-div. 1917 – Gwendolyn Wickersham (1888-1963) |
| | M/2 – 1919 – Diane de Lemee (1891-1940) |
| Address: | Everit Avenue, Hewlett Harbor |
| Name of estate: | *Homewood* |
| Year of construction: | |
| Style of architecture: | |
| Architect(s): | |
| Landscape architect(s): | |
| House extant: unconfirmed | |
| Historical notes: | |

The *Social Register Summer, 1915* lists Albert J. and Gwendolyn Wickersham Akin as residing in Hewlett [Hewlett Harbor].

He was the son of Albro and Emma Reed Akin of *The Homestead* in Quaker Hill, NY.

Gwendolyn Wickersham Akin was the daughter of George Woodward and Mildred Wendell Wickersham of *Marshfield* in Lawrence. Gwendolyn subsequently married Henry Ives Cobb, Jr. with whom she resided in Hewlett.

Albert John and Gwendolyn Wickersham Akin, Sr.'s son Albert John Akin III married Dorothy Murray Forbes, the daughter of Murray Forbes of Wellesley, MA. Their daughter Mildred married Russell Lynes and resided in Bryn Mawr, PA.


### Albert, Judith Florence Carman (1938-1998)

| | |
|---|---|
| Occupation(s): | artist |
| | inventor - TANA, a painting technique which bonded texture-rich packing material with glue and covered it in bright acrylic color |
| | doll designer - Arranbee Doll Corp., Hicksville, 1958; |
| | Valentine Doll Corp., Brooklyn, 1958-1959; |
| | Ideal Toy Corp, Hollis, 1959-1981; |
| | design consultant, Galoob Toy Corp., South San Francisco, CA, 1990-1992; |
| | Tyco Toys, Inc., Mount Laurel, NJ; |
| | Direct Connect, Inc., 1991-1992; |
| | Ideal Viewmaster Corp., 1987-1988; |
| | Roseart Industries, Inc., Orange, NJ |
| | president, Alberts Design Co., Inc., Oyster Bay |
| Marriage(s): | M/1 – Joseph P. Paruolo |
| | M/2 – 1975-1998 – Arthur Albert |
| | - marketer, Alberts Design Co., Inc., Oyster Bay |
| Address: | *[unable to determine street address]*, Franklin Square |
| Name of estate: | |
| Year of construction: | |
| Style of architecture: | |
| Architect(s): | |
| Landscape architect(s): | |
| House extant: unconfirmed | |
| Historical notes: | |

Judith Florence Carman Albert was raised in Franklin Square and was a graduate of Sewanhaka High School in Floral Park. She was the daughter of Ernest A. and Ruth Ott Carman.

Judith's doll designs included Betsy Wetsy, Tiny Tears, Tiffany Taylor, Chrissie, Puffalumps, Singing Bouncy Baby, Happy Hugs, and Cabbage Patch.

The Alberts resided in Mill Neck.

### Alexandre, Frederick Francis, Sr. (1894-1968)

| | |
|---|---|
| Occupation(s): | financier - partner, Gude, Winmill, and Co. (stock brokerage firm) |
| | capitalist - member, board of governors, and vice-president, Aqueduct Race Track, Jamaica, NY |
| Civic Activism: | member, board of governors, Turf & Field Club; |
| | vice-president, Hunts Racing Association; |
| | member, race committee, Rockaway Steeplechase Association, 1937 |
| Marriage(s): | 1916-1957 – Regina Mathilde Saportas (1899-1957) |
| | - merchant - vice-president and director, Mainbocher, NYC (couturiers) |
| Address: | White's Lane, Lawrence |
| Name of estate:` | *Nieman* |
| Year of construction: | |
| Style of architecture: | |
| Architect(s): | |
| Landscape architect(s): | |
| House extant: unconfirmed | |
| Historical notes: | |

The *Long Island Society Register, 1929* lists Frederick F. and Regina M. Saportas Alexandre [Sr.] as residing at *Nieman* in Lawrence.

He was the son of James Henry and Elizabeth Boyce Lawrence Alexandre, Sr. of Hempstead.

Regina Mathilde Saportas Alexandre was the daughter of George Arthur and Renia Brown Saportas.

Frederick Francis and Regina Mathilde Saportas Alexandre, Sr.'s daughter Elizabeth married H. Wisner Miller, Jr. of Lawrence. Their son Lawrence married Beverly Burger, the daughter of Van Vechten Burger of Lawrence. Their daughter Joan married Walter Russell Herrick, Jr. of Lawrence. Their son Anthony married Louisa Gilbert, the daughter of Roger Gilbert of Greenwich, CT.

*[See following entry for additional family information.]*

*James Henry Alexandre, Sr. residence, front facade, 2000*

### Alexandre, James Henry, Sr. (1848-1912)

| | |
|---|---|
| Occupation(s): | shipping - president, Provincial Steam-ship Co.; president, Alexandre Steamship Line |
| Marriage(s): | M/1 – Gertrude Jerome (1853-1883) |
| | M/2 – 1888 – Elizabeth Boyce Lawrence (1862-1906) |
| | M/3 – 1910-1912 – Pauline Garcia Onativia (1871-1950) |
| Address: | 170 Cathedral Avenue, Hempstead |
| Name of estate: | |
| Year of construction: | c. 1928 |
| Style of architecture: | Colonial Revival |
| Architect(s): | |
| Landscape architect(s): | |
| House extant: yes | |
| Historical notes: | |

The house was built by James Henry Alexandre, Sr.

He was the son of Francis Alexandre, the founder of Alexandre Steamship Line.

Gertrude Jerome Alexandre was the daughter of Thomas Atwater and Emma Vanderbilt Jerome. Her sister Kate married Clarence Gray Dinsmore.

James Henry and Gertrude Jerome Alexandre, Sr.'s son James Henry Alexandre, Jr., who resided at *Valleybrook Farm* in Old Brookville, married Ann Loomis and, subsequently, Olivia D. Wheeler. [*See* Spinzia, *Long Island's Prominent North Shore Families, vol. I* – Alexandre entry.] Their daughter Gertrude married Samuel Adams Clark, Jr. and resided in Cedarhurst.

Elizabeth Boyce Lawrence Alexandre was the daughter of Frederick Newbold and Elizabeth Boyce Lawrence of Bayside and Manhattan. Elizabeth's sister Mary married Frank Worth White and, subsequently, Foxhall Parker Keene with whom she resided at *Rosemary Hall* in Old Westbury. [*See* Spinzia, *Long Island's Prominent North Shore Families, vol. I* – Keene entry.]

James Henry and Elizabeth Boyce Lawrence Alexandre, Sr.'s daughter Mary married Nathaniel Edward Caldwell Rutter, Sr. and resided in Lawrence. Their son Frederick married Regina Mathilde Saportas and resided in Lawrence. Their daughter Virginia remained unmarried.

The *Long Island Society Register, 1929* lists Pauline Onativia Alexandre as residing at 170 Cathedral Avenue, Hempstead.

She was the daughter of José Victorio and Georgiana Jones Onativia, Sr. of Manhattan. Pauline had previously been married to John Richard Townsend of Newport, RI, and Manhattan. Their son Robert Tailer Townsend, Sr. married Mary H. Frieze and resided in Hempstead. Pauline's brother José Victorio Onativia, Jr., who resided in Southampton and at *Cross Roads Cottage* in Millbrook, NY, married Clare Wright Barclay, Jean Clarisse Coudert, and, subsequently, Maria Adele Montant. [*See* Spinzia, *Long Island's Prominent North Shore Families, vol. II* – Nast entry; *Long Island's Prominent South Shore Families* – de Coppet entry; and *Long Island's Prominent Families in the Town of Southampton* – Onativia entry.] Pauline's sister Vera married Dana de Peyster Whipple, Sr. and resided in Hempstead.

*[See previous entry for additional family information.]*

*Dr. Benjamin Roy Allison residence,
front facade, 2006*

### Allison, Dr. Benjamin Roy (1889-1981)

| | |
|---|---|
| Occupation(s): | physician - Chief of Medicine, Nassau Hospital (later, Winthrop University Hospital; now NYU Langone Hospital – Long Island) |
| Civic Activism: | chairman, Nassau County Board of Health; president, Nassau County Medical Society; a founder, Meadowbrook Hospital, Hempstead (later, Nassau County Medical Center) |
| Marriage(s): | Ruth Hovey (1890-1986)<br>- nurse - anesthetist<br>Civic Activism: was awarded the Croix de Guére and the Bronze Star for her service as a Red Cross combat nurse during World War I |
| Address: | 26 Ives Road, Hewlett Bay Park |
| Name of estate: | |
| Year of construction: | 1922 |
| Style of architecture: | Colonial Revival |
| Architect(s): | |
| Landscape architect(s): | |
| House extant: yes | |
| Historical notes: | |

The *Long Island Society Register, 1929* lists Dr. Benjamin R. and Mrs. Ruth Hovey Allison as residing on Ives Road, Hewlett [Hewlett Bay Park].

Ruth Hovey Allison was the daughter of Henry Russell and Alice Eliza Huntley Hovey.

Dr. Benjamin Roy and Mrs. Ruth Hovey Allison's daughter Mary married Daniel Caldwell Millett, the son of Daniel A. Millett of Denver, CO. Their son Huntly married Virginia Perry Schauffler, the daughter of Harry Klock Schauffler of Pelham Manor, NY.


### Almirall, Raymond Francis (1869-1939)

| | |
|---|---|
| Occupation(s): | architect* - partner with brother-in-law, Philip Allain Cusachs, Almirall and Cusachs |
| Civic Activism: | member, Tenement House Commission (appointed by Governor Theodore Roosevelt in 1900) |
| Marriage(s): | 1897-1939 – Marguerite Allain Cusachs (1876-1961) |
| Address: | Fulton Avenue, Hempstead |
| Name of estate: | *Ma Chaumière* |
| Year of construction: | |
| Style of architecture: | |
| Architect(s): | |
| Landscape architect(s): | |
| House extant: unconfirmed | |
| Historical notes: | |

The *Social Register Summer, 1921* lists Raymond F. and Marguerite A. Cusachs Almirall as residing at *Ma Chaumière* in Hempstead. The *Long Island Society Register, 1929* lists them as residing on Fulton Avenue, Hempstead.

He was the son of Joseph Janer and Ida Gunn Almirall of Brooklyn.

Marguerite Allain Cusachs Almirall was the daughter of Pierre Leon Cusachs of New Orleans, LA. Marguerite's brother Philip married Helen Krech, the daughter of Alvin William and Angeline Sherwood Jackson Krech of *Hedgerow* in Southampton and resided in East Islip. [*See* Spinzia, *Long Island's Prominent Families in the Town of Southampton* – Krech entry – and *Long Island's Prominent South Shore Families* – Cusachs entry.]

Raymond Francis and Marguerite Allain Cusachs Almirall's son Joseph Janer Almirall II married Madeline Marvin–Smith, the daughter of George Valentine Smith of Rye, NY, and resided in Old Westbury. Their daughter Raymonde married Don Morrison Kelley, the son of Albert Tevis Kelly of New York, and resided in Syosset. Their daughter Marguerite died in 1901 at the age of three.

*Among their numerous commissions, Almirall designed the Fordham and Gouveneur Hospitals in New York City; Sea View Hospital on Staten Island; a sanitarium in East Moriches; and the Roman Catholic churches in Oyster Bay and Glen Cove.

### Almy, Frederick, Jr. (1849-1917)

| | |
|---|---|
| Occupation(s): | merchant - linens |
| Marriage(s): | 1885-1917 – Millicent Magruder (1856-1940)<br>  - Civic Activism: chair, Lawrence division, YMCA Committee to raise money for the erection of Hostess Houses at Camp Upton, Yaphank, during World War I |
| Address: | Broadway, Lawrence |
| Name of estate: | |
| Year of construction: | |
| Style of architecture: | |
| Architect(s): | |
| Landscape architect(s): | |
| House extant: unconfirmed | |
| Historical notes: | |

   He was the son of Frederick and Susan Henrietta Niles Almy, Sr.
   Millicent Magruder Almy was the daughter of Dr. William Beans. and Mrs. Sarah Van Wyck Magruder.
   Frederick and Millicent Magruder Almy, Jr.'s son William married Dorothy Greer, the daughter of Lawrence Greer. Their daughter Elizabeth married John Yates Gholson Walker, the son of Norman Stewart and Georginia F. Gholson Walker of Llewellyn Park, West Orange, NJ, and resided at *Eagleridge* in Llewellyn Park, West Orange, NJ. Their daughter Millicent married Henri Laurent Laussucq, the son of Pascal Laussucq of Dax, France, and, later, Philip Warner with whom she resided in Salisbury, CT. Their son Frederick Almy III married the Baroness Michelham, the daughter of Octavius Bradshaw of *Powerham Castle* in England. They were only married one month when his wife died leaving him the bulk of her estate which was estimated at $50 million. Frederick, who was known as "the cowboy millionaire" because of his obsession with The West, subsequently married June Dibble, the daughter of General Dibble of the British army. [*The New York Times* January 2, 1927, p. 27, and February 19, 1927, p. 1.]


### Amerman, William H. H., Jr. (1877-1935)

| | |
|---|---|
| Occupation(s): | financier - president, Amerman & Patterson (customs and insurance broker) |
| Marriage(s): | 1907-1935 – Helen Barton Mandeville (1885-1964) |
| Address: | 476 Fulton Avenue, Hempstead |
| Name of estate: | |
| Year of construction: | |
| Style of architecture: | |
| Architect(s): | |
| Landscape architect(s): | |
| House extant: no | |
| Historical notes: | |

   The *Long Island Society Register, 1929* lists William H. H. and Helen Mandeville Amerman, Jr. as residing on Fulton Avenue in Hempstead.
   He was the son of William H. H. and Elizabeth Armitage Amerman.
   Helen Barton Mandeville Amerman was the daughter of Harry Ellsworth and Elizabeth Barton Mandeville of Hazleton, PA.

### Anderson, Ellery Oswald (1875-1942)

| | |
|---|---|
| Occupation(s): | attorney |
| | capitalist - president and treasurer, 36th Street and First Avenue Corp. |
| Civic Activism: | trustee, Catholic Youth Organization |
| Marriage(s): | 1900-1942 – Melicent Stebbins Duryea (1876-1951) |
| Address: | Fulton Avenue, Hempstead |
| Name of estate: | *Waycroft* |
| Year of construction: | |
| Style of architecture: | |
| Architect(s): | |
| Landscape architect(s): | |
| House extant: unconfirmed | |
| Historical notes: | |

The *Long Island Society Register, 1929* lists Ellery O. and Melicent S. Duryea Anderson as residing at *Waycroft* on Fulton Avenue, Hempstead.

He was the son of Edward H. and Josephine Allen Anderson.

Melicent Stebbins Duryea Anderson was the daughter of Civil War General Hiram and Mrs. Laura Dewey Duryea. Hiram's regiment was known as "Duryea's Zouaves." Melicent's father was murdered in his Bay Ridge, Brooklyn, home by Melicent's deranged brother Chester. Her brother Harry, who married Minga Pope and resided in Old Brookville, died from a self-inflicted gunshot wound in his Manhattan office. The incident occurred after Melicent filed court papers requesting an audit of their father's trust, which Harry was administrating. [*See* Spinzia, *Long Island's Prominent North Shore Families, vol. I* – Duryea entry.]

Ellery Oswald and Melicent Stebbins Duryea Anderson's daughter Melicent married Cedric Culbertson French, Jr., the son of Culbertson French, Sr. of New York.

### Anderson, Roy Bennett, Sr. (1892-1969)

| | |
|---|---|
| Occupation(s): | industrialist - president, Brooklyn Varnish and Paint Co. |
| Marriage(s): | 1920-1969 – Agnes Adelaide England (1891-1974) |
| Address: | 129 Kilburn Road, Garden City |
| Name of estate: | |
| Year of construction: | 1924 |
| Style of architecture: | American Craftsman |
| Architect(s): | |
| Landscape architect(s): | |
| House extant: yes | |
| Historical notes: | |

The *Long Island Society Register, 1929* lists Roy Bennett and Agnes Adelaide England Anderson [Sr.] as residing at 129 Kilburn Road, Garden City.

He was the son of William James and Sadie Wilson Anderson of Brooklyn.

Roy Bennett and Agnes Adelaide English Anderson, Sr.'s son Roy Bennett Anderson, Jr. was killed in World War II. Their daughter Adelaide married Paul Sheppard Eckhoff, the son of Arnold Eckhoff of Palisades Park, NJ, and resided in Syosset.

*front facade, 2001*

### Anderton, Dr. William Bancroft (1857-1917)

| | |
|---|---|
| Occupation(s): | physician - consulting physician, St. Joseph Hospital, Far Rockaway |
| Civic Activism: | trustee, Francis Asbury Palmer Fund |
| Marriage(s): | 1885-1917 – Elizabeth Story Palmer (1863-1953)<br> - Civic Activism: member, Woman's Auxiliary, Orthopaedic Hospital<br>suffragist* |
| Address: | Ocean Avenue, Lawrence |
| Name of estate: | *Ye Corners* |
| Year of construction: | |
| Style of architecture: | |
| Architect(s): | |
| Landscape architect(s): | |
| House extant: unconfirmed | |
| Historical notes: | |

    The *Brooklyn Blue Book and Long Island Society Register, 1921* lists Elizabeth S. Palmer Anderton as residing in Cedarhurst [Lawrence].
    She was the daughter of Walter Bowne and Mary Elizabeth Story Palmer.
    Dr. William Bancroft Anderton was the son of Ralph Leigh and Sarah H. Knapp Anderton.
    Dr. William Bancroft and Mrs. Elizabeth Story Palmer Anderton's daughter Alice married Louis Townsend Montant, the son of Auguste P. Montant. Their daughter Ruth married William Garnet Chiscolm, the son of William E. Chiscolm of Baltimore, MD, and resided in Manhattan. Their son Walter married Ethel Welles Kingsland and resided in Manhattan. Their daughter Dorothy married Edward Sailsbury Bentley, Sr. and resided at *Cherrygarth* in Lawrence. Their daughter Frances died in 1900 at the age of eleven.
    *For other Long Islanders involved in the suffrage movement *see* Raymond E. Spinzia, "Winning the Franchise: Long Island Activists in the Fight for Woman's Suffrage and Their Opponents, Long Island's Anti-Suffragists." wwwspinzialongislandestates.com.


### Arledge, Roone Pinckney, Jr. (1931-2002)

| | |
|---|---|
| Occupation(s): | capitalist - president, ABC News, 1977-1998;<br>    president, ABC Sports, 1968-1998<br>writer - *Roone, a Memoir*, 2003 |
| Marriage(s): | M/1 – 1953-div.1971 – Joan Dorothy Heise<br>M/2 – 1975-div. 1985 – Ann Fowler (b. 1948)<br>   - former Miss Alabama, 1969<br>M/3 – 1994-2002 – Gisele N. Shaw (1952-2010) |
| Address: | *[unable to determine street address]*, Merrick |
| Name of estate: | |
| Year of construction: | |
| Style of architecture: | |
| Architect(s): | |
| Landscape architect(s): | |
| House extant: unconfirmed | |
| Historical notes: | |

    Roone Pinckney Arledge, Jr. grew up in Merrick and graduated from Wellington C. Mepham High School in Bellmore. He was the son of Roone Pinckey and Gertrude Agnes Stritmater Arledge, Sr.
    Joan Dorothy Heise Arledge was the daughter of Benjamin Ryer Heise of Wantagh. She subsequently married Arthur John Spring, Jr.
    Roone Pinckey and Joan Dorothy Heise Arledge, Jr.'s daughter Susan married Lee William Weston, the son of Warren and Barbara Weston of Carefree, AZ. Their daughter Patricia married Robert J. Loonie, Jr. and resided in New Canaan, CT, and Bridgehampton.
    Ann Fowler was the daughter of N. W. Fowler of Birmingham, AL.
    Arledge, who won thirty-seven Emmy Awards, created "Monday Night Football," "Wide World of Sports," "Nightline," "World News Tonight Primetime," and "20/20."

### Aten, Courtenay Nixon, Sr. (1895-1971)

| | |
|---|---|
| Occupation(s): | industrialist - director, United States Tobacco Co. |
| | merchant - director, John G. Paton Co. (food merchant and broker) |
| Marriage(s): | M/1 – 1919-1930 – Helen Jackson Page (1899-1930) |
| | - Civic Activism: recording secretary, Faith Home For the Incurables, Brooklyn, 1925; sold Liberty Bonds during World War I |
| | M/2 – *[unable to determine name]* |
| Address: | 69 Third Street, Garden City |
| Name of estate: | |
| Year of construction: | 1908 |
| Style of architecture: | Modified Dutch Colonial Revival |
| Architect(s): | |
| Landscape architect(s): | |
| House extant: yes | |
| Historical notes: | |

*front facade, 2008*

The *Long Island Society Register, 1929* lists Courtenay Nixon and Helen Jackson Page Aten [Sr.] as residing at 69 Third Street, Garden City.

He was the son of Dr. William H. and Mrs. Mae Emma Greene Aten of Brooklyn.

Helen Jackson Page Aten was the daughter of Frank C. Bauman and Henrietta Jackson Page, who resided at *Elmcroft* in Upper Brookville. [*See* Spinzia, *Long Island's Prominent North Shore Families, vol. II* – Page entry.] Helen's sister Ruth married Franklin E. Burke, Jr.

Courtenay Nixon and Helen Jackson Page Aten, Sr.'s daughter Ruth married Karl Dravo Pettit, Jr. of *Cherry Hill Farm* in Princeton, NJ. Their daughter Barbara married Charles S. White, the son of R. E. White of Seaford, VA. Their son Courtenay Nixon, Jr., who died in a plane crash in 1945, married Anita Roberts of Riverside, CA.

In 1977 the house was remodeled.


### Atwater, Albert Leonard (1867-1954)
### aka Bert L. Atwater

| | |
|---|---|
| Occupation(s): | industrialist - vice-president for sales, director, and chairman of board, William Wrigley, Jr., Co., Chicago, IL (chewing gum manufacturer) |
| | financier - director, Garden City Bank and Trust Co. |
| Marriage(s): | Blanche Cox (1877-1959) |
| Address: | 168 Nassau Boulevard, Garden City |
| Name of estate: | |
| Year of construction: | |
| Style of architecture: | Mediterranean |
| Architect(s): | |
| Landscape architect(s): | |
| House extant: yes | |
| Historical notes: | |

*side / front facade, 2001*

The *Long Island Society Register, 1929* lists Bert L. and Blanche Cox Atwater as residing at 168 Nassau Boulevard, Garden City.

He was the son of Albert and Margaret Carswell Atwater.

Blanche Cox Atwater was the daughter of Amariah Cox, who resided at *Maryland* in Pasadena, CA.

Albert Leonard and Blanche Cox Atwater's son Amariah George Cox Atwater, Sr., who married Betty Ann Bergmann, Marjorie Elizabeth Millsap, Angelita Kay Harmes, and Nancy Fuller, resided in Garden City. Their daughter Helen married Philip K. Wrigley and resided in Chicago, IL. Their daughter Olive married George F. Getz, Jr. of Chicago, IL.

*[See following entry of additional family information.]*

The house is now the Garden City Jewish Center.

**Atwater, Amariah George Cox, Sr. (1910-1997)**

| | |
|---|---|
| Occupation(s): | industrialist - vice president for sales, William Wrigley, Jr., Co., Chicago, IL (chewing gum manufacturer); director, William Wrigley, Jr., Co., Ltd., Canada intelligence agent - head of the Office of Strategic Services for Middle Eastern Theater during World War II |
| Civic Activism: | president, Tavern Club, Arlington Racetrack; president, Post and Paddock Club, Arlington Racetrack |
| Marriage(s): | M/1 – 1932-div. 1936 – Betty Ann Bergmann (1913-1998) <br> M/2 – 1936-div. 1939 – Marjorie Elizabeth Millsap (1911-1999) (aka Dorothy Lee) <br> - entertainers and associated professions - motion picture comedian <br> M/3 – 1941-div. 1949 – Angelita Kay Harmes (1915-2004) <br> - model <br> entertainers and associated professions - radio singer <br> M/4 – Nancy Fuller (1925-1975) |
| Address: | 174 Roxbury Road, Garden City |
| Name of estate: | |
| Year of construction: | 1929 |
| Style of architecture: | Colonial Revival |
| Architect(s): | |
| Landscape architect(s): | |
| House extant: yes | |
| Historical notes: | |

Amariah George Cox Atwater, Sr. was the son of Albert Leonard and Blanche Cox Atwater of Garden City.

In 1932 Amariah George Cox and Betty Ann Bergmann Atwater, Sr. were residing at the Roxbury Road address. [*The Brooklyn Daily Eagle* March 16, 1932, p. 21.]

Their daughter Claire married David Daniel Stuart.

Marjorie Elizabeth Millsap Atwater was the daughter of Homer and Bess Millsap. Marjorie had previously been married to Robert Booth, Jimmy Fidler, and Marshall Duffield. After her divorce from Atwater, she married Frank John Bersbach, Jr. and, subsequently, Charles Calderni.

Angelita Kay Harmes Atwater was the daughter of John Albert Ray and Leonora Angeline Conant Harmes. Angelita had previously been married to Seymour Laney.

Amariah George Cox and Angelita Kay Harmes Atwater, Sr.'s son Amariah George Cox Atwater, Jr. married Donna Johnson, the daughter of Donn E. and Beverly Jean Streedain Johnson. After Angelita's divorce from Amariah, she married William Rasmussen.

Nancy Fuller Atwater was murdered by her husband's forty-year-old male nurse Daniel Bedelian. Bedelian stabbed and bludgeoned Mrs. Atwater in her California home and stuffed her body into a fifty-five-gallon steel barrel which he then filled with concrete and dumped in a Pacoima, CA, junkyard. [*The New York Times* February 7, 1975, p. 11; *The Los Angeles Times* March 8, 1975, p. C9, April 18, 1975, p. D8, July 3, 1975, p. OCA2, and December 12, 1975, p. E1.]

*[See preceding entry for additional family information.]*

In 2005 the 2,588-square-foot house sold for $1,385,800.

*front facade*

### Atwell, George Joseph, Sr. (1873-1944)

| | |
|---|---|
| Occupation(s): | financier - director, National Safety Bank & Trust Co., |
| | director, Consolidated Indemnity & Insurance Co.; |
| | director, Lefcourt Normandie National Bank; |
| | president and director, Prudence Securities Corp.; |
| | member, advisory board, American Mutual Liberty Insurance Co. |
| | capitalist - president, Thompson–Starrett Co., Inc. (construction firm)*; |
| | president and director, Nelson Towers Realty Corp.; |
| | director, Walsh, Atkinson, Kier, & Co.; |
| | director, New York City Omnibus Corp. |
| Marriage(s): | Mary Hogan (1885-1954) |
| Address: | Broadway and Oak Street, Woodmere |

Name of estate:
Year of construction:
Style of architecture:
Architect(s):
Landscape architect(s):
House extant: unconfirmed
Historical notes:

The *Long Island Society Register, 1929* lists George J. Atwell as residing at Broadway and Oak Street, Woodmere.

His daughter Mary married Francis C. E. Hitchcock, the son of Thomas and Louise Eustis Hitchcock, Sr., who resided at *Broad Hollow Farm* in Old Westbury, and, subsequently, William Mairs Duryea, Sr., the son of Walter Bartow and Ella Louise Mairs Duryea of East Hampton. [*See* Spinzia, *Long Island's Prominent North Shore Families, vol. I* – Hitchcock entry– and *Long Island's Prominent Families in the Town of East Hampton* – Duryea entry.] His daughter Edwina married Esmond Bradley Martin, Sr. and resided at *Knole* in Old Westbury. [*See* Spinzia, *Long Island's Prominent North Shore Families, vol. I* – Martin entry.] Edwina later married Robert Whiton Stuart, Sr. Atwell's son George Joseph Atwell, Jr., who resided at *Greenridge* in Roslyn, married Jean Cochran, the daughter of Gifford A. and Princess Hohenlohe–Schillingsfurst Cochran of Manhattan. His daughter Angelia married John Krimsky, Sr., the son of Dr. Joseph Krimsky of Brooklyn.

*Thompson–Starrett Co., Inc. built a portion of the New York City subway system.

[For Atwell's Old Westbury residence, see Spinzia, *Long Island's Prominent North Shore Families, vol. I* – Atwell entry.]

### Auchincloss, Joseph Howland, Sr. (1886-1968)

| | |
|---|---|
| Occupation(s): | attorney - partner, Stetson, Jennings, and Russell |
| | financier - J. P. Morgan and Co. (now, J. P. Morgan Chase) (investment banking firm) |
| Marriage(s): | 1911-1968 – Priscilla Dixon Stanton (1888-1972) |
| Address: | *[unable to determine street address]*, Lawrence |

Name of estate:
Year of construction:
Style of architecture:
Architect(s):
Landscape architect(s):
House extant: unconfirmed
Historical notes:

The *Social Register Summer, 1915* and *Long Island Society Register, 1928* list J. Howland and Priscilla D. Stanton Auchincloss [Sr.] as residing in Lawrence. The *Social Register Summer, 1932* lists J. Howland and Priscilla D. Stanton Auchincloss [Sr.] as residing in Locust Valley [Matinecock]. [*See* Spinzia, *Long Island's Prominent North Shore Families, vol. I* – Auchincloss entry.] The *Social Register Summer, 1949* lists them as residing in Southampton. [*See* Spinzia, *Long Island's Prominent Families in the Town of Southampton* – Auchincloss entry.]

He was the son of John Winthrop and Joanna Russell Auchincloss of Manhattan.

Priscilla Dixon Stanton Auchincloss was the daughter of Louis Lee and Pauline Williams Dixon Stanton, Sr. of Lawrence. Priscilla's brother Louis Lee Stanton, Jr. married Helena Parsons La Fetra and resided in Lawrence. Her brother William Tillinghast Stanton, who resided at *Dina House* in Hong Kong, married Elsa Burgess, the daughter of William H. Burgess. She had previously been married to Frank Fearson of New York and Robert Jardine Paterson of Shanghai, China.

Joseph Howland and Priscilla Dixon Stanton Auchincloss, Sr.'s son John Winthrop Auchincloss II married Audrey Maynard. Their son Joseph Howland Auchincloss, Jr. married Sarah Sedgwick Knapp. Their son Louis Stanton Auchincloss, the well-known writer, married Adele Lawrence. Their daughter Priscilla married William F. Pederson.

**Auchincloss, Samuel Sloan, Sr. (1873-1934)**

| | |
|---|---|
| Occupation(s): | merchant - member, Auchincloss Brothers, NYC (textile merchant) |
| | financier - partner, Auchincloss, Joust, and Patrick (stock brokerage firm) |
| Marriage(s): | M/1 – 1898-1905 – Anna Stavely Agnew (1873-1905) |
| | M/2 – 1910-div. 1915 – Emma Guidet (1870-1953) |
| | M/3 – 1918-div. 1932 – Anna M. Christian (1876-1956) |
| Address: | 350 Ocean Avenue, Lawrence |
| Name of estate: | *Whale Acres* |
| Year of construction: | c. 1914 |
| Style of architecture: | Neo-Federal |
| Architect(s): | William Adams, Jr. designed the house (for Perkins) |

Landscape architect(s):
House extant: yes
Historical notes:

The house, originally named *Whale Acres*, was built by Norton Perkins.

Samuel Sloan Auchincloss, Sr. was the son of Edgar Sterling and Maria La Grange Sloan Auchincloss.

Anna Stavely Agnew Auchincloss was the daughter of Dr. Cornelius Rea and Mrs. Mary Nash Agnew of Montauk. [*See* Spinzia, *Long Island's Prominent Families* in the Town of East Hampton – Agnew entry.]

Samuel Sloan and Anna Stavely Agnew Auchincloss, Sr.'s son Samuel Sloan Auchincloss II, who resided in Sands Point, married Dorothy Milburn, the daughter of John George and Madeleine Scratcherd Milburn, Jr., who resided at *Wychwood* in North Hills, and, subsequently, Lydia Knight Garrison, the daughter of Philip McKim and Marian Knight Garrison of Llewellyn Park, West Orange, NJ. [*See* Spinzia, *Long Island's Prominent North Shore Families, vol. I* – Auchincloss and Milburn entries.]

Auchincloss also had an estate, *Shadow Meade,* in Garrison, NY.

Emma Guidet Auchincloss had previously been married to Gustavus Abell Duryee, the son of Henry William and Mary Gertrude Abell Duryee.

The *Long Island Society Register, 1928* lists Samuel Sloan and Anna Christian Auchincloss [Sr.] as residing at *Whale Acres* in Lawrence.

She was the daughter of John Augustus and Mary Ellen Hall Christian. Anna subsequently married Roderick Don O'Connor and resided in Roslyn.

*front facade, 1918*

**Auerbach, John Hone, Sr. (1883-1962)**

| | |
|---|---|
| Occupation(s): | financier - partner, Auerbach, Pollak, and Richardson, NYC (stock brokerage firm) |
| Marriage(s): | M/1 – 1909-1925 – Dorothy Pennington Toler (1889-1925) |
| | M/2 – 1927-div. 1944 – Frederica Stevens (1907-2000) |
| | - Civic Activism: head of motor corps, Women's Voluntary Services, New York, during World War II |
| | M/3 – 1945-div. 1952 – Margaret Ines Zolnay (1905-2000) |
| Address: | Club Drive, Hewlett Harbor |
| Name of estate: | *Seawane* |
| Year of construction: | c. 1914 |
| Style of architecture: | Modified Neo-Georgian |
| Architect(s): | |
| Landscape architect(s): | |
| House extant: yes | |
| Historical notes: | |

The house, originally named *Seawane*, was built by Joseph Smith Auerbach.

John Hone Auerbach, Sr. was the son of Joseph Smith and Katharine Hone Auerbach.

John Hone and Dorothy Pennington Toler Auerbach, Sr.'s son John Hone Auerbach, Jr. married Carol Janet Praker, the daughter of Howard C. Praker of Tonawanda, NY.

The *Long Island Society Register, 1929* lists John Hone and Frederica Stevens Auerbach [Sr.] as residing at *Seawane* in Hewlett [Hewlett Harbor.]

She was the daughter of Frederic William and Alice Caroline Seely Stevens. Frederica later married Philippe Bernard and resided in Paris, France.

John Hone and Frederica Stevens Auerbach, Sr.'s daughter Mary married Howard Neeham, the son of Carl L. Needham of San Francisco, CA. Their daughter Eugenie married Jean Paul Angles, the son of Raoul and Madeline Angles of Paris, France. Their son Philip married Joelle Denize, the daughter of Robert Denize of Paris, France. Their daughter Joan married LeRoy King, Jr. of *Indian Spring* in Newport, RI. Their daughter Frederica married Robert Weir Barney, the son of James E. Barney of Great Neck.

Margaret Zolnay Auerbach was the daughter of George Julian and Abigail Rowan Gillim Zolnay of Manhattan. She had previously been married to John Churchill Newcomb.

The main residence is now the clubhouse of the Seawane Golf Club.

By 1939 the Auerbachs had relocated to *Sunninghill* in Glen Head.

*[See following entry for additional family information.]*

*front / side facade*

## Auerbach, Joseph Smith (1855-1944)

| | |
|---|---|
| Occupation(s): | attorney - partner, Davies, Auerbach, Cornell, and Hardy, NYC |
| | capitalist - director, City & Suburban Homes Co.; |
| | director, Long Island Rail Road |
| | financier - trustee, Mutual Life Insurance Co.; |
| | director, Queen Bank; |
| | director, Knickerbocker Trust Co.; |
| | director, Lawyers Mortgage Insurance Co.; |
| | director, Audit Company of New York |
| | industrialist - director, Mechanical Rubber Co. |
| | writer - *The Lessons of Bishop Potter's Life*, 1912; |
| | *Essays and Miscellanies*, 1914-1923 (3 vols.); |
| | *The Bible and Modern Life*, 1914; |
| | *A Club*, 1915; |
| | *DeLancey Nicoll: An Appreciation*; |
| | *The Bar of Other Days*, 1940 |
| Civic Activism: | trustee, Village of Hewlett Harbor |
| Marriage(s): | 1881-1923 – Catharine Hone (1858-1923) |
| Address: | Club Drive, Hewlett Harbor |
| Name of estate: | *Seawane* |
| Year of construction: | c. 1914 |
| Style of architecture: | Modified Neo-Georgian |
| Architect(s): | |
| Landscape architect(s): | |
| House extant: yes | |
| Historical notes: | |

The house, originally named *Seawane*, was built by Joseph Smith Auerbach.

The *Long Island Society Register, 1929* lists Joseph S. Auerbach as residing in Hewlett [Hewlett Harbor.]

He was the son of Dr. Julius and Mrs. Alice Ann Cornell Auerbach of New York.

Catharine Hone Auerbach was the daughter of John P. and Susan J. Miller Hone and the granddaughter of New York City Mayor Philip Hone.*

Joseph Smith and Catharine Hone Auerbach's son John, who inherited the house, continued to call it *Seawane*. Their daughter Helen, who also resided at *Seawane*, married Herman LeRoy Emmet II. The Emmets later relocated to Erie, PA.

The estate's main residence is now the clubhouse of the Seawane Golf Club.

*Honesdale, PA, is named in honor of Philip Hone.

*[See previous entry for additional family information.]*

*rear facade*

**Ayer, Frederick, II (1908-1998)**

| | |
|---|---|
| Occupation(s): | educator - member, physics department, New York University, NYC; |
| | member, physics department, University of Colorado, Boulder, CO; |
| | member, physics department, Sarah Lawrence College, Bronxville, NY |
| | scientist - physicist, energy research, Brookhaven National Laboratory, Upton, NY |
| | writer - *Memories of an Unplanned Life*, 1988 (autobiography); |
| | articles on his experiences collecting orchids in Ethiopia; |
| | compiled grammar on Balinese language; |
| | wrote chapter in Air Force's report, "Scientific Study of Unidentified Flying Objects," 1969 |
| Civic Activism: | a benefactor and trustee, Masters and Johnson Institute, St. Louis, MO; |
| | funded research into UFOs; |
| | funded research for corneal transplants; |
| | funded research for connection between emotional disturbance and cancer; |
| | funded DNA research at Burke Museum of Natural History and Culture, University of Washington, Seattle, WA; |
| | trustee, American Geographic Society, NY; |
| | founder, Ayer Foundation; |
| | trustee, A Contemporary Theater, Seattle, WA; |
| | trustee, Seattle Symphony, Seattle, WA |
| Marriage(s): | M/1 – 1930- div.1946 – Elizabeth Jenney (1909-2000) |
| | M/2 – 1946-div. 1966 – Marcella Flood (1913-2009) |
| | - model |
| | M/3 – 1966-1998 – Rosa Hahn (1924-2000) |
| | - entertainers and associated professions - |
| | a founder, The Playcrafters, Bellport, NY, theater group; |
| | summer stock actress and singer |
| | Civic Activism: trustee, Seattle Repertory Theater, Seattle, WA; |
| | trustee, Seattle Opera, Seattle WA |
| Address: | Stevenson Road, Hewlett |
| Name of estate: | |
| Year of construction: | |
| Style of architecture: | Colonial Revival |
| Architect (s): | |
| Landscape architect(s): | |
| House extant: unconfirmed` | |
| Historical notes: | |

   The *Social Register New York, 1933* lists Frederick and Betty Jenney Ayer II as residing on Stevenson Road, Hewlett.
   He was the son of Dr. James Cook and Mrs. May Candee Hancock Ayer of *Shadowland* in Glen Cove. [*See* Spinzia, *Long Island's Prominent North Shore Families, vol. I* – Ayer entry.] His brother Richard married Mary Eleanore Potter, the daughter of Edward Clarkson and Emily Blanche Havemeyer Potter, Sr., who resided in Glen Cove. [*See* Spinzia, *Long Island's Prominent North Shore Families, vol. II* – Potter entry.]
   Elizabeth Jenney was the daughter of William Sherman and Nina Bevan Jenney of *Little Close* in East Hampton. Elizabeth subsequently married Richard Draper Richards and resided at *Little Too Close* in East Hampton. [*See* Spinzia, *Long Island's Prominent Families in the Town of East Hampton* – Jenney and Richards entries.]
   Frederick and Elizabeth Jenney Ayer II's son Anthony married Roberta Still, the daughter of Professor Richard R. Still of Syracuse, NY, and, later, Nancy Sumwalt with whom he resides on Orcas Island in Eastsound, WA. Their son James, who married Jutta Eisold and, later, Elizabeth Tyler, resides in Marblehead, MA. Their son Frederick Ayer III married Claire Sylvie Labourel, the daughter of André Labourel of Paris, France, and resides in East Hampton. [*See* Spinzia, *Long Island's Prominent Families in the Town of East Hampton* – Ayer entry.]
   Rosa Hahn Ayer was the daughter of Dr. James Pendleton Hahn of Hartington, NE. She had previously been married to Frederick Paine and Dwain Houston White with whom she resided in Bellport.
   [For information about Frederick's Locust Valley residence, *see* Spinzia, *Long Island's Prominent North Shore Families, vol. I* – Ayer entry.]

*front facade, 1932*

### Backus, Henry Clinton (1848-1908)

Occupation(s): attorney - partner, Beebe, Wilcox, and Hobbs

Marriage(s): 1891-1908 – Harriet Ivins Davis (d. 1941)
- Civic Activism: vice-president, Woman's Municipal League
(anti-suffrage organization);
actively opposed woman's suffrage*;
member, Association Opposed to Woman's
Suffrage;
member of board, New York Colored Orphan
Asylum

Address: 111 Seventh Street, Garden City
Name of estate:
Year of construction:
Style of architecture: Condominium
Architect(s):
Landscape architect(s):
House extant: yes
Historical notes:

The *Long Island Society Register, 1929* lists Harriet Ivins Davis Bachus as residing at 111 Seventh Street, Garden City.
Henry Clinton Backus was the son of Charles Chapman and Harriet Newell Baldwin Backus of Utica, NY.
Harriet Ivins Davis Backus was the daughter of Wilmer and Jane Hastings Davis.
Henry Clinton and Harriet Ivins Davis Backus' son Clinton, a bachelor, died at the age of thirty-five. Their daughter Harriet was an infant at the time of her death.
*For other Long Islanders involved in the suffrage movement *see* Raymond E. Spinzia, "Winning the Franchise: Long Island Activists in the Fight for Woman's Suffrage and Their Opponents, Long Island's Anti-Suffragists." wwwspinzialongislandestates.com.
[For information about the Backus' East Hampton residence, *see* Spinzia, *Long Island's Prominent families in the Town of East Hampton* – Backus entry.]


### Baker, Elwood Wilson (b. 1882)

Occupation(s): industrialist - manager, Condé Nast Engravers, Inc.;
member, Offset Printing Co.;
president, Baker Offset Co.

Marriage(s): 1924 – Winifred Tate (b. 1888)

Address: 12 Euston Road, Garden City
Name of estate:
Year of construction: 1923
Style of architecture: Colonial Revival

Architect(s):
Landscape architect(s):
House extant: yes
Historical notes:

*front facade, 2000*

The *Long Island Society Register, 1929* lists Elwood W. and Winifred Tate Baker as residing at 12 Euston Road, Garden City.
He was the son of Elwood Thomas Baker of Brooklyn.
Elwood Wilson and Winifred Tate Baker's son Elwood Tate Baker married Leonie de Milhau Vosburgh, the daughter of Peter C. Vosburgh of Northampton, MA. The younger Baker was serving aboard the USS *Missouri* when the representatives of the Emperor of Japan signed the instrument of surrender.

### Baldwin, William Mood (1862-1942)

| | |
|---|---|
| Occupation(s): | industrialist - president, New York Tanning Extract Co., (later, American Dyewood Co.); |
| | director, American Dyewood Co.; |
| | vice-president and treasurer, Argentine Quebracho; |
| | director, International Products Co. |
| Civic Activism: | chairman of trustees, State Institute of Applied Agriculture, Farmingdale; |
| | chairman, fund-raising committee, Flower Hospital; |
| | president, executive committee, Nassau Hospital, Mineola; |
| | a founder, first president, and director, Cherry Valley Club, Garden City, 1916 |
| Marriage(s): | 1887-1938 – Lydia Perry Cowl (1858-1938) |
| | - Civic Activism: a founder, Nassau Hospital, Mineola; |
| | chairman, training school committee, Nassau Hospital, Mineola; |
| | a founder, Working Girls Vacation Society |
| Address: | Cathedral Avenue, Garden City |
| Name of estate: | *Seven acres* |
| Year of construction: | |
| Style of architecture: | Neo-Tudor |
| Architect(s): | |
| Landscape architect(s): | Hicks Nursery supplied the Red Cedar plantings for a windbreak (for Baldwin) |
| House extant: unconfirmed | |

*c. 1908*

Historical notes:

The *Social Register Summer, 1910* lists William M. and Lydia P. Cowl Baldwin as residing in Garden City.

He was the son of Joseph Clark and Emma Jane Mood Baldwin of Manhattan.

Lydia Perry Cowl Baldwin was the daughter of William Henry and Mary Ann Augusta Yeomans Cowl.

William Mood and Lydia Perry Cowl Baldwin's daughter Ruth married Colonel Roger G. Alexander. Their daughter Dorothy married Dr. Edgar Lorrington Gilcreest; James William Walsh III of Lawrence; and, subsequently, Thomas Buel with whom she resided in Manhattan. Their daughter Alice married Francis W. Murphy. Their daughter Mary married Conrad Godwin Goddard and resided at *Montrose* in Roslyn Harbor. Conrad Godwin Goddard was son of Frederick M. and Minna Goodwin, who resided at *Clovercroft* in Roslyn Harbor. [*See* Spinzia, *Long Island's Prominent North Shore Families, vol. 1* – Goddard entry.]

In 1924, Baldwin sold his seven-acre estate to Edward Quinby McVitty for a reputed $135,000. [*The Brooklyn Daily Eagle* April 23, 1924, p. 21.] McVitty renamed the estate *Garstead*.

### Ballantine, Herbert Wilgus, Sr. (1893-1979)

| | |
|---|---|
| Occupation(s): | industrialist - chairman of board and treasurer, Neptune Meter Co. (later, Neptune International Corp.) |
| Marriage(s): | 1918 – Marguerite Louise Small (b. 1897) |
| Address: | 17 Piermont Avenue, Hewlett Bay Park |
| Name of estate: | *Meadowview* |
| Year of construction: | |
| Style of architecture: | |
| Architect(s): | |
| Landscape architect(s): | |
| House extant: no | |

Historical notes:

The *Social Register Summer, 1937* lists Herbert W. and Marguerite Louise Small Ballantine [Sr.] as residing in Hewlett [Hewlett Bay Park]. The 1930 Census lists them at this address.

He was the son of John Herbert and Lois Naomi Wilgus Ballantine of Lawrence.

Marguerite Louise Small Ballantine was the daughter of Charles Small of Brooklyn and *Beach Hill* in Westhampton Beach. Marguerite's sister Carol married Edwin Shuttleworth, Jr. and resided in Westhampton Beach and Quiogue. [*See* Spinzia, *Long Island's Prominent Families in the Town Southampton* – Shuttleworth and Small entries.] Her sister Suzanne married Lewis P. Buckner, the son of Walter Buckner of Manhattan.

Herbert Wilgus and Marguerite Louise Small Ballantine, Sr.'s daughter Marguerite married Emlen Williams Holmes II, the son of the president of New York Law School Jabish Holmes, Sr. of Manhattan; Neilson Olcott; and, subsequently, Haven Putnam, Sr. Their daughter Alice married William Harold Bush, the son of Henry Bush of Lexington, KY. Their son Herbert Wilgus Ballantine, Jr. married Elizabeth Frances Irving, the daughter of Dr. Albert J. Irving of Manhattan.

*[See other Ballantine entries for additional family information.]*

### Ballantine, John Herbert, II (1867-1946)

| | |
|---|---|
| Occupation(s): | industrialist - president, Neptune Meter Co. (later, Neptune International Corp.); president, American Pastry Manufacturing Co. |
| Marriage(s): | M/1 – 1890-1919 – Lois Naomi Wilgus (d. 1919) <br> M/2 – Gertrude Williams Drake (1870-1958) |
| Address: | Albro Lane, Lawrence |
| Name of estate: | |
| Year of construction: | c. 1915 |
| Style of architecture: | Neo-Tudor |
| Architect(s): | |
| Landscape architect(s): | |
| House extant: unconfirmed | |
| Historical notes: | |

The house was built by John Herbert Ballantine, II.

His father John Holme Ballantine, Sr. was the founder of the Ballantine Brewery.

Lois Naomi Wilgus Ballantine was the daughter of John Butler and Margaret Standart Wilgus of Cleveland, OH.

John Herbert and Lois Naomi Wilgus Ballantine II's son John, who resided at *Holmeridge* in Woodsburgh, married Helen Ridgely Morgan and, later, Dorothy Bortz. Their son Herbert married Marguerite Louise Small and resided in Hewlett Bay Park.

The *Long Island Society Register, 1929* lists John Herbert and Gertrude W. Drake Ballantine [II] as residing at *Holmdene* in Kings Point. [*See* Spinzia, *Long Island's Prominent North Shore Families, vol. I* – Ballantine entry.]

*[Other Ballantine entries precede and follow. See those entries for additional family information.]*

*front facade*

### Ballantine, John Holme, II (1892-1976)

| | |
|---|---|
| Occupation(s): | industrialist - president and director, Neptune Meter Co. (later, Neptune International Corp.) |
| Marriage(s): | M/1 – 1915-1963 – Helen Ridgely Morgan (1896-1963) <br> M/2 – Dorothy Bortz |
| Address: | South End Road, Woodsburgh |
| Name of estate: | *Holmeridge* |
| Year of construction: | |
| Style of architecture: | |
| Architect(s): | |
| Landscape architect(s): | |
| House extant: unconfirmed | |
| Historical notes: | |

The *Long Island Society Register, 1929* lists John Holme and Helen Ridgely Morgan Ballantine [II] as residing at *Holmeridge* in Woodmere [Woodsburgh]. The 1930 Census lists the Ballantines at this address.

He was the son of John Herbert and Lois Naomi Wilgus Ballantine II.

Helen Ridgely Morgan Ballantine was the daughter of Lancaster and Letitia Goodwin Morgan III of Manhattan.

John Holme and Helen Ridgely Morgan Ballantine II's daughter Helen married Wentworth Smith, the son of Stuart Smith of Lexington, MA, and resided at *Greenfield Hill* in Fairfield, CT. Their son Morgan died in 1926 at the age of five.

The *Social Register Summer, 1932* lists the Ballantines as residing at *Overbrook Farm* in Southbury, CT.

*[See other Ballantine entries for additional family information.]*

### Banks, Harold Purdy (1887-1968)

| | |
|---|---|
| Occupation(s): | engineer -  president, Banks & Sons (engineering firm) |
| | industrialist -  manager, metal ore department, W. R. Grace & Co., NYC; |
| | manager, Frank Samuel & Co., Philadelphia, PA |
| Marriage(s): | 1919-1968 – Amo Pauline Sessions (1894-1967) |
| Address: | 4 Combs Avenue, Woodmere |
| Name of estate: | |
| Year of construction: | |
| Style of architecture: | |
| Architect(s): | |
| Landscape architect(s): | |
| House extant: yes | |
| Historical notes: | |

The *Long Island Society Register, 1929* lists Harold P. and Amo P. Sessions Banks as residing on Combs Avenue, Hewlett [Woodmere].

He was the son of John H. and Emilie S. Hultsch Banks of Manhattan.

Harold Purdy and Amo Pauline Sessions Banks' son John married Jean Paige Flanagan, the daughter of John Roberts Flanagan, and resided in Rowayton, CT. Their daughter Emilie married Arthur Damarest Dague, the son of Bryon Scott Dague.

At the time of his death, Banks was residing at 150 Woodside Drive, Hewlett Bay Park. [*The New York Times* October 12, 1968, p. 37.]

*150 Woodside Drive,
front / side facade, 2000*

### Bannerman, Parry Elwood (1892-1951)

| | |
|---|---|
| Occupation(s): | industrialist -  sales executive, Murphy Varnish Co. |
| Marriage(s): | 1917-1951 – Marion Tiffany Marsh (1894-1980) |
| Address: | 610 Front Street, Hempstead |
| Name of estate: | |
| Year of construction: | c. 1928 |
| Style of architecture: | Colonial Revival |
| Architect(s): | |
| Landscape architect(s): | |
| House extant: yes | |
| Historical notes: | |

The house was built by Parry Elwood Bannerman.

The *Long Island Society Register, 1929* lists Parry Elwood and Marion Tiffany Marsh Bannerman as residing on Front Street, Hempstead.

*front facade, 2008*

Marion Tiffany Marsh Bannerman was the daughter of Darius Augustus and Prudence Estelle Tiffany Marsh.

Parry Elwood and Marion Tiffany Marsh Bannerman's daughter Jean married Richard Marchand Hesselman, the son of Leo W. Hesselman of Kilburn Road, Garden City. Their daughter Ruth married William Roxbury Hart, the son of William Henry Hart of Manhattan.

The Bannermans' daughter Lois married Harold John Henrich; John L. Senior, Jr.; and, later, Howard Crawford. At the age of ten, Lois fought off would be kidnappers with her roller skates and managed to escape from their car. By the time Lois was fifteen, she was winning major awards as a harpist and at the age of sixteen was invited to perform at the White House. She had a long career as a harpist, appearing with major orchestras, and performing on television and on Broadway.

At the time of his death, Parry Elwood Bannerman was residing at 610 Front Street, Hempstead. [*The New York Times* May 22, 1951, p. 31.]

### Barnard, John Augustus (1871-1958)

| | |
|---|---|
| Occupation(s): | financier - director, Home Life Insurance Co., NYC; partner, Dominick & Dominick Co., NYC |
| | industrialist - director, Crosley Radio Co. |
| Civic Activism: | trustee, Museum of The City of New York, 1937-1958; |
| | trustee, Clear Pool Camp, Carmel, NY (summer camp for underprivileged children) |
| Marriage(s): | M/1 – 1911-1948 – Margaret Ruth Lawrence Walsh (1883-1948) |
| | M/2 – 1949 – Ruth Alms |
| | - Civic Activism - donated paintings to the Metropolitan Museum of Art, NYC |
| Address: | Bannister Lane, Lawrence |
| Name of estate: | *Tigh-na-Curach* |
| Year of construction: | |
| Style of architecture: | |
| Architect(s): | Stanford White designed the house* |
| Landscape architect(s): | |
| House extant: unconfirmed | |
| Historical notes: | |

The *Social Register Summer, 1929* lists J. Augustus and Margaret R. L. Walsh Barnard as residing at *Tigh-na-Curach* in Lawrence.

He was the son of Horace B. and Louisa Augusta Zerega Barnard of Manhattan and a descendant of Augustus Porter Barnard for whom Barnard College in New York City is named.

Margaret Lawrence Walsh Barnard was the daughter of James W. and Susan Newbold Lawrence Walsh, Jr., who resided in Lawrence.

John Augustus and Margaret Ruth Lawrence Walsh Barnard's son John Lawrence Barnard married Diana Kissel. *[See following entry for additional family information.]*

Ruth Alms was the daughter of John Sorgel Alms of Cincinnati, OH.

*John Lawrence Barnard. *Gently Down the Stream: Notes from an Endangered Species*. (New York: Walker and Co., 1976), p. 8.

### Barnard, John Lawrence (1912-1977)

| | |
|---|---|
| Occupation(s): | diplomat - United States Consul, Antwerp, Belgium, 1954-1959; |
| | United States Consul General, Aruba, 1960; |
| | United States Consul General, Bahamas, 1960-1966 |
| | intelligence agent - military intelligence during World War II; |
| | member, Office of Intelligence Research, United States Department of State |
| | writer - *Revelry By Night*, 1941 (novel); *Land of Promise*, 1942 (novel); |
| | *Gently Down the Stream: Notes from an Endangered Species*, 1976 (autobiography) |
| Marriage(s): | 1938-1977 – Diana Kissel (1919-2009) |
| Address: | Albert Place, Lawrence |
| Name of estate: | |
| Year of construction: | |
| Style of architecture: | |
| Architect(s): | |
| Landscape architect(s): | |
| House extant: unconfirmed | |
| Historical notes: | |

In 1941 John Lawrence Barnard rented the house of Albert Ralph Stephan. [*The Brooklyn Daily Eagle* May 11, 1941, p. B3.]

He was the son of John Augustus and Margaret Ruth Lawrence Walsh Barnard of *Tigh-na-Curach* in Lawrence.

Diana Kissel Barnard was the daughter of Rudolph Hermann and Irene Turnure Kissel, Jr.

John Lawrence and Diana Kissel Barnard's daughter Daphne married Michael Hamilton Davis, the son of Daniel A. Davis of Manhattan, and resided in Stonington, CT. Their daughter Sylvia married Meredith Mason Brown, the son of John Mason Brown II. Their daughter Pamela married Jeffrey Fraiser Ruzicka, the son of James Ruzicka of Wisconsin, and resided in Stonington, CT.

*[See previous entry for additional family information.]*

### Barnes, Roderic Barbour (1882-1954)

| | |
|---|---|
| Occupation(s): | architect* |
| Marriage(s): | 1911-1954 – Rose Marie Naething (1891-1987) |
| Address: | Ocean Avenue and Briarwood Crossing, Lawrence |

Name of estate:
Year of construction:
Style of architecture:
Architect(s):
Landscape architect(s):
House extant: unconfirmed
Historical notes:

    The *Long Island Society Register, 1929* lists Roderic Barbour and Rose Marie Naething Barnes as residing in Lawrence. The *Social Register Summer, 1932* lists the Barneses as residing at *Belle Hill* in Washington, CT.
    He was the son of Richard Storrs and Harriet Day Barbour Barnes.
    Rose Marie Naething Barnes was the daughter of Charles Frederick and Mary Louise Bingham Naething.
    Roderic Barbour and Rose Marie Naething Barnes' daughter Louise married Jessie Angell Hall, the son of John Raymond and Louise Twichell Hall of Washington, CT. Their daughter Rosemary married Ernest Allan Akins, the son of Ernest Norwood and Elizabeth Allison Howard Akins. Their son Richard married Katherine Ward Watkins, the daughter of Edward Francis and Louise Ward Watkins.
    *Barnes designed the Tower Club building at Princeton and the library in Great Barrington, MA. [*The New York Times* May 14, 1954, p. 23.]

### Barnum, Joshua Willets (1847-1906)

| | |
|---|---|
| Occupation(s): | merchant - Joshua Barnum & Son (later, S. C. Barnum & Co.) |
| Civic Activism: | president, Queens County Game Association |
| Marriage(s): | Mary Richmond Taylor (1848-1931) |
| Address: | Merrick Avenue, East Meadow |
| Name of estate: | *Meadow Brook Farm* |

Year of construction:
Style of architecture:
Architect(s):
Landscape architect(s):
House extant: unconfirmed
Historical notes:

    He was the son of Peter Crosby and Sarah Ann Baldwin Barnum from whom he inherited *Meadow Brook Farm*.
    Mary Richmond Taylor Barnum was the daughter of Joseph Burnap and Sarah Felthausen Taylor.
    Joshua Willets and Mary Richmond Taylor Barnum's daughter Maie married Frederick Leighton Harris of Brooklyn, who died some six months after their marriage due to complications from an appendicitis operation. [*The New York Times* March 8, 1908, p. 7.] Maie then married Leo Frederick Florian Warner and, subsequently, Hiram D. West.

### Barnum, Peter Crosby (1816-1889)

| | |
|---|---|
| Occupation(s): | merchant - partner, Joshua Barnum & Son (later, Joshua Barnum & Son and, subsequently, S. C. Barnum & Co.); capitalist - director, New York and Hempstead Railroad |
| Civic Activism: | president, Queens County Agricultural Society |
| Marriage(s): | M/1 – Frances Maria Barnum (1819-1844) |
| | M/2 – Sarah Ann Baldwin (1814-1893) |
| | - Civic Activism*: chair, Ladies Visiting Committee, Barnum Island Poor Farm; chair, Queens County Agricultural Society Ladies Aid |
| Address: | Merrick Avenue, East Meadow |
| Name of estate: | *Meadow Brook Farm* |
| Year of construction: | |
| Style of architecture: | |
| Architect(s): | |
| Landscape architect(s): | |
| House extant: unconfirmed | |
| Historical notes: | |

    Peter Crosby Barnum was the son of Stephen Crosby and Hannah Rundle Barnum.
    Sarah Ann Baldwin Barnum was the daughter of Thomas and Susan Baldwin of Baldwin. Sarah had previously been married to Samuel Carman.
    *Hearing that a syndicate wanted to purchase Hog Island to construct a summer hotel, Sarah rode ten miles to the island in a snowstorm and purchased the island for $13,360, outwitting the syndicate which was, purportedly, offering $75,000. She then sold the island to Queens County for use as a farm for the poor. The island was renamed Barnum Island in her honor. It was later the site of a smallpox hospital.
    Sarah was also instrumental in convincing the county's farmers to vote for a bill that would allow Queens County to permit the sale of the county's common land thereby enabling A. T. Stewart to purchase land in what would become the Village of Garden City. The farmers' vote was a slim victory, 650 to 630, but an Island-changing vote nonetheless.
    Peter Crosby and Sarah Ann Baldwin Barnum's daughter Kate remained unmarried. Their son Joshua, who inherited *Meadow Brook Farm*, married Mary Richmond Taylor.
*[See previous entry for additional family information.]*

### Barrett, Gilbert Conklin, Sr. (1889-1967)

| | |
|---|---|
| Occupation(s): | financier - president and chairman of board, Brooklyn Savings Bank |
| Civic Activism: | director, American Red Cross, Brooklyn chapter; trustee and assistant treasurer, Brooklyn Hospital; trustee, Brooklyn Institute of Arts and Sciences; trustee, St. Christopher Hospital for Babies; chairman, governing committee, Brooklyn Children's Museum; member, advisory board, The Salvation Army |
| Marriage(s): | 1916 – Marguerite Simmons (b. 1889) |
| Address: | Nassau Place, Hempstead |
| Name of estate: | |
| Year of construction: | |
| Style of architecture: | |
| Architect(s): | |
| Landscape architect(s): | |
| House extant: unconfirmed | |
| Historical notes: | |

    The *Long Island Society Register, 1929* lists Gilbert Conklin and Marguerite Simmons Barrett [Sr.] as residing on Nassau Place, Hempstead.
    He was the son of Harry Freeman and Helen H. Conklin Barrett of Brooklyn.
    Marguerite Simmons Barrett was the daughter of Francis Rutledge Simmons of Brooklyn.
    Gilbert Conklin and Marguerite Simmons Barrett, Sr.'s daughter Jean married Maurice Joseph Fitzgerald, the son of Maurice Fitzgerald of Fort Smith, AR. Their son Gilbert Conklin Barrett, Jr. resided in Connecticut.

### Bateson, Edgar Farrar, Sr. (1887-1962)

| | |
|---|---|
| Occupation(s): | attorney |
| Civic Activism: | member, Manhattan County Bar Committee on Aeronautical Law, 1939; member, Manhattan Draft Board, 1940 |
| Marriage(s): | 1914-1962 - Rosina H. Otis (d. 1978) |
| Address: | Osborne Avenue, Lawrence |
| Name of estate: | *South Wind* |
| Year of construction: | |
| Style of architecture: | |
| Architect(s): | |
| Landscape architect(s): | |
| House extant: unconfirmed | |
| Historical notes: | |

Edgar Farrar Bateson, Sr. was the son of Charles Edward and Mary McLaughlin Stamps Bateson, who resided in NYC. His mother was a great-niece of Jefferson Davis, President of the Confederate States of America. [*The New York Times* March 24, 1950, p. 25.]

The *Long Island Society Register, 1929* lists E. Farrar and Rosina H. Otis Bateson [Sr.] as residing at *South Wind* in Lawrence. The *Social Register Summer, 1937* lists E. Farrar and Rosina H. Otis Bateson [Sr.] as residing at *Deramore* in Cold Spring Harbor. [*See* Spinzia, *Long Island's Prominent North Shore Families, vol. 1* – Bateson entry.] The *Social Register, 1978* lists Rosina H. Otis Bateson, then residing on East Gate Road, Lloyd Harbor.

Edgar Farrar and Rosina Hoyt Otis Bateson, Sr.'s daughter Rosina Elizabeth married Francis Jamison Rue of Manhattan. Their daughter Florence married Loren Curtis Berry and resided in Cold Spring Harbor. Their son Edgar Farrar Bateson, Jr. married Virginia Moffat, whose parents Douglas Maxwell and Gertrude Mali Moffat resided at *Annandale* in Cold Spring Harbor. [*See* Spinzia, *Long Island's Prominent North Shore Families, vol. 1* – Moffat entry.]


### Beadleston, Chauncey Perry (1886-1940)

| | |
|---|---|
| Occupation(s): | financier - partner, Teft and Co. (bond brokerage firm); partner, McDonnell and Co. (stock brokerage firm) |
| Civic Activism: | member, race committee, Rockaway Steeplechase Association, 1937; director, Atlantic Beach Club, 1937 |
| Marriage(s): | 1917-1940 – Eleanor Baxter (1895-1954) |
| Address: | Everit Avenue, Hewlett Bay Park |
| Name of estate: | |
| Year of construction: | |
| Style of architecture: | |
| Architect(s): | |
| Landscape architect(s): | Louise Payson, 1930 (for Beadleston) |
| House extant: unconfirmed | |
| Historical notes: | |

The *Long Island Society Register, 1929* lists the Beadlestons as residing in Hewlett [Hewlett Bay Park].

He was the son of William Henry and Susan Annie Colwell Beadleston of East Hampton.

Eleanor Baxter Beadleston was the daughter of the Territorial Governor of Wyoming (1886) George White Baxter and Mrs. Margaret White McGhee Baxter of East Hampton. [*See* Spinzia, *Long Island's Prominent Families in the Town of East Hampton* – Baxter entry.] Eleanor subsequently married James Clarke Milholland of Hewlett Harbor. Her sister Cornelia married Hugh Tevis, Sr. of San Francisco, CA, and, later, Evelyn Toulimin of London, England. Her sister Margaret married Albert Volney Foster and resided in Lake Forest, IL. Her sister Katharine married Russell Burrage of Boston, MA. Her brother Charles married Marcella Virginia Andrews, the daughter of Matthew Andrews of Cleveland, OH.

Chauncey Perry and Eleanor Baxter Beadleston's daughter Margaret married Evarts Ziegler, the son of Edmé Ziegler of NYC. Their daughter Edith married Francis Inman Amory III, the son of Francis Inman and Margaret Mae Perin Amory, Jr.

### Becker, Claude M. (1876-1960)

| | |
|---|---|
| Occupation(s): | publisher - business manager, Tablet Publishing Co. (Catholic weekly newspaper) |
| Civic Activism: | member, Brooklyn Chamber of Commerce; president, Catholic Press Association, 1920-1922; secretary and president, The Cathedral Club, Brooklyn, 1902-1904 (Roman Catholic Lay Organization); director, Roman Catholic Orphan Asylum Society; director, Emerald Society |
| Marriage(s): | 1907-1960 – Mary Collord O'Connor (1883-1963) |
| Address: | 116 Fourth Street, Garden City |
| Name of estate: | |
| Year of construction: | 1918 |
| Style of architecture: | Georgian Revival |
| Architect(s): | |
| Landscape architect(s): | |
| House extant: yes | |
| Historical notes: | |

*front facade*

The *Long Island Society Register, 1929* lists Mrs. Claude M. Becker as residing on Fourth Street, Garden City.

She was the daughter of Michael Edmund and Francis Miller O'Connor of Brooklyn.

Claude M. Becker was the son of Joseph F. Becker of Brooklyn.

Claude M. and Mary Collord O'Connor Becker's daughter Frances married Joseph A. Keenan, Jr. of Brooklyn and resided in Arlington, VA. Their son David married Ruth Louise Collord, the daughter of Frank Mortimer Collord.

### Beebe, Henry Ward (1887-1960)

| | |
|---|---|
| Occupation(s): | financier - director, Brown, Harriman, and Co., Inc. (later, Harriman, Ripley, and Co.) (investment banking firm); vice-president and director, Harriman, Ripley, and Co. (investment banking firm); trustee, The Green Point Savings Bank |
| Civic Activism: | chairman, District Committee 13, National Security Dealers Inc.; member, board of governors, National Security Dealers Inc. |
| Marriage(s): | Edna Alice Eldridge (b. 1889) <br> - Civic Activism: chair, Garden City–Hempstead Community Club, 1944 |
| Address: | 87 Second Street, Garden City |
| Name of estate: | |
| Year of construction: | 1957 |
| Style of architecture: | Split-Level |
| Architect(s): | |
| Landscape architect(s): | |
| House extant: yes | |
| Historical notes: | |

Edna Alice Eldridge Beebe was the daughter of John Kingsley Eldridge of Freeport.

Henry Ward and Edna Alice Eldridge Beebe's son John married Margaret Sands Hubbell, the daughter of Sherwood and Helen Sands Nostrand Hubbell of Garden City and resided in Garden City.

*[See following entry for additional family information.]*

In 1970 the house was remodeled.

*front facade, 2008*

**Beebe, John Eldridge, Sr. (1923-2016)**

Occupation(s): financier - vice-president and director, Paine, Webber, Jackson, and Curtis (stock brokerage firm)

Marriage(s): 1945-2016 – Margaret Sands Hubbell (b. 1927)

Address: 118 Euston Road, Garden City
Name of estate:
Year of construction: 1930
Style of architecture: Colonial Revival
Architect(s):
Landscape architect(s):
House extant: yes
Historical notes:

   John Eldridge Beebe, Sr. was the son of Henry Ward and Edna Alice Eldridge Beebe of Garden City.
   Margaret Sands Hubbell Beebe was the daughter of Sherwood and Helen Sands Nostrand Hubbell of Garden City.
   John Eldridge and Margaret Sands Hubbell Beebe, Sr.'s daughter Martha married Kenneth Emerson Knowles III of Oyster Bay. Their son John Eldridge Beebe, Jr. married Ravenel Weekes, the daughter of Bradford Gage Weckes of Oyster Bay.
   By 1975 the Beebes had relocated to Oyster Bay.
*[See previous entry of additional family information.]*
   In 2019, the four-bedroom, five-bath, 2,496-square-foot-house sold for $1.3 million.

*front facade, 2009*

### Belcher, Edwin Willoughby, Jr. (1864-1929)

Occupation(s): industrialist - secretary, treasurer, and director, American Hard Rubber, Co., Brooklyn

Marriage(s): Mary Halsey Seymour (b. 1865)
- Civic Activism: vice-president, Guild of the Cathedral of the Incarnation, Garden City

Address: 88 Eleventh Street, Garden City
Name of estate:
Year of construction:
Style of architecture:
Architect(s):
Landscape architect(s):
House extant: no
Historical notes:

The *Long Island Society Register, 1929* lists Mary Halsey Seymour Belcher as residing on Eleventh Street, Garden City.

Edwin Willoughby and Mary Halsey Seymour Belcher, Jr.'s son Stephen married Arline B. Cadmus, the daughter of George G. Cadmus. Their son Edwin Seymour Belcher married Helen Elizabeth Hull, the daughter of George Frederick Hull of Larchmont, NY.

At the time of his death, Edwin W. Belcher, Jr. was residing at 88 Eleventh Street, Garden City. [*The New York Times* January 3, 1929, p. 21.]

*August Belmont II's estate, Blemton Manor, front facade*

**Belmont, August, II (1853-1924)**

| | |
|---|---|
| Occupation(s): | financier - partner, Belmont and Co. (investment banking firm); trustee, Bank for Savings, NYC |
| | capitalist - chairman of board, Interborough Rapid Transit Co.; chairman of board, Rapid Transit Subway Construction Co.; president, Boston, Cape Cod, and New York Canal Co. |
| Marriage(s): | M/1 – 1881-1898 – Elizabeth Hamilton Morgan (1862-1898)* |
| | M/2 – 1910-1924 – Eleanor Robson (1879-1979) |
| | - entertainers and associated professions - actress |
| | writer - *The Fabric of Memory,* 1957 |
| | Civic Activism: |
| | a founder, Working Girls Vacation Association; |
| | founder, SPUGS, Society for the Prevention of Useless Giving; |
| | assistant to Red Cross War Council during World War I; |
| | chairman, National Council for Home Nursing Courses; |
| | chairman, Women's Division of the Emergency Unemployment Relief; |
| | a founder and chairman, Adopt–a–Family Committee; |
| | chairman, Nurses' House Committee for the Association for Improving the Condition of the Poor; |
| | founder and president, Metropolitan Opera Guild, NYC; |
| | president, Motion Picture Research Council; |
| | a founder and chairman of board, Northeast Harbor Library, Northeast, MA |
| Address: | Fulton Avenue, Hempstead |
| Name of estate: | *Blemton Manor* |
| Year of construction: | c. 1865 |
| Style of Architecture: | Colonial Revival |
| Architect(s): | |
| Landscape architect(s): | |
| House extant: | no** |
| Historical notes: | |

 August Belmont, Jr. [II] was the son of August and Caroline Slidell Perry Belmont, Sr., who resided at *Nursery Stud Farm* in North Babylon. His mother was the daughter of Commodore Matthew Perry, who opened Western trade with Japan. When August Belmont, Sr. died in 1890, his son dropped the designation Jr. and made his eight-year-old son August Belmont, Jr. [Harry W. Havemeyer, *Along the Great South Bay: From Oakdale to Babylon, The Story of a Summer Spa 1840 to 1940* (Mattituck, NY: Amereon House, 1996), pp. 298-299.]

 August Belmont II's brother Perry married Jessie Robbins. His brother Raymond Rogers Belmont I, a bachelor, committed suicide. His sister Jane was also unmarried at the time of her death in 1875. His sister Frederika married Samuel Howland. His brother Oliver Hazard Perry Belmont, known as OHP, married Sarah Swan Whiting and, subsequently, Alva Erskine Smith Vanderbilt, the wife of his close friend William Kissam Vanderbilt, Sr., who resided at *Idlehour* in Oakdale. [*See* Spinzia, *Long Island's Prominent South Shore Families* – Vanderbilt entry.] OHP and Alva Belmont resided at *Brookholt* in East Meadow. Alva Belmont subsequently resided at *Beacon Towers* in Sands Point and in Paris.

 Elizabeth Hamilton Morgan Belmont was the daughter of Edward Morgan.

 August and Elizabeth Hamilton Morgan Belmont's son Morgan married Margaret F. Andrews. Their son Raymond Rogers Belmont II married Ethel Helen Linda, whose stage name was Ethel Loraine; Caroline Hubbard of Virginia; and, subsequently, Marie Muurling, the daughter of I. J. R. Muurling, and resided with her at *Belray Farms* in Middleburg, VA. Raymond's daughter Bettina married Newell Jube Ward, Jr., the son of Newell Jube and Ethel L. Conderman Ward, Sr. of East Hampton, and resided at *Valley View Farm* in Middleburg. [*See* Spinzia, *Long Island's Prominent Families in the Town of East Hampton* – Ward entry.] Their son August Belmont III married Alice Wall de Goicouria, the daughter of Valentine and Mary Cecelia Wall de Goicouria of Islip, and resided in Bay Shore. Alice subsequently married John Daniel Wing, who resided in Southampton. [*See* Spinzia, *Long Island's Prominent North Shore Families, vol. 1,* and *Long Island's Prominent South Shore Families* – Belmont and de Goicouria entries; and *Long Island's Prominent Families in the Town of Southampton* – Wing entry.]

 *A memorial window in St. George's Episcopal Church, Hempstead, honors Elizabeth Morgan Belmont.

 **The house became the Hempstead Elks Lodge prior to being demolished for the construction of the County Estates Apartments.

**Belmont, Oliver Hazard Perry (1858-1908)**

| | |
|---|---|
| Occupation(s): | financier - partner, August Belmont & Co. (investment banking firm)<br>publisher - *The Verdict*<br>politician - member, United States Congress, 13th district, 1901-1903 |
| Marriage(s): | M/1 – 1882-div. 1885 – Sarah Swan Whiting (1861-1924)<br>M/2 - 1896-1908 – Alva Erskine Smith (1853-1933)<br>  - writer - *Melinda and Her Sisters* (suffragist opera/with Elsa Maxwell); *One Month's Log of the Seminole*, 1916; two unpublished autobiographies, 1917, 1933<br>  journalist - numerous newspaper and magazine articles<br>  Civic Activism:<br>    woman's suffrage* - founder and president, Political Equality Association, NYC;<br>      first president, National Woman's Party;<br>    purchased building in Washington, DC, for National Woman's Party [now, known as the Sewall–Belmont House];<br>    primary benefactor and president of board, Hempstead Hospital, Hempstead [not the present-day hospital also named Hempstead Hospital];<br>    established, Brookholt School of Agriculture for Women at East Meadow estate;<br>    built and supported, Sea Side Hospital for Sick Children, Great River;<br>    built mission church for Our Lady of Loretto Roman Catholic Church, 1904, Hempstead;<br>    paid for rectory furnishing for St Mark's Episcopal Church, Islip (the church was financed by her first husband, William Kissam Vanderbilt, Sr.) |
| Address: | Front Street, East Meadow |
| Name of estate: | *Brookholt* |
| Year of construction: | c. 1897 |
| Style of architecture: | Colonial Revival |
| Architect(s): | Richard Howland Hunt designed the 1897 house (for O. H. P. Belmont)<br>John Russell Pope designed a Georgian-style farmhouse, 1906 (for O. H. P. Belmont)* |
| Landscape architect(s): | Hicks Nursery supplied plantings (for O. H. P. Belmont) |

House extant: no; destroyed by fire, 1934
Nassau County Museum Collection has photographs of the estate.
Historical notes:

    The house, originally named *Brookholt*, was built by Oliver Hazard Berry Belmont. It contained nine master bedrooms, nine bathrooms, and thirteen bedrooms for servants.
    He was the son of August and Caroline Slidell Perry Belmont, Sr. of *Nursery Stud Farm* in North Babylon.
    Sarah Swan Whiting Belmont was the daughter of Augustus and Sarah Swan Whiting, Sr. of Newport, RI. She separated from Oliver during their Paris honeymoon because of his excessive drinking and his affair with a French dancer. Oliver refused to recognize their daughter Natica as his child and disinherited her. In 1907, Natica married William Proudfit Burden. She died of asphyxiation in 1908 due to a faulty gas line to a lamp. Natica had been adopted by Sarah's second husband George Lockhart Rives. Sarah and George's son Francis married Helen Leigh Hunt, the daughter of Leigh Smith James and Jessie Nobel Hunt, and resided at *Mapleglades* in Hewlett Bay Park.
    *[See previous entry for information on the Belmont family.]*
    The estate was subsequently owned by Alexander Smith Cochran, who sold it in 1923 to the Cold Stream Golf Club. [*The New York Times* November 18, 1923, p. XII.]
    [For information about Alva Erskine Smith (Vanderbilt) Belmont's North and South Shore estates, *see* Spinzia, *Long Island's Prominent North Shore Families, vol. I* – Belmont entry – and *Long Island's Prominent South Shore Families* – Vanderbilt entry.]
    The 1906 Georgian-style farmhouse on the estate property was demolished.
    *For other Long Islanders involved in the suffrage movement *see* Raymond E. Spinzia, "Winning the Franchise: Long Island Activists in the Fight for Woman's Suffrage and Their Opponents, Long Island's Anti-Suffragists." wwwspinzialongislandestates.com.
    [For information about Alva Erskine Smith (Vanderbilt) Belmont, see Raymond E. Spinzia, "In Her Wake: The Story of Alva Smith Vanderbilt." *The Long Island Historical Journal* 6 (Fall 1993):96-105 and www.spinzialongislandestates.com.]

## Oliver Hazard Perry Belmont residence, *Brookholt*

*rear facade, 1902*

*side/front facade*

*dining room*

*side / front facade, 1902*

*stables*

**Belsterling, Charles Starne (1874-1959)**

| | |
|---|---|
| Occupation(s): | attorney - partner of Charles McVeagh, who became U. S. Ambassador to Japan in 1925 |
| | industrialist - vice-president and general commerce manager, U. S. Steel Corp. (now, USX); manager, A & P Products Inc., Philadelphia, PA (later, American Bridge Co.; then, U. S. Steel Corp., and now, USX); |
| | capitalist - director, Pittsburgh, Bessemer, & Lake Erie Railroad Co.; director, Marquette & Bessemer Dock and Navigation Co. |
| | shipping - director, Isthmian Steamship Co. |
| | writer - *History of Industrial Railway Cases*, 1933; *Legislative History of Commodities Clause of the Interstate Commerce Act*, 1934; *William Preston of Newcastle-Upon-Tyme, England and Philadelphia, Pennsylvania, and Allied Families*, 1934; *Digest of Transit Privileges*, 1912; *Paternal Ancestors of Florence Fries Belsterling*, 1938; numerous articles in genealogical and historical publications |
| Marriage(s): | M/1 – 1898-1910 – Florence Fries (1876-1910) |
| | M/2 – 1931-1959 – Helen Gunter |
| Address: | 370 Ocean Avenue, Lawrence |
| Name of estate: | |
| Year of construction: | 1923 |
| Style of architecture: | Neo-Tudor with Flemish elements |
| Architect(s): | |
| Landscape architect(s): | |
| House extant: yes | |
| Historical notes: | |

    In 1941 Belsterlong purchased the house from Mrs. Albert Samuel Roberts, Jr. [*The New York Times* November 12, 1941, p. 41.]
    He was the son of William Franklin and Ida Julia Sutterle Belsterling of Philadelphia, PA.
    Florence Fries Belsterling was the daughter of Edgar Fries of Philadelphia, PA.
    Charles Starne and Florence Fries Belsterling's daughter Edna married Harold Gilman Dow, Sr. and resided in Garden City. Their daughter Florence married Sturges Mason Schley and resided in Kennebunkport, ME. Their daughter Ruth, who resided in Manhattan, remained unmarried.
    Helen Gunter Belsterling was the daughter of William Adams Gunter of Montgomery, AL. She had previously been married to ____ Jackson.

*front facade, 2008*

### Bené, John Raymond (1893-1965)

| | |
|---|---|
| Occupation(s): | industrialist - secretary and treasurer, John Bené and Sons, Inc., Brooklyn |
| Marriage(s): | 1915-1965 – Madeline Brown (1896-1971) |
| Address: | 126 Whitehall Boulevard, Garden City |
| Name of estate: | |
| Year of construction: | 1927 |
| Style of architecture: | Dutch Colonial Revival |
| Architect(s): | |
| Landscape architect(s): | |
| House extant: yes | |
| Historical notes: | |

The house was built by John Raymond Bené.

The *Long Island Society Register, 1929* lists John Raymond and Madeline Brown Bené as residing on Whitehall Boulevard, Garden City.

He was the son of John Bené of Brooklyn.

Madeline Brown Bené was the daughter of William Atherton and Rebecca E. Koop Brown of Quogue. [*See* Spinzia, *Long Island's Prominent Families in the Town of Southampton* – Brown entry.]

John Raymond and Madeline Brown Bené's daughter Janice married Lombard Fortson and resided in Augusta, GA.

In 1937 the house was remodeled.

*front facade, 2001*

### Benedict, Le Grand Lockwood, Sr. (1855-1923)

| | |
|---|---|
| Occupation(s): | financier - partner, Lockwood and Co. (stock brokerage firm); a founder and partner, Benedict Brothers (later, Benedict & Co.) (stock brokerage firm); governor, New York Stock Exchange |
| Marriage(s): | 1881-1923 – Sarah Collier Blaine (1856-1939) |
| Address: | Hollywood Crossing, Lawrence |
| Name of estate: | *Nooke* |
| Year of construction: | |
| Style of architecture: | |
| Architect(s): | |
| Landscape architect(s): | |
| House extant: unconfirmed | |
| Historical notes: | |

The *Social Register Summer, 1910* lists Le Grand L. and Sarah C. Blaine Benedict [Sr.] as residing at *Nooke* in Cedarhurst [Lawrence].

He was the son of James Hoyt and Mary Elizabeth Andrews Benedict.

Le Grand Lockwood and Sarah Collier Blaine Benedict, Sr.'s daughter Louise married Francis B. T. Thurber, Jr. Their son Le Grand Lockwood Benedict, Jr. married Urling Harper, the daughter of Joseph Henry and Mary Say Hoe Harper of *Brightside* in Lawrence.

### Benkard, Henry Horton (1879-1928)

| | |
|---|---|
| Occupation(s): | financier - partner, J. P. Benkard & Co. (stock brokerage firm); partner, F. B. Keech & Co. (stock brokerage firm) |
| Marriage(s): | 1903-1928 – Bertha King Bartlett (1877-1945) |
| | - Civic Activism: president general, Colonial Dames of America; first woman trustee, The New York Genealogical & Biographical Society, 1941; member, Fine Arts Committee for the decoration of the White House; vice-chair, Women's Committee of the Museum of the City of New York; vice president, Sanitarium for Aged, NYC; president, North Country Garden Club; numerous gifts to various museums; * |
| Address: | *[unable to determine street address]*, Garden City |
| Name of estate: | |
| Year of construction: | |
| Style of architecture: | |
| Architect(s): | |
| Landscape architect(s): | |
| House extant: | unconfirmed |
| Historical notes: | |

The *Long Island Society Register, 1928* lists Henry Horton and Bertha K. Bartlett Benkard as residing in Garden City. The *Social Register Summer, 1937* lists Harry Horton and Bertha K. Bartlett Benkard as residing in Oyster Bay [Upper Brookville].

He was the son of James Julius and Fanny Gage Horton Benkard. Henry's brother James married Edith Lake, the daughter of Louis L. Lake of Manhattan, and resided in Babylon. [*See* Spinzia, *Long Island's Prominent South Shore Families*, – Benkard entry.]

Bertha King Bartlett Benkard was the daughter of Franklin and Bertha King Post Bartlett.

*Mrs. Benkard was an authority on and collector of antique furniture. She donated her furniture collection to the Metropolitan Museum of Art.

Henry Horton and Bertha King Bartlett Benkard's daughter Bertha married Reginald Perry Rose and resided in Garden City, Syosset, and, later, in Upper Brookville. The Benkards' son Franklin married Laura Derby Dupee, the daughter of William Arthur Dupee of Boston, MA. [*See* Spinzia, *Long Island's Prominent North Shore Families, vol. I* – Benkard and Mackay entries – and *Long Island's Prominent North Shore Families, vol. II* – Rose entry.]

**Bentley, Edward Manross (1858-1936)**

| | |
|---|---|
| Occupation(s): | attorney - partner, Betts, Sheffield, Bentley, and Betts |
| | industrialist - a founder, Bentley–Knight (built first electric street car system in the United States in Cleveland, OH); manager, patent department, General Electric Co. |
| Civic Activism: | trustee, Village of Lawrence |
| Marriage(s): | 1888-1936 – Mary H. Merrill (1854-1938) |
| Address: | 232 Broadway, Lawrence |
| Name of estate: | *Cherrygarth* |
| Year of construction: | |
| Style of architecture: | |
| Architect(s): | |
| Landscape architect(s): | |
| House extant: no | |
| Historical notes: | |

The *Social Register Summer, 1910* lists Mr. and Mrs. Edward M. and Mary H. Merrill Bentley as residing at *Cherrygarth* in Cedarhurst [Lawrence].

He was the son of The Reverend Edward Warren and Mrs. Emily Humphrey Bentley of Ellenville, NY.

Mary H. Merrill Bentley was the daughter of Daniel Ford and Luella Bell Merrill.

Edward Manross and Mary H. Merrill Bentley's son Edward Sailsbury Bentley, Sr. married Dorothy Anderton and resided at *Cherrygarth* in Lawrence.

At the time of his death, Bentley was residing at 232 Broadway, Lawrence.

*[See following entry for additional family information.]*


**Bentley, Edward Sailsbury, Sr. (1893-1975)**

| | |
|---|---|
| Occupation(s): | attorney |
| | financier - director, Lawrence–Cedarhurst Bank |
| Marriage(s): | 1919-1968 – Dorothy Anderton (1894-1968) |
| Address: | 232 Broadway, Lawrence |
| Name of estate: | *Cherrygarth* |
| Year of construction: | |
| Style of architecture: | |
| Architect(s): | |
| Landscape architect(s): | |
| House extant: no | |
| Historical notes: | |

The *Long Island Society Register, 1929* lists Edward S. and Dorothy Anderton Bentley [Sr.] as residing at *Cherrygarth* in Lawrence.

He was the son of Edward Manross and Mary H. Merrill Bentley of Lawrence.

Dorothy Anderton Bentley was the daughter of Dr. William Bancroft and Mrs. Elizabeth Story Palmer Anderton, who resided at *Ye Corners* in Lawrence.

Edward Sailsbury and Dorothy Anderton Bentley, Sr.'s son William married Phoebe Meredith Frey, the daughter of Dr. W. Guernsey Frey of Forest Hills Gardens, Queens, and resided in Manhattan. Their daughter Mary married Richard Kilcullen, the son of William Kilcullen of Manhattan, and resided in Manhattan.

In 1943, during World War II, their son Edward Sailsbury Bentley, Jr., a Navy Seal, died when his ship sunk off the coast of Tunisia.

*[See previous entry for additional family information.]*

### Berdell, Theodore Van Duzer (1888-1950)

| | |
|---|---|
| Occupation(s): | financier - a founder and partner, with his brother Charles, Berdell Brothers (jobber to other stock exchange brokerage houses) |
| Marriage(s): | 1913-1950 – Jean Bryan (1891-1961) |
| Address: | 84 Third Street, Garden City |
| Name of estate: | |
| Year of construction: | |
| Style of architecture: | |
| Architect(s): | |
| Landscape architect(s): | |
| House extant: no | |
| Historical notes: | |

The *Long Island Society Register, 1929* lists Mrs. and Mrs. Theodore [Van Duzer] Berdell as residing at 84 Third Street, Garden City.

He was the son of Charles Prescott and Ann Van Duzer Gott Berdell. Theodore's brother Charles Prescott Berdell married Katherine S. Curtiss and resided at *The Wilderness* in St. James. Their grandfather Robert Berdell was president of the Erie Railroad from 1864 to 1867.

Jean Bryan Berdell was the daughter of Manhattan builder William Bryan.

Theodore Van Duzer and Jean Bryan Berdell's daughter Anne married Kenneth Heron Hannon.


### Bernstein, Lester (1920-2014)

| | |
|---|---|
| Occupation(s): | capitalist - vice-president, NBC; vice-president, RCA |
| | journalist - motion picture critic, *The New York Times*; managing editor, *Newsweek*; editor-in-chief, *Newsweek* |
| Marriage(s): | 1946-2014 – Jacqueline Lipscomb (1925-2014) (aka Mimi Talbot) - artist |
| Address: | 44 Buxton Street, Lido Beach |
| Name of estate: | |
| Year of construction: | 1926 |
| Style of architecture: | Contemporary |
| Architect(s): | |
| Landscape architect(s): | |
| House extant: yes | |
| Historical notes: | |

*front / side facade, 2019*

Lester and Jacqueline Lipscomb Bernstein were residing in Lido Beach at the time of their deaths.

He was the son of Isidore and Rebecca Axelrod Bernstein.

Jacqueline predeceased Lester by eight days.

Lester and Jacqueline Lipscomb Bernstein's daughter Nina married Andress A. Huyssen, the son of Arnold O. Huyssen of Baden-Baden, Germany. Their son Daniel died, in 1978, at the age of twenty-five. Their daughter Lynn married ____ Brenner and, later, Gerald McKelvey.

In 2016 the 2,080-square-foot house sold for $575,000.

### Bertschmann, Jean Jacques (d. 1938)

| | |
|---|---|
| Occupation(s): | capitalist - real estate holdings |
| Marriage(s): | M/1 – 1924-div. 1934 – Constance Hatch Banks |
| | M/2 – 1934-1938 – Mary Elliott |
| Address: | Auerbach Avenue, Hewlett |
| Name of estate: | |
| Year of construction: | |
| Style of architecture: | |
| Architect(s): | |
| Landscape architect(s): | |
| House extant: | unconfirmed |
| Historical notes: | |

The *Long Island Society Register, 1929* lists Jean Jacques and Constance H. Banks Bertschmann as residing on Auerbach Avenue, Hewlett.

He was the son of Louis and Maude Smith Bertschmann of Manhattan. Jean's brother Louis Frederick Bertschmann, who resided at *Les Bouleaux* in Muttontown, married Maude M. Smith, and, later, Constance Percival. [*See* Spinzia, *Long Island's Prominent North Shore Families, vol. I* – Bertschmann entry.]

Constance Hatch Banks Bertschmann was the daughter of David Banks of Manhattan. Her sister Cecilia married William Wakeman, the son of Stephen H. Wakeman of Manhattan.

Jean Jacques and Constance Hatch Banks Bertschmann's daughter Shelagh married David Hall McConnell III, the son of David Hall and Marjorie Anderson McConnell, Jr., and resided in East Hampton. [*See* Spinzia, *Long Island's Prominent Families in the Town of East Hampton* – McConnell entry.] Shelagh later married Ralph Strother Richards, Jr.


### Bierwirth, John Edward (1895-1978)

| | |
|---|---|
| Occupation(s): | capitalist - vice-president and director, Thompson–Starrett Co., Inc., NYC (contractor); |
| | director, Warner Brothers Pictures, Inc. |
| | financier - president and director, The New York Trust Co.; |
| | director, Northern Insurance Co. |
| | industrialist - president, National Distillers Products Corp.; |
| | director, Avco Manufacturing Co.; |
| | director, Owens–Corning Fiberglass Corp.; |
| | director, Bell Aircraft Corp.; |
| | director, Panhandle Eastern Pipe Line Co. |
| | merchant - director, Mercantile Stores Inc. |
| Marriage(s): | 1922-1978 – Alice Marguerite Von Bernuth (1898-1978) |
| Address: | Briarwood Crossing, Lawrence |
| Name of estate: | |
| Year of construction: | c. 1927 |
| Style of architecture: | Neo-Federal |
| Architect(s): | James Monroe Hewlett designed his own house |
| Landscape architect(s): | |
| House extant: | yes |
| Historical notes: | |

*front/side facade, 1978*

The house was designed and built by James Monroe Hewlett. It was subsequently owned by Bierwirth.

The *Long Island Society Register, 1929* lists John E. Bierwirth as residing on Marbridge Road, Lawrence.

He was the son of Dr. Julius Carl and Mrs. Nettie Gerhardine Cocks Bierwirth of Lawrence.

Alice Marguerite Von Bernuth Bierwirth was the daughter of August Von Bernuth.

John Edward and Alice Marguerite Von Bernuth Bierwirth's daughter Nancy married Robert Connell Baldridge and resided in Lawrence. Their daughter Alice married Delos Walker Wainwright, the son of Carroll Livingston and Nina Walker Wainwright, Jr. of East Hampton, and resided in East Hampton. [*See* Spinzia, *Long Island's Prominent Families in the Town of East Hampton* – Wainwright entry.]

*[See following entry for additional family information.]*

The house was later owned by Anthony Marmo.

### Bierwirth, Dr. Julius Carl (1856-1921)

Occupation(s): physician

Marriage(s): 1889-1921 – Nettie Gerhardine Cocks (1871-1946)

Address: Meadow Lane, Lawrence
Name of estate:
Year of construction:
Style of architecture:
Architect(s):
Landscape architect(s):
House extant: unconfirmed
Historical notes:

   The *Long Island Society Register, 1929* lists Nettie Gerhardine Cocks Bierwirth as residing on Meadow Lane, Lawrence.
   She was the daughter of John James and Florence Hutchinson Cocks.
   Julius Carl and Nettie Gerhardine Cocks Bierwith's daughter Florence married Clarence Franklin Pritchard, the son of Alfred Pritchard of New Rochelle, NY, and resided in Lawrence.
*[See previous entry for additional family information.]*


### Bigelow, Bushnell (1880-1969)

Occupation(s): industrialist - treasurer, New Jersey Zinc Co,

Marriage(s): 1906-1967 – Sophie Louise Himley (1880-1967)

Address: Meadowview Road, Hewlett Bay Park
Name of estate:
Year of construction:
Style of architecture:
Architect(s):
Landscape architect(s):
House extant: unconfirmed
Historical notes:

   The *Long Island Society Register, 1929* lists Bushnell and Louise Himley Bigelow as residing in Woodmere [Hewlett Bay Park]. The 1920 Census lists the Bigelows at this address.
   He was the son of Edward P. Bigelow of Manhattan.
   Sophie Louise Himley Bigelow was the daughter of Henry Alexander Himley of Far Rockaway and a cousin of Mrs. Reginald Vanderbilt.
   Bushnell and Sophie Louise Hemley Bigelow's daughter Louise married William Parsons and resided in Cold Spring Harbor.

### Bird, Oliver William, Jr. (1862-1932)

| | |
|---|---|
| Occupation(s): | real estate agent -   Pease & Elliman |
| | capitalist -   built International Polo Field at the Meadowbrook Club |
| Civic Activism: | steward, Meadow Brook Hunt Club |
| Marriage(s): | 1889-1932 – Clara Sutton Gautier (1864-1928) |
| | - Civic Activism:  chair, women's auxiliary fund-raising committee for Hempstead, Nassau Hospital |
| Address: | 50 Fulton Avenue, Uniondale |
| Name of estate: | *Greenhedge* |
| Year of construction: | |
| Style of architecture: | |
| Architect(s): | |
| Landscape architect(s): | |
| House extant:  no | |
| Historical notes: | |

   The *Social Register Summer, 1910* lists Oliver W. and Clara S. B. Gautier Bird [Jr.] as residing at *Greenhedge* in Hempstead [Uniondale]. The *Long Island Society Register, 1929* lists the address as Fulton Avenue, Hempstead.
   He was the son of Oliver William and Mary E. Bird, Sr. of Mount Auburn, MA.
   Clara Gautier Bird was the daughter of Dr. Josiah Hornblower and Mrs. Mary Louisa Gregory Gautier.
   Oliver William and Clara Sutton Gautier Bird, Jr.'s son Oliver William Bird III married Lois V. Hewett, the daughter of Harvey J. Hewitt of Manhattan, and resided in Manhattan. Their son Dudley married Ruth Merritt Gaynor, the daughter of New York City Mayor William Jay and Mrs. Augusta C. Mayer Gaynor of *Deepwells* in St. James. [*See* Spinzia, *Long Island: A Guide to New York's Suffolk and Nassau Counties – Deepwells Farm* – Estate of William Jay Gaynor – Deepwells, St. James.] Their daughter Claire married Reginald Minturn Lewis, the son of Frederick Lewis. Their daughter Marie married Bernard N. Jackson, the son of F. Nevill Jackson of London, England.

### Bishop, Clifford Monroe (1883-1960)

| | |
|---|---|
| Occupation(s): | merchant -   president, Bishop, McCormick, & Bishop, Brooklyn, Long Island City, and Jamaica (Dodge and Plymouth automotive dealership) |
| | industrialist -   director, Dodge Brothers (automobile manufacturing firm) |
| Civic Activism: | chairman, Brooklyn Safety Council; |
| | chairman, Automobile Old Timers; |
| | director, Better Business Bureau of New York; |
| | chairman, Long Island Highway Commission of Brooklyn Chamber of Commerce |
| Marriage(s): | 1912 – Grace Goodwin |
| Address: | 84 Third Street, Garden City |
| Name of estate: | *Shadowland* |
| Year of construction: | |
| Style of architecture: | |
| Architect(s): | |
| Landscape architect(s): | |
| House extant:  no | |
| Historical notes: | |

   The *Long Island Society Register, 1929* lists Clifford Monroe and Grace Goodwin Bishop as residing at *Shadowland*, 84 Third Street, Garden City.
   He was the son of Eli H. and Fanny Heritage Bishop of Grand Avenue, Rockville Centre, and Brooklyn.
   Grace Goodwin Bishop was the daughter of Richard Goodwin of Brooklyn.
   Clifford Monroe and Grace Goodwin Bishop's daughter Jane married ____ Holbrook.

### Black, Archibald (1888-1943)

| | |
|---|---|
| Occupation(s): | engineer -  Curtiss Aeroplane & Motor Co.; |
| |     chief engineer, L–W–F Engineering Co., NYC; |
| |     president, Black & Bigelow (engineering firm); |
| |     engineer, Republic Aviation Corp.; |
| |     engineer, Snead & Co. |
| | writer - *Transport Aviation*, 1926; |
| |     *Civil Airports and Airways*, 1929; |
| |     *The Story of Bridges*, 1936; |
| |     *The Story of Tunnels*, 1937 (2nd edition, 1943) |
| Civic Activism: | secretary, Aeronautic Division, American Society of Mechanical Engineers |
| Marriage(s): | 1929-1943 – Dorothy Eleanor Stricker (b. 1903) |
| Address: | 25 Brixton Road, Garden City |
| Name of estate: | |
| Year of construction: | 1908 |
| Style of architecture: | American Craftsman |
| Architect(s): | |
| Landscape architect(s): | |
| House extant: yes | |
| Historical notes: | |

*front facade, 2001*

The *Long Island Society Register, 1929* lists Archibald Black as residing at 25 Brixton Road, Garden City.

He was the son of John and Marjorie Robb Black of Brixton Road, Garden City.

Dorothy Eleanor Stricker Black was the daughter of John F. Stricker of Sackville Road, Garden City.

### Blackwood, Arthur Temple (1892-1953)

| | |
|---|---|
| Occupation(s): | diplomat -  assistant naval attaché, British Embassy, Washington, DC, during World War I; |
| |     British vice-consul in Baltimore during World War II |
| | industrialist -  member, Ross Brothers (linen manufacturing firm); |
| |     member, Gribbon Co. (linen manufacturing firm) |
| Civic Activism: | president, Scottish Linen Guild (industrial trade association) |
| Marriage(s): | 1923-1953 – Sarah Goodwin Robinson (1902-1982) |
| |   - Civic Activism:  a founder, Junior League, Hartford, CT; |
| |     trustee, Gunston School; |
| |     lieutenant, American Red Cross during World War II |
| Address: | Smith Lane, Hewlett Neck |
| Name of estate: | |
| Year of construction: | |
| Style of architecture: | |
| Architect(s): | |
| Landscape architect(s): | |
| House extant: unconfirmed | |
| Historical notes: | |

In 1920 Blackwood purchased the ten-room house from Hampton Robb. [*The New York Times* June 5, 1930, p. 50.]

Sarah Robinson Blackwood was the daughter of Henry Seymour and Sarah Morgan Goodwin Robinson, Sr. of Hartford, CT.

Arthur Temple and Sarah Goodwin Robinson Blackwood's son Matthew married Helen Stokes Morris, the daughter of Sidney Sharp Morris of Berwin, PA, and resided in Hartford, CT. Their son Terence married Elizabeth Dawson, the daughter of Bernard and Veronica Dawson of Syracuse, NY.

### Blagden, Thomas (1882-1959)

| | |
|---|---|
| Occupation(s): | merchant - vice-president, Ichabod T. R. Williams & Sons, NYC (dealers in exotic woods and veneers) |
| Civic Activism: | president, Lawrence Association |
| Marriage(s): | M/1 – 1911-1947 – Mary E. Prentiss (1877-1947) |
| | M/2 – Mary DeLaney (1877-1962) |
| Address: | 218 Causeway, Lawrence |
| Name of estate: | |
| Year of construction: | 1937 |
| Style of architecture: | Contemporary |
| Architect(s): | |
| Landscape architect(s): | |
| House extant: yes | |
| Historical notes: | |

*front facade, 2009*

The *New York Social Register, 1939* lists Thomas and Mary Prentiss Blagden as residing at 218 Causeway, Lawrence. She had previously been married to James P. Hastings.

Mary DeLaney Blagden was the daughter of James Edward DeLaney of Brooklyn. She had previously been married to Dr. William J. Maroney and Dr. Aquin S. Kelly.

In 2007 the 6,375-square-foot house sold for $2.4 million.

### Blaine, Graham Burt, Sr. (1894-1978)

| | |
|---|---|
| Occupation(s): | financier - chairman of board, Manhattan Trust Co., NYC (later, Chase–Manhattan Bank, NYC); |
| | chairman of board, Chase–Manhattan Bank, NYC; |
| | vice-president, Kidder, Peabody Acceptance Corp., Boston, MA; |
| | partner, Tucker, Anthony, and R. L. Day, NYC (investment banking firm) |
| | industrialist - director, Burlington Mills, Inc. |
| Civic Activism: | trustee, National Academy of Religion and Mental Health; |
| | chairman, horse inspector committee for the South Shore villages; |
| | trustee, Village of Hewlett Harbor, 1935 and 1941; |
| | treasurer, America First Committee, 1940 |
| Marriage(s): | 1918-1968 – Katharine Winthrop Tweed (1888-1968) |
| | - Civic Activism: president, board of trustees, Spence School, NYC; |
| | president, board of trustees, Peninsula Community Library; |
| | member, campaign committee, Community Chest; |
| | patroness, Cedarhurst Dramatic Club; |
| | chair, Your Books for Your Boys Committee of the America First Committee |
| Address: | Causeway, Lawrence |
| Name of estate: | |
| Year of construction: | |
| Style of architecture: | |
| Architect(s): | |
| Landscape architect(s): | |
| House extant: unconfirmed | |
| Historical notes: | |

The *Long Island Society Register, 1929* lists Graham B. and Katharine W. Tweed Blaine [Sr.] as residing on Causeway, Lawrence.

He was the son of Charles Hodge and Emma J. Burt Blaine of Tauton, MA.

Katharine Winthrop Tweed Blaine was the daughter of Charles Harrison and Helen Minerva Evarts Tweed of New York City. Her grandfather Maxwell Evarts was Secretary of State in the Hayes administration.

Graham Burt and Katharine Winthrop Tweed Blaine, Sr.'s daughter Katharine married Eugene L. Swan, Jr. and resided in Farmington, CT. Their daughter Charlotte married James Hurd Vaughn, the son of Harry D. Vaughn of Atherton, CA, and resided in Woodside, CA. Their daughter Lorna married Tasker Howard, Jr. of Brooklyn and, subsequently, Albert Halper with whom she resided in Pawling, NY. Their son Dr. Graham Burt Blaine, Jr. married Patricia Smallwood and resided in South Kent, CT.

By 1935 the Blaines were residing in Hewlett.

### Blanchard, George Holmes (1875-1948)

| | |
|---|---|
| Occupation(s): | merchant - president, Blanchard & Co., Hempstead (distributors of advertising specialties) |
| Civic Activism: | first president, Hempstead Association of Commerce |
| Marriage(s): | M/1 – Margaret Eleanor Brown (b. 1887) |
| | M/2 – Genevieve Cadmus (1880-1947) |
| |    - Civic Activism: president, Morning Choral Society; president, Mundell Choral Society |
| Address: | 141 Meadbrook Road, Garden City |
| Name of estate: | |
| Year of construction: | 1921 |
| Style of architecture: | Neo-Tudor |
| Architect(s): | Olive Frances Tjaden designed the house |
| Landscape architect(s): | |
| House extant: yes | |
| Historical notes: | |

The *Long Island Society Register, 1929* lists George H. Blanchard as residing in Hempstead.

George Holmes and Margaret Eleanor Brown Blanchard's son Robert married Helen Page Thompson, the daughter of Roy Thompson, and resided in Hartford, CT. Their son Webster married Andrea Vining Arrighi, the daughter of Roswell Smith Arrighi, and resided in Hempstead.

Genevieve Cadmus Blanchard had previously been married to George W. Berry.

At the time of their deaths, George Holmes and Genevieve Cadmus Blanchard was residing at 141 Meadowbrook [sic] Road, Garden City. [*The New York Times* September 11, 1947, p. 27.]

*front facade, 2008*

### Blanchard, Walter Scott, Sr. (c. 1902-1953)

| | |
|---|---|
| Occupation(s): | capitalist - president, Blanchard Lumber Co. |
| Civic Activism: | director, Atlantic Beach Club, 1937 |
| Marriage(s): | M/1 – 1924-div. 1932 – Elizabeth Percival (1904-1967) (aka Lydia Percival) |
| | M/2 – Evelyn Evans (b. 1909) |
| Address: | Cedar Avenue, Hewlett Bay Park |
| Name of estate: | |
| Year of construction: | c. 1927 |
| Style of architecture: | Colonial Revival |
| Architect(s): | |
| Landscape architect(s): | Louise Payson, 1928 (for W. S. Blanchard, Sr.) |
| House extant: unconfirmed | |
| Historical notes: | |

The *Long Island Society Register, 1929* lists W. Scott and Lydia Percival Blanchard as residing in Hewlett Bay Park. He was the son of Millard F. and Mary B. O'Neill Blanchard.

The house was purchased by Blanchard in 1927. [*The New York Times* April 22, 1927, p. 37.]

Elizabeth Percival Blanchard was the daughter of David Crowell Percival of Boston, MA. Her sister Constance married Louis Frederick Bertschmann and resided at *Les Boulaux* in Muttontown. [*See* Spinzia, *Long Island's Prominent North Shore Families, vol. I* – Bertschmann entry.] Elizabeth later married Charles George Moller III of Lawrence.

Walter Scott and Elizabeth Percival Blanchard, Sr.'s daughter Elizabeth married William Grannis Tankoos, the son of Samuel and Mary Margaret Walsh Tankoss.

Evelyn Evans Blanchard was the daughter of Harman Kuhn Evans of Manhattan. She subsequently married John Burghart Wright and resided in Hewlett Bay Park.

Walter Scott and Evelyn Evans Blanchard, Sr.'s son Walter Scott Blanchard, Jr. married Wanda M. White, the daughter of Austin W. White.

### Bloomer, James Ralph (1880-1963)

| | |
|---|---|
| Occupation(s): | financier - a founder and partner, with William F. Forepaugh, J. R. Bloomer & Co. (stock brokerage firm)<br>industrialist - president, New Mexican Silver-Mining Co.; president, San Juan Mines Co.<br>real estate agent - treasurer, Howard Cole & Co. (Florida, Louisiana, and Pacific Coast properties)<br>politician - Deputy Collector of Customs, Port of New York |
| Marriage(s): | |
| Address: | 167 Nassau Boulevard, Garden City |
| Name of estate: | |
| Year of construction: | 1911 |
| Style of architecture: | Colonial Revival |
| Architect(s): | |
| Landscape architect(s): | |
| House extant: | yes |
| Historical notes: | |

The *Long Island Society Register, 1929* lists James Ralph Bloomer as residing at 167 Nassau Boulevard, Garden City.

He was the son of James Frank and Ada M. Bare Bloomer of Cincinnati, OH.

*rear facade, 2001*

### Boardman, Andrew H. (1880-1963)

| | |
|---|---|
| Occupation(s): | attorney |
| Civic Activism: | president and director, Midland Golf Club, Garden City |
| Marriage(s): | Sarah Greenly Johnson (1878-1968)<br>- Civic Activism: president and recording secretary, Garden City Women's Club |
| Address: | 19 Beech Street, Garden City |
| Name of estate: | |
| Year of construction: | 1913 |
| Style of architecture: | Dutch Colonial Revival |
| Architect(s): | |
| Landscape architect(s): | |
| House extant: | yes |
| Historical notes: | |

The *Long Island Society Register, 1929* lists Mr. and Mrs. Andrew H. Boardman as residing on Magnolia Avenue, Garden City.

Sarah Greenly Johnson Boardman was the daughter of Lee and Frances Augusta Nicoll Johnson of East Islip and Garden City. [*See* Spinzia, *Long Island's Prominent South Shore Families* – Johnson entry.]

Andrew H. and Sara Greenly Johnson Boardman's daughter Cordelia married ____ Keys.

At the time of his death, Andrew H. Boardman was residing at 19 Beech Street, Garden City. [*The New York Times* July 6, 1963, p. 15.]

*front facade, 2001*

### Bodine, William Henry Johnson (1893-1968)

| | |
|---|---|
| Occupation(s): | real estate agent - president, William Bodine & Co., NYC |
| Marriage(s): | 1918-1962 – Helen Jeannette Pierson (1896-1962) |
| Address: | 141 Euston Road, Garden City |
| Name of estate: | |
| Year of construction: | 1917 |
| Style of architecture: | Colonial Revival |
| Architect(s): | |
| Landscape architect(s): | |
| House extant: yes | |
| Historical notes: | |

*front facade, 2001*

The *Long Island Society Register, 1929* lists William H. J. and Helen Jeannette Pierson Bodine as residing at 141 Euston Road, Garden City.

He was the son of William Henry and Mehitable J. Swan Bodine of Staten Island, NY.

Helen Jeannette Pierson Bodine was the daughter of Eihu Halsey and Minnie Adelaide Lloyd Pierson of Brooklyn.

At the time of his death, William Henry Johnson Bodine was residing in Great Neck. [*The New York Times* January 24, 1968, p. 45.]

William Henry Johnson and Helen Jeannette Pierson Bodine's daughter Helen married Frank B. Gill, the son of Benjamin Gill of Reno, NV. Their daughter Doris married Sherman Nott Dowsett, the son of Herbert M. Dowsett.

### Bogert, Henry Lawrence, Jr. (1883-1965)

| | |
|---|---|
| Occupation(s): | financier - member, Eastman, Dillon, and Co. (stock brokerage firm) |
| | capitalist - director, Rochester Ice & Cold Storage Utilities Inc. |
| Civic Activism: | trustee, New York Institute for the Education of the Blind |
| Marriage(s): | 1910-1959 – Elizabeth Blodget Sanford (1892-1959) |
| Address: | Cedarhurst Avenue, Lawrence |
| Name of estate: | |
| Year of construction: | |
| Style of architecture: | |
| Architect(s): | |
| Landscape architect(s): | |
| House extant: unconfirmed | |
| Historical notes: | |

The *Long Island Society Register, 1929* lists Henry L. and Elizabeth B. Sanford Bogert, Jr. as residing on Cedarhurst Avenue, Cedarhurst [Lawrence].

He was the son of Henry Lawrence and Caroline Lawrence Osgood Bogert, Sr. of Lawrence. His brother Edward married Esther Jean Bochman and, later, Elizabeth Wood, the daughter of Robert Williams and Gertrude Ames Wood of East Hampton, and resided in East Hampton. [*See* Spinzia, *Long Island's Prominent Families in the Town of East Hampton* – Bogert and Wood entries.]

Elizabeth Blodget Sanford Bogert was the daughter of George Baylies and Caroline Blodget Sanford, who resided at *The Byways* in Lawrence. Elizabeth's sister Genevieve married William Frederic Philips, the son of Frederic D. and Jessie M. Taylor Philips, and resided at *Fairway* in Lawrence.

Henry Lawrence and Elizabeth Blodget Sanford Bogert, Jr.'s daughter Cardine married Thomas Hildt, Jr. of Black Point, CT, and resided in Littleton, CO. Their daughter Caroline married Grenville Kane McVickar, the son of Henry Lansing McVickar of Tuxedo Park, NY, and resided in Tuxedo Park, NY. Their daughter Lucretia married Reginald Radcliffe Frost, Jr. of Far Hills, NJ, and, later, ____ Abbott with whom she resided in Gates Mills, OH. Their son Henry Lawrence Bogert III married Brigid Lee Cunningham and resided in New York.

### Bond, Walter Huntington (1878-1965)

| | |
|---|---|
| Occupation(s): | attorney - partner, Bond and Babson |
| | industrialist - director, Republic Coal; |
| |     director, Consolidated Coal Co.; |
| |     director, New York Die Co.; |
| |     director, United States and Santo Domingo Knitting Co.; |
| |     director, Arch Crown Manufacturing Co. |
| | publisher - director, Field & Stream Publishing Co.; |
| | capitalist - director, American Incorporation Co.; |
| |     director, Henry A. Gould Co. |
| Civic Activism: | governor, Order of the Founders and Patriots of America |
| Marriage(s): | M/1 – 1914-1934 – Mary Madeline Morgan (1882-1934) |
| | M/2 – 1941-1965 – Florence Steward Thompson (1889-1971) |
| Address: | 126 Stewart Avenue, Garden City |
| Name of estate: | |
| Year of construction: | |
| Style of architecture: | |
| Architect(s): | |
| Landscape architect(s): | |
| House extant: | no |
| Historical notes: | |

    The *Long Island Society Register, 1929* lists Walter H. and Mary Madeline Morgan Bond as residing at 126 Stewart Avenue, Garden City.
    He was the son of David Taylor and Emma Gertrude Bigelow Bond of Waltham, MA.
    Mary Madeline Morgan Bond was the daughter of Richard J. Morgan, who resided at *Cottenham Plantation* in Keller, GA. She had previously been married to \_\_\_\_ Bottome.
    Walter Huntington and Mary Madeline Morgan Bond's daughter Madeline married Robert Charles Picoli, the son of Henry Picoli of Garden City. Their son David married Jane Howie Arnold, the daughter of Dr. Douglas Perkins Arnold of Buffalo, NY.
    By 1942 the Bonds were residing at 10 Kilburn Road, Garden City.

*Bond's Kilburn Road residence*

**Bonner, Douglas Griswold, Sr. (1902-1960)**

| | |
|---|---|
| Occupation(s): | financier - partner, Bonner and Gregory (stock brokerage firm) |
| Civic Activism: | vice-chairman, board of trustees, Museum of the American Indian, NYC; trustee, Huntington Free Library |
| Marriage(s): | M/1 – 1924-div. – Ethel Sanders Hays (1901-1962) <br> M/2 – Kathleen H. Curtis |
| Address: | Railroad Avenue, Hewlett |
| Name of estate: | |
| Year of construction: | |
| Style of architecture: | |
| Architect(s): | |
| Landscape architect(s): | |
| House extant: | unconfirmed |
| Historical notes: | |

The *Long Island Society Register, 1929* lists Douglas Griswold and Ethel S. Hays Bonner [Sr.] as residing on Railroad Avenue, Hewlett. The *Social Register, 1937* lists their residence as *Thorne Lane* in Locust Valley.

He was the son of Paul Edward and Theodora Hall Bonner.

Ethel Sanders Hays Bonner was the daughter of William Henry and Mary N. Sanders Hays of Manhattan.

The *Social Register Summer, 1949* lists Douglas G. and Kathleen Curtis Bonner [Sr.] as residing at *Meadow Cottage* on Duck Pond Road, Glen Cove [Matinecock].

Kathleen H. Curtis Bonner had previously been married to Alfred Wagstaff III. Their daughter Audrey Curtis Wagstaff married James Hampden Robb, Jr., the son of James Hampden and Cornelia Van Rensselaer Thayer Robb, Sr. of *The Dolphins* in Southampton, and resided in Beverly Farms, MA. [*See* Spinzia, *Long Island's Prominent Families in the Town of Southampton* – Robb entry.] Mrs. Bonner subsequently married James A. Moffett II, whose father George Monroe Moffett, Sr. resided at *Les Bois* in Old Brookville.

The *Social Register New York 1964* lists Kathleen H. Curtis Bonner as married to James A. Moffett II and residing at 620 Park Avenue, NYC.

[*See* Spinzia, *Long Island's Prominent North Shore Families, vol. I* – Bonner entry – and *Long Island's Prominent South Shore Families* – Wagstaff entry.]

*Louis Bossert's West Bay Shore estate, The Oaks, c. 1923*

### Bossert, John (1870-1944)

| | |
|---|---|
| Occupation(s): | capitalist - partner, Gage & Tarvell (real estate developer of Nassau Boulevard section of Garden City); |
| | partner, with his stepmother Philippine and half-brother Charles, Hotel Bossert, Brooklyn Heights; |
| | real estate developer, Long Beach* |
| | industrialist - partner, with his half-brother Charles, Bossert Lumber Co., Brooklyn** |
| | financier - a founder and trustee, Roosevelt Savings Bank of Brooklyn |
| Civic Activism: | a founder, Arion Society, Brooklyn |
| Marriage(s): | Mary A. Jones |
| Address: | 229 Stewart Avenue, Garden City |
| Name of estate: | |
| Year of construction: | |
| Style of architecture: | |
| Architect(s): | |
| Landscape architect(s): | |
| House extant: no | |
| Historical notes: | |

John Bossert was the son of Louis Bossert, who resided at *The Oaks* in West Bay Shore. His sister Harriet married Frederick Max Huber, Sr. and resided in Bay Shore. His sister Josephine married Dr. Henry Moser of Brooklyn. His brother Charles married Natalie Taylor and resided in Sayville. His sister Bienie married Carroll Trowbridge Cooney, the son of John J. Cooney of Brooklyn, and resided in Plandome. [*See* Spinzia, *Long Island's Prominent South Shore Families* – Bossert and Huber entries.]

John and Mary A. Jones Bossert did not have children.

*Bossert and his partner New York State Senator Reynolds built houses and the original beach boardwalk in Long Beach.

**The Bossert Lumber Company, which was one of the largest lumber companies in the country, filed for bankruptcy during the Depression. Bossert subsequently relocated to Jamaica, Queens, and worked for $25-a-week as a real estate appraiser for a bank. [Liz Howell, *Continuity: Biography 1819-1934* (Sister Bay, WI: The Dragonsbreath Press, 1993), pp. 364-65.]


### Boulton, Howard Sr. (1886-1936)

| | |
|---|---|
| Occupation(s): | financier - member, W. B. Franklin Co. (stock brokerage firm); |
| | partner, Howard Boulton and Co. (stock brokerage firm); |
| | member, J. Lawrence and Sons (stock brokerage firm) |
| Marriage(s): | 1910-1925 – Grace Russell Jones (d. 1925) |
| Address: | Lefferts Road, Hewlett Bay Park |
| Name of estate: | |
| Year of construction: | |
| Style of architecture: | |
| Architect(s): | |
| Landscape architect(s): | |
| House extant: unconfirmed | |
| Historical notes: | |

The *Long Island Society Register, 1929* lists Howard Boulton [Sr.] as residing in Hewlett [Hewlett Bay Park.]

He was the son of William Bowen and Louisa Kuhl Kelly Boulton, Sr., who resided at *Avila* in Lawrence.

Grace Russell Jones Boulton was the daughter of William Strother and Mary Grace Russell Jones of Manhattan.

Howard and Grace Russell Jones Boulton, Sr.'s daughter Grace married Charles Dean Stearns, the son of Dr. Alfred E. Stearns, the headmaster of Phillips Andover Academy. Their son Howard Boulton, Jr. married Helen Schley Yates, the daughter of John Carrington and Linda L. Lindeberg Yates of East Hampton, and, subsequently, Mary Augusta Fosdick, the daughter of Clark Fosdick of Hewlett. [*See* Spinzia, *Long Island's Prominent Families in the Town of East Hampton* – Yates entry.]

*[See following entry for additional family information.]*

### Boulton, William Bowen, Sr. (1859-1922)

| | |
|---|---|
| Occupation(s): | financier - trustee, Atlantic Mutual Insurance Co.; director, United States Mortgage and Trust Co.; president, Morristown Trust Co.; director, Mechanics National Bank |
| Marriage(s): | 1881-1922 – Louisa Kuhl Kelly (1860-1929) |
| Address: | *[unable to determine street address]*, Lawrence |
| Name of estate: | *Avila* |
| Year of construction: | c. 1898 |
| Style of architecture: | Neo-Tudor |
| Architect(s): | Thomas Henry Randall designed the house (for Boulton) |

Landscape architect(s):
House extant: no; demolished c. 1950
Historical notes:

The house, originally named *Avila*, was built by William Bowen Boulton, Sr.
He was the son of William G. and Mary E. Boulton.
Louisa Kuhl Kelly Boulton was the daughter of Henry Kuhl and Louisa Warner Hard Kelly.
William Bowen and Louisa Kelly Boulton, Sr.'s daughter Anita married John Grenville Bates, the son of Alfred W. Bates. Their son Howard married Grace Russell Jones and resided in Hewlett. Their daughter Pauline married Newbold Lawrence Herrick, Sr. and resided in Woodsburgh. Their son William Bowen Boulton, Jr. married Adele Hager, who had previously been married to William Henry Harrison II. Their son Anson Hard Boulton died at the age of fourteen. [*The New York Times* February 28, 1905, p. 9.]
*[See previous entry for additional family information.]*

*rear facade, c. 1902*

**Bowker, Horace, Sr. (1877-1954)**

| | |
|---|---|
| Occupation(s): | industrialist -  president, Bowker Chemical Co.; president and chairman of board, American Agricultural Chemical Co. |
| | financier -  member, Newberger, Henderson, and Loeb (bond brokerage firm) |
| Civic Activism: | trustee, Village of Lawrence; |
| | member, commission to purchase chemicals during World War I; |
| | director, National Fertilizer Association; |
| | director, Five Towns Community House; |
| | director, Community Chest; |
| | director, Peninsula Public Library, Lawrence |
| Marriage(s): | M/1 – 1901-1938 – Adelaide Kent Greene (1879-1938) |
| | M/2 – 1939-1954 – Laurence Hewlett (1903-1987) |
| | - real estate agent -  a founder and president, Burr & McCauley, Hewlett |
| Address: | 290 Ocean Avenue, Lawrence |
| Name of estate: | |
| Year of construction: | 1908 |
| Style of architecture: | Modified Shingle |
| Architect(s): | |
| Landscape architect(s): | |
| House extant: yes | |
| Historical notes: | |

*front facade, 2007*

The *Social Register, 1933* lists Horace and Adelaide K. Greene Bowker [Sr.] as residing at 290 Ocean Avenue, Lawrence.

He was the son of William Henry and Charlotte Jeanette Ryder Bowker of Boston, MA.

Adelaide Kent Greene Bowker was the daughter of Albert T. Greene of Cambridge, MA.

Horace and Adelaide Kent Greene Bowker, Sr.'s daughter Rosmand married Elmer G. Thompson, the son of Henry F. Thompson of Manhasset. Their daughter Alice married John West La Pice.

Laurence Hewlett Bowker was the daughter of James Monroe and Anna Willets Hewlett, who resided in Lawrence. Laurence had previously been married to Robert Page Burr, Sr. with whom she resided in Lawrence.

In 1994 the house was remodeled.

**Bowman, Archibald (1879-1955)**

| | |
|---|---|
| Occupation(s): | accountant -  partner, Peat, Marwick, Mitchell, and Co., NYC |
| Civic Activism: | member, several technical committees of American Institute of Accountants; |
| | member, board of managers, St. Andrew's Society of New York State |
| Marriage(s): | Maude Pickthall (b. 1878) |
| | - Civic Activism:  member, Long Island Choral Society |
| Address: | 121 Brompton Road, Garden City |
| Name of estate: | |
| Year of construction: | 1913 |
| Style of architecture: | Eclectic |
| Architect(s): | |
| Landscape architect(s): | |
| House extant: yes | |
| Historical notes: | |

*front facade, 2018*

The *Long Island Society Register, 1929* lists Mr. and Mrs. Archibald Bowman as residing on Brompton Road, Garden City.

Their son Arthur married Electra Waggoner, the daughter of Edward Waggoner of Fort Worth, TX, and, later, Jeanne Turner, the daughter of Dr. George Turner of El Paso, TX.

In 2018 the five-bedroom, three-and-a-half-bath, 3,251-square-foot house sold for $1.215 million.

### Bradford, George Dexter (1897-1971)

| | |
|---|---|
| Occupation(s): | attorney |
| Marriage(s): | M/1 – 1923 – Dorothy Wainwright Maupin (1901-1986) |
| | M/2 – Margaret Elliott |
| Address: | Brower Point Road, Woodsburgh |
| Name of estate: | |
| Year of construction: | |
| Style of architecture: | |
| Architect(s): | |
| Landscape architect(s): | |
| House extant: unconfirmed | |
| Historical notes: | |

The *Long Island Society Register, 1929* lists George D. and Dorothy W. Maupin Bradford as residing in Woodmere [Woodsburgh].

He was the son of William Henry and Mary Kingsland Bradford, Sr. and a descendant of Colonial Governor William Bradford of Plymouth Colony.

Dorothy Wainwright Maupin Bradford was the daughter of Robert Washington and Florence Smith Maupin.

George Dexter and Dorothy Wainwright Maupin Bradford's daughter Dorothy married Martin Vogel Frank, the son of Stuart H. Frank of Manhattan; Geoffrey C. Doyle; Richard L. Strous; and Oscar Manuel Alonso. Their daughter Priscilla married Henry Baldwin Hyde Ripley, Jr. of *Ochre Point* in Newport.

### Braman, Chester Alwyn, Jr. (1902-1964)

| | |
|---|---|
| Occupation(s): | industrialist - president, A. D. Juillard Co., Inc. (textile manufacturer) |
| | financier - partner, Phelps and McKee (stock brokerage firm); |
| | partner, Delafield and Delafield (stock brokerage firm) |
| Marriage(s): | M/1 – 1925-div. 1941 – Anna Eleanor Roosevelt Hall (1903-1988) |
| | M/2 – 1941-1964 – Gladys Pomeroy Jenkins (1904-1995) |
| Address: | Woodside Drive, Hewlett Bay Park |
| Name of estate: | |
| Year of construction: | 1927 |
| Style of architecture: | Half-timber Neo-Tudor |
| Architect(s): | Polhemus and Coffin designed the house |
| Landscape architect(s): | |
| House extant: unconfirmed | |
| Historical notes: | |

The *Long Island Society Register, 1929* lists Chester A. and Anna E. R. Hall Braman, Jr. as residing at Woodside Drive and Cedar Avenue, Woodmere [Hewlett Bay Park].

Braman bought the house in 1927. [*The New York Times* April 22, 1927, p. 37.]

He was the son of Chester Alwyn and Mary Richards Butler Braman, Sr.

Anna Eleanor Roosevelt Hall Braman was the daughter of Edward Ludlow and Josephine Zabriskie Hall and the cousin of First Lady Anna Eleanor (Roosevelt) Roosevelt, for whom she was named.

Charles Alwyn and Anna Eleanor Roosevelt Hall Braman, Jr.'s daughter Eleanor married Thomas Arthur McGraw, the son of the Arthur Butler McGraw of Gross Point, MI; later, Graham H. R, Jenkins; and, subsequently, Dr. Thomas A. Grasso. Their daughter Mary married Arthur Frances Murray, the son of Matthew T. Murray of Lawrence, and resided in Lawrence. Their son Chester Alwyn Braman III married Sally Lane, the daughter of Frank Thatcher Lane of New Haven, CT, and resided in Darien, CT.

Gladys Pomeroy Jenkins Braman was the daughter of James Sinclair and Aurelia Gladys Pomeroy Jenkins of Stamford, CT. Gladys had previously been married to William Dixon Stevens of Hewlett Neck. After Braman's death, Gladys married Rector Kerr Fox, Jr.

In 1930 Braman purchased the George Baylies Sanford house *The Byways* in Lawrence.

### Breck, Duer du Pont (1870-1917)

Occupation(s): financier - assistant secretary, Mutual Life Insurance Co.

Marriage(s): 1905-1917 – Sydney Sewall Manley (1874-1951)

Address: 21 Franklin Court, Garden City
Name of estate:
Year of construction: 1912
Style of architecture: Neo-Tudor Townhouse
Architect(s): Ford, Butler, and Oliver designed the house*

Landscape architect(s):
House extant: yes
Historical notes:

The *Long Island Society Register, 1929* lists Mrs. Duer du Pont Breck as residing at 21 Franklin Court, Garden City. She was the daughter of Joseph Homan and Susan Hannah Cony Manley of Augusta, GA.

Duer du Pont Breck was the son of Charles du Pont and Mary Duer Breck. Duer du Pont and Sydney Sewall Manley Breck's daughter Susan married Douglas Dearborn, the son of George S. and Bessie Douglas Dearborn of Manhattan, and also resided in Manhattan. Their daughter Manley married William A. Smith, Jr.

Duer died of a self-inflicted gunshot wound. [*The New York Times* August 4, 1917, p. 14.]

*The houses were built by Doubleday, Page, and Company as rentals.

*Franklin Court complex, 2009*

### Breed, William Constable, Sr. (1871-1951)

| | |
|---|---|
| Occupation(s): | attorney - partner, Breed, Abbott and Morgan |
| | industrialist - director, Armco Steel Corp.; |
| |     director, National Distillers Products Corp.; |
| |     director, American Rolling Mill Co.; |
| |     director, Dictaphone Corp. |
| | politician - member, St. Lawrence Waterways Commission in the Coolidge administration; |
| |     chairman of board, New York State Economic Council |
| Civic Activism: | director, New York Chapter of American Red Cross; |
| | chairman, Greater New York Red Cross World War II Fund Drive; |
| | chairman, Greater New York Red Cross Committee for Disaster Relief; |
| | chairman and president, New York State Bar Association; |
| | treasurer, American Citizens Relief Committee of London; |
| | president, Merchants Association of New York; |
| | trustee, executive committee of lawyers, United Fund Drive; |
| | associate chairman, committee to modernize YMCA of Greater New York; |
| | chairman, committee to raise funds for stadium concerts; |
| | vice-president, Legal Aid Society; |
| | vice-president, New York City Bar Association; |
| | trustee, Amherst College, Amherst, MA; |
| | director, Commerce and Industry Association of New York |
| Marriage(s): | M/1 – 1896 – Emma Wise Ryder (b. 1873) |
| | M/2 – 1931-1951 – Eugenia S. Grigorcea (1892-1974) |
| Address: | 350 Ocean Avenue, Lawrence |
| Name of estate: | *Whale Acres* |
| Year of construction: | c. 1914 |
| Style of architecture: | Neo-Federal |
| Architect(s): | William Adams designed the house (for Perkins) |
| Landscape architect(s): | |
| House extant: yes | |
| Historical notes: | |

*front facade, 1918*

   The house, originally named *Whale Acres*, was built by Norton Perkins. It was rented by Breed.
   The *Long Island Society Register, 1929* lists William Constable and Emma Ryder Breed [Sr.] as residing at *Whales Acre* [sic] in Lawrence.
   He was the son of Charles Webster and Eweretta McVickar Breed of Malone, NY.
   Emma Wise Ryder Breed was the daughter of Edwin Lynden and Mary Wise Ryder.
   William Constable and Emma Wise Ryder Breed, Sr.'s son Alan married Rosilla M. Hornblower, whose parents George Sanford and Dorothy Marshall Hornblower resided at *Laurel Top* in Laurel Hollow. Their son William Constable Breed, Jr. married Ellen Harvey Whitman, the daughter of Eben Esmond and Jane Whitthorne Harvey Whitman of Lawrence, and resided in Manhattan and New Canaan, CT.
   The *Social Register Summer, 1937* lists William Constable and Eugenia S. Grigorcea Breed [Sr.] as residing at *Normandy Farms* in Glen Head [Old Brookville].
   [*See* Spinzia, *Long Island's Prominent North Shore Families, vol. I* – Hornblower and Breed entries.]
   Eugenia was the daughter of Emmanuel and Rose Singlianu Grigorcea. Eugenia had previously been married to Maris Veron Stiles.

### Brett, George Platt, Jr. (1893-1984)

| | |
|---|---|
| Occupation(s): | publisher -   chairman, American division, Macmillan Publishing Co.* |
| Civic Activism: | secretary, Peninsular Club, 1924; |
| | commissioner, Hewlett Bay Fire Department, 1929 |
| Marriage(s): | 1916-1978 – Isabella Stevenson Yeomans (1896-1978) |
| | - publisher -  member, trade advertising department, Macmillan Publishing Co.; |
| | member, educational department, Macmillan Publishing Co.; |
| | head, children's department, Macmillan Publishing Co. |
| Address: | Ocean Avenue, Woodmere |
| Name of estate: | *Justamere Cottage* |

Year of construction:
Style of architecture:
Architect(s):
Landscape architect(s):
House extant:  unconfirmed
Historical notes:

   The *Long Island Society Register, 1929* lists George Platt and Isabella Stevenson Yeomans Brett, Jr. as residing at *Justamere Cottage* on Ocean Avenue, Woodmere.
   He was the son of George Platt and Marie Louise Tostevin Brett, Sr. of New York City.
   Isabella Stevenson Yeomans Brett was the daughter of George Dallas and May Baldwin Stoddard Yeomans of Manhattan and Brooklyn.
   George Platt and Isabella Stevenson Yeomans Brett, Jr.'s son Bruce married Jacqueline Dewey, the daughter of DeWitt Greaves Dewey of Brooklyn. Their son George Platt Brett III married Katharine Irons, the daughter of Harry Stuart Irons of Bridgeport, CT, and resided in Dover, DE.
   The *Social Register Summer, 1937* lists George Platt and Isabella Stevenson Yeomans Brett, Jr. as residing at *Dennecote* in Fairfield, CT.
   *Brett arranged for the publication of Margaret Michell's *Gone With the Wind*.
   By 1932 the Bretts had relocated to Woodside Drive in Hewlett Bay Park.

### Briggs, Albert Martin (1875-1932)

| | |
|---|---|
| Occupation(s): | advertising executive -   vice-president, Outdoor Advertising, Inc., New York City, Cleveland, and Chicago |
| Civic Activism: | trustee, St. Giles Hospital for Crippled Children; |
| | a founder, Advertising Association of the World; |
| | governor, Lambs Club; |
| | governor, Question Club |
| Marriage(s): | Anna Howard Alden (1879-1960) |
| | - Civic Activism:  president, Y.W.C.A., Nassau County |
| Address: | 24 Cathedral Avenue, Garden City |

Name of estate:
Year of construction:
Style of architecture:
Architect(s):
Landscape architect(s):
House extant:  no
Historical notes:

   The *Long Island Society Register, 1929* lists Mr. and Mrs. Albert M. Briggs as residing at 24 Cathedral Avenue, Garden City.
   Anna Howard Alden Briggs was the daughter of John Byron and Caroline Amerlia Ball Alden of Jamestown, NY.
   Albert Martin and Anna Howard Alden Briggs' daughter Priscilla resided in Bemus Point, NY.

### Brisbane, Arthur (1864-1936)

| | |
|---|---|
| Occupation(s): | journalist - reporter, *New York Sun*, 1883-1887; |
| | managing editor, *Evening Sun*, 1887-1890; |
| | managing editor, *New York World*, 1890-1897; |
| | managing editor, *Evening Journal*, 1897-1921; |
| | editor, *Chicago Herald and Examiner* |
| | publisher - owner, *Washington Times*, 1917-1919; |
| | owner, *Evening Wisconsin*, 1918-1919 |
| | capitalist - extensive Manhattan real estate holdings; |
| | built and owned Ritz Tower Apartment Building, NYC |
| | writer - *Mary Baker Glover Eddy*, 1908 |
| Civic Activism: | a founder, Museum of the City of New York; |
| | suffragist* |
| Marriage(s): | 1912-1936 – Phoebe Cary (1890-1967) |
| | - Civic Activism: suffragist* - a founder and president, Westbury Suffrage Club, 1915; |
| | deeded 1,200 acres to State of New Jersey for the establishment of Allaire State Park and Historic Village** |
| Address: | Newbridge Road and Hempstead Turnpike, East Meadow |
| Name of estate: | |
| Year of construction: | |
| Style of architecture: | |
| Architect(s): | Hicks Nursery supplied plantings (for Brisbane) |
| Landscape architect(s): | |

House extant: no; demolished in 1946 for a housing development
Historical notes:

The *Long Island Society Register, 1929* lists Arthur and Phoebe Cary Brisbane as residing on East Meadow Road [Newbridge Road], Hempstead [East Meadow].

He was the son of Albert and Sarah White Brisbane of Buffalo, NY.

Phoebe Cary Brisbane was the daughter of Seward and Emily Scatcherd Cary of Buffalo and Hempstead, NY.

Arthur and Phoebe Cary Brisbane's daughter Sarah married John Reagan "Tex" McCrary, Jr. and resided in Manhasset. [*See* Spinzia, *Long Island's Prominent North Shore Families, vol. I* – McCrary entry.] Sarah subsequently married Chase Mellen, Jr., the son of Chase and Lucy Cony Manley Mellen, Sr. of Garden City. Their daughter Eleanor married Solon Chester Kelly III and, subsequently, Ewing Reginald Philbin, Jr., the son of Ewing Reginald and Harriet Mary Woodward Philbin, Sr. of *Pine Tree House* in Hewlett Bay Park. Their daughter Alice married E. Haring Chandor, the son of Reginald M. Chandor and, subsequently, David Dows, Jr. Their daughter Emily remained unmarried. Their son Seward married Doris Fauser and resided in Upper Brookville.

*For other Long Islanders involved in the suffrage movement *see* Raymond E. Spinzia, "Winning the Franchise: Long Island Activists in the Fight for Woman's Suffrage and Their Opponents, Long Island's Anti-Suffragists." wwwspinzialongislandestates.com.

**The Historic Village at Allaire in Allaire State Park is an interpretive restoration of an early 19th-century New Jersey iron producing community.

[For information about Brisbane's Montauk residence, *see* Spinzia, *Long Island's Prominent Families in the Town of East Hampton* – Brisbane entry.]

### Bromfield, Percy Butler (1857-1933)

| | |
|---|---|
| Occupation(s): | publisher -  a founder, *Success Magazine* |
| | advertising executive -   advertising manager, *The Christian Herald*; |
| | president, Bromfield & Field Inc.; |
| | president, Bromfield & Co. |
| Civic Activism: | trustee, Village of Hempstead; |
| | a founder and vice-president, Nassau Hospital, Mineola; |
| | known as the "Father of Fulton Park" for the conversion of a cemetery into the park |
| Marriage(s): | 1876-1929 – Emma Martin Rushmore (1854-1929) |
| Address: | 375 Fulton Avenue, Hempstead |
| Name of estate: | |
| Year of construction: | |
| Style of architecture: | |
| Architect(s): | |
| Landscape architect(s): | |
| House extant: no | |
| Historical notes: | |

   The *Long Island Society Register, 1929* lists Percy B. and Emma Martin Rushmore Bromfield as residing on Fulton Avenue, Hempstead. The 1910 Census lists the Bromfields at this address.
   He was the son of The Reverend Edward T. and Mrs. Georgiana Musgrave Bromfield.
   Emma Martin Rushmore Bromfield was the daughter of Elbert and Sarah Frances Fanning Rushmore.
   Percy Butler and Emma Martin Rushmore Bromfield's son Thomas married Mary Powell and resided in Garden City. Their son Percy married Florence Payntar and resided in Hempstead.
*[See following entry for additional family information.]*

### Bromfield, Percy Rushmore (1877-1953)

| | |
|---|---|
| Occupation(s): | advertising executive -   vice-president, United States Advertising Corp, NYC |
| Civic Activism: | member, Hempstead Draft Board, 1943 |
| Marriage(s): | 1901-1951 – Florence Payntar (1878-1951) |
| | - Civic Activism:  treasurer, Hempstead Public Library |
| Address: | 64 Hilton Avenue, Hempstead |
| Name of estate: | |
| Year of construction: | 1902 |
| Style of architecture: | Colonial Revival |
| Architect(s): | |
| Landscape architect(s): | |
| House extant: yes | |
| Historical notes: | |

   The *Long Island Society Register, 1929* lists Percy R. Bromfield as residing on Hilton Avenue, Hempstead.
   He was the son of Percy Butler and Emma Martin Rushmore Bromfield of Hempstead.
   Florence Payntar Bromfield was the daughter of George W. Payntar of Fulton Street, Hempstead.
   Percy Rushmore and Florence Payntar Bromfield's son Horace resided in Elizabeth, NJ.
*[See previous entry for additional family information.]*
   The house is now a commercial property.

*front facade, 2008*

### Brooks, Ernest, Sr. (1879-1957)

| | |
|---|---|
| Occupation(s): | architect -   partner, Starrett & Van Vleck* |
| Marriage(s): | Jeanne L. Marion (d. 1944)<br>    - Civic Activism:  president, Lawrence Garden Club |
| Address: | Club Lane, Lawrence |
| Name of estate: | *The Moorings* |
| Year of construction: | |
| Style of architecture: | |
| Architect(s): | |
| Landscape architect(s): | |
| House extant: | unconfirmed |
| Historical notes: | |

    The *Long Island Society Register, 1929* lists Ernest and Jeanne Marion Brooks [Sr.] as residing at *The Moorings* in Cedarhurst [Lawrence].
    Their son Ernest Brooks, Jr. married Mary Caroline Schoyer, the daughter of William E. Schoyer of Pittsburgh, PA, and resided in Manhattan.
    *The firm of Starrett and Van Vleck specialized in department store architectural designs. They designed the Lord and Taylor department store on Manhattan's Fifth Avenue and also Manhattan's Saks Fifth Avenue and Bloomingdale stores.


### Brower, Howard Stanley (1884-1968)

| | | |
|---|---|---|
| Occupation(s): | merchant - | president, Nassau Lumber Co.*;<br>president, Browner Lumber Co.;<br>president, Reserve Supply Corp., Mineola |
| | educator - | acting president, Hofstra Memorial Nassau College,<br>    Hempstead (now, Hofstra University) |
| | financier - | a founder, West Hempstead Bank |
| Civic Activism: | | a founder and chairman of board of trustees, Hofstra Memorial<br>    Nassau College, Hempstead (now, Hofstra University) |
| Marriage(s): | | 1906-1968 – Edna Dawson (1887-1981) |
| Address: | | Long Drive, West Hempstead |
| Name of estate: | | *Longdrive* |
| Year of construction: | | |
| Style of architecture: | | |
| Architect(s): | | |
| Landscape architect(s): | | |
| House extant: | unconfirmed | |
| Historical notes: | | |

    The *Long Island Society Register, 1929* lists Howard S. Brower as residing at *Longdrive* in West Hempstead. The 1930 Census lists the Browers at this address.
    He was the son of Richard and Elizabeth Jackson Brower of Hempstead.
    Howard Stanley and Edna Dawson Bower's daughter Mildred married Fillmore Samuel Frock and resided in West Palm Beach, FL. Their daughter Jean Ann married ____ Gustafson and resided in Waterford, NY.
    *Brower was William Sake Hofstra's partner in the Nassau Lumber Company and the co-executor of Mrs. Hofstra's will.

### Brown, Albert Winton, Sr. (1873-1937)

Occupation(s): attorney - partner, Campbell and Brown
financier - a founder and secretary, Mortgage Holding Corporation of Nassau County, 1908
capitalist - a founder, Baldwin Building Co., 1915

Marriage(s): Margaret Baldwin

Address: 143 Hampton Road, Hempstead
Name of estate:
Year of construction: 1931
Style of architecture: Neo-Tudor
Architect(s):
Landscape architect(s):
House extant: yes
Historical notes:

*Brown's Hampton Road residence, front facade, 2013*

The *Long Island Society Register, 1929* lists Mr. and Mrs. Albert Winton Brown [Sr.] as residing at 131 Hilton Avenue, Hempstead.

Their daughter Margaret married Langley William Isom and resided in Belmont, MA. Their son Major General Arthur Brown was a judge advocate in the United States Army. Their son David married Helen Catherine Whitney, the daughter of Arthur Edward and Florence Colgate Craig Whitney of Garden City, and resided in Lloyd Harbor.

At the time of Albert's death, he was residing at 143 Hampton Road in Garden City.


### Brown, Arthur Alvin, Sr. (1879-1972)

Occupation(s): industrialist - treasurer, Beck Hazard Shoe Co.

Marriage(s): 1905-1956 – Estelle Lupton Wiswell (1883-1956)

Address: 122 Stratford Avenue, Garden City
Name of estate:
Year of construction: 1893
Style of architecture: Colonial Revival
Architect(s):
Landscape architect(s):
House extant: yes
Historical notes:

The *Long Island Society Register, 1929* lists Mr. and Mrs. Arthur A. Brown [Sr.] as residing at 122 Stratford Road [Avenue], Garden City.

Estelle Lupton Wiswell Brown was the daughter of Stephen A. and Hannah Maria Drake Wiswell.

Arthur Alvin and Estelle Lupton Wiswell Brown, Sr.'s son Stanley married Margaret Jamieson Hanemann, the daughter of Edward Louis and Edna Cranmer Hanemann of Hempstead, and, later, Cynthia Robin. Their daughter Shirley married James Cyril Maille, the son of John E. Maille of Brooklyn. In 1911, their one-year-old son Arthur Alvin Brown, Jr. died

In 1929 Brown sold his ten-room house to Leonard H. Bick of Brooklyn and relocated to Stewart Avenue, between Brixton and Kensington Streets. [*The New York Times* June 21, 1930, p. 32, and October 19, 1929, p. 35.]

*front facade, 2001*

### Brown, Frederick Rhinelander (1889-1941)

| | |
|---|---|
| Occupation(s): | capitalist - owned apartment buildings in The Bronx |
| | financier - member, Deering, Milliken Co. (cotton brokerage firm); |
| | member, Amory Brown (cotton brokerage firm) |
| Civic Activism: | Special Deputy Sheriff, Nassau County |
| Marriage(s): | 1913-div. – Laura Pelton Hazard (1891-1970) |
| Address: | *[unable to determine street address],* Cedarhurst |
| Name of estate: | |
| Year of construction: | |
| Style of architecture: | |
| Architect(s): | |
| Landscape architect(s): | |
| House extant: | unconfirmed |
| Historical notes: | |

    The *Long Island Society Register, 1929* lists Frederic [sic] and Laura P. Hazard Brown as residing in Cedarhurst.
He was the son of Frederick Tilden and Mary Crosby Renwick Brown of Lawrence.
    Laura Pelton Hazard Brown was the daughter of William Ayrault and Laura Abell Pelton Hazard, who resided at *Meadow Hall* in Lawrence.
    Frederick Rhinelander and Laura Pelton Hazard Brown's daughter Frederica married Joseph Kenneth Lincoln, the son of George S. Lincoln of Wiscasset, ME. Their daughter Laura married A. Philippe Montant, the son of Louis T. Montant of Ridgewood, NJ, and resided in Manhattan. Their daughter Nathalie married William Goodby Lawrence, the son of Robert C. Lawrence of Red Bank, NJ. Their son Frederick Tilton Brown II married Katherine Cerf, the daughter of Louis Amadee Cerf of Quogue. [*See* Spinzia, *Long Island's Prominent Families in the Town of Southampton* – Cerf entry.]
    *[See following entry for additional family information.]*


### Brown, Dr. Frederick Tilden (1853-1910)

| | |
|---|---|
| Occupation(s): | physician |
| Marriage(s): | 1884-1910 – Mary Crosby Renwick (1849-1921) |
| Address: | Broadway, Woodmere |
| Name of estate: | *By-the-Way* |
| Year of construction: | |
| Style of architecture: | |
| Architect(s): | |
| Landscape architect(s): | |
| House extant: | unconfirmed |
| Historical notes: | |

    The *Social Register Summer, 1915* lists Mary C. Renwick Brown as residing at *By-the-Way* on Broadway in Woodmere.
    She was the daughter of William Rhinelander and Eliza Smedes Crosby Renwick. Mary had previously been married to Henry Tunstall Strong.
    Dr. Frederick Tilden Brown was the son of David Tilden and Cornelia Welles Brown.
    Dr. Frederick Tilden and Mrs. Mary Crosby Renwick Brown's daughter Margaret married Hans Carl Stricker, the son of Ludwig and Josefine Josefa Grossman Stricker, and resided at *The Orchard* in Woodmere. Their son Frederick Rhinelander Brown married Laura Pelton Hazard and resided in Cedarhurst.
    By 1920 Mary had relocated to *Windward* on Bannister Lane in Lawrence. It was a fifteen-acre estate with a large main residence and service buildings. [*The Standard Union* October 20, 1920, p. 14.]
    *[See previous entry for additional family information.]*

**Brown, Lewis Dean (1920-2001)**

| | | |
|---|---|---|
| Occupation(s): | diplomat - | United States Vice-Consul, Leopoldville, Belgian Congo, 1946-1948; |
| | | United States Vice-Consul, Ottawa, Canada, 1948-1952; |
| | | United States Second Secretary-Consul, Paris France, 1955-1958; |
| | | United States Ambassador to Senegal, 1967-1970*; |
| | | United States Ambassador to Gambia, 1967-1970*; |
| | | United States Ambassador to Jordan, 1970-1973; |
| | | United States Special Envoy to Cyprus, 1974; |
| | | United States Special Envoy to Lebanon, 1975 |
| | statesman - | member, Foreign Affairs Office, United States Department of State, 1952-1955; |
| | | member, International Relations Office, United States Department of State, 1958-1961; |
| | | Under-Secretary of State for Management, United States Department of State, 1973-1975** |
| Civic Activism: | | president, Middle East Institute; |
| | | director, American Academy of Diplomacy; |
| | | director, Institute for Islamic Affairs |
| Marriage(s): | | June Vereker Farquhar (1922-1986) |
| Address: | | 53 Pine Street, Garden City |
| Name of estate: | | |
| Year of construction: | | 1925 |
| Style of architecture: | | Victorian Revival |
| Architect(s): | | |
| Landscape architect(s): | | |
| House extant: yes | | |
| Historical notes: | | |

The house was built by Lewis Philip Brown.

Lewis Dean Brown was the son of Lewis Philip and Elizabeth Amy Crossley Brown and a graduate of Garden City High School.

June Vereker Farquhar Brown's parents resided in Hempstead.

Lewis Dean and June Vereker Farquhar Brown's son Michael married Karen Marie Huter, the daughter of Robert O. and Josephine Maidana Huter of Chicago, IL, and resides in Gordes, France.

Brown was no stranger to dangerous situations having taken part in the Normandy landings. As a diplomat and because of the high risk of several of his postings, Brown kept a pistol handy stating, "I would hope that I would not be an embarrassment to the United States government by being held hostage."

*Brown was United States Ambassador to Senegal and Gambia simultaneously.

**He was one of Secretary of State Henry Kissinger's "diplomatic dozen" that reorganized the Department of State. At the end of the Vietnamese War Brown organized and supervised the airlift of Americans and friendly Vietnamese from Saigon.

In 1994 the house was remodeled.

*front facade, 2009*

### Brownback, Garrett Arthur, Sr. (1882-1972)

| | |
|---|---|
| Occupation(s): | attorney -   member, Roberts and Montgomery |
| | industrialist -  director, Moto-Meter, Co. |
| | financier -   member, Field, Glore, and Co. (investment banking firm) |
| Marriage(s): | 1914-1961 – Lillian B. Hunter (1888-1962) |
| Address: | 3 Albro Lane, Lawrence |
| Name of estate: | |
| Year of construction: | |
| Style of architecture: | |
| Architect(s): | |
| Landscape architect(s): | |
| House extant: no | |
| Historical notes: | |

The *Long Island Society Register, 1929* lists Garrett A. and Lillian Hunter Brownback as residing at 3 Albro Lane, Cedarhurst [Lawrence].

He was the son of Garrett Elwood and Emma E. Evans Brownback.

Lillian B. Hunter Brownback was the daughter of Lida Gertrude Connely Hunter of Philadelphia.

Garret Arthur and Lillian B. Hunter Brownback, Sr.'s son Garrett Arthur Brownback, Jr. married Sharon Kay Arrick. Their daughter Sarah married Lewis G. Solomon, the son of Ferdinand L. Solomon of Woodmere.

By 1938 the Brownbacks were residing at 150 Albro Lane, Lawrence. [*Nassau Daily Review* September 30, 1938, p. 12, section 2.]

*150 Albro Lane, front facade, 2007*

### Browne, Curtis Northrop (1890-1946)

| | |
|---|---|
| Occupation(s): | advertising executive -   vice-president and director, Albert Frank – Guenther Law, NYC |
| Civic Activism: | clerk and mayor, Village of Hewlett Harbor; president, Badminton Association |
| Marriage(s): | 1917-1946 – Winifred Wheelwright Chisolm (b. 1896) |
| Address: | Oakwood Avenue, Cedarhurst |
| Name of estate: | |
| Year of construction: | |
| Style of architecture: | |
| Architect(s): | |
| Landscape architect(s): | |
| House extant: unconfirmed | |
| Historical notes: | |

The *Long Island Society Register, 1929* lists Curtis Northrop and Winifred W. Chisolm Browne as residing on Oakwood Avenue, Cedarhurst. In 1930 they relocated to Hewlett Harbor.

He was the son of Junius Henri Browne of Manhattan.

Winifred Wheelwright Chisolm Browne was the daughter of Benjamin Ogden and Bessie Rhoades Chisolm of New York City.

Curtis Northrop and Winifred Wheelwright Chisolm Browne's son Peter married Jeanne Hancock, the daughter of John Hancock of Cedarhurst, and resided in Saranac Lake, NY. Their daughter Sheila married Thomas Dwyer, the son of Martin and Mary Baker Tredwell Dwyer of Hewlett.

In 1930 the Brownes had relocated to Hewlett Harbor. [*Nassau Daily Review* March 19, 1942, p. 10.]

### Brush, Gilbert Palmer (1887-1967)

| | |
|---|---|
| Occupation(s): | attorney - partner, Brush and Block, NYC |
| Marriage(s): | 1912-1967 – Mildred Miller (1892-1968) |
| Address: | 155 Kensington Road, Garden City |
| Name of estate: | |
| Year of construction: | 1926 |
| Style of architecture: | Dutch Colonial Revival |
| Architect(s): | |
| Landscape architect(s): | |
| House extant: yes | |
| Historical notes: | |

*front facade, 2001*

The *Long Island Society Register, 1929* lists Gilbert Palmer and Mildred Miller Brush as residing at 155 Kensington Road, Garden City.

He was the son of Daniel Scofield and Margaret J. Stewart Brush.

Mildred Miller Brush was the daughter of William Henry and Martha Forker Miller.

Gilbert Palmer and Mildred Miller Brush's daughter Dorothy married William Kenneth Eastham, the son of William Eastham.

### Buck, Harold Winthrop (1873-1958)

| | |
|---|---|
| Occupation(s): | engineer - chief electrical engineer, Niagara Falls Power Co., Niagara Falls, NY; a founder and vice president, Viele, Blackwell, & Buck, NYC (engineering firm) |
| | inventor - co-inventor, with E. M. Newlen, of an electrical suspension insulator system |
| Marriage(s): | M/1 – 1902-1936 – Charlotte Ross Porter (1879-1936) |
| | M/2 – 1941 – Mary McEwen |
| Address: | Piermont Avenue, Hewlett Bay Park |
| Name of estate: | |
| Year of construction: | |
| Style of architecture: | Neo-Georgian |
| Architect(s): | |
| Landscape architect(s): | |
| House extant: unconfirmed | |
| Historical notes: | |

The *Long Island Society Register, 1929* lists Harold Winthrop and Charlotte R. Porter Buck as residing in Lawrence [Hewlett Bay Park].

He was the son of Albert Henry and Laura Salucia Abbott Buck of Manhattan.

Charlotte Ross Porter Buck was the daughter of Albert Augustus Porter of Niagara Falls, NY.

Harold Winthrop and Charlotte Ross Porter Buck's son Winthrop Porter Buck married Dorothy Higginson Weekes, the daughter of Arthur Delano and Dorothy Lee Higginson Weekes, Jr. who resided at *The Anchorage* in Oyster Bay Cove. [*See* Spinzia, *Long Island's Prominent North Shore Families, vol. II* – Weekes entry.] Their son Gordon married Loranda Prochnik, the daughter of the Austrian Minister. Their son Gurdon married Elizabeth Jackson, the daughter of James Jackson of Boston, MA.

*rear facade*

### Burr, Robert Page, Sr. (1897-1923)

| | |
|---|---|
| Occupation(s): | financier - member, Watson and White (stock brokerage firm) |
| Marriage(s): | 1921-1923 – Laurence Hewlett (1903-1987)<br>- real estate agent - a founder and president, Burr & McAuley, Hewlett |
| Address: | Martin's Lane, Lawrence |
| Name of estate: | |
| Year of construction: | |
| Style of architecture: | |
| Architect(s): | |
| Landscape architect(s): | |

House extant: unconfirmed
Historical notes:

The *Long Island Society Register, 1929* lists Mrs. Robert Page Burr as residing in Lawrence.

She was the daughter of James Monroe and Anna Willets Hewlett of Lawrence. Laurence, subsequently, married Horace Bowker, Sr. with whom she resided in Lawrence.

Robert Page Burr, Sr. was the son of Winthrop and Frances Page Burr, Sr., who resided at *Orchard Hall* in Lawrence.

Robert Page and Laurence Hewlett Burr, Sr.'s son Robert Page Burr, Jr. married Marian Hodges, the daughter of John King Hodges of Manhattan and, subsequently, Elizabeth J. Long, the daughter of William Henderson and Dorothy J. Smith Long, Jr. of *Moranda* in Hewlett Harbor, with whom he resided in Lloyd Harbor.

*[See following entry for additional family information.]*

### Burr, Winthrop, Sr. (1864-1929)

| | |
|---|---|
| Occupation(s): | financier - partner, Parkinson and Burr (stock brokerage firm); governor, New York Stock Exchange |
| Civic Activism: | chairman, arbitration committee, New York Stock Exchange; trustee, Society for the Reforming of Juvenile Delinquents; governor, president, and treasurer, Rockaway Hunting Club, Lawrence |
| Marriage(s): | 1887-1929 – Frances Page (1865-1939)<br>- Civic Activism: suffragist - member, state committee, Woman's Political Union* |
| Address: | Causeway, Lawrence |
| Name of estate: | *Orchard Hall* |
| Year of construction: | c. 1900 |
| Style of architecture: | Neo-Jacobean |
| Architect(s): | Thomas Henry Randall designed the house (for Burr) |
| Landscape architect(s): | Hicks Nursery supplied the Norway Maples, Japanese Poplars, Pin Oaks, and Silver Maples (for W. Burr, Sr.) |

House extant: no; demolished in 1968
Historical notes:

The house, originally named *Orchard Hall*, was built by Winthrop Burr, Sr.

The *Social Register Summer, 1910* lists Winthrop and Frances Page Burr [Sr.] as residing in Lawrence.

He was the son of Isaac Tucker and Ann Frances Hardon Burr of Newton, MA.

Frances Page Burr was the daughter of Joseph French Page of Philadelphia, PA.

Winthrop and Frances Page Burr, Sr.'s daughter Rosamund married Albert Boardman Kerr. Their daughter Frances married Alfred Ely. Their son Winthrop Burr, Jr. married Nathalie Audrey Randolph and resided in Shoreham. Their son Robert married Laurence Hewlett and resided in Lawrence.

*[See previous entry for more family information.]*

The house was subsequently owned by Henry Greenberg.

*For other Long Islanders involved in the suffrage movement *see* Raymond E. Spinzia, "Winning the Franchise: Long Island Activists in the Fight for Woman's Suffrage and Their Opponents, Long Island's Anti-Suffragists." wwwspinzialongislandestates.com.

*Orchard Hall, c. 1900*

### Burtis, Divine Franklin, III (1872-1907)

| | |
|---|---|
| Occupation(s): | real estate agent -   De Selden Brothers, Manhattan & Brooklyn |
| Marriage(s): | 1898-1907 – Florence Lockitt (d. 1948)<br>   - Civic Activism:  president, Woman's Board of Church Charity Foundation;<br>      chairman, women's board, St. John's Hospital, Brooklyn |
| Address: | 91 Salisbury Avenue, Garden City |
| Name of estate: | |
| Year of construction: | 1935 |
| Style of architecture: | Colonial Revival |
| Architect(s): | |
| Landscape architect(s): | |
| House extant:  yes | |
| Historical notes: | |

*91 Salisbury Avenue, Garden City, front facade, 2001*

The *Long Island Society Register, 1929* lists Divine Franklin and Florence Lockitt Burtis [III] as residing at 98 Clinton Road, Garden City.

He was the son of Divine Franklin Burtis, Jr. of Brooklyn and Bay Shore. The Burtises were Brooklyn shipbuilders and it was their firm that built the *General Slocum* in 1891, which subsequently burned to the water line in the East River. More than 1,000 people died in the accident on June 15, 1904 making it the single worst civilian loss-of-life until the attacks on the World Trade Towers on September 11, 2001.

Florence Lockitt Burtis was the daughter of Clement Lockitt of Brooklyn. Her sister Fanny married Charles Abercrombie Bryant and resided in Garden City.

At the time of her death, Florence was residing at 91 Salisbury Avenue, Garden City. [*The New York Times* March 19, 1948, p. 23.]

The Burtises did not have children.

### Burton, John Howes (1869-1946)

| | |
|---|---|
| Occupation(s): | capitalist -   owned Manhattan real estate;<br>      director, Woodmere Realty Co.<br>industrialist -   partner, Burton Brothers (cotton manufacturing firm) |
| Civic Activism: | chairman, Save New York Committee;<br>chairman, Thirty-Eighth Street Tunnel Committee;<br>governor, Woodmere Club;<br>member, executive committee, Rockaway Steeplechase Association, 1937 |
| Marriage(s): | 1902-1946 – Marie Digna Brooks (1871-1959) |
| Address: | Burton Lane, Lawrence |
| Name of estate: | *Albro House* |
| Year of construction: | c. 1900 |
| Style of architecture: | Georgian Revival |
| Architect(s): | Joseph H. Taft designed the house (for R. L. Burton) |
| Landscape architect(s): | Hicks Nursery supplied plantings (for R. L. Burton) |
| House extant:  no; demolished c. 1945 | |
| Historical notes: | |

*front facade*

The house, originally named *Albro House,* was built by Robert Lewis Burton.

The *Long Island Society Register, 1929* lists John Howes and Marie D. Brooks Burton as residing at *Albro House* in Cedarhurst [Lawrence].

He was the son of Josiah and Lucia Maria Clark Burton. His brother Robert built *Albro House*.

Marie Digna Brooks Burton was the daughter of Ernest August and Elisabeth Ann Douglas Arzola Brooks of Santiago, Cuba.

John Howes and Marie Digna Brooks Burton's son Howes married Sarah E. Dexter and resided in East Islip as did their son Ernest, who married Lucy F. Falkiner.

*[See following entry for additional family information.]*

Burton was residing at *The Farm* in East Islip at the time of his death. [*The New York Times* August 2, 1946, p. 13.]

### Burton, Robert Lewis (1860-1927)

| | |
|---|---|
| Occupation(s): | industrialist -  partner, Burton Brothers (cotton manufacturing firm) |
| | capitalist -   Woodmere Land Association (residential developer of the Village of Woodmere) |
| Civic Activism: | governor, Rockaway Hunting Club, Lawrence |
| Marriage(s); | 1884-1927 – Florence Southwick (1861-1937) |
| Address: | Burton Lane, Lawrence |
| Name of estate: | *Albro House* |
| Year of construction: | c. 1900 |
| Style of architecture: | Georgian Revival |
| Architect(s): | Joseph H. Taft designed the house (for R. L. Burton) |
| Landscape architect(s): | Hicks Nursery supplied plantings (for R. L. Burton) |

House extant:  no; demolished c. 1945
Historical notes:

The house, originally named *Albro House,* was built by Robert Lewis Burton.
The *Social Register Summer, 1915* lists Robert L. and Florence Southwick Burton as residing at *Albro House* in Cedarhurst [Lawrence].
He was the son of Josiah and Lucia Maria Clark Burton.
Florence Southwick Burton was the daughter of Richard Augustus and Anna Crawford Southwick.
Robert Lewis and Florence Southwick Burton's daughter Florence married Stephen Holladay Philbin and resided in Old Lyme, CT. Their daughter Louise married Wendell Phillips Blagden of Manhattan and, subsequently, George Lawson Wren with whom she resided at *Zee-in-Duin* in Southampton. [*See* Spinzia, *Long Island's Prominent Families in the Town of Southampton* – Wrenn entry.] Their son Crawford married Hariet Bullock and, later, Gertrude Harris, the daughter of John Francis and Gertrude Burbank Harris of *Storm-a-Long* in Southampton, and resided at *Pikes Inveraray* in Garrison, MD. [*See* Spinzia, *Long Island's Prominent Families in the Town of Southampton* – Harris entry.]
  [*See previous entry for more family information.*]

*rear facade, c. 1900*

### Cady, Everett Ware, Sr. (1902-1964)

Occupation(s): financier - partner, Cady, Roberts, and Co., NYC
industrialist - director, Budd Co., Philadelphia, PA;
    director, Nesco, Chicago, IL
capitalist - director, Electric Ferries, NY

Marriage(s): 1925-1964 – Clarissa Hurd (b. 1904)

Address: 220 Woodside Drive, Hewlett Bay Park
Name of estate:
Year of construction: 1923
Style of architecture: Mediterranean
Architect(s):
Landscape architect(s):
House extant: yes
Historical notes:

*rear facade, 2006*

The house was built by Everett Ware Cady, Sr.
The *Long Island Society Register, 1929* lists Everett Ware and Clarissa Hurd Cady [Sr.] as residing in Woodmere [Hewlett Bay Park].
He was the son of Bertha Ware Rhoades Cady.
Clarissa Hurd Cady was the daughter of George Arthur and Emily Lea Gazzam Hurd of Manhattan.
Everett Ware and Clarissa Hurd Cady, Sr.'s daughter Clarissa, who resided in New Haven, CT, married James Leslie, Jr. Their son Everett Ware Cady, Jr. married Ruth A. Payan and, later, Nancy Farr.

### Cameron, Walter Scott (1875-1932)

Occupation(s): sportsman
Civic Activism: master of hounds, Meadow Brook pack

Marriage(s): M/1 – 1902-div. 1920 – Rosalie de Goicouria (1878-1959)
M/2 – 1926-1932 – Cicely Mary Hilger (b. 1892)

Address: Fulton Avenue, Hempstead
Name of estate:
Year of construction:
Style of architecture:
Architect(s):
Landscape architect(s):
House extant: unconfirmed
Historical notes:

Walter Scott Cameron was the son of Adam Scott and Julia Elizabeth Sewell Cameron of Manhattan.
Rosalie de Goicouria Cameron was the daughter of Albert Valentine and Mary Cecelia Wall de Goicouria of Islip. Rosalie subsequently married Benjamin Curtis Allen of Philadelphia, PA. Rosalie's sister Alice married August Belmont III with whom she resided in Bay Shore. Alice subsequently married John Daniel Wing of Southampton. [*See* Spinzia, *Long Island's Prominent South Shore Families* – Belmont and de Goicouria entries – and *Long Island's Prominent Families in the Town of Southampton* – Wing entry.]
Walter Scott and Rosalie de Goicouria Cameron's daughter Rhoda married John Balfour Clark with whom she resided at *Hickory Hill* in Old Westbury and, subsequently, Ivan Henning Wichfield. [*See* Spinzia, *Long Island's Prominent North Shore Families, vol. I* – Clark entry.]
The *Long Island Society Register, 1929* lists W. Scott and Cicely Hilger Cameron as residing in Southampton.
She was the daughter of John Hilger of St. Louis, MO. She later married Oscar Moech Burke of East Hampton. [*See* Spinzia, *Long Island's Prominent Families in the Town of East Hampton* – Burke entry.]
[For information about Walter Scott Cameron's East End residences, *Wee Home* in Southampton and in East Hampton, see Spinzia, *Long Island's Prominent Families in the Town of Southampton* and *Long Island's Prominent Families in the Town of East Hampton* – Cameron entries.]

## Cammann, Herbert Schuyler (1884-1965)

| | |
|---|---|
| Occupation(s): | real estate agent |
| Civic Activism: | governor, Merrick Civic League, 1925 |
| Marriage(s): | 1911-1965 – Katharine Van Rensselaer Fairfax (1888-1978) |
| | - Civic Activism: director, Seamen's Church Institute, NYC; |
| | vice-president, auxiliary, Episcopal Church of the Holy Redeemer; |
| | president, Church Women's League for Patriotic Services, 1940; |
| | trustee and corresponding secretary, Young Women's Christian Association of Nassau County, 1933; |
| | director, Women's Auxiliary to Long Island Dioceses, 1936 |
| Address: | Merrick Road, Merrick |
| Name of estate: | *Lindenmere* |
| Year of construction: | |
| Style of architecture: | |
| Architect(s): | |
| Landscape architect(s): | |
| House extant: | unconfirmed |
| Historical notes: | |

The house, originally named *Lindenmere*, was built by Herbert's father Herman Henry Cammann.

The *Social Register Summer, 1937* lists H. Schuyler and Katharine V. R. Fairfax Cammann as residing at *Lindenmere* in Merrick.

Herbert was the great-grandson of the inventor of the steamboat Robert Fulton.

Katharine Van Rensselaer Fairfax Cammann was the daughter of Hamilton Rogers and Eleanor Ceclia Van Rensselaer Fairfax.

Herbert Schuyler and Katharine Van Rensselaer Fairfax Cammann's daughter Katharine married Howard Schuyler Lipson, Jr. and resided in Huntington. Their son Schuyler married Marcia de Forest Post and, later, Mary Lyman Cox.

*[See following Cammann entries for additional family information.]*


## Cammann, Herman Henry (1845-1930)

| | |
|---|---|
| Occupation(s): | capitalist - real estate developer in New York City and Long Island; president, Cammann, Voorhees, & Floyd |
| Civic Activism: | trustee, Columbia University, NYC; |
| | governor, New York Presbyterian Hospital, NYC; |
| | controller, Trinity Protestant Episcopal Parish, NYC |
| Marriage(s): | 1873-1919 – Ella Cornelia Crary (1843-1919) |
| Address: | Merrick Road, Merrick |
| Name of estate: | *Lindenmere* |
| Year of construction: | |
| Style of architecture: | |
| Architect(s): | |
| Landscape architect(s): | |
| House extant: | unconfirmed |
| Historical notes: | |

The house, originally named *Lindenmere*, was built by Herman Henry Cammann.

The *Social Register Summer, 1910* lists Herman H. and Ella C. Crary Cammann as residing at *Lindenmere* in Merrick.

He was the son of Dr. George Philip and Mrs. Anna Catharina Lorillard Cammann.

Ella Cornelia Crary Cammann was the daughter of Edward Charles and Cornelia Livingston Crary.

Herman Henry and Ella Cornelia Crary Cammann's son Herbert, who later owned *Lindenmere*, married Katharine Van Rensselaer Fairfax. Their son Edward married Helena Van Kortlandt Clarkson and resided on Byron Road in Merrick.

*[See other Cammann entries for additional family information.]*

**Cammann, Schuyler Van Rensselaer (1912-1991)**

| | | |
|---|---|---|
| Occupation(s): | educator - | Yale-in China, Changsha, Hunan, 1935-1937; |

assistant professor of Oriental Studies, University of Pennsylvania, Philadelphia, PA, 1949-1950;
associate professor, University of Pennsylvania, Philadelphia, PA, 1950-1956;
professor of Oriental Studies, University of Pennsylvania, Philadelphia, PA, 1966-1982;
professor, North American Treaty Organization, Denmark University, Copenhagen, Denmark, 1969;
professor, International School American Around the World, 1962-1963;
associate curator of Eastern Asian Collection, University Museum, University of Pennsylvania, Philadelphia, PA

entertainer and associated professions -
    panelist, "What in the World?" 1951-1955 (television program);
    narrator, "Southeastern Asia" (television series)

journalist - editor, *Journal of American Oriental Society*

writer - four books and 379 articles

Civic Activism:
vice-president, Oriental Society;
president, Philadelphia Anthropological Society;
president, Oriental Club of Philadelphia;
fellow, American Learned Societies;
fellow, American Anthropological Society;
director, Council for Old World Archeology;
director, Far Eastern Society

Marriage(s):
M/1 – 1943-div. 1972 – Marcia de Forest Post (1920-1994)
  - intelligence agent - member, Naval Intelligence during World War II
  educator - Shipley School, Bryn Mawr, PA;
    Bryn Mawr College
M/2 – 1980-1991 – Mary Lyman Cox (1923-c. 2009)

Address: Merrick Road, Merrick
Name of estate: *Lindenmere*
Year of construction:
Style of architecture:
Architect(s):
Landscape architect(s):
House extant: unconfirmed
Historical notes:

    Schuyler was the son of Herbert Schuyler and Katharine Van Rensselaer Fairfax Cammann of *Lindenmere*.
    Marcia de Forest Post Cammann was the daughter of Charles Addison and Marcia de Forest Post.
    Schuyler Van Rensselaer and Marcia de Forest Post Cammann's son Stephen married Margurite Judith Morinelli, the daughter of A. F. Morinelli of Marple, PA, and resided in Marple, PA. Their son Hamilton resided in Chilmark, MA. Their son William resided in Long Beach Island, NJ. Their daughter Frances married ____ Hrynio and resided in Sugar Hill, NH.
    Mary Lyman Cox Cammann was the daughter of John Lyman Cox of Philadelphia. She had previously been married to John Brinley Muir, the son of John Wallingford and Mary Frothingham Brinley Muir.
    *[See other Cammann entries for additional family information.]*

## Camprubi, Jose Aymar (1879-1942)

| | |
|---|---|
| Occupation(s): | engineer - worked on building of Hudson tubes from Manhattan to New Jersey for Hudson & Manhattan Railroad Co.; worked on electrification of New York Central Railroad |
| | publisher - president, *La Prensa*, NYC (Spanish language newspaper) |
| Civic Activism: | president, *Union Benefica Espanola* (Spanish charitable society) |
| Marriage(s): | 1909-1942 – Agnes Ethel Leaycraft (1882-1958) |
| Address: | Irving Place, Woodmere |
| Name of estate: | |
| Year of construction: | |
| Style of architecture: | |
| Architect(s): | |
| Landscape architect(s): | |
| House extant: unconfirmed | |
| Historical notes: | |

The *Long Island Society Register, 1929* lists Jose Aymar and A. Ethel Leaycraft Camprubi as residing on Irving Place, Woodmere.

He was the son of Raimundo Escudero and Isabel Aymar y Lucca Camprubi of Puerto Rico.

Agnes Ethel Leaycraft Camprubi was the daughter of Charles Russell Leaycraft of Essex Fells, NJ, and a descendant of Nicholas Roosevelt.

Jose Aymar and Agnes Ethel Leaycraft Camprubi's daughter Inis married John Scott Mabon, the son of The Reverend Arthur F. Mabon of Manhattan and Madison, CT. Their daughter Leontine married Dr. Gerhard Tintner, the son of Leopold Tintner of Vienna, Austria, and Ames, IA.

By 1935 the Camprubis were residing at 956 Central Avenue, Woodmere. [*The Brooklyn Daily Eagle* October 13, 1935, p. 4B.]


## Candler, Flamen Ball (1838-1914)

| | |
|---|---|
| Occupation(s): | attorney - partner, Van Winkle, Candler, and Jay |
| | educator - first president, Department of Law, Brooklyn Institute of Arts and Sciences; |
| Civic Activism: | trustee, Long Island Historical Society (later, Brooklyn Historical Society) |
| Marriage(s): | 1865-1914 – Marcia Lillian Welch (1845-1917) |
| Address: | Smith Lane, Woodmere |
| Name of estate: | |
| Year of construction: | |
| Style of architecture: | |
| Architect(s): | |
| Landscape architect(s): | |
| House extant: unconfirmed | |
| Historical notes: | |

Flamen Ball Candler was the son of Samuel Marsden and Elizabeth Cecilia Ball Candler of Cincinnati, OH.

Marcia Lillian Welch Candler was the daughter of Robert William and Marcia Alden Packard Welch.

Flamen Ball and Marcia Lillian Welch Candler's daughter Edith married George Ledyard Stebbins, Sr. and resided in Woodmere. Their son Duncan married Beatrice de Trobriand Post, the daughter of Charles Alfred and Marie Caroline de Trobriand Post who resided at *Strandhome* in Bayport. [*See* Spinzia, *Long Island's Prominent South Shore Families* – Post entry.]

### Carl, James Harvey, Jr. (1893-1956)

Occupation(s): industrialist - head, sales department, Ashville–Schoonmaker Mica Co.;
president, Mica Company of Canada

Marriage(s): 1917-1927 – Helen Cowperthwaite Eilbeck (d. 1927)

Address: 110 Fifth Street, Garden City
Name of estate:
Year of construction: 1923
Style of architecture: English Cottage Style with Victorian elements
Architect(s):
Landscape architect(s):
House extant: yes
Historical notes:

*front facade, 2009*

The house was built by James Harvey Carl, Jr.
The *Long Island Society Register, 1929* lists James H. Carl, Jr. as residing at 110 Fifth Street, Garden City.
He was the son of James Harvey Carl, Sr. of Garden City.
Helen Cowperthwaite Eilbeck Carl was the daughter of John Herbert and Mabelle Eilbeck of Manhattan.

### Carlin, George Andrew (1890-1945)

Occupation(s): attorney
journalist - reporter, *Brooklyn Daily Eagle*, 1911-1912;
reporter, *Brooklyn Standard Union*, 1912-1916;
reporter, *New York Sun*, 1916-1917, 1919-1920;
London correspondent, Edward Marshall Syndicate, 1920-1921;
reporter, *New York Herald*, 1921-1922;
editor, Metro Newspaper Service, 1928-1930
manager, United Feature Syndicate, NYC
educator - teacher, Patillas, Puerto Rico

Marriage(s): 1922-1945 – Mary Carr (b. 1892)

Address: 44 Hilton Avenue, Garden City
Name of estate:
Year of construction: 1888
Style of architecture: Victorian
Architect(s):
Landscape architect(s):
House extant: yes
Historical notes:

*front facade, 2018*

The *Long Island Society Register, 1929* lists George A. and Mary Carr Carlin as residing at 50 Cruickshank Avenue, Hempstead. By 1932 the Carlins were residing at 74 Cathedral Avenue, Hempstead. [*The Brooklyn Daily Eagle* August 5, 1932, p. 15.] At the time of George's death, the Carlins were residing at 44 Hilton Avenue, Garden City. [*Nassau Daily Review–Star* November 29, 1945, p. 1.]
He was the son of Frederick William and Joan Driscoll Carlin of Brooklyn.
Mary Carr Carlin was the daughter of New York State Supreme Court Judge William J. Carr.
George Andrew and Mary Carr Carlin's daughter Joan married John Alden. Their daughter Julia married Peter Anthony Vischer, the son of Peter Leonhard Vischer, who resided at *Chateau de Wildenstein* in Bale–Campagne, Switzerland.
George's funeral was attended by First Lady Eleanor Roosevelt.
In 2018, the six-bedroom, four-and-a-half-bath, 3,650-square-foot house sold for $1.546 million.
In 2001 the house was remodeled.

### Carpenter, Edward Novell (1920-2011)

| | |
|---|---|
| Occupation(s): | financier - member, Jessup and Lamont (stock brokerage firm) |
| Marriage(s): | M/1 – 1942-1971 – Katherine Van Duzer Eaton (d. 1971) |
| | M/2 – 1973-2011 – Margaret Arnold Owen |
| Address: | 275 Barrett Road, Lawrence |
| Name of estate: | |
| Year of construction: | 1905 |
| Style of architecture: | Colonial Revival |
| Architect(s): | |
| Landscape architect(s): | |
| House extant: yes | |
| Historical notes: | |

*front facade, 2013*

The *Social Register New York, 1951* lists Edward N. and Katherine Van D. Eaton Carpenter as residing on Longwood Crossing, Cedarhurst [Lawrence].

He was the son of George and Dorothy Millen Carpenter.

Katherine Van Duzer Eaton Carpenter was the daughter of Walter Bradley and Margaret Burton Eaton, who resided at *The Corral* in Cedarhurst.

Edward Novell and Katherine Van Duzer Eaton Carpenter's daughter Katherine married Glasgow-born actor David Keith McCallum, Jr., well-known for his role in the *Great Escape* and as Illya Kuryakin in the 1960s television series *The Man From U.N.C.L.E.* McCallum is the son of David Keith McCallum, Sr., violinist and concertmaster of the London Philharmonic. The Carpenters' son George was killed in the Vietnam War. Their son Jake married Donna Gaston.

By 1984 Edward Novell and Margaret Arnold Owen Carpenter were residing at 275 Barrett Road, Lawrence.

She was the daughter of Stephen Cooke Owen of Lawrence. She had previously been married to Hendrick Barnard Van Rensselaer, Jr.

In 2013 the house sold for $1.510 million.


### Carroll, Royall Phelps (1862-1922)

| | |
|---|---|
| Occupation(s): | yachtsman |
| Marriage(s): | 1891-1922 – Marion Landon (1864-1949) |
| | - Civic Activism: member, ladies committee of board of governors, Newport Golf Club |
| Address: | Front Street, Hempstead |
| Name of estate: | |
| Year of construction: | |
| Style of architecture: | |
| Architect(s): | |
| Landscape architect(s): | |
| House extant: unconfirmed | |
| Historical notes: | |

Royall Phelps Carroll was the son of Governor John Lee and Mrs. Anita Georgiana Phelps Carroll of Maryland and a descendant of Charles Carroll, a signer of the Declaration of Independence. His sister ____ married Baron de la Grande of France. His sister Marie married Count Jean de Kergorlay of Paris, France. His sister Helen married Herbert Daniel Robbins and resided in Paris, France. His sister Anne married Howard Townsend and resided at *Overedge* in Northeast Harbor, ME.

Marion Landon Carroll was the daughter of Eugene and Harriet Lowndes Landon. Marion was the step-daughter of General Philip S. Schuyler of *Nevis* in Irvington, NY, and descendant of John Jacob Astor.

Royall Phelps and Marion Landon Carroll's daughter Dorothea married Avery Claflin, the son of Alan A. Claflin of Winchester, MA, and resided in Cedarhurst.

### Carter, Russell Steenback (1878-1944)

| | |
|---|---|
| Occupation(s): | industrialist - assistant manager, New York Office, Ingersoll–Rand Co. |
| Marriage(s): | 1907-1944 – Florence Bates (1880-1964) <br> - Civic Activism: donated her collection of 17th- and 18th-century English pottery to the Metropolitan Museum of Art, NYC |
| Address: | 91 Cedar Avenue, Hewlett Bay Park |
| Name of estate: | *The Villa Blue* |
| Year of construction: | c. 1910 |
| Style of architecture: | 20th Century Eclectic |
| Architect(s): | Albro and Lindeberg designed the house (for Carter) |
| Landscape architect(s): | |
| House extant: yes | |
| Historical notes: | |

*front facade, 1911*

The house, originally name *The Villa Blue*, was built by Russell Steenback Carter.
The *Long Island Society Register, 1929* lists Russell S. and Florence Bates Carter as residing in Hewlett [Hewlett Bay Park].
He was the son of Dr. Henry Skelton and Mrs. Florence Russell Carter. Russell's brother Jarvis married Harriet Coleman Delafield, the daughter of Maturn and Mary Coleman Livingston Delafield, Sr. of *Fieldstone* in Riverdale-on-Hudson, NY, and resided at *Sunswyck* in Westhampton Beach. [*See* Spinzia, *Long Island's Prominent Families in the Town of Southampton* – Carter entry.]
Florence Bates Carter was the daughter of Charles Bates of Manhattan.
Russell Steenback and Florence Bates Carter's daughter Mary died in 1928 at the age of twenty.
In 1984 the house was remodeled.

### Cartwright, Henry Rogers, Jr. (1879-1941)

| | |
|---|---|
| Occupation(s): | financier - member, United Services Life Insurance Co. |
| Marriage(s): | 1915-1941 – Mildred Gould Patton (1891-1955) <br> - Civic Activism: vice-president, publicity committee, Community Chest |
| Address: | Piermont Avenue, Hewlett |
| Name of estate: | *Applecot* |
| Year of construction: | |
| Style of architecture: | Colonial Revival |
| Architect(s): | |
| Landscape architect(s): | |
| House extant: unconfirmed | |
| Historical notes: | |

The *Long Island Society Register, 1929* lists Henry R. and Mildred G. Patton Cartwright, Jr. as residing at *Applecot* in Hewlett. The *Social Register New York, 1939* lists the Cartwrights' address as Piermont Road [Avenue], Hewlett.
He was the son of Henry Rogers and Julia Smith Cartwright, Sr. of Philadelphia, PA.
Mildred Gould Patton Cartwright was the daughter of John Woodbridge and Florence B. Crew Patton of Philadelphia, PA.
Henry Rogers and Mildred Gould Patton Cartwright, Jr.'s daughter Mildred married Thomas Comins Hart, Jr. of Sharon, CT, and, later, Carl Mitchell Light, the son of Benjamin Light of Trenton, NJ. Their son John married Joan Baldwin, the daughter of Alexander T. Baldwin of Bedford Hills, NY.
In 1946 the house was purchased by Alden Rodney Ludlow, Jr. [*The Brooklyn Daily Eagle* June 2, 1946, p. 29, and *Nassau Daily Review–Star* June 6, 1946, p. 8.]

**Casey, William Joseph, Jr. (1913-1987)**

| | |
|---|---|
| Occupation(s): | attorney -   partner, Hall, Casey, Dickler, and Howley |
| | intelligence agent -   member of Office of Strategic Services (OSS) during World War II; |
| | director, Central Intelligence Agency, 1981-1987 |
| | statesman - Under Secretary of State for Economic Affairs in Nixon administration, 1973-1974 |
| | politician -   campaign manager, Ronald Reagan presidential campaign, 1980 |
| | financier -  chairman, U. S. Export–Import Bank |
| | writer -   *Tax Sheltered Investments*, 1952; *Estate Planning Book*, 1956; *Lawyers Desk Book*, 1965; *Forms of Business Agreements*, 1966; *Accounting Desk Book*, 1967; *Armchair Guide to the American Revolution*, 1976; *The Secret War Against Hitler*, 1988 |
| | capitalist -   director, The Bechtel Group (a San Francisco–based international construction firm)* |
| Civic Activism: | chairman of board, Long Island Association of Industry and Commerce; trustee, Fordham University, The Bronx, NYC |
| Marriage(s): | 1941-1987 – Sophia Bernadette Kurz (1909-2000) |
| Address: | 422 Midwood Avenue, Bellmore |
| Name of estate: | |
| Year of construction: | 1924 |
| Style of architecture: | Colonial Revival |
| Architect(s): | |
| Landscape architect(s): | |
| House extant: yes | |
| Historical notes: | |

   William Joseph Casey, Jr. was raised in this house. He was the son of William Joseph and Blanche Agnes LaVigne Casey, Sr.
   William Joseph and Sophia Bernadette Kurz Casey, Jr.'s daughter Bernadette married Owen Telfair Smith and resided in Laurel Hollow.
   In 1948 Casey relocated to Roslyn Harbor, purchasing an 1855 Victorian home he called *Mayknoll* for $50,000. [*See* Spinzia, *Long Island's Prominent North Shore Families, vol. 1* – Casey entry – and *Long Island's Prominent North Shore Families, vol. II* – Smith entry.]
   *Over the years Bechtel has constructed such diverse projects as: the Hoover Dam; the English Channel Tunnel; the Hong Kong airport; Boston Central Road Artery and Tunnel; the AT&T wireless network expansion; the Ankara–Gerede highway in Turkey; and the Kirkuck–Syria pipeline in Iraq. The contract to rebuild Kuwait's oil fields after the 1991 Gulf War went to Bechtel. After the Iraq War of 2003 Bechtel was awarded the contract to rebuild two international airports and three domestic airports, to reconstruct electric power plants, to repair roads, railroads, schools, hospitals, and irrigation and drinking water systems in Iraq. [*The New York Times* April 18, 2003, p. A1 and B7.]
   In 2012 the 1,402-square-foot Bellmore house sold for $283,000.

*front facade, 2001*

## Chalfant, Edward Newton (1891-1964)

| | |
|---|---|
| Occupation(s): | advertising executive - partner, McMullen, Sterling, and Chalfant (later, Gotham Advertising Co.); vice-president, Gotham Advertising Co. |
| Marriage(s): | M/1 – 1916 – Mary McKean (b. 1892) <br> M/2 – Jane N. *[unable to determine maiden name]* (d. 1955) |
| Address: | 51 Roxbury Road, Garden City |
| Name of estate: | |
| Year of construction: | 1908 |
| Style of architecture: | Four Square |
| Architect(s): | |
| Landscape architect(s): | |
| House extant: yes | |
| Historical notes: | |

The *Brooklyn Blue Book and Long Island Society Register, 1922* lists Edward N. Chalfant as residing at 51 Roxbury Road, Garden City.

The son of The Reverend Frank Herring and Mrs. Jane A. Martin Chalfant, Edward was born in Wei-hein, China.

Edward Newton Chalfant's daughter Patricia married Andrew Fred Frey, the son of Fred Frey of Hollis. His daughter Carolyn married Rex D. Crump and resided in Buffalo, NY.

In 2004, the three-bedroom, 3,043-square-foot house sold for $1.275 million.

*front facade, 2012*

## Chamberlin, Dr. William Taylor (1873-1945)

| | |
|---|---|
| Occupation(s): | physician - surgeon, Nassau Hospital, Mineola; surgeon, Meadow Brook Hospital, Hempstead; resident physician, County Home, East Hempstead <br> capitalist - director, Calderon Theatre Corp., Hempstead <br> financier - director, Second National Bank & Trust Co., Hempstead |
| Civic Activism: | president, Village of Hempstead, 1927; mayor, Village of Hempstead, 1928-1935 (first village mayor) |
| Marriage(s): | Bessie Shenton (1882-1957) <br>    - Civic Activism:  a founder, Visiting Nurse Service, Garden City |
| Address: | 359 Fulton Avenue, Hempstead |
| Name of estate: | |
| Year of construction: | |
| Style of architecture: | |
| Architect(s): | |
| Landscape architect(s): | |
| House extant: no | |
| Historical notes: | |

The *Long Island Society Register, 1929* lists Dr. W. Taylor and Mrs. Bessie Shenton Chamberlin as residing at 359 Fulton Avenue, Hempstead.

He was the son of James Sutphin Chamberlin of Ottawa, Canada.

Dr. William Taylor and Mrs. Bessie Shenton Chamberlin's daughter Dorothy married Charles Sigmund Roever with whom she resided in Garden City.

## Chambers, Jay (1877-1922)
## aka James A. Chambers

| | |
|---|---|
| Occupation(s): | artist - bookplate illustrator;<br>graphic artist, *New York World* |
| Civic Activism: | directed and designed sets for numerous local and Brooklyn theatrical productions;<br>designed sets for General Organization of South Side High School, 1915;<br>donated 800 modern American and foreign bookplates to the Flatbush Branch of the New York Public Library |
| Marriage(s): | 1900-1922 – Laha Whittaker (1872-1958)<br>- Civic Activism: involved in numerous local school and community theatrical productions;<br>president, Mothers Club of Lynbrook;<br>a founder, Lynbrook Public Library |
| Address: | 228 Earle Avenue, Lynbrook |
| Name of estate: | |
| Year of construction: | 1915 |
| Style of architecture: | Long Island Farmhouse |
| Architect(s): | |
| Landscape architect(s): | |
| House extant: yes | |
| Historical notes: | |

James A. Chambers was the son of James Slater and Elizabeth Mendora Chambers.

Laha Whittaker Chambers was the daughter of Charles and Mary Blanchard Chambers. Her name was Malaysian for princess.

James A. and Laha Whittaker Chambers' family was totally dysfunctional. James did not want or like children and seldom spoke to his sons. In spite of the fact that he made a good salary as an artist, he refused to repair the house or purchase adequate furniture. The kitchen was created by moving a service building against the house. The juncture of the two buildings leaked for ten or twelve years until his son Richard was old enough to climb onto the roof and repair it. The wallpaper in the house was old, faded and peeling. The ceiling in the living room/dining room collapsed revealing the laths. The yellow paint on the exterior of the house was faded and peeling.

In 1926, their twenty-three-year-old son Richard, who had taken to drink, committed suicide in the kitchen by turning on the stove's gas jets.

Their son Jay Vivian Chambers (aka Whittaker Chambers and David Whittaker Chambers), who was bi-sexual, married Esther Shemitz. He became a Soviet spy and testified before the House UnAmerican Activities Committee of Congress that Alger Hiss, who would later reside in East Hampton, was a member of the Communist Party. [*See* Spinzia, *Long Island's Prominent Families in the Town of East Hampton* – Hiss entry – and Whittaker Chambers, *Witness: Whittaker Chambers*. (New York: Random House, 1952).]

*front facade, 2000*

### Chambers, William Ely, Sr. (1895-1972)

| | |
|---|---|
| Occupation(s): | financier - vice-president, First National City Bank |
| Marriage(s): | Hazel Nesbitt Wiseman (1895-1973) |
| Address: | 2 Ives Road, Hewlett |
| Name of estate: | *Cornerware* |
| Year of construction: | |
| Style of architecture: | |
| Architect(s): | |
| Landscape architect(s): | |
| House extant: unconfirmed | |
| Historical notes: | |

The *Social Register New York, 1934* lists William Ely and Hazel N. Wiseman Chambers as residing at *Cornerware* in Hewlett. By 1935 they were residing on Ives Road, Hewlett.

He was the son of Dr. Porter Flewellen and Mrs. Alice Ely Chambers, who resided at *Bon Acre* in Southampton. William's brother Ambrose resided at *Sandhurst* in Southampton. [*See* Spinzia, Long Island's Prominent Families in the Town of Southampton – Chambers entries.]

William Ely and Hazel Nesbitt Wiseman Chambers, Sr.'s son William Ely Chambers, Jr. married Eleanor Virginia Neill, the daughter of Dr. Thomas Edwin Neill of Middleburg, VA, and resided in Scarsdale, NY. Their daughter Cathleen married Mark D'Ashby Farrington, the son of Joseph P. Farrington of Lawrence.


### Chapman, Gilbert Whipple, Sr. (1902-1979)

| | |
|---|---|
| Occupation(s): | capitalist - president, American Water Works and Electric Co.; president, Sutton Place South Corp., NYC |
| | industrialist - president, Yale & Towne Manufacturing Co. |
| Civic Activism: | president, board of trustees, New York Public Library; first chairman, National Book Committee; first president, Council on Library Resources; a founder and director, Lincoln Center for the Performing Arts, NYC; secretary, Lawrence Beach Club |
| Marriage(s): | M/1 – 1925-1949 – Katharine Bright (1903-1949) |
| | - Civic Activism: treasurer, Lawrence Garden Club; chair, parents' committee, Lawrence School |
| | M/2 – 1950-1979 – Elizabeth Fuller (1893-1980) |
| | - Civic Activism: president, Arts Club of Chicago, 1932-1940 |
| Address: | 92 Burton Avenue, Woodmere |
| Name of estate: | |
| Year of construction: | |
| Style of architecture: | |
| Architect(s): | |
| Landscape architect(s): | |
| House extant: no | |
| Historical notes: | |

The *Long Island Society Register, 1929* lists Gilbert Whipple and Katharine Bright Chapman as residing at 92 Burton Avenue, Woodmere.

He was the son of Henry Otis and Harriet Louise Murphey Chapman, Sr. of Woodmere.

Katharine Bright Chapman was the daughter of Osborn Wyckoff and Joanna Hayes Shepard Bright.

Gilbert Whipple and Katharine Bright Chapman, Sr.'s daughter Harriet married H. Worthington Kalt. Their son Gilbert Whipple Chapman, Jr. married Judith Rodel Coste, the daughter of Felix Wilkins Coste of Manhattan, and resided in Locust Valley.

Elizabeth Fuller Chapman was the daughter of Dr. Charles Gordon Fuller. She had previously been married to Charles Barnett Goodspeed.

*[See following entry for additional family information.]*

### Chapman, Henry Otis, Sr. (1862-1929)

| | |
|---|---|
| Occupation(s): | architect - partner, Barney and Chapman;* |
| | partner, Henry Otis Chapman & Son* |
| Civic Activism: | trustee, Village of Woodsburgh |
| Marriage(s): | Harriet Louise Murphey (1866-1947) |
| Address: | Woodmere Boulevard, South Woodsburgh |
| Year of construction: | c. 1902 |
| Style of architecture: | Neo-Tudor |
| Architect(s): | Henry Otis Chapman, Sr. designed his own house |
| Landscape architect(s): | |
| House extant: | no |

*front facade, 1904*

Historical notes:

Henry Otis Chapman, Sr. designed and built his own residence.

The *Long Island Society Register, 1929* lists Henry Otis and Harriet M. [sic] Murphey Chapman [Sr.] as residing in Woodmere.

He was the son of Henry and Frances C. Otis Chapman.

Henry Otis and Harriet Louise Murphey Chapman, Sr.'s son Gilbert, who resided in Woodmere, married Katharine Bright and, later, Elizabeth Fuller. Their son Henry Otis Chapman, Jr. married Virginia Morrill, the daughter of Arthur Putnam Morill of Concord, NH, and resided in Lawrence. Virginia later married Schuyler Merritt II with whom she resided in Lawrence. Their son Coolidge married Helen Gross Hume, the daughter of John Charlick Hume, and resided in Tacoma, WA.

*See architect appendix for Chapman's commission in the Town of Hempstead. *See also* architect appendices in Spinzia, *Long Island's Prominent North Shore Families, vol. II*, and *Long Island's Prominent Families in the Town of Southampton*.

In 1928 the house was remodeled.


### Chenault, Dr. Hortenius (1910-1990)

| | |
|---|---|
| Occupation(s): | physician - dental surgeon with Hempstead and Rockville Centre offices, 1939-1987 |
| Marriage(s): | 1942-1990 – Anne Naomi Quick (1914-2012) |
| | - dental hygienist, Department of Health, City of New York |
| | Civic Activism: vice-president, Women's Fellowship; |
| | secretary, Friends of Hempstead Library |
| Address: | 25 Dietz Street, Hempstead |
| Name of estate: | |
| Year of construction: | 1948 |
| Style of architecture: | Cape Cod |
| Architect(s): | |
| Landscape architect(s): | |
| House extant: | yes |

Historical notes:

Dr. Hortenius Chenault was first in his class at Howard University Dental School, passed the New York State dental exam with the highest score to date, and was the recipient of the Guggenheim Award from the John Simon Guggenheim Memorial Foundation.

Anne Naomi Quick Chenault was the daughter of Oscar and Louise Quick of South Carolina. Anne was first in her class at the School of Dental Hygiene of Howard University.

Dr. Hortenius and Mrs. Anne Naomi Quick Chenault's daughter resides in Hempstead. Their son Arthur, who was the Building Superintendent of the Village of Hempstead, resides in Great Neck. Their son Stephen, who is the director of Science Development at the New York Botanical Garden, did not marry and resides in Brooklyn. Their son Kenneth married Kathryn Cassell and resides in New Rochelle, NY.

*[See following entry for additional family information.]*

### Chenault, Kenneth Irvine (b. 1951)

| | |
|---|---|
| Occupation(s): | attorney - member, Rogers and Wells, 1977-1979 |
| | capitalist - director, Airbnb; |
| |     director, Facebook (now, Meta Platforms, Inc.); |
| |     director, Berkshire Hathaway; |
| |     director, Brooklyn Union Gas Co. |
| | industrialist - director, International Business Machine; |
| |     director, Quaker Oats |
| | financier - director, strategic planning, American Express Co.; |
| |     general manager and vice president for Merchandise Services, American Express Co.; |
| |     vice-president, Am Ex Travel Related Services, American Express Co.; |
| |     executive vice-president and, later, president, Consumer Card and Financial Service Group, American Express Co.; |
| |     president, American Express USA; |
| |     vice-chairman, American Express USA; |
| |     CEO, American Express USA |
| Civic Activism: | trustee, New York Medical Center; |
| | trustee, Bowdoin College; |
| | trustee, NCAA; |
| | trustee, Arthur Ash Institute for Urban Health; |
| | chairman, advisory council, Smithsonian National Museum of African History and Culture; |
| | trustee, Harvard Corporation (university's fiduciary authority); |
| | funding donor, Art for Justice Fund; |
| | member, executive committee, Business Roundtable; |
| | member, executive committee, The Business Council |
| Marriage(s): | Kathryn Cassell |
| |   - attorney - United Negro College Fund |
| |     Civic Activism: funding donor, Art For Justice Fund |
| Address: | 25 Dietz Street, Hempstead |
| Name of estate: | |
| Year of construction: | 1948 |
| Style of architecture: | Cape Cod |
| Architect(s): | |
| Landscape architect(s): | |
| House extant: yes | |
| Historical notes: | |

Kenneth was raised in this 2,334-square-foot, five-bedroom, two-bath house by his parents Dr. Hortenius and Mrs. Anne Naomi Quick Chenault.

He was the third African-American to serve as a CEO of a Fortune 500 company and first to serve on the board of Facebook.

*[See previous entry for additional family information.]*

*front facade, 2000*

### Childs, Edwards Herrick (1869-1944)

| | |
|---|---|
| Occupation(s): | attorney |
| Marriage(s): | 1900-1944 – Frances Aimee LaFarge (1874-1951) |
| Address: | Cedar Avenue, Hewlett Bay Park |
| Name of estate: | |
| Year of construction: | |
| Style of architecture: | Colonial Revival |
| Architect(s): | |
| Landscape architect(s): | |
| House extant: unconfirmed | |
| Historical notes | |

The *Long Island Society Register, 1929* lists Edwards Herrick and Frances Aimee LaFarge Childs as residing in Hewlett [Hewlett Bay Park].

He was the son of Oscar A. and Mary Edwards Childs of Cleveland, OH.

Frances Aimee LaFarge Childs was one of nine children, the daughter of the noted artist and stained-glass designer John LaFarge and his wife the former Margaret Mason Perry, whose grandfather Commodore Matthew Calbriath Perry opened Japan to trade and whose great-uncle was Commodore Oliver Hazard Perry. The LaFarges had homes in Middletown and Newport, RI, and in Glen Cove. Frances' eldest brother Christopher Grant LaFarge was a noted architect. He designed the original Byzantine-style Cathedral of St. John the Divine, the Astor Court Buildings, the Bronx Zoo, and St. Anthony Hall at Yale University as well as designing many North Shore estate houses. [*See* Spinzia, *Long Island's Prominent North Shore Families, vol. II*, architect appendix.] Her brother John was a Jesuit priest who wrote the papal encyclical against Nazi polices, *Humani Generis Unitas*, for Pope Pius XI. Unfortunately, the pope died just three weeks after receiving the encyclical and never acted upon it. It remained buried in the Vatican archives.

Edwards Herrick and Frances Aimee LaFarge Childs' daughter Frances remained unmarried.

*front facade*

### Childs, John Lewis (1856-1921)

| | |
|---|---|
| Occupation(s): | capitalist - president, John Lewis Childs, Inc. (wholesale floral and seed company)* |
| | publisher - Childs Seed Catalog; |
| | founder and president, *The Schoolmate* (children's magazine); |
| | *Floral Guide and Mayflower* (horticultural industry magazine) |
| | politician - member, New York State Senate, 1894-1895 |
| Civic Activism: | president, Floral Park School Board; |
| | a founder, Village of Floral Park; |
| | first president, Village of Floral Park; |
| | member of board, Jamaica Board of Trade |
| Marriage(s): | 1886-1921 – Caroline Goldsmith (1867-1937) |
| | - capitalist - president, John Lewis Childs, Inc. |
| | publisher - editor, *The Schoolmate*; |
| | manager, Mayflower Publishing Co. |
| | writer - *Lost Lineage* (novel); |
| | *The Sword Fell* (novel) |
| | Civic Activism: a founder and president, Hempstead Woman's Club; |
| | a founder and director, Nassau Hospital, Mineola (later, Winthrop–University Hospital; now, NYU Langone Hospital – Long Island); |
| | president, Floral Park Woman's Club; |
| | president, New York State Sunshine Club; |
| | member, Hoover National Food Commission; |
| | Suffragist** |
| Address: | 91 Tulip Avenue, Floral Park |
| Name of estate: | |
| Year of construction: | |
| Style of architecture: | Eclectic with Victorian elements |
| Architect(s): | |
| Landscape architect(s): | |
| House extant: no; demolished in 1950 | |
| Historical notes: | |

The house was built by John Lewis Childs.
He was the son of Stephen and Lydia Chandler Childs of North Jay, ME.
Caroline Goldsmith Childs was the daughter of Rienzi A. and Julia Norris Goldsmith of Washingtonville, NY.
John Lewis and Caroline Goldsmith Childs' son Vernon married Clarice Hunt and resided in Floral Park. Their son John married Fanny Hutcheson Hamlet and also resided in Floral Park.
*John Lewis Childs, Inc. had some three hundred acres in Floral Park and an additional eight hundred acres at Flowerfield in Suffolk County under cultivation.
The house was inherited by the Childses' daughter Norma and son-in-law John Francis Schwieters.
**For other Long Islanders involved in the suffrage movement *see* Raymond E. Spinzia, "Winning the Franchise: Long Island Activists in the Fight for Woman's Suffrage and Their Opponents, Long Island's Anti-Suffragists." wwwspinzialongislandestates.com.

*side facade*

**Chu, Steven (b. 1948)**

| | |
|---|---|
| Occupation(s): | statesman - United States Secretary of Energy (Obama administration)<br>educator - professor of physics and molecular and cellular biology, University of California, Berkeley, CA;<br>    chairman and professor of physics, Stanford University, Stanford, CA, 1990-1993, 1999-2001<br>scientist*- director, quantum electronics research department, Bell Laboratories, Holmdel, NJ, 1983;<br>    director, Lawrence Berkeley National Laboratory, Berkeley, CA, 2004<br>writer - published over 260 academic papers<br>inventor - holds 10 patents |
| Marriage(s): | M/1 – 1980 – Lisa Louise Thielbar<br>  - scientist - astrobiologist<br>    public relations - director, Multimedia Communications, NASA Ames Research Center<br>  writer - scientific articles<br>  Civic Activism: president, board of directors, Kamuela Philharmonic Orchestra, Kamuela, HI<br>M/2 – 1997 – Jean Holmes (b. 1937)<br>  - scientist - physicist<br>    educator - assistant professor of physics, San Jose University, San Jose, CA;<br>    associate director, Center for Teaching and Learning, Stanford University;<br>    assistant to two presidents, Stanford University<br>    Dean of Undergraduate Admissions, Stanford University;<br>    Associate Dean of Graduate Studies and Research, Stanford University<br>  writer - *Questions and Admissions: Reflection on 100,000 Admission Decisions at Stanford*, 1995 |
| Address: | 34 Linden Street, Garden City |
| Name of estate: | |
| Year of construction: | 1950 |
| Style of architecture: | Ranch |
| Architect(s): | |
| Landscape architect(s): | |
| House extant: yes | |
| Historical notes: | |

  Steven's parents Ju Chin and Ching Chen Li Chu built the house.

  *In 1997 Steven shared the Nobel Prize for Physics with Claude Cohen–Tannoudji and William Daniel Phillips. Steven is the first Nobel Prize winner to be appointed to a cabinet position.

  Jean Holmes Chu had previously been married to Alexander L. Fetter who was Professor Emeritus of Physics and Applied Physics, Stanford University, Stanford, CA,

*front facade, 2009*

### Claflin, Avery (1898-1979)

| | |
|---|---|
| Occupation(s): | financier - president, French American Banking Corp.<br>composer - *The Fall of Usher* (opera);<br>*La Grande Breteche* (opera);<br>*Hester Prynne* (opera) |
| Civic Activism: | president, Nassau Taxpayers League;<br>treasurer, American Composers Alliance;<br>member of board, Contemporary Music Society;<br>a founder, Leopold Stokowski's American Symphony Orchestra;<br>chairman of board, Composers Recording Inc.;<br>director, Long Island Symphony Association, 1939 |
| Marriage(s): | 1922-1979 – Dorothea Carroll (1893-1978)<br>  - writer -  librettist, *Hester Prynne* |
| Address: | Maple Avenue, Cedarhurst |
| Name of estate: | |
| Year of construction: | |
| Style of architecture: | |
| Architect(s): | |
| Landscape architect(s): | |
| House extant: unconfirmed | |
| Historical notes: | |

The *Long Island Society Register, 1929* lists Avery and Dorothea Carroll Claflin as residing on Maple Avenue, Cedarhurst. The 1940 Census has them residing on Everit Avenue, Hewlett Harbor.

He was the son of Alan A. Claflin of Winchester, MA.

Dorothea Carroll Claflin was the daughter of Royall Phelps and Marion Landon Carroll of Hempstead.

Avery and Dorothea Carroll Claflin's daughter Barbara married Alfred Randall Heath, Jr. of Manhattan.

### Clark, Samuel Adams, Sr. (1875-1931)

| | |
|---|---|
| Occupation(s): | architect -  partner, Warren and Clark* |
| Marriage(s): | 1899-1931 – Gertrude Jerome Alexandre (1880-1949)<br>  - Civic Activism:  president, social services auxiliary, Cancer Institute;<br>organizer, social services, Throat, Nose and Lung<br>    Hospital, St. Luke's Hospital;<br>chairman, Merchant Marine Library Association;<br>chairman, Women's Emergency Aid Committee,<br>    Salvation Army |
| Address: | 190 Cedarhurst Avenue, Lawrence |
| Name of estate: | |
| Year of construction: | |
| Style of architecture: | |
| Architect(s): | |
| Landscape architect(s): | |
| House extant: no | |
| Historical notes: | |

The *Social Register Summer, 1937* lists Gertrude Jerome Alexandre Clark as residing at 190 Cedarhurst Avenue, Cedarhurst [Lawrence].

She was the daughter of James Henry and Gertrude Jerome Alexandre, Sr. of Hempstead and a second cousin of Winston Churchill. Gertrude's brother James Henry Alexandre, Jr., who resided at *Valleybrook Farm* in Old Brookville, married Anne Loomis and, subsequently, Olivia Dulany Wheeler, the daughter of John Harold and Olivia Donaldson Dulany Wheeler, Jr. of Baltimore, MD. [*See* Spinzia, *Long Island's Prominent North Shore Families, vol. I* – Alexandre entry.] Her half-brother Frederick married Regina M. Saportas and resided at *Nieman* in Lawrence. Her sister Virginia remained unmarried. Her sister Mary married N. Edward C. Rutter, Sr. and resided in Lawrence.

Samuel Adams Clark, Sr. was the son of Henry and Mary E. Davenport Clark of Somerville, NJ.

Samuel Adams and Gertrude Jerome Alexandre Clark, Sr.'s son Samuel Adams Clark, Jr. married Elizabeth Fenno, the daughter of William E. Fenno, and resided in Manhattan.

*See Spinzia, *Long Island's Prominent North Shore Families, vol. II*, architect appendix, for list of firm's North Shore commissions.

### Clute, Frank M. (1860-1940)

| | |
|---|---|
| Occupation(s): | attorney -   partner, Hatch and Clute |
| | capitalist -  trustee, Brevoort Building Co., Brooklyn (real estate development company); |
| | director, New York Connecting Railroad Co.; |
| | director, Arverne-by-the-Sea, Queens County (real estate development company) |
| Civic Activism: | a founder, Garden City Country Club; |
| | trustee, Village of Garden City; |
| | member, board of governors, New York Athletic Club, NYC |
| Marriage(s): | Emma Anna Amerman (b. 1862) |
| Address: | 105 Stewart Avenue, Garden City |
| Name of estate: | |
| Year of construction: | |
| Style of architecture: | |
| Architect(s): | |
| Landscape architect(s): | |
| House extant:  no | |
| Historical notes: | |

    The *Long Island Society Register, 1929* lists Mr. and Mrs. Frank M. Clute as residing at 105 Stewart Avenue, Garden City.
    He was the son of John Marcy and Elizabeth Powers Clute of Brooklyn.
    Frank M. and Emma Anna Amerman Clute's son Tracy married Virginia Thornton Bailey, the daughter of Frederick J. Bailey of NYC, and resided in Garden City.
    At the time of his death, Frank M. Clute was residing at 223 Seventh Street, Garden City. [*The New York Times* May 1, 1940, p. 29.]

### Cobb, Boughton, Sr. (1894-1974)

| | |
|---|---|
| Occupation(s): | industrialist - vice-president and director, Esmond Mills; vice-president and director, Clarence Whitman & Sons; director, Beacon Manufacturing Co. |
| Civic Activism: | trustee, Village of Hewlett Bay Park; director, Long Island Symphony Association, 1939 |
| Marriage(s): | 1918-1974 – Edith McKeever (1895-1977) |
| Address: | Woodside Drive, Hewlett Bay Park |
| Name of estate: | *The Chimney Corner* |
| Year of construction: | |
| Style of architecture: | |
| Architect(s): | |
| Landscape architect(s): | |

Nassau County Museum Collection has photographs of the estate.
House extant: unconfirmed
Historical notes:

The *Society Register New York, 1933* lists Boughton and Edith McKeever Cobb [Sr.] as residing at *The Chimney Corner* on Woodside Drive, Hewlett [Hewlett Bay Park].

He was the son of Henry Ives and Emma Martin Smith Cobb, Sr. of Brookline, MA, and East Hampton. [*See* Spinzia, *Long Island's Prominent Families in the Town of East Hampton* – Cobb entry.] His brother Henry Ives Cobb, Jr., who resided in Hewlett, married Carolyn Satterlee Postlethwaite and, subsequently, Gwendolyn Wickersham.

Edith McKeever Cobb was the daughter of Isaac Chauncey and Julia Draper McKeever of *Red Top Farm* in Southampton. Edith's sister Marianne married Edmund Steuart Davis, Sr. and resided at *Wooley Creek Farm* in Southampton. [*See* Spinzia, *Long Island's Prominent Families in the Town of Southampton* – Davis and McKeever entries.] Edith's sister Frances married Walter L. Carey and resided in Manhattan.

Boughton and Edith McKeever Cobb, Sr.'s daughter Ann married Francis Burritt Thorne, Jr., the son of Francis Burritt and Hildegarde Kobbe Thorne, Sr. of *Brookwood* in East Islip, and resided in Bay Shore. [*See* Spinzia, *Long Island's Prominent South Shore Families* – Thorne entries.] Their son Boughton Cobb, Jr. married Barbara Woodruff Benjamin, the daughter of William Wallace and Candace C. Woodruff Benjamin III of East Hampton, and, subsequently, Margaret Hamilton with whom he resided in Cold Spring Harbor. [*See* Spinzia, *Long Island's Prominent Families in the Town of East Hampton* – Benjamin entry.]

*[See following entry for additional family information.]*

In 1934 Cobb sold the house to William D. Yergason. [*The New York Times* June 27, 1934, p. 36.]

*living room, 1923*

**Cobb, Henry Ives, Jr. (1883-1974)**

Occupation(s): architect
Civic Activism: donated John La Farge's sketches to Avery Architectural and Fine Arts Library, Columbia University, NYC

Marriage(s): M/1 – 1906-div. 1915 – Carolyn Satterlee Postlethwaite (1883-1960)
M/2 – 1920-1963 – Gwendolyn Wickersham (1888-1963)

Address: Everit and Cedar Avenues, Hewlett Bay Park
Name of estate: *Homewood*
Year of construction:
Style of architecture:
Architect(s):
Landscape architect(s):
Nassau County Museum Collection has photographs of the estate.
House extant: unconfirmed
Historical notes:

Henry Ives Cobb, Jr. was the son of Henry Ives and Emma Martin Smith Cobb, Sr. of East Hampton and Brookline, MA. [*See* Spinzia, *Long Island's Prominent Families in the Town of East Hampton* – H. I. Cobb, Sr. entry.] His brother Boughton married Edith McKeever and resided in Hewlett Bay Park.

Carolyn Satterlee Postlethwaite Cobb was the daughter of The Reverend William Morton and Mrs. Sallie Tweed Ellis Postlethwaite.

Henry Ives and Carolyn Sattlerleee Postlethwaite Cobb, Jr.'s daughter Margaret married Frederick Talbot Fairchild and, later, ____Westervelt and resided in Rowayton, CT. Their son Henry Ives Cobb III married Evelyn Whitehouse, the daughter of Henry J. Whitehouse of Mount Kisco, NY, and resided in Mount Kisco.
*[See previous entry for additional family information.]*

The *Long Island Society Register, 1929* lists Henry Ives and Gwendolyn Wickersham Cobb, Jr. as residing in Hewlett.

She was the daughter of George Woodward and Mildred Wendell Wickersham, who resided at *Marshfield* in Lawrence. Gwendolyn had previously been married to Albert John Akin II with whom she resided at *Homewood* in Hewlett Harbor.

[For information about Cobb's Southampton residence *Fair Lea, see* Spinzia, *Long Island's Prominent Families in the Town of Southampton* – H. I. Cobb, Jr. entry.]

In 1921 the estate was sold to Mrs. Ellen Hale Boulton. [*The Brooklyn Daily Eagle* January 5, 1921, p. 17.]

*living room, 1922*

## Cochran, Alexander Smith (1874-1929)

| | |
|---|---|
| Occupation(s): | industrialist - president, Alexander Smith and Sons Co., Yonkers, NY (carpet manufacturer) |
| | capitalist - director, Northern Pacific Railroad; created summer resort near Cascade, CO |
| Civic Activism: | * |
| | major benefactor, Yale University; |
| | benefactor, St. John's Riverside Hospital, Yonkers, NY; |
| | donated fully equipped ambulance to American Volunteer Ambulance during World War I; |
| | donated land for Y.W.C.A. building; |
| | donated land for Municipal Tuberculosis Hospital |
| Marriage(s): | 1920-div. 1922 – Ganna Walka (1887-1984) |
| | - entertainers and related professions - opera singer |
| Address: | Front Street, East Meadow |
| Name of estate: | |
| Year of construction: | c. 1897 |
| Style of architecture: | Colonial Revival |
| Architect(s): | Richard Howland Hunt designed the house (for O. H. P. Belmont) |
| | John Russell Pope designed a Georgian-style farmhouse, 1906 (for O. H. P. Belmont) |
| Landscape architect(s): | Hicks Nursery supplied plantings (for O. H. P. Belmont) |

House extant: no; destroyed by fire, 1934
Historical notes:

    The house with nine master bedrooms, thirteen servants' bedrooms, and nine bathrooms, originally named *Brookholt*, was built by Oliver Hazard Perry Belmont. It was later owned by Cochran.

    Alexander Smith Cochran was the son of William Francis and Eva Smith Cochran, Sr. of Yonkers, NY. His sister Anne married Thomas Ewing, Jr. His brother William Francis Cochran, Jr. resided in Baltimore, MD. Self-described as a Christian Socialist, in 1915 William asked for suggestions on how he should give away his fortune. [*The New York Times* March 7, 1915, p. SM11.]

    *Cochran gave the carpet company employees semi-annual bonuses of 5-10-percent for twenty-eight years.

    His yacht *Vanitie* was a contender in the America Cup race against Thomas Lipton's *Shamrocks* which was subsequently defeated by *Resolute* in the race to represent the United States. Cochran's three-masted, 214-foot yacht *Sea Call* was launched in April 1915. In August 1915 it was scrapped due to poor construction. In 1917 the British government purchased his yacht *Warrior* and converted it into a cruiser. [*The New York Times* February 23, 1917, p. 9.]

    Ganna Walka Cochran had previously been married to Baron Archadie d' Eignhorne of Russia and Dr. Julius Fraenkel of New York. She subsequently married Harold Fowler McCormick and Theos Bernard.

    In 1923 Cochran sold his estate to the Coldstream Golf Club. [*The New York Times* November 18, 1923, p. XII.]

    Alexander had previously resided in Old Westbury. After selling his East Meadow estate, he relocated to Brookville. [*See* Spinzia, *Long Island's Prominent North Shore Families, vol. I* – Cochran entry.]

*front facade, 1907*

## Coe, Elmore Holloway (1868-1939)

| | |
|---|---|
| Occupation(s): | industrialist - president, E. Frank Coe & Co., NYC (fertilizer firm) |
| Marriage(s): | 1904-1939 – Elizabeth Wright Davie (1875-1958) |
| Address: | Everit Avenue, Hewlett Bay Park |
| Name of estate: | |
| Year of construction: | |
| Style of architecture: | Colonial Revival |
| Architect(s): | |
| Landscape architect(s): | |
| House extant: | unconfirmed |
| Historical notes: | |

*front facade*

The *Long Island Society Register, 1929* lists E. Holloway and Elizabeth W. Davie Coe as residing in Hewlett [Hewlett Bay Park].

He was the son of Elmore Frank and Emma Harmstead Coe of Brooklyn. His sister Selina, who resided at *Fithian House* in East Hampton, married Chauncey F. Kerr and, subsequently, Charles Weaver Bailey, the son of Joseph Trowbridge and Caroline Goddard Bailey, Jr. of Philadelphia. [*See* Spinzia, *Long Island's Prominent Families in the Town of East Hampton* – Kerr entry.] In the fall of 1900, prior to her marriage to Bailey, Selina and Bailey were canoeing in the Adirondacks when they were mistaken for a deer by a hunter. The hunter's bullet entered Bailey's back and was deflected into Selina's leg. They both recovered but Selina's leg had to be amputated. Not long after the incident, Selina and Bailey were married. Their two-year marriage ended when Selina filed for divorce charging Bailey with adultery. Bailey, who claimed the other woman's affidavit was false, sued Elmore Holloway Coe for allegedly conspiring to alienate the affections of his wife. [*The New York Times* October 16, 1902, p. 3, and January 26, 1904, p. 1.]

Elizabeth Wright Davie Coe was the daughter of James and Alice Powell Davie.

Elmore Holloway and Elizabeth Wright Davie Coe's daughter Elizabeth married Daniel Aylesbury Finlayson, Jr. of Hewlett Bay Park and, subsequently, William French Prescott, the son of George J. Prescott of Boston, MA, with whom she resided at *Still Pond* in East Islip. [*See* Spinzia, *Long Island's Prominent South Shore Families* – Prescott entry.] Their daughter Marjorie married Daniel Leslie Monroe, the son of Roland G. Monroe of Manhattan. Their daughter Bertha married Sumner H. Foster, the son of John W. Foster of Cedarhurst.

## Coffin, William Haskell, Sr. (1878-1941)
### aka Haskell Coffin

| | |
|---|---|
| Occupation(s): | artist - portrait painter;<br>poster and magazine illustrator |
| Marriage(s): | M/1 – 1908-1918 – Ida Ashhurst Bremen (1880-1918)<br>M/2 – 1920-div. 1930 – Frances Grant Starr (1880-1973)<br>- entertainers and associated professions -<br>Broadway and television actress |
| Address: | 120 Roxbury Road, Garden City |
| Name of estate: | |
| Year of construction: | 1913 |
| Style of architecture: | Modified Dutch Colonial Revival |
| Architect(s): | |
| Landscape architect(s): | |
| House extant: | yes |
| Historical notes: | |

*front facade, 2000*

The *Long Island Society Register, 1929* lists Mr. [William] Haskell Coffin as residing at 120 Roxbury Road, Garden City.

He was the son of George Mathews and Julia Ellen Haskell Coffin of Charleston, SC, and NYC.

Ida Ashhurst Bremen Coffin was the daughter of Martin W. and Donaciana Ashhurst Bremen.

William Haskell and Ida Ashhurst Bremen Coffin, Sr.'s son William Haskell Coffin, Jr. married Lillian Fraser.

Frances Starr Grant Coffin was the daughter of Charles Edward and Emma Grant Starr. Frances later married R. Golden Donaldson of Washington, DC, and Emil C. Wetten.

Coffin, despondent and destitute, committed suicide by plunging to the ground from the window of his third-floor hospital room in St. Petersburg, FL. [*The New York Times* May 13, 1941, p. 12.]

### Cohen, Bennett R. (b. 1951)

| | |
|---|---|
| Occupation(s): | industrialist - a founder, with Jerry Greenfield, and CEO, Ben and Jerry's Homemade Holdings, Inc. (ice cream manufacturing firm)* |
| | educator - craft teacher, private school for emotionally disturbed adolescents |
| Civic Activism: | a founder, Ben and Jerry's Foundation; |
| | a founder, One Percent for Peace; |
| | a founder, Business for Social Responsibility; |
| | board member, Social Venture Network; |
| | trustee, Hampshire College, Amherst, MA; |
| | board member, Oxfam; |
| | board member, Greenpeace |
| Marriage(s): | Cynthia *[unable to determine maiden name]* |
| | - psychologist |
| Address: | Millwood Lane, Merrick |
| Name of estate: | |
| Year of construction: | |
| Style of architecture: | Ranch |
| Architect(s): | |
| Landscape architect(s): | |
| House extant: unconfirmed | |
| Historical notes: | |

Bennett was raised in this house by his parents Irving and Frances Cohen.

*When it was decided that Ben's longtime friend and co-founder of the company Jerry Greenfield should be the first CEO, Ben's name was placed first on the ice cream container as a consolation prize.

### Combs, Clinton deRaismes, Sr. (1886-1953)

| | |
|---|---|
| Occupation(s): | attorney - member, Worcester, Williams, and Saxe; |
| | member, Root, Clark, Buckner, and Howland (later, Root, Clark, Buckner, and Ballantine) |
| Marriage(s): | 1915-1953 – Margery Gillespie (1883-1966) |
| Address: | 106 Fourth Street, Garden City |
| Name of estate: | |
| Year of construction: | 1915 |
| Style of architecture: | Colonial Revival |
| Architect(s): | |
| Landscape architect(s): | |
| House extant: yes | |
| Historical notes: | |

*front facade, 2020*

The *Long Island Society Register, 1929* lists Clinton deRaismes and Margery Gillespie Combes [Sr.] as residing at 106 Fourth Street, Garden City.

He was the son of Abbott Carson and Marie Louise deRaimes Combes of Newtown (now, Elmhurst), NY.

Margery Gillespie Combes was the daughter of Earl Augustus and Isabelle Booth Curtiss Gillespie of Woodhaven, NY.

Clinton deRaismes and Margery Gillespie Combs, Sr.'s daughter Isabelle married James Robert Orgain, Jr. Their son Clinton deRaismes Combs, Jr. married Jean Z. Hanabergh, the daughter of William Wheeler and Helen Hanabergh.

In 2020, the four-bedroom, three-and-a-half-bath house sold for $1.625 million.

### Connable, Arthur W. (b. 1863)

| | |
|---|---|
| Occupation(s): | financier - stockbroker |
| Marriage(s): | Clara P. *[unable to determine maiden name]* (b. 1880) |
| Address: | East Rockaway Road, Hewlett Bay Park |
| Name of estate: | *Boxwood* |
| Year of construction: | c. 1910 |
| Style of architecture: | Neo-Tudor |
| Architect(s): | |
| Landscape architect(s): | |
| House extant: unconfirmed | |
| Historical notes: | |

The house, originally named *Boxwood*, was built by Arthur W. Connable.

The 1910 Census lists the Connables at this address.

In 1914 the house was sold to Joseph Diver. [*The New York Times* May 20, 1914, p. 21.]

*front facade, c. 1913*

### Cooper, Leslie Bradford (1894-1944)

| | |
|---|---|
| Occupation(s): | industrialist - vice-president, Giro Associates, NY; Pitcairn–Larsen Autogiro Co., Inc.; Kellet Autogiro Co.; Curtiss–Wright Flying Service |
| Marriage(s): | 1916-1944 – Katharine Trumbull Thomas (1892-1979) |
| Address: | Raymond Place, Woodmere |
| Name of estate: | |
| Year of construction: | |
| Style of architecture: | |
| Architect(s): | |
| Landscape architect(s): | |
| House extant: unconfirmed | |
| Historical notes: | |

The *Long Island Society Register, 1929* lists Leslie B. and Katharine T. Thomas Cooper as residing on Raymond Place, Woodmere. The *Social Register, 1933* lists their address as Ocean Avenue, Lawrence.

He was the son of Rear Admiral Philip Henry and Mrs. Catherine Jardena Foote Cooper.

Katharine Trumbull Thomas Cooper was the daughter of William R. Thomas of Morristown, NJ.

Leslie Bradford and Katharine Trumbull Thomas Cooper's daughter Katharine married William Henry Moorhouse, the son of William L. Moorhouse of Wayne, PA, and, later, Burrows Barstow, Jr. Their son Leslie Trumbull Cooper married Cornelia Tilden Sinkler.

Leslie Bradford Cooper was killed when his twin engine training plane crashed. [*The New York Times* October 20, 1944, p. 8.]

### Cooper, Peter (1791-1883)

| | |
|---|---|
| Occupation(s): | industrialist - built the "Tom Thumb" (first American steam locomotive); owned a glue factory, Gowanda, NY; founder, Canton Iron Works, Baltimore, MD; owned an iron rolling mill, NY |
| | capitalist - invested in real estate; a founder, New York, Newfoundland, and London Telegraph Co.*; a founder, American Telegraph Co. |
| | politician - Greenbacks' presidential candidate for 1876 election |
| | inventor - developed new way to produce gelatin (sold it to firm for use in making Jell-O); developed new way to produce glue and cement; developed new way to use isinglass; designed first steel rocking chair |
| Civic Activism: | founder, Cooper Union for the Advancement of Science and Art (aka Cooper Union), NYC; a founder, Children's Village (aka New York Juvenile Asylum), 1851 (orphanage) |
| Marriage(s): | 1813-1869 – Sarah Bedell (1793-1869) |
| Address: | Clinton Street, Hempstead |
| Name of estate: | |
| Year of construction: | 1700s |
| Style of architecture: | Colonial |
| Architect(s): | |
| Landscape architect(s): | |
| House extant: yes | |

Historical notes:

Peter Cooper purchased the house from Gideon Nichols.

*front facade prior to relocation*

He was the son of John O. and Margaret Campbell Cooper of New York.

Peter and Sarah Bedell Cooper's son Edward, who served as Mayor of New York, married Cornelia Redmond, the daughter of James Morton and Anne Bowne Redmond. Their daughter Sarah married New York City Mayor Abram Stevens Hewitt, the son of John and Ann Gurnee Hewitt.

*Cooper, who was reputed to have been one of the richest men in New York City, supervised the laying of the first transatlantic telegraph cable.

In 1960 the house was moved to Old Bethpage Village Restoration.

### Corroon, George Aloysisus, Sr. (1913-2002)

| | |
|---|---|
| Occupation(s): | financier - a founder and partner, Coroon, Lichtenstein, and Co. (stock brokerage firm) |
| Marriage(s): | 1938-1991 – Gladys Adelaide Durand (1915-1991) |
| Address: | 210 Brixton Road, Garden City |
| Name of estate: | |
| Year of construction: | 1937 |
| Style of architecture: | Colonial Revival |
| Architect(s): | |
| Landscape architect(s): | |
| House extant: yes | |

Historical notes:

In 1940, George Aloysius and Gladys Adelaide Durand Corroon, Sr. were residing at 36 Kenwood Road, Garden City. By 1942 they had relocated to 210 Brixton Road.

*front facade, 2008*

He was the son of Richard Aloysisus and Margaret Veronica Teaken Corroon, Sr. of Massapequa.

Gladys Adelaide Durand Corroon was the daughter of Charles Aloysius and Irene J. Loving Durand, Sr. of Garden City.

George Aloysius and Gladys Adelaide Durand Corroon, Sr.'s daughter Carol married James Guy Pratt, the son of James J. Pratt of Westbury and Centre Island, and resided in Garden City.

In 2006, the 2,094-square-foot house sold for $985,000.

### Corwith, Lester F. (1882-1946)

| | |
|---|---|
| Occupation(s): | financier -  president, Corwith Brothers (insurance and real estate brokerage firm); trustee, Bushwick Savings Bank |
| Civic Activism: | president, Hempstead Board of Education; president of board, Lakemont Academy; director, Bay Colony Property Owners Association of Baldwin |
| Marriage(s): | Elsie Sauer (1880-1967) |
| Address: | 58 Hilton Avenue, Hempstead |
| Name of estate: | |
| Year of construction: | 1900 |
| Style of architecture: | Colonial Revival |
| Architect(s): | |
| Landscape architect(s): | |
| House extant: yes | |
| Historical notes: | |

The *Long Island Society Register, 1929* lists Mr. and Mrs. Lester F. Corwith as residing at 58 Hilton Avenue, Hempstead.

He was the son of William F. and Annie V. Schaffer Corwith of Hempstead.

Lester F. and Elsie Sauer Corwith's son Charles married Grace McKenney, the daughter of Daniel S. McKenney of Rockville Centre.

The house is now a commercial property.

*front facade, 2001*

### Cottone, Anthony (1905-1989)

| | |
|---|---|
| Occupation(s): | merchant -  founder and president, A. Cottone & Co., Inc., NYC (retail electronics firm) |
| Marriage(s): | 1934 – Rose Iovino (1905-1996) |
| Address: | 157 Lincoln Street, Garden City |
| Name of estate: | |
| Year of construction: | 1953 |
| Style of architecture: | ranch* |
| Architect(s): | |
| Landscape architect(s): | |
| House extant: yes | |
| Historical notes: | |

The house was built by Anthony Cottone.

He was the son of Philip and Rosalia Muratore Cottone of Lercara Friddi, Italy, and Brooklyn. His sister Margaret married Ralph Spinzia and resided in Garden City.

Anthony and Rose Iovino Cottone's daughter Lillian married Gilles Santeix of Rochforte, France, and resides in Paris, France. Their son Philip married Maureen Cuite, the daughter of Francis and Frances Connolly Cuite of Brooklyn, and resided in East Rockaway, Devin, PA, and, later, in Malvern, PA.

*The house was modified in 1963 by a subsequent owner to include a partial second story.

## Coupe, Frank J. (1878-1934)

| | |
|---|---|
| Occupation(s): | advertising executive - a founder, Andrews & Coupe; vice-president, Dorrance, Sullivan, & Co.; partner, Redfield–Coupe, Inc.; partner, Lewis & Coupe, Inc. |
| | industrialist - vice-president, Sonora Phonograph |
| Civic Activism: | a founder, Garden City Country Club |
| Marriage(s): | Louise Bennett (b. 1884) |
| Address: | 148 Brixton Road, Garden City |
| Name of estate: | |
| Year of construction: | 1928 |
| Style of architecture: | American Craftsman |
| Architect(s): | |
| Landscape architect(s): | |
| House extant: | yes |
| Historical notes: | |

*front facade, 2008*

The house was built by Frank J. Coupe.

The *Long Island Society Register, 1929* lists Mr. and Mrs. Frank J. Coupe as residing on Brixton Road, Garden City.

Frank J. and Louise Bennett Coup's daughter Norma married Andrew Francis Thompson, the son of Arthur F. Thompson of Garden City.

At the time of his death, Coupe was residing at 148 Brixton Road, Garden City. [*The New York Times* February 26, 1934, p. 17.]

## Courtenay, Adrian Henry, Sr. (1880-1939)

| | |
|---|---|
| Occupation(s): | attorney |
| | educator - superintendent, Hempstead School System; teacher, The Gunnery School, Washington, CT |
| | financier - a founder, Second National Bank of Hempstead; a founder, Hempstead Co-operative Building and Loan Association (later, First Federal Savings and Loan); president, Hempstead Bond & Mortgage Guarantee Co.; president, Commonwealth Funding Co. |
| Marriage(s): | 1908-1939 – Jane Kieffer Burhans (1881-1966) |
| Address: | 100 Phoenix Street, Hempstead |
| Name of estate: | |
| Year of construction: | 1920 |
| Style of architecture: | American Craftsman |
| Architect(s): | |
| Landscape architect(s): | |
| House extant: | yes |
| Historical notes: | |

*front facade, 2000*

The *Long Island Society Register, 1929* lists Mrs. Adrian H. Courtenay as residing on Phoenix Street, Hempstead.

Adrian Henry Courtenay, Sr. was the son of William Henry and Harriet LaCroix Courtenay of Redwood, NY.

Adrian Henry and Jane Kieffer Burhans Courtenay, Sr.'s daughter Catherine married Leslie Gould Cheshire. Their son Aldrich married Harriet Ann Tredwell, the daughter of Henry Hewlett Tredwell of East Williston.

In 1934, Adrian Henry Courtenay, Sr. was arraigned on two indictments of perjury for allegedly filing false statements to the New York State Insurance Department. [*The New York Times* October 24, 1934, p. 4.]

At the time of his death, he was residing at 100 Phoenix Street, Hempstead. [*The New York Times* November 27, 1939, p. 17.]

### Covert, Charles Edward (1872-1948)

| | |
|---|---|
| Occupation(s): | financier - trust officer, Williamsburgh Trust Co., Brooklyn; president, U. S. Title Guaranty Co., Brooklyn; vice-president, New York Title & Mortgage Co. |
| Marriage(s): | 1900-1948 – Magdalene Frances Vanderveer (1870-1955) |
| Address: | 108 Stewart Avenue, Garden City |
| Name of estate: | |
| Year of construction: | |
| Style of architecture: | |
| Architect(s): | |
| Landscape architect(s): | |
| House extant: | unconfirmed |
| Historical notes: | |

The *Long Island Society Register, 1929* lists Charles Edward and Magdalene F. Vanderveer Covert as residing at 108 Stewart Avenue, Garden City.

He was the son of Henry Aldrich and Amy Elizabeth Betts Covert of Maspeth.

Charles Edward and Magdalene Frances Vanderveer Covert's daughter Frances married Charles Vanderveer, Jr. Their daughter Florence married Henry Hewlett Tredwell.

In 1926, Charles Edward and Magdalene Frances Vanderveer Covert sold their house at 34 Nassau Boulevard, Garden City to Clayton Berrian. [*The New York Times* October 2, 1926, p. 33.]

In 1929 they relocated to Old Westbury. [*The New York Times* January 31, 1929, p. 45.]

### Cowdrey, Loren Montague (1880-1945)

| | |
|---|---|
| Occupation(s): | capitalist - importer |
| Civic Activism: | president, Garden City Club, 1923; secretary, Property Owners Association, Central Section, Garden City, 1923 |
| Marriage(s): | Gladys Pauline Watson (1884-1966) - Civic Activism: chairman, fund-raising committee, Nassau Hospital, Mineola; director, Garden City Branch, Needlework Guild of America, 1923 |
| Address: | 95 Ninth Street, Garden City |
| Name of estate: | |
| Year of construction: | 1875 |
| Style of architecture: | French Empire |
| Architect(s): | John Kellum designed the house* |
| Builder: | James L'Hommedieu |
| Landscape architect(s): | |
| House extant: | yes |
| Historical notes: | |

*front facade, 2008*

The *Long Island Society Register, 1929* lists Loren Montague and Gladys P. Watson Cowdrey as residing at 95 Ninth Street, Garden City.

He was the son of Nathaniel Ackley and Martha Jane Hartley Cowdrey.

Gladys Pauline Watson Cowdrey was the daughter of Arthur Wellesly and Anna Josephine Sutton Watson.

Loren Montague and Gladys Pauline Watson Cowdrey's daughter Gladys married Edward Rawson Godfrey, Jr. of Bangor, ME, and resided in Hartford, CT.

*The Cowdreys' house was one of the original "Disciple Houses" built by Alexander Turney Stewart.

### Cox, Daniel Hargate (1872-1955)

| | |
|---|---|
| Occupation(s): | naval architect - partner, Cox and Stevens, Inc. |
| Civic Activism: | manager, ship construction, United States Shipping Board Emergency Fleet Corp., 1917-1918; secretary and treasurer, Society of Naval Architects and Marine Engineers, 1910-1933 |
| Marriage(s): | 1903-1952 – Frances Lawrason Buckler (1882-1952) |
| Address: | 35 South Wood Lane, Woodsburgh |
| Name of estate: | |
| Year of construction: | 1908 |
| Style of architecture: | Neo-Georgian |
| Architect(s): | |
| Landscape architect(s): | |
| House extant: yes | |
| Historical notes: | |

*front facade, 2001*

The *Long Island Society Register, 1929* lists Daniel Hargate and Frances L. Buckler Cox as residing at 35 South Wood Lane, Woodmere [Woodsburgh].

He was the son of Daniel Townsend and Anna Helme Townsend Cox, Sr. of Manhattan. His brother Irving married Jane Eckstein and resided at *Meadow Farm* in Mill Neck. [*See* Spinzia, *Long Island's Prominent North Shore Families, vol. 1* – Cox entry.]

Frances Lawrason Buckler Cox was the daughter of Dr. Riggin and Mrs. Alice Lawrason Riggs Buckler of Baltimore, MD.

Daniel Hargate and Frances Lawrason Buckler Cox's daughter Anne married Samuel Ricker, Jr. of *Overlook Farm* in Red Bank, NJ. Their daughter Alice married Ernest M. Jonkiaas of Gampola, Ceylon [now, Sri Lanka].

The house was remodeled in 1962.

### Cox, Dr. Gerard Hutchinson, Sr. (1877-1952)

| | |
|---|---|
| Occupation(s): | physician - plastic surgeon, ophthalmologist and otorhinolaryngologist; associate visiting plastic surgeon, Bellevue Hospital, NYC; consulting plastic surgeon, Meadow Brook Hospital, Hempstead; visiting plastic surgeon, Nassau Hospital, Mineola (later, Winthrop – University Hospital; now, NYU Langone Hospital – Long Island); visiting ear, nose, and throat surgeon, Glen Cove Hospital |
| Civic Activism: | director, Nassau County Tuberculosis and Public Health Association |
| Marriage(s): | M/1 – 1907-div. 1937 – Maude E. Knapp |
| | M/2 – 1937-1951 – Alice Tweedy (1892-1951) |
| Address: | East Rockaway Road, Hewlett |
| Name of estate: | |
| Year of construction: | 1908 |
| Style of architecture: | Neo-Georgian |
| Architect(s): | |
| Landscape architect(s): | |
| House extant: yes | |
| Historical notes: | |

*front facade*

The *Long Island Society Register, 1921* lists Gerard H. and Maude E. Knapp Cox [Sr.] as residing in Lawrence. By 1926 they had relocated to Hewlett.

He was the son of John and Florence Hutchinson Cox of Brooklyn.

Dr. Gerard Hutchinson and Maude E. Knapp Cox, Sr.'s son Gerard Hutchinson Cox, Jr. married Edith Curtis Martin, the daughter of John C. Martin of *Wedgwood* in Wyncote, PA.

In 1926, Cox purchased the Clifford A. Dunning residence and relocated to Glen Cove. [*The Nassau Daily Review* March 3, 1931, p. 6.] [*See* Spinzia, *Long Island's Prominent North Shore Families, vol. 1* – Cox entry.]

Alice Tweedy Cox was the daughter of Robert Benedict Tweedy of Milwaukee, WI. She had previously been married to Walter Morgan Crunden.

### Crandall, Dr. Floyd Milford (1858-1919)

| | |
|---|---|
| Occupation(s): | physician - surgeon;<br>Bellevue Dispensary, NYC, 1886-1889;<br>Northwestern Dispensary, 1889-1890;<br>New York Skin and Cancer Hospital, 1890-1895;<br>Infant's Hospital, 1895-1898<br>educator - adjunct professor, Children's Hospital<br>journalist - editor, *New York Medical Journal*, 1889-1893;<br>editor, *Galliards Medical Journal*, 1893-1895;<br>editor, *Archives of Pediatrics*, 1895-1901<br>writer - *How to Keep Well*, 1903;<br>numerous articles in medical journals |
| Civic Activism: | secretary, Medical Society of the State of New York, 1919 |
| Marriage(s): | |
| Address: | Fulton Street and St. Paul's Road, Hempstead |
| Name of estate: | *The Pines* |
| Year of construction: | |
| Style of architecture: | Neo-Italianate |
| Architect(s): | |
| Landscape architect(s): | |
| House extant: no | |
| Historical notes: | |

Born in Belfast, Ireland, he was the son of Dr. Charles Milford and Mrs. Deborah J. Wood Crandall.

*front facade, 1913*

### Crane, Clinton Hoadley (1873-1958)

| | |
|---|---|
| Occupation(s): | naval architect - partner, Tams, Lemoine, and Crane<br>industrialist - president and chairman of board, St. Joseph Lead Co.*<br>capitalist - vice-president, Missouri–Illinois Railroad Co.<br>writer - *Clinton Crane's Yachting Memoirs*, 1952;<br>numerous articles on yachting |
| Civic Activism: | member, War Industries Board in the Wilson administration;<br>president, Lead Industries Association |
| Marriage(s): | 1900-1958 - Rebecca Riggs (1875-1960)<br>- artist |
| Address: | Cedar Avenue, Hewlett Bay Park |
| Name of estate: | |
| Year of construction: | |
| Style of architecture: | |
| Architect(s): | |
| Landscape architect(s): | |
| House extant: unconfirmed | |
| Historical notes: | |

The *Social Register Summer, 1915* lists Clinton Hoadley and Rebecca Riggs Crane as residing in Hewlett [Hewlett Bay Park.] The *Long Island Society Register, 1929* lists Clinton Hoadley and Rebecca Riggs Crane as residing on Shore Road [Crane Road], Cold Spring Harbor [Lloyd Harbor]. [*See* Spinzia, *Long Island's Prominent North Shore Families, vol. I* – Crane entry.]

He was the son of Jonathan H. and Elizabeth C. Hoadley Crane.

Rebecca Riggs Crane was the daughter of Dr. Benjamin Clapp and Mrs. Rebecca Fox Riggs of Baltimore, MD.

Clinton Hoadley and Rebecca Riggs Crane's daughter Rebecca married Duncan Van Norden of Greenwich, CT; John M. Eddison; and, subsequently, Laurence Tompkins.

*Under Crane's leadership St. Joseph Lead Co. became the largest single producer of lead in the United States. He received the William Lawrence Saunders Medal of the American Institute of Mining and Metallurgical Engineers for his contributions to the mining industry. [*The New York Times* December 12, 1958, p. 37.]

### Crane, Warren Seabury (1866-1931)

| | |
|---|---|
| Occupation(s): | financier -   partner, Crane and Webb (stock brokerage firm); partner, Greer, Crane, and Webb (investment banking firm); partner, DuVal, Green and Co. (investment banking firm) |
| Marriage(s): | 1899-1931 – Violet Lee Wallace (1872-1936) |
| Address: | Polo Avenue, Lawrence |
| Name of estate: | *East View* |
| Year of construction: | c. 1924 |
| Style of architecture: | Neo-Georgian |
| Architect(s): | Auguste Louis Noel designed the house (for W. S. Crane) |
| Landscape architect(s): | Annette Hoyt Flanders designed the flagstone terrace, shrubbery, lawns, and the vegetable and flower gardens, c. 1934 (for Mrs. W. S. Crane); (also for A. K. Peck) |

House extant:  yes
Historical notes:

The house, originally names *East View*, was built by Warren Seabury Crane.

The *Long Island Society Register, 1929* lists Warren Seabury and Violet L Wallace Crane as residing in Cedarhurst [Lawrence].

He was the son of John McDowell and Harriet H. Seabury Crane.

Violet Lee Wallace Crane was the daughter of Shippen and Laura Christina Barclay Wallace.

Warren Seabury and Violet Lee Wallace Crane's daughter Christiana married Arthur Chittenden Crunden, the son of Frank Payne Crunden of St. Louis, MO, and, subsequently, Arthur Knowlton Peck, Sr. The Pecks subsequently owned *East View*.

*rear facade, c. 1924*

### Cruikshank, James (1804-1895)

| | |
|---|---|
| Occupation(s): | financier -   president, New York Real Estate Exchange; a founder and director, Hempstead National Bank |
| Marriage(s): | M/1 – 1835 – Caroline Maria Wheeler (1818-1841)<br>M/2 – 1841 – Mary Ann Wheeler (1816-1888) |
| Address: | Greenwich Street, Hempstead |
| Name of estate: | |
| Year of construction: | |
| Style of architecture: | |
| Architect(s): | |
| Landscape architect(s): | |

House extant:  unconfirmed
Historical notes:

James Cruikshank was the son of William and Sarah Allen Cruikshank.

Caroline Maria Wheeler Cruikshank was the daughter of John and Caroline Cotterill Wheeler.

James and Caroline Maria Wheeler Cruikshank had two sons George and Edward W. Cruikshank.

James and Mary Ann Wheeler Cruikshank had three children – James W., Charles, and Harriet.

At the time of his death, Cruikshank was residing on Greenwich Street, Hempstead. [*The New York Times* August 31, 1895, p. 5.]

### Cruikshank, William Morris, Sr. (1870-1963)

| | |
|---|---|
| Occupation(s): | real estate agent - president, William M. Cruikshank & Sons, NYC (later, Cruikshank & Co.); chairman of board, Cruikshank & Co. |
| | financier - trustee, New York Life Insurance & Trust Co.; trustee, New York Guarantee Mortgage Corp.; director, Atlantic Mutual Insurance Co.; trustee, Bank of New York; trustee, Fifth Avenue Bank |
| Civic Activism: | a founder, secretary, and director, Cherry Valley Club, Garden City, 1916 |
| Marriage(s): | M/1 – Mary Dimick |
| | M/2 – 1906 – Edwina Richards Bigelow (b. 1877) |
| Address: | 385 Stewart Avenue, Garden City |
| Name of estate: | |
| Year of construction: | 1918 |
| Style of architecture: | Colonial Revival |
| Architect(s): | |
| Landscape architect(s): | |
| House extant: | yes |
| Historical notes: | |

The *Long Island Society Register, 1929* lists William Morris and Edwina Richards Bigelow Cruikshank [Sr.] as residing on Sixth Street, Garden City.

He was the son of William and Mary Ann Worley Cruikshank.

Edwina Richards Bigelow Cruikshank was the daughter of Elliot and Edwina H. Richards Bigelow.

William Morris and Edwina Richards Bigelow Cruikshank, Sr.'s daughter Edwina married Edward Daly Weatherhead, the son of Albert J. Weatherhead of Cleveland, OH. Their son William Morris Cruikshank, Jr. married Esther Gurney, the daughter of Thomas Nichol and Ethel Kirkman Gurney of Garden City.

At the time of his death, William Morris Cruikshank, Sr. was residing at 385 Stewart Avenue, Garden City. [*The New York Times* May 28, 1963, p. 37.]

*front facade, 2000*

## Curtiss, Glenn Hammond, Sr. (1878-1930)

| | |
|---|---|
| Occupation(s): | industrialist - founder, G. H. Curtiss Manufacturing Co., Hammondsport, NY (motorcycle manufacturer) (later, Herring–Curtiss Co., Hammondsport, NY); vice-president, Herring–Curtiss Co. (airplane manufacturer); president, Curtiss Aeroplane & Motor Co. (later, Curtiss–Wright Co.) (airplane manufacturer) |
| | inventor - designed and improved hydroaeroplane (seaplane), life boats, speedboats, and autoplanes |
| | writer - *The Curtiss Aviation Book*, 1912 |
| | capitalist - Florida land developer, Opa–Locka, Hialeah, and Miami Springs |
| Civic Activism: | director, National Aerial Experiment Association |
| Marriage(s): | 1898-1930 – Lena Pearl Neff (1879-1951) |
| Address: | Stewart Avenue, between Nassau Boulevard and Euston Road, Garden City |
| Name of estate: | |
| Year of construction: | 1908 |
| Style of architecture: | Mediterranean |
| Architect(s): | Oswald Hering designed the house (for Tarbell) |
| Landscape architect(s): | |

House extant: no; demolished in 1960s*
Historical notes:

   The house was built by Gage Eli Tarbell. In 1918 he sold the house to Curtiss. [Mildred H. Smith *Garden City, Long Island In Early Photographs* (New York: Dover Publications, Inc., 1987), p. 56.]
   Glenn Hammond Curtiss, Sr., known as the "father of naval aviation" and "founder of the American aircraft industry," was the son of Frank Richmond and Lua Andrews Curtiss of Hammondsport, NY.
   Lena Pearl Neff Curtiss was the daughter of Guy Neff of Hammondsport, NY. She subsequently married H. Sayre Wheeler.
   Glenn Hammond and Lena Pearl Neff Curtiss, Sr.'s son Glenn Hammond Curtiss, Jr. married Ada Howell and resided in Miami Springs, FL.
   *The house was demolished in the 1960s and replaced by a Unitarian Church building and some contemporary houses.

*front facade*

### Daingerfield, Algernon Gray (1867-1941)

| | |
|---|---|
| Occupation(s): | capitalist - secretary, Washington, DC, Jockey Club, 1901; assistant treasurer, New York Jockey Club, 1903*; secretary, Washington Park Jockey Club, Saratoga, NY |
| Marriage(s): | M/1 – 1886-div. – Elizabeth M. Thomas (1868-1931) <br> M/2 – 1902-1941 – Margaret P. Duncan (1874-1965) |
| Address: | 42 Hilton Avenue, Garden City |
| Name of estate: | |
| Year of construction: | 1873 |
| Style of architecture: | Colonial Revival |
| Architect(s): | |
| Landscape architect(s): | |
| House extant: | yes |

Historical notes:

Algernon Gray Daingerfield was the son of Foxhall Alexander Parker and Henrietta Henderson Gray Daingerfield.
Elizabeth M. Thomas Daingerfield had previously been married to George B. Ecker.
Algernon Gray and Elizabeth M. Thomas Daingerfield's son Foxhall did not marry.

The *Long Island Society Register, 1929* lists Algernon and Margaret Duncan Daingerfield as residing at 42 Hilton Avenue, Garden City. The 1920 Census lists the Daingerfields at 32 Hilton Avenue.

She was the daughter of Henry Timberlake and Elizabeth V. Brand Duncan, Jr. of Lexington, KY.

Algernon Gray and Margaret P. Duncan Daingerfield's daughter Margaret married John Kirkman Berry, Jr. of Greenwich, CT.

*Daingerfield was the undisputed boss of horse racing prior to the institution of state regulations. [*The New York Times* June 11, 1941, p. 21.]

*front facade, 2008*

### Dall, Charles Whitney, Sr. (1881-1972)

| | |
|---|---|
| Occupation(s): | industrialist - partner, Grinnell, Willis, & Co. (later, Ridley Watts Co.) <br> financier - director, Patriotic Insurance Co.; director, Sun Indemnity Co. |
| Civic Activism: | president, National Rayon Weavers Association; co-chairman, special gifts committee, Five Towns War Community Chest, 1942 |
| Marriage(s): | 1911-1972 – Emily Marshall Maurice (1887-1975) |
| Address: | Club Lane, Lawrence |
| Name of estate: | |
| Year of construction: | |
| Style of architecture: | |
| Architect(s): | |
| Landscape architect(s): | |
| House extant: | unconfirmed |

Historical notes:

The *Social Register Summer, 1915* and the *Long Island Society Register, 1929* list Charles Whitney and Emily M. Maurice Dall [Sr.] as residing in Cedarhurst [Lawrence].

He was the son of Dr. William Healey and Mrs. Annette Whitney Dall of Washington, DC.

Emily Marshall Maurice Dall was the daughter of Charles Stewart Maurice of Athens, PA.

Charles Whitney and Emily Marshall Maurice Dall, Sr.'s son Stewart married Margaret Meyerkort and resided in Cedarhurst. Their daughter Priscilla married Karl F. Mautner, the son of Stephen Mautner of New York, and, subsequently, ____ Krstuiovic. Their son Charles Whitney Dall, Jr. married Helen Mary Alice Watkins and, subsequently, Ruth Asire, the daughter of Judd D. Asire of Fostoria, OH, with whom he resided in Washington, DC.

*[See following entry for additional family information.]*

### Dall, Stewart Maurice, Sr. (1916-2004)

Occupation(s): industrialist - Sperry Gyroscope

Marriage(s): 1944-2004 – Margaret Meyerkort (1924-2006)

Address: 540 Atlantic Avenue, Lawrence
Name of estate:
Year of construction:
Style of architecture: Neo-Tudor
Architect(s):
Landscape architect(s):
House extant: no; demolished in 2007
Historical notes:

The *Social Register New York, 1965* lists Stewart and Margaret Meyerkort Dall [Sr.] as residing at 540 Atlantic Avenue, Cedarhurst.

He was the son of Charles Whitney and Emily Marshall Maurice Dall, Sr. of Lawrence.

Margaret Meyerkort Dall was the daughter of John and Edith Jacquelin Smith Meyerkort, Jr. of Lawrence.

Stewart Maurice and Margaret Meyerkort Dall, Sr.'s son Henry married Anne Morrill of Bradford, VT. Their son Stewart Meyerkort Dall, Jr. married Cynthia Louise Clark and resides in Vancouver, WA.

*[See previous entry for additional family information.]*

*front facade, 2001*

### Darlington, The Reverend Gilbert Sterling Bancroft (1892-1980)

Occupation(s): clergy - rector, Heavenly Rest Church, NYC
financier - director, Pan-American Trust Co.;
president and chairman of board, Harbor State Bank
capitalist - president, Astor Place Real Estate Co.;
vice-president and director, Fuller Building Corp.;
president, Nepahwin Inc.
Civic Activism: treasurer, Washington Square Home

Marriage(s): 1919-1971 – Elizabeth Remsen Thompson (1894-1971)

Address: Ocean Avenue, Lawrence
Name of estate:
Year of construction:
Style of architecture:
Architect(s):
Landscape architect(s):
House extant: unconfirmed
Historical notes:

The *Social Register Summer, 1921* and the *Long Island Society Register, 1929* list The Reverend Gilbert S. and Mrs. Elizabeth Remsen Thompson Darlington as residing on Ocean Avenue, Cedarhurst [Lawrence].

He was the son of The Right Reverend Dr. James Henry and Mrs. Ella Louise Bearns Darlington of Newport, RI. Dr. Darlington was the Bishop of the Episcopal Diocese of Harrisburg, PA. Gilbert's sister Eleanor married J. Ellis Fisher, Jr., the son of J. Ellis Fisher, Sr. of NYC.

Elizabeth Remsen Thompson Darlington was the daughter of Joseph TodHunter and Jane Remsen Thompson of *Holly Holm* in Lawrence. Her sister Jane, who married Earl H. Schultz, resided in Sands Point. He disappeared from the Fall River Line steamship SS *Providence*. Jane later married Charles James Irwin, Jr. Her brother Jonathan married Lillian P. MacLeod and resided in Babylon.

### Davidson, Thomas Charles, Sr. (b. 1888)

| | |
|---|---|
| Occupation(s): | financier - partner, A. M. Kidder Co. (stock brokerage firm); partner, Halstead and Harrison (stock brokerage firm)<br>industrialist - treasurer and vice-president, United Zinc Smelting |
| Marriage(s): | Marjorie M. *[unable to determine maiden name]* (b. 1894) |
| Address: | 33 Roxbury Road, Garden City |
| Name of estate: | |
| Year of construction: | 1924 |
| Style of architecture: | |
| Architect(s): | |
| Landscape architect(s): | |
| House extant: yes | |
| Historical notes: | |

Thomas Charles Davidson, Jr. married Helen Covert Vanderveer, the daughter of Charles and Frances Elizabeth Covert Vanderveer, Jr. of Hempstead.

In 1928 Davidson sold his house to J. H. Mears. [*The New York Times* November 15, 1928, p. 57.]

In 2015, the five-bedroom, four-bath, 2,500-square-foot house sold for $1.289 million.

*front / side facade, 2005*

### Davie, Preston, Sr. (1881-1967)

| | |
|---|---|
| Occupation(s): | attorney - partner, Humphrey, Davie, and Humphrey; partner, O'Brien, Boardman, and Platt (later, Conboy, Hewitt, O'Brien, and Boardman) |
| | capitalist - vice-president, Patterson & Browns, Inc., NYC; secretary, United States Distributing Corp, NYC; director, Godward Gas Generator; director, Universal Pictures, Inc. |
| | industrialist - director, Corn Products Refining Co.; director, Western New York Coal Co.; director, Sheridan–Wyoming Coal Co.; director, Talbot Coal Corp. |
| | shipping - director, United States Barge Corp.; director, Charleston Shipbuilding & Drydock Co. |
| Civic Activism: | Legal Aid Society; chairman and legal advisor, Council of National Defense |
| Marriage(s): | M/1 – 1910-div. 1928 – Emily Harriet Bedford (1882-1975) |
| | M/1 – 1930-1967 – Eugenie Mary Ladenburg (1895-1975) |
| | - politician - chairman, finance committee, Republican Party of New York State; delegate, GOP National Convention; assistant treasurer, Taft campaign for the presidency, 1952; member, Republican Party National Finance Committee |
| | Civic Activism: chairman of board, New York Heart Association; president, Robert Taft Institute of Government; director, The Pioneer Fund, 1974-1975 |
| Address: | Valentines Road, Salisbury |
| Name of estate: | *The Oasis* |
| Year of construction: | |
| Style of architecture: | Victorian |
| Architect(s): | |
| Landscape architect(s): | |

House extant: no; demolished in 1952 for housing development
Historical notes:

Preston Davie, Sr. was the son of George Montgomery and Margaret Howard Preston Davie of Louisville, KY.

Emily Harriet Bedford Davie was the daughter of Edward Thomas and Mary Ann Dingle Bedford. Emily later married Russell Ellis Sard, Sr., the son of Grange and Caroline S. Woolverton Sard, Jr. of Southampton, and, subsequently, Paulding Fosdick of *Old Trees* in Southampton. [*See* Spinzia, *Long Island's Prominent Families in the Town of Southampton* – Sard and Fosdick entries.]

Preston and Emily Harriet Bedford Davie, Sr.'s son Edward married Marilyn Morris Mathews, the daughter of Robert Morris and Alice Mathews of Winter Haven, FL, and, later, Diana Marion Wing. Their daughter Emily married Joseph Kornfeld.

The house, originally named *Heathcote*, was built by Adolph Landenburg. It was subsequently owned by his daughter Eugenie and son-in-law Preston Davie, Sr., who renamed it *The Oasis*.

Eugenie had inherited $10 million on her twenty-first birthday. [*The New York Times* August 7, 1958, p. 16.]

*side facade, 1910*

### Davies, Edward Livingston (1884-1951)

| | |
|---|---|
| Occupation(s): | engineer - construction engineer, United Gas Improvement Co., Philadelphia, PA;<br>gas engineer and operating manager, Queens Borough Gas & Electric Co., Far Rockaway;<br>gas operating manager, Long Island Lighting Co.;<br>vice-president and gas operating manager, Nassau–Suffolk Lighting Co. |
| Marriage(s): | 1917-1951 – Margaret Chapman Taylor (1881-1974) |
| Address: | 70 Third Street, Garden City |
| Name of estate: | |
| Year of construction: | 1923 |
| Style of architecture: | Colonial Revival |
| Architect(s): | |
| Landscape architect(s): | |
| House extant: yes | |
| Historical notes: | |

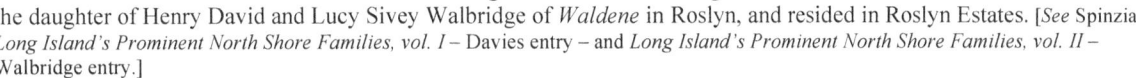

*front facade, 2008*

The *Long Island Society Register, 1929* lists Mr. and Mrs. Edward L. Davies as residing at 70 Third Street, Garden City.

He was the son of Richard Theodore and Mary Pinckney Gridley Davies of Manhattan. Edward's brother Ernest married Marguerite Helene Walbridge, the daughter of Henry David and Lucy Sivey Walbridge of *Waldene* in Roslyn, and resided in Roslyn Estates. [*See* Spinzia, *Long Island's Prominent North Shore Families, vol. I* – Davies entry – and *Long Island's Prominent North Shore Families, vol. II* – Walbridge entry.]

Margaret Chapman Taylor Davies was the daughter of Ransom Frederick and Virginia Byrd Chapman Taylor of Worcester, MA.

Edward Livingston and Margaret Chapman Taylor Davies' son Richard married Caryl Hackstaff Wood, the daughter of Howard Ogden and Caryl Hackstaff Wood, Jr. of Lawrence, and resided in Valley Stream.

### Davis, William Shippen, Sr. (1892-1962)

| | |
|---|---|
| Occupation(s): | financier - member, Blair S. Williams Co. (stock brokerage firm);<br>member, Blake Brothers and Co. (stock brokerage firm) |
| Civic Activism: | chairman, nominating committee, New York Stock Exchange;<br>trustee, gratuity fund, New York Stock Exchange |
| Marriage(s): | Frances Townsend Riker (1897-1965)<br>- Civic Activism: chair, Council of Social Agencies;<br>chair, volunteer services, Nassau chapter, American Red Cross, 1942 |
| Address: | Woodside Road, Hewlett Bay Park |
| Name of estate: | |
| Year of construction: | |
| Style of architecture: | |
| Architect(s): | |
| Landscape architect(s): | |
| House extant: unconfirmed | |
| Historical notes: | |

The *Long Island Society Register, 1929* lists W. Shippen and Frances T. Riker Davis [Sr.] as residing on Woodside Road, Lawrence [Hewlett Bay Park]. The *Social Register, 1973* lists their residence as on Albin Road, Hewlett.

He was the son of Howland and Anna Shippen Davis.

Frances Townsend Riker Davis was the daughter of Samuel and Frances Mortimer Townsend Riker.

William Shippen and Frances Townsend Riker Davis, Sr.'s son Samuel married Barbara T. Gould, the daughter of John H. Gould of *Mahkeenac Farm* in Lenox, MA, and resided in Katonah, NY. Their son Rodman married Eleanor Stuart Childs, the daughter of Dr. Edward Paterson Childs of Manhattan. Their son David married Gwenyth Olive Piper, the daughter of Richard Freeborn Piper, and resided in Manhattan. Their daughter Frances married Rollin B. Fisher II and resided in Kirkwood, MO. Their daughter Nina married William J. Jackson, the son of R. Arnold Jackson of Pelham Manor, NY, and resided in Exeter, NH. Their son William Shippen Davis, Jr. married Deborah Wood, the daughter of Benjamin Wood of Greenwich, CT, and resided in Shrewsbury, CT.

### de Aguilar, Elizabeth Pendleton Slattery (d. 1933)

| | |
|---|---|
| Civic Activism: | director, auxiliary, Martha Parsons' Children Hospital, St. Louis, MO |
| Marriage(s): | M/1 – 1893-1901 – Francis Beauregarde de Aguilar (d. 1901)<br>(aka Francis Beauregarde Aglar)<br>- industrialist – general manager, Interchangeable Brake Beam Co., St Louis, MO<br>M/2 – Frederick William Kendrick (b. 1877)<br>- financier - partner, R. L. Day and Co. (stock brokerage firm); partner, Mackay and Co. (stock brokerage firm) |
| Address: | *[unable to determine street address]*, Lawrence |
| Name of estate: | |
| Year of construction: | |
| Style of architecture: | |
| Architect(s): | |
| Landscape architect(s): | |
| House extant: | unconfirmed |
| Historical notes: | |

The *Social Register, 1905, 1908,* and *1911* list Elizabeth P. Slattery de Aguilar as residing in Lawrence.

She was the daughter of Dennis Paul and Elizabeth Wyman Leigh Slattery of St. Louis, MO. Her father was the commander of the USS *Vindicator* on the Mississippi River during the Civil War.

Francis Beauregarde de Aguilar was the son of James F. Aglar.

Francis Beauregarde and Elizabeth Pendleton Slattery de Aguilar's son Francis Paul de Aguilar resided in Garden City.

Frederick William Kendrick, who resided in Hempstead, was the son of Rufus Kendrick of Boston, MA.

*[See following entry for additional family information.]*


### de Aguilar, Francis Paul

| | |
|---|---|
| Occupation(s): | |
| Marriage(s): | M/1 – 1920-div. – Gladys Newbold Black (1893-1974)<br>M/2 – 1925-div. – Natalie Livingston Forbes (1896-1932) |
| Address: | 222 Stewart Avenue, Garden City |
| Name of estate: | |
| Year of construction: | 1918 |
| Style of architecture: | Neo-Tudor |
| Architect(s): | |
| Landscape architect(s): | |
| House extant: | yes |
| Historical notes: | |

The *Long Island Society Register, 1929* lists F. Paul and Natalie L. Forbes de Aguilar [Jr.] as residing at 222 Stewart Avenue, Garden City.

He was the son of Francis Beauregarde and Elizabeth Pendleton Slattery de Aguilar, Sr.

Gladys Newbold Black de Aguilar was the daughter of Henry McKeen and Nina Wolf Black, Sr., who resided at *Locust Hall Farm* in Jobstown, NJ. Gladys subsequently married John V. Bishop, the son of John Israel and Anna Ridgeway Bishop.

Natalie Livingston Forbes de Aguilar was the daughter of Arthur Holland and Jessica Livingston Forbes of *Garden Court* in Fairfield, CT. Natalie's father was president of the Forbes Publishing Company. Natalie had previously been married to Robert Beach and George Clinton McKesson Perry, the son of William Sumner and Ida Lefferts McKesson Perry of Manhattan. After her divorce from de Aguilar, Natalie married Harold S. Thompson with whom she resided in Honolulu, HI.

*[See previous entry for additional family information.]*

In 2006, the 5,256-square-foot house sold for $1.325 million.

*Francis Paul de Aguilar residence,
side facade, 2008*


### Dean, Howard Brush, Sr. (1897-1950)

| | |
|---|---|
| Occupation(s): | financier -  partner, Struthers and Dean (stock brokerage firm) |
| | capitalist -  vice-president, Pan American Airways; |
| | vice-president, Pan American Grace Airways |
| Civic Activism: | governor, Association of Stock Exchange Firms |
| Marriage(s): | 1920-1950 – Maria Fahys Cook (1900-1983) |
| Address: | 119 Fifth Street, Garden City |
| Name of estate: | |
| Year of construction: | |
| Style of architecture: | |
| Architect(s): | |
| Landscape architect(s): | |
| House extant: no | |
| Historical notes: | |

The *Long Island Society Register, 1929* lists the Deans as residing at 119 Fifth Street, Garden City.

He was the son of Herbert Hollingshead and Marion Atwater Brush Dean of *Deanlea* in Lattingtown.

Maria Fahys Cook Dean was the daughter of Henry Francis and Lena Marianna Fahys Cook of *Clench–Warton* in North Haven. Maria subsequently married Dudley DeVore Roberts, Jr. of East Hampton.

Howard Brush and Maria Fahys Cook Brush, Sr.'s daughter Marianne married William C. Felch. Their son Howard Brush Dean, Jr. married Andree Belden Maitland, the daughter of James William and Sylvia Wigglesworth Maitland of Hewlett Bay Park, and resided in East Hampton.

[*See* Spinzia, *Long Island's Prominent North Shore Families, vol. I* – Dean entry; *Long Island's Prominent Families in the Town of Southampton* – Cook entry; and *Long Island's Prominent Families in the Town of East Hampton* – Dean and Roberts entries.]

The Deans' grandson Dr. Howard Brush Dean III was Governor of Vermont from 1991-2003 and was unsuccessful in becoming the Democratic candidate for the presidency in the 2004 election. He then headed the Democratic National Committee through the 2008 election.

The house was subsequently owned by George Andrew Carlin.

### Delafield, Lewis Livingston, Jr. (1863-1944)

| | |
|---|---|
| Occupation(s): | attorney -   partner, Hawkins, Delafield, and Longfellow, NYC; |
| | judge, New York State Supreme Court |
| | financier -   director, City Bank Farmers Trust |
| Civic Activism: | member, New York State Charter Revision Commission, 1921-1922; |
| | secretary, Rapid Transit Commission, 1894-1899; |
| | member, Committee of Seventy, 1894*; |
| | member, Town of Hempstead Legislative Board; |
| | a founder, New York County Lawyers Association; |
| | chairman, local draft board No. 7231; |
| | director, New York Historical Society; |
| | secretary, Cedarhurst Yacht Club, 1936 |
| Marriage(s): | 1885-1944 – Charlotte Hoffman Wyeth (1859-1947) |
| | - Civic Activism:  vice-president, Colonial Dames of America; |
| | member, Nassau County Welfare Board; |
| | suffragist -  regional congressional leader, Congressional Union of Woman Suffrage** |
| Address: | Ocean Avenue, Lawrence |
| Name of estate: | *Norton Perkins Cottage* |
| Year of construction: | |
| Style of architecture: | |
| Architect(s): | |
| Landscape architect(s): | |
| House extant: | unconfirmed |
| Historical notes: | |

The *Social Register Summer, 1921* lists Lewis L. and Charlotte H. Wyeth Delafield [Jr.] as residing in Hewlett. The *Long Island Society Register, 1929* lists Lewis L. and Charlotte H. Wyeth Delafield [Jr.] as residing at *Norton Perkins Cottage* in Lawrence.

He was the son of Lewis Livingston and Emily Prime Delafield, Sr. of Manhattan.

Charlotte Hoffman Wyeth Delafield was the daughter of Leonard Jarvis and Charlotte Prime Wyeth of Manhattan.

Lewis Livingston and Charlotte Hoffman Wyeth Delafield, Jr.'s daughter Charlotte married Robert McCurdy Marsh. Their daughter Emily married Edmund Wetherbee Peaslee, Sr. and resided in Lawrence. Their son Lewis Livingston Delafield, Jr. [III], who married Ruth L. Manierre and, subsequently, Elsa Ringletaube, resided in Hewlett Bay Park.

*[See following entry of additional family information.]*

*The Committee of Seventy was instrumental in disbanding the notorious Tweed Ring.

**For other Long Islanders involved in the suffrage movement *see* Raymond E. Spinzia, "Winning the Franchise: Long Island Activists in the Fight for Woman's Suffrage and Their Opponents, Long Island's Anti-Suffragists." wwwspinzialongislandestates.com.

### Delafield, Lewis Livingston, III (1886-1957)

| | |
|---|---|
| Occupation(s): | attorney - partner, Delafield and Wood, NYC |
| Civic Activism: | trustee, Roosevelt Hospital, NYC; |
| | president, Indian Mountain School, Lakeville, CT; |
| | member, Governor's Commission on School Finance, 1925-1926; |
| | member, Governor's Commission on Construction of New York State Thruway, 1950; |
| | chairman, local Board of Selective Service, 1940-1946; |
| | chairman, Nassau Emergency Work Bureau, 1933-1934; |
| | member, Nassau County Board of Public Welfare, 1928; |
| | president, Five Towns Community Council; |
| | trustee, Village of Hewlett Bay Park |
| Marriage(s): | M/1 – 1921-1937 – Ruth Lockwood Manierre (d. 1937) |
| | - Civic Activism: president, Junior League |
| | M/2 – 1956-1957 – Elsa Ringletaube |
| Address: | 20 Piermont Avenue, Hewlett Bay Park |
| Name of estate: | |
| Year of construction: | |
| Style of architecture: | |
| Architect(s): | |
| Landscape architect(s): | |
| House extant: no | |
| Historical notes: | |

The *Long Island Society Register, 1929* lists Lewis L. and Ruth L. Manierre Delafield, Jr. [III] as residing in Hewlett [Hewlett Bay Park]. The 1930 Census lists them at this address.

He was the son of Lewis Livingston and Charlotte Hoffman Wyeth Delafield, Jr., who resided at *Norton Perkins Cottage* in Lawrence.

Ruth Lockwood Manierre Delafield was the daughter of Alfred Lee Manierre of NYC.

Lewis Livingston and Ruth Lockwood Manierre Delafield III's daughter Ruth married Clarkson Nott Potter, the son of John H. N. Potter of *Stone House Farm* in Mendham, NJ. Their son Lewis Livingston Delafield IV married Patricia Marie Russo, the daughter of Natal Y. Russo.

### Delafield, Maturin Livingston, II (1901-1945)

| | | |
|---|---|---|
| Occupation(s): | financier - | member, Kuhn, Loeb, and Co., NYC, 1926-1927 (investment banking firm); |
| | | member, Dominick and Dominick, Co., NYC, 1927-1937; |
| | | partner, Delafield and Delafield, NYC (stock brokerage firm); |
| | | vice-president, Delafield Allied Corp. |
| | capitalist - | chairman of board, Kansas City Southern Railway Co. |
| Civic Activism: | trustee, New York Dispensary, NYC | |
| Marriage(s): | 1924-1945 – Mary Peirce Lyon (1901-1986) | |
| Address: | 112 Irving Place, Woodmere | |
| Name of estate: | | |
| Year of construction: | | |
| Style of architecture: | | |
| Architect(s): | | |
| Landscape architect(s): | | |
| House extant: no | | |
| Historical notes: | | |

The *Long Island Society Register, 1929* lists Maturin Livingston and Mary P. Lyon Delafield II as residing at 112 Irving Place, Woodmere. The *Social Register, 1933* lists them residing in Hewlett.

He was the son of Edward Coleman and Margaretta Stockton Beasley Delafield of Manhattan.

Mary Peirce Lyon Delafield subsequently married John S. Williams and resided in Chatham, NY.

Maturin Livingston and Mary Peirce Lyon Delafield II's daughter Mary married Clinton Linwood Allen, Jr. of West Hartford, CT. Their son Maturin Livingston Delafield III married Barbara de Saussure Reed, the daughter of William Barton Reed of Omaha, NE.

### Delafield, Robert Hare, Jr. (1894-1945)

| | |
|---|---|
| Occupation(s): | capitalist -  vice-president, Columbia Gas & Electric Corp. |
| | financier -  manager, Boston, MA, branch, National City Bank |
| Civic Activism: | trustee and treasurer, Pomfret School; |
| | trustee, Village of Hewlett Bay Park |
| Marriage(s): | 1915-1945 – Jessie Hardy (1892-1959) |
| Address: | Hewlett Neck Road, Hewlett Neck* |

Name of estate:
Year of construction:
Style of architecture:
Architect(s):
Landscape architect(s):
House extant:  unconfirmed
Historical notes:

The *Social Register Summer, 1921* lists Robert Hare and Jessie Hardy Delafield [Jr.] as residing in Woodmere. The *Long Island Society Register, 1929* lists Robert Hare and Jessie Hardy Delafield [Jr.] as residing in Hewlett [Hewlett Neck].

He was the son of Robert Hare and Anne Shepherd Lloyd Delafield, Sr. of New York.

Robert Hare and Jessie Hardy Delafield, Jr.'s daughter Anne married Disque Dee Deane and, later, Donald Stuart, the son of George B. Stuart. Their son Robert Hare Delafield III married Sarah K. Rice of Hartford, CT, and resided in Ukiah, CA.

*Hewlett Neck Road was previously called Georges Boulevard.


### De Mercado, Frank Eliot (1892-1959)

| | |
|---|---|
| Occupation(s): | capitalist -  import/export business |
| | journalist -  reporter and book reviewer, *The New York Times* |
| Marriage(s): | 1921-1959 – Margaret Ludlow Harrison (1901-1962) |
| Address: | 116 Fifth Street, Garden City |

Name of estate:

| | |
|---|---|
| Year of construction: | 1913 |
| Style of architecture: | Contemporary Shingle |

Architect(s):
Landscape architect(s):
House extant:  yes
Historical notes:

The *Long Island Society Register, 1929* lists Mr. and Mrs. Frank De Mercado as residing at 116 Fifth Street, Garden City.

He was the son of Michael De Mercado of Manhattan.

Frank Eliot and Margaret Ludlow Harrison De Mercado's daughter Peggy married John R. Hansen III. Their daughter Barbara married John D. Smith and resided in Washington, DC.

*front facade, 2004*

**DeMille, Nelson Richard (b. 1943)**
**aka Jack Cannon, Kurt Ladner, and Brad Matthews\***

| | |
|---|---|
| Occupation(s): | writer - *The Sniper*, 1974; *The Hammer of God*, 1974; *The Agent of Death*, 1975; *The Smack Man*, 1975; *The Cannibal*, 1975; *The Night of the Phoenix*, 1975; *Hitler's Children: The True Story of Nazi Human Stud Farms*, 1976 [as Kurt Ladner]; *Killer Sharks: The Real Story*, 1977 [as Brad Mathews]; *By the Rivers of Babylon*, 1978; *Mayday*, 1979/1998 [with Thomas Block]; *Cathedral*, 1981; *The Talbot Odyssey*, 1984; *Word of Honor*, 1985; *The Charm School*, 1988; *The Gold Coast*, 1990; *The General's Daughter*, 1992; *Spencerville*, 1994; *Plum Island*, 1997; "Revenge and Rebellion," in *The Plot Thickens*, 1997 (ed. by Mary Higgins Clark); *The Lion's Game*, 2000; *Up Country*, 2002; *Night Fall*, 2004; *Wild Fire*, 2006; *The Gate House*, 2008; *The Quest* 1975 / 2013; *The Gate House*, 2008; *The Lion*, 2010; *The Panther*, 2012; *Radiant Angel*, 2015; *The Cuban Affair*, 2017; *The Deserter*, 2019; *The Maze*, 2022 |
| Civic Activism: | supported numerous charities |
| Marriage(s): | M/1 – 1971-div. 1987 – Ellen Wasserman<br>   - medical technologist<br>M/2 – 1988-div. 2004 – Virginia Sindel (b. 1947)<br>        (aka Virginia Maxine and Ginny Witte)<br>   - journalist - staff writer, *Pittsburgh Post–Gazzette*;<br>        contributor, feature articles in local newspapers, 1977-1979;<br>   public relations - public relations director, Greater Pittsburgh March of Dimes, 1978-1979;<br>        member, Marc & Company, Pittsburgh, PA, 1979-1983;<br>        member, O'Connell Associates, Garden City, 1984;<br>        founder and president, G. DeMille Public Relations, Garden City<br>M/3 – 2007-2018 – Sandra Jane Dillingham (1964-2018)<br>   - public relations - book publicist |
| Address: | Eleventh Street, Garden City |
| Name of estate: | |
| Year of construction: | 2003 |
| Style of architecture: | Neo-Tudor |
| Architect(s): | |
| Landscape architect(s): | |
| House extant: yes | |
| Historical notes: | |

The 9,731-square-foot house was built by Nelson Richard DeMille.
He is the son of Huron and Antonia Panzera DeMille of Elmont.
Virginia Sindel DeMille is the daughter of Roy Roger and Joanna Franks Sindel.
Sandra Jane Dillingham DeMille was the daughter of Robert and Joan Dillingham.
\*Several of Nelson DeMille's books have been written using these pen names.

*front / side facade, 2005*

## De Mott, Harry Mead (1868-1936)

| | |
|---|---|
| Occupation(s): | financier - president, Mechanics Bank, Brooklyn (later, Brooklyn Trust Co.); |
| | vice-president, Brooklyn Trust Co.; |
| | vice-president, Greater New York Savings Bank; |
| | director, Bank of Flatbush, Brooklyn; |
| | director, Brooklyn Safe Deposit Co.; |
| | director, Morris Plain Industrial Bank, NJ; |
| | director, New York Casualty Co. |
| | capitalist - vice-president, Brooklyn Dodgers (baseball team); |
| | director, Brooklyn Storage & Warehouse Co. |
| Civic Activism: | member, advisory council, State Superintendent of Banks; |
| | trustee, Tompkins Avenue Congregational Church, Brooklyn |
| Marriage(s): | 1893-1936 – Emma Cammeyer Heyberger (1871-1942) |
| Address: | 118 Hilton Avenue, Garden City |
| Name of estate: | |
| Year of construction: | 1927 |
| Style of architecture: | Colonial Revival |
| Architect(s): | |
| Landscape architect(s): | |
| House extant: yes | |
| Historical notes: | |

The house was built by Harry Mead De Mott.

The *Long Island Society Register, 1929* lists Mr. and Mrs. Harry M. De Mott as residing at 118 Hilton Avenue, Garden City.

Emma Cammeyer Hayberger De Mott was the daughter of William H. and Emma Cammeyer Heyberger.

The De Motts' daughter Mildred remained unmarried. Their daughter Blanche married Mortimer Brendon Kelly and resided in Morristown, NJ.

In 2001, the 3,500-square-foot house sold for $1.050 million.

*front facade, 2008*

## Denny, Archibald Marshall, Sr. (1887-1950)

| | |
|---|---|
| Occupation(s): | engineer - chemical |
| Marriage(s): | 1907-1950 – Katharine Varnum Kendall (1888-1965) |
| Address: | 37 Brompton Road, Garden City |
| Name of estate: | |
| Year of construction: | 1920 |
| Style of architecture: | American Craftsman |
| Architect(s): | |
| Landscape architect(s): | |
| House extant: yes | |
| Historical notes: | |

The *Long Island Society Register, 1929* lists Archibald Marshall and Katharine Varnum Kendall Denny [Sr.] as residing at 37 Brompton Road, Garden City.

He was the son of Harmar Denny and Elizabeth Bell Marshall Denny of Pittsburgh, PA.

*front facade, 2007*

Katharine Varnum Kendall Denny was the daughter of William Beals and Katharine Varnum Whitney Kendall of Garden City.

Archibald Marshall and Katharine Varnum Kendall Denny, Sr.'s daughter Katharine married Edgar Humphrey Cobb, the son of George Cobb of Brookline, MA. Their son Archibald Marshall Denny, Jr. married Marjorie Evans, the daughter of James Evans.

### Derby, Robert Mason, Sr. (1879-1966)

| | |
|---|---|
| Occupation(s): | mechanical engineer |
| | industrialist - Niles–Bemont–Pond Co. |
| Civic Activism: | conservationist |
| Marriage(s): | 1912-1957 – Ruth Rossiter Hubbell (1887-1957) |
| Address: | 92 Auerbach Lane, Lawrence |
| Name of estate: | |
| Year of construction: | 1891 |
| Style of architecture: | Modified Colonial Revival |
| Architect(s): | |
| Landscape architect(s): | |
| House extant: yes | |
| Historical notes: | |

The *Long Island Society Register, 1929* lists Robert Mason and Ruth R. Hubbell Derby [Sr.] as residing on Auerbach Lane, Cedarhurst [Lawrence]. The *Social Register, 1933* lists their address as 92 Auerbach Lane, Cedarhurst [Lawrence].

He was the son of Dr. Hasket and Mrs. Sarah Mason Derby of Boston, MA.

Ruth Rossiter Hubbell Derby was the daughter of Charles Bulkley and Emily Allen Chandler Hubbell of *Brookside Farm* in Williamstown, MA.

Robert Mason and Ruth Rossiter Hubbell Derby, Sr.'s son Robert Mason Derby, Jr. [III] married Elizabeth Murrell Millet, the daughter of Dr. John A. P. Millet of Stockbridge, MA, and resided in Fairfield, CT. In 1922, their four-year-old son, also named Robert Mason Derby, Jr., died. [*The North Adams Transcript* October 9, 1922, p. 9.]

In 2002, the 2,968-square-foot house sold for $550,000.

*front facade, 2001*

### de Saulles, Charles Augustus Heckscher, Sr. (1876-1962)

| | |
|---|---|
| Occupation(s): | industrialist -  manager, Gas City Plant of Prime Western Smelter |
| Marriage(s): | M/1 – 1905-div.1922 – Louise Margaret Hock (1882-1923) |
| | M/2 – Ann G. Barnitz |
| Address: | 143 Wellington Road, Garden City |
| Name of estate: | *The Box* |
| Year of construction: | c. 1906 |
| Style of architecture: | Shingle |
| Architect(s): | |
| Landscape architect(s): | |
| House extant: | no |
| Historical notes: | |

The *Social Register Summer, 1921* lists Charles A. H. and Louise M. Hoch de Saulles [Sr.] as residing at *The Box* in Westbury. Prior to relocating to Garden City, Charles had purchased *The Box* which was the residence of his brother John Gerard Longer de Saulles [I]. John was murdered by his wife Blanca Elena Errazurita Vergara de Saulles. Blanca had become despondent over her divorce from John, which implicated Rudolph Valentino, and shot John five times in front of their son. In spite of this, she was acquitted and subsequently married Fernando Santa Cruz Wilson. In 1940, she committed suicide in Vina del Mar. The de Saulles murder was the subject of Raul Walsh's 1918 silent film "The Woman and the Law."

Charles and John were the sons of Arthur Brice and Catherine M. Heckscher de Saulles.

Louise Margaret Hock de Saulles was the daughter of George M. and Elizabeth Regina Hertkorn Hock of Kansas.

Charles Augustus Heckscher and Louise Margaret Hoch de Saulles, Sr.'s son John Gerard Longer de Saulles II married Doris Elizabeth Slagle, the daughter of Joseph Ray and Maybell Kiper Slagle. Their son Charles Augustus Heckscher De Saulles, Jr. married Veronica Cecila Hefferman, the daughter of John J. and Mary M. Dillon Hefferman.

Charles Augustus Heckscher and Ann G. Barnitz de Saulles, Sr.'s son Norman married Christine Erb and resided in Smithtown.


### Deshler, Charles Franklin, Jr. (1877-1947)

| | |
|---|---|
| Occupation(s): | real estate agent -  sales agent for Davies, Auerbach, & Cornell (developers of Hewlett Bay Park and Hewlett Beach) |
| | financier -  trustee, American Savings Bank, NYC |
| Civic Activism: | member, Real Estate Board of New York |
| Marriage(s): | 1909-1947 – Lydia R. Hartshorne (b. 1879) |
| Address: | Everit Avenue, Hewlett Bay Park |
| Name of estate: | |
| Year of construction: | |
| Style of architecture: | |
| Architect(s): | |
| Landscape architect(s): | |
| House extant: | unconfirmed |
| Historical notes: | |

The *Long Island Society Register, 1929* lists Charles F. and Lydia R. Hartshorne Deshler [Jr.] as residing in Hewlett [Hewlett Bay Park].

He was the son of Dr. Charles Franklin and Mrs. Hannah Virginia Wyckoff Deshler, Sr. of Hightstown, NJ.

Lydia R. Hartshorne Deshler was the daughter of Richard Bowne Hartshorne of Manhattan.

Charles Franklin and Lydia R. Hartshorne Deshler, Jr.'s daughter Josephine married James Clifton Edgar. Their son Charles Franklin Deshler III resided in Scarsdale, NY.

### De Tienne, Dr. John Antoine (1871-1940)

| | |
|---|---|
| Occupation(s): | physician - osteopath |
| | financier - trustee, Brevoort Savings Bank, Brooklyn |
| Civic Activism: | regent, American Osteopathic Association |
| Marriage(s): | 1903-1940 – Maude Olive Waterman (1875-1948) |
| Address: | 43 Nassau Boulevard, Garden City |
| Name of estate: | |
| Year of construction: | 1916 |
| Style of architecture: | Shingle |
| Architect(s): | |
| Landscape architect(s): | |
| House extant: yes | |
| Historical notes: | |

*front facade, 2001*

The *Long Island Society Register, 1929* lists Dr. John A. and Mrs. De Tienne as residing at 43 Nassau Boulevard in Garden City.

He was the son of Henry P. and Mary Jane Duchant De Tienne.

Maude Olive Waterman De Tienne was the daughter of Elisha Silas Waterman and an heir to the Waterman fountain pen fortune.

Dr. John Antoine and Mrs. Maude Olive Waterman De Tienne's daughter Elizabeth married Henry Dudley Gerard, the son of Ernest Dudley and Emily A. Carpenter Gerard of Garden City, with whom she resided in Garden City. Elizabeth later married Raymond Pryor Ackerman, Jr., the son of Raymond Pryor and Mildred Chadbourn Irish Ackerman, Sr. of Garden City. Their daughter Maude married Robert Drake Martin, Sr. and resided in Garden City.

In 1990, the 3,027-square-foot house sold for $425,000.


### De Veau, George Putnam (1890-1964)

| | |
|---|---|
| Occupation(s): | |
| Marriage(s): | 1917-1964 – Maryanna Ludlow Lincoln (1897-1983) |
| Address: | Hollywood Crossings, Lawrence |
| Name of estate: | |
| Year of construction: | |
| Style of architecture: | |
| Architect(s): | |
| Landscape architect(s): | |
| House extant: unconfirmed | |
| Historical notes: | |

The *Long Island Society Register, 1929* and the *Social Register, 1951* list George Putnam and Maryanna L. Lincoln De Veau as residing on Hollywood Crossings, Cedarhurst [Lawrence].

He was the son of Frederic Clinton and Sarah Hunt De Veau of Manhattan.

Maryanna Ludlow Lincoln De Veau was the daughter of Lowell and Anna Jackson Steward Lincoln, Jr. of Manhattan.

George Putnam and Maryanna Ludlow Lincoln De Veau's daughter Phyllis married Reginald Endicott Francklyn, the son of Reginald Gebhard and Lilian Endicott Francklyn of Hewlett Harbor, and resided in Avon, CT. Their daughter Nancy married Joel Rathbone, the son of Hall Rathbone of Woodmere, and, subsequently, Wade Lamson, the son of Jarvis Lamson of Hewlett, and resided in Lawrence.

### Devereux, Alvin, II (1889-1983)

| | |
|---|---|
| Occupation(s): | attorney - member, Beekman, Menken, and Griscom |
| Civic Activism: | president, Intercollegiate Polo Association, 1925 |
| Marriage(s): | 1922 -1983 – Virginia H. Hagen (1890-1985)<br>- Civic Activism: treasurer, New York State Birth Control Federation; trustee, Long Island Biological Association, Cold Spring Harbor |
| Address: | *[unable to determine street address]*, Lawrence |
| Name of estate: | |
| Year of construction: | |
| Style of architecture: | |
| Architect(s): | |
| Landscape architect(s): | |
| House extant: | unconfirmed |
| Historical notes: | |

The *Long Island Society Register, 1929* lists Alvin and Virginia H. Hagen Devereux II as residing in Lawrence.
He was the son of Walter Bourchier and Mary Porter Gregory Devereux.
Virginia H. Hagen Devereux was the daughter of Winston Henry and Lucy Trotter Hagen of *Locust Knoll* in Oyster Bay.
By 1938 the Devereauxs had relocated to West Hills. [*See* Spinzia, *Long Island's Prominent North Shore Families, vol. I* – Devereux and Hagen entries.]

### Dixon, Courtland Palmer, II (1884-1943)

| | |
|---|---|
| Occupation(s): | financier - partner, Jacquelin and deCoppet (stock brokerage firm) |
| Marriage(s): | 1911-1943 – Hortense Howland (1886-1975) |
| Address: | Osborne Avenue, Lawrence |
| Name of estate: | *The Causeway* |
| Year of construction: | c. 1930 |
| Style of architecture: | Colonial Revival |
| Architect(s): | Louis Seabury Weeks, Sr. |
| Landscape architect(s): | |
| House extant: | yes |
| Historical notes: | |

*rear facade 1980*

The *Social Register, 1933* lists Courtland P. and Hortense Howland Dixon [II] as residing in Lawrence.
He was the son of William Palmer and Evelina Babcock Dixon, Sr. His sister Evelina married Eben Stevens and resided at *The Mount* in Lawrence. His brother William Palmer Dixon, Jr., who married Theodora Thorpe and, subsequently, Joan Deery, also resided in Lawrence.
Horstense Howland Dixon was the daughter of Louis Meredith and Virginia Lee Lawrence Howland of Bayside, Queens.
Courtland Palmer and Horstense Howland Dixon II's son Lawrence married Harriet Parker Merritt, the daughter of Schuyler Merritt II. Their son Courtland Palmer Dixon III married Penelope Allis Harrison, the daughter of William B. Harrison of Louisville, KY. Their daughter Marie married Arthur Mason Du Bois and resided in Lawrence.
*[See following entry for additional family information.]*

### Dixon, William Palmer, Jr. (1902-1968)

| | |
|---|---|
| Occupation(s): | financier - partner, Loeb, Rhodes, and Co. (investment banking firm); director, Rhoades International, Inc.; director, American Home Assurance Co.; director, International Life Assurance Co. of New York; director, United States Life Insurance Co.; director, Life Holding Corp.; director, Transatlantic Reinsurance Co. |
| Civic Activism: | trustee, The Lighthouse; director, American Field Service; trustee, Midtown Hospital, NYC; director, Atlantic Beach Club, 1937 |
| Marriage(s): | M/1 – 1925-div. – Theodora Thorpe (1906-1978)<br>   - Civic Activism: donated paintings to the Parrish Art Museum, Southampton<br>M/2 – 1941-1968 – Joan Deery (1911-1989)<br>   (aka Joan Wetmore)<br>   - entertainers and associated professions - actress |
| Address: | Causeway, Lawrence |
| Name of estate: | |
| Year of construction: | |
| Style of architecture: | |
| Architect(s): | |
| Landscape architect(s): | |
| House extant: unconfirmed | |
| Historical notes: | |

   The *Long Island Society Register, 1929* lists William Palmer and Theodora Thorpe Dixon [Jr.] as residing in Lawrence.
   He was the son of William Palmer and Evelina Franklin Babcock Dixon, Sr. His sister Evelina married Eben Stevens and resided at *The Mount* in Lawrence. His brother Courtland Palmer Dixon II, who married Hortense Howland, also resided in Lawrence.
   Theodora Thorpe Dixon was the daughter of Warren and Helen Prentiss Converse Thorpe, Sr. of Lawrence. She subsequently married Charles John Frederick Winn, the son of Baron Saint Oswald and Baroness Mabel Susan Forbes Winn of London, England. Theodora's brother Warren Thorpe, Jr. married Elizabeth Searles Greene, the daughter of Herbert and Elizabeth Searles Greene of Cedarhurst.
   Born in Australia, Joan Deery Dixon was the daughter of Arthur and Agness Thorn Deery. Joan had previously been married to William Wetmore. She portrayed elegant women in her nearly thirty-year career as a Broadway and television actress and was residing in Manhattan at the time of her death.
   At the time of his death, William Palmer Dixon, Jr. was residing in St. James. [*The New York Times* July 27, 1968, p. 27.]
*[See previous entry for additional family information.]*

**Doolittle, Frederick William, Jr. (1883-1950)**

| | |
|---|---|
| Occupation(s): | educator - instructor, mechanics and hydraulics, University of Illinois, Urbana–Champaign, IL; |
| | instructor, structural engineering, University of Colorado, Boulder, CO; |
| | assistant professor, mechanics, University of Wisconsin, Madison, WI |
| | capitalist - vice-president, North American Co. (engineering consulting firm); |
| | director, Cleveland Electric Illuminating Co.; |
| | director, Potomac Electric Power Co. |
| | writer - *Cost of Urban Transportation Service*, 1916; |
| | numerous articles in technical journals |
| Civic Activism: | member, Garden City Board of Education; |
| | member, Garden City Board of Zoning Appeals; |
| | member, Price Adjustment Board during World War II; |
| | treasurer, Transit Code Authority; |
| | secretary, Illinois Public Utilities Commission, 1913-1914; |
| | director, Bureau of Fare Research of American Railway Association; |
| | chairman, committee on public utilities, Commerce and Industry Association of New York |
| Marriage(s): | 1910-1950 – Madeleine Steele (1882-1966) |
| Address: | 79 Brompton Road, Garden City |
| Name of estate: | |
| Year of construction: | 1906 |
| Style of architecture: | Colonial Revival |
| Architect(s): | |
| Landscape architect(s): | |
| House extant: yes | |
| Historical notes: | |

   The *Long Island Society Register, 1929* lists Frederick W. Doolittle [Jr.] as residing at 79 Brompton Road, Garden City.
   He was the son of Frederick William and Mary Jane Russell Doolittle, Sr. of Hopkintown, IA.
   Madeleine Steele Doolittle was the daughter of Henry Pember Steele of Denver, CO.
   Frederick William and Madeleine Steele Doolittle, Jr.'s son Frederick William Doolittle III married Lora Louise Sharp, the daughter of David Gordon Sharp of Chapel Hill, NC. In 1925, their nine-year-old son Robert died.

*front facade, 2001*

### Dooman, Dr. David Stoddard (1894-1955)

| | |
|---|---|
| Occupation(s): | physician - heart specialist, Buffalo General Hospital, Buffalo, NY; Commissioner of Health, Garden City, 1927 |
| Civic Activism: | director, Japan Society of United States; a founder, Los Gatos Disabled American War Veterans |
| Marriage(s): | Kathleen Etherington (1901-1975) |
| Address: | 75 Whitehall Boulevard, Garden City |
| Name of estate: | |
| Year of construction: | c. 1928 |
| Style of architecture: | Neo-Tudor |
| Architect(s): | |
| Landscape architect(s): | |
| House extant: | yes |
| Historical notes: | |

The house was built by Dr. David Stoddard Dooman, who examined Charles Lindbergh just prior to his historic trans-Atlantic flight.

The *Long Island Society Register, 1929* lists Dr. D. Stoddard and Mrs. Kathleen Ethrington [sic] Dooman as residing at 75 Whitehall Boulevard, Garden City.

Their daughter Eleanor married Sidney Arthur Pritchard and resided in San Mateo, CA. Their daughter Margaret married Robert C. Hilpert and resided in Great Neck. Their daughter Kathleen married Charles Henry Hulburd and resided in Saratoga, CA.

*front facade 2005*

### Dow, Harold Gilman, Sr. (1896-1963)

| | |
|---|---|
| Occupation(s): | shipping - president, Dyson Shipping Co., Inc., NY; chairman of board, Pennsylvania–Maryland Steamship Co., Baltimore, MD |
| Marriage(s): | 1922-1963 – Edna Marion Belsterling (1899-1983) - Civic Activism: regent, Daughters of the American Revolution |
| Address: | 167 Kensington Road, Garden City |
| Name of estate: | |
| Year of construction: | 1930 |
| Style of architecture: | Georgian Revival |
| Architect(s): | |
| Landscape architect(s): | |
| House extant: | yes |
| Historical notes: | |

Edna Marion Belsterling Dow was the daughter of Charles Starne and Florence Fries Belsterling of Lawrence.

Harold Gilman and Edna Marion Belsterling Dow, Sr.'s daughter Jean married Robert Milton Taliaferro Deaner, the son of Frank Cleveland Deaner of Lynchburg, VA and resided in Allison Park, PA. Their son Harold Gilman Dow, Jr. married Mary Amanda Boles, the daughter of William T. Boles.

*front facade, 2000*

### Downer, Jesse Halsey, Sr. (1883-1971)

Occupation(s): financier - partner, Rutter and Co. (bond brokerage firm)

Marriage(s): Magdalene Schenck Johnstone (1892-1946)

Address: 105 Third Street, Garden City
Name of estate:
Year of construction:
Style of architecture:
Architect(s):
Landscape architect(s):
House extant: no
Historical notes:

   The *Long Island Society Register, 1929* lists J. Halsey and Magdalene Schenck Johnstone Downer [Sr.] as residing at 105 Third Street, Garden City.
   He was the son of John and Edith Halsey Strong Downer of Sag Harbor.
   Magdalene Schenck Johnstone Downer was the daughter of John and Jane Rapelyea Johnstone.
   Their daughter Dalene married George Henry Taylor, Jr. of Baltimore, MD. Their son Halsey married Jean A. Champlin, the daughter of George L. Champlin of Hartford, CT. Their son Jessie Halsey Downer, Jr. married Joan Ross Le Boeuf, the daughter of Randall James Le Boeuf of Old Westbury.


### Downey, E. Kelly (1880-1948)

Occupation(s): merchant - sales manager, Red Jacket Coal Sales Co., Columbus, OH

Marriage(s): Katherine Glanville (1879-1948)

Address: 150 Kilburn Road, Garden City
Name of estate:
Year of construction: 1917
Style of architecture: Dutch Colonial Revival
Architect(s):
Landscape architect(s):
House extant: yes
Historical notes:

   The *Long Island Society Register, 1929* lists Mr. and Mrs. E. Kelly Downey as residing on Kilburn Road, Garden City. The 1930 Census lists the Downeys at this address.

*front facade, 2001*

### Driggs, Edmund Hope, Jr. (1894-1957)

| | |
|---|---|
| Occupation(s): | financier - president, E. H. Driggs & Co. (insurance brokerage firm); vice-president, Marsh & Mc Lennan, Inc. (insurance brokerage firm) |
| Civic Activism: | treasurer, Adelphi Academy, Brooklyn |
| Marriage(s): | M/1 – 1917-div. – Elizabeth Hunter Watson (1896-1977) |
| | M/2 – 1938 – Shelia Elise Swan (1906-1994) |
| Address: | 12 Kilburn Road, Garden City |
| Name of estate: | |
| Year of construction: | 1924 |
| Style of architecture: | Long Island Farmhouse |
| Architect(s): | |
| Landscape architect(s): | |
| House extant: yes | |
| Historical notes: | |

The *Long Island Society Register, 1929* lists Edmund Hope and Elizabeth Hunter Watson Driggs, Jr. as residing at 12 Kilburn Road, Garden City.

He was the son of Edmund Hope and Emily Lavinia Walker Driggs, Sr. of Brooklyn.

Elizabeth Hunter Watson Driggs was the daughter of Henry D. Watson of Brooklyn. She subsequently married ____ Bluntschli.

Edmund Hope and Elizabeth Hunter Watson Driggs, Jr.'s son Edmund Hope Driggs III married Marie Knight, the daughter of William Knight, Jr, and, later, Audrey Simpson, the daughter of Ernest Aldrich Simpson and the stepdaughter of the Duchess of Windsor Wallis Simpson. Their son Dixon married Eulalia Turner, the daughter of Claude E. and Eulalia Rodriquez Turner of Plandome. Their daughter Patricia married Dr. Claude E. McGahey and, later, Robert Pratt Kelsey, Jr.

Shelia Elise Swan Driggs was the daughter of W. Harry and Kathleen Maude Drury Swan. Shelia had previously been married to Franklin Whitin Orvis, the son of George Alfred and Louise Simonds Orvis.

*front facade, 2000*

### Du Bois, Arthur Mason (1890-1979)

| | |
|---|---|
| Occupation(s): | financer -   insurance broker |
| Civic Activism: | treasurer, St. Nazaire Memorial Fund, St. Nazaire, France |
| Marriage(s): | M/1 – 1924-1943 – Marie Louise Dixon (1895-1943) |
| | M/2 – 1952-1956 – Cornelia Prime Coster (1901-1956) |
| Address: | 380 Broadway, Lawrence |

Name of estate:
Year of construction:
Style of architecture:
Architect(s):
Landscape architect(s):
House extant: no
Historical notes:

The *Long Island Society Register, 1929* lists Arthur M. and M. Louise Dixon DuBois [sic] as residing at 380 Broadway, Lawrence.

He was the son of Dr. Robert Ogden and Mrs. Alice Mason Du Bois.

Marie Louise Dixon Du Bois was the daughter of Courtland Palmer and Hortense Howland Dixon II, who resided at *The Causeway* in Lawrence.

Arthur Mason and Marie Louise Dixon Du Bois' son Dr. John Jay Du Bois married Adrienne Bansall Allan, the daughter of John C. Leighton Allan of Toronto, Canada, and resided in Rye, NY. Their daughter Louise married Edward Clifford Perkins, the son of Edward N. Perkins of Manhattan and resided in Bethlehem, PA.

Cornelia Prime Coster Du Bois was the daughter of Edward Livingston and Margaret Elizabeth Lowndes Coster, who resided at *Acorn Farm* in Mount Kisco, NY. Cornelia had previously been married to Phillips Lounsberg with whom she resided in Bedford, NY.

By 1938 DeBois had relocated to Cedar Avenue in Hewlett Bay Park.

### Duncan, Alexander Butler (1858-1920)

| | |
|---|---|
| Occupation(s): | capitalist -   a founder, The Butler–Duncan Land Co., 1890 |
| Civic Activism: | trustee, Institutional Care of the Insane of Butler Hospital, Providence, RI, 1906; |
| | vice-president, Butler Hospital, Providence, RI |
| Marriage(s): | 1907-1920 – Eloise Stevenson (1872-1948) |
| | - Civic Activism:  president, Ladies Kennel Association of America, 1903 |
| Address: | Fulton Avenue, Hempstead |
| Name of estate: | *The Meadows* |

Year of construction:
Style of architecture:
Architect(s):
Landscape architect(s):
House extant: no; demolished in 1927 for housing development
Historical notes:

The house, originally named *The Meadows*, was built by James Lorillard Kernochan.

*front entrance, 1911*

Alexander Butler Duncan was the son of William Butler and Jane Percy Sargent Duncan. His brother William married Blanche Havemeyer and resided at *Park Hill* in Sands Point. [*See* Spinzia, *Long Island's Prominent North Shore Families, vol. I* – Duncan entry – and *Long Island's Prominent South Shore Families* – Havemeyer entries.]

Alexander's Manhattan house was located at the corner of Eighth Street and Fifth Avenue. [Thomas Floyd–Jones, *Backward Glances; Reminiscences of an Old New Yorker* (New York: privately printed, 1914), p. 116.]

Eloise Stevenson Duncan was the daughter of Major Vernon King Stevenson, CSA, and Mrs. Anna Louisa Eve Stevenson, Jr. Eloise had previously been married to James Lorillard Kernochan. After her marriage to Duncan she continued to resided at *The Meadows*, eventually relocating to *Yonder House* in Westbury. [*See* Spinzia, *Long Island's Prominent North Shore Families, vol. I* – Duncan entry.] Eloise's brother Maxwell, who resided at *The Lodge* in Hempstead, married Caroline Elizabeth Livingston, the daughter of Robert Cambridge and Maria Whitney Livingston III of *Lakeside* in Islip, and, later, Anne Davis Richardson. [*See* Spinzia, *Long Island's Prominent South Shore Families* – Livingston entry.]

### Dunham, Carroll, III (1887-1948)

| | |
|---|---|
| Occupation(s): | financier - partner, Rutter and Co. (bond brokerage firm); member, Wood, Low, and Co. (stock brokerage firm); partner, Carrere and Co. (stock brokerage firm); partner, Dunham and Fletcher (stock brokerage firm) |
| Marriage(s): | 1915- 1948 – Ruth Harper Pilling (1890-1961) |
| Address: | 30 Sealy Drive, Lawrence |
| Name of estate: | *Stone Lodge* |
| Year of construction: | |
| Style of architecture: | |
| Architect(s): | |
| Landscape architect(s): | |
| House extant: | no |
| Historical notes: | |

The *Long Island Society Register, 1929* lists Carroll and Ruth H. Pilling Dunham III as residing at *Stone Lodge* in Cedarhurst [Lawrence]. The 1930 Census lists the Dunhams at this address.

He was the son of Carroll and Margaret Worcester Dows Dunham, Jr. of *Hillside* in Irvington, NY.

Ruth Harper Pilling Dunham was the daughter of James Constantine and Mary Lois Harper Pilling of Blue Ridge Summit, PA.

Carroll and Ruth Harper Pilling Dunham III's daughter Angela married William Francis Rogers III. Their son Carroll Dunham IV married Margaret W. Dows and resided in Pleasantville, NY. Their son Peter married M. Patricia Hopkinson and resided in New Canaan, CT.

### Dunnell, Frank Lyman, Sr. (1866-1942)

| | |
|---|---|
| Occupation(s): | financier - stockbroker |
| Civic Activism: | commodore, American Canoe Association, Brooklyn |
| Marriage(s): | 1901-1936 – Susette Bertha Barnes (1864-1936) |
| Address: | 7 Beech Street, Garden City |
| Name of estate: | |
| Year of construction: | 1923 |
| Style of architecture: | Dutch Colonial Revival |
| Architect(s): | |
| Landscape architect(s): | |
| House extant: | yes |
| Historical notes: | |

*front facade, 2001*

The *Long Island Society Register, 1929* and the *Social Register, 1933* list Frank Lyman and Susette B. Barnes Dunnell [Sr.] as residing at 7 Beech Street, Garden City.

He was the son of John Wanton and Mary Ann Taylor Dunnell of Brooklyn.

Susette Bertha Barnes Dunnell was the daughter of William and Jane Hull Barnes of Buffalo, NY. Susette had previously been married to Frank Lobdell Danforth of Buffalo, NY.

Frank Lyman and Susette Bertha Barnes Dunnell, Sr.'s daughter Clara married Francis Bacon Hamlin, Sr. and resided in Garden City.

In 1966 the house was remodeled.

### Dunning, Clarence Seymour, Sr. (1848-1931)

| | |
|---|---|
| Occupation(s): | financier - vice president and treasurer, South Brooklyn Savings Bank |
| Marriage(s): | Sarah C. Thomas (1857-1908) |
| Address: | 111 Seventh Street, Garden City |
| Name of estate: | |
| Year of construction: | |
| Style of architecture: | Condominium |
| Architect(s): | |
| Landscape architect(s): | |
| House extant: | yes |
| Historical notes: | |

The *Long Island Society Register, 1929* lists Clarence S. Dunning as residing at 111 Seventh Street, Garden City. He was the son of Czar and Elizabeth Alexander Dunning of Brooklyn.

Clarence Seymour and Sarah C. Thomas Dunning, Sr.'s daughter Ruth married Hamilton Henry Salmon, Jr. and resided in Garden City. In 1881 their son Franklin died at the age of three. In 1882 their one-year-old daughter Edith died. In 1930 their son Clarence Seymour, Jr. died.

### Dunstan, James Samuel (1879-1962)

| | |
|---|---|
| Occupation(s): | financier - partner, Hornblower and Weeks (stock brokerage firm) |
| | industrialist - director, Michigan Mining Co.; |
| | director, Mohawk Mining Co., Michigan; |
| | director, Wolverine Copper Mining Co., Michigan |
| Marriage(s): | 1904-1962 – Eda Louise Kempshall (1880-1982) |
| | - Civic Activism: member, executive committee, Nassau County chapter, American Red Cross |
| Address: | 255 Breezeway, Lawrence |
| Name of estate: | *Brightside* |
| Year of construction: | 1892 |
| Style of architecture: | Neo-Georgian |
| Architect(s): | Carrere and Hastings designed the house and stable (for J. H. Harper, Sr.) |
| Landscape architect(s): | |
| House extant: | yes |
| Historical notes: | |

The house, originally named *Brightside*, was built by Joseph Henry Harper, Sr. It was later owned by Dunstan, who continued to call it *Brightside*.

The *Long Island Society Register, 1929* and the *Social Register, 1933* list James S. and Eda L. Kempshall Dunstan as residing at *Brightside* in Lawrence.

He was the son of Thomas Bree and Mary A. MacDonald Dunstan of Houghton, MI.

James Samuel and Eda Louise Kempshall Dunstan's daughter Marian married John Mortimer Rutherfurd, the son of John Morris Livingston Rutherfurd of Sands Point. [*See* Spinzia, *Long Island's Prominent North Shore Families, vol. II*– Rutherfurd entry.] Their daughter Dorothy married Henry Wood Wiley, Jr. of Haverford, PA. Their daughter Joan married Guysbert B. Vroom, Jr. of Bath, ME. Their daughter Edna married Ichabod Thomas Williams, the son of Thomas Resolved and Dorothy S. Hinckley Williams of *Windmere* in Lawrence, and resided in Lawrence. Their daughter Alice married Harland Felch Baker, the son of Albert P. Baker.

The house was subsequently owned by Enos Thompson Throop IV.

*front facade, 2009*

### Durand, Celestin Aloysious, Jr. (1813-1978)

| | |
|---|---|
| Occupation(s): | financier - a founder, with his father, C. A. Durand & Son (stock brokerage firm) |
| Marriage(s): | 1935-1978 – Adele Marie Robinson (1914-1987)<br>- Civic Activism: chair, St. Joseph School Society, 1941 |
| Address: | Hilton Avenue, Garden City |
| Name of estate: | |
| Year of construction: | |
| Style of architecture: | |
| Architect(s): | |
| Landscape architect(s): | |
| House extant: unconfirmed | |
| Historical notes: | |

Celestin Aloysious Durand, Jr. was the son of Celestin Aloysious and Irene J. Sweeney Durand, Sr. of Garden City.

Adele Marie Robinson Durand was the daughter of Suffolk County Democratic Party leader John J. Robinson, Jr. and his wife Marie Metzner Robinson of Huntington Bay.

Celestin Aloysious and Adele Marie Robinson Durand, Jr.'s daughter Adele married Frederick C. Stutzmann, Jr. of Queens Village. Their son Celestin Aloysious Durand III married June Evelyn Edwards and resided in Garden City.

*[See other Durand entries for additional family information.]*


### Durand, Celestin Aloysious, Sr. (1885-1973)

| | |
|---|---|
| Occupation(s): | financier - a founder, with his son Celestin Aloysious Durand, Jr., and president, C. A. Durand and Son (stock brokerage firm) |
| Marriage(s): | Irene J. Sweeney (1889-1959)<br>- Civic Activism: president, women's auxiliary, St. Joseph's Roman Catholic Church, Garden City |
| Address: | 15 Cathedral Avenue, Garden City |
| Name of estate: | |
| Year of construction: | 1930 |
| Style of architecture: | Neo-Tudor |
| Architect(s): | |
| Landscape architect(s): | |
| House extant: yes | |
| Historical notes: | |

The *Long Island Society Register, 1929* lists Mr. and Mrs. C. A. Durand as residing at 111 Hilton Avenue, Garden City. They subsequently relocated to 15 Cathedral Avenue, Garden City.

Celestin Aloysious and Irene J. Sweeney Durand, Sr.'s daughter Gladys married George Aloysious Corroon, the son of Richard A. and Margaret Teaken Corroon of Massapequa, and resided in Garden City. Their son Celestin Aloysious Durand, Jr. married Adele Marie Robinson and resided in Garden City.

*[See other Durand entries for additional family information.]*

*side / front facade, 2009*

### Durand, Celestin Aloysious, III (1936-1997)

| | |
|---|---|
| Occupation(s): | financier - a founder, Durand and Cullen (stock brokerage firm); vice-president, Merrill Lynch (stock brokerage firm) |
| | capitalist - partner, Royal Line Stables |
| | merchant - director, World Fuel Service, Miami, FL (suppliers of fuel) |
| Civic Activism: | director, The Jockey Club Condominium Association |
| Marriage(s): | 1957-1990 – Jane Evelyn Edwards (1937-1990) |
| Address: | *[unable to determine street address]*, Garden City |
| Name of estate: | |
| Year of construction: | |
| Style of architecture: | |
| Architect(s): | |
| Landscape architect(s): | |
| House extant: | unconfirmed |
| Historical notes: | |

Celestin Aloysious III was the son of Celestin Aloysious and Adele Marie Robinson Durant, Jr. of Garden City. Jane Evelyn Edwards Durand was the daughter of Fred J. Edwards.
*[See other Durand entries for additional family information.]*


### Durand, James Francis, Sr. (1882-1953)

| | |
|---|---|
| Occupation(s): | financier - stockbroker |
| Civic Activism: | member, admissions committee, New York Stock Exchange |
| Marriage(s): | Elizabeth Lillian Garvin (1884-1959) |
| Address: | 127 Cherry Valley Road, Garden City |
| Name of estate: | |
| Year of construction: | 1926 |
| Style of architecture: | Colonial Revival |
| Architect(s): | |
| Landscape architect(s): | |
| House extant: | yes |
| Historical notes: | |

The house was built by James Francis Durand, Sr.

The *Long Island Society Register, 1929* lists Mr. and Mrs. James F. Durand [Sr.] as residing on Cherry Valley Road, Garden City.

James Francis and Elizabeth Lillian Garvin Durand, Sr.'s daughter Virginia remained unmarried. Their daughter Agnes married John J. Bradley, the son of John P. Bradley of Hempstead. Their daughter Vivianne married Howard Mott, the son of Charles E. Mott of Fairway Drive, Hempstead. Their daughter Helen married Adrian Arnold Scheiss, Jr. of Garden City.

At the time of his death James Francis Durand, Sr. was residing at 111 Seventh Street, Garden City. [*The New York Times* December 31, 1953, p. 19.]

*[See other Durand entries for additional family information.]*

*front facade, 2008*

**Duryea, William H. (1880-1936)**

Occupation(s): financier - New York Life Insurance Co.

Marriage(s): Ann J. *[unable to determine maiden name]*

Address: 16 Westbury Road, Garden City

Name of estate:
Year of construction: 1931
Style of architecture: Neo-Georgian
Architect(s): Olive Frances Tjaden designed
    the house (for W. H. Duryea)

Landscape architect(s):
House extant: yes
Historical notes:

   The house was built by William H. Duryea.
   By 1950 Mrs. Duryea had relocated to Hilton Avenue in Garden City.
   The house was later owned by Asa Warinner and, then, by Robert F. Hussey.

*front facade, 2001*

**Duryea, Wright, Jr. (1896-1961)**

| | |
|---|---|
| Occupation(s): | financier -   member, Dodge, Clark, and Co. (bond brokerage firm); partner, Glore, Forgan, and Co. (investment banking firm) |
| Civic Activism: | president, Meadowbrook Club |
| Marriage(s): | M/1 – 1925-div. – Cornelia De Lancey Cammann (1894-1985) |
| | M/2 – 1949-1961 – Ann R. Foster (d. 1961) |
| Address: | 558 Fulton Street, Hempstead |
| Name of estate: | *Shortacre* |
| Year of construction: | |
| Style of architecture: | |
| Architect(s): | |
| Landscape architect(s): | |
| House extant: no | |
| Historical notes: | |

The *Long Island Society Register, 1929* lists Wright and Cornelia DeL. Cammann Duryea as residing at *Shortacre* in Hempstead. The *Social Register 1933* lists them as residing at *Chestnut Vale* in Syosset.

He was the son of Francis Wright and Grace C. Wolcott Duryea, Sr. and the grandson of Hendrick Vanderbilt Duryea, the founder of Duryea Starch Works in Glen Cove. Wright's great uncle was General Hiram Duryea, commander of "Duryea's Zouaves" during the Civil War. [*See* Spinzia, *Long Island's Prominent North Shore Families, vol. 1* – Duryea entries.]

Cornelia De Lancy Cammann Duryea was the daughter of Charles Lewis and Estelle Wright Cammann. Cornelia had previously been married to William Samuel Fairchild, Jr. the son of Samuel William and Emily Justina Tappen Fairchild, Sr.

Wright and Cornelia De Lancey Cammann Duryea, Jr.'s daughter Cornelia married Huntington Lyman and, later, Michael Antony Telfer–Smollet, the son of General A. P. D. Telfer–Smollet of *Cameron House* in Lock Lomond, Scotland.

Ann R. Foster Duryea was the daughter of Herbert I. Foster. She had previously been married to Thomas Le Boutillier III of Old Westbury. [*See* Spinzia, *Long Island's Prominent North Shore Families, vol. 1* – Le Boutillier entry.]

[For information about Duryea's Southampton residence, see Spinzia, *Long Island's Prominent Families in the Town of Southampton* – Duryea entry.]

**d'Utassy, George (1870-1953)**
**aka George von d'Utassey**

| | |
|---|---|
| Occupation(s): | journalist -   business manager: *Motor Magazine; Cosmopolitan Magazine; Motor Boating Magazine; Hearst Magazine, Harper's Bazaar; Good Housekeeping Magazine; Nash's Magazine*, London, England; *Illustrated Daily News; Daily Mirror*, NYC; *New York Daily News*, NYC |
| | publisher -   co-owner, *Life* magazine |
| | capitalist -   president, Indian Refining Co. |
| Marriage(s): | 1904 – Florence Chapman (b. 1882) |
| | - merchant -   gift and book store, Cedarhurst |
| | Civic Activism:  instructor, surgical dressing, Five Towns chapter, American Red Cross, during World War II; |
| | member of board, Citizens Committee, Army and Navy, during World War II; |
| | member of board, Bundles for Britain during World War II |
| Address: | Broadway, Cedarhurst |
| Name of estate: | |
| Year of construction: | 1857 |
| Style of architecture: | |
| Architect(s): | |
| Landscape architect(s): | |
| House extant: yes | |
| Historical notes: | |

The *Long Island Society Register, 1929* lists Mr. and Mrs. George d'Utassy as residing on Broadway, Cedarhurst. Their house was the third oldest in the community. [*The Brooklyn Daily Eagle* September 5, 1943, p. 9.]

He was the son of Anton W. and Laura Galvin von d'Utassy of Philadelphia, PA.

George and Florence Chapman de'Utassy's daughter Babetta married William Anderson Castle II, the son of Clifford De Witt Castle of Springfield, MA, and resided in Phoenix, AZ. Their son Chapman married Ruth Katherine Hicks.

In 1943 the d'Utassys sold the house to Mr. Lawrence.

### Duval, William Hamlyn, III (1871-1933)

| | |
|---|---|
| Occupation(s): | merchant - a founder, Molten & Duval; partner, Duval, Cone, & Terhune; president, William H. Duval & Co., NYC |
| | capitalist - C. C. & S. Railroad Co. (first standard gage railroad in Alaska); a founder and vice-president, Alaska Telegraph & Telephone Co. |
| | industrialist - director, Melville Woolen Co. |
| | financier - director, Garden City Bank and Trust Co. |
| Marriage(s): | 1897-1933 – Louise Whiting Guindon (1871-1945) |
| Address: | 18 Cathedral Avenue, Garden City |
| Name of estate: | |
| Year of construction: | 1908 |
| Style of architecture: | Neo-Tudor |
| Architect(s): | |
| Landscape architect(s): | |
| House extant: yes | |
| Historical notes: | |

*front facade, 2000*

The *Long Island Society Register, 1929* lists William H. and Louise Whiting Guindon Duval [III] as residing on Cathedral Avenue, Garden City.

He was the son of William Hamlyn and Jane B. Miller Duval, Jr. of Utica, NY.

Louise Whiting Guindon Duval was the daughter of Eugene Whiting and Margaretta Morgan Van Horne Guindon.

In 1901, William Hamlyn and Louise Whiting Guindon Duval III's one-year-old son Guindon died. Their son William Guindon Duval married Marian Winona Baxendale.

In 1929 Duvall sold the twenty-room house to George Urban Tompers. [*The New York Times* January 31, 1929, p. 45.]


### Dwight, Philip J. (1892-1959)

| | |
|---|---|
| Occupation(s): | financier - partner, Wrenn Brothers and Co. (stock brokerage firm) |
| Civic Activism: | president of board, Nassau Industrial School, Inwood; treasurer, Village of Hewlett Neck; member, zoning and appeals board, Village of Hewlett Neck |
| Marriage(s): | 1920-1959 – Emily Thomas (1894-1971) |
| | - Civic Activism: volunteer in France, American Fund for French Wounded, during World War I; treasurer, Five Towns Women's Exchange, 1942 |
| Address: | 251 Adams Lane, Hewlett Neck |
| Name of estate: | |
| Year of construction: | c. 1926 |
| Style of architecture: | French Country |
| Architect(s): | Peabody, Wilson, & Brown designed the house (for Dwight) |
| Landscape architect(s): | |
| House extant: no | |
| Historical notes: | |

*front / side facade, 1927*

The house was built by Philip J. Dwight.

The *Long Island Society Register, 1929* lists Philip J. and Emily Thomas Dwight as residing in Hewlett. The *Social Register New York, 1939* lists their address as 251 Adams Lane, Hewlett [Hewlett Neck].

He was the son of James Dwight of Beacon Street, Boston, MA.

Emily Thomas Dwight was the daughter of Clark Thomas of Boston, MA.

Philip J. and Emily Thomas Dwight's daughter Veronica married Mark Gadd Richard, the son of Auguste and Hetly Lawrence Hemenway Richard of Hewlett Harbor and East Hampton. [*See* Spinzia, *Long Island's Prominent Families in the Town of East Hampton* – Richard entry.] Their son Philip Thomas Dwight married Alice Fort Milton, the daughter of George Fort and Alice Warner Milton.

## Dwyer, Martin, Sr. (1897-1973)

| | |
|---|---|
| Occupation(s): | industrialist - president and chairman of board, Aerial Products Industries, Merrick, NY (manufacturer of distress signals for the United States Armed Forces) |
| | capitalist - land developer |
| | publisher - *Air–Sea Safety* magazine |
| Civic Activism: | a founder and vice-treasurer, Naval Order of the United States |
| Marriage(s): | Mary Baker Tredwell (1899-1976) |
| Address: | Club Drive, Hewlett Harbor |
| Name of estate: | |
| Year of construction: | |
| Style of architecture: | |
| Architect(s): | |
| Landscape architect(s): | |
| House extant: | unconfirmed |
| Historical notes: | |

Mary Baker Tredwell Dwyer was the daughter of William Baker Treadwell

Martin and Mary Baker Tredwell Dwyer, Sr.'s son Thomas married Sheila Cornish Browne, the daughter of Curtis Northrop and Winifred Wheelwright Chisolm Browne of Cedarhurst. Their daughter Evelyn married Harry Aries Van Sciver of Philadelphia, PA. Their son Martin Dwyer, Jr. married Mary Noyes Thompson and resided in Laurel Hollow. [*See* Spinzia, *Long Island's Prominent North Shore Families, vol. I* – Dwyer entry.]

In 1948 the Dwyers relocated to Lawrence.


## Earle, Alexander Morse, Sr. (1881-1940)

| | |
|---|---|
| Occupation(s): | financier - charter member, New York Curb Exchange (stock brokerage firm) |
| Marriage(s): | 1907-1940 – Grace Eliza Young (1883-1972) |
| Address: | 7 Woodview Road, West Hempstead |
| Name of estate: | |
| Year of construction: | |
| Style of architecture: | |
| Architect(s): | |
| Landscape architect(s): | |
| House extant: | no |
| Historical notes: | |

The *Long Island Society Register, 1929* lists Alexander Morse and Grace Eliza Young Earle [Sr.] as residing in West Hempstead.

He was the son of Henry and Alice Morse Earle of Brooklyn. Alexander's mother Alice was a noted author who specialized in New England and Colonial life. She authored seventeen books and forty-two magazine articles.

Grace Eliza Young Earle was the daughter of James C. Young of Brooklyn.

Alexander Morse and Grace Eliza Young Earle, Sr.'s son Edwin died in 1910 at the age of six months. Their son Alexander Morse Earle married Valeria R____ and resided in Melbourne, FL. Their daughter Alice married ____ Gracey and resided in Sarasota, Fl.

### Earnshaw, Geoffrey S. (1891-1952)

| | |
|---|---|
| Occupation(s): | advertising executive - vice-president, General Outdoor Advertising, Inc., NYC |
| Marriage(s): | 1914 – Mary L. Harrington (b. 1896) |
| Address: | 41 Brixton Road, Garden City |
| Name of estate: | |
| Year of construction: | 1918 |
| Style of architecture: | Colonial Revival |
| Architect(s): | |
| Landscape architect(s): | |
| House extant: yes | |
| Historical notes: | |

*front facade, 2006*

The *Long Island Society Register, 1929* and the *Social Register, 1924* and *1933* list Geoffrey S. and Mary L. Harrington Earnshaw as residing at 41 Brixton Road, Garden City.

Their daughter Barbara married Kenneth Monroe Spencer, Jr. and resided in Boston, MA.

### Eaton, Walter Bradley (1888-1966)

| | |
|---|---|
| Occupation(s): | financier - stockbroker;<br>director, Peninsula National Bank, Cedarhurst;<br>director, East Rockaway National Bank |
| Civic Activism: | commissioner, Sanitary District No. 1;<br>president, South Shore Polo Club;<br>director, Long Island Symphony Association, 1939 |
| Marriage(s): | 1921-1966 – Margaret Burton (1899-1973)<br>- Civic Activism: chair, finance committee, Five Towns Women's Exchange |
| Address: | Cedarhurst Avenue, Lawrence |
| Name of estate: | *The Corral* |
| Year of construction: | |
| Style of architecture: | |
| Architect(s): | |
| Landscape architect(s): | |
| House extant: unconfirmed | |
| Historical notes: | |

The *Long Island Society Register, 1929* lists Walter B. and Margaret Burton Eaton as residing on Cedarhurst Avenue, Cedarhurst [Lawrence].

He was the son of Bradley Llewellyn Eaton of Manhattan.

Margaret Burton Eaton was the daughter of Frank Vincent and Katharine Sayre Van Duzer Burton, Sr. of Manhattan. Margaret's brother Van Duzer Burton, Sr., who married Amy F. Ashley Sparks, and, subsequently, Charlotte Rhodes, resided at *Pink Coat Cottage* in Syosset. Her brother Frank Vincent Burton, Jr. married Beatrice Boswell Eliott and resided at *Northlea* in Westbury. [*See* Spinzia, *Long Island's Prominent North Shore Families, vol. I* – Burton entries.]

Walter Bradley and Margaret Burton Eaton's daughter Barbara married Harold R. Tyler, Jr. of Waterville, NY, and resided in Bedford, NY. Their daughter Katherine married Edward Novell Carpenter, the son of George and Dorothy Millen Carpenter, and resided in Cedarhurst. Their daughter Sheila married Heyward Isham, the son of Ralph Heyward and Margaret Dorothy Hunt Isham of Glen Head, and resided at *Skyfields* in Sagaponack. [*See* Spinzia, *Long Island's Prominent North Shore Families, vol. I* – Isham entry – and *Long Island's Prominent Families in the Town of Southampton* – Isham entry.]

### Ebinger, Walter Dohrmann (1885-1945)

| | |
|---|---|
| Occupation(s): | merchant -  Ebinger Baking Co., Brooklyn (chain of 43 stores) |
| Civic Activism: | president, Flatbush Chamber of Commerce; |
| | president, Flatbush Boys Club; |
| | director, Brooklyn Association for Improving Conditions of the Poor |
| Marriage(s): | 1908-1945 – Ann Katherine Ottens (1890-1969) |
| Address: | 261 Stewart Avenue, Garden City |
| Name of estate: | |
| Year of construction: | 1919 |
| Style of architecture: | Neo-Tudor |
| Architect(s): | Olive Frances Tjaden designed the house (for Ebinger) |
| Landscape architect(s): | |
| House extant:  yes | |
| Historical notes: | |

*front facade, 2018*

The house was built by Walter Dohrmann Ebinger.

He was the son of George and Katherine M. Ebinger. Walter's brother Arthur married Carolyne M. Wingerath and resided in Westhampton Beach. [*See* Spinzia, *Long Island's Prominent Families in the Town of Southampton* – Ebinger entry.]

Ann Katherine Ottens Ebinger was the daughter of John F. H. and Adeheid Fricks Ottens of Brooklyn.

Walter Dohrmann and Ann Katherine Ottens Ebinger's daughter Lorraine married Jack Berner Porter, the son of Ernest Grove and Grace Irene Berner Porter, and resided in Garden City. Lorraine later married Ralston Lawrence Rundquist.

[For information about Ebinger's Bay Shore residence, *see* Spinzia, *Long Island's Prominent South Shore Families* – Ebinger entry.]

The house was later owned by Harold Francis Merritt, Sr.; Edward Jerome Fanning; and, then, by Mark Parbatusby.

In 2017, the 4,974-square-foot house, with six bedrooms and six and a half bathrooms, sold for $1.75 million.

### Eddy, William Higbie, Sr. (1879-1957)

| | |
|---|---|
| Occupation(s): | financier -  vice-president, Chase Securities Corp.; |
| | member, Halsey and Co. (investment banking firm); |
| | member, Emanuel Parker Co.; |
| | member, Estabrook Co.; |
| | vice-president, Equitable Trust Co. |
| Civic Activism: | chairman of board, New York Group of Investment Bankers' Association; |
| | trustee, Hobart College, Geneva, NY; |
| | trustee, Englewood, NJ, chapter, American Red Cross |
| Marriage(s): | 1923-1957 – Grace Cole Bissell (1894-1981) |
| Address: | 566 Atlantic Avenue, Lawrence |
| Name of estate: | |
| Year of construction: | 1913 |
| Style of architecture: | Modified Victorian |
| Architect(s): | |
| Landscape architect(s): | |
| House extant:  yes | |
| Historical notes: | |

The *Long Island Society Register, 1929* lists William Higbie and Grace C. Bissell Eddy [Sr.] as residing in Cedarhurst [Lawrence].

He was the son of Herbert Morton and Harriet Higbie Eddy.

Grace Cole Bissell Eddy was the daughter of John B. Bissell.

William Higbie and Grace Cole Bissell Eddy, Sr.'s daughter Clare married the renowned art collector Eugene Victor Thaw. Their son William Higbie Eddy, Jr., who was a noted wildlife conservationist, Peace Corp consultant, lecturer, and author, married Beryl Forbes and, later, Pamela Sisson.

In 1968 the house was remodeled.

*front facade, 2001*

### Edsell, Levi Perin (1874-1948)

| | |
|---|---|
| Occupation(s): | capitalist - real estate |
| | financier - insurance broker |
| Civic Activism: | clerk, Village of Cedarhurst, 1933-1934; |
| | one of the original members of Cedarhurst Zoning Board of Appeals; |
| | member, Long Island Real Estate Board; |
| | secretary, Peninsula Y.M.C.A., Cedarhurst |
| Marriage(s): | 1897-1948 – Harriet Armena Jones (1870-1960) |
| Address: | 595 Park Avenue, Cedarhurst |
| Name of estate: | |
| Year of construction: | |
| Style of architecture: | |
| Architect(s): | |
| Landscape architect(s): | |
| House extant: no | |
| Historical notes: | |

The *Long Island Society Register, 1929* lists Mr. and Mrs. L. P. Edsell as residing on Bayview Avenue, Lawrence. He was the son of Cyrus Phineas and Mary J. Edsell.

Harriet Armena Jones Edsell was the daughter of James Jones.

Levi Perin and Harriet Armena Jones Edsell's daughter Aida married Theodore Edward Warren and resided in Ohio. Their daughter Lily married Richard Stevens and also resided in Ohio. Their son Ralph James Edsell, Sr. resided in Cedarhurst.

At the time of her death, Mrs. Edsell was residing at 595 Park Avenue, Cedarhurst. [*The New York Times* March 21, 1960, p. 29.]

*[See following Edsell entries for additional family information.]*


### Edsell, Ralph James, Jr. (1923-1982)

| | |
|---|---|
| Occupation(s): | attorney - Internal Security Division, United States Department of Justice |
| | politician - chief counsel to Joseph F. Carlino, Speaker of the New York State Assembly; |
| | administrative assistant to Representative Norman F. Lent |
| Marriage(s): | M/1 – 1945 – Mary Elizabeth Essig |
| | M/2 – June Rohrer |
| Address: | 623 Central Avenue, Lawrence |
| Name of estate: | |
| Year of construction: | |
| Style of architecture: | |
| Architect(s): | |
| Landscape architect(s): | |
| House extant: no | |
| Historical notes: | |

Ralph James Edsell, Jr. was the son of Ralph James and Geraldine V. Dulfer Edsell, Sr. of Cedarhurst.

Mary Elizabeth Essig James was the daughter of Charles Hiram Essig of Royal Oak, MI.

The Jameses' daughter Lisa married Thomas O'Hare Evered, the son of John O'Hara Evered of Cinnaminson, NJ, and resided in New York City.

*[See other Edsell entries for additional family information.]*

### Edsell, Ralph James, Sr. (1899-1973)

| | |
|---|---|
| Occupation(s): | capitalist -  marketing executive, Radio Corporation of America (RCA) |
| Civic Activism: | president, Lawrence Public School Board; Republican committeeman (25 years) |
| Marriage(s): | 1923-1973 – Geraldine V. Dulfer (1903-1992)<br>   - Civic Activism:  trustee, Five Towns Child Care Center |
| Address: | 348 Washington Avenue, Cedarhurst |
| Name of estate: | |
| Year of construction: | 1918 |
| Style of architecture: | Victorian |
| Architect(s): | |
| Landscape architect(s): | |
| House extant:  yes | |
| Historical notes: | |

*front facade, 2000*

The *Long Island Society Register, 1929* lists Ralph J. Edsell [Sr.] as residing on Washington Avenue, Cedarhurst [Lawrence].

He was the son of Levi Perin and Harriet Armena Jones Edsell of Cedarhurst.

Geraldine V. Dulfer Edsell was the daughter of John Leonard and Anna O'Connell Dulfer of Richmond Hill, NY.

Ralph James and Geraldine V. Dulfer Edsell, Sr.'s daughter ____ married Richard Hevens. Their son Ralph James Edsell, Jr. married Elizabeth Essig and, later, June Rohrer with whom he resided in Lawrence.

*[See other Edsell entries for additional family information.]*


### Edwards, Jesse (1862-1936)

| | |
|---|---|
| Occupation(s): | industrialist -  president, Edwards & Crist Co., Philadelphia, PA (motorcycle and bicycle manufacturer)<br>accountant -  Gregory Wholesale Grocery Co.; Henry Horner Wholesale Grocery Co., Chicago |
| Civic Activism: | president, Cycles Jobbers Association of America; president, West Point Club of Chicago |
| Marriage(s): | 1888-1935 – Lotta Julia Eaton (1876-1935)<br>   - Civic Activism:  a founding regent, Lord Sterling Chapter, Hempstead, Daughters of the American Revolution;<br>   a founding regent, Colonel Aaron Ogen Chapter, Garden City, Daughters of the American Revolution |
| Address: | 514 East Front Street, Hempstead |
| Name of estate: | |
| Year of construction: | |
| Style of architecture: | |
| Architect(s): | |
| Landscape architect(s): | |
| House extant:  no | |
| Historical notes: | |

The *Long Island Society Register, 1929* lists Mr. and Mrs. Jesse Edwards as residing on East Front Street, Hempstead. She was the daughter of David H. Eaton.

Jesse and Lotta Julia Eaton Edward's daughter Amelia married Maurice Tassencourt and resided in Philadelphia and Paris, France. Their daughter Lotta (aka Lavinia Darvé) was a noted operatic singer who performed at the Opera Comique in Paris, the New York Opera Company, and La Scala in Milan, Italy.

### Egginton, Hersey (1875-1951)

| | |
|---|---|
| Occupation(s): | attorney - partner, Rathbone, Perry, and Drye, Brooklyn; partner, Joline, Larkin, and Rathbone; assistant district attorney, Kings County, NY |
| | financier - trustee, Greater New York Savings Bank |
| Civic Activism: | president, Methodist Hospital of Brooklyn, 1938-1948; counsel, Brooklyn Bureau of Social Service; counsel, Children's Air Society |
| Marriage(s): | Mary E. Benner (1875-1962) - Civic Activism: donated Childe Hassam etching to Hood Museum of Art, Dartmouth College, Hanover, NH |
| Address: | 85 Tenth Street, Garden City |
| Name of estate: | |
| Year of construction: | 1925 |
| Style of architecture: | Dutch Colonial Revival |
| Architect(s): | |
| Landscape architect(s): | |
| House extant: | yes |
| Historical notes: | |

*front facade, 2000*

Hersey Egginton was the son of William Henry and Mazey J. Smith Egginton.

Hersey and Mary E. Benner Egginton's son Hersey Benner Egginton married Mary Florence Twining, the daughter of Charles and Roberta Mary Braine Twining of *Iris Acre* in Garden City, and resided in Garden City. In 1925, their son Everett died at the age of twenty-five. Their daughter Elsie did not marry.

In 1994 the house was remodeled.


### Egly, Henry Harris (1893-1958)

| | |
|---|---|
| Occupation(s): | financier - vice-president, Dillon Read and Co. (investment banking firm); director, Merrick National Bank; director, South Shore Trust Co. |
| Civic Activism: | chairman, securities division, Securities and Exchange Commission, 1938-1939; trustee and chairman, underwriting committee, Beekman–Downtown Hospital (which was formed by the merger of Beekman Street Hospital and Downtown Hospital; trustee, Adelphi College (now, Adelphi University, Garden City); member, executive committee, New York Group of Investment Bankers Association |
| Marriage(s): | 1916-1958 – Matilda Anna Pasfield (1897-1971) |
| Address: | 420 Stewart Avenue, Garden City |
| Name of estate: | |
| Year of construction: | 1928 |
| Style of architecture: | Colonial Revival |
| Architect(s): | |
| Landscape architect(s): | |
| House extant: | no |
| Historical notes: | |

Henry Harris Egly was the son of Louis and Ema Bertha Maturns Egly of Brooklyn.

Henry Harris and Matilda Anna Pasfield Egly's daughter Jean married Harold Cole, the son of Charles Cole of Cold Spring Harbor and resided in Bellport. Their daughter Patricia did not marry.

[For information about Egly's Islip residence, *see* Spinzia, *Long Island's Prominent South Shore Families* – Ebinger entry.]

### Einhaus, Harry Madison (1884-1962)

| | |
|---|---|
| Occupation(s): | financier - treasurer, Greenwich Savings Bank |
| Marriage(s): | 1912-1962 – Grace Caroline Hageman (1887-1971) |
| Address: | 23 Chestnut Street, Garden City |
| Name of estate: | |
| Year of construction: | 1928 |
| Style of architecture: | Colonial Revival |
| Architect(s): | |
| Landscape architect(s): | |
| House extant: yes | |
| Historical notes: | |

In 1934, Harry Madison Einhaus purchased the house. [*The Brooklyn Daily Eagle* September 30, 1934, section E.]

He was the son of William Einhaus of Brooklyn.

Grace Caroline Hageman Einhaus was the daughter of Fred Thomas Hageman of Brooklyn.

Harry Madison and Grace Caroline Hageman Einhaus' son Gordon married Olive Vanderbilt Hodgson, the daughter of Robert John and Olive Vanderbilt Hodgson, Jr. of Garden City.

*front facade, 2009*

### Eldridge, Lewis Angevine, Sr. (1862-1931)

| | |
|---|---|
| Occupation(s): | shipping - partner, with his brother Roswell Eldridge and Harry Kearsarge Knapp, Sr.,* ferry service firm that operated ferries between Manhattan and Hoboken |
| Marriage(s): | 1898-1930 – Elizabeth Moore Huyck (1869-1950) |
| | - Civic Activism: suffragist - patron, Suffrage Memorial Fund, 1930** |
| Address: | 115 Greenwich Street, Hempstead |
| Name of estate: | |
| Year of construction: | |
| Style of architecture: | |
| Architect(s): | |
| Landscape architect(s): | Hicks Nursery supplied plantings (for L. A. Eldridge, Sr.) |
| House extant: no | |
| Historical notes: | |

The *Long Island Society Register, 1929* lists Louis A. and Elizabeth M. Huyck Eldridge [Sr.] as residing on Greenwich Street, Hempstead.

He was the son of Roswell and Ann Elizabeth Angevine Eldridge, Sr. of Hempstead. His brother Roswell Eldridge, Jr. married Louise Udall Skidmore and resided at *Udalls* in Saddle Rock. Roswell was the founder and first mayor of Saddle Rock. [*See* Spinzia, *Long Island's Prominent North Shore Families, vol. I* – R. Eldridge, Jr. entry.]

By 1932 Louis Angevine and Elizabeth Moore Huyck Eldridge, Sr. had relocated to *Redcote* in Saddle Rock.

Elizabeth Moore Huych Eldridge was the daughter of Francis Conkling and Emily Harriet Niles Huyck.

Lewis Angevine and Elizabeth Moore Huyck Eldridge, Sr.'s daughter Elizabeth married William Herbert Miller, Sr. and resided in Norwalk, CT. Their son William married Barbara Franklin Jones and resided in Mt. Kisco, NY. Their son Harry married Kate Larsen and resided in Albany, NY. Their son Lewis Angevine Eldridge, Jr. married Ruth Williamson, the daughter of Oren E. Williamson of Schoharie, NY.

*[For information on Knapp's East Islip estate *Brookwood*, see Spinzia, *Long Island's Prominent South Shore Families* – Knapp entries.]

[For information about L. A. Eldridge, Sr.'s Saddle Rock residence *Redcote*, see Spinzia, *Long Island's Prominent North Shore Families, vol. I* – L. A. Eldridge entry.]

**For other Long Islanders involved in the suffrage movement *see* Raymond E. Spinzia, "Winning the Franchise: Long Island Activists in the Fight for Woman's Suffrage and Their Opponents, Long Island's Anti-Suffragists." www.spinzialongislandestates.com.

### Elliman, Lawrence Bogert, Sr. (1876-1954)

| | |
|---|---|
| Occupation(s): | real estate agent - partner, Pell & Graves, 1897; a founder, president and chairman of board, Pease & Elliman Inc., 1901 |
| | financier - director, Commonwealth Insurance Co.; director, Homeland Insurance Co.; director, New York Title and Mortgage Co. |
| | capitalist - president, Hotel Barbizon, NYC; director, Palm Beach Harbor Co.; director, Farnal Realty Corp. |
| Civic Activism: | trustee and president, Genealogical and Biographic Society of New York; president, New York State Chamber of Commerce; president, New York State Association of Real Estate Boards; director, New York State Economic Council; trustee, St. Nicholas Society of Colonial Wars; trustee, New York History Society; director, First Avenue Association; director, Fifth Avenue Association |
| Marriage(s): | M/1 – 1902-1941 – Edyth Howard Coppell (1873-1941) - Civic Activism: a founder, Colony Club of New York; director, Children's Division of New York Orthopedic Hospital, NYC |
| | M/2 – 1944-1954 – Madelaine Chauncey (1878-1971) |
| Address: | Ocean Point Avenue, Cedarhurst |
| Name of estate: | *Cluny Lodge* |
| Year of construction: | |
| Style of architecture: | |
| Architect(s): | |
| Landscape architect(s): | |
| House extant: | unconfirmed |
| Historical notes: | |

   The *Long Island Society Register, 1929* lists Lawrence Bogert and Edyth Howard Coppell Elliman [Sr.] as residing at *Cluny Lodge* on Ocean Point Avenue, Cedarhurst.
   He was the son of William Benbow and Mary Lawrence Bogert Elliman of Flushing, Queens.
   Edyth Howard Coppell Elliman was the daughter of George and Helen Hoffman Gillingham Coppell.
   Lawrence Bogert and Edyth Howard Coppell Elliman, Sr.'s daughter Edyth married Edward Spring Knapp III of Bay Shore and Roslyn. [*See* Spinzia, *Long Island's Prominent South Shore Families* and *Long Island's Prominent North Shore Families, vol. 1* – Knapp entries.] She subsequently married Prentice Talmage with whom she resided in Lawrence. Their son Lawrence Bogert Elliman, Jr., who died in 1954 as a result of a fall over a second-story banister in his home, married Rhea Logan Munroe, the daughter of Charles A. Munroe of Greenwich, CT, and resided in Lattingtown.
   Madelaine Chauncey Elliman was the daughter of Daniel and Caroline Raymond Chauncey. Madelaine had previously been married to Edmund Ambrose Lynch, Sr. with whom she resided in Lawrence.
   [For information about the Ellimans' Bridgehampton residence *White Cottage, see* Spinzia, *Long Island's Prominent Families in the Town of Southampton* – Elliman entry.]

### Ellis, Ralph Nicholson, Sr. (1858-1930)

| | |
|---|---|
| Occupation(s): | attorney - never practiced law |
| Marriage(s): | 1906-1930 – Elizabeth Warder (1875-1952)<br>- Civic Activism: * |
| Address: | Valentines Road, Salisbury |

Name of estate:
Year of construction:
Style of architecture:
Architect(s):
Landscape architect(s):
House extant: unconfirmed
Historical notes:

    Ralph Nicholson Ellis, Sr. was the son of John Washington and Caroline Saterlee Lindley Ellis. He devoted himself to sports, the study of economics, and the collecting of rare books and jade. He had one of the finest collections of Chinese jade tomb horses in the United States.
    Elizabeth Warder Ellis was the daughter of Benjamin H. Warder of Washington, DC.
    By 1927 Ellis had relocated to *Bunga Fields* in Brookville. [*See* Spinzia, *Long Island's Prominent North Shore Families, vol. I* – Ellis entry.]
    *Elizabeth donated her collection of rare Chinese, African, and European artifacts to the Phoebe A. Hearst Museum of Anthropology, University of California, Berkeley, CA,


### Elwell, Richard Derby, Sr. (b. 1905)

| | |
|---|---|
| Occupation(s): | financier - member, McKinsey & Co., NYC (management consulting firm |
| Marriage(s): | M/1 – 1929-div. 1949 – Ethel Olive Joseph (1905-1999)<br>M/2 – 1949 – Ruth Brown<br>    - merchant – proprietor, dress shop, Cedarhurst |
| Address: | Barrett Road, Lawrence |

Name of estate:
Year of construction:
Style of architecture:
Architect(s):
Landscape architect(s):
House extant: unconfirmed
Historical notes:

    Richard Derby Elwell, Sr. was the son of Joseph Bowne and Helen Derby Elwell of Manhattan and a relative of Dr. Richard and Mrs. Ethel Carow Roosevelt Derby of *Old Adam* in Oyster Bay. Edith was the daughter of President Theodore and Mrs. Edith Kermit Carow Roosevelt of *Sagamore Hill* in Cove Neck. [*See* Spinzia, *Long Island's Prominent North Shore Families, vol. I* – Derby entry – and *Long Island's Prominent North Shore Families, vol. II* – Roosevelt entries.]
    In 1920, Richard's father Joseph was murdered by a 45 caliber gunshot to his head in a locked room of his Manhattan residence. Reputedly, the police identified some 1,000 people who had reason to kill Joseph. To this day, the murder has remained unsolved.
    Ethel Olive Joseph Elwell was the daughter of Henry Joseph of Montreal, Canada.
    Richard Derby and Ethel Olive Joseph Elwell, Sr.'s son Richard Derby Elwell, Jr. married Malleck Nonechalen, the daughter of Kleow and Mai An Nonechalen of Thailand.
    Ruth Brown Elwell was the daughter of Dan and Eva Brown of Fort Worth, TX. Ruth had previously been married to Alden R. Hatch, the son of Frederic Horace and May Palmer Daly Hatch of *Somerleas* in Lawrence.
    Richard Derby and Ruth Brown Elwell, Sr.'s son Daniel died in California at the age of sixty-six.

### Emmons, Walter Reed, Sr. (1875-1942)

| | |
|---|---|
| Occupation(s): | industrialist - partner, Walter R. Emmons, Inc., NYC (manufacturer of men's hats) |
| Marriage(s): | M/1 – 1909-1932 – Minnie Louise Teets (1886-1932) |
| | M/2 – 1938-1942 – Nancy Rachel Nichelson (1886-1947) |
| Address: | 39 Nassau Boulevard, Garden City |
| Name of estate: | |
| Year of construction: | 1919 |
| Style of architecture: | Dutch Colonial Revival |
| Architect(s): | |
| Landscape architect(s): | |
| House extant: yes | |
| Historical notes: | |

*front facade, 2001*

The *Long Island Society Register, 1929* lists Mr. and Mrs. Walter R. Emmons [Sr.] as residing on Seventh Street, Garden City. The 1920 Census lists Walter R. and Minnie Louise Teets Emmons as residing at 39 Nassau Boulevard, Garden City.

He was the son of Henry Ware and Mary Antoinette Reed Emmons.

Walter Reed and Minnie Louise Teets Emmons, Sr.'s daughter Mary married Harold Edward Ingraham, the son of Harold O. C. Ingraham of Greenwich, CT, and resided at *Old Orchard Farm* in Devon, PA. Their son Walter Reed Emmons, Jr. married Dorcas Spalding and resided in Carmel, CA.

Nancy Rachel Nichelson Emmons was the daughter of Andrew and Sina Smith Nichelson. Nancy had previously been married to Frank W. Bradsby. Bradsby's company manufactured the "Louisville Slugger" baseball bat. After Walter's death, Nancy married Carlyle Blackwell.

In 1973, the 4,170-square-foot house sold for $79,000.

### Enequist, John Theodore, Jr. (1885-1957)
### aka Johan Teodor Enequist, Jr.

| | |
|---|---|
| Occupation(s): | industrialist - president, Enequist Chemical Co., Brooklyn; |
| | a founder, with Rudolph Seldner, manager, and secretary, Seldner & Enequist, Inc. Brooklyn (chemical manufacturing firm) (later, Enequist Chemical Co.) |
| Civic Activism: | member, membership committee, Rotary Club of Brooklyn, 1926; |
| | member, sports committee, Garden City Country Club, 1929 |
| Marriage(s): | 1910-1957 - Carolyn Clewly Detrick (1886-1982) |
| Address: | 36 Brompton Road, Garden City |
| Name of estate: | |
| Year of construction: | 1931 |
| Style of architecture: | Colonial Revival |
| Architect(s): | |
| Landscape architect(s): | |
| House extant: yes | |
| Historical notes: | |

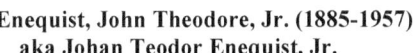

*front facade, 2019*

The *Long Island Society Register, 1929* lists John Theodore and Carolyn Clewly Detrick Enequist, Jr. as residing at 123 Seventh Street, Garden City. By 1933 they had relocated to Brompton Road.

He was the son of John Theodore Enequist, Sr. (aka Johan Teodor Enequist, Sr.) and Frances Elizabeth Parsons Enequist.

Carolyn Clewly Detrick Enequist was the daughter of George Detrick of Brooklyn.

John Theodore and Carolyn Clewly Detrick Enequist, Jr.'s son David married Pauline Gunnison, the daughter of Raymond M. Gunnison of Scarsdale, NY.

In 2019, the 2,197-square-foot house sold for $1.3 million.

*[See following entry for additional family information.]*

### Enequist, William Lars (1887-1956)

| | |
|---|---|
| Occupation(s): | real estate agent - president, William L. Enequist, Inc. |
| | industrialist - president, Selder & Enequist, Inc., Brooklyn (later, Enequist Chemical Co.) |
| Civic Activism: | president, Long Island Real Estate Board; |
| | chairman, Garden City Taxpayers' Association; |
| | chairman, New York State Convention Committee |
| Marriage(s): | 1915-1956 – Dorothy Kirkman (1894-1977) |
| Address: | 120 Whitehall Boulevard, Garden City |
| Name of estate: | |
| Year of construction: | 1925 |
| Style of architecture: | Colonial Revival |
| Architect(s): | |
| Landscape architect(s): | |
| House extant: yes | |
| Historical notes: | |

The house was built by William Lars Enequist.

The *Long Island Society Register, 1929* lists William Lars and Dorothy Kirkman Enequist as residing on Whitehall Boulevard, Garden City.

*front facade, 2001*

He was the son of John Theodore Enequist, Sr. (aka Johan Tedor Enequist, Sr.) and Frances Elizabeth Parsons Enequist.

Dorothy Kirkman Enequist was the daughter of John and Mary Louise Seaman Kirkman of Brooklyn.

William Lars and Dorothy Kirkman Enequist's daughter Beatrice married John Kenneth Strifert, the son of Albert Strifert of Bayside.

At the time of his death, Enequist was residing at 119 Second Street, Garden City. [*The New York Times* July 27, 1956, p. 21.]

*[See previous entry for additional family information.]*


### Englis, William Franklin, Sr. (1883-1957)

| | |
|---|---|
| Occupation(s): | engineer |
| Marriage(s): | 1913-1957 – Sybil Adel Genthner (1883-1969) |
| | - Civic Activism: director, vice-president, and chair of membership committee, Garden City Woman's Club |
| Address: | 11 Chestnut Street, Garden City |
| Name of estate: | |
| Year of construction: | 1915 |
| Style of architecture: | Modified Colonial Revival |
| Architect(s): | |
| Landscape architect(s): | |
| House extant: yes | |
| Historical notes: | |

The *Long Island Society Register, 1929* lists William Franklin and Sybil Adel Genthner [Sr.] as residing at 25 Meadow Street, Garden City. By 1938 they had relocated to Chestnut Street.

He was the son of William T. and Carrie E. Banks Brinckerhoff Englis.

Sybil Adel Genthner Englis was the daughter of Dr. and Mrs. Philip J. Genthner of Brooklyn.

William Franklin and Sybil Adel Genthner Englis, Sr.'s daughter Marilynn married John J. Reilly, Jr. of Hempstead. Their son William Franklin Englis, Jr. married Jeanne Drevet Snowden, the daughter of Robert E. Snowden of Garden City.

In 2010 the house sold for $682,500.

*front facade, 2010*

### English, William K.

| | |
|---|---|
| Occupation(s): | financier -   vice-president, Empire Trust Co.<br>capitalist -   director, Garden City Development Co.;<br>director, Realty Associates |
| Marriage(s): | |
| Address: | Stewart Avenue, Garden City |
| Name of estate: | |
| Year of construction: | |
| Style of architecture: | Neo-Georgian |
| Architect(s): | Kirby, Petit, and Green designed the house (for Gulick) |
| Landscape architect(s): | |
| House extant: unconfirmed | |
| Historical notes: | |

The house was built by Ernestus Schenck Gulick. It was later owned by English, who sold it in 1920. [*The New York Times* June 6, 1920, p. 101.]

*front facade, c. 1909*

### Engs, Russell Larned, Sr. (1888-1949)

| | |
|---|---|
| Occupation(s): | merchant -   president, Russell L. Engs, Inc., NYC (automotive dealership) |
| Marriage(s): | M/1 – Marion Everett Barling (1890-1934)<br>M/2 – Helen Owen |
| Address: | Tenth Street, Garden City |
| Name of estate: | |
| Year of construction: | |
| Style of architecture: | |
| Architect(s): | |
| Landscape architect(s): | |
| House extant: unconfirmed | |
| Historical notes: | |

The *Long Island Society Register, 1929* lists Russell L. and Marion Barling Hawkesworth Engs [Sr.] as residing on Tenth Street, Garden City.

He was the son of Samuel Franklin and Sarah M. Schenck Engs of Richmond Hill, NY.

Marion Everett Barling Engs had previously been married to John Hawkesworth, the son of James A. and Ella Zebley Hawkesworth.

Russell Larned and Marion Everett Barling Engs, Sr.'s son Samuel married Joan Ransom, the daughter of Philip Cox Ransom of Concord, NH, and resided in Riverdale, NY.

Helen Owen Engs was the daughter of John Owen, Jr. of Detroit, MI. She had previously been married to H. Stevens Gillespie of Detroit, MI.

### Erhart, William Herman (1868-1940)

| | |
|---|---|
| Occupation(s): | industrialist - chairman of board, Charles Pfizer Co., Brooklyn (chemical manufacturing firm) |
| | capitalist - director, American Water Works & Electric Co. |
| Marriage(s): | M/1 – 1894-1902 – Frances Lee Huntington (1870-1902) |
| | M/2 – 1904-1940 – Emma Henriette Graves (1874-1953) |
| Address: | Ocean Avenue, Lawrence |
| Name of estate: | *Five Oaks* |
| Year of construction: | c. 1906 |
| Style of architecture: | Neo-Tudor |
| Architect(s): | Freeman and Hesselman designed the house (for Erhart) |

Landscape architect(s):
House extant: no; demolished c. 1950
Historical notes:

The house, originally named *Five Oaks*, was built by William Herman Erhart.
He was the son of Charles Frederick and Fanny Pfizer Erhart of Brooklyn.
Frances Lee Huntington Erhart was the daughter of Benjamin Hoagland and Sarah Rebecca Haynes Huntington of Brooklyn.
William Herman and Frances Lee Huntington Erhart's son Charles, who resided in Mount Holly, SC, married Katherine Kent, the daughter of George Edward and Lillias Juanita Grace Kent of *Jericho House* in Jericho, and, subsequently, Joanna Bright, the daughter of Osborn Wyckoff Bright of Manhattan. [*See* Spinzia, *Long Island's Prominent North Shore Families, vol. 1* – Kent entry.] Their daughter Margaret married Andrea Geisser Celesia Di Vegliasco of Italy.
The *Long Island Society Register, 1929* lists William H. and Henrietta Graves as residing at *Five Oaks* in Cedarhurst.
She was the daughter of Robert and Cesarine Amelia Barbery Graves of *Pouch Mansion* in Brooklyn. Emma had previously been married to James Joseph Faye, Jr. with whom she resided at *Woodland Farms* in Sands Point. [*See* Spinzia, *Long Island's Prominent North Shore Families, vol. 1* – Faye entry.]
William Herman and Emma Henriette Graves Erhart's daughter Henriette married John Rathbone Ruggles and resided in Stamford, CT. Henrietta subsequently married Robert Forman Six, who later married the noted entertainers Ethel Merman and Audrey Meadows.

*rear facade*

**Eustis, George Peabody (1864-1936)**
**aka George Eustis Corcoran***

| | |
|---|---|
| Occupation(s): | capitalist - real estate - owner, Arlington Hotel, Washington, DC |
| Marriage(s): | M/1 – 1888-annulled 1901 – Marie Clarice Eustis (1866-1856) |
| | M/2 – 1908-1936 – Rosamond Kearny Street (1882-1966) |
| | - Civic Activism: member, advisory committee, Shop for Women's Work, NYC |
| Address: | Valentines Road, Salisbury |

Name of estate:
Year of construction:
Style of architecture:
Architect(s):
Landscape architect(s):
House extant: destroyed by fire in 1897
Historical notes:

    George Peabody Eustis was the son of George and Louise Morris Corcoran Eustis, Jr. His sister Louise married Thomas Hitchcock, Sr. and resided at *Broad Hollow Farm* in Old Westbury. [*See* Spinzia, *Long Island's Prominent North Shore Families, vol. I* – Hitchcock entry.]

    *Because his maternal grandfather William W. Corcoran did not have a male heir, Eustis, in 1921, changed his name to George Eustis Corcoran. [*The New York Times* January 6, 1921, p. 14.]

    Marie Clarice Eustis Eustis was the daughter of James Biddle and Ellen Eustis Buckner Eustis, Sr. of Salisbury. Marie subsequently married the noted classical pianist Josef Kazimierz Hofmann, aka Josef Casimer Hofmann.

    Marie and George Peabody Eustis were first cousins.

    George Peabody and Marie Clarice Eustis Eustis' son George Morris Eustis married Dorothy Harrison, the daughter of Charles Curtis and Ellen Nixon Harrison of Philadelphia, PA, and, later Grace Virginia Pomeroy Hendrick, the daughter of Alfred Elwood and Josephine Fanny Pomeroy Hendrick.

    Rosamond Kearny Street Eustis was the daughter of William Street of Manhattan and *The Hermitage* in Bright, NJ.

    George Peabody and Rosamond Street Eustis's daughter Lucinda married Dr. Edward Patterson Childs. Their son William married Gertrude Stadelman, the daughter of George M. Stadelman of *Grey Lodge* in Akron, OH.

*[See following entry of additional family information.]*


**Eustis, James Biddle, Sr. (1834-1899)**

| | | |
|---|---|---|
| Occupation(s): | attorney - | judge advocate, Confederate Army during Civil War |
| | politician - | member, U.S. Senate, from Louisiana, 1876-79, 1885-91; member, Louisiana House of Representatives, 1866; member, Louisiana Senate, 1874 |
| | diplomat - | United States Ambassador Extraordinary and Plenipotentiary to France, 1893-97 |
| | educator - | professor of civil law, Tulane University, New Orleans, LA |
| Marriage(s): | 1857-1895 – Ellen Eustis Buckner (1836-1895) | |
| Address: | Valentines Road, Salisbury | |

Name of estate:
Year of construction:
Style of architecture:
Architect(s):
Landscape architect(s):
House extant: destroyed by fire in 1897
Historical notes:

    James Biddle Eustis was the son of Louisiana Chief Justice George Eustis, Sr. and Mrs. Clarice Allain Biddle Eustis.

    Ellen Eustis Buckner Eustis was the daughter of Henry Sullivan and Catherine Allan Buckner of New Orleans, LA.

    James Biddle and Ellen Eustis Buckner Eustis' son William died in 1863 at the age of three. Their son James Biddle Eustis, Jr. married Nina Floyd Crosby, the daughter of Walter and Louise Gautier Sutton Crosby. Their son Newton married Margaret Hickey. Their son Henry died in 1876 at the age of fourteen. Their daughter Marie married George Peabody Eustis, aka George Eustis Corcoran, and, later, the noted classical pianist Josef Kazimierz Hofmann, aka Josef Casimir Hofmann. Their daughter Celestine married Charles Bohlen, the son of John and Priscilla Elizabeth Bohlen, Jr. Charles and Celestine's son Charles Eustis Bohlen was United States Ambassador to the U.S.S.R., 1953-1957; United States Ambassador to The Philippines, 1957-1959; and United States Ambassador to France, 1962-1968.

*[See previous entry for additional family information.]*

### Fairchild, Willard, Sr. (1887-1946)
### aka Charles Willard Fairchild, Sr.

| | |
|---|---|
| Occupation(s): | artist - illustrator |
| | art editor, *Time* magazine |
| | advertising executive - art director, Batten, Barton, Durstine, & Osborn, Inc., NYC; |
| | art director, Fuller, Smith, & Ross, Inc., NYC; |
| | art director, Tranquillini Advertising Art, NYC; |
| | art director, Carl Reimers, NYC |
| Civic Activism: | made USO tours to sketch wounded |
| Marriage(s): | 1917-1946 – Edith Clappe (1885-1973) |
| | - Civic Activism: volunteer, New York City chapter, American Red Cross |
| Address: | 26 Franklin Court, Garden City |
| Name of estate: | |
| Year of construction: | 1912 |
| Style of architecture: | Neo-Tudor Townhouse |
| Architect(s): | Ford, Butler, and Oliver designed the house* |
| Landscape architect(s): | |
| House extant: yes | |
| Historical notes: | |

The *Long Island Society Register, 1929* lists Mr. and Mrs. Willard Fairchild as residing at 26 Franklin Court, Garden City.

She was the daughter of Arthur Albert and Amy Chesswas Clappe.

Willard Fairchild, Jr. was killed at the age of twenty-two during an aircraft training exercise during World War II.

*The houses were built by Doubleday, Page, and Company as rentals.

*Franklin Court complex 2009*

### Fanning, Edward Jerome (1877-1944)

| | |
|---|---|
| Occupation(s): | attorney - partner, Elliott, Jones, and Fanning, Brooklyn |
| Civic Activism: | fund-raising committee, Mercy Hospital, Hempstead; |
| | director, Apollo Club, Brooklyn; |
| | police justice, Garden City |
| Marriage(s): | 1905-1944 – Genevieve Marie Shaw (1878-1966) |
| Address: | 261 Stewart Avenue, Garden City |
| Name of estate: | |
| Year of construction: | 1929 |
| Style of architecture: | Neo-Tudor |
| Architect(s): | Olive Frances Tjaden designed the house |
| Landscape architect(s): | |
| House extant: yes | |
| Historical notes: | |

The house was built by Walter Dohrmann Ebinger. It was later owned by Harold Francis Merritt, Sr. and, then, by Fanning.

The *Long Island Society Register, 1929* lists Mr. and Mrs. Edward J. Fanning as residing at 261 Stewart Avenue, Garden City.

He was the son of John James and Mary Ann McCasland Fanning.

Genevieve Marie Shaw Fanning was the daughter of Joshua A. and Catherine J. Cunningham Shaw of Brooklyn.

In 2017 the house sold for $1.75 million.

By 1939 the Fannings had relocated to 405 Stewart Avenue, Garden City.

The house was later owned by Mark Parbatusby.

In 2017, the 4,974-square-foot house, with six bedrooms and six and a half bathrooms, sold for $1.75 million.

*front facade, 2018*

### Farquhar, William Joslyn, Sr. (1868-1932)

Occupation(s): capitalist -  treasurer, Holmes Electric Protective Co.

Marriage(s): 1901-1932 – Cora Adelene Brightson (1873-1944)

Address: 125 Stratford Avenue, Garden City
Name of estate:
Year of construction: 1916
Style of architecture: Dutch Colonial Revival with American Craftsman elements
Architect(s):
Landscape architect(s):
House extant: yes
Historical notes:

*front facade, 2001*

The *Long Island Society Register, 1929* lists William Joslyn and Cora A. Brightson Farquhar [Sr.] as residing at 15 Stratford Avenue, Garden City.

He was the son of David Weber Farquhar of Brooklyn.

Cora Adelene Brightson Farquhar was the daughter of George Edgar and Susan Donnell Brightson, who resided at *Harbor Point* on Centre Island. [*See* Spinzia, *Long Island's Prominent North Shore Families, vol. I* – Brightson entry.] Cora's sister Suzanne married Charles B. Ketcham of Dover Plains, NJ.

William Joslyn and Cora Adelene Brightson Farquhar, Sr.'s daughter Elizabeth married Grenville Davies Braman of Los Angeles, CA. Their son William Joslyn Farquhar, Jr. resided in Pasadena, CA.


### Farr, John, Jr. (1887-1969)

Occupation(s): financier -  partner, Farr & Co. (sugar brokerage firm)
journalist -  "Beachcomber" column, *Southampton Press*

Marriage(s): 1918-1969 – Hazel S. Sims (1898-1978)

Address: *[unable to determine street address]*, Hewlett
Name of estate:
Year of construction:
Style of architecture:
Architect(s):
Landscape architect(s):
House extant: unconfirmed
Historical notes:

The *Long Island Society Register, 1929* lists John and Hazel S. Sims Farr, Jr. as residing in Hewlett.

He was the son of John and Frances Bartow Farr, Sr. of Southampton. His sister Edith married William Montague Geer, Jr. and resided in Lawrence. His brother Henry married Mildred Blair of Chicago, IL, and, subsequently, Selma Kraus.

Hazel S. Sims Farr was the daughter of Charles Pickett Sims of Spartanburg, SC.

John and Hazel S. Sims Farr, Jr.'s daughter Hazel married David Forgan Freeman, Sr., the son of Halstead Gurnee Freeman of Manhattan, and resided in Rumson, NJ. Their son Charles married Mary Randolph Rue, the daughter of Francis Rue of New York. Their son Francis married Edith G. Fincke, the daughter of Reginald Fincke of Manhattan, and resided in New York. Their son John Farr III was killed in an automobile accident in East Quogue.

By 1947 the Farrs were residing at *Breezy Lawn* on Main Street in Southampton. [*See* Spinzia, *Long Island's Prominent Families in the Town of Southampton* – Farr entries.]

### Fearey, Morton Lazell, Sr. (1876-1954)

| | |
|---|---|
| Occupation(s): | attorney - partner, Burlingham, Veeder, Fearey, Clark, and Hupper; partner, Fearey, Johnston, and Smythe; partner, Fearey and Powell |
| | shipping - trustee, Munson Steamship Line |
| Marriage(s): | 1905-1954 – Julia Lawrence |
| Address: | 243 Cathedral Avenue, Garden City |
| Name of estate: | |
| Year of construction: | |
| Style of architecture: | |
| Architect(s): | |
| Landscape architect(s): | |
| House extant: | unconfirmed |
| Historical notes: | |

  The *Long Island Society Register, 1929* lists Morton L. and Julia Lawrence Fearey as residing on First Street, Garden City. The *Social Register New York, 1933* lists their address as Cathedral Avenue, Garden City.
  He was the son of William Hartwell and Anna Eliza Shiland Fearey.
  Julia Lawrence Fearey was the daughter of The Right Reverend William Lawrence, Episcopal Bishop of Massachusetts. Her sister Ruth married Lansing Parmelee Reed and resided at *Windy Hill* in Lloyd Harbor. [*See* Spinzia, *Long Island's Prominent North Shore Families, vol. II* – Reed entry.]
  Morton Lazell and Julia Lawrence Fearey, Sr.'s son Morton Lazell Feary, Jr. married Mary Cowham Senior, the daughter of John L. Senior of Manhattan. Their son Gordon married Lydia Dwight, the daughter of Maitland Dwight, who resided at *Chipperkyle* in Bedford, NY. Their son John married Mary Lavell White, the daughter of Dr. William Crawford White of Newtown, CT. In 1913, their son William died at the age of two. Their son Robert married Shirley Granum, the daughter of Christian and Katherine Goll Granum.

### Feldstein, Martin Stuart (1939-2019)

| | |
|---|---|
| Occupation(s): | educator - professor of economics, Harvard University, Cambridge, MA |
| | financier - member, advisory board, Paulson & Co., Inc. (hedge fund); director, American International Group, Inc. (international insurance firm)*; director, J. P. Morgan/Chase (investment banking firm); director, Group of Thirty (financial advisory body); economic advisor, Brevan Howard Asset Management, LLP |
| | industrialist - economic advisor, Reliance Industries (oil and gas conglomerate); member, advisory board, Daimler AG (automotive manufacturing firm); director, Eli Lilly |
| | writer - over 300 articles** |
| Civic Activism: | governor, United States Federal Reserve; chairman, President's Council of Economic Advisors (Reagan administration)***; member, President's Foreign Intelligence Advisory Board (George W. Bush administration); member, President's Economic Recovery Board (Obama administration); consultant, United States Department of Defense; president, American Economic Association; president and CEO, National Bureau of Economic Research; director, Council on Foreign Relations; a founder, Climate Leadership Council; governor, Smith Richardson Foundation, Inc.; director, National Committee on United States–China Relations; member, President's Task Force on Tax Reform (Reagan administration); member of board, Belfer Center for Science and International Affairs; co-endowed, Kathleen and Martin Feldstein Paintings Conservation Fund, Museum of Fine Arts, Boston, MA |

**Feldstein, Martin Stuart** (cont'd)

| | |
|---|---|
| Marriage(s): | 1965-2019 – Kathleen Foley (b. 1941) |
| | - capitalist - director, Sherill House, Boston, MA (not-for-profit skilled nursing and rehabilitation center; |
| | director, Consolidated Rail Corp.; |
| | director, Partners HealthCare (hospital network); |
| | director, Knight–Ridder, Inc. (newspaper conglomerate); |
| | director, AT&T SportsNet Southwest (television network) |
| | financier - trustee, BlackRock Municipal 2020 Team Trust; |
| | trustee, BlackRock Corporate High Yield Fund III, Inc. |
| | Civic Activism: trustee, Catholic Charities of Boston; |
| | chair of board, McLean Hospital, Belmont, MA; |
| | trustee, Committee for Economic Development; |
| | trustee, Museum of Fine Arts, Boston, MA; |
| | co-endowed, Kathleen and Martin Feldstein Paintings Conservation Fund, Museum of Fine Arts, Boston, MA; |
| | member, visiting committee, Harvard Arts Museum; |
| | president, Economic Studies, Inc. |
| Address: | 31 Rugby Road, Rockville Centre |
| Name of estate: | |
| Year of construction: | 1931 |
| Style of architecture: | Neo-Tudor |
| Architect(s): | |
| Landscape architect(s): | |
| House extant: yes | |
| Historical notes: | |

Martin was raised in this house by his parents Meyer C. and Esther Gervarter Feldstein.
Kathleen Foley Feldstein is the daughter of Charles Joseph and Eleanor Croxon Foley.
Martin Stuart and Kathleen Foley Feldstein's daughter Margaret married Mark Borden. Their daughter Jane married Matt McKillop.
*Many believe that Martin's involvement in the collapse of AIG may have cost him the chairmanship of the Federal Reserve Board.
**He co-authored, with Charles Horioka, the investment behavior of various countries which later became known as the "Feldstein–Horioka Puzzle."
***Martin was President Reagan's chief economic advisor.
In 2011, he was included in *Bloomberg Margets* magazine as one of the fifty most influential people in global finance.
In 2006, the 1,826-square-foot house sold for $805.000.

*front facade, 2000*

### Fensterer, Dr. Gustave Adolf (1866-1945)

| | |
|---|---|
| Occupation(s): | physician - surgeon |
| Civic Activism: | a founder and chairman of medical board, Nassau Hospital, Mineola (later, Winthrop – University Hospital; now, NYU Langone Hospital – Long Island); |
| | first president, Nassau County Medical Society |
| Marriage(s): | Anna Marie Christ (1869-1950) |
| Address: | 120 Brixton Road, Garden City |
| Name of estate: | |
| Year of construction: | 1928 |
| Style of architecture: | American Craftsman |
| Architect(s): | |
| Landscape architect(s): | |
| House extant: yes | |
| Historical notes: | |

The house was built by Dr. Gustave Adolf Fensterer. The *Long Island Society Register, 1929* lists Dr. Gustave A. Fensterer as residing at 120 Brixton Road, Garden City.

Dr. Gustave Adolf and Mrs. Anna Marie Christ Fensterer's son Philip resided in Oyster Bay. Their son John resided in Garden City. Their son Gabriel resided in Bay Shore.

*front facade, 2008*

### Ferguson, David, Sr. (1887-1972)

| | |
|---|---|
| Occupation(s): | attorney -    partner, White and Chase |
| Civic Activism: | vice-president, secretary, and trustee, Myson and Anabel Taylor Foundation; |
| | trustee, John Jay and Eliza Jane Watson Foundation; |
| | member, Garden City branch, American Red Cross, during World War II |
| Marriage(s): | 1920-1968 – Marion M. Fitch (1892-1968) |
| Address: | 70 Washington Avenue, Garden City |
| Name of estate: | |
| Year of construction: | 1930 |
| Style of architecture: | Neo-Tudor |
| Architect(s): | Olive Francis Tjaden designed the house |
| Landscape architect(s): | |
| House extant: yes | |
| Historical notes: | |

In 1936, Ferguson purchased the house from Mrs. Bethune Wellington Jones. [*The Nassau Daily Review* October 2, 1936, p. 10, and Nassau County Department of Assessments records.]

He was the son of William J. Ferguson of Manchester, CT.

Marion M. Fitch Ferguson was the daughter of Walter S. Fitch of Brooklyn.

David and Marion M. Fitch Ferguson Sr.'s son David Ferguson, Jr. married Barbara Hopkins, the daughter of Irving George Hopkins of Richmond Hill, and resided in Garden City.

In 2017, the 5,200-square-foot house, with six bedrooms and three and a half bathrooms, sold for $1.7 million.

*front facade, 2010*

### Ferris, Dr. Henry Clay, Sr. (1870-1937)

| | |
|---|---|
| Occupation(s): | physician - dentist - orthodontist |
| Civic Activism: | member, Garden City Zoning Appeals Board; president, New York Society of Orthodontists; a founder and president, Eastern Property Owners Association, Inc. |
| Marriage(s): | Anna Jacobus Bennett (1869-1929) - Civic Activism: president, Garden City Woman's Club |
| Address: | Westbury Road, Garden City |
| Name of estate: | |
| Year of construction: | |
| Style of architecture: | |
| Architect(s): | |
| Landscape architect(s): | |
| House extant: unconfirmed | |
| Historical notes: | |

The *Long Island Society Register, 1929* lists Mr. and Mrs. Henry C. Ferris [Sr.] as residing on Westbury Road, Garden City.

He was the son of The Reverend and Mrs. Daniel Ostrander Ferris of Brooklyn.

Anna Jacobus Bennett Ferris was the daughter of George Washington and Margaret M. Whaley Bennett.

Dr. Henry Clay and Mrs. Anna Jacobus Bennett Ferris, Sr.'s daughter Margaret married Millard Stanley Brown, the son of Seth Stanley and Sarah E. Brown of *Anderson Acres* in Huron, OH, and resided in Manhattan. Their daughter Carolyn married Philip De Angelis and resided in New York. Their son William married Margery Jarvis, the daughter of Rodney Sheldon Jarvis of *Wild Goose Farm*, Shepherdstown, WV. Their son Dakin Bennet Ferris, Sr. resided in Hempstead. Their son Aubrey died in 1901 at the age of three. Their son Bertram died in 1901 at the age of four. Their son Henry Clay Ferris, Jr. died in 1901 at the age of six.

### Ferris, Morris Douw, Sr. (1884-1978)

| | |
|---|---|
| Occupation(s): | attorney - member, Hunt, Hill, and Betts shipping - director, Electric Ferries Inc. |
| Civic Activism: | secretary, National Association of Importers; member, United States Shipping Board; director, Emergency Fleet Corp, 1918-1919; treasurer, Association for the Protection of the Adirondacks; governor, Lawrence Association |
| Marriage(s): | 1913-1971 – Dorcas Williams (1886-1971) - Civic Activism: director, Nassau–Suffolk Y.M.C.A.; president, St. Elizabeth's Guild, St. John's Episcopal Church, Far Rockaway; chair, South Shore branch, Citizen's Committee for Army and Navy, Inc., during World War II |
| Address: | Ocean Avenue, Lawrence |
| Name of estate: | |
| Year of construction: | |
| Style of architecture: | |
| Architect(s): | |
| Landscape architect(s): | |
| House extant: unconfirmed | |
| Historical notes: | |

The *Long Island Society Register, 1929* lists Morris Douw and Dorcas Williams Ferris [Sr.] as residing in Lawrence.

He was the son of Morris Patterson and Mary Lanman Douw Ferris of Garden City.

Dorcas Williams Ferris was the daughter of Thomas and Emma Wells Scott Williams II of Lawrence. Dorcas' brother Thomas Resolved Williams married Dorothy S. Hinckley, the daughter of Samuel Parker and Rosalie Neilson Hinckley of *Elm Hall* in Lawrence, and also resided in Lawrence.

Morris Douw and Dorcas Williams Ferris' daughter Dorcas married Robert Lincoln Cummings, Jr. of Brookline, MA, and resided in Laurel Hollow. Their son Morris Douw Ferris, Jr. married Daphne Richardson, the daughter of Franklin Stanton Richardson of Manhattan, and, subsequently, Gloria Batten with whom he resided in Rumson, NJ.

*[See following entry for additional family information.]*

### Ferris, Morris Patterson (1855-1918)

| | |
|---|---|
| Occupation(s): | attorney |
| | writer - *Sleepy Hollow Church Records: Notes on the Hendrickson Family* |
| Civic Activism: | a founder and corresponding secretary, Brooklyn Young Republicans Club, 1881-1884; |
| | treasurer, Society of American Authors, 1898-1906; |
| | a founder and secretary, New York State Historical Association; |
| | president, Yonkers Historical and Library Association; |
| | a founder and president, Garden City Club; |
| | secretary, Sons of the Revolution; |
| | registrar, Society of the War of 1812; |
| | a founder and member of advisory board, Daughters of the Cincinnati* |
| Marriage(s): | 1879-1918 – Mary Lanman Douw (1855-1932) |
| | - writer - *Dutch Nursery Rhymes of Colonial Times*; |
| | *Random Rhymes of Old Dutch Times*; |
| | *The Van Courtlandt Mansion*; |
| | *Colonial Dames*; |
| | *History of Fort Crailo*; |
| | *The Schepan's Dream*; |
| | *Legend of New Year's Eve*; |
| | *Grandmother's Cake Basket*; |
| | *St. Nicholas' Church Legend* |
| | journalist - editor, *The American Authors* |
| | Civic Activism: chairman, Van Cortland Mansion Restoration Committee; |
| | a founder, Daughters of the Cincinnati* |

| | |
|---|---|
| Address: | Roxbury Road, Garden City |
| Name of estate: | |
| Year of construction: | |
| Style of architecture: | |
| Architect(s): | |
| Landscape architect(s): | |
| House extant: | unconfirmed |
| Historical notes: | |

Morris Patterson Ferris was the son of Isaac F. and Letita Storm Ferris of Manhattan.

Mary Lanman Douw Ferris was the daughter of John de Peyster and Marianna Chandler Lanman Douw, Jr. of Poughkeepsie, NY.

Morris Patterson and Mary Lanman Douw Ferris' daughter Mary married Joseph B. Roberts and, subsequently, Arthur A. Van Rensselaer Ferguson with whom she resided in Ridgewood, NJ. Their son Van Wyck married Elizabeth Gouverneur Morris Ramsay, the daughter of William Gouverneur and Caroline J. Canby Ramsay of Wilmington, DE, and resided at *Creekside* in Warwick, NY. Their son Morris Douw Ferris, Sr. married Dorcas Williams and resided in Lawrence.

At the time of her death, Mrs. Ferris was residing at *Windswept*, which was located at 551 Fulton Avenue, Hempstead. *[See previous entry for additional family information.]*

*The Daughters of the Cincinnati, a society for women descendants of Revolutionary War officers, was founded in 1894, in part, to encourage study of the American Revolution.

### Finch, Stephen Baker, Sr.

| | |
|---|---|
| Occupation(s): | financier - member, Hempshill, Noyes, and Co. (stock brokerage firm); partner, Prescott, Merrill, Turbin, and Co. (stock brokerage firm) |
| Marriage(s): | 1946 – Margaret Riker Whipple (1923-2002) - Civic Activism: trustee, New York City Mission Society |
| Address: | 70 Causeway, Lawrence |
| Name of estate: | |
| Year of construction: | 1897 |
| Style of architecture: | Eclectic |
| Architect(s): | William Adams, Jr. designed the house (for A. O. Norris) |
| Landscape architect(s): | |
| House extant: yes | |
| Historical notes: | |

The house was built by Alfred Oliphant Norris. It was then owned by William Adams III, who called it *Landfall*, and then by Finch.

The *Social Register New York, 1960* lists Stephen B. and Margaret R. Whipple Finch [Sr.] as residing at 70 Causeway, Lawrence.

He was the son of Henry LeRoy and Mary Farquhar Finch of Manhattan.

Margaret Riker Whipple Finch was the daughter of Julian Van Ness and Ruth Riker Whipple [Sr.] who resided at *Rustee Granit* in Hewlett. Margaret's sister Barbara married Joseph Wickes Welsh, Jr., the son of Joseph Wickes and Dorothy L. Kelly Welsh, Sr. of Lawrence, and resided in Hewlett. New York City's Riker Island was named after the Riker family.

Stephen Baker and Margaret Riker Whipple Finch Sr.'s son Stephen Baker Finch, Jr. married Louise Pinches, the daughter of Charles William Pinches of Lewiston, NY. Their daughter Margaret married Arthur Charrington Ames Nicol, the son of Carlyle Forrest Nicol, Jr.

In 2006 the house was remodeled.

*front facade, 2006*

### Finlayson, Daniel Aylesbury, Jr. (1903-1999)

| | |
|---|---|
| Occupation(s): | financier -  member, Lazard Freres and Co. (investment banking firm) |
| Marriage(s): | M/1 – 1932-div. 1939 – Elizabeth Harmsteadt Coe (1908-2002)<br>   - Civic Activism:  president, South Side Garden Club<br>M/2 – 1940 – Margaret Resler Warren (1898-1971)<br>   - merchant -  owner, Band Box, Cedarhurst (clothing store) |
| Address: | 116 Meadowview Avenue, Hewlett Bay Park |

Name of estate:
Year of construction:
Style of architecture:
Architect(s):
Landscape architect(s):
House extant:  unconfirmed
Historical notes:

   Daniel Aylesbury Finlayson, Jr. was the son of Daniel Aylesbury and Mary Archer Perkins Finlayson, Sr.
   Elizabeth Harmsteadt Coe Finlayson was the daughter of Elmore Holloway and Elizabeth Wright Davie Coe of Hewlett Bay Park. She subsequently married William French Prescott, the son of The Reverend George Jarvis and Mrs. Lucille F. Campbell Prescott of Boston, MA, with whom she resided at *Still Pond* in East Islip. [*See* Spinzia, *Long Island's Prominent South Shore Families* – Prescott entry.] Her sister Marjorie married Daniel Leslie Monroe, the son of Roland G. Monroe of Manhattan. Her sister Bertha married Sumner H. Foster, the son of John W. Foster of Cedarhurst.
   Daniel Aylesbury and Elizabeth Harmsteadt Coe Finlayson, Jr.'s daughter Elizabeth married Robert Hamilton Gregory, the son of George Mitchell and Marjorie Cooper Waddell Gregory of Bay Shore, and, later, William Hamilton Gregory III, the son of William Hamilton and Edith A. Crowley Gregory, Jr. of *Creekside* in East Islip, and resided in Glen Cove. [*See* Spinzia, *Long Island's Prominent South Shore Families* and *Long Island's Prominent North Shore Families, vol. 1* – Gregory entries.]
   The *Social Register New York, 1948* lists D. Aylesbury and Margaret Warren Finlayson, Jr. as residing at 116 Meadow View Road [sic], Hewlett [Hewlett Bay Park]. The *Social Register New York, 1922* lists their address as Lynn Place, Woodmere.
   She was the daughter of Charles Elliot and Anna Margaret Geissenhainer Warren, Sr., who resided at *Still Pond* in Hewlett Neck. Margaret had previously been married to Shannon Lord Meany, Sr. with whom she resided in Hewlett Bay Park.

### Fisher, Dr. Lamont H. (1877-1941)

| | |
|---|---|
| Occupation(s): | physician -  osteopath, Riverside Hospital |
| Civic Activism: | member, board of censors, Nassau County Medical Society |
| Marriage(s): | 1913-1938 – Dr. Millie Rhodes (1873-1938)<br>   - physician -  osteopath |
| Address: | Graham Avenue, Hempstead |

Name of estate:
Year of construction:
Style of architecture:
Architect(s):
Landscape architect(s):
House extant:  no
Historical notes:

   The *Long Island Society Register, 1929* lists Dr. Lamont H. and Mrs. [Dr.] Millie Rhodes Fisher as residing on Graham Avenue in Hempstead.
   He was the son of Joseph Lybrook and Mary Cinderella Flora Fisher.
   At the time of Mrs. Fisher's death, they were residing at 115 Henry Street in Hempstead.

### Fletcher, Thomas Clement (d. 1926)

| | |
|---|---|
| Occupation(s): | financier - Fidelity Trust Co., NYC;<br>    officer, Fidelity and Deposit Company of Maryland<br>attorney |
| Marriage(s): | Marie A. *[unable to determine maiden name]* (d. 1951) |
| Address: | 29 Kilburn Road, Garden City |
| Name of estate: | |
| Year of construction: | c. 1928 |
| Style of architecture: | Neo-Tudor |
| Architect(s): | |
| Landscape architect(s): | |
| House extant: yes | |
| Historical notes: | |

The *Long Island Society Register, 1929* lists Marie A. Fletcher as residing at 29 Kilburn Road, Garden City.

Thomas Clement Fletcher was the son of Judge Charles Carroll Fletcher of St. Louis, MO.

*front facade, 2001*

### Floyd, Nicoll, Jr. (1860-1950)

| | |
|---|---|
| Occupation(s): | financier - a founder and partner, Walsh and Floyd (stock brokerage firm);<br>    member, Colgate Hoyt and Co. (stock brokerage firm);<br>    member, J. P. Morgan and Co. |
| Civic Activism: | a founder, Garden City Golf Club |
| Marriage(s): | 1886-1934 – Margaret Otis Pott (1857-1934) |
| Address: | 105 Seventh Street, Garden City |
| Name of estate: | |
| Year of construction: | |
| Style of architecture: | Condominium |
| Architect(s): | |
| Landscape architect(s): | |
| House extant: yes | |
| Historical notes: | |

The *Long Island Society Register, 1929* lists Nicoll and Margaret Otis Pott Floyd [Jr.] as residing at 105 Seventh Street, Garden City.

He was the son of Nicoll and Cornelia Augusta DuBois Floyd, Sr., a descendant of William Floyd, a signer of the Declaration of Independence, whose estate in Mastic Beach is open to the public. [*See* Spinzia, *Long Island: A Guide to New York's Suffolk and Nassau Counties* – William Floyd Estate, Mastic Beach.]

Margaret Otis Pott Floyd was the daughter of Gideon Pott.

Nicoll and Margaret Otis Pott Floyd, Jr.'s daughter Helen married Dr. Henry Griffin Bullwinkel of Brooklyn and resided in Garden City. Their son Nicoll Floyd III married Elizabeth Donson and resided in Garden City. Their one-year-old son died in 1898.

*[See following entry for additional family information.]*

### Floyd, Nicoll, III (1887-1948)

| | |
|---|---|
| Occupation(s): | merchant -  president, Hubbard & Floyd, Inc., The Bronx (builders' supply firm) |
| Marriage(s): | Elizabeth Langry Donson (1894-1959) |
| Address: | 119 Cherry Valley Road, Garden City |
| Name of estate: | |
| Year of construction: | 1927 |
| Style of architecture: | Dutch Colonial Revival |
| Architect(s): | |
| Landscape architect(s): | |
| House extant: yes | |
| Historical notes: | |

The house was built by Nicoll Floyd III.

The *Long Island Society Register, 1929* lists Nicoll and Elizabeth L. Donson Floyd, Jr. [III] as residing at 119 Cherry Valley Road, Garden City.

He was the son of Nicoll and Margaret Otis Pott Floyd, Jr. of Garden City and a descendant of William Floyd of Mastic Beach, who was a signer of the Declaration of Independence. [*See* Spinzia, *Long Island: A Guide to New York's Suffolk and Nassau Counties* – William Floyd Estate, Mastic Beach.]

*[See previous entry for additional family information.]*

*front facade, 2009*

### Fogarty, James Francis, Sr. (1888-1960)

| | |
|---|---|
| Occupation(s): | capitalist -  president, North American Company, 1934-1939 (public utility holding company)*; chairman, finance committee, North American Company, 1939-1949; director, Detroit Edison Co. (electric utility company); director, General Corporation; director, Cleveland Electric Illuminating Co. |
| | financier -  director, Long Island Trust Co. |
| | industrialist -  director, Carriers Corp. (air conditioner manufacturing firm) |
| Civic Activism: | member, business advisory council, U. S. Department of Commerce; trustee, Eastern Garden City Association, 1938; trustee, Village of Garden City |
| Marriage(s): | Marian Esther O'Brien (1894-1960) |
| Address: | 106 Brixton Road, Garden City |
| Name of estate: | |
| Year of construction: | 1932 |
| Style of architecture: | Neo-Tudor |
| Architect(s): | Olive Frances Tjaden designed the house |
| Landscape architect(s): | |
| House extant: yes | |
| Historical notes: | |

*front facade, 2013*

James Francis and Marian Esther O'Brien Fogarty, Sr.'s son Robert married Jo Ann Textor. Their son James Francis Fogarty, Jr. married Frances Robb Fenn, the daughter of John Fleming Fenn of Winnetka, IL.

*In 1939, Fogarty was called before the U. S. Securities and Exchange Commission over the political activities and accounting methods of Union Electric, a division of North American Company. John Foster Dulles of Lloyd Harbor, who would later become Secretary of State in the Eisenhower administration, and Harrison Williams of *Oak Point* in Bayville, who was North American's board chairman, were also implicated in the alleged conspiracy. [*See* Spinzia, *Long Island's Prominent North Shore Families, vol. 1* – Dulles entry – and *vol. II* – Williams entries; *The St. Louis Star and Times* May 23, 1939, p. 5, and February 5, 1944, p. 3.]

The house was later owned by W. C. Hollis.

### Forman, Harold Baldwin (1890-1957)

Occupation(s):

Marriage(s): 1922- div. 1946 – Helaine Piatt Peters (1896-1986)
- Civic Activism: chair, Garden City branch, American Red Cross, 1943-1944;
vice-chair, Nassau County chapter, American Red Cross, 1944
chair, Garden City Red Cross War Emergency Production, 1944

Address: 125 Cherry Valley Road, Garden City
Name of estate:
Year of construction: 1926
Style of architecture: 20th Century
Architect(s):
Landscape architect(s):
House extant: yes
Historical notes:

*front facade, 2005*

The house was built by Harold Baldwin Forman.
The *Long Island Society Register, 1929* lists Harold Baldwin and Helaine Piatt Peters Forman as residing at 125 Cherry Valley Road, Garden City.
He was the son of Arthur Willis and Henrietta Baldwin Forman of Brooklyn and Westhampton Beach.
Helaine Piatt Peters Forman was the daughter of Ralph and Eleanor Hartshorn Goodman Peters, Sr. of Garden City. Helaine subsequently married Allen Supple. Her sister Eleanor married Argyll Rosse Parsons and resided in Rye, NY. Her sister Pauline married George Walker Pierpont, the son of Henry V. Pierpont of Chicago, IL. Her sister Dorothy married John Platt Hubbell of Garden City. Her sister Jane married Ford Wright. Her brother Ralph Peters, Jr. married Helen Louise Frew, the daughter of Walter Edwin and Ella Louise Carman Frew of Garden City.
In 1999 the house was remodeled.

### Forrest, Richard Earp (1877-1932)

Occupation(s): financier - member, W. R. K. Taylor & Co. (cotton brokerage firm)
capitalist - president, West India Co., Haiti (producer of castor beans)

Marriage(s): M/1 – 1902 – Louise Hollister (1882-1946)
M/2 – Harriet Louise Wright (1883-1969)
- Civic Activism: deputy commissioner, New York City Girl Scout Council;
director, National Board, Girl Scouts of the United States

Address: Longwood Crossing, Lawrence
Name of estate: *Longwood*
Year of construction: c. 1905
Style of architecture: Modified Shingle
Architect(s) Ewing and Chappell designed the house (for Forrest)
Landscape architect(s):
House extant: no
Historical notes:

*rear facade, c. 1908*

The house, originally named *Longwood*, was built by Richard Earp Forrest.
He was the son of Morton Hooks and Emma Louise Safford Forrest.
Louise Hollister Forrest was the daughter of Henry Hutchinson and Sarah Louise Howell Hollister, Sr. of Islip. In 1909 she married Landon Barrett Valentine with whom she resided in Islip. [*See* Spinzia, *Long Island's Prominent South Shore Families* – Hollister and Valentine entries.]
Harriet Louise Wright Forrest was the daughter of John W. and Carrie Hastings Wright.

**Forshay, Ralph Hoyt (1894-1946)**

Occupation(s): merchant - partner, Forshay Brothers, NYC (automobile accessories)

Marriage(s): 1916-1946 – Ruth Field (1895-1951)

Address: 21 Park Place, Hempstead
Name of estate:
Year of construction: 1933
Style of architecture: Neo-Tudor
Architect(s):
Landscape architect(s):
House extant: yes
Historical notes:

The *Long Island Society Register, 1929* lists Ralph H. and Ruth Field Forshay as residing at 45 Fairway Drive, Hempstead. At the time of Ralph's death, they were residing at 21 Park Place in Hempstead.

Ruth Field Forshay was the daughter of Frank Harvey and Mary Sniffen Field.

Ralph Hoyt and Ruth Field Forshay's son Richard married Jane Putnam Coakley, the daughter of John Coakley of Garden City. Their son Robert married Catherine A. Porrier.

In 2019, the four-bedroom, 2,800-square-foot house sold for $479,000.

*front facade, 2020*

**Fosdick, Clark (1879-1962)**

Occupation(s): industrialist - executive, Standard Oil Company of New Jersey
Civic Activism: a founder and director, Peninsula Club, Woodmere, 1919

Marriage(s): 1911-1962 – Linda H. Orne (1891-1978)

Address: Ocean Avenue, Woodmere
Name of estate:
Year of construction:
Style of architecture:
Architect(s):
Landscape architect(s):
House extant: unconfirmed
Historical notes:

The *Long Island Society Register, 1929* lists Clark and Lina [sic] H. Orne Fosdick as residing on Ocean Avenue, Woodmere. *Social Register New York, 1933* lists them as residing in Hewlett [Hewlett Bay Park.]

He was the son of Charles Barnard and Jenny Parkhurst Childs Fosdick, Jr. of *The Hedges* in Newport, RI.

Linda H. Orne Fosdick was the daughter of James Dwight and Emily Vale Orne.

Clark and Linda H. Orne Fosdick's daughter Mary married Howard Boulton, Jr., the son of Howard and Grace Russell Jones Boulton, Sr. of Hewlett. Their daughter Audrey married Thomas Donaldson Sloan, Jr., the son of Thomas Donaldson and Helen de R. Clark Sloan, Sr. of Lawrence, and, subsequently, Percy Rinde–Thorsen. Their daughter Jane married Arthur Ryle, Jr., the son of Arthur and Caroline Elizabeth Disher Ryle, Sr. who resided at *Whileaway* in Matinecock. [*See* Spinzia, *Long Island's Prominent North Shore Families, vol. II* – Ryle entry.]

### Fowler, Benjamin Kimball True (1885-1915)

Occupation(s): financier - insurance broker

Marriage(s): Rosemary O'Conor (1891-1944)

Address: 105 Franklin Court, Garden City
Name of estate:
Year of construction: 1912
Style of architecture: Neo-Tudor Townhouse
Architect(s): Ford, Butler, and Oliver
designed the house*

Landscape architect(s):
House extant: yes
Historical notes:

The *Long Island Society Register, 1929* lists Mrs. B. Kimball True Fowler as residing at 105 Franklin Court, Garden City.

Benjamin Kimball True and Rosemary O'Conor Fowler's daughter Harriet married William Mackall Wheeler, Jr. of Washington, DC.

*The houses were built by Doubleday, Page, and Company as rentals.

*Franklin Court complex, 2009*

### Fox, William (1879-1952)

Occupation(s): capitalist - president, Fox Film Corp (later, 20th Century Fox) (motion picture studio); president, Fox Circuit of Theatres

Marriage(s): 1900-1952 – Eva Leo (1880-1962)

Address: 100 Meadow Drive, Woodsburgh
Name of estate: *Fox Hall*
Year of construction: c. 1920
Style of architecture: Modified Colonial Revival
Architect(s):
Landscape architect(s):
Nassau County Museum Collection has photographs of the house.
House extant: no; demolished c. 1960
Historical notes:

The house, originally named *Fox Hall*, was built by William Fox.
He was the son of Michael and Anna Field Fox of Hungary.
Eva Leo Fox was the daughter of Max and Caroline Leo.
William and Eva Leo Fox's daughter Caroline married Douglas Nicholas Tauszig, the son of Douglas Nicholas and Matilda Wolf Tauszig. Their daughter Belle married Milton Schwartz.

*front facade*

### Francke, Albert, Sr. (1871-1945)

| | |
|---|---|
| Occupation(s): | financier - director, Peninsula National Bank, Cedarhurst; partner, Jacqueline and deCoppet (stock brokerage firm); partner, Carlisle and Jacqueline (stock brokerage firm); partner, L. H. and A. Francke (stock brokerage firm); governor, New York Stock Exchange |
| Civic Activism: | governor, Rockaway Hunting Club, Lawrence; member, executive committee, Rockaway Steeplechase Association, 1937 |
| Marriage(s): | 1898-1945 – Marian Doane Rand (1874-1962)<br>- Civic Activism: vice-president, Lawrence Garden Club; suffragist* |
| Address: | Meadow Lane, Lawrence |
| Name of estate: | |
| Year of construction: | c. 1899 |
| Style of architecture: | Colonial Revival |
| Architect(s): | William Adams, Jr. designed the house (for Francke) |
| Landscape architect(s): | Louise Payson, 1931 (for Francke); Hicks Nursery supplied plantings (for Francke) |

House extant: unconfirmed
Historical notes:

The house was built by Albert Francke, Sr.
The *Long Island Society Register, 1929* lists Albert and Marian Doane Rand Francke [Sr.] as residing in Lawrence.
He was the son of Jonas Robert and Sabiana Hernandez Francke. Albert's brother Luis married Jane Bush and resided at *Glenby* in Brookville. [*See* Spinzia, *Long Island's Prominent North Shore Families, vol. 1* – Francke entry.]
Marian Doane Rand Francke was the daughter of George Curtis and Eugenia Isabelle Elizabeth Blanchard Rand.
Albert and Marian Doane Rand Francke, Sr.'s son Albert Francke, Jr. married Eleanor Fitz Gerald, the daughter of Harold Fitz Gerald of Manhattan, and resided at *The Breezes* in Bridgehampton. [*See* Spinzia, *Long Island's Prominent Families in the Town of Southampton* – Francke entry.]
*For other Long Islanders involved in the suffrage movement *see* Raymond E. Spinzia, "Winning the Franchise: Long Island Activists in the Fight for Woman's Suffrage and Their Opponents, Long Island's Anti-Suffragists." wwwspinzialongislandestates.com.

*front facade, 1912*

### Francklyn, Reginald Gebhard (1889-1971)

Occupation(s): attorney
Civic Activism: secretary and treasurer, Nassau Taxpayers League, 1949

Marriage(s): M/1 – 1923-1928 – Lilian Endicott (1891-1928)
M/2 – 1931-1971 – Mary Culbertson Kilbreth (1889-1978)

Address: Harbor Road, Hewlett Harbor
Name of estate:
Year of construction:
Style of architecture:
Architect(s):
Landscape architect(s):
House extant: unconfirmed
Historical notes:

Reginald Gebhard Francklyn was the son of Reginald H. and Agnes Virginia Binsse Francklyn of New York. His sister Mary married John Dykers Nichols and resided at *Nicholyn* in Hewlett.

Lilian Endicott Francklyn was the daughter of Robert Endicott of Geneva, NY.

Reginald Gebhard and Lilian Endicott Francklyn's daughter Caroline married Campbell Locke, Jr., the son of Campbell and Ruth Cary Slattery Locke, Sr. of Lawrence, and resided in Bernardsville, NJ. Their son Reginald Endicott Francklyn married Phyliss De Veau, the daughter of George Putnam and Maryanna Ludlow Lincoln Culbertson De Veau of Lawrence, and resided in Avon, CT.

The *Social Register New York, 1951* lists Reginald G. and Mary C. Kilbreth Francklyn as residing on Harbor Road, Hewlett [Hewlett Harbor].

She was the daughter of John Culbertson Kilbreth of Hewlett. Her sister Anna married James Truesdell Kilbreth, Jr. and resided in Hewlett Bay Park.


### Fraser, Dougall Charles, Sr. (1912-1994)

Occupation(s): engineer - treasurer and secretary, Brace Engineering Co.
capitalist - director, Long Island Lighting Co.

Marriage(s):

Address: 129 Stratford Avenue, Garden City
Name of estate:
Year of construction: 1926
Style of architecture: Dutch Colonial Revival
Architect(s):
Landscape architect(s):
House extant: yes
Historical notes:

*front / side facade, 2013*

Dougall Charles Fraser, Sr. purchased the house from Dean Courtney Anderson in 1948. [*The Brooklyn Daily Eagle* April 11, 1948, p. 36.]

He was the son of Charles Edward and Helen Pettit Sweezy Fraser of Kew Gardens.

Dougall's son Dougall Charles Fraser, Jr. married Carol Catherine Valkenburgh, the daughter of Donald Newton and Carol Schauman Valkenburgh of Rochester, NY.

In 2013, the 3,718-square-foot house, with six bedrooms and three and a half bathrooms, sold for $1.5 million.

### Fraser, John W. (1863-1941)

| | |
|---|---|
| Occupation(s): | financier - president, Roosevelt Savings Bank, Brooklyn; trustee, Brooklyn Trust Co.; director, Morris Plains Industrial Bank, Morris Plains, NJ; president, Eastern District Savings Bank, Brooklyn (later, Roosevelt Savings Bank); assistant manager, Greenport branch, Corn Exchange Bank |
| Marriage(s): | Helen Sophia *[unable to determine maiden name]* (1869-1943) |
| Address: | 226 Stewart Avenue, Garden City |
| Name of estate: | |
| Year of construction: | 1920 |
| Style of architecture: | Modified Neo-Tudor |
| Architect(s): | |
| Landscape architect(s): | |
| House extant: yes | |
| Historical notes: | |

The *Long Island Society Register, 1929* lists Mr. and Mrs. John W. Fraser as residing on Stewart Avenue, Garden City.

His father John was killed at the Battle of Bull Run. His mother Harriet S. Fraser died in 1911.

In 2013, the six-bedroom, 4,957-square-foot house sold for $1.425 million.

*front facade, 2013*

### French, Seth Barton, Sr. (1889-1961)

| | |
|---|---|
| Occupation(s): | capitalist - real estate holdings |
| Marriage(s): | 1918-1961 – Mary Tyler Duffy (1899-1981) |
| Address: | 115 Ocean Avenue, Hewlett Neck |
| Name of estate: | |
| Year of construction: | 1920 |
| Style of architecture: | Modified Victorian |
| Architect(s): | |
| Landscape architect(s): | |
| House extant: yes | |
| Historical notes: | |

The *Long Island Society Register, 1929* lists Seth B. and Mary T. Duffy French [Sr.] as residing in Hewlett [Hewlett Neck].

He was the son of Dr. John Herndon French of New York.

Mary Tyler Duffy French was the daughter of Edward Duffy of Baltimore, MD.

Seth Barton and Mary Tyler Duffy French, Sr.'s daughter Chloe married John R. Winterbotham III of Chicago, IL. Their son Edward married Joan Francke Remick, the daughter of Joseph Gould and Eleanor Huntington Francke Remick of Woodmere, and resided in Chicago, IL. Their son John Herndon French II married Sarah Pierpont Fleurnoy Simpson, the daughter of Kenneth F. Simpson of Manhattan. Their son Seth Barton French, Jr., who resided in Manhattan, married Frederika Pearson Ripley, the daughter of Henry Baldwin Hyde and Lesley Frederika Pearson Ripley, Sr. of *Beech Bound* in Newport, RI.

At the time of his death, French was residing at 90 Cedar Avenue, Hewlett Bay Park. [*The New York Times* October 3, 1961, p. 39.]

In 1992 the house was remodeled.

*front facade, 2008*

### Frew, Walter Edwin (1864-1941)

| | |
|---|---|
| Occupation(s): | financier - trustee, Long Island City Savings Bank;<br>president, Queens County Bank of Long Island;<br>president, Corn Exchange Bank;<br>vice-president, Corn Exchange Safe Deposit Co.;<br>director, Bankers' Trust Co.;<br>director, Washington Trust Co.;<br>director, Dry Dock Savings Bank<br>industrialist - director, United Button Co. |
| Civic Activism: | chairman, Clearing House Association;<br>member, Loan Commission during Panic of 1907 |
| Marriage(s): | 1888 – Ella Louise Carman (b. 1866) |
| Address: | 6 Cathedral Avenue, Garden City |
| Name of estate: | |
| Year of construction: | 1893 |
| Style of architecture: | Modified Shingle |
| Architect(s): | |
| Landscape architect(s): | Hicks Nursery supplied plantings (for G. L. Hubbell, Sr.) |
| House extant: yes | |
| Historical notes: | |

*front facade, 2000*

The house was previously owned by George Loring Hubbell, Sr., who called it *Lonesomehurst*.
The *Long Island Society Register, 1929* lists Walter E. and Ella Louise Carman Frew as residing at 6 Cathedral Avenue, Garden City.
He was the son of George Edward and Amanda Ducker Crooker Frew of Brooklyn and Greenport.
Ella Louise Carman Frew was the daughter of Samuel Carman of Brooklyn.
Walter Edwin and Ella Louise Carman Frew's daughter Helen married Ralph Peters, Jr. and resided in Garden City.


### Frost, Newberry Halstead (1846-1900)

| | |
|---|---|
| Occupation(s): | capitalist - treasurer, Atlantic Avenue Railroad, Brooklyn |
| Civic Activism: | a founder, Brooklyn Riding and Driving Club |
| Marriage(s): | bachelor |
| Address: | Hilton Avenue, Hempstead |
| Name of estate: | |
| Year of construction: | |
| Style of architecture: | |
| Architect(s): | |
| Landscape architect(s): | |
| House extant: unconfirmed | |
| Historical notes: | |

Newberry Halstead Frost was the son of Jacob and Sarah Titus Frost of Manhattan. Newberry's sister Alice married William M. Van Anden, Sr. and resided in Islip. [*See* Spinzia, *Long Island's Prominent South Shore Families* – Van Anden entry.]
His sister Louise married George R. Read of Manhattan.

### Fuller, Paul, Jr. (1881-1947)

| | |
|---|---|
| Occupation(s): | attorney - partner, Coudert Brothers, NYC |
| Civic Activism: | director, War Trade Intelligence during World War I; |
| | acting director, Bureau of Enemy Trade during World War I; |
| | member, Censorship Board during World War I; |
| | chairman, Foreign Trade Commission of New York's Merchants' Association; |
| | president, Rockaway Hunting Club, Lawrence |
| Marriage(s): | 1905-1947 – Marie Augustine de Florez (1877-1974) |
| Address: | Cedar Avenue, Hewlett Bay Park |
| Name of estate: | *Four Winds* |
| Year of construction: | |
| Style of architecture: | |
| Architect(s): | |
| Landscape architect(s): | |
| House extant: | unconfirmed |
| Historical notes: | |

The *Long Island Society Register, 1929* lists Paul and Marie A. de Florez Fuller [Jr.] as residing in Hewlett [Hewlett Bay Park]. The *Social Register Summer, 1937* lists the name of their estate as *Four Winds*.

He was the son of Paul and Leonie Anne Julie Coudert Fuller, Sr.

Paul and Marie Augustine de Florez Fuller, Jr.'s daughter Cecile married John Hurd, the son of George Frederick and Mary Burnett Hurd of Lawrence. Their daughter Marie married Louis King Timolat, the son of James Guyon Timolat, Sr. of Red Bank, NJ. Their daughter Catherine married Donald Lee Norris, Sr., the son of Alfred Lockwood and Florence Middleton Lee Norris of Lawrence, and resided in Hewlett Bay Park. Their twenty-three-year-old son Peter was killed in an automobile accident. [*The New York Times* October 13, 1932, p. 3.] Their daughter Leonie married William Troy.

### Fulton, Ralph Whittier (1892-1967)

| | |
|---|---|
| Occupation(s): | advertising executive - advertising director, *Sports Afield* magazine; |
| | advertising director, *Cosmopolitan* magazine |
| Marriage(s): | M/1 – 1913-div – Helen Goodrich Dunlap (1894-1988) |
| | M/2 – Grace Fitzgerald |
| Address: | 124 Salisbury Avenue, Garden City |
| Name of estate: | |
| Year of construction: | c. 1928 |
| Style of architecture: | 20th Century Eclectic |
| Architect(s): | |
| Landscape architect(s): | |
| House extant: | yes |
| Historical notes: | |

The house was built by Ralph Whittier Fulton.

The *Long Island Society Register, 1929* lists Ralph Whittier and Helen Goodrich Dunlap Fulton as residing at 124 Salisbury Avenue, Garden City.

Born in Canton, Shunde, Guandong, China, he was the son of The Reverend Albert A. Fulton.

Helen Goodrich Dunlap Fulton was the daughter of George T. Dunlap of Manhattan and Pinehurst, NC. She later married Hugh Lockhart Forman.

Ralph Whittier and Helen Goodrich Dunlap Fulton's daughter Helen married John Robinson Miller, Jr. of Garden City with whom she resided in Garden City. Their son Dunlap married Marjorie Louise Sticker, the daughter of John Frederick and Mary Kathryn Daubert Sticker of Garden City, and resided in Huntington.

*side / front facade, 2001*

### Furst, Michael (1856-1934)

| | | |
|---|---|---|
| Occupation(s): | attorney - | partner, Furst, Schwartz, and Schwager, Brooklyn; corporation counsel, City of Brooklyn, 1894-1898 |
| | financier - | vice-president, Kings County Mortgage Co.; trustee, Greater New York Savings Bank; a founder, Montauk Bank; director, National Exchange Bank & Trust Co.; director, Mechanics Bank of Brooklyn; chairman of board, National Title Guaranty Co. |
| | capitalist - | director, Valley Stream Development Co.; chairman of board, Stockholders' Realty Corp. |

Civic Activism: trustee, Temple Israel;
president, Brooklyn Bar Association;
trustee, Denver Home for Consumptives;
trustee, Jewish Protectory of New York City;
a founder and president, Brooklyn Young Men's Hebrew Association*;
a founder and director, Brooklyn Federation of Jewish Charities;
director, Girls' Memorial Club;
director, Brooklyn Home for the Aged;
member, Aqueduct Commission, 1910;
member, condemnation commission, Brooklyn;
member, Brooklyn Real Estate Board

Marriage(s): bachelor

Address: 50 Wyckoff Place, Woodmere
Name of estate:
Year of construction:
Style of architecture:
Architect(s):
Landscape architect(s):
House extant: no
Historical notes:

The *Long Island Society Register, 1929* lists Michael Furst as residing in Woodmere.
*He was known as the father of the Brooklyn Young Men's Hebrew Association (Y.M.H.A.).


### Gamel, Isaac (1930-2014)

Occupation(s): capitalist - real estate developer; owner, Hollywood Beach Club

Marriage(s): Nancy Mezistrano (1933-2019)

Address: 580 Ocean Avenue, Lawrence
Name of estate:
Year of construction: c. 1900
Style of architecture: Neo-Tudor
Architect(s): Renwick, Aspinwall, and Owen designed the house (for R. A. Peabody)
Landscape architect(s):
House extant: yes
Historical notes:

The house, originally named *Terrace Hall*, was built by Richard Augustus Peabody. It was later owned by William Raymond, Sr., and, subsequently, by Gamel.

He was the son of Haim and Rivka Gamel of Brooklyn.

Nancy Mezistrano Gamel was the daughter of Benjamin and Matilda Mezistrano. Nancy later married Joseph Resnick.

*rear facade, 1901*

### Garde, John Franklin, Jr. (d. 1983)

| | |
|---|---|
| Occupation(s): | industrialist - sales, Scott Paper Co. 1938-1941 |
| | financier - member, The New York Trust, 1945-1950 |
| | capitalist - member, Sanderson & Porter Engineering Firm |
| Civic Activism: | trustee, Village of Lawrence; |
| | president of board, Five Towns Community Chest |
| Marriage(s): | M/1 – 1944-1975 – Katharine Delano Hamill (1921-1975) |
| | M/2 – *[unable to determine maiden name]* |
| Address: | Ocean Avenue, Lawrence |
| Name of estate: | |
| Year of construction: | |
| Style of architecture: | |
| Architect(s): | |
| Landscape architect(s): | |
| House extant: | unconfirmed |
| Historical notes: | |

The *Social Register New York, 1948* lists John F. and Katharine D. Hamill Garde, Jr. as residing on Ocean Avenue in Lawrence.

He was the son of John Franklin and Henrietta Lee White Garde, Sr.

Katharine Delano Hamill Garde was the daughter of Robert Lyon and Katharine Delano Porter Hamill, Sr. of Cedarhurst.

John Franklin and Katharine Delano Hamill Garde, Jr.'s son John Franklin Garde III married Harriet Parker Merritt, the daughter of Schuyler and Cornelia Kane McElroy Merritt II of Hewlett Bay Park.

### Gardner, Bertram (1871-1924)

| | |
|---|---|
| Occupation(s): | attorney |
| | politician - chief deputy, Collector of Internal Revenue, New York First District, Brooklyn; |
| | Nassau County Democratic State Committeeman, 1914-1918 |
| | financier - director, Citizens' National Bank, Freeport |
| Civic Activism: | president, National Tax Consultants; |
| | member, Advisory Board of Long Island Bankers, Inc. |
| Marriage(s): | 1904 – Gardina Greenleaf Yvelin (b. 1877) |
| Address: | 114 Sixth Street, Garden City |
| Name of estate: | |
| Year of construction: | 1876 |
| Style of architecture: | Victorian |
| Architect(s): | |
| Landscape architect(s): | |
| House extant: | yes |
| Historical notes: | |

The *Long Island Society Register, 1929* lists Mr. [sic] and Mrs. Bertram Gardner as residing on Sixth Street, Garden City.

He was the son of Alfred Hussey and Augusta Atwater Gardner.

Gardina Greenleaf Yvelin Gardner was the daughter of Garde Greenleaf and Cordelia E. Macpherson Yvelin.

Bertram and Gardina Greenleaf Yvelin Gardner's son Yvelin married Betty Stoddard, the daughter of Thomas A. Stoddard of Hempstead. Their daughter Ruth did not marry.

*front facade, 2006*

### Gaston, George Albert (1875-1968)

| | |
|---|---|
| Occupation(s): | attorney |
| | capitalist - director, American Transportation Co.; |
| | director, Grand Trunk and Western Railroad; |
| | director, Central Railroad of Vermont; |
| | a founder and president, Gaston, Williams, & Wegmore of New York (exporting, shipping, and banking firm) |
| | president, Gaston, Williams, & Wegmore of Canada; |
| | president, Gaston, Williams, & Wegmore of Far East; |
| | president, Gaston, Williams, & Wegmore of London* |
| | financier - director, American Merchant Marine Insurance |
| Marriage(s): | 1914 – Ethel Ada Ellis (b. 1883) |
| Address: | 93 Fifth Street, Garden City |
| Name of estate: | |
| Year of construction: | |
| Style of architecture: | Queen Anne |
| Architect(s): | |
| Landscape architect(s): | |
| House extant: yes | |
| Historical notes: | |

*front facade, 2000*

The *Long Island Society Register, 1929* lists Mr. and Mrs. George A. Gaston as residing at 93 Fifth Street, Garden City.

Gaston's World War I Draft Card lists his birth date as July 23, 1876. His 1921 passport application lists his birth date as July 23, 1875.

He was the son of George and Rachel Montgomery Gaston of East Liverpool, England.

*The firm supplied the Allies with munitions during World War I.

### Geer, Enos Throop, Sr. (1883-1968)

| | |
|---|---|
| Occupation(s): | attorney - partner, Glenn, Alley, Geer, and Roberts; partner, Iselin, Riggs, Ferris, and Myatt |
| Civic Activism: | treasurer, Corporation for Relief of Widows |
| Marriage(s): | 1916-1962 – Mary Savage Cleveland (1889-1962) |
| Address: | 39 Euston Road, Garden City |
| Name of estate: | |
| Year of construction: | c. 1928 |
| Style of architecture: | Colonial Revival |
| Architect(s): | |
| Landscape architect(s): | |
| House extant: yes | |
| Historical notes: | |

*front facade, 2000*

The house was built by Enos Throop Geer, Sr.

The *Long Island Society Register, 1929* lists Enos Throop and Mary Savage Cleveland Geer [Sr.] as residing at 39 Euston Road, Garden City.

He was the son of The Reverend William Montague and Mrs. Katharine Gridley Throop Geer, Sr. of Oyster Bay. Enos' brother Garrow, who resided at *Redbrook* in North Sea, married Marion L. Firth and, subsequently, Rose Kane. [*See* Spinzia, *Long Island's Prominent Families in the Town of Southampton* – Geer entry.] His brother William Montague Geer, Jr. married Edith Jaffray Farr and resided in Lawrence.

Mary Savage Cleveland Geer was the daughter of Samuel Bennett Cleveland of New Orleans, LA. Her sister Martha married Charles Longstreet Poor, Sr. and resided in Quogue. [*See* Spinzia, *Long Island's Prominent Families in the Town of Southampton* – Poor entry.]

Enos Throop and Mary Savage Cleveland Geer, Sr.'s son Enos Throop Geer, Jr. married Viola Tingle Culbertson, the daughter of John Dickey Culbertson of Sewickley, PA.

*[See following entry for additional family information.]*

### Geer, William Montague Jr. (1885-1954)

| | |
|---|---|
| Occupation(s): | attorney - partner, Everett, Clarke, and Benedict, NYC; financier - partner, Farr & Co. (sugar brokerage firm) |
| Marriage(s): | 1921-1954 – Edith Jaffray Farr (1894-1980) |
| Address: | 480 Ocean Avenue, Lawrence. |
| Name of estate: | |
| Year of construction: | |
| Style of architecture: | Modified Colonial Revival |
| Architect(s): | |
| Landscape architect(s): | |
| House extant: yes | |
| Historical notes: | |

The *Social Register New York, 1933* lists William Montague and Edith J. Farr Greer, Jr. as residing in Hewlett.

He was the son of The Reverend William Montague and Mrs. Katharine Gridley Throop Geer, Sr. of Oyster Bay.

Edith Jaffray Farr Geer was the daughter of John and Frances Bartow Farr, Sr. of Southampton. [*See* Spinzia, *Long Island's Prominent Families in the Town of Southampton* – Farr entry.] Edith's brother Henry married Mildred Blair of Chicago, IL, and, subsequently, Selma Kraus. Her brother John Farr, Jr. married Hazel S. Sims and resided in Hewlett.

William Montague and Edith Jaffray Farr Geer, Jr.'s son John married Carolyn V. Boston and resided in Manhattan. Their son William Montague Geer III married Barbara Helen Tyner, the daughter of Gerald Kerwin and Helen Virginia Kennedy Tyner of Garden City and Quogue, and resided in Duxbury, MA. [*See* Spinzia, *Long Island's Prominent Families in the Town of Southampton* – Tyner entry.]

Geer committed suicide in his car in his garage by shooting himself in the head. [*The New York Times* August 31, 1954, p. 22.]

*[See previous entry for additional family information.]*

*front facade, 2009*

### Geoghegan, Joseph Gregory (1876-1925)

| | |
|---|---|
| Occupation(s): | industrialist - partner, Gilles & Geoghegan, NYC (manufacturer of heating and ventilating equipment) |
| Marriage(s): | 1900-1925 – Ethel McCullogh (1881-1980) |
| Address: | 31 Wellington Road, Garden City |
| Name of estate: | |
| Year of construction: | c. 1928 |
| Style of architecture: | Scandinavian Cottage |
| Architect(s): | |
| Landscape architect(s): | |
| House extant: yes | |
| Historical notes: | |

The house was built by Joseph Gregory Geoghegan.

He was the son of Stephen Jeremiah and Ellen Foley Geoghegan. Joseph died as a result of an automobile accident.

The *Long Island Society Register, 1929* lists Mrs. Joseph G. Geoghegan as residing at 31 Wellington Road, Garden City. She later married Thaddeus K. MacIlroy.

*front facade, 2000*

Joseph Gregory and Ethel McCullogh Geoghegan's daughter Marion married Henry B. Clark and resided in Garden City. Their son Stephen married Josephine Genevieve Naisawald, the daughter of H. Louis Naisawald of Garden City.

In 1944 the house was remodeled.

### Gerard, Ernest Dudley (b. 1871)

Occupation(s): industrialist - treasurer and director, Empire City – Gerard (door, window, and molding manufacturer)

Marriage(s): Caroline B. *[unable to determine maiden name]* (1877-1958)

Address: 105 Tenth Street, Garden City
Name of estate:
Year of construction: 1910
Style of architecture: Mediterranean
Architect(s):
Landscape architect(s):
House extant: yes
Historical notes:

*front facade*

The *Long Island Society Register, 1929* lists Mr. and Mrs. Ernest D. Gerard as residing on Tenth Street, Garden City.

He was the son of George Henry and Emily A, Carpenter Gerard of Garden City.

Ernest Dudley and Caroline B. Gerard's son Henry married Elizabeth De Tienne, the daughter of Dr. John Antoine and Mrs. Maude Olive Waterman De Tienne, and resided in Garden City.

At the time of her death, Mrs. Gerard was residing at 105 Tenth Street, Garden City. [*The New York Times* December 10, 1958, p. 39.]

*[See other Gerard entries for additional family information.]*


### Gerard, George Henry (d. 1916)

Occupation(s): industrialist - a founder, with Ernest Dudley Gerard, G. H. Gerard, Greenpoint, NY (later, Young & Gerard; then, Empire City – Gerard) (door, window, and molding manufacturer)
capitalist - owned a lumber yard, Brookhaven
financier - president, Home Savings Bank, Greenpoint, NY; director, Mechanics and Traders Bank, Brooklyn; director, Greenpoint branch, Corn Exchange Bank; treasurer, Long Island Building and Loan Association

Civic Activism: a founder, school in western Canada

Marriage(s): Emily A. Carpenter (1851-1921)

Address: Cathedral Avenue and Second Street, Garden City
Name of estate:
Year of construction:
Style of architecture:
Architect(s):
Landscape architect(s):
House extant: no
Historical notes:

Emily A. Carpenter Gerard was the daughter of Nathaniel Carpenter of Babylon.

George Henry and Emily A. Carpenter Gerard's son Henry, who resided in Garden City, married Elizabeth De Tienne.

*[See other Gerard entries for additional family information.]*

**Gerard, Henry Dudley (1901-1972)**
**aka Dudley Gerard**

Occupation(s):

Marriage(s): 1928-div. – Elizabeth De Tienne (1904-1948)

Address: Cathedral Avenue, Garden City
Name of estate:
Year of construction:
Style of architecture:
Architect(s):
Landscape architect(s):
House extant: unconfirmed
Historical notes:

Henry Dudley Gerard was the son of Ernest Dudley and Caroline B. Gerard of Garden City.

Elizabeth De Tienne Gerard was the daughter of Dr. John Antoine and Mrs. Maude Olive Waterman De Tienne of Garden City. Elizabeth later married Raymond Pryor Ackerman, Jr., the son of Raymond Pryor and Mildred Chadbourn Irish Ackerman, Sr. of Garden City. *[See other Gerard entries for additional family information.]*

**Gerstner, Louis Vincent, Jr. (b. 1942)**

Occupation(s): capitalist - president, American Express;
chairman of board and CEO, American Express Travel Related Services;
director, The New York Times Co.;
director, McKinsey & Co., Inc. (management consulting firm)
financier - chairman of board, Carlyle Group
industrialist - director, Caterpillar, Inc.;
director, DaimlerChrysler (automobile manufacturing firm);
chairman of board, International Business Machine Corp;
chairman of board and CEO, R. J. Nabisco;
member, advisory board, Sony Corp.;
director, Bristol–Meyers Squibb Co.;
writer - *Who Says Elephants Can't Dance*;
co-author, *Reinventing Education*, 1994;

Civic Activism: chairman of board, Broad Institute of Massachusetts Institute of Technology, Cambridge, MA;
chairman of board of advisors, Columbia Medical Center Department of Ophthalmology, NYC;
member of board, Council on Foreign Affairs;
established Gerstner Family Foundation;
director, National Committee on United States–China Relations;
vice-chairman of board, Memorial Sloan Kettering Cancer Center, NYC;
vice-chairman of board, American Museum of Natural History, NYC;
chairman of board, Gerstner Sloan Kettering Graduate School of Biomedical Sciences, NYC

Marriage(s): 1968 – Elizabeth Robins Link

Address: 53 Fairfield Avenue, Mineola
Name of estate:
Year of construction: 1938
Style of architecture: Cape Cod
Architect(s):
Landscape architect(s):
House extant: yes
Historical notes:

*front facade, 2001*

Louis was raised in this house by his parents Louis Vincent and Marjorie Rutan Gerstner, Sr.

Elizabeth Robins Link Gerstner is the daughter of Harry Rollen Link of Danville, VA.

Louise Vincent and Elizabeth Robins Link Gerstner, Jr.'s son Louis Vincent Gerstner II, who married Mary Gervaise Lawthorne, choked to death in 2013 while dining in a restaurant at the age of forty-one. Their daughter Dr. Elizabeth Robins Gerstner married Dr. Neal Kush Lakdawala of Round Rock, TX.

In 1997, the 1,176-square-foot house sold for $214,500.

### Gesell, Dr. Herbert Ross, Sr. (1892-1946)

| | |
|---|---|
| Occupation(s): | physician - dentist - Kings County Hospital, Brooklyn; Meadow Brook Hospital, Hempstead; House of St. Giles, Garden City |
| Civic Activism: | treasurer, Nassau County Dental Society |
| Marriage(s): | M/1 – 1916-div. c. 1933 – Anna Margaretta Marie Eggers<br>M/2 – Doris M. Herdman (1898-1991)<br>    - educator - teacher<br>        Civic Activism: president, Hempstead Classroom Teachers Association |
| Address: | 114 Fifth Street, Garden City |
| Name of estate: | |
| Year of construction: | 1923 |
| Style of architecture: | Modified Shingle |
| Architect(s): | |
| Landscape architect(s): | |
| House extant: yes | |
| Historical notes: | |

The *Long Island Society Register, 1929* lists Dr. and Mrs. Herbert R. Gesell as residing at 114 Fifth Street, Garden City.

He was the son of Charles Lewis and Mary Elizabeth Kells Gesell, Sr.

Anna Margaretta Marie Eggers Gesell was the daughter of Rudolph and Sophie Eggers.

Doris M. Herdman Gesell was the daughter of Henry Wheeler and Ida Miers Herdman.

At the time of his death, Dr. Gesell was residing at 67 Hilton Avenue, Garden City. [*The New York Times* July 10, 1946, p. 23.]

*front facade, 2005*

### Gildersleeve, Raleigh Colston (1869-1944)

| | |
|---|---|
| Occupation(s): | architect<br>capitalist - president, Philipse Manor Co.;<br>vice-president and director, Alpha Realty Co.<br>(Manhattan apartment buildings) |
| Marriage(s): | 1915 – Elena Josepha Mariana de Apezteguia (1882-1952)<br>- writer - *Baby Epicure: Appetizing Dishes for Children and Invalids*, 1937 |
| Address: | 240 Causeway, Lawrence |
| Name of estate: | *Red House* |
| Year of construction: | 1883 |
| Style of architecture: | Shingle |
| Architect(s): | |
| Landscape architect(s): | |
| House extant: yes | |
| Historical notes: | |

*side facade, 2000*

The *Social Register Summer, 1921* and *Long Island Society Register, 1929* list Raleigh C. and Elena de Apezteguia Gildersleeve as residing at *Red House* in Lawrence. The *Social Register New York, 1933* lists their address as 240 Causeway, Lawrence.

He was the son of Basil Lanneau and Eliza Fisher Colston Gildersleeve.

Elena Josepha Mariana de Apezteguia Gildersleeve was the daughter of Julia Jose and Helen Seagrave Vincent de Apezteguia. Elena had previously been married to John Izard Middleton, Sr.

### Glass, Brent David (b. 1947)

| | |
|---|---|
| Occupation(s): | educator - executive director, North Carolina Humanities Council, 1983-1987;<br>executive director, Pennsylvania Historical and Museum Commission, 1987-2002;<br>executive director, Smithsonian National Museum of American History, 2002-2011<br>capitalist - founder, Brent D. Glass, LLC, 2001 (consulting firm to museum and history organizations)*<br>writer - *50 Great American Places*, 2016;<br>numerous articles in professional journals; |
| Civic Activism: | member of board, State Department's United States–Russian Working Group on Education, Culture, Sports, and Media;<br>United States State Department's Diplomatic Center Advisory Committee;<br>member of board, San Francisco Presido Heritage Advisory Board;<br>trustee, Lafayette College, Easton, PA;<br>federal commissioner, National Historical Publications and Records Commission;<br>member of board, National Council of American Association for State and Local History;<br>member of board, Flight 93 Memorial Advisory Commission, Shanksville, PA |
| Marriage(s): | M/1 – Barbara Martin<br>M/2 – Cathryn Keller |
| Address: | 991 Dartmouth Lane, Woodmere |
| Name of estate: | |
| Year of construction: | 1960 |
| Style of architecture: | Colonial Revival |
| Architect(s): | |
| Landscape architect(s): | |
| House extant: yes | |
| Historical notes: | |

*front facade, 2000*

Brent was raised in this house by his parents Joseph H. and Corinne Bernstein Glass.

*Brent has been the management consultant for over fifty cultural and educational museums.

### Gleason, Marshall Wilfred (1853-1955)

| | |
|---|---|
| Occupation(s): | industrialist - president, Gleason–Tiebout Glass Co., Brooklyn |
| | inventor - design for glass globes (shades) |
| Civic Activism: | a founder, Brooklyn Chamber of Commerce; |
| | president, American Glass Ware Association; |
| | member, executive committee, National Association of Glass Manufacturers |
| Marriage(s): | 1889-1928 – Alice Tiebout (1859-1928) |
| Address: | Seventh Street, Garden City |
| Name of estate: | |
| Year of construction: | |
| Style of architecture: | |
| Architect(s): | |
| Landscape architect(s): | |
| House extant: | unconfirmed |

Historical notes:

 The *Long Island Society Register, 1929* lists Marshall W. and Alice Tiebout Gleason as residing on Seventh Street, Garden City.

 He was the son of John Marshall and Mary Jane Baston Gleason of Weymouth, MA.

 Alice Tiebout Gleason was the daughter of Cornelius Henry and Maria Bosworth Cother Tiebout of Brooklyn.

 Marshall Wilfred and Alice Tiebout Gleason's son Charles married Helen Winchester Smith and resided in Garden City prior to relocating to Old Brookville. Their daughter Shirley married Joseph Lloyd Bailey and resided in Bronxville, NY.

### Glover, John Irwin (1828-1906)

| | |
|---|---|
| Occupation(s): | architect - designed the first building of Brooklyn Institute of Arts and Sciences |
| | capitalist - Brooklyn builder |
| Marriage(s): | 1849-1906 – Rhoda Ann Hallock (1826-1920) |
| | - Civic Activism: suffragist*; |
| | vice-president, Political Equality League of Queens–Nassau Counties; |
| | member, Baldwin School Board; |
| Address: | Foxhurst and Merrick Roads, Baldwin |
| Name of estate: | |
| Year of construction: | c. 1890 |
| Style of architecture: | Modified Italianate |
| Architect(s): | John Irwin Glover designed his own house and 1892 alterations |
| Landscape architect(s): | |
| House extant: | no |

*architectural sketch front facade, c. 1890*

Historical notes:

 The house was built by John Irwin Glover as his own residence.

 He was the son of Frederick and Susan Terry Glover of Southold.

 Rhoda Ann Hallock Glover was the daughter of Thomas and Christiana Pain Hallock of Mattituck.

 John Irwin and Rhoda Ann Hallock Glover's son Joseph died in 1862 at the age of four. Their son John Graham Glover, who was also an architect, married Emma Louise Prentice. Their daughter Anna, who was a suffragist, married Dr. Nathaniel Matson, the son of Stephen Johnson and Esther Van Bergen Matson, and resided at 1249 Pacific Street, Brooklyn. In 1897, their son John Wheeler Glover married Sarah Alberton and resided in Baldwin. He and Sarah divorced in 1911.

 Glover retired from business due to deafness.

 *Rhoda, who was reputed to be the oldest active Long Island suffragist, marched in the New York City Suffragist Parade at the age of eight-four. [*The Brooklyn Daily Eagle* October 11, 1912, p. 25, and October 7, 1920, p. 3.]

 [For other Long Islanders involved in the suffrage movement *see* Raymond E. Spinzia, "Winning the Franchise: Long Island Activists in the Fight for Woman's Suffrage and Their Opponents, Long Island's Anti-Suffragists." wwwspinzialongislandestates.com.]

 The Glovers' children offered to donate land for the site of an assembly hall and library as a memorial to their parents. [*South Side Messenger* February 5, 1909, p. 1.] In 1921, the twenty-acre estate was sold to Stephen P. Pettit who subdivided the property for business and residential sites. [*The Daily Review* September 3, 1921, p. 1.]

### Gluck, Louise Elizabeth (b. 1943)

| | |
|---|---|
| Occupation(s): | writer - poetry – |
| |         Pulitzer Prize for Poetry, 1993 |
| |         Bollinger Prize, 2001 |
| |         United States Poet Laureate, 2003-2004 |
| |         National Book Award, 2014 |
| |         National Humanities Medal, 2015 |
| |         Nobel Prize in Literature, 2020 |
| | educator - Rosenkranz Writer in Residence, Yale University; |
| |         English lecturer, Williams College, MA |
| | capitalist - director, New England Culinary Institute |
| Marriage(s): | M/1 – 1967-div. 1977 – Charles Schaeffer Hertz, Jr. |
| | M/2 – 1977-div. 1996 – John Dranow |
| |    - educator - started summer writing program, Goddard College, Plainfield, VT |
| |    capitalist - a founder, New England Culinary Institute |
| Address: | 966 Northfield Road, Woodmere |
| Name of estate: | |
| Year of construction: | |
| Style of architecture: | |
| Architect(s): | |
| Landscape architect(s): | |
| House extant: no | |
| Historical notes: | |

Louise is the daughter Daniel and Beatrice Grosby Gluck.


### Goadby, Arthur McMaster (1867-1958)

| | |
|---|---|
| Occupation(s): | financier - partner, W. H. Goadby (stock brokerage firm) |
| Marriage(s): | 1912-1955 – Joanna Adele Morgan (1885-1955) |
| Address: | 280 Narragansette Avenue, Lawrence |
| Name of estate: | *Wistaria* |
| Year of construction: | 1908 |
| Style of architecture: | Shingle |
| Architect(s): | |
| Landscape architect(s): | |
| House extant: yes | |
| Historical notes: | |

    The *Social Register New York, 1933* lists Arthur and Joanna A. Morgan Goadby as residing at *Wistaria* in Lawrence. He was the son of Thomas and Amelia Ann Wood Goadby of Manhattan.
    Joanna Adele Morgan Goadby was the daughter of William Rogers and Elizabeth W. Hunter Morgan, who resided at *Tudor Lodge* in Newport, RI.
    Arthur McMaster and Joanna Adele Morgan Goadby's daughter Dorothy married Robert Snyder Womrath, the son of Arthur Romain and Grace Snyder Womrath of *Saso Hill* in Southport, CT. Their daughter Elsie married Bernard Henry Wood III of Tuxedo Park, NY, and, later, William O. Bloom. Their son William married Giuliana Cinelli, the daughter of Giuseppe Cinelli of Old Greenwich, CT, and Florence, Italy.
    In 1999, the 5,326-square-foot house sold for $750,000.

*Arthur McMaster Goadby residence, front facade*

### Goodhue, Francis Abbot, Jr. (1883-1963)

| | |
|---|---|
| Occupation(s): | financier - president, Brookline Trust Co., Brookline, MA; |
| | president, Bank of the Manhattan Co. (later, Chase |
| |     National Bank; now, Chase Manhattan Bank); |
| | vice-president, First Bank of Boston, Boston, MA; |
| | a founder, French–American Banking Corp.; |
| | a founder and president, International Acceptance Bank, NYC; |
| | president, Bank of Manhattan Safe Deposit Co., NYC; |
| | trustee, Bank For Savings, NYC; |
| | chairman of board, Bank of Manhattan, NYC |
| Civic Activism: | trustee, Phillips Andover Academy, Andover, NH; |
| | chairman of trustees, Bellevue Medical Center, NYC; |
| | member, Interallied Commission for War Purchases and Finance, 1918; |
| | chairman, American Bankers Committee on International Negotiations |
| |     for the Settlement of Short-Term German Credits, 1934-1935 |
| Marriage(s): | 1913-1963 – Nora Forbes Thayer (1889-1988) |
| Address: | 16 Ives Road, Hewlett Bay Park |
| Name of estate: | |
| Year of construction: | |
| Style of architecture: | |
| Architect(s): | |
| Landscape architect(s): | |
| House extant: no | |
| Historical notes: | |

    The *Social Register New York, 1933* lists F. Abbot and Nora F. Thayer Goodhue [Jr.] as residing in Hewlett [Hewlett Bay Park].

    He was the son of Francis Abbot and Elizabeth Johnston Cushing Goodhue, Sr. of Brookline, MA.

    Nora Forbes Thayer Goodhue was the daughter of John Eliot and Evelyn Duncan Forbes Thayer of Massachusetts.

    Francis Abbot and Nora Forbes Thayer Goodhue, Jr.'s daughter Phoebe married Warren Winslow, the son of Charles Gibson Winslow, and, subsequently, Gerrish H. Milliken, Jr. Their son John married Charlotte Barton Streeter, the daughter of Edward and Charlotte L. Warren Streeter, Sr. of Kings Point, and resided in Katonah, NY. [*See* Spinzia, *Long Island's Prominent North Shore Families, vol. II* – Streeter entry.] Their son Stephen married Barbara J. Steed, the daughter of Ralph A. Steed of Bowden, GA, and, later, Judith Relles, the daughter of Nathan Relles. Their son Francis Abbot Goodhue III married Mary Elizabeth Brier, the daughter of Ernest Brier of Grosse Point Farms, MI, and resided in Mt. Kisco, NY.

**Goodwin, Doris Helen Kearns (b. 1943)**

| | |
|---|---|
| Occupation(s): | writer - *Lyndon Johnson and the American Dream*, 1977; *Wait Till Next Time: A Memoir*, 1997; *Character Above All: Ten Presidents From FDR to George Bush*, 1996; *History for No Ordinary Time: Franklin and Eleanor Roosevelt: The Home Front During World War II*, 1994 (for which she was awarded the Pulitzer Prize); *Every Four Years: Presidential Campaign Coverage from 1896-2000*, 2000; *The Fitzgeralds and the Kennedys*, 2002; *Team of Rivals: The Political Genius of Abraham Lincoln*, 2005 (for which she was awarded the Lincoln Prize); *The Bully Pulpit: Roosevelt, William Howard Taft, and the Golden Age of Journalism*, 2014 (for which she was awarded the Andrew Carnegie Medal for Excellence in Non-Fiction); *Leadership: In Turbulant Times*, 2018 |
| | capitalist - director, Northwest Airlines |
| | educator - professor of government and the American presidency, Harvard University, Cambridge, MA |
| | entertainer and associate professions - hostess, "What's the Big Idea?" (television program); presidential commentator, numerous television programs |
| | journalist - sports |
| Civic Activism: | member, Harvard Board of Overseers |
| Marriage(s): | 1975-2018 – Richard Naradof Goodwin (1931-2018) |
| | - attorney - clerked for United States Supreme Court Justice Felix Frankfurter |
| | educator - fellow, Wesleyan University, Middletown, CT; professor, Public Affairs, Massachusetts Institute of Technology, Cambridge, MA |
| | journalist - political editor, *Rolling Stone* |
| | statesman - Deputy Assistant Secretary of State for Inter-American affairs |
| | politician - Secretary General of International Peace Corps; |
| | writer - *The American Condition*; *Promises to Keep: A Call for a New American Revolution*, 1988; *Remembering America: A Voice From the Sixties* (a memoir); *Triumph or Tragedy*; numerous articles in journals |
| | Civic Activism: president, Harvard Law Review |
| Address: | 125 Southard Avenue, Rockville Centre |
| Name of estate: | |
| Year of construction: | 1927 |
| Style of architecture: | Neo-Tudor |
| Architect(s): | |
| Landscape architect(s): | |
| House extant: yes | |
| Historical notes: | |

Doris was raised in this house by her parents Michael Francis Aloysius and Helen Witt Miller Kearns.

Richard Naradof Goodwin was the son of Joseph C. and Belle Fisher Goodwin of Massachusetts. Richard had previously been married to Sandra Gail Leverant.

Richard Naradof and Doris Helen Kearns Goodwin's son Joseph married Victoria Bonney.

In 2004, the 1,840-square-foot house sold for $560,000.

*front facade, 2000*

### Goodwin, Robert Henning (1878-1929)

Occupation(s): shipping - president, Funch, Edye, & Co.

Marriage(s): 1903-1929 – Lucy Kathryna Auel (1876-1932)

Address: Piermont Avenue, Hewlett Bay Park
Name of estate: *Cedar Corners*
Year of construction:
Style of architecture:
Architect(s):
Landscape architect(s):
House extant: unconfirmed
Historical notes:

The *Long Island Society Register, 1929* lists Robert H. and Lucy K. Auel Goodwin as residing at *Cedar Corners* in Hewlett [Hewlett Bay Park].
He was the son of Robert Goodwin of Brooklyn.
Lucy Kathryna Auel Goodwin was the daughter of Charles Auel of Brooklyn.
Robert Henning and Lucy Kathryna Auel Goodwin's daughter Virginia married Edward Fitch Beddall II of Manhattan. Their son Robert Auel Goodwin married Anne Elaine Sokale.


### Gormley, John Vincent (1894-1946)

Occupation(s): financier - investment counsel, Mellon Securities Corporation
of New York

Marriage(s): 1920-1946 – Edna May Yenser (1897-1990)
- artists' model - 1915-1920
  real estate agent - member, Ben Kasper Realtors, Levittown
  Civic Activism: Gray Lady volunteer, American Red Cross,
  Mitchell Field, during World War II

Address: 41 Meadow Street, Garden City
Name of estate:
Year of construction: 1923
Style of architecture: Neo-Tudor
Architect(s):
Landscape architect(s):
House extant: yes
Historical notes:

At the time of John's death, the Gormleys were residing at 41 Meadow Street in Garden City.
John Vincent and Edna May Yenser Gormley's daughter Betty married Roger Wolcott Hubbell, the son of John Platt and Dorothy Peters Hubbell, Sr. of Garden City. Their daughter Barbara married Milton M. Ashley, the son of John D. Ashley of Swifton, AR, and, later, ____ Davis with whom she resided at Bay Village, OH.

*front facade, 2005*

### Gray, James McIlvaine (1872-1942)

| | |
|---|---|
| Occupation(s): | attorney - partner, Gray and Tomlin, Brooklyn*; <br> partner, Owens and Gray, Brooklyn; <br> partner, Owens, Gray, and Tomlin, Brooklyn |
| | industrialist - director and counsel, Buick Motor Co. <br> writer - *Fraudulent Conveyances*, 1896; <br> *Taxation of Railroads Under Federal Ownership*, 1906; <br> numerous articles in law reviews and magazines |
| Marriage(s): | 1904-1942 – Lillian De Mott (1879-1961) |
| Address: | 111 Ninth Street, Garden City |
| Name of estate: | |
| Year of construction: | 1927 |
| Style of architecture: | Modified Dutch Colonial Revival |
| Architect(s): | |
| Landscape architect(s): | |
| House extant: yes | |
| Historical notes: | |

*front facade, 2008*

The house was built by James McIlvaine Gray.

The *Long Island Society Register, 1929* lists James M. and Lillian DeMott Gray as residing at 111 Ninth Street, Garden City.

He was the son of The Reverend Joseph and Mrs. Mary A. Miller Gray.

*Gray was the attorney for the Brooklyn Dodgers Baseball Team.

He was killed in a railroad accident at the Garden City station of the Long Island Rail Road. [*The New York Times* February 2, 1942, p. 15.]

Lillian De Mott Gray was the daughter of John W. and Charlotte Davison DeMott.

In 1999 the house was remodeled.

### Greason, Samuel, Jr. (1887-1974)

| | |
|---|---|
| Occupation(s): | attorney - judge - First District Court <br> financier - director, Central National Bank of Mineola <br> politician - Nassau County Ombudsman, 1966-1971; <br> Nassau County Commissioner of Accounts |
| Civic Activism: | director, Garden City Country Club |
| Marriage(s): | 1918-1974 – Rita Leone Pomeroy (1892-1991) |
| Address: | 61 Whitehall Boulevard, Garden City |
| Name of estate: | |
| Year of construction: | 1926 |
| Style of architecture: | Cottage |
| Architect(s): | |
| Landscape architect(s): | |
| House extant: yes | |
| Historical notes: | |

The house was built by Samuel Greason, Jr.

The *Long Island Society Register, 1929* lists Samuel and Rita L. Pomeroy Greason, Jr. as residing at 61 Whitehall Boulevard, Garden City.

He was the son of Samuel and Elizabeth Monroe Gleason, Sr. of Brooklyn.

Rita Leone Pomeroy Greason was the daughter of Henry Childs and Ida Florence Pearce Pomeroy of Brooklyn.

Samuel and Rita Leone Pomeroy Greason, Jr.'s son Craig married Suzanne Bartlett, the daughter of William Lawson Bartlett.

*front facade, 2001*

### Green, Harry Thomas Sinclair (1864-1942)

| | |
|---|---|
| Occupation(s): | financier - vice-president, National City Bank; president, International Banking Corp. |
| | capitalist - president, Philippine Railway Co.; director, Sixty Wall Street |
| Marriage(s): | 1901-1929 – Winifred Rudge (1867-1929) |
| Address: | Woodside Drive and Coombs Avenue, Hewlett Bay Park |
| Name of estate: | |
| Year of construction: | |
| Style of architecture: | |
| Architect(s): | |
| Landscape architect(s): | Mary Rutherfurd Jay, 1920-1921 (for H. T. S. Green) |
| House extant: unconfirmed | |
| Historical notes: | |

The *Long Island Society Register, 1929* lists Harry T. S. and Winifred Rudge Green as residing at the intersection of Woodside Drive and Coombs Avenue in Hewlett [Hewlett Bay Park].

He was the son of Thomas and Jane Stewart Green.

Harry Thomas Sinclair and Winifred Rudge Green's daughter Claire married Charles Arland Maitland Freaks, the son of Sir Frederick Freaks of *Halford Manor* in Shipston-on-the-Stour, England. Their daughter Veronica married Werner Conrad von Clemm, the son of Baron Gustav Clemm von Hohenberg of Hesse, Germany, and resided in Syosset.

### Green, Walton Atwater, Sr. (1881-1954)

| | |
|---|---|
| Occupation(s): | attorney |
| | publisher - editor and publisher, *Boston Journal*, 1913-1917 |
| | financier - member, Hodges, Dunham and Co. (stock brokerage firm) |
| | writer - *Corsair* (novel made into a motion picture of the same title) |
| Civic Activism: | chief prohibition investigator, Washington, DC, 1925; chairman, Massachusetts Committee on State Constabulary, 1916-1917; member, Massachusetts Committee on Public Safety, 1917 |
| Marriage(s): | M/1 – 1904-div. 1933 – Eleanor Roberts Munroe (1884-1967) - journalist - *Boston Journal* |
| | M/2 – 1933-1954 – Elsie J. King (1904-1981) |
| Address: | Sealy Lane, Lawrence |
| Name of estate: | |
| Year of construction: | |
| Style of architecture: | |
| Architect(s): | |
| Landscape architect(s): | |
| House extant: unconfirmed | |
| Historical notes: | |

The *Long Island Society Register, 1929* lists Walter A. and Eleanor Munroe Green [Sr.] as residing on Sealy Lane, Cedarhurst [Lawrence]. The 1920 Census lists Walton Atwater and Eleanor Munroe Green as residing on Central Avenue, Lawrence.

He was the son of George Walton and Harriet Brodhead Atwater Green of Manhattan.

Eleanor Roberts Munroe Green was the daughter of Dr. Henry Smith Munroe. She later married James Freeman Curtis with whom she resided at *Willowmere* in Roslyn Harbor. [See Spinzia, *Long Island's Prominent North Shore Families, vol. 1* – Curtis entry.]

Walton Atwater and Eleanor Roberts Munroe Green, Sr.'s son Munroe was an infant at the time of his death in 1910. Their son George died in 1920 at the age of twelve. Their daughter Gloria married Donald Buckingham Gaddesden Horn, the son of William Gaddesden Horn. Their son Douglas married Cynthia Pruyn.

Elsie J. King Green was the daughter of Patrick D. King of New Haven, CT.

Walton Atwater and Elsie J. King Green, Sr.'s son Walton Atwater Green, Jr. married Martha Manheim, the daughter of Paul Earnest Mankeum of East Hampton.

The Smithsonian's Walton Atwater Green National Museum of Natural History was named in Green's honor.

### Greene, Herbert Gouverneur (1881-1974)

| | |
|---|---|
| Occupation(s): | attorney - partner, Arnold and Greene |
| Civic Activism: | assistant secretary and treasurer, Rockaway Hunting Club, 1946 |
| Marriage(s): | 1910-1962 – Elizabeth Porter Searles (1884-1962) |
| Address: | 67 Washington Avenue, Lawrence |
| Name of estate: | |
| Year of construction: | 1908 |
| Style of architecture: | Victorian |
| Architect(s): | |
| Landscape architect(s): | |
| House extant: yes | |
| Historical notes: | |

The *Long Island Society Register, 1929* lists Herbert G. and Elizabeth P. Searles Green [sic] as residing on Washington Avenue, Cedarhurst [Lawrence].

He was the son of Joseph Warren and Julia Strong Sherman Greene of Brooklyn.

Elizabeth Porter Searles Greene was the daughter of James Harvey and Eloise Katherine Rumney Searles of Rome, NY.

Herbert Gouverneur and Elizabeth Porter Searles Greene's daughter Eloise married Francis Everit Holbrook, the son of Arthur Holbrook of Manhattan. Their daughter Elizabeth married Warren Parsons Thorpe, Jr., the son of Warren Parsons and Helen Prentiss Converse Thorpe Sr. of Lawrence.

In 2000, the 2,973-square-foot house sold for $573,000.


### Greenfield, Jerry (b. 1951)

| | |
|---|---|
| Occupation(s): | a founder, with Bennett R. Cohen, and first CEO of Ben and Jerry's Homemade Holdings, Inc. (ice cream manufacturing firm)* |
| Civic Activism: | a founder, One Percent for Peace; a founder, Ben and Jerry's Foundation |
| Marriage(s): | 1987 – Elizabeth Skarie - psychologist |
| Address: | West Loines Avenue, Merrick |
| Name of estate: | |
| Year of construction: | |
| Style of architecture: | High Ranch |
| Architect(s): | |
| Landscape architect(s): | |
| House extant: yes | |
| Historical notes: | |

Jerry was raised in this house by his parents Malcolm and Mildred Kuperstein Greenfield.

*When it was decided that Jerry would be the first CEO of Ben and Jerry's, his longtime friend and co-founder of the company Ben would have his name placed first on the ice cream containers as a consolation prize.

### Greenleaf, John Cameron, Sr. (1878-1958)

| | |
|---|---|
| Occupation(s): | architect - a founder and partner, with J. Laying Mills, Mills & Greenleaf, NYC |
| Marriage(s): | 1907-1958 – Marion Constance Bacon (1886-1971)<br>- Civic Activism: vice-president, Five Towns Women's Exchange, 1936 |
| Address: | 37 Meadowview Avenue, Hewlett Bay Park |

Name of estate:
Year of construction:
Style of architecture:
Architect(s):
Landscape architect(s):
House extant: unconfirmed
Historical notes:

The *Long Island Society Register, 1929* lists John C. and M. Constance Bacon Greenleaf as residing in Hewlett [Hewlett Bay Park]. The 1930 Census lists the Greenleafs at this address.

He was the son of Dr. Richard Cranch and Mrs. Adeline Emma Stone Greenleaf, who resided at *Windyside* in Lenox, MA.

Marion Constance Bacon Greenleaf was the daughter of William B. Bacon and the niece of Secretary of State Robert Bacon, who resided at *Old Acres* in Old Westbury. [*See* Spinzia, *Long Island's Prominent North Shore Families, vol. I* – Bacon entry.] Marion's sister Elizabeth married Joseph Swain Lovering, who resided at *Sunny Ridge* in Hewlett Harbor.

John Cameron and Marion Constance Bacon Greenleaf, Sr.'s daughter Elizabeth married William B. Chappell and resided in Mount Kisco, NY. Their daughter Adeline married Alfred Oliphant Norris with whom she resided in Lawrence. Adeline later married Elias C. Atkins and resided in Bedford Village, NY. Their daughter Joan married Clifford Duke Wright. Their son John Cameron Greenleaf, Jr. resided in Tucson, AZ.

In 1941, the house was purchased from Greenleaf by Maurice L. Gaffney. [*The Brooklyn Daily Eagle* October 19, 1941, p. B3.]

### Grew, Henry Sturgis, Jr. (1901-1966)

| | |
|---|---|
| Occupation(s): | industrialist - director, Equinox Mills, Anderson, SC (textile manufacturing firm);<br>director, Millville Manufacturing Co., Millville, NJ (textile manufacturing firm)<br>merchant - vice-president and director, Wellington, Sears, & Co., NYC (wholesale textile merchant) |
| Marriage(s): | 1935-1966 – Selina Richards Wood (1911-2001) |
| Address: | 285 Breezyway, Lawrence |

Name of estate:
Year of construction:
Style of architecture:
Architect(s):
Landscape architect(s):
House extant: no
Historical notes:

In 1946, Grew purchased the house from James Henry Work, Jr. [*The New York Times* October 10, 1946, p. 48.]

The *Social Register New York, 1948* lists Henry S. and Selina R. Wood Grew, Jr. as residing at 285 Breeze Way [sic] in Lawrence.

He was the son of Henry Sturgis and Ethel Hooper Grew, Sr. of Boston, MA.

Selina Richards Wood Grew was the daughter of Richard Davis and Louisa Lawrence Schroeder Wood, Sr. of Philadelphia, PA. She subsequently married Roger Sanderson Hewlett of Hewlett Neck.

Henry Sturgis and Selina Richards Wood Grew, Jr.'s son Joseph married Sarah Winslow Loomis, the daughter of Luther Loomis of Sharon, CT. Their daughter Selina married W. Allen Rossiter, the son of Arthur Wickes Rossiter, Jr. of Lloyd Harbor, and resided in Lincoln, MA. [*See* Spinzia, *Long Island's Prominent North Shore Families, vol. II* – Rossiter entry.] Their son Robert married Stella Elizabeth Waugh, the daughter of Edward Walter Rail Waugh of Raleigh, NC, and resided in Chapel Hill, NC.

### Griffin, Dominic Bodkin, Jr. (1914-2014)

Occupation(s): shipping - Cunard White Star Line
industrialist - Grumman Aircraft Engineering Co., Bethpage, NY (later, Grumman Aerospace Corp.; now, Northrop Grumman); president, T. A. D. Jones Co. (Gulf Oil Corporation subsidiary)

Marriage(s): M/1 – 1940-1997 – Margaret L. Robinson (d. 1997)
M/2 – 2000-2014 – Jane Hutchinson (1921-2016)

Address: Kensington Road, Garden City
Name of estate:
Year of construction:
Style of architecture:
Architect(s):
Landscape architect(s):
House extant: unconfirmed
Historical notes:

Dominic Bodkin Griffin, Jr. was the son of Dominic Bodkin and Elizabeth Scott Kelly Griffin, Sr. of Garden City.
Margaret L. Robinson Griffin was the daughter of John J. Robinson of Garden City.
Dominic Bodkin and Margaret L. Robinson Griffin, Jr.'s daughter Ann married John R. Selinger, Sr. and resides in Washington, DC. Their son Dominic Bodkin Griffin III married Mary Archer Whitcombe of Suva, Fiji, and resides in Honolulu, HI.
Jane Hutchinson Griffin was the daughter of Charles F. and Elizabeth Keegan Hutchinson. Jane had previously been married to Arthur H. Munkenbeck, Jr. with whom she resided in Garden City.
As a youth, Dominic witnessed Charles Lindbergh's takeoff for his historic 1927 trans-Atlantic flight. [*See* Spinzia, *Long Island's Prominent North Shore Families, vol. I* – Lindbergh entry.]
*[See following entry for additional family information.]*


### Griffin, Dominic Bodkin, Sr. (1885-1948)

Occupation(s): attorney - counsel for Pennsylvania Railroad

Marriage(s): 1910 – Elizabeth Scott Kelly

Address: 49 Hilton Avenue, Garden City
Name of estate:
Year of construction: 1888
Style of architecture: French Empire
Architect(s):
Landscape architect(s):
House extant: yes
Historical notes:

*front facade, 2009*

The *Long Island Society Register, 1929* lists Dominic Bodkin and Elizabeth Scott Kelly Griffin [Sr.] as residing at 49 Hilton Avenue, Garden City.
He was the son of Dr. John Griffin of Brooklyn.
Elizabeth Scott Kelly Griffin was the daughter of Judge William J. and Mrs. Elizabeth A. Scott Kelly. Kelly served as Judge of the Appellate Division in the New York State Supreme Court.
Dominic Bodkin and Elizabeth Scott Kelly Griffin, Sr.'s daughter Mary married Emil Schiess, Jr. of Merrick and, later, Joseph F. Kern, Sr. with whom she resided in Garden City. Their son Domenic Bodkin Griffin, Jr. married Margaret L. Robinson and resided in Garden City. Their son William married Elizabeth Shoumatoff, the daughter of Leo Shoumatoff of *Hidden Garden* in Locust Valley.
*[See previous entry for additional family information.]*
In 2016, the 3,017-square-foot house sold for $1.9 million.

### Griswold, John Augustus, Sr. (1882-1940)

| | |
|---|---|
| Occupation(s): | capitalist -  secretary, Interborough–Metropolitan Co.<br>financier -  executive, Guaranty Trust Co. |
| Marriage(s): | 1909-1940 – Helene Robson (1886-1968) |
| Address: | 29 Piermont Avenue, Hewlett Bay Park |
| Name of estate: | |
| Year of construction: | 1908 |
| Style of architecture: | Colonial Revival |
| Architect(s): | |
| Landscape architect(s): | |
| House extant: | yes |
| Historical notes: | |

The *Long Island Society Register, 1929* lists John A. and Helen [sic] Robson Griswold [Sr.] as residing in Hewlett [Hewlett Bay Park]. The 1930 Census lists the Griswolds as residing on Franklin Avenue in Hewlett.

He was the son of John W. Griswold of Troy, NY.

John Augustus and Helene Robson Griswold, Sr.'s son John Augustus Griswold, Jr. married Agness Devens Osborne, the daughter of the Mayor of Auburn, NY, Charles Devens Osbourne. Agness' great-grandfather, David Munson Osborne; grandfather, Thomas Mott Osborne; and father, Charles Devens Osborne, served as mayors of Auburn, NY.

In 1924 the house was purchased by Ewing Reginald Philbin, Sr. [*The New York Times* August 26, 1924, p. 24.]

In 1967 the house was remodeled.

*front facade, 2006*

### Gross, Andre Eugene (1890-1954)

| | |
|---|---|
| Occupation(s): | financier -  head, bond department, Post and Flagg, NYC;<br>member, McDonnell and Co., NYC (brokerage firm);<br>member, McClure, Jones, and Reed (brokerage firm) |
| Civic Activism: | a founder, Junior Anti-Suffrage League |
| Marriage(s): | 1920 – Elinor Whitney Kendall<br>- Civic Activism:  member, Junior Anti-Suffrage League |
| Address: | 122 Salisbury Avenue, Garden City |
| Name of estate: | |
| Year of construction: | c. 1928 |
| Style of architecture: | Modified Colonial Revival |
| Architect(s): | |
| Landscape architect(s): | |
| House extant: | yes |
| Historical notes: | |

The house was built by Andre Eugene Gross.

The *Long Island Society Register, 1929* lists Andre E. and Elinor W. Kendall Gross as residing at 122 Salisbury Avenue, Garden City.

*front facade, 2015*

He was the son of Charles E. M. and Mary L. Miller Gross of New York City.

Elinor Whitney Kendall Gross was the daughter of William Beals and Katharine Varnum Whitney Kendall of Garden City. Elinor's sister Katharine married Marshall Denny, Sr. and resided in Garden City. Her sister Marjorie married Maitland Lathrop Bishop, Sr. and, subsequently, Howard Wainwright.

Andre Eugene and Elinor Whitney Kendall Gross's daughter Elinor married Frank Stephen Kochle, the son of Frank J. Kochle of Hempstead.

In 2015, the 2,600-square-foot house, with four bedrooms and two and a half bathrooms, sold for $900,100.

### Gruner, Otto Harry, Jr. (1903-1980)

Occupation(s):

Marriage(s): 1926-1980 – Harriot Hudson Coffin (1906-1981)
- Civic Activism: chair, toy center, Five Towns Community Chest

Address: 9 Combs Avenue, Woodmere
Name of estate:
Year of construction:
Style of architecture:
Architect(s):
Landscape architect(s):
House extant: unconfirmed
Historical notes:

Otto Harry Gruner, Jr. was the son of Otto Harry and Katharine Hays Drake Gruner, Sr. of Hewlett.
Harriot Hudson Coffin Gruner was the daughter of John Roberts Coffin.
Otto Harry and Harriot Hudson Coffin Gruner, Jr.'s daughter Harriot married Henry Lawrence Ross, Jr. and, later, Andrew Carnegie Rockefeller, the son of James Stillman and Nancy Campbell Sherlock Carnegie Rockefeller, Sr. Their son Otto Harry Gruner III married Nancy Vaughan Evans, the daughter of Dr. Frank Alexander and Mrs. Sara Elizabeth Fischer Evans.
*[See following entry for additional family information.]*


### Gruner, Otto Harry, Sr. (1880-1942)

Occupation(s): financier - member, New York Stock Exchange

Marriage(s): 1903-1942 – Katharine Hays Drake (1883-1968)

Address: *[unable to determine street address]*, Hewlett
Name of estate:
Year of construction:
Style of architecture:
Architect(s):
Landscape architect(s):
House extant: unconfirmed
Historical notes:

*The Brooklyn Daily Eagle* June 28, 1908, lists O. H. Gruner [Sr.] and family as renting the *Mohan Cottage* on Broadway in Hewlett. The *Social Register Summer, 1910* lists, O. Harry and Katharine H. Drake as residing at *Rose Bush Cottage* in Cedarhurst. The *Long Island Society Register, 1929* lists them as residing in Hewlett.
He was the son of Siegfried and Annie Josephine Dater des Garets Gruner. Otto's sister Charlotte married Dr. Louis Faugeres Bishop, Sr., the son of James and Mary Faugeres Ellis Bishop, and resided at *Bishopgate* in East Hampton. [*See* Spinzia, *Long Island's Prominent Families in the Town of East Hampton–* Bishop entry.]
Katharine Hays Drake Gruner was the daughter of Simeon Joseph and Katharine Hays Drake of Manhattan.
Otto Harry and Katharine Hays Drake Gruner, Sr.'s daughter Cathleen married Lyman Tibbals Whitehead, Jr. and resided in Locust Valley. Their son Otto Harry Gruner, Jr. married Harriet Hudson Coffin and resided in Woodmere.
*[See previous entry for additional family information.]*

### Gulick, Ernestus Schenck (1865-1913)

| | |
|---|---|
| Occupation(s): | real estate agent - a founder, Alger & Gulick, Brooklyn (real estate and insurance firm) (later, Lovett & Gulick; then Ernestus Gulick & Co.); president, Ernestus Gulick & Co., Brooklyn |
| | capitalist - president, Hempstead South Co.; vice-president, Garden City Estates; director, Montauk Theatre Co.; treasurer, Chaumont Co., Chaumont, NY; president, Long Island Estates |
| | financier - vice-president, Garden City Securities Co. |
| Marriage(s): | |
| Address: | Stewart Avenue, Garden City |
| Name of estate: | |
| Year of construction: | |
| Style of architecture: | Neo-Georgian |
| Architect(s): | Kirby, Petit, and Green designed the house (for Gulick) |
| Landscape architect(s): | |
| House extant: unconfirmed | |
| Historical notes: | |

The house was built by Ernestus Schenck Gulick.
He was the son of The Reverend Uriah de Hart and Mrs. Virginia Schenck Gulick.
The house was later owned by William K. English, who sold it in 1920. [*The New York Times* June 6, 1920, p. 101.]

*front facade, c. 1909*

### Gurney, Thomas Nichols (1877-1947)

| | |
|---|---|
| Occupation(s): | merchant - director, Lindsley Hanf & Co., Newark, NJ (commission merchants of woolen and worsted goods); president, Gurney Security Paper Co. (marketed paper for checks and securities) |
| | industrialist - vice-president, Kirkman Soap Co. (merged into Colgate–Palmolive–Peet Co. in 1930) |
| | inventor - created the special type of paper used for checks and securities |
| Marriage(s): | 1906-1947 – Ethel Kirkman (1879-1961) |
| Address: | 59 Third Street, Garden City |
| Name of estate: | |
| Year of construction: | 1924 |
| Style of architecture: | Modified Colonial Revival |
| Architect(s): | |
| Landscape architect(s): | |
| House extant: yes | |
| Historical notes: | |

The house was built by Thomas Nichols Gurney. [*The Garden City News* October 24, 1923, p. 3.]

The *Long Island Society Register, 1929* lists Thomas Nichols and Ethel Kirkman Gurney as residing on Rockaway Avenue, Garden City. The 1940 Census lists them at 59 Third Street, Garden City.

He was the son of Richard and Clara Nichols Gurney of Brooklyn.

Ethel Kirkman Gurney was the daughter of Alexander Samson and Esther Field Coleman Kirkman, Sr. of Brooklyn and Garden City.

Thomas Nichols and Ethel Kirkman Gurney's son John married Margaret Jane Peterkin, the daughter of DeWitt and Margaret Ella O'Brien Peterkin, Sr. of Garden City. Their daughter Esther married William Morris Cruikshank, Jr., the son of William Morris and Edwina Richards Bigelow Cruikshank, Sr. of Garden City. Their daughter Ethel married Franklin Drake Mooney, Jr., the son of Franklin Drake and Grace A. Munson Mooney, Sr. of Garden City.

In 2017, the 7,412-square-foot house, with ten bedrooms and five and a half bathrooms, sold for $2.3 million.

*front facade, 2008*

### Gwynne, Frederick Walker (1884-1935)

| | |
|---|---|
| Occupation(s): | financier - partner, Gwynne Brothers (stock brokerage firm) |
| Marriage(s): | 1916-1935 – Dorothy Goddard Ficken (1886-1978) |

- artist - "Sunny Jim," aka "Sun-ny ," posters and illustrations on
Force Cereal packaging*
entertainer and associated professions -
silent motion picture actress:
"A Suspicious Wife," 1914;
"A Yellow Streak," 1915;
"It May Be Your Daughter," 1916
Civic Activism: active in war relief

| | |
|---|---|
| Address: | Ocean Avenue, Woodmere |
| Name of estate: | |
| Year of construction: | |
| Style of architecture: | Colonial Revival |
| Architect(s): | |
| Landscape architect(s): | |
| House extant: unconfirmed | |
| Historical notes: | |

In 1921, Frederick Walker Gwynne purchased the house, which was situated on two acres, from the Frank Cotter Company. [*The Standard Union* May 29, 1921, p. 12.]

He was the son of The Reverend Dr. Walter and Mrs. Helen Lee Gwynne of Summit, NJ. Frederick's brother Arthur married Mildred Van Schaick and resided at *Mill Cove* in Lloyd Harbor. [*See* Spinzia, *Long Island's Prominent North Shore Families, vol. I* - Gwynne entry.] Frederick died due to complications of a sinus surgery.

Dorothy Goddard Ficken Gwynne was the daughter of Henry Edwards and Josephine Preston Hubbard Ficken.

Frederick Walker and Dorothy Goddard Ficken Gwynne's infant son Bowers died in 1917, Their daughter Dorothy died in 1919. Their son Frederick Hubbard Gwynne, aka Fred Gwynne, the noted motion picture, theater, and television actor, married Jean Rennard, the daughter of John Townsend and Ruth Merritt Gaynor Rennard of Uniondale. Jean was the granddaughter of New York City Mayor William Jay Gaynor whose estate *Deepwells Farm* was located in St. James. [*See* Spinzia, *Long Island: A Guide to New York's Suffolk and Nassau Counties – Deepwells Farm –* Estate of William Jay Gaynor – *Deepwells*, St. James.] Fred Gwynne subsequently married Deborah Flater.

*The Force Food Company of Buffalo, NY, became the A. C. Fincken & Co. Ltd. and eventually became a subsidiary of Nestle. In 2013 the manufacture of the whole wheat flake cereal ceased due to poor sales.

[*See following entry for additional family information.*]


### Gwynne, Walter Lee (1881-1955)

| | |
|---|---|
| Occupation(s): | financier - partner, Gwynne Brothers (stock brokerage firm) |
| Marriage(s): | 1926-1995 – Anita Ingersoll (1891-1970) |
| Address: | Piermont Avenue, Hewlett Bay Park |
| Name of estate: | |
| Year of construction: | |
| Style of architecture: | |
| Architect(s): | |
| Landscape architect(s): | |
| House extant: unconfirmed | |
| Historical notes: | |

The *Long Island Society Register, 1929* lists W. Lee and Anita Ingersoll Gwynne as residing in Manhattan. The *Social Register Summer, 1932* lists the Gwynnes as residing on Piermont Road, Hewlett [Hewlett Bay Park].

He was the son of The Reverend Dr. Walter and Mrs. Helen Bowers Lee Gwynne of Summit, NJ.

Anita Ingersoll Gwynne was the daughter of Judge Charles Dennis Ingersoll of Manhattan. She had previously been married to Roger Medina Minton, the son of Charles Telfair Minton of Manhattan. Roger Medina and Anita Ingersoll Minton's daughter Anita married Ricardo Angelo Mestres II and resided at *Bayberry Hill* in Upper Brookville. [*See* Spinzia, *Long Island's Prominent North Shore Families, vol. I* – Mestres entry.]

Walter Lee and Anita Ingersoll Gwynne's daughter Leeanne married Eugene Kimbark MacColl and resided in Portland, OR.

[*See previous entry for additional family information.*]

### Hadden, James Elnathan Smith (1852-1914)

| | |
|---|---|
| Occupation(s): | capitalist - Hadden & Co., NYC (silk importer) |
| | financier - banker, London, England |
| Marriage(s): | 1880-1914 – Emily Georgina Hamilton (d. 1925) |
| Address: | Jerusalem Avenue, Uniondale |
| Name of estate: | *Uniondale Farm* |

Year of construction:
Style of architecture:
Architect(s):
Landscape architect(s):
House extant: no
Historical notes:

   The *Social Register Summer, 1910* lists Mrs. and Mrs. J. E. Smith as residing at *Uniondale Farm* in Hempstead [Uniondale].
   He was the son of William Alexander and Frances Sanderson Smith Hadden of Manhattan.
   Emily Georgina Hamilton Hadden was the daughter of James Augustus and Mary W. Hamilton.
   James Elnathan Smith and Emily Georgina Hamilton Hadden's son Hamilton Hadden, Sr. married Anita Leslu Peabody, the daughter of Charles Augustus and Charlotte Damon Peabody, Jr. of Cold Spring Harbor, and resided at *Dogwood* in Jericho and, later, at *Harbor Lights* in Cold Spring Harbor. [*See* Spinzia, *Long Island's Prominent North Shore Families* – Hadden entries – and *Long Island's Prominent North Shore Families, vol. II* – Peabody entry.] Their daughter Frances remained unmarried.
   By 1918 Mrs. Hadden had relocated to her estate *Dogwood* in Jericho.


### Halsted, Gilbert Coutant, Jr. (1893-1974)

| | |
|---|---|
| Occupation(s): | industrialist - chairman of board, E. S. Halsted, Jersey City, NJ, and Brooklyn (cotton and burlap bag manufacturer) |
| Marriage(s): | 1916-1974 – Marjory Royce (1894-1994) |
| Address: | 58 Wellington Road, Garden City |

Name of estate:
Year of construction:
Style of architecture:
Architect(s):
Landscape architect(s):
House extant: no
Historical notes:

   The *Long Island Society Register, 1929* lists Mr. and Mrs. Gilbert C. Halsted as residing at 58 Wellington Road, Garden City.
   He was the son of Gilbert Coutant and Isabel Camerden Halsted, Sr. of Brooklyn. His brother Harold married Grace Ward Bower and resided in Garden City.
   Marjory Royce Halsted was the daughter of Henry Herbert and Elizabeth Monroe Royce of Brooklyn.
   Gilbert Coutant and Marjory Royce Halsted, Jr.'s daughter Nancy married Waldo Watson Simons, the son of William Butterfield Simons of Rockville Centre.
   *[See following entry for additional family information.]*

### Halsted, Harold Camerden (1891-1970)

| | |
|---|---|
| Occupation(s): | industrialist - chairman of board, E. S. Halsted, Jersey City, NJ, and Brooklyn (cotton and burlap bag manufacturer) |
| Marriage(s): | 1918-1968 – Grace Ward Bower (1898-1968) |
| Address: | 59 Wellington Road, Garden City |
| Name of estate: | |
| Year of construction: | c. 1928 |
| Style of architecture: | Colonial Revival |
| Architect(s): | |
| Landscape architect(s): | |
| House extant: yes | |
| Historical notes: | |

    The house was built by Harold Camerden Halsted.
    The *Long Island Society Register, 1929* lists Harold Camerden and Grace Ward Bower Halsted as residing at 59 Wellington Road, Garden City.
    He was the son of Gilbert Coutant and Isabel Camerden Halsted, Sr. of Brooklyn. His brother Gilbert married Marjory Royce and resided in Garden City.
    Grace Ward Bower Halsted was the daughter of George Hoyle Bower of Memphis, TN.
    Harold Camerden and Grace Ward Bower Halsted's daughter Barbara married Ernst Pfrunder, the son of Heinrich Pfrunder of Zurich, Switzerland. Their son William, who resided in Bellport, married Alice Osborn, the daughter of Franklin Osborn of Franklin, NJ, and, subsequently, Evelyn Lerch.
    By 1947 Harold Camerden and Grace Ward Bower Halsted had relocated to Glen Head. [*The New York Times* February 23, 1947, p. R3.]

*front facade, 2000*

## Hamill, Robert Lyon, Sr. (1899-1974)

| | |
|---|---|
| Occupation(s): | capitalist - president and director, The Lyon Co., Chicago, IL (timber, real estate, turpentine, and farming in Mississippi, Alabama, Florida, and Mexico); |
| | partner, Sanderson & Porter, NYC (later, Sanderson & Porter, Inc.) (engineering and construction firm); |
| | president and director, Sanderson & Porter, Inc.; |
| | president and director, The Hamill Corp.; |
| | president, The 700 Park Corp., NYC; |
| | director, Pan American World Airways, Inc.; |
| | director, Liberian Development Corp.; |
| | director, Bermuda Properties Ltd.; |
| | financier - director, Metropolitan Life Insurance Co.; |
| | chairman of board, Lawrence–Cedarhurst Bank |
| Civic Activism: | president, Sailor's Snug Harbor, NYC; |
| | mayor, Village of Lawrence; |
| | member, advisory council, New York State Department of Commerce, 1950-1952; |
| | trustee, Society of New York Hospitals, 1955-1960; |
| | president, Lawrence School Board; |
| | trustee, Miss Porter's School, Farmington, CT; |
| | chairman, advisory board, New York Exchange for Woman's Work, NYC; |
| | president, Nassau County Chapter, American Red Cross, during World War II |
| Marriage(s): | 1920-1973 – Katharine Delano Porter (1900-1973) |
| Address: | Longwood Crossing, Lawrence |
| Name of estate: | |
| Year of construction: | |
| Style of architecture: | |
| Architect(s): | |
| Landscape architect(s): | |
| House extant: unconfirmed | |
| Historical notes: | |

The *Long Island Society Register, 1929* lists Robert L. and Katherine [sic] D. Porter Hamill [Sr.] as residing in Cedarhurst [Lawrence].

He was the son of Robert Walbridge and Katharine Lyon Hamill of Chicago, IL.

Katharine Delano Porter Hamill was the daughter of Henry Hobart and Katharine Delano Porter, who resided at *Lauderdale* in Lawrence.

Robert Lyon and Katharine Delano Porter Hamill, Sr.'s daughter Katharine married John Franklin Garde, Jr. and resided in Cedarhurst. Their daughter Ann married John Lawrence Koehne, Jr., the son of John Lawrence and Laura Blue Koehne, Sr. of Lawrence, and resided in New Haven, CT. Their daughter Joan married Montgomery Meggs Atwater, the son of Maxwell W. Atwater of Salt Lake City, and, later, Robert Hollister Porter of Squaw Valley, CA. Their son Robert Lyon Hamill, Jr. married Wendy J. Knight Nunan and resided at *Sky Step Farm* in Clinton, NY.

### Hamilton, Campbell Thorpe (1865-1932)

| | |
|---|---|
| Occupation(s): | financier - partner, Benedict & Benedict (insurance firm) |
| Civic Activism: | president, Village of Garden City; |
| | mayor, Village of Garden City, 1929-1932 |
| Marriage(s): | M/1 – Gertrude Greene (d. 1900) |
| | M/2 – 1902-1932 – Helen Biddle de Raismes (1883-1953) |
| Address: | 54 Kilburn Road, Garden City |
| Name of estate: | |
| Year of construction: | 1910 |
| Style of architecture: | Italianate |
| Architect(s): | |
| Landscape architect(s): | |
| House extant: yes | |
| Historical notes: | |

*front facade, 2001*

The *Long Island Society Register, 1929* lists Campbell Thorpe and Helen Biddle de Raismes Hamilton as residing at 54 Kilburn Road, Garden City.

He was the son of John and Charlotte Sophia Filley Hamilton.

Helen Biddle de Raismes Hamilton was the daughter of Emile John and Eliza Eveline Biddle de Raismes of Brooklyn.

Campbell Thorpe and Helen Biddle de Raismes Hamilton's daughter Charlotte married Theodore Andrews Davidson of Chicago, IL. Their daughter Helen married Marion Griffin Irwin, the son of Louis Henry Irwin of Garden City, and resided in Garden City.

In 1991, the 3,502-square-foot house sold for $360,00.


### Hamlin, Francis Bacon, Sr. (1887-1955)

| | |
|---|---|
| Occupation(s): | attorney - partner, Hamlin, Hubbell, and Davis; |
| | member, Greene and Hurd, 1923-1937; |
| | partner, Hurd, Hamlin, and Hubbell |
| | financier - director, Garden City Bank and Trust Co.; |
| | director, Long Island Trust Co. |
| | capitalist - director, Elevator Supply Co. |
| Civic Activism: | trustee and mayor, Village of Garden City; |
| | police justice, Village of Garden City; |
| | president, Cherry Valley Golf Club, Garden City; |
| | director, Eastern Garden City Property Owners Association |
| Marriage(s): | 1911-1950 – Clara Barnes Danforth (1890-1950) |
| Address: | 21 Chestnut Street, Garden City |
| Name of estate: | |
| Year of construction: | 1921 |
| Style of architecture: | Modified Dutch Colonial Revival |
| Architect(s): | |
| Landscape architect(s): | |
| House extant: yes | |
| Historical notes: | |

*front facade, 2005*

The *Long Island Society Register, 1929* lists Francis B. and Clara B. Danforth Hamlin [Sr.] as residing at 21 Chestnut Street, Garden City.

He was the son of The Reverend Tenuis Slingerland and Mrs. Frances Ward Hamlin of Brooklyn.

Clara Barnes Danforth Hamlin was the daughter of Frank Lyman and Susette Bertha Barnes Danforth, Sr. of Garden City.

Francis Bacon and Clara Barnes Danforth Hamlin, Sr.'s daughter Susan remained unmarried. Their daughter Jane married Ernest Henderson Horton, the son of Chauncey T. and Helen Henderson Horton of Garden City. Their son Francis Bacon Hamlin, Jr. married Kathleen Bleecker Ripson, the daughter of Theodore Newland Ripson of Garden City.

### Hammond, Harry Stevens, Sr. (1884-1960)

| | |
|---|---|
| Occupation(s): | industrialist - sales engineer, Pressed Steel Car Co., Pittsburgh, PA; representative, National Tube Co. (subsidiary of United States Steel) |
| Marriage(s): | 1917-1960 – Helen Hoffstot (1890-1980) |
| Address: | 103 Tenth Street, Garden City |
| Name of estate: | |
| Year of construction: | 1903 |
| Style of architecture: | Dutch Colonial Revival |
| Architect(s): | Aymar Embury II designed the house (for Orr) |
| Landscape architect(s): | |
| House extant: yes | |
| Historical notes: | |

*front facade, 2000*

The house was built by Henry Steers Orr. It was later owned by Hammond.

The *Long Island Society Register, 1929* lists Harry S. and Helen Hoffstot Hammond [Sr.] as residing on Hilton Avenue, Garden City. By 1931 they had relocated to 103 Tenth Street, Garden City.

He was the son of Charles Lyman and Mary Electra Stevens Hammond of Crown Point, NY. His brother John married Hester Reilly and resided in Garden City.

Helen Hoffstot Hammond was the daughter of Frank Norton and Adelaide Whitier Shaffer Hoffstot, who resided at *Belcaro* in Sands Point. [*See* Spinzia, *Long Island's Prominent North Shore Families, vol. I* – Hoffstot entry.]

Harry Stevens and Helen Hoffstot Hammond, Sr.'s daughter Anne married William Moulton Graves. Their son Frank married Virginia Eldridge Thomas and resided in Washington, DC. Their son Harry Stevens Hammond, Jr. married Constance P. Johnston and resided in Branford, CT.


### Hammond, John Stevens, Sr. (1880-1939)

| | |
|---|---|
| Occupation(s): | capitalist - chairman of board, Madison Square Garden Corp., NYC; president, New York Rangers (hockey team); oil and land speculation |
| | military - colonel; American Legation, Argentina, Chile, Uruguay, and Paraguay |
| Marriage(s): | M/1 – 1907-1927 – Hester Reilly (1888-1927) |
| | M/2 – 1929 – Louise Schulze |
| Address: | 106 Sixth Street, Garden City |
| Name of estate: | |
| Year of construction: | 1874 |
| Style of architecture: | Colonial Revival with Italianate elements |
| Architect(s): | John Kellum designed the house* |
| Builder: | James L'Hommedieu |
| Landscape architect(s): | |
| House extant: yes | |
| Historical notes: | |

*front facade, 2009*

The *Long Island Society Register, 1929* lists Colonel John S. Hammond [Sr.] as residing at 106 Sixth Street, Garden City.

*The Hammonds' house was one of the earliest houses built in Garden City.

John Stevens Hammond, Sr. was the son of Charles Lyman and Mary Electra Stevens Hammond of Crown Point, NY. His brother Harry married Helen Hoffstot and resided in Garden City.

Hester Reilly Hammond was the daughter of Henry J. Reilly who was killed in China during the Boxer Rebellion of 1900.

John Stevens and Hester Reilly Hammond, Sr.'s son Orson married Kitty Canivet, the daughter of Jean Canivet.

Louise Schulze Hammond was the daughter of Theodore A. Schulze of Manhattan. She had previously been married to Theodore Pomeroy of Chicago, IL.

*[See previous entry for additional family information.]*

### Handy, Courtlandt Waite (1888-1973)

| | |
|---|---|
| Occupation(s): | industrialist - a founder, president, and chairman of board, Handy & Harman (processor of precious and specialty metals) |
| Civic Activism: | mayor, Village of Hewlett Neck, 1936-1938 |
| Marriage(s): | 1919-1973 – Julia Ireland Ramsey (1898-1975) |
| Address: | 140 Woodmere Boulevard South, Hewlett Neck |
| Name of estate: | |
| Year of construction: | 1924 |
| Style of architecture: | Georgian Revival |
| Architect(s): | |
| Landscape architect(s): | |
| House extant: | yes |
| Historical notes: | |

*front facade, 2008*

The house was built by Courtlandt Waite Handy. [*The Brooklyn Daily Eagle* April 28, 1923, p. 19.]

The *Long Island Society Register, 1929* lists Courtlandt W. and Julia I. Ramsey Handy as residing on South [sic] Woodmere Boulevard in Woodmere [Hewlett Neck].

He was the son of Parker Douglas and Ann Kissam Warner Handy, who resided at *Groendak* in Glen Cove. [*See* Spinzia, *Long Island's Prominent* North Shore Families, *vol. I* – Handy entry.] Courtlandt's sister Ruth married Ford Burchell and resided at *Milestone* in Port Chester, NY.

Julia Ireland Ramsey was the daughter of Robert and Marjorie Spring Ramsey of Manhattan.

Courtlandt Waite and Julia Ireland Ramsey Handy's daughter Marjorie married Dudley Foulke Cates, the son of Dudley Cates, and, later, Gouverneur Morris Nichols, the son of James Osgood Nichols of Short Hills, NJ. Their daughter Judith did not marry.

In 1941 Handy sold the house to Ralph Heymsfeld. [*The Brooklyn Daily Eagle* September 22, 1941, p. 6.]


### Hanemann, Edward Louis (1883-1940)

| | |
|---|---|
| Occupation(s): | financier - member, board of managers, Cotton Exchange, NYC; partner, Mohr & Hanemann (cotton brokerage firm) |
| Marriage(s): | 1908-1940 – Edna Cranmer (1881-1957)<br>- Civic Activism: member, Cathedral of the Incarnation Guild, Garden City |
| Address: | Jerusalem Avenue, Hempstead |
| Name of estate: | |
| Year of construction: | |
| Style of architecture: | |
| Architect(s): | |
| Landscape architect(s): | |
| House extant: | unconfirmed |
| Historical notes: | |

The *Long Island Society Register, 1929* lists Mr. and Mrs. Edward L. Hanemann as residing on Jerusalem Avenue, Hempstead. By 1935 they had relocated to Stewart Avenue in Garden City.

He was the son of Henry William and Ernestine Develle Hanemann. Edward's brother John married Frederica Carlotta Prentiss and resided at *Aboha Hanta* in Hewlett Bay Park.

Edward Louis and Edna Cranmer Hanemann's daughter Margaret married Stanley Wiswell Brown, the son of Arthur Alvin and Estelle Lupton Wiswell Brown, Sr. of Garden City.

*[See following entry for additional family information.]*

### Hanemann, John Theodore, Sr. (1880-1960)

| | |
|---|---|
| Occupation(s): | architect - partner with William J. Rogers (specialized in residential and church architecture) |
| | artist |
| | writer - *Architectural Composition* |
| Civic Activism: | Mayor's Commission on Architecture, NYC (LaGuardia administration) |
| Marriage(s): | 1918-1960 – Frederica Carlotta Prentiss (1883-1973) |
| | - Civic Activism: president, Women's Auxiliary of Trinity Church |
| Address: | 212 Cedar Avenue, Hewlett Bay Park |
| Name of estate: | *Aboha Hanta* |
| Year of construction: | 1919 |
| Style of architecture: | French Country |
| Architect(s): | |
| Landscape architect(s): | |
| House extant: yes | |
| Historical notes: | |

The *Social Register Summer, 1921* and the *Long Island Society Register, 1929* list John Theodore and Frederica Carlotta Prentiss Haneman [sic] [Sr.] as residing at *Aboha Hanta* in Hewlett [Hewlett Bay Park].

He was the son of Henry William and Ernestine Devell Hanemann.

Frederica Carlotta Prentiss Hanemann was the daughter of Frederick Charles and Lydia Smith Floyd Prentiss and was a descendant of William Floyd, a signer of the Declaration of Independence, whose estate in Mastic Beach is open to the public. [*See* Spinzia, *Long Island: A Guide to New York's Suffolk and Nassau Counties* – William Floyd Estate, Mastic Beach.] Frederica subsequently married Thomas Jefferson Haldeman of Greenport.

John Theodore and Frederica Carlotta Prentiss Hanemann, Sr.'s son William married Mary Elizabeth Breed, the daughter of Amos Francis Breed of Brookline, MA. Their son John Theodore Hanemann, Jr. married Isabel Scovill Wayland, the daughter of Thomas Chandler and Barbara Shedd Wayland of *Woodrising* in West Hills. [*See* Spinzia, *Long Island's Prominent North Shore Families, vol. II* – Wayland entry.]

*[See previous entry for additional family information.]*

*front facade, 2000*

### Hard, Anson Wales, Sr. (1840-1917)

| | |
|---|---|
| Occupation(s): | capitalist - partner, Wright, Maxwell, & Co. (coffee importer); partner, Hard & Rand (coffee importer) |
| | financier - trustee, Atlantic Mutual Insurance Co.; trustee, Norwich Union Fire Insurance Society; trustee, Seamen's Bank for Savings, NYC; director, Bank of New York; director, Indemnity Fire Insurance Co. |
| Marriage(s): | M/1 – 1870-1905 – Sarah Elizabeth Brown (1846-1905) |
| | M/2 – 1907-1912 – Ellen Whipple Brown (1849-1912) |
| Address: | Broadway and Lord Avenue, Lawrence |
| Name of estate: | *Driftwood* |
| Year of construction: | |
| Style of architecture: | Shingle |
| Architect(s): | |
| Landscape architect(s): | |
| House extant: unconfirmed | |
| Historical notes: | |

The *Social Register Summer, 1910* lists Anson W. Hard [Sr.] as residing in Lawrence.

He was the son of The Reverend Anson Bois and Mrs. Hester Yarnell Hard.

Sarah Elizabeth Brown was the daughter of James Muncaster and Julia Elizabeth Post Brown.

Anson Wales and Sarah Elizabeth Brown Hard, Sr.'s, daughter Laura married Henry von Lengerke Meyer, Sr. and resided at *Cobblestone Farm* in Suffern, NY. Their son DeCourcy married Marjorie Work and resided at *Briarwood* in Lawrence. Their daughter Nellie married John Kane Mills and resided at *Ruddington Farm* in Hackettstown, NJ. Their daughter Sarah married William Reed Kirkland Taylor, Sr. and resided in Lawrence. Their daughter Julia married Augustine Jacquelin Smith, the son of Lewis Jacquelin and Mary Campbell Smith, and resided at *Sunnyside* in Lawrence. Their son Anson Wales Hard, Jr., who resided at *Meadow Edge* in West Sayville, married Florence Bourne and, subsequently, Katherine Potter. Their son James married Leonor Landron de Guevara. In 1884, their one-year-old daughter Edith died.

Ellen Whipple Brown Hard and Sarah Elizabeth Brown Hard were sisters.

*[See following entry for additional family information.]*

The 1914 Belcher Hyde map shows Wales owning a large parcel of property at Broadway and Lord Avenue. Some sources list 18 Lord Avenue as owned by Hard. This is not possible as the Nassau County Assessment Office records that house as having been built in 1923 by which date Hard and all of his wives were deceased. It is not likely that his son Anson Wales Hard, Jr. built a house in Lawrence as, at that time, he had a large estate in West Sayville.

*sketch of Driftwood, 1899*

### Hard, DeCourcy Lawrence, Sr. (1888-1966)

| | |
|---|---|
| Occupation(s): | industrialist - a founder, Health Products Corp. (later, White Laboratories, Inc.); a founder and vice-president, White Laboratories, Kenilworth, NJ (pharmaceutical firm) |
| Civic Activism: | trustee, Village of Lawrence director, Rockaway branch Community Chest, 1934; rear-commodore, Cedarhurst Yacht Club, 1936 |
| Marriage(s): | 1912-1966 – Marjorie Work (1892-1984) - Civic Activism: co-chair, Peninsula branch, Citizens' Committee for Army and Navy war bonds, 1942; chair, medical-social work committee, Community Chest of the Villages, 1935 |
| Address: | Longwood Crossing, Lawrence |
| Name of estate: | *Briarwood* |
| Year of construction: | |
| Style of architecture: | |
| Architect(s): | |
| Landscape architect(s): | |
| House extant: unconfirmed | |
| Historical notes: | |

The *Social Register Summer, 1921* and *Long Island Society Register, 1929* list De Courcy [sic] L. and Marjorie Work Hard [Sr.] as residing at *Briarwood* in Cedarhurst [Lawrence].

He was the son of Anson Wales and Sarah Elizabeth Brown Hard, Sr., who resided at *Driftwood* in Lawrence.

Marjorie Work Hard was the daughter of James Henry and Marie Pierce Warner Work, Sr. of *The Gowans* in Lawrence. Marjorie's sister Alice married John L. Lawrence, Sr. and resided at *Moorlands* in Lawrence. Her sister Sally married Franklin Baker Lefferts and resided in Lawrence. Her brother James Henry Work, Jr. married Mary Laying Davies and resided at *Engleside* in Lawrence. Her sisters Mabel, Jean, and Marie remained unmarried.

DeCourcy Lawrence and Marjorie Work Hard, Sr.'s daughter Barbara married John Milton Urner, the son of Dr. Samuel Everitt Urner of Los Angeles, CA. Their son DeCourcy Lawrence Hard, Jr. married Kathryn Fitzsimmons, the daughter of Robert Fitzsimmons of *Bray House* in Dublin, Ireland. In 1921, their seven-year-old daughter Mary died.

*[See previous entry for additional family information.]*

### Harlow, Frank Strobridge (1866-1964)

| | |
|---|---|
| Occupation(s): | financier - trustee and secretary, Greenpoint Savings Bank |
| Civic Activism: | member, executive committee, Group 5 (represented all the savings banks in Brooklyn, Queens, and Long Island) |
| Marriage(s): | 1892-1944 – Edith L. Young (1870-1944) |
| Address: | 95 Fulton Avenue, Hempstead |
| Name of estate: | *Willisleigh* |
| Year of construction: | 1891 |
| Style of architecture: | Victorian |
| Architect(s): | |
| Landscape architect(s): | |
| House extant: yes* | |
| Historical notes: | |

*Willisleigh*

The house, originally named *Willisleigh*, was built by Willis Howard Young, Sr. [*The Brooklyn Citizen* September 21, 1890, p. 15.] It was later owned by his daughter Edith L. Young Harlow who continued to call it *Willisleigh*.

At the time of Edith's death, she was living in Forest Hills.

Frank Strobridge and Edith L. Young Harlow's son Willis resided on Roxbury Road in Garden City.

In 1921, Edith sold the house to the Sisters of St. Joseph who utilized it as the Sacred Heart Convent and School until 1949 when they relocated the convent and school to Brentwood. [*The Brooklyn Daily Eagle* September 11, 1921, p. 14.] The house is currently the Sisters of Saint Joseph Mission Office.

*In 1900, the barn was destroyed and carriage house was severely damaged by fire. [*The Brooklyn Times Union* June 7, 1900, p. 8.] In 1903, the house suffered nearly $35,000 damage from a fire. Work to restore the house was immediately started by Young. [*The Brooklyn Times Union* November 7, 1903, p. 9, and November 13, 1903, p. 10.]

*Frank Strobridge Harlow's residence,
Willisleigh*, 1902

### Harper, Joseph Abner (1833-1910)

Occupation(s):     publisher - partner, Harper & Brothers*

Marriage(s):     1854-1910 – Hannah Caroline Sackett (1836-1916)

Address:     *[unable to determine street address]*, Hempstead
Name of estate:
Year of construction:
Style of architecture:
Architect(s):
Landscape architect(s):
House extant: unconfirmed
Historical notes:

    Joseph Abner Harper was the son of John and Tammisin Higgins Harper.
    *He was associated with his brothers and uncles in the publishing firm which began as J. & J. Harper in 1817, changing its name to Harper & Brothers in 1833, the year in which Joseph Abner Harper was born. They published *Harper's New Monthly Magazine*, which became *Harper's Magazine*; *Harper's Weekly*, which became part of *The Independent* in 1916 and merged with *The Outlook* in 1928; and *Harper's Bazaar*, which was sold to William Randolph Hearst in 1913 and is today know as *Bazaar*. Harper & Brothers merged with Row, Peterson, & Co. to become Harper & Row, now part of Rupert Murdoch's News Corporation, surviving today as HarperCollins.
    Hannah Caroline Sackett Harper was the daughter of Amos Mead and Sarah Elisabeth Mead Sackett.
    Joseph Abner and Hannah Caroline Sackett Harper's son John married Fanny Ball Hoe. Their son Franklin married Gertrude Olivia Franks, the daughter of Edward and Cornelia Maria Woodruff Franks.
    At the time of his death, Harper and his wife were residing at their estate *Ingleside* in New Windsor, NY.

### Harper. Joseph Henry, Jr. (1888-1971)

| | |
|---|---|
| Occupation(s): | financier - partner, F. S. Smithers and Co. (stock brokerage firm); director, Chain Store Stock Inc. (investment trust) |
| Civic Activism: | secretary, Rockaway Hunting Club, Lawrence, 1906 |
| Marriage(s): | 1920-1969 – Margaret Moulton (1896-1969) |
| Address: | Woodside Drive, Hewlett Bay Park |
| Name of estate: | |
| Year of construction: | |
| Style of architecture: | |
| Architect(s): | |
| Landscape architect(s): | |
| House extant: | unconfirmed |
| Historical notes: | |

The *Long Island Society Register, 1929* lists J. Henry and Margaret Moulton Harper, Jr. as residing in Hewlett [Hewlett Bay Park].

He was the son of Joseph Henry and Mary Say Hoe Harper, Sr., who resided at *Brightside* in Lawrence.

Margaret Moulton Harper was the daughter of Franklin Woodruff and Edith Stockwell Moulton of *Interlaken* in Wakefield, RI.

Joseph Henry and Margaret Moulton Harper, Jr.'s son Fletcher married Prudence Oliver, the daughter of Peter Oliver. Their daughter Margaret married John Dalrymple, the son of Percival Dalrymple of London, England. Their three-year-old son Joseph Henry Harper III died in 1925.

*[See following entry for additional family information.]*


### Harper, Joseph Henry, Sr. (1850-1938)

| | |
|---|---|
| Occupation(s): | publisher - vice-president, Harper & Brothers (book publisher) |
| | writer - *The House of Harper: A Century of Publishing in Franklin Square*, 1912 |
| Civic Activism: | vice-president, Rockaway Hunting Club, Lawrence |
| Marriage(s): | 1874-1925 – Mary Say Hoe (1854-1925) |
| Address: | 255 Breezeway, Lawrence |
| Name of estate: | *Brightside* |
| Year of construction: | 1892 |
| Style of architecture: | Neo-Georgian |
| Architect(s): | Carrere and Hastings designed the house and stable (for J. H. Harper, Sr.) |
| Landscape architect(s): | |
| House extant: | yes |
| Historical notes: | |

*front facade, 2009*

The house, originally named *Brightside*, was built by Joseph Henry Harper, Sr.

He was the son of Joseph Wesley and Ellen Urling Smith Harper of Manhattan.

Mary Say Hoe Harper was the daughter of Richard March and Mary G. Howe Hoe.

Joseph Henry and Mary Say Hoe Harper, Sr.'s son Fletcher married Harriet T. Wadsworth and resided at *Friendship Farm* in The Plains, VA. Their son Richard married Mabel S. Bacon. Their daughter Mary married Langdon Barrett Valentine, the son of Henry C. Valentine. Langdon subsequently married Louise Hollister with whom he resided in Islip. [See Spinzia, *Long Island's Prominent South Shore Families* – Valentine entry.] Their son Joseph Henry Harper, Jr. married Margaret Moulton and resided in Hewlett Bay Park. Their daughter Urling married LeGrand Lockwood Benedict, Jr., the son of LeGrand Lockwood and Sarah Collier Blaine Benedict, Sr. of *Nooke* in Lawrence.

*[See previous two entries for additional family information.]*

The house was later owned by James Samuel Dunstan, who continued to call it *Brightside*, and, subsequently, by Enos Thompson Troop IV.

**Harrar, Dr. James Aitken (1877-1970)**

| | |
|---|---|
| Occupation(s): | physician - obstetrics and gynecology |
| | educator - associate professor, clinical obstetrics and gynecology, Cornell University Medical Center, NYC |
| Civic Activism: | director, Nursery and Child's Hospital |
| Marriage(s): | 1909-1959 – Florence Lakewood Humiston (1885-1959) |
| Address: | 25 Ives Road, Hewlett Bay Park |
| Name of estate: | |
| Year of construction: | 1922 |
| Style of architecture: | Modified Colonial Revival |
| Architect(s): | |
| Landscape architect(s): | |
| House extant: yes | |
| Historical notes: | |

The *Long Island Society Register, 1929* lists Dr. James A. and Mrs. Florence L. Humiston Harrar as residing on Ives Road, Hewlett [Hewlett Bay Park].

He was the son of Scott and Lillie R. Aitken Harrar of Williamsport, PA.

Florence Lakewood Humiston Harrar was the daughter of William Henry and Harriet Millar Humiston of Cleveland, OH.

Dr. James Aitkin and Mrs. Florence Lakewood Humiston Harrar's daughter Nancy married Dr. John Medwell Brown, the son of Stuart Albert Brown of *Hythe* in Kent, England, and resided in Cornwall, England. Their son William married Elisabeth Joyce Sanders, the daughter of Clarence Sanders of St. Paul, MN, and, subsequently, Tiffany Harper, the daughter of Herbert Harper of Memphis, TN.

In 2021, the 2,480 square-foot house, with five bedrooms and three and a half bathrooms, sold for $949,000.

*front facade*

## Harriman, Edward Henry (1848-1909)

| | | |
|---|---|---|
| Occupation(s): | financier - | founder, Harriman and Co. (investment banking firm); director, Northern Securities Co.; director, Equitable Life Assurance Society; director, National City Trust Co.; director, Guaranty Trust Co. |
| | capitalist - | director, Union Pacific Railroad; president and chairman of board, Southern Pacific Railroad; director, New York Central Railroad; director, Ogdensburg & Lake Champlain Railroad; vice-president, Illinois Railroad; director, Baltimore and Ohio Railroad; director, Sodus Bay & Southern Railroad; director, Wells Fargo & Co.; director, Western Union Telegraph Co. |
| | shipping - | director, Portland & Asiatic Steamboat Co.; director, Pacific Mail Steamship Co. |
| Civic Activism: | | founder, Boys' Club of New York; founder, Trudeau Tuberculosis Sanitarium, Saranac Lake, NY; vice president, Rockaway Hunting Club, Lawrence, 1903 |
| Marriage(s): | | 1879-1909 – Mary Williamson Averell (1851-1932) - Civic Activism: endowed E. H. Harriman Chair of Forestry, Yale University, New Haven, CT; established E. H. Harriman Medical & Research Fund; created Harriman Park on Hudson River with endowment of $1 million; member, National Red Cross Board; financed Eugenics Record Office, Cold Spring Harbor |

Address: 217 Peninsula Boulevard, Hempstead
Name of estate:
Year of construction: 1793
Style of architecture: Colonial
Architect(s):
Landscape architect(s):
House extant: yes
Historical notes:

 Edward Henry Harriman was the son of The Reverend Orlando and Mrs. Cornelia Neilson Harriman, Jr. He was born in the parsonage of Hempstead's St. George's Episcopal Church where his father served as the rector from 1844 to 1849.
[Rudy Abramson, *Spanning the Century: The Life of W. Averell Harriman* (New York: William Morrow and Co., Inc., 1992), p. 28.]
 Mary Williamson Averell Harriman was the daughter of William J. and Mary Lawrence Williamson Averell of Rochester, NY, and Ogdensburg, NY.
 Edward Henry and Mary Williamson Averell Harriman's son William Averell, who married Katharine Lanier Lawrance, Marie Norton, and Pamela Digby, owned two estates in Sands Point and one in Old Westbury. Their daughter Mary married Charles Cary Rumsey, Sr. and resided in Brookville, Sands Point, and at *The Plains* in Middleburg, VA.
[*See* Spinzia, *Long Island's Prominent North Shore Families, vol. I* – Harriman entries and *Long Island's Prominent North Shore Families, vol. II* – Rumsey and Smith entries.] The Harrimans' daughter Carol married Richard Penn Smith, Jr. of Old Westbury and, later, William Plunket Stewart with whom she resided in East Williston. Their daughter Cornelia married Robert Livingston Gerry and resided at *Aknusti* in Delhi, NY. Their son Edward Roland Noel married Gladys C. C. Fries and resided at *Arden Homestead* in Arden, NY. Their son Henry died in childhood.
[For a discussion of Mary Williamson Averell Harriman and Mary Harriman Rumsey, *see* Judith Ader Spinzia, "Women of Long Island: Mary Williamson Averell Harriman; her daughter, Mary Harriman Rumsey" *The Freeholder*, 12 (Spring 2008):8-9,16-20. Also available at www.spinzialongislandestates.com.]
 The house has been on the National Register of Historic Places since 1988.

### Harris, Tracy Hyde, Jr. (1864-1933)

| | |
|---|---|
| Occupation(s): | attorney - partner, with his brother Edward, Harris and Harris, NYC (specialized in real estate law) |
| | capitalist - president, Harcourt Realty Co.; president, Laneson Realty Co.; vice-president, Fellows Company of New York |
| [Civic Activism: | governor, Rockaway Hunting Club, Lawrence, 1911; president, Princeton Club |
| Marriage(s): | 1890-1931 – Laura Dudley Curtis (1870-1931) |
| Address: | East Rockaway Road, Hewlett Bay Park |
| Name of estate: | *Wistaria Lodge* |
| Year of construction: | |
| Style of architecture: | Modified Neo-Georgian |
| Architect(s): | Albro and Lindeberg designed the house (for Harris) |
| Landscape architect(s): | |
| House extant: unconfirmed | |
| Historical notes: | |

*front facade*

The house, originally named *Wistaria Lodge*, was built by Tracy Hyde Harris, Jr.

The *Social Register Summer, 1910* lists Tracy Hyde and Laura D. Curtis Hyde [Jr.] as residing in Hewlett. The *Long Island Society Register, 1929* lists Tracy Hyde and Laura D. Curtis Harris [Jr.] as residing at *Wistaria Lodge* in Hewlett [Hewlett Bay Park].

He was the son of Tracy Hyde and Hannah Virginia Wyckoff Hyde, Sr.

Laura Dudley Curtis Harris was the daughter of Jeremiah Winslow and Mary Estelle Schooley Curtis of West End, NJ.

The Harrises did not have children.


### Harrison, Milton Strong, Jr. (1890-1965)

| | |
|---|---|
| Occupation(s): | financier - member, Field, Glore, and Co. (stock brokerage firm); member, Page, Smith, and Remick (stock brokerage firm); member, Wood, Struthers, and Winthrop (stock brokerage firm) |
| Marriage(s): | 1917-1965 – Mary Constance Kittinger (1895-1973) |
| Address: | 562 Atlantic Avenue, Lawrence |
| Name of estate: | |
| Year of construction: | 1913 |
| Style of architecture: | Arts and Crafts |
| Architect(s): | |
| Landscape architect(s): | |
| House extant: yes | |
| Historical notes: | |

*front / side facade, 2001*

The 1940 Census lists Milton S. and Mary K. Harrison [Jr.] as residing at 562 Atlantic Avenue, Lawrence.

He was the son of Milton Strong and Eleanor Miller Harrison, Sr. of Manhattan.

Mary Constance Kittinger Harrison was the daughter of George B. and Mary Carroll Terry Kittinger of Seattle, WA.

Milton Strong and Mary Constance Kittinger Harrison, Jr.'s son Milton Strong Harrison III married Alice Hurley and resided in San Antonio, TX. Their daughter Mary married John Griswold Livingston, Jr., the son of John Griswold and Clara M. Dudley Livingston, Sr. of Lawrence. Their daughter Eleanor did not marry.

In 1999, the 3,281-square-foot house sold for $532,000.

### Hart, Alexander Richmond (1854-1938)

| | |
|---|---|
| Occupation(s): | attorney |
| | industrialist - president, New York Engraving and Printing Co. |
| | publisher - a founder, Fine Arts Publishing Co. (later, A. R. Hart Corporation) |
| | capitalist - a founder, Long Island Electric Railroad Co.; a founder, Queens–Nassau Light & Power Co. |
| Civic Activism: | a founder and vice-president, Union League Club |
| Marriage(s): | 1877-1926 – Caroline E. Snow (1858-1926) |
| Address: | 115 Whitehall Boulevard, Garden City |
| Name of estate: | |
| Year of construction: | 1930 |
| Style of architecture: | Colonial Revival |
| Architect(s): | |
| Landscape architect(s): | |
| House extant: yes | |
| Historical notes: | |

Alexander Richmond Hart was the son of Augustin Hart of Brooklyn and a descendant of John Hart, a signer of the Declaration of Independence.

Caroline E. Snow Hart was the daughter of Augustin and Harriet Louisa Butler Snow.

Alexander Richmond and Caroline E. Snow Hart's son Augustin also resided in Garden City.

*[See following entry for additional family information.]*

*front facade, 2001*

### Hart, Augustin Snow, Sr. (1879-1947)

| | |
|---|---|
| Occupation(s): | attorney - Brooklyn |
| | industrialist - a founder and director, Metal Company, NYC, 1909 (manufacturer of Metal products) |
| Civic Activism: | secretary, Crescent Athletic Club, Brooklyn |
| Marriage(s): | Alice O'Connor |
| Address: | 65 Whitehall Boulevard, Garden City |
| Name of estate: | |
| Year of construction: | |
| Style of architecture: | |
| Architect(s): | |
| Landscape architect(s): | |
| House extant: no | |
| Historical notes: | |

The *Long Island Society Register, 1929* lists Augustine [sic] S. Hart as residing in the Garden City Estates section of Garden City. The 1930 Census lists Hart at this address.

He was the son of Alexander Richmond and Caroline E. Snow Hart of Garden City.

Augustin and Alice O'Connor Hart, Sr.'s son Augustin Snow Hart, Jr., who was vice-chairman of the Quaker Oats Company, married Margaret Stuart, the daughter of R. Douglas and Harriet McClure Stuart of Lake Forest, IL, and resided in Lake Forest. Their daughter Natalie married Eliot Miller Wadsworth, the son of Oliver Fairfield and Rose Evelyn Miller Wadsworth, and resided in Boston, MA.

*[See previous entry for additional family information.]*

### Hastings, The Reverend A. Abbott (1887-1972)

| | |
|---|---|
| Occupation(s): | clergy - archdeacon, Episcopal Diocese of Albany, NY; warden, St. Michael's Mission to Arapahoes in Wyoming; dean, St. Mathews Cathedral, Troy, NY; associate rector, Christ Church, Shaker Heights, OH |
| Civic Activism: | founder, first Boy Scout troop in Boston, MA |
| Marriage(s): | 1912-1970 – Dorothy Quincy Turner (1890-1970) <br> - Civic Activism: vice-president, Garden City–Hempstead Community Club, 1926 |
| Address: | 109 Fifth Street, Garden City |
| Name of estate: | |
| Year of construction: | 1878 |
| Style of architecture: | |
| Architect(s): | |
| Landscape architect(s): | |
| House extant: yes | |
| Historical notes: | |

The *Long Island Society Register, 1929* lists A. Abbott and Dorothy Quincy Turner Hastings as residing at 109 Fifth Street, Garden City.

Dorothy Quincy Turner Hastings was the daughter of William Henry and Abigail Atkins Quincy Turner, Jr.

The Reverend A. Abbott and Mrs. Dorothy Quincy Turner Hastings' daughter Dorothy married The Reverend Frederick Myers Morris. Their son The Reverend William Bradford Turner Hastings married Virginia Floyd. Their son F. Murray Hastings was also a member of the clergy. Their son Abbott married Gretchen Weiland, the daughter of Adelbert A. Weiland.

In 1993, the 3,345-square-foot house sold for $591,000.


### Hatch, Alden R. (1898-1975)

| | |
|---|---|
| Occupation(s): | writer - over forty books, mostly biographies <br> journalist |
| Marriage(s): | M/1 – 1932-div. 1949 – Ruth Brown <br> - merchant - proprietor, dress shop, Cedarhurst <br> M/2 – 1950-1975 – Allene Pomeroy Gaty <br> - writer - *The Best of Times* <br> artist - literary illustrator – <br> *A Man Named John: The Life of Pope John XXIII*, 1963; <br> *The Circus King: Our Ringling Family*, 1963 |
| Address: | Polo Lane, Lawrence |
| Name of estate: | *Somerleas* |
| Year of construction: | c. 1928 |
| Style of architecture: | Neo-Tudor |
| Architect(s): | |
| Landscape architect(s): | |
| House extant: unconfirmed | |
| Historical notes: | |

Alden R. Hatch was the son of Frederic Horace and May Palmer Daly Hatch of Lawrence who previously owned *Somerleas*.

Ruth Brown Hatch was the daughter of Dan and Eva Brown of Fort Worth, TX. Ruth later married Richard Derby Elwell, Sr. of Lawrence.

Alden R. and Ruth Brown Hatch's son Alden Denison Hatch married Barbara Carol Florio, the daughter of Carl J. Florio of Hamden, CT, and later, Margaret Cook.

Allene Pomeroy Gaty Hatch was the daughter of Theodore Emmett Gaty of Clermont, NY, and a descendant of James Gettys, the founder of Gettysburg, PA.

*[See other Hatch entries for additional family information.]*

## Hatch, Eric Stow (1901-1973)

| | |
|---|---|
| Occupation(s): | financier - member, Frederic H. Hatch Co., NYC (stock brokerage firm)* |
| | capitalist - co-owner, with his wife E. Constance, WBIS radio station, Bristol, CT |
| | writer - numerous magazine articles; |
| | short stories; |
| | fiction and non-fiction books; |
| | plays; |
| | television and motion picture scripts** |
| Civic Activism: | chairman, Connecticut State Historical Commission, 1967; |
| | chairman, American Bicentennial Commission of Connecticut; |
| | director, Connecticut Horse Show Association; |
| | judge and steward, American Horse Shows; |
| | member, advisory committee, National Trust for Historic Preservation |
| Marriage(s): | M/1 – eloped 1921-div. 1929 – Silvia Whiton Stuart |
| | M/2 – 1929-div. 1945 – Mary Gertrude Thomas |
| | M/3 – 1945-1973 – E. Constance De Boer (1920-2007) |
| | - capitalist - co-owner with her husband Eric, WBIS radio station, Bristol, CT |
| | educator - taught English literature, University of Connecticut, Torrington |
| | Civic Activism: women's rights and food programs for the homeless |
| Address: | 70 Auerbach Lane, Lawrence |
| Name of estate: | |
| Year of construction: | 1898 |
| Style of architecture: | Shingle |
| Architect(s): | |
| Landscape architect(s): | |
| House extant: yes | |
| Historical notes: | |

   Eric Stow Hatch was the son of Frederic Horace and May Palmer Daly Hatch of *Semerleas* in Lawrence.
   Sylvia Whiton Stuart Hatch was the daughter of Jesse Paulmier and Mary Marshall Ogden Whiton Stuart of Manhattan and *Goodhope* in Greenwich, CT. Sylvia later married Lawrence Turnure and, then, Nelson Olcott with whom she resided in Millbrook, NY.
   Eric Stow and Sylvia Whiton Stuart Hatch's daughter Evelyn married Emlen Williams Holmes II and resided in Lawrence.
   Mary Gertrude Thomas Hatch was the daughter of George P. Thomas of Port Washington. In 1946 she married radio producer Frank Chase.
   E. Constance De Boer Hatch was the daughter of Dr. William and Mrs. Elizabeth Garner De Boer of Chicago, IL.
   Eric Stow and E. Constance De Boer Hatch's son Jonathan resided in New Preston, CT. Their son Eric Kent De Boer Hatch married Nancy Ellen Mack, the daughter of Edgar R. Mack of Litchfield, CT, and resided in Charlottesville, VA, and Litchfield, CT.
   *Eric withdrew from his career in finance to pursue one as an author.
   **Among Eric's many authorships were the scripts for the motion picture "Our Man Godfrey" and the television series "Topper."
*[See other Hatch entries for additional family information.]*
[For information on the Hatches' Hampton Bays residence *Westerly*, see Spinzia, *Long Island's Prominent Families in the Town of Southampton* – Hatch entry.]

*front facade, 2001*

### Hatch, Frederic Horace (1862-1930)

| | |
|---|---|
| Occupation(s): | financier - president and chairman of board, Frederic H. Hatch Co., NYC (stock brokerage firm) |
| Civic Activism: | a founder, Village of Woodsburgh, 1912; president and trustee, Village of Woodsburgh, 1914-1926; a founder and president, Unlisted Securities Dealers' Association; president, New York Stock Exchange; treasurer, Rockaway Hunting Club, Lawrence, 1917; deputy governor, Society of Mayflower Descendants |
| Marriage(s): | 1883-1930 – May Palmer Daly (1870-1952) - writer - short stories for magazines |
| Address: | Polo Lane, Lawrence |
| Name of estate: | *Somerleas* |
| Year of construction: | c. 1928 |
| Style of architecture: | Neo-Tudor |
| Architect(s): | |
| Landscape architect(s): | |
| House extant: unconfirmed | |
| Historical notes: | |

The *Long Island Society Register, 1929* lists Frederick [sic] H. and May Palmer Daly Hatch as residing at *Somerleas* in Cedarhurst [Lawrence]. They had previously resided on Channel Road in Woodsburgh.

He was the son of Alfrederick Smith and Theodasia Ruggles Hatch of Manhattan.

Frederic Horace and May Palmer Daly Hatch's son Eric, who resided in Lawrence, married Sylvia Whiton Stuart; Mary Gertrude Thomas; and, subsequently, E. Constance DeBoer. The Hatches' son Alden, who resided at *Somerleas* in Lawrence, married Ruth Brown and, subsequently, Allene Pomeroy Gaty.

*[See other Hatch entries for additional family information.]*


### Haughey, William Wallace (1878-1960)

| | |
|---|---|
| Occupation(s): | inventor - devised a process of treating distillery by-products, 1916; devised process of producing fertilizer material, 1916<br>industrialist - president, Distillery By-Products, 1917 |
| Civic Activism: | chairman of board, Church of Religious Science; donated, with his wife Irene, General Lew Wallace's sketches to the William Henry Smith Library of the Indiana State Historical Society |
| Marriage(s): | 1901-1960 – Irene Test (1878-1972) - Civic Activism: donated, with her husband William, General Lew Wallace's sketches to the William Henry Smith Library of the Indiana State Historical Society; suffragist - a founder and president, Garden City Suffrage Club, 1915; secretary, Nassau Assembly District, New York State Woman's Suffrage Party, 1914 |
| Address: | *[unable to determine street address]*, Garden City |
| Name of estate: | |
| Year of construction: | |
| Style of architecture: | |
| Architect(s): | |
| Landscape architect(s): | |
| House extant: unconfirmed | |
| Historical notes: | |

William Wallace Haughey was the son of Louis Chauncey and Zerelda Wallace Haughey.
Irene Test Haughey was the daughter of General Edward F. and Mrs. Rosa Dunham Test.
William Wallace and Irene Test Haughey's daughter Louisa married Lawrence Washington Lewis.

### Hawke, John Daniel, Jr. (1933-2022)

| | | |
|---|---|---|
| Occupation(s): | attorney - | general counsel, Federal Reserve Board of Governors; chairman of board, Arnold & Porter; |
| | educator - | taught law, Georgetown School of Law; taught law, Boston University School of Law |
| | journalist - | editor-in-chief, Columbia Law School Review |
| | financier - | director and chairman of risk committee, M & T Bank; United States Controller of the Currency (Clinton and George W. Bush administrations); director, Federal Deposit Insurance Corp. (FDIC) |
| | statesman - | United States Under Secretary of Treasury for Domestic Finance (Clinton administration) |
| Civic Activism: | | chairman of board of advisors, Morin Center for Banking Law Studies; director, Federal Examination Council; director, Basel Committee on Banking Supervision; a founder, Shadow Financial Regulatory Committee |
| Marriage(s): | | 1962-1991 – Josephine Marie Reddan (d. 1991) |
| Address: | | 40 Westminister Road, Rockville Centre |
| Name of estate: | | |
| Year of construction: | | 1928 |
| Style of architecture: | | Dutch Colonial Revival |
| Architect(s): | | |
| Landscape architect(s): | | |
| House extant: yes | | |
| Historical notes: | | |

John, who was known as the "Dean of American Bank Lawyers," was raised in this house by his parents John Daniel and Olga Buchbinder Hawke, Sr.

John Daniel and Josephine Marie Reddan Hawke, Jr.'s son John Daniel Hawke III married Jessica Anne Blake, the daughter of Dr. Thomas R. Blake of Amherst, MA.

In 2019, the 2,003-square-foot house sold for $860,00.

*front facade, 2012*

### Hazard, William Ayrault, Sr. (1854-1922)

| | |
|---|---|
| Occupation(s): | industrialist - president, Sterling Salt Co.;<br>president, Michigan Salt Works, Marine City, MI<br>capitalist - president, Halite and Northern Railroad;<br>president, River Transit Co., Marine City, MI<br>financier - trustee, Seaman's Bank for Savings, NYC |
| Civic Activism: | a founder, governor, and president, Rockaway Hunting Club, Lawrence, 1911 |
| Marriage(s): | 1885-1922 – Laura Abell Pelton (1863-1934) |
| Address: | Ocean Avenue, Lawrence |
| Name of estate: | *Meadow Hall* |
| Year of construction: | c. 1910 |
| Style of architecture: | Neo-Tudor |
| Architect(s): | |
| Landscape architect(s): | |
| House extant: | no; demolished, c. 1950 |
| Historical notes: | |

*Meadow Hall*

The house, originally named *Meadow Hall*, was built by William Ayrault Hazard, Sr.

The *Social Register Summer, 1910* lists William Ayrault and Laura Abell Pelton Hazard [Sr.] as residing at *Meadow Hall* in Cedarhurst [Lawrence.]

She was the daughter of William Tilden and Catherine E. Abell Pelton.

William Ayrault and Laura Abell Pelton Hazard, Sr.'s daughter Laura married Frederick Rhinelander Brown, the son of Frederick Tilden and Mary Crosby Renwick Brown of *By-the-Way* in Woodmere. Their daughter Jessie married Charles Reginald Leonard, Sr. and resided at *Walls of Jericho* in Jericho. Their daughter Mary married Duncan Argyle Holmes and resided in Brookville. [See Spinzia, *Long Island's Prominent North Shore Families, vol. I* – Leonard and Holmes entries.] Their son William Ayrault Hazard, Jr. married Ella Johnson, the postmistress of Cedarhurst and the daughter of Sylvanus Johnson, the deputy sheriff of Nassau County. Their daughter Katharine married Courtland Dixon Moss, Jr. and resided in Muttontown. [See Spinzia, *Long Island's Prominent North Shore Families, vol. I* – Moss entry.] Their son William Tilden Pelton Hazard married Silvie Livingston, the daughter of Johnston and Nathalie Fellows Moss Livingston of Hewlett.


### Heath, Cuyler (1889-1938)

| | |
|---|---|
| Occupation(s): | financier - ores and metal broker |
| Marriage(s): | Mildred Johnson (b. 1890) |
| Address: | 150 Wellington Road, Garden City |
| Name of estate: | |
| Year of construction: | 1920 |
| Style of architecture: | Dutch Colonial Revival |
| Architect(s): | |
| Landscape architect(s): | |
| House extant: | yes |
| Historical notes: | |

The *Long Island Society Register, 1929* lists Mr. and Mrs. Cuyler Heath as residing at 150 Wellington Road, Garden City.

He was the son of Henry Minor and Julia Cuyler Heath of Brooklyn.

Cuyler and Mildred Johnson Heath's son Albert married Enid Valerie St. John, the daughter of Frank Lamar and Enid Rice St. John of Garden City.

*front facade, 2001*

### Hendrickson, Charles Le Roy (1883-1973)

| | |
|---|---|
| Occupation(s): | attorney |
| | financier - partner, Hendrickson, Hall, and Co. (stock brokerage firm) |
| Civic Activism: | a founder and director, Cherry Valley Club, Garden City, 1916 |
| Marriage(s): | 1906-1972 – Marie Merritt (1883-1972) |
| Address: | 63 Second Street, Garden City |
| Name of estate: | |
| Year of construction: | 1928 |
| Style of architecture: | Neo-Georgian |
| Architect(s): | |
| Landscape architect(s): | |
| House extant: yes | |
| Historical notes: | |

The house was built by Charles Le Roy Hendrikson.
The *Long Island Society Register, 1929* lists C. LeRoy [sic] and Marie Merritt Hendrickson as residing at 63 Second Street, Garden City.

He was the son of George Skidmore and Elizabeth Frost Hendrickson of Floral Park.

Marie Merritt Hendrickson was the daughter of Israel John and Caroline Freytag Merritt, Jr. of Whitestone, NY.

Charles Le Roy and Marie Merritt Hendrickson's daughter Hazel married Kenneth Ryhs Williams of New York.

*front facade, 2001*

### Herrick, Harold (1853-1933)

| | |
|---|---|
| Occupation(s): | financier - president, Niagara Fire Insurance Co. |
| Civic Activism: | a founder, Linnean Society (an ornithology club) |
| Marriage(s): | 1878-1931 – Annie Trotter Lawrence (1853-1931) |
| Address: | Causeway, Lawrence |
| Name of estate: | *The Meadows* |
| Year of construction: | |
| Style of architecture: | |
| Architect(s): | |
| Landscape architect(s): | |
| House extant: unconfirmed | |
| Historical notes: | |

The *Social Register Summer, 1910* and the *Long Island Society Register, 1929* list Harold and Annie T. Lawrence Herrick as residing at *The Meadows* in Lawrence.

He was the son of Jonathan Kilham and Elizabeth Tiller Herrick of Manhattan.

Annie Trotter Lawrence Herrick was the daughter of Newbold and Anne Hough Trotter Lawrence. Annie's brother Newbold Trotter Lawrence married Isabella Gillet and resided at *Homewood* in Lawrence.

Harold and Annie Trotter Lawrence Herrick's daughter Gertrude married Ethelbert Ide Low and resided in Lawrence. Their daughter Anna remained unmarried. Their son Harold Edward Herrick married Pauline Bacon and resided in Woodmere. Their son Newbold married Pauline Esther Boulton and resided in Woodsburgh.

*[See other Herrick entries for additional family information.]*

### Herrick, Harold Edward, Sr. (1890-1975)

| | |
|---|---|
| Occupation(s): | attorney - partner, Sower, Herrick, and Black, NYC |
| | financier - director, Home Life Insurance Co. |
| Civic Activism: | trustee, St. Paul's Episcopal Church, Rome, Italy; |
| | trustee, St. James Episcopal Church, Florence, Italy |
| | trustee, Village of Hewlett Neck; |
| | member, Nassau County Mosquito Commission |
| Marriage(s): | 1918-1975 – Pauline Bacon (1897-1988) |
| | - Civic Activism: vice-president, Family Service Association, 1948 |
| Address: | 935 Smith Lane, Hewlett Neck |
| Name of estate: | |
| Year of construction: | 1922 |
| Style of architecture: | Colonial Revival |
| Architect(s): | |
| Landscape architect(s): | |
| House extant: yes | |
| Historical notes: | |

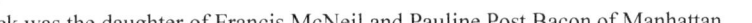

*side facade, 2005*

The *Long Island Society Register, 1929* lists Harold Edward and Pauline Bacon Herrick, Sr. as residing in Woodmere.

He was the son of Harold and Annie Trotter Lawrence Herrick of *The Meadows* in Lawrence.

Pauline Bacon Herrick was the daughter of Francis McNeil and Pauline Post Bacon of Manhattan.

Harold Edward and Pauline Bacon Herrick, Sr.'s daughter Eleanor married Albert Stickney, Jr. and resided at *Windy Hill* in Rockfall, CT. Their daughter Adeline married John Michael Alistair Bird of London, England, and resided in Rye, NY. Their son Newbold married Pauline Esther Boulton and resided in Woodmere. Their son Harold Edward Herrick, Jr. married Mary Hayden Williams, the daughter of Warren Williams of New Haven, CT.

*[See other Herrick entries for additional family information.]*

In 1988, the 4,265-square-foot house sold for $760,000.

In 1991 the house was remodeled.

### Herrick, Newbold Lawrence, Sr. (1885-1976)

| | |
|---|---|
| Occupation(s): | industrialist - director, White Rock Mineral Springs Co. |
| Civic Activism: | mayor, Village of Woodsburgh, 1937-1943; |
| | trustee, Village of Woodsburgh, 1943-1945 |
| | president, Community Chest Inc. of the Rockaways |
| Marriage(s): | 1910-1970 – Pauline Esther Boulton (1888-1970) |
| Address: | 151 Woodmere Boulevard, Woodsburgh |
| Name of estate: | |
| Year of construction: | |
| Style of architecture: | |
| Architect(s): | |
| Landscape architect(s): | |
| House extant: no | |
| Historical notes: | |

The *Social Register Summer, 1910* and the *Long Island Society Register, 1929* list Newbold L. and Pauline E. Boulton Herrick, Sr. as residing in Woodmere [Woodsburgh].

He was the son of Harold and Annie Trotter Lawrence Herrick of *The Meadows* in Lawrence.

Pauline Esther Boulton was the daughter of William Bowen and Louisa Kuhl Kelly Boulton, Sr. of *Avila* in Lawrence. Pauline's brother Howard married Grace Russell Jones and resided in Hewlett.

Newbold Lawrence and Pauline Esther Boulton Herrick, Sr.'s daughter Pauline married Thomas Foster Huntington, the son of Henry Strong Huntington of Chapel Hill, NC, and resided in Princeton, NJ. Their son Anson married Ruth Mary Burdett, the daughter of Gilbert Underhill Burdett of Englewood, NJ, and resided in East Hampton. [*See* Spinzia, *Long Island's Prominent Families in the Town of East Hampton* – Herrick entry.] Their daughter Louisa married William Smith Garnsey III of Denver, CO. Their son Newbold Lawrence Herrick, Jr. married Harriet Janet Thacher, the daughter of Sherman Day Thacher and a descendant of Roger Sherman, a signer of the Declaration of Independence.

*[See previous Herrick entries for additional family information.]*

### Hewitt, Thomas M.

Occupation(s):

Marriage(s): 1897 – Marcie Wilson

Address: 106 Kilburn Road, Garden City
Name of estate:
Year of construction: 1934
Style of architecture: Colonial Revival
Architect(s): Olive Frances Tjaden designed the house (for T. M. Hewitt)
Landscape architect(s):
House extant: yes
Historical notes:

The house was built by Thomas M. Hewitt.
He was the son of John Hewitt of Belfast, Ireland.
Marcie Wilson Hewitt was the daughter of William Wilson of Brooklyn.
Thomas M. and Marcie Wilson Hewitt's son William married Mildred Hegeman and resided in Garden City.
*[See following entry for additional family information.]*
In 2013, the 2,722-square-foot house, with four bedrooms and three and a half bathrooms, sold for $1,253,500.

*front facade*

### Hewitt, William Wilson, Sr. (b. 1900)

Occupation(s): financier - stock trader, Gilbert Eliott Co.;
a founder and partner, Clinton Gilbert and Co., 1930 (stock brokerage firm);
a founder and president, Hewitt and Satterfield, 1935 (stock brokerage firm);
member, Emanuel and Co., 1939 (stock brokerage firm)

Marriage(s): 1927 – Mildred Hegeman (b. 1901)

Address: 25 Hilton Avenue, Garden City
Name of estate:
Year of construction: 1934
Style of architecture: Georgian Revival
Architect(s):
Landscape architect(s):
House extant: yes
Historical notes:

*front facade, 2021*

The house was built by William Wilson Hewitt, Sr. [*The Brooklyn Daily Eagle* November 12, 1933, p. 36.] The 1940 Census lists the Hewitts at this address.
He was the son of Thomas M. and Marcie Wilson Hewitt of Garden City.
Mildred Hegeman Hewitt was the daughter of Frederick T. Hegeman of Brooklyn.
William Wilson and Mildred Hegeman Hewitt, Sr.'s son William Wilson Hewitt, Jr. married Suzanne Throckmorton. Their daughter Barbara married ____ McBride.
In 1940, the senior Hewitt was instrumental in preventing the assassination of Wendell Lewis Willkie at a rally in Madison Square Garden. [*Nassau Daily Review–Star* November 4, 1940, p. 23.]
*[See previous entry for additional family information.]*
In 2021, the 3,888-square-foot house, with six bedrooms and six and a half bathrooms, sold for $2.545 million.

### Hewlett, George H. (1866-1951)

| | |
|---|---|
| Occupation(s): | |
| Civic Activism: | trustee, Village of Lawrence, 1898-1900 |
| Marriage(s): | bachelor |
| Address: | 199 Broadway, Lawrence |
| Name of estate: | *Rock Hall* |
| Year of construction: | 1767 |
| Style of architecture: | Colonial |
| Architect(s): | |
| Landscape architect(s): | |
| House extant: | yes |
| Historical notes: | |

The *Social Register Summer, 1915* and the *Long Island Society Register, 1929* list George Hewlett as residing at *Rock Hall* in Lawrence.

He was the son of James Augustus and Mary Elizabeth Sanderson Hewlett. George bought out other family members who had shared in ownership of *Rock Hall*.

The house was built by Josiah Martin, a prosperous trader from Antigua, West Indies. Martin's land holdings consisted of six hundred acres extending from *Rock Hall* to the ocean front at Far Rockaway. During the Revolutionary War Martin was an active Loyalist whose ships were used to transport British soldiers to the area while the house became a haven for his daughter Elizabeth and her Loyalist husband who was the last colonial governor of North Carolina. In 1824 Thomas Hewlett purchased the house and its remaining 125 acres. The house, which is on The National Register of Historic Places, was donated to the Town of Hempstead in 1948, through the efforts of George H. Hewlett, for use as a museum. It is open to the public.

*[See other Hewlett entries for additional family information.]*

*rear facade, 2009*

### Hewlett, James Monroe (1868-1941)

| | |
|---|---|
| Occupation(s): | architect - partner, Lord & Hewlett |
| | *[See Architects appendix for selected list of commissions in the Town of Hempstead.]* |
| | artist - muralist* |
| Civic Activism: | director, American Academy, Rome, Italy; |
| | president, Architectural League of New York, 1919-1921; |
| | president, Society of Mural Painters, 1921-1926; |
| | member, executive committee, National Academy of Design; |
| | vice-president, American Institute of Architects; |
| | director, Fontainebleau School, Paris, France |
| Marriage(s): | M/1 – 1894-1920 – Anna Willets (1868-1920) |
| | M/2 – 1924-1941 – Estelle Rodgers (1888-1967) |
| Address: | 234 Briarwood Crossing, Lawrence |
| Name of estate: | |
| Year of construction: | 1927 |
| Style of architecture: | Neo-Federal |
| Architect(s): | James Monroe Hewlett designed his own house |
| Landscape architect(s): | |
| House extant: yes | |
| Historical notes: | |

The house was built by James Monroe Hewlett.

He was the son of James Augustus and Mary Elizabeth Sanderson Hewlett of Lawrence.

Anna Willets Hewlett was the daughter of Edward Bowne and Sarah Frances Carman Willets.

James Monroe and Anna Willets Hewlett's son Roger, who resided in Hewlett Neck, married Kathryn Charlotte Pierce, the daughter of Frank R. Pierce of Milwaukee, WI, and a relative of President Franklin Pierce, and, later, Selina Richards Wood, the daughter of Richard Davis Wood. The Hewletts' daughter Hester married James Britton Stearns, the son of Cooper Stearns of Lawrence. Their daughter Anne, who resided in Philadelphia, PA, married Richard Buckminster Fuller, the acclaimed designer, architect, poet, author, and inventor. The Hewletts' daughter Anglesea married George E. Abbot and resided in Andover, MA. Their daughter Laurence, who resided in Lawrence, married Robert Page Burr. Sr. and, later, Horace Bowker, Sr. Their daughter Hope married William Man Parkhurst and resided in Woodmere. Hope later married Harry D. Watts. Their son Arthur Thomas Hewlett II married Natalie Caroline Franz of Stockbridge, MA, and resided in Homer, AR. Their son James Augustus Hewlett, who resided in Jericho, married Marjorie Beard and, later, Mabel Pratt, the daughter of Charles Holden Pratt.

Estelle Rodgers Hewlett was the daughter of Harrie Oscar and Eva Lilien Funston Rogers.

*Hewlett painted the murals for the Willard Straight Memorial at Cornell University and the Elihu Root Memorial in Washington, DC. [*See* Spinzia, *Long Island's Prominent North Shore Families, vol. II* – Straight entry – and *Long Island's Prominent Families in the Town of Southampton* – Root entry.]

The house was later owned by John Edward Bierwirth and, then, by Anthony Marmo.

*front/side facade, 1978*

## Hewlett, Roger Sanderson (1911-1977)

| | |
|---|---|
| Occupation(s): | entertainers and associated professions -   actor |
| | writer -   playwright |
| | journalist -   contributing editor, Time, Inc.; |
| | senior sports editor, *Sports Illustrated* magazine |
| Civic Activism: | commodore, Cedarhurst Yacht Club |
| Marriage(s): | M/1 – 1937-1969 – Kathryn Charlotte Pierce (1907-1969) |
| | M/1 – 1970-1977 – Selina Richards Wood (1911-2001) |
| Address: | 178 Hewlett Neck Road, Hewlett Neck |
| Name of estate: | |
| Year of construction: | 1926 |
| Style of architecture: | Colonial Revival |
| Architect(s): | |
| Landscape architect(s): | |
| House extant:  yes | |

Historical notes:

   The house was built by Roger Sanderson Hewlett.
   The *Social Register New York, 1965* lists Roger S. and Kathryn C. Pierce Hewlett as residing at 178 Hewlett Neck Road, Lawrence [Hewlett Neck].
   He was the son of James Monroe and Anna Willets Hewlett of Lawrence.
   Kathryn Charlotte Pierce Hewlett was the daughter of Franklyn Roberts and Edna Charlotte Whitten Pierce, Jr. of Milwaukee, WI, and a descendant of President Franklin Pierce.
   Selina Richards Wood Hewlett was the daughter of Richard Davis and Louisa Lawrence Schroeder Wood of Philadelphia, PA. She had previously been married to Henry Sturgis Grew, Jr. with whom she resided in Lawrence.

*front facade, 2000*

## Hillman, Stanley (1887-1946)

| | |
|---|---|
| Occupation(s): | labor organizer - president, Amalgamated Clothing Workers of America; a founder, vice-president and CIO, Congress of Industrial Organizations; chief clerk, International Workers Union, 1914<br>politician - a founder, American Labor Party, 1936; a founder, Liberal Party of New York |
| Civic Activism: | member, National Defense Advisory Committee (FDR administration); associate director, Office of Production Management (FDR administration); head, labor division, War Production Board (FDR administration); member, Labor Advisory Board of National Recovery Administration (FDR administration); a founder, Labor's Non Partisan League; founder, Sidney Hillman Foundation |
| Marriage(s): | 1916-1946 – Bas Sheva Abramowitz (1889-1970)<br>- labor organizer - educational director, Laundry Workers Joint Board; a founder and vice president, Amalgamated Clothing Workers of America<br>Civic Activism: member, Presidential Commission on Status of Women (FDR administration) |
| Address: | 73 Union Place, Lynbrook |
| Name of estate: | |
| Year of construction: | 1913 |
| Style of architecture: | Colonial Revival |
| Architect(s): | |
| Landscape architect(s): | |
| House extant: | yes |
| Historical notes: | |

The Hillmans resided in Lynbrook from 1924 through the 1930s.

Sidney was born in Zagare, Lithuania, which at the time was part of Russia. Arrested for his anti-Czarist activities, he eventually arrived in the United States via Germany and Great Britain. In the United States, he worked in a warehouse, in Sears, Roebuck & Company's infant wear department, and as an apprentice garment cutter for Hart, Shaffner, & Marx.

Born in Linoveh, Grodno, Russia, Bas Sheva Abramowitz Hillman was the daughter of Emanuel and Sarah Rabinowitz Abramowitz. Bas Seva immigrated to America to escape marriage and found work as a button sewer at Hart, Shaffner, & Marx.

Stanley and Bas Sheva Abramowitz Hillman's daughter Philoine married Milton Fried of Brooklyn. Their daughter Sally married ____ Kraft.

In 2009, the 2,584-square-foot house sold for $510,000.

At the time of Sidney's death, the Hillmans were residing at 107 Glenwood Avenue, Point Lookout.

*front facade, 2013*

### Hinckley, Julian (1884-1955)

| | |
|---|---|
| Occupation(s): | architect |
| | writer -  *E*, 1914 (novel); |
| | *The Family Tradition*, 1918 (novel); |
| | numerous articles in periodicals |
| Civic Activism: | governor, Lawrence Association |
| Marriage(s): | M/1 – 1907 – Mildred Culver (b. 1888) |
| | M/2 – 1931-1955 – Isobel Catherine Bartlett (1907-1995) |
| | (aka Danah Bartlett) |
| | - Civic Activism:  vice-president, South Shore Division, League of Women Voters |
| Address: | 285 Longwood Crossing, Lawrence |
| Name of estate: | |
| Year of construction: | |
| Style of architecture: | |
| Architect(s): | |
| Landscape architect(s): | |
| House extant: no | |
| Historical notes: | |

Julian Hinckley was the son of Samuel Parker and Rosalie Neilson Hinckley, who resided at *Sunset Hall* in Lawrence. Mildred Culver Hinckley was the daughter of Frederick F. and Isobel Clark Culver.

The *Social Register, 1933* lists Julian and Danah Bartlett Hinckley as residing in Cedarhurst [Lawrence].

She was the daughter of Dr. Daniel Edwin and Mrs. Isobel Catherine Rose Bartlett of Litchfield, CT. Isobel subsequently married William Ebbets Lowe II and resided in Manhattan.

Julian and Isobel Catherine Bartlett Hinckley's daughter Isobel married Price Perkins Glover and resided in Manhattan. Their son Daniel married Maria Luisa Low, the daughter of Luis Low of New York, and resided in Boston, MA.

In 1941 the roof and second floor were severely damaged by fire. [*The New York Times* December 22, 1941, p. 21, and *The Brooklyn Daily Eagle* December 22, 1941, p. 6.]

*[See following Hinckley entries for additional family information.]*


### Hinckley, Samuel Neilson, Sr. (1881-1931)

| | |
|---|---|
| Occupation(s): | financier -  stockbroker |
| Marriage(s): | 1914-div. 1921 – Catherine Livingston Hamersley (1891-1977) |
| | - capitalist -  owned large tracts of land on Manhattan's Fifth Avenue |
| Address: | Ocean Avenue, Lawrence |
| Name of estate: | *Son Ridge* |
| Year of construction: | |
| Style of architecture: | |
| Architect(s): | |
| Landscape architect(s): | |
| House extant: unconfirmed | |
| Historical notes: | |

The *Long Island Society Register, 1929* lists Samuel Neilson Hinckley as residing at *Son Ridge* in Cedarhurst [Lawrence].

He was the son of Samuel Parker and Rosalie Neilson Hinckley of *Sunset Hall* in Lawrence.

Catherine Livingston Hamersley Hinckley, who was the first woman from America to visit Saudi Arabia's capital of Riyadh, was the daughter of James Hooker and Margaret Willing Chisholm Hamersley of Newport, RI. Catherine later married Henry Coleman Drayton and, subsequently, Charles Whitney Carpenter. Catherine's brother Louis married Hilles Morris, the daughter of Stuyvesant Fish and Elizabeth Hilles Wynkoop Morris, Jr. of Hewlett Bay Park, and resided in Southampton and at *The Moorings* in Sands Point. Hilles was the great-granddaughter of President Martin Van Buren. [*See* Spinzia, *Long Island's Prominent Families in the Town of Southampton* and *Long Island's Prominent North Shore Families, vol. I* – Hamersley entries.]

Samuel Neilson and Catherine Livingston Hamersley Hinckley Sr.'s son Samuel Neilson Hinckley, Jr. married Helen Pettit, the daughter of Howard Leslie Pettit of Flint, MI, and resided in California.

*[See other Hinckley entries for additional family information.]*

### Hinckley, Samuel Parker (1850-1935)

| | |
|---|---|
| Occupation(s): | industrialist - director, New England Phonograph Co. |
| | capitalist - real estate development in Manhattan, Lawrence, and Cedarhurst |
| Civic Activism: | trustee, Village of Lawrence, 1898 |
| Marriage(s): | 1881-div. 1910 – Rosalie Neilson (1858-1939) |
| Address: | Central Avenue, Lawrence |
| Name of estate: | *Sunset Hall* |
| Year of construction: | c. 1883 |
| Style of architecture: | Shingle |
| Architect(s): | Lamb and Rich designed the house (for S. P. Hinckley) |
| Landscape architect(s): | |
| House extant: | no |

Historical notes:

The house, originally named *Sunset Hall*, was built by Samuel Parker Hinckley. [*The New York Times* October 21, 1935, p. 27.]

The *Social Register Summer, 1910* lists Samuel Parker and Rosalie Neilson Hinckley as residing at *Sunset Hall* in Lawrence.

*front facade, 1886*

He was the son of Lyman and Anne Cutler Parker Hinckley of Boston, MA.

Rosalie Neilson Hinckley was the daughter of William Hude and Caroline Kane Neilson of Far Rockaway. Rosalie's sister Caroline married William Voss and resided at *Merriefield* in Hewlett Bay Park. Her sister Emilie married Middleton Schoolbred Burrill and resided at *Jericho Farms* in Jericho. [*See* Spinzia, *Long Island's Prominent North Shore Families, vol. 1* – Burrill entry.]

Samuel Parker and Rosalie Neilson Hinckley's daughter Rosalie married Cornelius Wendell Wickersham, Sr. and resided at *Briarwood* in Lawrence. Their daughter Dorothy married Thomas Resolved Williams and resided at *Windemere* in Lawrence. Their son Samuel Neilson Hinckley, Sr. married Catherine Livingston Hamersley and resided at *Son Ridge* in Lawrence. Their son Julian, who resided in Lawrence, married Mildred Culver and, later, Isobel Catherine Bartlett (aka Danah Bartlett).

*[See other Hinckley entries for additional family information.*

### Hoag, Charles H. (1869-1938)

| | |
|---|---|
| Occupation(s): | merchant - president, Star Towel Supply Co., Brooklyn |
| | industrialist - a founder, Quick Kleen Soap Co., Brooklyn |
| Marriage(s): | Sarah H. Keith |
| | - Civic Activism: recording secretary, Garden City Woman's Club, 1930; |
| | corresponding secretary, Garden City Woman's Club, 1932; |
| | vice president, Garden City Woman's Club, 1939 |
| Address: | 47 Roxbury Road, Garden City |
| Name of estate: | |
| Year of construction: | 1927 |
| Style of architecture: | Neo-Tudor |
| Architect(s): | |
| Landscape architect(s): | |
| House extant: | yes |

Historical notes:

The house was built by Charles H. Hoag.

The *Long Island Society Register, 1929* lists Charles H. and Sarah H. Keith Hoag as residing at 47 Roxbury Road, Garden City.

Charles H. and Sarah H. Keith Hoag's son Paul was an avid collector of material on Thomas Edison. Their daughter Lorena married Archie R. Cook and resided in Cortland, NY. Their daughter Bessie married ____ Shelly and resided in Farmingdale.

*front facade, 2000*

### Hodges, John King (1891-1935)

| | |
|---|---|
| Occupation(s): | financier - partner, Lock, Hodges, and Co. (stock brokerage firm); partner, Hodges, Dunham, and Co. (stock brokerage firm); partner, Stokes, Hodges, and Co. (stock brokerage firm); director, Distillers Securities Corp. |
| | writer - *The Girl Outside* (play)* |
| Marriage(s): | 1917-1935 – Rosamond Batchelder (1897-1935) |
| Address: | Briarwood Crossing, Lawrence |
| Name of estate: | |
| Year of construction: | |
| Style of architecture: | |
| Architect(s): | |
| Landscape architect(s): | |
| House extant: unconfirmed | |
| Historical notes: | |

The *Social Register Summer, 1921* and the *Long Island Society Register, 1929* list John K. and Rosamond Batchelder Hodges as residing in Cedarhurst [Lawrence].

He was the son of Amory Glazier and Alice Woodward Hodges of New York.

**The Girl Outside* was produced in October 1932. [Internet Broadway Database]

Rosamond Batchelder Hodges was the daughter of John L. Batchelder of Beacon Hill, Boston, MA.

John King and Rosamond Batchelder Hodges' daughter Rosamond married Sterling Shattuck Adams and resided in Milbrook, NY. Their daughter Marion married Roger Kirkland Hart, the son of Albert Edward Hart of Cedarhurst.

Grief stricken by the death of her husband, Mrs. Hodges committed suicide by leaping to her death from the seventh floor of a Washington, DC, hotel. [*The Washington Post* October 30, 1935, p. 1.]


### Hodges, Wetmore, Sr. (1887-1957)

| | |
|---|---|
| Occupation(s): | industrialist - a founder, Hodges Research and Development Co., Redwood City, CA (mechanical automotive engineering firm); a founder, Wetmore Hodges & Associates, Redwood City, CA (mechanical automotive engineering firm); director, General Foods Co.; chairman of board, General Sea Food Corp.; vice-president and secretary, American Radiator Co. |
| | financier - chairman of board and director, Interstate Equities Corp. |
| | educator - associate professor of business research, Graduate School of Business Administration, Harvard University, Cambridge, MA |
| Civic Activism: | vice-chairman, Business Advisory Council, Department of Commerce during World War II |
| Marriage(s): | 1914-1957 – Dorothy Miller Chapman (1889-1958) |
| Address: | Knota Road, Woodmere |
| Name of estate: | |
| Year of construction: | |
| Style of architecture: | |
| Architect(s): | |
| Landscape architect(s): | |
| House extant: unconfirmed | |
| Historical notes: | |

The *Long Island Society Register, 1929* lists Wetmore and Dorothy Chapman Hodges [Sr.] as residing in Woodmere.

He was the son of Charles W. and Eliza Kellog Wetmore.

Wetmore and Dorothy Miller Chapman Hodges, Sr.'s son William married Eleanor Elizabeth Root, the daughter of Louis Demman Root of Southampton. Their son Wetmore Hodges, Jr. married Charlena McAnarney, the daughter of Charles J. McAnarney of Phoenix, AZ, and resided at *Beverly Farms* in MA. Their son Henry married Emma Wagoner.

### Hodgson, Robert John, Jr. (1885-1949)

| | |
|---|---|
| Occupation(s): | merchant - president, Fine–Goods Sales Associates |
| Marriage(s): | 1918-1949 – Olive Vanderbilt (1887-1980) |
| Address: | 145 Euston Road, Garden City |
| Name of estate: | |
| Year of construction: | |
| Style of architecture: | Colonial Revival |
| Architect(s): | Olive Frances Tjaden designed the house (for Hodgson) |
| Landscape architect(s): | |
| House extant: yes | |
| Historical notes: | |

The house was built by Robert John Hodgson, Jr.

The *Long Island Society Register, 1929* lists Robert John and Olive Vanderbilt Hodgson, Jr. as residing at 145 Euston Road, Garden City.

He was the son of Robert John Hodgson, Sr. of Lewiston, ME.

Olive Vanderbilt Hodgson was the daughter of Joseph White and Philena Winslow Vanderbilt of Brooklyn and Old Brookville. [*See* Spinzia, *Long Island's Prominent North Shore Families, vol. II* – L. T. Vanderbilt entry.]

Robert John and Olive Vanderbilt Hodgson. Jr.'s daughter Barbara married Amherst W. Meeker. Their daughter Olive married Gordon Madison Einhaus, the son of Harry Madison Einhaus of Garden City.

*front facade, 2000*

### Hoffman, Horace E. (d. 1878)

| | |
|---|---|
| Occupation(s): | financier - member, Porter, Robjent, & Co., 1923 (public utility trading firm); founder, H. E. Hoffman and Co. (government securities trading firm); a founder and partner, with Leonard L. Maher, Hoffman & Maher, 1938 (government securities trading firm); a founder and partner, with William P. Neacy, Hoffman & Neacy (government securities trading firm); partner, Charles E. Quincy & Co. (government securities trading firm) |
| Marriage(s): | |
| Address: | 250 Stewart Avenue, Garden City |
| Name of estate: | |
| Year of construction: | 1932 |
| Style of architecture: | Neo-Tudor |
| Architect(s): | Olive Frances Tjaden designed the house (for H. E. Hoffman) |
| Landscape architect(s): | |
| House extant: yes | |
| Historical notes: | |

The house was built by Horace E. Hoffman.

It was later owned by John Francis Marini, Sr. and, then, by Jurge Cerriut.

*entrance, 2001*

### Hofheimer, Lester (1880-1936)

| | |
|---|---|
| Occupation(s): | industrialist - manager, Perth Amboy, NJ, factory, New Brunswick Cigar Co; |
| | manager, Hirschorn Mack Cigar Co. (later, General Cigar Co.) |
| Civic Activism: | president, Hofheimer Foundation, NY |
| Marriage(s): | 1913-1936 – Corinne Kodziesen (1892-1963) |
| | - Civic Activism: a founder, American Shakespeare Festival Theater and Academy, Stratford, CT |
| Address: | Woods Lane, Woodmere |
| Year of construction: | 1917 |
| Style of architecture: | Georgian Revival |
| Architect(s): | B. E. Stern designed the house (for Hofheimer) |
| Landscape architect(s): | |
| Builder: | John P. Streigler, Far Rockaway, framing |
| | Smith Brothers, Far Rockaway, plumbing and heating |

House extant: unconfirmed
Historical notes:

The house was built by Lester Hofheimer.

He was the son of Nathan and Helene Rosengart Hofheimer of *Long Acre Farm* in Warrenville, NJ, and an heir to the General Motors fortune.

Corinne Kodziesen Hofheimer was the daughter of Aaron and Jennie Spellman Kodziesen.

Lester and Corinne Kodziesen Hofheimer's son Lester Nathan Hofheimer, who was killed in World War II, bequeathed one million dollars to charity.

*front facade, 1918*

### Hofstra, William Sake (1861-1932)

| | |
|---|---|
| Occupation(s): | merchant - president, Nassau Lumber Co.*; president, Price & Co., Ltd., Canada (dealers in pulpwood) |
| Civic Activism: | trustee, Nassau County Police Relief Association |
| Marriage(s): | M/1 – 1881-div. c. 1885 – Anna Laura Morton (1863-1930) |
| | M/2 – Katharine Mason (1854-1933) |
| | - Civic Activism: vice-president, Bide-a-Wee Home for Animals, Wantagh; donated *The Netherlands* to be used "for the public good"; president, Atlantic Cat Club |
| Address: | Fulton Avenue, Hempstead |
| Name of estate: | *The Netherlands* |
| Year of construction: | c. 1904 |
| Style of architecture: | Modified Shingle |
| Architect(s): | H. Craig Severance designed the house (for Hofstra) |

Landscape architect(s):
House extant: yes
Interior and exterior photographs of the estate can be found in Special Collections, Axinn Library, Hofstra University. Interior photographs can be viewed at Hofstra University's Special Collection website.
Historical notes:

The house, originally named *The Netherlands*, was built by William Sake Hofstra.
He was the son of Sakee and Wilhelmina Zageweg Hofstra of Muskegan, MI.
William Sake and Anna Laura Morton Hofstra's fourteen-year-old daughter Laura died in 1896 of peritonitis. Their daughter Margaret married Olof Fredik Angelin of Stockholm, Sweden.
The *Long Island Society Register, 1929* lists William S. and Katharine Mason Hofstra as residing at *The Netherlands* in Hempstead.
She had previously been married to Morgan Williams of Leadville, CO.
William Sake and Katharine Mason Hofstra did not have children.
The estate is now Hofstra University. The house serves as administrative offices.
*Howard Stanley Bower, who resided at *Longdrive* in West Hempstead, was also president of the Nassau Lumber Co.

*front facade, 1992*

### Holmes, Emlen Williams, II (1914-1975)

| | |
|---|---|
| Occupation(s): | attorney -   partner, Holmes and Healy |
| Marriage(s): | M/1 – 1938-div. 1947 – Marguerite Ballantine (1919-2007) |
| | M/2 – Evelyn Ogden Hatch (1923-2011) |
| |     - journalist -  fashion editor, *Town and Country* magazine |
| Address: | 110 Berkshire Place, Lawrence |
| Name of estate: | |
| Year of construction: | 1890 |
| Style of architecture: | Modified Four Square |
| Architect(s): | |
| Landscape architect(s): | |
| House extant: yes | |
| Historical notes | |

   Emlen Williams Holmes II was the son of the president of the New York Law School Jabish Holmes, Sr.
   Marguerite Ballantine Holmes was the daughter of Herbert Wilgus and Marguerite Louise Small Ballantine of Hewlett Bay Harbor. Marguerite subsequently married Neilson Olcott, and, later, Haven Putnam, Sr.
   Emlen Williams and Marguerite Ballantine Holmes II's son Peter married Ann H. Jones and resided in Manhattan and Nantucket, MA. Their son Jabish married Barbara Elaine Swizal and resided in Dallas, TX. Their son Emlen Williams Holmes III resided in La Canada, CA.
   The *Social Register New York, 1968* lists E. Williams and Evelyn O. Hatch Holmes as residing at 110 Berkshire Place, Lawrence.
   She was the daughter of Eric Stow and Sylvia Whiton Stuart Hatch of Lawrence.

*front facade, 2014*

### Hoppin, Samuel Howland (1858-1932)

| | |
|---|---|
| Occupation(s): | attorney -   partner, Hoppin and Beard, NYC |
| Marriage(s): | 1916-1932 – Marie L. d'Ablemont (1863-1933) |
| Address: | 96 Albemarle Avenue, Hempstead |
| Name of estate: | |
| Year of construction: | 1919 |
| Style of architecture: | Colonial Revival |
| Architect(s): | |
| Landscape architect(s): | |
| House extant: yes | |
| Historical notes | |

   The *Social Register Summer, 1921* and the *Long Island Society Register, 1929* list Samuel Howland and Marie d'Ablemont Hoppin as residing at 96 Albemarle Avenue, Hempstead.
   He was the son of Hamilton and Louisa Howland Hoppin of Newport, RI.
   Marie L. d'Ablemont Hoppin was the daughter of Auguste Lazard and Charrise Lambert d'Ablemont. Marie had previously been married to Benjamin Leydier.

### Horton, Chauncey Todd, Sr. (1883-1969)

Occupation(s): merchant -  partner, with his brothers, Sheffield Farms Co. (dairy distributors)
industrialist -  purchasing agent, Horton Pilsner Brewing Co.

Marriage(s): M/1 – 1911-1919 – Grace Louise Duckworth (1884-1919)
M/2 – 1920 – Helen Henderson
  - president, Women's Catholic Club of Garden City, 1933;
    president, Woman's Auxiliary, St. Joseph's Church

Address: 25 Nassau Boulevard, Garden City
Name of estate:
Year of construction: 1920
Style of architecture: Colonial Revival
Architect(s):
Landscape architect(s):
House extant: yes
Historical notes:

*front facade, 2009*

Chauncey Todd Horton, Sr. was the son of Loton and Sarah Alice Todd Bailey Horton of Manhattan.

Grace Louise Duckworth Horton was the daughter of Walter Franklin Duckworth of Brooklyn.

Chauncey Todd and Grace Louise Duckworth Horton, Sr.'s son Chauncey Todd Horton, Jr. was the editor of the *Newman News* and the associate editor of the *Newman Literary Quarterly.*

The *Long Island Society Register, 1929* lists Chauncey T. and Helen Henderson Horton [Sr.] as residing at 25 Nassau Boulevard, Garden City.

She was the daughter of Ernest Kirtland Henderson of Manhattan.

Chauncey Todd and Helen Henderson Horton, Sr.'s son Donald married Patricia Anne Harrison, the daughter of George Harrison of Ridgefield, NJ. Their son Ernest married Jane Gordon Hamlin, the daughter of Francis Bacon and Clara Barnes Danforth Hamlin of Garden City.

By 1932 the Hortons had relocated to 25 Rockaway Avenue in Garden City.

At the time of his death, Horton was residing in Bay Shore. [*The New York Times* January 5, 1969, p. 77.]


### Houghton, Owen Edward, Jr.  (1892-1967)

Occupation(s): merchant -  president, bank supply company

Marriage(s): 1916 – Helen Hasbrouck Reeve (b. 1896)

Address: 140 Chestnut Street, Garden City
Name of estate:
Year of construction: 1924
Style of architecture: Eclectic with Dutch Colonial elements
Architect(s):
Landscape architect(s):
House extant: yes
Historical notes:

*front facade, 2001*

The *Long Island Society Register, 1929* lists Owen Edward and Helen Hasbrouck Reeve Houghton [Jr.] as residing at 140 Chestnut Street, Garden City.

He was the son of Dr. Owen Edward and Mrs. Nellie Alden Wattles Houghton, Sr. of Brooklyn.

Helen Hasbrouck Reeve Houghton was the daughter of Arthur Linwood Reeve of Brooklyn.

Owen Edward and Helen Hasbrouck Reeve Houghton, Jr.'s son Lawrence married Diane Cardelli, the daughter of Count Giovanni Guido Carlo and Countess Jacqueline Stewart Cardelli of *Orchard Cottage*, Centre Island, and of Water Mill. [*See* Spinzia, *Long Island's Prominent North Shore Families, vol. I* – Cardelli entry; *Long Island's Prominent North Shore Families, vol. II* – Stewart entry; and *Long Island's Prominent Families in the Town of Southampton* – Cardelli entry.]

In 1966 the house was remodeled.

### Howe, Wallis Eastburn, Jr. (1901-1976)

| | |
|---|---|
| Occupation(s): | publisher - editor and advertising manager, *The Garden City News*; sales manager, Pocket Books Inc.; vice-president, Henry M. Snyder Co.; vice-president and general manager, Samuel Gabriel Sons Co. (division of American Colortype Co.) |
| Marriage(s): | Louise Pratt (1902-1998) - Civic Activism: member, Garden City League of Helen Keller Services for the Blind; volunteer, Nassau Hospital, Mineola (later, Winthrop – University Hospital; now, NYU Langone Hospital – Long Island) |
| Address: | 43 Hilton Avenue, Garden City |
| Name of estate: | |
| Year of construction: | 1883 |
| Style of architecture: | Victorian |
| Architect(s): | |
| Landscape architect(s): | |
| House extant: | yes |
| Historical notes: | |

*front facade, 2008*

The *Long Island Society Register, 1929* lists Wallis E. and Louise Pratt Howe as residing at 6 Franklin Court, Garden City.

He was the son of the noted architect Wallis Eastburn Howe, Sr. and Mrs. Mary Emily Locke Howe of Bristol, RI.

Louise Pratt Howe was the daughter of Dr. Charles A. Pratt of New Bedford, MA.

Wallis Eastburn and Louise Pratt Howe, Jr.'s daughter Elizabeth married John Sanford Shannon, the daughter of Judge George Thomas and Mrs. Ruth Garrett Shannon of Florida.

At the time of his death, Howe was residing at 43 Hilton Avenue, Garden City. [*The New York Times* January 1, 1977, p. 12.]

In 1970 the house was remodeled.


### Hoxie, Isaac Richmond, Sr. (1879-1951)

| | |
|---|---|
| Occupation(s): | financier - member, Rhodes and Co., NYC (stock brokerage firm) |
| Marriage(s): | Eleanor Throop Brown (1881-1969) |
| Address: | 220 Ocean Avenue, Lawrence |
| Name of estate: | |
| Year of construction: | 1920 |
| Style of architecture: | Modified Colonial Revival |
| Architect(s): | |
| Landscape architect(s): | |
| House extant: | yes |
| Historical notes: | |

*rear facade, 2007*

The *Long Island Society Register, 1929* lists I. Richmond and Eleanor T. Brown Hoxie [Sr.] as residing at 220 Ocean Avenue, Lawrence.

He was the son of Timothy Wright and Abbie Elizabeth Richmond Hoxie.

Eleanor Throop Brown Hoxie was the daughter of William Fayette and Gertrude Hoyt Brown.

Isaac Richmond and Eleanor Throop Brown Hoxie, Sr.'s daughter Lenore married Marsden Bayard Chandler, the son of Robert Welch Chandler of Edgartown, MA. Their daughter Gertrude married Harvey Ladew Williams and resided in Greenwich, CT. Gertrude subsequently married Gordon S. Campbell. Their son Isaac Richmond Hoxie, Jr. married Elaine Mary Hine, the daughter of Arthur and Eva Tilly Pearsall Hine of Cedarhurst, and resided in Rockville Centre.

The house was subsequently owned by Lars Sellstedt, Jr.

## Hubbell, George Loring, Jr. (1894-1990)

| | |
|---|---|
| Occupation(s): | attorney - member, Greene and Hurd; partner, Hurd, Hamlin, and Hubbell; partner, Hubbell and Van de Walle |
| | financier - director, Garden City Bank and Trust Co.; director, West Hempstead National Bank; director, Roslyn National Bank and Trust Co.; chairman of board, Long Island Trust Co. |
| Civic Activism: | attorney, Village of Garden City; member, New York State Board of Regents, 1955-1965; member, Nassau County Charter Revision Committee |
| Marriage(s): | 1917-1974 – Sophie Milbank Young (1894-1974) |
| Address: | 103 Rockaway Avenue, Garden City |
| Name of estate: | |
| Year of construction: | 1920 |
| Style of architecture: | Colonial Revival |
| Architect(s): | |
| Landscape architect(s): | |
| House extant: yes | |
| Historical notes: | |

The *Long Island Society Register, 1929* lists George Loring and Sophie [Milbank] Young Hubbell, Jr. as residing at 2 Putting Lane, Garden City. Number 2 Putting Lane became 103 Rockaway Avenue. The *Social Register New York, 1980* lists the Hubbells as residing at 103 Rockaway Avenue, Garden City.

He was the son of George Loring and Eliza Strong Platt Hubbell, Sr. of *Lonesomehurst* in Garden City.

Sophie Milbank Young Hubbell was the daughter of John Manning Young of Manhattan.

George Loring and Sophie Milbank Young Hubbell, Jr.'s daughter Sophie married Granger Hall Collens, the son of Clarence Lynn Collens of Cleveland Heights, OH. Their daughter Elizabeth married The Reverend Edward Finch Parsons, the son of William Bowne Parsons of Flushing, Queens, and resided in Spokane, WA. Their daughter Susan married Donald Frederick Wohlers, the son of Frederick Wohlers of Hempstead, and resided in Basking Ridge, NJ. Their son William married Elizabeth Jane Smith, the daughter of Dwight Elgin Smith of Takoma Park, MD. Their daughter Barbara married Jay Murchison Field of Garden City, and resided in Lake Placid, FL. Their son George Loring III married Loretta McHugh and resided in Chazy, NY.

*[See other Hubbell entries for additional family information.]*

In 2013, the 4,949-square-foot house, with five bedrooms and four and a half bathrooms, sold for $1.9 million.

*rear facade. 2013*

## Hubbell, George Loring, Sr. (1865-1959)

| | |
|---|---|
| Occupation(s): | real estate agent - resident manager, Garden City Co. (real estate developer); agent, Hempstead Plains Co.; agent, Merillon Estates; president, Cathedral Avenue Realty Co. |
| | financier - a founder and director, Nassau County Trust Co.; a founder and president, Garden City Bank and Trust Co.; director, Nassau Suffolk Bond and Mortgage Guarantee Co. |
| | capitalist - secretary and treasurer, Hempstead Plains Aviation Co.; general purchasing agent, claims adjuster, and real estate agent, Long Island Railroad |
| Civic Activism: | first president, Village of Garden City; president, Garden City School Board; secretary and governor, Garden City Golf Club; president, Garden City Republican Club; Republican district leader, treasurer, and member of executive committee, Nassau County Republican Committee; governor and vice-president, Camp Fire Club; a founder and director, Cherry Valley Club, Garden City, 1916 |
| Marriage(s): | 1891-1955 – Eliza Strong Platt (1867-1955) - suffragist |
| Address: | 6 Cathedral Avenue, Garden City |
| Name of estate: | *Lonesomehurst* |
| Year of construction: | 1896 |
| Style of architecture: | Modified Shingle |
| Architect(s): | |
| Landscape architect(s): | Hicks Nursery supplied the plantings (for G. L. Hubbell, Sr.) |
| House extant: | yes |
| Historical notes: | |

The house, originally named *Lonesomehurst*, was built by George Loring Hubbell, Sr.

The *Social Register Summer, 1915* lists George Loring and Eliza S. Platt Hubbell [Sr.] as residing in Garden City. The *Long Island Society Register, 1929* lists George Loring and Eliza S. Platt Hubbell [Sr.] as residing at 6 Cathedral Avenue, Garden City.

He was the son of John Wolcott and Margaret Louise Beckwith Hubbell.

Eliza Strong Platt Hubbell was the daughter of John L. and Susan Sherwood Platt of Poughkeepsie, NY.

George Loring and Eliza Strong Platt Hubbell, Sr.'s son John married Dorothy Peters and resided in Garden City. Their son Sherwood married Helen Sands Nostrand and resided in Garden City. Their daughter Margaret married Philip Shumway Lord, Sr., the son of Alonzo Boardman Lord of Evanston, IL. Their daughter Elizabeth married Andrew Waldon Stone and resided in Garden City. Their son George Loring Hubbell, Jr. married Sophie Milbank Young and resided in Garden City.

*[See other Hubbell entries for additional family information.]*

The house was later owned by Walter Edwin Frew.

*rear facade*

### Hubbell, John Platt, Sr. (1893-1963)

| | |
|---|---|
| Occupation(s): | inventor - co-inventor, electro-galvanizing process for depositing zinc coatings |
| | engineer - chief chemical engineer, New Jersey Zinco Co.; partner, Singmaster & Breyer; assistant secretary, Keldur Corp. |
| Civic Activism: | mayor and trustee, Village of Garden City; Commissioner of Public Works, Village of Garden City |
| Marriage(s): | 1917-1963 – Dorothy Peters (1891-1986) |
| Address: | 106 Fifth Street, Garden City |
| Name of estate: | |
| Year of construction: | 1913 |
| Style of architecture: | Modified Shingle |
| Architect(s): | |
| Landscape architect(s): | |
| House extant: yes | |
| Historical notes: | |

*front facade, 2008*

The house was previously owned by Sterling Hollingshead Ivison, Sr.

The *Long Island Society Register, 1929* lists the Hubbells as residing at 106 Fifth Street, Garden City.

John Platt Hubbells, Sr. was the son of George Loring and Eliza Strong Platt Hubbell, Sr. of *Lonesomehurst* in Garden City.

Dorothy Peters Hubbell was the daughter of Ralph and Eleanor Hartshorn Goodman Peters of *Wyndymeede* in Garden City.

John Platt and Dorothy Peters Hubbell, Sr.'s daughter Dorothy married Frederick Quincy Gemmill of Hempstead, the son of Edwin Earle Gemmill of Salina, KS. Their son Ralph married Jane Snyder, the daughter of William R. Snyder, and resided in Garden City. Their son Roger married Mary Bertyne Gormley, the daughter of John Vincent and Edna May Yenser Gormley of Garden City. Their son Richard married Carol Marie Patterson, the daughter of Thomas Joseph Patterson of Garden City. Their son John Platt Hubbell, Jr. married Martha Gallison of Brookline, MA, and resided in Cambridge, MA.

By 1943 the Hubbells had relocated to Kilburn Road in Garden City.

*[See other Hubbell entries for additional family information.]*


### Hubbell, Ralph Peters, Sr. (1921-2015)

| | |
|---|---|
| Occupation(s): | sales executive for several textile firms |
| Civic Activism: | president, Clinton County, NY, Historical Society; trustee, United Way; trustee, Y.M.C.A.; volunteer, for twenty-two years, Champlain Valley Physicians Hospital |
| Marriage(s): | 1943 – Harriet Jane Snyder |
| Address: | 50 Meadow Street, Garden City |
| Name of estate: | |
| Year of construction: | 1927 |
| Style of architecture: | Bungalow with Victorian elements |
| Architect(s): | |
| Landscape architect(s): | |
| House extant: yes | |
| Historical notes: | |

*front facade, 2009*

The house was built by Ralph Peters Hubbell.

He was the son of John Platt and Dorothy Peters Hubbell, Sr. of Garden City.

Harriet Jane Snyder Hubbell was the daughter of William Robert and Emma Harriet Henry Snyder of Garden City.

Ralph Peters and Harriet Jane Snyder Hubbell, Sr.'s son William married Laura Louise Faires, the daughter of Hunter Faires, Jr. of El Paso, TX. Their daughter Beckey married John Riley.

In 1984 the Hubbells relocated to *Sunnywood* in Chazy, NY.

## Hubbell, Sherwood (1895-1991)

Occupation(s): real estate agent - member, George L. Hubbell (real estate and and insurance firm

Marriage(s): 1922-1991 – Helen Sands Nostrand (1895-1994)

Address: 107 Rockaway Avenue, Garden City
Name of estate:
Year of construction: 1928
Style of architecture: Colonial Revival
Architect(s):
Landscape architect(s):
House extant: yes
Historical notes:

*front facade, 2000*

The house was built by Sherwood Hubbell.

The *Long Island Society Register, 1929* lists Sherwood and Helen Sands Nostrand Hubbell as residing at 107 Rockaway Avenue, Garden City.

He was the son of George Loring and Eliza Strong Platt Hubbell, Sr. of *Lonesomehurst* in Garden City.

Helen Sands Nostrand Hubbell was the daughter of Frederick William and Martha Morris Nostrand.

Sherwood and Helen Sands Nostrand Hubbell's daughter Martha married The Reverend Hubert Stanley Wood, Jr., the son of The Very Reverend Hubert Wood, Sr. of Garden City. Their daughter Margaret married John Eldridge Beebe, Sr., the son of Henry Ward and Edna Alice Eldridge Beebe of Garden City, and resided in Garden City.


## Hunter, Fenley (1886-1965)
### aka Richard Fenley Hunter

Occupation(s): industrialist - president, Hunter Illuminated Car Sign Co., Flushing
Civic Activism: vice-president, Queens Chamber of Commerce;
*

Marriage(s): M/1 – 1911-div. 1933 – Jessie Lines (b. 1888)
M/2 – Hazel M. *[unable to determine maiden name]*

Address: 70 First Street, Garden City
Name of estate:
Year of construction:
Style of architecture:
Architect(s):
Landscape architect(s):
House extant: no
Historical notes:

Richard Fenley Hunter was the son of Lytle and Elizabeth Durbin Hunter who resided in Manhattan.

Jessie Lines Hunter was the daughter of Stephen V. and Frances Ellen Benham Lines of Canandaigua, NY. Jessie subsequently married King R. Graham.

Richard Fenley and Jessie Lines Hunter's daughter Virginia married Egbert Moxham, Jr. of Kings Point. Their son Durbin married Kathryn Gave Sucher, the daughter of Theodore Richard Sucher of Hamden, CT, and resided in Kings Point.

*The Hunters co-sponsored, with H. Scarritt, and accompanied a paleontological expedition to the Crazy Mountains in Montana for the American Museum of Natural History, NYC. [*The New York Times* May 23, 1935, p. 25, and October 11, 1935, p. 27.] Subsequently, they were part of a paleontological expedition to Saskatchewan, Canada, which discovered more than six hundred prehistoric animal remains. [*The New York Times* August 13, 1936, p. 25.]

In 1928, Hunter was residing at *Porto Bello* in Kings Point. [*See* Spinzia, *Long Island's Prominent North Shore Families, vol. I* – Hunter entry.]

In 1952, Hunter's house was replaced by a ranch-style residence.

### Huntington, Ellery Channing, Jr. (1893-1987)

| | |
|---|---|
| Occupation(s): | attorney |
| | industrialist - director, National Postal Meter Co. |
| | financier - chairman of board and director, Equity Corp. of New York; |
| |     director, United Founders Corp.; |
| |     director, General Alliance Corp.; |
| |     director, Reliance International Corp.; |
| |     president, Morris Group Plan |
| | intelligence agent - Deputy Director of Special Operations, Office of Strategic Services and, later, chief liaison to Marshall Tito during World War II |
| Marriage(s): | M/1 – 1917-div. 1929 – Hester Gordon Gibson (b. 1897) |
| | M/2 – 1945-1987 – Helen Catherine DuBois (1914-2005) |
| |     - intelligence agent - secretary for chief of Office of Strategic Services in Algeria during World War II |
| Address: | Tenth Street and Carteret Place, Garden City |
| Name of estate: | |
| Year of construction: | 1923 |
| Style of architecture: | |
| Architect(s): | Arthur William Blake Wood designed the house (for E. C. Huntington, Jr.) |
| Landscape architect(s): | |
| House extant: unconfirmed | |
| Historical notes: | |

    The house was built by Ellery Channing Huntington, Jr. [*The Brooklyn Standard Union* June 25, 1922, p. 29.]

    The *Social Register Summer, 1921* and the *Long Island Society Register, 1929* list Ellery C. and Hester G. Gibson Huntington, Jr. as residing at Tenth Street and Carteret Place, Garden City.

    He was the son of Dr. Ellery Channing and Mrs. Susan Blanton Tucker Huntington, Sr.

    Hester Gordon Gibson Huntington was the daughter of the noted architect Robert Williams Gibson and Mrs. Caroline Hammond Gibson of *North Point* in Cove Neck. [*See* Spinzia, *Long Island's Prominent North Shore Families, vol. I* – Gibson entry.] Hester subsequently married Oscar Fulton Davisson, Jr., whom she divorced in 1933. She was eliminated from the *Social Register* for bailing the Communist leader Nicholas Doxenberg (aka George Morris and Earl Browder) out of jail.

    Ellery Channing and Hester Gordon Gibson Huntington, Jr.'s daughter Hester married Byron Cleary Darling and resided in Stamford, CT. Their son Ellery Channing Huntington III was killed in action in Germany during World War II.

    Helen Catherine DuBois Huntington was the daughter of Barron Peter and Helen Catherine Hodgkins DuBois.

    Ellery Channing and Helen Catherine DuBois Huntington, Jr.'s son The Reverend Frederick DuBois Huntington resided in Burke, VA.

### Hurd, George Frederick (1880-1941)

| | |
|---|---|
| Occupation(s): | attorney -  partner, Green and Hurd; |
| | partner, Hurd, Hamlin, and Hubbell |
| | capitalist -  director, Burton–Fifth Avenue Corp.; |
| | director, Exchange Corp. |
| | industrialist -  director, Cutler Mail Chute Co. |
| Marriage(s): | M/1 – 1905-div. 1934 – Mary Burnett (1883-1964) |
| | M/2 – 1934-1941 – Patricia E. Kendall (1901-1973) |
| | - writer -  *Come With Me to India*, 1931 |
| Address: | Village Way, Lawrence |

Name of estate:
Year of construction:
Style of architecture:
Architect(s):
Landscape architect(s):
House extant: unconfirmed
Historical notes:

The *Social Register Summer, 1915* and the *Long Island Society Register, 1929* list George Fred and Mary Burnett Hurd as residing in Cedarhurst [Lawrence].

He was the son of Burrit Newton and Louise Harriet Rose Hurd of Titusville, PA.

Mary Burnett Hurd subsequently married Robert B. Whiting with whom she resided in North Colebrook, CT.

George Frederick and Mary Burnett Hurd's daughter Anne married Mahlon Hutchinson, Jr., of *Ashwood Farm* in Devon, PA, and resided in North Colebrook, CT. Their daughter Mary married Lloyd Renshaw and resided in West Chester, PA. Their son John married Cecile Fuller, the daughter of Paul and Marie Augustine de Florez Fuller, Jr. of *Four Winds* in Hewlett, and resided in North Colebrook, CT.


### Hurry, Renwick Clifton (1875-1954)

| | |
|---|---|
| Occupation(s): | merchant -  art dealer, NYC* |
| Marriage(s): | 1904-1950 – Lucy Washington Morss (1884-1950) |
| | - artist - water-colorist |
| Address: | 60 Greenwich Street, Hempstead |

Name of estate:
Year of construction:
Style of architecture:
Architect(s):
Landscape architect(s):
House extant: no
Historical notes:

The *Long Island Society Register, 1929* lists Renwick C. and Lucy Washington Morss Hurry as residing at 60 Greenwich Street, Hempstead.

He was the son of Edmond Abdy and Emily Ashton Hurry.

Lucy Washington Morss was the daughter of Foster Burton and Lucy Madison Morss and a descendant of President George Washington's brother Samuel. [*The New York Times* April 11, 1950, p. 31.]

Renwick Clifton and Lucy Washington Morss Hurry's son Renwick Washington Hurry married Anna Baily Stoddard, the daughter of Francis Russell and Eleanor Whipple Stoddard and resided at *Baywick* in Cold Spring Harbor. Their daughter Lucy remained unmarried. Their daughter Emily married Stephen Dow Fuller and resided at *Harewood* in Oyster Bay.

*Henry du Pont, Payne Whitney, and President Franklin Delano Roosevelt were among his prominent clients.

### Hussey, Thomas Jefferson (1860-1933)

Occupation(s): merchant - manager, Knickerbocker Co. (ice company)

Marriage(s): 1896 – Marian Waitt Haley (1873-1958)

Address: 130 Chestnut Street, Garden City
Name of estate:
Year of construction: 1924
Style of architecture: Modified Dutch Colonial Revival
Architect(s):
Landscape architect(s):
House extant: yes
Historical notes:

The *Long Island Society Register, 1929* lists Thomas J. and Marion Waitt Haley Hussey as residing at 130 Chestnut [Street], Garden City.

He was the son of Erwin Albert and Harriet Frances Southard Hussey, Jr. Thomas' sister Harriet Bishop Hussey married Charles Wyman Morse who was known as Tammany Hall's "Ice King" of Manhattan.

Marian Waitt Haley Hussey was the daughter of E. A. Haley.

Thomas Jefferson and Marian Waitt Haley Hussey's daughter Harriet married Robert James Paisley, the son of The Reverend John O. Paisley of Highlands, MA, and resided in Garden City.

*front facade, 2005*

### Hutchinson, William Furman (1877-1920)

Occupation(s): financier - insurance broker

Marriage(s): 1916-1920 – Dorothy Allen (1896-1961)

Address: 69 Hilton Avenue, Garden City
Name of estate:
Year of construction:
Style of architecture:
Architect(s):
Landscape architect(s):
House extant: no
Historical notes:

The *Long Island Society Register, 1929* lists Mrs. William F. Hutchinson as residing at 69 Hilton Avenue, Garden City.
She was the daughter of Frank Howard and Susan Easton Bishop Allen of San Francisco, CA.
William Furman Hutchinson was among those killed on September 16, 1920, by a terrorist bombing at the corner of Broad and Wall Streets. [*The New York Times* September 20, 1920, p. 3, and *The Brooklyn Daily Eagle* September 17, 1920, p. 2.] His left leg was severed below the knee and part of his head was torn away. A horse-drawn wagon was parked across the street from 23 Wall Street, the site of the headquarters of J. P. Morgan, Inc. The bomb inside the wagon, consisting of 100 pounds of dynamite with 500 pounds of heavy cast-iron slugs, was detonated by a timer. Thirty-eight people were killed, four hundred people were injured, and property damage estimated at about $2 million resulted. The damage on the front of 23 Wall Street is visible today. It was never proven absolutely, but it is believed to have been the work of Galleanists, followers of the Italian anarchist Luigi Galleani, in revenge for the arrest of Sacco and Vanzetti. [Thomas A. Bailey and David M. Kennedy, *The American Pageant* (D. C. Heath & Co., 1994).]
William Furman and Dorothy Allen Hutchinson's daughter Barbara married William Fisk Knehr, Sr. of Chicago, IL.

**Hyland, John Francis (1868-1936)**

| | |
|---|---|
| Occupation(s): | attorney - judge, New York City, 1906-1914; judge, County Court, 1915 |
| | politician - mayor, New York City, 1918-1925 |
| Marriage(s): | 1899 – Marian O'Hara |
| Address: | 84 South Maron Place, Rockville Centre |
| Name of estate: | |
| Year of construction: | 1887 |
| Style of architecture: | Modified Dutch Colonial Revival |
| Architect(s): | |
| Landscape architect(s): | |
| House extant: yes | |
| Historical notes: | |

The house was built by John Francis Hyland. He was the son of Thomas H. Hyland of Green County, NY. John Francis and Marian O'Hara Hyland's daughter Virginia married John Francis Sinnott.
In 2022, the 4,301-square-foot house sold for $940,000.

*front facade, 2022*

**Iger, Robert Allen (b. 1951)**

| | |
|---|---|
| Occupation(s): | capitalist -  president, ABC Television;<br>    CEO and chairman of board, The Walt Disney Co.;<br>    director, Genies, Inc. (technology firm)<br>industrialist -  director, Perfect Day, Inc. (dairy replacement firm) |
| Civic Activism: | donated $5 million to aid small businesses struggling due to the Covid-19 pandemic |
| Marriage(s): | M/1 – div. 1994 – Kathleen Susan Kiger (b, 1947)<br>  - capitalist -  executive producer, ABC Television, NBC Television; CNBC Television, and City College of New York, American Television<br>M/2 – 1995 – Kristine Carlin Bay (b. 1963)<br>  (aka Willow Bay)<br>  - - fashion model, Ford Modeling Agency<br>  capitalist -  executive producer and host, "Spotlight" (Live Time Television)<br>  entertainer and associated professions -<br>    spokesperson, Estee Lauder cosmetics, 1983-1989;<br>    correspondent, "Today Show" (NBC Television);<br>    co-anchor, "Good Morning America Sunday" (ABC Television);<br>    co-host, "NBA Inside Stuff";<br>    freelance anchor and correspondent, MSNBC Television and NBC News<br>  journalist -  senior editor, Huffington Post<br>  writer -  *Talking to Your Kids in Tough Times*, 2003 |
| Address: | 102 Virginia Avenue, Oceanside |
| Name of estate: | |
| Year of construction: | 1957 |
| Style of architecture: | Split Level |
| Architect(s): | |
| Landscape architect(s): | |
| House extant: | yes |
| Historical notes: | |

    Robert was raised in this house by his parents Arthur Lawrence and Miriam A. Tunick Iger. Arthur was a graduate of the Whartan School of Business, a professional jazz trumpeter in the 1940s, professor of marketing and advertising at New York Institute of Technology, and a publishing executive at Cunningham and Walsh, Macmillan Publishing Company and Greenvale Marketing Corporation. He was the author of *Music of the Golden Age 1900-1950 and Beyond* and served as president of the Oceanside School Board and the Southwest Civic Association.

    Robert Allen and Kathleen Susan Kiger Iger's daughter Kathleen married Jarrold Alan Cushing, the son of Alan Clarke and Mary-Anita Crean Cushing of Watertown, CT. Their daughter Amanda, to date, has not married.

    Robert Allen and Kristine Carlin Bay Iger have two children, Robert who was born in 1998 and William who was born in 2002.

    In 2015, Robert was inducted into the Broadcasting and Cable Hall of Fame and the Toy Industry Hall of Fame. In 2020, he was inducted into the Television Hall of Fame.

    In 2010, the 1,828-square-foot house sold for $415,000.

*front facade, 2000*

### Ingraham, Frederick, Sr. (1958-1929))

| | | |
|---|---|---|
| Occupation(s): | attorney - | counsel, Queens County Board of Supervisors; counsel, Nassau County Board of Supervisors; counsel, Village of Hempstead |
| | merchant - | director, E. V. Harman & Co. |
| | financier - | a founder and president, First National Bank of Hempstead |
| | capitalist - | director, New York and Manhattan Beach Railway Co.; developer, Ingraham Estates, Hempstead; a founder and director, Ingraham Corp., 1913 |

Marriage(s): 1884-1929 – Gertrude Julia Leverich (1855-1929)

Address: 571 Front Street, Hempstead
Name of estate:
Year of construction:
Style of architecture:
Architect(s):
Landscape architect(s):
House extant: no; demolished c. 1937
Historical notes:

The *Long Island Society Register, 1929* lists Frederick and Gertrude Leverich Ingraham as residing on Front Street, Hempstead.
He was the son of Richard and Jane Dikeman Ingraham, Sr.
Gertrude Julia Leverich Ingraham was the daughter of R. B. Leverich.
Frederick and Gertrude Julia Leverich Ingraham, Sr.'s son Richard married Anna Van Loan. In 1918, their son Frederick Ingraham, Jr. married Emilie Canfield, the daughter of James A. Canfield. Emilie died in 1918 of the Spanish Flu. [*The Brooklyn Daily Eagle* April 15, 1918, p. 7, and October 25, 1918, p. 4.]
*[See following entry for additional family information.]*


### Ingraham, Richard, III (1885-1961)

| | | |
|---|---|---|
| Occupation(s): | financier - | a founder and director, First National Bank of Hempstead |
| | attorney - | counsel, Title Guarantee and Trust Co. |

Marriage(s): 1912-1961 – Anna Van Loan (1884-1964)

Address: 571 Front Street, Hempstead
Name of estate:
Year of construction:
Style of architecture:
Architect(s):
Landscape architect(s):
House extant: no; demolished c. 1937
Historical notes:

Richard Ingraham was the son of Frederick and Gertrude Julia Ingraham of Hempstead.
Anna Van Loan Ingraham was the daughter of Frank Van Loan of Manhattan.
*[See previous entry for additional family information.]*

### Irwin, Louis Henry (b. 1865)

| | |
|---|---|
| Occupation(s): | financier - director, Terminal Bank of the City of New York |
| Marriage(s): | 1898 – Alice May Sherwood (1871-1966) |
| Address: | 145 Whitehall Boulevard, Garden City |
| Name of estate: | |
| Year of construction: | 1926 |
| Style of architecture: | Colonial Revival |
| Architect(s): | |
| Landscape architect(s): | |
| House extant: | yes |
| Historical notes: | |

The house was built by Louis Henry Irwin.

The *Long Island Society Register, 1929* lists Mr. and Mrs. Louis Henry Irwin as residing at 145 Whitehall Boulevard, Garden City. The 1930 Census lists the Irwins' address as 70 Whitehall Boulevard, Garden City.

He was the son of William Henry and Anna Maria Conselyea Irwin, Sr. of Brooklyn.

Alice May Sherwood Irwin was the daughter of Arthur and Harriet Jane Kemper Sherwood of Westport, CT.

Louis Henry and Alice May Sherwood Irwin's son Marion married Helen de Raismes Hamilton and resided in Garden City. Their son Louis Sherwood Irwin married Gertrude Bradley, the daughter of George Franklin Bradley of Brooklyn.

*[See following entry for additional family information.]*

*front facade, 2005*

### Irwin, Marion Griffin (1906-1971)

| | |
|---|---|
| Occupation(s): | financier - stockbroker |
| Marriage(s): | 1928-1971 – Helen de Raismes Hamilton (1905-1996) |
| Address: | 51 Chestnut Street, Garden City |
| Name of estate: | |
| Year of construction: | c. 1928 |
| Style of architecture: | Colonial Revival |
| Architect(s): | |
| Landscape architect(s): | |
| House extant: | yes |
| Historical notes | |

The house was built by Marion Griffin Irwin.

The *Long Island Society Register, 1929* lists Marion Griffin and Helen de Raismes Hamilton Irwin as residing on Chestnut Street, Garden City. The 1930 Census lists the Irwins at this address.

*front facade, 2006*

He was the son of Louis Henry and Alice May Sherwood Irwin of Garden City.

Helen de Raismes Hamilton Irwin was the daughter of Campbell Thorpe and Helen Biddle de Raismes Hamilton of Garden City.

Marion Griffin and Helen de Raismes Hamilton Irwin's son Campbell married Carolyn Studwell, the daughter of Joseph Colson Knapp and Carolyn M. Stafford Studwell of Garden City. Their daughter Sherwood married John Dowling, the son of John Joseph and Mary M. Dorkings Dowling. Their son Louis Henry Irwin II married Virginia Jane Johnson, the daughter of James L. Johnson, Sr. of Garden City.

In 2006 the house was remodeled.

### Ivison, Maynard Cady (1895-1979)

| | |
|---|---|
| Occupation(s): | financier - member, Anglo-American Commercial Corp., 1919-1920;<br>member, Foreign Commercial Corporation American, 1920-1921;<br>member, G. M. P. Murphy and Co., 1921-1923;<br>member, Mechanics and Metals Bank, 1923-1926;<br>manager, bond department, Chrisholm and Chapman, 1925-1926;<br>member, Chase National Bank, 1927-1929;<br>partner, Abbott, Hoppin, and Co., 1929-1934 (stock brokerage firm);<br>partner, Abbott, Proctor, Paine, 1934-1970 (stock brokerage firm);<br>member, Paine, Weber, Jackson, and Curtis, 1970-1979 |
| Civic Activism: | member, board of governors, New York Stock Exchange, 1954-1957 |
| Marriage(s): | 1919-1979 – Alice R. Thayer (b. 1890) |
| Address: | 209 Cedar Avenue, Hewlett Bay Park |
| Name of estate: | |
| Year of construction: | 1926 |
| Style of architecture: | Colonial Revival |
| Architect(s): | |
| Landscape architect(s): | |
| House extant: yes | |
| Historical notes: | |

*rear facade, 2021*

The *Long Island Society Register, 1929* lists Maynard C. and Alice R. Thayer Ivison as residing in Hewlett [Hewlett Bay Park]. The 1940 Census lists their address as 209 Cedar Avenue.

He was the son of William Crane and Celia Mae Cady Ivison of *Wilcemay Farm* in Lawrence.

Alice R. Thayer Ivison was the daughter of Benjamin Bowditch and Marie Cecile Renouard Thayer, Jr. of Lawrence. Alice's sister Cecile married Douglas Gibbons and resided at *The Annex* in Purchase, NY. Her sister Marie married Junius Alexander Richards, Sr. and resided in Lawrence.

Maynard Cady and Alice R. Thayer Ivison's daughter Audrey married Paul Day Pattinson, the son of Ismay Graham Pattinson of Arcadia, CA, and resided in Santa Monica, CA. Their son Maynard Thayer Ivison married Caroline Chester Curtis, the daughter of William John Curtis, Jr., and resided in Richfield, CT.

In 2021, the 3,800-square-foot, six-bedroom, six-bath house sold for $1.85 million

### Ivison, Sterling Hollingshead, Sr. (1892-1968)

| | |
|---|---|
| Occupation(s): | merchant - New York yacht broker |
| Marriage(s): | M/1 – 1917-div. 1928 – Lisbeth Moore Lyle (1894-1943)<br>M/2 – 1932 – Dorothy M. Droste (1895-1954) |
| Address: | 106 Fifth Street, Garden City |
| Name of estate: | |
| Year of construction: | 1913 |
| Style of architecture: | Modified Shingle |
| Architect(s): | |
| Landscape architect(s): | |
| House extant: yes | |
| Historical notes: | |

*front facade, 2008*

The *Long Island Society Register, 1928* lists Sterling H. and Lisbeth M. Lyle Ivison [Sr.] as residing at 106 Fifth Street, Garden City.

He was the son of Henry and Bertha May Hollingshead Ivison of Manhattan.

Lisbeth Moore Lyle Ivison was the daughter of Dr. Alexander Lyle. Lisbeth subsequently married Cecil P. Young.

Sterling Hollingshead and Lisbeth Moore Lyle Ivison, Sr.'s daughter Eleanor married Howard Pratt Wall, the son of William L. Wall of Philadelphia, PA, and, later, Joseph W. Jensen. Their son Sterling Hollingshead Ivison, Jr. married Katharine Phelps Brown, the daughter of Ledyard Maynadier and Katharine Ken Didier Brown.

Dorothy M. Droste Ivison was the daughter of George F. Droste of Bellport. She had previously been married to Benjamin Hatfield Tibbs of Garden City.

The house was later owned by John Platt Hubbell, Sr.

### Ivison, William Crane (1869-1951)

| | |
|---|---|
| Occupation(s): | financier -   member, Hopkins Brothers, NYC, 1892-1893 (investment banking firm); |
| | assistant treasurer, U. S. Mortgage & Trust Co., 1900-1907; |
| | partner, Chisholm and Capman, NYC, 1911-1941 (stock brokerage firm) |
| | industrialist -   vice president and director, Cady–Ivison Shoe Co., Cleveland, OH, 1894-1897; |
| | secretary and treasurer, Orinaco Iron Co. |
| | publisher -   vice-president, The G. & C. Merriam Co., Springfield, MA, 1923-1951; |
| | director, American Book Co., NYC |
| Civic Activism: | fellow in perpetuity, Metropolitan Museum of Art, NYC |
| Marriage(s): | M/1 – 1894-1930 – Celia May Cady (1873-1930) |
| | M/2 – 1937-1951 – Mabel Baylis |
| Address: | Kendridke Road, Lawrence |
| Name of estate: | *Wilcemay Farm* |
| Year of construction: | |
| Style of architecture: | |
| Architect(s): | |
| Landscape architect(s): | |
| House extant:  no | |
| Historical notes: | |

The *Social Register Summer, 1910* lists William Crane and Celia M. Cady Ivison as residing at *Wilcemay Farm* in Hewlett [Lawrence].

He was the son of David Brinckerhoff and Eveline Matilda Crane Ivison.

Celia May Cady Ivison was the daughter of George W. and Amanda L. Feusier Cady of Cleveland, OH.

William Crane and Celia May Cady Ivison's son Maynard married Alice R. Thayer and resided in Hewlett Bay Park.

Mabel Baylis Ivison was the daughter of Joseph Thomas and Katherine Jane Bagley Baylis of Baltimore, MD. Mabel had previously been married to Chauncey Eldridge, the son of Frederick Gideon and Alice Lee Goodrich Eldridge.

### Jackson, Rickard Gilbert (1889-1952)

| | |
|---|---|
| Occupation(s): | industrialist -   director, Benjamin Moore Paint Co. |
| Civic Activism: | trustee, Tiny Tim Society of the Home of St. Giles the Cripple |
| Marriage(s): | M/1 – 1916-1933 – Mildred Natalie Marier (d. 1933) |
| | M/2 – Helen Kate Henderson (1887-1935) |
| | M/3 – Alice Devereaux |
| Address: | 56 Third Street, Garden City |
| Name of estate: | |
| Year of construction: | 1930 |
| Style of architecture: | Georgian Revival |
| Architect(s): | |
| Landscape architect(s): | |
| House extant:  yes | |
| Historical notes: | |

*front facade, 2015*

The *Long Island Society Register, 1929* lists Mrs. Mildred N. Jackson as residing at 103 Stewart Avenue, Garden City.

She was the daughter of Joseph C. and Anna M. Marier of Brooklyn.

Rickard Gilbert Jackson was the son of Rickard and Marie Louise Gilbert Jackson of Brooklyn.

Rickard Gilbert and Mildred Natalie Marier Jackson's sixteen-year-old son William was shot to death while aboard a yacht in Nassau, Bahamas. [*The New York Times* January 8, 1942, p. 12, and January 10, 1942, p. 17.] Their daughter Geraldine married William Kistler Coors, the son of Adolph Herman Joseph and Alice May Kistler Coors, Jr. of Golden, CO. William was the grandson of the founder of Golden Brewery, later Adolph Coors Co. in 1873, and ultimately Coors Brewing Co.

Helen Kate Henderson Jackson was the daughter of Southmayd and Kate Shaffner Henderson of Brooklyn. Helen had previously been married to James McFadden with whom she resided in Garden City.

At the time of his death, Rickard was residing at 56 Third Street in Garden City.

In 2008, the 6,846-square-foot house sold for $1.725 million.

**Jacobi, Harold, Sr. (1884-1938)**

| | |
|---|---|
| Occupation(s): | merchant - a founder, United Grocery Stores |
| | industrialist - a founder, with his brother Sanford, and president, Schenley Distillers Corp. |
| | capitalist - president, Sam Thompson Gibson Distributing Co.; erected, in partnership with Jacob A. Voice and Sanford Jacobi, Inwood Beach Club |
| Civic Activism: | chairman, Greater New York campaign of the United Palestine Appeal; co-chairman, Palestine exhibit, New York World's Fair, 1939 |
| Marriage(s): | 1910-1939 – Freda Moritz (1886-1939) (aka Frederica Moritz) |

    - educator - teacher

    Civic Activism: honorary vice-president Juvenile Service League; took prominent part in aiding the country home of the Hospital for Joint Diseases, NYC; fund-raiser, Rockaway Branch, Community Chest; assisted her husband Harold, Greater New York Campaign of the United Palestine Appeal; member, Corresponding Council of the Federation for Support of Jewish Philanthropic Societies of New York City; active in Youth Aliyah (aid to children of Nazi victims)

| | |
|---|---|
| Address: | Short Cut Road, Woodmere |
| Name of estate: | |
| Year of construction: | 1931 |
| Style of architecture: | Norman Revival |
| Architect(s): | Olive Frances Tjaden designed the house, interior woodwork, several of interior color schemes, and greenhouse (for H. Jacobi) |
| Landscape architect(s): | |
| House extant: | no; demolished c. 1941 |
| Historical notes: | |

  The house was built by Harold Jacobi, Sr.
  He was the son of Emile H. and Sarah Simon Jacobi.
  Freda Moritz Jacobi was the daughter of Sigmund Moritz of Manhattan and Montgomery, AL.
  Harold and Freda Moritz Jacobi, Sr.'s daughter Alice married Arnold Schlossberg, Sr., the son of Maurice J. and Jennie Weinstein Schlossberg, and resided in Woodsburgh and, later, Roanoke, VA. Their son Harold Jacobi, Jr. married Margaret Bloom, the daughter of Warren J. Bloom of Scarsdale, NY. Their daughter Edith married Arthur D. Marks, Jr. and, later, Sol Nichtern.

*[See following entry for additional family information.]*

*front facade*

### Jacobi, Sanford (1879-1938)

| | |
|---|---|
| Occupation(s): | capitalist - erected, in partnership with Jacob A. Voice and Harold Jacobi, Inwood Beach Club |
| | industrialist - a founder, with his brother Harold, Schenley Distillers Corp.; |
| | president, Eastern Distillers Corp. (subsidiary of Schenley Distillers Corp. |
| Civic Activism: | member, New York Committee, National Jewish Hospital, Denver, CO; |
| | co-chairman, Joint Distribution Committee, Jewish Philanthropic Societies; |
| | vice-president and trustee, Hospital for Joint Diseases, NYC; |
| | trustee, Louis Heinsheimer Fund |
| Marriage(s): | Florence Harris |
| | - Civic Activism: honorary vice-president, Juvenile Service League |
| Address: | *[unable to determine street address]*, Hewlett Neck |
| Name of estate: | |
| Year of construction: | c. 1935 |
| Style of architecture: | |
| Architect(s): | Olive Frances Tjaden designed the house (for S. Jacobi) |
| Landscape architect(s): | Olive Frances Tjaden planted 10,000 tulip bulbs |

House extant: no; demolished c. 1941
Historical notes:

The house was built by Sanford Jacobi.
He was the son of Emil H. and Sarah Simon Jacobi of Montgomery, AL.
Florence Harris Jacobi later married James Weingarten.
Sanford and Florence Harris Jacobi's daughter Ethel married Stanley M. Roth, the son of Samuel and Etta Ungenleiden Roth of Manhattan.
*[See previous entry for additional family information.]*


### Jewell, John Voorhees, Jr. (1901-1982)

| | |
|---|---|
| Occupation(s): | financier - trustee and secretary, Williamsburgh Savings Bank; trustee, Kings County Trust Co. |
| Marriage(s): | 1940 – Marjorie Elizabeth Winter (b. 1903) |
| | - Civic Activism; vice-chair, door committee, Garden City–Hempstead Community Club; |
| | member, Cathedral Guild of Red Cross at Mitchel Field, 1946 |
| Address: | 113 Nassau Boulevard, Garden City |
| Name of estate: | |
| Year of construction: | 1921 |
| Style of architecture: | Colonial Revival |
| Architect(s): | |
| Landscape architect(s): | |

House extant: yes
Historical notes:

He was the son of John Voorhees and Adeline Wakeman Bennett Jewell, Sr. of Garden City.
Marjorie Elizabeth Winter Jewell was the daughter of Harry Zina Winter of Mamaroneck, NY.
*[See following entry for additional family information.]*
In 2014, the 4,360-square-foot house sold for $890,000.

*side / front facade*

### Jewell, John Voorhees, Sr. (1850-1937)

| | |
|---|---|
| Occupation(s): | financier - president, Twenty-Sixth Ward Bank of Brooklyn (later, Mechanics Bank); |
| | trustee, Nassau Trust Co. (later, Mechanics Bank); |
| | president and chairman of board, Williamsburgh Savings Bank; |
| | trustee, Gratuity Fund; |
| | trustee, Brooklyn Trust Co.; |
| | partner, D. Jewell & Son (New York Produce Exchange); |
| | director, Kings County Trust Co.; |
| | member, board of managers, New York Produce Exchange |
| | writer - *Historic Williamsburgh*, 1926 |
| Civic Activism: | trustee, Tiny Tim Society of the Home of St. Giles the Cripple |
| Marriage(s): | M/1 – 1871-1893 – Jennie E. Carll (1849-1893) |
| | M/2 – 1900-1937 – Adeline Wakeman Bennett (1869-1944) |
| Address: | 113 Nassau Boulevard, Garden City |
| Name of estate: | |
| Year of construction: | 1921 |
| Style of architecture: | Colonial Revival |
| Architect(s): | |
| Landscape architect(s): | |
| House extant: yes | |
| Historical notes: | |

*front facade, 2009*

John Voorhees Jewell, Sr. was the son of Ditmas and Joanna Kouwenhoven Voorhees Jewell of Brooklyn.

John Voorhees and Jennie E. Carll Jewell, Sr.'s daughter Grace married Joseph Edwin Hinds and, later, Henry L. Crane. Their daughter Alice married Cornelius Schenck Bevoise and resided in Cold Spring Harbor. Their son John Voorhees Jewell, Jr., who married Marjorie Elizabeth Winter, later owned the house.

*[See previous entry for additional family information.]*

The *Long Island Society Register, 1929* lists John V. and Addie W. Bennett Jewell [Sr.] as residing on Nassau Boulevard, Garden City.

### Johnson, Lee (1845-1895)

| | |
|---|---|
| Occupation(s): | capitalist - subdivided property in the Town of Islip for development; |
| | built and rented houses in the Town of Islip |
| | industrialist - partner, William M. Johnson & Sons (later, Johnson and Lazarus) (distilling and sugar refining) |
| Marriage(s): | 1874-1895 – Frances Augusta Nicoll (1849-1930) |
| Address: | *[unable to determine street address]*, Garden City |
| Name of estate: | |
| Year of construction: | |
| Style of architecture: | |
| Architect(s): | |
| Landscape architect(s): | |
| House extant: unconfirmed | |
| Historical notes: | |

Lee Johnson was the son of Edwin Augustus and Ellen A. Woodruff Johnson, Sr., who resided at *Deer Range Farm* in East Islip. [*See* Spinzia, *Long Island's Prominent South Shore Families* – Johnson entry.]

Frances Augusta Nicoll Johnson was the daughter of William and Sarah Augusta Nicoll VII of *Grange* in East Islip. [*See* Spinzia, *Long Island's Prominent South Shore Families* – Nicoll entry.] Francis' sister Sarah married Dr. Silias R. Corwith and resided in Bridgehampton. [*See* Spinzia, *Long Island's Prominent Families in the Town of Southampton* – Corwith entry.] Her sister Mary married Coryton Messenger Woodbury. Her brother Edward married Ella Lattling. Her brother William Greenly Nicoll, who married Phoebe Disbrow, and, subsequently, Kate Cornwall, resided in Babylon. Her brother Henry married Augusta Maltby and resided in Virginia. Her sister Helen married Charles Fiske Bound and resided in Manhattan.

Lee and Frances Augusta Nicoll Johnson's daughter Sarah married Andrew H. Boardman and resided in Garden City.

### Jones, Bethune Wellington (1870-1936)

| | |
|---|---|
| Occupation(s): | financier - member, Kidder, Peabody and Co.; secretary, vice-president, and director, Bankers Trust Co. industrialist - director, National Distillers Products Corp. entertainer and associated professions - member, Hoadley Orchestra, Brooklyn |
| Civic Activism: | executive secretary, War Credits Board; a founder, Police Relief Association of Nassau County |
| Marriage(s): | 1902-1936 – Alma Elizabeth Steiner (b. 1877) - Civic Activism: president, Hempstead Branch, Needlework Guild, 1936; member, executive board, Hempstead Branch, Nassau Hospital, Mineola (later, Winthrop–University Hospital; now, NYU Langone Hospital – Long Island) |
| Address: | 70 Washington Avenue, Garden City |
| Name of estate: | |
| Year of construction: | 1930 |
| Style of architecture: | Neo-Tudor |
| Architect(s): | Olive Tjaden designed the house |
| Landscape architect(s): | |
| House extant: yes | |
| Historical notes: | |

The *Long Island Society Register, 1929* lists Bettume [sic] Wellington and Alma Steiner Jones as residing at 167 Fulton Avenue, Hempstead.

By 1932 they had relocated to Garden City.

He was the son of Einathan Perry and Ades Memoria Brown Jones of Brooklyn.

Alma Elizabeth Steiner Jones was the daughter of Jacob Steiner of Brooklyn.

Bethune Wellington and Alma Elizabeth Steiner Jones' son Robert married Carrie Ellen Cameron of Nova Scotia, Canada. Their son Richard married Florence Gilhooly and resided at 35 Chestnut Street, Garden City.

In 1936 Alma sold the house to David Ferguson, Sr. *[The Nassau Daily Review* October 2, 1936, p. 10, and Nassau County Department of Assessment records.]

In 2017, the 5,200 square-foot house, with six bedrooms and three and a half bathrooms, sold for $1.7 million.

*front facade, 2017*

### Jones, Dr. Dunham Carroll (1877-1954)

| | |
|---|---|
| Occupation(s): | physician |
| | educator - member, medical faculty, McGill University, Montreal, Canada |
| Marriage(s): | 1899-1931 – Lily Margaret Richardson McConkey (1874-1931) (aka Madame Broville) |
| | - writer* |
| | artist - watercolorist |
| Address: | Cathedral Avenue, Hempstead |
| Name of estate: | *Bleak House* |
| Year of construction: | |
| Style of architecture: | |
| Architect(s): | |
| Landscape architect(s): | |
| House extant: | unconfirmed |
| Historical notes: | |

Dr. Dunham Carroll Jones was the son of Andrew and Frances Ann Good Jones.

Lily Margaret Richardson McConkey was the daughter of William Hudson and Charlotte Margaret Cotton McConkey of Ontario, Canada, and the granddaughter of Baron Alexander Cotton of England.

*Under the pen name Madame Broville, she published several scientific articles and many poems.

Dr. Dunham Carroll and Mrs. Lily Margaret Richardson McConkey Jones' daughter Sybil was an infant at the time of her death in 1906. Their daughter Lily did not marry. Their son Carroll married Florence Virginia Greene, the daughter of Arthur Greene of Salmon City, ID. Their daughter Christina married William Boyd Ricketts, the son of Arthur Ricketts of Hempstead.

### Jones, Howard S. (1863-1936)

| | |
|---|---|
| Occupation(s): | industrialist - president, Brooklyn Decorative Glass Co. |
| | financier - director, Bank of Manhattan |
| Marriage(s): | Minnie E. Weed (1868-1946) |
| Address: | 84 Nassau Boulevard, Garden City |
| Name of estate: | |
| Year of construction: | 1906 |
| Style of architecture: | Dutch Colonial Revival |
| Architect(s): | |
| Landscape architect(s): | |
| House extant: | yes |
| Historical notes: | |

The *Long Island Society Register, 1929* lists Howard S. and Minnie E. Weed Jones as residing at 84 Nassau Boulevard, Garden City.

He was the son of Thomas and Caroline M. Jones.

Minnie E. Weed Jones was the daughter of William A. and Emily Slawson Weed.

*front facade, c. 1909*

### Jones, Thomas Catesby, Sr. (1880-1946)

| | |
|---|---|
| Occupation(s): | attorney - partner, Bigham, Englar, Jones, and Houston |
| Civic Activism: | member, War Prize Commission after World War I; |
| | trustee, Hampden–Sydney College, Hampden–Sydney, VA |
| |    (all male college established in 1775); |
| | trustee, Kenyon College, Gambier, OH; |
| | trustee, Museum of Fine Arts, Richmond, VA |
| Marriage(s): | M/1 – 1911-1913 – Olga Hasbrouck (1884-1913) |
| | M/2 – 1916-1946 – Louisa Rebecca Brooke (1883-1967) |
| Address: | East Rockaway Road, Hewlett Bay Park |
| Name of estate: | *Green Plains* |
| Year of construction: | |
| Style of architecture: | |
| Architect(s): | |
| Landscape architect(s): | |
| House extant: unconfirmed | |
| Historical notes: | |

   Thomas Catesby Jones, Sr. was the son of Walter Nelson and Ada Virginia Vaughn Jones of Petersburg, VA.
   Olga Hasbrouck Jones was the daughter of Frank and Esther Jackman Hasbrouck.
   Thomas Catesby and Olga Hasbrouck Jones, Sr.'s son Thomas Catesby Jones, Jr. resided in Daytona Beach, FL.
   The *Long Island Society Register, 1929* lists T. Catesby and Louisa Brooke Jones as residing at *Green Plains* in Hewlett. The 1930 Census lists this address for Thomas Catesby and Louisa Brooke Jones.
   She was the daughter of Francis Key Brooke.


### Jordan, Edward Bailey, Jr. (1876-1955)

| | |
|---|---|
| Occupation(s): | industrialist - partner, Edward B. Jordan & Co., Brooklyn |
| |                (manufacturer of wood products) |
| Marriage(s): | 1899-1951 – Elise Eastman (1877-1951) |
| Address: | Merrick Avenue, East Meadow |
| Name of estate: | |
| Year of construction: | |
| Style of architecture: | |
| Architect(s): | |
| Landscape architect(s): | |
| House extant: unconfirmed | |
| Historical notes: | |

   The *Long Island Society Register, 1929* lists Edward Bailey and Elsie Eastman Jordan, Jr. as residing on Barnum Avenue [Merrick Avenue], East Hempstead [East Meadow].
   He was the son of Edward Bailey and Jennie A. Dumay Jordan, Sr. of Brooklyn. His sister Elizabeth married Henry Lascelles Maxwell, Sr., the son of John Rogers and Maria Louise Washburn Maxwell, Sr. of *Maxwelton* in Glen Cove, and resided in Glen Cove. [*See* Spinzia, *Long Island's Prominent North Shore Families, vol. I* – Maxwell entries.]
   Elsie Eastman Jordan was the daughter of Frederick Eastman of Brooklyn.
   Edward Bailey and Elsie Eastman Jordan, Jr.'s daughter Elsiette married Herbert Jenkins Pratt, the son of E. S. Pratt of Garden City, and resided in Port Washington. Their daughter Jennie married Deane Aston Libby.

### Kamen, Dean Lawrence (b. 1951)

| | |
|---|---|
| Occupation(s): | inventor - over 1,000 patents including that for the Segway PT (self-balancing human transporter) and the iBot (electric wheelchair) |
| | industrialist - a founder, DEKA (manufacturer of iBot and portable dialysis machines); a founder, Auto Syringe (manufacturer of drug infusion pump) |
| Civic Activism: | founder, For Inspiration; founder, Recognition of Science and Technology; founder, Advanced Regenerative Manufacturing Institute; founder, Foundry for American Biotechnology |
| Marriage(s): | bachelor |
| Address: | 99 Bulson Road, Rockville Centre |
| Name of estate: | |
| Year of construction: | 1949 |
| Style of architecture: | Colonial Revival |
| Architect(s): | |
| Landscape architect(s): | |
| House extant: yes | |
| Historical notes: | |

Dean was raised in this house by his parents Jack and Evelyn Kamen. In 2005, Dean was inducted into the National Inventors Hall of Fame. In 2008, the 2,567-square-foot house sold for $750,000.

*front facade, 2015*

### Kane, John Patrick, Jr. (1882-1949)

| | |
|---|---|
| Occupation(s): | merchant - president and chairman of board, General Builders Supply Corp.* |
| | capitalist - president, South River Trucking Corp. |
| | industrialist - president and treasurer, John P. Kane Co., Catskill, NY (manufacturers and distributors of Portland Cement); director, Patent Scaffolding Co. (manufacturer of scaffolds); president, Dennings Paint Brick Works; president, Newton Hook Brick Co.; director, American Machine Device Co. |
| Marriage(s): | 1908-1947 – Margaret A. Yauch (d. 1947) |
| Address: | East Rockaway Road, Hewlett Bay Park |
| Name of estate: | |
| Year of construction: | |
| Style of architecture: | |
| Architect(s): | |
| Landscape architect(s): | |
| House extant: unconfirmed | |
| Historical notes: | |

The *Social Register Summer, 1921* and the *Long Island Society Register, 1929* list John P. and Margaret A. Yauch Kane [Jr.] as residing in Hewlett [Hewlett Bay Park], while the *Social Register Summer, 1932* lists the Kanes' residence as Locust Valley [Matinecock].

He was the son of John P. and Mary T. Griffith Kane, Sr. of *Interbaien* in Huntington Bay. [*See* Spinzia, *Long Island's Prominent North Shore Families, vol. I* – Kane entries.]

Margaret A. Yauch Kane was the daughter of Arthur Yauch of Manhattan.

*United States Postmaster General James A. Farley was Kane's partner. [*The New York Times* January 15, 1949, p. 17.]

John Patrick and Margaret A. Yauch Kane, Jr.'s daughter Barbara married Samuel Wynn Mills, the son of Paul Dencka and Ellen Drexel Paul Mills of Old Brookville. [*See* Spinzia, *Long Island's Prominent North Shore Families, vol. I* – Mills entry.] Their daughter Marjorie married Elbridge T. Gerry, the son of Robert Livingston and Cornelia Averell Harriman Gerry, Sr. Elbridge's brother Robert Livingston Gerry, Jr. married Marleigh Kramer, the daughter of Albert Ludlow and Anna Bement Kramer of *Picket Farm* in Jericho and, later, Harriet Boynton Wells. [*See* Spinzia, *Long Island's Prominent North Shore Families, vol. I* – Gerry and Ludlow entries.]

### Karan, Donna Ivey Faske (b. 1948)

| | |
|---|---|
| Occupation(s): | fashion designer -   head of Ann Klein design team; CEO, designer and co-founder, with her husband Stephan, Dona Karan (line of clothes) |
| | writer -   *My Journey*, 2015 (autobiography) |
| Civic Activism: | co-founder, Urban Zen |
| Marriage(s): | M/1 – 1976-div. 1978 – Mark Karan |
| | - merchant -  boutique owner |
| | M/2 – 1983-2001 – Stephan Weis (d. 2001) |
| | - artist - sculptor and painter |
| | fashion designer -   co-founder, with his wife Donna, Donna Karan (clothes line) |
| Address: | *[unable to determine street address]*, Woodmere |
| Name of estate: | |
| Year of construction: | |
| Style of architecture: | |
| Architect(s): | |
| Landscape architect(s): | |
| House extant: | unconfirmed |
| Historical notes: | |

Donna was the daughter of Gabriel and Helen Rabinowitz Faske. She was raised in Woodmere by her mother and step-father Harold Flaxman.

Mark and Donna Ivy Faske Karan's daughter Gabby married Gian Palo DeFelice and resided in East Hampton as did Donna. [*See* Spinzia, *Long Island's Prominent Families in the Town of East Hampton* – DeFelice and Karan entries.]


### Keating, William J. (1894-1963)

| | |
|---|---|
| Occupation(s): | financier -   member, Hornblower and Weeks (stock brokerage firm); partner, Corlies and Booker (stock brokerage firm) |
| Marriage(s): | Anne Pierson (1893-1993) |
| Address: | 6 Carteret Place, Garden City |
| Name of estate: | |
| Year of construction: | |
| Style of architecture: | |
| Architect(s): | |
| Landscape architect(s): | |
| House extant: | no |
| Historical notes: | |

The *Long Island Society Register, 1929* lists Mr. and Mrs. William J. Keating as residing on Carteret Place, Garden City. The 1930 Census lists the Keatings at this address. They also had a residence in Remsenburg.

He was the son of Edward F. and Margaret Keating of Brooklyn.

Anne Pierson Keating was the daughter of Lewis Eugene and Blanche Thorne Pierson, Sr., who resided at *Thorncroft* in Westhampton Beach. [*See* Spinzia, *Long Island's Prominent Families in the Town of Southampton* – Keating and Pierson entries.]

William J. and Anne Pierson Keating's daughter Anne married James Lance Hurley, the son of James E. Hurley of Manhattan, and resided in Riverside, CT. Their son Pierson married Elizabeth Ann Nelson, the daughter of Arvid E. Nelson, and resided in Rye, NY. Their son Robert married Rosemary Ann Sullivan, the daughter of Joseph R. Sullivan, and resided in Glen Cove.

### Keene, James Robert (1838-1913)

| | |
|---|---|
| Occupation(s): | attorney |
| | capitalist - president, United States Graphotype Co.; Castleton Farm (thoroughbred race horse breeding farm in Kentucky)* |
| | publisher - owner and editor, *Examiner*, San Francisco, CA |
| | financier - president, San Francisco Stock Exchange; speculated in Nevada mining stocks |
| Marriage(s): | 1860-1913 – Sara Jay Daingerfield (1840-1916) |
| Address: | Ocean Avenue, Lawrence |
| Name of estate: | |
| Year of construction: | |
| Style of architecture: | |
| Architect(s): | |
| Landscape architect(s): | |
| House extant: unconfirmed | |
| Historical notes: | |

The *Social Register New York, 1907* and the *Social Register Summer, 1915* list Mr. and Mrs. James R. Keene as residing in Cedarhurst [Lawrence].

He was the son of James and Cecelia Jeanetta Gaughenlaugh Keen of London, England.

Sara Jay Daingerfield Keene was the daughter of Leroy Parker and Juliet Octavia Daingerfield, Sr. of Virginia.

James Robert and Sara Jay Daingerfield Keene's daughter Jessica married Talbot Jones Taylor, Sr. of *Talbot House* in Lawrence and, later, Edward Inglis Frost, the son of Mahlon Smith and Frances Harriet Foster Frost. Their son Foxhall married Mary Lawrence, the daughter of Frederick N. Lawrence of Manhattan, and resided at *Rosemary Hall* in Old Westbury. [*See* Spinzia, *Long Island's Prominent North Shore Families, vol. I* – Keene entry.] It is said that a chef at Delmonico's restaurant created a dish for the young Foxhall Keene, chicken a la Keene, a dish that became known as chicken a la king.

James Keene's horse, also named Foxhall, won the Grand Prix in Paris in 1881.

*In 2019 Keene was voted into the National Museum of Racing Hall of Fame.


### Keisler, Peter Douglas (b. 1960)

| | |
|---|---|
| Occupation(s): | attorney - partner, Sidley & Austin, LLP (later, Sidley, Austin, Brown, & Wood); Associate Council to the President (Reagan administration) |
| | statesmen - United States Acting Attorney General (George W. Bush administration); United States Assistant Attorney General for Civil Division (George W. Bush administration); United States Associate Attorney General (George W. Bush administration) |
| Civic Activism: | co-founder and director, Federalist Society (conservative think tank); chairman, Party of the Right, Yale University, New Haven, CT |
| Marriage(s): | Susan Gomory (b. 1963) |
| Address: | 350 Westwood Road, Woodmere |
| Name of estate: | |
| Year of construction: | 1926 |
| Style of architecture: | Colonial Revival with Victorian Elements |
| Architect(s): | |
| Landscape architect(s): | |
| House extant: yes | |
| Historical notes: | |

*front facade, 2000*

Peter was raised in this house by his parents William and Sydelle Prisand Keisler.

Peter clerked for United States Supreme Court Justice Anthony Kennedy and Judge Robert Bork of the District of Columbia Circuit Court. He was nominated by President George W. Bush in 2005 and again in 2006 to be a judge of the District of Columbia Circuit Court. The Senate, which was controlled by the Republicans and, then, by the Democrats, returned the nomination to the President both times without acting on it.

**Kellum, John (1809-1871)**

| | |
|---|---|
| Occupation(s): | architect - partner, King and Kellum, 1846-1859*; partner, with his son Hiram, John Kellum and Son** *[See Architects appendix for selected list of commissions in the Town of Hempstead.]* |
| Marriage(s): | 1831-1871 – Hannah Raynor (1811-1877) |
| Address: | Fulton Avenue, Hempstead |

Name of estate:
Year of construction:
Style of architecture:
Architect(s):
Landscape architect(s):
House extant: unconfirmed
Historical notes:

Hannah Raynor Kellum was the daughter of Benjamin and Abigail Smith Raynor.

John and Hannah Raynor Kellum's son John H. died of consumption the year following his father's death. Their daughter Hannah married Dr. Garret D. Van Vrankan and resided in Hempstead. Their son Hiram challenged his father's 1891 will, in which Kellum's widow Hannah was the sole beneficiary of the estate and the sole executrix. [*The Brooklyn Eagle* December 2, 1972, p. 4.] A second will, created from a draft in Kellum's own handwriting, had been found; it was unsigned. The second will designated different executors and divided his estate between his wife and children. [*The Brooklyn Eagle* April 18, 1972, p. 2.]

*John Kellum, a carpenter by trade and largely self-taught as an architect, began his association with Gamaliel King as his project foreman. As such, he supervised the building of Brooklyn City Hall in 1845 which since 1898 has been known as the Brooklyn Borough Hall. One of the significant commissions that was completed after King took Kellum into partnership was the design of the Italianate Friends Meeting House on Gramercy Park South in New York City in 1859 which now houses the Brotherhood Synagogue. They also designed and built the Cary Building between Chambers Street and Reade Street to house William H. Cary's dry-goods shop and warehouse in 1857. The Venetian Renaissance exterior was one of the first cast-iron-fronted buildings in the world.

**John Kellum served as the planner for Alexander Turney Stewart's ambitious municipal project that would eventually be Garden City, Long Island. He was the superintendent for all buildings erected in Garden City, laying out the village and designing many of the earlier houses, although it should be noted than many of these houses were not built until after his death. He designed the original twenty-five-room, mansard-roofed Garden City Hotel, which was begun in 1871 and completed in 1874. Other commissions of note by Kellum and Son were the New York County Courthouse [known as the Tweed Courthouse] on Chambers Street in Lower Manhattan, 1861; the Mutual Life Insurance Company building on Broadway in New York City; the Stock Exchange in Lower Manhattan; the Working Women's Hotel (later, the Park Avenue Hotel), New York City; the Herald Building, New York City; Union Ferry Iron Ferry Houses; A. T. Stewart's Department Store at the corner of Broadway and Tenth Street; and the Stewarts' Manhattan residence on the northeast corner of Fifth Avenue and Thirty-fourth Street.

Despite his portfolio as a successful architect, the American Institute of Architects denied Kellum membership because he was self-taught.

### Kelly, Dr. Aquin S. (1876-1948)

| | |
|---|---|
| Occupation(s): | physician - senior surgeon and chief of ophthalmological services, St. Vincent's Hospital, NYC, 1921-1945; honorary assistant surgeon, New York Eye and Ear Infirmary, NYC; consulting ophthalmologist, St. John's Hospital, Far Rockaway; consulting ophthalmologist, Meadowbrook Hospital, Hempstead |
| Civic Activism: | president, New York Ophthalmological Society |
| Marriage(s): | M/1 – Mary O'Donnell (d. 1924)<br>M/2 – Mary DeLaney |
| Address: | Bannister Lane, Lawrence |
| Name of estate: | |
| Year of construction: | |
| Style of architecture: | Colonial Revival |
| Architect(s): | |
| Landscape architect(s): | |
| House extant: yes | |
| Historical notes: | |

*front / side facade*

Born in Dublin, Ireland, Dr. Aquin S. Kelly was the son of James E. and Annie Kelly.

Dr. Aquin S. and Mary O'Donnell Kelly's daughter Marie married Ernesto Stagg, Jr., the son of Ernesto and Rosa Angela Icaza Overweg Stagg, Sr. of Cedarhurst. In 1918, the Kellys' twelve-year-old daughter Barbara died from the Spanish Flu. Their son Lawrence married Dorothea Veeder, the daughter of Paul Lansing and Grace Dorothea Thrallis Veeder of *Meadowood* in Hewlett Bay Park. Their son Thomas married June Hess, the daughter of Harry Bellas and Mabel Bingham Hess of *The Cedars* in Huntington Station, and resided in East Hampton. [*See* Spinzia, *Long Island's Prominent North Shore Families, vol. I* – Hess entry.]

Mary DeLaney Kelly was the daughter of James Edward DeLaney of Brooklyn. She had previously been married to Dr. William J. Maroney. After Aquin's death, she married Thomas Blagden with whom she resided in Lawrence.

Dr. Aquin S. and Mrs. Mary DeLaney Kelly's daughter Myra married Rowland Godfrey Freeman III of Massachusetts. Myra later married Edward Gardiner Rudd of Boston, MA.

### Kendall, William Beals (1857-1922)

| | |
|---|---|
| Occupation(s): | financier - partner, Hatch and Kendall (stock brokerage firm); partner, Kendall and Whitlock (stock brokerage firm); trustee, Brooklyn Trust Co.; trustee, Hamilton Trust Co. |
| Civic Activism: | trustee, Brooklyn Public Library |
| Marriage(s): | 1883-1922 – Katharine Varnum Whitney (1857-1942) |
| Address: | 110 Tenth Street, Garden City |
| Name of estate: | |
| Year of construction: | 1898 |
| Style of architecture: | Shingle |
| Architect(s): | |
| Landscape architect(s): | |
| House extant: yes | |
| Historical notes: | |

*front facade, 2000*

The *Long Island Society Register, 1929* lists Kate V. Whitney Kendall as residing at 37 Brompton Road, Garden City.

She was the daughter of Rufus Hayden Whitney.

William Beals Kendall was the son of Isaac Kendall. William's ancestor John Kendall was the Sheriff of Nottingham who was killed at the Battle of Bosworth in 1485 while fighting for Richard III.

Katharine Varnum Whitney Kendall was the daughter of Rufus Hayden Whitney.

William Beals and Katharine Varnum Whitney Kendall's daughter Elinor married Andre Eugene Gross and resided in Garden City. Their daughter Katharine, who resided in Garden City, married Archibald Marshall Denny, Sr. Their daughter Marjorie married Maitland Lathrop Bishop, Sr.; Howard Wainwright; and, later, Wallis Clinton Bird with whom she resided at *Farnsworth* in Upper Brookville. [*See* Spinzia, *Long Island's Prominent North Shore Families, vol. I* – Bird entry.]

At the time of his death, Kendall was residing at 110 Tenth Street, Garden City. [*The New York Times* January 28, 1922, p. 11.]

### Kendrick, Frederick William (b. 1877)

| | |
|---|---|
| Occupation(s): | financier - partner, R. L. Day and Co. (stock brokerage firm); partner, Mackay and Co. (stock brokerage firm) |
| Marriage(s): | 1916 – Elizabeth Pendleton Slattery (d. 1933) |
| | - Civic Activism: auxiliary director, Martha Parsons' Hospital, St. Louis, MO |
| Address: | 194 Cathedral Avenue, Hempstead |
| Name of estate: | *Boxley* |
| Year of construction: | 1924 |
| Style of architecture: | Colonial Revival |
| Architect(s): | |
| Landscape architect(s): | |
| House extant: yes | |
| Historical notes: | |

The *Long Island Society Register, 1929* lists Frederick K. [sic] and Elizabeth P. Slattery Kendrick as residing at *Boxley* in Hempstead. The 1930 Census lists the Kendricks at this address.

He was the son of Rufus Kendrick of Boston, MA.

Elizabeth Pendleton Slattery Kendrick was the daughter of Dennis Paul and Elizabeth Wyman Leigh Slattery of St. Louis, MO. Elizabeth had previously been married to Francis Beauregarde de Aguilar of Lawrence. Her son Francis Paul de Aguilar, who resided in Garden City, married Gladys Newbold Banks and, later, Natalie Livingston Forbes.

In 2018, the 2,201-square-foot house, with three bedrooms and two and a half bathrooms, sold for $585,000.

*front facade, 2018*

### Kennedy, Henry Van Rensselaer (1863-1912)

| | | |
|---|---|---|
| Occupation(s): | financier - | director, First National Bank of Hempstead; director, Farmers Loan and Trust Co.; director, Union Trust Co.; director, New York Life Insurance and Trust Co. |
| | capitalist - | director, Land and River Co.; director, Degnon Realty and Terminal Co. (construction firm)* |
| Civic Activism: | | trustee, Lenox Library, NYC; trustee, New York Public Library, NYC |
| Marriage(s): | | 1886-1912 – Marion Robbins (1862-1946) |
| Address: | | Greenwich Street, Hempstead |
| Name of estate: | | *Three Oaks* |
| Year of construction: | | 1902 |
| Style of architecture: | | Neo-Georgian |
| Architect(s): | | |
| Landscape architect(s): | | |

House extant: no; demolished in 1965
Historical notes:

The house, originally named *Three Oaks*, was built by Henry Van Rensselaer Kennedy.
The *Long Island Society Register, 1929* lists Mrs. H. Van Rensselaer Kennedy as residing at *Three Oaks* in Hempstead.
Henry Van Rensselaer Kennedy was the son of James Lenox and Cornelia Van Rensselaer Kennedy of Manhattan.
Marion Robbins Kennedy was the daughter of George A. Robbins of New York.
*Degnon Realty and Terminal Company built the Grand Central Station in Manhattan, the North and East River tunnels of the Long Island Rail Road, and part of Manhattan's Pennsylvania Station.

Henry Van Rensselaer and Marion Robbins Kennedy's daughter Maude married Eric S. Winston; Malcolm Stevenson, Sr. with whom she resided at *Two Maple Farm* in Old Westbury; and, subsequently, Stuart Bryce Wing with whom she resided at *Twin Oaks* in Old Westbury. [*See* Spinzia, *Long Island's Prominent North Shore Families, vol. II* – Stevenson and Wing entries.] Their daughter Marion married John Stewart Pettit. Their daughter Rachel married Frank B. Porter and, subsequently, Graeme Donald.

A memorial stained-glass window dedicated to Henry Van Rensselaer Kennedy can be found in Saint George's Episcopal Church in Hempstead. [*See* Spinzia, *Long Island: A Guide to New York's Suffolk and Nassau Counties* – Saint George's Episcopal Church, Hempstead.]

*front facade*

### Kernochan, James Lorillard (1868-1903)

Occupation(s):

Marriage(s): 1892-1903 – Eloise Stevenson (1872-1948)
- Civic Activism: president, Ladies Kennel Association of America, 1903

Address: Fulton Avenue, Hempstead
Name of estate: *The Meadows*
Year of construction:
Style of architecture:
Architect(s):
Landscape architect(s):
House extant: no; demolished in 1927 for housing development
Historical notes:

*front entrance, 1911*

The house, originally named *The Meadows*, was built by James Lorillard Kernochan. He died of injuries he sustained when his horse fell while taking a hurdle.

James was the son of James Powell and Katherine Lorillard Kernochan and heir to tobacco and Louisiana sugar plantation fortunes. His brother John married Louise Marshall and resided in Manhattan. His brother Frank married Abba E. Learned. His brother J. Frederick Kernochan married Mary S. Whitney and resided in Manhattan. His sister Katharine married Herbert Claiborne Pell without the consent of her parents.

The *Social Register New York, 1907* lists Eloise Stevenson Kernochan as residing at *The Meadows* in Hempstead.

Eloise Stevenson Kernochan was the daughter of Vernon King and Anna Louisa Eve Stevenson, Jr. Eloise subsequently married Alexander Butler Duncan and continued to reside at *The Meadows* prior to relocating to *Yonder House* in Westbury. [See Spinzia, *Long Island's Prominent North Shore Families, vol. 1* – Duncan entry.] Her sister _____ married Vernon K. Hugh.

James Lorillard and Eloise Stevenson Kernochan did not have children.


### Kilbreth, James Truesdell, Jr. (1873-1954)

Occupation(s): attorney - partner, Ouden, Kilbreth, and Schackno
Civic Activism: treasurer, Village of Hewlett Bay Park

Marriage(s): 1913-1954 – Anna Winston Kilbreth (1885-1971)

Address: 69 East Rockaway Road, Hewlett Bay Park
Name of estate: *Bush Corners*
Year of construction:
Style of architecture:
Architect(s):
Landscape architect(s):
House extant: no
Historical notes:

The *Social Register Summer, 1915* lists James T. and Anna W. Kilbreth [Jr.] as residing at *Bush Corners* in Hewlett [Hewlett Bay Park].

[For information about the Kilbreths' Southampton residence *Daisyfields*, see Spinzia, *Long Island's Prominent Families in the Town of Southampton* – Kilbreth entry.]

He was the son of James Truesdell and Sophie Josephine Agnus Kilbreth, Sr. of Southampton.

Anna Winston Kilbreth Kilbreth was the daughter of John Culbertson and Nora M. Murphy Kilbreth of Hewlett. Anna was her husband's second cousin.

James Truesdell and Anna Winston Kilbreth Kilbreth, Jr.'s daughter Sophie married Ernest Patrick Bernuth, the son of Oscar Bernuth of Cedarhurst, and resided in Lawrence. Their son James Truesdell Kilbreth III married Shirley Smith, the daughter of Dr. Lawrence Smith of Manhattan, and resided in Atlanta, GA.

**Kilmer, Dr. Theron Wendell, Sr. (1872-1946)**
**aka Theron Sylvester Norton, Jr.**

| | | |
|---|---|---|
| Occupation(s): | physician - | pediatrician; chief of clinic, Babies Hospital, NYC; attending physician, St. Vincent's Hospital, NYC; attending physician, St. Bartholomew's Clinic, NYC; attending physician, Metropolitan Throat Hospital, NYC; disease of children, West Side German Dispensary; surgeon, Roosevelt Hospital, NYC |
| | educator - | lecturer on diseases of children, New York Polyclinic Medical School; lecturer, Department of Education, NYC |
| | inventor - | Kilmer Test (determined if motorists were inebriated); Mensurgraph (photograph of a person or object by placing a screen with a scale over the negative) |
| | writer - | *The Practical Care of the Infant and Young Child*, 1903; *The Physical Examination of Infants and Young Children*, 1912; magazine articles on photography |
| Civic Activism: | | monitored German messages sent from Telephunken's trans-Atlantic radio station in West Sayville during World War I*; special duty sheriff, Nassau County; first aid and pistol instructor, Nassau County, Garden City, and Hempstead police departments; a founder and secretary, Riverside Practitioners Society, 1900 |
| Marriage(s): | | 1898-1946 – Angie Ransom (1875-1947) |
| Address: | | 215 Hilton Avenue, Hempstead |
| Name of estate: | | |
| Year of construction: | | 1890 |
| Style of architecture: | | Victorian |
| Architect(s): | | |
| Landscape architect(s): | | |
| House extant: | | yes |
| Historical notes: | | |

The *Long Island Society Register, 1929* lists Dr. Theron Wendell and Mrs. Angie Ransom Kilmer [Sr.] as residing at 215 Hilton Avenue, Hempstead.

He was the son of Theron Sylvester and Antoinella Wendell Norton, Sr.

Angie Ransom Kilmer was the daughter of Lewis Emot and Phebe Augusta Buckley Ransom of Manhattan and Hempstead and a cousin of President Ulysses S. Grant.

Dr. Theron Wendell and Mrs. Angie Ransom Kilmer, Sr.'s son Theron Wendell Kilmer, Jr. married Mona Ione Magness, the daughter of Perry Green and Sarah Walker Stockard Magness, and resided in Hempstead. Their daughter Gladys married Henry Learmonth and resided in Mineola.

*For information about German sabotage in the New York Metropolitan area during World War I, *see* Raymond E. Spinzia, "The Involvement of Long Islanders in the Events Surrounding German Sabotage in the New York City Metropolitan Area 1914-1917." @ spinzialongislandestates.com.

*side / front facade, 2012*

### Kimball, Frank Allan (1865-1926)

| | |
|---|---|
| Occupation(s): | financier - member, Corn, Schwartz Co. (coffee and sugar brokerage firm) |
| Marriage(s): | 1894-1926 – Ella Davis (1864-1948) |
| Address: | 86 Fourth Street, Garden City |
| Name of estate: | |
| Year of construction: | 1910 |
| Style of architecture: | Eclectic Victorian |
| Architect(s): | |
| Landscape architect(s): | |
| House extant: | yes |
| Historical notes: | |

The *Long Island Society Register, 1929* lists Mrs. Frank A. Kimball as residing on Fourth Street, Garden City. A 1920 passport application lists this address for Kimball.

Ella Davis Kimball was the daughter of Alson Chapin and Ella Stone Davis of Brooklyn.

Frank Allan and Ella Davis Kimball's son Heathcote married Sabra Parsons Mallett, the daughter of Percy Smith and Emily E. Parsons Mallett of Garden City. Their son Alson married Betsey Chamberlain Ohnewald, the daughter of George Henry and Betsey Chamberlain Ohnewald of Garden City.

*front facade, 2008*

### King, Hugh Purviance, Sr. (1874-1966)

| | |
|---|---|
| Occupation(s): | capitalist - export manager, Procter and Gamble Distributing Co. |
| Marriage(s): | 1907-1946 – Virginia Howard Miller (1878-1946) |
| Address: | 24 Everit Avenue, Hewlett Bay Park |
| Name of estate: | |
| Year of construction: | 1911 |
| Style of architecture: | Colonial Revival |
| Architect(s): | |
| Landscape architect(s): | |
| House extant: | yes |
| Historical notes: | |

The *Long Island Society Register, 1929* lists Hugh Purviance and Virginia Howard Miller King [Sr.] as residing on Everit Avenue, Hewlett [Hewlett Bay Park].

He was the son of Brevet General Adam Eckfeldt and Mrs. Frances Susan Purviance King.

Virginia Howard Miller King was the daughter of Decatur Howard Miller of Baltimore, MD.

Hugh Purviance and Virginia Howard Miller King, Sr.'s daughter Frances married Thomas Wentworth Boykin, Jr. of *Cedar Cliff* in Green Spring Valley, MD, and, later, Hugh Chester Montgomery with whom she resided in Greenwich, CT. Their son Hugh Purviance King, Jr. was killed in the battle of Saipan during World War II. Their daughter Agnes, who did not marry, resided in Rochester, NY.

*front facade, 2000*

### Kingsland, Harold Nutting (1889-1978)

| | |
|---|---|
| Occupation(s): | capitalist - president and director, W. J. Kingsland, Inc., NY (import-export firm) |
| Civic Activism: | road commissioner, Village of Hewlett Bay Park |
| Marriage(s): | 1919-1978 – Mathilde Marie Thieriot (1892-1979) <br> - real estate agent - member, Burr & McAuley, Hewlett <br> Civic Activism: treasurer, Five Towns War Chest, 1943; <br> trustee, District Nursing Association of the Branch Community Chest |
| Address: | 161 Ocean Avenue, Woodmere |
| Name of estate: | |
| Year of construction: | |
| Style of architecture: | |
| Architect(s): | |
| Landscape architect(s): | |
| House extant: no | |
| Historical notes: | |

The *Long Island Society Register, 1929* lists Harold N. and Mathilde M. Thieriot Kingsland as residing in Cedarhurst. The 1940 Census lists them as residing at 69 Elinor Road, Hewlett Bay Park. The *Social Register New York, 1967* lists their address as 161 Ocean Avenue, Woodmere.

The Kingslands' Woodmere residence had previously been owned by John Sise.

Harold Nutting Kingsland was the son of William Jacques and Olive Fair Kingsland of Carmel, CA.

Mathilde Marie Thieriot Kingsland was the daughter of Ferdinand Melly and Pauline Elise Henschell Thieriot.

Harold Nutting and Mathilde Marie Thieriot Kingsland's daughter Pauline married Mark Healey Dall, the son of Marion Dall of Brookline, MA, and resided in Darien, CT. Their daughter Mathilde married Charles Lowell Burnett, the son of Dr. Francis Burnett of Manchester, MA, and resided in Longmeadow, MA.


### Kingsley, Darwin Pearl, Jr. (1899-1987)

| | |
|---|---|
| Occupation(s): | attorney - partner, Clark, Carr, and Ellis, NYC <br> capitalist - director, Laramie Park and Western Railroad Co. |
| Civic Activism: | president, Metropolitan Squash Racquet Association; <br> mayor, Village of Hewlett Harbor |
| Marriage(s): | M/1 – 1926-div. 1932 – Heywood Mason Butler (1906-1945) <br> - entertainer and associate professions - singer <br> M/2 – 1935-1987 – Elizabeth Eckhart (1913-1999) <br> - Civic Activism: president, New York Vassar Club, 1957 |
| Address: | 34 Ablon Road, Hewlett Harbor |
| Name of estate: | *High Tide* |
| Year of construction: | |
| Style of architecture: | |
| Architect(s): | |
| Landscape architect(s): | |
| House extant: no | |
| Historical notes: | |

Darwin Pearl Kingsley, Jr. was the son of Darwin Pearl and Josephine Ignatius McCall Kingsley.

Heywood Mason Butler Kingsley was the daughter of Henry E. Butler of Rumson, NJ. She later married William H. Lieb and, subsequently, Edwin Willard prior to committing suicide in her South Salem, NY, home.

Darwin Pearl and Heywood Mason Butler Kingsley, Jr.'s son Darwin Pearl Kingsley III married Margaret Jane Cotton.

The *Social Register Summer, 1937* lists Darwin P. and Elizabeth Eckhart Kingsley [Jr.] as resided at *High Tide* on Ablon Road, Hewlett [Hewlett Harbor]. The 1940 Census lists Darwin Pearl and Elizabeth E. Kingsley as residing at 34 Ablon Road, Hewlett Harbor.

She was the daughter of Percy B. Eckhart of Chicago, IL.

Darwin Pearl and Elizabeth Eckhart Kingsley, Jr.'s son Charles married Gretchen Uppercu Hill, the daughter of the George Washington Hill, Jr. of Stanford, CT. Their daughter Judith married John Duncan.

### Kip, Ira Andruss, Jr. (1869-1960)
### aka Ira Andrew Kip

| | |
|---|---|
| Occupation(s) | industrialist - leather product manufacturer; vice-president, Salt's Textile Co.; president, Duratex Co, Newark, NJ (upholstery material manufacturing firm) |
| | financier - partner, Shonnard and Co. (stock brokerage firm); partner, Pope and Co. (stock brokerage firm) governor, New York Stock Exchange |
| | capitalist - member, Henry H. Crocker and Co. (East India importer); partner, with his father, Ira A. Kip and Co. (East India importer) |
| Civic Activism: | secretary, The Riding and Driving Club, East Orange, NJ, 1899; village president, South Orange, NJ |
| Marriage(s): | M/1 – 1893-div. 1918 – Katharine Fowler (1870-1951) |
| | - Civic Activism: donated their home in the Thousand Islands to the Canadian government for a convalescent hospital for WW I soldiers, 1917; founded, Golden Apple Tea Room, Gananoque, Ontario, Canada |
| | M/2 – 1918-1960 – Elizabeth Josephine Taylor (1884-1962) |
| Address: | Cedar Avenue and Meadowview Avenue, Hewlett Bay Park |
| Name of estate: | |
| Year of construction: | c. 1908 |
| Style of architecture: | Modified Cotswold |
| Architect(s): | Albro and Lindeberg designed the house (for Carroll Macy) |
| Landscape architect(s): | |
| House extant: | no |
| Historical notes: | |

The house, originally named *Birch Corners*, was built by Carroll Macy. In 1920 it was purchased by Kip.

The *Social Register New York, 1907* lists Ira A. and Katharine Fowler Kip, Jr. as residing at *Oakhall* in South Orange, NJ.

He was the son of Ira Andruss and Mary Roe Kip, Sr.

Katharine Fowler Kip, who later married Dr. Medford Runyon, was the daughter of John D. Fowler of New York.

Ira Andruss and Katharine Fowler Kip, Jr.'s daughter Mary was an infant at the time of her death in 1893. Their daughter Nathalie was fifteen years old when she died in 1921 after falling off a horse. Their son John was twenty-eight at the time of his death in 1924. Their daughter Katherine married David Avery Brenneman. Their son Ira Andruss Kip III married Flora MacMurch Rees.

The *Brooklyn Blue Book and Long Island Society Register, 1921* lists Ira A. and E. Josephine Taylor Kip, Jr. as residing in Hewlett [Hewlett Bay Park]. The Kips later relocated to East Hampton.

Elizabeth Josephine Taylor Kip was the daughter of William F. and Elizabeth Negus Taylor. She had previously been married to Selwyn Kip Farrington, Sr. Their son Selwyn Kip Farrington, Jr. married Sara H. Chisholm, the daughter of Edward de Clifford and Edith Seymour Johnson Chisolm of *Onadune* in East Hampton, and resided in East Hampton. [*See* Spinzia, *Long Island's Prominent Families in the Town of East Hampton* – Chisholm, Farrington, and Kip entries.]

The house was later owned by Danforth Miller, Jr., who also called it *Birch Corners*, and Laurence Anthony Slesinger, who purchased it from Miller in 1942 for $40,000. [*Nassau Daily Review–Star* July 27, 1942, p. 14, and *The New York Times* July 22, 1942, p. 33.]

In 1949 Slesinger placed the house on the market and relocated to Sands Point. [*Newsday* May 6, 1949, p. 45.]

*front facade, 1908*

### Kirkman, Alexander Sampson, Sr. (1844-1912)

| | |
|---|---|
| Occupation(s): | industrialist - founder and president, Kirkman & Son, Brooklyn (later, Colgate–Palmolive Peet Co.) (soap manufacturer) |
| Marriage(s): | 1868-1912 – Esther Field Coleman (1844-1937) |
| Address: | Rockaway Avenue, Garden City |
| Name of estate: | |
| Year of construction: | |
| Style of architecture: | |
| Architect(s): | |
| Landscape architect(s): | |
| House extant: | unconfirmed |
| Historical notes: | |

The *Long Island Society Register, 1929* lists Esther Field Coleman Kirkman as residing on Rockaway Avenue, Garden City.

She was the daughter of John Baxter and Lucy Hubbard Coleman.

Alexander Sampson Kirkman, Sr. was the son of John Kirkman, the founder of Kirkman & Sons.

Alexander Sampson and Esther Field Coleman Sampson Sr.'s daughter Ethel married Thomas Nichols Gurney of Lenox, MA, and resided in Garden City. Their son John married Louise Seaman. Their daughter Lucy died in 1874 at the age of two. Their son Alexander Sampson Kirkman, Jr. married Mary Lewis Evans.

*[See following entry for additional family information.]*


### Knapp, Robert Cole (1885-1924)

| | |
|---|---|
| Occupation(s): | real estate agent - partner, Webb & Knapp (later, real estate construction and holding company)* |
| Marriage(s): | 1908-1924 – Jessie Allen (1883-1941) |
| Address: | 94 Sixth Street, Garden City |
| Name of estate: | |
| Year of construction: | 1873 |
| Style of architecture: | French Empire |
| Architect(s): | |
| Landscape architect(s): | |
| House extant: | yes |
| Historical notes: | |

*side facade 2022*

The *Long Island Society Register, 1929* lists Mr. and Mrs. Robert C. Knapp as residing on Tenth Street, Garden City. The 1920 Census lists the Knapps' address as 94 Sixth Street, Garden City.

He was the son of Walter H. and Mary Cole Knapp.

Jessie Allen Knapp was the daughter of Dr. Cyrus Allen.

Robert Cole and Jessie Allen Knapp's daughter Barbara married John Hyde Preston, the son of George Hyde Preston of New Canaan, MA, and, later, Peter Cary.

*Webb and Knapp developed Roosevelt Field Shopping Center.

In 2022, the 3,535-square-foot house was for sale. The asking price was $2.1 million; the annual taxes were $30,158.

*front facade, 2022*

### Kniffin, Howard Summers, Sr. (1870-1929)

Occupation(s): financier - partner, Kniffin & Caffrey (hemp and jute brokerage firm)

Marriage(s): 1904-1929 – Florence May Aldrich (1874-1957)

Address: 515 Ocean Avenue, Lawrence
Name of estate: *Restleigh*
Year of construction: 1911
Style of architecture: Neo-Georgian
Architect(s): William Adams, Jr. designed the house (for Kniffin)
Landscape architect(s):
House extant: yes
Historical notes:

*front facade*

The house, originally named *Restleigh*, was built by Howard Summer Kniffin, Sr.
The *Long Island Society Register, 1929* lists Howard Summers and M. Aldrich Kniffin [Sr.] as residing on Ocean Avenue, Cedarhurst [Lawrence].
He was the son of Charles Edgar and Anna Wood Ogden Kniffin.
Florence May Aldrich Kniffin was the daughter of Judge Edgar Aldrich of Littleton, NH, and Boston, MA.
Howard Summers and Florence May Aldrich Kniffin, Sr.'s son Ogden married Catharine Ross Swan, the daughter of Robert O. Swan of *Con–Amore* in Hingham, MA, and granddaughter of Edward H. Swan of Oyster Bay, and John H. Ross of Boston, MA. [*See* Spinzia, *Long Island's Prominent North Shore Families, vol. II* – Swan entry.] Their son Edgar, who resided in St. James, married Agnes Means Laying, the daughter of James D. Laying, Jr. of *Round Top Farm* in Somers, NY, and, later, Jean Nolan. Their son Howard Summers, Jr. married Barbara Washburn, the daughter of Charles D. Washburn of Pittsfield, MA, and resided in Forest Hills, Queens.
The house was subsequently owned by Robert Morrow.

### Knopf, Samuel (1861-1932)

Occupation(s): publisher - treasurer and director, Alfred A. Knopf, Inc. (of which the Knopfs' son Alfred was the founder and president)
advertising executive - owner, advertising agency
financier - member, Pacific Bank
capitalist - treasurer and director, American Mercury Inc. (periodical distributor)

Marriage(s): M/1 – Ida Japhe (1864-1897)
- educator - school teacher
M/2 – 1898 – Lillian Harris (1865-1945)

Address: Lord Avenue, Lawrence
Name of estate:
Year of construction: c. 1910
Style of architecture: Modified Neo-Federal
Architect(s):
Landscape architect(s):
Nassau County Museum Collection has photographs of the house.
House extant: no; demolished c. 1950
Historical notes:

*front facade, c. 1916*

Samuel and Ida Japhe Knopf's son Alfred married Blanche Wolf, the daughter of Julius W. and Bertha Samuels Wolf of Manhattan, and resided in Hartsdale, NY. Their daughter Sophia married Alvin M. Josephy, Sr.
Despondent about being accused of being an adulteress, Ida committed suicide.
Samuel and Lillian Harris Knopf's son Edwin married Mary Elsas, the daughter of Herman Elsas of Manhattan, and resided in Beverly Hills, CA.

### Knowlton, Eben Joseph (1844-1938)

| | |
|---|---|
| Occupation(s): | industrialist - partner, William Knowlton & Sons, NYC (straw goods manufacturing firm) |
| Marriage(s): | 1874-1915 – Mary Holberton Beers (1849-1915) |
| Address: | 67 Woodmere Boulevard South, Woodsburgh |
| Name of estate: | |
| Year of construction: | 1918 |
| Style of architecture: | Modified Colonial Revival |
| Architect(s): | |
| Landscape architect(s): | |
| House extant: yes | |
| Historical notes: | |

The *Long Island Society Register, 1929* lists Eben J. Knowlton as residing in Woodmere [Woodsburgh]. He was the son of William and Caroline Taft Knowlton of Brooklyn.

Mary Holberton Beers Knowlton was the daughter of Jonathan P. and Mary Frances Nichols Beers.

Eben Joseph and Mary Holberton Beers Knowlton's daughter Ella married Arthur Nelson Peck and resided in Woodsburgh. Their daughter Grace married Burr Clark Chamberlin of Manhattan and Dalton, MA. Their son Eben Beers Knowlton married Violet Neil Richardson, the daughter of Thomas and Charlotte Seymour Annan Richardson. Their daughter Mabel was an infant at the time of her death in 1883.

*front facade, 2017*

### Kobbe, Carolyn Wheeler (d. circa 1953)

| | |
|---|---|
| Marriage: | 1892-1918 – Gustav Kobbe (1857-1918) |
| | - journalist - music critic, *New York Herald;* editor, *Musical Review* |
| | writer - a novel and several reference books about music and the theater, including *The Complete Opera Book*, 1919 |
| Address: | 120 Fifth Street, Garden City |
| Name of estate: | |
| Year of construction: | |
| Style of architecture: | |
| Architect(s): | |
| Landscape architect(s): | |
| House extant: no | |
| Historical notes: | |

Carolyn Wheeler Kobbe was the daughter of George Minor Wheeler of Scarsdale, NY.

Gustave Kobbe was the son of Carl Wilhelm Ludwig August and Sarah Lord Sistare Kobbe. Gustav was killed while sailing on the Great South Bay when the mast of his boat was struck by an airplane. [Harry W. Havemeyer, *Along the Great South Bay From Oakdale to Babylon: The Story of a Summer Spa 1984 to 1940* (Mattituck, NY: Amerion House, 1996.] Shorty prior to Gustav's death, the Kobbes relocated to Garden City. After Gustav's death, Mrs. Kobbe's new residence was in East Islip.

Gustav and Carolyn Wheeler Kobbe's daughter Beatrice married Raymond Demarest Little, the son of Joseph J. Little, and resided in Babylon. Their daughter Hildegarde married Joseph Hutchins Stevenson, the son of Richard W. Stevenson of Cedarhurst, and, later, Francis Burritt Thorne, Sr., with whom she resided at *Brookwood* in East Islip. Their daughter Carol married Robert Woodward Morgan, Sr., the son of Charles and Clara Woodward Morgan, Sr. and resided in East Islip. Carol subsequently married George Palen Snow, the son of Frederick Augustus and Mary Palen Snow of *Gardenside* in Southampton, and resided in Syosset. [*See* Spinzia, *Long Island's Prominent North Shore Families, vol. II* – Snow entry – and *Long Island's Prominent Families in the Town of Southampton* – Snow entry.] Their son George married Marjorie W. Goss, the daughter of Gustav Goss of Cincinnati, OH. Their daughter Virginia married Gerald Vanderbilt Hollins, Sr., with whom she resided at *The Hawks* in East Islip, and, subsequently, Henry Morgan.

[*See* Spinzia, *Long Island's Prominent South Shore Families* – Hollins, Kobbe, Little, Morgan, and Thorne entries.]

### Kobbe, Frederick William (1887-1946)

| | |
|---|---|
| Occupation(s): | attorney - member, Milbank, Tweed, Hope, and Webb, NYC; member, Masten and Nichols |
| | writer - several articles on bird and plant life |
| Civic Activism: | secretary, Genealogical and Biographical Society of New York |
| Marriage(s): | 1917-1946 – Helen Jay Du Bois (1893-1960) |
| Address: | Hewlett Neck Road, Hewlett Neck |
| Name of estate: | |
| Year of construction: | |
| Style of architecture: | |
| Architect(s): | |
| Landscape architect(s): | |
| House extant: unconfirmed | |
| Historical notes: | |

The *Long Island Society Register, 1929* lists Frederick William and Helen Jay DuBois Kobbe as residing in Woodmere. They later relocated to Hewlett Neck.

He was the son of Frederick and Georgiana Louise Schlotter Kobbe of New York.

Helen Jay Du Bois Kobbe was the daughter of Dr. Robert Ogden and Mrs. Alice Mason Du Bois. Helen's brother Arthur, who resided in Lawrence, married Marie Louise Dixon, the daughter of Courtland Palmer and Hortense Howland Dixon II of *The Causeway* in Lawrence, and, later, Cornelia Prime Coster, the daughter of Edward Livingston and Margaret Elizabeth Lowndes Coster of *Acorn Farm* in Mount Kisco, NY.

Frederick William and Helen Jay Du Bois Kobbe's daughter Alice married Farnham Gilbert, the son of Cass Gilbert, Jr. of Greenwich, CT, and resided in Wilton, CT. Their daughter Helen married Waldron Williams Proctor, the son of William Ross and Joy Waldron Williams Proctor, Jr. of Hewlett Bay Park, and resided in New Canaan, CT.

### Koehler, Robert Henry (1880-1962)

| | |
|---|---|
| Occupation(s): | attorney - member, Strong and Cadwalder; general counsel and director, Fifth Avenue Association; attorney for New York Furniture Exchange |
| | industrialist - director, Roselle Park Building & Loan Association |
| | capitalist - president, Fenimore Building Corp. |
| Civic Activism: | director, Nassau County Bar Association; a founder, Sayville Yacht Club |
| Marriage(s): | M/1 – 1905-1927 – Harriet A. Bischoff (d. 1927) |
| | M/2 – 1929-1950 – Ruth Allen Young (1896-1950) |
| | - second vice-president, Bayport chapter, American Red Cross |
| Address: | 158 Brixton Road, Garden City |
| Name of estate: | |
| Year of construction: | 1922 |
| Style of architecture: | Colonial Revival |
| Architect(s): | |
| Landscape architect(s): | |
| House extant: yes | |
| Historical notes: | |

Robert Henry Koehler was the son of Henry and Bertha Russell Koehler of Brooklyn. He had previously resided on Ocean Avenue in Bayport. [*See* Spinzia, *Long Island's Prominent South Shore Families* – Koehler entry.]

*front facade, 2001*

### Koehne, John Lawrence, Sr. (1896-1978)

Occupation(s): industrialist - president, Shamokin Woolen Mills, Shamokin, PA
Civic Activism: member, fund-raising committee, Berkshire Farm

Marriage(s): Laura Blue (1894-1965)

Address: 272 Victoria Place, Lawrence
Name of estate:
Year of construction: 1900
Style of architecture: Contemporary
Architect(s):
Landscape architect(s):
House extant: yes
Historical notes:

John Lawrence Koehne, Sr. was the son of Louis Koehne of Indianapolis, IN.
Laura Blue Koehne as the daughter of Percy Harris Blue.
John Lawrence and Laura Blue Koehne, Sr.'s son Richard married Laura Grinnell Martin. Their son John Lawrence Koehne, Jr. married Ann Porter Hamill, the daughter of Robert Lyon and Katharine Delano Porter Hamill of Lawrence, and resided in New Haven, CT.
*[See following entry for additional family information.]*

*front facade, 2017*

### Koehne, Richard Sperry, Sr. (1923-1999)

Occupation(s): financier - vice president, Chemical Bank

Marriage(s): 1946-1999 – Laura Grinnell Martin (1926-1999)

Address: 264 Victoria Place, Lawrence
Name of estate:
Year of construction: 1910
Style of architecture: Modified Shingle
Architect(s):
Landscape architect(s):
House extant: yes
Historical notes:

The *Social Register New York, 1965* lists Richard S. and Laura Grinnell Martin Koehne [Sr.] as residing at 264 Victoria Place, Lawrence.
He was the son of John Lawrence and Laura Blue Koehne, Sr. of Lawrence.
Laura Grinnell Martin Koehne was the daughter of Grinnell and Myra Tutt Fraser Martin, who resided at *Grey Cottage* in Cove Neck. [*See* Spinzia, *Long Island's Prominent North Shore Families, vol. I* – Martin entry.]
Richard Sperry and Laura Grinnell Martin Koehne, Sr.'s daughter Laura married Alexander Harvey Whitman, Jr. of Lawrence. Their daughter Sarah married Mark Scharfenaker, the son of William Joseph Scharfenaker of Dearborn, MI.
*[See previous entry for additional family information.]*
In 1958 the house was remodeled.

*front facade, 2000*

## Konta, Geoffrey (1887-1942)

| | |
|---|---|
| Occupation(s): | attorney* -  member, Simpson, Thacher and Bartlett, 1911-1915; partner, Konta, Kirchwey, France, and Michael, 1919-1923; a founder and partner, Konta, Kirchwey, and Engel, 1923; |
| Marriage(s): | 1912-1942 – Phyllis Goodhue (1890-1975) |
| Address: | Hempstead Turnpike and Newbridge Road, East Meadow |
| Name of estate: | *East Meadows* |
| Year of construction: | |
| Style of architecture: | |
| Architect(s): | |
| Landscape architect(s): | |

Nassau County Museum Collections has twelve uncatalogued photographs of the house.
House extant: unconfirmed
Historical notes:

The *Long Island Society Register, 1929* lists Geoffrey and Phyllis Goodhue Konta as residing at *East Meadows* in Hempstead [East Meadow].

He was the son of Alexander and Anne Lemp Konta of Manhattan.

Phyllis Goodhue Konta was the daughter of Charles E. Goodhue.

Geoffrey and Phyllis Goodhue Konta's daughter Anne married Enzo Rangoni Lucci, the son of Marchesa Alda Rangoni Lucci of Rome, Italy, and, subsequently, Wilfred R. Brewer with whom she resided in Locust Valley. Their daughter Phyllis married Renzo Olivieri, the son of Giovanni Olivieri of Florence, Italy.

*Konta, who specialized in corporate and personal income tax law, was William Randolph Hearst's personal attorney and that of his corporation. [*See* Spinzia, *Long Island's Prominent North Shore Families, vol. 1* and *Long Island's Prominent Families in the Town of* Southampton – Hearst entries.] Geoffrey was also Arthur Brisbane's attorney. [*See* Spinzia, *Long Island's Prominent Families in the Town of East Hampton* – Brisbane entry.]


## Koons, Franklin Stevenson (1887-1976)

| | |
|---|---|
| Occupation(s): | financier -  assistant treasurer, National City Bank; president, Plymouth Fund |
| | capitalist -  vice-president, Queens Borough Gas and Electric Co.; chairman, Suffolk County Water Authority; vice-president, Long Island Lighting Co.; director, Long Beach Gas Co., Inc. |
| Civic Activism: | mayor, Village of Garden City, 1937-1939; treasurer, Electrical and Gas Association; trustee, Village of Old Field; trustee, Village of Garden City, 1930-1937; trustee, Emma S. Clark Library, Setauket |
| Marriage(s): | M/1 – Bertha Eliza Niles (1887-1920) |
| | M/2 – Mary McKennan (1895-1989) |
| Address: | 119 Kensington Road, Garden City |
| Name of estate: | |
| Year of construction: | 1921 |
| Style of architecture: | Colonial Revival |
| Architect(s): | |
| Landscape architect(s): | |
| House extant: yes | |
| Historical notes: | |

*front facade, 2015*

The *Long Island Society Register, 1929* lists Franklin S. Koons as residing on Kensington Road, Garden City. The 1940 Census lists Mr. and Mrs. Koons as residing at 119 Kensington Road in Garden City.

He was the son of Benjamin Franklin and Hannah Jennie Stevenson Koons.

Bertha Eliza Niles Koons was the daughter of William Pitt and Mary A. Dudley Niles of Fairhaven, CT.

Mary McKennan Koons was the daughter of George Ethelbert and Mary Harris Owen McKennan. She had previously been married to Claude Ashburn Mayborn Hickman, the son of Maylon James and Mattie Brents Hickman.

By 1952 Koons had relocated to the Village of Old Field.

In 1991, the 2,722-square-foot Garden City house sold for $512,000.

**Krugman, Paul Robin (b. 1953)**

| | |
|---|---|
| Occupation(s): | educator - professor of economics, Yale University, New Haven, CT; professor of economics, Massachusetts Institute of Technology, Cambridge, MA; professor of economics, Stanford University, Stanford, CA; professor of economics, Princeton University, Princeton, NJ; professor of economics, London School of Economics, London, England; professor of economics, Graduate Center, City University of New York, NYC |
| | journalist - articles, editorials, and columns for several newspapers and periodicals |
| | writer - author or editor of twenty-seven books; over two hundred articles in professional journals |
| Civic Activism: | member, Council of Economic Advisors (Reagan administration); research associate, National Bureau of Economic Research; president, Eastern Economic Association; member, Group of Thirty (international economic body) |
| Marriage(s): | M/1 – div. – Robin Leslie Bergman<br>- artist<br>capitalist - founder, Robin Originals (women's clothing and accessory firm)<br>M/2 – Robin Wells (b. 1959)<br>- educator - professor of economics, Massachusetts Institute of Technology, Cambridge, MA;<br>journalist - *The New York Times*, *The Guardian* online, and *The Huffington Post*<br>writer - co-authored several books with her husband |
| Address: | 116 Hampton Way, Merrick |
| Name of estate: | |
| Year of construction: | 1950 |
| Style of architecture: | Contemporary |
| Architect(s): | |
| Landscape architect(s): | |
| House extant: | yes |
| Historical notes: | |

Paul was raised in this house by his parents David and Anita Krugman.

In 2008, Paul was awarded the Nobel Prize in Economic Sciences. In 2018, *Foreign Policy* named him one of the Top 100 Global Thinkers.

In 2018, the 2,375-square-foot house sold for $577,500.

*front facade, 2018*

**Ladd, William Fowle, Jr. (1885-1949)**

Occupation(s): financier - partner, Tilney, Ladd, and Co. (stock brokerage firm); partner, W. F. Ladd and Co. (stock brokerage firm)
capitalist - real estate holdings*

Civic Activism: director, Atlantic Beach Club, 1937

Marriage(s):
M/1 – 1910-div. 1930 – Cornelia Lee (1886-1969)
M/2 – 1935-div. – Beatrice Goelet Greenough (1908-1984)
M/3 – 1941-div. 1947 – Joan Marie Kaufman (b. 1907)
M/4 – 1948-1949 – Natalie Rathbone Jones

Address: Rutherford Lane, Lawrence
Name of estate:
Year of construction: c. 1920
Style of architecture: Neo-Tudor
Architect(s): Peabody, Wilson, and Brown designed the house in association with Carroll Ladd (for W. F. Ladd, Jr.)
Landscape architect(s):
House extant: no**
Historical notes:

The house was built by William Fowle Ladd, Jr.

The *Long Island Society Register, 1929* lists William F. and Cornelia Lee Ladd [Jr.] as residing in Cedarhurst [Lawrence] and Southampton. [*See* Spinzia, *Long Island's Prominent Families in the Town of Southampton* – Ladd entry.]

He was the son of William Fowle and Caroline Willis Ladd, Sr.

Cornelia Lee Ladd was the daughter of Charles Henry and Lucy Cushing Whitney Lee, who resided at *Westlawn* in Southampton. [*See* Spinzia, *Long Island's Prominent Families in the Town of Southampton* – Lee entry.] Cornelia subsequently married Payson McLean Merrill with whom she resided in Syosset. Her sister Elinor married Malcolm Douglas Sloan with whom she resided in Sands Point. Elinor subsequently married Albert Delmont Smith with whom she resided at *Keewayden* in Sands Point and, later, at *Mill Pond* in Lloyd Harbor. [*See* Spinzia, *Long Island's Prominent North Shore Families, vol. II* – Sloane and Smith entries.]

William Fowle and Cornelia Lee Ladd, Jr.'s son Charles married Phillis A. Howe, the daughter of Dudley Rogers and Ellen Mercer Atterbury Howe of Boston, MA, and resided in Needham, MA. Their daughter Elinor married William Ladd Storey, Sr., the son of Richard C. Storey of Boston, MA, and resided in Lloyd Harbor.

Beatrice Goelet Greenough Ladd was the daughter of William and Charlotte Warren Greenough. Beatrice had previously been married to William Townsend Adee, the son of Ernest Rufus and Geraldine Fitzgerald Adee. After her divorce from Ladd, Beatrice married John Anthony Marple, the son of Verne D. and Essie Bell Marple.

William Fowle and Beatrice Goelet Greenough Ladd, Jr.'s daughter Gabrielle, who married Stafford Morss, died in an airplane crash.

Joan Marie Kaufman Ladd was the daughter of Louis Graverael and Marie Julia Young Kaufman of Short Hills, NJ. Joan had previously been married to George Drexel Biddle of Philadelphia, PA; Joseph M. Wintersteen of Haverford, PA; and Frank F. Polk of Reno, NV.

Natalie Rathbone Jones Ladd was the daughter of Dr. Seabury Jones of New York. Prior to her marriage to Ladd, she had been married to James Daniel Hurd and, then, to James Lakeman Ward.

Despondent over his poor health, Ladd committed suicide by shooting himself in the mouth. [*The New York Times* June 2, 1949, p. 23.]

*Ladd was known as the "King of Nassau" because of his extensive holdings in the Bahamas.

**Only the service buildings are extant.

*c. 1930*

### Ladenburg, Adolph (1855-1896)
### aka Moritz Adolph Emil Ladenburg

| | |
|---|---|
| Occupation(s): | capitalist - real estate - trustee, Meadow Brook Park Co. (Hempstead land development company) |
| | financier - a founder and partner, Ladenburg, Thalmann, and Co. (investment banking firm) |
| Marriage(s): | Emily Louise Stevens (1864-1937) |
| Address: | Valentines Road, Salisbury |
| Name of estate: | *Heathcote* |
| Year of construction: | |
| Style of architecture: | Victorian |
| Architect(s): | |
| Landscape architect(s): | |
| House extant: | no; demolished in 1952 for housing development |
| Historical notes: | |

*side facade, 1910*

The house, originally named *Heathcote*, was built by Adolph Ladenburg. He was the son of Emil and Eugenie Adele Halphen Ladenburg.

Emily Louise Stevens Ladenburg was the daughter of Alexander Henry and Mary Alleyne Otis Stevens of Lawrence and a descendant of United States Secretary of the Treasury Albert Gallatin.

While traveling to Nassau in the Bahamas for a vacation aboard the SS *Niagara* Adolph was reported drowned. His body was never recovered. In 1908, he was reported to have been seen in Marienbad, Germany. Family and business associates said it was probably his brother or one of his cousins, who were still residing in Germany, that caused the identity confusion.

In 1906, the Ladenburgs' thirteen-year-old daughter Eugenie was the subject of an attempted kidnapping at *Heathcote*. Her screams alerted the gardener and a neighbor, Mrs. McDonald. They were able to frighten away the attacker. Eugenie married Preston Davie, Sr. and resided at *Heathcote*, which they renamed *The Oasis*.

In 1909, Mrs. Landenburg shocked society at Saratoga, NY, by introducing the split skirt for horseback riding.

In 1950, the Davies sold the estate which, at the time, consisted of a fourteen-room house, a stable, and a five-car garage. [*The New York Times* July 9, 1950, p. R.]


### La Mont, Herbert Murray (1877-1930)

| | |
|---|---|
| Occupation(s): | financier - member, Brown, Ryan, and Williams (stock brokerage firm); |
| | member, Clark, Childs and Co. (stock brokerage firm); |
| | member, Gray and Wilmerding (stock brokerage firm) |
| | capitalist - director, Rampo Water Co.; |
| | vice-president and treasurer, M. A. Shaw Co., Inc. |
| | industrialist - Westinghouse Electric & Manufacturing Co. |
| Marriage(s): | 1919-1930 – Mary Horsman (1880-1964) |
| Address: | Clark Place, Woodmere |
| Name of estate: | |
| Year of construction: | |
| Style of architecture: | |
| Architect(s): | |
| Landscape architect(s): | |
| House extant: | unconfirmed |
| Historical notes: | |

The *Long Island Society Register, 1929* lists Herbert Murray and Mary Horsman Swain La Mont as residing on Clark Place, Woodmere.

He was the son of Charles A. and Regina Holmes Warren La Mont.

Mary Horsman La Mont was the daughter of Edward Imeson and Florence Lewis Benton Horsman, Sr. of Brooklyn. Mary had previously been married to Robert Wilmarth Appleton of *Nid de Papillion* in East Hampton and Spencer Swain. [*See* Spinzia, *Long Island's Prominent Families in the Town of East Hampton* – Appleton entry.]

### La Montagne, Montaigu (1881-1938)

| | |
|---|---|
| Occupation(s): | industrialist - partner, with his brothers William, Morgan, and Rene La Montagne, Jr., Green River Distillery, Louisville, KY |
| | merchant - partner, with his brothers, R. La Montagne's Sons, NYC (wine and liquor distributors) |
| Marriage(s): | 1913-1938 – Hyldagarde Jurgensen |
| Address: | *[unable to determine street address]*, Cedarhurst |

Name of estate:
Year of construction:
Style of architecture:
Architect(s):
Landscape architect(s):
House extant: unconfirmed
Historical notes:

The *Social Register Summer, 1910* and the *Long Island Society Register, 1929* list Montaigu and Hyldagarde Jurgensen La Montagne as residing in Cedarhurst.

He was the son of Rene La Montagne, Sr., who founded the Green River Distillery.

Hyldagarde Jurgensen La Montage was the daughter of John Jurgensen of Manhattan.

During Prohibition the La Montagne brothers were known as the "society bootleggers." They were arrested, tried, convicted, and served jail sentences for their activities. [*The New York Times* January 30, 1938, p. 45.]

### Lamy, Henry Bernard, Jr. (1884-1957)

| | |
|---|---|
| Occupation(s): | financier - vice-president and director, Pacific Fire Insurance Co.; |
| | vice-president and director, Bankers and Shippers Insurance, Co.; |
| | director, Christiania General Insurance Co.; |
| | director, Metropolitan Fire Assurance Co.; |
| | director, Stand Holding Co.; |
| | manager and fire secretary, New Jersey Insurance Co. |
| | capitalist - secretary and director, Rhelaudo Building Corp. |
| Civic Activism: | chairman, Commerce and Industry Division, New York City Emergency Unemployment Committee, 1930-1934 |
| Marriage(s): | M/1 – 1916 – Helen Elizabeth Newland (1892-1982) |
| | M/2 – 1927-1957 – Mildred M. Simpson (b. 1885) |
| Address: | 73 First Street, Garden City |

Name of estate:
Year of construction:
Style of architecture:
Architect(s):
Landscape architect(s):
House extant: no
Historical notes:

The *Long Island Society Register, 1929* lists Henry B. and Mildred M. Simpson Lamy, Jr. as residing at 73 First Street, Garden City.

He was the son of Henry Bernard and Eglantine Huntsinger Green Lamy, Sr.

Helen Elizabeth Newland Lamy was the daughter of David and Sarah Tompkins Newland. Helen subsequently married Ned Douglass Biddison and, later, Charles Alonzo Russ.

Henry Bernard and Helen Elizabeth Newland Lamy, Jr.'s son Richard died at the age of sixteen. In 1939, their twenty-year-old son Douglass eloped with the eighteen-year-old Veronica Stearns whose stage name was Veronica Drake. She was the daughter Robert B. Stearns, a founder of the investment firm of Bear Sterns and the granddaughter of Isaac Stern, a founder of the Stern Brother Department Store. In 1945, Douglass, whose stage names were Douglass Newland, Douglass Drake, and Johnny Mitchell, attempted to murder Veronica. The thirty-two-year-old Douglass's body was found by his mother slumped on a sofa. Despondent over his separation from Veronica, he had committed suicide by placing a 22-caliber rifle between his legs and shooting himself in the forehead.

Mildred M. Simpson Lamy was the daughter of James Simpson of Brooklyn.

Henry Bernard and Mildred M. Simpson Lamy, Jr.'s daughter Ellen married William Edward Moore, the son of Harry Lawson Moore of Greenwich, CT, and resided in Pasadena, CA.

In 1933, the house was purchased by Warren J. Nissely. [*The Nassau Daily Review* February 18, 1933, p. 5.]

### Lancaster, John Edward, Jr. (1894-1964)

Occupation(s): financier - auditor, Irving Trust Co.

Marriage(s): 1921-1964 – Jean Saunders (1893-1974)

Address: Veeder Drive and Lefferts Road, Hewlett Bay Park
Name of estate:
Year of construction:
Style of architecture:
Architect(s):
Landscape architect(s):0
House extant: unconfirmed
Historical notes:

The *Long Island Society Register, 1929* lists John Edward and Jean Saunders Lancaster [Jr.] as residing in Hewlett [Hewlett Bay Park]. The 1930 Census lists the Lancasters at this address.

He was the son of John Edward and Agnes Fanning Lancaster, Sr. His sister Rosamund married Barclay Harding Warburton, Jr., the grandson of John Wanamaker of Philadelphia, PA. She later married William Kissam Vanderbilt, Jr. in a ceremony in the mayor's office in Paris, France, and resided with him at *Eagle's Nest* in Centerport. [*See* Spinzia, *Long Island's Prominent North Shore Families, vol. II* – Vanderbilt entry.]

Jean Saunders Lancaster was the daughter of William Lawrence and Eliza Morton Saunders of Plainfield, NJ. Jean had previously been married to Marsom I. Buttfield.

In 1940 Mrs. Lancaster sold the house to George F. Mitchell. [*The Brooklyn Daily Eagle* October 2, 1940, p. 23.]


### Lanman, Jonathan Trumbull, Sr. (1872-1952)

Occupation(s): financier - member, White, Weld, and Co. (investment banking firm); partner, Jones and Lanman (stock brokerage firm)

Marriage(s): 1896-1945 – Mary Ludlow Thomas (1872-1945)

Address: Causeway, Lawrence
Name of estate: *Orchard Hall*
Year of construction: c. 1900
Style of architecture: Neo-Jacobean
Architect(s): Thomas Henry Randall designed the house (for W. Burr, Sr.)
Landscape architect(s): Hicks Nursery supplied the Norway Maples, Pin Oaks, and Silver Maples (for W. Burr, Sr.)
House extant: no; demolished in 1968
Historical notes:

The house, originally named *Orchard Hall*, was built by Winthrop Burr, Sr.

The *Social Register Summer, 1910* lists Jonathan Trumbull and Mary Ludlow Thomas Lanman [Sr.] as residing at *Orchard Hall* in Lawrence.

He was the son of Trumbull Lanman.

Mary Ludlow Thomas Lanman was the daughter of Ludlow and Mary S. Thompson Thomas.

Jonathan Trumbull and Mary Ludlow Thomas Lanman Sr.'s daughter Sylvia remained unmarried. Their daughter Mary married Alexander Moss White, Jr. and resided at *Hickory Hill* in Oyster Bay Cove. [*See* Spinzia, *Long Island's Prominent North Shore Families, vol. II* – White entry.] Their son Jonathan Trumbull Lanman, Jr. married Sonia Laurie, the daughter of Oscar Laurie of St. Petersburg, Russia, and resided in Katonah, NY.

*Orchard Hall, c. 1900*

**Lannin, Joseph John (1866-1928)**

| | |
|---|---|
| Occupation(s): | capitalist - president, Lannin Realty Corp. (extensive real estate holdings); |
| | owner, Roosevelt Air Field, Hempstead Plains; |
| | owner, Salisbury Country Club, East Meadow; |
| | owner, Salisbury Golf Club, East Meadow; |
| | owner, Garden City Hotel; |
| | owner, Grenoble Hotel, NYC; |
| | owner, Granada Hotel, Brooklyn; |
| | manager, The Balsams Grand Resort Hotel, Dixville Notch, NH; |
| | owner, Boston Red Sox Baseball Team, 1913-1916; |
| | owner, Boston Braves Baseball Team; |
| | owner, Boston American League Baseball Club; |
| | owner, Providence Grays Baseball Club; |
| | owner, Buffalo Bisons, 1915-1920 (baseball club); |
| | owner, Newark Baseball Club |
| Civic Activism: | a founder and director, Mineola–Garden City Rotary Club |
| Marriage(s): | Hannah J. Furlong (1869-1954) |
| | - Civic Activism: volunteer, various Long Island military bases during World War I |
| Address: | 45 Seventh Street, Garden City |
| Name of estate: | |
| Year of construction: | 1901 |
| Style of architecture: | |
| Architect(s): | Stanford White designed the hotel |
| | Ford, Butler, and Oliver enlarged and remodeled the hotel, 1911 |

Landscape architect(s):
House extant: demolished, 1973
Historical notes:

The *Long Island Society Register, 1929* lists Mrs. Hannah J. Furlong Lannin as residing in the Garden City Hotel.

Joseph John Lannin was the son of John and Catherine Lannin of Lac Beauport, Quebec, Canada. Joseph, a fourteen-year-old penniless orphan walked from Lac Beauport to Boston, MA, to seek his fortune.

Hannah was buried in the "potter's field" on the grounds of Pilgrim State Hospital in Brentwood. The family plans to intern her with her husband Joseph in Holy Rood Cemetery in Westbury.

Joseph John and Hannah J. Furlong Lannin's daughter Dorothy married Harry Alphonse Tunstall, the son of Harry Gabriel and Jessie Gertrude Graham Tunstall of Garden City, and resided in East Meadow and Garden City. Their son Paul, who was a noted Broadway composer, conductor, lyricist, and musician remained a bachelor.

Joseph fell from a ninth-story window of the Granada Hotel. At the time of his death his fortune was estimated at $7-$8 million. [*The New York Times* May 16, 1929, p. 11.]

In 2004, he was inducted into The Canadian Baseball Hall of Fame and Museum.

*Garden City Hotel, front facade, 1901*
*(picture taken from the roof of The Cathedral of the Incarnation)*

### Larkin, John Adrian, Sr. (1891-1948)

| | |
|---|---|
| Occupation(s): | attorney -   clerk for Supreme Court Chief Justice Charles Evans Hughes |
| | industrialist -  director and secretary, Celanese Corp. |
| | financier -  chairman of board, Fulton Trust Co., NYC |
| Civic Activism: | established scholarship at Princeton University and art prize at Phillips Exeter Academy in memory of his son John Adrian Larkin, Jr. |
| Marriage(s): | 1915-1948 – Henrietta Rosa Kleberg (1889-1969) |
| | - capitalist – chair of board, King Ranch, Kingsville, TX |
| Address: | Woodside Drive, Hewlett Bay Park |
| Name of estate: | |
| Year of construction: | |
| Style of architecture: | |
| Architect(s): | |
| Landscape architect(s): | |
| House extant: unconfirmed | |
| Historical notes: | |

The *Long Island Society Register, 1929* lists John A. and Henrietta R. Kleberg Larkin [Sr.] as residing in Lawrence. They later relocated to Hewlett Bay Park.

He was the son of John and Ida Rahm Larkin of Manhattan.

Henrietta Rosa Kleberg Larkin was the daughter of Robert Justus and Alice Gertrudis King Kleberg, Sr. of the King Ranch in Kingsville, TX. After John's death Henrietta married Thomas Reeves Armstrong.

John Adrian and Henrietta Rosa Kleberg Larkin, Sr.'s daughter Henrietta married John Barkley Armstrong. Their daughter Ida married James Harrison Clement. Their son John Adrian Larkin, Jr., who was killed in World War II, was awarded the Silver Star.

### Lasher, Dr. Frank Hermance (1883-1946)

| | |
|---|---|
| Occupation(s): | physician -  ear, nose, and throat surgeon |
| Marriage(s): | 1920-1946 – Gladys Georgetta Bryan (1894-1946) |
| Address: | 57 Pine Street, Garden City |
| Name of estate: | |
| Year of construction: | 1904 |
| Style of architecture: | Contemporary |
| Architect(s): | |
| Landscape architect(s): | |
| House extant: yes | |
| Historical notes: | |

The 1940 Census lists Dr. Frank H. and Mrs. Gladys Bryan Lasher as residing at 57 Pine Street in Garden City.

He was the son of Warren P. and Almira J. Hermance Lasher.

Gladys Georgetta Bryan Lasher was the daughter of George Edward and Emma Selina Sind Bryan.

Dr. Lasher murdered his wife and mother-in-law, and wounded his twenty-one-year-old son Douglas prior to committing suicide in his Garden City house. [*The New York Times* October 26, 1946, pp. 1 and 3.]

In 2002, the 1,944-square-foot house sold for $630,000.

*front facade*

### Lawrence, Alfred Newbold, I (1813-1884)

| | |
|---|---|
| Occupation(s): | merchant - dry goods; wholesale druggist |
| Marriage(s): | 1837-1884 – Elizabeth Woodhull Lawrence (1817-1884) |
| Address: | *[unable to determine street address]*, Lawrence |
| Name of estate: | |
| Year of construction: | |
| Style of architecture: | |
| Architect(s): | |
| Landscape architect(s): | |
| House extant: | unconfirmed |
| Historical notes: | |

Alfred Newbold Lawrence I was the son of John Burling and Hannah Haines Newbold Lawrence.

Elizabeth Woodhull Lawrence was the daughter of John L. and Sarah Augusta Smith Lawrence and the granddaughter of John Tangier Smith and Revolutionary War General Nathaniel Woodhull of *The Manor of Saint George* in Mastic Beach. [*See* Spinzia, *Long Island: A Guide to New York's Suffolk and Nassau Counties – The Manor of Saint George*, Mastic Beach.]

Alfred Newbold and Elizabeth Woodhull Lawrence Lawrence I's daughter Hannah married Clarence Edwin Sherman of California. Their son John married Alice Warner Work, the daughter of James Henry and Marie Pierce Warner Work, Sr. of *The Gowans* in Lawrence, and resided at *Moorlands* in Lawrence.

*[See other Lawrence entries for additional family information.]*

### Lawrence, Clifford Winfield, Jr. (1891-1970)

| | |
|---|---|
| Occupation(s): | industrialist - assistant treasurer, Swift & Co. (food producer) |
| Marriage(s): | Florence Rue (1894-1978) |
| Address: | 78 Brompton Road, Garden City |
| Name of estate: | |
| Year of construction: | 1926 |
| Style of architecture: | Neo-Tudor |
| Architect(s): | |
| Landscape architect(s): | |
| House extant: | yes |
| Historical notes: | |

The house was built by Clifford Winfield Lawrence, Jr.

The *Long Island Society Register, 1929* lists Clifford W. and Florence Rue Lawrence [Jr.] as residing at 78 Brompton Road, Garden City.

He was the son of Josephine A. Weed Lawrence, who resided at 158 Roxbury Road, Garden City. Clifford had erroneously been placed on the federal government's "slacker list" of World War I deserters. He had actually served in the United States Navy from 1917-1918 and had been honorably discharged. [*The Evening World* August 26, 1921, p. 3.]

Florence Rue Lawrence was the daughter of Charles Halsey and Florence Teale Rue of Garden City.

Clifford Winfield and Florence Rue Lawrence, Jr.'s daughter Audrey married Richard Dunnette Link, the son of Rue S. Link of Seattle, WA. Their daughter Rue married Emory McMichael Clark, the son of Stuart Benson Clark of Riverton, NJ. Their daughter Ann married Dr. John Grove Rogers, the son of Dr. Harry L. Rogers of Riverton, NY.

*[See other Lawrence entries for additional family information.]*

*front / side facade, 2001*

### Lawrence, John L., Sr. (1857-1930)

| | |
|---|---|
| Occupation(s): | industrialist - vice-president, National Meter Co. |
| Civic Activism: | president, Village of Lawrence, 1898, 1904; |
| | fire commissioner, Lawrence Volunteer Fire Department, 1900 |
| Marriage(s): | 1895-1930 – Alice Warner Work (1875-1966) |
| Address: | Breezyway, Lawrence |
| Name of estate: | *Moorlands* |
| Year of construction: | |
| Style of architecture: | |
| Architect(s): | |
| Landscape architect(s): | Hick Nursery supplied a mature Pine Oak, |
| | Wild Cherry, Boxwood, and shrubs, 1897 |

Nassau County Museum Collection has eleven uncatalogued photographs of the house.
House extant: unconfirmed
Historical notes:

The *Social Register Summer, 1910, 1915*, and *1921* and the *Long Island Society Register, 1929* list John L. and Alice W. Work Lawrence [Sr.] as residing at *Moorlands* in Lawrence.

He was the son of Alfred Newbold and Elizabeth Woodhull Lawrence Lawrence I of Lawrence. John's sister Hannah married Charles Edwin Sherman and resided at *The Brae* in Lawrence.

Alice Warner Work Lawrence was the daughter of James Henry and Maria Pierce Warner Work, Sr., who resided at *The Gowans* in Lawrence. Alice's sister Sally married Franklin Baker Lefferts and resided in Lawrence. Her sister Marjorie married DeCourcy Lawrence Hard, Sr. and resided at *Briarwood* in Lawrence. Her sisters Mabel, Jean, and Marie remained unmarried. Her brother James Henry Work, Sr. married Mary Laying Davis and resided at *Engleside* in Lawrence.

John L. and Alice Warner Work Lawrence, Sr.'s son Alfred Newbold Lawrence II married Marianna T. Casserly, the daughter of John Bernard and Cecelia Cudahy Casserly, and, later, Else K. Johnson.

*[See other Lawrence entries for additional family information.]*

*Moorlands, 1897*

### Lawrence, Newbold Trotter, Sr. (1855-1928)

| | |
|---|---|
| Occupation(s): | real estate agent – member, H. H. Camman & Co. but later became an |
| | independent broker |
| | financier - director, Union Square Savings Bank |
| | writer - ornithological articles |
| Civic Activism: | governor and secretary, Rockaway Hunting Club, Lawrence, 1911; |
| | treasurer, St. John's Episcopal Church, Lawrence; |
| | bequeathed his bird collection to the Academy of Natural Sciences, |
| | Philadelphia, PA |
| Marriage(s): | 1887-1904 – Isabella Gillet (1860-1904) |
| Address: | 125 Barrett Road, Lawrence |
| Name of estate: | *Homewood* |
| Year of construction: | |
| Style of architecture: | |
| Architect(s): | |
| Landscape architect(s): | |

House extant: no
Historical notes:

The *Social Register New York, 1907* and the *Social Register Summer, 1910* and *1915* list Newbold T. Lawrence [Sr.] as residing at *Homewood* in Lawrence.

He was the son of Newbold and Anne Hough Lawrence.

Isabella Gillet Lawrence was the daughter of Noah and Eliza Winters Halleck Gillet.

Newbold Trotter and Isabella Gillet Lawrence Sr.'s daughter Annie married Harold Herrick and resided at *The Meadows* in Lawrence. Their son Newbold Trotter Lawrence, Jr. married Evelyn Cromwell, the daughter of Richard Cromwell, Jr. of Baltimore, MD, and resided in Lloyd Harbor. Their daughter Caroline did not marry.

*[See other Lawrence entries for additional family information.]*

### Lebaudy, Jacques (1868-1919)

| | |
|---|---|
| Occupation(s): | capitalist - owner, Huanchaca Silver Mine, Chile |
| Marriage(s): | 1896-1919 – Augustine Delliere (1873-1950)<br>  - entertainers and associated professions -   French actress |
| Address: | Valentine's Road, Salisbury |
| Name of estate: | *Phoenix Lodge* |
| Year of construction: | |
| Style of architecture: | Modified Colonial Revival |
| Architect(s): | |
| Landscape architect(s): | |
| House extant: | no* |
| Historical notes: | |

*front facade, c. 1919*

The house was previously owned by William Morrow Knox Olcott, who called it *Phoenix Lodge*. In 1913, Olcott sold the house to Lebaudy, who continued to call it *Phoenix Lodge*.

He was the son of French sugar refining magnet Jules Lebaudy and Amicie Piou Lebaudy. Jacques' sister was Countess Marie Teresa Jeanne Lebaudy de Fels.

In 1903, after inheriting $8 million from his parents, Jacques converted his yacht *Frasquita* into a battleship and sailed to North Africa where he proclaimed himself Jacques I Emperor of the Sahara. After being rebuffed by the French and Spanish governments, both of which laid claims to portions of North Africa, Lebaudy came to Long Island. Becoming increasingly unstable, he was confined to the state hospital in Amityville. He was released by a court order from the Amityville facility but was again institutionalized after assaulting his wife, but, then, again released. While his wife and eighteen-year-old daughter were on the second floor of their Long Island mansion, Lebaudy attempted to burn down the house. Hearing the noise, Mrs. Lebaudy came down the stairs and shot him five times, killing him instantly.

In 1922, Augustine Delliere Lebaudy married her bodyguard Henri Sudreau and took up residence in France.

The Lebaudys' daughter Marguerite married Henri Sudreau's son Roger and also resided in France.

*In 1926, the estate was purchased by Lannin Realty Company. In 1935, several of the estate's service buildings were destroyed by fire.

### Lefferts, Franklin Baker (1879-1906)

| | |
|---|---|
| Occupation(s): | architect -   partner, Lefferts and Smith, NYC;<br>                    specialized in the design of Brooklyn brownstone houses |
| Marriage(s): | 1902-1906 – Sally Duncan Work (1879-1972) |
| Address: | *[unable to determine street address]*, Lawrence |
| Name of estate: | |
| Year of construction: | |
| Style of architecture: | |
| Architect(s): | |
| Landscape architect(s): | |
| House extant: | unconfirmed |
| Historical notes: | |

The *Social Register New York, 1907* lists Franklin B. and Sally D. Work Lefferts as residing in Lawrence.

He was the son of Marshall Clifford and Carrie Ella Baker Lefferts, Sr., who resided at *Hedgewood* in Lawrence.

Sally Duncan Work Lefferts was the daughter of James Henry and Maria Pierce Warner Work, Sr., who resided at *The Gowans* in Lawrence. Sally's sister Alice married John L. Lawrence, Sr. and resided at *Moorlands* in Lawrence. Her sister Marjorie married DeCourcy Lawrence Hard, Sr. and resided at *Briarwood* in Lawrence. Her sisters Mabel, Jean, and Marie remained unmarried. Her brother James Henry Work, Jr. married Mary Laying Davis and resided at *Engleside* in Lawrence.

Franklin Baker and Sally Duncan Work Lefferts' daughter Dorothy married Lawrence Moore, the son of Frank Gardner Moore of Manhattan.

*[See following entry for additional family information.]*

### Lefferts, Marshall Clifford, Sr. (1848-1928)

| | |
|---|---|
| Occupation(s): | industrialist - president and chairman of board, Celluloid Manufacturing Co. |
| Civic Activism: | member, Committee of Seventy, 1892* |
| Marriage(s): | 1878-1926 – Carrie Ella Baker (1856-1926) |
| Address: | Ocean Avenue and Tanglewood Crossing, Lawrence |
| Name of estate: | *Hedgewood* |
| Year of construction: | c. 1905 |
| Style of architecture: | Shingle |
| Architect(s): | Lord and Hewlett designed the house (for M. C. Lefferts) |
| Landscape architect(s): | Hicks Nursery supplied plantings (for M. C. Lefferts, Sr.) |

House extant: unconfirmed
Historical notes:

*front / side facade, c. 1905*

The house, originally named *Hedgewood*, was built by Marshall Clifford Lefferts, Sr.

The *Social Register Summer, 1910* and *1915,* and the *Long Island Society Register, 1929* list Marshall Clifford Lefferts, Sr. as residing in Lawrence.

He was the son of Marshall and Mary Allen Lefferts of Manhattan.

Carrie Ella Baker Lefferts was the daughter of Peter C. and Malvina Lockwood Baker of New York.

Marshall Clifford and Carrie Ella Baker Lefferts, Sr.'s son Franklin married Sally Duncan Work and resided in Lawrence. Their daughter Mary married Henry Rawle, Jr. of Philadelphia, PA, and resided in Manhattan.

*[See previous entry for additional family information.]*

*The Committee of Seventy was instrumental in disbanding the notorious Tweed Ring.


### Lehrenkrauss, Charles Frederick (1903-1975)

| | |
|---|---|
| Occupation(s): | financier - member, J. Lehrenkrauss & Sons, Brooklyn (bond and mortgage firm)* |
| Civic Activism: | established Charles F. Lehrenkrauss Cup for high scholarship at Adelphi Academy, Brooklyn (later, Adelphi University, Garden City) |
| Marriage(s): | 1926-1975 – Arline Relyea French (1906-1975) |
| Address: | 121 Whitehall Boulevard, Garden City |
| Name of estate: | |
| Year of construction: | 1925 |
| Style of architecture: | Neo-Tudor |
| Architect(s): | |
| Landscape architect(s): | |

House extant: yes
Historical notes:

*front facade, 2017*

The house was built by Charles Frederick Lehrenkrauss.

The *Long Island Society Register, 1929* lists Charles F. and Arline R. French Lehrenkrauss as residing at 121 Whitehall Boulevard, Garden City.

He was the son of Charles H. and Katherine Madeline Bene Lehrenkrauss of Brooklyn.

Arline Relyea French Lehrenkrauss was the daughter of Arthur H. and Mabel Augusta Relyea French of Brooklyn.

*In 1934, Lehrenkrauss was indicted on alleged larceny charges. [*The New York Times* February 28, 1934, p. 5.]

In 2017, the 4,020-square-foot house sold for $1.975 million.

## Leighton, Alexander E. (1882-1961)

| | |
|---|---|
| Occupation(s): | financier - assistant comptroller, Williamsburgh Savings Bank |
| Civic Activism: | chairman, Saving Bank Advertising Association, 1935 |
| Marriage(s): | Charlotte Neuber (1879-1953) |
| Address: | Hilton Place, Hempstead |

Name of estate:
Year of construction:
Style of architecture:
Architect(s):
Landscape architect(s):
House extant: unconfirmed
Historical notes:

    The *Long Island Society Register, 1929* lists Alexander E. Leighton as residing on Hilton Place, Hempstead. The 1940 Census lists the Leightons at 17 Hilton Avenue in Hempstead.
    He was the son of Alexander and Elizabeth and Vollmer Leighton.
    Charlotte Neuber Leighton was the daughter of Charles F. Neuber, who was believed to have been the last surviving member of "Hawkin's Zouaves." Neuber's unit served in the Union Army during the Civil War. [*The New York Times* March 11, 1940, p. 19.]
    Alexander E. and Charlotte Neuber Leighton's son Robert married Jean Lalmart, the daughter of Eugene J. and Bertie McDonald Lalmart of Hempstead.


## Leighton, George Bridge (1864-1929)

| | | |
|---|---|---|
| Occupation(s): | industrialist - | director and vice president, American Steel Foundries; president, Leighton and Howard Steel Co., St. Louis, MO, 1897-1903; director, Bridge Beach Manufacturing Co.; director, Commonwealth Steel Co.; director, Alleghany-By-Products Coke Co. |
| | shipping - | president, Lone Star Shipbuilding Co. |
| | capitalist - | president, Los Angeles Terminal Railroad, 1890-1900; director, Hannibal Water Co.; director, New York Railways Co. |
| Civic Activism: | | member, New Hampshire State Forestry Commission; chairman, New Hampshire chapter, American Red Cross; president, New Hampshire State Historical Society |
| Marriage(s): | | 1893-1929 – Charlotte Kayser (1866-1934)<br>  - Civic Activism: chair, Women's Committee of Hempstead Democratic Club |
| Address: | | Fulton Avenue, Hempstead |

Name of estate:
Year of construction:
Style of architecture:
Architect(s):
Landscape architect(s):
House extant: unconfirmed
Historical notes:

    The 1930 Census lists the Leightons as residing on the Duncan Estate on Fulton Avenue.
    George Bridge Leighton was the son of George Eliot and Isabel Bridge Leighton I.
    Charlotte Kayser Leighton was the daughter of Henry and Emily Lassen Kayser of St. Louis, MO.
    George Bridge and Charlotte Kayser Leighton's son George Eliot Leighton II married Lisa Gilman Todd, the daughter of Henry Alfred Todd of Manhattan. Their son John married Alice B. Allen, the daughter of Ethan Allen of Manhattan.
*[See following entry for additional family information.]*

## Leighton, John Langdon (1896-1936)

Occupation(s): advertising executive
financier - member, Brown Brothers, NYC (investment banking firm);
member, Tucker, Anthony and Co., Boston, MA
(investment banking firm)
publisher - vice-president and editor, *Outlook* magazine
writer - *Simsadus: London: The American Navy in Europe*, 1920;
magazine articles in *Outlook*;
pamphlets and articles on economics, politics, and social
questions

Marriage(s): M/1 – 1926-div. 1930 – Alice B. Allen
M/2 – 1936-1936 – Helen *[not able to determine maiden name]*

Address: Fulton Avenue, Hempstead
Name of estate:
Year of construction:
Style of architecture:
Architect(s):
Landscape architect(s):
House extant: unconfirmed
Historical notes:

The *Long Island Society Register, 1929* lists John L. and Alice B. Allen Leighton as residing in Hempstead. The 1930 Census lists the Leightons as residing on the Duncan Estate on Fulton Avenue.

He was the son of George Bridge and Carlotte Kayser Leighton of Hempstead.

Alice B. Allen was the daughter of Ethan Allen of Manhattan and a descendant of Ethan Allen of Revolutionary War fame.

Three weeks after his second marriage, Leighton committed suicide on his honeymoon in Manhattan's Peter Cooper Hotel by hanging himself with his belt in the bathroom while his wife waited in the adjoining bedroom. [*The New York Times* September 12, 1936, p. 8, and *Daily News* September 12, 1936, pp. 3 and 27.]

Helen Leighton had previously been married to Reuben Senton Fisher.

*[See previous entry for additional family information.]*.

*George Morton Levy, Sr. residence,
front facade, 2000*

### Levy, George Morton, Sr. (1888-1977)

| | |
|---|---|
| Occupation(s): | attorney - partner, Smith and Levy; partner, with New York State Supreme Court Judge Townsend Scudder, Townsend Scudder, and George Morton Levy<br>capitalist - a founder and president, Roosevelt Raceway, Westbury<br>Civic Activism: president, Nassau Trotting Association |
| Marriage(s): | M/1 – 1915-div. – Frances Roberta Hendrickson (1893-1973)<br>M/2 – 1922-div. 1931 – Beatrice Baldwin<br>M/3 – 1937-div.1943 – Margaret Kinsella (1907-1987)<br>M/4 – 1949-1967 – Elise Huehle (1918-1967) |
| Address: | 266 Smith Street, Freeport |
| Name of estate: | |
| Year of construction: | 1920 |
| Style of architecture: | Bungalow |
| Architect(s): | |
| Landscape architect(s): | |
| House extant: yes | |
| Historical notes: | |

George Morton Levy, who was called the "Father of Modern Harness Racing," was the son of Adolph and Anna Katz Levy of Seaford and, later, Freeport.

Frances Roberta Hendrickson Levy was from Seaford. She later married Robert Harrison Candlish, the son of Robert and Julia Bellmer Candlish.

George Morton and Beatrice Baldwin Levy, Sr.'s son George Morton Levy, Jr. married Dolores Ann Van Keuren, the daughter of Mrs. Ellen M. Van Keuren of Merrick.

Margaret Kinsella Levy subsequently married the noted actor Richard Arlen.

Levy was known for his association with Mafia Dons. In 1936, he defended Lucky Luciano against prostitution charges. In 1951, he paid Frank Costello $60,000 to rid Roosevelt Racetrack of book makers [*Reno Gazette–Journal* March 12, 1951, p. 1.]

In 1966, Levy was inducted into the Hall of Fame of the Trotters.

### Levy, Isaac D. (1867-1934)

| | |
|---|---|
| Occupation(s): | capitalist - president, Oppenheim–Collins Realty Co.;<br>merchant - president, Oppenheim, Collins, & Co. (dry goods firm)* |
| Marriage(s): | 1902-1934 – Rosetta Davis (b. 1883) |
| Address: | Cedarhurst Avenue and West Broadway, Cedarhurst |
| Name of estate: | *Roselle Manor* |
| Year of construction: | c. 1900 |
| Style of architecture: | Neo-Jacobean |
| Architect(s): | Buchman and Fox designed the house (for Levy) |
| Landscape architect(s): | Lord and Burnham designed the conservatory (for Levy) |
| House extant: no; demolished c. 1960 | |
| Historical notes: | |

*front facade*

The house, originally named *Roselle Manor*, was built by Isaac D. Levy.

*Oppenheim, Collins, and Company was originally a ladies' skirt manufacturer. It later became a department store with locations in Manhattan, Brooklyn, Philadelphia, PA, Buffalo, NY, Pittsburgh, PA, Cleveland, OH, and Newark, NJ.

Levy was known as "the prince of merchant princes in the realm of ready-to-wear." [*The New York Times* September 10, 1934, p. 17.]

Isaac D. and Rosetta Davis Levy's son Robert married Doris Dawson. Their daughter Miriam married Martin Lewis Cohn, Jr. of Manhattan and, later, August Montulet with whom she resided at *Raymar Farms* in Long Branch, NJ. Their daughter Kathleen married Robert Kenton and resided in Manhattan.

In 1927 the Levys donated the house to St. Joseph's Hospital in Far Rockaway as a memorial to their daughter Dorothy. [*The New York Times* September 10, 1934, p. 17.]

### Lewis, Edison (1880-1942)

| | |
|---|---|
| Occupation(s): | capitalist - director and vice president, 435 Park Avenue Corp, NYC; |
| |            director and vice president, Ritz–Carlton Hotel Corp., NYC; |
| |            vice-president, Goelet Realty Co., NYC; |
| |            director and vice-president, Hotel Imperial Corp. |
| | industrialist - director, Tanamo Sugar Corp. |
| Marriage(s): | 1907-1942 – Edith Greenough (1881-1971) |
| |   - Civic Activism: vice-president, Lawrence Garden Club |
| Address: | Longwood Crossing, Lawrence |
| Name of estate: | |
| Year of construction: | |
| Style of architecture: | Colonial Revival |
| Architect(s): | |
| Landscape architect(s): | |
| House extant: unconfirmed | |
| Historical notes: | |

The *Long Island Society Register, 1929* lists Edison and Edith Greenough Lewis as residing on Longwood Crossing, Cedarhurst [Lawrence].

He was the son of Charles H. and Orianna Pendleton Lewis of Boston, MA.

Edith Greenough Lewis was the daughter of William and Alice Mary Patterson Greenough. Her sister Alice married Edward Mitchell Townsend II and resided at *Townsend Place* in Oyster Bay Cove. [*See* Spinzia, *Long Island's Prominent North Shore Families, vol. II* – Townsend entry.]

Edison and Edith Greenough Lewis' son John married Natalie Greene, the daughter of A. Crawford Greene of San Francisco, CA. Their son Charles married Mabel Burke Walker, the daughter of John Yates Gholson Walker of Llewellyn Park, West Orange, NJ.

### Lewis, Henry Llewellyn Daingerfield, Jr. (1877-1938)

| | |
|---|---|
| Occupation(s): | financier - partner, Pynchon and Co. (stock brokerage firm) |
| Marriage(s): | M/1 – 1916-div. 1924 – Lucy Reis |
| | M/2 – 1925 – Jessie Somerville Knox Voss |
| |     - artist |
| Address: | Pleasant Place, Hewlett Bay Park |
| Name of estate: | *Merriefield* |
| Year of construction: | |
| Style of architecture: | Colonial Revival with Long Island Farmhouse elements |
| Architect(s): | |
| Landscape architect(s): | |
| House extant: unconfirmed | |
| Historical notes: | |

*rear facade*

Henry Llewellyn Daingerfield Lewis, Jr. was the son of Henry Llewellyn Daingerfield and Carter Penn Freeland Lewis, Sr. of Piedmont, VA, and a great-great-grandson of Betty Washington, President George Washington's sister. Henry was also a great-grandson of Eleanor Parks Custis and related to the Byrd, Lee, and Carter families of Virginia.

Lucy Reis Lewis was the daughter of William E. Reis of Greenwich, CT.

The house, originally named *Merriefield*, had been previously owned by William Voss. It was subsequently owned by his daughter Jessie and son-in-law Henry Llewellyn Daingerfield Lewis, Jr., who continued to call it *Merriefield*.

The *Long Island Society Register, 1929* lists H. L. Daingerfield and Jessie S. K. Voss Lewis [Jr.] as residing in Hewlett [Hewlett Bay Park].

### Lissberger, Benjamin (1875-1937)

| | |
|---|---|
| Occupation(s): | financier - director, First National Bank of Rockville Centre |
| | industrialist - president and chairman of board, Federated Metals Division, American Smelting and Refining Co., |
| | director, American Smelting and Refining Co.; |
| | president, Summerville Iron Works; |
| | president, United Zinc Smelting and Refining Co.; |
| | a founder and chairman of board, B. Lissberger & Co. (smelting and refining firm) |
| Civic Activism: | director, American Zinc Institute |
| Marriage(s): | Juliet Waixel (1887-1943) |
| Address: | East Rockaway Road and Waverly Avenue, Hewlett Harbor |
| Name of estate: | *Twin Gables* |
| Year of construction: | |
| Style of architecture: | Eclectic |
| Architect(s): | |
| Landscape architect(s): | |
| House extant: unconfirmed | |
| Historical notes: | |

*Twin Gables*

In 1921, the estate, which consisted of a main residence, garage, service buildings, and nine acres, was purchased by Lissberger from George William and Julia McMahon Loft of *Lakeview* in Baldwin for $112,000. [*The Daily Review* April 14, 1921, p. 1.]

Benjamin and Juliet Waixel Lissberger's daughter Dorothy married Harold Masius, the son of Max L. Masius of Manhattan. Their daughter Marion married Henry L. Lambert.

In 1941 the estate was sold to Louis Kaplan. [*The New York Times* October 6, 1941, REAL 32.]

### Littleton, Martin Wilson, Sr. (1897-1966)
### aka Martin W. Littleton, Jr.

| | |
|---|---|
| Occupation(s): | attorney - partner, George Morton Levy of Freeport; |
| | member, legal department, Standard Oil; |
| | Nassau County District Attorney; |
| | member, Lamar Hardy |
| | capitalist - cattle ranch* |
| | writer - co-author, with Kyle Crichton, *My Partner – In-Law: The Life and Times of George Morton Levy*, 1957 |
| Marriage(s): | 1920-1966 – Marion Carroll (1902-1972) |
| Address: | 81 Westminister Road, Garden City |
| Name of estate: | |
| Year of construction: | 1930 |
| Style of architecture: | Colonial Revival |
| Architect(s): | |
| Landscape architect(s): | |
| House extant: yes | |
| Historical notes: | |

The *Social Register Summer, 1937* lists Martin Wilson and Marion Carroll Littleton [Sr.] as residing at 81 Westminister Road, Garden City.

He was the son of Martin Wiley and Maude E. Wilson Littleton of *Plandome Manor House* in Plandome Manor.

Marion Carroll Littleton was the daughter of Bradish Johnson and Marion Bowers Carroll and the granddaughter of Dr. Alfred Ludlow and Mrs. Lucy Ann Johnson Carroll of Bay Shore. [*See* Spinzia, *Long Island's Prominent North Shore Families, vol. I* – Littleton entry – and *Long Island's Prominent South Shore Families* – Carroll and Johnson entries.]

Martin Wilson and Marion Caroll Littleton, Sr.'s daughter Louise married K. Harrison Roberts and resided near Cody, WY. Their daughter Susan married John R. Peterson of Cody. WY. Their son Martin Wilson Littleton, Jr. married Ann Leigh.

*In 1940, Littleton moved to a ranch forty miles outside of Cody, WY.

In 2007, the 5,234-square-foot house sold for $2.515 million

*Martin Wilson Littleton, Sr. residence,
front facade, 2007*

### Livingston, John Griswold, Sr. (1872-1961)

| | |
|---|---|
| Occupation(s): | capitalist - purchasing agent, Lexington & Eastern Railroad, KY; general superintendent, Honduras Railroad Co.; president and treasurer, J. Livingston Co. (electrical contractor)* |
| Civic Activism: | governor, Rockaway Hunting Club, Lawrence, 1911; president, Rockaway Steeplechase Association, 1937 |
| Marriage(s): | 1903-1955 – Clara Miller Dudley (1875-1955) |
| Address: | 175 Causeway, Lawrence |
| Name of estate: | |
| Year of construction: | 1908 |
| Style of architecture: | Shingle |
| Architect(s): | |
| Landscape architect(s): | |
| House extant: yes | |
| Historical notes: | |

The *Social Register New York, 1933* lists John G. and Clara M. Dudley Livingston as residing at 175 Causeway in Lawrence.

He was the son of Robert Cambridge and Maria Whitney Livingston III of *Lakeside* in Islip. [*See* Spinzia, *Long Island's Prominent South Shore Families* – Livingston entry.] John's sister Maud married Henry Worthington Bull and resided in Islip and, later, in North Hills. [*See* Spinzia, *Long Island's Prominent South Shore Families* – Bull and Livingston entries – and *Long Island's Prominent North Shore Families, vol. I* – Bull entry.]

Clara Miller Dudley Livingston was the daughter of B. William and Maria Hunt Dudley.

John Griswold and Clara Miller Dudley Livingston, Sr.'s son William married Jane Edison, the daughter of John L. Edison of Sewickley, PA, and resided in Darien, CT. Their son Robert married Joan Ordway, the daughter of Samuel Gilman and Mildred O. Wurtele Ordway of *Dellwood* in East Hampton, and resided in New Canaan, CT. [*See* Spinzia, *Long Island's Prominent Families in the Town of East Hampton* – Ordway entry.] Their son John Griswold Livingston, Jr. married Mary Terry Harrison, the daughter of Milton Strong and Mary Constance Kittinger Harrison, Jr. of Cedarhurst, and, subsequently, Deborah Locke, the daughter of Campbell and Ruth Cary Slattery Locke, Sr. of Hewlett Neck.

*J. Livingston Company was reputed to be the largest electrical contracting firm in the country. In 1938 Livingston was arrested for allegedly failing to make material entries into the company's ledgers. [*The New York Times* July 15, 1938, p. 1.]

*front facade, 2000*

### Livingston, Johnston, II (1877-1939)
### aka Johnston Livingston, Jr.

| | |
|---|---|
| Occupation(s): | capitalist - founder, Johnston Livingston, Jr. and Co. (construction firm) |
| Marriage(s): | M/1 – 1901-1922 – Nathalie Fellows Moss (1879-1922) |
| | M/2 – 1923-1939 – Ruth Helene Moller (1893-1978) |
| Address: | East Rockaway Road and Union Avenue, Hewlett |
| Name of estate: | *Homeacre* |
| Year of construction: | |
| Style of architecture: | |
| Architect (s): | |
| Landscape architect(s): | |
| House extant: | unconfirmed |
| Historical notes: | |

The *Social Register New York, 1907* lists Johnston and Nathalie F. Moss Johnston, Jr. as residing in Cedarhurst. The *Social Register Summer, 1910* lists the name of their residence as *Homeacre*. By 1914 they had relocated to Hewlett.

He was the son of Robert Cambridge and Maria Whitney Livingston of *Lakeside* in Islip and a descendant of Philip Livingston who was a signer of the Declaration of Independence. [*See* Spinzia, *Long Island's Prominent South Shore Families* – Livingston entry.]

Nathalie Fellows Moss Livingston was the daughter of Courtland Dixon and Camilla Woodward Moss, Sr. Nathalie's brother Courtland Dixon Moss, Jr. married Katharine Hazzard, the daughter of William Ayrault and Laura Abell Pelton Hazzard, Sr. of *Meadow Hall* in Lawrence, and resided in Muttontown. [*See* Spinzia, *Long Island's Prominent North Shore Families, vol. I* – Moss entry.]

Johnston and Nathalie Fellows Moss Livingston II's daughter Camilla married Donald McVicker of *Pondacre* in East Norwich and, later, Daniel Peart Erwin with whom she resided in East Hampton. [*See* Spinzia, *Long Island's Prominent North Shore Families, vol. I* – McVicker entry – and *Long Island's Prominent Families in Town of East Hampton.* – Erwin entry.] Their daughter Silvie married William Tilden Pelton Hazzard of *Meadow Hall*, and, later, William Philander Hulbert.

The *Long Island Society Register, 1929* lists Johnston and Ruth H. Moller Livingston as residing at *Still Pond* in Huntington. [*See* Spinzia, *Long Island's Prominent North Shore Families, vol. I* – Livingston entry.] She was the daughter of Charles George and Helene Allen Moller, Jr. of Lawrence.

Johnston and Ruth Helene Moller Livingston II's daughter Silvie married Frank William Wall, the son of Harold M. and Helen M. K. Bond Wall of *The Taj* in Southampton. [*See* Spinzia, *Long Island's Prominent Families in Town of Southampton.* – Wall entry.]

By 1951 Ruth and her son Johnston Livingston III had relocated to East Hampton. [*See* Spinzia, *Long Island's Prominent Families in Town of East Hampton.* – Livingston entry.]


### Locke, Campbell, Sr. (1874-1950)

| | |
|---|---|
| Occupation(s): | attorney - partner, Alexander and Green, NYC |
| | industrialist - secretary and treasurer, Cerro de Pasco Copper Corp. |
| Civic Activism: | president, Men's Club, Trinity Episcopal Church, Hewlett, 1931 |
| Marriage(s): | 1905-1918 – Ruth Cary Slattery (1884-1918) |
| Address: | 150 Ocean Avenue, Lawrence |
| Name of estate: | |
| Year of construction: | 1923 |
| Style of architecture: | Colonial Revival |
| Architect(s): | |
| Landscape architect(s): | |
| House extant: | yes |
| Historical notes: | |

*front facade, 2016*

The *Long Island Society Register, 1929* lists Campbell Locke as residing on East Broadway, Hewlett Neck. By 1935 he had relocated to Ocean Avenue in Lawrence.

He was the son of Charles E. and Eleanor Brown Locke of Kansas City, MO.

Campbell and Ruth Cary Slattery Locke, Sr.'s daughter Deborah married Dudley Avery Coonley and, subsequently, John Griswold Livingston, Jr. of Lawrence. Their daughter Faith married Francis Hine Low, the son of Ethelbert Ide and Gertrude Herrick Low of Woodsburgh, and, subsequently, Charles S. Moffett. Their son Campbell Locke, Jr. married Caroline Agnes Francklyn, the daughter of Reginald Gebhard and Lilian Endicott Francklyn of Hewlett Harbor, and resided in Bernardsville, NJ.

### Loft, George William (1865-1943)

| | |
|---|---|
| Occupation(s): | industrialist - president, Loft Candy Co.<br>capitalist - founder, George W. Loft Realty Co.*;<br>      raised thoroughbred horses<br>merchant - founder, George W. Loft Markets, Inc. (Loft candy retail stores<br>      in White Plains, New Rochelle, Yonkers, and The Bronx)<br>politician - member, United States Congress representing New York's<br>      13th and 15th Districts, 1906, 1913-1917<br>financier - a founder, Emerald National Bank and Trust Co., NYC;<br>      a founder and president, South Shore Trust Co., Rockville Centre;<br>      chairman of board, County Federal Savings & Loan<br>          Association, Rockville Centre |
| Civic Activism: | chairman, New York City Mayor's Committee on National Defense, 1918;<br>member, New York State Racing Commission;<br>president, Harlem Board of Trade |
| Marriage(s): | M/1 – Elizabeth Marie Lyons (1871-1910)<br>M/2 – 1911-1943 – Julia McMahon (1885-1962)<br>  - Civic Activism: deputy police commissioner, New York City, 1921-1923;<br>      her charities included Mercy Hospital, Rockville<br>          Centre and St. Anthony's Convent, East Meadow |
| Address: | Merrick Road and Milburn Avenue, Baldwin |
| Name of estate: | *Lakeview* |
| Year of construction: | |
| Style of architecture: | |
| Architect(s): | |
| Landscape architect(s): | |
| House extant: unconfirmed | |

Historical notes:

   The house was built by the founder of the Village of Baldwin, Francis Baldwin. It was later owned by Loft.
*[South Side Messenger* May 12, 1911, p. 5.]

*Lakeside, 1919*

   He was the son of the founder of the Loft Candy Company, William Loft.

   George William and Elizabeth Marie Lyons Loft's son George Leon Loft, who was known on Broadway as "The Candy Kid," married Elizabeth Ahearn and, later, Ziegfeld girl Rose Gallagher.

   *In 1938 Loft sub-divided forty acres of his estate and erected twelve luxury homes.

### Logan, John Alexander, III (1890-1969)

| | |
|---|---|
| Occupation(s): | |
| Marriage(s): | 1913-1969 – Margaret Lauretta Powell (1893-1984) |
| Address: | Hewlett Neck Road, Hewlett Neck* |
| Name of estate: | |
| Year of construction: | |
| Style of architecture: | Colonial Revival |
| Architect(s): | |
| Landscape architect(s): | |
| House extant: unconfirmed | |

Historical notes:

   The *Long Island Society Register, 1929* lists John A. and Margaret L. Powell Logan [III] as residing in Hewlett Bay Park [Hewlett Neck]. The 1930 Census lists the Logans as residing on Georges Boulevard, Hewlett Neck.

   *Hewlett Neck Road was previously called Georges Boulevard.

   He was the son of John Alexander and Edith H. Andrews Logan II of Newport, RI, and the grandson of Grand Army of the Republic Commander in Chief General John Alexander Logan, Sr., who, by general order, officially established May 30th as Decoration Day in 1868 (renamed Memorial Day by presidential declaration). [*The New York Times* February 23, 1923, p. 13.] John Alexander Logan III's sister Edith married Dewees Wood Dilworth and resided at *Gloan House* in Old Westbury. [*See* Spinzia, *Long Island's Prominent North Shore Families, vol. I* – Dilworth entry.]

   Margaret Lauretta Powell Logan was the daughter of Robert Walter Powell, Jr. of St. Joseph, MO.

   John Alexander and Margaret Lauretta Powell Logan III's daughter Edith married Robert Earl Magoffin. Their daughter Margot married Herbert Karel Krumel. Their son Robert married Barbara Anne Koontz. Their son John Alexander Logan IV married Maxine Dolores McCarl and, later, Evagene Collard.

   In 1935 Logan relocated to Tucson, AZ, where he died.

### Long, William Henderson, Jr. (1892-1985)

| | |
|---|---|
| Occupation(s): | engineer - chairman of board, J. G. White Engineering Corp. |
| | financier - director, Empire Trust Co. |
| | advertising executive - president and chairman of board, Doremus & Co., NYC |
| Civic Activism: | police commissioner, Village of Hewlett Harbor; |
| | trustee, Village of Hewlett Harbor, 1948; |
| | chairman, advisory board, Seawaine Club |
| Marriage(s): | 1924-1971 – Dorothy Jacquelin Smith (1905-1971) |
| |   - writer - articles about dog breeding and training |
| |     Civic Activism: president, Long Island Kennel Club, 1949; |
| |         president, Westbury Kennel Association, 1941; |
| |         a founder and president, Long Island Obedience Training Club; |
| |         a founder and secretary, Dogs for Defense (trained dogs for duty during World War II); |
| |         president, Collie Club of America; |
| |         president, Buddies, Ind. (trained dogs for blind children); |
| |         co-founder, Meadowbrook Hounds Pony Club |
| Address: | Everit Avenue, Hewlett Harbor |
| Name of estate: | *Noranda* |
| Year of construction: | |
| Style of architecture: | |
| Architect(s): | |
| Landscape architect(s): | |
| House extant: | unconfirmed |
| Historical notes: | |

    The *Long Island Society Register, 1929* lists William H. and Dorothy J. Smith Long as residing at *Moranda* [sic] on Schenck Lane, Hewlett Harbor. The 1940 Census lists them as residing on Everit Avenue in Hewlett Harbor.

    He was the son of William Henderson and Letitia Bonbright Long, Sr. of Philadelphia, PA.

    Dorothy Jacquelin Smith Long was the daughter of Augustine Jacquelin and Julia Post Hard Smith of *Sunnyside* in Lawrence, and the great-granddaughter of Anson Wales Hard of *Driftwood* in Lawrence. Dorothy's sister Edith married John Meyerkort, Jr. and resided in Lawrence. Her sister Mary married Dr. DeWitt Hendee Smith, the son of Charles Hendee Smith of Lawrence, and resided in Princeton, NJ.

    William Henderson and Dorothy Jacquelin Smith Long, Jr.'s daughter Dorothy married John H. Hale, the son of Horace C. Hale of Canton, NY. Their daughter Elizabeth married Robert Page Burr, Jr., the son of Robert Page and Laurence Hewlett Burr, Sr. of Lawrence, and resided in Lloyd Harbor.

    By 1950 the Longs has relocated to Berry Hill Road in Syosset.

*Daniel de Forest Lord V's residence, Sosiego, garden, 1923*

### Lord, Daniel de Forest, V (1846-1899)

| | |
|---|---|
| Occupation(s): | attorney - partner, Lord, Day, and Lord, NYC |
| | financier - director, United States Trust Co.; |
| | director, Equitable Life Assurance Society; |
| | director, Fifth Avenue Trust Co. |
| Marriage(s): | 1868-1899 – Silvie Livingston Bolton (1846-1922) |
| Address: | Westover Place, Lawrence |
| Name of estate: | *Sosiego* |
| Year of construction: | |
| Style of architecture: | |
| Architect(s): | |
| Landscape architect(s): | Martha Brookes Brown Hutcheson (for D. Lord V) |
| House extant: | unconfirmed |
| Historical notes: | |

The house, originally named *Sosiego*, was built by Daniel de Forest Lord V.

The *Social Register New York, 1907* and the *Social Register Summer, 1910* and *1921* list Silvie Bolton Lord as residing at *Sosiego* in Lawrence.

She was the daughter of William Henry and Frances Howell Hewlett Bolton.

Daniel de Forest Lord V was the son of Daniel de Forest and Mary Howard Butler Lord IV of Manhattan. His brother Franklin married Josephine Gillet and resided in Lawrence. *[See following entry.]*

While visiting the 1893 Chicago World's Fair, the Lords' twenty-three-year-old son Daniel de Forest Lord VI fell from his fourth story bedroom window while sleepwalking. [*The New York Times* June 21, 1893.]

The house was subsequently owned by Lord's daughter Frances and son-in-law Origen Storrs Seymour II, who continued to call it *Sosiego*.

### Lord, Franklin Butler, Sr. (1850-1908)

| | |
|---|---|
| Occupation(s): | attorney - partner, Lord, Day, and Lord, NYC |
| | capitalist - director, Queens County Water Co.; |
| | vice-president and director, Cuba Railroad Co. |
| | financier - director, Lawyer's Title Insurance & Trust Co. |
| Civic Activism: | secretary and treasurer, Barnard College, NYC; |
| | trustee, Society for the Relief of Half Orphans and Destitute Children; |
| | president, Village of Lawrence |
| Marriage(s): | 1875-1908 – Josephine Gillet (1853-1909) |
| Address: | Causeway, Lawrence |
| Name of estate: | |
| Year of construction: | |
| Style of architecture: | |
| Architect(s): | |
| Landscape architect(s): | |
| House extant: | no |
| Historical notes: | |

Franklin Butler Lord, Sr. was the son of Daniel de Forest and Mary Howard Butler Lord IV of Manhattan. *[See previous and following entries for additional family information.]*

Josephine Gillet Lord was the daughter of Joseph and Mary Higgenbotham Gillet of New York City.

Franklin Butler and Josephine Gillet Lord, Sr.'s son George married Hazel Symington and resided in Woodmere and, later, at *Overfields* in Syosset. Their son Franklin Butler Lord II married Lillian Lee Fordyce Barker, the daughter of Fordyce Barker of Manhattan, and resided at *Meadowedge Farms* in Cedarhurst and *Cottsleigh* in Syosset. [*See* Spinzia, *Long Island's Prominent North Shore Families, vol. 1* – Lord entries.]

**Lord, George de Forest, Sr. (1892-1950)**

| | |
|---|---|
| Occupation(s): | attorney - partner, Lord, Day, and Lord, NYC |
| | financier - director, National Surety Corp.; |
| | director, National Surety Marine Insurance Co.; |
| | trustee, United States Trust Co.; |
| | director, Seaman's Bank for Savings |
| Civic Activism: | trustee, New York Public Library, NYC; |
| | president, Children's Aid Society; |
| | trustee, United Charities |
| Marriage(s): | 1914-1950 – Hazel Symington (1893-1965) |
| Address: | Ocean Avenue, Woodmere |
| Name of estate: | |
| Year of construction: | c. 1922 |
| Style of architecture: | Georgian Revival |
| Architect(s): | Beer and Farley designed the house (for G. de F. Lord, Sr.) |
| Landscape architect(s): | Charles W. Leavitt (for G. de F. Lord, Sr.) |
| Builder: | E. W. Howell |
| House extant: yes | |
| Historical notes: | |

The house was built by George de Forest Lord, Sr. By 1927 he had relocated to *Overfields* in Syosset. [*See* Spinzia, *Long Island's Prominent North Shore Families, vol. 1* – Lord entry.]

He was the son of Franklin Butler and Josephine Gillet Lord, Sr. of Lawrence.

Hazel Symington Lord was the daughter of Albert Symington of Manhattan.

George de Forest and Hazel Symington Lord, Sr.'s daughter Edith married Charles Garrison Meyer, Jr. and resided in Locust Valley. Their son George de Forest Lord, Jr. married Ruth du Pont and resided on Fishers Island and in New Haven, CT. Their son Edward Crary Lord II married Elizabeth H. McVitty.

*rear facade, 1922*

**Lovering, Joseph Swain, II (1882-1953)**

| | |
|---|---|
| Occupation(s): | electrical engineer |
| | financier - vice-president, Hanover Bank, NYC |
| Marriage(s): | M/1 – 1901-div.1905 – Elsie Richmond |
| | - entertainers and related professions - actress |
| | M/2 – 1907-1935 – Elizabeth Bacon (1883-1935) |
| Address: | 140 Everit Avenue, Hewlett Bay Park |
| Name of estate: | *Sunny Ridge* |
| Year of construction: | |
| Style of architecture: | |
| Architect(s): | |
| Landscape architect(s): | |
| House extant: no | |
| Historical notes: | |

Joseph Swain Lovering II was the son of Charles Taylor and Marian Shaw Sears Lovering of Boston, MA.

Elsie Richmond Lovering was the daughter of The Reverend W. C. Richmond of Boston, MA. She later married William S. Stinson and, subsequently, Alfred Evans.

The *Long Island Society Register, 1929* lists Joseph S. and Elsie Bacon Lovering [II] as residing at *Sunny Ridge* in Hewlett [Hewlett Bay Park]. The *Social Register New York, 1933* lists their address as Everit Avenue. The Bureau of Naval Personnel lists their address as 140 Everit Avenue, Hewlett.

She was the daughter of William Benjamin and Elizabeth Gardner Stone Bacon, Jr. and the niece of Secretary of State Robert Bacon, who resided at *Old Acres* in Old Westbury. [*See* Spinzia, *Long Island's Prominent North Shore Families, vol. 1* – Bacon entry.] Elizabeth's sister Marion married John Cameron Greenleaf, Sr. and resided in Hewlett.

Joseph Swain and Elizabeth Bacon Lovering, II's son William was killed at the battle of Midway in World War II. Their son Robert died in 1910 at the age of two. Their son Charles Taylor Lovering III married Anna Margaret Murray, the daughter of Herman Stump and Susanne Elizabeth Warren Murray of *Our House* in Woodmere. Their son Joseph Sears Lovering, Sr., who married Carol Stevenson, and, subsequently, Anne Valentine, resided in Islip. [*See* Spinzia, *Long Island's Prominent South Shore Families* – Lovering entry.]

*Richard Lowden residence, Carman – Lowden Homestead,*
*1887 painting by R. Bond*

### Low, Ethelbert Ide (1880-1946)

| | |
|---|---|
| Occupation(s): | attorney - partner, Low, Miller, and Low, NYC; partner, Hoes, Low, and Miller, NYC |
| | financier - president and chairman of board, Home Life Insurance Co.; director, Niagara Fire Insurance Co.; director, Continental Insurance Co.; director, Corn Exchange Bank Trust Co.; director, Fidelity and Casualty Co. of New York |
| Civic Activism: | trustee, Village of Woodsburgh, 1937-1941 |
| Marriage(s): | 1904-1946 – Gertrude Herrick (1882-1972) |
| | - Civic Activism: president, National Society of Colonial Dames of New York; trustee and vice-president, New York Genealogical and Biographical Society |
| Address: | Woodmere Boulevard, Woodsburgh |
| Name of estate: | |
| Year of construction: | |
| Style of architecture: | |
| Architect(s): | |
| Landscape architect(s): | |
| House extant: unconfirmed | |
| Historical notes: | |

Ethelbert Ide Low was the son of Ethelbert Mills and Mary Louise Ide Low of Brooklyn.

Gertrude Herrick Low was the daughter of Harold and Annie Trotter Lawrence Herrick of *The Meadows* in Lawrence.

Ethelbert Ide and Gertrude Herrick Low's son Ethelbert Herrick Low married Mary Holland, the daughter of Nelson Clarke Holland of *Holland Farm* in Belchertown, MA. Their son Francis married Faith Atherton Locke, the daughter of Campbell and Ruth Cary Slattery Locke Sr. of Lawrence, and, later, Susanne W. Murray, the daughter of Herman Stump and Susanne E. Warren Murray of *Our House* in Woodmere. Their daughter Gertrude married George Philip Lynch, Sr., the son of Edmund Ambrose and Madelaine Chauncey Lynch, Sr. of Lawrence, and resided in Lawrence and Bridgehampton. [*See* Spinzia, *Long Island's Prominent Families in the Town of Southampton* – Lynch entry.]

In 1977 the house was remodeled.

### Lowden, Richard (1841-1913)

| | |
|---|---|
| Occupation(s): | politician - unsuccessful candidate for Hempstead Superintendent of Highways |
| Civic Activism: | trustee, Hempstead School Board |
| Marriage(s): | 1867-1913 – Mary Ann Carman (1844-1921) |
| Address: | Hempstead Turnpike, East Meadow |
| Name of estate: | *Carman – Lowden Homestead* |
| Year of construction: | Long Island Farmhouse |
| Style of architecture: | |
| Architect(s): | |
| Landscape architect(s): | |
| House extant: no | |
| Historical notes: | |

Mary Ann Carman Lowden was the daughter of Sylvanus and Lydia M. Weeks Carman.

Richard and Mary Ann Carman Lowden's daughter Etta married John Whitman and resided in Bay Shore. Their son Walter married Blanche A. Greenfield, the daughter of Newman and Nina J. Hubbard Greenfield and, later, Eleanor Isabelle Kelly. Their daughter Lydia married George Van Nostrand and resided in Bay Shore.

*front facade*

### Ludlow, Alden Rodney, Jr. (1911-1998)

| | |
|---|---|
| Occupation(s): | industrialist - member, United States Alcohol Co., NYC; director and vice president, U. S. Industrial Chemicals Co. |
| Marriage(s): | 1935-1994 – Mabel Shives Whitman (1912-1994) |
| Address: | 100 Ocean Avenue, Lawrence |
| Name of estate: | |
| Year of construction: | 1940 |
| Style of architecture: | Ranch |
| Architect(s): | |
| Landscape architect(s): | |
| House extant: yes | |
| Historical notes: | |

The *Social Register New York, 1954* lists Alden R. and Mabel S. Whitman Ludlow [Jr.] as residing on Hewlett Neck Road, Woodmere [Hewlett Neck]. In 1946, the Ludlows purchased Henry Rogers Cartwright, Jr.'s residence *Applecot* in Hewlett. [*The Brooklyn Daily Eagle* June 2, 1946, p. 29, and *Nassau Daily Review–Star* June 6, 1946, p. 8.] At the time of his death Ludlow was residing at 100 Ocean Avenue, Lawrence.

He was the son of Alden Rodney and Alicia Gamble Ludlow, Sr., who resided in Mill Neck. [*See* Spinzia, *Long Island's Prominent Families North Shore Families, vol. 1* – Ludlow entry.]

Mabel Shives Whitman Ludlow was the daughter of Eben Esmond and Jane Whitthorne Harvey Whitman, Sr. of Lawrence. Mabel's sister Alicia married Lawrence Dunbar Cavanagh and resided in East Norwich, CT.

Alden Rodney and Mabel Shives Whitman Ludlow, Jr.'s son Eben married Hope Tompkins, the daughter of John Harrison and Hope Coffey Tompkins. Their son Alden Rodney Ludlow III married Karin Hepp.

*side facade, 2005*

### Ludlum, Dr. Charles Henry (1843-1930)

| | |
|---|---|
| Occupation(s): | physician |
| Civic Activism: | president, Hempstead Board of Education; regent, Royal Arcanum |
| Marriage(s): | 1868-1921 – Mary Jane White (1844-1921) |
| Address: | 34 Columbia Avenue, Hempstead |
| Name of estate: | |
| Year of construction: | |
| Style of architecture: | |
| Architect(s): | |
| Landscape architect(s): | |
| House extant: no | |
| Historical notes: | |

The *Long Island Society Register, 1929* lists Dr. Charles H. Ludlum as residing at 34 Columbia Avenue, Hempstead. He was the son of Daniel and Judith Smith Ludlum of Jamaica, NY.

Mary Jane White Ludlum was the daughter of Samuel White of Brooklyn.

At the time of Mary's death, she was residing at 145 Main Street, Hempstead.

Dr. Charles Henry and Mrs. Mary Jane White Ludlum's daughter Marion married Isaac Henry Kirby and resided in Hempstead. Their son Clinton married Sarah Perry Schell, the daughter of James P. and Margaret Melissa Plumer Schell and resided in Connecticut. Their son Walter married Addie Ireene Daniel, the daughter of William Munsell and Adalissa Harner Phillips Daniel, and resided in Manhattan. Their daughter Edith died in 1880 at the age of one.

### Lynch, Edmund Ambrose, Sr. (1870-1928)

Occupation(s): financier - member, New York Stock Exchange

Marriage(s): 1909-1928 – Madelaine Chauncey (1878-1971)

Address: Rutherford Lane, Lawrence
Name of estate:
Year of construction:
Style of architecture:
Architect(s):
Landscape architect(s):
House extant: unconfirmed
Historical notes:

The *Long Island Society Register, 1929* lists Edmund A. and Madelaine Chauncey Lynch [Sr.] as residing on Rutherford Lane, Cedarhurst [Lawrence].

He was the son of Philip and Mary Louise Lambert Lynch of Dublin, Ireland.

Madelaine Chauncey Lynch was the daughter of Daniel and Caroline Raymond Chauncey. Madelaine subsequently married Lawrence Bogert Elliman, Sr. of *Cluny Lodge* in Lawrence and *White Cottage* in Bridgehampton. [*See* Spinzia, *Long Island's Prominent Families in the Town of Southampton* – Elliman entry.]

Edmund Ambrose and Madelaine Chauncey Lynch, Sr.'s son George, who resided in Lawrence and Bridgehampton, married Gertrude Low, and, later, Sylvia Maitland. Their son Edmund Ambrose Lynch, Jr. married Florence Dodd Sullivan, the daughter of Leonard Sullivan of Cedarhurst.

*[See following entry for additional family information.]*

### Lynch, George Philip, Sr. (1913-1998)

Occupation(s): financier - partner, F. P. Ristine and Co. (stock brokerage firm); partner, Chauncey and Co. (stock brokerage firm)

Marriage(s): M/1 – 1936-1977 – Gertrude Herrick Low (1914-1977)
- Civic Activism: officer, Five Towns Women's Exchange
M/2 – Sylvia Maitland (1927-2007)

Address: 175 Briarwood Crossing, Lawrence
Name of estate:
Year of construction: 1908
Style of architecture: Modified French Chateau
Architect(s):
Landscape architect(s):
House extant: yes
Historical notes:

*front facade, 2005*

The *Social Register, 1977* lists G. Philip and Gertrude Low Lynch [Sr.] as residing at 175 Briarwood Crossing, Cedarhurst [Lawrence].

He was the son of Edmund Ambrose and Madelaine Chauncey Lynch, Sr., who resided in Lawrence.

Gertrude Low Lynch was the daughter of Ethelbert Ide and Gertrude Herrick Low of Woodsburgh.

George Philip and Gertrude Low Lynch, Sr.'s daughter Madelaine married Peter Arnold Karthaus Reese, the son of Charles Lee Reese, Jr. of Wilmington, DE, and resided in Chicago, IL. Their son Raymond married Maura Gaffney, the daughter of Maurice Gaffney of Cedarhurst. Their son George Philip Lynch, Jr. married Nina Braxton Carter, the daughter of Paul S. Carter of Bridgehampton, and resided in West Hartford, CT.

Sylvia Maitland Lynch was the daughter of James William and Sylvia Wigglesworth Maitland of Hewlett Bay Park. She had previously been married to Martin McGregor Horner, and resided with him in Lawrence.

*[See previous entry for additional family information.]*

In 2000 the house was remodeled.

[For information about the Lynches' Bridgehampton residence, *see* Spinzia, *Long Island's Prominent Families in the Town of Southampton* – Lynch entry.]

## Lyon, Edmund Burton (1862-1937)

| | |
|---|---|
| Occupation(s): | |
| Civic Activism: | member, executive committee, St. George's Society of New York |
| Marriage(s): | 1896-1913 – Emily Carlotta Vyse (1864-1913) |
| Address: | Fulton Avenue, Hempstead |
| Name of estate: | *Nearacre* |
| Year of construction: | c. 1907 |
| Style of architecture: | Colonial Revival |
| Architect(s): | Dwight James Baum designed the house (for Lyon) |
| Landscape architect(s): | |
| House extant: | no |
| Historical notes: | |

*front facade, 1922*

The house, originally named *Nearacre*, was built by Edmund Burton Lyon.

The *Social Register 1915* and *1921* list E. Burton Lyon as residing at *Nearacre* on Fulton Street in Hempstead.

He was the son of Thomas and Frances Alford Lyon.

Emily Carlotta Vyse Lyon was the daughter of Thomas A. Vyse of Staten Island. Vyse Avenue in The Bronx was named for her family.

Edward Burton and Emily Carlotta Vyse Lyon's son Cecil married Elizabeth Sturgis Grew, the daughter of Ambassador Joseph Clark Grew, and resided at *Harrow Hill* in Muttontown. [*See* Spinzia, *Long Island's Prominent Families North Shore Families, vol. I* – Lyon entry.] Their son William married Gwendolyn Constance McWhinney, the daughter of W. J. McWhinney of Toronto, Canada.


## Mabon, Samuel Clifton (1871-1957)

| | |
|---|---|
| Occupation(s): | financier - partner, Mabon & Co., NYC (later, Mabon, Nugent, and Co.; now, Mabon Securities) |
| Marriage(s): | 1917-1944 – Margaret Burnham Lunt (1890-1944) |
| Address: | 46 Second Street, Garden City |
| Name of estate: | |
| Year of construction: | 1930 |
| Style of architecture: | Georgian Revival |
| Architect(s): | |
| Landscape architect(s): | |
| House extant: | yes |
| Historical notes: | |

The house was built by Samuel Clifton Mabon.

The *Long Island Society Register, 1929* lists S. Clifton Mabon as residing on New Market Road, Garden City. By 1932 he had relocated to 46 Second Street, Garden City.

He was the son of Dr. William Van Vranken and Mrs. Emeline Sarah Deas Mabon.

Margaret Burnham Lunt Mabon was the daughter of Wilbur Fisk and Florence E. Hodgdon Lunt.

Samuel Clifton and Margaret Burnham Lunt Mabon's daughter Barbara married Malcolm MacKay Roberts. Their daughter Margaret married David Hurst Knott, Jr., the son of David Hurst and Agnes Gibson Geekie Knott, Sr. of Glen Cove. [*See* Spinzia, *Long Island's Prominent Families North Shore Families, vol. I* – Knott entry.] After her husband's death in World War II, Margaret married Everett Stevens Wise, the son of Paul T. Wise of Manhattan, and resided in Brookville. She subsequently married William E. Stockhausen, the son of Thomas C. Stockhausen of NYC. Their daughter Hope remained unmarried.

*Samuel Clifton Mabon residence,
front facade, 2001*

### MacDowell, Noah, Jr. (1884-1972)

Occupation(s): financier - director, William McGee & Co. Inc. (insurance underwriters);
member, bond department, Hallgarten & Co.;
partner, Noah MacDowell and Co. (investment banking firm)*
capitalist - director, W. F. Hall Printing Co.
merchant - director, McCrory Stores Corp.

Marriage(s): 1914-1971 – Christine Sawyer Taylor (1885-1971)

Address: 460 Fulton Avenue, Hempstead
Name of estate:
Year of construction:
Style of architecture:
Architect(s):
Landscape architect(s):
House extant: no
Historical notes:

    The *Long Island Society Register, 1929* lists Noah and Christine Taylor MacDowell, Jr. as residing at 460 Fulton Avenue, Hempstead.
    She was the daughter of George Miller Taylor of New Rochelle, NY.
    Noah and Christine Sawyer Taylor MacDowell, Jr.'s daughter Annetta married William Stuart Harrington of Manhattan.
    *MacDowell's partners were Charles Sabin, Jr. and Allan A. Ryan, Jr., the grandson of Thomas Fortune Ryan. [*See* Spinzia, *Long Island's Prominent Families in the Town of Southampton* – Sabin entry.]

## Macy, Carleton (1872-1949)

| | |
|---|---|
| Occupation(s): | capitalist - president and treasurer, Queens Borough Gas & Electric, NYC; president, Hewlett Bay Co. (later, Deed Realty Co.) (real estate developer of Hewlett Bay Park); vice-president, Deed Realty Co.; vice-president, General Electric Co.; vice-president and director, Hudson Co.; director, Lefferts Co. |
| | financier - director, National Bank of Far Rockaway; director, Hewlett–Woodmere National Bank; director, Anchor Capital & Closure Corp.; director, Anchor Capital Co. |
| | industrialist - director, Beaver Mills; director, Millwood Corp.; director, Martel Mills; director, Anchor Hocking Glass Corp. |
| Civic Activism: | trustee, Village of Hewlett Bay Park |
| Marriage(s): | M/1 – 1900-1936 – Helen Lefferts (1873-1936) |
| | M/2 – 1937-1949 – Winifred Earl Lefferts (1903-1995) |
| | - artist - illustrated books and designed dust jackets for books |
| | Civic Activism: founded Arms Acres, Carmel, NY (alcoholic treatment facility); donated 100 acres in Massachusetts to New England Forestry Foundation, 1972; donated a house in Blandford, MA, for the Town Hall; endowed a professorship in arts and humanities to Amherst College, Amherst, MA; donated seventy-two pieces of furniture to The Five College Museums Historic Deerfield Collection |
| Address: | 1261 Veeder Drive, Hewlett Bay Park |
| Name of estate: | *Meadowwood* |
| Year of construction: | c. 1908 |
| Style of architecture: | Modified Mediterranean |
| Architect(s): | Albro & Lindeberg designed the house (for Carlton Macy) |
| Landscape architect(s): | |
| House extant: | yes |
| Historical notes: | |

The house, originally named *Meadowwood*, was built by Carleton Macy.

He was the son of Josiah Henry and Jane Carpenter Macy of White Plains, NY. His sister Carroll resided at *Birch Corners* in Hewlett Bay Park *[See following entry.]*

Helen Lefferts Macy was the daughter of Oscar and Louise A. Hubbard Lefferts of Brooklyn.

The Macys did not have children.

*Meadowwood* was purchased from Macy for $70,000 in 1918 by Paul Lansing Veeder, who continued to call the estate *Meadowwood*.

The *Long Island Society Register, 1929* lists Carleton and Helen Lefferts Macy as residing at *Wonderwhy* in Hewlett [Hewlett Bay Park].

Winifred Earl Lefferts Macy was the daughter of Oscar and Winifred Wood Lefferts of Brooklyn. After Carlton's death, Winifred married Robert A. Arms, who was subsequently killed by a drunken driver.

*Meadowwood, rear facade*

### Macy, Miss Carroll (b. 1870)

| | |
|---|---|
| Marriage(s): | unmarried |
| Address: | Cedar Avenue and Meadowview Avenue, Hewlett Bay Park |
| Name of estate: | *Birch Corners* |
| Year of construction: | c. 1908 |
| Style of architecture: | Modified Cotswold |
| Architect(s): | Albro and Lindeberg designed the house (for Carroll Macy) |

Landscape architect(s):
House extant: no
Historical notes:

*Birch Corners*

The house, originally named *Birch Corners*, was built by Carroll Macy.

The *Social Register New York, 1933* lists Carroll Macy and Myra Moffat as residing at 81 Hamilton Avenue, New Rochelle, NY.

Carroll was the daughter of Josiah Henry and Jane Carpenter Macy of White Plains, NY. Her brother Carleton resided at *Meadowwood* and *Wonderwhy* in Hewlett Bay Park. *[See previous entry.]*

The house was later owned by Ira Andruss Kip, Jr., Danforth Miller, Jr., and Laurence Anthony Slesinger, who purchased the house from Miller in 1942 for $40,000. [*Nassau Daily Review–Star* July 27, 1942, p. 14, and *The New York Times* July 22, 1942, p. 33.] In 1949 Slesinger placed the house on the market and relocated to Sands Point. [*Newsday* May 6, 1949, p. 45.]

### Macy, George Henry (1858-1918)

| | | |
|---|---|---|
| Occupation(s): | capitalist - | president, Carter, Macy, & Co. (tea importer); |
| | | president, George H. Macy & Co. (tea importer); |
| | | director, St. Louis, Southwestern Railway; |
| | | director, Union Pacific Tea Co.; |
| | | director, Pacific Mail |
| | financier - | vice-president, Seaman's Bank for Savings, NYC (which became The Williamsburgh Savings Bank); |
| | | director, Atlantic Mutual Insurance Co.; |
| | | director, Commonwealth Co. |
| | industrialist - | director, Sterling Salt Co. |
| Marriage(s): | 1880-1918 – Kathleen Louise Carter (1860-1921) | |
| Address: | *[unable to determine street address]*, Lawrence | |
| Name of estate: | *The Bungalow* | |
| Year of construction: | c. 1910 | |
| Style of architecture: | Modified Shingle | |

Architect(s):
Landscape architect(s):
House extant: no; demolished c. 1950
Historical notes:

*The Bungalow*

George Henry Macy was the son of Silvanus Jenkins and Caroline Ridgeway Macy, Sr. of Manhattan. George's sister Margaret married Charles W. Pestalozzi, the son of W. Pestalozzi of Zurich, Switzerland.

Kathleen Louise Carter Macy was the daughter of Oliver Stanley and Elizabeth Hyde Carter.

George Henry and Kathleen Louise Carter Macy's son Oliver married Martha J. Law, the daughter of Walter W. Law of Scarborough, NY. Their son William Kingsland Macy, Sr. married Julia A. Henrietta Dick, the daughter of John Henry and Julia Theodora Mollenhauer Dick of *Allen Winden Farm* in Islip, and resided in Islip. Their daughter Kathleen married James Anthony Finn and resided in Islip. Their daughter Helen married Irving Hall and resided in Scituate, MA. Their son Thomas married Louise Pugh.

George Henry Macy also had a residence in Bay Shore. [*See* Spinzia, *Long Island's Prominent South Shore Families* – Dick and Macy entries.]

## Macy, Valentine Everit, Sr. (1871-1930)

| | |
|---|---|
| Occupation(s): | financier - director, Mechanics and Metal National Bank of Long Island; director, Union Trust Co.; director, Provident Loan Society; trustee, Title Guarantee and Title Co.; capitalist - director, Commercial Co.; director, Queensboro Gas & Electric Co.; director, Hewlett Bay Co. (later, Deed Realty Co.) (developer of Hewlett Bay Park) |
| Civic Activism: | treasurer, National Child Labor Committee; trustee, Teachers' College, Columbia University, NYC; trustee, Universal Settlement Society; trustee, Syrian Protestant College; trustee, People's Institute; member, executive committee, National Civic Federation; vice-president, New York State Child Labor Committee; president, National Civic Foundation suffragist* - member, men's advisory board, New York State Woman Suffrage Party, 1917; Commissioner of Public Welfare, Westchester County, NY; commissioner, Department of Charities and Corrections, Westchester County, NY; Commissioner of Parks, Westchester County, NY |
| Marriage(s): | 1896-1925 – Edith Wiesman Carpenter (1871-1925) - Civic Activism: suffragist* - delegate, National American Woman Suffrage Association Convention, 1917; chair, National Board of directors, Girl Scouts of America, 1919-1925; a founder, Cosmopolitan Club; a founder, Westchester County, Girl Scout Council; a founder and vice-president, Westchester County Children's Association; director, League of Women Voters, Westchester County, NY; member, board of managers, Bedford Reformatory; member, social services committee, Grasslands Hospital |
| Address: | *[unable to determine street address]*, Hewlett |
| Name of estate: | |
| Year of construction: | c. 1910 |
| Style of architecture: | Neo-Tudor |
| Architect(s): | Albro and Lindeberg designed the house (for V. E. Macy, Sr.) |
| Landscape architect(s): | |
| House extant: | no |
| Historical notes: | |

The house was built by Valentine Everit Macy, Sr.
He was the son of Josiah and Caroline Louise Everit Macy, Jr.
Edith Wiesman Carpenter Macy was the daughter of Miles B. Carpenter of Manhattan.
Valentine Everit and Edith Wiesman Carpenter Macy, Sr.'s daughter Editha married Burnham Lewis. Their son Josiah married Mary C. Emerson and resided in Morristown, NJ. Their son Valentine Everit Macy, Jr., who resided at *Wayside* in Southampton, married Lydia P. Bodrero, Alice Emily Yates, and, subsequently, Harriet Ayer Seymour. [*See* Spinzia, *Long Island's Prominent Families in the Town of Southampton* – Macy entry.]
*For other Long Islanders involved in the suffrage movement *see* Raymond E. Spinzia, "Winning the Franchise: Long Island Activists in the Fight for Woman's Suffrage and Their Opponents, Long Island's Anti-Suffragists." wwwspinzialongislandestates.com.

*Valentine Everit Macy, Sr. residence,
rear facade, c. 1912*

### Maitland, James William (1890-1968)

| | | |
|---|---|---|
| Occupation(s): | financier - | a founder, Hudson Fund Inc.; |
| | | member, Bonbright and Co. (investment banking firm); |
| | | trustee, New York Savings Bank, NYC |
| | capitalist - | director, Maine Central Railroad; |
| | | director, Portland Terminal Co.; |
| | | director, Hotel Lexington, Inc., NYC; |
| | | director, Central South West Corp., NYC; |
| | | director, Waldorf–Astoria Hotel Corp., NYC |
| Civic Activism: | | member, executive and race committees, Rockaway Steeplechase Association; |
| | | director, Atlantic Beach Club, 1937; |
| | | director, Long Island Symphony Association, 1929; |
| | | governor, Lawrence Association, 1940; |
| | | trustee, Village of Lawrence, 1941-1943; |
| | | director, Five Towns Community Chest, 1944 |
| Marriage(s): | | 1927 – Sylvia Wigglesworth (1897-1957) |
| | | - Civic Activism: treasurer, Five Towns branch, American Red Cross, 1940; chair, Five Towns branch, Citizens Committee of Army and Navy, Inc., 1941 |
| Address: | | Meadowview, Hewlett Bay Park |

Name of estate:
Year of construction:
Style of architecture:
Architect(s):
Landscape architect(s):
House extant: unconfirmed
Historical notes:

In 1920 Maitland purchased the house from Harold Baxter Rees, Sr. [*The New York Times* October 18, 1928, p. 50.]

The *Long Island Society Register, 1929* lists James W. and Sylvia Wigglesworth Maitland as residing on Meadow View [sic] in Hewlett [Hewlett Bay Park]. By 1933 they had relocated to Lawrence.

He was the son of Thomas Andrew and Helen Abby Van Voorhis Maitland of Manhattan.

Sylvia Wigglesworth Maitland was the daughter of Henry and Olive Gertrude Belden Wigglesworth of Garden City. Sylvia had previously been married to Chase Mellen, Jr., the son of Chase and Lucy Cony Manley Mellen, Sr. of Garden City.

James William and Sylvia Wigglesworth Maitland's daughter Helen married Robert Francis Corroon and resided in Manhattan. Their daughter Sylvia married Martin McGregor Horner, the son of Louis Horner of Newark, NJ, and resided in Lawrence. She later married George Philip Lynch, Sr., the son of Edmund Ambrose and Madelaine Chauncey Lynch, Sr. of Lawrence, and resided with George in Lawrence. Their daughter Andree married Howard Brush Dean, Jr., the son of Howard Brush and Maria Fahys Cook Dean, Sr. of Garden City, and resided in East Hampton. [*See* Spinzia, *Long Island's Prominent Families in the Town of East Hampton* – Dean entry.]

The Maitlands' grandson Dr. Howard Brush Dean III was Governor of Vermont from 1991-2003 and was unsuccessful in becoming the Democratic candidate for the presidency in the 2004 election. He then headed the Democratic National Committee through the 2008 election.

### Malcolm, George Ide, Jr., 1896-1958)

Occupation(s):

Marriage(s): 1920 – Dorothy Dudley Koues (b. 1893)

Address: Ward Place, Hewlett
Name of estate:
Year of construction:
Style of architecture:
Architect(s):
Landscape architect(s):
House extant: unconfirmed
Historical notes:

   The *Long Island Society Register, 1929* lists the Malcolms as residing on Ward Place, Hewlett.
   He was the son of George Ide and Beula Augusta Benham Malcolm, Sr. of Hewlett.
   Dorothy Dudley Koues Malcolm was the daughter of George Ellsworth and Mary Parmly Toby Koues.
   George Ide and Dorothy Dudley Koues Malcolm, Jr.'s son William married Elinor Bliss, the daughter of Henry Mather Bliss, of Chestnut Hill, MA, and resided in Concord, MA.
*[See following entry for additional family information.]*


### Malcolm, George Ide, Sr. (1857-1910)

Occupation(s): financier - partner, Malcolm and Coombe, NYC (stock brokerage firm);
          governor, New York Stock Exchange

Marriage(s): 1885-1910 – Beula Augusta Benham (1860-1931)

Address: *[unable to determine street address]*, Hewlett
Name of estate:
Year of construction:
Style of architecture:
Architect(s):
Landscape architect(s):
House extant: unconfirmed
Historical notes:

   Despondent over the death of his twelve-year-old son William, Malcolm committed suicide by jumping off the Fall River Line ship *Priscilla*. [*The New York Times* October 8, 1910, p. 5.]
   George Ide and Beula Augusta Benham Malcolm, Sr.'s son Julian, who resided in Manhattan, married Florence Scott of Rochester, NY, and, subsequently, Zelda M. Turner. Their son James married Georgiana Barber, the daughter of Charles Gibbs Barber of Manhattan; Louise Curtis Betterly, the daughter of Albert W. Betterly of Waterbury, CT; and, later, Sarah T. Waterford. Their son George Ide Malcolm, Jr. married Dorothy Dudley Koues and resided in Hewlett.
*[See previous entry for additional family information.]*

## Mallett, Percy Smith (1856-1936)

| | |
|---|---|
| Occupation(s): | financier - treasurer, Assured Association; secretary and director, Willcox, Peck, and Hughes (insurance firm); partner, Willcox, Peck, Brown, and Crosby (insurance firm); director, Knickerbocker Insurance Co.; trustee, South Brooklyn Savings Institute |
| | industrialist - secretary, The Scotia Gold Mining Co. |
| Civic Activism: | secretary, New York Southern Society; a founder and director, Fire Broker's Association |
| Marriage(s): | 1887-1946 – Emily Elizabeth Parsons (1864-1946) |
| Address: | 108 Ninth Street, Garden City |
| Name of estate: | |
| Year of construction: | 1888 |
| Style of architecture: | Italianate |
| Architect(s): | |
| Landscape architect(s): | |
| House extant: yes | |
| Historical notes: | |

The *Long Island Society Register, 1929* lists Percy S. and Emily E. Parsons Mallett as residing at 108 Ninth Street, Garden City.

He was the son of Lothrop Lewis Smith and Margaret Isabel Mallett.

Emily Elizabeth Parsons Mallett was the daughter of William John and Isabella Webb Parsons.

Percy Smith and Emily Elizabeth Parsons Malletts' daughter Sabra married Dr. Heathcote Mureson Harth Kimball, the son of Frank Allan and Ella Davis Kimball of Garden City. Their daughter Marguerite married Seymour Holbrook and, later, Henry Jarvis Raymond. Their son Guy married Virginia Katharine Evans.

*front facade, 2008*

## Mallouk, George Elias (1912-2006)

| | |
|---|---|
| Occupation(s): | merchant - partner, Chrysler–Plymouth dealership, Cairo, Egypt |
| | capitalist - president, Elias Mallouk Realty Corp. (owned apartment building complexes) |
| Civic Activism: | trustee, Winthrop University, Rock Hill, SC |
| | established the Roma and Jeff A. Marmon, Jr. Memorial Scholarships, Rhodes College, Memphis, TN |
| Marriage(s): | 1946-2006 – Ann Marmon (b. 1923) |
| | - educator - assistant to the president, Hofstra University, Hempstead, NY, 1974-1976; |
| | assistant director of admissions, Adelphi University, Garden City, 1980-1981; |
| | executive director, Family Life Center, 1981, 1988; |
| | supervisor, Interfaith Nutrition Network, Hempstead, 1989; |
| | assistant to the president, Hofstra University, Hempstead, NY, 1991 |
| | Civic Activism: chair of board of trustees, Hofstra University, Hempstead, NY; |
| | director, Planned Parenthood of Nassau County; |
| | member, advisory committee, Community Service Center; |
| | established Ann Mallouk Endowed Scholarship for Women in Science, Hofstra University, Hempstead, NY; |
| | established the Roma and Jeff A. Marmon, Jr. Memorial Scholarships, Rhodes College, Memphis, TN; |
| | recipient, Beatrice McClintock Planned Parenthood award, 1989; |
| | recipient, Estabrook Distinguished Service Award, Hofstra University, Hempstead, NY, 1990; |
| | Ann Mallouk Day proclaimed by Nassau County, March 22, 1987 |
| Address: | 25 Rockaway Road, Garden City |
| Name of estate: | |
| Year of construction: | 1926 |
| Style of architecture: | Neo-Tudor |
| Architect(s): | |
| Landscape architect(s): | |
| House extant: | yes |
| Historical notes: | |

George Elias Mallouk was the son of Elias and Katherine Mallouk of Brooklyn.

Ann Marmon Mallouk is the daughter of Jeff Audrey and Naomi Merrell Marmon of Memphis, TN.

George Elias and Ann Marmon Mallouk's son John, a bachelor, resides in Okeechobee, FL. Their son William, also a bachelor, resided in San Francisco, CA. Their son Jeff married Marie Brown of Virginia and resides in Princeton, NJ. Their son James married Arlene Norberg, the daughter of Edward and Florence Norberg of Bloomfield, NJ, and resides in Breckenridge, CO. Their son Thomas married Gael Galloway, the daughter of Kenneth and Muriel Galloway of El Cerrito, CA, and resides in State College, PA.

In 1968 the house was remodeled.

*front facade, 2005*

### Manice, de Forest (1799-1862)

Occupation(s): capitalist - partner, Manice, Gould, & Co. (importing firm); extensive Manhattan real estate holdings

Marriage(s): Catherine Marie Booth (1800-1878)

Address: Hempstead Turnpike, Elmont
Name of estate: *Oatlands*
Year of construction: c. 1840
Style of architecture: Gothic Revival with Tudor elements
Architect(s):
Landscape architect(s):
Nassau County Museum Collection has photographs of the estate.
House extant: no; demolished in 1956
Historical notes:

*Oatlands after 1926 remodeling*

The house, originally named *Oatlands*, was built by de Forest Manice. He was the son of William and Eunice de Forest Manice.
Catherine Marie Booth Manice was the daughter of William and Mary Ann Lewis Booth.
De Forest and Catherine Marie Booth Manice's daughter Caroline married Dr. Gabriel Grant and resided in Manhattan. Their daughter Frances married The Reverend James Tuttle Smith and resided in Manhattan. Their daughter Marie married Newbold LeRoy Edgar and resided in Southampton. [*See* Spinzia, *Long Island's Prominent Families in the Town of Southampton* – Edgar entry.] Marie subsequently married Count Alexander Mercati of Greece. Their son William married Jane Remsen and resided in Manhattan.
In 1865 de Forest Manice's son William, acting as his father's executor upon his father's death, placed the fifty-six-acre estate up for sale. At the time, the estate consisted of a main residence, a carriage house, stables, a gardener's cottage, and a greenhouse. [*The New York Times* May 19, 1865, p. 7.] The main residence later became the Turf and Field Clubhouse at Belmont Race Track.

### Mann, Samuel Vernon, Jr. (1873-1950)

Occupation(s): financier - partner, Mann, Pell, and Peake (stock brokerage firm)

Marriage(s): 1899-1932 – Helen Colgate (1874-1932)

Address: Harbor Road, Lawrence
Name of estate: *Grove Point*
Year of construction: c. 1905
Style of architecture: Neo-Federal
Architect(s):
Landscape architect(s): Beatrix Jones Farrand (for Mann)
Plantings were supplied by Hicks Nursery, Jericho

House extant: yes
Historical notes:

*Grove Point*

The house, originally named *Grove Point*, was built by Samuel Vernon Mann, Jr.
He was the son of Samuel Vernon and Harriet Cogswell Onderdonk Mann, Sr. of Flushing, Queens.
Helen Colgate Mann was the daughter of Robert and Henrietta Augusta Craig Colgate, Jr., who resided at *Sandacres* in Quogue. [*See* Spinzia, *Long Island's Prominent Families in the Town of Southampton* – Colgate entry.] Helen's brother Craig, who resided in Flushing and *Pen Craig* in Quogue, married Marion Goodall Townsend and, later, Sally Brigham. Her sister Roberta married William Fisher Howard and resided in St. James. Her sister Annette married Altmore Robinson, Sr. and resided at *Head of the River Farm* in Smithtown. Her sister Alice married Arthur Wickes Rossiter, Sr. and resided at *Cedarcroft* in Glen Cove.
The Mann's son Samuel Vernon Mann III married Elizabeth Standish Sizer and resided in Kings Point. Their son Robert married Margaret Stone, the daughter of Charles and Mary Stone, Sr. of Matinecock.
By 1927 the Manns had relocated to Kings Point. [*See* Spinzia, *Long Island's Prominent North Shore Families, vol. 1* – Mann entry – and *vol. II* – Sizer, Rossiter, and Stone entries.]
[For information about Mann's Quogue estate, *see* Spinzia, *Long Island's Prominent Families in the Town of Southampton* – Mann entry.]

**Mariani, John Francis, Sr. (1895-1972)**

Occupation(s): merchant - founder, Banfi Vintners

Marriage(s): 1928-1972 – Eva Barr (1907-1994)

Address: 250 Stewart Avenue, Garden City
Name of estate:
Year of construction: 1932
Style of architecture: Neo-Tudor
Architect(s): Olive Frances Tjaden designed the house (for Hoffman)
Landscape architect(s):
House extant: yes
Historical notes:

The house was built by Horace E. Hoffman. It was later owned by Mariani.

John Francis and Eva Barr Mariani, Sr.'s son Harry married Ann Marie Goetz and resided in Lloyd Harbor.

John's appreciation of fine wines and food was instilled in him by his aunt Teodolina Banfi who was the chef for Pope Pius XI. In 1919, he founded Banfi Vintners on Spring Street in Manhattan's "Little Italy" section. The company managed to survive prohibition by importing Italian spices and specialty items. Today it produces and imports wines from over eighty-five countries.

In 1979, Banfi Vintners purchased the former Sir Samuel Agar Salvage / Margaret Emerson / William Irving Lundy estate in Old Brookville for their corporate headquarters. [*See* Spinzia, *Long Island's Prominent North Shore Families, vol. I* – Emerson and Lundy entries – and *vol. II* – Salvage entry.]

The house was later owned by Jurge Cerriut.

*entrance, 2001*

## Marks, Arthur David, Jr. (1910-1997)

| | |
|---|---|
| Occupation(s): | financier - insurance broker |
| Civic Activism: | member of board, The Jewish Guild for the Blind; chairman of board, Five Towns Community Chest, 1955; trustee, Village of Woodsburgh, 1945-1952 |
| Marriage(s): | M/1 – 1933-div. –Edith C. Jacobi (1913-1988) |
| |    - Civic Activism: chair, Child Development Center, Jewish Board of Family & Children Services; directed social work programs at Metropolitan Hospital, NYC, and Beth Israel Hospital, NYC |
| |    a founder, Grandmothers Program (assistance to patients with babies suffering from HIV-AIDS) |
| | M/2 – Alice Oppenheimer |
| Address: | 69 Willow Road, Woodsburgh |
| Name of estate: | |
| Year of construction: | 1935 |
| Style of architecture: | French County |
| Architect(s): | Olive Frances Tjaden designed the house (for Marks) |
| Landscape architect(s): | |
| House extant: yes | |
| Historical notes: | |

   The house was built by Arthur David Marks, Jr.
   He was the son of Arthur David and Bessie Mae Hollander Marks, Sr.
   Edith C. Jacobi Marks was the daughter of Harold and Freda Moritz Jacobi, Sr. of Woodmere. Edith later married Sol Nichtern with whom she committed a double suicide by taking an overdose of sleeping pills in their Sutton Place South residence in Manhattan. [*The New York Times* June 12, 1988, p. 38.]
   Arthur David and Edith C. Jacobi Marks, Jr's son Arthur David Marks III married Gail Weisbard, the daughter of Marco Weisbard of Manhasset, and, later Terrell Flax, the daughter of Dr. Leo Flax of Denver, CO. Their daughter Alice married Jeffrey Michael Preston, the son of Harry A. Preston of Ridgewood, NJ. Their daughter Edith married Alan Seligson, the son of Maurice Seligson of Lawrence.
   In 2021, the 3,676-square-foot house sold for $1.8 million.

*front facade, 2000*

## Marshall, Charles Alexander (1883-1957)

| | |
|---|---|
| Occupation(s): | attorney - partner, Rearick, Dorr, Travis, and Marshall (later, Hine, Rearick, Dorr, Travis, and Marshall)<br>merchant - director, Atlantic Pacific Corp. |
| Civic Activism: | chairman, mission to Denmark for U. S. Economic Co-Operation Administration, 1948;<br>member, War Claims Board;<br>president, Village of Woodsburgh, 1926-1931 |
| Marriage(s): | 1911-1957 – Lillie H. Cunningham (1886-1973)<br>  - Civic Activism:  president, Lawrence Garden Club, 1938 |
| Address: | 161 Woodmere Boulevard South, Woodsburgh |

Name of estate:
Year of construction:
Style of architecture:
Architect(s):
Landscape architect(s):
House extant: no
Historical notes:

The *Long Island Society Register, 1929* lists Charles A. and Lillie H. Cunningham Marshall as residing at 161 South Woodmere Boulevard, Woodmere [Woodsburgh].

He was the son of Charles and Rebecca Snowden Marshall of Baltimore, MD, and a relative of Chief Justice John Marshall. Charles was the military secretary of General Robert E. Lee and the only Confederate officer with Lee at his meeting with General Ulysses S. Grant at Appomattox Courthouse. Charles drafted Lee's response to the surrender terms.

Lillie H. Cunningham Marshall was the daughter of Theodore Bliss Cunningham.

Charles Alexander and Lillie H. Cunningham Marshall's daughter Elizabeth married Wainwright Hardie Shepard, the son of Frederic White and Agnes O'Connor Shephard of Woodmere, and resided at *Driftway* in New Canaan, CT. Their daughter Ann Snowden Marshall, who remained unmarried, resided in London, England.

*[See following entry for additional family information.]*


## Marshall, James Markham, II (1871-1936)

| | |
|---|---|
| Occupation(s): | attorney - partner, Van Vorst, Marshall, and Smith, NYC;<br>partner, Underwood, Van Vorst, and Hoyt;<br>partner, Marshall and Wehle, NYC |
| Marriage(s): | 1911-1936 – Helen Denison (1879-1975) |
| Address: | Keene Lane, Woodsburgh |

Name of estate:
Year of construction:
Style of architecture:
Architect(s):

Landscape architect(s):
House extant: unconfirmed
Historical notes:

The *Long Island Society Register, 1929* lists James Markham and Helen Denison Marshall as residing on Keen [sic] Lane, Woodmere [Woodsburgh]. The *Social Register New York, 1933* lists their address as 945 Browers Point Road, Woodmere.

He was the son of Charles and Sarah Rebecca Snowden Marshall.

Helen Denison Marshall was the daughter of John Marcus and Sophia Augusta Pearce Denison of Baltimore MD.

*[See previous entry for additional family information.]*

## Marshall, Levin Rothrock, Sr. (1877-1935)

Occupation(s): financier - partner, Jacquelin and DeCoppet (stock brokerage firm)

Marriage(s): Martha Jacob (1876-1963)

Address: Waverly Avenue, Hewlett Harbor
Name of estate: *Hawkswood*
Year of construction:
Style of architecture: Colonial Revival
Architect(s): Albro and Lindeberg designed the house (for Marshall)
Landscape architect(s):
House extant: unconfirmed
Historical notes:

*front facade, 1915*

The house, originally named *Hawkswood*, was built by Levin Rothrock Marshall, Sr.

The *Social Register Summer, 1915* lists Levin R. and Martha Jacob Marshall [Sr.] as residing at *Hawkswood* in Hewlett [Hewlett Harbor].

He was the son of Stephen Duncan and Catharine Marie Calhoun Marshall and a descendent of Chief Justice John Marshall.

Martha Jacob Marshall was the daughter of Leonard Jacob, Sr. Her brother Leonard Jacob, Jr., a bachelor, resided at *Chale* in Bedminster, NJ.

Levin Rothrock and Martha Jacob Marshall, Sr.'s daughter Trina married Nathaniel Read Norton, Jr. and resided in Bedford Hills, NY. Their daughter Emma married William Ebbets Lowe II, the son of Gerald and Cora Towne Underhill Lowe of Bethayres, PA, and resided in East Williston. Emma later relocated to Sag Harbor. Their son Levin Rothrock Marshall, Jr. married Harriet McG. Woodbury and, later, Marie Glass. In 1945 he committed suicide. [*The New York Times* June 10, 1945, p. 30.] Their son Duncan married Mary Osborn.

By 1933 the Marshalls had relocated to *Silver Maples* in Roslyn Harbor. [*The New York Times* July 28, 1933, p. 12.]

[*See* Spinzia, *Long Island's Prominent North Shore Families, vol. I* – Marshall entry – and *Long Island's Prominent Families in the Town of East Hampton* – Lowe entry.]

## Marshall, May Louise Bamber (1865-1943)

Marriage(s): Chauncey Marshall, Sr. (1854-1915)
- capitalist - director and secretary, Brighton Beach Stadium Co., Brooklyn;
director and president, Brighton Beach Development Co., Brooklyn;
director and president, Manhattan Beach Development Co.;
director, E. W. Bliss Co.
industrialist - director and president, Black Rock Machine Co., Bridgeport, CT;
director, Union Bag and Paper Co.
financier - director, Williamsburgh City Fire Insurance Co., Brooklyn

Address: 105 Ocean Avenue, Lawrence
Name of estate: *Cedarcroft*
Year of construction: c. 1892
Style of architecture: Queen Anne
Architect(s):
Landscape architect(s):
House extant: no; demolished c. 1950
Historical notes:

The house was built by E. T. Palmer. It was later owned by Russell Sage who called it, alternately, *Cedarcroft* and *Cedar Croft*. In 1920, Mrs. Marshall purchased the twenty-acre estate which consisted of a main residence, garage, outbuildings, and a three-acre lake. [*The Brooklyn Daily Eagle* April 15, 1920, p. 18.]

*rear facade*

The *Social Register Summer, 1937* lists May L. Bamber Marshall as residing at *Cedarcroft*, 105 Ocean Avenue, Lawrence.

Chauncey Marshall Sr. was the son of William and Jane Montgomery Marshall.

Chauncey and May Louise Bamber Marshall, Sr.'s daughter Edith did not marry. Their son Chauncey Marshall, Jr. married Fay E. Lucas, the daughter of Mrs. Sarah M. Perkey Lucas.

### Martin, Thomas Stephen (1884-1954)

| | |
|---|---|
| Occupation(s): | capitalist - member, Wilmerding & Bisset (importing firm) |
| Marriage(s): | 1919-div. 1938– Edith Victoria Deacon (b. 1899) |
| Address: | 430 Meadow Way, Lawrence |
| Name of estate: | *Mistletoe Way* |
| Year of construction: | |
| Style of architecture: | |
| Architect(s): | |
| Landscape architect(s): | |
| House extant: | no |

Historical notes:

The *Long Island Society Register, 1929* lists Thomas Stephen and Edith V. Deacon Martin as residing at *Mistletoe Way* in Cedarhurst [Lawrence]. The 1930 Census lists the Martins at this address.

He was the son of William Martin of Dundee, Scotland.

Edith Victoria Deacon Martin was the daughter of Richard Deacon of *Kettering Lodge* in St. Louis, MO.

Thomas Stephen and Edith Victoria Deacon Martin's daughter Joan married John Hill Tyner, the son of Richard L. Tyner of Greenwich, CT, and resided in Lawrence.

### Massamino, Michael James (b. 1962)

| | |
|---|---|
| Occupation(s): | astronaut - NASA, 1996-2014; |
| | member STS-109 Columbia crew, 2002 (upgraded Hubble Space Telescope); |
| | member STS-125 Atlantis crew, 2009 (final upgrade of Hubble Space Telescope) |
| | inventor - two patents for human control of space robotics systems |
| | engineer - system engineer, IBM, 1984-1986; |
| | general engineer, NASA Headquarters, summer, 1987; |
| | research fellow, NASA Marshall Space Flight Center, summers 1988 and 1989; |
| | visiting research engineer, German Aerospace Center, summer 1990; |
| | research engineer, McDonnell Douglas Aerospace, Houston, TX |
| | educator - assistant professor, Rice University, 1992-1994; |
| | assistant professor, Georgia Tech, 1995; |
| | professor, mechanical engineering, Columbia University, current |
| | writer - *Spaceman: An Astronaut's Unlikely Journey to Unlock the Secrets of the Universe*, 2016 (autobiography); |
| | entertainer and associated professions - motion pictures and television |
| Civic Activism: | senior advisor of space programs, Intrepid Sea, Air, and Space Museum, NYC; |
| Marriage(s): | Carola P. Pardo |
| Address: | 32 Commonwealth Street, Franklin Square |
| Name of estate: | |
| Year of construction: | 1953 |
| Style of architecture: | Contemporary |
| Architect(s): | |
| Landscape architect(s): | |
| House extant: | yes |

Historical notes:

Michael was raised in this house by his parents C. Mario and Vincenza Gianferra Massimino.

In 2018, Michael was inducted into the Long Island Air and Space Hall of Fame.

In 2011, the 1,428-square-foot house sold for $327,000.

*front facade, 2000*

### Matthews, John (1891-1942)

| | |
|---|---|
| Occupation(s): | financier - stockbroker |
| Marriage(s): | 1916-1942 – Katie Schermerhorn (1895-1942) |
| Address: | *[unable to determine street address]*, Hewlett |
| Name of estate: | |
| Year of construction: | |
| Style of architecture: | |
| Architect(s): | |
| Landscape architect(s): | |
| House extant: unconfirmed | |
| Historical notes: | |

The *Long Island Society Register, 1929* lists John and Katie Schermerhorn Matthews as residing in Hewlett.
He was the son of John H. Matthews of Manhattan.
Katie Schermerhorn Matthews was the daughter of John Egmont Schermerhorn of Lenox, MA.
John and Katie Schermerhorn Matthews' daughter Joan married William L. F. Gildersleeve and resided in Montclair, NJ.
Despondent over financial affairs, Matthews murdered his wife in their Lenox, MA, home by shooting her in the back of her head while she was typing a letter in their bedroom and then committed suicide. [*The New York Times* May 16, 1942, p. 35.]


### McCrea, James Alexander, II (1875-1923)

| | |
|---|---|
| Occupation(s): | capitalist - general manager, Long Island Rail Road, 1911; vice-president, Pennsylvania Railroad, 1920 |
| | financier - vice-president, Bankers Trust Co., NYC |
| Civic Activism: | a founder, Village of Woodsburgh; president, Village of Woodsburgh, 1912,1914; trustee, Village of Woodsburgh, 1914-1918 |
| Marriage(s): | 1897-1923 – Mabel Clarke (1876-1957) |
| Address: | South End Road, Woodsburgh |
| Name of estate: | |
| Year of construction: | 1909 |
| Style of architecture: | Neo-Georgian |
| Architect(s): | Charles A. Platt designed the house (for McCrea) |
| Landscape architect(s): | Plantings were supplied by Hicks Nursery, Jericho |
| House extant: no; demolished c. 1960 | |
| Historical notes: | |

The house was built by James Alexander McCrea II.
The *Long Island Society Register, 1929* lists James A. and Mabel Clarke McCrea [II] as residing on South End Avenue [Road], Woodmere [Woodsburgh].
He was the son of James and Ada Montgomery McCrea of Philadelphia, PA.
Mabel Clarke McCrea was the daughter of Charles J. Clarke of Pittsburgh, PA.
James Alexander and Mabel Clarke McCrea II's son Charles married Josephine A. G. Scott, the daughter of Russell Scott of Manhattan, and resided in Greenwich, CT. Their daughter Agnes married Henry Lewis III and, subsequently, Eaton Greenwood Davis, the son of William Hammat Davis of New York.

*rear facade*

### McKee, Lanier (1872-1943)

| | |
|---|---|
| Occupation(s): | attorney - partner, Hervey, Barber, and McKee |
| | writer - *The Land of Nome*, 1902 |
| Civic Activism: | chairman, draft board |
| Marriage(s): | 1921-1943 – Elizabeth Lloyd Lee (b. 1882) |
| Address: | 46 Causeway, Lawrence |
| Name of estate: | *Recess* |
| Year of construction: | |
| Style of architecture: | |
| Architect(s): | |
| Landscape architect(s): | |
| House extant: no | |
| Historical notes: | |

The *Long Island Society Register, 1929* lists Lanier and Elizabeth L. Lee McKee as residing at *Recess* in Lawrence. Their address is listed in *Newsday* January 27, 1943, p. 24.

He was the son of David Richie and Frances Elizabeth Dunn McKee of Washington, DC.

Elizabeth Lloyd Lee McKee had previously been married to George Garr Henry, Sr., who died in 1917, at the age of thirty-six, from injuries he suffered at a polo game at the Whippany River Club.

### McKinny, Alexander, Jr. (1892-1932)

| | |
|---|---|
| Occupation(s): | engineer - member, Walter Kidde & Co. |
| Marriage(s): | 1920-1932 – Veronica Blackhall (b. 1896) |
| Address: | 104 Locust Street, Garden City |
| Name of estate: | |
| Year of construction: | 1928 |
| Style of architecture: | Neo-Tudor |
| Architect(s): | |
| Landscape architect(s): | |
| House extant: yes | |
| Historical notes: | |

The *Long Island Society Register, 1929* lists Alexander and Veronica Blackhall McKinny, Jr. as residing at 19 Meadow Street, Garden City.

He was the son of Alexander and Marcella Tevlin McKinny of Garden City. At the time of his death McKinny was residing at 104 Locust Street, Garden City. [*The New York Times* December 15, 1932, p. 19.]

Veronica Blackhall McKinny was the daughter of George C. Blackhall of Brooklyn and, later, Woodhaven.

Alexander and Veronica Blackhall McKinny, Jr.'s son John served in World War II as a navy torpedo pilot attached to the aircraft carrier USS *Franklin*. He participated in the Guam, Iwo Jima, Palu, Saipan, Okinawa, Formosa, Philippines, and Leyle Gulf campaigns and was awarded the Navy Cross for his participation in the sinking of a Japanese aircraft carrier. After the war, he participated in the Berlin Airlift. In 1950, he married Helen Louise Williams and resided in Coronado, CA.

*[See following entry for additional family information.]*

*front facade, 2001*

## McKinny, Alexander, Sr. (1861-1920)

| | |
|---|---|
| Occupation(s): | attorney - partner, Jones, McKinny, and Steinbrink, Brooklyn |
| | politician - Acting Collector of Internal Revenue (Cleveland administration) |
| Civic Activism: | chairman, New York City Parole Commission; |
| | trustee, Brooklyn Bar Association |
| Marriage(s): | Marcella Tevlin (1867-1934) |
| Address: | 34 Brompton Road, Garden City |
| Name of estate: | |
| Year of construction: | 1926 |
| Style of architecture: | Colonial Revival |
| Architect(s): | |
| Landscape architect(s): | |
| House extant: yes | |
| Historical notes: | |

The *Long Island Society Register, 1929* lists Mrs. Alexander McKinny as residing on Brompton Road, Garden City.

Alexander and Marcella Tevlin McKinny, Sr.'s daughter Margaret remained unmarried. Their son Alexander McKinny, Jr. married Veronica Blackhall and resided in Garden City. Their son Archibald married Ellen Ann Bouchard, the daughter of Frederick Bouchard of Brooklyn. Their daughter Marcella, who married Henry Amy, Jr. of Brooklyn, later resided with Henry in her parent's former residence. Their daughter Mary married William Harold Barnes, the son of State Senator William D. Barnes.

*[See previous entry for additional family information.]*

In 2005, the 2515 square-foot house sold for $920,000.

*front facade, 2016*

**McVitty, Edward Quinby, Sr. (1875-1954)**

| | |
|---|---|
| Occupation(s): | capitalist - breeder of polo and race horses |
| | industrialist - partner, with his brothers, Leas & McVitty, Inc., Philadelphia (leather tanning and manufacturing firm) |
| Civic Activism: | vice-president, Princeton Club of Nassau County 1936; |
| | assisted in all Liberty Loan and Red Cross drives during World War I; |
| | chairman, local draft board during World War I |
| Marriage(s): | M/1 – eloped 1902-div. 1905 – Elizabeth McFadden (b. 1883) |
| |   - artist model |
| | M/2 – 1913-1954 – Harriet Elizabeth Clausen (1887-1972) |
| |   - Civic Activism: chair, early diagnosis campaign, Nassau County Tuberculosis and Public Health Association, 1940; |
| |     director, Nassau County Tuberculosis and Public Health Association, 1944 |
| Address: | Cathedral Avenue, Garden City |
| Name of estate: | *Garstead* |
| Year of construction: | |
| Style of architecture: | Neo-Tudor |
| Architect(s): | |
| Landscape architect(s): | Hicks Nursery supplied Red Cedar plantings for windbreak (for Baldwin) |

House extant: unconfirmed
Historical notes:

    Edward Quinby McVitty, Sr. was the son of Thomas Edward and Phoebe Quinby McVitty of Philadelphia, PA.
    Elizabeth McFadden McVitty met Edward while she was a student at Bryn Mawr College. Edward's family objected to the marriage because of the social status of Elizabeth's family. They claimed that Edward was under the influence of liquor when he married Elizabeth and encouraged him to divorce her. He deserted Elizabeth two days after their marriage and disappeared, eventually relocating to San Francisco, CA, where Elizabeth found him in 1904. In 1906, Elizabeth was arrested along with Alvie M. King, a racetrack bookie, in connection with the robbery of $50,000 worth of jewels belonging to her friend Mrs. Halsey Corwin. [*Harrisburg Daily Independent* April 5, 1905, p. 4, and *The Leavenworth Times* July 24, 1906, p. 5.]
    In 1924, Edward Quinby McVitty, Sr. purchased William Mood Baldwin's seven-acre estate for a reputed $135,000 and renamed it *Garstead*. [*The Brooklyn Daily Eagle* April 23, 1924, p. 21.]
    Harriet Elizabeth Clausen had previously been married to ____ Baird.
    Edward Quinby and Harriet Elizabeth Clausen McVitty, Sr.'s daughter Elizabeth married Edward Crary Lord II, the son of George de Forest and Hazel Syminton Lord, Sr. of *Overfields* in Syosset, and resided in Syosset. [*See* Spinzia, *Long Island's Prominent North Shore Families, vol. I* – Lord entry.] Their son Howard married Suzanne Harrison Cushman, the daughter of Alvin A. Cushman and, later, Nancy Redmond, the daughter of Geraldyn Livingston and Katharine Elizabeth Register Redmond, Sr. of *Gray Horse Farm* in Upper Brookville. [*See* Spinzia, *Long Island's Prominent North Shore Families, vol. II* – Redmond entry.] Their son Herbert married Micheline Muselli, the daughter of Michel Muselli. Their son Bruce died in 1960 at the age of forty-one. Their son Edward Quinby McVitty, Jr. died in 1993 at the age of seventy-five.

*c. 1908*

### McWilliam, Culver B. (b. 1890)

| | |
|---|---|
| Occupation(s): | financier - partner, McWilliam, Wainwright, and Co. (stock brokerage firm) |
| Marriage(s): | 1916-div. 1937 – Eleanor Arnett Nash (1893-1969)<br>- journalist - articles for various publications<br>entertainer and associated professions - television personality<br>writer - *It Was Mary*, 1947 (novel);<br>*Bachelors Are Made* (novel);<br>*Footnote To Life*, 1944 (novel);<br>*The Woman in His Life* (novel);<br>*Beauty is Not an Age*, 1953 (novel);<br>*Kit Coreli: TV Stylist*, 1955 (novel);<br>*Lucky Miss Spaulding*, 1958 (novel) |
| Address: | Ocean Avenue, Lawrence |
| Name of estate: | |
| Year of construction: | |
| Style of architecture: | |
| Architect(s): | |
| Landscape architect(s): | |
| House extant: | unconfirmed |
| Historical notes: | |

    The *Long Island Society Register, 1929* lists Culver B. and Eleanor A. Nash McWilliam as residing in Cedarhurst [Lawrence]. McWilliam's World War I draft card registration lists this address.
    Eleanor Arnett Nash McWilliam was the daughter of Edmund Strudwick and Mattie Chenault Nash of Rye, NY. Her brother was [Frederic] Ogden Nash, the humorous poet, playwright, screenplay writer, radio personality, and lecturer, who married Frances Leonard and resided in Baltimore, MD. Ogden Nash wrote his first poem while employed as an editor by Garden City-headquartered Doubleday and Co., Inc. They were the descendants of the Nash family for whom Nashville, TN, is named.
    Culver B. and Eleanor Arnett Nash McWilliam's daughter Gwendolen married John Robert Barstow of Los Angeles, CA. Their daughter Eleanor married Walter McNeil Woodward, the son of John Taylor Woodward of Baltimore, MD. Their son Alexander married Dea Ann Wiley, the daughter of Walter W. Wiley of Goldens Bridge, NY.


### Meany, Shannon Lord, Sr. (1892-1951)

| | |
|---|---|
| Occupation(s): | artist |
| Marriage(s): | 1921-div. 1940 – Margaret Resler Warren (1898-1971)<br>- merchant - owner, Band Box, Cedarhurst (clothing store) |
| Address: | 968 East Broadway, Hewlett Bay Park |
| Name of estate: | |
| Year of construction: | |
| Style of architecture: | |
| Architect(s): | |
| Landscape architect(s): | |
| House extant: | no |
| Historical notes: | |

    The *Long Island Society Register, 1929* lists Shannon Lord and Margaret R. Warren Meany as residing at 968 East Broadway, Woodmere [Hewlett Bay Park].
    He was the son of Edward P. and Rosalie Behr Meany of *Alnwick Hall* in Convent Station, NJ.
    Margaret Resler Warren Meany was the daughter of Charles Elliot and Anna Margaret Geissenhainer Warren, Sr. of *Still Pond* in Hewlett Neck. Margaret subsequently married Daniel Aylesbury Finlayson, Jr. and resided in Hewlett Bay Park.
    Shannon Lord and Margaret Resler Warren Meany, Sr.'s son Shannon Lord Meany, Jr., who married Janice Marie Kelty, the daughter of John B. Kelly of Hewlett, was a marine combat correspondent who was killed in the Korean War.

### Meeker, Samuel Mundy, Jr. (1857-1939)

| | |
|---|---|
| Occupation(s): | attorney -   partner, Samuel Mundy and David Edward Meeker, Brooklyn |
| | financier -   vice-president and treasurer, Williamsburgh Savings Bank |
| Civic Activism: | vice-president, treasurer, and trustee, House of St. Giles the Cripple, Brooklyn; |
| | trustee, Church Mission of Help |
| | president, Brooklyn Kindergarten Society |
| Marriage(s): | M/1 – 1885-1889 – Ella Stoothoff (1856-1889) |
| | M/2 – 1891-1931 – Anna Wright (1863-1931) |
| Address: | 115 Hilton Avenue, Garden City |
| Name of estate: | |
| Year of construction: | 1926 |
| Style of architecture: | Colonial Revival |
| Architect(s): | |
| Landscape architect(s): | |
| House extant: yes | |
| Historical notes: | |

The house was built by Samuel Mundy Meeker, Jr.

He was the son of Samuel Mundy and Jane Elizabeth Wright Meeker, Sr. of Brooklyn.

Ella Stoothoff Meeker was the daughter of Ditmas and Phebe Jane Hulst Stoothoff.

The *Long Island Society Register, 1929* lists Samuel M. and Anna Wright Meeker [Jr.] as residing at 115 Hilton Avenue, Garden City.

Samuel Mundy and Anna Wright Meeker, Jr.'s son Amherst was killed in World War I.

*front facade, 2008*

### Meissner, William Christen (1879-1935)

| | |
|---|---|
| Occupation(s): | financier -   insurance broker |
| Marriage(s): | 1906-1935 – Louise Dall Aldrich (1880-1980) |
| Address: | 131 Salisbury Avenue, Garden City |
| Name of estate: | |
| Year of construction: | |
| Style of architecture: | |
| Architect(s): | |
| Landscape architect(s): | |
| House extant: no | |
| Historical notes: | |

The *Long Island Society Register, 1929* lists William C. and Louise Dall Aldrich Meissner as residing at 131 Salisbury Road, Garden City. The 1940 Census lists Mrs. Meissner's residence as 56 Whitehall Boulevard, Garden City.

He was the son of Karl Meissner of Hanover, Germany.

Louise Dall Aldrich Meissner was the daughter of Spencer and Harriette Holley Dall Aldrich, who resided at *Windemere* in Bay Shore. [*See* Spinzia, *Long Island's Prominent South Shore Families* – Aldrich entry.] Louise's brother Spencer Wyman Aldrich, who resided in East Hampton, married Imogene Gaither and, later, Lillian B. Turk. [*See* Spinzia, *Long Island's Prominent Families in the Town of East Hampton* – Aldrich entry.] Her sister Mary married Charles Malcolm Fraser. Her sister Helen married Talcott Hunt Clark. Her sister Maude married Stanley Matthews.

William Christen and Louise Dall Aldrich Meissner's daughter Helena married The Reverend George A. Palmer and resided in Springfield, MA. Their son William Aldrich Meissner married Ruth Courter, the daughter of Harry W. Courter of Manhattan.

## Mellen, Chase, Sr. (1863-1939)

| | |
|---|---|
| Occupation(s): | attorney - partner, Strong and Mellon; |
| | counsel, Metropolitan Street Railroad |
| | capitalist - director, Harvard Co.; |
| | director, James H. Dunham & Co. |
| Civic Activism: | trustee, Garden City Public School District; |
| | president, Twin County Association, 1924; |
| | a founder, vice-president, and director, Cherry Valley Club, Garden City, 1916 |
| Marriage(s): | 1893-1939 – Lucy Cony Manley (1869-1950) |
| Address: | *[unable to determine street address]*, Garden City |
| Name of estate: | |
| Year of construction: | |
| Style of architecture: | |
| Architect(s): | |
| Landscape architect(s): | |
| House extant: unconfirmed | |
| Historical notes: | |

The *Social Register New York, 1907* and the *Social Register Summer, 1921* list Chase and Lucy C. Manley Mellen [Sr.] as residing in Garden City.

He was the son of William Proctor and Ellen Seymour Clark Mellen of Cincinnati, OH.

Lucy Cony Manley Mellen was the daughter of Joseph Homan and Susan Hannah Cony Manley.

Chase and Lucy Cony Manley Mellen, Sr.'s son Joseph married Clara Standish Hawkins, the daughter of William Ashton Hawkins of La Luz, NM. Their son William married Bridget F. Hurt. Their daughter Susan married Stephen C. Millett, Jr. Their son Chase Mellen Jr. married Sylvia Wigglesworth, the daughter of Henry and Olive Gertrude Belden Wigglesworth of Garden City, and, subsequently, Sarah Brisbane, the daughter of Arthur and Phoebe Cary Brisbane of East Meadow and Montauk. [*See* Spinzia, *Long Island's Prominent Families in the Town of East Hampton* – Brisbane entry.] Sylvia subsequently married James William Maitland with whom she resided in Hewlett Bay Park. Sarah had previously been married to John "Tex" McCrary, Jr. with whom she resided in Manhasset. [*See* Spinzia, *Long Island's Prominent North Shore Families, vol. I* – McCrary entry.]

## Meneely, Charles Dickinson (1860-1922)

| | |
|---|---|
| Occupation(s): | capitalist - vice-president and treasurer, Brooklyn Rapid Transit Co. |
| | inventor - process of constructing tubular rollers, 1892 |
| | industrialist - partner, with his father, George R. Meneely & Son (manufacturers of car bearings); |
| | secretary and treasurer, Meneely Bearing Co., West Troy, NY |
| Civic Activism: | treasurer, Employees' Benefit Association |
| Marriage(s): | 1903-1922 – Emily Frances Gahn (1870-1941) |
| Address: | 65 Second Street, Garden City |
| Name of estate: | |
| Year of construction: | 1898 |
| Style of architecture: | Colonial Revival |
| Architect(s): | |
| Landscape architect(s): | |
| House extant: yes | |
| Historical notes: | |

The *Long Island Society Register, 1929* lists Charles Dickinson and Emily Frances Gahn Meneely as residing at 65 Second Street, Garden City.

He was the son of George Rodney and Achsah Bethiah Dickinson Meneely.

Charles Dickinson and Emily Frances Gahn Meneely's son George married Ethelioynne Eaton Underwood, the daughter of Enoch William and Alice Wyman Underwood of Garden City. Their daughter Eleanor married Clinton Blake Townsend, the son of Clinton Paul Townsend.

*front facade, 2008*

### Merrill, Payson, Sr. (1842-1933)

| | |
|---|---|
| Occupation(s): | attorney - partner, Merrill and Rogers, NYC |
| | financier - trustee, United States Savings Bank; vice-president and director, Union Mortgage and Realty Co.; director, Lawyers' Title Insurance & Trust Co. |
| Civic Activism: | chairman, executive committee, Association of the Bar of the City of New York, 1905-1906 |
| Marriage(s): | 1879-1925 – Emma Harrison Strong (1848-1925) |
| Address: | Clinton Road, Lawrence |
| Name of estate: | |
| Year of construction: | |
| Style of architecture: | Modified Neo-Tudor |
| Architect(s): | Delano and Aldrich designed the house (for Merrill) |
| Landscape architect(s): | |
| House extant: | unconfirmed |
| Historical notes: | |

The house was built by Payson Merrill, Sr.
The *Long Island Society Register, 1929* lists Payson Merrill [Sr.] as residing on Clinton Road, Lawrence.
He was the son of Phinebas and Abigall Rollins Merrill of Stratham, NH.
Emma Harrison Strong Merrill was the daughter of Theron Rudd and Abby Louisa Hart Strong.
Payson and Emma Harrison Strong Merrill, Sr.'s daughter Cornelia married John Vosburgh Irwin.


### Merritt, Edward Charles, Sr. (1861-1939)

| | |
|---|---|
| Occupation(s): | industrialist - vice-president of sales, Solvay Sales Corp. (subsidiary of Allied Chemical and Dye Corp |
| Marriage(s): | Grace B. Hollingsworth (1860-1951) |
| Address: | 169 Whitehall Boulevard, Garden City |
| Name of estate: | |
| Year of construction: | 1931 |
| Style of architecture: | Neo-Tudor |
| Architect(s): | Olive Frances Tjaden designed the house |
| Landscape architect(s): | |
| House extant: | yes |
| Historical notes: | |

Edward Charles Merritt, Sr. was the son of Francis J. Merritt of Astoria, NY.
Grace B. Hollingsworth Merritt was also from Astoria.
Edward Charles and Grace B. Hollingsworth Merritt, Sr.'s daughter Grace married Harold Douglas Pennington and resided in Garden City. Their son Harold, who also resided in Garden City, married Dorothy Calhoun Hearne and, later, Verona Ruth Oakley. Their three-year-old son Edward Charles Merritt, Jr. died in 1899.
*[See following entry for additional family information.]*
In 2010 the house sold for $1.78 million.

*front facade, 2016*

**Merritt, Harold Francis, Sr. (1891-1973)**

| | |
|---|---|
| Occupation(s): | industrialist - vice-president, Solvay Sales Corp., NYC (subsidiary of Allied Chemical and Dye Corp.) |
| Marriage(s): | M/1 – 1919-div. 1928 – Dorothy Calhoun Hearne (1894-1972) |
| | M/2 – 1929-1973 – Verona Ruth Oakley (1904-1987) |
| | (aka Verona Ruth DeMott) |
| | - entertainer and associated professions - Broadway actress |
| Address: | 261 Stewart Avenue, Garden City |
| Name of estate: | |
| Year of construction: | 1929 |
| Style of architecture: | Neo-Tudor |
| Architect(s): | Olive Frances Tjaden designed the house (for Ebinger) |
| Landscape architect(s): | |
| House extant: yes | |
| Historical notes: | |

The house was built by Walter Dohrmann Ebinger. In 1941, it was purchased by Merritt. [*Nassau Daily Review–Star* September 15, 1941, p. 5.]

He was the son of Edward Charles and Grace B. Hollingsworth Merritt, Sr. of Garden City.

Dorothy Calhoun Hearne Merritt was the daughter of Robert Joseph and Jean Cunningham Calhoun Hearne of Manhattan. Dorothy subsequently married Charles L. Bausher, Jr. with whom she resided in Westhampton. [*See* Spinzia, *Long Island's Prominent Families in the Town of Southampton* – Bausher entry.]

Verona Ruth Oakley Merritt was the daughter of the noted circus clown Frank Oakley whose stage name was "Silvers." In 1916 Frank committed suicide. Verona was, subsequently, adopted by the well-known bareback horse rider of the Barnum and Bailey Circus Josephine DeMott Robinson of West Hempstead.

Harold Francis and Verona Ruth Oakley Merritt, Sr.'s son Edward married Jeannette Helen Vogt, the daughter of Henry Ludwig Vogt of Fort Lauderdale, FL.

*[See previous entry for additional family information.]*

The house was later owned by Edward Jerome Merritt and, then, by Mark Barbatusly.

In 2017, the 4,974-square-foot house, with six bathrooms and six and one half bathrooms, sold for $1.75 million.

*side facade, 2018*

**Merritt, Schuyler, II (1899-1983)**

| | |
|---|---|
| Occupation(s): | financier - executive manager, Dillon, Read Co. (investment banking firm); vice-president, New York State Bank, Albany, NY; a founder, president, and CEO, Commerce & Industry Insurance Co. (later, Combined Insurance Company of America); director, Commerce and Industry Insurance Company of Canada; president, Reciprocal Managers Inc. (industrial and commercial fire insurance firm); president, Underwriters Exchange, Kansas City, MO |
| | industrialist - secretary, treasurer, and director McKesson and Robbins, Inc. (pharmaceutical firm) |
| Marriage(s): | M/1 – 1926-1972 – Cornelia Kane McElroy (1905-1972) - real estate agent - Burr & McAuley Civic Activism: president, Five Towns District Nursing Association |
| | M/2 – 1972 – Virginia Morrill |
| Address: | 250 Briarwood Crossing, Lawrence |
| Name of estate: | |
| Year of construction: | 1920 |
| Style of architecture: | Colonial Revival |
| Architect(s): | |
| Landscape architect(s): | |
| House extant: yes | |
| Historical notes: | |

The *Social Register New York, 1939* lists Schuyler and Cornelia K. McElroy Merritt II as residing on Meadowview Road, Hewlett [Hewlett Bay Park].

He was the son of Henry C. Merritt.

Cornelia Kane McElroy Merritt was the daughter of Charles Edward and Harriet Langdon Parker McElroy. Cornelia's aunt Mary Arthur McElroy was the sister of President Chester A. Arthur. She served as the hostess of the White House after President Arthur's wife died.

Schuyler and Cornelia Kane McElroy Merritt II's daughter Harriet married Lawrence Howland Dixon, the son of Courtland Palmer and Hortense Howland Dixon of *Causeways* in Lawrence. Harriet later married John Franklin Garde III, the son of John Franklin Garde, Jr. of Lawrence, and resided in Lawrence. Their daughter Cornelia married Norcross Sheldon Tilney, the son of Sheldon Tilney of Llewellyn Park, West Orange, NJ, and resided in Lawrence. Their daughter Camilla married Robert Milligan McLane, the son of Allan and Edith Gibb Pratt McLane, Jr. of *Home Wood* in Lattington. [*See* Spinzia, *Long Island's Prominent North Shore Families, vol. I* – McLane entry – and *Long Island's Prominent North Shore Families, vol. II* – Pratt entry.]

The *Social Register, 1982* lists Schuyler and Virginia Morrill Merritt II as residing at 250 Briarwood Crossing in Cedarhurst [Lawrence].

She had previously been married to Henry Otis Chapman, Jr., the son of Henry Otis and Harriet Louise Murphey Chapman, Sr. of Woodsburgh.

The Lawrence house was formerly owned by Henry Otis Chapman, Jr. In 1989 it sold for $569,000.

*front facade*

### Meyerkort, John, Jr. (1895-1950)
### aka Jack Meyerkort, Jr.

Occupation(s):
Civic Activism: quartermaster sergeant, Veterans of Foreign Wars of The Branch;
vice president, men's club, Trinity Church, Hewlett

Marriage(s): 1921-div. 1939 – Edith Jacquelin Smith (1900-1985)
- Civic Activism: board member, Lawrence–Cedarhurst Democratic Club, 1931;
secretary, Family Service Association of Lawrence;
district commissioner, Five Towns Council of Girl Scouts of America;
treasurer, Five Towns Women Exchange

Address: 190 Sage Avenue, Lawrence
Name of estate:
Year of construction:
Style of architecture:
Architect(s):
Landscape architect(s):
House extant: no
Historical notes:

The *Long Island Society Register, 1929* lists John and Edith Jacquelin Smith Meyerkort [Jr.] as residing at 190 Sage Avenue, Lawrence.

He was the son of John and Clara Oakley Meyerkort, Sr.

Edith Jacquelin Smith Meyerkort was the daughter of Augustine Jacquelin and Julia Post Hard Smith of *Sunnyside* in Lawrence and the great-granddaughter of Anson Wales Hard, Sr. of *Driftwood* in Lawrence. Edith's sister Dorothy married William Henderson Long, Jr. and resided at *Noranda* in Hewlett Harbor. Her sister Mary married Dr. DeWitt Hendee Smith, the son of Charles Hendee Smith of Lawrence, and resided in Princeton, NJ.

John and Edith Jacquelin Smith Meyerkort, Jr.'s daughter Margaret married Stewart Maurice Dall, the son of Charles Whitney and Emily Marshall Maurice Dall, Sr. of Lawrence, and resided in Lawrence.

*[See following entry for additional family information.]*


### Meyerkort, Clara Oakley (1864-1944)

Marriage(s): 1894-1907 – John Meyerkort (1859-1907)
- capitalist - founder, Meyerkort & Co. (commission cotton broker);
member, New York Cotton Exchange

Address: South Ocean and Clinton Avenues, Lawrence
Name of estate:
Year of construction: 1923
Style of architecture:
Architect(s): Henry Otis Chapman designed
the house (for C. O. Meyerkort)
Landscape architect(s):
House extant: no
Historical notes:

The house was built by Clara Oakley Meyerkort.

She was the daughter of William Henry and Adele Suydam Oakley. Clara's sister Louise married Albert Barnes Boardman of *Villa Mille Fiori* and *Windswept* in Southampton. [*See* Spinzia, *Long Island's Prominent Families in the Town of Southampton* – Boardman entries.]

John Meyerkort, Sr., who was born in Germany, was a cotton broker for several companies in Bremen, Germany, and Moscow, Russia, where he obtained the Crown Commission for importing cotton from Afghanistan from the Czar. [*The Commercial Appeal* April 17, 1955, p. 83.]

John and Clara Oakley Meyerkort, Sr.'s son John Meyerkort, Jr. married Edith Jacquelin Smith and resided in Lawrence.

*[See previous entry for additional family information.]*

**Milholland, James Clarke (1893-1954)**

Occupation(s):

Marriage(s): M/1 – 1919-div. 1936 – Florence Appleton (1899-1987)
M/2 – 1943-1954 – Eleanor Baxter (1896-1954)

Address: Adams Road, Hewlett Harbor
Name of estate:
Year of construction:
Style of architecture:
Architect(s):
Landscape architect(s):
House extant: unconfirmed
Historical notes:

   The *Long Island Society Register, 1929* lists James Clark [sic] and Florence Appleton Milholland as residing on Adams Road, Hewlett [Hewlett Harbor].
   He was the son of Harry Carter and Sarah Clarke Milholland, Sr. of Pittsburgh, PA.
   Florence Appleton Milholland was the daughter of Robert Walmarth and Mary Horsman Appleton of *Nid de Papillion* in East Hampton. She subsequently married John Mingus Dodd III with whom she resided in East Hampton. [*See* Spinzia, *Long Island's Prominent Families in the Town of East Hampton* – Appleton and Dodd entries.]
   James Clarke and Florence Appleton Milholland's daughter Anne married John William Kiser III, the son of John William and Mary Buford Peirce Kiser, Jr. of *Sunset Court / Westerly* in Southampton, and resided in East Hampton. [*See* Spinzia, *Long Island's Prominent Families in the Town of Southampton* and *Long Island's Prominent Families in the Town of East Hampton* – Kiser entries.] Their daughter Mary married Charles Mathews Dick, Jr. and resided in Lake Forest, IL. Their son Peter married Dorothy Keane, the daughter of John Redmore Keane, and resided in East Hampton. Their son Peter, who resided in East Hampton, married Dorothy M. Keane, the daughter of John Redmore Keene; Kathleen Hanley; Maura Mulligan; and Virginia Gennett.
   Eleanor Baxter Milholland was the daughter of the Territorial Governor of Wyoming George White Baxter and Mrs. Margaret White McGhee Baxter of *Cherokee Cottage* in East Hampton. [*See* Spinzia, *Long Island's Prominent Families in the Town of East Hampton* – Baxter entry.] Eleanor had previously been married to Chauncey Perry Beadleston with whom she resided in Hewlett Bay Park.

*Danforth Miller, Sr. estate,
Birch Corners*

## Miller, Danforth, Sr. (1893-1952)

| | |
|---|---|
| Occupation(s): | capitalist - vice-president, Cuban Aviation Corp. (holding company) |
| Civic Activism: | chairman, fund-raising committee, Lawrence–Cedarhurst fire department, 1937; member, fund-raising committee, Five Towns Community Chest, 1938 |
| Marriage(s): | 1917-1952 – Ann Talbot Day |
| | - Civic Activism: director and secretary, New York Exchange for Women's Work; chair, nurses aides, Five Towns branch, American Red Cross, 1942; vice-chair, Committee to Defend America by Aiding the Allies, 1941; chair, committee to collect aluminum for war effort, 1941; director, Far Rockaway Mothers' Health Center, 1938 |
| Address: | Cedar and Meadowview Avenues, Hewlett Bay Park |
| Name of estate: | *Birch Corners* |
| Year of construction: | c. 1908 |
| Style of architecture: | Modified Cotswold |
| Architect(s): | Albro and Lindeberg designed the house (for Carroll Macy) |
| Landscape architect(s): | |
| House extant: no | |
| Historical notes: | |

The house, originally named *Birch Corners*, was built by Carroll Macy. It was later owned by Ira Andruss Kip, Jr. and, then, by Miller, who also called it *Birch Corners*.

The *Long Island Society Register, 1929* lists Danforth and Ann Talbot Day Miller [Sr.] as residing at *Birch Corners* in Hewlett [Hewlett Bay Park].

She was the daughter of T. Ferman Day of Southampton.

Danforth and Ann Talbot Day Miller, Sr.'s son Danforth Miller, Jr. married Elizabeth Harriman Schaff, the daughter of Walter Schaff of Youngstown, OH, and resided in Farmington, CT.

The living room was decorated with sixteenth-century walnut paneling which Miller had brought from England. [*The New York Times* July 22, 1942, p. 33.]

In 1942, Miller sold the house to Laurence Anthony Slesinger for $40,000. [*Nassau Daily Review–Star* July 27, 1942, p. 14, and *The New York Times* July 22, 1942, p. 33.] In 1949, Slesinger placed the house on the market and relocated to Sands Point. [*Newsday* May 6, 1949, p. 45.]

*front facade, 1908*

**Miller, John Robinson, Sr. (1914-1982)**

| | |
|---|---|
| Occupation(s): | publisher - president, CEO, and director, Hearst Corp. (holding company for 10 radio and television stations, 20 magazines, 8 newspapers, and 3 book publishers)*; vice-chairman, finance committee, Hearst Corp.; chairman of board, National Magazine Co., Ltd., Great Britain; chairman, finance committee, National Magazine Co., Ltd, Great Britain |
| Civic Activism: | director, William Randolph Hearst Foundation of New York; director, William Randolph Hearst Foundation of California; director and vice-chairman of board, Audit Bureau of Circulation (monitors newspaper and magazine circulation); chairman of board, National Better Business Bureau; member of panel, American Arbitration Association; director, Boys' Club of America; director, United Cerebral Palsy Research and Educational Foundation; trustee, St. Paul's School, Garden City; trustee, St. Mary's School, Garden City |
| Marriage(s): | 1935-1982 – Helen Elizabeth Fulton (1914-2004) |
| Address: | *[unable to determine street address]*, Garden City |

Name of estate:
Year of construction:
Style of architecture:
Architect(s):
Landscape architect(s):
House extant: unconfirmed*
Historical notes:

He was the son of John Robinson and Helen Dora Smythe Miller, Sr. of Garden City. *[See following entry.]*

Helen Elizabeth Fulton Miller was the daughter of Ralph Whittier and Helen Goodrich Dunlop Fulton of Garden City.

John Robinson and Helen Elizabeth Fulton Miller, Jr.'s son John Robinson Miller, III married Kay Elizabeth Zoller, the daughter of Norman Charles Zoller of Lyndhurst, OH, and resided in Asharoken. [*See* Spinzia, *Long Island's Prominent North Shore Families, vol. I* – Miller entry.] Their son Mark married Linda Joyce Palmer, the daughter of John Edward Palmer of Oaklyn, NJ. Their daughter Dale married Robert Max Frehse, Jr. of Detroit, MI.

*[For W. R Hearst's estate *Saint Joan* in Sands Point, *see Long Island's Prominent North Shore Families, vol. I* – Hearst entry. For Mrs. Hearst's estate *Millhurst* in Southampton, *see Long Island's Prominent Families in the Town of Southampton*– Hearst entry.]

*[See following entry for additional family information.*

**Miller, John Robinson, Sr. (1879-1945)**

| | |
|---|---|
| Occupation(s): | financier - director, Garden City Bank and Trust Co. industrialist - vice-president in charge of sales, West Virginia Pulp & Paper Co. |
| Marriage(s): | Helen Dora Smythe (b. 1882) |
| Address: | 122 Stewart Avenue, Garden City |

Name of estate:
Year of construction:
Style of architecture:
Architect(s):
Landscape architect(s):
House extant: unconfirmed
Historical notes:

The *Long Island Society Register, 1929* lists Mr. and Mrs. John R. Miller as residing at 122 Stewart Avenue, Garden City. In 1945, their address was listed as 238 Stewart Avenue, Garden City. [*The Brooklyn Daily Eagle* March 16, 1945, p. 11.]

He was the son of N. S. Miller of Rockland, DE.

John Robinson and Helen Dora Smythe Miller's son John Robinson Miller, Jr. married Helen Elizabeth Fulton. Their daughter Gertrude married Herbert Ludlam Smith, Jr., the son of Herbert Ludlam and Marie Schoonmaker Smith, Sr. of Garden City and *Oliver's Point* on Centre Island. [*See* Spinzia, *Long Island's Prominent North Shore Families, vol. II* – Smith entry.] Their daughter Muriel married Julian Jordan Frey, the son of Frank Gustav and Harriet Jordan Frey of Baltimore, MD. Their son Douglas resided in San Francisco.

**Miller, Lawrence McKeever, Sr. (1889-1970)**

| | |
|---|---|
| Occupation(s): | financier - a founder and partner, Russell, Miller, and Co., 1922-1935 (stock brokerage firm) |
| | partner, E. F. Hutton, 1936 (investment banking firm) |
| Civic Activism: | trustee, Ruptured & Crippled Hospital (later, Hospital for Special Surgery of which he became chairman of executive committee) |
| Marriage(s): | M/1 – 1915-div. 1930 – Frances Tileston Breese (1893-1985) |
| | - artist - textile designer*; painter |
| | merchant - president, Frances T. Miller, Inc., NYC (contemporary home furnishings) |
| | writer - *"Tanty": Encounters With the Past*, 1979 (autobiography); |
| | *More About "Tanty": A Second Growing Up*, 1980 (autobiography); |
| | *"Tanty": The Daring Decades*, 1981 (autobiography); |
| | *The Green Fish and Other Haitian Folktales*; |
| | "Two Haitian Folktales," *Unicorn Journal*; |
| | "Sketches of a Childhood," *Long Island University Journal*; |
| | "Calling Day," *New York Magazine*, 1975** |
| | Civic Activism: chairman of board, Junior League, 1912; director, New York Exchange for Women's Work |
| | M/2 – 1933-1970 – Katharine Wyman Porter (1895-1970) |
| Address: | West Broadway, Hewlett |
| Name of estate: | |
| Year of construction: | |
| Style of architecture: | |
| Architect(s): | |
| Landscape architect(s): | |
| House extant: | unconfirmed |
| Historical notes: | |

    The *Long Island Society Register, 1929* lists Lawrence McKeever and Frances T. Breese Miller [Sr.] as residing in Hewlett.

    He was the son of Hoffman and Edith McKeever Miller of Tuxedo Park, NY. Lawrence's brother George married Flora Payne Whitney, the daughter of Harry Payne and Gertrude Vanderbilt Whitney of Old Westbury, and resided at *French House* in Old Westbury. [*See* Spinzia, *Long Island's Prominent North Shore Families, vol. I* – Miller entry – and *vol. II* – Whitney entries.]

    Frances Tileston Breese Miller was the daughter of James Lawrence and Frances Tileston Potter Breese, Sr., who resided at *The Orchard* in Southampton. She subsequently married Arsene Marius, a Haitian journalist with whom she resided in Mexico and at *The Sandbox* in Bridgehampton. [*See* Spinzia, *Long Island's Prominent Families in the Town of Southampton* – Breese and Miller entries.]

    Frances' inter-racial marriage to Arsene Marius was not well-received by all the residents and merchants of the Hamptons. This first encounter with racial prejudice caused Arsene to become insecure and to start drinking heavily. During these occasions he became violent, smashing furniture and even threatening Frances with a butcher knife. After their divorce, Frances returned to Long Island and continued to summer at *The Sandbox* while wintering in Sag Harbor.

    *In 1937 Frances was awarded a gold medal at the Paris International Exposition for her textile designs.

    **"Calling Day" was a short-story competition winner.

    Lawrence McKeever and Frances Tileston Breese Miller, Sr.'s daughter Edith married Lloyd Francis Roberts and resided in Vermont. Their son George married Carolyn Pickett. Their son Lawrence McKeever Miller, Jr. married Ruth Smedley Passmore, the daughter of John Willits and Hannah A. Wickersham Passmore of Pennsylvania, and resided in Doylestown, PA.

    Katharine Wyman Porter was the daughter of Thomas Wyman and Lillian Mary Ward Porter of Tuxedo Park, NY. Katharine had previously been married to George Hunt Pendleton.

### Miller, William Wilson (1870-1940)

| | |
|---|---|
| Occupation(s): | attorney - partner, Hornblower, Miller, Potter, and Earle, NYC; partner, Miller, Owen, Otis, and Bailley, NYC<br>industrialist - president and director, Houbigant, Inc.; president and director, Cheramay, Inc.; director, Otis Elevator Co.<br>capitalist - director, Carolina, Clinchfield, & Ohio Railroad |
| Civic Activism: | member, executive committee, Southern Society; member, advisory board, New York Foundling Hospital, NYC |
| Marriage(s): | 1914-1919 – Nanette C. Campbell (1893-1919)<br>- entertainers and associated professions - Broadway actress |
| Address: | 291 Ocean Avenue, Lawrence |
| Name of estate: | *Villa Nancy* |
| Year of construction: | 1920 |
| Style of architecture: | Modified Colonial Revival |
| Architect(s): | |
| Landscape architect(s): | |
| House extant: yes | |
| Historical notes: | |

*front facade, 2000*

The *Long Island Society Register, 1929* lists William Wilson Miller as residing at *Villa Nancy* in Lawrence.

He was the son of William John and Frances Marion Joyce Miller of Washington, DC.

Nanette C. Campbell Miller was the daughter of William Arthur and Nanette Long Campbell of Manhattan.

William Wilson and Nanette C. Campbell Miller's daughter Nancy married Edward Francis Cavanagh, Jr. and resided at *Naghward* in Old Brookville. [*See* Spinzia, *Long Island's Prominent North Shore Families, vol. 1* – Cavanagh entry.]

### Mills, Edward Shorrey (1883-1976)

| | |
|---|---|
| Occupation(s): | publisher - president, Longmans, Green, & Co., NYC (publishing firm) |
| Civic Activism: | president, National Association of Book Publishers |
| Marriage(s): | M/1 – 1907-1955 – Marion E. Partridge (1889-1955)<br>M/2 – 1957-1976 – Janet Cook (1899-1990) |
| Address: | Knote Road, Woodmere |
| Name of estate: | |
| Year of construction: | |
| Style of architecture: | |
| Architect(s): | |
| Landscape architect(s): | |
| House extant: unconfirmed | |
| Historical notes: | |

The *Long Island Society Register, 1929* lists Edward S. and Marion E. Partridge Mills as residing in Hewlett [Woodmere]. The 1920 Census lists the Millses at this address.

He was the son of Charles James and Mary F. Quimby Mills of Orange, NJ.

Marion E. Partridge Mills was the daughter of George H. and Adelaide W. Partridge of Minneapolis, MN.

Edward Shorrey and Marion E. Partridge Mills' son George married Evelyn Cary Smith, the daughter of Courtland and Elinor Cary Smith of Sands Point. Their son Charles married Dorothy Ordway, the daughter of Samuel Gilman and Mildred O. Wurtele Ordway of *Dellwood* in East Hampton. [*See* Spinzia, *Long Island's Prominent Families in the Town of East Hampton* – Ordway entry.]

Janet Cook Mills had previously been married to Howard Morris.

At the time of his death, Mills was residing on Quimby Lane, Bridgehampton. [*The New York Times* October 15, 1976, p. 22.]

[For information about his Bridgehampton residence *Annesden, see* Spinzia, *Long Island's Prominent Families in the Town of Southampton* – Mills entry.]

### Minton, Henry Miller (1898-1982)

| | |
|---|---|
| Occupation(s): | industrialist - president and chairman of board, Church & Dwight Co., Inc. (manufacturers of Arm & Hammer Baking Soda)* |
| Civic Activism: | trustee, Village of North Hills |
| Marriage(s): | 1922-1982 – Helen Dwight Church (1900-2005) |
| Address: | 159 Brixton Road, Garden City |
| Name of estate: | |
| Year of construction: | 1918 |
| Style of architecture: | Colonial Revival |
| Architect(s): | |
| Landscape architect(s): | |
| House extant: yes | |
| Historical notes: | |

The *Long Island Society Register, 1929* lists Henry Miller and Helen Dwight Church Minton as residing at 159 Brixton Road, Garden City, while the *Social Register Summer, 1932* lists the Mintons as residing at *Brookwood* on Old Courthouse Road, Great Neck [North Hills.].

He was the son of Dr. Henry Brewster Minton of Brooklyn.

Helen Dwight Church Minton was the daughter of Robert Elihu Dwight and Emma Vose Church, who resided in Westhampton Beach.

Henry Miller and Helen Dwight Church Minton's daughter Helen married John Burlinson Coleman, Jr. Their daughter Mary married Richard Nevins of Pasadena, CA. Their son Dwight married Suzanne Patricia Zezza, the daughter of Baron Francesco Zezza of Naples, Italy.

*Church & Dwight Co. is the largest manufacturer of baking soda in America. It was founded by Charles Thomas Church, Sr., who resided at *Three Brooks* in Mill Neck. Minton was instrumental in naming one of its divisions Arm & Hammer Baking Soda. [*The New York Times* April 30, 1982, p. 21.]

[For information on Charles Thomas Church's estate *Three Brooks* in Mill Neck; Minton's estate *Brookwood* in North Hills; and Elihu Dwight Church's estate in Westhampton Beach, see Spinzia, *Long Island's Prominent North Shore Families, vol. 1* – Church and Minton entries – and *Long Island's Prominent Families in the Town of Southampton* – Church entry.]

*side facade, 2001*

### Mixter, George, Sr. (1889-1968)

| | |
|---|---|
| Occupation(s): | capitalist - vice-president, Stone & Webster (construction firm); |
| | vice-president, American Balsa Corp.; |
| | director, Pan American Airways; |
| | director, Roosevelt Field Corp., Garden City |
| | industrialist - secretary, treasurer, and vice-president, United States Smelting, Refining, and Mining Co. |
| | financier - director, Ware Trust Co. |
| Civic Activism: | director, The West End House; |
| | director, Massachusetts Heart Association; |
| | trustee, American Child Guidance Foundation; |
| | trustee, Eaton & Howard Foundation; |
| | trustee, Village of Hewlett Harbor; |
| | trustee, Franklin Institute, Philadelphia, PA |
| Marriage(s): | 1914-1968 – Muriel Eaton (b. 1892) |
| | - Civic Activism: chair, Council of Social Agencies of The Branch Community Chest, 1933 |
| Address: | Seawane Drive, Hewlett Harbor |
| Name of estate: | *Strode* |
| Year of construction: | |
| Style of architecture: | |
| Architect(s): | |
| Landscape architect(s): | |
| House extant: unconfirmed | |
| Historical notes: | |

The *Social Register New York, 1933* lists George and Muriel Eaton Mixter [Sr.] as residing at *Strode* in Hewlett [Hewlett Harbor.]. In 1934 the Mixters relocated to Boston, MA.

George Mixter was the son of Samuel Jason and Wilhelmina Galloupe Mixter of Boston, MA.

George and Muriel Eaton Mixter, Sr.'s son Robert married Lucy Victoria Rusletvedt, the daughter of Trygve Rusletvedt of Denver, CO, and resided in Dobbs Ferry, NY. Their son James married Phebe Baker Perry, the daughter of Henry Eldridge Perry of Manchester, VT, and resided in Cincinnati, OH. Their son George Mixter, Jr. married Jane Sanford Warren, the daughter of Charles Appleton Warren of Kingston, NY, and resided in Chicago, IL.

### Moller, Charles George, Jr. (1870-1918)

| | |
|---|---|
| Occupation(s): | heir to sugar refining fortune |
| Marriage(s): | Helen Allen (1871-1945) |
| Address: | *[unable to determine street address]*, Lawrence |
| Name of estate: | *Wayside* |
| Year of construction: | |
| Style of architecture: | |
| Architect(s): | |
| Landscape architect(s): | |
| House extant: unconfirmed | |
| Historical notes: | |

The *Social Register Summer 1910* lists Charles G. and Helene Allen Moller, Jr. as residing at *Wayside* in Lawrence.

He was the son of Charles George and Elizabeth Furman Moller, Sr. and the grandson of Peter Moller, who was born in the Kingdom of Hanover, now part of Germany. Peter immigrated to America and climbed the corporate ladder while working for several refining firms. He eventually formed a partnership in the firm of Havemeyer & Moller with Henry Osborne Havemeyer of *Bayberry Point* in Islip. [*See* Spinzia, *Long Island's Prominent South Shore Families* – Havemeyer entry.] Peter then became a founding partner in the firm of Howlands & Moller and, subsequently, the president of the New York Steam Sugar Refining Company. At the time of his death, Peter was referred to as the "Sugar King of America." [*The New York Times* March 25, 1914, p. 3.]

Charles George and Helene Allen Moller, Jr.'s daughter Ruth married Johnston Livingston II of *Homeacre* in Lawrence. Their son Charles George Moller III, who also resided in Lawrence, married Mary Esther White and, later, Elizabeth Percival.

*[See following entry for additional family information.]*

### Moller, Charles George, III (1897-1966)

| | |
|---|---|
| Occupation(s): | capitalist - real estate |
| Marriage(s): | M/1 – 1918-div. 1933 – Mary Esther White (b. 1898) |
| | M/2 – 1934-1966 – Elizabeth Percival (1904-1967) |
| | (aka Lydia Percival) |
| Address: | Tanglewood Crossing, Lawrence |

Name of estate:
Year of construction:
Style of architecture:
Architect(s):
Landscape architect(s):
House extant: unconfirmed
Historical notes:

The *Long Island Society Register, 1929* lists Charles G. and Mary E. White Moller III as residing in Cedarhurst [Lawrence]. The 1930 Census lists the Mollers at this address.

He was the son of Charles George and Helene Allen Moller, Jr. of *Wayside* in Lawrence.

Mary Esther White Moller was the daughter of George Wagner White of Washington, DC. She subsequently married De Lancey Nicoll, Jr., the son of De Lancey and Maude Churchill Nicoll, Sr. of *Windymere* in Southampton, and resided in Hewlett Harbor. [*See* Spinzia, *Long Island's Prominent Families in the Town of Southampton* – Nicoll entry.]

Charles George and Mary Esther White Moller III's daughter Mary married Benjamin Franklin Lucas, Jr. of Baltimore, MD.

The *Social Register Summer, 1937* lists Charles G. and Elizabeth Percival Moller [III] as residing in Camden, SC.

She was the daughter of David Crowell Percival of Boston, MA. Elizabeth had previously been married to Walter Scott Blanchard, Sr. with whom she resided in Hewlett Bay Park. Her sister Constance married Louis Frederick Bertschmann of *Les Bouleaux* in Muttontown. [*See* Spinzia, *Long Island's Prominent North Shore Families, vol. I* – Bertschmann entry.]

### Moller, Hans Eskildsen (1865-1933)

| | |
|---|---|
| Occupation(s): | industrialist - director, Worthington Pump & Machinery Co.; |
| | president, Guanajuato Consolidated Mining & Milling Co.; |
| | secretary and treasurer, Cerro de Pasco Copper Co. |
| | capitalist - treasurer, Cerro de Pasco Railway Co.; |
| | president, several realty firms |
| Civic Activism: | treasurer, American Scandinavian Foundation |
| Marriage(s): | 1921-1933 – Helen Desmond Nelson |
| Address: | Stevenson Road, Hewlett |

Name of estate:
Year of construction:
Style of architecture:
Architect(s):
Landscape architect(s):
House extant: unconfirmed
Historical notes:

The *Long Island Society Register, 1929* lists Hans Eskildsen and Helen Desmond Nelson Moller as residing on Stevenson Road, Hewlett.

He was a native of Copenhagen, Denmark.

Helen Desmond Nelson Moller was the daughter of William Beebe Nelson of Manhattan and Amenia, NY.

### Mooney, Franklin Drake, Sr. (1874-1966)

| | |
|---|---|
| Occupation(s): | shipping - chairman of board, Atlantic and West Indies Steam Ship Lines; president, Ward Shipping Line; president, New York–Porto Rico Steamship Line; president, Clyde Steamship Co.; president, Agi Steamship Line |
| Civic Activism: | chairman, wage committee, American Steamship Association, 1919; vice-president, Harbor and Shipping Committee, New York State Chamber of Commerce; director, Maritime Association of the Port of New York |
| Marriage(s): | 1907-1962 – Grace A. Munson (1872-1962) |
| Address: | 25 Cathedral Avenue, Garden City |
| Name of estate: | |
| Year of construction: | 1906 |
| Style of architecture: | |
| Architect(s): | |
| Landscape architect(s): | |
| House extant: | yes |

Nassau County Museum Collection has ten uncatalogued photographs of the house.
Historical notes:

The 1930 Census lists the Mooneys at this address.
Franklin Drake Mooney, Sr. was the son of George Augustus and Annie E. Drake Mooney of Elizabeth, NJ.
Franklin Drake and Grace A. Munson Mooney, Sr.'s daughter Ruth married Thurston Huntting Smith, the son of Herbert Ludlam and Marie Schoonmaker Smith, Sr. of Garden City and *Oliver's Point* on Centre Island, and resided at *Upper Orchard* on Centre Island. [*See* Spinzia, *Long Island's Prominent North Shore Families, vol. II* – Smith entry.] Their son Franklin Drake Mooney, Jr. married Ethel Gurney, the daughter of Thomas Nichols and Ethel Kirkman Gurney of Garden City, and resided in Wantagh.
In 2010, the 6,259-square-foot house sold for $2.225 million.

### Moore, Arthur Standish (1880-1956)

| | |
|---|---|
| Occupation(s): | publisher - director, vice-president, treasurer, and general manager of Hearst Publications |
| Civic Activism: | director and treasurer, National Publisher's Association; a founder and president, North Fork Country Club, Cutchogue |
| Marriage(s): | M/1 – 1907-1918 – Anite Dumars (1886-1918)<br>M/2 – 192-1956 – Effe Jeanette Leary (1898-1985) |
| Address: | 105 Chester Avenue, Garden City |
| Name of estate: | |
| Year of construction: | c. 1928 |
| Style of architecture: | Colonial Revival |
| Architect(s): | |
| Landscape architect(s): | |
| House extant: | yes |
| Historical notes: | |

*front facade, 2000*

The house was built by Arthur Standish Moore.
He was the son of Stuart Hall and Myra Drake Moore of *Quawknest* in Cutchogue. Arthur's brother Douglas was the famous American composer who won the Pulitzer Prize in 1951 for his opera *Giants in the Earth* and the New York Critics Circle Award in 1958 for his opera *The Ballad of Baby Doe*. [*See* Spinzia, *Long Island: A Guide to New York's Suffolk and Nassau Counties* – Cutchogue Cemetery, Grave of Douglas Stuart Moore.]
Anite Dumars Moore was the daughter of Horace G. and Mary Elizabeth Contris Dumars of Glen Ridge, NJ.
Arthur Standish and Anite Dumars Moore's daughter Marjorie married Dr. Julian Scott Butterworth of Manhattan.
The *Long Island Society Register, 1929* lists Arthur Standish and Effe J. Laavy [sic] Moore as residing at 105 Chester Avenue, Garden City.
Arthur Standish and Effe Jeanette Leary Moore's son David was killed in World War II.

### Moore, Rufus Ellis (1840-1918)

| | |
|---|---|
| Occupation(s): | architect |
| | publisher - owner and publisher, *The American Churchman*, Chicago, IL |
| | merchant - founder, American Art Gallery; |
| Civic Activism: | director, Chicago Academy of Design (later, Chicago Institute of Art) |
| Marriage(s): | 1881-1918 – Mary Wright Stevens (1862-1932) |
| Address: | 222 Stewart Avenue, Garden City |
| Name of estate: | |
| Year of construction: | |
| Style of architecture: | |
| Architect(s): | |
| Landscape architect(s): | |
| House extant: unconfirmed | |
| Historical notes: | |

The *Long Island Society Register, 1929* lists Mary W. Stevens Moore as residing at 222 Stewart Avenue, Garden City.

Rufus Ellis Moore was the son of Don Loreno Bentevolee Voughley and Sarah Catherine Gay Moore of Greenfield, MA.

Rufus and Mary Wright Stevens Moore's son Edward married Catharine Gianini and, later, Margaret V. Willis, the daughter of Herbert Willis of Garden City. Their son Don married Edith Caroline Condict, the daughter of Henry Vail Condict of Essex Falls, NJ. Their son Charles married Marjory Watt, the daughter of William J. Watt of Manhattan.

### Moran, Michael Arthur (b. circa 1940)

| | |
|---|---|
| Occupation(s): | certified public accountant - Peat, Marwick, Mitchell, and Co., NYC |
| Marriage(s): | 1963 – Margaret Mary Stuberfield |
| Address: | 8 Andover Court, Garden City |
| Name of estate: | |
| Year of construction: | 1959 |
| Style of architecture: | Colonial Revival |
| Architect(s): | |
| Landscape architect(s): | |
| House extant: yes | |
| Historical notes: | |

Michael Arthur Moran is the son of Eugene Francis and Marie Josephine Staudt Moran, Jr., who resided at *Shadow Lawn* in Brightwaters. [*See* Spinzia, *Long Island's Prominent South Shore Families* – Moran entry.]

Margaret Mary Stuberfield Moran is the daughter of William Francis Stuberfield of Garden City.

Michael Arthur and Margaret Mary Stuberfield Moran's daughter Margaret married Hugh David Carmichael, Jr. of Alexandria, VA.

*front facade, 2001*

## Moran, Robert G. (1866-1933)

Occupation(s): shipping - a founder, United States and Australian Steamship Co.
financier - member, New York Produce Exchange;
member, New York Maritime Exchange

Marriage(s): 1891-1933 – Edith Parker (b. 1870)

Address: 123 Stratford Avenue, Garden City
Name of estate:
Year of construction: 1923
Style of architecture: Dutch Colonial Revival
Architect(s):
Landscape architect(s):
House extant: yes
Historical notes:

The *Long Island Society Register, 1929* lists Robert G. and Edith Parker Moran as residing at 123 Stratford Avenue, Garden City.

She was the daughter of John W. Parker of Brooklyn.

Robert G. and Edith Parker Moran's daughter Arvilla married George Leslie Mendes, Sr. and resided in Garden City. Their daughter Marjorie married Warren K. Rishel.

In 2001 the house was remodeled.

*side / front facade, 2001*

## Morehouse, David (1859-1940)

Occupation(s): financier - president and trustee, East Brooklyn Bank
merchant - A. B. Sands & Co. (wholesale pharmaceutical firm)

Marriage(s): Josephine S. Mead (1869-1931)

Address: 61 Kensington Road, Garden City
Name of estate:
Year of construction: 1912
Style of architecture: Dutch Colonial Revival
Architect(s):
Landscape architect(s):
House extant: yes
Historical notes:

The *Long Island Society Register, 1929* lists Mr. and Mrs. David Morehouse as residing on Kensington Road, Garden City.

He was the son of Sarah Riell Morehouse. At the time of his death, Morehouse was residing at 61 Kensington Road, Garden City. [*The New York Times* March 16, 1940, p. 20.]

In 1976 the house was remodeled.

*front facade, 2005*

### Morgenthau, Julius Caesar, Sr. (1858-1929)

| | |
|---|---|
| Occupation(s): | merchant - founder and president, J. C. Morgenthau & Co. (rare stamp merchant)* |
| | auctioneer - stamps |
| | capitalist - director, Woodmere Realty Co.; |
| | educator - teacher of philosophy, Greek, and Latin, College of the City of New York |
| Civic Activism: | president, Stamp Collectors Club of New York; |
| | president, first two international stamp exhibitions held in the United States, 1913 and 1926 |
| Marriage(s): | 1894-1929 – Regina Rose (1865-1935) |
| Address: | Woodmere Boulevard, Woodmere |
| Name of estate: | |
| Year of construction: | |
| Style of architecture: | |
| Architect(s): | |
| Landscape architect(s): | |
| House extant: unconfirmed | |
| Historical notes: | |

The *Long Island Society Register, 1929* lists J. C. Morgenthau [Jr.] as residing on Woodmere Boulevard, Woodmere. He was the son of Lazarus and Babette Guggenheim Morgenthau of Manheim, Germany.

Regina Rose Morgenthau was the daughter of Joseph and Caroline Brandeis Rose of New York.

Julius Caesar and Regina Rose Morgenthau, Sr.'s daughter Lucy married Bernard Heineman. In 1906, their nine-year-old son Julius Caesar Morgenthau, Jr. died.

*J. C. Morgenthau & Co. was the foremost stamp auction firm in the nation. In 1978 Morgenthau was inducted into the American Philatelic Society Hall of Fame.

*[See following entry for additional family information.]*

### Morgenthau, Maximilian, Sr. (1847-1936)

| | |
|---|---|
| Occupation(s): | attorney |
| | capitalist - a founder, Woodmere Realty Co.; |
| | president, Hudson Realty Co.; |
| | president, Sellwell Realty Co., NY, 1914; |
| | president, Owners' Syndicate, NY, 1909; |
| | president Park Realty Co., NY |
| | merchant - member, Ehrich Brothers, NYC (department store) |
| Civic Activism: | governor, Woodmere Club |
| Marriage(s): | 1872-1917 – Fanny Ehrich (1851-1917) |
| Address: | Willow Lane, Keene Lane, and Woodmere Boulevard, Woodsburgh |
| Name of estate: | |
| Year of construction: | |
| Style of architecture: | |
| Architect(s): | Ernest Flagg designed the house (for M. Morgenthau, Sr.) |
| Landscape architect(s): | |
| House extant: unconfirmed | |
| Historical notes: | |

Maximilian Morgenthau was the son of Lazarus and Babette Guggenheim Morgenthau of Manheim, Germany.

Fanny Ehrich Morgenthau was the daughter of Joseph and Rebecca Sporborg Ehrich.

Maximilian and Fanny Ehrich Morgentau, Sr.'s one-year-old daughter Brunhilda died in 1874. Their daughter Adele married James Frank, Sr., the son of Nathan and Mathilde Friedberger Frank. Their daughter Minna married Ludwig Mannheimer, Sr. Their daughter Alice married Leon A. Strauss, the son of Abraham and Ernestine Leopold Strauss. Their son Maximilian Morgenthau, Jr. married Rita A. Wallach, the daughter of Leopold and Therese Adelaide Luchtenstadter Wallach and, later, Mary Agnes Loraditch, the daughter of Edward Joseph and Mary Alice McKenzie Loraditch.

*[See previous entry for additional family information.]*

### Morrell, Robert Whiting (1887-1955)

| | |
|---|---|
| Occupation(s): | naval architect |
| Marriage(s): | 1912-1955 – Victoria Alexandra Carter (1891-1991) |
| Address: | 155 Euston Road, Garden City |
| Name of estate: | |
| Year of construction: | c. 1920 |
| Style of architecture: | Long Island Farmhouse |
| Architect(s): | Aymar Embury II designed the house |
| Landscape architect(s): | |
| House extant: | yes |
| Historical notes: | |

*front facade, 2001*

The *Long Island Society Register, 1929* lists Mr. and Mrs. Robert Whiting Morrell as residing at 111 Kilburn Road, Garden City. They previously resided at 155 Euston Road, Garden City.

He was the son of Joseph Barber and Harriett Whiting Morrell, who resided at *The Moorings* in Centerport. [*See* Spinzia, *Long Island's Prominent North Shore Families, vol. I* – Morrell entry.]

Victoria Alexander Carter Morrell was the daughter of A. G. Carter of Brooklyn.

Robert Whiting and Victoria Alexandra Carter Morrell's daughter Victoria married George Wilson Dunham, Jr. of Ann Arbor, MI. Their son Robert Carter Morrell married Mary Elizabeth Isaacson, the daughter of John W. Isaacson.

### Morris, Alfred Hennen (1864-1959)

| | |
|---|---|
| Occupation(s): | capitalist - treasurer, Morris Park, The Bronx (race track); director, New Orleans, Fort Jackson & Grand Isle Railway; president, Monmouth Park Association, Oceanport, NJ. (race track) |
| | politician - member, New York State Assembly, representing Westchester, NY, 1892-1893; supervisor, Town of Westchester, 1892-1904; Commissioner of Education, NYC |
| Marriage(s): | 1889-1952 – Jessie Harding (1865-1952) |
| Address: | Everit Avenue and Meadowview Avenue, Hewlett Bay Park |
| Name of estate: | |
| Year of construction: | |
| Style of architecture: | |
| Architect(s): | |
| Landscape architect(s): | |
| House extant: | unconfirmed |
| Historical notes: | |

The *Long Island Society Register, 1929* lists A. Hennen and Jessie Harding Morris as residing on Everit Avenue and Meadow View [sic] Avenue, Hewlett [Hewlett Bay Harbor].

He was the son of John Albert and Cora Hennen Morris of Throgs Neck, NY, Boston, MA, New Orleans, LA, and Bar Harbor, ME. John was known as the "Louisiana Lottery King."

Jessie Harding Morris was the daughter of William White Harding.

Alfred Hennen and Jessie Harding Morris' daughter Cora married Dr. Alfred H. Ehrenclou and resided in Camden, SC. Their son John Alfred Morris II married Edna Loew Brokaw, the daughter of Howard Crosby and Edna Goadby Loew Brokaw of *The Chimneys* in Muttontown. [*See* Spinzia, *Long Island's Prominent North Shore Families, vol. I* – Brokaw entry.]

### Morris, McLean Forman, Sr. (1885-1956)

| | |
|---|---|
| Occupation(s): | financier - United States Trust Co. |
| Civic Activism: | mayor, treasurer, and trustee, Village of Hewlett Neck |
| Marriage(s): | 1924-1956 – Lucy Evelyn Linderman (1892-1967) |
| Address: | 197 Hewlett Neck Road, Hewlett Neck |
| Name of estate: | |
| Year of construction: | 1926 |
| Style of architecture: | Colonial Revival |
| Architect(s): | |
| Landscape architect(s): | |
| House extant: yes | |
| Historical notes: | |

*front facade, 2000*

The house was built by McLean Forman Morris, Sr.

The *Long Island Society Register, 1929* lists McLean F. and Lucy E. Linderman Morris [Sr.] as residing at Hollywood Road and Ocean Avenue, Cedarhurst [Lawrence]. The *Social Register New York, 1939* lists their address as 197 Hewlett Neck Road, Woodmere [Hewlett Neck].

He was the son of Theodore Wilson and Frances Schanck Morris, Sr. of *The Vines* in Freehold, NJ. McClean's brother Theodore Wilson Morris, Jr. married Mary Maynadler Steele and resided in East Hampton. [*See* Spinzia, *Long Island's Prominent Families in the Town of East Hampton* – Morris entry.]

Lucy Evelyn Linderman Morris was the daughter of Robert Packer and Ruth Mae Sayre Linderman of Bethlehem, PA.

McLean Forman and Lucy Evelyn Linderman Morris, Sr.'s daughter Evelyn married Osterholt Gregory, the son of Edward S. Gregory of Hewlett. Their three-year-old son McLean Forman Morris, Jr. died in 1929.


### Morris, Stuyvesant Fish, Jr. (1877-1925)

| | |
|---|---|
| Occupation(s): | financier - partner, Morris, Freeman, and Co. (stock brokerage firm); president, Stuyvesant Fish Morris, Jr. and Co. (stock brokerage firm) |
| Marriage(s): | 1900-1925 – Elizabeth Hilles Wynkoop (1877-1957) |
| Address: | 235 Everit Avenue, Hewlett Bay Park |
| Name of estate: | |
| Year of construction: | |
| Style of architecture: | English Country |
| Architect(s): | William Adams Jr. designed the house (for S. F. Morris, Jr.) |
| Landscape architect(s): | |
| House extant: unconfirmed | |
| Historical notes: | |

*front facade*

The house was built by Stuyvesant Fish Morris, Jr.

The *Long Island Society Register, 1929* lists Mrs. Elizabeth H. Wynkoop Morris as residing in Hewlett [Hewlett Harbor].

She was the daughter of Geradus H. Wynkoop.

Stuyvesant Fish Morris, Jr. was the son of Dr. Stuyvesant Fish and Mrs. Ellen James Van Buren Morris, Sr., who resided at *Long Acre* in Quogue, and the great-grandson of President Martin Van Buren. His sister Elizabeth married Benjamin Woolsey Rogers. His sister Ellen married Francis Livingston Pell. His brother Richard married Carolyn W. Fellows and resided at *The Three Chimneys* in Southampton.

Stuyvesant Fish and Elizabeth Hilles Wynkoop Morris, Jr.'s son Martin Van Buren Morris, who resided at *Longacre* in Southampton, married Helen de Russy Sloan, the daughter of Thomas Donaldson and Helen de Russy Clark Sloan who resided at *Whilton Gables* in Lawrence. Their daughter Hilles married Louis Gordon Hamersley, Sr. of *The Moorings* in Sands Point and *The Moorings* in Southampton. Hilles later married George Leslie Bartlett with whom she resided in Tuxedo Park, NY, and, subsequently, Robert L. C. Timpson. Their son Stuyvesant Fish Morris III married Madeline White and resided in Babylon. [*See* Spinzia, *Long Island's Prominent North Shore Families, vol. I* – Hamersley entry; *Long Island's Prominent South Shore Families* – Morris entry; and *Long Island's Prominent Families in the Town of Southampton* – Hamersley and Morris entries.]

### Morrow, Dr. Albert Sidney, Sr. (1878-1960)

| | |
|---|---|
| Occupation(s): | physician - surgeon - Bellevue Hospital, NYC |
| | educator - adjunct professor of general surgery, New York Polyclinic Medical School and Hospital; associate professor of surgery, Columbia University, NYC |
| | writer - *The Immediate Care of the Injured*, 1906 (rev. 1917); *Diagnostic and Therapeutic Technique*, 1911 (rev. 1921); numerous articles in medical journals |
| Civic Activism: | director, New York City Cancer Committee |
| Marriage(s): | 1909-1960 – Marjorie Wyld (1884-1979) |
| Address: | 110 Fourth Street, Garden City |
| Name of estate: | |
| Year of construction: | 1916 |
| Style of architecture: | Modified Victorian |
| Architect(s): | |
| Landscape architect(s): | |
| House extant: yes | |
| Historical notes: | |

*front facade, 2005*

The *Long Island Society Register, 1929* lists Dr. Albert S. and Mrs. Marjorie Wyld Morrow [Sr.] as residing at 110 Fourth [Street], Garden City.

He was the son of Prince Albert and Lucy Bibb Slaughter Morrow of Madison, NJ.

Marjorie Wyld Morrow was the daughter of James and Blandia Hasbrouck Wyld of Brooklyn. Marjorie's brother Robert married Margaret Hart and resided in Garden City.

Dr. Albert Sidney and Mrs. Marjorie Wyld Morrow, Sr.'s daughter Alison remained unmarried. Their son Albert Sidney Morrow, Jr. married Barbara Merrill, the daughter of George Henry and Louise Alberta Wandell Merrill, and resided in Cornwall-on-Hudson, NY.

### Morse, Roy Bertram (1886-1953)

| | |
|---|---|
| Occupation(s): | merchant - marine hardware |
| | capitalist - partner, Morse Dry Dock and Repair Co., Brooklyn (later, United Dry Docks Inc. a division of Bethlehem Steel Co.) |
| Marriage(s): | Margaret J. Bixby (b. 1883) |
| Address: | 20 Cedar Place, Garden City |
| Name of estate: | |
| Year of construction: | 1936 |
| Style of architecture: | Colonial Revival |
| Architect(s): | |
| Landscape architect(s): | |
| House extant: yes | |
| Historical notes: | |

*front facade, 2000*

Roy Bertram Morse was the son of Edward Phinley and Ada Margaret Gavel Morse, Sr., who resided at *Red Gables* in Water Mill. [*See* Spinzia, *Long Island's Prominent Families in the Town of Southampton* – Morse entry.]

Roy's brother Edward Phinley Morse, Jr. was disinherited as a result of a law suit which he brought against their father for his share of the profits from their father's Brooklyn firm, the Morse Dry Dock and Repair Company.

\*At the time of Roy's death, United Dry Docks Inc. controlled fifty percent of all dry dock facilities in the Port of New York. [*Newsday* October 16, 1953, p. 125.]

Roy Bertram and Margaret Bixby Morse's daughter Ada married Haden Weller and resided in Northport.

## Moyers, Bill (b. 1934)

Occupation(s):
clergy - ordained Baptist minister
journalist - reporter, *Marshall News Messenger*, Marshall, TX, 1950;
reporter, *The Daily Texan*
publisher - *Newsday*, 1967-70
politician - personal assistant to Senator Lyndon Baines Johnson, 1960-61;
associate director of public affairs, Peace Corps, 1961-62;
deputy director, Peace Corps, 1963;
special assistant to President Lyndon Baines Johnson, 1963-67;
informal White House Chief of Staff, 1964-67;
White House Press Secretary, 1965-67
entertainers and associated professions -
assistant news editor, KTBC Radio and Television Station;
anchor, *USA: People and Politics*, 1976;
editor and chief correspondent, *CBS Reports*, 1976-80;
senior news analyst and commentator, *CBS Evening News With Dan Rather*, 1981-86;
executive editor and co-founder, with his wife Judith, Public Affairs Television, Inc., 1986 (television program production company);
host, *Bill Moyer's Journal*, PBS, 1971-76, 1978-81, 2007-2010;
host, *Now With Bill Moyers*, PBS;
host, *The Power of Myth*, PBS, 1988;
senior analyst and commentator, *NBC News*, 1995;
host, *Insight*, MSNBC, 1996;
host, *Wide Angle*, PBS, 2005;
host, *Faith and Reason*, PBS, 2006;
host, *Moyers on America*, PBS, 2006;
*
writer- *Listening To America: A Traveler Rediscovers His Country* (co-author), 1971;
*Of Kennedys and Kings: Making Sense of the Sixties* (co-author), 1980;
*Report From Philadelphia: The Constitutional Convention of 1787*, 1987;
*The Secret Government*, 1988;
*Joseph Campbell and the Power of Myth*, 1988;
*A World of Ideas II: Public Opinions From Private Citizens*, 1989;
*Healing and the Mind*, 1993;
*The Language of Life: A Festival of Poets*, 1995;
*Genesis: A Living Conversation* (co-author), 1996;
*Fooling With Words: A Celebration of Poets and Their Craft*, 1999

Civic Activism:
president, Schuman Center for Media and Democracy

Marriage(s):
1954 – Judith Suzanne Davidson
- entertainers and associated professions –
president and co-founder, with her husband Bill, Public Affairs Television, Inc., 1986 (television program production company)
capitalist - director, Columbia Residential Realty, Inc.;
director, Ogden Corporation (service-oriented firm)
financier - director of mutual funds, Capital Group, Pain Webber
Civic Activism: member, White House Commission on Children;
United States Commissioner to UNESCO;
trustee and vice-chairman, State University of New York;
trustee, Hofstra University, Hempstead;
director, Research Foundation of New York State;
director, Rockefeller Institute of Government;
a founder, Day Care Council of Nassau County;
member, National Governor's Association Task Force on Education and Economic Development

## Moyers, Bill (cont'd)

Address: 76 Fourth Street, Garden City
Name of estate:
Year of construction: 1932
Style of architecture: Dutch Colonial Revival
Architect(s):
Landscape architect(s):
House extant: yes
Historical notes:

Bill Moyers, born Billy Don Moyers, is the son of John Henry and Ruby Johnson Moyers of Marshall, TX.

Bill and Judith Suzanne Davidson Moyers' son William Cope Moyers married Kathleen Connolly Ahearne, the daughter of Allan J. Ahearne of Garden City.

*Moyers received the Lifetime Achievement Award of the National Television Academy. Over the years he has received over thirty Emmys and virtually every other major award for television journalism.

In 1968 the house was remodeled.

*front facade, 2008*

## Mulford, Charles William (c. 1825-1912)

Occupation (s):

Marriage(s): 1853-1909 – Deborah Wickes (c. 1825-1909)

Address: Fulton Avenue, Hempstead
Name of estate: *Langsyne*
Year of construction:
Style of architecture:
Architect(s):
Landscape architect(s): Ruth Bramley Dean, c. 1917
   (for F. Mulford)
House extant: unconfirmed
Nassau County Museum Collection has photographs of the estate.
Historical notes:

Charles William Mulford, who made his fortune in the 1849 California Gold Rush, was the son of Charles Lewis and Millie Cook Mulford of Rensselaerville, NY.

Deborah Wickes Mulford was the daughter of Dr. Platt and Mrs. Fanny Wickes of Rensselaerville, NY.

Charles William and Deborah Wickes Mulford's daughter Helen died in 1862 at the age of three. Their daughters Harriet and Fannie, who resided together at the estate after their parents died, never married.

*garden, c. 1921*

### Mumford, Philip Gurdon (1874-1951)

| | |
|---|---|
| Occupation(s): | industrialist - president and chairman of board, American Machine & Metals, Inc.; |
| | director, South Porto Rico Sugar Co.; |
| | president, Commercial Solvents Co.; |
| | director, Union Bag and Paper Co.; |
| | director, General Public Service Corp. |
| | financier - partner, William Schall Co. (investment banking firm); |
| | director, Peninsula National Bank, Cedarhurst |
| Marriage(s): | 1901-1951 – Carmen Atocha Davis (1874-1963) |
| Address: | Barret Road, Lawrence |
| Name of estate: | *Journey's End* |
| Year of construction: | |
| Style of architecture: | |
| Architect(s): | |
| Landscape architect(s): | |
| House extant: | unconfirmed |
| Historical notes: | |

The *Long Island Society Register, 1929* lists Philip G. and Carmen Atocha Davis Mumford as residing at *Journey's End* in Cedarhurst [Lawrence]. The 1930 Census lists the Mumfords at this address.

He was the son of George E. and Julia Emma Hills Mumford.

Carmen Atocha Davis Mumford was the daughter of George Whitefield and Caren Atocha Davis.

The Mumfords' daughter Carmen remained unmarried.

### Munson, Lawrence Josiah (1878-1950)
### aka Lauritz Josiah Munsen

| | |
|---|---|
| Occupation(s): | educator - director, Munson School of Music, Brooklyn |
| Civic Activism: | secretary, American Guild of Organists |
| Marriage(s): | M/1 – 1905-1929 – Anna Josephine Lee (1884-1929) |
| | (aka Anna Georgine Lee) |
| | M/2 – Claire Adele Burkhart (1884-1944) |
| | - Civic Activism: vice-president, Woman's Missionary Society of Marble Collegiate Church, NYC; |
| | vice-president, Women's Board for Missions of the Reformed Church of America; |
| | chairman and treasurer, Women's Personnel Service Relief Committee; |
| | recording secretary, New York branch, Women's Foreign Missionary Society |
| Address: | 117 Meadbrook Road, Garden City |
| Name of estate: | |
| Year of construction: | 1927 |
| Style of architecture: | Neo-Tudor |
| Architect(s): | |
| Landscape architect(s): | |
| House extant: | yes |
| Historical notes: | |

*front facade, 2003*

The *Long Island Society Register, 1929* lists Lawrence J. and Anne G. [sic] Lee Munson as residing at 117 Meadbrook Road, Garden City.

He was the son of Lewis Lauritz Christian and Anna Ingethal Josephine Pederadatter Halling Monsen.

Anna Josephine Lee Munson was the daughter Hans Halvorsen Skjold and Maren Jorgensen Wold Lee of Hempstead.

Lawrence Josiah and Anna Josephine Lee Munson's daughter Marion married Jean Pasquet, the son of Leon and Dorothy Ekart Pasquet, and resided in Garden City. Their daughter Anne married Charles Richards Leake III and resided in Radburn, NJ. Their son Henry married Monique Ghislaine Ruzette, the daughter of Baron Etienne Ruzette of Belgium, and resided in Manhattan. Their son Alexander married Bertha Louise Greer, the daughter of Eugene and Anne Bertha Dawson Greer, and resided in Lloyd Harbor. Their son Lawrence Shipley Munson married Gretchen Thannhauser, the daughter of Dr. Siegfried Joseph and Mrs. Franziska Reiner Thannhauser.

In 2003, the 2,352-square-foot house sold for $885,000.

Claire Adele Burkhart has previously been married to Fred A. Tucker.

### Murphy, William Gordon, Jr. (1885-1954)

| | |
|---|---|
| Occupation(s): | attorney - partner, Olin, Clark, and Phelps |
| | capitalist - president and director, various real estate corporations |
| | financier - trustee, Williamsburgh Savings Bank |
| Civic Activism: | mayor, Village of Garden City; |
| | trustee and secretary, Wesleyan University, Middletown, CT |
| Marriage(s): | 1911 – Mary Billings Stoddard (b. 1888) |
| Address: | Seventh Street, Garden City |
| Name of estate: | |
| Year of construction: | |
| Style of architecture: | |
| Architect(s): | |
| Landscape architect(s): | |
| House extant: unconfirmed | |
| Historical notes: | |

The *Long Island Society Register, 1929* lists William Gordon and Mary B. Stoddard Murphy [Jr.] as residing on Seventh Street, Garden City.

He was the son of William Gordon and Mary Hett Shepherd Murphy, Sr. of Brooklyn.

Mary Billings Stoddard Murphy was the daughter of Orrin Edward Stoddard of Middletown, CT,

William Gordon and Mary Billings Stoddard Murphy, Jr.'s daughter Martha married Henry Lee Ferguson, Jr. of Fishers Island. Their son Gordon married Nancy Mulford, the daughter of Allen and Marion Bush Mulford of Manhattan.


### Murray, Francis King (1895-1929)

| | |
|---|---|
| Occupation(s): | educator - master, Phillips Andover Academy, Andover, MA |
| Marriage(s): | 1920-1929 – Dorothy Maitland Lee Fuller Griggs (1899-1958) |
| Address: | 41 Hilton Avenue, Garden City |
| Name of estate: | |
| Year of construction: | 1883 |
| Style of architecture: | French Empire |
| Architect(s): | |
| Landscape architect(s): | |
| House extant: yes | |
| Historical notes: | |

The *Long Island Society Register, 1929* lists Francis King and Dorothy M. L. Griggs Murray as residing at 41 Hilton Avenue, Garden City.

He was the son of Augustus Taber and Nella Howland Gifford Murray of Palo Alto, CA.

Dorothy Maitland Lee Fuller Griggs Murray was the daughter of Maitland Fuller Griggs of Ardsley-on-Hudson, NY.

Francis King and Dorothy Maitland Lee Fuller Griggs Murray's son Douglas, who resided in Fort Collins, CO, married Pauline Kirkpatrick; Kathryn Parker; and, subsequently, Molly Brown. Their daughter Mary, who resided in California, married Dr. L. Martin Griffin, Jr., and, later, Clinton Jones III.

*front facade, 2006*

### Murray, Herman Stump (1888-1965)

Occupation(s): capitalist - president, Kalak Water Co., NY
industrialist - president, Oriental Silk Printing Co.

Marriage(s): 1916-1965 – Susanne Elizabeth Warren (1893-1971)
- Civic Activism: vice-president, Lawrence Garden Club, 1938

Address: 993 East Broadway, Woodmere
Name of estate: *Our House*
Year of construction: 1916
Style of architecture: 20th Century
Architect(s):
Landscape architect(s):
House extant: yes
Historical notes:

*front facade, 2000*

The *Long Island Society Register, 1929* lists Herman S. and Susanne E. Warren Murray as residing at *Our House* in Woodmere.
He was the son of Russell and Rosa Neilson Murray.
Susanne Elizabeth Warren Murray was the daughter of Charles Elliott and Anna Margaret Geissenhainer Warren, Sr. of *Still Pond* in Hewlett Neck.
Herman Stump and Susanne Elizabeth Warren Murray's daughter Susanne married Francis Hine Low, the son of Ethelbert Ide and Gertrude Herrick Low of Lawrence. Their daughter Anna married Charles Taylor Lovering III, the son of Joseph Swaine and Elizabeth Bacon Lovering II of *Sunny Ridge* in Hewlett Harbor. Their son Russell Murray II married Sally Gardiner, the daughter of George N. Gardiner.

### Myers, Charles (1848-1935)

Occupation(s): financier - Mutual Life Insurance Co.;
a founder, Federal Insurance Company of Jersey City;
trustee, Marine Insurance Company Ltd., London, England

Marriage(s): 1877-1920 – Anna Freeborn (1857-1920)

Address: Fulton Avenue, Hempstead
Name of estate:
Year of construction:
Style of architecture:
Architect(s):
Landscape architect(s):
House extant: unconfirmed
Historical notes:

The *Social Register New York, 1906* lists Charles and Anna Freeborn Myers as residing in Hempstead.
He was the son of William B. and Julia Myers of Hempstead.
Charles and Ann Freeborn Myers' daughter Jeannett married Colgate Hoyt, Jr., the son of Colgate and Lida Sherman Hoyt, Sr. of *Eastover* on Centre Island, and resided at *Meadow Spring* in Glen Cove. [*See* Spinzia, *Long Island's Prominent North Shore Families, vol. 1* – Hoyt entries.] Their daughter Mary married Alden S. Blodget, the son of Henry Townsend Blodget, and resided in Setauket. Their daughter Annie married Latham Ralston Reed, the son of Latham Gallup and Mary Newbold Welsh Reed of Manhattan, and resided at *Fair Lea Villa* in Southampton. [*See* Spinzia, *Long Island's Prominent Families in the Town of Southampton* – Reed entry.] In 1887, their son Charles Freeborn Myers died at the age of nine. Their daughter Lucy died at the age of fourteen months in 1894. Their son Arthur, who died in 1917 at the age of thirty-one, was discharged from the army suffering from shell shock.

### Naething, Charles Frederick (1852-1913)

| | |
|---|---|
| Occupation(s): | attorney |
| Marriage(s): | 1880-1913 – Mary Louise Bingham (1855-1938)<br>- Civic Activism: chairman, Ways and Means Committee, Interdenominational Guild for the Aid of Crippled Children of the Poor |
| Address: | 111 Seventh Street, Garden City |
| Name of estate: | |
| Year of construction: | |
| Style of architecture: | Condominium |
| Architect(s): | |
| Landscape architect(s): | |
| House extant: yes | |
| Historical notes: | |

The *Long Island Society Register, 1929* lists Mrs. Charles Frederick Naething as residing at 111 Seventh Street, Garden City.
    She was the daughter of Samuel Dexter and Mary Heister Keyser Bingham, Sr.
    Charles Frederick Naething was the son of John and Maria Elizabeth Seil Naething of NYC.
    Charles Frederick and Mary Louise Bingham Naething's daughter Rose married Roderic Barbour Barnes, the son of Richard S. Barnes of Manhattan, and resided at *Abbot House* in Washington, CT. Rose later married Arthur Cort Holden, the son of Edwin Babcock and Alice Cort Holden. Their son Foster married Frances Witter Lyon, the daughter of Daniel L. and Lina T. Lyon and, later Frances Mary Newman, the daughter of Robert Morris and Kate Smith Newman.


### Neilson, Robert Hude (1882-1940)

| | |
|---|---|
| Occupation(s): | attorney - member, Cravath, Henderson, and de Gersdorff, NYC;<br>    partner, Wickes and Neilson, NYC;<br>industrialist - director, Thomas Strahan Co., Chelsea, MA;<br>    director, White Rock Mineral Springs Co.;<br>    director, Blue Ridge Slate Corp. |
| Civic Activism: | trustee, Rutgers University, New Brunswick, NJ;<br>president of board, Harlem House, NYC;<br>trustee, Home for Old Men and Aged Couples, NYC;<br>trustee, Public Education Association;<br>director, Legal Aid Society, 1930-1940 |
| Marriage(s): | 1908-1931 – Sarah Elizabeth Russell (1885-1931) |
| Address: | *[unable to determine street address]*, Woodmere |
| Name of estate: | |
| Year of construction: | |
| Style of architecture: | |
| Architect(s): | |
| Landscape architect(s): | |
| House extant: unconfirmed | |
| Historical notes: | |

The *Long Island Society Register, 1929* lists Robert Hude and Sarah E. Russell Neilson as residing in Woodmere.
    He was the son of Henry Augustus and Joanna Bayard Neilson of New Brunswick, NJ.
    Sarah Elizabeth Russell Neilson was the daughter of Joseph B. Russell of Cambridge, MA.
    Robert Hude and Sarah Elizabeth Russell Neilson's daughter Lillian married George H. Day II and, subsequently, George Mason Newick with whom she resided in Providence, RI. Their daughters Joanna and Sarah remained unmarried.

### Newton, Arthur Ulysses (1892-1978)

| | |
|---|---|
| Occupation(s): | merchant - founder and owner, Arthur U. Newton Galleries, NYC |
| Civic Activism: | member, Inter-Allied Plebiscite and Government Commission, Upper Silesia, 1920-1922 |

Marriage(s):
- M/1 – 1926-1958 – Grace Hamilton (d. 1958)
- M/2 – 1959-1960 – Margaret Wood (1893-1960)
  - (aka Margot White)
  - artist*
- M/3 – 1962-1975 – Helen Davidson (d. 1975)

Address: Chauncey Lane, Lawrence
Name of estate:
Year of construction:
Style of architecture:
Architect(s):
Landscape architect(s):
House extant: unconfirmed
Historical notes:

Arthur Ulysses Newtown was the son of Adolph and Kate Mehesy Newton of Manhattan.

Margaret Wood Newton was the daughter of Dr. Robert Williams and Gertrude Ames Wood, Jr. of East Hampton. [*See* Spinzia, *Long Island's Prominent Families in the Town of East Hampton* – Wood entry.] Margaret had previously been married to Victor Gerald White, Sr. with whom she resided in Lawrence. Her sister Elizabeth married Edward Osgood Bogart and resided in East Hampton. [*See* Spinzia, *Long Island's Prominent Families in the Town of East Hampton* – Bogart entry.]

*Margaret's painting of President Franklin Delano Roosevelt is in the Harvard Club in New York City. She also did paintings of Gordon Hoxie, the provost of C. W. Post College of Long Island University, and Truden Thomas, a dean of Hofstra University.

Helen Davidson Newton had previously been married to ____ Craig and to E. Kellogg Baird.


### Nichols, John Dykers (1891-1964)

Occupation(s):

Marriage(s): 1918-1964 – Mary Delia Francklyn (1892-1977)

Address: Johnson Place, Woodmere
Name of estate: *Nicholyn*
Year of construction:
Style of architecture:
Architect(s):
Landscape architect(s):
House extant: unconfirmed
Historical notes:

The *Long Island Society Register, 1929* lists John Dykers and Mary D. Francklyn Nichols as residing at *Nicholyn* in Hewlett [Woodmere]. The 1920 Census lists the Nicholses at this address.

He was the son of Romaine Charles and Amelia Echeverria Nichols of Bernardsville, NJ, and a descendant of Sir Richard Nichols, First Colonial Governor of New York.

Mary Delia Francklyn Nichols was the daughter of Reginald H. and Agnes Virginia Binsse Francklyn of New York. Mary's brother Reginald Gebhard Francklyn, who resided in Hewlett Harbor, married Lilian Endicott and, subsequently, Mary Culbertson Kilbreth.

John Dykers and Mary Delia Franklyn Nichols' daughter Leta married Hugh Montgomery Adams, the son of Thomas S. Adams of Rumson, NJ. Their daughter Anna married Charles F. Schaefer, the son of Charles Schaefer of Hewlett Harbor. Their daughter Helen married Ashton Harvey Baker, the son of David S. and Dorothy Harvey Baker, Sr. Their daughter Virginia married Robert J. Pike, the son of Frederick H. Pike of Hewlett. Their daughter Nancy married John T. Savage.

## Nichols, John Treadwell (1883-1958)

| | |
|---|---|
| Occupation(s): | scientist - ichthyologist - |
| |     assistant, Department of Mammals, American Museum of Natural |
| |         History, NYC, 1907-1908; |
| |     assistant. United States Bureau of Fishes, 1908-1909; |
| |     assistant, Department of Fishes, American Museum of Natural |
| |         History, NYC, 1909-1918; |
| |     associate curator, American Museum of Natural History, NYC, |
| |         1919-1927; |
| |     curator, American Museum of Natural History, NYC |
| | writer - *Long Island Fauna and Flora,* 1913 (co-author); |
| |     *Long Island Fauna,* 1916; |
| |     *Fresh Water Fishes of the Congo Basin Obtained by the* |
| |         *American Museum,* 1917; |
| |     *Fishes of the Vicinity of New York City,* 1918; |
| |     *On a Collection of Marine Fishes From Peru,* 1922 (co-author); |
| |     *Representative North American Fresh Water Fishes,* 1942; |
| |     *Fresh Water Fishes of China,* 1943; |
| |     *Fishes and Shells of the Pacific World,* 1945; |
| |     over 950 articles in scientific journals |
| Marriage(s): | 1910-1958 – Cornelia DuBois Floyd (1881-1977) |
| Address: | 116 Ninth Street, Garden City |
| Name of estate: | |
| Year of construction: | |
| Style of architecture: | |
| Architect(s): | |
| Landscape architect(s): | |
| House extant: no | |
| Historical notes: | |

    The *Long Island Society Register, 1929* lists John Treadwell and Cornelia DuBois Floyd Nichols as residing at 116 Ninth Street, Garden City.
    He was the son of John White Treadwell and Mary Blake Slocum Nichols, who resided at *The Kettles* in Cove Neck. His brother George Nichols, Sr., who resided at *Uplands* in Cold Spring Harbor, married Jane N. Morgan, the daughter of John Pierpont and Jane Grew Morgan, Jr. of *Matinecock Point* on East Island in Glen Cove. His sister Elizabeth married Edwin Pemberton Taylor, Jr. and resided at *White Oaks* in Oyster Bay Cove. His sister Susan married Harold Trowbridge Pulsifer, the son of Nathan Trowbridge and Almira Houghton Valentine Pulsifer, and resided at *Cooper's Bluff* in Cove Neck. His brother William married Isabel Bruce and resided at *Four Winds* in Laurel Hollow. His sister Helen married Mansfield Esterbrook. [*See* Spinzia, *Long Island's Prominent North Shore Families, vol. I* – Morgan entry – and *vol. II* – Nichols, Pulsifer, and Taylor entries.]
    Cornelia DuBois Floyd Nichol was a descendent of William Floyd of Mastic Beach, a signer of the Declaration of Independence. The Floyds' Mastic Beach estate is open to the public under the auspices of the National Park Service. [*See* Spinzia, *Long Island: A Guide to New York's Suffolk and Nassau Counties* – William Floyd Estate, Mastic Beach.]
    John Treadwell and Cornelia DuBois Floyd Nichols' daughter Mary married David Weld, the son of Francis Minot and Margaret Low White Weld, Jr. of *Lulworth* in Lloyd Harbor, and resided in Nissequogue. [*See* Spinzia, *Long Island's Prominent North Shore Families, vol. II* – Weld entry.] Their son John Slocum Nichols, Sr. married Jarvis Gilbert, the daughter of Cass Gilbert, Jr. of Greenwich, CT. Their son William Floyd Nichols married Catherine Gallatin Gay, the daughter of Charles Merrick Gay of Philadelphia, PA. Their son David Gelston Nichols married Monique Robert Le Braz, the daughter of Marius Robert Le Braz of Paris, France.

### Nicoll, De Lancey, Jr. (1892-1957)

| | |
|---|---|
| Occupation(s): | attorney - counsel for United States Mail Steamship Co., Ford Motor Co., and General Motors Corp. |
| | capitalist - established muskrat farm in Calverton |
| Civic Activism: | president, board of trustees (1927) and mayor, Village of Hewlett Harbor |
| Marriage(s): | M/1 – 1913-div. 1934 – Alma C. Hayde (1891-1963) |
| | M/2 – 1934-div. 1945 – Mary Esther White (b. 1898) |
| | M/2 – 1945-1957 – Fern Newbern (1904-2004) |
| Address: | Auerbach Avenue, Hewlett Harbor |
| Name of estate: | *Three Acres* |
| Year of construction: | |
| Style of architecture: | |
| Architect(s): | |
| Landscape architect(s): | |
| House extant: unconfirmed | |
| Historical notes: | |

The *Long Island Society Register, 1929* lists DeLancey [sic] and Alma C. Hyde [sic] Nicoll as residing at *Three Acres* in Hewlett [Hewlett Harbor].

He was the son of De Lancey and Maud Churchill Nicoll, Sr. of *Windymere* in Southampton. [*See* Spinzia, *Long Island's Prominent Families in the Town of Southampton* – Nicoll entry.]

Alma C. Hayde Nicoll was the daughter of John Hayde.

De Lancey and Alma C. Hayde Nicoll, Jr.'s daughter Cuyler married Dexter Spear French and resided in Coconut Grove, FL. Their daughter Alma married R. Palmer Baker, Jr. and resided in Manhattan. Their son De Lancey Nicoll III married Alice V. Fullerton and resided at *White Haven* in Church Creek, MD. Their daughter Mary married Benjamin F. Lucas.

Mary Esther White Nicoll was the daughter of George Wagner White of Washington, DC. She had previously been married to Charles George Moller III with whom she resided in Lawrence.

Fern Newbern Nicoll was the daughter of Frederick L. and Addie May Newbern. Fern later married Brian J. Ingoldsby, Sr.

### Niles, George Casper (1872-1960)

| | |
|---|---|
| Occupation(s): | capitalist - secretary, Ann Arbor Railroad Co., MI; Detroit, Southern Railroad Co.; and Detroit, Toledo, Ironton Railroad Co. |
| Marriage(s): | 1903-1947 – Maud Louise Nicholas (1879-1947) |
| Address: | 74 Auerbach Lane, Lawrence |
| Name of estate: | |
| Year of construction: | |
| Style of architecture: | |
| Architect(s): | |
| Landscape architect(s): | |
| House extant: no | |
| Historical notes: | |

The *Long Island Society Register, 1929* lists G. Casper and Maud L. Nicholas Niles as residing at *Cross Cottage* in Bridgehampton. [*See* Spinzia, *Long Island's Prominent Families in the Town of Southampton* – Niles entry.] The *Social Register New York, 1939* lists their residence as 74 Auerbach Lane, Lawrence.

He was the son of George E. Niles of Boston, MA.

Maud Louise Nicholas Niles was the daughter of Harry Ingersoll and Alice Hollins Nicholas, Sr. of *Virginia Farm* in Babylon. Maude's brother Harry Ingersoll Nicholas II married Dorothy Snow, the daughter of Frederick A. and Mary Palen Snow of *Gardenside* in Southampton, and resided at *Rolling Hill Farm* in Muttontown. Her sister Beatrice married Edward Nicoll Townsend, Jr. of Garden City. Her sister Rita married Uriel Atwood Murdock II and resided in Babylon. Her sister Daisy married Grosvenor Nicholas and resided in Old Westbury. Her sister Elsie married Alonzo Potter II and resided at *Harbor House* in St. James and *Westmoor* in Southampton. Her sister Evelyn married Alexander Duncan Cameron Arnold, Sr. of West Islip and, subsequently, Joseph Hutchinson Stevenson with whom she resided at *The Farm* in Hewlett Bay Park. [*See* Spinzia, *Long Island's Prominent North Shore Families, vol. II* – Nicholas entry; *Long Island's Prominent South Shore Families* – Arnold, Murdock, and Nicholas entries; and *Long Island's Prominent Families in the Town of Southampton* – Potter and Snow entries.]

George Casper and Maud Louise Nicholas Niles' son Nicholas married Marian Lawrence Freeman, the daughter of Leon S. Freeman of Morristown, NJ, and resided in Mendham, NJ. Their daughter Elsie married David Henry McWayne, the son of Henry Page and Clara May Fisher McWayne. Their daughters Maude and Marjorie did not marry.

### Norris, Alfred Lockwood (1868-1933)

| | |
|---|---|
| Occupation(s): | financier -   partner, James M. Oliphant Brokerage Co. |
| Civic Activism: | a founder, National Golf Club, Southampton |
| Marriage(s): | 1901-1933 – Florence Middleton Lee (1877-1961) |
| Address: | 250 Causeway, Lawrence |
| Name of estate: | |
| Year of construction: | |
| Style of architecture: | |
| Architect(s): | |
| Landscape architect(s): | |
| House extant: | no |
| Historical notes: | |

    The *Long Island Society Register, 1929* lists Alfred Lockwood and Florence M. Lee Norris as residing in Lawrence. The 1930 Census lists the Norrises at this address.
    He was the son of John Brodhead and Mary Reynard Norris of Brooklyn.
    Florence Middleton Lee Norris was the daughter of Donald Stevens Lane Lee.
    Alfred Lockwood and Florence Middleton Lee Norris' son Donald married Catherine Fuller and resided in Hewlett Bay Park. Their son Alfred Oliphant Norris married Adeline Emily Greenleaf and resided in Lawrence. Their daughter Florence married Robert Sage Sloan II, the son of Thomas Donaldson and Helen de Russy Clark Sloan of *Wilton Gables* in Lawrence, and resided in Georgetown, VA. Their son Nathaniel married Adel Reynal, the daughter of Eugene Sugny Reynal of New York, and resided at *Twin Harbor* in Bayville.
*[See following two entries for additional family information.]*


### Norris, Alfred Oliphant (b. 1901)

| | |
|---|---|
| Occupation(s): | capitalist -   American Water Co., Havana Cuba |
| Marriage(s): | 1929 – Adeline Emily Greenleaf (b. 1908) |
| Address: | 70 Causeway, Lawrence |
| Name of estate: | |
| Year of construction: | 1897 |
| Style of architecture: | Eclectic |
| Architect(s): | William Adams, Jr. designed the house (for A. O. Norris) |
| Landscape architect(s): | |
| House extant: | yes |
| Historical notes: | |

*front facade, 2008*

    The house was built by Alfred Oliphant Norris.
    The *Social Register New York, 1933* lists Alfred Oliphant and Adeline Emily Greenleaf Norris as residing at 70 Causeway, Lawrence.
    He was the son of Alfred Lockwood and Florence Middleton Lee Norris of Lawrence.
    Adeline Emily Greenleaf Norris was the daughter of John Cameron and Marion Constance Bacon Greenleaf, Sr. of Hewlett. Adeline subsequently married Elias C. Atkins with whom she resided in Bedford Village, NY.
    Alfred Oliphant and Adeline Emily Greenleaf Norris' daughter Emily married Cornelius Oscar Alig, Jr. of Indianapolis, IN, and, later, Gilbert S. Daniels.
*[See previous and following entries for additional family information.]*
    The house was later owned by William Adams III, who called it *Landfall*, and, subsequently, by Stephen Baker Finch. In 2006 the house was remodeled.

### Norris, Donald Lee, Sr. (1903-1967)

| | |
|---|---|
| Occupation(s): | financier - partner, James M. Oliphant and Co. (stock brokerage firm) |
| Marriage(s): | 1930 – Catherine Fuller (1907-2004) |
| Address: | Woodside Drive, Hewlett Bay Park |
| Name of estate: | |
| Year of construction: | |
| Style of architecture: | |
| Architect(s): | |
| Landscape architect(s): | |
| House extant: | unconfirmed |

Historical notes:

The *Social Register New York, 1951* lists Donald Lee and Catherine Fuller Norris [Sr.] as residing on Woodside Drive, Hewlett [Hewlett Bay Park].

He was the son of Alfred Lockwood and Florence Middleton Lee Norris of Lawrence.

Catherine Fuller Norris was the daughter of Paul and Marie Augustine de Florez Fuller, Jr. of *Four Winds* in Hewlett. Her sister Cecile married John Hurd, the son of George Fred and Mary Burnett Hurd of Lawrence. Her sister Marie married Louis King Timolat, the son of James Guyon Timolat, Sr. of Red Bank, NJ.

Donald Lee and Catherine Fuller Norris, Sr.'s daughter Catrina married John Powell Garvey, the son of Clifford P. Garvey, and, later, Walter Russell Herrick, Jr. Their son Donald Lee Norris, Jr. married Martha Loretta Young.

*[See previous two entries for additional family information.]*

### O'Brien, Justin Cameron (1890-1957)

| | |
|---|---|
| Occupation(s): | capitalist - president, O'Brien Homes, Inc. (construction firm)*; president, Justin C. O'Brien Co. (construction firm)**; director and vice-president, Madison Avenue Corp; director and vice-president, Fifth Street Co.; president, Nellis–O'Brien Realty Development Corp.; president, Hamilton Realty Association |
| | financier - director, United States Bond and Mortgage Co. |
| | publisher - director, Hamilton Press |
| Marriage(s): | 1926-1957 – Dorothy Buck (1895-1974) |
| Address: | Garfield Street, Garden City |
| Name of estate: | |
| Year of construction: | c. 1940 |
| Style of architecture: | |
| Architect(s): | |
| Landscape architect(s): | |
| Builder: | O'Brien Homes, Inc. |
| House extant: | unconfirmed |

Historical notes:

The house was built by Justin Cameron O'Brien.

The *Long Island Society Register,* 1929 list Justin Cameron and Dorothy Buck O'Brien as residing in Southampton. Both of their residences, *Eastwind* and *Westwind,* were on Beach Road, Southampton.

He was the son of Judge Morgan Joseph and Mrs. Rose Mary Crimmins O'Brien, Jr. of *Rosecrest* in Hampton Bays and *Villa Mille Fiori* in Southampton. Judge O'Brien served on New York State's Supreme Court and, New York State's Appellate Court. Justin's brother Kenneth married Katherine Mackay, the daughter of Charles Hungerford and Katherine Duer Mackay of *Harbor Hill* in Roslyn, and resided at *Chateau O'Brien* in Southampton. Their brother Esmond, who resided in Southampton, married Mary P. Weightman and, later, Charlotte Troope. Their sister Rosalie married Dr. Henry James, Sr. and resided at *Grey Cottage* in Southampton. Their sister Madeline married Stuart Duncan Preston, Sr., the son of William D. and Annie Fargo Preston, and resided at *Miramichi* in Southampton. [*See* Spinzia, *Long Island's Prominent North Shore Families, vol. 1* – Mackay entry – and *Long Island's Prominent Families in the Town of Southampton* – James, O'Brien, and Preston entries.]

Dorothy Buck O'Brien was the daughter of the vice-president and director of Bethlehem Steel Company Charles Austin Buck and his wife Josephine Martha Reinch Buck of Bethlehem, PA.

Justin Cameron and Dorothy Buck O'Brien's daughter Patricia married Jerome Edward Shaw, the son of Jerome T. Shaw of Westport, CT. Their daughter Rosemary married Huntington Lyman and, later, Peter Van Slyck of Niantic, CT.

*O'Brien Homes, Inc. is reputed to have built one hundred and fifty homes in Garden City. [*The Brooklyn Daily Eagle* July 28, 1940, p. 27.]

**The Justin C. O'Brien Company is reputed to have built three hundred and twenty-five four-room houses on Larkin Street, Farmingdale Road, and Melville Road in Farmingdale. The architect for the homes was H. Douglas Fiedler of Springfield, MA. [*The New York Times* April 13, 1941, p. RE2.]

**123 Stewart Avenue, Garden City**
*built by* O'Brien Homes Incorporated

*1940*

*front facade, 2000*

**125 Stewart Avenue, Garden City**
*built by* **O'Brien Homes Incorporated**

**IN GARDEN CITY** — T. F. Fletcher, an official of E. R. Squibb & Sons, has purchased this new home in the O'Brien Homes, Inc., development on Garfield St., Garden City. It was designed by Walter D. Spelman, architect.

*1940*

*front facade, 2000*

*1941*

## O'Connor, Eugene Franklin, Jr. (1876-1945)

| | |
|---|---|
| Occupation(s): | attorney - judge |
| Marriage(s): | 1912-1945 – Merrilee Durham (b. 1890) |
| Address: | 145 Brompton Road, Garden City |
| Name of estate: | |
| Year of construction: | 1925 |
| Style of architecture: | Dutch Colonial Revival |
| Architect(s): | |
| Landscape architect(s): | |
| House extant: yes | |
| Historical notes: | |

*front facade, 2001*

The *Long Island Society Register, 1929* lists Eugene F. O'Connor, Jr. as residing at 73 Hilton Avenue, Garden City.

He was the son of Eugene Franklin O'Connor, Sr. of Brooklyn.

Merrilee Durham O'Connor was the daughter of J. Wesley Durham of Philadelphia, PA.

Eugene Franklin and Merrilee Durham O'Connor, Jr.'s daughter Josephine married Victor Neils Agather, the son of Alfonso August Agather of Kalispell, MT. Their son Eugene Franklin O'Connor III married Nancy Benedict Harrison, the daughter of Walter Jones Harrison of Leesburg, VA.

At the time of his death, Eugene Franklin O'Connor, Jr. was residing at 145 Brompton Road, Garden City. [*The New York Times* June 27, 1945, p. 19.]

The Hilton Avenue house was purchased by Mabel Beatrice Littig and, later, by Benjamin Swan Young.

### Ohnewald, George Henry (1880-1925)

| | |
|---|---|
| Occupation(s): | real estate agent - secretary and treasurer, John Reis Co., Brooklyn |
| | capitalist - president, Midwood Associates, Brooklyn (construction firm) |
| Civic Activism: | member, Brooklyn Real Estate Board |
| Marriage(s): | M/1 – 1907 – Lalla Rookh Lewis |
| | M/2 – Betsy Chamberlin |
| Address: | 31 Cathedral Avenue, Garden City |
| Name of estate: | |
| Year of construction: | 1903 |
| Style of architecture: | Neo-Tudor |
| Architect(s): | |
| Landscape architect(s): | |
| House extant: yes | |
| Historical notes: | |

The *Long Island Society Register, 1929* lists Mrs. George H. Ohnewald as residing at 31 Cathedral Avenue, Garden City.

Betsy Chamberlin Ohnewald subsequently married Joseph Terry McCaddon.

George Henry and Betsy Chamberlin Ohnewald's daughter Betsy married Alson Davis Kimball, the son of Frank Allan and Ella Davis Kimball of Garden City. Their daughter Jeanette married John H. White of Douglaston.

*front facade, 2008*

## Olcott, William Morrow Knox (1862-1933)

| | |
|---|---|
| Occupation(s): | attorney - New York District Attorney, 1896-1898; |
| | judge - New York City Court, 1898-1899; |
| | partner, Olcott, Gruber, Bonynge, and McManus; |
| | partner, Olcott, Olcott, and Bonynge |
| | politician - treasurer, Suffolk County, NY; |
| | alderman, New York City, 1894-1896 |
| | capitalist - vice-president, Lawyers Engineering & Surveying Co. |
| | shipping - director, Mary Powell Steamboat Co.; |
| | director, Hudson River Day Line; |
| | director, Hudson River Steamboat Co. |
| | financier - trustee, Maiden Lane Savings Bank |
| | industrialist - vice-president, James Everard's Breweries; |
| | director, James Everard's Companies, Inc. |
| Marriage(s): | M/1 – 1888-1930 – Jessie Augusta Baldwin (1863-1930) |
| | M/2 – 1931-1933 – Florence A. Cobbette (d. 1951) |
| Address: | Valentines Road, Salisbury |
| Name of estate: | *Phoenix Lodge* |
| Year of construction: | |
| Style of architecture: | Modified Colonial Revival |
| Architect(s): | |
| Landscape architect(s): | |
| House extant: | no* |

Historical notes:

William Morrow Knox Olcott headed Harry K. Thaw's legal defense in the Stanford White murder case. [For other Long Island attorneys involved in the case, *see* Spinzia, *Long Island's Prominent North Shore Families, vol. I* – Littleton entry – and *Long Island's Prominent South Shore Families* – Stanchfield entry.]

He was the son of John Nathaniel and Euphema Helen Knox Olcott of New York City.

Jessie Augusta Baldwin Olcott was the daughter of Jessie H. Baldwin.

William Morrow Knox and Jessie Augusta Baldwin Olcott's son Neilson Olcott II married Mary Lattin, the daughter of Homer Arthur and Florence Whitehouse Lattin of Brooklyn.

Florence A. Cobbette Olcott was the daughter of Richard Cobbette.

[For information about the Olcott's estate in Quogue, *see* Spinzia, *Long Island's Prominent Families in the Town of Southampton* – Olcott entry.]

In 1913, Olcott sold the house to Jacques Lebaudy, who continued to call it *Phoenix Lodge*.

*In 1926, the estate was purchased by Lannin Realty Company. In 1935, several of the estate's service buildings were destroyed by fire.

*front facade, c. 1919*

## Olena, Alfred Douglas (1886-1949)

| | |
|---|---|
| Occupation(s): | attorney - partner, Merchant, Olena, and Merchant (later, Merchant, Olena, Buck, and Santomenna) |
| | financier - trustee, Citizens Savings Bank of New York (later, Manhattan Savings Bank) |
| Civic Activism: | chairman, Garden City Board of Zoning Appeals, 1923-1943*; |
| | director, New York State Planning Association; |
| | vice-chairman, Nassau County Commission on Governmental Revision; |
| | chairman, Nassau County Civil Service Commission; |
| | chairman, Garden City Chapter, Boy Scouts of America |
| Marriage(s): | 1914 – Mildred McDonald Armour (b. 1885) |
| Address: | 123 Kensington Road, Garden City |
| Name of estate: | |
| Year of construction: | 1921 |
| Style of architecture: | Colonial Revival |
| Architect(s): | |
| Landscape architect(s): | |
| House extant: | yes |
| Historical notes: | |

*front facade, 2001*

The *Long Island Society Register, 1929* lists Alfred Douglas and Mildred McDonald Armour Olena as residing at 123 Kensington Road, Garden City.

He was the son of Theophilus Douglas and Harriet Hyde Olena of Brooklyn.

Mildred McDonald Armour Olena was the daughter of Theodore Short and Mary Jane McDonald Armour of Manhattan.

Alfred Douglas and Mildred McDonald Armour Olena's daughter Audrey married James Platt Wilderson. Their son Arnold married Nathalie Hawthorne French.

*Olena was chairman of the village commission that drew up Garden City's first zoning ordinance in 1923.

## Olney, Peter Butler, Jr. (1891-1968)

| | |
|---|---|
| Occupation(s): | attorney - Assistant United States District Attorney, Southern District of New York |
| | financier - federal bankruptcy referee, 1922-1949* |
| Civic Activism: | treasurer, Village of Lawrence |
| Marriage(s): | M/1 – 1912 – Amy Cruger (1889-1927) |
| | M/1 – Elizabeth Kirkland Ralph (1886-1947) |
| Address: | Washington Avenue, Lawrence |
| Name of estate: | |
| Year of construction: | |
| Style of architecture: | |
| Architect(s): | |
| Landscape architect(s): | |
| House extant: | unconfirmed |
| Historical notes: | |

The *Long Island Society Register, 1929* lists Peter Butler Olney, Jr. as residing in Cedarhurst [Lawrence].

He was the son of Peter Butler and Mary Sigourney Butler Olney, Sr. of *Meadowside* in Lawrence.

Amy Cruger Olney was the daughter of James Pendleton and Amy Nevans Shepard Cruger.

Peter and Amy Cruger Olney's daughter Amy married Winston Ralph Johnson, the son of Edwin Johnson of Santa Maria, CA, and, later, David Bruce Dell. Their son Peter Butler Olney IV married Elinor Bowman and resided in MA.

In 1921 the Olneys' children, Peter Butler Olney III, age six, and Cornelia, age eight, drowned in the Bouquet River near Elizabethtown, NJ. [*The New York Times*, September 6, 1921, p. 1.]

*[See following two Olney entries for additional family information.]*

*Olney succeeded his father as a federal bankruptcy referee.

### Olney, Peter Butler, Sr. (1843-1922)

| | |
|---|---|
| Occupation(s): | attorney - partner, Olney and Comstock; District Attorney of New York County, 1883-1885 |
| | financier - federal bankruptcy referee, 1898-1922 |
| Civic Activism: | member of commission that revised New York City laws, 1882; trustee, Teachers' College |
| Marriage(s): | 1879-1922 – Mary Sigourney Butler (1850-1928) |
| Address: | Washington Avenue, Lawrence |
| Name of estate: | *Meadowside* |
| Year of construction: | |
| Style of architecture: | |
| Architect(s): | |
| Landscape architect(s): | |
| House extant: unconfirmed | |
| Historical notes: | |

Peter Butler Olney, Sr. was the son of Wilson and Eliza L. Butler Olney of Oxford, MA. Peter's brother Richard was Secretary of State in the administrations of Presidents Cleveland and McKinley.

Peter Butler and Mary Sigourney Butler Olney, Sr.'s son Sigourney married Elizabeth H. Powel and resided in Hewlett. Their son Wilson resided in Hampton, NH. Their son Peter Butler Olney, Jr., who married Amy Cruger and, subsequently, Elizabeth Kirkland Ralph, resided in Lawrence.

In 1921 three of the Olneys' grandchildren drowned in the Bouquet River near Elizabethtown, NJ: Peter Butler Olney III, age six; Cornelia, age eight, and Wilson Olney, Jr., age eight.

*[See previous and following Olney entries for additional family information.]*


### Olney, Sigourney Butler, Sr. (1888-1956)

| | |
|---|---|
| Occupation(s): | attorney - partner, Cullen and Dykeman |
| | capitalist - director, General Public Services Corp. (utility firm) |
| | financier - director, Brooklyn Saving Bank |
| Civic Activism: | director, Legal Aid Society; trustee, Polytechnic Institute of Brooklyn |
| Marriage(s): | 1922-1956 – Elizabeth Hare Powel (1888-1956) |
| Address: | East Rockaway Road, Hewlett Bay Park |
| Name of estate: | |
| Year of construction: | |
| Style of architecture: | |
| Architect(s): | |
| Landscape architect(s): | |
| House extant: unconfirmed | |
| Historical notes: | |

The *Long Island Society Register, 1929* lists Sigourney Butler and Elizabeth H. Powell [sic] Olney [Sr.] as residing on East Rockaway Road, Hewlett [Hewlett Bay Park].

He was the son of Peter Butler and Mary Sigourney Butler Olney, Sr. of *Meadowside* in Lawrence.

Elizabeth Hare Powel Olney was the daughter of Robert J. and Elizabeth Crosby Powel, Sr. of Newport. She had previously been married to William Baillie Fraser Campbell.

Sigourney Butler and Elizabeth Hare Powel Olney, Sr.'s son John resided in Santa Monica, CA. Their son Robert married Joan Paton, the daughter of Dr. R. Townley Paton of New York, and resided in Cold Spring Harbor. Their son Sigourney Butler Olney, Jr. married Ardella Louise Hanman, the daughter of Earl L. Hanman of St. Catherines, Ontario, Canada, and resided on Mercer Island, WA.

At the time of his death, Olney was residing in St. James. [*The New York Times* June 22, 1956, p. 23.]

*[See previous two Olney entries for additional family information.]*

### Orr, Henry Steers (1871-1934)

| | |
|---|---|
| Occupation(s): | merchant - president, John C. Orr Co., Brooklyn (lumber firm) |
| Civic Activism: | a founder and director, Mercy Hospital, Hempstead, 1913; president, Garden City Club, 1911; chairman, Democratic Committee of the Town of Hempstead, 1914; a founder and director, Cherry Valley Club, Garden City, 1916 |
| Marriage(s): | Mary Keenan (b. 1877) - Civic Activism: vice-president, Barat Settlement; director, The Lots for Little Shop; president, Shedowa Garden Club, 1914 |
| Address: | 103 Tenth Street, Garden City |
| Name of estate: | |
| Year of construction: | 1903 |
| Style of architecture: | Dutch Colonial Revival |
| Architect(s): | Aymar Embury II designed the house (for Orr) |
| Landscape architect(s): | |
| House extant: yes | |
| Historical notes: | |

*front facade, 2000*

The house was built by Henry Steers Orr. By 1930 the Orrs had relocated to Old Westbury.

He was the son of John Clifton and Mary Louise Steers Orr, Sr. of Amityville. [*See* Spinzia, *Long Island's Prominent South Shore Families* – Orr entry.]

Mary Keenan Orr was the daughter of John and Delia Gorman Keenan.

Henry Steers and Mary Keenan Orr's son John Clifton Orr II married Cora Legg, the daughter of George Albert Legg of Manhattan, and resided in Mt. Kisco, NY. Their daughter Marie remained unmarried.

Orr sold the house to Harry Steven Hammond, Sr.

### Orvis, Schuyler Adams, Sr. (1892-1976)

| | |
|---|---|
| Occupation(s): | financier - partner, Schuyler A. Orvis and Co., NYC (stock brokerage firm) |
| Civic Activism: | vice-president, New York Chapter, Sons of the American Revolution |
| Marriage(s): | M/1 – 1915-div. – Ina Leland (1890-1948) - Civic Activism: a founder, New York Defense Corp (women ambulance and bus drivers for metropolitan areas during World War I) <br> M/2 – 1929 – Virginia Schnebly (b. 1898) |
| Address: | Oakwood Avenue, Cedarhurst |
| Name of estate: | |
| Year of construction: | |
| Style of architecture: | |
| Architect(s): | |
| Landscape architect(s): | |
| House extant: unconfirmed | |
| Historical notes: | |

The *Long Island Society Register, 1929* lists Schuyler A. Orvis [Sr.] as residing on Oakwood Avenue, Cedarhurst.

He was the son of Edwin Waitstill and Carrie Emerton Orvis.

Ina Leland Orvis subsequently married Thomas Smith.

Schuyler Adams and Ina Leland Orvis, Sr.'s son Schuyler Adams Orvis, Jr. married Pauline St. John, the daughter of Albert St. John of Norwalk, CT, and resided in Norwalk, CT.

Virginia Schnebly Orvis was the daughter of Robert Cox and Katherine Craig Schnebly of Los Angeles, CA. Virginia had previously been married to ____ Ruggles.

### Osborne, Lawrence Woodhull (1879-1960)

| | |
|---|---|
| Occupation(s): | financier -   vice-president, secretary, treasurer, and director, General Electric Employees Security Corp. |
| | capitalist -   a founder and director, Hempstead Plains Co., 1910 (real estate development firm) |
| Civic Activism: | a founder and director, Cherry Valley Club, Garden City, 1916 |
| Marriage(s): | Elizabeth W. Strain (1878-1956) |
| Address: | 109 Arthur Street, Garden City |
| Name of estate: | |
| Year of construction: | 1910 |
| Style of architecture: | Colonial Revival |
| Architect(s): | |
| Landscape architect(s): | |
| House extant: yes | |
| Historical notes: | |

*side / front facade, 2000*

The *Long Island Society Register, 1929* lists Mr. and Mrs. Lawrence Woodhull Osborne as residing on Arthur Street, Garden City.

He was the son of Frank Sayre and Louise Nicoll Smith Osborne.

Elizabeth W. Strain Osborne was the daughter of James K. and Mary H. Smith Strain.

Lawrence Woodhull and Elizabeth W. Strain Osborne's daughter Louise married William Langmore, the son of Wilfred B. Langmore of Manhattan, and resided in Garden City. Their son James married Edith Mortimer, the daughter of Lawrence Mortimer of Garden City, and resided in North Stamford, CT.

At the time of his death, Osborne was residing at 109 Arthur Street, Garden City. [*The New York Times* March 14, 1960, p. 29.]

In 1970 the house was remodeled.


### Osborne, Robert Klipfel (1896-1955)

| | |
|---|---|
| Occupation(s): | financier -   banker |
| Marriage(s): | M/1 – 1917-div. 1935 – Martha S. Warren (1894-1937) |
| | M/2 – 1935-div. – Elizabeth Barrows (1895-1968) |
| | M/3 – 1940-1955 – Irene Ashley (b. 1904) |
| Address: | Broadway, Hewlett Bay Park |
| Name of estate: | |
| Year of construction: | |
| Style of architecture: | |
| Architect(s): | |
| Landscape architect(s): | |
| House extant: unconfirmed | |
| Historical notes: | |

The *Long Island Society Register, 1929* lists Robert K. and Martha S. Warren Osborne as residing in Hewlett [Hewlett Bay Park]. The 1920 Census lists the Osbornes as residing at this address.

He was the son of Thomas Mott and Agnes Devens Osborne of Auburn, NY. Robert's father Thomas Mott Osborne, his grandfather David Munson Osborne, and his brother Charles Devens Osborne served as mayors of Auburn, NY.

Martha S. Warren Osborne was the daughter of Frederick and Estelle Ward Cary Warren of New Haven, CT.

Robert Klipfel and Martha S. Warren Osborne's daughter Anne married Carl Eric Almstrom, the son of Knut Almstrom of Stockholm, Sweden, and, later, ____ Chase with whom she resided in Concord, MA.

Elizabeth Barrows Osborne was the daughter of Howard A. and Anna Ridley Barrows. Elizabeth had previously been married to Theodore E. Pennock, the son of James W. and Amelia Wilson Pennock of Rochester, NY. After her divorce from Robert, she married Arthur Jay Schamehorn, the son of Stephen and Jemima V. Lee Schamehorn.

By 1940 the Osbornes had relocated to Rochester, NY.

### Ossman, John, Jr. (1886-1972)

Occupation(s): merchant - vice-president, James H. Bell & Co., NYC

Marriage(s): 1917-1957 – May Tompkins (1897-1957)
- Civic Activism: treasurer, Garden City–Hempstead Community Club

Address: 65 Kensington Road, Garden City
Name of estate:
Year of construction: 1926
Style of architecture: Colonial Revival
Architect(s):
Landscape architect(s):
House extant: yes
Historical notes:

The house was built by John Ossman, Jr.
The *Long Island Society Register, 1929* lists John and May Tompkins Ossman [Jr.] as residing at 65 Kensington Road, Garden City.
She was the daughter of Charles Carter and Adele L. Lummis Tompkins of Brooklyn.
John and May Tompkins Ossman, Jr.'s daughter Jean married William C. Kerchof of Bogata, NJ.
In 1998 the house was remodeled.

*front facade, 2001*

### Osterhout, Howard (1889-1972)

Occupation(s): attorney
politician - private secretary to New York State Secretary of State Francis M. Hugo
diplomat - member, United States Peace Commission (Hoover administration)

Civic Activism: president, Nassau County Bar Association

Marriage(s): 1921-1959 – Edna Suydam Davison (1894-1959)

Address: 6 Cedar Place, Garden City
Name of estate:
Year of construction: 1918
Style of architecture: Colonial Revival
Architect(s):
Landscape architect(s):
House extant: yes
Historical notes:

The *Long Island Society Register, 1929* lists Howard and Edna Suydam Davison Osterhout as residing at 6 Cedar Place, Garden City.
He was the son of William Burgess Osterhout of Freeport.
Edna Suydam Davison Osterhout was the daughter of The Reverend Dr. William L. Davison of Brooklyn.
Howard and Edna Suydam Davison Osterhout's daughter Miriam married Frederic Rosengarten, Jr. of Chestnut Hill, Philadelphia, PA.
In 1966 the house was remodeled.

*front facade, 2009*

## Otto, Carl Ludwig, Sr. (1877-1972)

Occupation(s): architect - banks and churches*
financier - trustee, Roosevelt Savings Bank, Brooklyn

Marriage(s): 1908-1972 – Lena Martina Retter (1882-1983)
- Civic Activism: vice-president and director, Garden City–
Hempstead Community Club;
donated their historic house to Nassau
County Parks Department**

Address: 225 Mayfair Avenue, Garden City
Name of estate:
Year of construction: c. 1772
Style of architecture: Colonial
Architect(s): Carl Ludwig Otto Sr. designed alterations to his house
Landscape architect(s):
House extant: yes
Nassau County Museum Collection has six uncatalogued photographs of the house.
Historical notes:

*front facade, c. 1926
after Otto's alterations*

Carl Ludwig Otto was the son of John Martin and Agnes Wilhelmina Roehr Otto of Brooklyn.

Lena Martina Retter Otto was the daughter of Wilhelm Julius Arwed and Hallie Josephine Hollingsworth Retter.

Carl Ludwig and Lena Martina Retter Otto, Sr.'s son Carl Ludwig Otto, Jr. was a retired design engineer at the time of his death in 1974. He was residing on Lummi Island in Washington State.

*Carl designed the Church of Notre Dame on Morningside Drive, Manhattan; Brooklyn's Bushwick Presbyterian Church of Peace, Menahan Street; St. John's Church at Covert and Linden Streets, Brooklyn; the Prudential Savings Bank at Broadway and Vernon Avenue, Brooklyn; the Hamburg Savings Bank at Myrtle Avenue and Bleecker Street, Brooklyn; and the Roosevelt Savings Bank at Gates Avenue and Broadway, Brooklyn. [*The New York Times* January 21, 1972, p. 46.]

**The house was originally located in West Hempstead. It was moved Garden City by Otto and was later relocated to Old Bethpage Village Restoration Complex.

*front facade
at Old Bethpage Village Restoration Complex*

**Page, Walter Hines, Sr. (1855-1918)**

| | |
|---|---|
| Occupation(s): | journalist - editor, *Age*; |
| | editor, *Daily Gazette*, St. Louis, MO; |
| | literary editor, *New York World*; |
| | managing editor, *Forum*; |
| | editor, *Atlantic Monthly* |
| | writer - *The Autobiography of a Southerner* [under pseudonym Nicholas Worth] |
| | publisher - a founder, *State Chronicle*, Raleigh, NC; a founder, with Frank Nelson Doubleday, Doubleday, Page, & Co., Garden City (which became Doubleday & Co., Inc.) |
| | diplomat - United States Ambassador to the Court of St. James in Wilson administration |
| Civic Activism: | trustee, Peabody Fund; |
| | member, Southern Education Board; |
| | member, General Education Board |
| Marriage(s): | 1880-1918 – Willa Alice Wilson (1858-1942) |
| Address: | 32 Cathedral Avenue, Garden City |
| Name of estate: | |
| Year of construction: | 1888 |
| Style of architecture: | French Empire |
| Architect(s): | |
| Landscape architect(s): | |
| House extant: yes | |
| Historical notes: | |

Walter Hines Page Sr. was residing in Garden City at the time of his death. [*Who Was Who, vol. 1*, p. 939.] Mildred Smith's *History of Garden City* lists the Pages' address as Cathedral Avenue. He had previously resided on Ocean Avenue in Bay Shore. [*See* Spinzia, *Long Island's Prominent South Shore Families* – Page entry.]

Page was the son of Allison Francis and Catherine Frances Raboteau Page.

Willa Alice Wilson Page was the daughter of Dr. William Wilson of Michigan.

Walter Hines and Willa Alice Wilson Page, Sr.'s daughter Katherine married Charles G. Loring of Boston, MA. Both King George and Queen Mary of Great Britain attended their wedding. [*The New York Times* June 28, 1915, p. 9.] Their son Arthur married Mollie W. Hall and resided at *County Line Farm* in West Hills. [*See* Spinzia, *Long Island's Prominent North Shore Families, vol. II* – Page entry.]

*front facade, 2005*

### Paine, Edward Stetson (1882-1943)

| | |
|---|---|
| Occupation(s): | attorney - partner, Rounds, Hatch, Dillingham, and Debevoise |
| | industrialist - director and secretary, South Porto Rico Sugar; |
| | director, Fabrica Dominica de Tejidos; |
| | director, Humaco Fruit Co.; |
| | a founder, Pan American Industries |
| | capitalist - director, Antilles Navigation Co.; |
| | director, Newport Packing Co. |
| | financier - member, William Schall and Co. (investment banking firm) |
| Marriage(s): | 1907-1929 – Florence Margaret Bragg (1883-1929) |
| Address: | East Rockaway Road, Hewlett Harbor |
| Name of estate: | |
| Year of construction: | |
| Style of architecture: | |
| Architect(s): | |
| Landscape architect(s): | |
| House extant: unconfirmed | |
| Historical notes: | |

The *Long Island Society Register, 1929* lists Edward S. and Florence M. Bragg as residing in Hewlett Bay Park [Hewlett Harbor].

He was the son of Levi Leonard and Jeanette Holmes Paine of Bangor, ME.

Florence Margaret Bragg Paine was the daughter of Charles Frederick and Florence Emma Wingate Bragg of Bangor, ME.

Edward Stetson and Florence Margaret Bragg Paine's son Leonard was killed in the Pacific theater during World War II. Their son Wingate married Mona Maraguita Hewitt, the daughter of Joseph F. and Violet J. Hewitt. In 1911, their one-year-old daughter Jeannette died. Their son Edward Bragg Paine married Louise Mary Mitchell, the daughter of T. Garvey Mitchell of Flushing. Louise later married George Washington Vanderbilt IV, the son of Alfred Gwynne and Margaret Emerson Vanderbilt of *Rynwood* in Old Brookville. [*See* Spinzia, *Long Island's Prominent North Shore Families, vol. I* – Emerson entry]. After his divorce from Louise, Edward married the president of the Bundles for Britain Program Natalie S. Wales, the daughter of Nathaniel B. Wales, Sr. After Edward's death, Natalie married Lord Malcolm Douglas–Hamilton.


### Palmer, E. T. (1816-1906)

| | |
|---|---|
| Occupation(s): | military |
| Marriage(s): | |
| Address: | 105 Ocean Avenue, Lawrence |
| Name of estate: | *Cedarcroft* |
| Year of construction: | c. 1892 |
| Style of architecture: | Queen Anne |
| Architect(s): | |
| Landscape architect(s): | |
| House extant: no; demolished c. 1950 | |
| Historical notes: | |

The house was built by retired British naval officer E. T. Palmer.

It was later owned by Russell Sage who called it, alternately, *Cedarcroft* and *Cedar Croft*. In 1920, May Louise Bamber Marshall purchased the twenty-acre estate which consisted of a main residence, garage, outbuildings, and a three-acre lake and called it *Cedarcroft*. [*The Brooklyn Daily Eagle* April 15, 1920, p. 18.]

*front / side facade*

### Pancake, Carl Oakley (1888-1950)

| | |
|---|---|
| Occupation(s): | financier - assistant secretary, Guaranty Trust Company of New York; chairman, cable department, Guaranty Trust Company of New York |
| Civic Activism: | chairman, telegraph and cable department of the International Chamber of Commerce, 1933; United States technical radio advisor, International Telegraph Conference, Brussels, Belgium, 1928; delegate, National Trade Council to international conference on cable and wire rates, 1938 |
| Marriage(s): | 1912-1950 – Clara Pauline Hoover (1890-1980) |
| Address: | 81 Brompton Road, Garden City |
| Name of estate: | |
| Year of construction: | 1932 |
| Style of architecture: | Neo-Tudor |
| Architect(s): | Olive Frances Tjaden designed the house (for Pancake) |
| Landscape architect(s): | |
| House extant: yes | |
| Historical notes: | |

*front facade, 2001*

The house was built by Carl Oakley Pancake.
He was the son of Henry Wiley and Effie Gertrude Blain Pancake of Ohio.
Clara Pauline Hoover Pancake was the daughter of Peter J. and Melissa Jane Johanna Mault Hoover of Ohio.
Carl Oakley and Clara Pauline Hoover Pancake's son Robert married Edwina Howard Hansfield, the daughter of Frederick H. Hansfield of Garden City.
In 2018, the 3,587-square-foot house, with six bedrooms and three full and two half bathrooms, sold for $1.365 million.

### Pardee, Dr. Ensign Bennett (1853-1917)

| | |
|---|---|
| Occupation(s): | physician |
| Marriage(s): | 1882-1917 – Clara Bigelow Burton (1858-1951) |
| Address: | Ocean Avenue, Lawrence |
| Name of estate: | *Edgewater Cottage* |
| Year of construction: | |
| Style of architecture: | |
| Architect(s): | |
| Landscape architect(s): | |
| House extant: unconfirmed | |
| Historical notes: | |

The *Social Register Summer, 1923* and the *Long Island Society Register, 1929* list Clara B. Burton Pardee as residing at *Edgewater Cottage* in Lawrence.
She was the daughter of Aaron B. Burton of Philadelphia, PA.
Dr. Ensign Bennett Pardee was the son of Dr. Walter Bennett Pardee of New York City.
Dr. Ensign Bennett and Mrs. Clara Bigelow Burton Pardee's son Harold married Dorothy Dwight Porter and resided at *The Wild Oat* in Cedarhurst. Their daughter Gertrude married Frank Russell, Jr. of Pittsburgh, PA, and resided in Manhattan. Their son Irving, who married Margaret Estelle Trevor and, subsequently, Abigail Rockefeller, resided at *Edgewater Cottage*.
*[See following two entries for additional family information.]*

**Pardee, Dr. Harold Ensign Bennett (1886-1972)**

| | |
|---|---|
| Occupation(s): | physician - heart disease and circulation specialist - New York Hospital, NYC; Polyclinic Hospital, NYC; Women's Hospital, NYC |
| | educator - instructor, clinical medicine, Cornell University Medical School, NYC |
| | writer - *Essentials of Physiology: Prepared Especially for Students of Medicine*, 1916 (co-author); *Clinical Aspects of Electrocardiogram*, 1924 (4th ed. 1941); *What you Should Know About Heart Disease*, 1928; *Criteria for the Classification and Diagnosis of Heart Disease*, 1934 (co-author); *The Field of the Various Methods of Cardiac Diagnosis*; numerous articles in professional journals |
| Marriage(s): | 1918-1972 – Dorothy Dwight Porter (1892-1985) |
| Address: | Cedar Lane, Cedarhurst |
| Name of estate: | *The Wild Oat* |
| Year of construction: | |
| Style of architecture: | |
| Architect(s): | |
| Landscape architect(s): | |
| House extant: unconfirmed | |
| Historical notes: | |

The *Social Register Summer, 1955* lists Dr. Harold E. B. and Mrs. Dorothy D. Porter Pardee as residing at *The Wild Oat* on Cedar Lane, Lawrence [Cedarhurst].

He was the son of Dr. Ensign Bennett and Mrs. Clara Bigelow Burton Pardee of *Edgewater Cottage* in Lawrence.

Dorothy Dwight Porter was the daughter of Henry Hobart and Katharine Delano Porter, Jr. of *Lauderdale* in Lawrence.

Dr. Harold Ensign Bennett and Mrs. Dorothy Dwight Porter Pardee's daughter Pamela married Ranald Hugh MacDonald III, the son of Ranald Hugh and Anne Hunter Thompson MacDonald, Jr. of Upper Brookville. [*See* Spinzia, *Long Island's Prominent North Shore Families, vol. I* – MacDonald entry.]

*[See previous and following entries for additional family information.]*

### Pardee, Dr. Irving Hotchkiss (1892-1949)

| | |
|---|---|
| Occupation(s): | physician - neurologist, St. Luke's Hospital, NYC |
| Marriage(s): | M/1 – 1916-div. 1945 – Margaret Estelle Trevor (1893-1990) |
| | M/2 – 1946-div. 1949 – Abigail Rockefeller (1903-1976) |
| | - Civic Activism: trustee, Memorial Sloan–Kettering Cancer Center, NYC; |
| | donated Greenacre Park to New York City |
| Address: | Ocean Avenue, Lawrence |
| Name of estate: | *Edgewater Cottage* |
| Year of construction: | |
| Style of architecture: | |
| Architect(s): | |
| Landscape architect(s): | |
| House extant: unconfirmed | |
| Historical notes: | |

The *Long Island Society Register, 1929* lists Dr. Irving H. and Mrs. Margaret E. Trevor Pardee as residing in Lawrence [Cedarhurst].

He was the son of Dr. Ensign Bennett and Mrs. Clara Bigelow Burton Pardee of *Edgewater Cottage* in Lawrence.

Margaret Estelle Trevor Pardee was the daughter of Henry Graff and Margaret Helen Schieffelin Trevor of *Meadowmere* in Southampton. A Tiffany window in St. Andrew's Dune Church in Southampton is dedicated to Margaret Helen Schieffelin [Trevor]. [*See* Spinzia, *Long Island: A Guide to New York's Suffolk and Nassau Counties* – St. Andrew's Dune Church, Southampton.] Margaret's sister Helen married Charles James Coulter, Jr. and resided at *Wee Wak* in Southampton. Her sister Louise, who also resided in Southampton, married James Couper Lord, Sr.; Lewis Spencer Morris; and, subsequently, Charles Henry Mellon. [*See* Spinzia, *Long Island's Prominent Families in the Town of Southampton* – Trevor and Coulter entries.]

Dr. Irving Hotchkiss and Mrs. Margaret Estellle Trevor Pardee's daughter Margaret married Dr. Talcott Bates, the son of The Reverend H. Roswell Bates, and resided in Monterey, CA. Their son S. Trevor Pardee married Elthea Peale, the daughter of Rembrandt Peale of Greenwich, CT. Their daughter Deborah married David M. Stewart, the son of Charles Morton Stewart III of Manhattan, and resided in Wilton, CT.

Abigail Rockefeller Pardee was the daughter of John D. and Abigail Greene Aldrich Rockefeller, Jr. and the sister of Nelson and David Rockefeller. She had previously been married to David Meriwether Milton. In 1953 she married Jean Mauze and resided at *Laurel Hill* in Mill Neck. [*See* Spinzia, *Long Island's Prominent North Shore Families, vol. I* – Mauze entry – and *vol. II* – O'Neill entry.]

*[See previous two entries for additional family information.]*

### Parker, Carleton Allen (1894-1956)

| | |
|---|---|
| Occupation(s): | industrialist - motor rebuilding firm |
| Marriage(s): | 1923-1932 – Dorothy Dumont Cragin (1892-1932) |
| Address: | 101 Long Drive, West Hempstead |
| Name of estate: | *Stonehouse* |
| Year of construction: | 1923 |
| Style of architecture: | English Cottage |
| Architect(s): | |
| Landscape architect(s): | |
| House extant: yes | |
| Historical notes: | |

The house, originally named *Stonehouse*, was built by Carleton Allen Parker. It was built of fieldstone and had a thatched roof. [*Brooklyn Life* April 19, 1924, p. 12.]

The *Long Island Society Register, 1929* lists Carleton Allen and Dorothy Dumont Cragin Parker as residing at *Stonehouse* on Long Drive, West Hempstead.

She was the daughter of Edwin Moore and Sarah Dumont Cragin of Brooklyn.

In 2021 the house sold for $600,000.

*front facade, 2000*

### Parker, Don M., Sr. (1881-1936)

| | |
|---|---|
| Occupation(s): | advertising executive -   vice-president, United States Advertising Co., NYC |
| | publisher -  assistant to S. S. McClure of *McClure's* magazine; advertising manager, Century Publishing Co.; a founder, with Grantland Rice and Innis Brown, *American Golfer* magazine* |
| Civic Activism: | a founder, president, secretary, and treasurer, New York State Golf Association |
| Marriage(s): | Katherine Harris (1878-1979) |
| Address: | 149 Brixton Road, Garden City |
| Name of estate: | |
| Year of construction: | 1909 |
| Style of architecture: | Colonial Revival |
| Architect(s): | |
| Landscape architect(s): | |
| House extant: yes | |
| Historical notes: | |

*front facade, 2007*

The *Long Island Society Register, 1929* lists Mr. and Mrs. Don M. Parker [Sr.] as residing on Brixton Road, Garden City. The 1930 Census lists the Parkers at this address.

Don M. and Katherine Harris Parker, Sr.'s son Don M. Parker, Jr. married Jeanne Bailwitz, daughter of Alexander Bailwitz.

In 1964 the house was remodeled.

*[For information about Grantland Rice's East Hampton residence, which is on the National Register of Historic Places, see Spinzia, *Long Island's Prominent Families in the Town of East Hampton* – Rice entry.]

### Parker, Glowacki Redfield (1882-1956)

| | |
|---|---|
| Occupation(s): | politician -  director, Region #4, Social Security Board |
| Civic Activism: | director, Eastern United States, National Recovery Act |
| Marriage(s): | 1911-1954 – Emily Stewart Bowers Davis (1882-1954) |
| Address: | 109 Ninth Street, Garden City |
| Name of estate: | |
| Year of construction: | 1868 |
| Style of architecture: | Victorian |
| Architect(s): | |
| Landscape architect(s): | |
| House extant: yes | |
| Historical notes: | |

*front facade, 2008*

The *Long Island Society Register, 1929* lists Glowacki Redfield and Emily Davis Parker as residing at 109 Ninth Street, Garden City.

He was the son of LeRoy and Elizabeth Lowler Chandler Parker of Batavia, NY.

Emily Stewart Bowers Davis Parker was the daughter of Charles L. and Margaretta S. Bowers Davis.

Glowacki Redfield and Emily Stewart Bowers Davis Parker's son Stewart Redfield Parker resided in Schenectady, NY.

### Parker, Henry Seabury, Sr. (1882-1975)

| | |
|---|---|
| Occupation(s): | financier - partner, Joseph Walker and Sons (stock brokerage firm) |
| Marriage(s): | 1910-1971 – Marion Stevenson (1888-1971)<br>- Civic Activism: director, The Singers and Players Club, 1935 |
| Address: | East Rockaway Road, Hewlett Bay Park |
| Name of estate: | *The Farm* |
| Year of construction: | |
| Style of architecture: | |
| Architect(s): | |
| Landscape architect(s): | |
| House extant: | unconfirmed |
| Historical notes: | |

The house, originally named *The Farm*, was owned by Marion's parents Richard Wilson and Martha Cowles Hutchinson Stevenson, Jr.

The *Long Island Society Register, 1929* lists Henry Seabury and Marion Stevenson Parker [Sr.] as residing on Cedarhurst Avenue, Hewlett [Cedarhurst]. By 1939 they had relocated to *The Farm* on East Rockaway Road, Hewlett Bay Park.

Henry was the son of Henry Ainsworth and Mary Seabury Parker of Boston, MA.

Henry Seabury and Marion Stevenson Parker, Sr.'s daughter Marion married Ren Van Aiken Myers, the son of Eugene Van Aiken Myers of East Orange, NJ. Their son Richard married Sarah Meade Price, the daughter of Philip Price of Philadelphia, PA. Their son Henry Seabury Parker, Jr. married Ruth Weyburn, the daughter of Lyon Weyburn of Boston, MA.

The Parkers relocated to Cold Spring Harbor. [*The New York Times* April 8, 1975, p. 40.]


### Parkhurst, William Man (1904-1987)

| | |
|---|---|
| Occupation(s): | attorney*- partner, Man and Man, NYC;<br>partner, Shattuck, Bangs, and Davis, NYC;<br>partner, Ferris, Bangs, Davis, Trafford, and Syz |
| Civic Activism: | president and trustee, The Boys Brotherhood Republic, NY (boys' club);<br>chairman of trustees, The Kosciuszko Foundation |
| Marriage(s): | M/1 – 1930-div. 1943 – Hope Hewlett (1908-1991)<br>M/2 – 1943-1987 – Mary Elizabeth Sherman (1915-1988) |
| Address: | 151 Willis Court, Woodmere |
| Name of estate: | |
| Year of construction: | 1918 |
| Style of architecture: | Modified Colonial Revival |
| Architect(s): | |
| Landscape architect(s): | |
| House extant: | yes |
| Historical notes: | |

*front facade, 2005*

The *Social Register New York, 1941* lists William M. and Hope Hewlett Parkhurst as residing at 151 Willis Court, Woodmere.

He was the son of Edwin B. and Harriet Man Parkhurst of Albany, NY.

Hope Hewlett Parkhurst was the daughter of James Monroe and Anna Willets Hewlett of Lawrence. Hope later married Harry D. Watts.

William Man and Hope Hewlett Parkhurst's daughter Hope married Arthur Atwater Kent, Jr. of Philadelphia, PA, and resided in Palm Beach, FL. Their daughter Angelsea married Charles Ingersoll Newman, the son of John E. Newman, Sr. of Orange, NJ, and resided in Essex Fells, NJ. Their daughter Anita died at the age of twenty-three.

*William was the attorney for the noted designer, architect, poet, author, and inventor Richard Buckminster Fuller.

The exterior of the house has been extensively modified.

### Parsons, Argyll Rosse, Sr. (1880-1961)

Occupation(s): financier - director, Excelsior Bank of New York
capitalist - treasurer, Hotel Pierre, NYC;
treasurer, Hotel Lexington, NYC
real estate agent - director and vice-president, Douglas L. Elliman & Co.

Marriage(s): 1912-1961 – Eleanor Hartshorn Peters (1884-1962)

Address: 42 Hilton Avenue, Garden City
Name of estate:
Year of construction: 1873
Style of architecture: Victorian
Architect(s):
Landscape architect(s):
House extant: yes
Historical notes:

*front facade, 2008*

The *Long Island Society Register, 1929* lists Argyll Rosse and Eleanor H. Peters Parsons [Sr.] as residing at 42 Hilton Avenue, Garden City.

He was the son of Albert Rosse and Alice Schuyler Van Ness Parsons. Argyll's sister Ethel married Donald Cuyler Vaughan, Sr. and resided in Garden City.

Eleanor Hartshorn Peters Parsons was the daughter of Ralph and Eleanor Hartshorn Goodman Peters, Sr. of *Wynymeede* in Garden City.

Argyll Rosse and Eleanor Hartshorn Peters Parsons, Sr.'s daughter Eleanor married Dr. Harmon Jackson Bailey, the son of Claude E. Bailey of Kirksville, MO. Their son Douglas married Monte Hyatt Nicholson, the daughter of William Shepard Nicholson. Their son Argyll Rosse Parsons, Jr. married Suzanne Brevoort Siebrecht, the daughter of Benjamin Siebrecht of Chappaqua, NY.


### Paterson, Basil Alexander (1926-2014)

Occupation(s): attorney - partner, Meyer, Suozzi, English, and Klein, Garden City
politician - member, New York State Senate, 1965-1970 (represented
Upper West Side of New York City and Harlem);
unsuccessful candidate for New York State Lieutenant
Governor, 1970;
Deputy Mayor of New York City for Labor Relations and
Personnel (Koch administration);
New York State Secretary of State, 1979-1983 (Carey
administration)

Marriage(s): 1953-2014 – Portia Hairston

Address: Carolina Avenue, Hempstead
Name of estate:
Year of construction: 1947
Style of architecture: 20th Century Colonial Revival
Architect(s):
Landscape architect(s):
House extant: yes
Historical notes:

The Patersons resided at this residence from the early 1950s to 1988.

Basil Alexander Paterson was the son of Leonard James and Evangeline Alicia Rondon Paterson. Basil was the first African-American New York State Secretary of State and the first African-American vice-chairman of the National Democratic Party.

Basil Alexander and Portia Hairston Paterson's son David, who became Governor of New York in 2008, married Michell R. Paige and, later, Mary Alexander.

*[See following entry for additional family information.]*

*Basil Alexander Paterson home,
front facade, 2008*

**Paterson, David Alexander (b. 1954)**

| | |
|---|---|
| Occupation(s): | politician* -   member, New York State Senate, 1985- (represented Upper West Side of New York City and Harlem); minority leader, New York State Senate, 2003; lieutenant governor, New York State, 2007-2008; governor, New York State, 2008-2010 |
| | educator -   professor, School for International and Public Affairs, Columbia University, NYC |
| Marriage(s): | M/1 – 1992-div. 2014 – Michelle R. Paige (b. 1961) |
| | - financier -   director, integrative wellness, external affairs, and contributions, Health Insurance Plan of New York (HIP) |
| | politician -   lobbyist, North General Hospital, NYC |
| | M/2 – 2019 – Mary Alexander |
| | - entertainer and associated professions -   radio talk-show host |
| Address: | Carolina Avenue, Hempstead |
| Name of estate: | |
| Year of construction: | 1947 |
| Style of architecture: | 20th Century Colonial Revival |
| Architect(s): | |
| Landscape architect(s): | |
| House extant: yes | |
| Historical notes: | |

David Alexander Paterson resided at this residence with his parents Basil Alexander and Portia Hairston Paterson until 1988.

*David was the youngest member of the New York State Senate when elected (1985); the first African-American legislative leader in New York State (2003); the first blind person to address the Democratic National Convention (2004); the first legally blind African-American Lieutenant Governor of New York State (2007); and the first legally blind African-American Governor of New York State (2008), when he succeeded to the governorship with the resignation of Governor Eliot Spitzer due to Spitzer's involvement in a prostitution scandal.

Michelle R. Paige Paterson is the first African-American First Lady of New York State.

Mary Alexander Paterson had previously been married to the founder of the Guardian Angels Curtis Sliwa.

*[See previous entry for additional family information.]*

### Patterson, Edward Liddon (1866-1930)

| | |
|---|---|
| Occupation(s): | attorney - partner, Brownell and Patterson, NYC; member, Davis, Polk, Wardwell, Gardiner, and Reed, NYC |
| Civic Activism: | member, War Trade Board during World War I |
| Marriage(s): | 1903-1930 – Frances Louise Hewlett (1879-1967) |
| Address: | 199 Broadway, Lawrence |
| Name of estate: | *Rock Hall* |
| Year of construction: | 1767 |
| Style of architecture: | Colonial |
| Architect(s): | |
| Landscape architect(s): | |
| House extant: yes | |
| Historical notes: | |

*rear facade, 2009*

*Rock Hall*, which is on the National Register of Historic Places, was built by Josiah Martin, a prosperous trader from Antigua, West Indies. Martin's land holdings consisted of six hundred acres extending from *Rock Hall* to the ocean front at Far Rockaway. During the Revolutionary War Martin was an active Loyalist whose ships were used to transport British soldiers to the area while the house became a haven for his daughter Elizabeth and her Loyalist husband who was the last colonial governor of North Carolina. In 1824 Thomas Hewlett purchased the house and its remaining 125 acres. The house was donated to the Town of Hempstead in 1948, through the efforts of George H. Hewlett, for use as a museum. It is open to the public.

The *Social Register Summer, 1923* and the *Long Island Society Register, 1929* list the Pattersons as residing at *Rock Hall* in Lawrence.


### Peabody, Richard Augustus (1860-1910)

| | |
|---|---|
| Occupation(s): | financier - partner, Knapp and Peabody (stock brokerage firm) |
| Marriage(s): | 1895-1910 – Mary Chester Miller (1872-1950) |
| Address: | 580 Ocean Avenue, Lawrence |
| Name of estate: | *Terrace Hall* |
| Year of construction: | c. 1900 |
| Style of architecture: | Neo-Tudor |
| Architect(s): | Renwick, Aspinwall, and Owen designed the house (for R. A. Peabody) |
| Landscape architect(s): | |
| House extant: yes | |
| Historical notes: | |

*rear facade, 1901*

The house, originally named *Terrace Hall*, was built by Richard Augustus Peabody.

The *Social Register Summer 1910* lists Richard A, and Mary C. Peabody as residing at *Terrace Hall* in Cedarhurst [Lawrence].

He was the son of Augustus Stephen and Harriet Sanderson Peabody of NYC.

Mary Chester Miller Peabody was the daughter of George Walbridge and Kate Chester Miller. Mary later married Augustus Rene Moen II of *Renwood* in Cove Neck. [*See* Spinzia, *Long Island's Prominent North Shore Families, vol. I* – Moen entry.]

Richard Augustus and Mary Chester Miller Peabody's daughter Constance married Matthew James Looram, Sr., the son of Matthew M. and Minnie Looram.

The house was later owned by William Raymond, Sr. and, subsequently, by Isaac Gamel.

### Peabody, Rushton, Sr. (1867-1954)

| | |
|---|---|
| Occupation(s): | financier -   partner, Peabody, Slawson, & Smythe (insurance brokerage firm) |
| Marriage(s): | M/1 – 1902-1915 – Helen Troth Mange (1878-1915) <br> M/2 – 1919-div. 1929 – Veron Marguerite Magoffin (1886-1956) |
| Address: | Waverly Avenue, Hewlett Harbor |
| Name of estate: | *Cherry Bounce* |
| Year of construction: | |
| Style of architecture: | |
| Architect(s): | |
| Landscape architect(s): | |
| House extant: | unconfirmed |

Historical notes:

The *Long Island Society Register, 1929* lists Rushton Peabody [Sr.] as residing at *Cherry Bounce* in Hewlett [Hewlett Harbor].

He was the son of Enoch Wood and Cornelia Marshall Peabody.

Rushton and Helen Troth Mange Peabody, Sr.'s son Charles, who resided in Wilton, CT, married Maisie K. Gill Wylie and, subsequently, Virginia Wilkinson, the daughter of Arthur H. Wilkinson of Forest Hills, Queens. Their daughter Eugenia married George Leary, Jr., the son of George and Julia Crofton Leary, Sr. of *Hawthorne House* in Southampton, and resided in Wilton, CT. [*See* Spinzia, *Long Island's Prominent Families in the Town of Southampton* – Leary entry.] Their son Rushton Peabody, Jr. married Katharine Walker Neilson, the daughter of Louis Neilson of Jericho.

Veron Marguerite Magoffin Peabody was the daughter of Samuel McAfee and Elizabeth Moran Rogers Magoffin of Kentucky. Veron had previously been married to Chester Peter Siems. After her divorce from Peabody, she married George Drexel Biddle Steel, the son of William Thomas Steel.


### Peace, Arthur W. (1880-1959)

| | |
|---|---|
| Occupation(s): | real estate agent -   president, A. Peace & Sons, Brooklyn |
| Civic Activism: | director, Brooklyn Real Estate Board |
| Marriage(s): | Jessie N. Irwin (1882-1925) <br>     - Civic Activism:  chair, lung motor committee, Hempstead branch, American Red Cross |
| Address: | 91 Brook Street, Garden City |
| Name of estate: | |
| Year of construction: | 1922 |
| Style of architecture: | Dutch Colonial Revival |
| Architect(s): | |
| Landscape architect(s): | |
| House extant: | yes |

Historical notes:

The *Long Island Society Register, 1929* lists Arthur W. Peace as residing at 91 Brook Street, Garden City.

Jessie N. Irwin Peace was the daughter of Henry and Anna M. Irwin.

Arthur W. and Jessie N. Irwin Peace's daughter Dorothy married Allen Van Pelt Suydam, the son of James Lambert Suydam of Tarrytown, NY.

In 1988 the house was remodeled.

*front facade, 2005*

### Peacock, Grant Allen, Sr. (d. 1977)

| | |
|---|---|
| Occupation(s): | merchant - partner, Charlton & Co., Inc., NYC (jewelry firm); founder and president, Grant A. Peacock, Inc., NYC |
| Marriage(s): | 1917 – Frances Antonio Emmons (1895-1985) |
| Address: | 91 Tenth Street, Garden City |
| Name of estate: | |
| Year of construction: | c. 1928 |
| Style of architecture: | Neo-Federal |
| Architect(s): | |
| Landscape architect(s): | |

House extant: yes

*front facade, 2000*

Historical notes:

The house was built by Grant Allen Peacock, Sr.

The *Long Island Society Register, 1929* lists Mrs. and Mrs. Grant A. Peacock [Sr.] as residing at 91 Tenth Street, Garden City.

He was the son of Alexander Peacock of Pittsburgh, PA.

Frances Antonio Emmons Peacock was the daughter of George Thornton Emmons of *Greenholm* in Princeton, NJ, and the granddaughter of Rear Admiral George Foster Emmons for whom the destroyer USS *Emmons* was named.

Grant Allen and Frances Antonio Emmons Peacock, Sr.'s daughter Janet married William Charles Clapp, Jr. and Stuart E. Knowlton, the son of Roger and Gwendolen Duclow Knowlton. Their son George married Marian McKenzie. Their son Grant Allen Peacock, Jr. married Jo Ann Mary Rowles, the daughter of Harry Charles and Irene Letitia McLauglin Rowles.

In 1933, Peacock was involved in a legal dispute with Arthur Severin Bourne, Sr. over the quality of the jewelry that he had sold to Bourne. [*The New York Times* February 5, 1933, p. 26, and Spinzia, *Long Island's Prominent South Shore Families* – Arthur Severin Bourne entry.]

In 1998 the house was remodeled.

### Pearce, Arthur Williams, Sr. (1874-1927)

| | |
|---|---|
| Occupation(s): | mining engineer - Venture Corp. |
| | financier - founder and partner, Simpson, Pearce, and Co. (investment banking firm) |
| | industrialist - treasurer, Williams–Hartley Corp. (tin smelting) |
| Civic Activism: | member, Liberty Loan committee, 1918; treasurer, Rockaway Hunting Club, Lawrence, 1919 |
| Marriage(s): | 1908-1927 – Lucy Inman (1875-1950) |
| Address: | Schencks, Lane, Hewlett Harbor |
| Name of estate: | |
| Year of construction: | c. 1911 |
| Style of architecture: | Neo-Georgian |
| Architect(s): | |
| Landscape architect(s): | Plantings were supplied by Hicks Nursery, Jericho (for Pearce) |

House extant: unconfirmed

*front facade*

Historical notes:

The house was built by Arthur Williams Pearce, Sr.

The *Social Register Summer, 1915* lists Arthur Williams and Lucy Inman Pearce [Sr.] as residing in Hewlett [Hewlett Harbor].

He was the son of Richard and Amelia Elizabeth Hawkin Pearce.

Lucy Inman Pearce was the daughter of John Hamilton and Margaret McKinney Coffin Inman, Jr. of Manhattan. Lucy's sister Nannie married Clifford Vail Brokaw, Sr. and resided at *The Elms* in Glen Cove. Nannie subsequently married Milton D. Brown with whom she continued to reside at *The Elms*. [*See* Spinzia, *Long Island's Prominent North Shore Families, vol. I* – Brokaw and Brown entries.]

Arthur Williams and Lucy Inman Pearce, Sr.'s son John married Jane Webster and resided in Princeton, NJ. Their son Richard married Estelle Patricia Pittman, the daughter of Ernest Wetmore and Estelle Young Romeyn Pittman of Lawrence, and resided in Old Lyme, CT, and East Hampton. [*See* Spinzia, *Long Island's Prominent Families in the Town of East Hampton* – Pittman entry.] Their son Arthur Williams Pearce, Jr. married Marion Gengler, the daughter of Joseph D. and Maria Bohner Gengler of Westhampton Beach, and resided in Norwalk, CT. [*See* Spinzia, *Long Island's Prominent Families in the Town of Southampton* – Gengler entry.]

### Pearsall, Harris Montgomery (1874-1940)

| | |
|---|---|
| Occupation(s): | financier - member, Consolidated Stock Exchange |
| | politician - Commission of Deeds, State of New Jersey, 1897 |
| Marriage(s): | 1916-1940 – Anna Watson O'Connor (1879-1959) |
| Address: | 113 Fourth Street, Garden City |
| Name of estate: | |
| Year of construction: | 1916 |
| Style of architecture: | 20th Century |
| Architect(s): | |
| Landscape architect(s): | |
| House extant: yes | |
| Historical notes: | |

front facade, 2008

The *Long Island Society Register, 1929* lists Mr. and Mrs. Harris Montgomery Pearsall as residing on Stewart Avenue, Garden City. In 1916 the Pearsalls were residing at 113 Fourth Street, Garden City. [*Brooklyn Life* October 16, 1916, p. 15.]

He was the son of Thomas E. Pearsall of Brooklyn. At the time of his death, Harris was residing in Bellport. [*The Brooklyn Daily Eagle* February 26, 1940, p. 11.]

Anna Watson O'Connor Pearsall was the daughter of Thomas O'Connor of Brooklyn. She had previously been married to Warren Bynner Nash, the son of William Alexander Nash of Manhattan.


### Pease, Walter Albert, Jr. (1871-1940)

| | |
|---|---|
| Occupation(s): | real estate agent - president, Pease and Elliman; |
| | vice-president, Walter N. Lawrence Co. |
| Marriage(s): | 1895-1936 – Martha Chamberi Rodgers (1876-1936) |
| Address: | Fulton Avenue, Hempstead |
| Name of estate: | *Bethpage* |
| Year of construction: | |
| Style of architecture: | Italianate |
| Architect(s): | |
| Landscape architect(s): | |
| House extant: unconfirmed* | |
| Historical notes: | |

front facade

The *Social Register Summer 1910* and *1915* list W. Albert and Martha C. Rodgers Pease [Jr.] as residing at *Bethpage* in Hempstead. The *Long Island Society Register, 1929* lists them as residing in Southampton and on Fulton Avenue, Hempstead. [*See* Spinzia, *Long Island's Prominent Families* in the Town of Southampton – Pease entry.]

He was the son of Walter Albert and Mary Louisa Hollister Pease, Sr. of New York. His brother Henry married Katharine B. N. Di Pollone and resided in Lenox, MA.

Martha Chamberi Rodgers Pease was the daughter of Admiral Rogers and the granddaughter of Commodore Matthew Calbraith and Mrs. Jane Slidell Perry. The Rodgers were related to Mrs. August Belmont, Sr. of *Nursery Stud Farm* in North Babylon.

Walter Albert and Martha Chamberi Rodgers Pease, Jr.'s daughter Martha married Lewis Mills Gibbs, Jr., the son of Lewis Mills and Anna Pinkerton Gibbs, Sr. of Bay Shore, and resided at *Cedarholme* in Bay Shore. Martha later married Richard Franklin Babcock of *Hark Away* in Woodbury. [*See* Spinzia, *Long Island's Prominent South Shore Families* – Belmont and Gibbs entries – and *Long Island's Prominent North Shore Families, vol. I* – Babcock entry.] Their son Perry, who resided at *Elmhurst* in Bridgehampton, married Mary Trimble, the daughter of Richard and Cora Randolph Trimble, Sr. who resided in Old Westbury. Her brother Richard Trimble, Jr., who married Winifred Lowe, also resided in Old Westbury. [*See* Spinzia, *Long Island's Prominent North Shore Families, vol. II* – Trimble entries – and *Long Island's Prominent Families in the Town of Southampton* – Pease entry.]

*In 1905 Pease's kennels and stables were destroyed by fire. [*The New York Times* November 21, 1905, p. 1.]

Mrs. Pease died after falling from the second floor bedroom window of her Park Avenue apartment. [*The New York Times* October 7, 1936, p. 24.]

**Peck, Arthur Knowlton, Sr. (1905-1990)**

| | |
|---|---|
| Occupation(s): | financier - vice-president and director, Robb, Peck, McCooey, and Co., NYC (stock brokerage firm); |
| | partner, Lockwood, Peck, and Co., NYC (stock brokerage firm); |
| | partner, Steven and Legg, NYC (stock brokerage firm); |
| | partner, Walters, Peck, and Co., NYC (stock brokerage firm) |
| | industrialist - vice-president, Republic Aviation, Farmingdale |
| Marriage(s): | M/1 – 1933-1973 – Christiana Wallace Crane (1900-1973) |
| | M/2 – 1973-1990 – Jane Cochran (1910-1999) |
| Address: | Polo Lane, Lawrence |
| Name of estate: | |
| Year of construction: | c. 1924 |
| Style of architecture: | Neo-Georgian |
| Architect(s): | Auguste Louis Noel designed the house (for W. S. Crane) |
| Landscape architect(s): | Annette Hoyt Flanders designed the flagstone terrace, shrubbery, lawns, and the vegetable and flower gardens, c. 1934 (for Mrs. W. S. Crane); (also for A. K. Peck) |

House extant: yes
Historical notes:

The house, originally named *East View*, was built by Warren Seabury Crane. It was subsequently owned by his daughter Christiana and son-in-law Arthur Knowlton Peck, Sr.

Arthur was the son of Arthur Nelson and Ella F. Knowlton Peck of Woodsburgh.

Christiana Wallace Crane Peck was the daughter of Warren Seabury and Violet Lee Wallace Crane. She had previously been married to Arthur Chittenden Crunden, the son of Frank Payne Crunden of St. Louis, MO.

Arthur Knowlton and Christiana Wallace Crane Peck, Sr.'s son Lee married Victoria Deacon Tyner and, subsequently, Kristey Ann Gunnell with whom he resided in Lawrence.

Jane Cockran Peck was the daughter of William S. Cochran of Houston, TX. She had previously been married to Stewart P. Coleman.

*[See following two entries for additional family information.]*

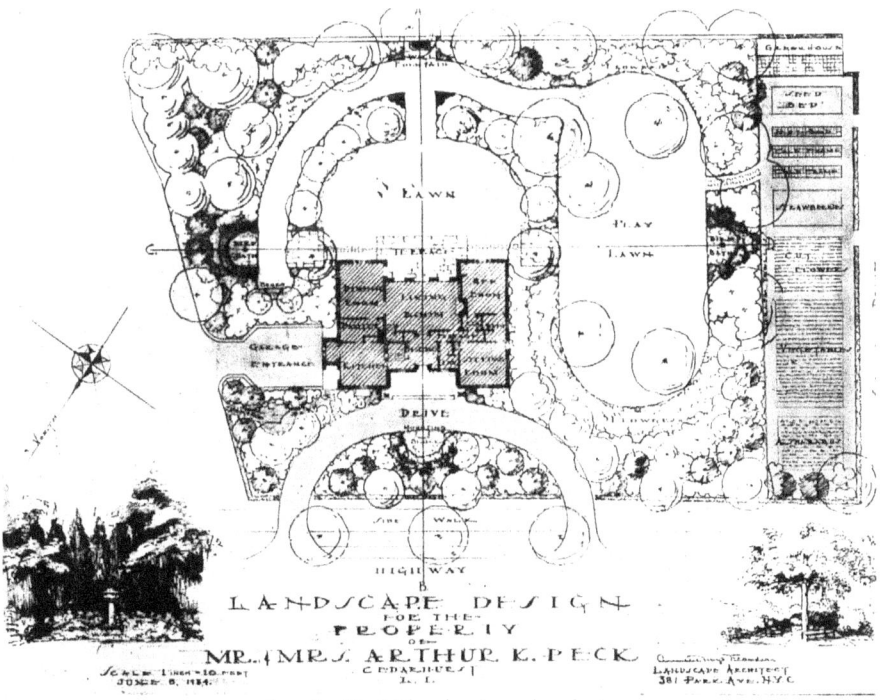

*Annette Hoyt Flanders' garden design*

### Peck, Arthur Nelson (1875-1940)

| | |
|---|---|
| Occupation(s): | financier - president, Walters, Peck, and Co. (stock brokerage firm) |
| Civic Activism: | a founder, Village of Woodsburgh, 1912 |
| Marriage(s): | 1904-1940 – Ella F. Knowlton (1875-1972) |
| Address: | Channel Road, Woodsburgh |
| Name of estate: | |
| Year of construction: | 1910 |
| Style of architecture: | Neo-Federal |
| Architect(s): | William Adams, Jr. designed the house (for A. N. Peck) |
| Landscape architect(s): | |
| House extant: unconfirmed | |
| Historical notes: | |

The house was built by Arthur Nelson Peck.

The *Social Register Summer 1910* and *1915* and the *Long Island Society Register, 1929* list Arthur N. and Ella F. Knowlton Peck as residing in Woodmere [Woodsburgh].

He was the son of Norman and Laura A. Martin Peck, Sr.

Ella F. Knowlton Peck was the daughter of Eben Joseph and Mary Holberton Beers Knowlton of Woodsburgh.

Arthur Nelson and Ella F. Knowlton Peck's son Arthur Knowlton Peck, Sr., who resided in Lawrence, married Christiana Wallace Crane and, later, Jane Cochran. Their daughter Ruth married David Horton Carnahan, Sr. and resided at *Island Ranch* in Big Horn, WY.

*[See other Peck entries for additional family information.]*

*front facade, 1912*

### Peck, Lee Wallace (1939-1984)

| | |
|---|---|
| Occupation(s): | financier - partner, Walters, Peck, and Co. (stock brokerage firm) |
| | merchant - president, Hassel Motors Inc., Freeport |
| Marriage(s): | M/1 – 1966-div. – Victoria Deacon Tyner (b. 1945) |
| | M/2 – 1975-1984 – Kristey Ann Gunnell |
| Address: | 115 Ocean Avenue, Lawrence |
| Name of estate: | |
| Year of construction: | 1954 |
| Style of architecture: | Cape Cod |
| Architect(s): | |
| Landscape architect(s): | |
| House extant: yes | |
| Historical notes: | |

Lee Wallace Peck was the son of Arthur Knowlton and Christiana Wallace Crane Peck, Sr. of Lawrence.

Victoria Deacon Tyner Peck was the daughter of John Hill and Joan Kettering Martin Tyner of Lawrence. Victoria later married Lars Sellstedt Potter, Jr. and, subsequently, Henry Thomas Kilburn, Jr.

The *Social Register, 1978* lists Lee W. and Kristey A. Gunnell Peck as residing at 115 Ocean Avenue, Lawrence.

She was the daughter of Elias Gunnell of Manitowoc, WI.

*[See previous Peck entries for additional family information]*

*front facade, 2000*

### Pell, Walden, Jr. (1875-1949)

| | |
|---|---|
| Occupation(s): | financier - partner, Mann, Bill, and Co., NYC (stock brokerage firm); partner, Pell, Peake, and Co., NYC (stock brokerage firm) |
| Civic Activism: | secretary, Diocesan Investment Trust Fund of Diocese of New York |
| Marriage(s): | 1918-1949 – Gladys Bruce Mumford (1890-1966) |
| Address: | 86 Auerbach Lane, Lawrence |
| Name of estate: | *Oak Lawn* |
| Year of construction: | 1910 |
| Style of architecture: | Long Island Farmhouse |
| Architect(s): | |
| Landscape architect(s): | |
| House extant: yes | |
| Historical notes: | |

The *Social Register New York, 1954* lists Walden and Gladys B. Mumford Pell [Jr.] as residing at 86 Auerbach Lane, Cedarhurst [Lawrence].

He was the son of Walden and Melissa Augusta Hyatt Pell, Sr.

Gladys Bruce Mumford Pell was the daughter of Blodgett Mumford.

Walden and Gladys Bruce Mumford Pell, Jr.'s daughter Mary married Charles J. Marsh, Jr. of Montclair, NJ, and resided in Shrewsbury, NJ. Their daughter Gladys married Donald E. Ward, the son of William Hoffman Ward of Baltimore, MD, and resided in Fredrick, MA. Their daughter Dorinda married William H. Cruikshank, Jr. and resided in Wellesley, MA.

*front facade, 2001*

### Pell, William Watson (1882-1930)

| | |
|---|---|
| Occupation(s): | financier - member, James H. Oliphant & Co. (stock brokerage firm); member, Carlisle, Millick & Co. (stock brokerage firm); partner, Richards, Pell, & Hume (stock brokerage firm); special partner, Harp, Tierney, & Co. (stock brokerage firm); member, H. N. Whitney & Sons (stock brokerage firm) |
| Marriage(s): | 1914-1930 – Louise Elder Pitt (1883-1971) |
| Address: | 260 Stewart Avenue, Garden City |
| Name of estate: | |
| Year of construction: | |
| Style of architecture: | |
| Architect(s): | |
| Landscape architect(s): | |
| House extant: unconfirmed | |
| Historical notes: | |

The *Long Island Society Register, 1929* lists William Watson and Louise Elder Pitt Pell as residing at 260 Stewart Avenue, Garden City.

He was the son of Roston and Mary Sebring Brooks Pell of Brooklyn.

Louise Elder Pitt Pell was the daughter of William Augustus and Emma Tracy Pitt and a descendant of William Pitt. Louise had previously been married to Thomas Jacob Biggs.

William Watson and Louise Elder Pitt Pell's daughter Dorothy married Hugh Murray Savage, the son of John Richard Savage, Sr. of Garden City. Their daughter Katharine married Hayward Headden, the son of John Headden III of Jersey City, NJ, and, later, Harry D. Rothrock.

### Pennington, Charles Gordon (1885-1943)

| | |
|---|---|
| Occupation(s): | capitalist - general passenger agent, Pennsylvania Railroad |
| Marriage(s): | M/1 – 1913-1918 – Lulu Dell Allison (d. 1918) |
| | M/2 – Edith Berta Fritz (1892-1975) |
| Address: | 106 Kilburn Road, Garden City |
| Name of estate: | |
| Year of construction: | 1934 |
| Style of architecture: | Colonial Revival |
| Architect(s): | Olive Frances Tjaden designed the house |
| Landscape architect(s): | |
| House extant: yes | |
| Historical notes: | |

Charles Gordon Pennington was the son of Charles Gordon Douglas Edward and Sarah Caroline Whitney Pennington of Hollis.

Lulu Dell Allison Pennington was the daughter of George Wallace Allison of *Holliswood* in Hollis.

Charles Gordon and Lulu Dell Allison Pennington's son Richard married Jean Swan, the daughter of A. E. Swan.

Edith Bertha Fritz Pennington was the daughter of George and Carrie Rinklin Fritz.

Charles drowned while swimming off Montauk.

*[See following entry for additional family information.]*

In 2013, the 2,722-square-foot house sold for $1.3 million.

*front facade, 2013*

### Pennington, Harold Douglas (b. 1892)

| | |
|---|---|
| Occupation(s): | financier - partner and director, Brown Brothers Harriman and Co. (investment banking firm) |
| Marriage(s): | 1920 – Grace Marion Merritt (b. 1895) |
| | - Civic Activism: president, Women's League of St. Gabriel's Church, Hollis; |
| | member, nominating committee, Cathedral of the Incarnation Club, Garden City, 1941 |
| Address: | 94 Third Street, Garden City |
| Name of estate: | |
| Year of construction: | 1936 |
| Style of architecture: | Colonial Revival |
| Architect(s): | Olive Frances Tjaden designed the house |
| Landscape architect(s): | |
| House extant: yes | |
| Historical notes: | |

Harold Douglas Pennington was the son of Charles Gordon Douglas Edward and Sarah Caroline Whitney Pennington of Hollis.

Grace Marion Merritt Pennington was the daughter of Edward Charles and Grace B. Hollingsworth Merritt, Sr. of Garden City.

Harold Douglas and Grace Marion Merritt Pennington's son Harold Edward Pennington married Helene Marjorie Hogan, the daughter of Bernard F. Hogan of Garden City.

*[See previous entry for additional family information.]*

In 2021, the house sold for $2.153 million.

*front facade, 2021*

### Perkins, Charles Lawrence, Jr. (1857-1919)

| | |
|---|---|
| Occupation(s): | capitalist - railroads |
| | publisher - director, University Press |
| | financier - director, Knickerbocker Trust Co. |
| Marriage(s): | 1882-1919 – Margaret Grandy (1854-1920) |
| Address: | *[unable to determine street address]*, Woodmere |
| Name of estate: | |
| Year of construction: | c. 1912 |
| Style of architecture: | Shingle |
| Architect(s): | William Adams, Jr. designed the house (for C. L. Perkins) |
| Landscape architect(s): | |
| House extant: unconfirmed | |
| Historical notes: | |

The house was built by Charles Lawrence Perkins, Jr.
He was the son of Charles Lawrence and Elizabeth West Perkins, Sr.
Margaret Grandy Perkins was the daughter of Sheppard and Elizabeth Brooks Grandy.
Charles Lawrence and Margaret Grandy Perkins, Jr.'s son John married Lydia Helen Logan.

*rear facade, 1912*

### Perkins, Norton (1876-1925)

| | |
|---|---|
| Occupation(s): | attorney - partner, McCurdy and Yard, NYC |
| Civic Activism: | police justice, Village of Lawrence, 1906; |
| | trustee, Village of Lawrence, 1914; |
| | trustee, Five Points House of Industry |
| Marriage(s): | 1903- 1925 – Ethel Whitney Holbrooke (1876-1961) |
| | - Civic Activism: director, Long Island Symphony Association, 1941 |
| Address: | 350 Ocean Avenue, Lawrence |
| Name of estate: | *Whale Acres* |
| Year of construction: | c. 1914 |
| Style of architecture: | Neo-Federal |
| Architect(s): | William Adams, Jr. designed the house (for Perkins) |
| Landscape architect(s): | |
| House extant: yes | |
| Historical notes: | |

The house, originally named *Whale Acres*, was built by Norton Perkins.
The *Long Island Society Register, 1929* lists Ethel W. Holbrook [sic] Perkins as residing at *Whale Acres* in Lawrence.
He was the son of Edward Henry and Mary Norton Perkins.
Ethel Whitney Holbrooke Perkins was the daughter of Stephen Holbrooke of Buffalo, NY.
The Perkinses did not have children.
The house was later owned by Samuel Sloan Auchincloss, Sr., who continued to call it *Whale Acres*.

*front facade, 1914*

### Persell, Harry Alexander (1881-1958)

| | |
|---|---|
| Occupation(s): | military - colonel; Chief of United States Army Personnel, National Guard Bureau |
| Marriage(s): | 1905-1958 – Mabel Elizabeth Fornof (1886-1967)<br>- politician - Republican Committee Woman, Nassau County<br>Civic Activism: parliamentarian, Garden City Women's Club; credentials chair, 91st convention, Long Island Federation of Women's Clubs, 1951; director, Garden City chapter, Delphian Society of Y.M.C.A., 1928<br>president, Cathedral of the Incarnation Guild, Garden City, 1942 |
| Address: | 37 Brixton Road, Garden City |
| Name of estate: | |
| Year of construction: | 1928 |
| Style of architecture: | Modified Dutch Colonial Revival |
| Architect(s): | |
| Landscape architect(s): | |
| House extant: | yes |
| Historical notes: | |

*front facade, 2001*

The house was built by Harry Alexander Persell.

The *Long Island Society Register, 1929* lists Harry A. Persell as residing at 37 Brixton Road, Garden City.

He was a veteran of the Spanish American War, the Mexican border campaign, and both World Wars.

Mabel Elizabeth Fornof Persell was the daughter of George Fornof of Wilkinsburg, PA.

### Peterkin, DeWitt, Sr. (1884-1954)

| | |
|---|---|
| Occupation(s): | industrialist - sales consultant, Pacific Mills (textile manufacturer) |
| Civic Activism: | vice-president, Cherry Valley Club, Garden City, 1943 |
| Marriage(s): | 1912-1952 – Margaret Ella O'Brien (1891-1952) |
| Address: | 81 Nassau Boulevard, Garden City |
| Name of estate: | |
| Year of construction: | 1920 |
| Style of architecture: | Colonial Revival |
| Architect(s): | |
| Landscape architect(s): | |
| House extant: | yes |
| Historical notes: | |

*front facade, 2022*

The *Long Island Society Register, 1929* lists DeWitt and Margaret Ella O'Brien Peterkin [Sr.] as residing at 55 Washington Avenue, Garden City. The 1940 Census lists the Peterkins as residing at 81 Nassau Boulevard, Garden City.

He was the son of Gilbert C. Peterkin of Brooklyn.

Margaret Ella O'Brien Peterkin was the daughter of Dr. Henry Lewis and Mrs. May Ella Thall O'Brien of Brooklyn.

DeWitt and Margaret Ella O'Brien Peterkin, Sr.'s daughter Margaret married John Kirkman Gurney, the son of Thomas Nichols and Ethel Kirkman Gurney of Garden City. Their son DeWitt Peterkin, Jr. married Jane Parks and resided in Darien, CT. Their son John married Kathleen McCormick, the daughter of Chesley McCormick of Wichita, KS, and, later, Helen Minton, the daughter of Henry Miller Minton of North Hills.

At the time of his death, DeWitt Peterkin, Sr. was residing in Westhampton Beach. [*The New York Times* August 22, 1954, p. 93.]

In 2022, the seven-bedroom, 4,909-square-foot house was for sale. The asking price was $1.399 million.

**Peters, Ralph, Jr. (1887-1957)**

| | |
|---|---|
| Occupation(s): | financier - vice-president, Corn Exchange Bank, NYC (later, Corn Exchange Bank Trust Co.); director, Corn Exchange Bank Trust Co., NYC; trustee, Franklin Savings Bank, Franklin Square |
| Civic Activism: | chairman, finance committee, North Country Community Hospital, Glen Cove; director, Woodlawn Cemetery, The Bronx |
| Marriage(s): | 1915-1957 – Helen Louise Frew (1891-1971) |
| Address: | 65 Third Street, Garden City |
| Name of estate: | |
| Year of construction | 1913 |
| Style of architecture: | Colonial Revival |
| Architect(s): | |
| Landscape architect(s): | |
| House extant: yes | |
| Historical notes: | |

The *Long Island Society Register, 1929* lists Ralph and Helen Louise Frew Peters [Jr.] as residing at 65 Third Street, Garden City.

He was the son of Ralph and Eleanor Hartshorn Goodman Peters, Sr. of Garden City.

Helen Louise Frew Peters was the daughter of Walter Edwin and Ella Louise Carman Frew of Garden City.

Ralph and Helen Louise Frew Peters, Jr.'s son Ralph Frew Peters married Diana Joyce Clayton. Their daughter Helen married Martin Victor, the son of Royall and Anna Romeyn Varcik Martin Victor, Sr. of Lattingtown and Muttontown, and resided in Locust Valley. [*See* Spinzia, *Long Island's Prominent North Shore Families, vol. II* – Victor entry.]

[*See following entry for additional family information.*]

*front facade, 2008*

365

**Peters, Ralph, Sr. (1853-1953)**

| | |
|---|---|
| Occupation(s): | capitalist - president, Cincinnati, Georgetown, & Portsmouth Railroad; president, Long Island Rail Road |
| | financier - director, Nassau–Suffolk Bond and Mortgage Guarantee Co.; trustee, Corn Exchange Bank, NYC (later, Corn Exchange Bank Trust Co.) |
| Civic Activism: | chairman, Committee on Railway Mail Pay; member, Brooklyn Grade Crossing and Atlantic Avenue Improvement Commission |
| Marriage(s): | 1882-1949 – Eleanor Hartshorn Goodman (1863-1949) |
| Address: | 7 Carteret Place, Garden City |
| Name of estate: | *Wyndymeede* |
| Year of construction: | c. 1908 |
| Style of architecture: | Modified Dutch Colonial Revival |
| Architect(s): | Aymar Embury II designed the house (for R. Peters, Sr.)* |
| Landscape architect(s): | |
| House extant: yes | |
| Historical notes: | |

The house, originally named *Wyndymeede*, was built by Ralph Peters, Sr.

The *Social Register Summer, 1910* lists Ralph and Eleanor H. Goodman Peters [Sr.] as residing at *Wyndemeede* in Garden City.

He was the son of Richard and Mary Jane Thompson Peters.

Eleanor Hartshorn Goodman Peters was the daughter of William Augustus and Lucy Ann Grandin Goodman of Cincinnati, OH.

Ralph and Eleanor Hartshorn Goodman Peters, Sr.'s daughter Eleanor married Argyll Rosse Parsons, Sr. and resided in Garden City. Their daughter Pauline married George Walker Pierpont, the son of Henry V. Pierpont of Chicago, IL. Their daughter Dorothy married John Platt Hubbell, Sr., the son of George Loring and Eliza Strong Platt Hubbell, Sr. of Garden City, and resided in Garden City. Their daughter Helaine married Harold Baldwin Forman, the son of Arthur Willis and Henrietta Baldwin Forman of Brooklyn and Westhampton, and resided in Garden City. Helaine later married Allen Supple. Their daughter Jane married Ford Wright. Their son Ralph Peters, Jr. married Helen Louise Frew and resided in Garden City.

*[See previous entry for additional family information.]*

*[For information about Embury's East Hampton residence, *see* Spinzia, *Long Island's Prominent Families in the Town of East Hampton* – Embury entry.]

In 2021, the 10,700-square-foot house, with eight bedrooms and seven full and two half bathrooms, was for sale. The asking price was $3.9 million.

*front facade, c. 1909*

### Pettit, Townsend Baldwin, Sr. (b. 1880)

| | |
|---|---|
| Occupation(s): | capitalist - owned real estate in Village of Hempstead |
| | merchant - whole woolen business |
| | industrialist - secretary, Empire State Bag Co., Brooklyn |
| Marriage(s): | Clara Post (1887-1969) |
| Address: | 15 Westbury Road, Garden City |
| Name of estate: | |
| Year of construction: | 1933 |
| Style of architecture: | Colonial Revival |
| Architect(s): | |
| Landscape architect(s): | |
| House extant: yes | |
| Historical notes: | |

*front facade, 2011*

The *Long Island Society Register, 1929* lists Mr. and Mrs. Townsend B. Pettit as residing on Cathedral Avenue, Hempstead. The 1940 Census lists their residence as 15 Westbury Road, Garden City.

He was the son of Seaman Lemanuel and Henrietta Augusta Hobby Pettit of Hempstead.

Clara Post Pettit was the daughter of Jotham Post.

Townsend Baldwin and Clara Post Pettit, Sr.'s son Townsend Baldwin Pettit, Jr. married Ann Lloyd Savage, the daughter of Dr. Francis J. Savage of St. Paul, MN, and resided in Garden City.

In 2011, the 4,921-square-foot house, with six bedrooms and three and a half bathrooms, sold for $2 million.

### Philbin, Ewing Reginald, Sr. (1889-1957)
### aka Erving Reginald Philbin

| | |
|---|---|
| Occupation(s): | attorney |
| Civic Activism: | member, War Loan Staff, 1922; |
| | mayor, Village of Hewlett Bay Park, 1942 |
| Marriage(s): | 1917 – Harriet Mary Woodward (b. 1891) |
| Address: | West Broadway, Hewlett Bay Park |
| Name of estate: | *Pine Tree House* |
| Year of construction: | |
| Style of architecture: | |
| Architect(s): | |
| Landscape architect(s): | |
| House extant: unconfirmed | |
| Historical notes: | |

In 1924, Philbin purchased the house of John Augustus Griswold, Sr., which was located at 29 Piermont Avenue, Hewlett Bay Park. [*The New York Times* August 26, 1924, p. 24.]

The *Long Island Society Register, 1929* lists Ewing R. and Harriet M. Woodward Philbin [Sr.] as residing at *Pine Tree House* on West Broadway in Hewlett [Hewlett Bay Park].

He was the son of Eugene Ambrose and Jessie Margarite Holladay Philbin of Manhattan. Ewing's brother Stephen, who resided in Hewlett, married Florence S. Burton and, later, Elizabeth S. Hoyt. His brother Jessie married Elizabeth Parker and resided in Lawrence. His sister Eugenie married Louis Wetmore and, subsequently, Alexander Tuck.

Harriet Mary Woodward Philbin was the daughter of Edwin Campbell Woodward of Middleton, OH.

Ewing Reginald and Harriet Mary Woodward Philbin, Sr.'s daughter Carolyn married Dr. Richard Bache Duane, Jr., the son of Richard Bache and Felicity C. Clark Duane of *Ups & Downs* in Locust, NJ, and resided at *Ups & Downs*. Their son Ewing Reginald Philbin, Jr. married Cynthia Soles, the daughter of Louis C. Soles, and, subsequently, Elinor Brisbane, the daughter of Arthur and Phoebe Cary Brisbane of East Meadow and Montauk. [*See* Spinzia, *Long Island's Prominent Families in East Hampton* – Brisbane entry].

*[See following two Philbin entries for additional family information.]*

### Philbin, Jessie Holladay (1890-1969)

| | |
|---|---|
| Occupation(s): | attorney |
| Marriage(s): | 1917-1964 – Elizabeth Parker (1891-1964) |
| Address: | 480 Ocean Avenue, Lawrence |
| Name of estate: | |
| Year of construction: | 1910 |
| Style of architecture: | Colonial Revival with Federal elements |
| Architect(s): | |
| Landscape architect(s): | |
| House extant: yes | |

*front facade, 2000*

Historical notes:

The *Long Island Society Register, 1929* lists Jessie Holladay and Elizabeth Parker Philbin as residing on Ocean Avenue, Cedarhurst [Lawrence]. The 1930 Census lists the Philbins at this address.

He was the son of Eugene Ambrose and Jessie Margarite Holladay Philbin of Manhattan.

Elizabeth Parker Philbin was the daughter of Frederic Parker of Boston, MA.

Jessie Holladay and Elizabeth Parker Philbin's daughter Mary married Watson Bradley Dickerman, Jr., the son of Bradley Watson and Florence Calkin Dickerman, Sr. of *Hillendale* in Mill Neck, and resided in Manhattan. [*See* Spinzia, *Long Island's Prominent North Shore Families, vol. 1* – Dickerman entry]. Their daughter Jessie married Ledyard Blair Clark, the son of William Clark of Princeton, NJ, and resided in Pembroke, NH.

*[See previous and following Philbin entries for additional family information.]*

In 1999 the house was remodeled.

### Philbin, Stephen Holladay (1888-1973)

| | |
|---|---|
| Occupation(s): | attorney -   member, Baker, Botts, Parker, and Garwood, Houston, TX; partner, Fish, Richardson, and Neave, NYC; partner, Fish and Neave, NYC |
| | writer -   "Judge Learned Hand and the Law Patents and Copyrights," *Harvard Law Review,* February 1947; "Patent Litigation," *Canadian Patent Reporter*, August 1957 |
| Civic Activism: | general counsel, Civilian Defense Volunteer Office of the City of New York during World War II; counsel, New York City Office of Civil Defense during Korean Conflict |
| Marriage(s): | M/1 – 1919-1957 – Florence Southwick Burton (1888-1957) <br> - Civic Activism: <br> trustee, Neurological Institute; <br> trustee, School of Nursing at Presbyterian Hospital; <br> trustee, New York Eye and Ear Infirmary, NYC; <br> trustee, Soldiers, Sailors, and Airmen's Club, NYC <br> M/2 – 1966-1973 – Elizabeth Sherman Hoyt (1891-1984) |
| Address: | *[unable to determine street address]*, Hewlett |
| Name of estate: | |
| Year of construction: | |
| Style of architecture: | |
| Architect(s): | |
| Landscape architect(s): | |
| House extant: unconfirmed | |

Historical notes:

The *Long Island Society Register, 1929* lists Stephen H. and Florence S. Burton Philbin as residing in Hewlett.

He was the son of Eugene Ambrose and Jessie Margarite Holladay Philbin of Manhattan.

Florence Southwick Burton Philbin was the daughter of Robert L. and Florence Southwick Burton of Millbrook, NY.

Stephen Holladay and Florence Southwick Burton Philbin's daughter Florence married Alfred C. Coxe, Jr. of NY.

Elizabeth Sherman Hoyt Philbin was the daughter of Henry Reese and Emy Lydig Otto Hoyt, Sr. of Manhattan. Prior to her marriage to Philbin she had been married to Thomas Harris Frothingham, the son of Theodore and Lucy Harris Frothingham, Sr. of Philadelphia, PA, and, later, to William Adams Walker Stewart II. She resided with Stewart at *Edgeover* in Cold Spring Harbor. [*See* Spinzia, *Long Island's Prominent North Shore Families, vol. II* – Stewart entry.] Elizabeth's brother Henry Reese Hoyt, Jr. married Mary Hills Foote and resided at *Arbeety Farm* in West Hills. [*See* Spinzia, *Long Island's Prominent North Shore Families, vol. 1* – Hoyt entry.]

*[See previous two Philbin entries for additional family information.]*

### Philips, Frederic Dimon (1860-1945)

| | |
|---|---|
| Occupation(s): | attorney |
| Civic Activism: | member, advisory board, St. Hilda's Guild; governor, Rockaway Hunting Club, Lawrence, 1911 |
| Marriage(s): | 1889-1945 – Jessie Matheson Taylor (1863-1947)<br>- Civic Activism: established the Kenneth Matherson Taylor Fund at Harvard University*<br>suffragist - member, state committee, Woman's Political Union, 1912 |
| Address: | 365 Ocean Avenue, Lawrence |
| Name of estate: | *Greyhouse* |
| Year of construction: | c. 1896 |
| Style of architecture: | Neo-Jacobean |
| Architect(s): | Thomas Henry Randall designed the house (for F. D. Philips) |
| Landscape architect(s): | |
| House extant: | yes |
| Historical notes: | |

The house, originally named *Greyhouse*, was built by Frederic Dimon Philips.

The *Social Register New York, 1907* and the *Social Register Summer, 1910* list Frederic D. and Jessie M. Taylor Philips as residing at *Greyhouse* in Lawrence.

He was the son of William H. and Susan Elizabeth Dimon Philips.

Jessie Matheson Taylor Philips was the daughter of John and Jessie Matheson Taylor.

Frederic Dimon and Jessie Matheson Taylor Philips' daughter Alison married Charles E. Van der Burgh of Minneapolis, MN, and resided in Paris, France. Their son John married Janet H. Freeman and resided in Woodmere. Their son Kenneth, who resided in Pittsburgh, married Mary Spencer, the daughter of Seth S. Spencer of Manhattan; Lynda Hansen; and, subsequently, Harriet Hansen, the daughter of John Morrison Hansen of Pittsburgh, PA. Their son William, who resided at *Fairway* in Lawrence, married Genevieve Leland Sandford and, subsequently, Dorothy Britton Longman.

*The Kenneth Matherson Taylor Fund was established in 1899 with a donation by Mrs. Philips of $50,000 in honor of her brother Kenneth.

*[See following entry for additional family information.]*

In 1924 Philips sold the house to Helen R. Wardwell. [*The New York Times* December 16, 1924, p. 46.]

*front facade, c. 1900*

### Philips, William Frederic (1890-1963)

| | |
|---|---|
| Occupation(s): | financier - partner, Abbott, Hoppin, and Co. (stock brokerage firm); partner, Abbott, Proctor, and Paine (stock brokerage firm); governor, New York Curb Exchange, 1935 |
| Civic Activism: | member, Selective Service Board |
| Marriage(s): | M/1 – 1917 – Genevieve Leland Sanford (b. 1892) |
| | M/2 – 1955 – Dorothy Britton Longman (1899-1982) |
| Address: | 597 Club Lane, Lawrence |
| Name of estate: | *Fairway* |
| Year of construction: | |
| Style of architecture: | |
| Architect(s): | |
| Landscape architect(s): | |
| House extant: no | |
| Historical notes: | |

The *Long Island Society Register, 1929* lists William F. and Genevieve L. Sanford Philips as residing at *Fairway* in Cedarhurst [Lawrence]. The 1930 Census lists the Philipses at this address.

He was the son of Frederick Dimon and Jessie Matheson Taylor Philips of *Greyhouse* in Lawrence.

Genevieve Leland Sanford Philips was the daughter of George Baylies and Cardine Granger Blodget Sanford of *The Byways* in Lawrence. Genevieve's sister Elizabeth married Henry Lawrence Bogert, Jr., the son of Henry Lawrence and Caroline L. Osgood Bogert, Sr. of Flushing, Queens, and resided in Cedarhurst.

William Frederic and Genevieve Leland Sanford Philips' daughter Genevieve married George Meredith Whitehouse, the son of Edward Whitehouse of Manhasset, and resided in Glen Cove.

Dorothy Britton Longman Philips was the daughter of Samuel Tremper and Charlotte Florence Britton Longman of Brooklyn. Dorothy had previously been married to Stuart English Kimball of Brooklyn.

*[See previous entry for additional family information.]*


### Pidgeon, Ashley E. (1889-1964)

| | |
|---|---|
| Occupation(s): | financier - a founder, president, and chairman of board, deWilt Conklin Organization (a stockholder relations specialist firm); a founder and partner, Hanning, Conklin, & Pidgeon, Inc., 1929 (wholesalers of investment securities) |
| Marriage(s): | 1921-1964 – Charlotte Stege (b. 1897) |
| Address: | 122 Fourth Street, Garden City |
| Name of estate: | |
| Year of construction: | 1926 |
| Style of architecture: | Modified Dutch Colonial Revival |
| Architect(s): | |
| Landscape architect(s): | |
| House extant: yes | |
| Historical notes: | |

*front facade, 2001*

The house was built by Ashley E. Pidgeon.

The *Long Island Society Register, 1929* lists Ashley E. and Charlotte Stege Pidgeon as residing at 122 Fourth Street, Garden City.

She was the daughter of George H. and Ida C. Stege, Sr. of Brooklyn.

Ashley E. and Charlotte Stege Pidgeon's daughter Charlotte married Donald Stokes, the son of Hubert Stokes of England. Their daughter Mary married Philip Albright Small Franklin III and resided in Mill Neck. [*See* Spinzia, *Long Island's Prominent North Shore Families, vol. 1 –* Franklin entry.]

In 1937 the house was remodeled.

### Piel, Rudolph Alfred (1892-1961)

| | |
|---|---|
| Occupation(s): | capitalist - owned a cattle ranch in Florida |
| Marriage(s): | 1919-1958 - Margarita Erwina Schile (1896-1958) |
| Address: | 50 Locust Street, Garden City |
| Name of estate: | |
| Year of construction: | 1928 |
| Style of architecture: | French Country |
| Architect(s): | Frances Olive Tjaden designed the house |
| Landscape architect(s): | |
| House extant: yes | |
| Historical notes: | |

Rudolph Alfred Piel was the son of Michael and Maria Gertrud Heermann Piel of Brooklyn and an heir to the Piel Brothers' Beer Fortune.

Margarita Erwina Schile Piel was the daughter of John Jerome and Anna Schmitt Schile of Hempstead.

Rudolph Alfred and Margarita Erwina Schile Piel's daughter Margarita married Alfred M. McCoy, Jr.

In 2012, the five-bedroom, two-bath, 2,232-square-foot house sold for $790,000.

*front facade, 2001*

### Pier, Roy (1880-1971)

| | |
|---|---|
| Occupation(s): | industrialist - cotton industry |
| Marriage(s): | 1910-1971 – Anne Terry Gardiner (1887-1982) |
| | - Civic Activism: chairman, Lenox Picture House, NYC (theater for children); president, St. John's Church Auxiliary, 1953 |
| Address: | Albon Road, Hewlett Harbor |
| Name of estate: | *Breezy Way* |
| Year of construction: | |
| Style of architecture: | |
| Architect(s): | |
| Landscape architect(s): | |
| House extant: unconfirmed | |
| Historical notes: | |

The *Long Island Society Register, 1929* lists Roy and Anne T. Gardiner Pier as residing in Hewlett [Hewlett Harbor].

He was the son of William Stanwood and Alciphron Moore Pier.

Anne Terry Gardiner Pier was the daughter of James Terry and Eliza Greene Gardiner of *Ye Haven* in Bar Harbor, ME.

Roy and Anne Terry Gardiner Pier's daughter Katharine married Fred Whitecomb Farwell, the son of Herman Waldo Farwell, Sr. of Leonia, NJ, and resided in Norwalk, CT. Their son Gardiner married Emily Dick, the daughter of Evans Dick of Boston, MA; Penelope Carver; and, subsequently, Erlita Sason. Their son William married Reinette Plimpton, the daughter of Theodore Barnet Plimpton of Boston, MA, and, later, Joan Cotton Dick.

The *Social Register New York, 1948* lists Roy and Anne T. Gardiner Pier as residing at *Pierfields* in Williamstown, MA.

### Pierce, Walter Bryant, Jr. (1899-1954)

| | |
|---|---|
| Occupation(s): | financier - member, Jewett, Pierce, and Sheehan, NYC (stock brokerage firm); |
| | member, R. F. Baby and Co., NYC (stock brokerage firm); |
| | partner, Walter Bryant Pierce and Co. (stock brokerage firm); |
| | partner, Wenman, Pierce, and Brown (stock brokerage firm) |
| Marriage(s): | M/1 – 1923-div. 1930 – K. Janavince Kerens |
| | - merchant - proprietor, gift shop, Los Angeles, CA |
| | M/2 – Pauline Jeanne Lautier |
| Address: | Colonial Road, Hewlett Bay Park |
| Name of estate: | |
| Year of construction: | 1923 |
| Style of architecture: | |
| Architect(s): | |
| Landscape architect(s): | |
| House extant: unconfirmed | |
| Historical notes: | |

The *Long Island Society Register, 1929* lists Walter Bryant and K. Janavince Kerns Pierce [Jr.] as residing in Hewlett Bay Park.

He was the son of Walter Bryant and Emily Guest Pierce, Sr.

K. Janavince Kerens Pierce was the daughter of Vincent and Janet Kerens and the granddaughter of Richard C. Kerens, the United States Ambassador to the Austro-Hungarian Empire. Janavince subsequently married Eskill Florman.

Pauline Jeanne Lautier Pierce had previously been married to De Courcy Browne, who lost his fortune, attempted suicide after suing Pierce for alienation of his wife's affections, and was, subsequently, employed by the WPA for thirty dollars a week. [*The New York Times* February 13, 1931, p. 3, and *The Philadelphia Inquirer* November 14, 1942, p. 107.]

Walter Bryant Pierce, Jr. committed suicide after being charged with allegedly transporting $87,000 in stolen securities. [*The New York Times* October 2, 1954, p. 8.]


### Pinkus, Frederick S. (1844-1927)
#### aka Salomon Friederick Pinkus; Frederick Salo Pinkus

| | |
|---|---|
| Occupation(s): | financier - partner, Jaffe & Pinkus (member of Foreign Fruit Exchange) |
| | industrialist - Frederick Solo Pinkus (linen importing and manufacturing firm) |
| Marriage(s): | 1869-1914 – Laura Amelia Ball (1844-1914) |
| Address: | Ocean Avenue, Lawrence |
| Name of estate: | |
| Year of construction: | |
| Style of architecture: | |
| Architect(s): | |
| Landscape architect(s): | |
| House extant: unconfirmed | |
| Historical notes: | |

The *Social Register Summer, 1914* lists Frederick S. and Laura A. Ball Pinkus as residing in Cedarhurst.

He was the son of Heimann Chaim and Blumele Dorothea Proskauer Pinkus.

Alice Laura Ball Pinkus was the daughter of Flamen and Evelina Candler Ball, Jr. Laura had previously been married to Charles Adea.

Frederick S. and Alice Laura Amelia Ball Pinkus' son Walter married E. Augusta Wight and resided in West Hempstead. Their daughter Alice married Rene Carillo de Albornoz.

In 1905, Frederick was arrested and charged with smuggling and attempted bribery of a customs official. [*The Sun* January 13, 1905, p. 1.]

At the time of his death, Frederick was residing in Bay Shore. [*The New York Times* July 31, 1927, p. E11.]

**Pittman, Ernest Wetmore (1889-1970)**

| | |
|---|---|
| Occupation(s): | industrialist - president, Rathbone Sard & Co., 1922-1926; director and chairman of board, Interchemical Corp. |
| | engineer - apprentice, Niles, Bement, Pond, and Co, 1912-1914; engineer, Dillon, Read, and Co., 1922-1926 |
| Civic Activism: | trustee, Memorial Hospital, NYC; chief, United States Rubber Mission to the Soviet Union, 1942; fund chairman, Hook Pond Associates |
| Marriage(s): | 1915-1970 – Estelle Young Romeyn (1894-1980) - Civic Activism: secretary, Garden Club of East Hampton |
| Address: | Osborn Avenue, Lawrence |

Name of estate:
Year of construction:
Style of architecture:
Architect(s):
Landscape architect(s):
House extant: unconfirmed
Historical notes:

    The *Long Island Society Register, 1929* lists Ernest Wetmore and Estelle Romeyn Pittman as residing in Lawrence. He was the son of Lansing Mizner and Annette Phelps Steuart Pittman of Detroit, MI.
    Estelle Young Romeyn Pittman was the daughter of Charles William and Estelle Young Romeyn of Manhattan. Her sister Rosalind married William Everdell, Jr. and resided in North Hills. [*See* Spinzia, *Long Island's Prominent North Shore Families, vol. 1* – Everdell and Horace Havemeyer, Jr. entries – and *Long Island's Prominent South Shore Families* – Horace Havemeyer, Jr. entry.]
    Ernest Wetmore and Estelle Young Romeyn Pittman's son Steuart, who was Assistant Secretary of Defense in the Kennedy and Johnson administrations, married Antoinette Eno Pinchot, the daughter of Amos Richards Eno and Ruth Pickering Pinchot and niece of Governor Gifford Pinchot of Pennsylvania. Antoinette's sister Mary married Cord Meyer IV, the son of Cord and Katharine Blair Thaw Meyer III of *Little River Farm* in North Hampton, NH, and grandson of Cord and Cornelia M. Covert Meyer II of *The Cove* in Kings Point. [*See* Spinzia, *Long Island's Prominent North Shore Families, vol. 1* – Meyer entry.] Cord Meyer IV was Chief of Covert Action Staff of the Directorate of Plans for the CIA's worldwide clandestine activities. His wife Mary was murdered in 1964 while walking along the former tow path of the Chesapeake and Ohio Canal in Georgetown, VA. [*See* Raymond E. Spinzia, "Adultery, Drugs, Murder, Untimely Deaths, and Long Island's Prominent Families: A Tangled Web." www.spinzialongislandestates.com and Judith Ader Spinzia, "Women of Long Island: Cornelia Bryce Pinchot, Feminist, Social-Activist – The Long Islander Who Became First Lady of Pennsylvania." www.spinzialongislandestates.com.] Steuart later married Barbara Milburn White, the daughter of Will Walter White. Antoinette subsequently married Benjamin Crowninshield Bradlee, Sr. of *Grey Gardens* in East Hampton. [*See* Spinzia, *Long Island's Prominent Families in the Town of East Hampton* – Bradlee entry.] The Pittmans' daughter Estelle married Richard Inman Pearce, the son of Arthur Williams and Lucy Inman Pearce of Hewlett. [*See* Spinzia, *Long Island's Prominent Families in the Town of Hempstead* – Pearce entry.]
    For information about Pittman's East Hampton residence, *see* Spinzia, *Long Island's Prominent Families in the Town of East Hampton* – Pittman entry.

**Plunkett, Henry Willoughby (1867-1951)**
**aka Harry Plunkett Grattan**

| | |
|---|---|
| Occupation(s): | entertainers and associated professions - British actor writer - playwright |
| Civic Activism: | a founder, American Actor Benevolent Fund |
| Marriage(s): | 1889 – Constance Elizabeth Frances Leveson (b. 1866) |
| Address: | 8 Euston Road, Garden City |
| Name of estate: | |
| Year of construction: | c. 1928 |
| Style of architecture: | Modified Victorian Farmhouse |
| Architect(s): | |
| Landscape architect(s): | |
| House extant: | yes |
| Historical notes: | |

The house was built by Henry Willoughby Plunkett.

The *Long Island Society Register, 1929* lists Mr. and Mrs. Harry P. Grattan as residing at 8 Euston Road, Garden City.

Harry Plunkett Grattan (stage name) made his debut in 1871 at the age of four, appearing with his two brothers and five sisters in *Uncle Tom's Cabin*. At the age of seven, he joined the company of George Edwardes' Gaity Theatre in London. [*The New York Times* September 26, 1951, p. 31.] At the age of nine he appeared with his sister Amelia, two years his senior who performed under the stage name of Emily Grattan, as one of the two children in *Rip Van Winkle* at the Princess' Theater in London to positive critical reviews. [*The Era*, London, August 13, 1876, p. 10c.] They were the children of actor and dramatic author Henry Willoughby Grattan and Elizabeth Shaw Plunkett, who resided in England. Henry Plunkett, who also used the stage name of Harry Grattan, wrote several vehicles for Master Harry, as he was then known, and his siblings.

At the time of his death, Henry Willoughby Plunkett was living in San Isidro, Argentina, to which he had relocated in 1931. [*The New York Times* September 26, 1951, p. 31.]

Constance Elizabeth Frances Leveson Plunkett was the daughter of The Reverend Charles Augustus and Mrs. Eliza Bayley Ashton Leveson.

*front facade, 2000*

### Polk, Frank Lyon, Sr. (1871-1943)

| | |
|---|---|
| Occupation(s): | politician - member, Civil Service Commission of New York, 1907-1909; president, Civil Service Commission of New York, 1908-1909 |
| | attorney - counselor United States Department of State, 1915-1919; partner, Davis, Polk, Wardwell, Gardiner, and Reed (which became Davis, Polk, Wardwell, Sunderland, and Kiendl)* |
| | statesman - Acting Secretary of State, 1918-1919; Under Secretary of State, 1919-1920 |
| | diplomat - United States Plenipotentiary to negotiate peace, 1919; chairman, United States delegation to Paris Peace Conference, 1919 |
| | capitalist - director, Erie Railroad Co. |
| | financier - director, United States Trust; director, Park Bank; trustee, Bowery Savings Bank; trustee, Mutual Life Insurance Co. of New York |
| | intelligence agent** |
| Civic Activism: | member of board, New York Board of Education; president, American Friends of Yugoslavia, Inc.; vice-president, British War Relief Society; vice-president, Woodrow Wilson Foundation; vice-president, Church Pension Fund of Protestant Episcopal Church; trustee, Cathedral of St. John the Divine, NYC; president, board of trustees, New York Public Library, NYC; trustee, Manhattan Maternity and Orthopedic Hospital, NYC |
| Marriage(s): | 1908-1943 – Elizabeth Sturgis Potter (1886-1960) |
| Address: | *[unable to determine street address]*, Lawrence |
| Name of estate: | |
| Year of construction: | |
| Style of architecture: | |
| Architect(s): | |
| Landscape architect(s): | |
| House extant: unconfirmed | |
| Historical notes: | |

Frank Lyon Polk, Sr., was the son of William Mecklenburg and Ida A. Lyon Polk of NYC and a great-nephew of President James Knox Polk.

*Democratic candidate for President of the United States John William Davis, who resided at *Mattapan* in Lattingtown, was also a partner in the law firm.

**During World War I, Polk and his assistant Gordon Auchincloss, Sr., who resided in Glen Cove and at *Ronda* in Matinecock, were in charge of coordinating United States intelligence operations. [*See* Spinzia, *Long Island's Prominent North Shore Families, vol. I* – Auchincloss and Davis entries.]

The *Long Island Society Register, 1929* lists Frank Lyon and Elizabeth Sturgis Potter Polk [Sr.] as residing in Lawrence while both the *Social Register Summer, 1932* and *1937* list the Polks as residing in Syosset [Muttontown]. The *Social Register New York, 1948* lists Elizabeth S. Potter Polk as residing at 817 Fifth Avenue, NYC, while the *Social Register New York, 1959* lists her residence as 3 East 71st Street, NYC.

The Polks' daughter Elizabeth married Raymond Richard Guest, Sr. who resided at *Roslyn Manor* in Brookville. Their daughter Alice married Winthrop Rutherfurd, Jr. and resided at *Stone House* in Allamuchy, NJ. The Polks' sons married sisters; Frank Lyon Polk II married Katharine Hoppin Salvage and James Potter Polk, Sr. married Margaret Smith Salvage. Both of the Polks' daughters-in-law were the daughters of Sir Samuel Agar and Mary Katharine Richmond Salvage, who resided at *Rynwood* in Old Brookville. [*See* Spinzia, *Long Island's Prominent North Shore Families, vol. II* – Polk and Salvage entries.] Their son John married Virginia Brand, the daughter of Robert H. Brand of *Eydon Hall* in Northamptonshire, England.

## Porter, Henry Hobart, Jr. (1865-1947)

| | |
|---|---|
| Occupation(s): | capitalist - chairman of board and director, American Water Works & Electric Co.; |
| | chairman of board, West Penn Electric; |
| | vice-president, Espertanza Land Corp.; |
| | director, Monongahela Power Co.; |
| | director, Brooklyn–Manhattan Transit Corp.; |
| | director, Hudson & Manhattan Railroad Co.; |
| | director, Ann Arbor Railroad Co.; |
| | director, Brooklyn–Queens Transit Co.; |
| | director, West Penn Railways Co. |
| | merchant - director, McLellan Stores Co.; |
| | director, United Stores Corp. |
| | financier - director, Mercantile Insurance of America; |
| | director, North British & Mercantile Insurance Corp.; |
| | director, Chemical Bank & Trust Co. |
| | industrialist - director, Tobacco Products Co. |
| Civic Activism: | trustee, Columbia University, NYC; |
| | trustee, New York Botanical Garden; |
| | president, Village of Lawrence, 1906; |
| | governor and vice-president, Rockaway Hunting Club, Lawrence, 1911 |
| Marriage(s): | 1891-1945 – Katharine Delano (1869-1945) |
| Address: | 375 Ocean Avenue, Lawrence |
| Name of estate: | *Lauderdale* |
| Year of construction: | c. 1900 |
| Style of architecture: | Neo-Tudor |
| Architect(s): | Barney and Chapman designed the house (for H. H. Porter, Jr.) |
| Landscape architect(s): | Martha Brookes Brown Hutcheson (for H. H. Porter, Jr.) |

House extant: yes
Historical notes:

The house, originally named *Lauderdale*, was built by Henry Hobart Porter, Jr.

The *Long Island Society Register, 1929* lists H. Hobart and Katherine [sic] D. Porter [Jr.] as residing at *Lauder Dale* [sic] in Lawrence.

He was the son of Henry Hobart and Annie Metcalf Dwight Porter, Sr.

Henry Hobart and Katharine Delano Porter, Jr.'s daughter Katharine married Robert Lyon Hamill, Sr. of Chicago, IL, and resided in Lawrence. Their daughter Dorothy married Dr. Harold Ensign Bennett Pardee and resided at *The Wild Oat* in Cedarhurst. Their son Seton married Frederica Virginia Berwind, the daughter of Charles Frederick and Anita B. Berwind of Philadelphia, PA, and resided at *Still House* in Matinecock. [*See* Spinzia, *Long Island's Prominent North Shore Families, vol. II* – Porter entry.]

*front facade, c. 1900*

### Post, Stephen Rushmore (1830-1899)

| | |
|---|---|
| Occupation(s): | financier - director, Marine National Bank;<br>member, New York Produce Exchange<br>capitalist - extensive real estate holdings in Brooklyn |
| Marriage(s): | 1869-1899 – Caroline Bulkeley Morgan (1844-1935) |
| Address: | *[unable to determine street address]*, Cedarhurst |
| Name of estate: | |
| Year of construction: | |
| Style of architecture: | |
| Architect(s): | |
| Landscape architect(s): | |
| House extant: | unconfirmed |
| Historical notes: | |

The *Long Island Society Register, 1929* lists Caroline Bulkeley Morgan Post as residing in Cedarhurst.

Stephen Rushmore Post was the son of Edmund and Mary Rushmore Post, Jr.

Stephen Rushmore and Caroline Bulkeley Morgan Post's son Charles married Julia Swift Gilbert, the daughter of Cass Gilbert. Their daughter Helen married Arthur Lincoln Frothingham, Jr., the son of Arthur Lincoln and Jessie Bolles Frothingham, Sr. Their son Henry married Mary Riker Haskell, the daughter of J. Amory Haskell of Manhattan.

### Potter, Lars Sellstedt, Jr. (1923-1983)

| | |
|---|---|
| Occupation(s): | financier - secretary, Blue Cross–Blue Shield for Western New York State |
| Marriage(s): | M/1 – 1946-div. – Brenda Adele Timpson<br>M/2 – 1973 – Victoria Deacon Tyner (b. 1945) |
| Address: | 220 Ocean Avenue, Lawrence |
| Name of estate: | |
| Year of construction: | 1920 |
| Style of architecture: | Modified Colonial Revival |
| Architect(s): | |
| Landscape architect(s): | |
| House extant: | yes |
| Historical notes: | |

The house was previously owned by Isaac Richmond Hoxie, Sr.

The *Social Register, 1960* lists Lars Sellstedt and Brenda A. Timpson Potter, Jr. as residing at 220 Ocean Avenue, Lawrence.

He was the son of Lars Sellstedt and Mary Gaddis Plum Potter, Sr. of Buffalo, NY.

Brenda Adele Timpson Potter was the daughter of Carl William and Marcelle E. Vallon Timpson, Sr., who resided at *Windy Top* in Hewlett Harbor. Brenda later married Andre O. Keohn. Her brother James married Annadel Beckers, the daughter of William Kurt Beckers of Manhattan. Her brother Carl William Timpson, Jr. married Patricia White and resided in Locust Valley.

Lars Sellstedt and Brenda Adele Timpson Potter, Jr.'s son Lars Sellstedt Potter III married Deborah Mae Shamel. Their daughter Hope married George S. Woodward IV.

Victoria Deacon Tyner Potter was the daughter of John Hill and Joan Kettering Martin Tyner of Lawrence. Victoria had previously been married to Lee Wallace Peck of Lawrence. She subsequently married Henry Thomas Kilburn, Jr.

*front facade, 2007*

### Pratt, Frederick Theodore (1899-1994)

Occupation(s): financier - member, Stone and Webster (investment banking firm)

Marriage(s): 1924-1989 – Anne D'Esterre French (1901-1989)

Address: Colonial Road and Ives Road, Hewlett Bay Park
Name of estate:
Year of construction:
Style of architecture:
Architect(s):
Landscape architect(s):
House extant: unconfirmed
Historical notes:

The *Long Island Society Register, 1929* lists Frederick T. and Anne D'Esterre French Pratt as residing at Colonial Road and Ives Road, Hewlett [Hewlett Bay Park].
   He was the son of Frederick Sanford Pratt, Sr.
   Anne D'Esterre French Pratt was the daughter of Henry Cormerais French.
   Frederick Theodore and Anne D'Esterre French Pratt's daughter Anne married Richard Le Baron Goodwin, the son of Lewis Le Baron Goodwin of Detroit, MI, and, subsequently, Dr. Stephen Alexander Fisher. Their daughter Lydia married Pierre Louis Elissabide, the son of Rene B. Elissabide of Mauleon–Soule, France, and, later, Dr. Robert W. Speir with whom she resided in Manhattan. Their son Frederick Sanford Pratt II died at the age of twenty-eight.


### Pratt, James Edward (b. 1934)

Occupation(s): attorney

Marriage(s): 1956 – Geraldine Marie McCabe

Address: 195 Kildare Road, Garden City
Name of estate:
Year of construction: 1954
Style of architecture: Cape Cod
Architect(s):
Landscape architect(s):
House extant: yes
Historical notes:

   James Edward Pratt is the son of Robert Edward and Marie Pratt, Sr. of Garden City.
   Geraldine Marie McCabe Pratt is the daughter of Bernard T. McCabe of Riverdale, NY.
   In 1964 the house was remodeled.

*front facade, 2000*

### Pratt, James Guy (b. 1938)

| | |
|---|---|
| Occupation(s): | capitalist -  president, Guy Pratt, Inc., Holtsville (construction firm)* |
| Marriage(s): | 1959 – Carol Ann Corroon (1939-2012) |
| Address: | 406 Stewart Avenue, Garden City |
| Name of estate: | |
| Year of construction: | 1968 |
| Style of architecture: | Colonial Revival |
| Architect(s): | |
| Landscape architect(s): | |
| House extant: yes | |
| Historical notes: | |

James Guy Pratt is the son of James J. Pratt, Jr. of Westbury and Centre Island.

Carol Ann Corroon Pratt was the daughter of George Aloysius and Gladys Adelaide Durand Corroon, Sr. of Garden City.

*The firm of Guy Pratt, Inc. constructed many of Long Island's roads, bridges, and parkways.

*front facade, 2001*

### Pratt, Reginald Tyler (1883-1978)

| | |
|---|---|
| Occupation(s): | electrical engineer -   Queens–Brooklyn Gas and Electric Co. |
| Marriage(s): | M/1 – Winifred L. Sealy (b. 1885) |
| | M/2 – 1929 – Edna Mary Halloram (b. 1904) |
| Address: | 49 Sealy Drive, Lawrence |
| Name of estate: | |
| Year of construction: | |
| Style of architecture: | |
| Architect(s): | |
| Landscape architect(s): | |
| House extant: no | |
| Historical notes: | |

The *Long Island Society Register, 1929* lists Reginald Pratt as residing in Lawrence.

Winifred L. Sealy was the daughter of Robert E. and Lillian Dawson Sealy.

Reginald Tyler Pratt's daughter Cora married G. Forrest Gillet, the son of Walter Noble Gillet of Kenilworth, IL, and, later, Stanhope Adams. His daughter Mary married Henry Wiggleworth Mellen, the son of Joseph Manley Mellen of Bowdoinham, ME, and, later, Henry W. Putnam. His son John married Susan Marie Smith, the daughter of Wallace Wyniard Smith of Lunenberg, SC, and resided in Greenwich, CT.

### Pratt, Robert Edward, Sr. (1902-1957)

| | |
|---|---|
| Occupation(s): | financier - president and director, Institutional Securities Corp. |
| | attorney - Assistant United States District Attorney, Southern District of New York, 1935-1940 |
| Civic Activism: | member, Enemy Alien Hearing Board during World War II |
| Marriage(s): | Marie E. *[unable to determine maiden name]* (b. 1906) |
| Address: | 26 St. James Street, Garden City |
| Name of estate: | |
| Year of construction: | 1954 |
| Style of architecture: | Ranch |
| Architect(s): | |
| Landscape architect(s): | |
| House extant: yes | |
| Historical notes: | |

Robert Edward and Marie Pratt, Sr.'s daughter Mary married William Andrew Nugent, Jr. Their son Daniel married Cathleen Grace Cullen, the daughter of Thomas W. Cullen. Their son Robert Edward Pratt, Jr. married Martha Ann Parker, the daughter of Ward F. Parker of Plandome. Their son James married Geraldine Marie McCabe and resided in Garden City.

[For information about the Pratt's East Quogue residence, *see* Spinzia, *Long Island's Prominent Families in the Town of Southampton* – Pratt entry.]

*front facade, 2001*

### Prescott, William French (1893-1969)

| | |
|---|---|
| Occupation(s): | financier - partner, Parr and Co. (stock brokerage firm); treasurer, New York Coffee & Sugar Exchange; bond salesman, F. S. Mosely & Co., Boston, MA, 1917 |
| Marriage(s): | M/1 – 1926-div. 1938 – Mary Agnes Worle (1899-1982) |
| | M/2 – 1939-1969 – Elizabeth Harmsteadt Coe (1908-2002) |
| | - Civic Activism: president, South Side Garden Club |
| Address: | 81 Park Row, Lawrence |
| Name of estate: | |
| Year of construction: | 1928 |
| Style of architecture: | Colonial Revival |
| Architect(s): | |
| Landscape architect(s): | |
| House extant: yes | |
| Historical notes: | |

*front facade*

The *Long Island Society Register, 1929* lists William F. and Mary A. Worle Prescott as residing on Park Row, Cedarhurst [Lawrence].

He was the son of The Reverend George Jarvis and Mrs. Lucille F. Campbell Prescott of Boston, MA.

Mary Agnes Worle Prescott was the daughter of Charles and Catherine Donovan Worle. Mary subsequently married Douglass Ball Simonson, the son of William Abram and Elizabeth Ball Simonson.

Elizabeth Coe Prescott was the daughter of Elmore Holloway and Elizabeth Wright Davie Coe of Hewlett. Elizabeth had previously been married to Daniel Aylesbury Finlayson, Jr. of Hewlett Bay Park.

At the time of his death, Prescott was residing at *Still Pond* in East Islip. [*See* Spinzia, *Long Island's Prominent South Shore Families* – Prescott entry.]

In 2013, the 2,577 square-foot house sold for $750,000.

### Pritchard, Clarence Franklin (1885-1963)

| | |
|---|---|
| Occupation(s): | capitalist - secretary, Warner Brothers |
| Civic Activism: | member, savings bond division, New York State Committee of Treasury, 1946 |
| Marriage(s): | 1914-1960 – Florence Helen Bierwirth (1890-1960) |
| Address: | 87 Meadow Road, Lawrence |

Name of estate:
Year of construction:
Style of architecture:
Architect(s):
Landscape architect(s):
House extant: no
Historical notes:

    The *Long Island Society Register, 1929* lists Clarence Franklin and Florence Helen Bierwirth Pritchard as residing on Meadow Road, Lawrence.
    He was the son of Alfred Pritchard of New Rochelle, NY.
    Florence Helen Bierwirth Pritchard was the daughter of Dr. Julius Carl and Mrs. Nettie Gerherdine Cocks Bierwirth of Brooklyn and Lawrence.
    Clarence Franklin and Florence Helen Bierwirth Pritchard's daughter Jane married Gilbert Barnes, the son of Frank Goffe Barnes of New Haven, CT.


### Proctor, William Ross, Jr. (1893-1979)

| | |
|---|---|
| Occupation(s): | financier - partner, Abbott, Hoppin, and Co., NYC (stock brokerage firm); partner, Abbott, Proctor, and Paine (stock brokerage firm) |
| Civic Activism: | director, American Kennel Club; president, Westminister Kennel Club, 1947-1950; a founder and governor, Leash Club |
| Marriage(s): | 1917-1977 – Joy Waldron Williams (1895-1977) |
| Address: | Cedar Avenue, Hewlett Bay Park |

Name of estate:
Year of construction:
Style of architecture:
Architect(s):
Landscape architect(s):
House extant: unconfirmed
Historical notes:

    The *Long Island Society Register, 1929* lists William Ross and Joy W. Williams Proctor, Jr. as residing in Hewlett [Hewlett Bay Park]. The 1930 Census lists the Proctors at this address.
    He was the son of William Ross and Elizabeth Singer Proctor.
    Joy Waldron Williams Proctor was the daughter of Waldron and Josephine Hotchkiss Williams of *Stone House* in Rye, NY.
    William Ross and Joy Waldron Williams Proctor, Jr.'s daughter Barbara married Derek Richardson and resided in Westport, CT. Their daughter Joy married William Jay Schieffelin III of Ashville, ME, and resided in New Haven, CT. Their son William Ross Proctor III married Cathleen Patricia Dugan, the daughter of Howard F. Dugan of Bronxville, NY, and resided in Greenwich, CT. Their son Waldron married Helen Jay Kobbe, the daughter of Frederick William Kobbe of Hewlett Neck, and resided in New Canaan, CT.

### Putnam, Hobart Hayes (1882-1965)

| | |
|---|---|
| Occupation(s): | industrialist - sales manager, United States Cast Iron Pipe & Foundry Co., NYC; vice-president, secretary, and director, Empire Pipe Corp., Brooklyn |
| Marriage(s): | M/1 – 1910-1923 – Natalie Maie Miller (d. 1923) <br> M/2 – 1937-1959 – Marie Schoonmaker (d. 1959) |
| Address: | 152 Wellington Road, Garden City |
| Name of estate: | |
| Year of construction: | 1920 |
| Style of architecture: | Colonial Revival |
| Architect(s): | |
| Landscape architect(s): | |
| House extant: | yes |
| Historical notes: | |

The *Long Island Society Register, 1929* lists Hobart Hayes Putnam as residing at 152 Wellington Road, Garden City.
He was the son of Dr. Thomas Jay and Mrs. Emma Katherine Hayes Putnam of Springfield, MA.
Natalie Maie Miller Putnam was the daughter of Matthew Kane and Saletta Pressinger Miller.
Hobart Hayes and Natalie Maie Miller Putnam's daughter Marjorie married James Lawrence Maxwell, the son of Howard Washburn and Helen Stark Young Maxwell, Sr. of *Maxwelton* in Glen Cove, and resided on Centre Island. [*See* Spinzia, *Long Island's Prominent North Shore Families, vol. I* – Maxwell entries – and *Long Island's Prominent South Shore Families* – Maxwell entry.]

Marie Schoonmaker Putnam had previously been married to Herbert Ludlam Smith, Sr. with whom she resided at *Oliver's Point* on Centre Island and, later, in Garden City. [*See* Spinzia, *Long Island's Prominent North Shore Families, vol. II* – Smith entry.]

*front facade, 2006*

### Quinby, John Gurley, Jr. (1893-1960)

| | |
|---|---|
| Occupation(s): | merchant - member, Clarence Whitman & Sons (textile commission merchants) |
| Marriage(s): | M/1 – 1917-div. 1929 – Margaret Slocum <br> M/2 – Jane Gillespie (1901-1979) |
| Address: | *[unable to determine street address]*, Lawrence |
| Name of estate: | |
| Year of construction: | |
| Style of architecture: | |
| Architect(s): | |
| Landscape architect(s): | |
| House extant: | unconfirmed |
| Historical notes: | |

The *Long Island Society Register, 1929* lists John G. and Margaret Slocum Quinby [Jr.] as residing in Lawrence.
He was the son of John Gurley and Mary S. Eaton Quinby, Sr. of New York.
Margaret Slocum Quinby was the daughter of William H. Slocum of Boston, MA. She later married James O. Stafford and, subsequently, Edward L. Stevenson.
John Gurley and Margaret Slocum Quinby, Jr.'s daughter Louise married William Whitney Pinney, Jr. Their daughter Ann married Dr. Peter F. Warfield and resided in Montclair, NJ. Their son John Gurley Quinby III married Joyce Estelle Easman, the daughter of James Elwood Easman, Jr. of Newburgh, NY.

### Rasmus, Carl Gerhard (d. 1957)

| | |
|---|---|
| Occupation(s): | financier - vice-president and treasurer, United States Mortgage & Trust Co., NYC |
| | founder, Rasmus and Co. (stock brokerage firm) |
| Marriage(s): | 1901-1957 – Helen Hale (1875-1960) |
| Address: | Maple Avenue, Cedarhurst |
| Name of estate: | |
| Year of construction: | |
| Style of architecture: | |
| Architect(s): | |
| Landscape architect(s): | |
| House extant: unconfirmed | |
| Historical notes: | |

 The *Long Island Society Register, 1929* lists Carl G. and Helen Hale Rasmus as residing in Cedarhurst. The 1920 Census lists the Rasmuses as residing on Mapel [sic] Avenue.
 She was the daughter of Henry Safford and Frances Emogene Kilburn Hale of Philadelphia, PA. The Hale's family fortune was severely constricted when Carl's brother-in-laws took his advice to invest in German war bonds.
 Carl Gerhard and Helen Hale Rasmus' daughter Rhoda married Donald Bedell Miller, the son of Kelton B. Miller of Pittsfield, MA. Their daughter Stephanie married George Maurice Churcher, the son of George Churcher of Suffolk, England. Their daughter Frances, who resided in Santa Barbara, CA, did not marry.


### Rawlins, George Foster (1875-1932)

| | |
|---|---|
| Occupation(s): | financier - partner, Rawlins, White, and Co. (stock brokerage firm) |
| Marriage(s): | M/1 – 1904-1905 – Helen Beadleston (1880-1905) |
| | M/2 – 1908 – Amelia Bowers (1877-1933) |
| Address: | Fulton Avenue, Hempstead |
| Name of estate: | |
| Year of construction: | |
| Style of architecture: | |
| Architect(s): | |
| Landscape architect(s): | |
| House extant: unconfirmed | |
| Historical notes: | |

 George Foster Rawlins was the son of Henry and Emily Dale Rawlins.
 Helen Beadleston Rawlins was the daughter of Alfred Nash and Mary Elizabeth Phipps Rawlins of Manhattan.
 The *Long Island Society Register, 1929* lists G. Foster and Amy [sic] Bowers Foster as residing on Fulton Avenue, Hempstead.
 Amelia Bowers Rawlins was the daughter of Henry and Mary Christie Bowers of Brooklyn. Amelia had previously been married to Lucius Trowbridge Martin, the son of William Royal Henry and Elizabeth Bulford Martin.

### Rawlins, Herbert Noel, Jr. (1904-1956)

| | |
|---|---|
| Occupation(s): | financier -   partner, Rhoades and Co. (stock brokerage firm) |
| | industrialist -  Madison Glass Co. |
| Marriage(s): | 1937-1956 – Doris Terhune |
| Address: | 26 Chestney Road, Cedarhurst |

Name of estate:
Year of construction:
Style of architecture:
Architect(s):
Landscape architect(s):
House extant:  no
Historical notes:

   Herbert Noel Rawlins, Jr. was the son of Herbert Noel and Nathalie Hatch Rawlins, Sr., who resided in Cedarhurst and Southampton. Herbert won the national amateur squash racquet championship in 1928 and the Canadian championship in 1929. He was the club champion of New York's Racquet and Tennis Club from 1928 through 1931.
   Doris Terhune Rawlins was the daughter of Ten Broeck Monroe and Florence Mabel Wilson Terhune of Manhattan.
*[See following entry for additional family information.]*


### Rawlins, Herbert Noel, Sr. (1879-1947)

| | |
|---|---|
| Occupation(s): | financier -   partner, Batcheller and Adee (stock brokerage firm) |
| Marriage(s): | M/1 – 1904-1927 – Nathalie Hatch (d. 1927) |
| | M/2 – Josephine Norman |
| Address: | Ocean Avenue, Cedarhurst |

Name of estate:
Year of construction:
Style of architecture:
Architect(s):
Landscape architect(s):
House extant:  unconfirmed
Historical notes:

   The *Long Island Society Register, 1929* lists Herbert Noel Rawlins [Sr.] as residing in Southampton. [*See* Spinzia, *Long Island's Prominent Families in the Town of Southampton* – Rawlins entry.]
   Nathalie Hatch Rawlins was the daughter of Nathaniel W. T. and Mary Riggs Hatch of New York.
   Herbert Noel and Nathalie Hatch Rawlins, Sr.'s daughter Mary married Bingham Willing Morris, the son of John B. Morris of New York, and resided at *Pra–Qua–Les* in Southampton. [*See* Spinzia, *Long Island's Prominent Families in the Town of Southampton* – Morris entry.] Their daughter Rosalie married Gerald Hamilton Moran, the son of William E. Moran of Manhattan, and resided in Cold Spring Harbor. Their son Herbert Noel Rawlins, Jr. married Doris Terhune and resided in Cedarhurst.
*[See previous entry for additional family information.]*

### Raymond, William, Sr. (1871-1944)

| | |
|---|---|
| Occupation(s): | financier -  partner, Chauncey and Co. (stock brokerage firm) |
| Marriage(s): | 1906-1944 – Marian Ward Low (1879-1971) |
| Address: | 580 Ocean Avenue, Lawrence |
| Name of estate: | |
| Year of construction: | c. 1900 |
| Style of architecture: | Neo-Tudor |
| Architect(s): | Renwick, Aspinwall, and Owen designed the house (for R. A. Peabody) |
| Landscape architect(s): | |
| House extant: | yes |
| Historical notes: | |

*rear facade, 1901*

The house, originally named *Terrace Hall,* was built by Richard Augustus Peabody. It was later owned by Raymond and, subsequently, by Isaac Gamel.

The *Long Island Society Register, 1929* lists William and Marian Ward Low Raymond [Sr.] as residing in Cedarhurst [Lawrence].

He was the son of James and Henrietta Ketchum Raymond. William's sister Caroline married Samuel Sloan Chauncey.

Marian Ward Low Raymond was the daughter of Abbot Augustus and Marian Ward Low, Sr.

William and Marian Ward Low Raymond, Sr.'s daughter Marian married George Winter Dean, the son of William John and Laura Winter Dean of St. Paul, MN. Their daughter Carolyn married Thomas Frederick Vietor, Jr., the son of Thomas Frederick and Elizabeth Bacon Allen Vietor, Sr., and resided in Manhattan. Their son William Raymond, Jr. married Mary Elizabeth Shonk, the daughter of Herbert Bronson and Sarah Gertrude Knight Shonk, of Scarsdale, NY, and resided in Manhattan.

### Recht, William, Sr. (1894-1983)

| | |
|---|---|
| Occupation(s): | industrialist -  export manager, Fuchs and Lang Manufacturing Co.; manager, Rutherford Machinery Co. (lithograph and printing machinery firm); vice-president and director, Sun Chemical Co.; founder and president, William Recht Co., Inc. (manufacturer of printing ink); president, Gaetjens, Berger, & Wirth (manufacturers of printing ink) |
| | inventor -  latex lining for bottle caps; coating for inside of toothpaste and cold cream tubes. |
| Civic Activism: | judge, New York State Boxing Commission |
| Marriage(s): | 1930 – Rosalie Adelaide Flebbe (b. 1899) |
| Address: | 955 Bentron Street, Woodmere |
| Name of estate: | |
| Year of construction: | 1938 |
| Style of architecture: | Contemporary |
| Architect(s): | Olive Frances Tjaden designed the house (for W. Recht, Sr.) |
| Landscape architect(s): | |
| House extant: | yes |
| Historical notes: | |

*front facade*

The house was built by William Recht, Sr.

He was the son of Marcus and Adhaid Elisabetha Kraus Recht.

Rosalie Adelaide Flebbe Recht was the daughter of Ernest August William and Annie Griffin Flebbe.

William and Rosalie Adelaide Flebbe Recht, Sr.'s son William Recht, Jr. married Patricia Hathaway Powers, the daughter of John Robert Powers of Beverly Hills, CA. Powers was the founder of the John Robert Powers Agency whose clients included Lucille Ball, Barbara Walters, Henry and Jane Fonda, John Wayne, and First Lady Betty Ford.

In 1991, the 2,664-square-foot house sold for $332,500.

### Rees, Harold Baxter, Sr. (1873-1936)

| | |
|---|---|
| Occupation(s): | industrialist - Rees' Sons (leather manufacturer) |
| Marriage(s): | 1896-1938 – Elizabeth Somervell Compton (1871-1962) |
| Address: | Meadow Lane, Lawrence |
| Name of estate: | |
| Year of construction: | |
| Style of architecture: | |
| Architect(s): | |
| Landscape architect(s): | |
| House extant: | unconfirmed |
| Historical notes: | |

The *Long Island Society Register, 1929* lists Harold B. and Elizabeth S. Compton Rees [Sr.] as residing on Meadow Lane, Cedarhurst [Lawrence].
   He was the son of Arthur F. Rees, Sr.
   Elizabeth Somervell Compton Rees was the daughter of Barnes and Margaret Hollyday Sothoron Compton, Sr.
   Harold Baxter and Elizabeth Somervell Compton Rees, Sr.'s son Compton married Katharine Hoppin Richmond, the daughter of Lewis Martin and Sarah Thacher Richmond of *Sunninghill* in Old Brookville, and, later, Myrna Guadalupe Bolio. [*See* Spinzia, *Long Island's Prominent North Shore Families, vol. II* – Richmond entry.] In 1924, their son Harold Baxter Rees, Jr., a college freshman, died of injuries sustained while playing hockey.
   In 1928 the house was purchased from Rees by James William Maitland. [*The New York Times* October 18, 1928, p. 50.]


### Reeves, Edward Duer, Sr. (b. 1880)

| | |
|---|---|
| Occupation(s): | industrialist - vice-president, Esso Research and Engineering Co., NY (affiliate of Standard Oil Co., of New Jersey) |
| Marriage(s): | 1908 – Beatrice Meserole Oltrogge (1887-1967) |
| Address: | 55 Brixton Road, Garden City |
| Name of estate: | |
| Year of construction: | 1923 |
| Style of architecture: | Dutch Colonial Revival |
| Architect(s): | |
| Landscape architect(s): | |
| House extant: | yes |
| Historical notes: | |

*front facade, 2001*

The *Long Island Society Register, 1929* lists Beatrice Meserole Oltrogge Reeves as residing at 55 Brixton Road, Garden City.
   She was the daughter of John F. Oltrogge of Manhattan. Beatrice subsequently married Edward Nicoll Townsend, Jr. and resided in Cold Spring Harbor. She later married Robert Newton Gilmore, Sr., the son of William Guy and Mary Jane Cochran Gilmore, Sr. of *My Fancy* in West Babylon, with whom she resided in Dix Hills. [*See* Spinzia, *Long Island's Prominent South Shore Families* – Gilmore entry.]
   Edward Duer and Beatrice Meserole Oltrogge Reeves, Sr.'s son John married Harriet Hoyt Phillips, the daughter of John Frank Phillips of Tarrytown, NY. Their daughter Meserole married John Daniel Haney, Jr. Their son Edward Duer Reeves, Jr. married Marjorie Ann Mixon, the daughter of Charles M. Mixon of Summit, NJ.

### Remick, Joseph Gould (1898-1962)

| | |
|---|---|
| Occupation(s): | financier - partner, Edey and Gibson, NYC (stock brokerage firm); partner, Paige, Smith, and Remick, NYC (stock brokerage firm); partner, Stillman, Maynard, and Co., NYC (later, Maynard, Oakley, and Lawrence) (stock brokerage firm); governor, New York Stock Exchange |
| Civic Activism: | president, Association of Stock Exchange Firms |
| Marriage(s): | 1922-1962 – Eleanor Huntington Francke (1902-1993) |
| Address: | Ocean Avenue, Woodmere |

Name of estate:
Year of construction:
Style of architecture:
Architect(s):
Landscape architect(s):
House extant: unconfirmed
Historical notes:

The *Long Island Society Register, 1929* lists Joseph Gould and Eleanor Huntington Francke Remick as residing in Woodmere.

He was the son of Joseph and Anne Gould Remick of Boston, MA.

Eleanor Huntington Francke Remick was the daughter of Leopold Hernandez and Elise Irving Huntington Francke of Lawrence. Eleanor's sister Mary married George West Van Siclen and resided in Woodsburgh.

Joseph Gould and Eleanor Huntington Francke Remick's daughter Joan married Edward Duffy French, the son of Seth Barton and Mary Tyler Duffy French, Sr. of Hewlett Neck, and resided in Chicago, IL. Their daughter Eleanor married Douglas Seaman, the son of Irving Seaman of Milwaukee, WI, and resided in Milwaukee.

### Rennard, John Townsend (1893-1958)

| | |
|---|---|
| Occupation(s): | financier - stockbroker |
| Marriage(s): | 1921-div. 1936 – Ruth Merritt Gaynor (1903-1977) |
| Address: | Fulton Avenue, Uniondale |

Name of estate:
Year of construction:
Style of architecture:
Architect(s):
Landscape architect(s):
House extant: unconfirmed
Historical notes:

The *Long Island Society Register, 1929* lists John Townsend and Ruth M. Gaynor Rennard as residing on Fulton Avenue, Hempstead. The 1930 Census lists the Rennards at this address.

He was the son of John Clifford and Mary Lockwood Townsend Rennard of Kings Point. His sister Dorothy married Henry Rogers Benjamin, Sr. and resided at *Lake House* in Southampton. [*See* Spinzia, *Long Island's Prominent Families in the Town of Southampton* - Benjamin entry.] Dorothy subsequently married George Hyde Clarke of *Hyde Hall* in Cooperstown, NY.

Ruth Merritt Gaynor Rennard was the daughter of New York City Mayor William Jay and Mrs. Augusta C. Mayer Gaynor, who resided at *Deepwells* in St. James. [*See* Spinzia, *Long Island: A Guide to New York's Suffolk and Nassau Counties – Deepwells Farm – Estate of William Jay Gaynor – Deepwells*, St. James.] Ruth subsequently married Dudley Gautier Bird with whom she resided in Westbury. He was the son of Oliver William and Clara Gautier Bird, Jr., who resided at *Green Hedge* in Uniondale. Ruth's sister Gertrude married William Seward D. Webb, Jr. and resided in Old Westbury. Her sister Marion married Ralph Heyward Isham of Glen Head and, later, Congrove Jackson of Oyster Bay; and, subsequently, Frank C. Hurt. [*See* Spinzia, *Long Island's Prominent North Shore Families, vol. I* - Isham entry; *Long Island's Prominent North Shore Families, vol. II* - Webb entry; and *Long Island's Prominent South Shore Families* - Gulden entry.] Her sister Helen married Edward T. Bedford II and, later, Whitney Kernochan, the son of J. Frederick Kernochan of Manhattan. Her sister Edith married Henry Kermit Vingut of St. James and, later, James Park, the son of William Gray and Elizabeth Sweitzer Park of *Turnpike Cottage* in Old Westbury, and resided at *Goodwill Farm* in Monkton, MD. Her brother Norman married Betsy Page, the daughter of The Reverend Page of Fairfax, VA. Betsey subsequently married Auguste Julien Cordier, Jr. of *Kyalami* in East Hampton [*See* Spinzia, *Long Island's Prominent Families* in East Hampton – Cordier entry.]

John Townsend and Ruth Merritt Gaynor Rennard's daughter Ruth married Frederick Hubbard Gwynne, Jr., the noted actor known as Fred Gwynne who was son of Frederick Walker and Dorothy Goddard Ficken Gwynne, Sr. of Woodmere.

### Rhett, William Brisbane, Sr. (1863-1942)

Occupation(s): industrialist - secretary and treasurer, Lorillard Tobacco Co.

Marriage(s): 1899-1942 – Elizabeth Tyler (1871-1966)

Address: 124 Hilton Avenue, Garden City
Name of estate:
Year of construction: 1910
Style of architecture: Colonial Revival
Architect(s):
Landscape architect(s):
House extant: yes
Historical notes:

   The *Long Island Society Register, 1929* lists William Brisbane and Elizabeth Tyler Rhett [Sr.] as residing on Hilton Avenue, Garden City. *The Brooklyn Daily Eagle* December 19, 1931, p. 5 lists their address as 124 Hilton Avenue.
   He was the son of Roland Smith and Julia Lowndes Brisbane Rhett, Sr.
   Elizabeth Tyler Rhett was the daughter of Nathaniel Tyler.
   William Brisbane and Elizabeth Tyler Rhett, Sr.'s daughter Elizabeth married Walter Murphy, Jr. of Garden City. Their son Edward married Elizabeth Louise Good, the daughter of John Good of Westbury. Their son William Brisbane Rhett, Jr. married Cornelia Ludlam Anderson, the daughter of Goodwin Anderson of Ridgewood, NY.
   In 2004, the 4,463-square-foot house sold for $1.85 million.

*front facade, 2012*

## Richard, Auguste (1890-1980)

| | |
|---|---|
| Occupation(s): | industrialist -   partner, Lawrence & Co., NYC (textile commission firm); |
| | treasurer and general manager, Ipswich Mills, MA |
| | (hosiery manufacturer); |
| | president, Spool Cotton Co.; |
| | president and director, Crown Fastener Corp., Warren, RI; |
| | director, Clark Thread Co., Newark, NJ; |
| | director, J. & P. Coates, Inc., Pawtucket, RI |
| | financier -   director, Bank of the Manhattan Co., NYC; |
| | partner, F. Eberstadt and Co. (investment banking firm) |
| Civic Activism: | trustee, Pomfret School, Pomfret, CT; |
| | president, Five Towns Community Chest, 1936; |
| | director, Manhattan Eye, Ear, and Throat Hospital, NYC; |
| | director, Merchants Association of New York; |
| | director, Cotton Thread Institute; |
| | director, American Management Association; |
| | director, Foundation House; |
| | chairman, Army & Navy Munitions Board, 1942; |
| | trustee, Village of Hewlett Harbor |
| Marriage(s): | M/1 – 1917-1961 – Hetty Lawrence Hemenway (1890-1961) |
| | - writer -   "Four Days" (short story) |
| | Civic Activism:   co-chairman, Mercy Ships for Children |
| | Committee, 1940; |
| | trustee, Spence–Chapin Adoption Service; |
| | co-founder, Fountain House Foundation, Inc. |
| | (West Side New York mental rehabilitation |
| | center) |
| | M/2 – 1970-1980 – Rita Conway |
| Address: | Causeway, Lawrence |
| Name of estate: | *Tenant Farm* |
| Year of construction: | |
| Style of architecture: | |
| Architect(s): | |
| Landscape architect(s): | |
| House extant: | unconfirmed |
| Historical notes: | |

In 1923, Auguste Richard purchased James Slee's colonial-styled residence and one acre of land on Causeway in Lawrence. [*The Brooklyn Daily Eagle* August 17, 1923, p. 14.]

The *Long Island Society Register, 1929* lists Auguste and Hetty L. Hemenway Richard as residing at *Tenant Farm* in Lawrence. They later relocated to Glen Eyre, PA. The *Social Register, 1937* lists the Richards as residing at *Witsend* in Glen Eyre, PA.

He was the son of Edwin Auguste and Alice Moore Richard of Manhattan.

Hetty Lawrence Hemenway Richard was the daughter of Edward Augustus Holyoke and Harriett Dexter Lawrence Hemenway of Readville, MA.

Auguste and Hetty Lawrence Hemenway Richard's daughter Harriett married Lindsay Coates Herkness, Jr. of Meadow Brook, PA, and, resided in Lawrence. Harriett later married ____ Dawson. Their daughter Elvine married John Holmes Magruder III; Paul Scott Rankine with whom she resided in Washington, DC; and, subsequently, ____ King. Their son Mark married Veronica Dwight, the daughter of Philip J. and Emily Thomas Dwight of Hewlett Neck, and resided in East Hampton.

By 1973 Auguste and Rita Conway Richard were also summering in East Hampton. [*See* Spinzia, *Long Island's Prominent Families in the Town of East Hampton* – Richard entries.]

Rita Conway had previously been married to Thomas A. Clark.

### Richards, Junius Alexander, Sr. (1892-1964)

| | |
|---|---|
| Occupation(s): | financier - partner, H. H. Whitney, Goadby, and Co. (stock brokerage firm); partner, Smith, Barney, and Co. (formerly, Harris Upham and Co.; Smith, Barney, Harris, Upham and Co.; Salomon Smith Barney; now, MorganStanley SmithBarney) (wealth management firm); partner, Edward B. Smith and Co. (stock brokerage firm) |
| | industrialist - director, Rayoner, Inc. (manufacturer of wood cellulose); director, Philip Morris Co. (now part of Altria Group, Inc.) (tobacco products manufacturing firm) |
| | merchant - director, Atlantic & Pacific International Corp. (supermarkets) |
| | capitalist - director, Equitable Office Building Corp. |
| Civic Activism: | trustee, New York Institute of Education of the Blind; director, Beekman–Downtown Hospital, NYC (which was formed by the merger of Beekman Street and Downtown Hospitals) |
| Marriage(s): | M/1 – 1923-div. 1942 – Marie Renouard Thayer (b. 1896) |
| | M/2 – 1957-1964 – Monawee Allen (1912-1994) |
| Address: | 84 Cedarhurst Avenue, Lawrence |
| Name of estate: | |
| Year of construction: | |
| Style of architecture: | |
| Architect(s): | |
| Landscape architect(s): | |
| House extant: no | |
| Historical notes: | |

The *Long Island Society Register, 1929* lists Junius A. and Marie R. Thayer Richards [Sr.] as residing on Park Row, Cedarhurst [Lawrence]. The 1930 Census lists the Richardses at 84 Cedarhurst Avenue, Lawrence.

He was the son of Reuben Francis and Marie Louisa Alexander Richards.

Marie Renouard Thayer Richards was the daughter of Benjamin Bowditch and Marie Cecile Renouard Thayer, Jr. of Lawrence. Marie's sister Alice married Maynard Cady Ivison and resided in Hewlett Bay Park. Her sister Cecile married Douglas Gibbons and resided at *The Annex* in Purchase, NY.

Junius Alexander and Marie Renouard Thayer Richards, Sr.'s son Rubin married Elizabeth Hamilton Brady, the daughter of James Cox Brady of Fall Hills, NJ, and resided in Fall Hills. Their son Junius Alexander Richards, Jr. married Virginia Beal, the daughter of Gerald Fessenden Beal of Manhattan, and resided in East Hampton, CT. Junius later married Ruth Arline Hall, the daughter of Charles Henry and Sarah Luella Maude Cameron Hall.

In 1939, Richards had the dubious distinction of becoming the first stockbroker to be suspended by the Securities and Exchange Commission for stock manipulation. [*The New York Times* March 28, 1939, p. 31.]

Monawee Allen Richards was the daughter of George Raymond Allen.

**Ridder, Joseph Edward, Sr. (1886-1966)**

| | |
|---|---|
| Occupation(s): | publisher - staff member, Staats–Zeitung, NYC (German language newspaper of which his father was the publisher); |
| | general manager, International Typesetting Co., Brooklyn (family-owned firm); |
| | co-publisher, with his brothers Victor and Bernard, Staats–Zeitung, NYC; |
| | president, Ridder Brothers, NYC (later, Ridder Publications); |
| | chairman of board, Ridder Publications (chain of twenty-four newspapers); |
| | president, Ridder–Johns Inc., NYC |
| | inventor - Intertype Composing Machine |
| | industrialist - chairman of board, American Bosch Co.; director, Sonotone Corporation of America |
| | capitalist - director, Fifth Avenue Coach Co. |
| Civic Activism: | chairman, North Hempstead Housing Authority during World War II; |
| | member, Price Adjustment Board during World War II; |
| | president of board, North Shore Hospital |
| Marriage(s): | M/1 – 1911-1960 – Hedwig Ottilia Schneider (1889-1960) |
| | M/2 – 1961-1966 – Irma Saltzseider (1899-1971) |
| Address: | East Rockaway Road, Hewlett Bay Park |
| Name of estate: | |
| Year of construction: | |
| Style of architecture: | |
| Architect(s): | |
| Landscape architect(s): | |
| House extant: unconfirmed | |
| Historical notes: | |

Joseph Edward Ridder, Sr.'s World War I draft registration card lists this address.
He was the son of Herman and Mary Amend Ridder of Manhattan.
Hedwig Ottilia Schneider Ridder was the daughter of Otto and Marie Lindenmeyer Schneider of New York City.
Joseph Edward and Hedwig Ottilia Schneider Ridder, Sr.'s daughter Hedwig married Orin Leach and resided in Laurel Hollow. Their daughter Barbara married Thomas Long and resided in Rutherford, NJ. Their son Eric, who resided in Lattingtown, married Ethelette French Tucker and, subsequently, Florence Madeleine Graham. [*See* Spinzia, *Long Island's Prominent North Shore Families, vol. II* – Ridder entry.] Their son Joseph Edward Ridder, Jr. was four months old at time of death in 1912.
The *Social Register New York, 1939* lists Joseph E. and Hedwig Schneider Ridder [Sr.] as residing on Old Courthouse Road, New Hyde Park.
Irma Saltzseider Ridder was the daughter of Frederick Wilhelm and Marie Lindenmeyr Saltzseider.

### Ripley, Joseph Pierce (1889-1974)

| | |
|---|---|
| Occupation(s): | financier - secretary, W. A. Harriman (investment banking firm); chairman of board and president, Brown, Harriman, and Co. (later, Drexel, Harriman, and Co.) (investment banking firm); director, Harriman, Ripley, and Co., Ltd. (Canada) |
| | capitalist - vice-president, National City Co. (later, City Company of New York); director, United Aircraft Corp.; director, United Airlines Transportation Corp. |
| | industrialist - director, Virginia Pulp & Paper Co.; director, Remington Rand (later, Sperry Rand Corp); director, Cannon Mills; director, Hershey Chocolate Corp.; director, Clupak Inc. |
| Civic Activism: | member, United States Treasury Department financial and commercial commission to Central American countries; trustee, Cornell University, Ithaca, NY; member, joint administrative board, New York Hospital–Cornell Medical College |
| Marriage(s): | 1916-1974 – Florence Guild Albro (1888-1974) |
| Address: | 120 Kensington Road, Garden City |
| Name of estate: | |
| Year of construction: | 1924 |
| Style of architecture: | Colonial Revival |
| Architect(s): | |
| Landscape architect(s): | |
| House extant: yes | |
| Historical notes: | |

The *Long Island Society Register, 1929* lists Joseph P. and Florence Albert [sic] Ripley as residing at 120 Kensington Road, Garden City.

He was the son of Joseph Trescott and Harriet Theresa Konantz Ripley of Oak Park, IL.

Florence Guild Albro Ripley was the daughter of Clark Billings and Hettie Guild Albro of Chicago, IL.

Joseph Pierce and Florence Guild Albro Ripley's son John married Nancy Howell.

*front facade, 2001*

## Ripley, Sidney Dillon, Sr. (1863-1905)

| | |
|---|---|
| Occupation(s): | financier - treasurer, Equitable Life Assurance Society of the United States; |
| |     a founder and director, First National Bank of Hempstead; |
| |     director, Mercantile Trust Co.; |
| |     director, Mount Morris Bank |
| | industrialist - director, Taylor Iron and Steel Co.; |
| |     director, Mananese Steele Safe, Co. |
| | capitalist - director, Union Pacific Railroad* |
| Marriage(s): | 1885-1905 – Mary Baldwin Hyde (1867-1938) |
| |   - Civic Activism: vice president, Sea Cliff Home for Convalescent Babies; |
| |     president, Lisa Day Nursery |
| Address: | California Avenue and Fulton Avenue, Uniondale |
| Name of estate: | *The Crossways* |
| Year of construction: | 1889 |
| Style of architecture: | Queen Anne |
| Architect(s): | |
| Landscape architect(s): | Hicks Nursery supplied Scotch Pines (for S. D. Ripley, Sr.) |

House extant: no; destroyed by fire in 1934
Historical notes:

    The forty-eight-room house, originally named *The Crossways*, was built by Sidney Dillon Ripley, Sr.

    The *Social Register New York, 1903* lists Sidney Dillon and Mary B. Hyde Ripley [Sr.] as residing at *The Crossways* in Hempstead [Uniondale]. They were included on Ward McAllister's list of society's elite "400."

    He was the son of Joseph Dwight and Juliet Elizabeth Dillon Ripley. Sidney's brother Julien married Helen Adell Bell and resided at *Three Corners Farm* in Muttontown. [*See* Spinzia, *Long Island's Prominent North Shore Families, vol. II* – Ripley entry.]

    Mary Baldwin Hyde Ripley was the daughter of Henry Baldwin and Annie Fitch Hyde, Sr., who resided at *The Oaks* in West Bay Shore. Mary subsequently married Charles Robert Scott and continued to reside at *The Crossways*. Her brother James Hazen Hyde, who inherited *The Oaks*, married Marthe Leishman and, later, Helen Ella Walker.

    Sidney Dillon and Mary Baldwin Hyde Ripley, Sr.'s son James Hazen Ripley married Marguerite Doubleday, the daughter of George Doubleday, and resided in Salisbury, CT. Their son Henry Baldwin Hyde Ripley, Sr. married Lesley Fredericka Pearson, the daughter of Frederick A. Pearson of *Ochre Point* in Newport, RI, and resided at *Beech Bound* in Newport, RI. Their son Sidney Dillon Ripley, Jr. married Betsy Ann Sherry, the daughter of Henry Sherry of New York City. Their daughter Annah married Count Pierre de Viel Castel of Orleans, France. During World War II, the de Viel Castels' house was occupied by the German Army. Because of her impeccable French and German, the Germans never suspected that Annah was an American. She was able to eavesdrop on the German conversations and pass the information on to the French resistance in a basket of eggs that she took to a local village for sale in the market. Annah's cousin Henry Baldwin Hyde II was the chief of the Office of Strategic Services in France and, later, in Switzerland, during World War II. [*See* Spinzia, *Long Island's Prominent South Shore Families* – Hyde entries.]

    *Ripley's grandfather Sidney Dillon was a founder and the president of the Union Pacific Railroad.

[*See also* Spinzia, *Long Island's Prominent Families in the Town of Southampton* – Wyckoff entry.]

*The Crossways, 1902*

### Rives, Francis Bayard (1890-1969)

| | |
|---|---|
| Occupation(s): | attorney -   member, Olin, Clark, and Phelps, NYC, 1916-1919; member, Winthrop, Stimson, Putnam, and Roberts, NYC, 1919-1928 |
| | intelligence agent -   chief of Strategic Services for France during World War II |
| Civic Activism: | trustee, Barnard College, NYC |
| Marriage(s): | 1917-1969 – Helen Leigh Hunt (1893-1996) |
| Address: | East Rockaway Road, Hewlett Bay Park |
| Name of estate: | *Mapleglades* |
| Year of construction: | |
| Style of architecture: | |
| Architect(s): | |
| Landscape architect(s): | |
| House extant: | unconfirmed |
| Historical notes: | |

The *Long Island Society Register, 1929* lists F. Bayard and Helen L. Hunt Rives as residing at *Mapleglades* in Hewlett [Hewlett Bay Park]. Rives' passport application lists this address.

He was the son of George Lockhart and Sarah Whiting Rives. Sarah had previously been married to Oliver Hazzard Perry Belmont of *Brookholt* in East Meadow, the son of August and Caroline Slidell Perry Belmont, Sr. of *Nursery Stud Farm* in North Babylon. [*See* Spinzia, *Long Island's Prominent South Shore Families* – Belmont entry – and O. H. P. Belmont entry in this book.]

Helen Leigh Hunt Rives was the daughter of Leigh Smith James and Jessie Noble Hunt.

Francis Bayard and Helen Leigh Hunt Rives' daughter Margaret married Laurance Blanchard Rand and, later, Robert Charles Kellam. Their son George married Emily Jane Eyre, the daughter of Beverley Montagu and Mary Ludlow Smedberg Weeks Eyre of Bay Shore. [*See* Spinzia, *Long Island's Prominent South Shore Families* – Eyre entry.] Their daughter Margaret married Laurance Blanchard Rand, Jr. of Southport, CT.


### Robb, Hampton (1895-1956)

| | |
|---|---|
| Occupation(s): | capitalist -   vice-president, Francis H. Leggett Co. |
| Marriage(s): | M/1 – 1918-div. 1929 – Elizabeth Wiley (1896-1978) |
| | M/2 – 1933-div.1939 – Miriam Fortune Ryan (1907-1980) |
| Address: | Smith Lane, Hewlett Neck |
| Name of estate: | |
| Year of construction: | |
| Style of architecture: | |
| Architect(s): | |
| Landscape architect(s): | |
| House extant: | unconfirmed |
| Historical notes: | |

The *Long Island Society Register, 1929* lists Hampton and Elizabeth Wiley Robb as residing in Hewlett Neck.

He was the son of Dr. Hunter and Mrs. Isabel Adams Robb of Philadelphia, PA.

Elizabeth Wiley Robb was the daughter of Admiral Henry Aristo and Mrs. Roberts Morgan Wood Wiley.

Hampton and Elizabeth Wiley Robb's daughter Elisabeth married William C. Evers who was killed in action at Iwo Jima and, later, Gilbert Bettman, Jr. of Cincinnati, OH.

Miriam Fortune Ryan Robb was the daughter of Allan Aloysius and Sarah Dunn Tack Ryan, Sr. and the granddaughter of Thomas Fortune Ryan. Miriam had previously been married to Jacques R. Herbert of Montreal, Canada. After her divorce from Hampton, she married Robert Herbert Ellinger, the son of Max Ellinger.

Hampton and Miriam Fortune Ryan Robb's son Theodore married Margaret Mary Armstrong, the daughter of William Edward Armstrong.

In 1930, Robb sold the ten-room house to Arthur Temple Blackwood. [*The New York Times* June 5, 1930, p. 50.]

### Roberts, Albert Samuel, Jr. (1880-1935)

| | |
|---|---|
| Occupation(s): | industrialist - vice-president and director, White Rock Mineral Spring Co. (soda manufacturing firm); |
| Civic Activism: | a founder and first president, Five Towns Community Chest; chairman, Emergency Work Bureau of Nassau County; member, board of Commissioners, Sanitary District #1 (sewer system for Five Towns area) |
| Marriage(s): | 1914-1935 – Nathalie Harrison (1892-1976) |
| Address: | 370 Ocean Avenue, Lawrence |
| Name of estate: | *Longwood Hall* |
| Year of construction: | 1923 |
| Style of architecture: | Neo-Tudor with Flemish elements |
| Architect(s): | |
| Landscape architect(s): | |
| House extant: yes | |

*front facade, 2008*

Historical notes:

In the 1920s Roberts purchased the house from Jennie McComb Taylor. [*The New York Times* June 24, p. 26.]

The *Long Island Society Register, 1929* lists Albert S. and Nathalie Harrison Roberts [Jr.] as residing at *Longwood Hall*, Cedarhurst [Lawrence]. The 1930 Census lists the Robertses at this address.

He was the son of General Albert Samuel Roberts, Sr. of Austin, TX.

Nathalie Harrison Roberts was the daughter of Mitchell and Virginia Norris Harrison of Philadelphia, PA.

Albert Samuel and Nathalie Harrison Roberts, Jr.'s daughter Natalie married Reginald William Elings, the son of John J. Elings of Chicago, IL. Their son Albert Samuel Roberts III married Marie Louise Slocum, the daughter of Dr. Morris Slocum of Pittsburgh, PA. Their son K. Harrison Roberts married Louise Willard Littleton and resided at *D Cross Ranch* in Kaycee, WY. Louise was the daughter of Martin Wilson Littleton and the granddaughter of Martin Wiley and Maude E. Wilson Littleton of *Plandome Manor House* in Plandome Manor. [*See* Spinzia, *Long Island's Prominent North Shore Families*, vol. I – Littleton entry.]

In 1941 Mrs. Roberts sold the house to Charles Starne Belsterling. [*The New York Times* November 12, 1941, p. 41.]

### Robins, Samuel Davis, Sr. (1899-1972)

| | |
|---|---|
| Occupation(s): | inventor - oscillating sander |
| | industrialist - president, Robins Conveying Belt Co., Passaic, NJ (later, Hewitt–Gutta Percha Rubber Corp.; Hewitt–Robins, Inc., manufacturer of transmission belts and rubber foam used in mattresses and upholstery; and finally, Litton Industries) |
| | capitalist - a founder, with Juan Trippe, Long Island Airways (later, Pan-American Airways) |
| Marriage(s): | M/1 – 1925-div. 1932 – Emma Lawrence Jacob (1904-1992) |
| | M/2 – 1933 – Elizabeth Dexter Spencer (1910-1986) |
| Address: | Adams Street, Hewlett Bay Park |
| Name of estate: | |
| Year of construction: | |
| Style of architecture: | |
| Architect(s): | |
| Landscape architect(s): | |
| House extant: unconfirmed | |

Historical notes:

The *Long Island Society Register, 1929* lists S. Davis and Emma L. Jacob Robins as residing on Prospect, Woodmere.

By 1938 Robins had relocated to Hewlett Bay Park. [*The New York Times* May 30, 1938, p. 23.]

He was the son of Thomas and Winifred Howard Tucker Robins III of *Saddle Rock House* in Stamford, CT. Samuel's brother Thomas Robins IV, who resided in Hewlett, married Louisa Winslow Cogswell and, subsequently, Eileen Burden.

Emma Lawrence Jacob Robins was the daughter of Bartholomew Jacob of *Whitewell Farm* in Darien, CT.

Samuel Davis and Emma Lawrence Jacob Robins, Sr.'s daughter Lydia died at the age of five. Their daughter Elizabeth married John French MacKay, Jr. of Syosset, and resided in Lloyd Harbor. Their son Samuel Davis Robins, Jr. married Ann Symington Willis, the daughter of Herbert Tiernan Willis of Amagansett, and, later, Ruth Rose, the daughter of Harold Clement and Ruth Miner Rose of Greenwich, CT. Samuel and Ruth also resided in Greenwich, CT.

*[See following entry for additional family information.]*

**Robins, Thomas, IV (1896-1977)**

| | | |
|---|---|---|
| Occupation(s): | industrialist - | sales manager, Robins Conveying Belt Co., Passaic, NJ (later, Hewitt–Gutta Percha Rubber Corp.; Hewitt–Robins, Inc.; and finally, Litton Industries) |
| | | president, Hewitt–Robins, Inc. (manufacturer of transmission belts and rubber foam used in mattresses and upholstery); |
| | | director, Niagara Slate Corp. |
| | financier - | chairman of board, Federal Reserve Bank of Buffalo; |
| | | director, Marine Trust Co., Buffalo, NY |

Civic Activism: director, Joint Charities and Community Fund;
director, Family Service Society;
trustee, National Urban League;
trustee, Spence–Chapin Adoption Nursery;
member, advisory board, National Security Resources Board during World War II

Marriage(s): M/1 – 1918 – Louisa Winslow Cogswell (1898-1962)
M/2 – 1963-1970 – Eileen Burden (1911-1970)

Address: *[unable to determine street address]*, Hewlett
Name of estate:
Year of construction:
Style of architecture:
Architect(s):
Landscape architect(s):
House extant: unconfirmed
Historical notes:

    The *Long Island Society Register, 1929* lists Thomas and Louisa W. Cogswell Robins, Jr. as residing in Hewlett.
    He was the son of Thomas and Winifred Howard Tucker Robins III of *Saddle Rock House* in Stamford, CT. Thomas' brother Samuel, who resided in Hewlett Bay Park, married Emma Lawrence Jacob and, later, Elizabeth Dexter Spencer.
    Louisa Winslow Cogswell Robins was the daughter of Cullen Van Rennselaer and Agnes Eugenie Nickerson Cogswell.
    Thomas and Louisa Winslow Cogswell Robins IV's daughter Mary, who resided in Darien, CT, married Dr. Stephen Goodyear, the son of Anson Conger and Mary Martha Forman Goodyear who resided in Old Westbury. Mary subsequently married Julian Davies McKee, the son of Henry Sellers and Alice Martin Davies McKee II of Babylon. [*See* Spinzia, *Long Island's Prominent North Shore Families, vol. I* – Goodyear entry – and *Long Island's Prominent South Shore Families* – McKee entry.] Their daughter Louisa married Austin Goodyear and resided at *White Oak Shade* in New Canaan, CT. Their daughter Anna married Evan W. Thomas II, the son of Norman Mattoon and Frances Violet Stewart Thomas of Cold Spring Harbor, and resided in Cold Spring Harbor. [*See* Spinzia, *Long Island's Prominent North Shore Families, vol. II* – Thomas entry.]
    Eileen Burden Robins was the daughter of Arthur Scott and Cynthia Burke–Roche Burden of Brookville. Eileen had previously been married to Walter Maynard, the son of Walter Effingham and Eunice Ives Maynard, who resided at *Haut Bois* in Brookville. [*See* Spinzia, *Long Island's Prominent North Shore Families, vol. I* – Burden and Maynard entries.]
    *[See previous entry for additional family information.]*

### Robinson, Beverley Randolph (1876-1951)

| | |
|---|---|
| Occupation(s): | attorney - member, Strong and Cadwalader; member, Masten and Nichols; member, Milbank, Tweed, Hope, and Hadley, NYC |
| | industrialist - director, Borden Co.; director, Borden Farm Products, Co.; director, Drake Bakeries, Inc. |
| | financier - director, Lincoln Trust Co. |
| | politician - member, New York City Board of Aldermen, 1904-1905; member, New York State Assembly, 1907-1909; member, executive committee, Nassau County Republican Committee, 1911-1912; assistant treasurer, Republican National Committee, 1916; chairman, Nassau County Bridge Authority |
| Civic Activism: | trustee, American Museum of Natural History, NYC; trustee, Five Points House of Industry; president, Museum of the City of New York; vice-president, New York Genealogical and Biographical Society; bequeathed a large collection of naval prints to the United States Naval Academy, Annapolis, MD; president, Union Club, NYC; trustee, Harvard Club of New York; trustee, Downtown Association |
| Marriage(s): | 1917-1951 – Gladys Endicott (1887-1972) |
| Address: | Cedar Lane, Lawrence |
| Name of estate: | |
| Year of construction: | |
| Style of architecture: | |
| Architect(s): | |
| Landscape architect(s): | |
| House extant: | unconfirmed |
| Historical notes: | |

The *Long Island Society Register, 1929* lists Beverley R. and Gladys Endicott Robinson as residing in Lawrence.
He was the son of Beverley and Anna Eliza Foster Robinson of Manhattan.
Gladys Endicott Robinson was the daughter of Robert and Caroline Stewart Endicott of Manhattan.
The Robinsons did not have children.

## Robinson, Charles M. (b. 1856)

Occupation(s): business manager, Barnum and Baily Circuses
politician - member, Ohio State Assembly

Marriage(s): 1891-div. 1912 - Josephine DeMott (1865-1948)
- entertainer and associate professions –
circus bareback horse performer, Robinson Circus and Barnum and Baily Circus;
uncredited stunt circus performer for May Marsh in the motion picture "Polly of the Circus," 1932;
performed shoulder stands on a moving horse in Billy Rose's "Jumbo," Hippodrome, NY, 1936
capitalist - trained horses to perform in the circus;
owner, horse riding school for girls, Garden City;
owner, dance studio, Fulton and Franklin Streets, Hempstead
educator - director of fashion and posture, Traphagen School of Fashion, NYC, 1934-1944
writer - *A Women's Story of the Gold Rush*, 1921 (autobiography published in McCall's magazine);
*The Circus Lady*, 1926 (autobiography);
co-author, *Five Girls Who Dared*, 1930;
Civic Activism: suffragist* - founder, Women of Barnum and Bailey Equal Rights Society, 1912;
president, local suffragist club;
participated in Mineola to Hempstead Suffrage Parade, 1913;
participated in Suffrage Aviation Parade, Hempstead Field, 1913

Address: between Nassau and Hempstead Avenues, West Hempstead
Name of estate:
Year of construction: c. 1855
Style of architecture:
Architect(s):
Landscape architect(s):
House extant: no
Historical notes:

The house was built by Samuel E. Johnson. He served as a Kings County judge, Brooklyn school superintendent, and New York State Assemblyman. The fourteen-acre farm was later purchased by the Robinsons.

Charles M. Robinson was the son of the Robinson Circus owner John Robinson.

Josephine DeMott Robinson, who was a third-generation circus performer, was the daughter of James and Josephine Tourniaire DeMott.

The Robinsons did not have children. Josephine would later adopt Verona Ruth Oakley, who married Harold Francis Merritt, Sr. and resided in Garden City. [*See* Merritt entry.]

In 1917, Josephine sold the house and property to William Collins, who, in 1940, sold it to a developer who drained the farm's pond and built the Hempstead Manor housing development. A portion of the property became the site of the Hebrew Academy of Nassau County.

*For other Long Islanders involved in the suffrage movement *see* Raymond E. Spinzia, "Winning the Franchise: Long Island Activists in the Fight for Woman's Suffrage and Their Opponents, Long Island's Anti-Suffragists." wwwspinzialongislandestates.com

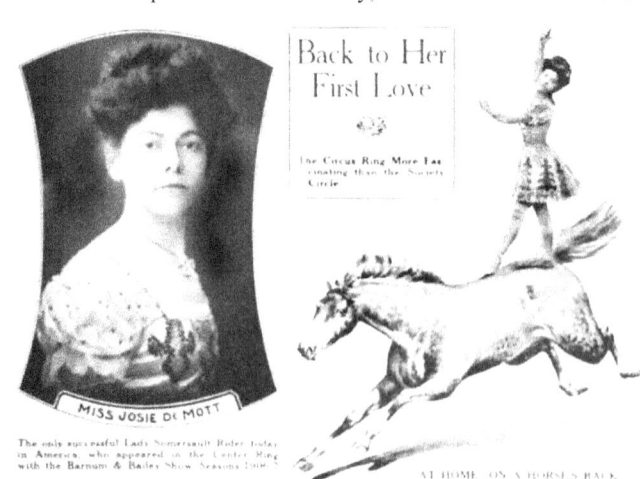

### Roche, The Reverend Spencer Summerfield (1949-1916)

| | |
|---|---|
| Occupation(s): | clergy - chancellor, Cathedral of the Incarnation, Garden City, 1897-1916; Saint Mark's Episcopal Church, Brooklyn, 1875-1912; examining chaplain, 1883-1911 |
| | writer - *The Life and Sermons of John Alexander Roche*; *Commemorative Discourses, Biographical and Civic Activism*; *St. Mark's Sixtieth Anniversary, 1850-1910*; *Cathedral Stones and Other Discourses*, 1917; *St. Mark's Church in the City of Brooklyn: The Story of the Rectory and Chancel*, 1908 |
| Civic Activism: | chairman, Church Pension Fund of Long Island |
| Marriage(s): | 1889-1916 – Emma Clark Henrickson (1865-1950) |
| Address: | 29 Hilton Avenue, Garden City |
| Name of estate: | |
| Year of construction: | 1923 |
| Style of architecture: | Colonial Revival |
| Architect(s): | |
| Landscape architect(s): | |
| House extant: | yes |
| Historical notes: | |

*front facade, 2008*

The *Long Island Society Register, 1929* lists Mrs. Spencer Summerfield and Emma Clark Hendrickson Roche as residing at 29 Hilton Avenue, Garden City.
   She was the daughter of John B. Henrickson.
   Spencer Summerfield Roche was the son of The Reverend John Alexander and Mrs. Mary Caroline Roche.
   The Reverend Spencer Summerfield and Mrs. Emma Clark Henrickson Roche's son Ernest, a stockbroker who committed suicide in 1929, married Florence Marguerite Menges, the daughter of Frederick Menges of Saratoga, NY, and resided in Garden City. Their son Austin married Jeananne Lafay O'Neill.
   In 1936 the house was remodeled.


### Roever, Charles Sigmund (b. 1900)

| | |
|---|---|
| Occupation(s): | publisher - member, Reinhold Publishing Co.; member, Ziff–Davis Publishing Co. |
| Marriage(s): | 1923-1947 – Dorothy Taylor Chamberlin (1902-1947) |
| Address: | 68 Garden Street, Garden City |
| Name of estate: | |
| Year of construction: | 1929 |
| Style of architecture: | Neo-Tudor |
| Architect(s): | |
| Landscape architect(s): | |
| House extant: | yes |
| Historical notes: | |

*front facade, 2001*

The *Long Island Society Register, 1929* lists Charles Sigmund and Dorothy Taylor Chamberlin as residing at 505 Fulton Avenue, Hempstead. The 1940 Census lists them at 68 Garden Street in Garden City.
   Dorothy Taylor Chamberlain Roever was the daughter of Dr. W. Taylor and Mrs. Bessie Shenton Chamberlin of Hempstead.
   In 1947, Dorothy committed suicide by inhaling gas from the kitchen stove. She left a note on the front door "Gas – Careful." She was found by her twenty-three-year-old son Charles. [*The New York Times* August 12, 1947, p. 14.]
   Charles Sigmund and Dorothy Taylor Chamberlin Roever's daughter Dorothy married Edward Cooper Sprague, Jr. of Hempstead.

### Rogers, Edward Sidney (1875-1949)

| | |
|---|---|
| Occupation(s): | attorney - specialized in unfair competition and trademarks* |
| | writer - *Good Will Trademarks and Unfair Trading*, 1915 |
| | industrialist - chairman of board, Sterling Drug, Inc. |
| Civic Activism: | delegate, International–American Conference to Negotiate Trademarks and Commercial Names; |
| | United States representative, International–American Committee, International Law Association; |
| | chairman, Brand Names Foundation; |
| | member, Patent, Trademark, and Copyright Board, Federal Trade Commission; |
| | delegate, Inter–American Trademark Conference |
| Marriage(s): | 1901-1949 – Eva Thompson (1875-1962) |
| Address: | Broadway, Lawrence |
| Name of estate: | |
| Year of construction: | c. 1900 |
| Style of architecture: | Colonial Revival |
| Architect(s): | Thomas Henry Randall designed the house (for Rogers) |
| Landscape architect(s): | |
| House extant: | no |
| Historical notes: | |

The house was built by Edward Sidney Rogers.
He was the son of James Harriman and Susan Fisher Rogers.
Eva Thompson Rogers was the daughter of William Nelson Thompson.
*Edward was often referred to as the "Father of Fair Trade."
[*The Cincinnati Enquirer* May 23, 1949, p. 13.]
Edward Sidney and Eva Thompson Rogers' son James married Sarah Dorothea Cholmeley–Jones, the daughter of Edward Cholmeley–Jones of *Seven Oaks* in Brommall, PA, and resided in Chicago, IL. Their son Edward Alden Rogers married Barbara Eldridge, the daughter of Harold Eldridge.

*front facade, c. 1900*

### Rolston, Brown, Sr. (1887-1971)

| | |
|---|---|
| Occupation(s): | industrialist - a founder, United States Metal Door and Trim Co. |
| Civic Activism: | president, American Importers Association |
| Marriage(s): | 1911-1971 – Mabel Brooks Hooley (1889-1944) |
| Address: | Evert Avenue, Hewlett Harbor |
| Name of estate: | |
| Year of construction: | |
| Style of architecture: | |
| Architect(s): | |
| Landscape architect(s): | |
| House extant: | unconfirmed |
| Historical notes: | |

The *Long Island Society Register, 1929* lists Brown and Mabel B. Hooley Rolston as residing in Hewlett [Hewlett Harbor].
He was the son of William Henry and Mary Adele Highet Rolston of New York.
Mabel Brooks Hooley Rolston was the daughter of Edwin Strange and Mabel Canfield Hooley of Plainfield, NJ.
Brown and Mabel Brooks Hooley Rolston, Sr.'s son Jared married Marion Louise Strickler, the daughter of Dr. Alfred Desch Strickler. Their son Brown Rolston, Jr. married Mary Donnelly Robb, the daughter of Hugh Montgomery Robb, and, later, Virginia Frances Whitmore.

### Roosevelt, Elliott, Sr. (1860-1894)

| | |
|---|---|
| Occupation(s): | capitalist - partner, Meadow Brook Park Company (Hempstead land development Co.); partner, Ludlow Real Estate; partner, Robinson, Russell, & Roosevelt (Manhattan real estate firm); financier - member, Roosevelt and Sons (investment banking firm) |
| Marriage(s): | 1883-1892 – Anna Rebecca Livingston Hall (1863-1892) |
| Address: | Salisbury Park Drive, Salisbury |
| Name of estate: | *Half Way Nirvana* |
| Year of construction: | 1887 |
| Style of architecture: | |
| Architect(s): | |
| Landscape architect(s): | |
| House extant: | unconfirmed |
| Historical notes: | |

The house, originally named *Half Way Nirvana*, was built by Elliott Roosevelt, Sr. [Joseph P. Lask, *Eleanor and Franklin: The Story of Their Relationship, Based on Eleanor Roosevelt's Private Papers* (New York: W. W. Norton & Co., Inc.), p. 32.]

He was the son of Theodore and Martha Bullock Roosevelt, Sr., who resided at *Tranquility* in Oyster Bay Cove. Elliott's brother President Theodore Roosevelt, who resided at *Sagamore Hill* in Cove Neck, married Alice Lee and, subsequently, Edith Kermit Carow. His sister Anna married William Cowles. His sister Corinne married Douglas Robinson.

Anna Rebecca Livingston Hall Roosevelt was the daughter of Valentine Gill and Mary Livingston Ludlow Hall, Jr., who resided at *Oak Terrace* in Tivoli, NY. Anna's sister Edith married William Forbes Morgan, Jr. and resided in Manhattan. Her brother Edward married Josephine B. Zabriskie, the daughter of Augustus and Josephine B. Booraem Zabriskie of Roslyn. Her sister Elizabeth married Stanley Mortimer and resided at *Roslyn Hall* in Old Westbury. [*See* Spinzia, *Long Island's Prominent North Shore Families, vol. I* – Mortimer entry.] Her sister Maude married Lawrence Waterbury with whom she resided in Pelham, NY, and, later, David Gray. The Grays resided at *Gray House* in Portland, ME.

Elliott and Anna Rebecca Livingston Hall Roosevelt, Sr.'s son Elliott died at the age of five. Their son Gracie Hall Roosevelt married Margaret Richardson and, subsequently, Dorothy Kemp. Their daughter Anna Eleanor married President Franklin Delano Roosevelt. [*See* Spinzia, *Long Island's Prominent North Shore Families, vol. II* – Roosevelt entry.]

[For a discussion of the life of Elliott Roosevelt, Sr., *see* Raymond E. Spinzia "Elliott Roosevelt, Sr. – A Spiral into Darkness: The Influences." *The Freeholder*, 12 (Fall 2007), pp. 3-7, 15-17.]

*Elliott Roosevelt, Sr. and Anna Eleanor at Half Way Nirvana*

## Roosevelt, Oliver Wolcott, Sr. (1890-1953)

| | |
|---|---|
| Occupation(s): | financier -  vice-president, Gregory and Son, Inc. (investment banking firm); |
| | assistant treasurer, Bankers Trust Co.; |
| | vice-president, Dry Dock Savings Bank |
| Civic Activism: | trustee, Savings Bank Life Insurance Fund (division of New York State Banking Department); |
| | president, Mortgage Conference of New York; |
| | member, executive committee, American Bankers Association; |
| | chairman, deposit committee, Savings Bank Association; |
| | trustee, Village of Hewlett Neck |
| Marriage(s): | M/1 – 1916-div. 1920 – Grace Helen Temple Olmstead (1894-1977) |
| | - nobility |
| | M/2 – 1921-1953 – Mary De Verdery Akin (1888-1976) |
| | - Civic Activism:  served in France with the Red Cross during World War I |
| Address: | 171 Ocean Avenue, Hewlett Neck |
| Name of estate: | |
| Year of construction: | 1920 |
| Style of architecture: | Colonial Revival |
| Architect(s): | |
| Landscape architect(s): | |
| House extant:  yes | |
| Historical notes: | |

Oliver Wolcott Roosevelt, Sr. was the son of Dr. James West and Mrs. Laura Henrietta d'Oremieulx Roosevelt of *Waldeck* in Cove Neck. [*See* Spinzia, *Long Island's Prominent North Shore Families, vol. II* – J. W. Roosevelt entry.]

Grace Helen Temple Olmstead Roosevelt was the daughter of Chauncey Lockhardt Olmstead. She subsequently married Baron Emanuel d'Astier de la Vigerie.

Oliver Wolcott and Grace Helen Temple Olmstead Roosevelt, Sr.'s son James West Roosevelt II married Eillene Joan Horan, the daughter of Timothy J. Horan.

The *Long Island Society Register, 1929* lists Oliver Wolcott and Mary De Verdery Akin Roosevelt [Sr.] as residing on Roger Avenue, Woodmere. The *Social Register New York, 1939* lists their address as 171 Ocean Avenue, Woodmere [Hewlett Neck].

She was the daughter of John Wesley and Frances Trippe Johnson Akin of Atlanta, GA. Mary had previously been married to Paul Stanley McMichael.

Oliver Wolcott and Mary De Verdery Akin Roosevelt, Sr.'s son Oliver Wolcott Roosevelt, Jr. married Ann Taylor, the daughter of Charles Lincoln and Hannah Chamberlin Taylor.

Roosevelt fell out of the window of his apartment which was located at 71 East 77th Street, NYC. [*The New York Times* July 16, 1953, p. 21.]

*side / rear facade, 2000*

### Rose, Reginald Perry (1903-1978)

| | |
|---|---|
| Occupation(s): | financier - partner, DeCoppet and Doremus (stock brokerage firm)<br>capitalist - theatrical producer |
| Marriage(s): | 1926-1978 – Bertha Benkard (1906-1982)<br>- Civic Activism: chairperson, committee that refurnished the principal rooms in President Theodore Roosevelt's home *Sagamore Hill*;<br>trustee, Henry Francis du Pont Museum;<br>trustee, New York Historical Society;<br>director, Museum of the City of New York;<br>trustee, Society for the Preservation of Long Island Antiquities;<br>chair, restoration committee, Joseph Lloyd Manor, Lloyd Harbor |
| Address: | 1 Franklin Court, Garden City |
| Name of estate: | |
| Year of construction: | 1912 |
| Style of architecture: | Neo-Tudor Townhouse |
| Architect(s): | Ford, Butler, and Oliver designed the house* |

Landscape architect(s):
House extant: unconfirmed
Nassau County Museum Collection has photographs of the house.
Historical notes:

The *Long Island Society Register, 1929* lists Reginald P. and Bertha Benkard Rose as residing at 1 Franklin Court, Garden City. The *Social Register New York,* 1975 list the Roses as residing on Mill River Road, Oyster Bay [Upper Brookville]. They relocated to Syosset prior to moving to Upper Brookville.

He was the son of George and Mary Josephine Maginnis Rose II, who resided in both Glen Head at *Overland Farm* and Old Westbury at *Overland House.* His sister Josephine was married to John William Mackay III and resided in Lattingtown and at *Happy House* in East Hills. His brother George Rose III married Jeannette T. Ross and resided at *Four Corners* in Lake Success and *On The Way* in Westbury.

Bertha Benkard Rose was the daughter of Henry Horton and Bertha King Benkard, who resided in Garden City and, later, in Muttontown.

Reginald Perry and Bertha Benkard Rose's son Reginald Peter Rose, who resided at 75 Mill River Road in Upper Brookville, married Margaret Beirne Waters, Marilyn H. Lipter, and Jeanne H. Chick. Their son George H. Rose resided on Bayville Road, Lattingtown. [*See* Spinzia, *Long Island's Prominent North Shore Families, vol. I* – Benkard and Makay entries – and *vol. II* – Rose entries.]

*The houses were built by Doubleday, Page, and Company as rentals.

*front facade of Franklin Court houses, 1912*

### Roth, Arthur Thomas (1905-1997)

| | |
|---|---|
| Occupation(s): | financier - CEO, chairman of board, and director, Franklin National Bank, Franklin Square*; chairman of board, Bank of Suffolk County (later, North Fork Bank) |
| | capitalist - director, Long Island Rail Road; director, Webb and Knapp (developers of Roosevelt Field) |
| Civic Activism: | president, Long Island Association; trustee, Long Island University – C. W. Post trustee, LaSalle Military Academy, Oakdale |
| Marriage(s): | 1930-1997 – Genevieve Kolezynski (1907-1998) |
| Address: | 344 Harvard Avenue, Rockville Centre |
| Name of estate: | |
| Year of construction: | 1937 |
| Style of architecture: | Contemporary |
| Architect(s): | |
| Landscape architect(s): | |
| House extant: yes | |
| Historical notes: | |

Born in The Bronx to Bavarian immigrants, Arthur Thomas Roth was known as "Mr. Long Island."

Arthur Thomas and Genevieve Kolezynski Roth's daughter Carolyn married John Powers Madigan, Jr. of Rockville Centre and resided in Oldwick, NJ. Their son Donald married Patricia Ann Mincieli, the daughter of Victor D. Mincieli of East Williston, and resided in East Setauket.

*Under Roth's leadership the Franklin National Bank became the twentieth largest bank in the nation and the largest on Long Island. It was the first bank to issue credit cards and to institute outdoor teller machines and drive-up teller windows.

In 2006, the 2,476-square-foot house sold for $1.25 million.

*front facade, 2000*

### Rowe, Reginald Manchester, Sr. (1887-1942)

| | |
|---|---|
| Occupation(s): | industrialist - assistant manager, Atlantic Branch, National Lead Co. |
| Marriage(s): | 1920-1942 – Lucia Virginia Malone (1894-1974) |
| Address: | 140 Kensington Road, Garden City |
| Name of estate: | |
| Year of construction: | 1913 |
| Style of architecture: | American Craftsman |
| Architect(s): | |
| Landscape architect(s): | |
| House extant: yes | |
| Historical notes: | |

The *Long Island Society Register, 1929* lists Reginald M. and Lucia Virginia Malone Rowe as residing at 140 Kensington Road, Garden City.

He was the son of Reginald Perch and Jane Louise Munn Rowe of Brooklyn.

Lucia Virginia Malone Rowe was the daughter of John F. Malone of Buffalo, NY.

Reginald Manchester and Lucia Virginia Malone Rowe, Sr.'s son Reginald Manchester Rowe, Jr. married Jan Tips.

At the time of his death, Rowe was residing at 92 Third Street, Garden City. [*The New York Times* October 8, 1942, p. 27.]

*front facade, 2001*

### Ruperti, Justus (1862-1944)

| | |
|---|---|
| Occupation(s): | capitalist -  president, G. Amsinck & Co. (importing and exporting firm) |
| | financier -  vice-president, Maritime Exchange; |
| | member, Coffee and Sugar Exchange |
| Civic Activism: | a founder, Clearwater Nursery School |
| Marriage(s): | 1893-1944 – Sarah Payne Nicoll (1865-1955) |
| Address: | 340 Ocean Avenue, Lawrence |
| Name of estate: | *Marigolds* |
| Year of construction: | |
| Style of architecture: | |
| Architect(s): | |
| Landscape architect(s): | |
| House extant: | no |

Historical notes:

   The *Long Island Society Register, 1929* lists Justus and Sallie P. Nicoll Ruperti as residing at *Marigolds* in Cedarhurst [Lawrence].

   He was the son of Oska and Ida Marianne Amsinck Ruperti.

   Sarah Payne Nicoll Ruperti was the daughter of William Courtland and Eliza Nicoll.

   Justus and Sarah Payne Nicoll Ruperti's daughter Florence married Allan Gerdau, the son of Otto Gerdau of Manhattan, and resided in Manhattan. Their daughter Ida married Charles Russell Marshall, the son of Charles Clinton Marshall, and resided in Manhattan. Their daughter Sallie married Charles Ketcham Clisby, the son of Dr. Alfred Clisby of Alabama, and, later, George Springmeyer, the son of Hermann Heinrich and Wilhelmine Katherine Springmeyer. Their son Justus Oscar Ruperti married Winifred Donaldson, the daughter of Austin Smith Donaldson of Panama.

### Russell, Frank Henry (1878-1947)

| | |
|---|---|
| Occupation(s): | industrialist -  Talon, Inc. (zipper manufacturer); |
| | general manager, Wright Brothers Co., Dayton, OH |
| | (airplane manufacturer); |
| | president, Burgess Aeroplane Co., Marblehead, MA |
| | (amphibian and training craft manufacturing firm) |
| | (merged into Curtiss Aeroplane & Motor Co.)*; |
| | president, Curtiss Asset Co.; |
| | vice-president and director, Curtiss Aeroplane & Motor Co.; |
| | president, Automatic Hook & Eye Co.; |
| | vice-president and director, Edward G. Budd Co. (lightweight, |
| | stainless steel, diesel, electric-powered train manufacturer) |
| Civic Activism: | a founder, president, and director, Manufacturers Aircraft Association, NYC; |
| | president, Montauk Club; |
| | vice-commodore, Manhasset Bay Yacht Club |
| Marriage(s): | M/1 – 1902-1924 – Marietta Holley Ford (1878-1924) |
| | M/2 – 1925-1947 – Constance B. Thompson (1885-1968) |
| Address: | 152 Prospect, Hempstead |
| Name of estate: | |
| Year of construction: | |
| Style of architecture: | |
| Architect(s): | |
| Landscape architect(s): | |
| House extant: | no |

Historical notes:

   Frank Henry Russell was the son of The Reverend Francis M. and Mrs. Aurelia Squier Henry Russell.

   Marietta Holley Ford Russell was the daughter of The Reverend James and Mrs. Frances R. Minar Ford.

   Frank Henry and Marietta Holley Ford Russell's daughter Katharine married Edward Wright Wootton, the son of Dr. Herbert Wright Wootton of Manhattan. Their son Frank Ford Russell married Ruth Oliver Kingsbury, the daughter of Howard Thayer and Alice Cary Bussing Kingsbury of *Rivombra* in Sands Point; Dorothy Milburn, the daughter of John George and Madeleine Scatcherd Milburn, Jr. who resided at *Wychwood* in North Hills; and, subsequently, Alice Abely. [*See* Spinzia, *Long Island's Prominent North Shore Families, vol. I* – Kingsbury and Milburn entries.]

   The *Long Island Society Register, 1929* lists Frank Henry and Constance B. Thompson as residing at 152 Prospect, Hempstead.

   *In 1912 Burgess Company built their first hydroplane aircraft.

### Russell, Dr. Thomas Hendrick (1885-1947)

| | |
|---|---|
| Occupation(s): | physician - director of surgery, New York Post Graduate Medical School and Hospital; director of surgery, Gouverneur Hospital |
| | educator - professor of clinical surgery, New York Post Graduate Medical School and Hospital |
| | writer - numerous articles on surgery |
| Marriage(s): | 1916 – Amelia Randall (b. 1893) |
| Address: | Everit Avenue, Hewlett Bay Park |
| Name of estate: | *Channel's End* |
| Year of construction: | |
| Style of architecture: | |
| Architect(s): | |
| Landscape architect(s): | |
| House extant: | unconfirmed |
| Historical notes: | |

The *Long Island Society Register, 1929* lists Dr. Thomas Hendrick and Mrs. Amelia Randall Russell as residing at *Channel's End* in Hewlett [Hewlett Bay Park].

He was the son of Edison H. and Mary Leakie Boyd Russell.

Amelia Randall Russell was the daughter of Darley Randall of Manhattan.

Dr. Thomas Hendrick and Mrs. Amelia Randall Russell's daughter Ella married Lynne Rhodes.


### Rutter, John Alexandre, Sr. (1922-2008)

| | |
|---|---|
| Occupation(s): | industrialist - Liberty Aircraft Corp., Farmingdale |
| | capitalist - E. W. Howell & Co., Babylon (construction firm)*; Long Island Construction Co., Floral Park |
| Marriage(s): | 1942-2008 – Ann Katharine Scharman |
| Address: | 385 Barrett Road, Lawrence |
| Name of estate: | |
| Year of construction: | 1923 |
| Style of architecture: | Shingle with Dutch Colonial elements |
| Architect(s): | |
| Landscape architect(s): | |
| House extant: | yes |
| Historical notes: | |

*front facade, 2007*

The *Social Register, 1977* lists John A. and Ann K. Scharman Rutter [Sr.] as residing at 385 Barrett Road, Cedarhurst [Lawrence].

He was the son of Nathaniel Edward Caldwell and Mary Elizabeth Alexandre Rutter, Sr. of Lawrence.

Ann Katharine Scharman Rutter was the daughter of August C. Scharman of Rockville Centre.

John Alexandre and Ann Katharine Scharman Rutter, Sr.'s son John Alexandre Rutter, Jr. married Pamela Stark Butler, the daughter of John Grier Butler of *September Farm* in Menton, OH, and resided at *Idle Times* in Gates Mills, OH. Their son Charles married Nancy Anne Harrington, the daughter of Martin Harrington, and resided in North Carolina.

*[See following entry for additional family information.]*

In 1963 the house was remodeled.

*E. W. Howell & Co. built a number of the large estate homes located on Long Island.

### Rutter, Nathaniel Edward Caldwell, Sr. (1890-1947)

| | |
|---|---|
| Occupation(s): | financier - Abbott, Proctor, Paine, and Co. (investment banking firm) |
| Civic Activism: | master of hounds, Millbrook Hunting Club |
| Marriage(s): | 1917-1947 – Mary Elizabeth Alexandre (1894-1970) |
| Address: | Ocean Avenue, Lawrence |
| Name of estate: | |
| Year of construction: | |
| Style of architecture: | |
| Architect(s): | |
| Landscape architect(s): | |
| House extant: unconfirmed | |
| Historical notes: | |

The *Long Island Society Register, 1929* lists N. Edward and Mary Alexandre Rutter [Jr.] as residing in Cedarhurst. By 1937 they had relocated to Lawrence.

He was the son of Nathaniel Edward and Sarah Caldwell Rutter.

Mary Elizabeth Alexandre Rutter was the daughter of James Henry and Elizabeth Boyce Lawrence Alexandre of Hempstead and a second cousin of Winston Churchill. Mary's sister Gertrude married Samuel Adams Clark, Sr. and resided in Cedarhurst. Her brother James Henry Alexander, Jr., who resided at *Valleybrook Farm* in Old Brookville, married Ann Loomis and, subsequently, Olivia D. Wheeler. [*See* Spinzia, *Long Island's Prominent North Shore Families*, vol. I – Alexandre entry.] Her half-brother Frederick married Regina M. Saportas and resided at *Nieman* in Lawrence.

Nathaniel Edward Caldwell and Mary Elizabeth Alexandre Rutter, Sr.'s daughter Mary married Kennedy Smith, the son of Raymond Templeton Smith of Pittsburgh, PA. Their daughter Nancy married David H. Green, Sr., the son of Burton Green. Their son John married Ann Katharine Scharman and resided in Lawrence. Their daughter Virginia married William Bradford White, the son of Victor Gerald and Margaret Wood White, Sr. of Lawrence.

*[See previous entry for additional family information.]*


### Sage, Russell (1816-1906)

| | | |
|---|---|---|
| Occupation(s): | * | |
| | financier - | member, New York Stock Exchange; |
| | | director, Fifth Avenue Bank, NYC; |
| | | director, Importers' and Traders' National Bank; |
| | | director, Mercantile Trust Co. |
| | capitalist - | president, Milwaukee and St. Paul Railroad; |
| | | president, Iowa Central Railroad; |
| | | vice-president, La Crosse Railroad; |
| | | director, Missouri Pacific Railroad; |
| | | director, Union Pacific, Wabash Railroad; |
| | | director, Troy and Boston Railroad; |
| | | director, Troy and Bennington Railroad; |
| | | director, German–American Real Estate Title Guarantee Co. |
| | shipping - | director, Mail Steamship Co. |
| | merchant - | partner, wholesale grocery firm, Troy, NY |
| | politician - | alderman, Troy, NY, 1841; |
| | | treasurer, Rensselaer County, NY; |
| | | member, United States House of Representatives, 1853-1857 |
| Civic Activism: | donated Sage Hall, Emma Willard Seminary, Troy, NY (later, Emma Willard School) | |

**Sage, Russell (1816-1906)** (cont'd)

| | |
|---|---|
| Marriage(s): | M/1 – 1840-1867 – Marie Winne (1819-1867) |
| | M/2 – 1869-1906 – Margaret Olivia Slocum (1828-1918) |

- Civic Activism:
  **
  established Russell Sage Foundation with an endowment of $10 million, to improve social and living conditions in the United States;
  first president, Emma Willard Association;
  trustee, Emma Willard School, Troy, NY;
  bequeathed $1 million to Emma Willard School;
  donated $1 million to Rensselaer Polytechnic Institute, Troy, NY;
  donated $800,000 to Cornell University, Ithaca, NY;
  donated $250,000 to Berea College, Berea, KY;
  donated $350,000 to the Y.M.C.A.;
  donated $500,000 to the Methodist Episcopal Church;
  donated Constitution Island at West Point to the United States government;
  donated $150,000 to Sag Harbor Public Schools;
  donated $150,000 to American Seamen's Fund Society;
  donated $300,000 to Sage Institute of Pathology of City Hospital;
  donated $250,000 to home for indigent women;
  vice president, New York Exchange for Women's Work
  suffragist - financial benefactor;
  hosted suffrage discussions in her home

*Russell Sage was identified with twenty-seven corporations and over forty railroads.
**Mrs. Sage's total philanthropy is estimated at between $75 and $80 million.

| | |
|---|---|
| Address: | 105 Ocean Avenue and Mallow Way, Lawrence |
| Name of estate: | *Cedarcroft / Cedar Croft* * |
| Year of construction: | c. 1892 |
| Style of architecture: | Queen Anne |
| Architect(s): | |
| Landscape architect(s): | |
| House extant: | no; demolished c. 1950 |
| Historical notes: | |

*rear facade, 1911*

The house was built by E. T. Palmer.

It was later owned by Sage, who, alternately called it *Cedarcroft* and *Cedar Croft*.

He was the son of Elisha and Prudence Risley Sage of Shenandoah, NY.

Marie Winne Sage was the daughter of Mores I. and Maria Lansing Winne of Troy, NY.

Margaret Olivia Slocum Sage was the daughter of Joseph and Margaret Pierson Jermain Slocum of Syracuse, NY.

The Sages did not have children.

*The *Social Register Summer, 1910* lists Margaret O. Slocum Sage as residing at *Cedarcroft* in Lawrence while the *Social Register Summer, 1915* lists the estate's name as *Cedar Croft*.

In 1920, May Louise Bamber Marshall purchased the twenty-acre estate which consisted of a main residence, garage, outbuildings, and a three-acre lake. [*The Brooklyn Daily Eagle* April 15, 1920, p. 18.]

[For information about the Sages' Sag Harbor residence *Harbor Home*, see Spinzia, *Long Island's Prominent Families in the Town of Southampton* – Sage entry – and *Long Island: A Guide to New York's Suffolk and Nassau Counties* – Sag Harbor Whaling and Historical Museum, Sag Harbor.]

[For information about the Sage Memorial window, created by Louis Comfort Tiffany, in Far Rockaway, see Spinzia, *Long Island: A Guide to New York's Suffolk and Nassau Counties* – First Presbyterian Church, Far Rockaway.]

***For other Long Islanders involved in the suffrage movement *see* Raymond E. Spinzia, "Winning the Franchise: Long Island Activists in the Fight for Woman's Suffrage and Their Opponents, Long Island's Anti-Suffragists." wwwspinzialongislandestates.com.

### St. John, Edward Atkinson (1869-1937)

| | |
|---|---|
| Occupation(s): | financier - a founder and president, National Surety Co., NYC (a mortgage firm); president, Joyce and Co., Chicago, IL; president, Chicago Surety Association; director, Bankers Bond and Mortgage Guarantee Co.; director, Independence Fund of North America; director, Garden City Bank and Trust Co. |
| Civic Activism: | president, Casualty Surety Club of New York; president, National Association of Casualty and Surety Agents; president, International Association of Casualty and Surety Underwriters |
| Marriage(s): | M/1 – Helen B. Harmon (1871-1927)<br>M/2 – 1928-1937 – Helen Knapp (b. 1884) |
| Address: | 117 Brixton Road, Garden City |
| Name of estate: | |
| Year of construction: | 1903 |
| Style of architecture: | Modified American Craftsman |
| Architect(s): | |
| Landscape architect(s): | |
| House extant: yes | |
| Historical notes: | |

*front facade, 2001*

Edward Atkinson St. John was the son of William James and Rose Wren St. John.

Helen B. Harmon St. John was the daughter of James and Honora Giles Harmon of Michigan.

The *Long Island Society Register, 1929* lists John Edward and Helen Knapp St. John as residing at 117 Brixton Road, Garden City.

She was the daughter of William Harvey Knapp and had previously been married to Clement E. Dunbar.

In 1977 the house was remodeled.


### St. John, Frank Lamar, Jr. (1892-1950)

| | |
|---|---|
| Occupation(s): | financier - stockbroker |
| Marriage(s): | M/1 – 1917 – Margery Aletta Boyd (b. 1894)<br>M/2 – Enid Rice |
| Address: | 7 Butler Place, Garden City |
| Name of estate: | |
| Year of construction: | 1918 |
| Style of architecture: | Colonial Revival |
| Architect(s): | |
| Landscape architect(s): | |
| House extant: yes | |
| Historical notes: | |

*front facade, 2004*

The *Long Island Society Register, 1929* lists Frank Lamar and Margery A. Boyd St. John [Jr.] as residing at 7 Butler Place, Garden City.

He was the son of Frank Lamar and Fannie Stanton St. John, Sr. of Brooklyn

Margery Aletta Boyd St. John was the daughter of Archibald Boardman Boyd of Brooklyn.

Enid Rice St. John was the daughter of George Trowbridge Rice of Brooklyn. She had previously been married to Charles Stanton Higgins of New Haven, CT.

Frank Lamar and Enid Rice St. John, Jr.'s daughter Enid married Albert Robert Heath, the son of Cuyler Heath of Garden City.

### Salmon, Hamilton Henry, Jr. (1861-1943)

| | |
|---|---|
| Occupation(s): | capitalist - president, H. H. Salmon & Co., NYC (fertilizer import and export firm) |
| | industrialist - president, Little Giant Fire Extinguisher Co. |
| | merchant - treasurer, Fertilizer Material Supply Co. |
| Civic Activism: | vice-president, Brooklyn Riding and Driving Club; judge, national horse shows |
| Marriage(s): | 1889-1934 – Jessie Barber Sweetland (1869-1934) |
| Address: | 61 Hilton Avenue, Garden City |
| Name of estate: | |
| Year of construction: | |
| Style of architecture: | Condominium |
| Architect(s): | |
| Landscape architect(s): | |
| House extant: yes | |
| Historical notes: | |

   The *Long Island Society Register, 1929* lists Hamilton H. and Jessie B. Sweetland Salmon [Jr.] as residing on Hilton Avenue, Garden City.
   He was the son of Hamilton Henry and Emily Morris Butler Salmon, Sr. of Brooklyn.
   Jessie Barber Sweetland Salmon was the daughter of Henry D. Sweetland of Brooklyn.
   Hamilton Henry and Jessie Barber Sweetland, Jr.'s son Hamilton Henry Salmon III married Ruth Estelle Dunning and resided in Garden City.
*[See following entry for additional family information.]*


### Salmon, Hamilton Henry, III (1893-1962)
### aka Hamilton Henry Salmon, Jr.

| | |
|---|---|
| Occupation(s): | financier - partner, Johnson & Higgins, NYC (maritime insurance firm) |
| Marriage(s): | 1917-1962 – Ruth Estelle Dunning (d. 1968) |
| Address: | 124 Oxford Boulevard, Garden City |
| Name of estate: | |
| Year of construction: | 1952 |
| Style of architecture: | Ranch |
| Architect(s): | |
| Landscape architect(s): | |
| House extant: yes | |
| Historical notes: | |

   The *Long Island Society Register, 1929* lists Hamilton H. and Ruth E. Dunning Salmon, Jr. [III] as residing at 111 Hilton Avenue, Garden City.
   He was the son of Hamilton Henry and Jessie Barber Sweetland Salmon, Jr., who resided in Garden City.
   Ruth Estelle Dunning Salmon was the daughter of Clarence Seymour and Sarah C. Thomas Dunning, Sr. of Garden City.
   Hamilton Henry and Ruth Estelle Dunning Salmon III's son Hamilton Henry Salmon IV (aka Hamilton Henry Salmon III) married Frances Colt Sinclair, the daughter of Dr. Donald B. Sinclair of Princeton, NJ, and, subsequently, Barbara Thompson Welch.
   At the time of his death, the Salmons were residing at 124 Oxford Boulevard, Garden City. [*The New York Times* September 16, 1962, p. 86.]
*[See previous entry for additional family information.]*

*front facade, 2001*

**Sampson, Sally Phillips Blagden (1842-1909)**

Civic Activism: corresponding secretary, Female Bible Society, Boston, MA

Marriage(s): M/1 – John Dixwell Thompson (c. 1836-1875)
- industrialist - partner, with Henry M. Clarke, H. M. Clarke & Co. (paper manufacturing firm); a founder and partner, with H. McK. Twombly, Thompson, Twombly, & Co. (paper manufacturing firm)
M/2 – 1883-1909 – Edward Cobb Sampson (1836-1916)

Address: Causeway, Lawrence
Name of estate:
Year of construction: c. 1900
Style of architecture: Shingle
Architect(s): William Adams Jr. designed the house (for S. P. B. Sampson)
Landscape architect(s):
House extant: unconfirmed
Historical notes:

*front facade, c. 1906*

The house was built by Sally Phillips Blagden Sampson.
She was the daughter of The Reverend George Washington and Mrs. Miriam Phillips Blagden.
John Dixwell and Sally Phillips Blagden Thompson's son Phillips married Marion McKeever, the daughter of James Lawrence and Mary Augusta Townsend McKeever, Sr. of *Red Top Farm* in Southampton, and resided at *Red Top Farm*. [*See* Spinzia, *Long Island's Prominent Families in the Town of Southampton* – McKeever and Thompson entries.]
Edward Cobb Sampson was the son of Alden and Sarah Taber Pope Sampson.


**Sanford, George Baylies (1861-1930)**

Occupation(s): industrialist - president, Sanford & Russell, Inc. (woolen manufacturing firm)
Civic Activism: president, American Association of Woolen and Worsted Manufacturers

Marriage(s): 1887-1930 – Cardine Granger Blodget (1964-1935)

Address: Barrett Road and Tanglewood Crossing, Lawrence
Name of estate: *The Byways*
Year of construction:
Style of architecture:
Architect(s):
Landscape architect(s):
House extant: unconfirmed
Historical notes:

The *Long Island Society Register, 1929* lists George Baylies and Cardine G. Blodget Sanford as residing at *The Byways* in Lawrence.
He was the son of Baylies and Elizabeth B. Cobb Sanford.
Cardine Granger Blodget Sanford was the daughter of Henry T. and Lucretia W. W. Leland Blodget.
George Baylies and Cardine Granger Blodget Sanford's daughter Elizabeth married Henry Lawrence Bogert, Jr., the son of Henry Lawrence and Caroline Lawrence Osgood Bogert, Sr. of Flushing, NY, and resided in Cedarhurst. Their daughter Genevieve married William Frederic Philips, the son of Frederic Dimon and Jessie Matheson Taylor Philips of *Greyhouse*, and resided at *Fairway* in Lawrence.
In 1930 the house was purchased by Chester Alwyn Braman, Jr. [*The New York Times* August 23, 1930, p. 26.]

### Sargent, Charles Sprague, Jr. (1880-1959)

| | |
|---|---|
| Occupation(s): | financier - director, Peninsula National Bank of Cedarhurst; member, Kidder Peabody & Co. (stock brokerage firm); governor, New York Stock Exchange |
| Civic Activism: | governor, Lawrence Association |
| Marriage(s): | 1912-1959 – Dagmar Wetmore (1888-1984)<br>- Civic Activism: vice-president, Peninsula Community Library |
| Address: | Hollywood Crossing, Lawrence |
| Name of estate: | |
| Year of construction: | |
| Style of architecture: | |
| Architect(s): | |
| Landscape architect(s): | |
| House extant: unconfirmed | |
| Historical notes: | |

The *Long Island Society Register, 1929* lists Charles S. and Dagmar Wetmore Sargent [Jr.] as residing on Hollywood Crossing, Cedarhurst [Lawrence].

He was the son of Charles Sprague and Mary Allen Robeson Sargent, Sr. of Brookline, MA.

Dagmar Wetmore Sargent was the daughter of William Boerum and Annette Butler Wetmore.

Charles Sprague and Dagmar Wetmore Sargent, Jr.'s son Charles Sprague Sargent III married Bridget McBurney, the daughter of Dr. Malcolm and Mrs. Dorothy Moran McBurney, who resided in East Islip. [*See* Spinzia, *Long Island's Prominent South Shore Families* – McBurney entry.] Their son John married Neltje Doubleday, the daughter of Nelson and Ellen George McCarter Doubleday, Sr. of *Barberrys* in Mill Neck. [*See* Spinzia, *Long Island's Prominent North Shore Families, vol. 1* – Doubleday entry.] Their daughter Mary married Henry Michell Havemeyer, the son of John F. Havemeyer of Ardsley-on-Hudson, NY. Their son Winthrop married Eileen Johnson and, later, Peggy Joyce Baker.

### Sayer, Murray (b. 1877)

| | |
|---|---|
| Occupation(s): | industrialist - secretary, Colonial Sugars, Co., 1902-1906<br>diplomat - secretary to auditor, Government of Porto Rico, 1906-1907; vice consul, Stockholm, Sweden, 1917-1919<br>capitalist - director, Scandinavian Trade Co. |
| Marriage(s): | 1911-1955 – Edith Burritt Conn (1881-1955) |
| Address: | 93 Fourth Street, Garden City |
| Name of estate: | |
| Year of construction: | 1903 |
| Style of architecture: | Modified Dutch Colonial Revival |
| Architect(s): | |
| Landscape architect(s): | |
| House extant: yes | |
| Historical notes: | |

The *Long Island Society Register, 1929* and the 1940 Census list Murray and Edith B. Conn Sayer as residing at 93 Fourth Street, Garden City.

He was the son of Edmund Sears and Mary Elizabeth Dick Sayer of Meadville, PA.

Edith Burritt Conn Sayer was the daughter of Frank W. and Alice Burritt Conn of Brooklyn.

Murray and Edith Burritt Conn Sayer's daughter Elizabeth married Everett W. Hoyt, the son of Charles W. Hoyt of Garden City.

*front facade, 2008*

### Schieffelin, John Jay, Sr. (1897-1987)

| | |
|---|---|
| Occupation(s): | financier - member, Chubb & Sons (insurance firm) |
| Civic Activism: | president, English Speaking Union of the United States |
| Marriage(s): | M/1 – 1923-div. 1931 – Eleanor Curtis Beggs (1899-1996) |
| | M/2 – 1932-1987 – Lois Lindon Smith (1911-2007) |
| Address: | 90 Burton Avenue, Woodmere |
| Name of estate: | |
| Year of construction: | 1928 |
| Style of architecture: | Colonial Revival |
| Architect(s): | |
| Landscape architect(s): | |
| House extant: yes | |
| Historical notes: | |

*front facade, 2000*

The house was built by John Jay Schieffelin, Sr.

The *Long Island Society Register, 1929* lists John Jay and Eleanor C. Beggs Schieffelin [Sr.] as residing at 90 Burton Avenue, Woodmere.

He was the son of William Jay and Maria Louisa Shepard Schieffelin, Sr. and a descendant of both Cornelius Vanderbilt and United States Supreme Court Justice John Jay.

Eleanor Curtis Beggs Schieffelin was the daughter of Joseph Patterson and Eleanor Hughes Beggs of Pittsburgh, PA. She later married Thomas Blythe Scott and, subsequently, Dean Kirkham Worcester.

John Jay and Eleanor Curtis Beggs Schieffelin, Sr.'s daughter Sally married John Richard Babich, the son of Richard Babich of Albuquerque, NM, and, subsequently, George Potter, Jr. Their son Joseph married Marilyn Preusse, the daughter of Herbert Preusse of Lincoln, NE, and resided in Lakewood, CO. Their daughter Eleanor did not marry.

Lois Lindon Smith Schieffelin was the daughter of Joseph Lindon and Corinna Haven Putnam Smith of Manhattan.

John Jay and Lois Lindon Smith Schieffelin, Sr.'s son John Jay Schieffelin, Jr. married Sherry Elizabeth Bragdon, the daughter of Clifford R. Bragdon of Northampton, MA.

### Schill, Emil (b. 1878)

| | |
|---|---|
| Occupation(s): | capitalist - owned Manhattan tenements |
| | industrialist - secretary and president, Continental Gas Compressor Co. |
| | inventor - improved process for making gasoline from heat gas |
| Marriage(s): | 1915-div. 1939 – Florence A. Kelley (1883-1965) |
| Address: | 980 Benton Street, Woodmere |
| Name of estate: | |
| Year of construction: | 1928 |
| Style of architecture: | Colonial Revival |
| Architect(s): | |
| Landscape architect(s): | |
| House extant: yes | |
| Historical notes: | |

The house was built by Emil Schill.

The *Long Island Society Register, 1929* lists Emil and Florence A. Kelley Schill as residing at 980 Benton Avenue [sic], Woodmere.

He was from Stuttgart, Germany.

Florence A. Kelley Schill was the daughter of Albert Tevis Kelley of Manhattan. She had previously been married to Amadee Valle Reyburn, Jr. of St. Louis, MO.

*front facade, 2000*

### Schley, Buchanan, Jr. (1870-1926)

| | |
|---|---|
| Occupation(s): | financier -  member, New York Cotton Exchange |
| | politician -  deputy collector, Port of Baltimore (Cleveland administration) |
| Civic Activism: | member, Stone Mountain Confederate Monumental Association |
| Marriage(s): | 1904-1926 – Edith Nathalie Selbie (1883-1927) |
| Address: | *[unable to determine street address]*, Cedarhurst |

Name of estate:
Year of construction:
Style of architecture:
Architect(s):
Landscape architect(s):
House extant:  unconfirmed
Historical notes:

    The *Long Island Society Register, 1929* lists Mr. and Mrs. Buchanan Schley, Jr. as residing in Cedarhurst.
    He was the son of Buchanan and Rebecca Roman Schley, Sr. of Hagerstown, MD.
    Edith Nathalie Selbie Schley was the daughter of John H. and Mollie A. Selbie of Watertown, CT.
    Buchanan and Edith Nathalie Selbie Schley, Jr.'s son Buchanan Schley III married Bonnie Bullock, the daughter of Judge Adam Henry Bullock of Johnson City, TN.
    Four months after the death of her husband Mrs. Schley fell to her death from the fifteenth floor of a Manhattan hotel.
[*The Washington Post* March 11, 1927, p. 5.]


### Schley, Henry Spaulding, Sr. (1878-1953)

| | |
|---|---|
| Occupation(s): | accountant |
| Marriage(s): | 1904-1953 – Adele Sturges Mason (1881-1954) |
| |    - politician -  corresponding secretary, Women's National Republican Club of New York |
| |    Civic Activism:  president, Garden City Women's Club |
| Address: | 91 St. James Street, Garden City |

Name of estate:
Year of construction:
Style of architecture:
Architect(s):
Landscape architect(s):
House extant:  unconfirmed
Historical notes:

    The *Long Island Society Register, 1929* lists Henry Spaulding and Adele S. Mason Schley [Sr.] as residing on St. James Street, Garden City. The 1940 Census lists them at this address.
    He was the son of Dr. James Monfort and Mrs. Margaret Thompson Schley.
    Adele Sturges Mason Schley was the daughter of Ebenezer Sturges and Abbie Low Ranlett Mason of Manhattan.
    Henry Spaulding and Adele Sturges Mason Schley, Sr.'s son Sturges married Florence Dorothy Belsterling, the daughter of Charles Starne Belsterling, and, subsequently, Kathleen Falconer, the daughter of Archibald C. Falconer of Port Washington. Their son Henry Spaulding Schley, Jr. married Arline Leach Bennett, the daughter of George Bennett of Park Ridge, NJ.

## Schlossberg, Arnold, Sr. (1908-1992)

| | |
|---|---|
| Occupation(s): | attorney |
| Civic Activism: | member, Roanoke Charter Commission, 1946; |
| | member, Roanoke School Board, 1947-1948; |
| | president, Roanoke Mental Hygiene Society, 1956; |
| | first general counsel, Legal Aid Society, Roanoke Valley, 1966-1968; |
| | co-chairman, professional division, Roanoke Valley United Fund, 1974; |
| | institutional chairman, Israel Bonds, 1970-1976 |
| Marriage(s): | secretly eloped 1932; formal wedding, 1933-1937 – Alice Hermine Jacobi (1912-1987) |
| | - probation officer, Juvenile Court, Roanoke, VA |
| |     Civic Activism: member of board, Virginia Council of Social Welfare |
| Address: | 75 Willow Road, Woodsburgh |
| Name of estate: | |
| Year of construction: | 1935 |
| Style of architecture: | Modified Norman Revival |
| Architect(s): | Olive Frances Tjaden designed the house (for Schlossberg) |
| Landscape architect(s): | |
| House extant: yes | |
| Historical notes: | |

   The house was built by Arnold Schlossberg, Sr.
   He was the son of Maurice J. and Jennie Weinstein Schlossberg.
   Alice Hermine Jacobi Schlossberg was the daughter of Harold and Freda Moritz Jacobi, Sr. of Woodmere.
   Arnold and Alice Hermine Jacobi Schlossberg, Sr.'s daughter Nancy married Robert A. Giannasi, the son of Louis Giannasi of Highwood, IL, and resided in Manassas, VA. Their daughter Deda married Roger E. Miller of Philadelphia, PA, and resided in Colorado Springs, CO. Their son Major General Arnold Scholossberg, Jr. married Jolene Sutter and resided in Burke, VA.
   In 1940 the Schlossbergs relocated to Roanoke, VA.
   In 2020, the 3,940-square-foot house sold for $1.8 million.

*front facade*

### Schultz, Albert Bigelow, Sr. (1883-1952)

| | |
|---|---|
| Occupation(s): | attorney |
| | financier -   vice-president, Peninsula National Bank, Cedarhurst; |
| |     partner, Horn, Ogilvie, & Co., NYC (insurance firm) |
| Civic Activism: | mayor, Village of Hewlett Bay Park; |
| | director, Beekman Street Hospital, NYC (which merged with Downtown |
| |     Hospital to become Beekman–Downtown Hospital); |
| | co-president, Community Chest of Five Towns; |
| | member of board, Hewlett–Woodmere Public Library, 1949 |
| Marriage(s): | 1912-1952 – Winifred Houghton King (1886-1967) |
| |   - Civic Activism:  a founder and secretary, Dispensary Aid Society of |
| |         the Tuberculosis League of Pittsburgh, 1908 |
| Address: | 1117 Broadway, Hewlett Bay Park |
| Name of estate: | |
| Year of construction: | |
| Style of architecture: | |
| Architect(s): | |
| Landscape architect(s): | |
| House extant: no | |
| Historical notes: | |

  The *Long Island Society Register, 1929* lists Albert B. and Winifred H. King Schultz [Sr.] as residing in Hewlett [Hewlett Bay Park].
  In 1945, he purchased the fifteen-room house from Mrs. John T. Phillips. [*The New York Times* February 27, 1945, p. 31.]
  Albert Bigelow Schultz, Sr. was the son of Albert Louis and Virginia Clay Bigelow Schultz of Pittsburgh, PA.
  Winifred Houghton King Schultz was the daughter of Henry Holdship King of Pittsburgh, PA.
  Albert Bigelow and Winifred Houghton King Schultz, Sr.'s daughter Hildegard married Dr. William S. Norton II and resided in Manhattan. Their daughter Alice married Robert John Wickett Sculthorpe, the son of Robert E. Sculthorpe of Port Hope, Ontario, Canada. Their son Albert Bigelow Schultz, Jr. married Virginia Trenholme Barbour, the daughter of Robert Leland Barbour of Millington, NJ.
  At the time of Albert's death, the Schultzes were residing at 1117 Broadway. [*Nassau Daily Review–Star* August 27, 1952, p. 19.]

### Schwieters, John Francis (1891-1973)

| | |
|---|---|
| Occupation(s): | attorney -   member, Fraser, Speir, and Meyer, NYC |
| Marriage(s): | 1919-1973 – Norma Dee Childs (1891-1988) |
| Address: | 91 Tulip Avenue, Floral Park |
| Name of estate: | |
| Year of construction: | |
| Style of architecture: | Eclectic with Victorian elements |
| Architect(s): | |
| Landscape architect(s): | |
| House extant: no; demolished in 1950 | |
| Historical notes: | |

  The house was built by John Lewis Childs. It was inherited by his daughter Norma and son-in-law John Francis Schwieters. Norma's brother Vernon married Clarice Hunt and resided in Floral Park. Her brother John married Fanny Hutcheson and also resided in Floral Park.

*front facade*

### Scott, Charles Robert (1869-1947)

| | |
|---|---|
| Occupation(s): | financier - representative, International Banking Corporation of New York |
| Marriage(s): | 1912-1938 – Mary Baldwin Hyde (1867-1938)<br>- Civic Activism: vice-president, Sea Cliff Home for Convalescent Babies;<br>president, Lisa Day Nursery |
| Address: | California and Fulton Avenues, Uniondale |
| Name of estate: | *The Crossways* |
| Year of construction: | 1889 |
| Style of architecture: | Queen Anne |
| Architect(s): | |
| Landscape architect(s): | Hicks Nursery supplied Scotch Pines (for S. D. Ripley, Sr.) |

House extant: no; destroyed by fire in 1934
Historical notes:

*The Crossways, 1902*

The forty-eight-room house, originally named *The Crossways*, was built by Sidney Dillon Ripley, Sr.

Mary Baldwin Hyde was the daughter of Henry Baldwin and Annie Fitch Hyde, Sr., who resided at *The Oaks* in West Bay Shore. [*See* Spinzia, *Long Island's Prominent South Shore Families* – Hyde entries.] Mary had previously been married to Ripley. She continued to reside at *The Crossways* after her marriage to Scott.

*[See Ripley entry for additional family information.]*

Charles Robert Scott was the son of Robert and Dora Adelaide Mansell Scott of Ireland.

### Scott, Henry Clarkson, Sr. (1901-1979)

| | |
|---|---|
| Occupation(s): | financier - partner, Bouvier, Bishop, and Co. (stock brokerage firm);<br>industrialist - vice-president, West Indies Sugar, 1956-1960<br>capitalist - manager for development, Pan American World Airways;<br>president and director, Inter-Continental Hotel Corp.;<br>superintendent, Thompson–Starrett Co., NY, 1925-1930<br>(construction firm)* |
| Marriage(s): | M/1 – 1926-div. – Michelle Caroline Bouvier (1905-1987)<br>M/2 – Jean M. Kelly |
| Address: | Allen Lane, Woodmere |
| Name of estate: | |
| Year of construction: | |
| Style of architecture: | |
| Architect(s): | |
| Landscape architect(s): | |

House extant: unconfirmed
Historical notes:

The *Social Register New York, 1933* lists Henry Clarkson and Michelle C. Bouvier Scott [Sr.] as residing on Allen Lane, Woodmere.

He was the son of W. Samuel Scott of St. Louis, MO.

Michelle Caroline Bouvier Scott was the daughter of John Vernou and Maude Frances Sergeant Bouvier, Jr. of *Lasata* and *Little House* in East Hampton. Michelle subsequently married Harrington Putnam and resided in East Hampton. Her sister Edith married Phelan Beale, Sr. and resided at *Gray Gardens* in East Hampton. Her brother William married Emma Louise Stone, who resided in Southampton. [*See* Spinzia, *Long Island's Prominent Families in the Town of Southampton* – Bouvier entry.] Her sister Maude married John E. Davis and resided in Ridgefield, CT. Her brother John Vernou Bouvier III married Janet Norton Lee and resided at *Rowdy House* and, later, *Little House*, in East Hampton. They were the parents of First Lady Jacqueline Bouvier Kennedy [later, Onassis]. [*See* Spinzia, *Long Island's Prominent Families in the Town of East Hampton* – Beale, Bouvier, and Putnam entries.]

Henry Clarkson and Michelle Caroline Bouvier Scott, Sr.'s daughter Michelle married William McIntosh Crouse, Jr. of Scarsdale, NY, and resided in Darien, CT. Their son Henry Clarkson Scott, Jr. married Elizabeth Winslow, the daughter of Dr. Robert M. Winslow of Ridgefield, CT, and resided in Scottsdale, AZ.

*Scott's construction firm took part in the construction of Manhattan's Waldorf–Astoria Hotel, and Paramount Theater as well as over thirty hotels around the world.

### Scott, John Frederick (1853-1934)

| | |
|---|---|
| Occupation(s): | financier - member, Morton, Bliss, and Co., NY, 1870-1872 (investment banking firm); |
| | member, Jay, Cook, McCullough, and Co., 1873-1875 (investment banking firm); |
| | member, W. B. Scott and Co., NY, 1877-1884 (stock brokerage firm); |
| | member, A. E. Scott and Co., NY, 1884 (stock brokerage firm) |
| | real estate agent - member, Pease & Elliman |
| Marriage(s): | 1879-1934 – Caroline Virginia Woodworth (1857-1939) |
| Address: | *[unable to determine street address],* Hewlett Bay Park |
| Name of estate: | *Rosebank* |
| Year of construction: | |
| Style of architecture: | Neo-Federal |
| Architect(s): | William Adams, Jr. designed the house (for J. F. Scott) |
| Landscape architect(s): | |
| House extant: unconfirmed | |
| Historical notes: | |

The house, originally named *Rosebank*, was built by John Frederick Scott.

The *Social Register Summer, 1915* and *1920* list John F. and C. Virginia Woodworth Scott as residing at *Rosebank* in Hewlett [Hewlett Bay Park.]

John Frederick and Caroline Virginia Woodworth Scott's daughter Caroline did not marry.

*dining room, 1918*

*front facade, 1918*

### Searle, John Endicott, Sr. (1885-1966)

| | |
|---|---|
| Occupation(s): | attorney |
| | capitalist - director, Film Securities Corp. (formerly, Fox Films Corp.) |
| | industrialist - director, Kelly–Springfield Tire Co. |
| Civic Activism: | trustee and mayor, Village of Hewlett Neck |
| Marriage(s): | 1923-1966 – Jeanne Hortense Schroers (1899-1971) |
| Address: | Smith Lane, Hewlett Neck |

Name of estate:
Year of construction:
Style of architecture:
Architect(s):
Landscape architect(s):
House extant: unconfirmed
Historical notes:

   The *Social Register New York, 1933* lists John Endicott and Jeanne H. Schroers Searle [Sr.] as residing on Smith Place [Lane], Woodmere [Hewlett Neck].
   He was the son of Charles Putnam and Cora Anne W. Hogg Searle, Sr. of Boston, MA.
   Jeanne Hortense Schroers Searle was the daughter of John Schroers of St. Louis, MO.
   John Endicott and Jeanne Hortense Schroers Searle, Sr.'s son John Endicott, Jr. married Linda Saunders Bailey, the daughter of Clifford Sherwood Bailey of New Canaan, CT, and resided in Marblehead, MA.
   In 1942 Searle purchased Martin Goodman's twenty-room house in Hewlett Neck. [*The New York Times* May 7, 1942, p. 35.]

### Sellar, Norrie, Sr. (1872-1932)

| | |
|---|---|
| Occupation(s): | financier - cotton broker* |
| | capitalist - director, General Talking Pictures Corp. |
| Marriage(s): | 1904 – Sybil Katherine Sherman (1875-1954) |
| | - merchant - president, Sybil Shop (women's clothing) |
| Address: | Auerbach Avenue, Hewlett Harbor |

Name of estate:
Year of construction:
Style of architecture:
Architect(s):
Landscape architect(s):
House extant: unconfirmed
Historical notes:

   The *Long Island Society Register, 1929* lists Norrie and Sybil W. Sherman Sellar as residing in Hewlett [Hewlett Harbor].
   He was the son of David Plenderleath and Mary Van Horne Norrie Sellar.
   Sybil Katherine Sherman Sellar was the daughter of William Watts and Anna Perry Wetmore Sherman of NYC. Sybil had previously been married to John Ellis Hoffman.
   Norrie and Sybil Katherine Sherman Sellar, Sr.'s daughter Iris, who resided in Hewlett Neck, married Francis Lansing Veeder, the son of Paul Lansing and Grace Thralls Coleman Veeder who resided at *Meadowwood* in Hewlett Bay Park. Their daughter Daphne married W. Radford Bascome, Jr. of Manhattan. Their son Norrie Sellar, Jr. married Rita Dolan, the daughter of Clarence W. Dolan of Rosemont, PA.
   *In 1910 Sellar was investigated by United States Attorney General George Woodward Wickersham of *Marshfield* in Lawrence for allegedly being part of a conspiracy to corner the cotton crop. [*The New York Times* April 20, 1910, p. 2.]

## Seymour, Origen Storrs, II (1872-1940)

| | |
|---|---|
| Occupation(s): | attorney - partner, Taylor, Anderson, and Seymour, NYC; |
| | partner, Huntington, Rhinelander, and Seymour, NYC; |
| | partner, Sprague, Seymour, and Sprague, NYC; |
| | judge - court of common pleas, State of Connecticut |
| | financier - director, Litchfield Mutual Fire Insurance Co.; |
| | director, Church Life Insurance Co.; |
| | director, Peninsula National Bank, Cedarhurst |
| | industrialist - director, British American Metals Co. |
| | capitalist - director, Queens Water Co.; |
| | vice-president, North American Copper Co. |
| Civic Activism: | trustee, Norwich State Hospital, Norwich, CT; |
| | trustee, General Theological Seminary, NYC; |
| | member, Litchfield Board of Education, Litchfield, CT; |
| | chairman, ethics committee, Association of the Bar of the City of New York; |
| | trustee, Village of Lawrence; |
| | trustee, New York State Training School for Deconesses; |
| | trustee, National Industrial School |
| Marriage(s): | 1899-1940 – Frances Bolton Lord (1871-1962) |
| Address: | Broadway, Lawrence |
| Name of estate: | *Sosiego* |
| Year of construction: | |
| Style of architecture: | |
| Architect(s): | |
| Landscape architect(s): | Martha Brookes Brown Hutcheson |
| | (for D. Lord V) |
| House extant: yes | |
| Historical notes: | |

The house, originally named *Sosiego*, was built by Daniel de Forest Lord V.

The *Long Island Society Register, 1929* lists Origen S. and Frances Bolton Lord Seymour [II] as residing at *Sosiego* in Lawrence.

He was the son of Morris Woodruff and Charlotte Tyler Sanford Seymour of Bridgeport, CT.

Frances Bolton Lord Seymour was the daughter of Daniel de Forest and Silvie Livingston Bolton Lord V, from whom she inherited *Sosiego*.

Origen Storrs and Frances Bolton Lord Seymour II's daughter Silvia married Darnall Wallace and, subsequently, Beverly Kennon Sinclair. Their daughter Frances married Miles Hodsdon Vernon.

*Sosiego, garden, 1923*

### Shaw, Munson Gallaudet, Sr. (1877-1951)

| | |
|---|---|
| Occupation(s): | capitalist - president, Alexander D. Shaw & Co., NYC (later, Munson G. Shaw Co.) (importer of liquors and wines); president, treasurer and chairman of board, Munson G. Shaw Co. |
| Civic Activism: | member, executive committee, Conference of Alcoholic Beverage Industry; chairman, Licensed Beverage Industries Inc. |
| Marriage(s): | 1901-1951 – Nettie Clinton McGuire (1880-1954) |
| Address: | *[unable to determine street address]*, Cedarhurst |

Name of estate:
Year of construction:
Style of architecture:
Architect(s):
Landscape architect(s):
House extant: unconfirmed
Historical notes:

The *Long Island Society Register, 1929* lists Munson G. and Nettie C. McGuire Shaw as residing in Cedarhurst.
He was the son of Alexander David and Caroline Budd Gallaudet Shaw.
Nettie Clinton McGuire Shaw was the daughter of Thomas McGuire of New York City.
Munson Gallaudet and Nettie Clinton McGuire Shaw, Sr.'s daughter Caro married Dave Hennen Coddington and, later, William Liseter Austin, Jr. with whom she resided in Atlantic Beach, LI. Their daughter Sibyl married Julian McCarty Boit, the son of Edward D. Boit, and resided in Greenwich, CT. Their son Munson Gallaudet Shaw, Jr. married Jeannette Conroy and resided in Cedarhurst.


### Shepard, Frederic White (1898-1954)

| | |
|---|---|
| Occupation(s): | attorney - for New York City |
| | politician - chairman, Nassau County Democratic Committee |
| Civic Activism: | president, Nassau County Bar Association; president and treasurer, Lawyers Club of Brooklyn; secretary, alumni association, Columbia Law School; secretary, Baywater Yacht Club |
| Marriage(s): | Agnes O'Connor |
| Address: | Singleton Avenue, Woodmere |

Name of estate:
Year of construction:
Style of architecture:
Architect(s):
Landscape architect(s):
House extant: unconfirmed
Historical notes:

The *Long Island Society Register, 1929* lists Frederic White and Agnes O'Connor Shepard as residing on Singleton Avenue, Woodmere.
He was the son of Dr. Charles H. Shepard of Brooklyn and a descendant of William Bradford, the second governor of Plymouth Colony.
Agnes O'Connor Shepard was the daughter of William P. O'Connor.
Frederic White and Agnes O'Connor Shepard's daughter Cornelia married Dr. John L. Riker, the son of Henry Ingersoll Riker of Manhattan, and resided in Rumson, NJ. Their son Wainwright Hardie Shepard married Elizabeth Cunningham Marshall, the daughter of Charles Alexander and Lillie H. Cunningham Marshall of Woodsburgh, and resided at *Driftway* in New Canaan, CT.

### Sherman, Charles Edwin (1841-1927)

Occupation(s):

Marriage(s): 1900-1925 – Hannah Newbold Lawrence (1852-1925)
- Civic Activism: vice-president, New York Exchange for Woman's Work;
treasurer, Daughters of Cincinnati;
donated a building to the Infirmary for Women and Children

Address: Causeway, Lawrence
Name of estate: *The Brae*
Year of construction:
Style of architecture:
Architect(s):
Landscape architect(s):
House extant: unconfirmed
Historical notes:

The *Long Island Society Register, 1929* lists Charles E. Sherman as residing in Lawrence.
He was the son of Charles Selden and Martha Esther Williams Sherman.
Hannah Newbold Lawrence Sherman was the daughter of Alfred Newbold and Elizabeth Woodhull Lawrence Lawrence and the great-great granddaughter of Revolutionary War hero Nathaniel Woodhull. [*See* Spinzia, *Long Island: A Guide to New York's Suffolk and Nassau Counties* – Woodhull Cemetery, Grave of Nathaniel Woodhull, Mastic Beach.] Hannah's brother John married Alice Warner Work, the daughter of James Henry and Marie Pierce Warner Work, Sr. of *The Gowans* in Lawrence, and resided at *Moorlands* in Lawrence.


### Silvers, Robert Benjamin (1929-2017)

Occupation(s): journalist - editor, *New York Review of Books*, 1963-2017;
editor, *The Paris Review*;
associate editor, *Harper's Magazine*

Marriage(s): bachelor

Address: 7 Bedford Avenue, Rockville Centre
Name of estate:
Year of construction: 1927
Style of architecture: Colonial Revival with Victorian Elements
Architect(s):
Landscape architect(s):
House extant: yes
Historical notes:

Robert was raised in this house by his parents James J. and Rose Roden Silvers.
Robert was the recipient of the National Book Foundation's Literarian Award, the American Academy of Arts and Letters Award for Distinguished Service to the Arts, the Ivan Sandrof Award for Lifetime Achievement in Publishing, and the National Humanities Medal.
In 1987, the 2,571-square-foot house sold for $243,000.

*front facade*

### Sise, John (1898-1942)

| | |
|---|---|
| Occupation(s): | financier - member, Kidder, Peabody and Co. (stock brokerage firm); partner, Abbott, Hoppin, and Co. (stock brokerage firm); partner, Abbott, Proctor, and Paine (stock brokerage firm) |
| Civic Activism: | director, Long Island Symphony Association, 1939 |
| Marriage(s): | 1925-1942 – Mary Cornelia Hebard (1901-1979) |
| Address: | 161 Ocean Avenue, Woodmere |
| Name of estate: | |
| Year of construction: | |
| Style of architecture: | |
| Architect(s): | |
| Landscape architect(s): | |
| House extant: | no |
| Historical notes: | |

The *Long Island Society Register, 1929* lists John and Mary C. Hebard Sise as residing at 161 Ocean Avenue, Woodmere.

He was the son of Frederick March Sise of Portsmouth, NH.

Mary Cornelia Hebard Sise was the daughter of Daniel Learned and Julia Kennedy Hebard of Philadelphia, PA. Mary subsequently married David Henner Morris, Jr., the son of Dave Henner and Alice Louise Vanderbilt Shepard Morris, Sr.

John and Mary Cornelia Hebard Sise's son Daniel married Cornelia Donaldson Ford, the daughter of Frank Richardson Ford, Jr. of *Driftway* in Southport, CT.

The house was subsequently owned by Harold Nutting Kingsland.


### Sizer, Theodore (1892-1967)

| | |
|---|---|
| Occupation(s): | capitalist - import–export firm, 1915-1917, 1919-1922<br>educator - lecturer, Western Reserve Univ., Cleveland, OH, 1924-1927; professor of art history, Yale Univ., New Haven, CT, 1927-1931; associate director, Yale University Art Gallery; curator, Cleveland Museum of Art, 1922-1927<br>artist - oil and watercolor landscapes |
| Civic Activism: | trustee, Textile Museum, Washington, DC; member, Monuments, Fine Arts, and Architecture Section, United States Army during World War II (saving art treasures in Italy) |
| Marriage(s): | 1916-1967 – Caroline Wheelwright Foster (1896-1985) |
| Address: | Franklin Place, Hewlett |
| Name of estate: | |
| Year of construction: | 1922 |
| Style of architecture: | |
| Architect(s): | |
| Landscape architect(s): | |
| House extant: | unconfirmed |
| Historical notes: | |

The house was built by Theodore Sizer. [*The Brooklyn Daily Eagle* September 10, 1921, p. 19.]

The *Long Island Society Register, 1929* lists Theodore and Caroline W. Foster Sizer as residing in Cedarhurst [Hewlett].

He was the son of Robert Ryland and Mary Theodora Thomsen Sizer, Sr. of *Norwood* in Plandome Manor. [*See* Spinzia, *Long Island's Prominent North Shore Families, vol. II* – Sizer entry.]

Caroline Wheelwright Foster Sizer was the daughter of Charles Henry Wheelwright and Mabel Chase Hill Foster of Boston, MA.

Theodore and Caroline Wheelwright Foster Sizer's daughter Caroline married Alexander S. Cochran, the son of William F. and Nina Gill Cochran of Baltimore, MD. Their daughter Hilda married Sturgis Warner, the son of Roger S. Warner of Boston, MA. Their daughter Mary married John Edwin Ecklund. Their daughter Elizabeth married Yorke Allen, Jr. Their daughter Alice married Caleb Warner. Their son Theodore Ryland Sizer II married Nancy Ellen Faust, the daughter of Harold E. Faust.

### Sklar, Dr. Leo

Occupation(s): physician

Marriage(s):

Address: Central Avenue, Lawrence
Name of estate: *Byrnewood*
Year of construction: c. 1918
Style of architecture: Modified Neo-Federal
Architect(s):
Landscape architect(s):
House extant: yes
Historical notes:

The house, originally named *Byrnewood*, was built by Dr. Leo Sklar.

*front facade*

### Skelos, Dean George (b. 1948)

Occupation(s): attorney - member, Ruskin, Moscou, Evans, and Faltischek
politician - member, New York State Senate, 1985-2015; New York State Senate Majority Leader, 2008 and 2011-2015

Marriage(s): M/1 – 1974-div – Nancy Elizabeth Moffitt
- capitalist - managing director, Holiday Inn, Rockville Centre
M/2 – 1990 – Gail M. Bernhardt (b. 1950)
- politician - legislative coordinator for Ralph Marino
real estate agent - manager, Rockville Centre Realty Corp.

Address: 31 Roxen Road, Rockville Centre
Name of estate:
Year of construction: 1933
Style of architecture: Neo-Tudor
Architect(s):
Landscape architect(s):
House extant: yes
Historical notes:

Dean George Skelos is the son of Basil and Ann Stratigos Skelos of Rockville Centre. Dean was convicted for corruption and sentenced to four years and three months in prison. In 2020, he was given house arrest because of testing positive for Covid-19.

Nancy Elizabeth Moffitt Skelos is the daughter of Thomas F. Moffitt, Jr. of Rockville Centre. She subsequently married ____ Duka.

Dean George and Nancy Elizabeth Moffitt Skelos' adopted son Adam, who was also convicted of corruption, married Ann Marie Diaz in 2011 and resided in Rockville Centre.

*front facade*

**Slade, Francis Henry (1833-1890)**

| | |
|---|---|
| Occupation(s): | merchant - John Slade & Co. (dry goods firm) |
| Marriage(s): | M/1 – 1863-1875 – Elizabeth James Stokes (1839-1875) |
| | M/2 – 1880-1890 – Amelia Mallory Strong (1840-1926) |
| Address: | Mistletoe Way and Hollywood Crossing, Lawrence |
| Name of estate: | |
| Year of construction: | c. 1884 |
| Style of architecture: | Victorian |
| Architect(s): | Henry Martyn Congdon designed the house and stables (for F. H. Slade) |

Landscape architect(s):
House extant: unconfirmed
Historical notes:

The house was built by Francis Henry Slade.
He was the son of John and Lucy Lord Slade.
Elizabeth James Stokes Slade was the daughter of James Boulter and Caroline Olivia Phelps Stokes of *Clifton Cottage* in Manhattan.

Francis Henry and Elizabeth James Stokes Slade's son James died in 1869 at the age of four. Their daughter Mabel married William Reierson Arbuthnot, Jr. of England. Their son Francis Louis Slade married Caroline McCormick.

Amelia Mallory Strong Slade was the daughter of New York State Supreme Court Associate Judge William and Mrs. Priscilla Lee Strong.

*architectural drawing of stables, 1883*

*architectural drawing, 1883*

## Slade, Prescott (1869-1913)

Occupation(s): financier - member, Taylor, Smith, and Hard (investment banking firm)

Marriage(s): 1902 -1913 – Josephine Bissell Roe (1877-1954)

Address: Ocean Point Avenue, Cedarhurst
Name of estate:
Year of construction:
Style of architecture:
Architect(s):
Landscape architect(s):
House extant: unconfirmed
Historical notes:

The Slades were residing in Cedarhurst at the time of Prescott Slade's death.

He was the son of John Milton and Gertrude Cook Slade. Prescott Slade's brother John Slade, Sr., who resided at *Underhill House* in Upper Brookville and at *Berry Hill Farm* in Oyster Bay Cove, married Alice Bell, the daughter of Samuel Peters and Lydia Seabury Bell, and, later, Edith Bradford Weekes, the daughter of Arthur Delano and Lily Underhill Weekes, Sr. and a descendant of the Indian fighter Captain John Underhill. Edith's brother Arthur Delano Weekes, Jr. married Dorothy Lee Higginson, the daughter of James J. Higginson of Boston, MA, and resided at *The Anchorage* in Oyster Bay Cove. Her brother Harold married Louisine Peters with whom he resided at *Wereholme* in Islip and, subsequently, Frances Stokes with whom he resided at *Valentine Farm* in Old Brookville.

Josephine Bissell Roe Slade was the daughter of General Charles Francis and Mrs. Catherine Bissell Bogert Roe of Highland Falls, NY. By 1937 Josephine had relocated to Mill Neck.

Prescott and Josephine Bissell Roe Slade's daughter Katherine, who married Henry Dennison Babcock II of Mill Neck and, subsequently, Eugene Maxwell Geddes, Sr. of *Punkin Hill* in Matinecock later owned the Cedarhurst house. [*See* Spinzia, *Long Island's Prominent North Shore Families, vol. 1* – Babcock and Geddes entries; *Long Island's Prominent North Shore Families, vol. II* – Slade and Weekes entries; *Long Island's Prominent South Shore Families* – Weekes entry; *Long Island: A Guide to New York's Suffolk and Nassau Counties* – Underhill Burying Ground, Grave of Captain John Underhill, Mill Neck – and – Whitaker Historical Collection, Southold Free Library, Southold.]


## Slee, James Noah, Jr. (1893-1974)

Occupation(s): financier - partner, Williamson, Gilbert, and Co. (stock brokerage firm);
partner, Grover, O'Neill, and Co. (stock brokerage firm)

Marriage(s): 1917-1974 – Anna Wright Benoist (1893-1981)

Address: *[unable to determine street address]*, Hewlett Bay Park
Name of estate:
Year of construction:
Style of architecture:
Architect(s):
Landscape architect(s):
House extant: unconfirmed
Historical notes:

The *Long Island Society Register, 1929* lists James Noah and Anna W. Benoist Slee [Jr.] as residing in Woodmere [Hewlett Bay Park].

He was the son of James Noah and Mary Roosevelt West Slee, Sr. and an heir to the Three-in-One Oil fortune. His stepmother was the noted birth control crusader Margaret Sanger. His sister Elizabeth married Walter Irving Willis and resided in Westhampton Beach. [*See* Spinzia, *Long Island's Prominent Families in the Town of Southampton* – Willis entry.]

Anna Wright Benoist Slee was the daughter of Theodore and Mary Emily Hunt Benoist of St. Louis, MO.

James Noah and Ann Wright Benoist Slee, Jr.'s daughter Mary married Robert Van Leer Simpson, the son of William S. Simpson of St. Louis, MO, and resided in Ashville, NC.

### Slesinger, Laurence Anthony (1893-1960)

| | |
|---|---|
| Occupation(s): | industrialist - founder, L. A. Slesinger, Inc. (textile manufacturing firm); president, Valentine Textile Co. |
| Civic Activism: | chief, cotton and leather division, War Production Board during World War II |
| Marriage(s): | Estelle Warner (1894-1986) (aka Ruth Stuyvesant) <br> - journalist - fashion editor, *New York Herald Tribune* <br> capitalist - proprietor, Renrew Kennels, Sands Point <br> Civic Activism: judge, dog shows |
| Address: | Cedar Avenue and Meadowview Avenue, Hewlett Bay Park |
| Name of estate: | |
| Year of construction: | c. 1908 |
| Style of architecture: | Modified Cotswold |
| Architect(s): | Albro and Lindeberg designed the house (for Carroll Macy) |
| Landscape architect(s): | |
| House extant: | no |

*front facade, 1908*

Historical notes:

The house, originally named *Birch Corners*, was built by Carroll Macy. It was later owned by Ira Andruss Kip, Jr. and, then, by Danforth Miller, Sr., who also called in *Birch Corners*. In 1942, Slesinger purchased the house from Danforth Miller, Sr. for $40,000. [*Nassau Daily Review–Star* July 27, 1942, p. 14, and *The New York Times* July 22, 1942, p. 33.] In 1949, Slesinger placed the house on the market and relocated to Sands Point. [*Newsday* May 6, 1949, p. 45.] The living room contained sixteenth-century walnut paneling which Miller brought from England [*The New York Times* July 22, 1942, p. 33.]

Laurence was the son of Anthony and Augusta Singer Slesinger of Manhattan. Laurence's sister Theresa, the noted novelist and screenwriter Tess Slesinger, was a Communist sympathizer. Theresa married Herbert Solow and, later, Hollywood director and screenwriter Frank Davis. Their brother Stephen, who married Hollywood marketer Shirley Ann Basso, obtained the rights for Winnie-the-Pooh, Dick Tracy, Tarzan, and Blondie and was also the creator of the Red Ryder comic strip.

Laurence Anthony and Estelle Warner Slesinger's daughter Priscilla, who was the model for Tess in the Red Ryder comic series, married Dr. William H. Victor, the son of A. W. Victor of Rockaway Beach and, later, Arthur Eichelbaum, the son of Abraham Eichelbaum of Norfolk, VA.

At the time of his death, Slesinger was residing in Sands Point.

### Sloan, Benson Bennett, Sr. (1867-1958)

| | |
|---|---|
| Occupation(s): | financier - partner, Post and Flagg (stock brokerage firm) <br> capitalist - director, Fort Wayne and Jackson Railroad; director, Valley Railroad |
| Marriage(s): | M/1 – 1889-1912 – Anna Lydia Worth (1867-1912) <br> M/2 – 1913-1958 – Margaret Milligan Sloane (1888-1961) |
| Address: | 415 Ocean Avenue, Lawrence |
| Name of estate: | *Ballyracket* |
| Year of construction: | |
| Style of architecture: | |
| Architect(s): | |
| Landscape architect(s): | |
| House extant: | no |

Historical notes:

Benson Bennett Sloan, Sr. was the son of Samuel Sloan and Margaret Elmendorf Sloan, Sr. of Manhattan.

Anna Lydia Worth Sloan was the daughter of Francis W. Worth.

The *Long Island Society Register, 1929* lists Benson Bennett and Margaret M. Sloane Sloan [Sr.] as residing at *Ballyracket* in Lawrence.

She was the daughter of Milligan Sloane of Manhattan.

Benson Bennett and Margaret Milligan Sloane Sloan, Sr.'s son Samuel Sloan III married Marion Baker, the daughter of Newcombe Chandler Baker of Rumson, NJ. Their son William married Margaret MacKenzie Treadway, the daughter of Heaton Ives Treadway of Stockbridge, MA, and resided at *Oolagiskit* in Dublin, NH. Their son Benson Bennett Sloan, Jr. married Virginia F. Stephens, the daughter of Franklin E. Stephens of Clovis, NM, and resided in Edgartown, MA.

### Sloan, Robert Sage, Sr. (1859-1926)

| | |
|---|---|
| Occupation(s): | military - lieutenant commander; chief of staff, NYS Naval Militia, 1898; executive officer, USS *Stranger*, during Spanish–American War |
| | financier - trustee, American Surety Co.; director, Peninsula National Bank, Cedarhurst |
| | industrialist - trustee, Fitzgibbons Boiler Co. |
| Civic Activism: | a founder, Village of Woodsburgh, 1912; trustee, Village of Woodsburgh, 1918-1926 |
| Marriage(s): | 1883-1926 – Ethel Donaldson (1860-1933) |
| Address: | Channel Road, Woodsburgh |
| Name of estate: | *Chilton Gables* |
| Year of construction: | |
| Style of architecture: | |
| Architect(s): | |
| Landscape architect(s): | |
| House extant: unconfirmed | |
| Historical notes: | |

   The *Long Island Society Register, 1929* lists Robert Sage and Ethel Donaldson Sloan [Sr.] as residing at *Chilton Gables* in Woodmere [Woodsburgh].
   He was the son of George Beale and Alvira Crane Sloan of Oswego, NY.
   Ethel Donaldson Sloan was the daughter of Thomas and Mary Pickering Elizabeth Dorsey Donaldson.
   Robert Sage and Ethel Donaldson Sloan, Sr.'s daughter Ethel married John Sinclair Liddell and, subsequently, Baron Ernest George Porcelli di' Sant'Andrea. Their son Thomas married Helen de Russy Clark and resided at *Whilton Gables* in Lawrence.

*[See following entry for additional family information.]*


### Sloan, Thomas Donaldson, Sr. (b. 1884)

| | |
|---|---|
| Occupation(s): | military - colonel, United States Army |
| | industrialist - assistant treasurer, Fitzgibbons Boiler Co. |
| Marriage(s): | 1909 – Helen de Russy Clark |
| Address: | 233 Narraganset Avenue, Lawrence |
| Name of estate: | *Wilton Gables* |
| Year of construction: | 1928 |
| Style of architecture: | Modified Georgian |
| Architect(s): | |
| Landscape architect(s): | |
| House extant: yes; remodeled in 1968 | |
| Historical notes: | |

   The house, originally named *Wilton Gables*, was built by Thomas Donaldson Sloan, Sr.
   The *Long Island Society Register, 1929* lists T. Donaldson and Helen de R. Clark Sloan [Sr.] as residing at *Wilton Gables* in Lawrence.
   He was the son of Robert Sage and Ethel Donaldson Sloan, who resided at *Chilton Gables* in Woodsburgh.
   Helen de Russy Clark Sloan was the daughter of Charles Hobart and Helen Maxwell de Russy Clark.
   Thomas Donaldson and Helen de Russy Clark Sloan, Sr.'s daughter Ethel married Prescott Morris–Smith, the son of Preston Morris–Smith of Detroit. Their daughter Miriam married James Dimpsey, the son of Thomas J. Dimpsey of Pittsburgh, PA. Their daughter Helen married Martin Van Buren Morris, the son of Stuyvesant Fish and Elizabeth Hilles Wynkoop Morris, Jr. of Hewlett Harbor, and resided at *Longacre* in Southampton. She later married Byron Lee Newton. [*See* Spinzia, *Long Island's Prominent Families in the Town of Southampton* – Morris entry.] Their eighteen-year-old son Charles committed suicide. [*The New York Times* March 21, 1935, p. 3.] Their son Robert Sage Sloan II married Florence Middleton Norris, the daughter of Alfred Lockwood and Florence M. Lee Norris of Lawrence, and resided in Georgetown, VA.

*[See previous entry for additional family information.]*

*Thomas Donaldson Sloan, Sr. residence,
front facade 2007*

**Slocum, Henry Warner, Jr. (1862-1949)**

Occupation(s): attorney
financier - member, New York Stock Exchange
Civic Activism: president, United States Lawn Tennis Association*

Marriage(s): 1888-1949 – Grace Edsall (1867-1949)

Address: *[unable to determine street address]*, Cedarhurst
Name of estate:
Year of construction:
Style of architecture:
Architect(s):
Landscape architect(s):
House extant: unconfirmed
Historical notes:

    The *Brooklyn Blue Book and Long Island Society Register, 1918* lists Henry Warner and Grace Edsall Slocum [Jr.] as residing in Cedarhurst.
    He was the son of Civil War General Henry Warner and Mrs. Clara Rice Slocum, Sr. of Brooklyn. The steamboat *General Slocum*, which sank in the East River in 1904, was named for the general.
    Grace Edsall Slocum was the daughter of Henry and Mary Emma Jerome Edsall of Manhattan.
    Henry Warner and Grace Edsall Slocum, Jr.'s daughter Nathalie married G. Albert Smith, Jr. of Louisville, KY. Their daughter Gertrude married William Herbert Adams of Lawrence.
    *In 1955 Slocum was inducted into the Tennis Hall of Fame.

### Smith, Augustine Jacquelin (1872-1943)

| | |
|---|---|
| Occupation(s): | industrialist - partner, Augustine Smith & Co. (paper manufacturing firm);<br>financier - director, National Nassau Bank (later, Irving Trust Co.); partner, Taylor, Smith, and Hard (stock brokerage firm) |
| Civic Activism: | governor and secretary, New York Hospital, NYC;<br>member and secretary, New York County Grand Jury panel for 10 years;<br>member, executive committee, New York Institute for the Education of the Blind |
| Marriage(s): | 1899-1943 – Julia Post Hard (1876-1953) |
| Address: | 430 Mistletoe Way, Lawrence |
| Name of estate: | *Sunnyside* |
| Year of construction: | |
| Style of architecture: | Modified Dutch Colonial Revival |
| Architect(s): | |
| Landscape architect(s): | |
| House extant: no | |
| Historical notes: | |

The *Long Island Society Register, 1929* lists Augustine J. and Julia Post Hard Smith as residing in Lawrence. He was the son of Lewis Jacquelin and Mary Campbell Smith.

Julia Post Hard Smith was the daughter of Anson Wales and Sarah Elizabeth Brown Hard, Sr. of *Driftwood* in Lawrence. Julia's brother DeCourcy married Marjorie Work, the daughter of James Henry and Mary L. Davies Work, Sr. of *Engleside* in Lawrence, and resided at *Briarwood* in Lawrence. Her sister Sarah married William Reed Kirkland Taylor, Sr. and resided in Lawrence. Her sister Nellie married John Kane Mills and resided at *Ruddington Farm* in Hackettstown, NJ. Her sister Laura married Henry von Lengerke Meyer, Sr. and resided at *Cobblestone Farm* in Suffern, NY. Her brother Anson Wales Hard, Jr., who resided at *Meadow Edge* in West Sayville, married Florence Bourne, the daughter of Frederick Gilbert and Emma Sparks Keeler Bourne of *Indian Neck Hall* in Oakdale, and, subsequently, Katherine Potter. [*See* Spinzia, *Long Island's Prominent South Shore Families* – Bourne and Hard entries.] Her brother James married Leonor Landron de Guevara.

Augustine Jacquelin and Julia Post Hard Smith's daughter Dorothy married William Henderson Long, Jr. and resided at *Noranda* in Hewlett Harbor. Their daughter Mary married Dr. DeWitt Hendee Smith, the son of Charles Hendee Smith of Lawrence, and resided in Princeton, NJ. Their daughter Edith married John Meyerkort, Jr. and resided in Lawrence.

Smith shot and killed himself in his private room at New York Hospital where he had just undergone eye surgery. [*The New York Times* January 8, 1943, p. 10.]

*front facade*

### Smith, Clarence Browning (1875-1959)

| | |
|---|---|
| Occupation(s): | military - lieutenant colonel; adjutant, Military District of Washington, DC<br>diplomat - unofficial United States delegate to Austrian Reparation Commission after World War I |
| Marriage(s): | M/1 – 1900-1953 – Anna Gertrude Jones (1875-1953)<br>- educator - chair, mathematics and astronomy department, Female College, Columbia, SC; chair, mathematics, department, South Carolina College, Columbia, SC; chair, mathematics department, San Antonio Female College, San Antonio, TX<br>Civic Activism: a founder, Save the Children Federation<br>M/2 – Marjorie Marsden |
| Address: | 141 Kensington Road, Garden City |
| Name of estate: | |
| Year of construction: | 1911 |
| Style of architecture: | American Craftsman |
| Architect(s): | |
| Landscape architect(s): | |
| House extant: yes | |
| Historical notes: | |

*front facade, 2001*

The *Long Island Society Register, 1929* lists Clarence Browning and Anne [sic] Gertrude Jones Smith as residing at 141 Kensington Road, Garden City.

He was the son of Joel Franklin and Alice Browning Smith, Jr.

Anna Gertrude Jones Smith was the daughter of James Ira Jones.

Clarence Browning and Anna Gertrude Jones Smith's daughter Alice married Count George Hoyes, the son of Count Edgar Hoyes of *Castle Soos on the Danube*, Vienna, Austria. Alice subsequently married John Conover Ten Eyck III of Manhattan, and resided in Hewlett. The Smiths' daughter Margaret married Charles Secor Risdon, the son of Alfred Risdon of New York City.


### Smith, Cyrus Porter, Sr. (1896-1982)

| | |
|---|---|
| Occupation(s): | financier - member, Spencer, Trask, and Co. (bond brokerage firm) |
| Civic Activism: | trustee, Village of Garden City |
| Marriage(s): | 1920-div. 1942 – Eileen Morrison O'Brien (1897-1981) |
| Address: | 122 Cherry Valley Road, Garden City |
| Name of estate: | |
| Year of construction: | |
| Style of architecture: | |
| Architect(s): | |
| Landscape architect(s): | |
| House extant: no | |
| Historical notes: | |

The *Long Island Society Register, 1929* lists Cyrus Porter and Eileen M. O'Brian Smith as residing on Cherry Valley Road, Garden City.

He was the son of B. Herbert Smith of Brooklyn.

Eileen Morrison O'Brien Smith was the daughter of Dr. Henry Lewis and Mrs. Mary Ella Thall O'Brien of Brooklyn.

Cyrus Porter and Eileen Morrison O'Brien Smith, Sr.'s daughter Eileen married Stephen Barker, Jr. of Short Hills, NJ. Their son Cyrus Porter Smith, Jr. married Deborah Steuart Myers, the daughter of William Nelson Myers of Williamsburg, VA. Their daughter Sarah married C. Malcolm Murphy, the son of Walter Murphy of Garden City.

### Smith, Herbert Ludlam, Sr. (1875-1927)

Occupation(s): financier - partner, Smith and Lewis (stock brokerage firm); vice-president and director, Garden City Bank and Trust Co.

Marriage(s): 1902-1927 – Marie Schoonmaker (d. 1959)

Address: Cathedral Avenue, Garden City
Name of estate:
Year of construction:
Style of architecture:
Architect(s):
Landscape architect(s):
House extant: unconfirmed
Historical notes:

By 1927 the Smiths had relocated from their Centre Island estate *Oliver's Point* to Cathedral Avenue, Garden City. [*See* Spinzia, *Long Island's Prominent North Shore Families, vol. II* – Smith entry.] The *Long Island Society Register, 1929* lists Marie Schoonmaker Smith as residing on Second Street, Garden City.

Herbert Ludlam Smith, Sr. was the son of Isaac and Cornelia Parish Ludlam Smith.

Herbert Ludlam and Marie Schoonmaker Smith, Sr.'s son Thurston married Ruth Eleanor Mooney, the daughter of Franklin Drake Mooney of Garden City. Their son Herbert Ludlam Smith, Jr. married Gertrude Louise Miller, the daughter of John Robinson Miller Sr. of Garden City.

In 1937, Marie Schoonmaker Smith married Hobart Hayes Putnam and continued to reside in Garden City.


### Smith, James Clinch (1856-1912)

Occupation(s): an heir to A. T. Stewart's Department Store fortune

Marriage(s): 1895-1912 – Bertha Ludington Barnes (1870-1913)

Address: Eisenhower Park, East Meadow
Name of estate:
Year of construction: 1903
Style of architecture:
Architect(s):
Landscape architect(s):
House extant: no; destroyed by fire, 1905
Historical notes:

The house was built by James Clinch Smith, who was included on Ward McAllister's list of society's elite "400."

He was the son of Judge John Lawrence and Mrs. Sarah Nicoll Smith of Smithtown and a descendant of the founder of Smithtown Richard "Bull" Smith. [*See* Spinzia, *Long Island: A Guide to New York's Suffolk and Nassau Counties* – Judge J. Lawrence Smith House – *The Homestead*, Village of the Branch.] His sister Cornelia Stewart Smith married Prescott Hall Butler. A painting of Cornelia Stewart Smith Butler hangs in The Smithtown Library. His sister Bessie married the controversial architect Stanford White and resided at *Box Hill* in Head of the Harbor. [*See* Spinzia, *Long Island: A Guide to New York's Suffolk and Nassau Counties* – Stanford White Estate – *Box Hill*, Head of the Harbor.] His sister Louisa married Frank Sayre Osborne. His sister Kate married The Reverend J. Bloomfield Wetherill.

Bertha Ludington Barnes Smith was the daughter of Charles Joseph and Mary Louise Ludington Barnes of New York and Chicago, IL. The Chicago Historical Society has an 1889 painting of Mrs. Smith by the artist M. Cordiginai.

James Clinch Smith died with the sinking of the *Titanic*. A stained-glass window, designed by Stanford White and executed by John LaFarge in Saint James Episcopal Church in St. James, stands as a memorial to James Clinch Smith. [*See* Spinzia, *Long Island: A Guide to New York's Suffolk and Nassau Counties* – Saint James Episcopal Church, St. James.]

### Snyder, William Robert (1887-1982)

| | |
|---|---|
| Occupation(s): | industrialist - manager, Manhattan branch, Thomaston Mills, Inc. |
| Civic Activism: | a founder, Georgia Tech Glee Club |
| Marriage(s): | 1916 – Emma Harriet Henry (1893-1968) |
| Address: | 1 Kilburn Road, Garden City |
| Name of estate: | |
| Year of construction: | 1927 |
| Style of architecture: | Neo-Tudor |
| Architect(s): | |
| Landscape architect(s): | |
| House extant: yes | |
| Historical notes: | |

*front facade, 2000*

William Robert Snyder was the son of William and Dora Wanner Snyder of Atlanta, GA.

Emma Harriet Henry Snyder was the daughter of John and Elizabeth Ballard Henry.

William Robert and Emma Harriet Henry Snyder's daughter Elizabeth married Harry Howard Wallace, Jr. of West Hartford, CT, and resided in Bethesda, MD. Their daughter Harriet married Ralph Peters Hubbell, Sr., the son of John Platt and Dorothy Peters Hubbell, Sr. of Garden City, and resided in Garden City.

### Southgate, Richard (1893-1946)

Occupation(s): diplomat - served in: United States Embassy in Paris, 1917-1918;
United States Embassy in Rome, 1919-1921;
United States Legation in Guatemala, 1921-1922;
United States Embassy in Constantinople, 1922-1923;
United States Embassy in Havana, 1925-1926;
Chief of Protocol and Chief of International Conferences, 1929-1939;
member, American delegation to Limitation of Armaments Conference, 1921;
member, London Naval Conference, 1935;
member, Aviation Conference, 1937;
Chief of Protocol, United States Department of State
capitalist - regional director in Europe, Pan American Airways
financier - banker

Marriage(s): 1927-1946 – Lila Lancashire (d. 1970)

Address: *[unable to determine street address]*, Hewlett
Name of estate:
Year of construction:
Style of architecture:
Architect(s):
Landscape architect(s):
House extant: unconfirmed
Historical notes:

The *Long Island Society Register, 1929* lists Richard and Lila Lancashire Southgate as residing in Hewlett.

He was the son of Louis Warren and Clara Brigham Southgate of Osterville, MA.

Lila Lancashire Southgate was the daughter of Dr. James Henry and Mrs. Sarah Hale Wright Lancashire of Manhattan and *Graftonwood* in Manchester, MA.

Richard and Lila Lancashire Southgate's daughter Patricia married Peter Matthiessen, the son of Erard A. Matthiessen of Stamford, CT. Their daughter Sarita married Edward R. Tallman, the son of Dr. Frank F. Tallman of Los Angeles, CA. Their son Richard Wright Southgate married Anna Fisher Hart, the daughter of Harry Carlton Hart of Princeton, NJ.

## Southworth, Theodore (1897-1974)

Occupation(s): merchant - president, Kings County Buick, Inc. (Brooklyn automobile dealer)

Civic Activism: state committee, Automobile Merchant's Association of New York; director, Long Island Chamber of Commerce, 1931; president, Motor Vehicle Retailing Code Administration, 1933

Marriage(s): Muriel Coddington (1897-1987)

Address: 135 Hampton Road, Garden City
Name of estate:
Year of construction: 1927
Style of architecture: Neo-Georgian
Architect(s):
Landscape architect(s):
House extant: yes
Historical notes:

*front facade, 2005*

The house was built by Theodore Southworth.
The *Long Island Society Register, 1929* lists Theodore and Muriel Coddington Southworth as residing at 135 Hampton Road, Garden City.
He was the son of Augustus Glidden and Lillian May Reynell Southworth of Englewood, NJ.
Muriel Coddington Southworth was the daughter of Alpheus and Elizabeth Dixon Roosa Coddington of Kingston, NY.
Theodore and Muriel Coddington Southworth's daughter Joan married David McLean Appleton and resided in Manhattan. Their daughter Jacelyn married William Edgar Mayer Jr. of Buffalo, NY.

## Sperry, Lawrence Burst, Sr. (1892-1923)

Occupation(s): industrialist - a founder, Lawrence Sperry Aircraft Co., Farmingdale*
inventor**

Marriage(s): 1918-1923 – Winifred Allen Kelly (1896-1943)
(aka Winifred Allen)
- entertainers and associated professions - silent film actress

Address: Atlantic Avenue, Garden City
Name of estate:
Year of construction:
Style of architecture:
Architect(s):
Landscape architect(s):
House extant: unconfirmed
Historical notes:

Lawrence Burst Sperry, Sr. was the son of Elmer Ambrose and Zula Goodman Sperry, Sr. of Bellport.
Winifred Allen Kelly Sperry was the daughter of Henry d'Arcy and Winfred Barclay Kelly. She was a star at Triangle Films Corp., whose cadre of stars included Mary Pickford, Lillian Gish, Douglas Fairbanks, Sr., and Roscoe "Fatty" Arbuckle.
In 1916, Lawrence made the first night flight over water in the country flying from Moriches to Amityville. He died while attempting to cross the English Channel from England to The Netherlands.
*Sperry commuted to his Farmingdale factory in a plane he garaged across the street from his house in Garden City.
[Mildred. H. Smith, *History of Garden City*. (Garden City, NY: Garden City Historical Society, 1980), p. 119.]
**He held twenty-three patents including those for the aircraft autopilot, turn and bank indicator, retractable landing gear, and the parachute pack.

### Spinzia, Peter (1896-1957)

| | |
|---|---|
| Occupation(s): | industrialist - founder and president, Peter Spinzia Dress Corp., NYC (women's clothing manufacturer); capitalist - founder and president, SILPA (olive oil importing firm). |
| Marriage(s): | 1932-1957 – Rose DeGregorio (1906-1984) |
| Address: | 423 Woodmere Boulevard, Woodmere |
| Name of estate: | |
| Year of construction: | 1928 |
| Style of architecture: | Colonial Revival |
| Architect(s): | |
| Landscape architect(s): | |
| House extant: yes | |
| Historical notes: | |

*front facade, 2000*

The house was built by Peter Spinzia.

He was the son of Dr. Joseph Anthony and Mrs. Angelica Sama Spinzia of Guardavalle, Italy.

Rose DeGregorio Spinzia was the daughter of Vincent and Genevieve Rabino DeGregorio of Brooklyn.

Peter and Rose De Gregorio Spinzia's daughter Norma Rita married New York State Supreme Court Judge Robert Roberto, Jr. and resides in Manhasset. Their son Dr. Joseph Arnold Spinzia, who resides in Southampton, married Barbara Kraft, the daughter of Harold and Ruth Jackson Kraft of Cristal Lake, IL, and, subsequently, Susan Hergert, the daughter of Frederick and Laura Hergert of Manhattan. [See Spinzia, *Long Island's Prominent Families in the Town of Southampton* – Spinzia entry.]

*[See following entry for additional family information.]*

In 2013, the 1,950-square-foot house sold for $499,000.


### Spinzia, Ralph (1906-1957)

| | |
|---|---|
| Occupation(s): | industrialist - founder and president, Ralph Spinzia & Co., NYC (women's clothing manufacturer)* |
| Marriage(s): | 1934-1957 – Margaret Cottone (1899-1977) |
| Address: | 111 Stewart Avenue, Garden City |
| Name of estate: | |
| Year of construction: | 1955 |
| Style of architecture: | Split-level |
| Architect(s): | |
| Landscape architect(s): | |
| House extant: yes | |
| Historical notes: | |

The house was built by Ralph Spinzia.

He was the son of Dr. Joseph Anthony and Mrs. Angelica Sama Spinzia of Guardavalle, Italy. His brother Peter married Rose DeGregorio and resided in Woodmere. His sister Carmella married Joseph Pacetta, the son of Cosmo and Maria Catherina Guardleone Pacetta of Guardavalle, Italy, and resided in Far Rockaway.

Margaret Cottone Spinzia was the daughter of Philip and Rosalia Muratore Cottone of Lercara Friddi, Italy, and Brooklyn. Her brother Anthony married Rose Iovino and resided in Garden City.

Ralph and Margaret Cottone Spinzia's son Raymond married Judith Kathryn Ader, the daughter of Richard Frederick and Myrtle Kathryn Waugh Ader of Rochester and Huntington, NY, and Tucson AZ, and resides at *Guardavalle* in White Deer Township, PA.

*[See previous entry for additional family information.]*

*Ralph Spinzia & Co. manufactured the women's tailored suit line of Christian Dior.

*front facade, 1960*

### Stanton, Louis Lee, Jr. (1897-1981)

| | |
|---|---|
| Occupation(s): | financier - partner, Carlisle and Jacquelin (stock brokerage firm) |
| Marriage(s): | 1923-1981– Helena Parsons LaFetra (1900-1998) |
| Address: | Washington Avenue, Lawrence |
| Name of estate: | |
| Year of construction: | |
| Style of architecture: | |
| Architect(s): | |
| Landscape architect(s): | |
| House extant: unconfirmed | |
| Historical notes: | |

The *Long Island Society Register, 1929* lists Louis Lee and Helena P. LaFetra Stanton [Jr.] as residing on Washington Avenue, Cedarhurst [Lawrence].

He was the son of Louis Lee and Pauline Williams Dixon Stanton, Sr. of Lawrence.

Helena Parsons LaFetra Stanton was the daughter of Dr. Linnaeus Edford LaFetra of New Canaan, CT.

Louis Lee and Helena Parsons LaFetra Stanton, Jr.'s daughter Ann married Charles Morgan Post, Jr. and resided in New Canaan, CT. Ann subsequently married Allen Farish Maulsby, the son of David Lee Maulsby III. Their son Dixon married Barbara Hadley, the daughter of Morris and Katherine Cumnock Blodgett Hadley of Glen Cove and *Whitewood* in Lloyd Harbor, and resided in Seal Harbor, ME. [*See* Spinzia, *Long Island's Prominent North Shore Families, vol. I* – Hadley entries.] Their son Louis Lee Stanton III married Phoebe Rentschler, the daughter of Gordon Sohn and Mary S. Coolidge Rentschler of Matinecock and *Waveland* in Old Brookville, and resided in New Canaan, CT. [*See* Spinzia, *Long Island's Prominent North Shore Families, vol. II* – Rentschler entry.] Louis later married Berit Rask, the daughter of Bror Rask of Sweden.

*[See following entry for additional family information.]*

### Stanton, Louis Lee, Sr. (1859-1911)

| | |
|---|---|
| Occupation(s): | capitalist - director, Staten Island Rapid Transit; director, Erie Rapid Transit |
| | financier - director, Electric Bond and Share Co.; vice-president and director, Standard Safe Deposit Co.; president, Standard Trust Co. |
| | industrialist - treasurer and director, American Malting Co. |
| Marriage(s): | 1887 – Pauline Williams Dixon (b. 1862) |
| Address: | *[unable to determine street address]*, Lawrence |
| Name of estate: | |
| Year of construction: | |
| Style of architecture: | |
| Architect(s): | |
| Landscape architect(s): | |
| House extant: unconfirmed | |
| Historical notes: | |

Louis Lee Stanton, Sr. was the son of Edmund Denison and Louise Babcock Stanton.

Pauline Williams Dixon Stanton was the daughter of Courtland Palmer and Hannah Elizabeth William Dixon of Brooklyn.

Louis Lee and Pauline Williams Dixon Stanton, Sr.'s daughter Priscilla married Joseph Howland Auchincloss, Sr., the son of John Winthrop and Joanna Russell Auchincloss, and resided in Lawrence, Matinecock, and Southampton. [*See* Spinzia, *Long Island's Prominent North Shore Families, vol. I*, and *Long Island's Prominent Families* in the Town of Southampton – Auchincloss entries.] Their son William Tillinghast Stanton, who resided at *Dina House* in Hong Kong, married Elsa Burgess, the daughter of William H. Burgess. She had previously been married to Frank Low Fearson of New York and Robert Jardine Paterson of Shanghai, China. Their son Louis Lee Stanton, Jr. married Helena Parsons LaFetra and resided in Lawrence.

### Stebbins, George Ledyard, Sr. (1862-1952)

| | |
|---|---|
| Occupation(s): | capitalist - real estate developer, Seal Harbor, ME |
| Civic Activism: | helped establish Arcadia National Park, ME |
| Marriage(s): | 1903-1952 – Edith Alden Candler (1865-1953) |
| Address: | Woodmere Boulevard, Woodsburgh |
| Name of estate: | |
| Year of construction: | |
| Style of architecture: | |
| Architect(s): | |
| Landscape architect(s): | |
| House extant: | unconfirmed |
| Historical notes: | |

    George Ledyard Stebbins was the son of Charles and Mary Mairs Dows Stebbins.
    Edith Alden Candler Stebbins was the daughter of Flamen Ball and Marcia Lillian Welch Candler of Woodmere. Her brother Duncan married Beatrice de Trobriand Post, the daughter of Charles Alfred and Marie Caroline de Trobriand Post, who resided at *Standhome* is Bayport. [*See* Spinzia, *Long Island's Prominent South Shore Families* – Post entry.]
    George Ledyard and Edith Alden Candler Stebbins' son George Ledyard Stebbins, Jr., the noted botanist who resided in Davis, CA, married Margaret Goldsborough Chamberlaine and, subsequently, Barbara Jean Brumley.

### Steinberg, Julius (1915-1978)

| | |
|---|---|
| Occupation(s): | capitalist - a founder, Leasco Data Processing Equipment Co., 1961 (leased computers) (later, Reliance Group); member, executive committee, Reliance Group; treasurer, Leasco Capital Equipment Co. |
| | industrialist - a founder, Utility Tire Co., 1947; president, Ideal Rubber Company, Brooklyn |
| | financier - director, Reliance Insurance Co. |
| Civic Activism: | trustee, Long Island Medical Center, Queens, NY |
| Marriage(s): | 1938-1978 – Anne Cohen (1917-2012) |
| Address: | 162 Cedar Avenue, Hewlett Bay Park |
| Name of estate: | |
| Year of construction: | 1955 |
| Style of architecture: | |
| Architect(s): | |
| Landscape architect(s): | |
| House extant: | yes |
| Historical notes: | |

    Julius Steinberg was the son of Morris and Sarah Kletzkin Steinberg.
    Ann Cohen Steinberg was the daughter of Samuel and Gussie Woodman Cohen.
    Julius and Anne Cohen Steinberg's son Robert married Kathryn Joanne Newman, the daughter of Fred and Madelon Newman and resided in East Hampton. [*See* Spinzia, *Long Island's Prominent Families in the Town of East Hampton* – Steinberg entry.] Their son Saul married Laura Sconocchia; Barbara Herzog, the daughter of Abraham Isaac and Frieda Hoose Herzog; and later, Gayfryd McNabb. Their daughter Roni married Bruce Leslie Sokoloff, the son of Jessie B. Sokoloff, and resided in Bedford, NY.
    In 1984, the 8,009-square-foot house sold for $1.15 million.

### Stephan, Albert Ralph (1892-1967)

| | |
|---|---|
| Occupation(s): | capitalist -  purchased and rented houses in Five Towns area |
| | politician -  commissioner, sanitary district Number 1 |
| Civic Activism: | mayor, Village of Hewlett Neck |
| Marriage(s): | Elizabeth Jane Beason (1895-1976) |
| |   - Civic Activism: recording secretary, Lawrence Garden Club, 1938; |
| |                     secretary, Family Service Association of Lawrence |
| |                         division of the Community Chest; |
| |                     chair, open house committee, Kennebunkport |
| |                         Historical Society, 1953 |
| Address: | Phillips Lane, Hewlett Neck |
| Name of estate: | |
| Year of construction: | |
| Style of architecture: | |
| Architect(s): | |
| Landscape architect(s): | |
| House extant: | unconfirmed |
| Historical notes: | |

  Albert Ralph Stephan was the son of Albert and Eustena Augusta Pfiel Stephan of Kennebunkport, ME.
Elizabeth Jane Beason Stephan was the daughter of Charles Boardman and Elizabeth Lord Beason.


### Stevens, Alexander Henry (1834-1916)

| | |
|---|---|
| Occupation(s): | merchant -  partner, with his brother Albert, Stevens and Angelo Co., |
| |                 1857-1868 (sugar commission firm) |
| | financier -  vice-president, Gallatin National Bank of NY, 1880; |
| |               president, Sixth National Bank, 1890 (later, Astor |
| |                 National Bank); |
| |               vice-president, Astor National Bank, 1899 |
| | capitalist -  president, Samuel Stevens Realty Co.; |
| |               director, Mobile and Olio Railroad; |
| |               director, St. Paul and Duluth Railroad |
| Marriage(s): | 1860-1916 – Mary Alleyne Otis (1833-1918) |
| Address: | Broadway, Lawrence |
| Name of estate: | |
| Year of construction: | |
| Style of architecture: | |
| Architect(s): | |
| Landscape architect(s): | |
| House extant: | yes |
| Historical notes: | |

  The *Social Register Summer 1910* and *1915* list Alexander H. and Mary A. Otis Stevens as residing in Lawrence.
  He was the son of Byam Kirby and Frances Gallatin Stevens, Sr. and grandson of Secretary of the Treasury and United States Ambassador to the United Kingdom and France Albert Gallatin.
  Mary Alleyne Otis Stevens was the daughter of William Foster and Emily Marshall Otis.
  Alexander Henry and Mary Alleyne Otis Stevens' daughter Emily married Adolph Ladenburg (aka Moritz Adolph Emil Ladenburg), the son of Emil and Eugenie Adele Halphen Ladenburg, and resided at *Heathcote* in Salisbury. Their daughter Frances married Harrington Swann, the son of John Bellinton Swann of Great Britain. In 1869, their son William died at the age of two. Their daughter Elizabeth did not marry. Their son Eben married Evelena Babcock Dixon, the daughter of William Palmer and Evelena Franklin Dixon, Sr. In 1883, their son Alexander Eliot Stevens died at the age of ten. Their son Francis married Elizabeth Shaw Oliver, the daughter of General Robert Oliver and Mrs. Marion Lucy Rathbone Oliver.

## Stevens, Byam Kirby, III (1897-1967)

| | |
|---|---|
| Occupation(s): | financier - partner, Stevens and Legg (stock brokerage firm) |
| Civic Activism: | member, nominating committee, New York Stock Exchange |
| Marriage(s): | 1923 – Clare Charlton Reynders (1901-1990)<br>- writer - *A Life's Journey* (autobiography)<br>  artist - painter |
| Address: | 41 Auerbach Lane, Lawrence |
| Name of estate: | |
| Year of construction: | 1926 |
| Style of architecture: | Modified Shingle |
| Architect(s): | |
| Landscape architect(s): | |
| House extant: yes | |
| Historical notes: | |

The house was built by Byam Kirby Stevens III.

The *Long Island Society Register, 1929* lists Byam K. and Clare C. Reynders Stevens [III] as residing in Cedarhurst [Lawrence]. The 1930 Census lists the Stevenses at this address.

He was the son of Eben and Evelina Babcock Dixon Stevens, who resided at *The Mount* in Lawrence.

Clare Charlton Reynders Stevens was the daughter of John Van Wicherin and Clare Charlton Reynders of Manhattan.

Byam Kirby and Clare Charlton Reynders Stevens III's daughter Clare married Daniel Winthrop Ingersoll, Jr. of Charlestown, MD. Their daughter Evelena married Richard Albert Kenworthy III of Youngstown, OH, and, subsequently, James Lowell Oakes of Brattleboro, VA. Their son Byam Kirby Stevens IV married Priscilla Gilpin Lucas, the daughter of Clinton Mansfield Lucas of Rock Hall, MD, and resided at *Kirby Hill* in Muttontown. [*See* Spinzia, *Long Island's Prominent North Shore Families, vol. II* – Stevens entry.]

*[See following two Stevens entries for additional family information.]*

*front facade, 2009*

## Stevens, Eben (1871-1926)

| | |
|---|---|
| Occupation(s): | financier - partner, Stevens and Legg (stock brokerage firm) |
| Marriage(s): | 1896-1926 – Evelena Babcock Dixon (1873-1935) |
| Address: | Ocean Avenue, Lawrence |
| Name of estate: | *The Mount* |
| Year of construction: | |
| Style of architecture: | |
| Architect(s): | |
| Landscape architect(s): | |
| House extant: | unconfirmed |
| Historical notes: | |

The *Long Island Society Register, 1929* lists Evelena B. Dixon Stevens as residing at *The Mount* in Lawrence.

Eben Stevens was the son of Alexander Henry and Mary Allyne Otis Stevens of Lawrence.

Evelena Babcock Dixon Stevens was the daughter of William Palmer and Evelena Babcock Dixon, Sr. Her brother William Palmer Dixon, Jr., who resided in Lawrence, married Theodora Thorpe and, subsequently, Joan Deery. Her brother Courtland married Hortense Howland and resided in Lawrence.

Eben and Evelena Babcock Dixon Stevens' son William resided in Hewlett Neck. Their son Byam resided in Lawrence.

*[See previous and following Stevens entries for additional family information.]*

In 1935, Mrs. Stevens fell from the window of her fourteen-room apartment at 405 Park Avenue. [*The New York Times* November 20, 1935, p. 19.]

## Stevens, William Dixon (1901-1960)

| | |
|---|---|
| Occupation(s): | financier - partner, Stevens and Legg (stock brokerage firm); partner, Jacquelin and Co. (stock brokerage firm) |
| Civic Activism: | trustee, Village of Hewlett Neck |
| Marriage(s): | M/1 – 1927-div. 1938 – Gladys Pomeroy Jenkins (1904-1995) |
| | M/2 – 1941-div. – Dorothy Michelson (1906-1995) |
| Address: | Hewlett Neck Road, Hewlett Neck* |
| Name of estate: | |
| Year of construction: | |
| Style of architecture: | |
| Architect(s): | |
| Landscape architect(s): | |
| House extant: | unconfirmed |
| Historical notes: | |

The *Long Island Society Register, 1929* lists William Dixon and Gladys P. Jenkins Stevens as residing on Georges Boulevard, Hewlett [Hewlett Neck].

*Hewlett Neck Road was previously called Georges Boulevard.

He was the son of Eben and Evelena Babcock Dixon Stevens of *The Mount* in Lawrence.

Gladys Pomeroy Jenkins Stevens was the daughter of James Sinclair and Aurelia Gladys Pomeroy Jenkins of Stanford, CT. Gladys later married Chester Alwyn Braman, Jr. of Hewlett Bay Park and, subsequently, Rector Kerr Fox, Jr. Braman had previously been married to Anna Eleanor Roosevelt Hall, a cousin of First Lady Mrs. Franklin Delano Roosevelt.

William Dixon and Gladys Pomeroy Jenkins Stevens' daughter Gladys married James Foster Thacher, the son of Thomas A. Thacher of San Francisco, CA, and resided in San Francisco. Their daughter Mary married William Vaughn Moody Fawcett, Jr. of Newton, MA, and, subsequently, Thomas McNulty with whom she resided in Boston, MA.

Dorothy Michelson Stevens was the daughter of Albert Abraham Michelson. She had previously been married to Sheldon Dick and John Fred Bitter. After her divorce from William, she married Goodhue Livingston, Jr., the son of Goodhue and Louisa Robb Livingston, Sr. of *Old Trees* in Southampton. [*See* Spinzia, *Long Island's Prominent Families in the Town of Southampton* – Livingston entry.]

*[See previous two Stevens entries for additional family information.]*

In 1941 the twelve-room house with four bathrooms was purchased from Stevens by Samuel Bradford Stewart, Jr.

### Stevenson, Joseph Hutchinson (b. 1887)

| | |
|---|---|
| Occupation(s): | financier - stockbroker |
| Marriage(s): | M/1 – 1908-div. 1917 – Hildegarde Kobbe (1889-1959) |
| | M/2 – 1921-1930 – Evelyn Hollins Nicholas (1895-1930) |
| Address: | East Rockaway Road, Hewlett Bay Park |
| Name of estate: | *The Farm* |
| Year of construction: | |
| Style of architecture: | |
| Architect(s): | |
| Landscape architect(s): | |
| House extant: | unconfirmed |
| Historical notes: | |

The house named *The Farm*, was owned by Joseph's parents Richard Wilson and Martha Cowles Hutchinson Stevenson, Jr.

Hildegarde Kobbe Stevenson was the daughter of Gustav and Carolyn Wheeler Kobbe of Babylon. Hildegarde subsequently married Francis Burritt Thorne, Sr. of *Brookwood* in East Islip. Her sister Beatrice married Raymond Demarest Little, the son of Joseph J. Little, and resided in Babylon. Her sister Carol married Robert Woodward Morgan, Sr., the son of Charles Morgan, and resided in East Islip. Carol subsequently married George Palen Snow, the son of Frederick Augustus and Mary Palen Snow of *Gardenside* in Southampton, and resided in Syosset. Her brother George married Marjorie W. Goss, the daughter of Gustav Goss of Cincinnati, OH. Her sister Virginia married Gerald Vanderbilt Hollins, Sr., with whom she resided at *The Hawks* in East Islip, and, subsequently, Henry Morgan.

Joseph Hutchinson and Hildegarde Kobbe Stevenson's daughter Carol married Joseph Sears Lovering, Sr. of Islip and, later, Max Stuart Roesler of Cos Cob, CT. Their daughter Hildegarde married Frederick Hard, the son of Anson Wales and Florence Bourne Hard, Jr. of *Meadow Edge* in West Sayville.

[*See* Spinzia, *Long Island's Prominent South Shore Families* – Hard, Hollins, Kobbe, Little, Lovering, Morgan, and Thorne entries; *Long Island's Prominent North Shore Families, vol. II* – G. P. Snow entry; and *Long Island's Prominent Families in the Town of Southampton* – F. A. Snow entry.]

The *Long Island Society Register, 1929* lists Joseph H. and Evelyn H. Nicholas Stevenson as residing at *The Farm* in Hewlett [Hewlett Bay Park].

Evelyn Hollins Nicholas Stevenson was the daughter of Harry Ingersoll and Alice McKim Hollins Nicholas, Sr., who resided at *Virginia Farm* in Babylon. Evelyn had previously been married to Alexander Duncan Cameron Arnold, Sr. with who she resided in West Islip. Her brother Harry Ingersoll Nicholas II married Dorothy Snow and resided in *Rolling Hill Farm* in Muttontown. Her sister Beatrice married Edward Nicholl Townsend, Jr. of Garden City. Her sister Rita married Uriel Atwood Murdock II and resided in Babylon. Her sister Daisy married Grosvenor Nicholas and resided in Old Westbury. Her sister Elsie married Alonzo Potter II and resided at *Harbor House* in St. James and at *Westmoor* in Southampton. Her sister Maud married George Casper Niles and resided at *Cross Cottage* in Bridgehampton. [*See* Spinzia, *Long Island's Prominent South Shore Families* – Arnold, Murdock, and Nicholas entries; *Long Island's Prominent North Shore Families, vol. II* – Nicholas entry; and *Long Island's Prominent Families in the Town of Southampton* – Niles and Potter entries.]

### Stevenson, Maxwell (1880-1951)

| | |
|---|---|
| Occupation(s): | capitalist - president, Maxwell Building Co. (residential developer)* |
| Civic Activism: | chairman, board of stewards, Inter-Collegiate Rowing Association, 1924-1941 |
| Marriage(s): | M/1 – 1901-div. – Caroline Elizabeth Livingston (1881-1964) |
| | M/2 – 1917-1951 – Anne Davis Richardson (1877-1954) |
| Address: | East Fulton Avenue, Hempstead |
| Name of estate: | *The Lodge* |
| Year of construction: | 1923 |
| Style of architecture: | |
| Architect(s): | |
| Landscape architect(s): | |
| House extant: | unconfirmed |
| Historical notes: | |

Maxwell Stevenson was the son of Major Vernon King Stevenson, CSA, and Anna Louisa Eve Stevenson, Jr. Maxwell's sister Eloise married James Lorillard Kernochan and, later, Alexander Butler Duncan of *The Meadows* in Hempstead. She eventually relocated to *Yonder House* in Westbury. [*See* Spinzia, *Long Island's Prominent North Shore Families, vol. 1* – Duncan entry.]

Caroline Elizabeth Livingston Stevenson was the daughter of Robert Cambridge and Maria Whitney Livingston III of *Lakeside* in Islip. [*See* Spinzia, *Long Island's Prominent South Shore Families* – Livingston entry.] Caroline later married Dr. Harold Woods Baker and, subsequently, Frank Hinchman Platt.

The *Social Register Summer, 1921* and the *Long Island Society Register, 1929* list Maxwell and Anne D. Richardson Stevenson as residing at *The Lodge* in Hempstead.

Anne was the daughter of James Benagh and Sallie Evans Richardson. She had previously been married to William Harding Jackson, Sr. of *Belle Meade Plantation* in Nashville, TN. The Jacksons' son William Harding Jackson II was the Deputy Director of the Central Intelligence Agency. He married Elisabeth Lyman, Mary Leet Pitcairn, and Irma M. Hanley May and resided in West Hills. [*See* Spinzia, *Long Island's Prominent North Shore Families, vol. 1* – Jackson entry.]

*In 1937, Stevenson built twenty residences adjacent to the campus of Hofstra University. [*The New York Times* June 6, 1937, p. 96.]


### Stevenson, Richard Wilson, Jr. (1854-1918)

| | |
|---|---|
| Occupation(s): | attorney |
| Marriage(s): | 1885-1918 – Martha Cowles Hutchinson (1856-1927) |
| Address: | East Rockaway Road, Hewlett Bay Park |
| Name of estate: | *The Farm* |
| Year of construction: | |
| Style of architecture: | |
| Architect(s): | |
| Landscape architect(s): | |
| House extant: | yes |
| Historical notes: | |

The *Social Register Summer, 1910* lists Richard W. and Mattie C. Hutchinson Stevenson, Jr. as residing at *The Farm* in Hewlett [Hewlett Bay Park].

He was the son of Richard Wilson and Ellen Leah Duryee Stevenson, Sr.

Martha Cowles Hutchinson Stevenson was the daughter of Joseph Cowles and Susan Huntington Benedict Hutchinson.

Richard Wilson and Martha Cowles Hutchinson Stevenson, Jr.'s son Philip married Janet Atlantis Marshall, the daughter of John Carter and Atlantis Octavia McClendon Marshall. Their son Joseph and daughter Marion also resided at *The Farm* with their spouses. Joseph married Hildegarde Kobbe, the daughter of Gustav and Carolyn Wheeler Kobbe of Babylon, and, later, Evelyn Hollins Nicholas, the daughter of Harry Ingersoll and Alice McKim Hollins Nicholas, Sr. of *Virginia Farm* in Babylon. [*See* Spinzia, *Long Island's Prominent South Shore Families* – Hollins and Kobbe entries.] Their daughter Marion married Henry Seabury Parker, Sr., the son of Henry Ainsworth and Mary Seabury Parker of Boston, MA.

## Stewart, John Henderson, Jr. (1891-1939)

| | |
|---|---|
| Occupation(s): | financier - vice-president, Hambleton and Co., Baltimore, MD (investment banking firm);<br>vice-president, Continental Illinois Co. (securities firm);<br>vice-president, Lawrence Stern and Co. (investment banking firm);<br>vice-president, Cassatt and Co. (investment banking firm) |
| Civic Activism: | director, Atlantic Beach Club, 1937 |
| Marriage(s): | M/1 – 1913-div. 1935 – Marjorie Cooper Weeks (1893-1980)<br>M/2 – 1936-1939 – Eleanor Sprague (1898-1959) |
| Address: | 174 Hollywood Crossing, Lawrence |
| Name of estate: | |
| Year of construction: | 1900 |
| Style of architecture: | Colonial Revival |
| Architect(s): | |
| Landscape architect(s): | |
| House extant: yes | |
| Historical notes: | |

*front / side facade, 2009*

The *Long Island Society Register, 1929* lists John Henderson and Marjorie C. Weeks Stewart [Jr.] as residing in Cedarhurst [Lawrence].

He was the son of John Henderson and Virginia Eleanor Hay Stewart, Sr. of Baltimore, MD, and Pittsburgh, PA.

Marjorie Cooper Weeks Stewart was the daughter of Herbert Augustus and Marjorie Cooper Howe Weeks, who resided at *Meenahga* in Lawrence. She subsequently married Dudley Crews and Francis A. Phillips.

John Henderson and Marjorie Cooper Weeks Stewart, Jr.'s daughter Marjorie married William Morrison Tingue, the son of William James Tingue of Manhattan, and resided in Manhattan. Their son John Henderson Stewart III married Helen Franchot Douw Cary, the daughter of Hudson Cary of *Ampthill House* in Richmond, VA, and resided in Manhattan.

Eleanor Sprague Stewart was the daughter of Charles Franklin and Mary Bryant Pratt Sprague. Eleanor had previously been married to Dr. Wilfred Sefton, the son of Frederick and Maude Fitch Sefton of Brooklyn. After Stewart's death, she married Edward Taylor Hunt Talmage, Jr., the son of Edward Taylor Hunt and Mary Bliss Prentice Talmage, Sr. of Brooklyn.

## Stewart, Samuel Bradford, Jr. (1908-1995)

| | |
|---|---|
| Occupation(s): | attorney - partner, Blake and Voorhees (later, Blake, Voorhees, and Stewart);<br>member, Cravath, de Gersdorff, Swaine, and Wood<br>financier - vice-president and chairman of board, Bank of America National Trust and Savings Association, San Francisco, CA;<br>vice-chairman of board, Bank America Corp.<br>merchant - director, Longs Drug Stores, Inc. |
| Civic Activism: | trustee, Golden Gate University, San Francisco, CA;<br>trustee, Salk Institute;<br>chairman of board, North California Presbyterian Homes, Inc.;<br>member, board of governors, San Francisco Symphony |
| Marriage(s): | 1934-1995 – Celeste Dorwin (1911-2009)<br>- Civic Activism: docent for 24 years, Asian Art Museum, San Francisco, CA |
| Address: | Hewlett Neck Road, Hewlett Neck* |
| Name of estate: | |
| Year of construction: | |
| Style of architecture: | |
| Architect(s): | |
| Landscape architect(s): | |
| House extant: unconfirmed | |
| Historical notes: | |

*Hewlett Neck Road was previously called Georges Boulevard.

In 1941 Stewart purchased the twelve-room house with four bathrooms from William Dixon Stevens.

Samuel Bradford Stewart, Jr. was the son of Samuel Bradford and Dora Amanda Pryor Stewart, Sr.

Samuel Bradford and Celeste Dorwin Stewart, Jr.'s daughter Linda married James F. Dickerson and resided in Pasadena, CA.

### Stoddard, Caswell Wheeler (1885-1962)

Occupation(s): financier - partner, Henderson and Co. (stock brokerage firm)

Marriage(s): 1912-1962 – Gertrude Brooke (1886-1976)

Address: 45 Hilton Avenue, Garden City
Name of estate:
Year of construction: 1883
Style of architecture: Victorian
Architect(s):
Landscape architect(s):
House extant: yes
Historical notes:

*front facade, 2008*

The *Long Island Society Register, 1929* lists Caswell W. and Gertrude Brooke Stoddard as residing on Hilton Avenue in Garden City. The 1930 Census lists the Stoddards at this address.

He was the son of John H. and Lucy Emma Wheeler Stoddard of Brooklyn.

Gertrude Brooke Stoddard was the daughter of William T. Brooke of Germantown, PA.

Caswell Wheeler and Gertrude Brooke Stoddard's son Brooke married Gracey Hobbs Luckett, the daughter of Gracey Hobbs and Edmonia Hopkins Rankin Luckett. Their son John married Jean McKenney, the daughter of Richard I. McKenney of Manhattan and a direct descendant of General William Irving who served on George Washington's staff and who later was a member of the Third United States Congress of 1793.


### Stone, Herman Foster (1874-1933)

Occupation(s): financier - partner, Blair and Co. (investment banking firm);
industrialist - director, Bridgeport Bronze Co.
inventor - improvements to bootjacks (the V-shaped devices for removing boots)

Marriage(s): 1906-1933 – Florence Scofield (1887-1961)
- Civic Activism: trustee, Frontier Nursing Service, Inc.;
treasurer, The Relief Association of Lawrence, Inwood, Cedarhurst, Woodmere, and Hewlett, 1915

Address: Bannister Lane, Lawrence
Name of estate: *The Moorings*
Year of construction:
Style of architecture:
Architect(s):
Landscape architect(s):
House extant: unconfirmed
Historical notes:

In 1909, Herman Foster Stone purchased the house from Mr. A. Clifford Tower. [*The Brooklyn Daily Eagle* January 29, 1909, p. 3.]

The *Long Island Society Register, 1929* lists Herman Foster and Florence Scofield Stone as residing at *The Moorings* in Lawrence.

He was the son of George Eliot and Madeline Post Stone.

Florence Scofield Stone was the daughter of Ebenezer and Mary Ellen Lippincott Scofield of Manhattan. Her sister Helen married Gordon Russell Thayer and resided in Tuxedo Park, NY.

Herman Foster and Florence Scofield Stone's son Bromley, who resided at *Twin Oaks* in Oyster Bay, married Mary Cliff Jones Williams, the daughter of Lewis Alfred and Marion Hills McCutcheon Williams of *Oak Hill* in Plainfield, NJ. Bromley subsequently married Eleanor Ridgely Flick, the daughter of Reuben Jay and Henrietta M. Ridgely Flick of Lenox, MA.

### Strauss, Peter, Sr. (1929-1911)

| | |
|---|---|
| Occupation(s): | capitalist - proprietor, hotel on Rockaway Beach; proprietor, Montauk Hotel, Far Rockaway; proprietor, Rossmore Hotel |
| Marriage(s): | Mary Hysing |
| Address: | West Broadway and Washington Avenue, Lawrence |
| Name of estate: | |
| Year of construction: | |
| Style of architecture: | eclectic with Dutch Colonial elements |
| Architect(s): | |
| Landscape architect(s): | |
| House extant: | unconfirmed |
| Historical notes: | |

The house, which was known locally as *The Ark*, was built by Peter Strauss, Sr.

He fought in Florida's Seminole War and at the Battles of Fredericksburg, Antietam, Fair Oaks, The Wilderness, and Bull's Run in the Civil War.

Peter and Mary Hysing Strauss Sr.'s daughter Mary married George Colton.

Strauss died in this house. [*The Brooklyn Daily Eagle* November 29, 1911, p. 6.]

*front facade*

### Stray, Edward James, Sr. (1895-1979)

| | |
|---|---|
| Occupation(s): | financier - stockbroker |
| Marriage(s): | Ellen M. *[unable to determine maiden name]* (1902-1951) |
| Address: | 16 Vassar Place, Rockville Centre |
| Name of estate: | |
| Year of construction: | 1933 |
| Style of architecture: | Colonial Revival |
| Architect(s): | Olive Frances Tjaden designed the house (for Stray) |
| Landscape architect(s): | |
| House extant: | yes |
| Historical notes: | |

The house was built by Edward James Stray, Sr.

Edward James and Ellen M. Stray, Sr.'s son Edward James Stray, Jr. married Florence Hughes, the daughter of Dr. Edgar Hamil Hughes and Mrs. Florence Ada Martindale Hughes, Sr. of Brooklyn.

In 2022, the 4,000-square-foot house sold for $1.9 million.

*front facade, 2022*

### Stricker, Hans Carl (1880-1927)

| | |
|---|---|
| Occupation(s): | capitalist - representative, Schenker & Co. (transportation firm) |
| | financier - member, F. A. Smithers (investment banking firm) |
| Civic Activism: | chairman, Austrian Red Cross in America |
| Marriage(s): | 1909-1927 – Margaret Renwick Brown (1886-1957) |
| Address: | Franklin Place, Woodmere |
| Name of estate: | *The Orchard* |
| Year of construction: | |
| Style of architecture: | |
| Architect(s): | |
| Landscape architect(s): | |
| House extant: unconfirmed | |
| Historical notes: | |

The *Long Island Society Register, 1929* lists Margaret Renwick Brown Stricker as residing at *The Orchard* in Woodmere.
She was the daughter of Frederick Tilden and Mary Crosby Renwick Brown of *By-the-Way* in Woodmere.
Hans Carl Stricker was the son of Ludwig and Josefine Josefa Grossman Stricker.


### Stricker, John Fritz (1879-1925)

| | |
|---|---|
| Occupation(s): | attorney - partner, Sparks, Fuller, and Strickler, Brooklyn |
| Marriage(s): | 1902-1925 – Dorothy Letitia Whalley (1880-1946) |
| Address: | 160 Euston Road, Garden City |
| Name of estate: | |
| Year of construction: | 1922 |
| Style of architecture: | Colonial Revival |
| Architect(s): | |
| Landscape architect(s): | |
| House extant: yes | |
| Historical notes: | |

John Fritz Stricker was the son of William and Sophie Louise Tritz Stricker.
John Fritz and Dorothy Letitia Whalley Stricker's daughter Dorothy married Archibald Black, the son of John and Marjorie Robb Black of Garden City, and resided in Garden City. Their daughter Lenore married Richard J. Holland, the son of Frank Holland of Freeport.
In 1997, the 2,371-square-foot house sold for $455,000.

*front facade, 2001*

### Strong, Edwin Allen (1877-1931)

Occupation(s): financier - member, Harris, Winthrop, and Co. (stock brokerage firm)

Marriage(s): 1903-1931 – Theodoria Helene Beinecke (1883-1940)

Address: Cedar and Piermont Avenues, Hewlett Bay Park
Name of estate:
Year of construction:
Style of architecture:
Architect(s):
Landscape architect(s):
House extant: unconfirmed
Historical notes:

   The *Long Island Society Register, 1929* lists Edwin A. and Theodoria H. Beinecke Strong as residing in Cedarhurst [Hewlett Bay Park]. The 1914 Belcher–Hyde map lists T. Strong as residing at Cedar and Piermont Avenues, Hewlett Bay Park.
   He was the son of Edwin and Annie Forbes Strong of Hartford, CT.
   Theodoria Helene Beinecke Strong was the daughter of Johann Bernard Georg Beinecke, who was the chairman of the board of the Plaza Hotel in New York City, and Mrs. Johanna Elizabeth Weigle Beinecke.
   Edwin Allen and Theodoria Helene Beinecke Strong's daughter Elizabeth died at the age of twenty-eight, only three weeks after the death of her father Edwin.
   Mrs. Strong plunged to her death from the twelfth floor of the Hotel Plaza.


### Stuberfield, William Francis (1909-1995)

Occupation(s): capitalist - secretary and director, Sherry–Netherland Hotel, NYC

Marriage(s): 1935 – Edith Marie Haggerty (1912-2005)

Address: 37 Laurel Street, Garden City
Name of estate:
Year of construction:
Style of architecture:
Architect(s):
Landscape architect(s):
House extant: no
Historical notes:

   William Francis Stuberfield was the son of Alvin Howard and Margaret V. Burke Stuberfield.
   William Francis and Edith Marie Haggerty Stuberfield's daughter Margaret, who resided in Garden City, married Michael Arthur Moran, the son of Eugene Francis and Marie Josephine Standt Moran, Jr., who resided at *Shadow Lawn* in Brightwaters. [*See* Spinzia, *Long Island's Prominent South Shore Families* – Moran entry.]

### Studwell, Joseph Colson Knapp (1883-1953)

| | |
|---|---|
| Occupation(s): | real estate agent |
| Marriage(s): | 1918-1953 – Carolyn M. Stafford (1894-1958) |
| Address: | 53 Willow Street, Garden City |
| Name of estate: | |
| Year of construction: | 1918 |
| Style of architecture: | Colonial Revival |
| Architect(s): | |
| Landscape architect(s): | |
| House extant: yes | |

*front facade, 2001*

Historical notes:

The *Long Island Society Register, 1929* lists Joseph Colson Knapp and Carolyn M. Stafford Studwell as residing on Willow Street, Garden City. The 1930 Census lists the Studwells at this address.

He was the son of Alexander Hamilton and Hannah Amelia Haines Studwell.

Carolyn M. Stafford Studwell was the daughter of Charles Morton and Josephine Norris Simonds Stafford of Brooklyn.

Joseph Colson Knapp and Caroline M. Stafford Studwell's daughter Carolyn married Campbell Hamilton Irwin, the son of Marion Griffin and Helen de Raismes Hamilton Irwin of Garden City. Their son Earl married Constance Barbara Lambert, the daughter of Frederick Stafford Tagg and Ellamee Cheshire Lambert. Their son Robert married Marlies Seiden, the daughter of Ludwig and G. Hennegsen Seiden; Gertrude Marston; and, subsequently, Joyce Ralalsky.

### Sturgis, Henry Sprague, Sr. (1892-1973)

| | |
|---|---|
| Occupation(s): | financier - vice-president, First National City Bank, NYC |
| | capitalist - chairman, executive board committee, Erie Railroad |
| | industrialist - director, General Mills Inc.; |
| | director, Curtis Wright Corp.; |
| | director, Pullman, Inc. |
| Civic Activism: | assistant to governor of Arizona for Industrial Development; |
| | trustee, St. Joseph Hospital, Phoenix, AZ; |
| | member, National Industrial Conference Board; |
| | president, Rockaway Hunting Club, Lawrence; |
| | director, United States Golf Association; |
| | president, Lawrence Beach Club |
| Marriage(s): | M/1 – 1916-div. 1941 – Gertrude Cutts Lovett (1896-1981) |
| | - Civic Activism: president, Everybody's Thrift Shop, 1939; commissioner - Five Towns Council of Girl Scouts, 1939 |
| | M/2 – 1941-1973 – Catharine Bartholomay (1899-1991) |
| Address: | Albro Lane, Lawrence |
| Name of estate: | |
| Year of construction: | |
| Style of architecture: | |
| Architect(s): | |
| Landscape architect(s): | Alice Recknagel Ireys designed perennial, bulb, and rose gardens; shrubbery and tree placement (for H. S. Sturgis, Sr.) |
| House extant: unconfirmed | |

*Ireys' garden design*

Historical notes:

In 1921 Sturgis purchased the house from Mary Rutherfurd. [*The New York Times* March 1, 1921, p. 32.]

The *Long Island Society Register, 1929* lists Henry Sprague and Gertrude Lovett Sturgis [Sr.] as residing on Albro Lane, Cedarhurst [Lawrence].

He was the son of William and Anna Louise Sprague Sturgis, Jr. of Merrick.

Gertrude Cutts Lovett Sturgis was the daughter of Dr. Robert Williamson and Mrs. Elizabeth Moorfield Storey Lovett.

Henry Sprague and Gertrude Cutts Lovett Sturgis, Sr.'s daughter Elizabeth married Thomas Suffern Tailer, Jr., who resided at *Beaupre* in Lattingtown. [*See* Spinzia, *Long Island's Prominent North Shore Families, vol. II* – Tailer entry.] Their son Robert married Beatrice Seabury, the daughter of Howland Seabury of Massachusetts.

Catharine Bartholomay Sturgis was the daughter of Henry Conrad and Clara Seipp Bartholomay. Catharine had previously been married to Nathan Green Osborne.

*[See following entry for additional family information.]*

### Sturgis, William Jr. (1843-1936)

| | |
|---|---|
| Occupation(s): | industrialist - oil wells, Yellowstone National Park, WY, and Denver, CO |
| | capitalist - cattle ranches, Missouri and Wyoming |
| Marriage(s): | 1888-1936 – Anna Louisa Sprague (1858-1940) |
| Address: | Beverly Road, Merrick |

Name of estate:
Year of construction:
Style of architecture:
Architect(s):
Landscape architect(s):
House extant: unconfirmed
Historical notes:

*Sturgis residence, Cheyenne, WY*

William Sturgis, Jr., who fought in the Union Army at Gettysburg, was the son of William and Elizabeth Knight Hinckley Sturgis, Sr.

Anna Louisa Sprague Sturgis was the daughter of Edward Dowse and Anna Shaw Auchincloss Sprague of Boston, MA.

William and Anna Louise Sprague Sturgis, Jr.'s daughter Anna married Edward Needles Wright III and resided in Germantown, PA. Their daughter Elizabeth married Hebard Paine, the son of Francis Hebard Paine of New York. Their son Henry, who resided in Lawrence, married Gertrude Cutts Lovett and, later Catharine Bartholomay. Their son William Sturgis III married Margaret Suzanne Cantwell. In 1897, their daughter Edith died at the age of three.

*[See previous entry for additional family information.]*


### Sturgis, William James, Sr. (1877-1968)

| | |
|---|---|
| Occupation(s): | financier - chairman of board, Parkinson and Burr (stock brokerage firm); |
| | vice-president, W. A. Harriman and Co. (became Brown Brothers–Harriman) (investment banking firm) |
| Marriage(s): | M/1 – 1915-div. – Ellen Daniel Yuile (1895-1986) |
| | M/2 – 1925-div. 1938 – Margaret Teackle Quinby (1905-1985) |
| | M/3 – 1939-div. – Jean Allison Maxwell (1884-1972) |
| Address: | Briarwood Crossing, Lawrence |

Name of estate:
Year of construction:
Style of architecture:
Architect(s):
Landscape architect(s):
House extant: unconfirmed
Historical notes:

William James Sturgis, Sr. was the son of Joseph Rogers and Alice Ellen Bradshaw Sturgis.

Ellen Daniel Yuile Sturgis was the daughter of Thomas Burks and Nancy Williams Long Yuile. Ellen subsequently married Wolcott Blair and resided in Muttontown. Her sister Melissa married Harry Payne Bingham, Sr. of *Ivycroft* in Old Westbury. [*See* Spinzia, *Long Island's Prominent North Shore Families*, vol. 1 – Bingham and Blair entries.]

The *Long Island Society Register, 1929* lists William J. and Margaret T. Quinby Sturgis [Sr.] as residing on Briarwood Crossing, Cedarhurst [Lawrence].

She was the daughter of Littleton Dennis Teackle and Lula Belle Hemphill Quinby.

William James and Margaret Teackle Quinby Sturgis, Sr.'s son Upshur married Nancy Lee Linke of Homestead, FL, and resided in Davie, FL, and, later, Charleston, SC. Their son William James Sturgis, Jr. married Doris Elaine Stahl, the daughter of Charles Paul and Amelia May Hunt Stahl.

Jean Allison Maxwell Sturgis was the daughter of Lawrence and Clara Moseley Barry Maxwell. Jean had previously been married to William Horace Schmidlapp, the son of Jacob Godfrey and Emilie Balke Schmidlapp. After her divorce from William, Jean married Truman Laurance Sanders, the son of Truman Wilcox and Lucy C. Titsworth Sanders.

### Swett, The Reverend Canon Paul Flynn, Sr. (1861-1922)

Occupation(s): clergy - private secretary to Bishop Frederick Burgess, 1902-1904;
precentor, Cathedral of the Incarnation, Garden City, 1902-1914

Civic Activism: trustee and treasurer, House of St. Giles the Cripple, Brooklyn; superintendent, Church Charity Foundation, 1904-1922

Marriage(s): 1905-1922 – Louise Poole Thompson (1874-1951)

Address: 82 Cathedral Avenue, Garden City
Name of estate:
Year of construction:
Style of architecture:
Architect(s):
Landscape architect(s):
House extant: no
Historical notes:

The *Long Island Society Register, 1929* lists Louise Pool Thompson Swett as residing on Cathedral Avenue, Garden City. The 1930 Census lists Mrs. Swett at 820 Sixth Street, Garden City.

The Reverend Canon Paul Flynn Swett, Sr. was the son of The Reverend Josiah and Lucy Miranda Wheeler Swett.

The Reverend Canon Paul Flynn and Louise Poole Thompson Swett, Sr.'s son Paul Flynn Swett, Jr. married Joan Decatur, the daughter of Arthur Garfield Decatur.


### Sylvester, Peter Charles (1889-1958)

Occupation(s):

Marriage(s): Rosina Besold (1900-1975)

Address: 73 Washington Avenue, Garden City
Name of estate:
Year of construction: 1929
Style of architecture: Neo-Tudor
Architect(s): Olive Frances Tjaden designed the house
Landscape architect(s):
House extant: yes
Historical notes:

Peter Charles and Rosina Besold Sylvester's son Peter G. Sylvester died in 1921 at the age of one. Their daughter Alice married Dolphin Alston Davis IV of Roland Park, Baltimore, MD.

In 2021, the 3,446-square-foot house sold for $1,557,500.

*front facade, 2021*

### Talmage, John Frelinghusen

| | |
|---|---|
| Occupation(s): | real estate agent - member, Douglas, Gibbons, Hollyday, & Ives |
| Marriage(s): | 1969 – Susanna Ludlum Migel |
| Address: | 91 Park Row, Lawrence |
| Name of estate: | |
| Year of construction: | 1912 |
| Style of architecture: | Dutch Colonial Revival |
| Architect(s): | |
| Landscape architect(s): | |
| House extant: yes | |
| Historical notes: | |

The *Social Register New York, 1971* lists John F. and Susanna L. Migel Talmage as residing at 91 Park Row, Cedarhurst [Lawrence].

He was the son of Prentice and Edyth Coppell Elliman Talmage, Sr. of Cedarhurst.

Susanna Ludlum Migel Talmage was the daughter of Richard Migel of Monroe, NY.

John Frelinghusen and Susanna Ludlum Migel Talmage's son John Elliman Talmage married Eleanor C. Larson and resided in Hollywood, FL.

*[See following entry for additional family information.]*

*front facade, 2001*

### Talmage, Prentice, Sr. (1900-1954)

| | |
|---|---|
| Occupation(s): | financier - member, Terry & Co. (insurance firm) |
| Marriage(s): | M/1 – 1925-div. 1935 – Sarah W. Williams (b. 1906) |
| | M/2 – 1936-1954 – Edyth Coppell Elliman (1906-1979) |
| Address: | Kenridge Road, Lawrence |
| Name of estate: | |
| Year of construction: | |
| Style of architecture: | |
| Architect(s): | |
| Landscape architect(s): | |
| House extant: unconfirmed | |
| Historical notes: | |

Prentice Talmage, Sr. was the son of Edward Taylor Hunt and Mary Bill Prentice Talmage, Sr. of Brooklyn.

Sarah W. Williams Talmage was the daughter of Richard H. Williams of Morristown, NJ.

Prentice and Sarah W. Williams Talmage, Sr.'s son Prentice Talmage, Jr. married Sylvia Gorton Woolworth, the daughter of Chester M. Woolworth of Lancaster, PA, and resided in Far Hills, NJ.

The *Social Register New York, 1951* lists Prentice and Edyth C. Elliman Talmage [Sr.] as residing on Kenridge Road, Cedarhurst [Lawrence].

She was the daughter of Lawrence Bogert and Edyth Howard Coppell Elliman, Sr., who resided at *Cluny Lodge* in Cedarhurst and *White Cottage* in Bridgehampton. Edyth had previously been married to Edward Spring Knapp III of Roslyn. [*See* Spinzia, *Long Island's Prominent North Shore Families, vol. I* – Knapp entry – and *Long Island's Prominent Families in the Town of Southampton* – Elliman entry.]

Prentice and Edyth Coppell Elliman Talmage, Sr.'s son John married Susanna Ludlum Migel, the daughter of Richard Migel of Monroe, NY, and resided in Lawrence. Their daughter Caroline married Robert Norris Sloan, the son of Robert Sage and Florence M. Norris Sloan, Jr.

*[See previous entry for additional family information.]*

### Tapscott, Ralph Henry (1885-1967)

| | |
|---|---|
| Occupation(s): | engineer - assistant electrical engineer, Edison Co., 1917-1924 |
| | capitalist - president and CEO, Consolidated Edison Co.; |
| | vice-president, United Electric Light Co.; |
| | president, Consolidated Edison of New York; |
| | president, New York and Queens Electric Light and Power Co.; |
| | director, Realty Hotels; |
| | director, Long Island Rail Road; |
| | director, Telegraph and Electrical Subway Co.; |
| | director, New York Steam Co.; |
| | president, Brooklyn Edison; |
| | director, Westchester Light Co.; |
| | director, Yonkers Electric Light and Power |
| Civic Activism: | member, Garden City School Board |
| Marriage(s): | 1912-1967 – Dorothea Van Voast (1888-1972) |
| Address: | 115 Fourth Street, Garden City |
| Name of estate: | |
| Year of construction: | 1916 |
| Style of architecture: | Eclectic |
| Architect(s): | |
| Landscape architect(s): | |
| House extant: yes | |
| Historical notes: | |

   The *Long Island Society Register, 1929* lists Ralph Henry and Dorothea Van Voast Tapscott as residing at 115 Fourth Street, Garden City.
   He was the son of Frank Livingston and Emily Louise Brown Tapscott of Brooklyn.
   Dorothea Van Voast Tapscott was the daughter of James and Mary Ward Van Voast.
   Ralph Henry and Dorothea Van Voast Tapscott's son Adrian was killed in action during World War II. Their son Robert married Leslie Hart Fenn, the daughter of Hart Conklin Fenn.

*front facade, 2000*

## Tarbell, Gage Eli (1856-1936)

| | |
|---|---|
| Occupation(s): | attorney |
| | capitalist - a founder and president, Garden City Estates Corporation (developer of the eastern section of Garden City); president and treasurer, Anvil Iron Mining Co. |
| | financier - vice-president, Equitable Life Assurance Society of the United States, NYC; trustee, Equitable Trust Co.; trustee, Hibernian Bank and Trust Co., New Orleans, LA |
| Civic Activism: | director, Fifth Avenue Association; a founder, Garden City Country Club; director, Aero Club of Long Island, 1911 |
| Marriage(s): | 1881-1936 – Ella Swift (1861-1950) |
| Address: | Stewart Avenue, between Nassau Boulevard and Euston Road, Garden City |
| Name of estate: | |
| Year of construction: | 1908 |
| Style of architecture: | Mediterranean |
| Architect(s): | Oswald Hering designed the house (for Tarbell) |

Landscape architect(s):
House extant: no; demolished in 1960s*
Historical notes:

    The house was built by Gage Eli Tarbell.
    He was the son of Charles Parker and Mabel Tillotson Tarbell.
    Ella Swift Tarbell was the daughter of George Lucien and Louisa Hunt Swift.
    Gage Eli and Ella Swift Tarbell's daughter Louise married Dr. Lester B. Rogers and resided in Manhattan. Their son Swift married Virginia Marguerite Whitcomb, the daughter of James A. and Virginia Huner Whitcomb of Boston, MA.
    In 1918 Tarbell sold the house to Glenn Hammond Curtiss, Sr. [Mildred H. Smith, *Garden City, Long Island In Early Photographs* (New York: Dover Publications, Inc., 1987), p. 56.]
    *The house was replaced by the Unitarian church and contemporary homes.

*front facade*

### Taylor, Dr. Quintard, Sr. (1887-1951)

| | |
|---|---|
| Occupation(s): | physician |
| Marriage(s): | Marjorie Parker Armstrong (1891-1968) |
| Address: | 86 Sixth Street, Garden City |
| Name of estate: | |
| Year of construction: | 1873 |
| Style of architecture: | Victorian* |
| Architect(s): | John Kellum designed the house* |
| Builder: | James L'Hommedieu |
| Landscape architect(s): | |
| House extant: no | |
| Historical notes: | |

The *Long Island Society Register, 1929* lists Dr. and Mrs. Quintard Taylor as residing at 86 Sixth Street, Garden City. Majorie Parker Armstrong Taylor was the daughter of George R. and Caroline Judson Clark Armstrong.

Dr. Quintard and Mrs. Marjorie Parker Armstrong Taylor, Sr.'s daughter Sarah married William Reynolds Freeman, the son of William C. and Ann K. Freeman. Their twenty-two-year-old son Quintard Taylor, Jr. was killed in World War II. Their son Carter married Penelope Harding Thompson, the daughter of John Walker Thompson of Barrington, IL. Their daughter Sally married Norman K. Toerge, Jr., the son of Norman K. and Elinor Gates Toerge, Sr. of *The Hitching Post* in Matinecock. [*See* Spinzia, *Long Island's Prominent North Shore Families, vol. II* – Toerge entry.]

*The house, owned by the Cathedral Corporation and on the grounds of St. Mary's Cathedral School for Girls, was one of the earliest houses built in Garden City. Although this house had been modified, the original A. T. Stewart era portion of the house still had the red brick basement floor and wooden beams in 1976. At the time of the survey, the brick supporting arch also survived.

### Taylor, Talbot Jones, Jr. (1865-1938)

| | |
|---|---|
| Occupation(s): | financier - partner, Talbot J. Taylor and Co. (stock brokerage firm)* |
| Marriage(s): | M/1 – 1892-div. 1908 – Jessica Harwar Keene (1868-1950) |
| | M/2 – 1909-1938 – Maria Isabella Zane (1876-1951) |
| Address: | Longwood Crossing, Lawrence |
| Name of estate: | *Talbot House* |
| Year of construction: | c. 1895 |
| Style of architecture: | Neo-Tudor |
| Architect(s): | Lamb and Rich designed the house (for T. J. Taylor, Jr.) |
| Landscape architect(s): | |
| House extant: no; demolished c. 1914** | |
| Historical notes: | |

The house, originally named *Talbot House*, was built by Talbot Jones Taylor, Jr.

*front facade, c. 1904*

He was the son of Talbot Jones and Lavina Kirkland Taylor, Sr. of Cantonsville, Baltimore, MD. His brother William, who resided in Lawrence, married Sarah Anson Hard and, subsequently, Mary Bill Prentice. His brother James married Lydia Anne Thorne and resided at *Ivy Hall* in Jericho and *Sunset House* in Cove Neck. [*See* Spinzia, *Long Island's Prominent North Shore Families, vol. II*– Taylor entries.]

Jessica Harwar Keene Taylor was the daughter of James Robert and Sara Jay Daingerfield Keene of Lawrence. Her brother Foxhall married Mary Lawrence, the daughter of Frederick N. Lawrence of Manhattan, and resided at *Rosemary Hall* in Old Westbury. Jessica subsequently married Edward Inglis Frost, the son of Mahlon Smith and Frances Harriet Foster Frost.

Talbot Jones and Jessica Harwar Keene Taylor, Jr.'s son Talbot Jones Taylor III married Louise Tiffany Frank and resided in Lawrence. Their daughter Dorothy married Valentino James Molina. Their son Foxhall married Helen Holmes Chamberlain.

Maria Isabella Zane Taylor was the daughter of Edmund Platoff and Maria Louisa Loughborough Zane. She had previously been married to William Northrop Cowles of Boston, MA.

*Taylor was in partnership with his brother James Blackstone Taylor, Sr. of Jericho and brother-in-law Foxhall Parker Keene of Old Westbury. [*See* Spinzia, *Long Island's Prominent North Shore Families, vol. I* – Keene entry – and *vol. II* – Taylor entry.]

**The stables survive and has been converted into a residence.

*[See following entry for additional family information.]*

## Talbot Jones Taylor, Jr. residence, *Talbot House*

*hall, 1906*

*drawing room, 1906*

*master suite, northwest bedroom, 1906*

*dining room, 1906*

*library, 1906*

*Talbot Jones Taylor, Jr. estate,
eighteenth century sculpture of the infant Bacchus, 1906*

### Taylor, Talbot Jones, III (1894-1971)

| | |
|---|---|
| Occupation(s): | real estate agent |
| Marriage(s): | M/1 – 1915 – Louise Tiffany Frank (1895) |
| | M/2 – Aletta Golding (1905-1985) |
| Address: | Ocean Avenue, Lawrence |
| Name of estate: | |
| Year of construction: | |
| Style of architecture: | |
| Architect(s): | |
| Landscape architect(s): | |
| House extant: unconfirmed | |
| Historical notes: | |

The *Brooklyn Blue Book and Long Island Society Register, 1921* lists Talbot Jones Taylor, Jr. [III] as residing in Cedarhurst [Lawrence]. The 1920 Census lists the Taylors at this address.

He was the son of Talbot Jones and Jessica Harwar Keene Taylor, Jr., who resided at *Talbot House* in Lawrence.

Louise Tiffany Frank Taylor was the daughter of Charles Augustus and Louise Clark Read Frank, Sr., who resided at *Charlon House* in Glen Cove. She subsequently married James Christy Bell, Jr. with whom she resided at *Stramore* in Upper Brookville. [*See* Spinzia, *Long Island's Prominent North Shore Families, vol. 1* – Bell and Frank entries.]

Talbot Jones and Louise Tiffany Frank Taylor III's son John married Patricia L'Amoureux Green, the daughter of Kneeland L. Green.

Talbot Jones and Aletta Golding Taylor III's daughter Alice married Sherwood Lovejoy, the son of Joseph Lovejoy, Jr. of *Greens Farms* in Southport, CT, and resided in Fairfield, CT.

*[See previous entry for additional family information.]*

### Taylor, Willard Underhill, Sr. (1868-1940)

| | |
|---|---|
| Occupation(s): | attorney - partner, MacFarland, Taylor, and Costello; partner, Choate, Henderson, and Taylor |
| | capitalist - president, Apex Equipment Co.; director, Undercliff Terminal and Warehouse Co.; director, Atlantic Timberland Corp.; director, Mercantile Corp.; director, American Commercial Corp.; president and director, Brunswick Marine Construction Corp.; president and director, Trade and Commerce Corp.; president and director, Lortay Corp. |
| Civic Activism: | vice-president and counsel, Underhill Society of America, Brooklyn, 1916-1917 |
| Marriage(s): | 1922-1940 – Evelyn Wood Keeler (1896-1966) |
| Address: | 83 Eleventh Street, Garden City |
| Name of estate: | |
| Year of construction: | |
| Style of architecture: | |
| Architect(s): | |
| Landscape architect(s): | |
| House extant: no | |
| Historical notes: | |

The *Long Island Society Register, 1929* lists Willard U. and Evelyn W. Keeler Taylor [Sr.] as residing at 83 Eleventh Street, Garden City. Their summer home *Ettington* was in North Haven.

He was the son of William Delling and Mary Morgan Underhill Taylor and a descendant of the colonial Indian fighter Captain John Underhill of Mill Neck. His brother Myron married Anabell Stevens Mack and resided at *Killingworth* in Lattingtown. [*See* Spinzia, *Long Island's Prominent North Shore Families, vol. II* – Taylor entry – and *Long Island: A Guide to New York's Suffolk and Nassau Counties* – Underhill Burying Ground, Grave of Captain John Underhill, Mill Neck – and – Whitaker Historical Collection, Southold Free Library, Southold.]

Evelyn Wood Keeler Taylor was the daughter of Ralph Richard and Annie Dennis Wood Keeler of Auburn, NY. She subsequently married Frederick Kenneth Stephenson of Garden City.

Willard Underhill and Evelyn Wood Keeler Taylor, Sr.'s son Willard Underhill Taylor, Jr. married Katherine Dickey Stevens, the daughter of Arthur Chambers Stevens of Savannah, GA.

**Taylor, William Reed Kirkland, Sr.** (1870-1936)

| | |
|---|---|
| Occupation(s): | financier -  partner, W. R. K. Taylor and Co. (stock brokerage firm); partner, Taylor, Smith, and Hard (stock brokerage firm); partner, Taylor, Smith, and Evans (stock brokerage firm) |
| Civic Activism: | trustee, Presbyterian Hospital; trustee, Loomes Sanitarium; trustee, Peabody Home |
| Marriage(s): | M/1 – 1896-1929 – Sarah Anson Hard (1875-1929)<br>M/2 – 1935-1936 – Mary Bill Prentice (1871-1964) |
| Address: | Causeway, Lawrence |

Name of estate:
Year of construction:
Style of architecture:
Architect(s):
Landscape architect(s):
House extant: unconfirmed
Historical notes:

The *Social Register New York, 1907* lists William R. K. and Sarah A. Hard Taylor [Sr.] as residing in Lawrence.

He was the son of Talbot Jones and Lavina Kirkland Taylor, Sr. of Cantonsville, Baltimore, MD. His brother Talbot Jones Taylor, Jr., who resided at *Talbot House* in Lawrence, married Jessica Harwar Keene and, subsequently, Marie Isabell Zane. His brother James married Lydia Anne Thorne and resided at *Ivy Hall* in Jericho and *Sunset House* in Cove Neck. [*See* Spinzia, *Long Island's Prominent North Shore Families, vol. II* – Taylor entry.]

Sarah Anson Hard Taylor was the daughter of Anson Wales and Sarah Elizabeth Brown Hard, Sr., who resided at *Driftwood* in Lawrence. Her sister Laura married Henry von Lengerke Meyer, Sr. and resided at *Cobblestone Farm* in Suffern, NY. Her brother DeCourcy married Marjorie Work and resided at *Briarwood* in Lawrence. Her sister Nellie married John Kane Mills and resided at *Ruddington Farm* in Hackettstown, NJ. Her sister Julia married Augustine Smith and resided at *Sunnyside* in Lawrence. Her brother Anson Wales Hard, Jr., who resided at *Meadow Edge* in West Sayville, married Florence Bourne, the daughter of Frederick Gilbert and Emma Sparks Keeler Bourne who resided at *Indian Neck Hall* in Oakdale, and, subsequently, Katherine Potter. [*See* Spinzia, *Long Island's Prominent South Shore Families* – Bourne and Hard entries.]

William Reed Kirkland and Sarah Anson Hard Taylor, Sr.'s daughter Marjorie married Edward Van V. Sands and resided in Greenwich, CT. Marjorie subsequently married John M. Denison with whom she resided at *Mosswood* in Fallston, MD. Their son DeCourcey married Elizabeth Ruth Cauthra and resided in Greenwich, CT. Their son Anson Wales Hard Taylor married Caroline Young and resided in Greenwich, CT. Their son William Reed Kirkland Taylor, Jr. married Elsie G. Lathrop and resided at *The Oaks* in Roslyn.

Mary Bill Prentice Taylor was the daughter of John and Caroline Bill Prentice. She had previously been married to Edward Taylor Hunt Talmage, Sr. Their son Prentice Talmage, Sr., who resided in Cedarhurst, married Sarah W. Williams and, subsequently, Edyth Coppell Elliman.

### Terry, Thomas Henry (1860-1914)

| | |
|---|---|
| Occupation(s): | capitalist - real estate agent; officer, Brooklyn Bridge Corporation*; president, Hempstead Farm Company** |
| Civic Activism: | president, American Pointers Club, 1895; secretary, Westminister Kennel Club, 1895; treasurer, United States Horse and Cattle Show Society, 1892; secretary, Meadowbrook Hunt Club, 1890 |
| Marriage(s): | 1890 – Caroline Cecilia Estevez (aka Carolina Estevez) |
| Address: | Hempstead Turnpike, East Meadow |
| Name of estate: | *Hempstead Farm* |
| Year of construction: | |
| Style of architecture: | |
| Architect(s): | |
| Landscape architect(s): | |
| House extant: no | |
| Historical notes: | |

In 1889, Thomas Henry Terry purchased Charles Rowell's sixty-acre farm in East Meadow for $8,000. [*The Brooklyn Daily Eagle* May 18, 1889, p. 1.]

The *Social Register August, 1895* lists Thomas H. and Caroline Eztevez Terry as residing at *Hempstead Farm* in Hempstead [East Meadow].

He was the son of Thomas Gamble and Matilda Dixon Terry of Brooklyn.

Caroline Cecilia Estevez Terry came from a wealthy Cuban family.

Thomas Henry and Caroline Cecilia Estevez Terry's son Thomas Estevez Terry married Katharine Morgan, the daughter of James K. and Edna B. Morgan of a Cuban sugar fortune.

In 1906, *Hempstead Farm*, which consisted of two residences, a mile racetrack, a steeplechase, and dog kennels, sold to a real estate syndicate for $127,800. [*The Brooklyn Daily Eagle* March 17, 1906, p. 10.]

In 1912, the kennels were destroyed by fire. [*The Brooklyn Daily Eagle* April 24, 1912, p. 6.]

*Thomas H. Terry was in charge of collecting rentals for the Brooklyn Bridge Corporation.

**Hempstead Farm Company kenneled prize dogs and stabled racing and hunting horses. [*The Brooklyn Daily Eagle* February 17, 1895, p. 20.]

### Tew, Benjamin Taylor (1871-1921)

| | |
|---|---|
| Occupation(s): | merchant - proprietor, sporting goods store, Hempstead<br>capitalist - proprietor, bowling alleys, Hempstead; proprietor, billiard parlors, Hempstead<br>politician - member, Hempstead Town Board of Audit |
| Civic Activism: | a founder and director, Hempstead Country Club |
| Marriage(s): | 1901-1921 – Ida Douglas (1871-1944) |
| Address: | Cruikshank Avenue, Hempstead |
| Name of estate: | |
| Year of construction: | |
| Style of architecture: | |
| Architect(s): | |
| Landscape architect(s): | |
| House extant: unconfirmed | |
| Historical notes: | |

The *Long Island Society Register, 1929* lists Mrs. Benjamin Taylor Tew as residing on Cruikshank Avenue, Hempstead.

She was descendant of Stephen A. Douglas, the noted orator and senator from Illinois.

Benjamin Taylor and Ida Douglas Tew's daughter Doris married Arthur Stuart Vaughan, Jr. of Garden City, and resided in Short Hills, NJ. Their daughter Myrtle married Hubert Biays Chappell, the son of Ralph Hubert Chappell of Kensington, MA, and resided in Manhattan.

The Tews also had a house in Newport, RI.

### Thayer, Benjamin Bowditch, Jr. (1862-1933)

| | |
|---|---|
| Occupation(s): | industrialist - director, Anaconda Wire & Cable Co.; |
| | president, Anaconda Copper Mining Co.; |
| | president, Raritan Copper Works; |
| | president, Electrolytic Zinc Process Co.; |
| | president, Santiago Mining Co.; |
| | director, International Smelting Co.; |
| | director, Chile Copper Co.; |
| | director, International Lead Refining Co.; |
| | director, Andes Copper Mining Co.; |
| | director, American Brass Co. |
| | capitalist - director, Potrerillos Railroad Co.; |
| | director, Butte Water Co.; |
| | director, Anaconda & Pacific Railway |
| Civic Activism: | chairman, Naval Consulting Board, 1915; |
| | president, American Institute of Mining and Metallurgical Engineers; |
| | governor, India House; |
| | president, Harvard Society of Engineers, 1912; |
| | president, Engineers Club, 1925, 1926 |
| Marriage(s): | 1890-1933 – Marie Cecile Renouard (1860-1950) |
| Address: | Ocean Avenue, Lawrence |
| Name of estate: | |
| Year of construction: | |
| Style of architecture: | |
| Architect(s): | |
| Landscape architect(s): | |
| House extant: unconfirmed | |
| Historical notes: | |

   Benjamin Bowditch Thayer, Jr. was the son of Benjamin Bowditch and Lucy Wilde Phipps Thayer, Sr.
   Marie Cecile Renouard Thayer was the daughter of Hyacinthe and Cecile Tesson Renouard.
   Benjamin Bowditch and Marie Cecile Renouard Thayer, Jr.'s daughter Alice married Maynard Cady Ivison and resided in Hewlett Bay Park. Their daughter Marie married Junius Alexander Richards, Sr. and resided in Lawrence. Their daughter Cecile married Douglas Gibbons and resided at *The Annex* in Purchase, NY.

### Thomas, Edward Clarke Oertel (1891-1975)

| | |
|---|---|
| Occupation(s): | attorney - partner with United States Assistant Postmaster Ambrose O'Connell |
| | military - colonel, United States Army; |
| | director, Civilian Protection, Nassau County and New York State during World War II |
| Civic Activism: | chief of Nassau County's War Council, 1942; |
| | chairman, National Defense Committee, Nassau County American Legion; |
| | director Nassau County Civilian Defense Council; |
| | director, Civilian Protection, 1944 |
| Marriage(s): | 1919-1975 – Ruth Woodland (1896-1977) |
| | - Civic Activism: president, Garden City Community Club, 1946 |
| Address: | 110 Chester Avenue, Garden City |
| Name of estate: | |
| Year of construction: | 1910 |
| Style of architecture: | Dutch Colonial Revival |
| Architect(s): | |
| Landscape architect(s): | |
| House extant: yes | |
| Historical notes: | |

*front facade, 2000*

   The *Long Island Society Register, 1929* lists Edward C. O. and Ruth Woodland Thomas as residing at 110 Chester Avenue, Garden City.
   He was the son of Ernest Edward and Jennie E. Oertel Thomas of Brooklyn.
   Ruth Woodward Thomas was the daughter of Edward Simonson and Minnie Jane Pretz Woodland of Brooklyn.
   Edward Clarke Oertel and Ruth Woodland Thomas' daughter Jane married ____ Folk.

### Thomas, Theodore Gaillard, III (1890-1963)

| | |
|---|---|
| Occupation(s): | attorney |
| | financier - partner, T. Gaillard Thomas II (later, Thomas, Torrey, and Griffith) (stock brokerage firm)* |
| Marriage(s): | M/1 – 1925-div. 1929 – Dorothy A. Donovan (1905-1938) |
| | (aka Dorothy Hale; Malan Cullen) |
| | - entertainers and associated professions - |
| | stage and motion picture actress |
| | M/2 – 1934 – Mary Sargent Spencer (b. 1904) |
| | M/3 – 1950-1963 – Elizabeth Everett Ward |
| Address: | Auerbach Avenue, Hewlett Harbor |
| Name of estate: | |
| Year of construction: | |
| Style of architecture: | |
| Architect(s): | |
| Landscape architect(s): | |
| House extant: unconfirmed | |
| Historical notes: | |

The *Long Island Society Register, 1929* lists T. Gaillard and Dorothy A. Donovan Thomas II as residing on Auerbach Lane [Avenue], Hewlett [Hewlett Harbor].

He was the son of John Metcalfe and Louisa Carroll Jackson Thomas of Southampton. [*See* Spinzia, *Long Island's Prominent Families in the Town of Southampton* – Thomas entry.]

Dorothy A. Donovan Thomas was the daughter of James Patrick and Emma Swain Anderson Donovan, Sr. of Pittsburgh, PA. Dorothy subsequently married Chicago artist Gardiner Hale, who was killed in 1931 when his car drove off a five-hundred-foot cliff in California. Dorothy, who at the time of her death was rumored to be engaged to President Franklin Delano Roosevelt's political advisor Harry Hopkins, plunged sixteen floors to her death from her apartment in the Hampshire House opposite New York's Central Park.

Mary Sargent Spencer Thomas was the daughter of Seth Sylvester and Martha Miner Norton Spencer, Jr. of *Box Hill* in Litchfield, CT. Mary had previously been married to Kenneth T. Philips of Woodmere. After her divorce from Thomas, Mary married Frank Oliver of Norwich, England, and resided at *Seaboard Cottage* in Boca Grande, FL.

Elizabeth Everett Ward Thomas was the daughter of Holcombe Ward of Red Bank, NJ.

*Thomas was suspended from the New York Stock Exchange for three years for alleged violation of its rules by his firm. [*The New York Times* January 26, 1938, p. 20.]

*Dr. Benjamin Franklin Thompson's 1826 house*

### Thompson, Dr. Benjamin Franklin (1784-1849)

| | |
|---|---|
| Occupation(s): | attorney - Queens County District Attorney, 1826-1836 |
| | physician |
| | politician - member, New York State Assembly, 1812-1814 |
| | writer - *History of Long Island: From Its Discovery and Settlement to the Present Time*, 1839* |
| Marriage(s): | 1810-1849 – Mary Howard Greene (1794-1868) |
| Address: | Fulton Avenue, Hempstead |
| Name of estate: | |
| Year of construction: | 1837 |
| Style of architecture: | Eclectic with Queen Anne elements |
| Architect(s): | |
| Landscape architect(s): | |
| House extant: no | |
| Historical notes: | |

*1837 house*

The house was built west of Burley Pond by Dr. Benjamin Franklin Thompson. [*The Brooklyn Daily Eagle* June 6, 1886, p. 1.]

He was the son of Dr. Samuel and Mrs. Phoebe and Satterly Thompson of Setauket.

Mary Greene Thompson was the daughter of The Reverend Zachariah and Mrs. Abigail Howard Greene.

In 1824, the Thompsons relocated from Setauket to Hempstead. Their Setauket homestead, which is on the National Register of Historic Places, is owned by Preservation Long Island and is open to the public. [*See* Spinzia, *Long Island: A Guide to New York's Suffolk and Nassau Counties* – Thompson House, Setauket.]

Dr. Benjamin Franklin and Mrs. Mary Howard Greene Thompson's daughter Harriet married Jacob T. Vanderhoof. Their son Edward married Mary Elizabeth Lush.

*Thompson's *History of Long Island* is considered the authoritative source for the early history of the Island.
*[See previous page for illustration of his original 1826 residence.]*


### Thompson, James Walter (1847-1928)

| | |
|---|---|
| Occupation(s): | advertising executive - founder and president, J. Walter Thompson Co. (international advertising firm; largest in the United States)* |
| Marriage(s): | 1879-1928 – Margaret Riggs Bogle (1852-1932) |
| | - Civic Activism: chair, Women's Liberty Loan Committee during World War I |
| Address: | Club Drive, Hewlett Harbor |
| Name of estate: | |
| Year of construction: | |
| Style of architecture: | |
| Architect(s): | |
| Landscape architect(s): | |
| House extant: unconfirmed | |
| Historical notes: | |

The *Long Island Society Register, 1929* lists J. Walter and Margaret R. Bogle Thompson as residing in Hewlett [Hewlett Harbor].

He was the son of Alonzo Decalvis and Cornelia Ann Roosevelt Thompson of Pittsfield, MA.

Margaret Riggs Bogle Thompson was the daughter of James and Rebecca Riggs Bogle of Brooklyn.

James Walter and Margaret Riggs Bogle Thompson's son Walter married Adele Kelley.

*James is credited with being "the father of modern magazine advertising in the United States."

### Thompson, Joseph TodHunter (1860-1900)

Occupation(s):

Marriage(s): 1884-1900 – Jane Remsen (1852-1932)

Address: Kenridge Road, Lawrence
Name of estate: *Holly Holm*
Year of construction:
Style of architecture:
Architect(s):
Landscape architect(s):
House extant: unconfirmed
Historical notes:

The *Social Register Summer, 1921* lists Joseph Todhunter [sic] and Jane Remsen Thompson as residing on Kenridge Road, Cedarhurst [Lawrence]. The *Long Island Society Register, 1929* lists Jane Remsen Thompson as residing at *Holly Holm* in Cedarhurst [Lawrence].

She was the daughter of William Remsen. Jane's sister Sarah married William Manice, the son of William de Forest Manice, and resided in Manhattan.

Joseph TodHunter Thompson was the son of Jonathan and Catherine TodHunter Thompson.

Joseph TodHunter and Jane Remsen Thompson's daughter Jane, who disappeared from the Fall River Line steamship SS *Providence*, married Carl H. Schultz and resided in Sands Point. Their son Jonathan Thompson II married Lillian P. MacLeod and resided in West Islip. Their daughter Elizabeth married The Reverend Gilbert Sterling Bancroft Darlington, the son of The Right Reverend James Henry Darlington, Bishop of the Diocese of Central Pennsylvania, and resided in Lawrence.

At the time of his death, Thompson was residing at *Windymeade* in East Hampton. [*The New York Times* July 10, 1900, p. 7.]


### Thorpe, Warren Parsons, Sr. (1878-1958)

Occupation(s): merchant - director, Keystone Materials Co. (dealers in raw materials and building supplies)
financier - partner, Henderson and Co., NYC (later, Henderson, Harrison, and Struthers) (stock brokerage firm)

Civic Activism: mayor, Village of Lawrence

Marriage(s): 1905-1958 – Helen Prentiss Converse (b. 1880)

Address: Bannister Lane, Lawrence
Name of estate:
Year of construction:
Style of architecture:
Architect(s):
Landscape architect(s):
House extant: unconfirmed
Historical notes:

The *Social Register Summer, 1921* and the *Long Island Society Register, 1929* list Warren and Helen P. Converse Thorpe [Sr.] as residing in Lawrence.

He was the son of Charles Newbold and Mary Warren Thorpe.

Helen Prentiss Converse Thorpe was the daughter of John Heman and Elizabeth Perkins Thompson Converse.

Warren Parsons and Helen Prentiss Converse Thorpe, Sr.'s daughter Theodoria married William Palmer Dixon, Jr. and resided in Lawrence. Theodoria later married Charles Winn of London, England. Their son Warren Parsons Thorpe, Jr. married Elizabeth Searles Greene, the daughter of Herbert Gouveneur and Elizabeth Porter Searles Greene of Lawrence.

### Throop, Enos Thompson, IV (1908-1993)

| | |
|---|---|
| Occupation(s): | capitalist - partner, Ichabod T. Williams & Sons (importer of wood and veneer) |
| | financier - member, Charles A. Frank and Co. (stock brokerage firm) |
| Marriage(s): | 1939-1993 – Barbara Williams (1913-1999) |
| Address: | 255 Breezeway, Lawrence |
| Name of estate: | |
| Year of construction: | c. 1892 |
| Style of architecture: | French Country |
| Architect(s): | Carrere and Hastings designed the house and stable (for J. H. Harper, Sr.) |
| Landscape architect(s): | |
| House extant: yes | |
| Historical notes: | |

The house, originally named *Brightside*, was built by Joseph Henry Harper, Sr. It was later owned by James Samuel Dunstan, who continued to call it *Brightside*, and, subsequently, by Throop.

He was the son of Enos Thompson and Bessie Sands Tyler Throop III of Brooklyn.

Barbara Williams Throop was the daughter of Thomas Resolved and Dorothy Strong Hinckley Williams, who resided at *Windemere* in Lawrence. Barbara's brother Ichabod married Eda Marie Dunstan, the daughter of James Samuel and Eda Louise Kempshall Dunstan who resided in Lawrence and who had formerly owned this house.

Enos Thompson and Barbara Williams Throop IV's son Enos Thompson Throop V married Anne Sherrill Davidson, the daughter of George Donnell Davidson of Charlotte, NC, and, subsequently, Muriel Bradshaw, the daughter of Thomas F. Bradshaw of Wilmington, NC. Their son Garrow married Amelia LeClair, the daughter of Leopold J. LeClair of Peterborough, NH.

*front facade, 2009*

### Tibbs, Benjamin Hatfield (b. 1886)

| | |
|---|---|
| Occupation(s): | capitalist - partner, Accombamuck Land Co. (Bellport development company) |
| Civic Activism: | a founder and director, Old Inlet Club, Bellport, 1910; |
| | secretary and treasurer, Bellport Bay Yacht Club, 1911 |
| Marriage(s): | 1920 – Dorothy M. Droste (1895-1954) |
| Address: | 104 Fifth Street, Garden City |
| Name of estate: | |
| Year of construction: | 1913 |
| Style of architecture: | Modified Shingle |
| Architect(s): | |
| Landscape architect(s): | |
| House extant: yes | |
| Historical notes: | |

*front facade, 2008*

The *Long Island Society Register, 1929* lists Mr. and Mrs. Benjamin H. Tibbs as residing at 104 Fifth Street, Garden City.

He was the son of Joseph Parker and Emma Storey Tibbs, Sr.

Dorothy M. Droste Tibbs was the daughter of George F. Droste of Bellport. Dorothy subsequently married Sterling Hollingshead Ivison, Sr. of Garden City and Bellport.

Benjamin Hatfield and Dorothy M. Droste Tibbs' daughter Nancy married Edward Ljungqvist, the son of Adolf E. Ljungqvist of Great River. Their daughter Barbara married Frederick Geller Horan, Sr., the son of Stanley Gray Horan of Great River, and resided in Short Hills, NJ.

### Tilford, Frank (1852-1924)

| | | |
|---|---|---|
| Occupation(s): | merchant - | vice-president, Park & Tilford (grocery firm) |
| | financier - | director, Sixth National Bank, NYC; |
| | | member, New York Real Estate Exchange; |
| | | trustee, North River Savings Bank; |
| | | a founder and vice-president, Bank of New Amsterdam; |
| | | a founder, Fifth Avenue Trust Co.; |
| | | a founder and vice-president, Lincoln Trust Co.; |
| | | president and director, Union Trust Co. of New York |
| | capitalist - | Manhattan real estate speculator; |
| | | director, Consolidated Gas Co. |

Civic Activism: director, New Amsterdam Eye and Ear Hospital, NYC;
member, executive committee, Grant Monument Association, NYC;
director, New York School of Applied Design;
director, New York Historical Society;
director, Eye, Ear, and Throat Hospital, NYC;
commodore, Atlantic Yacht Club, 1903

Marriage(s): 1881-1924 – Julia Greer (1859-1946)

Address: *[unable to determine street address]*, Cedarhurst
Name of estate:
Year of construction: 1891
Style of architecture: Shingle
Architect(s): A. J. Harris designed
   the house (for Tilford)
Landscape architect(s):
House extant: no
Historical notes:

   The house was built by Frank Tilford. [*The Brooklyn Daily Eagle* November 8, 1890, p. 1, and *The Brooklyn Times Union* May 26, 1891, p. 5.]
   He was the son of John M. Tilford of New York City.
   Julia Greer Tilford was the daughter of James A. and Almira Shepard Greer.
   Frank and Julia Greer Tilford's daughter Elsie married Edward Conover Wilson.


### Timpson, Carl William, Sr. (b. 1896)

Occupation(s): merchant - wholesale lumber
Civic Activism: trustee, Village of Hewlett Harbor

Marriage(s): 1922 – Marcelle E. Vallon (1898-1999)

Address: Seawane Drive, Hewlett Harbor
Name of estate: *Windy Top*
Year of construction:
Style of architecture:
Architect(s):
Landscape architect(s):
House extant: unconfirmed
Historical notes:

   The *Long Island Society Register, 1929* lists Carl W. and Marcelle Vallon Timpson [Sr.] as residing in Hewlett [Hewlett Harbor].
   He was the son of James and Adele M. Rasmus Timpson of Woodsburgh.
   Marcelle E. Vallon Timpson was the daughter of Raoul Vallon of New Orleans, LA.
   Carl William and Marcelle E. Vallon Timpson, Sr.'s daughter Brenda married Lars Sellstedt Potter, Jr. of Buffalo, NY, and resided in Lawrence. Brenda later married Andre O. Keohn. Their son James married Annadell Beckers, the daughter of William Kurt and Annadell Beckers of East Hampton. [*See* Spinzia, *Long Island's Prominent Families in the Town of East Hampton – Beckers entry.*] James later married Priscilla Rea. Their son Carl William Timpson, Jr. married Patricia White and resided in Locust Valley.
   *[See following entry for additional family information.]*

**Timpson, Carl William, Sr. (b. 1896)**

| | | |
|---|---|---|
| Occupation(s): | capitalist - | director, Brooklyn City Railroad; |
| | | director, Brooklyn Heights Railroad |
| | financier - | director, United States Mortgage and Trust Co.; |
| | | director, United Stated Safe Deposit Co.; |
| | | vice-chairman and director, Mercantile Insurance Company of Edinburgh; |
| | | director, Mercantile Insurance Company of North America; |
| | | director, Mercantile Insurance Company of London; |
| | | director, National Bank of Commerce; |
| | | president and general manager, Mutual Insurance Co. |

Civic Activism: a founder, Village of Woodsburgh, 1912; trustee, Village of Woodsburgh, 1920-1928

Marriage(s): 1895-1928 – Adele M. Rasmus (1871-1956)

Address: Willow Road, Woodsburgh
Name of estate:
Year of construction:
Style of architecture:
Architect(s):
Landscape architect(s):
House extant: unconfirmed
Historical notes:

   The *Social Register Summer, 1910* and *1921* list James and Adele M. Rasmus Timpson as residing in Woodmere [Woodsburgh].
   She was the daughter of William Rasmus of Brooklyn.
   James and Adele M. Rasmus Timpson's son Carl married Marcelle E. Vallon and resided at *Windy Top* in Hewlett Harbor.
   *[See previous entry for additional family information.]*

### Tjaden, Olive Frances (1904-1997)

| | |
|---|---|
| Occupation(s): | architect - *[See Architects appendix for selected list of commissions in the Town of Hempstead.]* * |
| Civic Activism: | director, Museum of Fine Arts, Fort Lauderdale, FL; inspector, Federal Housing Administration; vice-president, Alumnae Association of College of Architecture, Art, and Planning, Cornell University, Ithaca, NY; member, business ethics committee, Town of Hempstead Zonta Club; recording secretary, American Association of University Women, 1972; publicity chair, Cornell Women's Club of Long Island; bequeathed the major portion of her $12 million estate to Cornell University |
| Marriage(s): | M/1 – 1945-div.1969 – Carl Johnson<br>   - architect<br>     capitalist - real estate developer<br>M/2 – Roswell Charles Van Sickle (d. 1995)<br>   - electrical engineer; worked on the Manhattan project that developed the atomic bomb<br>     inventor - hydraulically operated circuit breaker with tandem piston construction |
| Address: | 104 Eleventh Street, Garden City |
| Name of estate: | |
| Year of construction: | |
| Style of architecture: | Norman Revival |
| Architect(s): | Olive Frances Tjaden designed her own residence |
| Landscape architect(s): | Olive Frances Tjaden designed her own landscaping |
| House extant: yes | |
| Historical notes: | |

  The house was built by Olive Frances Tjaden Johnson. She designed over two thousand buildings, four hundred of which were on Long Island. In addition, she planned the house for the 1939 World's Fair, Inwood Country Club in Atlantic Beach, apartment buildings in Lawrence, and the remodeling of the Congregational Church in Garden City.

  Olive Tjaden entered Cornell University at the age of fifteen and completed the university's five-year architectural degree in four years. She was the only woman in her class of 1928 to graduate with an architectural degree and was the youngest registered architect in New York State. The university's Tjaden Hall and Van Sickle Art Gallery are named in her honor. In 1938, Olive was the first woman to be inducted into the American Institute of Architects and, for over two decades, was considered to be the most prominent woman architect in the Northeast. [Sarah Allaback, *The First American Women Architects* (Urbana, IL: University of Illinois Press, 2008), p. 40.]

  She was the daughter of John and Hilda Francke Tjaden of Queens Village, NY.

  *Although married twice, Tjaden used her maiden name professionally.

  Her Garden City office was located at 109 Seventh Street.

  She relocated to Florida in 1945.

  Carl Johnson was the son of Alfred Johnson.

*front facade, 2009*

# Olive Frances Tjaden residence

*main floor peacock stained-glass door*

*Hilda Francke Tjaden (Mrs. John Tjaden)*

*patio, outside peacock stained-glass door*

# Olive Frances Tjaden residence

*rear garden*

*rear garden*

*sun room*

### Tompers, George Urban (1876-1936)

| | |
|---|---|
| Occupation(s): | financier - president and director, National Liberty Insurance Co.; president and director, Financial and Industrial Securities Corp., NYC |
| | industrialist - president and director, Tower Manufacturing Co.; president and director, Sterling Piano Co.; president, Huntington Piano Co.; president, Riedel and Co. (pharmaceutical firm); president, F. A. Ritcher and Co. (pharmaceutical firm) |
| Marriage(s): | 1900-1936 – Lucie Margaret Hartt (1874-1938) |
| Address: | 18 Cathedral Avenue, Garden City |
| Name of estate: | |
| Year of construction: | 1908 |
| Style of architecture: | Neo-Tudor |
| Architect(s): | |
| Landscape architect(s): | |
| House extant: yes | |
| Historical notes: | |

In 1929, Tompers purchased the twenty-room house from William Hamlyn Duval III. [*The New York Times* January 31, 1929, p. 45.]

George Urban and Lucie Margaret Hartt Tompers' daughter Jacqueline married Dr. H. Easton McMahon, the son of Henry E. McMahon of Brooklyn.

*front facade, 2000*

### Townley, The Reverend Frank Maxwell (1869-1940)

| | |
|---|---|
| Occupation(s): | clergy - rector, St. Bartholomew's Episcopal Church, Merrick |
| Civic Activism: | trustee, dioceses estate; vice-president, Church Charity of Long Island |
| Marriage(s): | M/1 – 1895-1896 – Edith Kathleen Thompson (d. 1896) |
| | M/2 – 1899-1940 – Ada Isabella Pearson (b. 1870) |
| Address: | 108 Roxbury Road, Garden City |
| Name of estate: | |
| Year of construction: | 1913 |
| Style of architecture: | Victorian |
| Architect(s): | |
| Landscape architect(s): | |
| House extant: yes | |
| Historical notes: | |

The Reverend Frank Maxwell and Mrs. Edith Kathleen Thompson Townley's daughter Edith married Van Cortland Stoutenburgh.

The *Long Island Society Register, 1929* lists The Reverend Frank Maxwell and Mrs. Ada Isabella Pearson Townley as residing at 108 Roxbury Road, Garden City.

He was the son of John Maxwell and Caroline Townley.

Ada Isabella Pearson Townley was the daughter of James McKenzie Pearson of Dublin, Ireland.

The Reverend Frank Maxwell and Mrs. Ada Isabella Pearson Townley's daughter Gladys married Henry Buechner Garnaus. Their daughter Ruth married Percy Heilner Buchanan. Their daughter Francis married Donald Roseborough Keller.

In 2001 the house was remodeled.

*front facade, 2005*

**Townsend, Edward Nicoll, Jr. (1887-1960)**

| | |
|---|---|
| Occupation(s): | merchant - member, E. N. Townsend Co. (dry goods firm) |
| | financier - vice-president and director, West Hempstead National Bank; director, Great Northern Investment Co.; partner, Curtis and Sanger, NYC (stock brokerage firm); a founder, Garden City Bank |
| Civic Activism: | a founder, Garden City Volunteer Fire Department; a founder and commissioner, Garden City Fire Department; a founder, Cherry Valley Country Club, Garden City |
| Marriage(s): | M/1 – 1912 – Beatrice Nicholas (b. 1891) |
| | M/2 – 1933 – Beatrice Meserole Oltrogge (1887-1967) |
| Address: | 112 Hilton Avenue, Garden City |
| Name of estate: | |
| Year of construction: | 1878 |
| Style of architecture: | Victorian |
| Architect(s): | |
| Landscape architect(s): | |
| House extant: yes | |
| Historical notes: | |

In 1922 Edward Nicoll Townsend, Jr. purchased the house. [*The Brooklyn Standard Union* June 25, 1922, p. 29.]

The *Long Island Society Register, 1929* lists Edward Nicoll and Beatrice Nicholas Townsend [Jr.] as residing at 112 Hilton Avenue, Garden City.

He was the son of Edward Nicoll and Margaret Livingston Douw Townsend, Sr. of Garden City.

Beatrice Nicholas Townsend was the daughter of Harry Ingersoll and Alice McKim Hollins Nicholas, Sr. of *Virginia Farm* in North Babylon. Beatrice's sister Rita married Uriel Atwood Murdock II and resided in Babylon. Her sister Daisy married Grosvenor Nicholas and resided in Old Westbury. Her sister Elsie married Alonzo Potter II and resided at *Harbor House* in St. James and *Westmoor* in Southampton. Her sister Evelyn married Alexander Duncan Cameron Arnold, Sr. of West Islip and, subsequently, Joseph Hutchinson Stevenson with whom she resided at *The Farm* in Hewlett Bay Park. Her brother Harry Ingersoll Nicholas II married Dorothy Snow, the daughter of Frederick Augustus and Mary Palen Snow of *Gardenside* in Southampton, and resided at *Rolling Hill Farm* in Muttontown. Her sister Maude married George Casper Niles and resided at *Cross Cottage* in Bridgehampton. [*See* Spinzia, *Long Island's Prominent North Shore Families, vol. II* – Vietor entry.] Their son Robert married Elizabeth Benziger, the granddaughter of Adelrick Benziger of *Diamond Trail Bar Ranch* in Jelm, WY.

Edward Nicoll and Beatrice Nicholas Townsend, Jr.'s son Killian married Mary Campbell, the daughter of Willis Everett Campbell, Jr. Their son Edward Nicoll Townsend III married Eleanor Vietor, the daughter of Dr. John Adolf and Mrs. Eleanore Emily Woodward Vietor, Sr. of *Cherrywood* in Matinecock, while she was still a minor. [*See* Spinzia, *Long Island's Prominent South Shore Families* – Arnold, Murdock, and Nicholas entries – and *Long Island's Prominent North Shore Families, vol. II* – Nicholas entry.]

Beatrice Meserole Oltrogge Townsend was the daughter of John Frederick and Hannah M. Shonard Oltrogge of Manhattan. Beatrice had previously been married to Edward Duer Reeves, Sr. of Garden City.

Edward and Beatrice Oltrogge Townsend relocated to Cold Spring Harbor after their 1933 marriage. By 1945 Townsend was residing in Plandome.

*[See following entry for additional family information.]*

In 1970 the seven-bedroom house was remodeled.

It was for sale in 2008. The asking price was $1.8; the taxes were $23,324.

*front facade, 2006*

### Townsend, Edward Nicoll, Sr. (1858-1914)

| | |
|---|---|
| Occupation(s): | publisher - owner and editor: *The Oyster Bay Pilot*; *The Hempstead Republican*; *The Nassau County Republican* |
| | capitalist - a founder, The Oyster Bay Land Improvement Co., 1888 |
| Marriage(s): | 1883-1914 – Margaret Livingston Douw (1858-1953) |
| Address: | 106 Tenth Street, Garden City |
| Name of estate: | |
| Year of construction: | 1906 |
| Style of architecture: | Dutch Colonial Revival |
| Architect(s): | |
| Landscape architect(s): | |
| House extant: yes | |
| Historical notes: | |

The *Long Island Society Register, 1929* lists Margaret Livingston Douw Townsend as residing at 106 Tenth Street, Garden City.

She was the daughter of John de Peyster and Marianna Chandler Laman Douw.

At the time of her death, she was residing at 78 Magnolia Street, Garden City. [*The New York Times* March 23, 1953, p. 23.]

Edward Nicoll Townsend, Sr. was the son of Solomon Samuel and Helene De Kay Townsend II of *Townsend House* in Oyster Bay. [*See* Spinzia, *Long Island's Prominent North Shore Families, vol. II –* Townsend entries.] His brother Robert married Edythe Earle, the daughter of Edward and Clara Noble Earle, and resided at *The Patch* in Garden City.

Edward Nicoll and Margaret Livingston Douw Townsend, Sr.'s son Mohannes married Ada Bryce Gray and resided at *Sunny Acres* in Old Westbury. Their daughter Anne married Edward B. MacKellar, the son of Daniel MacKellar of Garden City. Their son Edward Nicoll Townsend, Jr., who resided in Garden City, Cold Spring Harbor, and Plandome, married Beatrice Nicholas and, subsequently, Beatrice Meserole Oltrogge, the former wife of Edward Duer Reeves, Sr. of Garden City.

*[See previous entry for additional family information.]*

*front facade, 2006*

**Townsend, Frances Mary Fragos (b. 1961)**

| | | |
|---|---|---|
| Occupation(s): | attorney - | partner, Baker Botts LLP, 2004-2208; |
| | | assistant district attorney, Brooklyn; |
| | | member, United States Attorney Office, Southern District of New York; |
| | | Chief of Staff to United States Attorney General (George W. Bush administration); |
| | | counsel to the United States Attorney General for Intelligence Policy (George W. Bush administration) |
| | capitalist - | vice-president, secretary, chief compliance officer, Activision Blizzard; |
| | | vice-chair, general counsel, and chief administrative officer, MacAndrews and Forbes; |
| | | director, Freeport McMo Ran |
| | entertainer and associated professions - | |
| | | senior national security analyst, CBS news |
| | statesman - | member, President's Advisory Board, 1985; |
| | | Deputy Assistant to the President for Homeland Security and Counterterrorism (George W. Bush administration); |
| | | Assistant Commandant for Intelligence, United States Coast Guard |
| Civic Activism: | | director, International Republican Institute; |
| | | director, Council on Foreign Affairs; |
| | | director, Transatlantic Commission; |
| | | trustee, Atlantic Council; |
| | | trustee, Center for Strategic and International Studies; |
| | | trustee, Intrepid Sea, Air, and Space Museum, NYC; |
| | | trustee, McCain Institute; |
| | | trustee, New York City Foundation; |
| | | president, Counter Extremism Project |
| Marriage(s): | | 1994 – John Michael Townsend |
| | | - attorney -   partner, Hughes, Hubbard, and Reed, Washington, DC |
| Address: | | *[unable to determine street address]*, Wantagh |
| Name of estate: | | |
| Year of construction: | | |
| Style of architecture: | | |
| Architect (s): | | |
| Landscape architect(s): | | |
| House extant:  no | | |
| Historical notes: | | |

Francis was raised in Wantagh by her parents John and Dorothy Fragos.

### Townsend, Robert (1853-1915)

| | |
|---|---|
| Occupation(s): | attorney - Assistant District Attorney, NYC (for fifteen years) |
| | military - colonel, member of Governor Grover Cleveland's military staff |
| Marriage(s): | 1896-1915 – Edythe Earle (1876-1934) |
| | - restaurateur - owned cafeteria in Mineola Court House* |
| Address: | 124 Seventh Street, Garden City |
| Name of estate: | *The Patch* |
| Year of construction: | 1924 |
| Style of architecture: | |
| Architect (s): | |
| Landscape architect(s): | |
| House extant: no | |
| Historical notes: | |

The *Long Island Society Register, 1929* lists Edythe Earle Townsend as residing at *The Patch* at 124 Seventh Street, Garden City.

She was the daughter of Edward and Clara Noble Earle.

Robert Townsend was the son of Solomon Samuel and Helene De Kay Townsend II of *Townsend House* in Oyster Bay. [*See* Spinzia, *Long Island's Prominent North Shore Families, vol. II* – Townsend entries.] His brother Edward married Margaret Livingston Douw, the daughter of John de Peyster and Marianna Chandler Laman Douw, and resided in Garden City.

*After the death of her husband, Mrs. Townsend lost most of her fortune. Despondent over poor health, she committed suicide in her home by turning on the gas jets. At the time of her death she was operating the court house cafeteria.

Prior to relocating to Garden City the Townsends resided on West Shore Drive, Mill Neck.


### Townsend, Robert Tailer, Sr. (b. 1891)

| | |
|---|---|
| Occupation(s): | financier - stock broker |
| Marriage(s): | 1916 – Mary H. Frieze (1898-1950) |
| Address: | 72 Cathedral Avenue, Hempstead |
| Name of estate: | |
| Year of construction: | 1924 |
| Style of architecture: | |
| Architect (s): | |
| Landscape architect(s): | |
| House extant: yes | |
| Historical notes: | |

The *Social Register of New York, 1939* lists R. Tailer and Mary H. Frieze Townsend [Sr.] as residing at 72 Cathedral Avenue, Hempstead.

He was the son of John Richard and Pauline Garcia Onativia Townsend. Pauline subsequently married James Henry Alexandre, Sr. and resided in Hempstead.

Mary H. Frieze Townsend was the daughter of Lyman Bowers and Mary Savage Crowell Frieze, Jr. of New Brighton, Staten Island, NY.

Robert Tailer and Mary H. Frieze Townsend, Sr.'s son Robert Tailer Townsend, Jr. married Shirley Clark, the daughter of John S. Clark of Lloyd Harbor. Their son John married Mary Nell Rogers, the daughter of Henry Nelson Rogers of Earle, AR.

### Townsend, Stephen Van Rensselaer, Sr. (1860-1901)

| | |
|---|---|
| Occupation(s): | attorney |
| Marriage(s): | 1888-1899 – Janet Eckford King (1866-1899) |
| Address: | 10 Greenwich Street, Hempstead |
| Name of estate: | |
| Year of construction: | |
| Style of architecture: | |
| Architect (s): | |
| Landscape architect(s): | |
| House extant: | no |
| Historical notes: | |

   Stephen Van Rensselaer Townsend, Sr. was the son of Dr. Howard and Mrs. Justine Van Rensselaer Townsend, Sr. of Albany, NY. His sister Harriet married Thomas Henry Barber, Sr. and resided at *Claverack House* in Southampton. His brother Howard Townsend, Jr., who resided in Southampton, married Sophie Witherspoon Dickey and, later, Ann Lowndes Langdon. [*See* Spinzia, *Long Island's Prominent Families in the Town of Southampton* – Barber and Townsend entries.]
   Janet Eckford King Townsend was the daughter of Cornelius Low and Janet DeKay King.
   Stephen Van Rensselaer and Janet Eckford King Townsend, Sr.'s daughter Margaret Schuyler married Arthur Boynton Glidden and resided in Dover, MA. Their unmarried daughter Justine resided in Manhattan and at *Spring Creek Ranch* in Cottonwood, AZ. Their daughter Janet remained unmarried. Their two-year-old son Stephen Van Rensselaer Townsend, Jr. died in 1893.

### Tucker, St. George Brooke (1875-1963)

| | |
|---|---|
| Occupation(s): | politician - member, New York City Board of Assessors (Mayor John Purroy Mitchel administration); acting treasurer, New York County Republican Committee |
| | capitalist - Mizer Development Corp. |
| | financier - assistant treasurer, Guaranty Trust Co.; vice-president, Eastern Exchange Bank; vice-president and director, Seward National Bank |
| Civic Activism: | president, Nassau County Association |
| Marriage(s): | 1916-1959 – Grace Hollingsworth (1882-1959) |
| Address: | Hewlett Neck Road, Hewlett Neck* |
| Name of estate: | |
| Year of construction: | |
| Style of architecture: | |
| Architect(s): | |
| Landscape architect(s): | |
| House extant: | unconfirmed |
| Historical notes: | |

   The *Long Island Society Register, 1929* lists St. George Brooke and Grace Hollingsworth Tucker as residing on Georges Boulevard, Hewlett [Hewlett Neck].
   *Hewlett Neck Road was previously called Georges Boulevard.
   He was the son of Judge Charles Frederick and Mrs. Mary Sydnor Jones Tucker of Dallas, TX.
   Grace Hollingsworth Tucker was the daughter of William Hollingsworth of Manhattan.
   St. George Brooke and Grace Hollingsworth Tucker's son Beverly married Marjory Goodridge Spencer, the daughter of Henry Morgan Spencer of West Hartford, CT, and resided in Dallas, TX.

### Tunmore, John Septimus (1874-1946)

| | |
|---|---|
| Occupation(s): | financier - president, John S. Tunmore Insurance Agency, NYC; general agent, New York, Provident Mutual Life Insurance Co. |
| Civic Activism: | president, Property Owners Association of Garden City |
| Marriage(s): | Harriet Gibbons (b. 1885) |
| Address: | 91 Ninth Street, Garden City |
| Name of estate: | |
| Year of construction: | 1893 |
| Style of architecture: | Eclectic Shingle |
| Architect(s): | |
| Landscape architect(s): | |
| House extant: yes | |
| Historical notes: | |

The *Long Island Society Register, 1929* lists John Septimus and Harriet Gibbons Tunmore as residing at 91 Ninth Street, Garden City.

Their son John married Anna May Voege, the daughter of Harry William and Ida Lauman Voege, Sr. of Brooklyn and Garden City. Their son Harry married Priscilla Alden Rowe, the daughter of Henry W. Rowe of Greenwich, CT.

The five-bedroom house was for sale in 2008. The asking price was $2.2 million; the taxes were $23,699.

*front facade, 2008*

### Turnbull, John Gourlay, Jr. (1890-1969)

| | |
|---|---|
| Occupation(s): | attorney |
| Marriage(s): | 1915-1939 – Harriette Boden Hutchinson (1890-1939) |
| Address: | 125 Nassau Boulevard, Garden City |
| Name of estate: | |
| Year of construction: | |
| Style of architecture: | |
| Architect(s): | |
| Landscape architect(s): | |
| House extant: no | |
| Historical notes: | |

The *Long Island Society Register, 1929* lists John Gourlay and Harriette Boden Hutchinson Turnbull [Jr.] as residing at 129 [sic] Nassau Boulevard, Garden City. The 1930 Census lists the Turnbulls as residing at 125 Nassau Boulevard.

He was the son of John Gourley and Josephine Sherwood Turnbull, Sr. of *The Pines* in Brightwaters. [*See* Spinzia, *Long Island's Prominent South Shore Families* – Turnbull entry.] His sister Marjorie married Wallace MacNab Waddell, Sr. and also resided in Garden City.

Harriette Boden Hutchinson Turnbull was the daughter of David Wallace Hutchinson of Brooklyn.

### Tunstall, Harry Alphonse (1903-1959)

| | |
|---|---|
| Occupation(s): | real estate agent -   member, Carstens & Linnekin, NYC |
| Marriage(s): | 1929-1950 – Dorothy Ann Lannin (1894-1950) (aka Dorothea Ann Lannin) - Civic Activism:  volunteer, various Long Island military bases |
| Address: | Eisenhower Park, East Meadow |
| Name of estate: | |
| Year of construction: | 1930 |
| Style of architecture: | Neo-Tudor |
| Architect(s): | |
| Landscape architect(s): | |
| House extant: yes | |
| Historical notes: | |

Joseph John Lannin commissioned Olive Frances Tjaden to design the first 1928 house as a wedding present for his daughter Dorothy and his son-in-law Harry on the site of the former James Clinch Smith estate. [East Meadow Public Library, *East Meadow Past and Present 1658-1976*. East Meadow, NY, nd, p. 33.] Upon return from their honeymoon, the Tunstalls discovered their house and its furnishings had been destroyed by fire. [*The Nassau Daily Review* October 16, 1929, pp. 1 and 12.] They immediately built a new house on the site.

Harry Alphonse Tunstall was the son of Harry Gabriel and Jessie Gertrude Graham Tunstall of Garden City.

Dorothy Ann Lannin Tunstall was the daughter of Joseph John and Hannah J. Furlong Lannin of Garden City.

Harry Alphonse and Dorothy Ann Lannin Tunstall's daughter Dorothy married Edward W. Kirchner, the son of William E. Kirchner of Huntington. Their son Harry Paul Tunstall married Emily Jane Conroy. Their son John married Jeanne R. Lyman, the daughter of Burton Alvin and Jannette Julia Thorburn Lyman, Jr. of Brooklyn.

The main residence was later owned by Max Staller who, in 1955, sold it to Nassau County. In 1961, the house became the site of the Nassau County Historical Museum.  It is currently the Long Island headquarters of the Women's Sports Foundation. The estate's carriage house currently is the headquarters of the COPE Foundation.

At the time of her death, Mrs. Turnstall was residing at 142 Whitehall Boulevard in Garden City.

*front facade*

### Tunstall, Harry Gabriel (b. 1873)

Occupation(s): financier - a founder and partner, with E. Hope Norton, Norton and Tunstall, 1896;
a founder and partner, with Charles A. Wainwright, Tunstall and Co., 1899

Marriage(s): Jessie Gertrude Graham (b. 1881)

Address: 86 Roxbury Road, Garden City
Name of estate:
Year of construction: 1926
Style of architecture: Contemporary
Architect(s):
Landscape architect(s):
House extant: yes
Historical notes:

Harry Gabriel Tunstall was the son of Alphonse Gabriel and Corrine Yonge Tunstall.

Harry Gabriel and Jessie Gertrude Graham Tunstall's son Harry Alphonse Tunstall married Dorothy Ann Lannin and resided in East Meadow and Garden City.

In 1997, the 1,446-square-foot house sold for $70,000.


### Twining, Charles (1866-1941)

Occupation(s): industrialist - treasurer, secretary, and director, Federated Textiles Inc., NYC;
treasurer and director, American Bleached Goods Co., NYC

Marriage(s): 1908-1941 – Roberta Mary Braine (1876-1947)

Address: 124 Cherry Valley Road, Garden City
Name of estate: *Iris Acre*
Year of construction: 1900
Style of architecture: Modified Shingle
Architect(s):
Landscape architect(s):
House extant: yes
Historical notes:

The *Social Register Summer, 1921* and the *Long Island Society Register, 1929* list Charles and Roberta M. Braine Twining as residing at *Iris Acre*, 124 Cherry Valley Road, Garden City.

He was the son of Edward C. and Elizabeth Whitman Twining of Halifax, Nova Scotia, Canada.

Roberta Mary Braine Twining was the daughter of Robert Speir and Mary Burnett Carter Braine.

Charles and Roberta Mary Braine Twining's daughter Mary married Hersey Benner Egginton, the son of Hersey Egginton of Garden City, and resided in Garden City.

*front facade, 2008*

### Tyner, Gerald Kerwin (1896-1953)

| | |
|---|---|
| Occupation(s): | financier - partner, Benedict and Benedict (insurance brokerage firm) |
| Marriage(s): | 1923-1953 – Helen Virginia Kennedy (b. 1897) |
| Address: | 136 Wellington Road, Garden City |
| Name of estate: | |
| Year of construction: | 1923 |
| Style of architecture: | Colonial Revival |
| Architect(s): | |
| Landscape architect(s): | |
| House extant: yes | |
| Historical notes: | |

The *Long Island Society Register, 1929* lists Mr. and Mrs. Gerald Kerwin Tyner as residing on Quantuck Lane, Quogue. [*See* Spinzia, *Long Island's Prominent Families in the Town of Southampton*– Tyner entry.]

He was the son of Charles Legge and Emma Cranston Tyner of East Orange, NJ.

Helen Virginia Kennedy Tyner was the daughter of Dr. James Charles and Mrs. Margaret O'Rourke Kennedy of Brooklyn.

Gerald Kerwin and Helen Virginia Kennedy Tyner's daughter Geraldine married Thomas A. Dent III and resided in Lake Forest, IL. Their daughter Barbara married William Montague Geer III, the son of William Montague and Edith J. Farr Geer, Jr. of Lawrence, and resided in South Salem, MA.

*front facade, 2001*

### Tyner, John Hill (1920-1989)

| | |
|---|---|
| Occupation(s): | merchant - president, Edwin Jackson, Inc. (dealers in antique mantels and fireplace equipment)<br>industrialist - director, Bristol–Myers Co.; director, National Biscuit Co. |
| Marriage(s): | 1942-1989 – Joan Kettering Martin (1922-2012) |
| Address: | Briarwood Crossing, Lawrence |
| Name of estate: | |
| Year of construction: | |
| Style of architecture: | |
| Architect(s): | |
| Landscape architect(s): | |
| House extant: unconfirmed | |
| Historical notes: | |

The *Social Register New York, 1954* lists John H. and Joan K. Martin Tyner as residing on Briarwood Crossing, Cedarhurst [Lawrence].

He was the son of Richard L. Tyner of Greenwich, CT.

Joan Kettering Martin Tyner was the daughter of Thomas Stephens and Edith Victoria Deacon Martin of *Mistletoe Way* in Lawrence.

John Hill and Joan Kettering Martin Tyner's daughter Victoria married Lee Wallace Peck, the son of Arthur Knowlton and Christine Wallace Crane Peck, Sr. of Lawrence; Lars Sellstedt Potter, Jr.; and subsequently, Harry Thomas Kilburn, Jr. Their daughter Sandra married Lawrence Sumner Heath III.

Tyner committed suicide. He had suffered from depression for twenty years. [*The New York Times* December 6, 1989, p. D27.]

### Underhill, Enoch William (1878-1958)

| | |
|---|---|
| Occupation(s): | industrialist -  general manager, Arbuckle Brothers, Brooklyn (sugar refining firm) |
| | capitalist -  manager, Buffalo division, Erie Railroad; owner, Westward Farms, Farmington, MN (large dairy farm) |
| Marriage(s): | 1903-1956 – Alice Wyman (1877-1956) |
| Address: | 58 Third Street, Garden City |
| Name of estate: | |
| Year of construction: | 1928 |
| Style of architecture: | Modified Dutch Colonial |
| Architect(s): | |
| Landscape architect(s): | |
| House extant: | yes |
| Historical notes: | |

*front facade, 2015*

The house was built by Enoch William Underhill.

The *Long Island Society Register, 1929* lists Enoch William and Alice Wyman Underhill as residing at 58 Third Street, Garden City.

He was the son of Frederick Douglas and Sarah Smith Underhill.

Alice Wyman Underhill was the daughter of James Thomas Wyman of Minneapolis, MN.

Enoch William and Alice Wyman Underhill's daughter Betty married Dr. Jefferson Weed, the son of Leroy Jefferson and Mabel Scott Weed of Garden City. Their daughter Harriet married Lynne Anderson Warren. Their daughter Ethelwynne married George Rodney Meneely, the son of Charles Dickinson and Emily Frances Gahn Meneely of Garden City.

In 2021, the 4,646-square-foot house sold for $2.995 million.

### Underhill, Rawson Kip, Sr. (1890-1954)

| | |
|---|---|
| Occupation(s): | financier -  stockbroker |
| | real estate agent -  a founder, Rawson K. Underhill Realty Corp, Hempstead, 1926 |
| Marriage(s): | 1913 – Aurelia Phelan (1891-1948) |
| Address: | 20 Roxbury Road, Garden City |
| Name of estate: | |
| Year of construction: | |
| Style of architecture: | |
| Architect(s): | |
| Landscape architect(s): | |
| House extant: | no |
| Historical notes: | |

The *Long Island Society Register, 1929* lists Rawson K. Underhill as residing at 20 Roxbury Road, Garden City.

He was the son of Rawson and Justina Mills Crowley Underhill of Manhattan.

Aurelia Phelan was the daughter of George W. Phelan of Garden City.

## Vanderveer, Charles, Jr. (1895-1968)

Occupation(s):

Marriage(s): 1923-1968 – Frances Elizabeth Covert (1901-1986)

Address: 83 Cathedral Avenue, Hempstead
Name of estate:
Year of construction: 1924
Style of architecture: Colonial Revival
Architect(s):
Landscape architect(s):
House extant: no
Historical notes:

   The house was built by Charles Vanderveer, Jr. [*The Brooklyn Daily Eagle* November 2, 1923, p. 7.]
   The *Long Island Society Register, 1929* lists Charles and Frances Elizabeth Covert Vanderveer, Jr. as residing at 83 Cathedral Avenue, Hempstead.
   He was the son of Charles and Helen Wyckoff Ditmas Vanderveer, Sr. of Hollis, Queens.
   Frances Elizabeth Covert Vanderveer was the daughter of Charles Edward and Magdalene Frances Vanderveer Covert of Garden City.
   Charles and Frances Elizabeth Covert Vanderveer, Jr.'s daughter Shirley married Thomas Charles Davidson, Jr. Their son Charles Vanderveer III married Natalie Ann Lunn, the daughter of James Snow Lunn of Hempstead, and resided in Bridgehampton. Charles subsequently married Gertrude Mercer Altemus, the daughter of James Dobson and Rosalie S. Pillot Altemus.

*front facade, 2000*

## Vandewater, Benjamin Cornelius (1876-1955)

Occupation(s): financier - vice-president, Corn Exchange Bank
Civic Activism: chairman, finance committee, Queens Chamber of Commerce

Marriage(s): 1920-1926 – Hester Elizabeth Smith (1883-1926)

Address: 123 Prospect Avenue, Cedarhurst
Name of estate:
Year of construction: 1925
Style of architecture: Modified Neo-Federal
Architect(s):
Landscape architect(s):
House extant: yes
Historical notes:

   The *Long Island Society Register, 1929* lists Benjamin C. Vandewater as residing on Prospect Avenue, Cedarhurst.
   He was the son of Peter Cooper and Elizabeth Hewlett Vandewater.
   Hester Elizabeth Smith Vandewater was the daughter of William Skidmore Smith.
   In 2012, the 2,680-square-foot house sold for $685,000.

*front facade, 2012*

### Vandewater, James Horatio Poole (1855-1911)

| | |
|---|---|
| Occupation(s): | politician - highway commissioner, Town of Hempstead |
| Civic Activism: | a founder, Village of Cedarhurst, 1910; president, Village of Cedarhurst |
| Marriage(s): | 1884-1911 – Emeline Waters (1864-1934) |
| Address: | Linwood Avenue, Cedarhurst |
| Name of estate: | |
| Year of construction: | c. 1853 |
| Style of architecture: | |
| Architect(s): | |
| Landscape architect(s): | |
| House extant: | no; demolished in 1953* |
| Historical notes: | |

    James Horatio Poole Vanderwater was the son of Cornelius and Elizabeth Scull Vandewater.
    Emeline Waters Vandewater was the daughter of Isaac Snedeker and Imogene Shepherd Waters.
    James Horatio Poole and Emeline Waters Vandewater's son Neil also resided at the Vandewater homestead. Their daughter Dorothy married Francis Gould Hoyt.
    *The one-hundred-year-old Vandewater homestead was demolished for the construction of an apartment building. [*The New York Times* June 14, 1953, p. R1.]
    *[See following entry for additional family information.]*


### Vandewater, Neil Horatio (1886-1930)

| | |
|---|---|
| Occupation(s): | attorney |
| Marriage(s): | 1914-1930 – Laura Scull (1889-1973) |
| Address: | Linwood Avenue, Cedarhurst |
| Name of estate: | |
| Year of construction: | c. 1853 |
| Style of architecture: | |
| Architect(s): | |
| Landscape architect(s): | |
| House extant: | no; demolished in 1953* |
| Historical notes: | |

    The *Long Island Society Register, 1929* lists Neil H. Vandewater as residing on Linwood Avenue, Cedarhurst.
    He was the son of James Horatio Poole and Emeline Waters Vandewater of Cedarhurst who had also resided at the Vandewater homestead on Linwood Avenue.
    Laura Scull Vandewater was the daughter of Thomas E. and Anna Risley Scull.
    *The one-hundred-year-old Vandewater homestead was demolished for the construction of an apartment building. [*The New York Times* June 14, 1953, p. R1.]
    *[See previous entry for additional family information.]*

### Van Rensselaer, Bernard Sanders (1886-1977)

| | |
|---|---|
| Occupation(s): | attorney -   Deputy Assistant District Attorney |
| Civic Activism: | general industrial negotiator, Office of Industry Cooperation, 1948; |
| | director, senior citizens' committee, Republican National Committee, 1959-74; |
| | branch chief, Southeast Asia, Mutual Securities Administration; |
| | vice-chair, Mayor's Committee on Housing for the Elderly, Washington, DC; |
| | president, New York Society of the Cincinnati, 1963; |
| | Marshall Plan advisor |
| Marriage(s): | M/1 – 1915 – Rose Carolina Tillotson (1887-1945) |
| | - journalist -  editor, women's page, *Evening Telegram* |
| | M/2 – 1948-1977 – Charlotte Mary Southmayd (1912-1993) |
| Address: | East Rockaway Road, Hewlett Bay Park |
| Name of estate: | |
| Year of construction: | |
| Style of architecture: | |
| Architect(s): | |
| Landscape architect(s): | |
| House extant: | unconfirmed |
| Historical notes: | |

The *Long Island Society Register, 1929* lists Bernard S. and Rose Tillotson Van Rensselaer [Jr.] as residing on East Rockaway Road, Hewlett [Hewlett Bay Park].
   He was the son of Maunsell and Isabella Mason Van Rensselaer, Jr., who resided at *The Haven* in Hewlett Neck.
   Rose Carolina Tillotson Van Rensselaer was the daughter of James Knox Tillotson of Manhattan.
   Charlotte Mary Southmayd Van Rensselaer was the daughter of LeRoy Southmayd, Sr. of Great Falls, MT.
*[See other Van Rensselaer entries for additional family information.]*


### Van Rensselaer, Kiliaen Maunsell, II (1898-1981)

| | |
|---|---|
| Occupation(s): | merchant -   proprietor, Toy and Yarn Shop, Albuquerque, NM |
| Marriage(s): | M/1 – 1923-1981 – Elizabeth West Post (1904-1981) |
| Address: | Adams Lane, Hewlett Neck |
| Name of estate: | |
| Year of construction: | |
| Style of architecture: | |
| Architect(s): | |
| Landscape architect(s): | |
| House extant: | unconfirmed |
| Historical notes: | |

The *Long Island Society Register, 1929* lists Kiliaen M. and Elizabeth W. Post Van Rensselaer [II] as residing in Woodmere [Hewlett Neck].
   He was the son of Maunsell and Isabella Mason Van Rensselaer, Jr. of *The Haven* in Hewlett Neck.
   Elizabeth West Post Van Rensselaer was the daughter of Waldron Kintzing and Mary Lawrence Post, who resided at *Standhome* in Bayport. [*See* Spinzia, *Long Island's Prominent South Shore Families* – Post entry.]
*[See other Van Rensselaer entries for additional family information.]*

### Van Rensselaer, Maunsell, Jr. (1859-1952)

| | |
|---|---|
| Occupation(s): | |
| Marriage(s): | 1884-1952 – Isabella Mason (1861-1955) |
| Address: | Philips Lane, Hewlett Neck |
| Name of estate: | *The Haven* |
| Year of construction: | |
| Style of architecture: | |
| Architect(s): | |
| Landscape architect(s): | |
| House extant: unconfirmed | |
| Historical notes: | |

The *Long Island Society Register, 1929* lists Maunsell and Isabella Mason Van Rensselaer [Jr.] as residing at *The Haven* on Philips Lane, Woodmere [Hewlett Neck].

He was the son of The Reverend Manunsell and Mrs. Sarah Ann Taylor Van Rensselaer, Sr.

Isabella Mason Van Rensselaer was the daughter of The Reverend Arthur Mason.

Maunsell and Isabella Mason Van Rensselaer, Jr.'s son Bernard, who resided in Hewlett Bay Park, married Rose Carolina Tillotson and, subsequently, Charlotte Mary Southmayd. Their son Alexander married Constance Edith Henwood, the daughter of The Reverend William Henwood of Yorkshire, England. Their son Arthur, who contracted infantile paralysis while serving on the Mexican border in 1916, remained a bachelor. Among Arthur's inventions was a three wheel-electric automobile which was controlled entirely by hand. President Franklin Delano Roosevelt purchased one of his automobiles for his private use. Their daughter Maude did not marry. Their son Kiliaen, who resided in Hewlett Neck and later in Albuquerque, NM, married Elizabeth West Post.

*[See other Van Rensselaer entries for additional family information.]*


### Van Siclen, George West (1896-1958)

| | |
|---|---|
| Occupation(s): | capitalist - partner, Hersch & Van Siclen (importing firm) |
| Marriage(s): | 1917-1958 – Mary Irving Francke (1897-1978) |
| | - capitalist - founder and president, Tapin & Tew (secretarial service) |
| Address: | 49 Neptune Avenue, Woodsburgh |
| Name of estate: | |
| Year of construction: | 1916 |
| Style of architecture: | Modified Cape Cod |
| Architect(s): | |
| Landscape architect(s): | |
| House extant: yes | |
| Historical notes: | |

The *Long Island Society Register, 1929* lists George West and Mary Irving Francke Van Siclen as residing at 49 Neptune Avenue, Woodmere [Woodsburgh].

He was the son of Arthur James and Florence Benton Horsman Van Siclen.

Mary Irving Francke Van Siclen was the daughter of Leopold Hernandez and Elise Irving Huntington Francke of Lawrence. Her sister Eleanor married Joseph Gould Remick and resided in Woodmere.

George West and Mary Irving Francke Van Siclen's daughter Elise married William Arthur Boeger, Jr. of Flushing, Queens, and resided in New Canaan, CT.

Van Siclen died as a result of a fall from the window of his fifth-floor room in Doctor's Hospital. [*The New York Times* March 24, 1958, p. 52.]

*front facade, 2000*

### Van Tine, Addison Allen (1886-1953)

| | |
|---|---|
| Occupation(s): | attorney - member, O'Gormath, Battle, and Vandiver, NYC |
| Marriage(s): | 1921-1953 – Elizabeth Janes Gunn (1895-1971)<br>- writer - poetry |
| Address: | Woodside Drive, Hewlett Bay Park |
| Name of estate: | |
| Year of construction: | |
| Style of architecture: | |
| Architect(s): | |
| Landscape architect(s): | |
| House extant: unconfirmed | |
| Historical notes: | |

The *Long Island Society Register, 1929* lists Addison A. and Elizabeth J. Gunn Van Tine as residing in Woodmere [Hewlett Bay Park].
He was the son of Thomas Hartwell and Adelaide Allen Van Tine, Jr.
Elizabeth Janes Gunn Van Tine was the daughter of James Newton Gunn. Her sister Eleanor married the noted architect William O'Connor, Sr. and resided in Syosset. [*See* Spinzia, *Long Island's Prominent North Shore Families, vol. II* – O'Connor entry.]
Addison Allen and Elizabeth Janes Gunn Van Tine's daughter Priscilla married Harold Koutze, Jr. of Denver, CO. Their daughter Allen married Eyre Davis Gaillard, the son of William E. G. Gaillard, and resided in Delmar, NY. Their daughter Joy married Allison Buel Hart, the son of Donald Hart, and resided in Bernardsville, NJ.

### Van Vranken, Dr. Garrett Daniel (1841-1901)

| | |
|---|---|
| Occupation(s): | veterinarian<br>financier - director, Hempstead Bank; |
| Civic Activism: | trustee, Hempstead Methodist Church;<br>president, Queens County Sunday School Association, 1883 |
| Marriage(s): | 1877-1901 – Hannah Kellum (1844-1915) |
| Address: | Fulton Avenue and Rockaway Road, Hempstead |
| Name of estate: | |
| Year of construction: | |
| Style of architecture: | Colonial Revival |
| Architect(s): | |
| Landscape architect(s): | |
| House extant: unconfirmed | |
| Historical notes: | |

*front facade, 1920*

The house was built by Dr. Garrett Daniel Van Vranken. The seventy-five-acre estate was situated on the corner of Fulton Avenue and Rockaway Road. It extended north on the east side of Rockaway Road to First Street.
Hannah Kellum Van Vranken was the daughter of John and Hannah Raynor Kellum of Hempstead. Kellum was the architect engaged by Alexander Turney Stewart to plan Garden City.
The estate was inherited by the Van Vrankens' son John Kellum Van Vranken, Sr., who sold it in 1920.
*[See the following entry for additional family information.]*

### Van Vranken, John Kellum, Sr. (1880-1951)

| | |
|---|---|
| Occupation(s): | attorney |
| | financier - vice-president and director, Hempstead Bank; insurance broker |
| | capitalist - real estate |
| Marriage(s): | M/1 – 1912-1939 – Marjorie Chapin (1884-1939) |
| | M/2 – 1943-1951 – Isobel Beckwith (1900-1983) |
| Address: | 89 Tenth Street, Garden City |
| Name of estate: | |
| Year of construction: | 1898 |
| Style of architecture: | Neo-Federal |
| Architect(s): | |
| Landscape architect(s): | |
| House extant: yes | |
| Historical notes: | |

*front facade, 2005*

The house was built by Frederick P. Morris.

The *Long Island Society Register, 1929* lists John K. and Marjorie Chapin Van Vranken [Sr.] as residing on Rockaway Road, Hempstead. The 1930 Census lists John K. and Marjorie C. Van Vranken as residing at 89 Tenth Street, Garden City.

She was the daughter of Albert King and Emily Antoinette Schenck Chapin of Brooklyn and Lakeville, CT.

John Kellum and Marjorie Chapin Van Vranken, Sr.'s daughter Jean married David Austin Comstock, the son of Dr. George Comstock of Rockville Centre, and resided in Wilton, CT. Their son John Kellum Van Vranken, Jr., who also resided in Wilton, CT, married Theodora DeVinne Goldsmith, the daughter of Ellsworth H. Goldsmith of Manhattan.

Isobel Beckwith Van Vranken had previously been married to Watson Ranney Monroe.

*[See previous entry for additional family information.]*


### Van Zandt, Frederick Neville (1876-1954)

| | |
|---|---|
| Occupation(s): | attorney - corporation attorney, American Tobacco Co.; corporation attorney, General Electric |
| Civic Activism: | president, Nassau County Bar Association |
| Marriage(s): | Mary T. *[unable to determine maiden name]* (1880-1959) |
| Address: | 117 Kensington Road, Garden City |
| Name of estate: | |
| Year of construction: | 1923 |
| Style of architecture: | Dutch Colonial Revival |
| Architect(s): | |
| Landscape architect(s): | |
| House extant: yes | |
| Historical notes: | |

The *Long Island Society Register, 1929* lists Frederick N. Van Zandt as residing at 117 Kensington Road, Garden City.

*front facade, 2001*

### Varlet, Viscount René Georges (b. 1904)

| | |
|---|---|
| Occupation(s): | nobility - Viscount de Kergoet of Brittany, France |
| | financier - stockbroker* |
| Marriage(s): | M/1 – 1926-div. 1934 – Mildred Gautier Rice (1891-1971) |
| | - nobility |
| | M/2 – Hollis Nelson |
| | M/3 – 1938 – Barbara Douglas (b. 1911) |
| Address: | 944 East Broadway, Hewlett Neck |
| Name of estate: | |
| Year of construction: | |
| Style of architecture: | |
| Architect(s): | |
| Landscape architect(s): | |
| House extant: | no |
| Historical notes: | |

The *Long Island Society Register, 1929* lists René G. and Mildred G. Rice Newton Varlet as residing at 944 East Broadway, Woodmere [Hewlett Neck].

She was the daughter of William Low and Elsie Gautier French Rice of Cleveland, OH. William Low Rice was murdered by an unidentified assailant. [*The New York Times* August 30, 1910, p. 1.] Mildred had previously been married to Richard Heber Newton, Jr. of *Box Farm* in Water Mill. After her divorce from Varlet, she married John Oakley Radway and, subsequently, Francesco A. Zara of Hewlett Bay Park and Southampton. [*See* Spinzia, *Long Island's Prominent Families in the Town of Southampton* – Newton and Zara entries.]

Barbara Douglas Varlet was the daughter of Ernest Douglas of Pebble Beach, CA.

*During the Depression, Varlet was unable to find employment as a stockbroker. He relocated to Pasadena, CA, where he became the butler for James Darsie, the set dresser for the motion picture "Robin Hood," and the manager of the La Quinta Resort and Club in La Quinta, CA. [*The New York Times* May 25, 1935, p. A3; *Chico Record* October 3, 1927, pp. 1 and 3; and *Los Angeles Daily News* November 4, 1935, p. 15.]

### Vaughan, Donald Cuyler, Sr. (1884-1959)

| | |
|---|---|
| Occupation(s): | merchant - advertising manager, Brooks Brothers (clothing store chain); |
| | general manager, Mitchell Kennerley (rare book store) |
| | journalist - editor-in-chief, Nassau Literary Magazine |
| | publisher - partner, D. Appleton & Co. |
| Civic Activism: | trustee, New York Society Library; |
| | a founder, American Badminton Association |
| Marriage(s): | 1909-1959 – Ethel Thorne Parsons (b. 1885) |
| Address: | 48 Hilton Avenue, Garden City |
| Name of estate: | |
| Year of construction: | 1873 |
| Style of architecture: | Victorian |
| Architect(s): | |
| Landscape architect(s): | |
| House extant: | yes |
| Historical notes: | |

*front facade, 2006*

The *Brooklyn Blue Book and Long Island Society Register, 1922* lists Donald Cuyler and Ethel Thorne Parsons Vaughan [Sr.] as residing at 48 Hilton Avenue, Garden City.

He was the son of Arthur C. and Ida Morrison Kimball Vaughan.

Ethel Thorne Parsons Vaughan was the daughter of Albert Rosse and Alice Schuyler Van Ness Parsons, Sr. Ethel's brother Argyll married Eleanor Hartshorn Peters, the daughter of Ralph and Eleanor Hartshorn Goodman Peters, Sr. of *Wynymeede*, and resided in Garden City.

Donald Cuyler and Ethel Thorne Parsons Vaughan, Sr.'s son Donald Cuyler Vaughan, Jr. married Rachel Lacy, the daughter of Frank R. Lacy of Dubuque, IA, and, subsequently, Elizabeth Danforth.

## Veeder, Francis Lansing (1905-1973)

Occupation(s): financier - stockbroker

Marriage(s): 1932-1973 – Iris Sellar (c. 1909-1983)

Address: 1147 East Broadway, Hewlett Neck
Name of estate:
Year of construction:
Style of architecture:
Architect(s):
Landscape architect(s):
House extant: no
Historical notes:

The *Social Register New York, 1933* lists Francis L. and Iris Sellar Veeder as residing at 1147 East Broadway, Hewlett [Hewlett Neck].

He was the son of George Lansing and Grace Dorothea Thralls Coleman. After his father's death, his mother married Paul Lansing Veeder with whom she resided at *Meadowwood* in Hewlett Bay Park.

Iris Sellar Veeder was the daughter of Norrie and Sybil Katherine Sherman Sellar, Sr. of Hewlett Harbor.

Francis Lansing and Iris Sellar Veeder's daughter Georgette married Edward Collins Hinchliff, Jr.; Peter Ogden Kilbourn, the son of Orrin P. Kilbourn of West Hartford, CT; and, subsequently, ____ Richards.

*[See following entry for additional family information.]*


## Veeder, Paul Lansing (1884-1942)

Occupation(s): industrialist - a founder and vice-president, Boyce Motor Meter Co. (manufacturer of dashboard gauges for automobiles);
treasurer, Boyce–Veeder Corp., Long Island City (manufacturer of fire extinguishers)
attorney

Marriage(s): Grace Dorothea Thralls (1885-1966)

Address: 1261 Veeder Drive, Hewlett Bay Park
Name of estate: *Meadowwood*
Year of construction: c. 1908
Style of architecture: Modified Mediterranean
Architect(s): Albro & Lindeberg designed the house (for Carleton Macy)
Landscape architect(s):
House extant: unconfirmed
Historical notes:

*side / front facade*

The house, originally named *Meadowwood*, was built by Carleton Macy. It was purchased from Macy for $70,000 in 1918 by Veeder, who continued to call it *Meadowwood*.

The *Long Island Society Register, 1929* lists Paul Lansing and Grace Thralls Coleman Veeder as residing at *Meadowwood* in Hewlett [Hewlett Bay Park].

He was the son of Albert Henry and Helen Lovett Duryee Veeder.

Grace Dorothea Thralls was the daughter of Marion and Amanda Thralls. Grace had previously been married to George Lansing Coleman. Their son Francis, who was adopted by Paul Lansing Veeder, married Iris Sellar and resided in Hewlett Neck.

Paul Lansing and Grace Dorothea Thralls Veeder's daughter Dorothea married Maurice M. Condon and, subsequently, Lawrence J. Kelly, the son of Dr. Aquin S. and Marie O'Donnell Kelly of Lawrence.

*[See previous entry for additional family information.]*

## Veitch, Charles Whitely (1874-1948)

Occupation(s): capitalist - secretary and treasurer, Texas Pacific Railroad

Marriage(s): Emily *[unable to determine maiden name]* (b. 1880)

Address: 146 Wellington Road, Garden City
Name of estate:
Year of construction: 1918
Style of architecture: Colonial Revival
Architect(s):
Landscape architect(s):
House extant: yes
Historical notes:

The *Long Island Society Register, 1929* lists Mr. and Mrs. Charles W. Veitch as residing at 146 Wellington Road, Garden City.

*front facade, 2001*

## Voege, Harry William (1878-1952)

Occupation(s): merchant - Herman Kornahrens, Inc., NYC (wholesale housewares firm)

Marriage(s): Ida Lauman (b. 1881)

Address: 113 Stratford Avenue, Garden City
Name of estate:
Year of construction: 1923
Style of architecture: Colonial Revival
Architect(s):
Landscape architect(s):
House extant: yes
Historical notes:

Harry William and Ida Lauman Voege's daughter Anna married John J. Tunmore, the son of John Septimus and Harriet Gibbons Tunmore of Garden City.

At the time of his death, Harry William Voege was residing at 113 Stratford Avenue, Garden City. [*The New York Times* January 25, 1952, p. 21.]

*front facade, 2001*

### Vogel, Henry John (1848-1907)

| | |
|---|---|
| Occupation(s): | financier - trustee, Williamsburg Dime Savings Bank (later, The Dime Savings Bank of Brooklyn) |
| | industrialist - partner, William Vogel & Brothers, Brooklyn (tin plate manufacturer) |
| | capitalist - large real estate holdings in Brooklyn and Long Island |
| Civic Activism: | trustee, Eastern District Hospital; |
| | trustee, Brooklyn Bureau of Charities; |
| | vice-president, Manufacturers Association of New York; |
| | established fresh air home on Henry Street in Hempstead enabling poor children and aged to spend two weeks in the country, 1901; |
| | established fresh air home in Jamesport for children, 1904 |
| Marriage(s): | 1871-1907 – Emilie Sherwood (1851-1927) |
| | - Civic Activism: member, board of managers, Methodist Home for Aged, Brooklyn; |
| | vice-president, northern branch, Brooklyn Bureau of Charities |
| Address: | Fulton Avenue, East Meadow |
| Name of estate: | |
| Year of construction: | 1895 |
| Style of architecture: | Queen Anne |
| Architect(s): | |
| Landscape architect(s): | |
| Builder: | George B. Collyer |
| House extant: unconfirmed | |
| Historical notes: | |

The house was built by Henry John Vogel. [*Brooklyn Times Union* January 25, 1895, p. 8.]

He was the son of John and Catherine Vogel of Brooklyn.

Henry John and Emilie Sherwood Vogel's daughter Maria married Harry M. Edwards. Their daughter Irma married Herbert Jackson Braham. In 1888, their son Harry died at the age of twelve.

### Voss, William (1845-1928)

| | |
|---|---|
| Occupation(s): | financier - stockbroker |
| Civic Activism: | a founder and treasurer, Rockaway Hunting Club, Lawrence |
| Marriage(s): | Caroline Kane Neilson (1854-1941) |
| Address: | Pleasant Place, Hewlett Bay Park |
| Name of estate: | *Merriefield* |
| Year of construction: | |
| Style of architecture: | Colonial Revival with Long Island Farmhouse elements |
| Architect(s): | |
| Landscape architect(s): | |
| House extant: unconfirmed | |
| Historical notes: | |

*front facade*

The *Social Register Summer, 1910* and the *Long Island Society Register, 1929* list William and Caroline Kane Neilson Voss as residing at *Merriefield* in Hewlett [Hewlett Bay Park].

He was the son of Benjamin Franklin and Elizabeth Hobson Voss.

Caroline Kane Neilson Voss was the daughter of William Hude and Caroline Kane Neilson of Far Rockaway. Her sister Rosalie married Samuel Parker Hinckley and resided at *Sunset Hall* in Lawrence. Her sister Emilie married Middleton Schoolbred Burrill and resided at *Jericho Farms* in Jericho. [*See* Spinzia, *Long Island's Prominent North Shore Families, vol. I* – Burrill entry.]

William and Caroline Kane Neilson Voss' son William Hude Neilson Voss married Alice Marston McKim and resided at *Bannister Cottage* in Lawrence. Their son, the noted artist Franklin Brooke Voss, resided at *Merriefield Farm* in Monkton, MD. Their son Edward married the sculptress Elsa Horne. Their daughter Jessie, who was also an artist specializing in portraiture, married Henry Llewellyn Daingerfield, Jr.

The house was subsequently owned by Voss's daughter Jessie and son-in-law Henry Llewellyn Daingerfield, Jr., who continued to call it *Merriefield*.

*[See following entry for additional family information.]*

### Voss, William Hude Neilson (1875-1937)

Occupation(s): capitalist - real estate developer

Marriage(s): 1902-1937 – Alice Marston McKim (1876-1953)

Address: Waverly Avenue, Hewlett Harbor
Name of estate:
Year of construction:
Style of architecture:
Architect(s):
Landscape architect(s):
House extant: unconfirmed
Historical notes:

The *Long Island Society Register, 1929* lists W. H. Neilson and Alice M. McKim Voss as residing at *Bannister Cottage* in Lawrence.

He was the son of William and Caroline Kane Neilson Voss, who resided at *Merriefield* in Hewlett Bay Park.

Alice Marston McKim Voss was the daughter of The Reverend Haslett McKim of Manhattan.

William Hude Neilson and Alice Marston McKim Voss' daughter Alice married Robert Edward Lee Lewis, Jr., a descendant of George Washington's sister Betty who had married Fielding Lewis.

At the time of his death, Voss was residing on Waverly Avenue, Hewlett Harbor.

*[See previous entry for additional family information.]*


### Waddell, Wallace MacNab, Sr. (1885-1927)

Occupation(s): financier - member, O. J. Brand and Co. (stock brokerage firm); member, Frazier, Jelke, and Co. (stock brokerage firm)

Marriage(s): 1910-1927 – Marjorie Turnbull (1886-1957)

Address: 131 Nassau Boulevard, Garden City
Name of estate:
Year of construction: 1925
Style of architecture: Neo-Tudor
Architect(s):
Landscape architect(s):
House extant: yes
Historical notes:

The house was built by Wallace MacNab Waddell, Sr.

The *Long Island Society Register, 1929* lists Marjorie Turnbull Waddell as residing at 131 Nassau Boulevard, Garden City.

He was the son of Henry Alexander and Catherine Maria Joselin Waddell of New York.

Marjorie Turnbull Waddell was the daughter of John Gourlay and Josephine Sherwood Turnbull, Sr. of Garden City and *The Pines* in Brightwaters. [*See* Spinzia, *Long Island's Prominent South Shore Families* – Turnbull entry.] Marjorie's brother John Gourlay Turnbull, Jr. married Harriette Boden Hutchinson and resided in Garden City.

Wallace MacNab and Marjorie Turnbull Waddell, Sr.'s daughter Doris married Frank Earle Toors, Jr. of Brooklyn.

*front facade, 2001*

### Wainwright, Loudon Snowden, Sr. (1898-1942)

| | |
|---|---|
| Occupation(s): | financier - partner, Wainwright & Page, Inc. (insurance firm) |
| Marriage(s): | 1923-1942 – Eleanor Painter Sloan (1903-1985) |
| | - Civic Activism: director and secretary, Five Towns Women's Exchange |
| Address: | Georges Creek and Adams Lane, Hewlett Neck |

Name of estate:
Year of construction:
Style of architecture:
Architect(s):
Landscape architect(s):
House extant: unconfirmed
Historical notes:

 The *Long Island Society Register, 1929* lists Loudon S. and Eleanor P. Sloan Wainwright [Sr.] as residing in Woodmere [Hewlett Neck]. The 1930 Census lists the Wainwrights at this address.

 He was the son of Stuyvesant and Caroline Smith Snowden Wainwright, Sr. of Rye, NY. Caroline subsequently married Dr. Carl F. Wolff and resided at *Shadowmere* in East Hampton. Loudon's brother Carroll, who resided at *Gullcrest* in East Hampton, married Edith Gould, an heir to the Gould fortune and the daughter of George Gould. [*See* Spinzia, *Long Island's Prominent Families in the Town of East Hampton* – Wainwright and Wolff.] His brother Stuyvesant Wainwright, Jr. married Louise Flinn and resided in Bay Shore and Hampton Bays. [*See* Spinzia, *Long Island's Prominent Families in the Town of Southampton* – Wainwright entry.] Their grandfather Archibald Loudon Snowden was the director of the United States Mint in Philadelphia, PA.

 Eleanor Painter Sloan Wainwright was the daughter of Burrows and Eleanor Painter Sloan, who resided at *Orchard Hill* in Ardmore, PA.

 Louden Snowden and Eleanor Painter Sloan Wainwright, Sr.'s son Louden Snowden Wainwright, Jr. married Martha H. Taylor, the daughter of Walter H. Taylor of Atlanta, GA, and resided in Manhattan.


### Wallace, Edward Secomb (1897-1964)

| | |
|---|---|
| Occupation(s): | educator - Pan American University, Edinburgh, TX; Northeastern University, Boston MA; South Kent School, South Kent, CT |
| | writer - *Monterey's Forgotten Hero*; *The Story of the U. S. Cavalry*; *The Great Reconnaissance*; *Destiny and Glory*, 1957; numerous articles in historical journals |
| Marriage(s): | M/1 – 1925-div. – Elsie Dow (d. 1968) |
| | M/2 – Elizabeth Alden (1903-1995) |
| | - merchant - manager, The Personal Book, Cambridge, MA; manager, Olde Corner Store, Cambridge, MA |
| Address: | 1039 East Broadway, Hewlett Neck |

Name of estate:
Year of construction:
Style of architecture:
Architect(s):
Landscape architect(s):
House extant: no
Historical notes:

 The *Long Island Society Register, 1929* lists Edward S. and Elsie Dow Wallace as residing at 1039 East Broadway, Woodmere [Hewlett Neck].

 He was the son of Frederick William and Grace Mary Secomb Wallace of Manhattan.

 Elsie Dow Wallace was the daughter of Richard S. Dow of Boston, MA.

 Edward Secomb and Elsie Dow Wallace's daughter Sarah married Manfred L. Kreiner, the son of Erwin Kreiner of Graz, Austria, and resided in Manhattan. Their son Hugh married Phyllis Stothert.

 Elizabeth Alden Wallace was the daughter of John and Alice M. Nichols Alden. Elizabeth had previously been married to Allen Kazlett Bucknell and Roy Kenneth Hack. After Edward's death, she married Nathan Tufts.

### Walsh, James William, Jr. (1852-1908)

Occupation(s): financier - partner, Walsh and Floyd (stock brokerage firm)

Marriage(s): 1882-1908 – Susan Newbold Lawrence (1856-1923)

Address: Broadway, Lawrence
Name of estate:
Year of construction:
Style of architecture:
Architect(s):
Landscape architect(s):
House extant: unconfirmed
Historical notes:

The 1900 Census lists the Walshes at this address.
Susan Newbold Lawrence Walsh was the daughter of George Newbold and Anna Hough Trotter Lawrence.
James William and Susan Newbold Lawrence Walsh, Jr.'s daughter Margaret married John Augustus Barnard, the son of Horace and Louisa Zerega Barnard of Manhattan, and resided at *Tigh-na-Curach* in Lawrence. Their son James William Walsh III married Dorothy Baldwin and resided in Lawrence.
*[See following entry for additional family information.]*


### Walsh, James William, III (1887-1958)

Occupation(s):

Marriage(s): div. 1933 – Dorothy Baldwin (1888-1981)
- Civic Activism: member, New York unit in France, American Red Cross, during World War I

Address: 96 Bannister Lane, Lawrence
Name of estate:
Year of construction: 1888
Style of architecture: Victorian
Architect(s):
Landscape architect(s):
House extant: yes
Historical notes:

The *Long Island Society Register, 1929* lists James W. and Dorothy Baldwin Walsh [III] as residing on Bannister Lane, Lawrence. The 1930 Census lists the Walshes at this address.
He was the son of James William and Susan Newbold Lawrence Walsh, Jr., who resided in Lawrence.
Dorothy Baldwin Walsh was the daughter of William Mood and Lydia Perry Cowl Baldwin of *Seven Acres* in Garden City. Dorothy had previously been married to Dr. Edgar Lorrington Gilcreest of California. After her divorce from James, she married Thomas Buel, the son of Clarence Clough and Alice Snow Buel.
James William and Dorothy Baldwin Walsh III's son James William Walsh IV married Madeleine Curtis, the daughter of Eliot Curtis of Manhattan.
*[See previous entry for additional family information.]*
In 1998, the 4,378-square-foot house sold for $825,000.
In 2004 the house was remodeled.

*side facade, 2004*

## Ward, Rodney Allen (1862-1925)

| | |
|---|---|
| Occupation(s): | financier - a founder, Holland Trust Co. |
| | capitalist - a founder and director, Worcester Salt Co. |
| | industrialist - president, Maltine Manufacturing Co., Brooklyn |
| Civic Activism: | a founder, Crescent Athletic Club; |
| | a founder, Brooklyn Riding and Driving Club |
| Marriage(s): | 1886-1925 – Harriette Jane Woodruff (1866-1937) |
| Address: | 91 Cathedral Avenue, Hempstead |
| Name of estate: | |
| Year of construction: | |
| Style of architecture: | |
| Architect(s): | |
| Landscape architect(s): | |
| House extant: no | |
| Historical notes: | |

The *Long Island Society Register, 1929* lists Mrs. Harriette Woodruff Ward as residing at 91 Cathedral Avenue, Hempstead, and at *Snug Harbor* in Westhampton [Westhampton Beach].

She was the daughter of John and Harriet Jane Lester Woodruff of New Haven, CT. Harriette's brother Timothy, who served as New York State Lieutenant Governor, resided in Garden City.

Rodney Allen Ward was the son of Rodney C. and Anna Allen Ward.

Rodney Allen and Harriette Woodruff Ward's son Hugh married Margaret Bradshaw Alling, the daughter of Wilbur Merwin and Winifred Estelle Cowles Alling of Westhampton Beach. Their daughter Josephine married Bogert Greenwood Southack, the son of Frank Tilden Southack of Manhattan, and, subsequently, Perry David Bogue, the son of Morton David Bogue. Their daughter Dorothy remained unmarried. Their daughter Anne married Joseph H. Parsons.

[*See* Spinzia, *Long Island's Prominent Families in the Town of Southampton* – Alling and Ward entries.]

## Ward, Sylvanus Dwight (1880-1971)

| | |
|---|---|
| Occupation(s): | attorney - member, Steward and Bisbee, 1911-1914; |
| | legal assistant to Judge Townsend Scudder II*; |
| | judge - Appellate Division, New York State Supreme Court, 1928-1936; |
| | partner, Ward and Palzer |
| | capitalist - director, Westbury Holding Co. |
| Civic Activism: | a founder, Central New York Music Festival, Syracuse, NY |
| Marriage(s): | 1912-1964 – Mary Ellen Sedgwick (1879-1964) |
| Address: | 146 Nassau Boulevard, Garden City |
| Name of estate: | |
| Year of construction: | 1937 |
| Style of architecture: | Colonial Revival |
| Architect(s): | |
| Landscape architect(s): | |

Nassau County Museum Collection has six uncatalogued photographs of the house.

House extant: yes
Historical notes:

*front facade, 2001*

The *Long Island Society Register, 1929* lists Mr. and Mrs. S. Dwight Ward as residing on Kilburn Road, Garden City. By 1938 they had relocated to Nassau Boulevard, Garden City.

He was the son of Thomas and Katharine Ward of London, England.

Mary Ellen Sedgwick Ward was the daughter of Charles Hamilton and Marcia Antoinette Fenton Sedgwick and a direct descendant of General Robert Sedgwick, a founder of Boston, MA. Mary had previously been married to James H. Gould of Flushing.

Sylvanus Dwight and Mary Ellen Sedgwick Ward's son Thomas married Janet Movius Sicard, the daughter of George Hallum and Katharine Burrell Sicard of Buffalo and Utica, NY. Their daughter Sylvia married John Francis Juraschek, the son of Francis and Laura Juraschek. Their daughter Margery married Ernest S. Newell. Their daughter Nan married Charles Lediard Ward, the son of David S. and Helene L. Ward.

*[*See* Spinzia, *Long Island's Prominent North Shore Families, vol. II* – Scudder entry.]

In 2016, the 4,181-square-foot house sold for $1.4 million.

## Ward–Smith, Kenneth, Sr. (1881-1940)
### aka Kenneth Ward Smith

| | |
|---|---|
| Occupation(s): | financier - treasurer, Guaranty Company; |
| | partner, Lindley and Company (stock brokerage firm); |
| | partner, E. H. H. Simmons and Company (stock brokerage firm); |
| | member, McKay and Co. (stock brokerage firm) |
| | capitalist - assistant treasurer and assistant secretary, Southern Bell Telephone Co. |
| Marriage(s): | 1907-1940 – Elizabeth Dallas (1885-1946) |
| Address: | 105 Newmarket Road, Garden City |
| Name of estate: | |
| Year of construction: | 1922 |
| Style of architecture: | Neo-Tudor |
| Architect(s): | |
| Landscape architect(s): | |

Nassau County Museum Collection has six uncatalogued photographs of the house.
House extant: yes
Historical notes:

The *Long Island Society Register, 1929* lists Mr. Kenneth Ward–Smith [Sr.] as residing on Newmarket Street, Garden City.
He was the son of Robert McPhall and Letitia Trimble Smith of Tennessee.
Elizabeth Dallas Ward–Smith was the daughter of Trevanion Barlow and Ida Bonner Dallas of Nashville, TN.
Kenneth and Elizabeth Dallas Ward–Smith, Sr.'s daughter Lilias married Orville Wilbur Prescott, Jr. of New York. Their son Kenneth Ward–Smith, Jr. married Mildred Harris of Nashville, TN.
In 1999, the 2,400-square-foot house sold for $680,000.

*front facade*

### Warren, Charles Elliott, Sr. (1864-1945)

| | |
|---|---|
| Occupation(s): | financier - president, Lincoln National Bank, 1910-1920 (later, Irving Trust Co.); vice-president and chairman of board, Irving Trust Co. |
| | military - general, New York National Guard |
| | capitalist - president, Erie & Kalamazoo Railroad Co.; president, Lake Shore & Michigan Southern Railroad Co.; treasurer and director, Eastern Power Co. |
| | industrialist - president, Nestor Manufacturing Co. |
| Civic Activism: | treasurer and director, Lutheran Cemetery, NY; vice-governor, War Credits Board, 1917-1918; trustee, Village of Hewlett Neck; president, New York State Bankers Association, 1915-1916; member, Military and Naval Aviation Committee, Aero Club of America, 1916; treasurer, Duryea War Relief, 1918 |
| Marriage(s): | 1892-1945 – Anna Margaret Geissenhainer (1867-1953) |
| Address: | Hewlett Neck Road, Hewlett Neck |
| Name of estate: | *Still Pond* |
| Year of construction: | |
| Style of architecture: | |
| Architect(s): | |
| Landscape architect(s): | |
| House extant: | unconfirmed |
| Historical notes: | |

    The *Long Island Society Register, 1929* lists Charles Elliott and Anna Margaret Geissenhainer Warren [Sr.] as residing at *Still Pond* in Hewlett [Hewlett Neck].
    He was the son of Dr. George William and Mrs. Mary Elizabeth Pease Warren of Manhattan.
    Anna Margaret Geissenhainer Warren was the daughter of New Jersey Congressman J. A. Geissenhainer.
    Charles Elliott and Anna Margaret Geissenhainer Warren, Sr.'s daughter Margaret married Shannon Lord Meany and resided in Hewlett Bay Park. Margaret subsequently married Daniel Aylesbury Finlayson, Jr. with whom she resided in Hewlett Bay Park. Their daughter Susanne married Herman Stump Murray and resided at *Our House* in Woodmere. Their son Charles Elliott Warren, Jr. married Jean W. Murray and, subsequently, Susan Dunscombe.

**Warren, Northam, Sr. (1878-1962)**

| | |
|---|---|
| Occupation(s): | industrialist - secretary to William M. Warren and, later, member, import export division, Parke, Davis & Co. (pharmaceutical manufacturing firm); |
| | founder, Northam Warren's Special Products Co. (later, Northam Warren Corp, NYC (manufacturer of Phoebe Snow, Cutex, Dr. J. Parker Pray's, Elcaya Face Creams, Glazo Polishes, Peggy Sage, and Odo-Ro-No lines of beauty and personal care items; |
| | sole supplier of electrical conductors for United States aircraft during World War II*; |
| | produced anodized metal for aircraft during World War II; |
| | produced Sniff Kits to train personnel in the smell of dangerous chemicals during World War II |
| Civic Activism: | governor, South Side Yacht Club (later, Sayville Yacht Club); |
| | governor, Sayville Yacht Club; |
| | governor, Sayville Golf Club; |
| | Sayville chairman, Japan Relief Committee, South Suffolk chapter, American Red Cross, 1923 |
| Marriage(s): | Edna Louise O'Brien (1882-1962) |
| | - Civic Activism: trustee, Sayville Garden Club |
| Address: | Cherry Valley Road, Garden City |
| Name of estate: | |
| Year of construction: | c. 1934 |
| Style of architecture: | |
| Architect(s): | |
| Landscape architect(s): | |
| House extant: unconfirmed | |
| Historical notes: | |

The house was built by Northam Warren, Sr.

The *Long Island Society Register, 1929* lists Northam and Edna Louise O'Brien Warren [Sr.] as residing in Garden City.

He was the son of The Reverend Leroy and Mrs. Fannie Louise Wadsworth Warren of Kansas.

Edna Louise O'Brien Warren was the daughter of Edward O'Brien of Chicago, IL.

Northam and Edna Louise O'Brien Warren, Sr.'s daughter Agnes married Karl Wilhelm Illigen, the son of Wilhelm Illigen and resided in Harrisburg, PA. Their son Northam Warren, Jr. married Dorothy Calwell of Lawton, OK, and resided in Connecticut.

[For information about Warren's Sayville estate *Sandy Point*, see Spinzia, *Long Island's Prominent South Shore Families* – Warren entry.]

### Weed, Leroy Jefferson (1878-1961)

| | |
|---|---|
| Occupation(s): | educator - history teacher, Mercersburg Academy, Mercersburg, PA, 1901-1903; |
| | publisher - director, Ginn & Co., 1903-1952 |
| | financier - director, Long Island Trust Co., Garden City |
| | politician - member, New York State Assembly, 1911-1914 |
| Civic Activism: | trustee, Union College, Schenectady, NY; |
| | chairman of trustees, Hofstra College, Hempstead (later, Hofstra University)* |
| Marriage(s): | 1906-1947 – Mabel Scott (1880-1947) - physician |
| Address: | 23 Hilton Avenue, Garden City |
| Name of estate: | |
| Year of construction: | |
| Style of architecture: | Four-Square |
| Architect(s): | |
| Landscape architect(s): | |
| House extant: yes | |
| Historical notes: | |

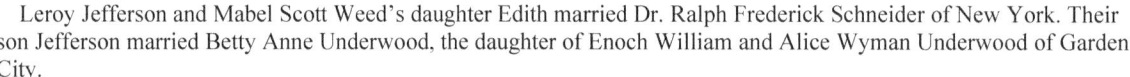

*front facade, 2016*

The 1940 Census lists Leroy J. and Mabel S. Weed as residing at 23 Hilton Avenue, Garden City.

He was the son of Seth R. and Annabelle William Weed of Ithaca, NY.

Mabel Scott Weed was the daughter of John B. Scott.

Leroy Jefferson and Mabel Scott Weed's daughter Edith married Dr. Ralph Frederick Schneider of New York. Their son Jefferson married Betty Anne Underwood, the daughter of Enoch William and Alice Wyman Underwood of Garden City.

In 2016, the 2,464-square-foot house sold for $899,999.

*Hofstra's Leroy J. Weed Hall was named in his honor.

### Weeks, Herbert Augustus (1859-1941)

| | |
|---|---|
| Occupation(s): | capitalist - built railroad line from Port Antonio to Spanish Town on the island of Jamaica; |
| | built first electrical powerhouse in New York City; |
| | built Pratt Chemical Laboratory, Brooklyn |
| Marriage(s): | 1891-1971 – Marjorie Cooper Howe (1868-1948) |
| Address: | Hollywood Crossing, Lawrence |
| Name of estate: | *Meenahga* |
| Year of construction: | |
| Style of architecture: | |
| Architect(s): | |
| Landscape architect(s): | |
| House extant: unconfirmed | |
| Historical notes: | |

The *Long Island Society Register, 1929* lists Herbert A. and Marjorie C. Howe Weeks as residing on Hollywood Crossing in Cedarhurst [Lawrence].

He was the son of Edward A. and Lucy Payne Weeks of Oyster Bay.

Marjorie Cooper Howe Weeks was the daughter of Lindsay Irving and Gertrude Nott Howe.

Herbert Augustus and Marjorie Cooper Howe Weeks' daughter Marjorie married John Henderson Stewart, Jr., the son of John Henderson and Virginia Hay Stewart, Sr., and resided in Lawrence. She subsequently married Dudley Crews and Francis A. Phillips. Their son Dr. Carnes Weeks, who resided in Manhattan, married Margaret Shoemaker, the daughter of Charles Shoemaker of Pittsburgh, PA, and subsequently, Ellen E. Jordan.

### Weeks, Louis Seabury, Sr. (1881-1971)

| | |
|---|---|
| Occupation(s): | architect - designed several buildings worldwide for International Telephone and Telegraph Co.; the Federal Electric Manufacturing Co. plant, Nutley, NJ; and the Drydock Savings Bank, Lexington Avenue and 59th Street, NYC; municipal architect, Village of Lawrence |
| Civic Activism: | trustee, Village of Lawrence |
| Marriage(s): | 1913 – Isabel Elise Coxe (b. 1883) |
| Address: | Auerbach Lane, Lawrence |
| Name of estate: | |
| Year of construction: | |
| Style of architecture: | |
| Architect(s): | |
| Landscape architect(s): | Louise Payson (for L. S. Weeks, Sr.) |
| House extant: unconfirmed | |
| Historical notes: | |

The *Long Island Society Register, 1929* lists Louis S. and Isabel E. Coxe Weeks as residing on Auerbach Lane, Cedarhurst [Lawrence].

He was the son of James and Kezia Seabury Weeks.

Isabel Elise Coxe Weeks was the daughter of Alfred Conklin and Maryette Andrews Doolittle Coxe.

Louis Seabury and Isabel Elise Coxe Weeks' son Howard married Annabel Caner, the daughter of Gerald Wayne Caner of Roxborough, PA, and resided in Syosset. Their son Louis Seabury Weeks, Jr. married Teresa Herring and resided in Lawrence. Their daughter Ann remained unmarried.

At the time of his death, Louis was residing at 264 Albert Place, Lawrence. [*Daily News* February 28, 1971, p. 114.]

*For Weeks' commissions in the Town of Southampton, *see* Architect appendix in Spinzia, *Long Island's Prominent Families in the Town of Southampton*.

### Weisselberg, Allen Howard (b. 1947)

| | |
|---|---|
| Occupation(s): | financier - accountant, Fred Trump's real estate holdings, 1973; CFO, Trump Organization, 2000-2022; manager, with Eric Trump and Donald J. Trump, Jr., Trump Organization, 2017-2022; trustee, Trump Organization; CFO and vice-president, Trump Hotels and Casino Resorts |
| Civic Activism: | trustee and treasurer, Donald J. Trump Foundation |
| Marriage(s): | Hilary S. *[unable to determine maiden name]* (b. 1950) |
| Address: | 1108 McLean Avenue, Wantagh |
| Name of estate: | |
| Year of construction: | 1951 |
| Style of architecture: | Ranch |
| Architect(s): | |
| Landscape architect(s): | |
| House extant: yes | |
| Historical notes: | |

In 2022 Allen pleaded guilty to fifteen felonies.

Allen Howard and Hilary S. Weisselberg's son Jack, who is a loan organization executive at Ladder Capital which loaned money to the Trump Organization, married Erica Devon Zucker, the daughter of Donald and Lynn Zucker of Englewood Cliffs, NJ. Their son Barry manages the Trump Wollman Rink in Manhattan's Central Park. Barry's former wife Jennifer gave Manhattan prosecutors of the Trump Organization boxes filled with family and company financial documents.

In 2013, Allen and his wife sold the house for $468,000 and relocated to the Trump Organization luxury apartment building on the Upper West Side of Manhattan.

*front facade, 2013*

### Weller, Augustus Noble (1836-1901)

| | |
|---|---|
| Occupation(s): | attorney - judge - Queens County Surrogate |
| Civic Activism: | trustee, St. Paul's School, Garden City; |
| | trustee, St. Mary's Cathedral School, Garden City; |
| | president, Nassau County Bar Association, 1899; |
| | member, Committee of Seventy* |
| Marriage(s): | 1873-1888 – Katharine Ward Onderdonk (1852-1888) |
| Address: | 304 Fulton Avenue, Hempstead |
| Name of estate: | |
| Year of construction: | |
| Style of architecture: | |
| Architect(s): | |
| Landscape architect(s): | |
| House extant: | no |
| Historical notes: | |

   Augustus Noble Weller was the son of Benjamin T. Weller of Pittsfield, MA.
   Katharine Ward Onderdonk Weller was the daughter of Henry Moscrop Onderdonk of Hempstead.
   Augustus Noble and Katharine Onderdonk Weller's daughter Katharine married Charles Lambert Addison and resided in Hempstead.
   *The Committee of Seventy was instrumental in disbanding the notorious Tweed Ring.


### Welsh, Joseph Wickes, Jr. (1911-2001)

| | |
|---|---|
| Occupation(s): | financier - vice-president, *Banque Francaise du Commerce Ertereur*, Paris, France; |
| | vice-president, Continental Illinois Bank of Chicago |
| Civic Activism: | governor, Union Club, NYC; |
| | commodore, Cedarhurst Yacht Club; |
| | director, Visiting Nurse Association, Vero Beach, FL |
| Marriage(s): | M/1 – 1946-1974 – Barbara Riker Whipple (1921-1974) |
| | M/1 – 1975-2001 – Mary Ellen Louise Restrepo (1926-2007) |
| Address: | 41 Trinity Place, Hewlett |
| Name of estate: | |
| Year of construction: | 1926 |
| Style of architecture: | Modified Colonial Revival |
| Architect(s): | |
| Landscape architect(s): | |
| House extant: | yes |
| Historical notes: | |

*front facade, 2000*

   The *Social Register Summer, 1959* lists Joseph Wickes and Barbara R. Whipple Welsh, Jr. as residing at 41 Trinity Place, Hewlett.
   He was the son of Joseph Wickes and Dorothy Lehman Kelly Welsh, Sr., who resided in Lawrence.
   Barbara Riker Whipple Welsh was the daughter of Julian Van Ness and Ruth Riker Whipple, who resided at *Rustee Granit* in Hewlett. Barbara's sister Margaret married Stephen Baker Finch, the son of Henry LeRoy Finch of New York City, and resided in Lawrence. New York City's Riker's Island was named for the Riker family.
   Mary Ellen Louise Restrepo Welsh was the daughter of Luciano Restrepo of Columbia. She had previous been married to ____ de Uribe.
   *[See following entry for additional family information.]*

### Welsh, Joseph Wickes, Sr. (1870-1932)

| | |
|---|---|
| Occupation(s): | attorney - partner, Carter, Ledyard, and Milburn, NYC |
| Marriage(s): | 1908-1932 – Dorothy Lehman Kelly (1883-1967) |
| Address: | Bannister Lane, Lawrence |

Name of estate:
Year of construction:
Style of architecture:
Architect(s):
Landscape architect(s):
House extant: unconfirmed
Historical notes:

The *Social Register Summer, 1923* and the *Long Island Society Register, 1929* list Joseph Wickes and Dorothy L. Kelly Welsh [Sr.] as residing in Lawrence.

He was the son of William Henry and Sarah Augusta Wickes Welsh of Charlestown, MA.

Dorothy Lehman Kelly Welsh was the daughter of Philip Frances Kelly of Philadelphia, PA. She subsequently married Theodosius Fowler Stevens, the son of Francis Bowes Stevens.

Joseph Wickes and Dorothy Lehman Kelly Welsh, Sr.'s daughter Carola married Savile Crossley Hardy, the son of John Gardiner Hardy of Quogue, and resided in Manhattan. Their daughter Virginia married Mark Leavenworth Sperry II, the son of Leavenworth Porter Sperry of Waterbury, CT, and resided in Waterbury. Their son Joseph Wickes Welsh, Jr., who resided in Hewlett, married Barbara Riker Whipple and, subsequently, Mary Ellen Louise Restrepo.

*[See previous entry for additional family information.]*


### Welton, Dr. Thurston Scott (1885-1961)

| | |
|---|---|
| Occupation(s): | physician - gynecologist, Williamsburg Hospital, Brooklyn |
| | educator - professor of obstetrics and gynecology, Long Island College of Medicine |
| | publisher - editor, *American Journal of Surgery* |
| | writer - *The Modern Method of Birth Control*, 1935 |
| Civic Activism: | president, Brooklyn Medical Society; |
| | president, Brooklyn Gynecologist Society; |
| | president, Kings County Medical Society |
| Marriage(s): | M/1 – 1912 -1927– Edith Roberts Schultz (d. 1927) |
| | M/2 – 1928-1961 – Margaret Roberts (b. 1901) |
| Address: | 129 Oxford Boulevard, Garden City |

Name of estate:
Year of construction: 1921
Style of architecture: Colonial Revival
Architect(s):
Landscape architect(s):
House extant: yes
Historical notes:

The *Long Island Society Register, 1929* lists Dr. T. S. Welton as residing at 129 Oxford Boulevard, Garden City.

He was the son of Dr. Robert Bradlee and Mrs. Henrietta Louise Phillips Welton.

Dr. Thurston Scott and Mrs. Edith Roberts Schultz Welton's daughter Edith married Dr. Ernest Ellsworth Keet, Jr.

*front facade, 2001*

### Whipple, Dana de Peyster, Sr. (1890-1958)

| | |
|---|---|
| Occupation(s): | real estate agent - member, William A. White & Sons, NYC; member, Bulkley and Horton Co. |
| Marriage(s): | 1918-1958 – Vera Onativia (1889-1972) |
| Address: | 99 East Graham Avenue, Hempstead |
| Name of estate: | |
| Year of construction: | 1922 |
| Style of architecture: | |
| Architect(s): | |
| Landscape architect(s): | |
| House extant: | yes |
| Historical notes: | |

The *Long Island Society Register, 1929* lists Dana de Peyster and Vera Onativia Whipple as residing at 99 Graham Avenue, Hempstead. The 1940 Census lists the Whipples as residing at this address.

He was the son of Napoleon Dana and Roberta Parker Whipple of Flushing and a descendant of William Whipple, a signer of the Declaration of Independence.

Vera Onativia Whipple was the daughter of José Victorio and Georgiana Jones Onativia, Sr. of Manhattan. Her sister Pauline married John Richard Townsend of Newport, RI, and, subsequently, James Henry Alexandre, Sr. who resided in Hempstead. Her brother José Onativia, Jr., who resided at *Cross Roads Cottage* in Millbrook, NY, and in Southampton, married Clara Wright Barclay, Jean Clarisse Coudert, and, subsequently, Marie Adele Montant. [*See* Spinzia, *Long Island's Prominent North Shore Families*, vol. II – Nast entry; *Long Island's Prominent South Shore Families* – deCoppet entry; and *Long Island's Prominent Families in the Town of Southampton* – Onativia entry.]

Dana de Peyster and Vera Onativia Whipple, Sr.'s son Dana de Peyster Whipple, Jr. married Eugenia Jennings, the daughter of Ufford Jennings of Spartanburg, SC. In 1945 he was awarded the Silver Star posthumously.

In 2000, the 1,443-square-foot house sold for $170,000.

*front facade*

### Whipple, Julian Van Ness (1879-1932)

| | |
|---|---|
| Occupation(s): | capitalist - real estate holdings |
| Marriage(s): | 1920-1932 – Ruth Riker (1893-1962) |
| Address: | East Broadway, Hewlett |
| Name of estate: | *Rustee Granit* |

Year of construction:
Style of architecture:
Architect(s):
Landscape architect(s):
House extant: yes
Historical notes:

In 1925, Julian Van Ness Whipple purchased Henry Ives Cobb, Jr.'s stone residence on East Broadway. [*The Brooklyn Daily Eagle* September 10, 1925, p. 15.]

The *Long Island Society Register, 1929* lists Julian Van Ness and Ruth Riker Whipple as residing at *Rustee Granit* in Hewlett.

He was the son of Napoleon Dana and Roberta Parker Whipple and a descendant of William Whipple, a signer of the Declaration of Independence.

Ruth Riker Whipple was a descendant of the family for which Riker's Island was named.

Julian Van Ness and Ruth Riker Whipple's daughter Margaret married Stephen Baker Finch, the son of Henry LeRoy Finch of Manhattan, and resided in Lawrence. Their daughter Barbara married Joseph Wickes Welsh, Jr., the son of Joseph Wickes and Dorothy Lehman Kelly Welsh, Sr. of Lawrence, and resided in Hewlett.


### White, Thomas Francis, Jr. (1882-1945)

| | |
|---|---|
| Occupation(s): | industrialist - president, Andrel Co. (soap manufacturer); vice-president, Products Manufacturing Co. |
| | capitalist - director, Good Homes Realty Co.; president, White Export Co., NYC |
| | financier - director, Peninsula National Bank, Cedarhurst |
| Civic Activism: | director, West Hills Racing Association |
| Marriage(s): | 1916-1945 – Ethel J. Croker (b. 1888) |
| Address: | 65 White's Lane, Lawrence |

Name of estate:
Year of construction:
Style of architecture:
Architect(s):
Landscape architect(s):
House extant: unconfirmed
Historical notes:

Thomas Francis White, Jr. was the son of Thomas Francis and Katherine J. Swift White, Sr. of Lawrence.

Ethel J. Crocker White had previously been married to her riding instructor John J. Breen, with whom she had eloped to Hoboken, NJ, in 1910. After a public and messy divorce, she married White. She was the daughter of Tammany Hall "Boss" Richard Welstead Crocker, Sr. and his wife Elizabeth Frazer Croker. In 1914, Ethel's father Richard married his second wife Beulah Edmonson, a Native-American artist, teacher, lecturer who unsuccessfully ran for Congress in 1934. When Richard gave Beulah power of attorney, he effectively disinherited his children causing them to institute unsuccessful litigation in New York, Florida, and Irish courts slandering Beulah and questioning Richard's competency. At stake was his fortune, a castle in Ireland, and an estate in Palm Beach. The litigation, which lasted from 1923 to 1943, resulted in Beulah filing for bankruptcy in 1937.

Thomas Francis and Ethel J. Croker White, Jr.'s son Thomas Fleetwood White, who was a graduate of LaSalle Military Academy in Oakdale, NY, married Priscilla Adams Bunn, the daughter of William Malcolm Bunn of Cedarhurst.

*[See following entry for additional family information.]*

## White, Thomas Francis, Sr. (1864-1904)

| | |
|---|---|
| Occupation(s): | capitalist - Brooklyn's contractor to remove dead animals, soil, and offal, 1896; |
| | a founder, White Export Co., NYC; |
| | built and rented houses in Lawrence |
| | industrialist - Sanitary Fertilization Co., Barren Island; |
| | Offal Co., Barren Island; |
| | president, P. White & Co., Barren Island, 1896; |
| | partner, with Andrew White, Fertilizing Oil and Guano Co., Barren Island |
| | politician - Brooklyn Police and Excise Commissioner |
| Civic Activism: | member, Brooklyn Board of Education; |
| | member, committee to investigate the establishment of a lighting district, Town of Hempstead, 1897 |
| Marriage(s): | Katherine J. Swift (d. 1930) |
| | - capitalist - rentals* |
| Address: | Between Broadway and Central Avenue, Lawrence |
| Name of estate: | |
| Year of construction: | |
| Style of architecture: | Shingle |
| Architect(s): | |
| Landscape architect(s): | |
| House extant: | unconfirmed |
| Historical notes: | |

Thomas Francis White, Sr. was the son of Patrick White.

Katherine J. Swift White was the daughter of Francis Swift of Lawrence.

Thomas Francis and Katherine J. Swift White, Sr.'s daughter Rosemary married Andrew Clancy Feeney, the son of Patrick Henry and Mary Teresa Flynn Feeney, and resided in Lawrence. Their son Thomas Francis White, Jr. married Ethel J. Crocker and resided in Lawrence. Their daughter Gertrude married Howard Croker.

*[See previous entry for additional family information.]*

*In 1914, Katherine owned thirteen house in Lawrence including *Rosemond Cottage*, *Edgemere*, *Maple Copse*, *Homeland*, and *Hickory Hall*. In 1915, *Hickory Hall* was rented by the German Ambassador to the United States Count Johann Heinrich von Bernstorff. [*See* Raymond E. Spinzia, "The Involvement of Long Islanders in the Events Surrounding German Sabotage in the New York City Metropolitan Area 1914-1917." @ spinzialongislandestates.com.]

*front facade*

## White, Victor Gerald, Sr. (1891-1954)

| | |
|---|---|
| Occupation(s): | artist - portraits and murals* |
| Marriage(s): | Margaret Wood (1893-1960) (aka Margot White) - artist** |
| Address: | 186 Hollywood Crossing, Lawrence |
| Name of estate: | |
| Year of construction: | 1936 |
| Style of architecture: | Colonial Revival |
| Architect(s): | |
| Landscape architect(s): | |
| House extant: | no |
| Historical notes: | |

The *Social Register New York, 1954* lists Victor Gerald and Margaret Wood White [Sr.] as residing at 186 Hollywood Crossing, Cedarhurst [Lawrence].

He was the son of Peter White of Dublin, Ireland.

Margot Wood White was the daughter of Robert Williams and Gertrude Ames Wood, Jr. of Princeton, NJ, and East Hampton. She subsequently married Arthur Ulysses Newton and resided in Lawrence. Margaret's sister Elizabeth married Edward Osgood Bogert and resided in East Hampton. [*See* Spinzia, *Long Island's Prominent Families in the Town of East Hampton* – Bogert and Wood entries.]

Victor Gerald and Margaret Wood White, Sr.'s daughter Christine married Alrick H. Man III of Forest Hills, and resided in Fairfield, CT. Their son William married Virginia Rutter, the daughter of Nathaniel Edward Caldwell and Mary Elizabeth Alexandre Rutter, Sr. of Lawrence. Their son Paul, who resided in Manhattan, married Marie Willer, the daughter of Herman E. Willer of East Orange, NJ, and, subsequently, Arden Kip duBois. Their son Victor married Virginia Elliot, the daughter of Edwin Day Elliot of West Falmouth, MA.

*Victor created the murals in *Three Ponds*, the estate of Victor Morawetz in Woodbury, now the main clubhouse of the Town of Oyster Bay Golf Course. [*See* Spinzia, *Long Island's Prominent North Shore Families, vol. I* – Morawetz entry.] He also painted the murals in the Waldorf–Astoria Hotel; International Telephone and Telegraph buildings in NYC; Grumman Aircraft Corp. in Bethpage; and the Rockville Centre post office.

**Margaret's painting of President Franklin Delano Roosevelt hangs in the Harvard Club in New York City. She also did portraits of Gordon Hoxie, the provost of C. W. Post College of Long Island University, and Truden Thomas, a dean of Hofstra University.

*front facade, 2009*

### Whitlock, Bache McEvers, Jr. (1889-1948)

| | |
|---|---|
| Occupation(s): | financier - partner, Farr and Co. (sugar brokerage firm) |
| Marriage(s): | 1915-1947 – Dorothy Gibb (1889-1947) |
| Address: | Franklin Avenue, Hewlett |
| Name of estate: | *Meadowview* |

Year of construction:
Style of architecture:
Architect(s):
Landscape architect(s):
House extant: unconfirmed
Historical notes:

The *Long Island Society Register, 1929* lists Bache McEvers and Dorothy Gibb Whitlock [Jr.] as residing at *Meadowview* in Hewlett.

He was the son of Bache McEvers and Emily Ogden Simonds Whitlock, Sr. Bache's brother Frederick, who resided in Southampton, married Marion E. de Rham, the daughter of Henry Casimir and Georgina Berryman de Rham of Tuxedo Park, NY, and Newport, RI. [*See* Spinzia, *Long Island's Prominent Families in the Town of Southampton* – Whitlock entry.]

Dorothy Gibb Whitlock was the daughter of John Richmond and Emily Mathews Gibb, Sr. [*See* Spinzia, *Long Island's Prominent North Shore Families, vol. 1*– Arthur Gibb entry.] Dorothy's sister Ruth married Harold Whitfield Carhart of Lattingtown and, later, Harry Messiter Addinsell. [*See* Spinzia, *Long Island's Prominent North Shore Families, vol. 1* – Carhart entry.]

Bache McEvers and Dorothy Gibb Whitlock, Jr.'s son Emmet married Patricia Cumming Quinn, the daughter of Jones Quinn of Sarasota, FL, and, later, Gloria Welch with whom he resided in Syosset. [*See* Spinzia, *Long Island's Prominent Families in the Town of East Hampton* – Laughlin entry.] Their daughter Cynthia, who married Harold Mitchell Von Husan, Jr. of Manhattan, resided in Manhattan. Their son Bache McEvers Whitlock III married Philbin Heath, the daughter of Alfred R. Heath of Hewlett.

### Whitman, Alexander Harvey, Sr. (1919-2004)

| | |
|---|---|
| Occupation(s): | financier - vice-president, Maritime Brokers, Inc. |
| Marriage(s): | 1942-2004 – Sylvia Choate (1922-2008) |
| Address: | Burton Lane, Lawrence |

Name of estate:
Year of construction:
Style of architecture:
Architect(s):
Landscape architect(s):
House extant: unconfirmed
Historical notes:

The *Social Register New York, 1956* lists Alexander H. and Sylvia Choate Whitman [Sr.] as residing on Burton Lane, Cedarhurst [Lawrence].

He was the son of Eben Esmond and Jane Whitthorne Harvey Whitman, Sr., who resided in Lawrence.

Sylvia Choate Whitman was the daughter of Robert Burnett and Katharine Schuyler Choate.

Alexander Harvey and Sylvia Choate Whitman, Sr.'s son Alexander Harvey Whitman, Jr. married Laura Grinnell Koehne, the daughter of Richard Sperry and Laura Grinnell Martin Koehne of Lawrence.

### Whitman, Eben Esmond, Sr. (1880-1934)

| | |
|---|---|
| Occupation(s): | industrialist -  vice-president and director, William Whitman Co., Inc., NYC (textile manufacturing firm) |
| Marriage(s): | 1905-1934 – Jane Whitthorne Harvey (1883-1961) |
| Address: | 404 Ocean Avenue, Lawrence |

Name of estate:
Year of construction:
Style of architecture:
Architect(s):
Landscape architect(s):
House extant:  unconfirmed
Historical notes:

The *Long Island Society Register, 1929* lists Eben Esmond and Jane W. Harvey Whitman [Sr.] as residing in Cedarhurst [Lawrence].

He was the son of William and Jane Dole Hallett Whitman, Sr. of Brookline, MA.

Jane Whitthorne Harvey Whitman was the daughter of Alexander and Ella Mayes Whitthorne Harvey.

Eben Esmond and Jane Whitthorne Harvey Whitman, Sr.'s daughter Mabel married Alden Rodney Ludlow, Jr., the son of Alden Rodney and Alicia Gamble Ludlow, Sr. of Mill Neck, and resided in Lawrence. [*See* Spinzia, *Long Island's Prominent North Shore Families, vol. I* – Ludlow entry.] Their son Alexander married Sylvia Choate and resided in Lawrence. Their son Eben Esmond Whitman, Jr., who resided in Sharon, CT, married Betty Gardner Neustadt, the daughter of Robert Gardner Neustadt of Santa Barbara, CA, and, subsequently, Hilda Stedman, the daughter of John W. Stedman. Their daughter Ellen married William Constable Breed, Jr., the son of William Constable and Emma Wise Ryder Breed, Sr. of *Whale Acres* in Lawrence, and resided in Manhattan and New Canaan, CT.


### Whitney, Arthur Edward (1876-1966)

| | |
|---|---|
| Occupation(s): | financier -  partner, H. N. Whitney and Sons (investment banking firm); partner, Whitney, Goadby, and Co. (investment banking firm); director, Garden City Bank and Trust Co. |
| Civic Activism: | a founder and director, Cherry Valley Club, Garden City, 1916 |
| Marriage(s): | M/1 – 1906 – Florence Colgate Craig<br>M/2 – Alice Sutherland |
| Address: | 31 Rockaway Avenue, Garden City |

Name of estate:
Year of construction: 1888
Style of architecture: French Empire
Architect(s):
Landscape architect(s):
House extant:  yes; remodeled in 1930
Historical notes:

*front facade, 2008*

The *Long Island Society Register, 1929* lists Arthur E. and Florence Colgate Craig Whitney as residing at 31 Rockaway Road [sic], Garden City.

He was the son of Henry Norris and Catherine L. Shipman Whitney.

Florence Colgate Craig Whitney was the daughter of Thomas H. Craig of Colorado Springs, CO.

The Whitney's son Craig married Ann Van Duzer Ward, the daughter of Stanley Ward, and resided in Mount Kisco, NY. Their daughter Helen married David Winton Brown, the son of Albert Winton Brown, Sr. of Hempstead, and resided in Lloyd Harbor. Their daughter Margaret married George Edward Diethelm and resided in Locust Valley.

**Whiton, Henry Devereux (1871-1930)**

| | |
|---|---|
| Occupation(s): | industrialist - president and treasurer, Union Sulphur Co.; director, Sulphur Export Co. |
| | financier - director, Seaboard National Bank, NYC |
| Civic Activism: | vice-president, New York Zoological Society |
| Marriage(s): | M/1 – 1902-div. 1921 – Frieda Frasch (1879-1951) - nobility |
| | M/2 – 1922-1930 – Gwendolen Harris (1895-1972) |
| Address: | 291 Meadowview Road, Hewlett Bay Park |
| Name of estate: | |
| Year of construction: | c. 1890 |
| Style of architecture: | Stuart Revival |
| Architect(s): | Alfred Charles Bossom designed the house (for Whiton) |
| Landscape architect(s): | |
| House extant: yes | |
| Historical notes: | |

The house was built by Henry Devereux Whiton.

He was the son of Edward Nathan and Mary Devereux Whiton.

Frieda Frasch Whiton was the daughter of "The Sulphur King" Herman Frasch and his wife Elizabeth Frasch of Cleveland, OH. Frieda later married Count David Augustus Costantini with whom she resided at *Tulip Hill* in Lattingtown, and, subsequently, Baron Carl Gottlieb von Seidlitz. [*See* Spinzia, *Long Island's Prominent North Shore Families, vol. I* – Costantini entry.]

Henry Devereux and Frieda Frasch Whiton's son Herman married Emelyn Thatcher Leonard, the daughter of Charles Reginald and Jessie A. Hazzard Leonard, Sr. of *Walls of Jericho* in Jericho, and, later, Katherine Margaret O'Brien. [*See* Spinzia, *Long Island's Prominent North Shore Families, vol. I* – Leonard entry.]

Gwendolen Harris Whiton was the daughter of Edward Henry and Sallie Craig Whiton Harris of Piermont, NY.

*In 1920 the house was purchased by the Lawrence Country Day School which merged with the Woodmere Academy in 1990 to form Lawrence Woodmere Academy and relocated to 336 Woodmere Boulevard, Woodmere. The Whiton house was purchased in 1992 by the Hebrew Academy of Long Beach for the site of its Stella K. Abraham High School for Girls.

*library*

# Henry Devereux Whiton residence

*front facade, c. 1914*

*rear facade*

*entrance hall*

*living room*

*conservatory*

**Wickersham, Cornelius Wendell, Sr. (1885-1968)**

| | |
|---|---|
| Occupation(s): | attorney - partner, Wickersham and Taft, NYC |
| | military - general, New York National Guard; deputy governor, United States zone in Germany after World War II |
| | writer - *Towards Two Centuries at the New York Bar* |
| Civic Activism: | member, New York State Board of Regents; a founder, American Legion |
| Marriage(s): | 1909-1968 – Rosalie Neilson Hinckley (1887-1981) |
| Address: | 235 Briarwood Crossing, Lawrence |
| Name of estate: | *Briarwood* |
| Year of construction: | 1920 |
| Style of architecture: | Georgian Revival |
| Architect(s): | |
| Landscape architect(s): | |
| House extant: yes | |
| Historical notes: | |

   The *Long Island Society Register, 1929* lists Cornelius Wendell and Rosalie N. Hinckley Wickersham [Sr.] as residing at *Briarwood* in Cedarhurst [Lawrence].
   He was the son of George Woodward and Mildred Wendell Wickersham, who resided at *Marshfield* in Lawrence.
   Rosalie Neilson Hinckley Wickersham was the daughter of Samuel Parker and Rosalie Neilson Hinckley of *Sunset Hall* in Lawrence.
   Cornelius Wendell and Rosalie Neilson Hinckley Wickersham, Sr.'s son The Reverend George Woodward Wickersham II married Elizabeth Wistar Craighill, the daughter of The Reverend G, Peyton Craighill of Leesburgh, VA. Their son Cornelius Wendell Wickersham, Jr. married Elizabeth Terry Savage, the daughter of The Reverend Fiske and Mrs. May Halsted Terry Savage of Lloyd Harbor, and resided at 459 Woodbury Road, Cold Spring Harbor. [*See* Spinzia, *Long Island's Prominent North Shore Families, vol. II* – Savage and Wickersham entries.]
   *[See following entry for additional family information.]*

*front facade, 2000*

## Wickersham, George Woodward (1858-1936)

| | |
|---|---|
| Occupation(s): | statesman - United States Attorney General (Taft administration)*; |
| | attorney - partner, Strong and Cadwalader; |
| | partner, Cadwalader, Wickersham, and Taft |
| | diplomat - special commissioner to Cuba, United States War Trade Board during World War I |
| | journalist - special correspondent, *The New York Tribune*, at Paris Peace Conference, 1919 |
| Civic Activism: | chairman, National Commission on Law Observance & Enforcement (Wickersham Commission), 1928-1931; |
| | president, New York Association for Improving Condition of the Poor; |
| | president, Council on Foreign Relations, 1933-1936; |
| | president, League of National Association, 1928; |
| | member, President Wilson's Industrial Conference, 1919; |
| | chairman, Harvard Research Committee on International Justice; |
| | president, American Law Institute; |
| | president, National Probation Association; |
| | president, American Prison Association; |
| | anti-suffragist** |
| Marriage(s): | 1883-1936 – Mildred Wendell (1854-1944) |
| | - Civic Activism: member, Junior anti-suffrage League, 1917 |
| Address: | Hollywood Crossing, Lawrence |
| Name of estate: | *Marshfield* |
| Year of construction: | c. 1904 |
| Style of architecture: | Neo-Georgian |
| Architect(s): | Foster, Gade, and Graham designed a house (for G. Wickersham)*** |
| Landscape architect(s): | Mary Rutherfurd Jay designed the Japanese garden, 1914 (for G. Wickersham) |

House extant: no
Historical notes:

*front facade*

The house, originally named *Marshfield*, was built by George Woodward Wickersham.

The *Long Island Society Register, 1929* lists George W. and Mildred Wendell Wickersham as residing at *Marshfield*, Hollywood Crossing, Cedarhurst [Lawrence].

He was the son of Samuel Morris and Elizabeth Cox Woodward Wickersham of Pittsburgh, PA.

Mildred Wendell Wickersham was the daughter of Cornelius and Mary Hinckley Wendell of Washington, DC.

George Woodward and Mildred Wendell Wickersham's daughter Gwendolyn married Albert John Akin II and resided at *Homewood* in Hewlett Harbor. She subsequently married Henry Ives Cobb, Jr. with whom she resided in Hewlett. Their son Cornelius married Rosalie Neilson Hinckley and resided at *Briarwood* in Lawrence. Their daughter Constance, who was also an anti-suffragist, remained unmarried.

*[See previous entry for additional family information.]*

*Wickersham prepared the income tax amendment to the United States Constitution, 1913, thereby legalizing the federal income tax.

**In 1915, Harriot Stanton Blatch referred to George as "the arch enemy of suffragists." For other Long Islanders involved in the suffrage movement *see* Raymond E. Spinzia, "Winning the Franchise: Long Island Activists in the Fight for Woman's Suffrage and Their Opponents, Long Island's Anti-Suffragists." wwwspinzialongislandestates.com.

***Foster, Gade, and Graham designed a small shingle-style cottage for the estate.

*Marshfield, Japanese garden*

*Marshfield, gardens and windmill*

## Wigglesworth, Henry (1866-1945)

| | |
|---|---|
| Occupation(s): | industrialist - vice-president, Benroi Products Co.; director and manager, research department, General Chemical Co. (heavy metal firm) |
| Civic Activism: | member, New York City General Reception Committee |
| Marriage(s): | M/1 – 1895-1909 – Olive Gertrude Belden (1874-1909) |
| | M/2 – 1918-div. 1935 – Beatrice Murphy |
| | - Civic Activism: director, New York State Woman's Land Army, 1918 |
| Address: | 24 Rockaway Avenue, Garden City |
| Name of estate: | |
| Year of construction: | 1873 |
| Style of architecture: | French Empire |
| Architect(s): | |
| Landscape architect(s): | |
| House extant: yes | |
| Historical notes: | |

Born in Belfast, Ireland, Henry Wigglesworth was the son of Alfred and Selina Hardy Wigglesworth.

Olive Gertrude Belden was the daughter of Mead and Gertrude Woolson Belden.

Henry and Olive Gertrude Belden Wigglesworth's daughter Sylvia married Chase Mellen, Jr., the son of Chase and Lucy Cony Manley Mellen, Sr. of Garden City, and, later, James William Maitland, the son of Thomas Andrew and Helen Abby Van Voorhees Maitland of Manhattan, and resided in Hewlett Bay Park and Lawrence. Their son Belden married Olive Leon Brogan and, later, Doris Drake. Their son Gardner married Viola Parry and resided in Chestfield, England. The Wigglesworth's great-grandson Dr. Howard Brush Dean III was Governor of Vermont from 1991-2003 and was unsuccessful in becoming the Democratic candidate for the presidency in the 2004 election. He then headed the Democratic National Committee through the 2008 election.

Beatrice Murphy Wigglesworth was the daughter of Henry M. and Nina G. Murphy.

By 1928 Wigglesworth had relocated to Lakeville. [*The Brooklyn Daily Eagle* April 15, 1928, p. 107.]

In 1960 the house was remodeled.

*front facade, 2007*

## Wildermuth, George C. (1883-1981)

| | |
|---|---|
| Occupation(s): | attorney - Garden City Police judge |
| | financier - trustee, Kings County Trust Co.; |
| | trustee, Dime Savings Bank of Brooklyn, 1893 |
| Civic Activism: | a founder, first president, and chairman of board, Dodger Knott-Hole Club; |
| | chairman, community division, Brooklyn United Service Organization, 1941; |
| | president, Protestant Lawyers Association; |
| | president, Brooklyn Bar Association; |
| | director and counsel, Downtown Brooklyn Association; |
| | member, grievance committee, State Bar Association; |
| | chairman, tax revision committee, Brooklyn Real Estate Board; |
| | vice-chairman, Brooklyn Cancer Committee; |
| | director, Brooklyn Tuberculosis and Health Association; |
| | chairman, Brooklyn Advisory Board, Salvation Army; |
| | president, Municipal Club of Brooklyn, 1949; |
| | president, Brooklyn Rotary Club; |
| | chairman, community division, USO, 1941 |
| Marriage(s): | M/1 – 1919-1945 – Mildred Sturges Keep (1894-1945) |
| | M/2 – Marguerite Handwright (1899-1972) |
| Address: | 57 Brompton Road, Garden City |
| Name of estate: | |
| Year of construction: | 1933 |
| Style of architecture: | Contemporary |
| Architect(s): | Olive Frances Tjaden designed the house |
| Landscape architect(s): | |
| House extant: yes | |
| Historical notes: | |

George C. Wildermuth was the son of Gottlob and Mary Bremer Wildermuth of Brooklyn.

Mildred Sturges Keep Wildermuth was the daughter of Charles Davis Keep of Elmira, NY.

At the time of Mildred's death, the Wildermuths were residing at 57 Brompton Road. [*Nassau Daily Review–Star* March 29, 1945, p. 5.]

Marguerite Handwright Wildermuth was the daughter of Edward F. and Mary E. Handwright of Tarrytown, NY.

*front facade*

### Williams, Ichabod Thomas, II (1907-1987)

| | |
|---|---|
| Occupation(s): | merchant - secretary, Ichabod T. Williams & Sons, NYC (dealers in exotic woods and veneers) |
| Civic Activism: | trustee, Village of Lawrence |
| Marriage(s): | 1930-1987 – Edna Marie Dunstan (1908-2003) |
| Address: | Sage Avenue, Lawrence |
| Name of estate: | |
| Year of construction: | |
| Style of architecture: | |
| Architect(s): | |
| Landscape architect(s): | |
| House extant: unconfirmed | |
| Historical notes: | |

The *Social Register New York, 1965* lists Ichabod Thomas and Edna M. Dunstan Williams [II] as residing on Sage Avenue, Lawrence.

He was the son of Thomas Resolved and Dorothy Strong Hinckley Williams of *Windemere* in Lawrence.

Edna Marie Dunstan Williams was the daughter of James Samuel and Edna Louise Kempshall Dunstan, who resided at *Brightside* in Lawrence. Edna's sister Marian married John Mortimer Rutherfurd, the son of John Morris Livingston Rutherfurd, and resided in Sands Point. [*See* Spinzia, *Long Island's Prominent North Shore Families, vol. II* – Rutherfurd entry.] Her sister Dorothy married Henry Wood Wiley, Jr. of Haverford, PA. Her sister Joan married Guysbert B. Vroom, Jr. of Bath, ME.

Ichabod Thomas and Edna Marie Dunstan Williams II's son Samuel married Susan Darienne Welch, the daughter of Garrison Bulkley Welch of Bevans, NJ. Their son Thomas married Barbara Cluett, the daughter of William Gorham Cluett.

*[See other Williams entries for additional family information.]*

### Williams, Thomas, II (1856-1935)

| | |
|---|---|
| Occupation(s): | financier - trustee, Mutual Life Insurance Co.; director, Guaranty Trust Co.; director, Chemical Bank and Trust Co.; director, Niagara Fire Insurance Co. |
| Civic Activism: | trustee, Charity Organization Society of New York; chairman, planning commission, Village of Lawrence; trustee, Northern Dispensary; trustee, Nassau Industrial School, Inwood; a founder and chairman, distribution committee, New York Community Chest |
| Marriage(s): | 1880-1935 – Emma Wells Scott (1859-1959) |
| Address: | Bannister Lane, Lawrence |
| Name of estate: | |
| Year of construction: | |
| Style of architecture: | Colonial Revival |
| Architect(s): | |
| Landscape architect(s): | |
| House extant: unconfirmed | |
| Historical notes: | |

*front facade, 1927*

The *Long Island Society Register, 1929* lists Thomas and Emma W. Scott Thomas [II] as residing in Lawrence.

He was the son of Ichabod Thomas and Elizabeth Skeldon Thomas, Sr. of Manhattan.

Thomas and Emma Wells Scott Williams II's son Thomas Resolved Williams married Dorothy Strong Hinckley and resided at *Windemere* in Lawrence. Their daughter Dorcas married Morris Douw Ferris, Sr., the son of Morris Patterson and Mary Lanman Douw Ferris of Garden City, and resided in Lawrence. Their daughter Edith married Vail Blydenburgh, the son of Jessie S. and Josephine Vail Blydenburgh of Smithtown, and resided in the Village of the Branch, Smithtown.

*[See other Williams entries for additional family information.]*

## Williams, Thomas Resolved (1881-1982)

| | |
|---|---|
| Occupation(s): | merchant - president, Icahabod T. Williams & Sons, NYC (dealers in exotic woods and veneers)<br>financier - director, Niagara Fire Insurance Co.; director, Chemical Bank and Trust Co. |
| Civic Activism: | director, New York Community Chest |
| Marriage(s): | 1905 – Dorothy Strong Hinckley (b. 1883) |
| Address: | 290 South Ocean Avenue, Lawrence |
| Name of estate: | *Windemere* |
| Year of construction: | c. 1883 |
| Style of architecture: | Shingle |
| Architect(s): | Lamb and Rich designed the house (for S. P. Hinckley) |
| Landscape architect(s): | |
| House extant: | no |
| Historical notes: | |

The house was built by Samuel Parker Hinckley.

The *Long Island Society Register, 1929* lists Thomas Resolved and Dorothy S. Hinckley Williams as residing at *Windemere* in Cedarhurst [Lawrence].

He was the son of Thomas and Emma Wells Scott Williams II, who resided in Lawrence.

Dorothy Strong Hinckley Williams was the daughter of Samuel Parker and Rosalie Neilson Hinckley, who resided at *Sunset Hall* in Lawrence. Dorothy's sister Rosalie married Cornelius Wendell Wickersham, Sr. and resided at *Briarwood* in Lawrence. Her brother Samuel Neilson Hinckley, Sr. married Catherine Livingston Hamersley and resided at *Son Ridge* in Cedarhurst. Her brother Julian, who resided in Lawrence, married Mildred Culver and, later, Danah Bartlett.

Thomas Resolved and Dorothy Strong Hinckley Williams' daughter Barbara married Enos Thompson Troop IV and resided in Lawrence. Their daughter Sybil married Dr. James Patton Miller and, subsequently, ____ Dukehart with whom she resided in Jarretville, MD. Their son Ichabod married Eda Marie Dunstan and resided at *Brightside* in Lawrence. Their daughter Anne married Robert Wallace Tilney, Jr. of Far Hills, NJ, and resided at *White Oak* in Far Hills. Their daughter Rosalie married James Otis Post, Jr. of Morristown, NJ.

*[See other Williams entries for additional family information.]*

The house has been extensively remodeled.

*rear facade*

### Wilson, Marshall Orme, Sr. (1860-1926)

| | |
|---|---|
| Occupation(s): | financier - partner, R. T. Wilson and Co. (investment banking firm founded by his father); director, Central Hanover Bank<br>industrialist - director, Mathieson Alkali Co. |
| Marriage(s): | 1884-1926 – Caroline Schermerhorn Astor (1861-1948) |
| Address: | 83 Eleventh Street, Garden City |
| Name of estate: | |
| Year of construction: | |
| Style of architecture: | |
| Architect(s): | |
| Landscape architect(s): | |
| House extant: no | |
| Historical notes: | |

The *Long Island Society Register, 1929* lists Caroline S. Astor Wilson [Sr.] as residing at 83 Eleventh [Street], Garden City.

Marshall Orme Wilson, Sr. was the son of Richard Thornton and Melissa Clementine Johnson Wilson, Sr. of Georgia. The Metropolitan Museum of Art, NYC, has a painting of Wilson by the French artist Leon Bonnat.

Caroline Schermerhorn Astor Wilson was the daughter of William Blackhouse and Caroline Schermerhorn Astor, Jr. Known as "Mystic Rose," Mrs. Astor was the undisputed arbiter of society's elite "Four Hundred."

[For additional Schermerhorn family information, *see* Spinzia, *Long Island's Prominent South Shore Families* – Suydam and Welles entries.]

Marshall Orme and Caroline Schermerhorn Astor Wilson, Sr.'s son Marshall Orme Wilson, Jr. married Alice Elise Borland, the daughter of John Nelson and Alice Haven Borland.


### Winkhaus, John Theodore, Sr. (1882-1950)

| | |
|---|---|
| Occupation(s): | financier - partner, Reynolds, Fish, and Co. (stock brokerage firm); partner, Jacquelin and deCoppet (stock brokerage firm); partner, Carlisle and Jacquelin (stock brokerage firm) |
| Marriage(s): | Mary Edna Smith (1880-1964) |
| Address: | 84 Eleventh Street, Garden City |
| Name of estate: | |
| Year of construction: | 1927 |
| Style of architecture: | Neo-Tudor |
| Architect(s): | |
| Landscape architect(s): | |
| House extant: yes | |
| Historical notes: | |

The *Long Island Society Register, 1929* lists John T. and Mary Edna Smith Winkhaus [Sr.] as residing at 84 Eleventh Street, Garden City.

He was the son of Frederick and Augusta C. Andresen Winkhaus.

John Theodore and Mary Edna Smith Winkhaus, Sr.'s son John Theodore Winkhaus, Jr. married Kathryn Charline Mayfield, the daughter of Charles Rufus Mayfield of Dallas, TX, and resided in Garden City.

In 2019, the 5,490-square-foot house sold for $2.75 million.

*front facade, 2019*

## Wood, Arthur William Blake (1875-1930)

| | |
|---|---|
| Occupation(s): | architect - partner, Wood and Whitaker, NYC (specialized in country homes and churches)* |
| | artist |
| | Garden City Building Inspector, 1924 |
| Marriage(s): | Alice Isabell Dayton (1883-1980) |
| Address: | Carteret Place, Garden City |
| Name of estate: | |
| Year of construction: | 1923 |
| Style of architecture: | Neo-Georgian |
| Architect(s): | Arthur William Blake Wood designed his own residence |
| Landscape architect(s): | |
| House extant: | unconfirmed |
| Historical notes: | |

The house was built by Arthur William Blake Wood [*The Brooklyn Standard Union* June 25, 1922, p. 29.]

The *Long Island Society Register, 1929* lists Mr. and Mrs. Arthur W. B. Wood as residing on Carteret Place, Garden City.

He was the son of Frederick J. and Margaretta Maxwell Wood of Garden City.

Arthur William Blake and Alice Isabell Dayton Wood's daughter Marghretta married Samuel A. Datlowe and resided in Essex, CT.

*[See following entry for additional family information.*

In 1929, the house was purchased from Wood by Mildred C. Harryman of Kew Gardens. [*The Brooklyn Daily Eagle* December 8, 1929, p. 2D.]

[For information about Wood's Montauk residence, *see* Spinzia, *Long Island's Prominent Families in the Town of East Hampton* – Wood entry.]

*Among Wood's commissions were *Olivia Cottage* (1914), Tomkins Cove, NY, for Mrs. Russell Sage. [*Buffalo Sunday Morning News* June 7, 1914, p. T8.]; a residence for Mrs. Edith Mortimer (1923) on Eleventh Street in Garden City. [*The Brooklyn Standard Union* November 26, 1922, p. 32.]; a residence for Ellery Channing Huntington, Jr. (1923) on Tenth Street and Carteret Place, Garden City. [*The Brooklyn Standard Union* June 25, 1922, p. 29.]; and a bank (1924) on Franklin Avenue in Garden City. [*The Brooklyn Standard Union* April 20, 1924, p. 27.] He designed houses for the Amherst Construction Company (1925) at Washington Street and Clowes Avenue in Hempstead. [*The Brooklyn Daily Eagle* December 4, 1925, p. 24.] and a brick automobile exhibition building (1925) on the Mineola Fair Grounds. [*The Brooklyn Times Union* August 16, 1925, p. 74.]. In addition, the design of a residence (1927) in Montauk for Carl Graham Fisher is attributed to Wood. [*See* Spinzia, *Long Island's Prominent Families in East Hampton* – Fisher entry.]

*front facade, 1929*

## Wood, Frederick J. (b. 1830)

Occupation(s):

Marriage(s): Margaretta Maxwell (1835-1915)

Address: Hilton Avenue and Fifth Street, Garden City
Name of estate:
Year of construction:
Style of architecture:
Architect(s):
Landscape architect(s):
House extant: unconfirmed
Historical notes:

At the time of her death, Margaretta Maxwell Ward had been a resident of Garden City for twenty-five years. [*Brooklyn Times Union* August 2, 1915, p. 7.]

She was the daughter of James and Margaret Dunlap Maxwell and the cousin of Henry William Maxwell of *Scrub Oaks* in Bay Shore and John Rogers Maxwell, Sr. of *Maxwelton* in Glen Cove. [*See* Spinzia, *Long Island's Prominent South Shore Families* – Maxwell entry – and *Long Island's Prominent North Shore Families, vol. 1* – Maxwell entry.]

Frederick J. and Margaretta Maxwell Wood's son Arthur married Alice Isabel Dayton and resided in Merrick and, later, Garden City.

*[See previous entry for additional family information.]*


## Wood, Howard Ogden, Jr. (1894-1964)

Occupation(s): financier - partner, Wood, Walker, and Co. (stock brokerage firm)

Marriage(s): 1918-1957 – Caryl Hackstaff (1895-1957)

Address: Meadow Drive, Lawrence
Name of estate:
Year of construction:
Style of architecture:
Architect(s):
Landscape architect(s):
House extant: unconfirmed
Historical notes:

The *New York Summer Social Register, 1919* lists Howard Ogden and Caryl Hackstaff Wood, Jr. as residing at *Tarriawyle* in East Hampton. The *Long Island Society Register, 1929* lists the Woods as residing on Meadow Lane [sic], Cedarhurst [Lawrence].

He was the son of Howard Ogden and Julia Curtis Twichell Wood, Sr., who resided in East Hampton. [*See* Spinzia, *Long Island's Prominent Families in the Town of East Hampton* – Wood entries.]

Caryl Hackstaff Wood was the daughter of Charles Ludovic and Margaret Euphemia Hoffman Hackstaff of *Tarriawyle* in East Hampton. [*See* Spinzia, *Long Island's Prominent Families in the Town of East Hampton* – Hackstaff entry.] Caryl's sister Mai married Dr. John B Walker, the son of The Reverend Avery S. Walker of Wellesley, MA. Her sister Margaret married Albert Gallatin II and resided in Southampton. [*See* Spinzia, *Long Island's Prominent Families in the Town of Southampton* – Gallatin entry.]

Howard Ogden and Caryl Hackstaff Wood, Jr.'s daughter Caryl married Richard Livingston Davies, the son of Edward Livingston and Margaret Chapman Taylor Davies of Garden City, and resided in Valley Stream. Their son Howard Ogden Wood III married Sarah Jane Fraser, the daughter of George C. Fraser of Hastings-on-Hudson, NY.

### Woodruff, Timothy Lester (1858-1913)

| | |
|---|---|
| Occupation(s): | politician - Commissioner of Parks, Brooklyn, 1895; New York State Lieutenant Governor, 1897-1902; chairman, New York State Republican Party, 1906-1910 |
| | capitalist - a founder and president, Garden City Estates Corp. (real estate development firm) |
| | industrialist - trustee, Worcester Salt Co.; a founder and president, Maltine Co.; president, Smith Premier Type-writer Co.; chairman of board, A. J. White, Ltd., London, England; director, Duncan Paper Co., Mechanicsville, NY |
| | financier - president, The Provident Life Assurance Society; director, Hamilton Trust Co.; director, Mechanics Exchange Bank; a founder, Holland Trust Co., Brooklyn |
| Civic Activism: | first president, board of trustees, Adelphi College, Brooklyn |
| Marriage(s): | M/1 – 1880-1904 – Cora Eastman (1858-1904) |
| | M/2 – 1905-1913 – Isabel Morrison |
| Address: | Stewart Avenue, Garden City |
| Name of estate: | |
| Year of construction: | 1908 |
| Style of architecture: | Dutch Colonial Revival |
| Architect(s): | Augustus N. Allen designed the house (for Woodruff) |
| Landscape architect(s): | |
| House extant: unconfirmed | |
| Historical notes: | |

*front facade, c. 1909*

The house was built by Timothy Lester Woodruff.

He was the son of John and Harriet Jane Lester Woodruff of New Haven, CT. Timothy's sister Harriette married Rodney Allen Ward, the son of Rodney and Anna Allen Ward, and resided in Hempstead and at *Snug Harbor* in Westhampton. [*See* Spinzia, *Long Island's Prominent Families in the Town of Southampton* – Ward entry.]

Cora Eastman Woodruff was the daughter of J. M. Eastman of Poughkeepsie, NY.

Timothy Lester and Cora Eastman Woodruff's son John married Eugenie Gray Watson.

Isabel Morrison Woodruff was the daughter of John E. Morrison of Manhattan.

### Woodward, William G., Sr. (1883-1947)

| | |
|---|---|
| Occupation(s): | journalist - advertising department, *The New York Press*; advertising manager, *The New York Tribune*; advertising manager, *The World*; advertising manager, *The New York American* |
| | merchant - advertising executive, S. S. Kresge Co. (department store chain) |
| Marriage(s): | Lilian Nelson (b. 1883) |
| Address: | 64 Euston Road, Garden City |
| Name of estate: | |
| Year of construction: | c. 1928 |
| Style of architecture: | Dutch Colonial Revival |
| Architect(s): | |
| Landscape architect(s): | |
| House extant: yes | |
| Historical notes: | |

*front facade, 2000*

The house was built by William G. Woodward, Sr.

The *Long Island Society Register, 1929* lists William G. and Lilian Nelson Woodward [Sr.] as residing at 64 Euston Road, Garden City.

### Woolverton, William Henderson, Jr. (1891-1969)

| | |
|---|---|
| Occupation(s): | capitalist - president and director, Frederick H. Cone Co. (importing and exporting firm); president and director, American Railway Supply Co.; vice-president, New York Transfer Co.; director, Gamewell Fire Alarm Telephone Co.; director, Union Transfer Co. |
| Civic Activism: | vice-president, National Council of American Importers |
| Marriage(s): | M/1 – 1917 – Frances Curtis (b. 1895)<br>M/2 – 1968 – Ethel Long Manville |
| Address: | Hollywood Crossing, Lawrence |
| Name of estate: | |
| Year of construction: | |
| Style of architecture: | |
| Architect(s): | |
| Landscape architect(s): | |
| House extant: | unconfirmed |
| Historical notes: | |

   The *Long Island Society Register, 1929* lists William Henderson and Frances Curtis Woolverton [Jr.] as residing on Hollywood Crossing, Cedarhurst [Lawrence].
   He was the son of William Henderson and Edith Beaver Woolverton, Sr. of Manhattan.
   Frances Curtis Woolverton was the daughter of Nelson Curtis of Boston, MA.
   William Henderson and Frances Curtis Woolverton, Jr.'s son William Henderson Woolverton III, who was a member of the Office of Strategic Services during World War II, married Joan Newton, the daughter of Maurice Newton of New York, and resided in Sands Point. Their son The Reverend John F. Woolverton married Margaret Ann Richardson, the daughter of Arthur Berry Richardson of Manhattan, and resided in Austin, TX.
   Ethel Long Manville was the daughter of Hiram Edward and Ethel B. Schniewind Manville, Jr. and an heir to the Johns Manville Manufacturing Company fortune. She had previously been married to Chalmers Handy, the son of Truman Parker and Charlotte Chalmers Handy of Lyme, CT.

### Work, James Henry, Jr. (1890-1954)

| | |
|---|---|
| Occupation(s): | financier - partner, McClure, Jones, and Co. (stock brokerage firm); director, Bankers Trust Co. of New York |
| Civic Activism: | trustee, Village of Lawrence. |
| Marriage(s): | 1916-1954 – Mary Laying Davis (1895-1970) |
| Address: | 285 Breezeway, Lawrence |
| Name of estate: | *Engleside* |
| Year of construction: | |
| Style of architecture: | |
| Architect(s): | |
| Landscape architect(s): | |
| House extant: | no |
| Historical notes: | |

   The *Long Island Society Register, 1929* lists James Henry and Mary L. Davies [sic] Work [Jr.] as residing at *Engleside* in Lawrence.
   He was the son of James Henry and Maria Pierce Warner Work, Sr., who resided at *The Gowans* in Lawrence.
   Mary Laying Davis Work was the daughter of Nathan Hatfield and Nancy Harlan Doll Davis of Philadelphia, PA.
   James Henry and Mary Laying Davis Work, Jr.'s daughter Nancy married Morgan Macy, the son of Silvanus Jenkins Macy, who resided at *Race Way Lodge* in Caledonia, NY, and, later, Alfred Severin Bourne, Sr., the son of Frederick Gilbert and Emma Sparks Keeler Bourne of *Indian Neck Hall* in Oakdale, with whom Nancy resided in Oakdale. [*See* Spinzia, *Long Island's Prominent South Shore Families* – Bourne entry.] Nancy subsequently married John L. Gray, Jr. of Greenwich, CT. The Works' daughter Margaret married W. Ware Lynch, the son of L. Ware Lynch of Greenwich, CT.
   In 1946 the house was purchased from Work by Henry Sturgis Grew, Jr. [*The New York Times* October 10, 1946, p. 48.]
   *[See following entry for additional family information.]*

### Work, James Henry, Sr. (1846-1916)

| | |
|---|---|
| Occupation(s): | attorney - partner, Davies, Work, and McNamee* |
| Marriage(s): | 1874-1919 – Maria Pierce Warner (1851-1927) |
| Address: | Broadway, Lawrence |
| Name of estate: | *The Gowans* |
| Year of construction: | |
| Style of architecture: | |
| Architect(s): | |
| Landscape architect(s): | |
| House extant: | unconfirmed |
| Historical notes: | |

The *Social Register New York, 1907* lists J. Henry and Marie Warner Work [Sr.] as residing at *The Gowans* in Lawrence. The 1900 Census lists the Works at this address.

James Henry and Maria Pierce Warner Work, Sr.'s daughter Alice married John L. Lawrence, Sr. and resided at *Moorlands* in Lawrence. Their daughter Sally married Franklin Baker Lefferts and resided in Lawrence. Their daughter Marjorie, who resided at *Briarwood* in Lawrence, married DeCourcy Lawrence Hard, Sr., the son of Anson Wales and Sarah Elizabeth Brown Hard, Sr. of *Driftwood* in Lawrence. Their daughters Mabel, Jean, and Marie remained unmarried. Their son James Henry Work, Jr. married Mary Laying Davis and resided at *Engleside* in Lawrence.

*Work was indicted for allegedly defrauding the Marine National Bank which caused the bank's failure and the bankruptcy of the brokerage firm of Grant and Ward, in which President Ulysses S. Grant was a partner. [*The New York Times* July 1, 1885, p. 2, and October 24, 1916, p. 13.]

### Wright, Mary Eliza Bedford (1826-1907)

| | |
|---|---|
| Marriage(s): | Isaac Merritt Wright, Sr. (1815-1868) |
| | - diplomat - United States Representative to Austro–Hungarian Empire |
| | shipping - partner, Liverpool packet ships; partner, Black Ball Line (shipping firm); partner, Wright & Co. (shipping firm) |
| Address: | 90 Greenwich Street, Hempstead |
| Name of estate: | *The Box* |
| Year of construction: | c. 1800 |
| Style of architecture: | Colonial Revival with Greek Revival elements |
| Architect(s): | |
| Landscape architect(s): | |
| House extant: | no |
| Historical notes: | |

*front facade, 1930*

The *Social Register Summer, 1907* lists Mary Bedford Wright as residing at *The Box* in Hempstead.

She was heir to the Gunning S. Bedford and Lord Beresford fortunes.

Isaac Merritt Wright, Sr. was the son of William M. Wright who was known as the "Quaker Merchant." William was the founder of a line of packet ships. Isaac's brother John D. Wright was a founder of The New York Society for the Prevention of Cruelty to Children.

Isaac Merritt and Mary Eliza Bedford Wright, Sr.'s daughter Clara married Henry Pennington Tailer, the son of Henry Austin and Sophia Clapham Pennington Tailer, and resided at *Caprice* in Roslyn Harbor. [*See* Spinzia, *Long Island's Prominent North Shore Families, vol. II* – Tailer entry.] Their daughters Mary Constance, known as Constance who inherited the house, and Florence did not marry. Their son William Merritt Wright, Jr. married May Payne of Ohio.

In 1941, Our Lady of Loretto Roman Catholic Church purchased the house for use as a parish center [*Nassau Daily Review–Star* September 18, 1941, p. 2, and August 13, 1942, p. 12.]

*rear facade, 1930*

### Wright, John B. (1898-1974)

| | |
|---|---|
| Occupation(s): | financier - vice-president, General Motors Acceptance Corp., 1960 |
| | industrialist - salesman, Financial Sales Dept., General Motors, 1924; |
| |     manager, Financial Sales Dept., General Motors, 1926; |
| |     assistant manager, Bank Relations Dept., General Motors, 1935; |
| |     assistant manager, Domestic Bank Relations, General Motors, 1951 |
| | intelligence agent - director of intelligence, First Air Division, during World War II |
| Marriage(s): | 1955-1974 – Evelyn Evans |
| Address: | 206 Ocean Avenue, Woodmere |
| Name of estate: | Cape Cod |
| Year of construction: | 1920 |
| Style of architecture: | |
| Architect(s): | |
| Landscape architect(s): | |
| House extant: yes | |
| Historical notes: | |

*front facade*

In 1942 John B. Wright was residing at 206 Ocean Avenue, Woodmere. [*The Brooklyn Daily* Eagle June 1, 1942, p. 6.]

He was the son of Thomas Addison Wright of San Francisco, CA.

Evelyn Evans Wright was the daughter of Hartman Kuhn Evans of Manhattan. She had previously been married to Walter Scott Blanchard, Sr. of Hewlett Bay.

At the time of his death, Wright was residing at 233 Sands Lane, Hewlett Bay Park. [*The New York Times* October 23, 1974, p. 48.]

In 2020, the 2,384-square-foot house sold for $982,500.

### Wright, Wilfred La Salles (1877-1947)

| | |
|---|---|
| Occupation(s): | industrialist - president and chairman of board, Savage Arms Corp., Utica, NY; |
| |     director, Stevens Arms Co., Chicoppee, MA; |
| |     director, Davis Arms Co.; |
| |     director, Crescent Firearms Co.; |
| |     vice-president, Wharton Iron & Steel Co.; |
| |     director, Worcester Lawn Mower Co.; |
| |     director, Gorham Manufacturing Co.; |
| |     chairman of board, Sipp–Eastwood Corp., Patterson, NJ |
| | financier - director, Garden City Bank & Trust Co.; |
| |     director, West Hempstead [NY] National Bank |
| Civic Activism: | chairman, Cornell's endowment fund committee, New York Semi-Centennial |
| Marriage(s): | 1903-1947 – Margery Rich White (1884-1965) |
| | - Civic Activism: suffragist - patron, Suffrage Memorial Fund, 1930; |
| |     member, program committee, Garden City–Hempstead Community Club, 1946; |
| |     member, hostess committee, Nassau County Republican Committee, 1936 |
| Address: | Hempstead Avenue, Hempstead |
| Name of estate: | |
| Year of construction: | |
| Style of architecture: | |
| Architect(s): | |
| Landscape architect(s): | |
| House extant: unconfirmed | |
| Historical notes: | |

The *Long Island Society Register, 1929* lists Wilfred L. and Margery White Wright as residing on Hempstead Avenue, Hempstead. By 1936 they had relocated to Cherry Valley Road, Hempstead.

He was the son of Craig La Salles and Katherine Perry Van Dyke Wright.

Margery Rich White Wright was the daughter of Hamilton Salisbury White of Syracuse, NY.

Wilfred La Salles and Margery Rich White Wright's son Craig married Marie Anne Kranefuses, the daughter of Albert Kranefuses of Boston, MA.

### Wyeth, Leonard Jarvis, IV (1890-1968)

| | |
|---|---|
| Occupation(s): | financier - member, F. S. Smithers and Co. (stock brokerage firm); vice-president, Bank of Manhattan Trust Co. |
| Marriage(s): | 1914-1968 – Priscilla Mullins Bull (1894-1981) |
| Address: | 170 Cedarhurst Avenue, Lawrence |
| Name of estate: | |
| Year of construction: | |
| Style of architecture: | |
| Architect(s): | |
| Landscape architect(s): | |
| House extant: | no |
| Historical notes: | |

The *Long Island Society Register, 1929* lists Leonard J. and Priscilla M. Bull Wyeth [IV] as residing in Cedarhurst [Lawrence].

He was the son of Leonard Jarvis and Louise Alley Wyeth III of Manhattan.

Priscilla Mullins Bull Wyeth was the daughter of James Edgar Bull of New York City. Her sister Marion married Butler Whiting and resided in Union Deep River, CT.

Leonard Jarvis and Priscilla Mullins Bull Wyeth IV's daughter Priscilla married Arthur Zebriskie Gray, the son of Arthur R. Gray of Garrision, NY, and resided in Armonk, NY. Their son Leonard Jarvis Wyeth V married Pamela Evans, the daughter of Tyrell Langley Evans of Asuncion, Paraguay.


### Wyld, Robert Hasbrouck (1881-1975)

| | |
|---|---|
| Occupation(s): | engineer and sales manager, Power Specialty Co., 1905-1927; sales manager, Foster Wheeler Corp., 1927-1934; consulting engineer and vice-president, Burns and Roe, Inc. |
| Civic Activism: | member, Garden City School Board; chairman, cultural committee, garden department, Garden City–Hempstead Community Club, 1930 |
| Marriage(s): | 1911 – Margaret Rebecca Hart (1884-1979) |
| Address: | 72 Second Street, Garden City |
| Name of estate: | |
| Year of construction: | 1925 |
| Style of architecture: | Colonial Revival |
| Architect(s): | |
| Landscape architect(s): | |
| House extant: | yes |
| Historical notes: | |

*front facade, 2006*

The house was built by Robert Hasbrouck Wyld.

The *Long Island Society Register, 1929* lists Mrs. Robert H. Wyld as residing on Second Street, Garden City.

She was the daughter of Dr. Robert Singleton and Rebecca Wason Hart of Pisgah, NY.

Robert Hasbrouck Wyld was the son of James and Blandina Hasbrouck Wyld of Brooklyn. Robert's sister Marjorie married Dr. Albert Sidney Morrow, Sr. and resided in Garden City.

Robert Hasbrouck and Margaret Rebecca Hart Wyld's son James was one of the great pioneers of American rocketry. Between 1938 and 1941 he invented, built, and tested the first successful VS regeneratively cooled rocket motor. A crater on the Moon is named in his honor. Their daughter Anne married John Risque Blizard, Jr., the son of John and Ethel Risque Blizard of Garden City, and resided in Corning, NY.

In 2000 the house was remodeled.

**Young, Benjamin Swan (1883-1965)**

Occupation(s):　　　　　　financier -　bond broker;
　　　　　　　　　　　　　　　　　　　　trustee, Chase Manhattan Bank

Marriage(s):　　　　　　　1922 – Susanne Meredith Bottomley (b. 1892)
　　　　　　　　　　　　　　 - Civic Activism:　chair of programs, Garden Department, Garden
　　　　　　　　　　　　　　　　　　　　　　　　City–Hempstead Community Club, 1930;
　　　　　　　　　　　　　　　　　　　　　　　　Red Cross and canteen work during World War I

Address:　　　　　　　　　15 Franklin Court, Garden City
Name of estate:
Year of construction:
Style of architecture:　　　Neo-Tudor Townhouse
Architect(s):　　　　　　　Ford, Butler, and Oliver
　　　　　　　　　　　　　　　designed the house*
Landscape architect(s):
House extant:　yes
Historical notes:

　The *Long Island Society Register, 1929* lists Benjamin S. and Susanne M. Bottomley Young as residing at 15 Franklin Court, Garden City. The 1940 Census lists them at 73 Hilton Avenue, Garden City.
　He was the son of Thomas Sears and Caroline E. Swan Young of Oyster Bay.
　Susanne Meredith Bottomley Young was the daughter of John and Susan Amelia Steers Bottomley of *Head O'Pond* in Southampton. [*See* Spinzia, *Long Island's Prominent Families in the Town of Southampton* – Bottomley entry.] Susan's brother William, the noted architect, married Harriet Bailey Campbell Townsend, the daughter of James Mulford and Harriet Bailey Campbell Townsend II of Mill Neck. [*See* Spinzia, *Long Island's Prominent North Shore Families, vol. I* – Bottomley entry – and *vol. II* – Townsend entry.]
　Benjamin Swan and Susanne Meredith Bottomley Young's daughter Caroline married Robert Bradley Rheault, Sr., the son of Charles Auguste and Roseamond Bradley Rheault. The character Colonel Walter Kutz in Francis Ford Coppola's motion picture "Apocalypse Now" was loosely based on Robert.
　*The houses were built by Doubleday, Page, and Company as rentals.

*Franklin Court Complex 2009*

**Young, Willis Howard, Sr. (1844-1917)**

| | |
|---|---|
| Occupation(s): | financier - a founder, Hempstead Bank; a founder and president, Long Island Bond and Guarantee Co., Jamaica; director and vice-president, Queens County Trust Co., Jamaica; director, Greenport Savings Bank |
| | capitalist - real estate developer in Jamaica and Queens |
| | industrialist - a founder and partner, Young and Gerard Co., Greenpoint (later, Empire City – Gerard Co.) (sash and door manufacturing firm) |
| Civic Activism: | trustee, Village of Hempstead; a founder and first president, Hempstead Athletic Association, 1888 |
| Marriage(s): | 1869-1912 – Mary Wickham Conklin (1847-1912) - Civic Activism: manager, secretary, and treasurer, Hempstead Subscription Library; vice-president, Hempstead Library Association, 1909 |
| Address: | 95 Fulton Avenue, Hempstead |
| Name of estate: | *Willisleigh* |
| Year of construction: | 1891 |
| Style of architecture: | Victorian |
| Architect(s): | |
| Landscape architect(s): | |
| House extant: yes* | |
| Historical notes: | |

The house, originally named *Willisleigh*, was built by Willis Howard Young, Sr. [*The Brooklyn Citizen* September 21, 1890, p. 15.]

He was the son of Jonathan Franklin and Mary E. Terry Young of Riverhead.

Mary Wickham Conklin Young was the daughter of Nathaniel Conklin of Brooklyn.

Willis Howard and Mary Wickham Conklin Young, Sr.'s son Willis Howard Young, Jr. died in 1879 at the age of eight. In 1883, their nine-year-old daughter Milla died. Their daughter Edith, who later owned *Willisleigh*, married Frank Strobridge Harlow of Brooklyn.

In 1921, Edith sold the house to the Sisters of St. Joseph who utilized it as the Sacred Heart Convent and School until 1949 when they relocated the convent and school to Brentwood. [*The Brooklyn Daily Eagle* September 11, 1921, p. 14.] The house is currently the Sisters of Saint Joseph Mission Office.

*In 1900, the barn was destroyed and the carriage house was severely damaged by fire. [*The Brooklyn Times Union* June 7, 1900, p. 8.] In 1903, the house suffered nearly $35,000 damage by a fire. Work to restore the house was immediately started by Young. [*The Brooklyn Times Union* November 7, 1903, p. 9, and November 13, 1903, p. 10.]

*Willisleigh*

**Youngs, William Jones (1851-1916)**

| | |
|---|---|
| Occupation(s): | journalist - editor, *The Hempstead Inquirer* |
| | attorney - United States District Attorney for Eastern District (Theodore Roosevelt and William Howard Taft administrations) |
| | politician - member, New York State Assembly, 1870-1880; New York State Deputy Superintendent of Banking (Theodore Roosevelt administration); United States Commissioner, Eastern District; private secretary, New York State Governor Theodore Roosevelt |
| Marriage(s): | M/1 – 1879-1883 – Eleanor Youngs (1854-1883) |
| | M/2 – Helen Louise Mason (1858-1889) |
| | M/3 – 1891-1916 – Mary Benson Emory (1867-1947) |
| Address: | 26 Cathedral Avenue, Garden City |
| Name of estate: | |
| Year of construction: | 1906 |
| Style of architecture: | Colonial Revival |
| Architect(s): | |
| Landscape architect(s): | |
| House extant: | yes |
| Historical notes: | |

William Jones Youngs was the son of Daniel Kelsey and Sarah Elizabeth Smith Youngs.
Eleanor Youngs Youngs was the daughter of David Jones and Cornelia Townsend Youngs.
William Jones and Eleanor Youngs Youngs' daughter Mary did not marry.
Helen Louise Mason Youngs was the daughter of James and Marie Louise Youngs Mason.
William Jones and Helen Louise Mason Youngs' daughter Helen married Russell Wheeler Strong, the son of Selah Brewster Strong of Setauket.
Mary Benson Emory Youngs was the daughter of George Washington and Susan Emilia Searing Emory of Mineola.
In 1893, William Jones and Mary Benson Emory Youngs' son Daniel Kelsey Youngs II died at the age of three months.
In 1999, the 5,103-square-foot house sold for $843,750. The same year, the house was remodeled.

*front facade, 2009*

## Zara, Francesco A. (1889-1987)

| | |
|---|---|
| Occupation(s): | financier - assistant vice-president, Bank of New York |
| Civic Activism: | president, Southampton Horse Show |
| Marriage(s): | M/1 – Eleanor Rogers Wood (1891-1945) |
| | M/2 – 1953-1971 – Mildred Gautier Rice (1894-1971) |
| |    - nobility |
| Address: | Cedar Avenue, Hewlett Bay Park |
| Name of estate: | |
| Year of construction: | |
| Style of architecture: | |
| Architect(s): | |
| Landscape architect(s): | |
| House extant: unconfirmed | |
| Historical notes: | |

   The *Long Island Society Register, 1929* lists Francesco and Eleanor R. Wood Zara as residing in Hewlett Park [Hewlett Bay Park].
   He was the son of The Reverend Michael C. and Mrs. Mary Cameron Adams Zara of Philadelphia, PA.
   Eleanor Rogers Wood Zara was the daughter of Thomas D. Wood of Philadelphia, PA.
   Francesco A. and Eleanor Rogers Wood Zara's son Michael married Mathilde Alexandre and resided in Frogmore, SC. Their daughter Mai married Peitro Colla of Milan, Italy, and, subsequently, Philip James with whom she resided in Manhattan.
   Mildred Gautier Rice Zara was the daughter of William Low and Elsie Gautier French Rice of Cleveland, OH. William Low Rice was murdered by an unidentified assailant. [*The New York* Times August 30, 1910, p. 1.] Mildred had previously been married to Richard Heber Newton, Jr. of *Box Farm* in Water Mill; Rene Georges Varlet, the Viscount de Kergoet of Brittany, France, with whom she resided in Hewlett Neck; and John Oakley Radway.
   By 1959 Zara had relocated to *Corner Gate* in Southampton.
   [*See* Spinzia, *Long Island's Prominent Families in the Town of Southampton* – Newton and Zara entries.]

## Ziegler, Frederick J. (1886-1966)

| | |
|---|---|
| Occupation(s): | industrialist - director, Steinway & Sons, Astoria, NY (piano manufacturer) |
| | merchant - director and vice-president, N. Stetson Co., Philadelphia, PA |
| |             (representative of Steinway & Sons) |
| | artist - sculptor |
| Civic Activism: | chairman, Ziegler Foundation; |
| | member, sculpture committee, Parish Art Museum, Southampton |
| Marriage(s): | 1930-1966 – Alice Cantwell (1900-1978) |
| Address: | 171 Woodmere Boulevard South, Woodsburgh |
| Name of estate: | |
| Year of construction: | |
| Style of architecture: | |
| Architect(s): | |
| Landscape architect(s): | |
| House extant: unconfirmed | |
| Historical notes: | |

   Frederick J. Ziegler was the son of Henry Ludwig W. and Albertine Helene Sophia Vogel Ziegler of Woodsburgh.
   Alice Cantwell Ziegler was the daughter of John Andrew Cantwell of Utica, NY.
   Frederick J. and Alice Cantwell Ziegler's son John married Carter Caroll, the daughter of Philip Acosta Carroll of *Doughoregan Manor* in Ellicot, MD, and, later, Marie Clair Montanari. Their son Henry married Patricia Blackmore and, later, Jourdan Arpelle. Their daughter Elenita married Henry Sears Lodge, the son of Ambassador Henry Cabot Lodge, Jr.
   [*See following entry for additional family information.*]
   For information about the Zieglers' Southampton residence *Street House*, see Spinzia, *Long Island's Prominent Families in the Town of Southampton* – Ziegler entry.]

### Ziegler, Henry Ludwig W. (1857-1930)

| | |
|---|---|
| Occupation(s): | industrialist - director and vice-president, Steinway & Sons, Astoria, NY (piano manufacturer) |
| | inventor - improvements in piano scale and resonating properties of sound board |
| Civic Activism: | a founder, Village of Woodsburgh, 1912 |
| Marriage(s): | 1881-1930 – Albertine Helene Sophia Vogel (1863-1934) |
| Address: | 171 Woodmere Boulevard South, Woodsburgh |
| Name of estate: | |
| Year of construction: | |
| Style of architecture: | |
| Architect(s): | |
| Landscape architect(s): | |
| House extant: unconfirmed | |
| Historical notes: | |

    The *Long Island Society Register, 1929* lists Henry Ziegler as residing in Woodmere [Woodsburgh].
    He was the son of Heinrick Jacob and Johanna Dosrettee Juliane Steinway [aka Steinweg] Ziegler.
    Albertine Helen Sophia Vogel Ziegler was the daughter of Theodore C. and Johanna Henrietta Wilhelmina Steinway (aka Steinweg) Vogel.
    Henry Ludwig W. and Albertine Helene Sophia Vogel Ziegler's daughter Eleanor married James Alexander Hill in 1902 and died two months later at the age of nineteen. [*The Daily Standard Union* July 1, 1902, p. 2.] Their son Frederick married Alice Cantwell and resided in Woodsburgh.
    *[See previous entry for additional family information.]*

# APPENDICES

# Mary Eliza Bedford Wright residence, *The Box*, architectural drawings

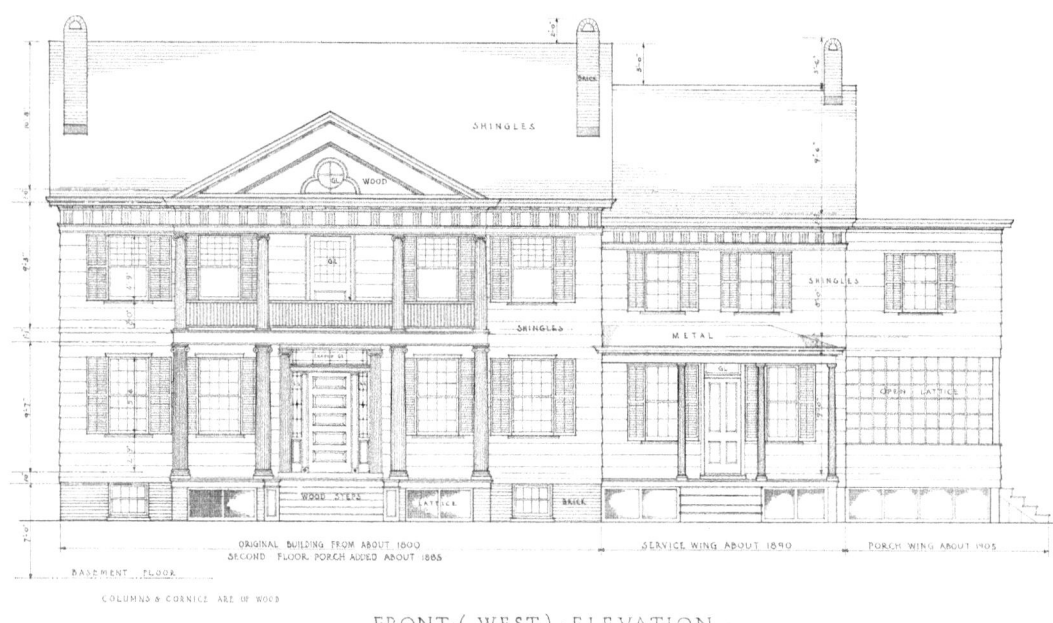

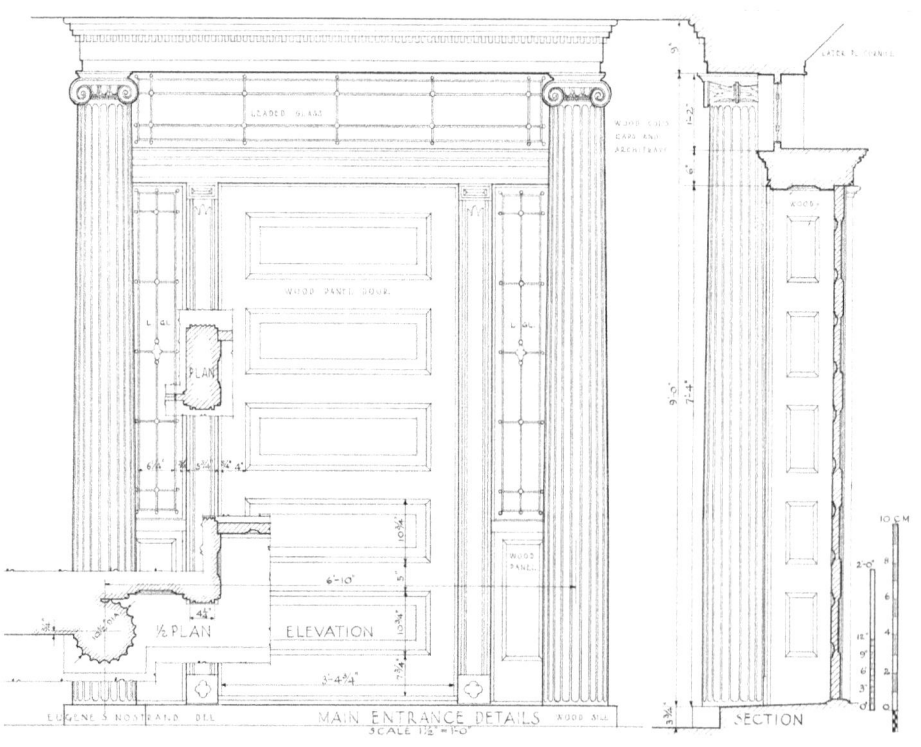

## Table of Contents for Appendices

| | |
|---|---|
| Architects | 533 |
| Civic Activism | 539 |
| Estate Names | 549 |
| Golf Courses on Former Town of Hempstead Estates | 555 |
| Landscape Architects | 557 |
| Maiden Names | 561 |
| Occupations | 591 |
| Rehabilitative Secondary Uses of Surviving Estate Houses | 613 |
| Statesmen and Diplomats Who Resided in the Town of Hempstead | 615 |
| Village Locations of Estates | 619 |
| America's First Age of Fortune: A Selected Bibliography | 629 |
| Selected Bibliographic References to Individual Town of Hempstead Estate Owners | 639 |
| Biographical Sources Consulted | 647 |
| Maps Consulted for Estate Locations | 649 |
| Illustration Credits | 651 |

*Architects*

## Mary Eliza Bedford Wright residence, *The Box*, architect's floor plan

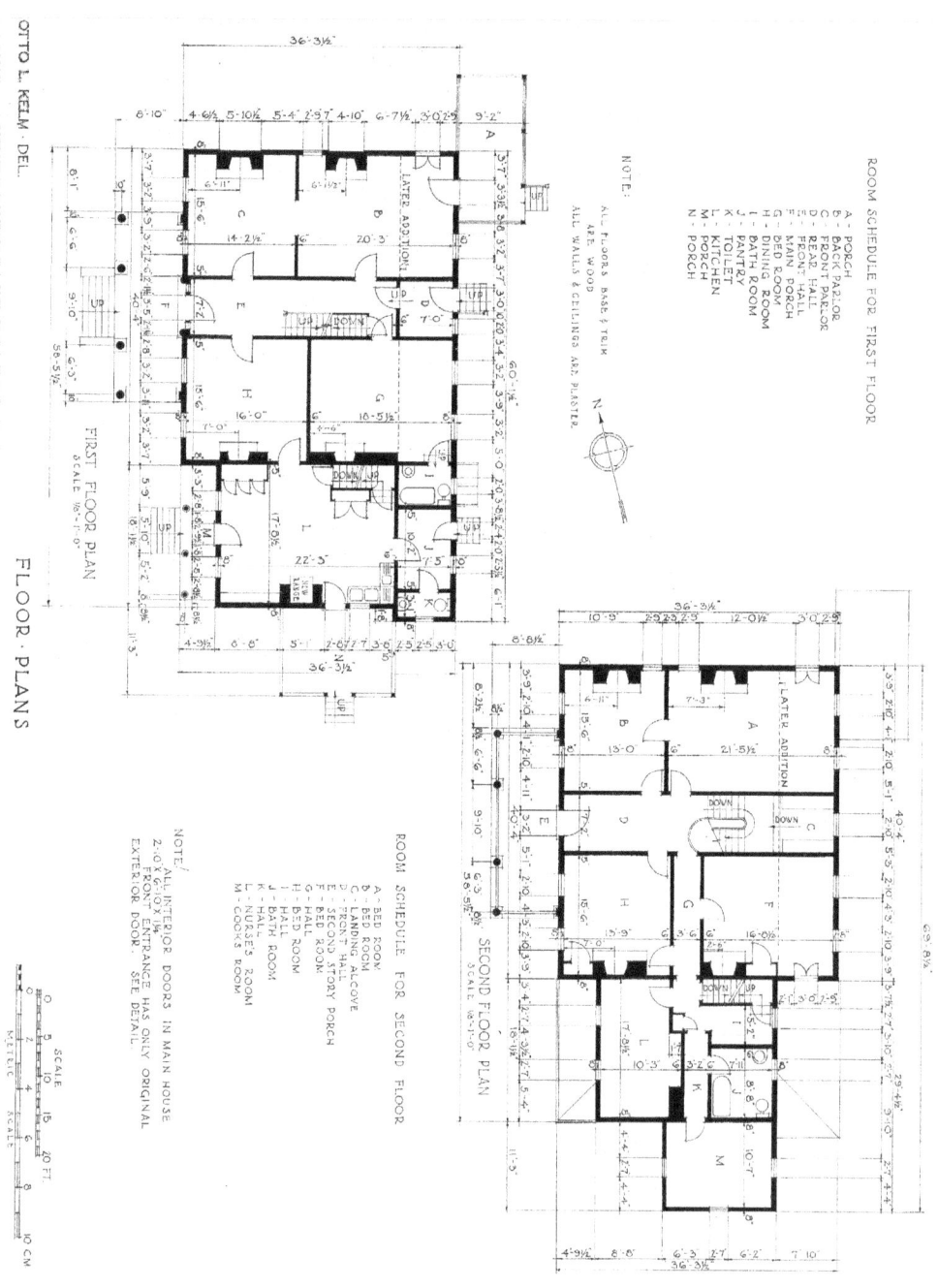

*Architects*

See the surname entry to ascertain if more than one architect was involved in designing the various buildings on an estate. This list reflects their commissions in the Town of Hempstead and includes the original and subsequent owners of the estates. When the owner who contracted with the architect is known, it is indicated by an asterisk.

**William Adams, Jr.**

| | | | |
|---|---|---|---|
| * | Adams, William, Jr. | | Lawrence |
| | Adams, William, III | *Landfall* | Lawrence |
| | Auchincloss, Samuel Sloan | *Whale Acres* | Lawrence |
| | Finch, Stephen Baker, Sr. | | Lawrence |
| * | Francke, Albert | | Lawrence |
| * | Kniffin, Howard Summers, Sr. | *Restleigh* | Lawrence |
| * | Morris, Stuyvesant Fish, Jr. | | Hewlett Bay Park |
| | Morrow, Robert | | Lawrence |
| * | Norris, Alfred Oliphant | | Lawrence |
| * | Peck, Arthur Nelson | | Woodsburgh |
| * | Perkins, Charles Lawrence, Jr. | | Woodmere |
| * | Perkins, Norton | *Whale Acres* | Lawrence |
| * | Sampson, Sally Phillips Blagden | | Lawrence |
| * | Scott, John Frederick | *Rosebank* | Hewlett Bay Park |

**Albro and Lindeberg**

| | | | |
|---|---|---|---|
| * | Carter, Russell Steenback | *The Villa Blue* | Hewlett Bay Park |
| * | Harris, Tracy Hyde, Jr. | *Wistaria Lodge* | Hewlett Bay Park |
| | Kip, Ira A., Jr. | | Hewlett Bay Park |
| * | Macy, Carlton | *Meadowwood* | Hewlett Bay Park |
| * | Macy, Carroll | *Birch Corners* | Hewlett Bay Park |
| * | Macy, Valentine Everit | | Hewlett |
| * | Marshall, Levin Rothrock | *Hawkswood* | Hewlett Harbor |
| | Miller, Danforth, Sr. | *Birch Corners* | Hewlett Bay Park |
| | Slesinger, Laurence Anthony | | Hewlett Bay Park |
| | Veeder, Paul Lansing | *Meadowwood* | Hewlett Bay Park |

**Barney and Chapman**

| | | | |
|---|---|---|---|
| * | Meyerkort, Clara Oakley | | Lawrence |
| * | Porter, Henry Hobart, Jr. | *Lauderdale* | Lawrence |

**Dwight James Baum**

| | | | |
|---|---|---|---|
| * | Lyon, Edmund Burton | *Nearacre* | Hempstead |

**Beer and Farley**

| | | | |
|---|---|---|---|
| * | Lord, George de Forest | | Woodmere |

**Alfred C. Bossom**

| | | | |
|---|---|---|---|
| * | Whiton, Henry Devereux | | Hewlett Bay Park |

*Architects*

**Buchman and Fox**
    * Levy, Isaac D.          *Roselle Manor*          Cedarhurst
                            (designed the conservatory)

**Carrere and Hastings**
    Dunstan, James Samuel      *Brightside*      Lawrence
    * Harper, Joseph Henry, Sr.      *Brightside*      Lawrence
    Throop, Enos Thompson, IV      Lawrence

**Henry Otis Chapman, Sr.**
    * Chapman, Henry Otis, Sr.      Woodsburgh

**Henry Martyn Congdon**
    * Slade, Francis Henry      (house and stables)      Lawrence

**Delano and Aldrich**
    * Merrill, Payson, Sr.      Lawrence

**Aymar Embury II**
    Hammond, Harry Stevens, Sr.      Garden City
    Morrell, Robert Whiting      Garden City
    * Orr, Henry Steers      Garden City
    * Peters, Ralph, Sr.      Garden City

**Ewing and Chappell**
    * Forrest, Richard Earp      *Longwood*      Lawrence

**Ernest Flagg**
    * Morgenthau, Maximilian, Sr.      Woodsburgh

**Ford, Butler, and Oliver**
    Breck, Duer du Pont      Garden City
    Fairchild, Willard, Sr.      Garden City
    Fowler, Rosemary O'Connor      Garden City
    Rose, Reginald Perry      Garden City
    Young, Benjamin Swan      Garden City

**Foster, Gade, and Graham**
    * Wickersham, George Woodward      *Marshfield*      Lawrence

**Freeman and Hesselman**
    * Erhart, William Herman      *Five Oaks*      Lawrence

**John Irwin Glover**
    * Bennett, A. B.      Baldwin
    * Glover, John Irwin      Baldwin

**A. J. Harris**
    * Tilford, Frank      Cedarhurst

*Architects*

**Oswald Hering**

    Curtiss, Glenn Hammond, Sr.                                                                   Garden City

  * Tarbell, Gage Eli                                                                            Garden City

**James Monroe Hewlett**

    Bierwirth, John Edward                                                                    Lawrence

  * Hewlett, James Monroe                                                                Lawrence

    Marmo, Anthony                                                                             Lawrence

**Richard Howland Hunt**

  * Belmont, Oliver Hazard Perry                    *Brookholt*                    East Meadow

    Cochran, Alexander Smith                                                           East Meadow

**John Kellum**

    Cowdrey, Loren Montague                                                       Garden City

    Hammond, John Stevens, Sr.                                                Garden City

    Taylor, Dr. Quintard, Sr.                                                           Garden City

**Kirby, Petit, and Green**

    English, William K.                                                                   Garden City

  * Gulick, Ernestus Scheneck                                                      Garden City

**Lamb and Rich**

  * Hinckley, Samuel Parker                                   *Sunset Hall*                Lawrence

  * Taylor, Talbot Jones, Jr.                                      *Talbot House*             Lawrence

    Williams, Thomas Resolved                                  *Windemere*               Lawrence

**Lord and Hewlett**

  * Lefferts, Marshall Clifford, Sr.                            *Hedgewood*             Lawrence

**Auguste Louis Noel**

  * Crane, Warren Seabury                                         *East View*                 Lawrence

    Peck, Arthur Knowlton, Sr.                                                   Lawrence

**Carl Ludwig Otto, Sr.**

  * Otto, Carl Ludwig, Sr.                                            (alterations)            Garden City

**Peabody, Wilson, and Brown**

  * Dwight, Philip J.                                                                      Hewlett Neck

  * Ladd, William Fowle, Jr.                                                         Lawrence

**Charles A. Platt**

  * McCrea, James Alexander                                                   Woodsburgh

**Polhemus and Coffin**

    Braman, Chester Alwyn, Jr.                                               Hewlett Bay Park

*Architects*

**John Russell Pope**

    \* Belmont, Oliver Hazard Perry      *Brookholt*      East Meadow
                                                (1906 farmhouse)

    Cochran, Alexander Smith      (1906 farmhouse)      East Meadow

**Thomas Henry Randall**

    \* Boulton, William Bowen, Sr.      *Avila*      Lawrence
    \* Burr, Winthrop, Sr.      *Orchard Hall*      Lawrence
    Greenberg, Henry      Lawrence
        *[See E. Burr, Sr. entry.]*
    Lanman, Jonathan Trumball, Sr.      *Orchard Hall*      Lawrence
    \* Philips, Frederic Dimon      *Greyhouse*      Lawrence
    \* Rogers, Edward Sidney      Lawrence
    Wardwell, Helen R.      Lawrence
        *[See F. D. Philps entry.]*

**Renwick, Aspinwall, and Owen**

    Gamel, Isaac      Lawrence
    \* Peabody, Richard Augustus      *Terrace Hall*      Lawrence
    Raymond, William, Sr.      Lawrence

**H. Craig Severance**

    \* Hofstra, William Sake      *The Netherlands*      Hempstead

**B. E. Stern**

    \* Hofheimer, Lester      Woodmere

**Joseph H. Taft**

    \* Burton, Robert Lewis      *Albro House*      Lawrence

**Olive Frances Tjaden**

    Barbatusby, Mark      Garden City
        *[See Ebinger entry.]*
    Blanchard, George Holmes      Garden City
    \* Duryea, William H.      Garden City
    \* Ebinger, Walter Dohrmann      Garden City
    Fanning, Edward Jerome      Garden City
    Ferguson, David, Sr.      Garden City
    Fogarty, James Francis, Sr.      Garden City
    \* Hammond, ____      Garden City
    \* Hewitt, Thomas M.      Garden City
    \* Hodgson, Robert John, Jr.      Garden City
    \* Hoffman, Horace E.      Garden City
    Hollis, W. C.      Garden City
        *[See Fogarty entry.]*
    Hussey, Robert F.      Garden City
        *[See W. H. Duryea entry.]*

*Architects*

**Olive Frances Tjaden** (cont'd)

| | | | |
|---|---|---|---|
| * | Jacobi, Harold, Sr. | (designed house, interior woodwork, several of house's interior color schemes, & greenhouse) | Woodmere |
| * | Jacobi, Sanford | | Hewlett Neck |
| | Jones, Bethune Wellington | | Garden City |
| * | Lannin, Joseph J. | | East Meadow |
| | Mariani, John Francis, Sr. | | Garden City |
| * | Marks, ____ | | Garden City |
| * | Marks, Arthur David, Jr. | | Woodsburgh |
| | Merritt, Edward Charles, Sr. | | Garden City |
| | Merritt, Harold Francis, Sr. | | Garden City |
| * | Pancake, Carl Oakley | | Garden City |
| | Pennington, Charles Gordon | | Garden City |
| | Pennington, Harold Douglas | | Garden City |
| | Piel, Rudolph Alfred | | Garden City |
| * | Recht, William, Sr. | | Woodmere |
| * | Schlossberg, Arnold, Sr. | | Woodsburgh |
| * | Stray, Edward James, Sr. | | Rockville Centre |
| | Sylvester, Peter Charles | | Garden City |
| * | Tjaden, Olive Frances | | Garden City |
| | Tunstall, Harry Alphonse | | East Meadow |
| | Warinner, Asa *[See W. H. Duryea entry.]* | | Garden City |
| | Wildermuth, George C. | | Garden City |

**Louis Seabury Weeks, Sr.**

| | | | |
|---|---|---|---|
| | Dixon, Courtland Palmer, II | *The Causeway* | Lawrence |

**Stanford White**

| | | | |
|---|---|---|---|
| | Barnard, John Augustus | *Igh-na-Curah* | Lawrence |

**Arthur William Blake Wood**

| | | | |
|---|---|---|---|
| * | Huntington, Ellery Channing, Jr. | | Garden City |
| * | Mortimer, Mrs. Edith *[See A. W. B. Wood entry.]* | | Garden City |
| * | Wood, Arthur William Blake | | Garden City |

## Mary Eliza Bedford Wright residence, *The Box,* elevation drawings

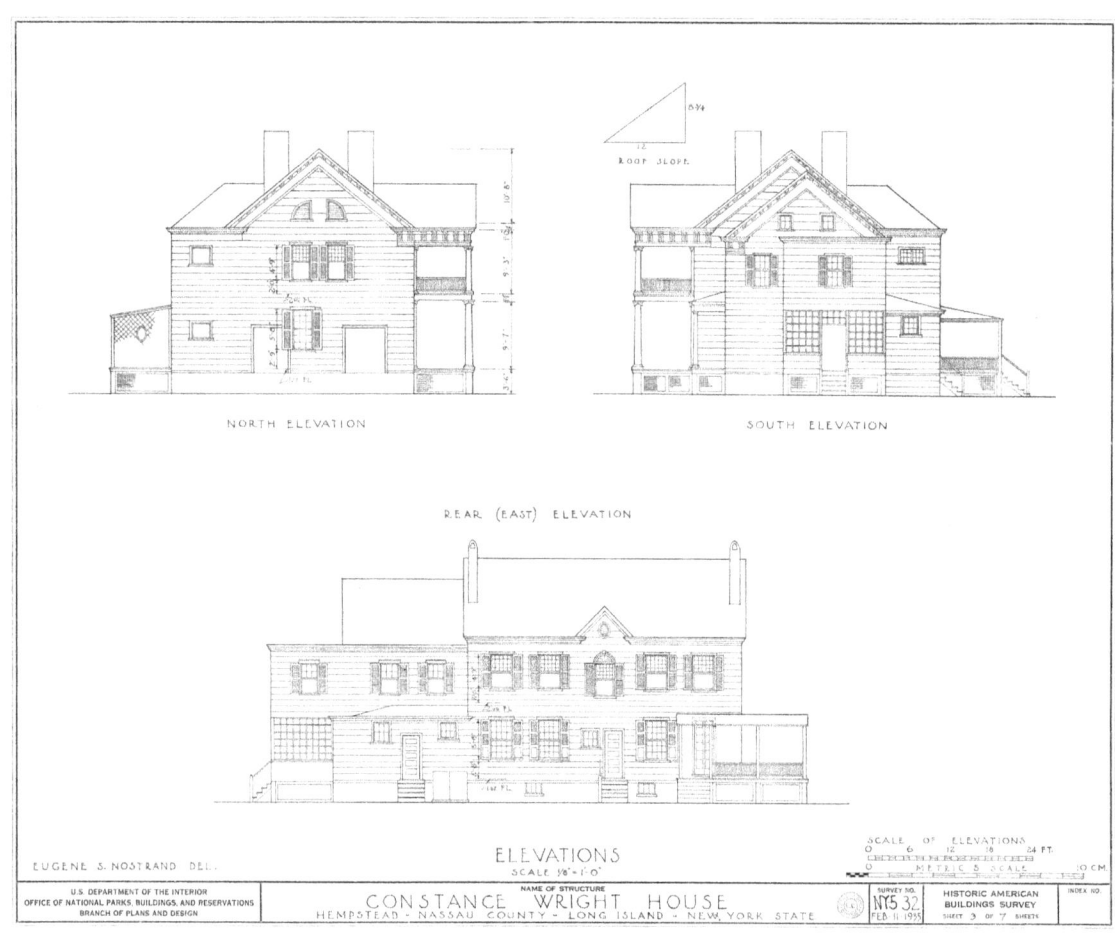

## *Civic Activism*

See the surname entry to ascertain specific civic activism information.

Adams, Alice Cameron Greenleaf
Adams, Charles Closson, Sr.
Adams, John Trevor
Adams, William, Jr.
Addison, Charles Lambert
Addison, James, Jr.
Akin, Albert John, II
Alexandre, Frederick Francis, Sr.
Allison, Dr. Benjamin Roy
Allison, Ruth Hovey
Almirall, Raymond Francis
Almy, Millicent Magruder
Anderson, Ellery Oswald
Anderton, Elizabeth Story Palmer
Anderton, Dr. William Bancroft
Aten, Helen Jackson Page
Atwater, Amariah George Cox, Sr.
Auerbach, Frederica Stevens
Auerbach, Joseph Smith
Ayer, Frederick, II
Ayer, Rosa Hahn
Backus, Harriet Ivins Davis
Baldwin, Lydia Perry Cowl
Baldwin, William Mood
Barnard, John Augustus
Barnard, Ruth Alms
Barnum, Joshua Willets
Barnum, Peter Crosby
Barnum, Sarah Ann Baldwin
Barrett, Gilbert Conklin, Sr.
Bateson, Edgar Farrar, Sr.
Beadleston, Chauncey Perry
Becker, Claude M.
Becker, Mary Collord
Beebe, Edna Alice Eldridge
Beebe, Harry W.
Belcher, Mary Halsey Seymour
Belmont, Alva Erskine Smith

Belmont, Eleanor Robson
Benkard, Bertha King Bartlett
Bentley, Edward Manross
Bird, Clara Sutton Gautier
Bird, Oliver William, Jr.
Bishop, Clifford Monroe
Black, Archibald
Blackwood, Arthur Temple
Blackwood, Sarah Goodwin
Blagden, Thomas
Blaine, Graham Burt, Sr.
Blaine, Katharine Winthrop Tweed
Blanchard, Genevieve Cadmus
Blanchard, George Holmes
Blanchard, Walter Scott, Sr.
Boardman, Andrew H.
Boardman, Sara Greenly Johnson
Bogert, Henry Lawrence, Jr.
Bond, Walter Huntington
Bonner, Douglas Griswold, Sr.
Bossert, John
Bowker, Horace, Sr.
Bowman, Archibald
Bowman, Maude Pickthall
Breed, William Constable, Sr.
Brett, George Platt, Jr.
Briggs, Albert Martin
Briggs, Anna Alden
Brisbane, Arthur
Brisbane, Phoebe Cary
Bromfield, Florence Payntar
Bromfield, Percy Butler
Bromfield, Percy Rushmore
Brooks, Jeanne Marion
Brower, Howard Stanley
Brown, Frederick Rhinelander
Brown, Lewis Dean
Browne, Curtis Northrop

## Civic Activism

Burr, Frances Page
Burr, Winthrop, Sr.
Burton, John Howes
Burton, Robert Lewis
Cammann, Herbert Schuyler
Cammann, Herman Henry
Cammann, Katharine Van Renssalaer Fairfax
Cammann, Schuyler Van Rensselaer
Camprubi, Jose Aymar
Candler, Flamen Ball
Carroll, Marion Landon
Carter, Florence Bates
Cartwright, Mildred Gould Patton
Casey, William Joseph, Jr.
Chamberlin, Bessie Shenton
Chamberlin, Dr. William Taylor
Chambers, Jay
  (aka James A. Chambers)
Chambers, Laha Whittaker
Chapman, Elizabeth Fuller
Chapman, Gilbert Whipple, Sr.
Chapman, Henry Otis, Sr.
Chapman, Katharine Bright
Chenault, Anne Naomi Quick
Chenault, Kathryn Cassell
Chenault, Kenneth Irvine
Childs, Caroline Goldsmith
Childs, John Lewis
Chu, Lisa Louise Thiebar
Clafin, Avery
Clute, Frank M.
Cobb, Boughton, Sr.
Cobb, Henry Ives, Jr.
Cochran, Alexander Smith
Cohen, Bennett R.
Cooper, Peter
Corwith, Lester F.
Coupe, Frank J.
Cowdrey, Gladys Pauline Watson
Cowdrey, Loren Montague
Cox, Daniel Hargate
Cox, Dr. Gerald Hutchinson, Sr.

Crandall, Dr. Floyd Milford
Crane, Clinton Hoadley
Cruikshank, William Morris, Sr.
Curtiss, Glenn Hammond, Sr.
Dall, Charles Whitney, Sr.
Darlington, The Reverend Gilbert Sterling Bancroft
Davie, Eugenie Mary Ladenburg
Davie, Preston, Sr.
Davis, Frances Townsend Riker
Davis, William Shippen, Sr.
de Aguilar, Elizabeth Pendleton Slattery
Dean, Howard Brush, Sr.
Delafield, Charlotte Hoffman Wyeth
Delafield, Lewis Livingston, Jr.
Delafield, Maturin Livingston, II
Delafield, Robert Hare, Jr.
Delafield, Ruth L. Manierre
DeMille, Nelson Richard
De Mott, Harry Mead
Derby, Robert Mason, Sr.
Deshler, Charles Franklin, Jr.
De Tienne, Dr. John Antoine
Devereux, Alvin, II
Devereux, Virginia H. Hagen
Dixon, Theodora Thorpe
Dixon, William Palmer, Jr.
Doolittle, Frederick William, Jr.
Dooman, Dr. David Stoddard
Dow, Edna Marion Belsterling
Driggs, Edmund Hope, Jr.
Du Bois, Arthur Mason
Duncan, Alexander Butler
Duncan, Eloise Stevenson
Dunnell, Frank Lyman, Sr.
Dunstan, Eda Louise Kempshall
Durand, Adele Marie
Durand, Celestin Aloysious, III
Durand, Irene J. Sweeney
Durand, James Francis
Duryea, Wright, Jr.
Dwight, Emily Thomas
Dwight, Philip J.

*Civic Activism*

Dwyer, Martin, Sr.
Eaton, Margaret Burton
Eaton, Walter Bradley
Ebinger, Walter Dohrmann
Eddy, William Higbie, Sr.
Edsell, Geraldine V. Dulfer
Edsell, Levi Perin
Edsell, Ralph James, Sr.
Edwards, Jesse
Edwards, Lotta Julia Eaton
Egginton, Hersey
Egginton, Mary E.
Egly, Henry Harris
Eldridge, Elizabeth Moore Huyck
Elliman, Edyth Howard Coppell
Elliman, Lawrence Bogert, Sr.
Enequist, William Lars
Englis, Sybil Adel Genthner
Fairchild, Edith Clappe
Fairchild, Willard, Sr.
   (aka Charles Willard Fairchild)
Fanning, Edward Jerome
Fanning, Genevieve Marie Shaw
Feldstein, Kathleen Foley
Feldstein, Martin Stuart
Fensterer, Dr. Gustave Adolf
Ferguson, David, Sr.
Ferris, Anna Jacobus Bennett
Ferris, Dorcas Williams
Ferris, Dr. Henry Clay, Sr.
Ferris, Mary Lanman Douw
Ferris, Morris Douw, Sr.
Ferris, Morris Patterson
Finch, Margaret Riker Whipple
Finlayson, Elizabeth Harmsteadt Coe
Fisher, Dr. Lamont H.
Floyd, Nicoll, Jr.
Fogarty, James Francis, Sr.
Forman, Helaine Piatt Peters
Forrest, Harriet Louise Wright
Francklyn, Reginald Gebhard
Frew, Walter Edwin

Frost, Newberry Halstead
Fuller, Paul, Jr.
Furst, Michael
Garde, John Franklin, Jr.
Gardner, Bertram
Gerard, George Henry
Gerstner, Louis Vincent, Jr.
Gesell, Doris M. Herdman
Gesell, Dr. Herbert Ross, Sr.
Geer, Enos Throop, Sr.
Glass, Brent David
Gleason, Marshall Wilfred
Glover, Rhoda Ann Hallock
Goodhue, Francis Abbot
Goodwin, Doris Helen Kearns
Goodwin, Richard Naradof
Greason, Samuel, Jr.
Green, Walton Atwater, Sr.
Greene, Herbert Gouverneur
Greenfield, Jerry
Greenleaf, Constance Bacon
Gross, Andre Eugene
Gross, Elinor Whitney Kendall
Gruner, Harriot Hudson Coffin
Gwynne, Dorothy Goddard Ficken
Hamill, Robert Lyon, Sr.
Hamilton, Campbell Thorpe
Hamlin, Francis Bacon, Sr.
Handy, Courtland Waite
Hanemann, Edna Cranmer
Hanemann, Frederica Carlotta Prentiss
Hanemann, John Theodore, Sr.
Hard, DeCourcy Lawrence, Sr.
Hard, Marjorie Work
Harlow, Frank Strobridge
Harper, Joseph Henry, Jr.
Harper, Joseph Henry, Sr.
Harrar, Dr. James Aitken
Harriman, Edward Henry
Harriman, Mary Williamson Averell
Harris, Tracy Hyde, Jr.
Hart, Alexander Richmond

## Civic Activism

Hastings, The Reverend A. Abbott
Hastings, Dorothy Quincy Turner
Hatch, E. Constance De Boer
Hatch, Eric Stow
Hatch, Frederic Horace
Haughey, Irene Test
Haughey, William Wallace
Hawke, John Daniel, Jr.
Hendrickson, Charles Le Roy
Herrick, Harold
Herrick, Harold Edward, Sr.
Herrick, Newbold Lawrence, Sr.
Herrick, Pauline Bacon
Hewlett, George H.
Hewlett, Roger Sanderson
Hewlett, James Monroe
Hillman, Bas Sheva Abramowitz
Hillman, Stanley
Hinckley, Isobel Catherine Bartlett
  (aka Danah Bartlett)
Hinckley, Julian
Hinckley, Samuel Parker
Hoag, Sara H. Keith
Hodges, Wetmore, Sr.
Hofheimer, Corinne Kodziesen
Hofheimer, Lester
Hofstra, Katharine Mason
Hofstra, William Sake
Horton, Helen Henderson
Howe, Louise Pratt
Hubbell, Eliza Strong Platt
Hubbell, George Loring, Jr.
Hubbell, George Loring, Sr.
Hubbell, John Platt, Sr.
Hubbell, Ralph Peters, Sr.
Hunter, Fenley
  (aka Richard Fenley Hunter)
Iger, Robert Allen
Ivison, Maynard Cady
Ivison, William Crane
Jackson, Rickard Gilbert
Jacobi, Florence Harris

Jacobi, Harold, Sr.
Jacobi, Sanford
Jewell, John Voorhees, Sr.
Jewell, Marjorie Elizabeth Winter
Jones, Alma Elizabeth Steiner
Jones, Bethune Wellington
Jones, Thomas Catesby, Sr.
Kamen, Dean Lawrence
Karan, Donna Ivy Faske
Keisler, Peter Douglas
Kelly, Dr. Aquin S.
Kendall, William Beals
Kendrick, Elizabeth Pendleton Slattery
Kennedy, Henry Van Rensselaer
Kernochan, Eloise Stevenson
Kilbreth, James Truesdell, Jr.
Kilmer, Dr. Theron Wendell, Sr.
  (aka Theron Sylvester Norton, Jr.)
Kingsland, Harold Nutting
Kingsland, Mathilde Marie Thieriot
Kingsley, Darwin Pearl, Jr.
Kingsley, Elizabeth Eckhart
Kingsley, Heywood Mason Butler
Kip, Ira Andruss
Kip, Katharine Fowler
Kobbe, Frederick William
Koehler, Robert Henry
Koehler, Ruth Allen Young
Koehne, John Lawrence, Sr.
Koons, Franklin Stevenson
Krugman, Paul Robin
Ladd, William Fowle, Jr.
Lamy, Henry Bernard, Jr.
Lannin, Hannah J. Furlong
Lannin, Joseph John
Larkin, John Adrian, Sr.
Lawrence, John L.
Lawrence, Newbold Trotter, Sr.
Lefferts, Marshall Clifford, Sr.
Lehrenkrauss, Charles Frederick
Leighton, Alexander E.
Leighton, Charlotte Kayser

## Civic Activism

Leighton, George Bridge
Levy, George Morton, Sr.
Lewis, Edith Greenough
Lissberger, Benjamin
Livingston, John Griswold, Sr.
Locke, Campbell, Sr.
Loft, George William
Loft, Julia McMahon
Long, Dorothy Jacquelin Smith
Long, William Henderson, Jr.
Lord, Franklin Butler, Sr.
Lord, George de Forest, Sr.
Low, Ethelbert Ide
Low, Gertrude Herrick
Lowden, Richard
Ludlum, Dr. Charles Henry
Lynch, Gertrude Low
Lyon, Edmund Burton
Macy, Carleton
Macy, Edith Wiesman Carpenter
Macy, Valentine Everit, Sr.
Macy, Winifred Earl Lefferts
Maitland, James William
Maitland, Sylvia Wigglesworth
Mallett, Percy Smith
Mallouk, Ann Marmon
Mallouk, George Elias
Marks, Arthur David, Jr.
Marks, Edith C. Jacobi
Marshall, Charles Alexander
Marshall, Lillie H. Cunningham
Massimino, Michael James
McCrea, James Alexander, II
McKee, Lanier
McKinny, Alexander, Sr.
McVitty, Edward Quinby, Sr.
McVitty, Harriet Elizabeth Clausen
Meeker, Samuel Mundy, Jr.
Mellen, Chase, Sr.
Meneely, Charles Dickinson
Merrill, Payson, Sr.
Merritt, Cornelia Kane McElroy

Meyerkort, Edith Jacquelin Smith
Meyerkort, John, Jr.
  (aka Jack Meyerkort, Jr.)
Miller, Ann Talbot Day
Miller, Danforth, Sr.
Miller, Frances Tileston Breese
Miller, John Robinson, Jr.
Miller, Lawrence McKeever, Sr.
Miller, William Wilson
Mills, Edward Shorrey
Minton, Henry Miller
Mixter, George, Sr.
Mixter, Muriel Eaton
Moller, Hans Eskildsen
Mooney, Franklin Drake, Sr.
Moore, Arthur Standish
Moore, Rufus Ellis
Morgenthau, Julius Caesar, Sr.
Morgenthau, Maximilian, Sr.
Morris, McLean Forman, Sr.
Morrow, Dr. Albert Sidney, Sr.
Moyers, Bill
Moyers, Judith Suzanne Davidson
Mulford, Miss Fannie
Munson, Claire Adele Burkhart
Munson, Lawrence Josiah
  (aka Lauritz Josiah Monsen)
Murphy, William Gordon, Jr.
Murray, Susanne Elizabeth Warren
Naething, Mary Louise Bingham
Neilson, Robert Hude
Newton, Arthur Ulysses
Nicoll, De Lancey, Jr.
Norris, Alfred Lockwood
Ohnewald, George Henry
Olena, Alfred Douglas
Olney, Peter Butler, Jr.
Olney, Peter Butler, Sr.
Olney, Sigourney Butler, Sr.
Orr, Henry Steers
Orr, Mary Keenan

## Civic Activism

Orvis, Ina Leland
Orvis, Schuyler Adams, Sr.
Osborne, Lawrence Woodhull
Ossman, Mary Tompkins
Osterhout, Howard
Otto, Lena Martina Retter
Page, Walter Hines, Sr.
Pancake, Carl Oakley
Pardee, Abby Rockefeller
Parker, Don M., Sr.
Parker, Glowacki Redfield
Parker, Marion Stevenson
Parkhurst, William Man
Patterson, Edward Liddon
Peace, Arthur W.
Peace, Jessie N. Irwin
Pearce, Arthur Williams, Sr.
Peck, Arthur Nelson
Pell, Walden, Jr.
Pennington, Grace Marion Merritt
Perkins, Ethel Holbrooke
Perkins, Norton
Persell, Mabel Elizabeth Fornof
Peterkin, DeWitt, Sr.
Peters, Ralph, Jr.
Peters, Ralph, Sr.
Philbin, Ewing Reginald, Sr.
  (aka Erving Reginald Philbin, Sr.)
Philbin, Florence S. Burton
Philbin, Stephen Holladay
Philips, Frederic Dimon
Philips, Jessie Matheson Taylor
Philips, William Frederic
Pittman, Ernest Wetmore
Pittman, Estelle Young Romeyn
Plunkett, Henry Willoughby
  (aka Harry Plunkett Gratton)
Polk, Frank Lyon, Sr.
Porter, Henry Hobart, Jr.
Pratt, Robert Edward, Sr.
Prescott, Elizabeth Harmsteadt Coe
Pritchard, Clarence Franklin

Proctor, William Ross, Jr.
Recht, William, Sr.
Remick, Joseph Gould
Richard, Auguste
Richard, Hetty Lawrence Hemenway
Richards, Junius Alexander, Sr.
Ridder, Joseph Edward, Sr.
Ripley, Joseph Pierce
Ripley, Mary Baldwin Hyde
Rives, Francis Bayard
Roberts, Albert Samuel, Jr.
Robins, Thomas, IV
Robinson, Beverley Randolph
Robinson, Josephine DeMott
Roche, The Reverend Spencer Summerfield
Rogers, Edward Sidney
Rolston, Brown, Sr.
Roosevelt Mary De Verdery Akin
Roosevelt, Oliver Wolcott, Sr.
Rose, Bertha Benkard
Roth, Arthur Thomas
Ruperti, Justus
Russell, Frank Henry
Rutter, Nathaniel Edward Caldwell, Sr.
Sage, Margaret Olivia Slocum
Sage, Russell
St. John, Edward Atkinson
Salmon, Hamilton Henry, Jr.
Sampson, Sally Phillips Blagden
Sanford, George Baylies
Sargent, Charles Sprague, Jr.
Sargent, Dagmar Wetmore
Schieffelin, John Jay, Sr.
Schley, Adele Sturges Mason
Schley, Buchanan, Jr.
Schlossberg, Alice Hermine Jacobi
Schlossberg, Arnold, Sr.
Schultz, Albert Bigelow, Sr.
Schultz, Winifred Houghton King
Scott, Mary Baldwin Hyde
Searle, John Endicott, Sr.
Seymour, Origen Storrs, II

*Civic Activism*

Shaw, Munson Gallaudet, Sr.
Shepard, Frederic White
Sherman, Hannah Newbold Lawrence
Sizer, Theodore
Slesinger, Estelle Werner
  (aka Ruth Stuyvesant)
Slesinger, Laurence Anthony
Sloan, Robert Sage, Sr.
Slocum, Henry Warner, Jr.
Smith, Anna Gertrude Jones
Smith, Augustine Jacquelin
Smith, Cyrus Porter, Sr.
Snyder, William Robert
Southworth, Theodore
Stebbins, George Ledyard, Sr.
Steinberg, Julius
Stephan, Albert Ralph
Stephan, Elizabeth Jane Beason
Stevens, Byam Kirby, III
Stevens, William Dixon
Stevenson, Maxwell
Stewart, Celeste Dorwin
Stewart, John Henderson, Jr.
Stewart, Samuel Bradford, Jr.
Stone, Florence Scofield
Stricker, Hans Carl
Sturgis, Gertrude Cutts Lovett
Sturgis, Henry Sprague, Sr.
Swett, The Reverend Canon Paul Flynn, Sr.
Tapscott, Ralph Henry
Tarbell, Gage Eli
Taylor, Willard Underhill, Sr.
Taylor, William Reed Kirkland, Sr.
Terry, Thomas Henry
Tew, Benjamin Taylor
Thayer, Benjamin Bowditch, Jr.
Thomas, Edward Clarke Oertel
Thomas, Ruth Woodland
Thompson, Margaret Riggs Bogle
Thorpe, Warren, Sr.
Tibbs, Benjamin Hatfield
Tilford, Frank

Timpson, Carl William
Timpson, James
Tjaden, Olive Frances
Townley, The Reverend Frank Maxwell
Townsend, Edward Nicoll, Jr.
Tucker, St. George Brooke
Tunmore, John Septimus
Tunstall, Dorothy Ann Lannin
  (aka Dorothea Ann Lannin Tunstall)
Vandewater, Benjamin Cornelius
Vandewater, James Horatio Poole
Van Rensselaer, Bernard Sanders
Van Vranken, Garrett Daniel
Van Zandt, Frederick Neville
Vaughan, Donald Cuyler, Sr.
Vogel, Emilie Sherwood
Vogel, Henry John
Voss, William
Wainwright, Eleanor Painter Sloan
Walsh, Dorothy Baldwin
Ward, Rodney Allen
Ward, Sylvanus Dwight
Warren, Charles Elliott, Sr.
Warren, Northam, Sr.
Weed, Leroy Jefferson
Weeks, Louis Seabury, Sr.
Weisselberg, Allen Howard
Weller, Augustus Noble
Welsh, Joseph Wickes, Jr.
Welton, Dr. Thurston Scott
White, Thomas Francis, Jr.
Whitney, Arthur Edward
Whiton, Henry Devereux
Wickersham, Cornelius Wendell, Sr.
Wickersham, George Woodward
Wickersham, Mildred Wendell
Wigglesworth, Beatrice Murphy
Wigglesworth, Henry
Wildermuth, George C.
Williams, Ichabod Thomas, II
Williams, Thomas, II
Williams, Thomas Resolved

*Civic Activism*

Woodruff, Timothy Lester
Woolverton, William Henderson, Jr.
Work, James Henry, Jr.
Wright, Margery Rich White
Wright, Wilfred La Salles
Wyld, Robert Hasbrouck
Young, Mary Wickham Conklin

Young, Susanne Meredith Bottomley
Young, Willis Howard, Sr.
Zara, Francesco A.
Ziegler, Frederick J.
Ziegler, Henry Ludwig W.

Brook Russell Astor,
chairman of the Astor Foundation and widow of William Vincent Astor,
quipped on the concept of *noblesse oblige:*

"*Money is like manure, it should be spread around.*"

*Ruth Hovey Allison*
*(Mrs. Benjamin Roy Allison)*

*Civic Activism*

## Anti – Suffragists:

**Backus**, Harriet Ivins Davis
(Mrs. Henry Clinton Backus)
**111 Seventh Street, Garden City**

**Gross**, Andre Eugene
**122 Salisbury Avenue, Garden City**

**Gross**, Elinor Whitney Kendell
(Mrs. Andre Eugene Gross)
**122 Salisbury Avenue, Garden City**

**Wickersham**, Mildred Wendell
(Mrs. George Woodward Wickersham)
*Marchfield*, **Hollywood Crossing, Lawrence**

**Wickersham**, George Woodward
*Marshfield*, **Hollywood Crossing, Lawrence**

**Wickersham**, Miss Constance
*[See G. W. Wickersham entry.]*
*Marshfield*, **Hollywood Crossing, Lawrence**

## Suffragists:

**Anderton**, Elizabeth Story Palmer
(Mrs. William Bancroft Anderton)
*Ye Corners*, **Ocean Avenue, Lawrence**

**Belmont**, Alva Erskine Smith
(Mrs. William Kissam Vanderbilt, Sr.;
Mrs. Oliver Perry Belmont)
*Idlehour* [I], **Idle Hour Boulevard, Oakdale**;
*Brookholt*, **Front Street, East Meadow**;
*Beacon Towers*, **Sands Light Road, Sands Point**

**Brisbane**, Arthur
**Newbridge Road and Hempstead Turnpike, East Meadow**

**Brisbane**, Phoebe Cary
(Mrs. Arthur Brisbane)
**Newbridge Road and Hempstead Turnpike, East Meadow**

**Burr**, Frances Page
(Mrs. Winthrop Burr, Sr.)
*Orchard Hall*, **Causeway, Lawrence**

**Childs**, Caroline Goldsmith
(Mrs. John Lewis Childs)
**91 Tulip Avenue, Floral Park**

**Delafield**, Charlotte Hoffman Wyeth
(Mrs. Lewis Livingston Delafield, Jr.)
*Norton Perkins* **Cottage, Ocean Avenue, Lawrence**

**Eldridge**, Elizabeth Moore Huyck
(Mrs. Lewis Angevine Eldridge)
**115 Greenwich Street, Hempstead**

**Francke**, Marian Doane Rand
(Mrs. Albert Francke, Sr.)
**Meadow Lane, Lawrence**

**Glover**, Anna Elizabeth
(Mrs. Nathaniel Matson)
*[See Glover entry.]*
**Foxhurst and Merrick Roads, Baldwin;
1249 Pacific Street, Brooklyn**

**Glover**, Rhoda Ann Hallock
(Mrs. John Irvin Glover)
**Foxhurst and Merrick Roads, Baldwin**

**Haughey**, Irene Test
(Mrs. William Wallace Haughey)
**Garden City**

## Civic Activism

**Hubbell**, Elza Strong Platt
(Mrs. George Loring Hubbell, Sr.)
*Lonsomehurst*, **6 Cathedral Avenue, Garden City**

**Macy**, Edith Wiesman Carpenter
(Mrs. Valentine Everit Macy, Sr.)
**Hewlett**

**Macy**, Valentine Everit, Sr.
**Hewlett**

**Philips**, Jessie Matheson Taylor
(Mrs. Frederic Dimon Philips)
*Greyhouse*, **365 Ocean Avenue, Lawrence**

**Robinson**, Josephine DeMott
(Mrs. Charles M. Robinson)
**between Nassau and Hempstead Avenues, West Hempstead**

**Sage**, Margaret Olivia Slocum
(Mrs. Russell Sage)
*Cedarcroft / Cedar Croft*, **105 Ocean Avenue and Mallow Way, Lawrence**

**Wright**, Margery Rich White
(Mrs. Wilfred La Salles Wright)
**Hempstead Avenue, Hempstead**

*Suffragist parade, New York, City, 1916*

### *Estate Names*

When the owner who contracted with the architect is known, it is indicated by an asterisk.
Multiple owners are listed in chronological order of ownership, not alphabetically by surname.
Ownership of estates is listed only for those that used that particular estate name.
See the surname entry to ascertain names used by other owners of the same estate.

| | | | |
|---|---|---|---|
| *Aboha Hanta* | | Hanemann, John Theodore, Sr. | Hewlett Bay Park |
| *Albro House* | | Burton, John Howes | Lawrence |
| | * | Burton, Robert Lewis | |
| *Applecot* | | Cartwright, Henry Rogers, Jr. | Hewlett |
| *Avila* | * | Boulton, William Bowen, Sr. | Lawrence |
| *Ballyracket* | | Sloan, Benson Bennett, Sr. | Lawrence |
| *Bethpage* | | Pease, Walter Albert, Jr. | Hempstead |
| *Birch Corners* | * | Macy, Carroll | Hewlett Bay Park |
| | | Miller, Danforth, Sr. | |
| *Bleak House* | | Jones, Dr. Dunham Carroll | Hempstead |
| *Blemton Manor* | | Belmont, August, II | Hempstead |
| *The Box* | | Wright, Mary Eliza Bedford | Hempstead |
| *Boxley* | | Kendrick, Frederick William | Hempstead |
| *Boxwood* | * | Connable, Arthur W. | Hewlett Bay Park |
| *The Brae* | | Sherman, Charles Edwin | Lawrence |
| *Breezy Way* | | Pier, Roy | Hewlett Harbor |
| *Briarwood* | | Hard, DeCourcy Lawrence, Sr. | Lawrence |
| *Briarwood* | | Wickersham, Cornelius Wendell, Sr. | Lawrence |
| *Brightside* | * | Harper, Joseph Henry, Sr. | Lawrence |
| | | Dunstan, James Samuel | |
| *Brookholt* | * | Belmont, Oliver Hazard Perry | East Meadow |
| *The Bungalow* | | Macy, George Henry | Lawrence |
| *Bush Corners* | | Kilbreth, James Truesdell, Jr. | Hewlett Bay Park |
| *By-the-Way* | | Brown, Dr. Frederick Tilden | Woodmere |
| *The Byways* | | Sanford, George Baylies | Lawrence |
| *Carman – Lowden Homestead* | | Lowden, Richard | East Meadow |
| *The Causeway* | | Dixon, Courtland Palmer, II | Lawrence |
| *Cedar Corners* | | Goodwin, Robert Henning | Hewlett Bay Park |
| *Cedarcroft / Cedar Croft* | | Sage, Russell | Lawrence |
| | | Marshall, May Louise Bamber | |
| *Channel's End* | | Russell, Dr. Thomas Hendrick | Hewlett Bay Park |
| *Cherry Bounce* | | Peabody, Rushton, Sr. | Hewlett Harbor |
| *Cherrygarth* | | Bentley, Edward Manross | Lawrence |
| | | Bentley, Edward Sailsbury, Sr. | |
| *Chilton Gables* | | Sloan, Robert Sage, Sr. | Woodsburgh |
| *The Chimney Corner* | | Cobb, Boughton, Sr. | Hewlett Bay Park |
| *Cluny Lodge* | | Elliman, Lawrence Bogert, Sr. | Cedarhurst |
| *Corral* | | Eaton, Walter Bradley | Lawrence |
| *Cornerware* | | Chambers, William Ely, Sr. | Hewlett Bay Park |

549

*Estate Names*

| | | |
|---|---|---|
| *The Crossways* | * Ripley, Sidney Dillon, Sr. | Uniondale |
| | Scott, Charles Robert | |
| *Driftwood* | Hard, Anson Wales, Sr. | Lawrence |
| *East View* | * Crane, Warren Seabury | Lawrence |
| *East Meadows* | Konta, Geoffrey | East Meadow |
| *Edgewater Cottage* | Pardee, Dr. Ensign Bennett | Lawrence |
| | Pardee, Dr. Irving Hotchkiss | |
| *Engleside* | Work, James Henry, Jr. | Lawrence |
| *Fairway* | Philips, William Frederic | Lawrence |
| *The Farm* | Stevenson, Richard Wilson, Jr. | Hewlett Bay Park |
| | Stevenson, Joseph Hutchinson | |
| | Parker, Henry Seabury, Sr. | |
| *Five Oaks* | * Erhart, William Herman | Lawrence |
| *Four Winds* | Fuller, Paul, Jr. | Hewlett Bay Park |
| *Fox Hall* | * Fox, William | Woodsburgh |
| *Garstead* | McVitty, Edward Quinby, Sr. | Garden City |
| *The Gowans* | Work, James Henry, Sr. | Lawrence |
| *Greenhedge* | Bird, Oliver William, Jr. | Uniondale |
| *Green Plains* | Jones, Thomas Catesby, Sr. | Hewlett Bay Park |
| *Greyhouse* | * Philips, Frederic Dimon | Lawrence |
| *Grove Point* | * Mann, Samuel Vernon, Jr. | Lawrence |
| *Half Way Nirvana* | * Roosevelt, Elliott, Sr. | Salisbury |
| *The Haven* | Van Rensselaer, Maunsell, Jr. | Hewlett Neck |
| *Hawkswood* | Marshall, Levin Rothrock, Sr. | Hewlett Harbor |
| *Heathcote* | * Ladenburg, Adolph | Salisbury |
| | (aka Moritz Adolph Emil Ladenburg) | |
| *Hedgewood* | * Lefferts, Marshall Clifford, Sr. | Lawrence |
| *Hempstead Farm* | Terry, Thomas Henry | East Meadow |
| *High Tide* | Kingsley, Darwin Pearl, Jr. | Hewlett Harbor |
| *Holly Holm* | Thompson, Joseph TodHunter | Lawrence |
| *Holmeridge* | Ballantine, John Holme, II | Woodsburgh |
| *Homeacre* | Livingston, Johnston, II | Hewlett |
| | (aka Johnston Livingston, Jr.) | |
| *Homewood* | Akin, Albert John, II | Hewlett Harbor |
| *Homewood* | Lawrence, Newbold Trotter, Sr. | Lawrence |
| *Iris Acre* | Twining, Charles | Garden City |
| *Journey's End* | Mumford, Philip Gurdon | Lawrence |
| *Justamere Cottage* | Brett, George Platt, Jr. | Woodmere |
| *Lakeview* | Loft, George William | Baldwin |
| *Landfall* | Adams, William, III | Lawrence |
| *Langsyne* | Mulford, Charles William | Hempstead |
| | Mulford, Fannie | Hempstead |
| | Mulford, Harriet | Hempstead |
| *Lauderdale* | * Porter, Henry Hobart, Jr. | Lawrence |

*Estate Names*

| | | |
|---|---|---|
| *Lindenmere* | * Cammann, Herman Henry<br>Cammann, Herbert Schuyler | Merrick |
| *The Lodge* | Stevenson, Maxwell | Hempstead |
| *Lonesomehurst* | * Hubbell, George Loring, Sr. | Garden City |
| *Longdrive* | Brower, Howard Stanley | West Hempstead |
| *Longwood* | * Forrest, Richard Earp | Lawrence |
| *Longwood Hall* | Roberts, Albert Samuel, Jr. | Lawrence |
| *Ma Chaumiere* | Almirall, Raymond Francis | Hempstead |
| *Mapleglades* | Rives, Francis Bayard | Hewlett Bay Park |
| *Marigolds* | Ruperti, Justus | Lawrence |
| *Marshfield* | * Wickersham, George Woodward | Lawrence |
| *Meadow Brook Farm* | Barnum, Peter Crosby<br>Barnum, Joshua Willets | East Meadow |
| *Meadow Hall* | * Hazard, William Ayrault, Sr. | Lawrence |
| *The Meadows* | * Kernochan, James Lorillard<br>Duncan, Alexander Butler | Hempstead |
| *Meadowside* | Olney, Peter Butler, Sr. | Lawrence |
| *Meadowview* | Whitlock, Bache McEvers, Jr. | Hewlett |
| *Meadowwood* | * Macy, Carleton<br>Veeder, Paul Lansing | Hewlett Bay Park |
| *Meenahga* | Weeks, Herbert Augustus | Lawrence |
| *Merriefield* | Voss, William<br>Lewis, Henry Llewellyn Daingerfield, Jr. | Hewlett Bay Park |
| *Mistletoe Way* | Martin, Thomas Stephen | Lawrence |
| *The Moorings* | Brooks, Ernest, Sr. | Lawrence |
| *The Moorings* | Stone, Herman Foster | Lawrence |
| *Moorlands* | Lawrence, John L., Sr. | Lawrence |
| *The Mount* | Stevens, Eben | Lawrence |
| *Nearacre* | * Lyon, Edmund Burton | Hempstead |
| *The Netherlands* | * Hofstra, William Sake | Hempstead |
| *Nicholyn* | Nichols, John Dykers | Woodmere |
| *Nieman* | Alexandre, Frederick Francis, Sr. | Lawrence |
| *Nooke* | Benedict, Le Grande Lockwood, Jr. | Lawrence |
| *Noranda* | Long, William Henderson, Jr. | Hewlett Harbor |
| *Norton Perkins Cottage* | Delafield, Lewis Livingston, Jr. | Lawrence |
| *Oak Lawn* | Pell, Walden, Jr. | Lawrence |
| *Oak Lodge* | Adams, Charles Closson, Sr. | Lawrence |
| *The Oasis* | Davie, Preston, Sr. | Salisbury |
| *Oatlands* | * Manice, de Forest | Elmont |
| *The Orchard* | Stricker, Hans Carl | Woodmere |
| *Orchard Hall* | * Burr, Winthrop, Sr.<br>Lanman, Jonathan Trumball, Sr. | Lawrence |
| *Our House* | Murray, Herman Stump | Hewlett Neck |

*Estate Names*

| | | |
|---|---|---|
| *The Patch* | Townsend, Robert | Garden City |
| *Phoenix Lodge* | Olcott, William Morrow Knox<br>Lebaudy, Jacques | Salisbury |
| *The Pines* | Crandall, Dr. Floyd Milford | Hempstead |
| *Pine Tree House* | Philbin, Ewing Reginald, Sr.<br>(aka Erving Reginald Philbin, Sr.) | Hewlett Bay Park |
| *Red House* | Gildersleeve, Raleigh Colston | Lawrence |
| *Restleigh* | * Kniffin, Howard Summers, Sr. | Lawrence |
| *Rock Hall* | Patterson, Edward Liddon | Lawrence |
| *Rosebank* | * Scott, John Frederick | Hewlett Bay Park |
| *Roselle Manor* | * Levy, Isaac D. | Cedarhurst |
| *Rustee Granit* | Whipple, Julian Van Ness | Hewlett |
| *Seawane* | * Auerbach, Joseph Smith<br>Auerbach, John Hone, Sr. | Hewlett Harbor |
| *Seven Acres* | Baldwin, William Mood | Garden City |
| *Shadowland* | Bishop, Clifford Monroe | Garden City |
| *Shortacre* | Duryea, Wright, Jr. | Hempstead |
| *Somerleas* | Hatch, Frederic Horace<br>Hatch, Alden R. | Lawrence |
| *Sosiego* | * Lord, Daniel de Forest, V<br>Seymour, Origen Storrs, II | Lawrence |
| *South Wind* | Bateson, Edgar Farrar, Sr. | Lawrence |
| *Still Pond* | Warren, Charles Elliott, Sr. | Hewlett Neck |
| *Stonehouse* | * Parker, Carleton Allen | West Hempstead |
| *Stone Lodge* | Dunham, Carroll, III | Lawrence |
| *Strode* | Mixter, George, Sr. | Hewlett Harbor |
| *Sunny Ridge* | Lovering, Joseph Swain, II | Hewlett Bay Park |
| *Sunnyside* | Smith, Augustine Jacquelin | Lawrence |
| *Sunset Hall* | * Hinckley, Samuel Parker | Lawrence |
| *Talbot House* | * Taylor, Talbot Jones, Jr. | Lawrence |
| *Tenant Farm* | Richard, Auguste | Lawrence |
| *Terrace Hall* | * Peabody, Richard Augustus | Lawrence |
| *Three Acres* | Nicoll, De Lancey, Jr. | Hewlett Harbor |
| *Three Oaks* | * Kennedy, Henry Van Rensselaer | Hempstead |
| *Tigh-na-Curach* | Barnard, John Augustus | Lawrence |
| *Twin Gables* | Lissberger, Benjamin | Hewlett Harbor |
| *Uniondale Farm* | Hadden, James E. Smith | Uniondale |
| *The Villa Blue* | * Carter, Russell Steenback | Hewlett Bay Park |
| *Villa Nancy* | Miller, William Wilson | Lawrence |
| *Waycroft* | Anderson, Ellery Oswald | Hempstead |
| *Wayside* | Moller, Charles George, Jr. | Lawrence |
| *Whale Acres* | * Perkins, Norton<br>Auchincloss, Samuel Sloan, Sr.<br>Breed, William Constable, Sr. | Lawrence |

*Estate Names*

| | | |
|---|---|---|
| *Wilcemay Farm* | Ivison, William Crane | Lawrence |
| *The Wild Oat* | Pardee, Dr. Harold Ensign Bennett | Cedarhurst |
| *Willisleigh* | \* Young, Willis Howard, Sr.<br>Harlow, Frank Strobridge | Hempstead |
| *Wilton Gables* | \* Sloan, Thomas Donaldson, Sr. | Lawrence |
| *Windemere* | Williams, Thomas Resolved | Lawrence |
| *Windward* | Brown, Mary Crosby Renwick | Lawrence |
| *Windy Top* | Timpson, Carl William, Sr. | Hewlett Harbor |
| *Wistaria* | Goadby, Arthur McMaster | Lawrence |
| *Wistaria Lodge* | \* Harris, Tracy Hyde, Jr. | Hewlett Bay Park |
| *Wonderwhy* | \* Macy, Carleton | Hewlett Bay Park |
| *Wyndymeede* | \* Peters, Ralph, Sr. | Garden City |
| *Ye Corners* | Anderton, Dr. William Bancroft | Lawrence |

### Tracy Hyde Harris, Jr. residence, *Wistaria Lodge*

*front facade*

*rear facade*

*William Herman Erhart residence, Five Oaks,
1906*

*William Voss residence, Merriefield,
rear facade*

## Golf Courses

The estate that is presently a golf course is identified by the
original owner. For subsequent estate owners, see surname entry.

Seawane Golf Course　　　　　　　　　　　Joseph Smith Auerbach estate,
　　　　　　　　　　　　　　　　　　　　　　*Seawane*, Hewlett Harbor

*William Fox residence, Fox Hall*

*George Woodward Wickersham residence, Marshfield, 1914*

## *Landscape Achitects*

When the date of landscaping is known, it has been included in brackets. Since, in some instances, more than one landscape architect worked on an estate and, in some rare instances, the architect who designed the house also designed the estate's grounds, the surname entry should be consulted to determine if anyone else was involved in designing the estate grounds. When the estate owner who contracted for landscaping is known, it is indicated by an asterisk. Original and subsequent estate owners are included in the list.

**Ruth Bramley Dean**

    Mulford, Charles William      *Langsyne*      Hempstead
                                                 (c. 1917)

\*   Mulford, Miss Fannie      *Langsyne*      Hempstead
                                                 (c. 1917)

    Mulford, Harriet      *Langsyne*      Hempstead
                                                 (c. 1917)

**Beatrix Jones Farrand**

\*   Mann, Samuel Vernon, Jr.      *Grove Point*      Lawrence

**Annette Hoyt Flanders**

\*   Crane, Mrs. Warren Seabury      *East View*      Lawrence
                                          (designed flagstone terrace, shrubbery, lawns, and vegetable and flower gardens, c. 1934)

\*   Demarest, F. C.      (c. 1925)      Rockville Centre

\*   Peck, Arthur Knowlton, Sr.      (designed formal gardens)      Lawrence

    Peck, Arthur Knowlton, Sr.      (designed flagstone terrace, shrubbery, lawns, and vegetable and flower gardens, c. 1934)      Lawrence

**Hicks Nursery**

\*   Baldwin, William Mood      *Seven Acres* (supplied Red Cedar windbreak)      Garden City

\*   Belmont, Oliver Hazard Perry      *Brookholt* (supplied plantings)      East Meadow

\*   Brisbane, Arthur      (supplied plantings)      East Meadow

\*   Burr, Winthrop, Sr.      *Orchard Hall* (supplied Norway Maples, Japanese Poplars, Pin Oaks, and Silver Maples)      Lawrence

\*   Burton, Robert Lewis      *Albro House* (supplied plantings)      Lawrence

    Corchran, Alexander Smith      (supplied plantings)      East Meadow

\*   Eldridge, Lewis Angevine, Sr.      (supplied plantings)      Hempstead

\*   Francke, Albert, Sr.      (supplied plantings)      Lawrence

    Frew, Walter Edwin      (supplied plantings)      Lawrence

    Greenberg, Henry      *Orchard Hall* (supplied Norway Maples, Japanese Poplars, Pin Oaks, and Silver Maples)      Lawrence
        *[See W. Burr, Sr. entry.]*

\*   Hubbell, George Loring, Sr.      *Lonesomehurst* (supplied plantings)      Garden City

*Landscape Architects*

**Hicks Nursery** (cont'd)

|  |  |  |
|---|---|---|
| Lanman, Jonathan Trumball, Sr. | *Orchard Hall* (supplied Norway Maples, Japanese Poplars, Pin Oaks, and Silver Maples) | Lawrence |
| * Lawrence, John L. | *Moorlands* (supplied mature Pin Oaks, Wild Cherry, boxwood, and shrubs, 1897) | Lawrence |
| * Lefferts, Marshall Clifford, Sr. | *Hedgewood* (supplied plantings) | Lawrence |
| * Mann, Samuel Vernon, Jr. | *Grove Point* (supplied plantings) | Lawrence |
| * McCrea, James Alexander, II | (supplied plantings) | Woodsburgh |
| McVitty, Edward Quinby, Sr. | *Garstead* (supplied Red Cedar windbreak) | Garden City |
| * Pearce, Arthur Williams, Sr. | (supplied plantings) | Hewlett Harbor |
| * Ripley, Sidney Dillon, Sr. | *The Crossroads* (supplied Scotch Pines) | Uniondale |
| Scott, Charles Robert | *The Crossroads* (supplied Scotch Pines) | Uniondale |

**Martha Brookes Brown Hutcheson**

|  |  |  |
|---|---|---|
| * Lord, Daniel de Forest, V | *Sosiego* | Lawrence |
| * Porter, Henry Hobart, Jr. | *Lauderdale* | Lawrence |
| Seymour, Origen Storrs, II | *Sosiego* | Lawrence |

**Alice Recknagel Ireys**

|  |  |  |
|---|---|---|
| * Sturgis, Henry Sprague, Sr. |  | Lawrence |

**Mary Rutherfurd Jay**

|  |  |  |
|---|---|---|
| * Green, Harry Thomas Sinclair | (1920-1921) | Hewlett Bay Park |
| * Livingston, Mrs. John T. | (1915-1916) | Woodmere |
| * Wickersham, George Woodward | *Marshfield* (designed Japanese garden, 1914) | Lawrence |

**Charles W. Leavitt**

|  |  |  |
|---|---|---|
| * Lord, George de Forest, Sr. |  | Woodmere |

**Lord and Burnham**

|  |  |  |
|---|---|---|
| * Levy, Isaac D. |  | Cedarhurst |

**Olmsted**

|  |  |  |
|---|---|---|
| * Miller, George Clinton | (1911) | Lawrence |
| * Remick, Mrs. | (1917) | Garden City |
| * Schenck, J. F. |  | Lawrence |

**Louise Payson**

|  |  |  |
|---|---|---|
| * Beadleston, Chauncey Perry | (1930) | Hewlett Bay Park |
| * Blanchard, Walter Scott, Sr. | (1928) | Hewlett Bay Park |

*Landscape Architects*

**Louise Payson** (cont'd)

| | | | |
|---|---|---|---|
| * | Francke, Albert, Sr. | (1931) | Lawrence |
| * | Phillips, Kenneth | (1927) | Woodmere |
| * | Weeks, Louis Seabury, Sr. | | Lawrence |
| * | Whitman  
*[unable to determine first name]* | | Cedarhurst |

**Olive Frances Tjaden**

| | | | |
|---|---|---|---|
| * | Jacobi, Sanford | (planted 10,000 tulip bulbs) | Hewlett Neck |
| * | Tjaden, Olive Frances | | Garden City |

*Samuel Knopf residence,  
1916*

*Sara Swan Whiting*
*(Mrs. Oliver Hazard Perry Belmont)*

*Natica Belmont (aka Natica Rives)*
*– daughter of Oliver Hazard Perry and Sara Swan Whitney Belmont –*
*(Mrs. William Proudfit Burden)*

*Maiden Names*

The following list of maiden names of women associated with estates in the Town of Hempstead was compiled from various biographical sources, social registers, and newspaper obituaries. It should be noted that women occasionally gave surnames from previous marriages to editors, without designating them as such. If there were multiple marriages, husbands are listed in chronological order. Please note that the women included in this list were either the homeowners or spouses of homeowners. Women of subsequent generations are not included unless they assumed ownership of the house.

| | | |
|---|---|---|
| **Abramowitz**, Bas Sheva | *married* | **Hillman**, Sidney |
| **Agnew**, Anna Stavely | | **Auchincloss**, Samuel Sloan, Sr. |
| **Akin**, Mary De Verdery | | **McMichael**, Paul Stanley |
| | | **Roosevelt**, Oliver Wolcott, Sr. |
| **Albro**, Florence Guild | | **Ripley**, Joseph Pierce |
| **Alden**, Anna | | **Briggs**, Albert Martin |
| **Alden**, Elizabeth | | **Bucknell**, Allen Kazlett |
| | | **Hack**, Roy Kenneth |
| | | **Wallace**, Edward Secomb |
| | | **Tufts**, Nathan |
| **Aldrich**, Florence May | | **Kniffin**, Howard Summers, Sr. |
| **Aldrich**, Louise Dall | | **Meissner**, William Christen |
| **Alexander**, Mary | | **Sliwa**, Curtis |
| | | **Paterson**, David Alexander |
| **Alexandre**, Gertrude Jerome | | **Clark**, Samuel Adams, Sr. |
| **Alexandre**, Mary E. | | **Rutter**, Nathaniel Edward, Jr. |
| **Allen**, Alice B. | | **Leighton**, John Langdon |
| **Allen**, Dorothy | | **Hutchinson**, William Furman |
| **Allen**, Helene | | **Moller**, Charles George, Jr. |
| **Allen**, Jessie | | **Knapp**, Robert Cole |
| **Allen**, Monawee | | **Richards**, Junius Alexander, Sr. |
| **Allison**, Lulu Dell | | **Pennington**, Charles Gordon |
| **Alms**, Ruth | | **Barnard**, John Augustus |
| **Amerman**, Emma Anna | | **Clute**, Frank M. |
| **Anderton**, Dorothy | | **Bentley**, Edward Sailsbury, Sr. |
| **Appleton**, Florence | | **Molholland**, James Clark |
| | | **Dodd**, John Mingus |
| **Armour**, Mildred McDonald | | **Olena**, Alfred Douglas |
| **Armstrong**, Marjorie Parker | | **Taylor**, Dr. Quintard, Sr. |
| **Ashley**, Irene | | **Osborne**, Robert Klipfel |
| **Astor**, Caroline Schermerhorn | | **Wilson**, Marshall Orme, Sr. |
| **Auel**, Lucy Kathryna | | **Goodwin**, Robert Henning |
| **Averell**, Mary Williamson | | **Harriman**, Edward Henry |
| **Bacon**, Elizabeth | | **Lovering**, Joseph Swain, II |
| **Bacon**, Marion Constance | | **Greenleaf**, John Cameron, Sr. |
| **Bacon**, Pauline | | **Herrick**, Harold Edward, Sr. |
| **Baker**, Carrie Ella | | **Lefferts**, Marshall Clifford, Sr. |

*Maiden Names*

**Baldwin**, Beatrice — **Levy**, George Morton, Sr.

**Baldwin**, Dorothy — **Gilcreest**, Dr. Edgar Lorrington
**Walsh**, James William, III
**Buel**, Thomas

**Baldwin**, Jessie Augusta — **Olcott**, William Morrow Knox

**Baldwin**, Margaret — **Brown**, Albert Winton, Sr.

**Baldwin**, Sarah Ann — **Carman**, Samuel
**Barnum**, Peter Crosby

**Ball**, Laura Amelia — **Pinkus**, Frederick S.
   (aka Salomon Friederick Pinkus;
   Frederick Salo Pinkus)

**Ballantine**, Marguerite — **Holmes**, Emlen Williams, II
**Olcott**, Neilson
**Putnam**, Haven, Sr.

**Bamber**, May Louise — **Marshall**, Chauncey, Sr.

**Banks**, Constance Hatch — **Bertschmann**, Jean Jacques

**Barling**, Marion Everett — **Hawkesworth**, John
**Engs**, Russell Larned, Sr.

**Barnes**, Bertha Ludington — **Smith**, James Clinch

**Barnes**, Susette Bertha — **Danforth**, Frank Lobdell
**Dunnell**, Frank Lyman, Sr.

**Barnitz**, Ann G. — **de Saulles**, Charles Augustus Heckscher, Sr.

**Barnum**, Frances Maria — **Barnum**, Peter Crosby

**Barr**, Eva — **Mariani**, John Francis, Sr.

**Barrows**, Elizabeth — **Pennock**, Theodore E.
**Osborne**, Robert Klipfel
**Schamehorn**, Arthur Jay

**Bartholomay**, Catharine — **Osborne**, Nathan Green
**Sturgis**, Henry Sprague, Sr.

**Bartlett**, Bertha King — **Benkard**, Henry Horton

**Bartlett**, Isobel Catherine — **Hinckley**, Julian
  (aka Danah Bartlett) — **Lowe**, William Ebbets, II

**Bathchelder**, Rosamond — **Hodges**, John King

**Bates**, Florence — **Carter**, Russell Steenback

**Baxter**, Eleanor — **Beadleston**, Chauncey Perry
**Milholland**, James Clarke

**Bay**, Kristine Carlin — **Iger**, Robert Allen
  (aka Willow Bay)

**Baylis**, Mabel — **Eldridge**, Chauncey
**Ivison**, William Crane

**Beadleston**, Helen — **Rawlins**, George Foster

**Beason**, Elizabeth Jane — **Stephan**, Albert Ralph

**Beckwith**, Isobel — **Monroe**, Watson Ranney
**Van Vranken**, John Kellum, Sr.

**Bedell**, Sarah — **Cooper**, Peter

*Maiden Names*

**Bedford**, Emily Harriet

**Bedford**, Mary Eliza

**Beers**, Mary Holberton

**Beggs**, Eleanor Curtis

**Beinecke**, Theodoria Helene

**Belden**, Olive Gertrude

**Belsterling**, Edna Marion

**Benham**, Beula Augusta

**Benkard**, Bertha

**Benner**, Mary E.

**Bennett**, Adeline Wakeman

**Bennett**, Anna Jacobus

**Bennett**, Louise

**Benoist**, Anna Wright

**Bergman**, Betty Ann

**Bergman**, Robin Leslie

**Bernhardt**, Gail M.

**Besold**, Rosina

**Bierwirth**, Florence Helen

**Bigelow**, Edwina Richards

**Bingham**, Mary Louise

**Bischoff**, Harriet

**Bissell**, Grace Cole

**Bixby**, Margaret J.

**Black**, Gladys Newbold

**Blackhall**, Veronica

**Blagden**, Sally Phillips

**Blaine**, Sarah Collier

**Blodget**, Cardine Granger

**Blue**, Laura

**Bogle**, Margaret Riggs

**Bolton**, Silvie Livingston

**Booth**, Catherine Marie

**Bortz**, Dorothy

**Bottomley**, Susanne Meredith

**Boulton**, Pauline Esther

**Davie**, Preston, Sr.
**Sard**, Russell Ellis
**Fosdick**, Pauling

**Wright**, Isaac Merritt, Sr.

**Knowlton**, Eben Joseph

**Schieffelin**, John Jay, Sr.
**Scott**, Thomas Blythe
**Worcester**, Dean Kirkham

**Strong**, Edwin Allen

**Wigglesworth**, Henry

**Dow**, Harold Gilman, Sr.

**Malcolm**, George Ide, Sr.

**Rose**, Reginald Perry

**Egginton**, Hersey

**Jewell**, John Voorhees, Sr.

**Ferris**, Dr. Henry Clay, Sr.

**Coupe**, Frank J.

**Slee**, James Noah, Jr.

**Atwater**, Amarah George Cox, Sr.

**Krugman**, Paul Robin

**Skelos**, Dean George

**Sylvester**, Peter Charles

**Pritchard**, Clarence Franklin

**Cruikshank**, Willliam Morris, Sr.

**Naething**, Charles Frederick

**Koehler**, Robert Henry

**Eddy**, William Higbie, Sr.

**Morse**, Roy Bertram

**deAguilar**, Francis Paul
**Bishop**, John V.

**McKinny**, Alexander, Jr.

**Thompson**, John Dixwell
**Sampson**, Edward Cobb

**Benedict**, Le Grand Lockwood, Sr.

**Sanford**, George Baylies

**Koehne**, John Lawrence, Sr.

**Thompson**, James Walter

**Lord**, Daniel de Forest, V

**Manice**, de Forest

**Ballantine**, John Holme, II

**Young**, Benjamin Swan

**Herrick**, Newbold Lawrence, Sr.

*Maiden Names*

**Bouvier**, Michelle Caroline — **Scott**, Henry Clarkson, Sr.
**Putnam**, Harrington

**Bower**, Grace Ward — **Halsted**, Harold Camerden

**Bowers**, Amelia — **Martin**, Lucius Trowbridge
**Rawlins**, George Foster

**Boyd**, Margery Aletta — **St. John**, Frank Lamar, Jr.

**Bragg**, Florence Margaret — **Paine**, Edward Stetson

**Braine**, Roberta Mary — **Twining**, Charles

**Breese**, Frances Tileston — **Miller**, Lawrence McKeever, Sr.
**Marius**, Arsene

**Breman**, Ida Ashhurst — **Coffin**, William Haskell, Sr.
  (aka Haskell Coffin)

**Bright**, Katharine — **Chapman**, Gilbert Whipple, Sr.

**Brightson**, Cora Adelene — **Farquhar**, William Joslyn, Sr.

**Brooke**, Gertrude — **Stoddard**, Caswell Wheeler

**Brooke**, Louisa Rebecca — **Jones**, Thomas Catesby, Sr.

**Brooks**, Marie Digma — **Burton**, John Howes

**Brown**, Eleanor Throop — **Hoxie**, Isaac Richmond, Sr.

**Brown**, Ellen Whipple — **Hard**, Anson Wales, Sr.

**Brown**, Madeline — **Bené**, John Raymond

**Brown**, Margaret Eleanor — **Blanchard**, George Holmes

**Brown**, Margaret Renwick — **Stricker**, Hans Carl

**Brown**, Ruth — **Hatch**, Alden R.
**Elwell**, Richard Derby, Sr.

**Brown**, Sarah Elizabeth — **Hard**, Anson Wales, Sr.

**Bryan**, Gladys Georgetta — **Lasher**, Dr. Frank Hermance

**Bryan**, Jean — **Berdell**, Theodore Van Duzer

**Buck**, Dorothy — **O'Brien**, Justin Cameron

**Buckler**, Frances Lawrason — **Cox**, Daniel Hargate

**Buckner**, Ellen Eustis — **Eustis**, James Biddle, Sr.

**Bull**, Priscilla Mullins — **Wyeth**, Leonard Jarvis, IV

**Burden**, Eileen — **Maynard**, Walter
**Robins**, Thomas, IV

**Burhans**, Jane Kieffer — **Courtenay**, Adrian Henry, Sr.

**Burkhart**, Claire Adele — **Tucker**, Fred A,
**Munson**, Lawrence Josiah
  (aka Lauritz Josiah Monsen)

**Burnett**, Mary — **Hurd**, George Frederick
**Whiting**, Robert B.

**Burton**, Clara Bigelow — **Pardee**, Dr. Ensign Bennett

**Burton**, Florence Southwick — **Philbin**, Stephen Holladay

**Burton**, Margaret — **Eaton**, Walter Bradley

**Butler**, Heywood Mason — **Kingsley**, Darwin Pearl, Jr.
**Lieb**, William H.
**Willard**, Edwin

*Maiden Names*

**Butler**, Mary Sigourney — **Olney**, Peter Butler, Sr.

**Cadmus**, Genevieve — **Berry**, George W.
　**Blanchard**, George Holmes

**Cady**, Celia May — **Ivison**, William Crane

**Cammann**, Cornelia De Lancy — **Fairchild**, William Samuel
　**Duryea**, Wright, Jr.

**Campbell**, Nanette C. — **Miller**, William Wilson

**Candler**, Edith Alden — **Stebbins**, George Ledyard, Sr.

**Cantwell**, Alice — **Ziegler**, Frederick J.

**Carll**, Jennie E. — **Jewell**, John Voorhees, Sr.

**Carman**, Ella Louise — **Frew**, Walter Edwin

**Carman**, Judith Florence — **Paruolo**, Joseph P.
　**Albert**, Arthur

**Carman**, Mary Ann — **Lowden**, Richard

**Carpenter**, Edith Wiesman — **Macy**, Valentine Everit, Sr.

**Carpenter**, Emily A. — **Gerard**, George Henry

**Carr**, Mary — **Carlin**, George Andrew

**Carroll**, Dorothea — **Claflin**, Avery

**Carroll**, Marion — **Littleton**, Martin Wilson, Sr.
　(aka Martin W. Littleton, Jr.)

**Carter**, Kathleen Louise — **Macy**, George Henry

**Carter**, Victoria Alexandra — **Morrell**, Robert Whiting

**Cary**, Phoebe — **Brisbane**, Arthur

**Cassell**, Kathryn — **Chenault**, Kenneth Irvine

**Chamberlin**, Betsy — **Ohnewald**, George Henry

**Chamberlin**, Dorothy Taylor — **Roever**, Charles Sigmund

**Chapin**, Marjorie — **Van Vranken**, John Kellum, Sr.

**Chapman**, Dorothy Miller — **Hodges**, Wetmore, Sr.

**Chapman**, Florence — **d'Utassy**, George
　(aka George von d'Utassy)

**Chauncey**, Madelaine — **Lynch**, Edmund Ambrose, Sr.
　**Elliman**, Lawrence Bogert, Sr.

**Childs**, Norma Dee — **Schwieters**, John Francis

**Chisolm**, Winifred Wheelwright — **Browne**, Curtis Northrop

**Choate**, Sylvia — **Whitman**, Alexander Harvey, Sr.

**Christ**, Anna Marie — **Fensterer**, Dr. Gustave Adolf

**Christian**, Anna M. — **Auchincloss**, Samuel Sloan
　**O'Connor**, Don

**Church**, Helen Dwight — **Minton**, Henry Miller

**Clappe**, Edith — **Fairchild**, Willard, Sr.
　(aka Charles Willard Fairchild)

**Clark**, Helen de Russy — **Sloan**, Thomas Donaldson, Sr.

**Clarke**, Mabel — **McCrea**, James Alexander, II

*Maiden Names*

**Clausen**, Harriet Elizabeth	**Baird**, ____
	**McVitty**, Edward Quinby, Sr.

**Cleveland**, Mary Savage	**Geer**, Enos Throop, Sr.

**Cobbette**, Florence A.	**Olcott**, William Morrow Knox

**Cochran**, Jane	**Coleman**, Stewart P.
	**Peck**, Arthur Knowlton, Sr.

**Cocks**, Nettie Gerhardine	**Bierwirth**, Dr. Julius Carl

**Coddington**, Muriel	**Southworth**, Theodore

**Coe**, Elizabeth Harmsteadt	**Finlayson**, Daniel Aylesbury, Jr.
	**Prescott**, William French

**Coffin**, Harriot Hudson	**Gruner**, Otto Harry, Jr.

**Cogswell**, Louisa Winslow	**Robins**, Thomas, IV

**Cohen**, Anne	**Steinberg**, Julius

**Coleman**, Esther Field	**Kirkman**, Alexander Sampson, Sr.

**Colgate**, Helen	**Mann**, Samuel Vernon, Jr.

**Compton**, Elizabeth Somervell	**Rees**, Harold Baxter, Sr.

**Conklin**, Mary Wickham	**Young**, Willis Howard, Sr.

**Conn**, Edith Burritt	**Sayer**, Murray

**Converse**, Helen Prentiss	**Thorpe**, Warren Parsons, Sr.

**Conway**, Rita	**Clark**, Thomas A.
	**Richard**, Auguste

**Cook**, Janet	**Morris**, Howard
	**Mills**, Edward Shorrey

**Cook**, Maria Fahys	**Dean**, Howard Brush, Sr.
	**Roberts**, Dudley DeVose, Jr.

**Coppell**, Edyth Howard	**Elliman**, Lawrence Bogert, Sr.

**Corroon**, Carol Ann	**Pratt**, James Guy

**Coster**, Cornelia Prime	**Lounsberg**, Phillips
	**Du Bois**, Arthur Mason

**Cottone**, Margaret	**Spinzia**, Ralph

**Covert**, Frances Elizabeth	**Vanderveer**, Charles, Jr.

**Cowl**, Lydia Perry	**Baldwin**, William Mood

**Cox**, Blanche	**Atwater**, Albert Leonard
	  (aka Bert L. Atwater)

**Cox**, Mary Lyman	**Muir**, John Brinley
	**Cammann**, Schuyler Van Rensselaer

**Coxe**, Isabel Elise	**Weeks**, Louis Seabury, Sr.

**Cragin**, Dorothy Dumont	**Parker**, Carleton Allen

**Craig**, Florence Colgate	**Whitney**, Arthur Edward

**Crane**, Christiana Wallace	**Crunden**, Arthur Chittenden
	**Peck**, Arthur Knowlton, Sr.

**Cranmer**, Edna	**Hanemann**, Edward Lewis

**Crary**, Ella Cornelia	**Cammann**, Herman Henry

**Croker**, Ethel J.	**Breen**, John J.
	**White**, Thomas Francis, Jr.

*Maiden Names*

**Cruger**, Amy — **Olney**, Peter Butler, Jr.
**Culver**, Mildred — **Hinckley**, Julian
**Cunningham**, Lillie H. — **Marshall**, Charles Alexander
**Curtis**, Frances — **Woolverton**, William Henderson, Jr.
**Curtis**, Kathleen H. — **Wagstaff**, Alfred, III
    **Bonner**, Douglas Griswold, Sr.
    **Moffett**, James A., II
**Curtis**, Laura Dudley — **Harris**, Tracy Hyde, Jr.
**Cusachs**, Marguerite Allain — **Almirall**, Raymond Francis
**d'Albemont**, Marie L. — **Leydier**, Benjamin
    **Hoppin**, Samuel Howland
**Daingerfield**, Sara Jay — **Keene**, James Robert
**Dallas**, Elizabeth — **Ward–Smith**, Kenneth, Sr.
**Daly**, May Palmer — **Hatch**, Frederic Horace
**Danforth**, Clara B. — **Hamlin**, Francis Bacon, Sr.
**Davidson**, Judith Suzanne — **Moyers**, Bill
**Davie**, Elizabeth W. — **Coe**, Elmore Holloway
**Davis**, Carmen Atocha — **Mumford**, Philip Gurdon
**Davis**, Ella — **Kimball**, Frank Allan
**Davis**, Emily Stewart Bowers — **Parker**, Glowacki Redfield
**Davis**, Harriet Ivins — **Backus**, Henry Clinton
**Davis**, Mary Laying — **Work**, James Henry, Jr.
**Davis**, Rosetta — **Levy**, Isaac D.
**Davison**, Edna Suydam — **Osterhout**, Howard
**Dawson**, Edna — **Brower**, Howard Stanley
**Day**, Ann Talbot — **Miller**, Danforth, Sr.
**Dayton**, Alice Isabell — **Wood**, Arthur William Blake
**Deacon**, Edith Victoria — **Martin**, Thomas Stephen
**de Apeztieguia**, Elena Josefa Mariana — **Middleton**, John Izard
    **Gildersleeve**, Raleigh Colston
**De Boer**, E. Constance — **Hatch**, Eric Stow
**Deery**, Joan (aka Joan Wetmore) — **Wetmore**, William
    **Dixon**, William Palmer, Jr.
**de Florez**, Marie Augustine — **Fuller**, Paul, Jr.
**de Goicouria**, Rosalie — **Cameron**, Walter Scott
    **Allen**, Benjamin Curtis
**DeGregorio**, Rose — **Spinzia**, Peter
**DeLaney**, Mary — **Maroney**, Dr. William J.
    **Kelly**, Dr. Aquin S.
    **Blagden**, Thomas
**Delano**, Katharine — **Porter**, Henry Hobart, Jr.
**Delliere**, Augustine — **Lebaudy**, Jacques
    **Sudreau**, Henri
**de Lemee**, Diane — **Akin**, Albert John, II

*Maiden Names*

**DeMott**, Josephine    **Robinson**, Charles M.
**De Mott**, Lillian    **Gray**, James McIlvaine
**Denison**, Helen    **Marshall**, James Markham, II
**de Raismes**, Helen Biddle    **Hamilton**, Campbell Thorpe
**De Tienne**, Elizabeth    **Gerard**, Henry Dudley
    (aka Dudley Gerard)
   **Ackerman**, Raymond Pryor, Jr.

**Detrick**, Carolyn Clewly    **Enequist**, John Theodore, Jr.
**Devereaux**, Alice    **Jackson**, Rickard Gilbert
**Dillingham**, Sandra Jane    **DeMille**, Nelson Richard
**Dimick**, Mary    **Cruickshank**, William Morris, Sr.
**Dixon**, Evelena Babcock    **Stevens**, Eben
**Dixon**, Marie Louise    **Du Bois**, Arthur Mason
**Dixon**, Pauline Williams    **Stanton**, Louis Lee, Sr.
**Donaldson**, Ethel    **Sloan**, Robert Sage, Sr.
**Donovan**, Dorothy A.    **Thomas**, Theodore Gillard, III
    (aka Dorothy Hale; Malan Cullen)    **Hale**, Gardiner
**Donson**, Elizabeth Langry    **Floyd**, Nicoll, III
**Dorwin**, Celeste    **Stewart**, Samuel Bradford, Jr.
**Douglas**, Barbara    **Varlet**, Viscount René Georges
**Douglas**, Ida    **Tew**, Benjamin Taylor
**Douw**, Margaret Livingston    **Townsend**, Edward Nicoll, Sr.
**Douw**, Mary Lanman    **Ferris**, Morris Patterson
**Dow**, Elsie    **Wallace**, Edward Secomb
**Drake**, Gertrude Williams    **Ballantine**, John Herbert, II
**Drake**, Katharine Hays    **Gruner**, Otto Harry, Sr.
**Droste**, Dorothy M.    **Tibbs**, Benjamin Hatfield
   **Ivison**, Sterling Hollingshead, Sr.
**Du Bois**, Helen Catherine    **Huntington**, Ellery Channing, Jr.
**Du Bois**, Helen Jay    **Kobbe**, Frederick William
**Duckworth**, Grace Louise    **Horton**, Chauncey Todd, Sr.
**Dudley**, Clara Miller    **Livingston**, John Griswold, Sr.
**Duffy**, Mary Tyler    **French**, Seth Barton, Sr.
**Dulfer**, Geraldine V.    **Edsell**, Ralph James, Sr.
**Dumars**, Anite    **Moore**, Arthur Standish
**Duncan**, Margaret P.    **Daingerfield**, Algernon Gray
**Dunlap**, Helen Goodrich    **Fulton**, Ralph Whittier
   **Forman**, Hugh Lockhart
**Dunning**, Ruth Estelle    **Salmon**, Hamilton Henry, III
    (aka Hamilton Henry Salmon, Jr.)
**Dunstan**, Edna Marie    **Williams**, Ichabod Thomas, II
**Durand**, Gladys Adelaide    **Corroon**, George Aloysius, Sr.
**Durham**, Merrilee    **O'Connor**, Eugene Franklin, Jr.

*Maiden Names*

**Duryea**, Milicent Stebbins — **Anderson**, Ellery Oswald
**Earle**, Edythe — **Townsend**, Robert
**Eastman**, Cora — **Woodruff**, Timothy Lester
**Eastman**, Elise — **Jordan**, Edward Bailey, Jr.
**Eaton**, Katherine Van Duzer — **Carpenter**, Edward Novell
**Eaton**, Lotta Julia — **Edwards**, Jesse
**Eaton**, Muriel — **Mixter**, George, Sr.
**Eckart**, Elizabeth — **Kingsley**, Darwin Pearl, Jr.
**Edsall**, Grace — **Slocum**, Henry Warner, Jr.
**Edwards**, Jane Evelyn — **Durand**, Celestin Aloysious, III
**Eggers**, Margarethia Marie — **Gesell**, Dr. Herbert Ross, Sr.
**Ehrich**, Fanny — **Morgenthau**, Maximilian, Sr.
**Eilbeck**, Helen Cowperthwaite — **Carl**, James Harvey, Jr.
**Eldridge**, Edna Alice — **Beebe**, Henry Ward
**Elliman**, Edyth Coppell — **Knapp**, Edward Spring, Jr.
    **Talmage**, Prentice, Sr.

**Elliott**, Margaret — **Bradford**, George Dexter
**Elliott**, Mary — **Bertschmann**, Jean Jacques
**Ellis**, Ethel Ada — **Gaston**, George Albert
**Emmons**, Frances Antonio — **Peacock**, Grant Allen, Sr.
**Emory**, Mary Benson — **Youngs**, William Jones
**Endicott**, Gladys — **Robinson**, Beverley Randolph
**Endicott**, Lilian — **Francklyn**, Reginald Gebhard
**England**, Agnes Adelaide — **Anderson**, Roy Bennett, Sr.
**Essig**, Mary Elizabeth — **Edsell**, Ralph James, Jr.
**Estevez**, Caroline Cecilia — **Terry**, Thomas Henry
    (aka Carolina Estevez)
**Etherington**, Kathleen — **Dooman**, Dr. David Stoddard
**Eustis**, Marie Clarice — **Eustis**, George Peabody
    (aka George Eustis Corcoran)
    **Hofmann**, Josef Kazimierz
    (aka Josef Casimer Hofmann)

**Evans**, Evelyn — **Blanchard**, Walter Scott, Sr.
    **Wright**, John B.

**Fairfax**, Katharine Van Renssalaer — **Cammann**, Herbert Schuyler
**Farquhar**, June Vereker — **Brown**, Lewis Dean
**Farr**, Edith Jaffray — **Geer**, William Montague, Jr.
**Ficken**, Dorothy Goddard — **Gwynne**, Frederick Walker
**Field**, Ruth — **Forshay**, Ralph Hoyt
**Fitch**, Marion M. — **Ferguson**, David, Sr.
**Fitzgerald**, Grace — **Fulton**, Ralph Whittier
**Flebbe**, Rosalie Adelaide — **Recht**, William, Sr.
**Flood**, Marcella — **Ayer**, Frederick, II

*Maiden Names*

**Floyd**, Cornelia DuBois — **Nichols**, John Treadwell
**Foley**, Kathleen — **Feldstein**, Martin Stuart
**Forbes**, Natalie Livingston — **Beach**, Robert
  **Perry**, George Clinton McKesson
  **de Aguilar**, Francis Paul
  **Thompson**, Harold S.
**Ford**, Marietta Holley — **Russell**, Frank Henry
**Fornof**, Mabel Elizabeth — **Persell**, Harry Alexander
**Foster**, Ann R. — **Le Boutillier**, Thomas, III
  **Duryea**, Wright, Jr.
**Foster**, Caroline Wheelwright — **Sizer**, Theodore
**Fowler**, Ann — **Arledge**, Roone Pinckney, Jr.
**Fowler**, Katharine — **Kip**, Ira A., Jr.
  **Runyon**, Dr. Medford
**Fragos**, Frances Mary — **Townsend**, John Michael
**Francke**, Eleanor Huntington — **Remick**, Joseph Gould
**Francke**, Mary Irving — **Van Siclen**, George West
**Francklyn**, Mary Delia — **Nichols**, John Dykers
**Frank**, Louise Tiffany — **Taylor**, Talbot Jones, III
  **Bell**, James Christy, Jr.
**Frasch**, Frieda — **Whiton**, Henry Devereux
  **Costantini**, Count David Augustus
  **von Seidlitz**, Baron Carl Gottlieb
**Freeborn**, Anna — **Myers**, Charles
**French**, Anne D'Esterre — **Pratt**, Frederick Theodore
**French**, Arline Relyea — **Lehrenkrauss**, Charles Frederick
**Frew**, Helen Louise — **Peters**, Ralph, Jr.
**Fries**, Florence — **Belsterling**, Charles Starne
**Frieze**, Mary H. — **Townsend**, R. Tailer, Sr.
**Fritz**, Edith Bertha — **Pennington**, Charles Gordon
**Fuller**, Catherine — **Norris**, Donald Lee, Sr.
**Fuller**, Elizabeth — **Goodspeed**, Charles Barnett
  **Chapman**, Gilbert Whipple, Sr.
**Fuller**, Nancy — **Atwater**, Amarah George Cox, Sr.
**Fulton**, Helen Elizabeth — **Miller**, John Robinson, Jr.
**Furlong**, Hannah J. — **Lannin**, Joseph John
**Gahn**, Emily Frances — **Meneely**, Charles Dickinson
**Gardiner**, Anne Terry — **Pier**, Roy
**Garvin**, Elizabeth Lillian — **Durand**, James Francis, Sr.
**Gaty**, Allene Pomeroy — **Hatch**, Alden R.
**Gautier**, Clara Sutton — **Bird**, Oliver William, Jr.
**Gaynor**, Ruth Merritt — **Rennard**, John Townsend
  **Bird**, Dudley Gautier
**Geissenhainer**, Anna Margaret — **Warren**, Charles Elliott, Sr.

*Maiden Names*

| | |
|---|---|
| **Genthner**, Sybil Adel | **Englis**, William Franklin, Sr. |
| **Gibb**, Dorothy | **Whitlocke**, Bache McEvers, Jr. |
| **Gibbons**, Harriet | **Tunmore**, John Septimus |
| **Gibson**, Hester Gordon | **Huntington**, Ellery Channing, Jr. |
| | **Davisson**, Oscar Fulton |
| **Gillespie**, Jane | **Quinby**, John Gurley, Jr. |
| **Gillespie**, Margery | **Combs**, Clinton deRaismes, Sr. |
| **Gillet**, Isabella | **Lawrence**, Newbold Trotter, Sr. |
| **Gillet**, Josephine | **Lord**, Franklin Butler, Sr. |
| **Glanville**, Katherine | **Downey**, E. Kelly |
| **Gluck**, Louise Elizabeth | **Hertz**, Charles Schaeffer, Jr. |
| | **Dranow**, John |
| **Golding**, Aletta | **Taylor**, Talbot Jones, III |
| **Goldsmith**, Caroline | **Childs**, John Lewis |
| **Gomory**, Susan | **Keisler**, Peter Douglas |
| **Goodhue**, Phyllis | **Konta**, Geoffrey |
| **Goodman**, Eleanor Hartshorn | **Peters**, Ralph, Sr. |
| **Goodwin**, Grace | **Bishop**, Clifford Monroe |
| **Gordon**, Grace | **Bishop**, Clifford Monroe |
| **Graham**, Jessie Gertrude | **Turnstall**, Harry Gabriel |
| **Grandy**, Margaret | **Perkins** Charles Lawrence, Jr. |
| **Graves**, Emma Henriette | **Faye**, James Joseph |
| | **Erhart**, William Herman |
| **Greene**, Adelaide | **Bowker**, Horace, Sr. |
| **Greene**, Gertrude | **Hamilton**, Campbell Thorpe |
| **Greene**, Mary Howard | **Thompson**, Dr. Benjamin Franklin |
| **Greenleaf**, Adeline Emily | **Norris**, Alfred Oliphant |
| | **Atkins**, Elias C. |
| **Greenleaf**, Alice Cameron | **Adams**, William, Jr. |
| **Greenough**, Beatrice Goelet | **Adee**, William Townsend |
| | **Ladd**, William Fowle, Jr. |
| | **Marple**, John Anthony |
| **Greenough**, Edith | **Lewis**, Edison |
| **Greer**, Julia | **Tilford**, Frank |
| **Griggs**, Dorothy Maitland Lee Fuller | **Murray**, Francis King |
| **Grigorcea**, Eugenia S. | **Stiles**, Maris Veron |
| | **Breed**, William Constable, Sr. |
| **Guidet**, Emma | **Duryee**, Gustavus Abeel |
| | **Auchincloss**, Samuel Sloan, Sr. |
| **Guindon**, Louise Whiting | **Duval**, William Hamlyn, III |
| **Gunn**, Elizabeth Janes | **Van Tine**, Addison Allen |
| **Gunnell**, Kristey Ann | **Peck**, Lee Wallace |
| **Gunter**, Helen | **Jackson**, ____ |
| | **Belsterling**, Charles Star |

*Maiden Names*

**Hackstaff**, Caryl — **Wood**, Howard Ogden, Jr.

**Hageman**, Grace Caroline — **Einhaus**, Harry Madison

**Hagen**, Virginia H. — **Devereux**, Alvin, II

**Haggerty**, Edith Maria — **Stuberfield**, William Frances

**Hahn**, Rosa — **Paine**, Frederick
**White**, Dwain Houston
**Ayer**, Frederick, II

**Hairston**, Portia — **Paterson**, Basil Alexander

**Hale**, Helen — **Rasmus**, Carl Gerhard

**Haley**, Marian Waitt — **Hussey**, Thomas Jefferson

**Hall**, Anna Rebecca Livingston — **Roosevelt**, Elliott, Sr.

**Hall**, Anna Roosevelt — **Braman**, Chester Alwyn, Jr.

**Hallock**, Rhoda Ann — **Glover**, John Irwin

**Halloram**, Edna Mary — **Pratt**, Reginald Tyler

**Hamersley**, Catherine Livingston — **Hinckley**, Samuel Neilson, Sr.
**Drayton**, Henry Coleman
**Carpenter**, Charles Whitney

**Hamill**, Katharine Delano — **Garde**, John Franklin, Jr.

**Hamilton**, Emily Georgina — **Hadden**, James E. Smith

**Hamilton**, Grace — **Newton**, Arthur Ulysses

**Hamilton**, Helen de Raismes — **Irwin**, Marion Griffin

**Handwright**, Marguerite — **Wildermuth**, George C.

**Hard**, Julia Post — **Smith**, Augustine Jacquelin

**Hard**, Sarah Anson — **Taylor**, William Reed Kirkland, Sr.

**Harding**, Jessie — **Morris**, Alfred Hennen

**Hardy**, Jessie — **Delafield**, Robert Hare, Jr.

**Harmes**, Angelita Kay — **Laney**, Seymour
**Atwater**, Amarariah George Cox, Sr.
**Rasmussen**, William

**Harmon**, Helen B. — **St. John**, Edward Atkinson

**Harrington**, Mary L. — **Earnshaw**, Geoffrey S.

**Harris**, Florence — **Jacobi**, Sanford
**Weingarten**, James

**Harris**, Katherine — **Parker**, Don M., Sr.

**Harris**, Lillian — **Knopf**, Samuel

**Harrison**, Margaret Ludlow — **De Mercado**, Frank Eliot

**Harrison**, Nathalie — **Roberts**, Albert Samuel, Jr.

**Hart**, Margaret Rebecca — **Wyld**, Robert Hasbrouck

**Hartshorne**, Lydia R. — **Deshler**, Charles Franklin, Sr.

**Hartt**, Lucie Margaret — **Tompers**, George Urban

**Harvey**, Jane Whitthorne — **Whitman**, Eben Esmond, Sr.

**Hasbrouck**, Olga — **Jones**, Thomas Catesby, Sr.

**Hatch**, Evelyn Ogden — **Holmes**, Emlen Williams, II

*Maiden Names*

**Hatch**, Nathalie — **Rawlins**, Herbert Noel, Sr.

**Hayde**, Alma C. — **Nicoll**, De Lancey, Jr.

**Haynes**, Helen Dunham — **Adams**, John Trevor, Sr.

**Hays**, Ethel Sanders — **Bonner**, Douglas Griswold, Sr.

**Hazard**, Laura Pelton — **Brown**, Frederick Rhinelander

**Hearne**, Dorothy Calhoun — **Merritt**, Harold Francis, Sr.
**Bauscher**, Charles L., Jr.

**Hebard**, Mary Cornelia — **Sise**, John
**Morris**, David Henner, Jr.

**Hegeman**, Mildred — **Hewitt**, William Wilson, Sr.

**Heise**, Joan Dorothy — **Arledge**, Roone Pinckney, Jr.
**Spring**, Arthur John, Jr.

**Hemenway**, Hetty Lawrence — **Richard**, Auguste

**Henderson**, Helen — **Horton**, Chauncey Todd, Sr.

**Henderson**, Helen Kate — **McFadden**, James
**Jackson**, Rickard Gilbert

**Henrickson**, Emma Clark — **Roche**, The Reverend Spencer Summerfield

**Hendrickson**, Frances Roberta — **Levy**, George Morton, Sr.
**Candlish**, Robert Harrison

**Henry**, Emma Harriet — **Snyder**, William Robert

**Herdman**, Doris M. — **Gessell**, Dr. Herbert Ross, Sr.

**Herrick**, Gertrude — **Low**, Ethelbert Ide

**Herrington**, Netta Alice — **Adams**, Charles Closson, Sr.

**Hewlett**, Frances Louise — **Patterson**, Edward Liddon

**Hewlett**, Hope — **Parkhurst**, William Man
**Watts**, Harry D.

**Hewlett**, Laurence — **Burr**, Robert Page, Sr.
**Bowker**, Horace, Sr.

**Heyberger**, Emma Cammeyer — **De Mott**, Harry Mead

**Hilger**, Cicely Mary — **Cameron**, Walter Scott

**Himley**, Sophie Louise — **Bigelow**, Bushnell

**Hinckley**, Dorothy Strong — **Williams**, Thomas Resolved

**Hinckley**, Rosalie Neilson — **Wickersham**, Cornelius Wendell, Sr.

**Hoch**, Louise Margaret — **de Saulles**, Charles Augustus Heckscher, Sr.

**Hoe**, Mary Say — **Harper**, Joseph Henry, Sr.

**Hoffstot**, Helen — **Hammond**, Harry Stevens, Sr.

**Hogan**, Mary — **Atwell**, George Joseph, Sr.

**Holbrooke**, Ethel Whitney — **Perkins**, Norton

**Hollingsworth**, Grace — **Tucker**, St. George Brooke

**Hollingsworth**, Grace B. — **Merritt**, Edward Charles, Sr.

**Hollister**, Louise — **Forrest**, Richard E.
**Valentine**, Landon Barrett

**Holmes**, Jean — **Fetter**, Alexander L.
**Chu**, Steven

*Maiden Names*

**Hone**, Catharine — **Auerbach**, Joseph Smith

**Hooley**, Mabel Brooks — **Rolston**, Brown, Sr.

**Hoover**, Clara Pauline — **Pancake**, Carl Oakley

**Horsman**, Mary — **Appleton**, Robert Wilmarth
**Swain**, Spencer
**La Mont**, Herbert Murray

**Hovey**, Ruth — **Allison**, Dr. Benjamin Roy

**Howe**, Marjorie Cooper — **Weeks**, Herbert Augustus

**Howland**, Hortense — **Dixon**, Courtland Palmer, II

**Hoyt**, Elizabeth Sherman — **Frothingham**, Thomas Harris
**Stewart**, William Adams Walker, II
**Philbin**, Stephen Holladay

**Hubbell**, Margaret Sands — **Beebe**, John Eldridge, Sr.

**Hubbell**, Ruth Rossiter — **Derby**, Robert Mason, Sr.

**Huehle**, Elise — **Levy**, George Morton, Sr.

**Humiston**, Florence Lakewood — **Harrar**, Dr. James Aitken

**Hunt**, Helen Leigh — **Rives**, Francis Bayard

**Hunter**, Lillian — **Brownback**, Garrett A.

**Huntington**, Frances Lee — **Erhart**, William Herman

**Hurd**, Clarissa — **Cady**, Everett Ware, Sr.

**Hutchinson**, Harriette Boden — **Turnbull**, John Gourlay, III

**Hutchinson**, Jane — **Munkenbeck**, Arthur H., Jr.
**Griffin**, Dominic Bodkin, Jr.

**Hutchinson**, Martha Cowles — **Stevenson**, Richard Wilson, Jr.

**Huyck**, Elizabeth Moore — **Eldridge**, Lewis Angevine, Sr.

**Hyde**, Mary Baldwin — **Ripley**, Sidney Dillon, Sr.
**Scott**, Charles Robert

**Hysing**, Mary — **Strauss**, Peter, Sr.

**Ingersoll**, Anita — **Minton**, Roger Medina
**Gwynne**, Walter Lee

**Inman**, Lucy — **Pearce**, Arthur Williams, Sr.

**Iovino**, Rose — **Cottone**, Anthony

**Irish**, Mildred Chadbourn — **Ackerman**, Raymond Pryor, Sr.

**Irwin**, Jessie N. — **Peace**, Arthur W.

**Jacob**, Emma Lawrence — **Robins**, Samuel Davis, Sr.

**Jacob**, Martha — **Marshall**, Levin Rothrock, Sr.

**Jacobi**, Alice Hermine — **Schlossberg**, Arnold, Sr.

**Jacobi**, Edith C. — **Marks**, Arthur David, Jr.
**Nichtern**, Sol

**Japhe**, Ida — **Knopf**, Samuel

**Jenkins**, Gladys Pomeroy — **Stevens**, William Dixon
**Braman**, Chester Alwyn, Jr.
**Fox**, Rector Kerr, Jr.

**Jenny**, Elizabeth — **Ayer**, Frederick, II
**Richards**, Richard Draper

*Maiden Names*

**Jerome**, Gertrude — **Alexandre**, James Henry, Sr.
**Johnson**, Mildred — **Heath**, Cuyler
**Johnson**, Sarah Greenly — **Boadman**, Andrew H.
**Johnstone**, Magdalene Schenck — **Downer**, Jesse Halsey, Sr.
**Jones**, Anna Gertrude — **Smith**, Clarence Browning
**Jones**, Grace Russell — **Boulton**, Howard, Sr.
**Jones**, Harriet Armena — **Edsell**, Levi Perin
**Jones**, Mary A. — **Bossert**, John
**Jones**, Natalie Rathbone — **Hurd**, James Daniel
    **Ward**, James Lakeman
    **Ladd**, William Fowle, Jr.
**Joseph**, Ethel Olive — **Elwell**, Richard Derby, Sr.
**Jurgensen**, Hyldagarde — **La Montagne**, Montaigu
**Kaske**, Donna Ivy — **Karan**, Mark
    **Weis**, Stephan
**Kaufman**, Joan Marie — **Biddle**, George Drexel
    **Wintersteen**, Joseph M.
    **Polk**, Frank F.
    **Ladd**, William Fowle, Jr.
**Kayser**, Charlotte — **Leighton**, George Bridge
**Kearns**, Doris Helen — **Goodwin**, Richard Naradof
**Keeler**, Evelyn Wood — **Taylor**, Willard Underhill, Sr.
    **Stephenson**, Frederick Kenneth
**Keenan**, Mary — **Orr**, Henry Steers
**Keene**, Jessica Harwar — **Taylor**, Talbot Jones, Jr.
    **Frost**, Edward Ingles
**Keep**, Mildred Sturges — **Wildermuth**, George C.
**Keith**, Sarah H. — **Hoag**, Charles H.
**Keller**, Cathryn — **Glass**, Brent David
**Kelley**, Florence A. — **Reyburn**, Amadee Valle, Jr.
    **Schill**, Emil
**Kellum**, Hannah — **Van Vranken**, Dr. Garrett Daniel
**Kelly**, Dorothy Lehman — **Welsh**, Joseph Wickes, Sr.
    **Stevens**, Theodosius Fowler
**Kelly**, Elizabeth Scott — **Griffin**, Dominic Bodkin, Sr.
**Kelly**, Jean M. — **Scott**, Henry Clarkson, Sr.
**Kelly**, Louisa Kuhl — **Boulton**, William Bowen, Sr.
**Kelly**, Winifred Allen (aka Winifred Allen) — **Sperry**, Lawrence Burst, Sr.
**Kempshall**, Eda Louise — **Dunstan**, James S.
**Kendall**, Elinor Whitney — **Gross**, Andre Eugene
**Kendall**, Katharine Varnum — **Denny**, Archibald Marshall, Sr.
**Kendall**, Patricia E. — **Hurd**, George Frederick
**Kennedy**, Helen Virginia — **Tyner**, Gerald Kerwin

*Maiden Names*

**Kerens**, K. Janavince — **Pierce**, Walter Bryant, Jr.
**Florman**, Eskill

**Kiger**, Kathleen Susan — **Iger**, Robert Allen
**Kilbreth**, Anna Winston — **Kilbreth**, James Truesdell, Sr.
**Kilbreth**, Mary Culbertson — **Francklyn**, Reginald Gebhard
**King**, Elsie J. — **Green**, Walton Atwater, Sr.
**King**, Janet Eckford — **Townsend**, Stephen Van Rensselaer, Sr.
**King**, Winifred Houghton — **Schultz**, Albert Bigelow, Sr.
**Kinsella**, Margaret — **Levy**, George Morton, Sr.
**Kirkman**, Dorothy — **Enequist**, William Lars
**Kirkman**, Ethel — **Gurney**, Thomas Nichols
**Kissel**, Diana — **Barnard**, John Lawrence
**Kittinger**, Mary Constance — **Harrison**, Milton Strong, Jr.
**Kleberg**, Henrietta Rosa — **Larken**, John Adrian, Sr.
**Armstrong**, Thomas Reeves

**Knapp**, Helen — **Dunbar**, Clement E.
**St. John**, Edward Atkinson

**Knapp**, Maude — **Cox**, Dr. Gerard Hutchinson, Sr.
**Knowlton**, Ella F. — **Peck**, Arthur Nelson
**Kobbe**, Hildegarde — **Stevenson**, Joseph Hutchinson
**Thorne**, Francis Burritt, Sr.

**Kodziesen**, Corrine — **Hofheimer**, Lester
**Kolezynski**, Genevieve — **Roth**, Arthur Thomas
**Koues**, Dorothy Dudley — **Malcolm**, George Ide, Jr.
**Kurz**, Sophia Bernadette — **Casey**, William Joseph, Jr.
**Ladenburg**, Eugenie Mary — **Davie**, Preston, Sr.
**LaFarge**, Frances Aimee — **Childs**, Edward Herrick
**LaFetra**, Helena Parsons — **Stanton**, Louis Lee, Jr.
**Lancashire**, Lila — **Southgate**, Richard
**Landon**, Marion — **Carroll**, Royall Phelps
**Lannin**, Dorothy Ann — **Tunstall**, Harry Alphonse
  (aka Dorothea Ann Lannin)
**Lauman**, Ida — **Voege**, Harry William
**Lautier**, Pauline Jeanne — **Browne**, De Courcy
**Pierce**, Walter Bryant, Jr.

**Lawrence**, Annie Trotter — **Herrick**, Harold
**Lawrence**, Elizabeth Boyce — **Alexandre**, James Henry, Sr.
**Lawrence**, Elizabeth Woodhull — **Lawrence**, Alfred Newbold, I
**Lawrence**, Hannah Newbold — **Sherman**, Charles Edwin
**Lawrence**, Julia — **Fearey**, Morton Lazell, Sr.
**Lawrence**, Susan Newbold — **Walsh**, James William, Jr.
**Leary**, Effe J. — **Moore**, Arthur Standish
**Leaycraft**, Agnes Ethel — **Camprubi**, Jose Aymar

*Maiden Names*

**Lee**, Anna Josephine
   (aka Anna Georgine Lee)     **Munson**, Lawrence Josiah
   (aka Lauritz Josiah Monsen)

**Lee**, Cornelia     **Ladd**, William Fowle, Jr.
   **Merrill**, Payson McL.

**Lee**, Dorothy     **Atwater**, A. G. Cox, Sr.

**Lee**, Elizabeth Lloyd     **Henry**, George Garr
   **McKee**, Lanier

**Lee**, Florence Middleton     **Norris**, Alfred Lockwood

**Lefferts**, Helen     **Macy**, Carleton

**Lefferts**, Winifred Earl     **Macy**, Carleton
   **Arms**, Robert A.

**Leland**, Ina     **Orvis**, Schuyler Adams, Sr.
   **Smith**, Thomas

**Leo**, Eva     **Fox**, William

**Leverich**, Gertrude Julia     **Ingraham**, Frederick, Sr.

**Leveson**, Constance Elizabeth Frances     **Plunkett**, Henry Willoughby
   (aka Harry Plunkett Grattan)

**Lewis**, Lalla Rookh     **Ohnewald**, George Henry

**Lincoln**, Maryanna Ludlow     **De Veau**, George Putnam

**Linderman**, Lucy Evelyn     **Morris**, McLean Forman, Sr.

**Lines**, Jessie     **Hunter**, Fenley
   (aka Richard Fenley Hunter)

**Link**, Elizabeth Robins     **Gerstner**, Louis Vincent, Jr.

**Lipscomb**, Jacqueline
   (aka Mimi Talbot)     **Bernstein**, Lester

**Livingston**, Caroline Elizabeth     **Stevenson**, Maxwell
   **Baker**, Dr. Harold Woods
   **Platt**, Frank Hinchman

**Lockitt**, Florence     **Burtis**, Divine Franklin, III

**Longman**, Dorothy Britton     **Kimball**, Stuart English
   **Philips**, William Frederic

**Lord**, Frances Bolton     **Seymour**, Origen Storrs, II

**Lovett**, Gertrude Cutts     **Sturgis**, Henry Sprague, Sr.

**Low**, Gertrude Herrick     **Lynch**, George Philip, Sr.

**Low**, Marian Ward     **Raymond**, William, Sr.

**Lunt**, Margaret Burnham     **Mabon**, Samuel Clifton

**Lyle**, Lisbeth Moore     **Ivison**, Sterling Hollingshead, Sr.
   **Young**, Cecil P.

**Lyon**, Mary Peirce     **Delafield**, Maturin Livingston, II
   **Williams**, John S.

**Lyons**, Elizabeth Marie     **Loft**, George William

**Macy**, Miss Carroll

**Magoffin**, Veron Marguerite     **Siems**, Chester Peter
   **Peabody**, Rushton, Sr.
   **Steel**, George Drexel Biddle

**Magruder**, Millicent     **Almy**, Frederick, Jr.

*Maiden Names*

**Maitland**, Sylvia — **Horner**, Martin McGregor
**Lynch**, George Philip, Sr.

**Malone**, Lucia Virginia — **Rowe**, Reginald Manchester, Sr.

**Mandeville**, Helen Barton — **Amerman**, William H. H., Jr.

**Mange**, Helen Troth — **Peabody**, Rushton, Sr.

**Manierre**, Ruth Lockwood — **Delafield**, Lewis Livingston, III

**Manley**, Lucy Cony — **Mellen**, Chase, Sr.

**Manley**, Sidney Sewall — **Breck**, Duer du Pont

**Manville**, Ethel Long — **Handy**, Chalmers
**Woolverton**, William Henderson, Jr.

**Marier**, Mildred Natalie — **Jackson**, Rickard Gilbert

**Marion**, Jeanne — **Brooks**, Ernest, Sr.

**Marmon**, Ann — **Mallouk**, George Elias

**Marsden**, Marjorie — **Smith**, Clarence Browning

**Marsh**, Marion Tiffany — **Bannerman**, Parry Elwood

**Martin**, Barbara — **Glass**, Brent David

**Martin**, Joan Kettering — **Tyner**, John Hill

**Martin**, Laura Grinnell — **Koehne**, Richard Sperry, Sr.

**Mason**, Adele Sturges — **Schley**, Henry Spaulding, Sr.

**Mason**, Helen Louise — **Youngs**, William Jones

**Mason**, Isabella — **Van Rensselaer**, Maunsell, Jr.

**Mason**, Katharine — **Williams**, Morgan
**Hofstra**, William Sake

**Maupin**, Dorothy Wainwright — **Bradford**, George Dexter

**Maurice**, Emily Marshall — **Dall**, Charles Whitney, Sr.

**Maxwell**, Jean Allison — **Schmidlapp**, William Horace
**Sturgis**, William James, Sr.
**Sanders**, Truman Laurance

**Maxwell**, Margaretta — **Wood**, Frederick J.

**McCabe**, Geraldine Marie — **Pratt**, James Edward

**McConkey**, Lily Margaret Richardson (aka Madame Broville) — **Jones**, Dr. Durham Carroll

**McCullogh**, Ethel — **Geoghegan**, Joseph Gregory
**MacIlroy**, Thaddeus K.

**McElroy**, Cornelia Kane — **Merritt**, Schuyler, II

**McEwen**, Mary — **Buck**, Harold Winthrop

**McFadden**, Elizabeth — **McVitty**, Edward Quinby, Sr.

**McGuire**, Nettie Clinton — **Shaw**, Munson Gallaudet, Sr.

**McKean**, Mary — **Chalfant**, Edward Newton

**McKeever**, Edith — **Cobb**, Boughton, Sr.

**McKennan**, Mary — **Hickman**, Claude Ashburn Mayborn
**Koons**, Franklin Stevenson

**McKim**, Alice Marston — **Voss**, William Hude Neilson

**McMahon**, Julia — **Loft**, George William

*Maiden Names*

**Mead**, Josephine S. — **Morehouse**, David
**Merrill**, Mary H. — **Bentley**, Edward Manross
**Merritt**, Grace Marion — **Pennington**, Harold Douglas
**Merritt**, Marie — **Hendrickson**, Charles Le Roy
**Meyerkort**, Margaret — **Dall**, Stewart Maurice, Sr.
**Mezistrano**, Nancy
    **Gamel**, Isaac
    **Resnick**, Joseph

**Michelson**, Dorothy
    **Dick**, Sheldon
    **Bitter**, John Fred
    **Stevens**, William Dixon
    **Livingston**, Goodhue, Jr.

**Migel**, Susanna Ludlum — **Talmage**, John Frelinghusen
**Miller,** Mary Chester
    **Peabody**, Richard Augustus
    **Moen**, Augustus Rene II

**Miller**, Mildred — **Brush**, Gilbert Palmer
**Miller**, Natalie Maie — **Putnam**, Hobart Hayes
**Miller**, Virginia Howard — **King**, Hugh Purviance, Sr.
**Millsap**, Marjorie Elizabeth (aka Dorothy Lee)
    **Booth**, Robert
    **Fidler**, Jimmy
    **Duffield**, Marshall
    **Atwater**, Amariah George Cox, Sr.
    **Bersbach**, Frank John, Jr.
    **Calderni**, Charles

**Miner**, Mary — **Adams**, William Herbert
**Moffitt**, Nancy Elizabeth
    **Skelos**, Dean George
    **Duka**, ____

**Moller**, Ruth Helene — **Livingston**, Johnston, II (aka Johnston Livingston, Jr.)

**Morgan**, Elizabeth Hamilton — **Belmont**, August, II
**Morgan**, Helen Ridgely — **Ballantine**, John Holme, II
**Morgan**, Joanna Adele — **Goadby**, Arthur McMaster
**Morgan**, Mary Madeline
    **Bottome**, ____
    **Bond**, Walter Huntington

**Moritz**, Freda (aka Frederica Moritz) — **Jacobi**, Harold, Sr.

**Morrill**, Virginia
    **Chapman**, Henry Otis, Jr.
    **Merritt**, Schuyler, II

**Morrison**, Isabel — **Woodruff**, Timothy Lester
**Morss**, Lucy Washington — **Hurry**, Renwick Clifton
**Morton**, Anna Laura — **Hofstra**, William Sake
**Moss**, Nathalie Fellows — **Livingston**, Johnston, II (aka Johnston Livingston, Jr.)

**Moulton**, Margaret — **Harper**, Joseph Henry, Jr.
**Munroe**, Eleanor Roberts — **Green**, Walton Atwater, Sr.
**Munson**, Grace A. — **Mooney**, Franklin Drake, Sr.
**Mumford**, Gladys Bruce — **Pell**, Walden, Jr.

*Maiden Names*

| | |
|---|---|
| **Murphey**, Harriet Louise | **Chapman**, Henry Otis, Sr. |
| **Murphy**, Beatrice | **Wigglesworth**, Henry |
| **Naething**, Rose Marie | **Barnes**, Roderic Barbour |
| **Nash**, Eleanor Arnett | **McWilliam**, Culver B. |
| **Neff**, Lena Pearl | **Curtiss**, Glenn Hammond, Sr. |
| | **Wheeler**, H. Sayre |
| **Neilson**, Caroline Kane | **Voss**, William |
| **Neilson**, Rosalie | **Hinckley**, Samuel Parker |
| **Nelson**, Helen Desmond | **Moller**, Hans Eskildsen |
| **Nelson**, Hollis | **Varlet**, Viscount René Georges |
| **Nelson**, Lilian | **Woodward**, William G., Sr. |
| **Neuber**, Charlotte | **Leighton**, Alexander E. |
| **Newbern**, Fern | **Nicoll**, De Lancey, Jr. |
| | **Ingoldsby**, Brian J., Sr. |
| **Newland**, Helen Elizabeth | **Lamy**, Henry Bernard, Jr. |
| | **Biddison**, Ned Douglass |
| | **Russ**, Charles Alonzo |
| **Nichelson**, Nancy Rachel | **Bradsby**, Frank W. |
| | **Emmons**, Walter Reed, Sr. |
| | **Blackwell**, Carlyle |
| **Nicholas**, Beatrice | **Townsend**, Edward Nicoll, Jr. |
| **Nicholas**, Evelyn Hollins | **Arnold**, Alexander Duncan Cameron, Sr. |
| | **Stevenson**, Joseph Hutchinson |
| **Nicholas**, Maud Louise | **Niles**, George Casper |
| **Nicoll**, Frances Augusta | **Johnson**, Lee |
| **Nicoll**, Sarah Payne | **Ruperti**, Justus |
| **Niles**, Bertha Eliza | **Koons**, Franklin Stevenson |
| **Norman**, Josephine | **Rawlins**, Herbert Noel, Sr. |
| **Nostrand**, Helen Sands | **Hubbell**, Sherwood |
| **Oakley**, Clara | **Meyerkort**, John, Sr. |
| **Oakley**, Verona Ruth (aka Verona Ruth DeMott) | **Merritt**, Harold Francis, Sr. |
| **O'Brien**, Edna Louise | **Warren**, Northam, Sr. |
| **O'Brien**, Eileen Morrison | **Smith**, Cyrus Porter, Sr. |
| **O'Brien**, Margaret Ella | **Peterkin**, DeWitt, Sr. |
| **O'Connor**, Agnes | **Shepard**, Frederic White |
| **O'Connor**, Alice | **Hart**, Augustin Snow, Sr. |
| **O'Connor**, Anna Watson | **Nash**, Warren Bynner |
| | **Pearsall**, Harris Montgomery |
| **O'Connor**, Mary Collord | **Becker**, Claude M. |
| **O'Conor**, Rosemary | **Fowler**, Benjamin Kimball True |
| **O'Donnell**, Mary | **Kelly**, Dr. Aquin S. |
| **O'Hara**, Marian | **Hyland**, John Francis |

*Maiden Names*

**Olmstead**, Grace Helen Temple — **Roosevelt**, Oliver Wolcott, Sr.
**de la Vigerie**, d'Astier

**Oltrogge**, Beatrice Meserole — **Reeves**, Edward Duer, Sr.
**Townsend**, Edward Nicoll, Jr.
**Gilmore**, Robert Newton, Sr.

**Onativia**, Pauline Garcia — **Townsend**, John Richard
**Alexandre**, James Henry, Sr.

**Onativia**, Vera — **Whipple**, Dana de Peyster, Sr.

**Onderdonk**, Katharine Ward — **Weller**, Augustus Noble

**Oppenheimer**, Alice — **Marks**, Arthur David, Jr.

**Orne**, Linda H. — **Fosdick**, Clark

**Otis**, Mary Alleyne — **Stevens**, Alexander Henry

**Otis**, Rosina Hoyt — **Bateson**, Edgar Farrar, Sr.

**Ottens**, Ann Katherine — **Ebinger**, Walter Dohrmann

**Owen**, Helen — **Gillespie**, H. Stevens
**Engs**, Russell Larned, Sr.

**Page**, Frances — **Burr**, Winthrop, Sr.

**Page**, Helen Jackson — **Aten**, Courtenay Nixon, Sr.

**Paige**, Michelle R. — **Paterson**, David Alexander

**Palmer**, Elizabeth Story — **Anderton**, Dr. William Bancroft

**Pardo**, Carola P. — **Massimino**, Michael James

**Parker**, Edith — **Moran**, Robert G.

**Parker**, Elizabeth — **Philbin**, Jessie Holladay

**Parsons**, Emily Elizabeth — **Mallett**, Percy Smith

**Parsons**, Ethel Thorne — **Vaughan**, Donald Cuyler, Sr.

**Partridge**, Marion E. — **Mills**, Edward Shorrey

**Pasfield**, Matilda Anna — **Egly**, Henry Harris

**Patton**, Mildred Gould — **Cartwright**, Henry Rogers, Jr.

**Payntar**, Florence — **Bromfield**, Percy Rushmore

**Pearson**, Ada Isabella — **Townley**, The Reverend Frank Maxwell

**Pelton**, Laura Abell — **Hazard**, William Ayrault, Sr.

**Percival**, Elizabeth
(aka Lydia Percival) — **Blanchard**, Walter Scott, Sr.
**Moller**, Charles George, III

**Peters**, Dorothy — **Hubbell**, John Platt, Sr.

**Peters**, Eleanor Hartshorn — **Parsons**, Argyll Rosse, Jr.

**Peters**, Helaine Piatt — **Forman**, Harold Baldwin
**Supple**, Allen

**Petrie**, Mima — **Addison**, James, Jr.

**Phelan**, Aurelia — **Underhill**, Rawson Kip, Sr.

**Pickthall**, Maude — **Bowman**, Archibald

**Pierce**, Kathryn Charlotte — **Hewlett**, Roger Sanderson

**Pierson**, Anne — **Keating**, William J.

**Pierson**, Helen Jeannette — **Bodine**, William Henry Johnson, Jr.

## Maiden Names

| | |
|---|---|
| **Pilling**, Ruth Harper | **Dunham**, Carroll, III |
| **Pitt**, Louise Elder | **Briggs**, Thomas Jacob |
| | **Pell**, William Watson |
| **Platt**, Eliza Strong | **Hubbell**, George Loring, Sr. |
| **Pomeroy**, Rita Leone | **Greason**, Samuel, Jr. |
| **Porter**, Charlotte Ross | **Buck**, Harold Winthrop |
| **Porter**, Dorothy Dwight | **Pardee**, Dr. Harold Ensign Bennett |
| **Porter**, Katharine Delano | **Hamill**, Robert Lyon, Sr. |
| **Porter**, Katharine Wyman | **Pendleton**, George Hunt |
| | **Miller**, Lawrence McKeever, Sr. |
| **Post**, Clara | **Pettit**, Townsend Baldwin, Sr. |
| **Post**, Elizabeth West | **Van Rensselaer**, Kiliaen Maunsell, II |
| **Post**, Marcia de Forest | **Cammann**, Schuyler Van Rensselaer |
| **Postlethwaite**, Carolyn Satterlee | **Cobb**, Henry Ives, Jr. |
| **Pott**, Margaret Otis | **Floyd**, Nicoll, Jr. |
| **Potter**, Elizabeth Sturgis | **Polk**, Frank Lyon, Sr. |
| **Powel**, Elizabeth Hare | **Campbell**, William Baillie Fraser |
| | **Olney**, Sigourney Butler, Sr. |
| **Powell**, Margaret Lauretta | **Logan**, John Alexander, III |
| **Pratt**, Louise | **Howe**, Wallis Eastburn, Jr. |
| **Prentice**, Mary Bill | **Talmage**, Edward Taylor Hunt, Sr. |
| | **Taylor**, William Reed Kirkland, Sr. |
| **Prentiss**, Frederica Carlotta | **Hanemann**, John Theodore, Sr. |
| | **Haldeman**, Thomas Jefferson |
| **Prentiss**, Mary E. | **Hastings**, James P. |
| | **Blagden**, Thomas |
| **Quick**, Anne Naomi | **Chenault**, Dr. Hortenius |
| **Quinby**, Margaret Teackle | **Sturgis**, William James, Sr. |
| **Ralph**, Elizabeth Kirkland | **Olney**, Peter Butler, Jr. |
| **Ramsey**, Julia Ireland | **Handy**, Courtlandt Waite |
| **Rand**, Marian Doane | **Francke**, Albert, Sr. |
| **Randall**, Amelia | **Russell**, Dr. Thomas Hendrick |
| **Randolph**, Alice | **Ritter**, Carlos T. |
| | **Adams**, John Trevor, Sr. |
| **Ransom**, Angie | **Kilmer**, Dr. Theron Wendell, Sr. (aka Theron Sylvester Norton, Jr.) |
| **Rasmus**, Adele M. | **Timpson**, James |
| **Raymond**, Grace Sinclair | **Adams**, William, III |
| **Raynor**, Hannah | **Kellum**, John |
| **Reddan**, Josephine Marie | **Hawke**, John Daniel, Jr. |
| **Reeve**, Helen Hasbrouck | **Houghton**, Owen Edward, Jr. |
| **Reilly**, Hester | **Hammond**, John Stevens, Sr. |
| **Reis**, Lucy | **Lewis**, Henry Llewellyn Daingerfield, Jr. |
| **Remsen**, Jane | **Thompson**, Joseph TodHunter |

*Maiden Names*

**Renouard**, Marie Cecile — **Thayer**, Benjamin Bowditch, Jr.

**Renwick**, Mary Crosby — **Brown**, Dr. Frederick Tilden

**Restrepo**, Mary Ellen Louise — **de Uribe**, ____
**Welsh**, Joseph Wickes, Jr.

**Retter**, Lena Martina — **Otto**, Carl Ludwig, Sr.

**Reynders**, Clare Charlton — **Stevens**, Byam Kirby, III

**Rhodes**, Dr. Millie — **Fisher**, Dr. Lamont H.

**Rice**, Enid — **Higgins**, Charles Stanton
**St. John**, Frank Lamar, Jr.

**Rice**, Mildred Gautier — **Newton**, Richard Heber, Jr.
**Varlet**, Viscount René Georges
**Radway**, J. Oakley
**Zara**, Francesco A.

**Richardson**, Anne Davis — **Jackson**, William Harding, Sr.
**Stevenson**, Maxwell

**Richmond**, Elsie — **Lovering**, Joseph Swain, II
**Stinson**, William S.
**Evans**, Alfred

**Riggs**, Rebecca — **Crane**, Clinton Hoadley

**Riker**, Frances Townsend — **Davis**, William Shippen, Sr.

**Riker**, Ruth — **Whipple**, Julian Van Ness

**Ringletaube**, Elsa — **Delafield**, Lewis Livingston, III

**Robbins**, Marion — **Kennedy**, Henry Van Rensselaer

**Roberts**, Margaret — **Welton**, Dr. Thurston Scott

**Robinson**, Adele Marie — **Durand**, Celestin Aloysious, Jr.

**Robinson**, Margaret L. — **Griffin**, Dominic Bodkin, Jr.

**Robinson**, Sarah Goodwin — **Blackwood**, Arthur Temple

**Robson**, Eleanor — **Belmont**, August, II

**Robson**, Helen — **Griswold**, John Augustus, Sr.

**Rockefeller**, Abigail — **Milton**, David Meriwether
**Pardee**, Dr. Irving Hotchkiss
**Mauze**, Jean

**Rodgers**, Martha Chamberi — **Pease**, Walter Albert, Jr.

**Roe**, Josephine Bissell — **Slade**, Prescott

**Rohrer**, June — **Edsell**, Ralph James, Jr.

**Romeyn**, Estelle Young — **Pittman**, Ernest Wetmore

**Rose**, Regina — **Morgenthau**, Julius Caesar, Sr.

**Royce**, Marjory — **Halsted**, Gilbert Coutant, Jr.

**Rudge**, Winifred — **Green**, Harry Thomas Sinclair

**Rue**, Florence — **Lawrence**, Clifford Winfield, Jr.

**Rushmore**, Emma Martin — **Bromfield**, Percy Butler

**Russell**, Sarah Elizabeth — **Neilson**, Robert Hude

**Ryan**, Miriam Fortune — **Herbert**, Jacques R.
**Robb**, Hampton
**Ellinger**, Robert Herbert

*Maiden Names*

**Ryder**, Emma Wise — **Breed**, William Constable, Sr.

**Sackett**, Hannah Caroline — **Harper**, Joseph Abner

**Saltzseider**, Irma — **Ridder**, Joseph Edward, Sr.

**Sanford**, Elizabeth Blodget — **Bogert**, Henry Lawrence, Jr.

**Sanford**, Genevieve Leland — **Philips**, William Frederic

**Saportas**, Regina Mathilde — **Alexandre**, Frederick Francis, Sr.

**Sauer**, Elsie — **Corwith**, Lester F.

**Saunders**, Jean — **Buttfield**, Marsom I.
**Lancaster**, John Edward, Jr.

**Scharman**, Ann Katharine — **Rutter**, John Alexandre, Sr.

**Schermerhorn**, Katie — **Matthews**, John

**Schile**, Margarita Erwina — **Piel**, Rudolph Alfred

**Schnebly**, Virginia — **Ruggles**, ____
**Orvis**, Schuyler Adams, Sr.

**Schneider**, Hedwig Ottilia — **Ridder**, Joseph Edward, Sr.

**Schoonmaker**, Marie — **Smith**, Herbert Ludlam, Sr.
**Putnam**, Hobart Hayes

**Schroers**, Jeanne Hortense — **Searle**, John Endicott, Sr.

**Schultz**, Edith Roberts — **Welton**, Dr. Thurston Scott

**Schulze**, Louise — **Pomeroy**, Theodore
**Hammond**, John Stevens, Sr.

**Scofield**, Florence — **Stone**, Herman Foster

**Scott**, Emma Wells — **Williams**, Thomas, II

**Scott**, Dr. Mabel — **Weed**, Leroy Jefferson

**Scull**, Laura — **Vandewater**, Neil Horatio

**Sealy**, Winifred L. — **Pratt**, Reginald Tyler

**Searles**, Elizabeth Porter — **Greene**, Herbert Gouverneur

**Sedgwick**, Mary Ellen — **Gould**, James H.
**Ward**, Sylvanus Dwight

**Selbie**, Edith Nathalie — **Schley**, Buchanan, Jr.

**Sellar**, Iris — **Veeder**, Francis Lansing

**Sessions**, Amo Pauline — **Banks**, Harold Purdy

**Seymour**, Mary Halsey — **Belcher**, Edwin Willoughby, Jr.

**Shaw**, Gisele N. — **Arledge**, Roone Pinckney, Jr.

**Shenton**, Bessie — **Chamberlin**, Dr. William Taylor

**Sherman**, Mary Elizabeth — **Parkhurst**, William Man

**Sherman**, Sybil Katherine — **Hoffman**, John Ellis
**Sellar**, Norrie, Sr.

**Sherwood**, Alice May — **Irwin**, Louis Henry

**Sherwood**, Emilie — **Vogel**, Henry John

**Simmons**, Marguerite — **Barrett**, Gilbert Conklin, Sr.

**Simpson**, Mildred M. — **Lamy**, Henry Bernard, Jr.

**Sims**, Hazel S. — **Farr**, John, Jr.

*Maiden Names*

**Sindel**, Virginia
   (aka Virginia Maxine Sindel; Ginny Witte)

**DeMille**, Nelson Richard

**Skarie**, Elizabeth

**Greenfield**, Jerry

**Slattery**, Elizabeth Pendleton

**de Aguilar**, Francis Beauregarde
   (aka Francis Beauregarde Agiar)
**Kendrick**, Frederick William

**Slattery**, Ruth Cary

**Locke**, Campbell, Sr.

**Sloan**, Eleanor Painter

**Wainwright**, Loudon Snowden, Sr.

**Sloane**, Margaret Milligan

**Sloan**, Benson Bennett, Sr.

**Slocum**, Gertrude

**Adams**, William Herbert

**Slocum**, Margaret

**Quinby**, John Gurley, Jr.
**Stafford**, James O.
**Stevenson**, Edward L.

**Slocum**, Margaret Olivia

**Sage**, Russell

**Small**, Marguerite Louise

**Ballantine**, Herbert Wilgus, Sr.

**Smith**, Alva Erskine

**Vanderbilt**, William Kissam, Sr.
**Belmont**, Oliver Hazard Perry

**Smith**, Dorothy Jacquelin

**Long**, William Henderson, Jr.

**Smith**, Edith Jacquelin

**Meyerkort**, John, Jr.
   (aka Jack Meyerkort, Jr.)

**Smith**, Hester Elizabeth

**Vandewater**, Benjamin Cornelius

**Smith**, Lois Lindon

**Schieffelin**, John Jay, Sr.

**Smith**, Mary Edna

**Winkhaus**, John Theodore, Sr.

**Smythe**, Helen Dora

**Miller**, John Robinson, Sr.

**Snow**, Caroline E.

**Hart**, Alexander Richmond

**Snyder**, Harriet Jane

**Hubbell**, Ralph Peters, Sr.

**Southmayd**, Charlotte Mary

**Van Rensselaer**, Bernard Sanders

**Southwick**, Florence

**Burton**, Robert Lewis

**Spencer**, Elizabeth Dexter

**Robins**, Samuel Davis, Sr.

**Spencer**, Mary Sargent

**Philips**, Kenneth T.
**Thomas**, Theodore Gaillard, III
**Oliver**, Frank

**Spillin**, Elizabeth K.

**Adams**, Charles Closson, Sr.

**Sprague**, Anna Louisa

**Sturgis**, William, Jr.

**Sprague**, Eleanor

**Sefton**, Dr. Wilfred
**Stewart**, John Henderson, Jr.
**Talmage**, Edward Taylor Hunt, Jr.

**Stafford**, Carolyn M.

**Studwell**, Joseph Colson Knapp

**Stanton**, Priscilla Dixon

**Auchincloss**, Joseph Howland, Sr.

**Starr**, Frances Grant

**Coffin**, William Haskell, Sr.
   (aka Haskell Coffin)
**Donaldson**, R. Golden

**Steele**, Madeleine

**Doolittle**, Frederick William, Jr.

**Stege**, Charlotte

**Pidgeon**, Ashley E.

**Steiner**, Alma Elizabeth

**Jones**, Bethune Wellington

*Maiden Names*

**Stevens**, Emily Louise — **Ladenburg**, Adolph
   (aka Moritz Adolph Emil Ladenburg)

**Stevens**, Frederica — **Auerbach**, John Hone, Sr.
   **Bernard**, Philippe

**Stevens**, Mary Wright — **Moore**, Rufus Ellis

**Stevenson**, Eloise — **Kernochan**, James Lorillard
   **Duncan**, Alexander Butler

**Stevenson**, Marion — **Parker**, Henry Seabury, Sr.

**Stoddard**, Mary Billings — **Murphy**, William Gordon, Jr.

**Stokes**, Elizabeth James — **Slade**, Francis Henry

**Stoothoff**, Ella — **Meeker**, Samuel Mundy, Jr.

**Strain**, Elizabeth W. — **Osborne**, Lawrence Woodhull

**Street**, Rosamond Kearny — **Eustis**, George Peabody
   (aka George Eustis Corcoran)

**Stricker**, Dorothy Eleanor — **Black**, Archibald

**Strong**, Amelia Mallory — **Slade**, Francis Henry

**Strong**, Emma Harrison — **Merrill**, Payson, Sr.

**Stuart**, Sylvia Whiton — **Hatch**, Eric Stow
   **Turnure**, Lawrence
   **Olcott**, Neilson

**Stuberfield**, Margaret Mary — **Moran**, Michael Arthur

**Sutherland**, Alice — **Whitney**, Arthur Edward

**Swan**, Shelia Elise — **Orvis**, Franklin Whitin
   **Driggs**, Edmund Hope, Jr.

**Sweeney**, Irene J. — **Durand**, Celestin Aloysious, Sr.

**Sweetland**, Jessie Barber — **Salmon**, Hamilton Henry, Jr.

**Swift**, Ella — **Tarbell**, Gage Eli

**Swift**, Katherine J. — **White**, Thomas Francis, Sr.

**Symington**, Hazel — **Lord**, George de Forest, Sr.

**Tate**, Winifred — **Baker**, Elwood Wilson

**Taylor**, Christine Sawyer — **MacDowell**, Noah, Jr.

**Taylor**, E. Josephine — **Farrington**, Selwyn K., Sr.
   **Kip**, Ira A., Jr.

**Taylor**, Jessie Matheson — **Philips**, Frederic Dimon

**Taylor**, Margaret C. — **Davies**, Edward Livingston

**Taylor**, Mary Richmond — **Barnum**, Joshua Willets

**Teets**, Minnie Louise — **Emmons**, Walter Reed, Sr.

**Terhune**, Doris — **Rawlins**, Herbert Noel, Jr.

**Test**, Irene — **Haughey**, William Wallace

**Tevlin**, Marcella — **McKinny**, Alexander, Sr.

**Thayer**, Alice R. — **Ivison**, Maynard Cady

**Thayer**, Marie Renouard — **Richards**, Junius Alexander, Sr.

**Thayer**, Nora Forbes — **Goodhue**, Francis Abbot

**Thielbar**, Lisa Louise — **Chu**, Steven

*Maiden Names*

**Thieriot**, Mathilde Marie — **Kingsland**, Harold Nutting

**Thomas**, Elizabeth M. — **Ecker**, George B.
**Daingerfield**, Algernon Gray

**Thomas**, Emily — **Dwight**, Philip J.

**Thomas**, Katharine Trumbull — **Cooper**, Leslie Bradford

**Thomas**, Mary Gertrude — **Hatch**, Eric Stow
**Chase**, Frank

**Thomas**, Mary Ludlow — **Lanman**, Jonathan Trumbull, Sr.

**Thomas**, Sarah C. — **Dunning**, Clarence Seymour, Sr.

**Thompson**, Constance B. — **Russell**, Frank Henry

**Thompson**, Edith Kathleen — **Townley**, The Reverend Frank Maxwell

**Thompson**, Elizabeth Remsen — **Darlington**, The Reverend Gilbert Sterling Bancroft

**Thompson**, Eva — **Rogers**, Edward Sidney

**Thompson**, Florence Steward — **Bond**, Walter Huntington

**Thompson**, Louise Poole — **Swett**, The Reverend Canon Paul Flynn, Sr.

**Thorpe**, Theodora — **Dixon**, William Palmer, Jr.
**Winn**, Charles John Frederick

**Thralls**, Grace Dorothea — **Coleman**, George Lansing
**Veeder**, Paul Lansing

**Tiebout**, Alice — **Gleason**, Marshall Wilfred

**Tillotson**, Rose Carolina — **Van Rensselaer**, Bernard Sanders

**Timpson**, Brenda Adele — **Potter**, Lars Sellstedt, Jr.
**Keohn**, Andre O.

**Tjaden**, Olive Frances — **Johnson**, Carl
**Van Sickle**, Roswell Charles

**Toler**, Dorothy Pennington — **Auerbach**, John Hone, Sr.

**Tompkins**, May — **Ossman**, John, Jr.

**Tredwell**, Mary Baker — **Dwyer**, Martin, Sr.

**Trevor**, Margaret Estelle — **Pardee**, Dr. Irving Hotchkiss

**Turnbull**, Marjorie — **Waddell**, Wallace MacNab, Sr.

**Turner**, Dorothy Quincy — **Hastings**, The Reverend A. Abbott

**Tweed**, Katharine Winthrop — **Blaine**, Graham Burt, Sr.

**Tweedy**, Alice — **Crunden**, Walter Morgan
**Cox**, Dr. Gerard Hutchinson, Sr.

**Tyler**, Elizabeth — **Rhett**, William Brisbane, Sr.

**Tyner**, Victoria Deacon — **Peck**, Lee Wallace
**Potter**, Lars Sellstedt, Jr.
**Kilburn**, Henry Thomas, Jr.

**Vallon**, Marcelle E. — **Timpson**, Carl William, Sr.

**Vanderbilt**, Olive — **Hodgson**, Robert John, Jr.

**Vanderveer**, Magdalene Frances — **Covert**, Charles Edward

**Van Loan**, Anna — **Ingraham**, Richard, III

**Van Voast**, Dorothea — **Tapscott**, Ralph Henry

**Vogel**, Albertine Helene Sophia — **Ziegler**, Henry Ludwig W.

*Maiden Names*

**Von Bernuth**, Alice Marguerite — **Bierwirth**, John Edward

**Voss**, Jessie Somerville Knox — **Lewis**, Henry Llewellyn Daingerfield, Jr.

**Vyse**, Emily Carlotta — **Lyon**, Edmund Burton

**Waixel**, Juliet — **Lissberger**, Benjamin

**Walka**, Ganna — **d'Eignhorne**, Baron Archadie
**Fraenkel**, Dr. Julius
**Cochran**, Alexander Smith
**McCormick**, Harold Fowler
**Bernard**, Theos

**Wallace**, Violet Lee — **Crane**, Warren Seabury

**Walsh**, Margaret Ruth Lawrence — **Barnard**, John Augustus

**Ward**, Elizabeth Everett — **Thomas**, Theodore Gillard, III

**Warder**, Elizabeth — **Ellis**, Ralph Nicholson, Sr.

**Warner**, Maria Pierce — **Work**, James Henry, Sr.

**Warren**, Margaret Resler — **Meany**, Shannon Lord, Sr.
**Finlayson**, Daniel Aylesbury, Jr.

**Warren**, Martha S. — **Osborne**, Robert Klipfel

**Warren**, Susanne Elizabeth — **Murray**, Herman Stump

**Wasserman**, Ellen — **DeMille**, Nelson Richard

**Waterman**, Maude Olive — **De Tienne**, Dr. John Antoine

**Waters**, Emeline — **Vandewater**, James Horatio Poole

**Watson**, Elizabeth Hunter — **Driggs**, Edmund Hope, Jr.
**Bluntschli**, ____

**Watson**, Gladys P. — **Cowdrey**, Loren Montague

**Weed**, Minnie E. — **Jones**, Howard S.

**Weeks**, Marjorie Cooper — **Stewart**, John Henderson, Jr.
**Crews**, Dudley
**Phillips**, Francis A.

**Welch**, Marcia Lillian — **Candler**, Flamen Ball

**Weller**, Katharine Onderdonk — **Addison**, Charles Lambert

**Wells**, Robin — **Krugman**, Paul Robin

**Wendell**, Mildred — **Wickersham**, George Woodward

**Werner**, Estelle (aka Ruth Stuyvesant) — **Slesinger**, Laurence Anthony

**Wetmore**, Dagmar — **Sargent**, Charles Sprague, Jr.

**Whalley**, Dorothy Letita — **Stricker**, John Fritz

**Wheeler**, Caroline Maria — **Cruikshank**, James

**Wheeler**, Carolyn — **Kobbe**, Gustave

**Wheeler**, Mary Ann — **Cruikshank**, James

**Whipple**, Barbara Riker — **Welsh**, Joseph Wickes, Jr.

**Whipple**, Ellen — **Hard**, Anson Wales, Sr.

**Whipple**, Margaret Riker — **Finch**, Stephen Baker, Sr.

**White**, Margery Rich — **Wright**, Wilfred La Salles

*Maiden Names*

| | |
|---|---|
| **White**, Mary Esther | **Moller**, Charles George, III<br>**Nicoll**, De Lancey, Jr. |
| **White**, Mary Jane | **Ludlum**, Dr. Charles Henry |
| **Whiting**, Sarah Swan | **Belmont**, Oliver Hazard Perry<br>**Rives**, George Lockhart |
| **Whitman**, Mabel Shives | **Ludlow**, Alden Rodney, Jr. |
| **Whitney**, Katharine Varnum | **Kendall**, William Beals |
| **Whittaker**, Laha | **Chambers**, Jay<br>    (aka James A. Chambers) |
| **Wickersham**, Gwendolyn | **Akins**, Albert John, II<br>**Cobb**, Henry Ives, Jr. |
| **Wickes**, Deborah | **Mulford**, Charles William |
| **Wigglesworth**, Sylvia | **Mellen**, Chase, Jr.<br>**Maitland**, James William |
| **Wilbur**, Estelle Rodgers | **Hewlett**, James Monroe |
| **Wiley**, Elizabeth | **Robb**, Hampton |
| **Wilgus**, Lois Naomi | **Ballantine**, John Herbert, II |
| **Willets**, Anna | **Hewlett**, James Monroe |
| **Williams**, Barbara | **Throop**, Enos Thompson |
| **Williams**, Dorcas | **Ferris**, Morris Douw, Sr. |
| **Williams**, Joy Waldron | **Proctor**, William Ross, Jr. |
| **Williams**, Sarah W. | **Talmage**, Prentice, Sr. |
| **Wilson**, Marcie | **Hewitt**, Thomas M. |
| **Wilson**, Willa Alice | **Page**, Walter Hines, Sr. |
| **Winne**, Marie | **Sage**, Russell |
| **Winter**, Marjorie Elizabeth | **Jewell**, John Voorhees, Jr. |
| **Wiseman**, Hazel Nesbitt | **Chambers**, William Ely, Sr. |
| **Wiswell**, Estelle Lupton | **Brown**, Arthur Alvin, Sr. |
| **Wood**, Eleanor Rogers | **Zara**, Francesco A. |
| **Wood**, Margaret<br>    (aka Margot White) | **White**, Victor Gerald, Sr.<br>**Newton**, Arthur Ulysses |
| **Wood**, Selina Richards | **Grew**, Henry Sturgis, Jr.<br>**Hewlett**, Roger Sanderson |
| **Woodland**, Ruth | **Thomas**, Edward Clarke Oertel |
| **Woodruff**, Harriette Jane | **Ward**, Rodney Allen |
| **Woodward**, Harriet Mary | **Philbin**, Ewing Reginald, Sr.<br>    (aka Erving Reginald Philbin, Sr.) |
| **Woodworth**, Caroline Virginia | **Scott**, John Frederick |
| **Work**, Alice Warner | **Lawrence**, John L., Sr. |
| **Work**, Marjorie | **Hard**, DeCourcy Lawrence, Sr. |
| **Work**, Sally Duncan | **Lefferts**, Franklin Baker |
| **Worle**, Mary Agnes | **Prescott**, William French |
| **Worth**, Anna Lydia | **Sloan**, Benson Bennett, Sr. |
| **Wright**, Anna | **Meeker**, Samuel Mundy, Jr. |

## Maiden Names

| | |
|---|---|
| **Wright**, Harriet Louise | **Forrest**, Richard Earp |
| **Wyeth**, Charlotte Hoffman | **Delafield**, Lewis Livingston, Jr. |
| **Wyld**, Marjorie | **Morrow**, Dr. Albert Sidney, Sr. |
| **Wyman**, Alice | **Underhill**, Enoch William |
| **Wynkoop**, Elizabeth Hilles | **Morris**, Stuyvesant Fish, Jr. |
| **Yauch**, Margaret A. | **Kane**, John Patrick, Jr. |
| **Yenser**, Edna May | **Gormley**, John Vincent |
| **Yeomans**, Isabella Stevenson | **Brett**, George Platt, Jr. |
| **Young**, Edith L. | **Harlow**, Frank Strobridge |
| **Young**, Grace Eliza | **Earle**, Alexander Morse, Sr. |
| **Young**, Ruth Allen | **Koehler**, Robert Henry |
| **Young**, Sophie Milbank | **Hubbell**, George Loring, Jr. |
| **Youngs**, Eleanor | **Youngs**, William Jones |
| **Yuile**, Ellen Daniel | **Sturgis**, William James, Sr.<br>**Blair**, Wolcott |
| **Yvelin**, Gardina Greenleaf | **Gardner**, Bertram |
| **Zane**, Maria Isabella | **Cowles**, William Northrop<br>**Taylor**, Talbot Jones, Jr. |
| **Zolnay**, Margaret | **Newcomb**, John Churchill<br>**Auerbach**, John Hone, Sr. |

*Margaret Resler Warren*
*(Mrs. Daniel Aylesbury Finlayson)*

*Dorothy Ann Lannin*
*(Mrs. Harry Alphonse Tunstall)*

*Occupations*

See the surname entry to ascertain if an individual is listed under several occupational headings.

**ACCOUNTANTS**

Bowman, Archibald

Moran, Michael Arthur

Schley, Henry Spaulding, Sr.

**ADVERTISING EXECUTIVES**

Briggs, Albert Martin

Bromfield, Percy Butler

Bromfield, Percy Rushmore

Browne, Curtis Northrop

Chalfant, Edward Newton

Coupe, Frank J.

Earnshaw, Geoffrey S.

Fairchild, Willard, Sr.
  (aka Charles Willard Fairchild)

Fulton, Ralph Whittier

Knopf, Samuel

Leighton, John Langdon

Long, William Henderson, Jr.

Parker, Don M., Sr.

Thompson, James Walter

**ARCHITECTS**

Adams, William, Jr.

Almirall, Raymond Francis

Barnes, Roderic Barbour

Brooks, Ernest, Sr.

Chapman, Henry Otis, Sr.

Clark, Samuel Adams, Sr.

Cobb, Henry Ives, Jr.

Gildersleeve, Raleigh Colston

Glover, John Irwin

Greenleaf, John Cameron, Sr.

Hanemann, John Theodore, Sr.

Hewlett, James Monroe

Hinckley, Julian

Johnson, Carl
  [See Tjaden entry.]

Kellum, John

Lefferts, Franklin Baker

Moore, Rufus Ellis

Otto, Carl Ludwig, Sr.

Tjaden, Olive Frances

Weeks, Louis Seabury, Sr.

Wood, Arthur William Blake

**ARTISTS**

Albert, Judith Florence Carman

Bernstein, Jacqueline Lipscomb
  (aka Mimi Talbot)

Chambers, Jay
  (aka James A. Chambers)

Coffin, William Haskell, Sr.
  (aka Haskell Coffin)

Crane, Rebecca Riggs

Fairchild, Willard, Sr.
  (aka Charles Willard Fairchild)

Hanemann, John Theodore, Sr.

Hatch, Allene Pomeroy Gaty

Hewlett, James Monroe

Krugman, Robin Leslie Bergman

Macy, Winifred Earl Lefferts

Meany, Shannon Lord, Sr.

Miller, Frances Tileston Breese

Sizer, Theodore

Stevens, Clare Charlton Reynders

Weis, Stephan
  [See Karan entry.]

White, Victor Gerald, Sr.

White, Margaret Wood
  (aka Margot White)

Wood, Arthur William Blake

Ziegler, Frederick J.

**ASTRONAUTS**

Massimino, Michael James

*Occupations*

**ATTORNEYS**

Adams, William Herbert
Anderson, Ellery Oswald
Auchincloss, Joseph Howland, Sr.
Auerbach, Joseph Smith
Backus, Henry Clinton
Bateson, Edgar Farrar, Sr.
Belsterling, Charles Starne
Bentley, Edward Manross
Bentley, Edward Sailsbury, Sr.
Boardman, Andrew H.
Bond, Walter Huntington
Bradford, George Dexter
Breed, William Constable, Sr.
Brown, Albert Winton, Sr.
Brownback, Garrett A.
Brush, Gilbert Palmer
Candler, Flamen Ball
Carlin, George Andrew
Casey, William Joseph, Jr.
Chenault, Kathryn Cassell
Chenault, Kenneth Irvine
Childs, Edwards Herrick
Clute, Frank M.
Combs, Clinton deRaismes, Sr.
Courtenay, Adrian Henry, Sr.
Davie, Preston, Sr.
Delafield, Lewis Livingston, Jr.
Delafield, Lewis Livingston, III
Devereux, Alvin, II
Edsell, Ralph James, Jr.
Egginton, Hersey
Ellis, Ralph Nicholson, Sr.
Eustis, James Biddle, Sr.
Fanning, Edward Jerome
Fearey, Morton Lazell, Sr.
Ferguson, David, Sr.
Ferris, Morris Douw, Sr.
Ferris, Morris Patterson
Fletcher, Thomas Clement
Francklyn, Reginald Gebhard
Fuller, Paul, Jr.
Furst, Michael
Gardner, Bertram
Gaston, George Albert
Geer, Enos Throop, Sr.
Geer, William Montague, Jr.
Goodwin, Richard Naradof
Gray, James McIlvaine
Greason, Samuel, Jr.
Green, Walton Atwater, Sr.
Greene, Herbert Gouverneur
Griffin, Dominic Bodkin, Sr.
Hamlin, Francis Bacon, Sr.
Harris, Tracy Hyde, Jr.
Hart, Alexander Richmond
Hart, Augustin Snow, Sr.
Hawke, John Daniel, Jr.
Hendrickson, Charles Le Roy
Herrick, Harold Edward, Sr.
Holmes, Emlen Williams, II
Hoppin, Samuel Howland
Hubbell, George Loring, Jr.
Huntington, Ellery Channing, Jr.
Hurd, George Frederick
Hyland, John Francis
Ingraham, Frederick, Sr.
Ingraham, Richard, III
Jones, Thomas Catesby, Sr.
Keene, James Robert
Keisler, Peter Douglas
Kilbreth, James Truesdell, Jr.
Kingsley, Darwin Pearl, Jr.
Kobbe, Frederick William
Koehler, Robert Henry
Konta, Geoffrey
Larkin, John Adrian, Sr.
Levy, George Morton, Sr.
Littleton, Martin Wilson, Sr.
  (aka Martin W. Littleton, Jr.)
Locke, Campbell, Sr.
Lord, Daniel de Forest, V

*Occupations*

**ATTORNEYS** (cont'd)

Lord, Franklin Butler, Sr.
Lord, George de Forest, Sr.
Low, Ethelbert Ide
Marshall, Charles Alexander
Marshall, James Markham, II
McKee, Lanier
McKinny, Alexander, Sr.
Meeker, Samuel Mundy, Jr.
Mellen, Chase, Sr.
Merrill, Payson, Sr.
Miller, William Wilson
Morgenthau, Maximilian, Sr.
Murphy, William Gordon, Jr.
Naething, Charles Frederick
Neilson, Robert Hude
Nicoll, De Lancey, Jr.
O'Connor, Eugene Franklin, Jr.
Olcott, William Morrow Knox
Olena, Alfred Douglas
Olney, Peter Butler, Jr.
Olney, Peter Butler, Sr.
Olney, Sigourney Butler, Sr.
Osterhout, Howard
Paine, Edward Stetson
Parkhurst, William Man
Paterson, Basil Alexander
Patterson, Edward Liddon
Perkins, Norton
Philbin, Ewing Reginald, Sr.
   (aka Erving Reginald Philbin, Sr.)
Philbin, Jessie Holladay
Philbin, Stephen Holladay
Philips, Frederic Dimon
Polk, Frederic D.
Polk, Frank Lyon, Sr.
Pratt, James Edward
Pratt, Robert Edward, Sr.
Rives, Francis Bayard
Robinson, Beverley Randolph
Rogers, Edward Sidney

Schlossberg, Arnold, Sr.
Schultz, Albert Bigelow, Sr.
Schwieters, John Francis
Searle, John Endicott, Sr.
Seymour, Origen Storrs, II
Shepard, Frederic White
Skelos, Dean George
Slocum, Henry Warner, Jr.
Stebbins, George Ledyard, Sr.
Stevenson, Richard Wilson, Jr.
Stewart, Samuel Bradford, Jr.
Strickler, John Fritz
Tarbell, Gage Eli
Taylor, Willard Underhill, Sr.
Thomas, Edward Clarke Oertel
Thomas, Theodore Gaillard, III
Thompson, Dr. Benjamin Franklin
Townsend, Frances Mary Fragos
Townsend, John Michael
Townsend, Robert
Townsend, Stephen Van Rensselaer, Sr.
Turnbull, John Gourlay, III
Vandewater, Neil Horatio
Van Rensselaer, Bernard Sanders
Van Tine, Addison Allen
Van Vranken, John Kellum, Sr.
Van Zandt, Frederick Neville
Ward, Sylvanus Dwight
Weller, Augustus Noble
Welsh, Joseph Wickes, Sr.
Wickersham, Cornelius Wendell, Sr.
Wickersham, George Woodward
Wildermuth, George C.
Work, James Henry, Sr.
Youngs, William Jones

**CAPITALISTS**

Adams, Charles Closson, Sr.
Adams, John Trevor, Sr.
Adams, William, III
Addison, Charles Lambert

*Occupations*

**CAPITALISTS** (cont'd)

Addison, James, Jr.
Alexandre, Frederick Francis, Sr.
Anderson, Ellery Oswald
Arledge, Roone Pinckney, Jr.
Atwell, George Joseph, Sr.
Auerbach, Joseph Smith
Barnum, Peter Crosby
Belmont, August, II
Belsterling, Charles Starne
Bernstein, Lester
Bertschmann, Jean Jacques
Bierwirth, John Edward
Bird, Oliver William, Jr.
Blanchard, Walter Scott, Sr.
Bogert, Henry Lawrence, Jr.
Bond, Walter Huntington
Bossert, John
Brisbane, Arthur
Brown, Albert Winton, Sr.
Brown, Frederick Rhinelander
Burton, John Howes
Burton, Robert Lewis
Cady, Everett Ware, Sr.
Cammann, Herman Henry
Casey, William Joseph, Jr.
Chamberlin, Dr. William Taylor
Chapman, Gilbert Whipple, Sr.
Chenault, Kenneth Irvine
Childs, Caroline Goldsmith
Childs, John Lewis
Clute, Frank M.
Cochran, Alexander Smith
Cooper, Peter
Cowdrey, Loren Montague
Crane, Clinton Hoadley
Curtiss, Glenn Hammond, Sr.
Daingerfield, Algernon Gray
Darlington, The Reverend Gilbert Sterling Bancroft
Davie, Preston, Sr.
Dean, Howard Brush, Sr.

Delafield, Maturin Livingston, II
Delafield, Robert Hare, Jr.
De Mercado, Frank Eliot
De Mott, Harry Mead
Doolittle, Frederick William, Jr.
Dranow, John
　*[See Gluck entry.]*
Duncan, Alexander Butler
Durand, Celestin Aloysious, III
d'Utassy, George
　(aka George von d'Utassy)
Duval, William Hamlyn, III
Dwyer, Martin, Sr.
Edsell, Levi Perin
Edsell, Ralph James, Sr.
Elliman, Lawrence Bogert, Sr.
English, William K.
Erhart, William Herman
Eustis, George Peabody
　(aka George Eustis Corcoran)
Farquhar, William Joslyn, Sr.
Feldstein, Kathleen Foley
Fogarty, James Francis, Sr.
Forrest, Richard Earp
Fox, William
Fraser, Dougall Charles, Sr.
French, Seth Barton, Sr.
Frost, Newberry Halstead
Furst, Michael
Gamel, Isaac
Garde, John Franklin, Jr.
Gaston, George Albert
Gerard, George Henry
Gerstner, Louis Vincent, Jr.
Gildersleeve, Raleigh Colston
Glass, Brent David
Glover, John Irwin
Gluck, Louise Elizabeth
Goodwin, Doris Helen Kearns
Green, Harry Thomas Sinclair
Griswold, John Augustus, Sr.
Gulick, Ernestus Schenck

*Occupations*

**CAPITALISTS** (cont'd)

Hadden, James E. Smith
Hamill, Robert Lyon, Sr.
Hamlin, Francis Bacon, Sr.
Hammond, John Stevens, Sr.
Hard, Anson Wales, Sr.
Harriman, Edward Henry
Harris, Tracy Hyde, Jr.
Hart, Alexander Richmond
Hatch, E. Constance De Boer
Hatch, Eric Stow
Hazard, William Ayrault, Sr.
Hinckley, Catherine Livingston Hamersley
Hinckley, Samuel Parker
Hubbell, George Loring, Sr.
Hurd, George Frederick
Iger, Kathleen Susan Kiger
Iger, Robert Allen
Ingraham, Frederick, Sr.
Jacobi, Harold, Sr.
Jacobi, Sanford
Johnson, Carl
   *[See Tjaden entry.]*
Johnson, Lee
Kane, John Patrick, Jr.
Keene, James Robert
Kennedy, Henry Van Rensselaer
King, Hugh Purviance, Sr.
Kingsland, Harold Nutting
Kingsley, Darwin Pearl, Jr.
Kip, Ira Andruss
Knopf, Samuel
Koehler, Robert Henry
Koons, Franklin Stevenson
Krugman, Robin Leslie Bergman
Ladd, William Fowle, Jr.
Ladenburg, Adolph
   (aka Moritz Adolph Emil Landenberg)
La Mont, Herbert Murray
Lamy, Henry Bernard, Jr.
Lannin, Joseph John
Larkin, Henrietta Rosa Kleberg

Lebaudy, Jacques
Leighton, George Bridge
Levy, George Morton, Sr.
Levy, Isaac D.
Lewis, Edison
Littleton, Martin Wilson, Sr.
   (aka Martin W. Littleton, Jr.)
Livingston, John Griswold, Sr.
Livingston, Johnston, II
   (aka Johnston Livingston, Jr.)
Loft, George William
Lord, Franklin Butler, Sr.
MacDowell, Noah, Jr.
Macy, Carleton
Macy, George Henry
Macy, Valentine Everit, Sr.
Maitland, James William
Mallouk, George Elias
Manice, de Forest
Marshall, Chauncey, Sr.
Martin, Thomas Stephen
McCrea, James Alexander, II
McVitty, Edward Quinby, Sr.
Mellen, Chase, Sr.
Meneely, Charles Dickinson
Meyerkort, John, Sr.
Miller, Danforth, Sr.
Miller, Lawrence McKeever, Sr.
Miller, William Wilson
Mixter, George, Sr.
Moller, Charles George, III
Moller, Hans Eskildsen
Morgenthau, Julius Caesar, Sr.
Morgenthau, Maximilian, Sr.
Morris, Alfred Hennen
Morse, Roy Bertram
Moyers, Judith Suzanne Davidson
Murphy, William Gordon, Jr.
Murray, Herman Stump
Nicoll, De Lancey, Jr.
Niles, George Casper
Norris, Alfred Oliphant

*Occupations*

**CAPITALISTS** (cont'd)

O'Brien, Justin Cameron
Ohnewald, George Henry
Olcott, William Morrow Knox
Olney, Sigourney Butler, Sr.
Osborne, Lawrence Woodhull
Paine, Edward Stetson
Parsons, Argyll Rosse, Sr.
Paterson, Mary Alexander
Pennington, Charles Gordon
Perkins, Charles Lawrence, Jr.
Peters, Ralph, Sr.
Pettit, Townsend Baldwin, Sr.
Piel, Rudolph Alfred
Polk, Frank Lyon, Sr.
Porter, Henry Hobart, Jr.
Post, Stephen Rushmore
Pratt, James Guy
Pritchard, Clarence Franklin
Richards, Junius Alexander, Sr.
Ridder, Joseph Edward, Sr.
Ripley, Joseph Pierce
Ripley, Sidney Dillon, Sr.
Robb, Hampton
Robins, Samuel Davis, Sr.
Robinson, Josephine DeMott
Roosevelt, Elliott, Sr.
Rose, Reginald Perry
Roth, Arthur Thomas
Ruperti, Justus
Rutter, John Alexandre
Sage, Russell
Salmon, Hamilton Henry, Jr.
Sayer, Murray
Schill, Emil
Scott, Henry Clarkson, Sr.
Searle, John Endicott, Sr.
Sellar, Norrie, Sr.
Seymour, Origen Storrs, II
Shaw, Munson Gallaudet, Sr.
Sizer, Theodore

Skelos, Nancy Elizabeth Moffitt
Slesinger, Estelle Werner
 (aka Ruth Stuyvesant)
Sloan, Benson Bennett, Sr.
Spinzia, Peter
Southgate, Richard
Stanton, Louis Lee, Sr.
Steinberg, Julius
Stephan, Albert Ralph
Stevens, Alexander Henry
Stevenson, Maxwell
Strauss, Peter, Sr.
Stricker, Hans Carl
Stuberfield, William Francis
Sturgis, Henry Sprague, Sr.
Sturgis, William, Jr.
Tapscott, Ralph Henry
Tarbell, Gage Eli
Taylor, Willard Underhill, Sr.
Terry, Thomas Henry
Tew, Benjamin Taylor
Thayer, Benjamin Bowditch, Jr.
Throop, Enos Thompson, IV
Tibbs, Benjamin Hatfield
Tilford, Frank
Timpson, James
Townsend, Edward Nicoll, Sr.
Townsend, Frances Mary Fragos
Tucker, St. George Brooke
Underhill, Enoch William
Van Siclen, George West
Van Siclen, Mary Irving Francke
Van Vranken, John Kellum, Sr.
Veitch, Charles Whitely
Vogel, Henry John
Voss, William Hude Neilson
Ward, Rodney Allen
Ward, Sylvanus Dwight
Ward–Smith, Kenneth, Sr.
Warren, Charles Elliott, Sr.
Weeks, Herbert Augustus

*Occupations*

**CAPITALISTS** (cont'd)

Whipple, Julian Van Ness
White, Katherine J. Swift
White, Thomas Francis, Jr.
White, Thomas Francis, Sr.
Woodruff, Timothy Lester
Woolverton, William Henderson, Jr.
Young, Willis Howard, Sr.

**CLERGY**

Darlington, The Reverend Gilbert Sterling Bancroft
Hastings, The Reverend A. Abbott
Moyers, The Reverend Bill
Roche, The Reverend Spencer Summerfield
Swett, The Reverend Canon Paul Flynn, Sr.
Townley, The Reverend Frank Maxwell

**COMPOSERS**

Clafin, Avery

**DIPLOMATS**

Barnard, John Lawrence
Blackwood, Arthur Temple
Brown, Lewis Dean
Eustis, James Biddle, Sr.
Osterhout, Howard
Page, Walter Hines, Sr.
Polk, Frank Lyon, Sr.
Sayer, Murray
Smith, Clarence Browning
Southgate, Richard
Wickersham, George Woodward
Wright, Isaac Merritt, Sr.

**EDUCATORS**

Ayers, Frederick, II
Brower, Howard Stanley
Cammann, Marcia de Forest Post
Cammann, Schuyler Van Rensselaer
Carlin, George Andrew
Chu, Jean Holmes
Chu, Steven
Cohen, Bennett R.
Courtenay, Adrian Henry, Sr.
Crandall, Dr. Floyd Milford
Doolittle, Frederick William, Jr.
Dranow, John
   *[See Gluck entry.]*
Eustis, James Biddle, Sr.
Feldstein, Martin Stuart
Gesell, Doris M. Herdman
Glass, Brent David
Gluck, Louise Elizabeth
Goodwin, Doris Helen Kearns
Goodwin, Richard Naradof
Harrar, Dr. James Aitkin
Hatch, E. Constance De Boer
Hawke, John Daniel, Jr.
Hodges, Wetmore, Sr.
Kilmer, Dr. Theron Wendell, Sr.
   (aka Theron Sylvester Norton, Jr.]
Knopf, Ida Japhe
Krugman, Paul Robin
Krugman, Robin Wells
Mallouk, Ann Marmon
Massimino, Michael James
Morgenthau, Julius Caesar, Sr.
Morrow, Dr. Albert Sidney, Sr.
Munson, Lawrence Josiah
   (aka Lauritz Josiah Monsen)
Murray, Francis King
Pardee, Dr. Harold Ensign Bennett
Paterson, David Alexander
Robinson, Josephine DeMott
Russell, Dr. Thomas Hendrick
Sizer, Theodore
Smith, Anna Gertrude Jones
Wallace, Edward Secomb
Weed, Leroy Jefferson
Welton, Dr. Thurston Scott

*Occupations*

**ENTERTAINERS AND ASSOCIATED PROFESSIONS**

Adams, John Trevor, Sr.

Adams, William Herbert

Atwater, Angelita Kay Harmes

Atwater, Marjorie Elizabeth Millsap
  (aka Dorothy Lee)

Ayer, Rosa Hahn

Belmont, Eleanor Robson

Cammann, Schuyler Van Rensselaer

Cochran, Ganna Walka

Coffin, Frances Grant Starr

Dixon, Joan Deery
  (aka Joan Wetmore)

Goodwin, Doris Helen Kearns

Gwynne, Dorothy Goddard Ficken

Hewlett, Roger Sanderson

Iger, Kristine Carlin Bay
  (aka Willow Bay)

Kingsley, Heywood Mason Butler

Lebaudy, Augustine Delliere

Lovering, Elsie Richmond

Massimino, Michael James

McWilliams, Eleanor Arnett Nash

Merritt, Verona Ruth Oakley
  (aka Verona Ruth DeMott)

Miller, Nanette C. Campbell

Moyers, Bill

Moyers, Judith Suzanne Davidson

Plunkett, Henry Willoughby
  (aka Harry Plunkett Grattan)

Robinson, Josephine DeMott

Sperry, Winifred Allen Kelly
  (aka Winifred Allen Thomas)

Thomas, Dorothy A. Donovan
  (aka Dorothy Hale; Malan Cullen)

Townsend, Frances Mary Fragos

**FASHION DESIGNERS**

Karan, Donna Ivy Faske

Weis, Stephan
  *[See Karan entry.]*

**FINANCIERS**

Ackerman, Raymond Pryor, Sr.

Adams, Charles Closson, Sr.

Addison, James, Jr.

Alexandre, Frederick Francis, Sr.

Amerman, William H. H., Jr.

Atwater, Albert Leonard
  (aka Bert L. Atwater)

Atwell, George Joseph, Sr.

Auchincloss, Joseph Howland, Sr.

Auchincloss, Samuel Sloan, Sr.

Auerbach, John Hone, Sr.

Auerbach, Joseph Smith

Barnard, John Augustus

Barrett, Gilbert Conklin, Sr.

Beadleston, Chauncey Perry

Beebe, Henry Ward

Beebe, John Eldridge, Sr.

Belmont, August, II

Belmont, Oliver Hazard Perry

Benedict, Le Grand Lockwood, Sr.

Benkard, Henry Horton

Bentley, Edward Sailsbury, Sr.

Berdell, Theodore Van Duzer

Bierwirth, John Edward

Bird, Oliver William, Jr.

Blaine, Graham Burt, Sr.

Bloomer, James Ralph

Bogert, Henry Lawrence, Jr.

Bonner, Douglas Griswold, Sr.

Bossert, John

Boulton, Howard, Sr.

Boulton, William Bowen, Sr.

Bowker, Horace, Sr.

Braman, Chester Alwyn, Jr.

Breck, Duer du Pont

Brower, Howard Stanley

Brown, Albert Winton, Sr.

Brown, Frederick Rhinelander

Brownback, Garrett A.

Burr, Robert Page, Sr.

*Occupations*

**FINANCIERS** (cont'd)
Burr, Winthrop, Sr.
Cady, Everett Ware, Sr.
Cartwright, Henry Rogers, Jr.
Casey, William Joseph, Jr.
Chamberlin, Dr. William Taylor
Chambers, William Ely, Sr.
Chenault, Kenneth Irvine
Claflin, Avery
Connable, Arthur W.
Corroon, George Aloysius, Sr.
Corwith, Lester F.
Courtenay, Adrian Henry, Sr.
Covert, Charles Edward
Crane, Warren Seabury
Cruikshank, James
Cruikshank, William Morris, Sr.
Dall, Charles Whitney, Sr.
Darlington, The Reverend Gilbert Sterling Bancroft
Davidson, Thomas Charles, Sr.
Davis, William Shippen, Sr.
Dean, Howard Brush, Sr.
Delafield, Lewis Livingston, Jr.
Delafield, Maturin Livingston, II
Delafield, Robert Hare, Jr.
De Mott, Harry Mead
Deshler, Charles Franklin, Jr.
De Tienne, Dr. John Antoine
Dixon, Courtland Palmer, II
Dixon, William Palmer, Jr.
Downer, Jesse Halsey, Sr.
Driggs, Edmund Hope, Jr.
Du Bois, Arthur Mason
Dunham, Carroll, III
Dunnell, Frank Lyman, Sr.
Dunning, Clarence Seymour, Sr.
Dunstan, James Samuel
Durand, Celestin Aloysious, Jr.
Durand, Celestin Aloysious, Sr.
Durand, Celestin Aloysious, III
Durand, James Francis, Sr.

Duryea, William H.
Duryea, Wright, Jr.
Duval, William Hamlyn, III
Dwight, Philip J.
Earle, Alexander Morse, Sr.
Eaton, Walter Bradley
Eddy, William Higbie, Sr.
Edsell, Levi Perin
Egginton, Hersey
Einhaus, Harry Madison
Elliman, Lawrence Bogert, Sr.
Elwell, Richard Derby, Sr.
Ely, Henry Harris
English, William K.
Farr, John, Jr.
Feldstein, Kathleen Foley
Feldstein, Martin Stuart
Finch, Stephen Baker, Sr.
Finlayson, Daniel Aylesbury, Jr.
Fletcher, Thomas Clement
Floyd, Nicoll, Jr.
Fogarty, James Francis, Sr.
Forrest, Richard Earp
Fowler, Benjamin Kimball True
Francke, Albert, Sr.
Fraser, John W.
Frew, Walter Edwin
Furst, Michael
Garde, John Franklin, Jr.
Gardner, Bertram
Gaston, George Albert
Geer, William Montague, Jr.
Gerard, George Henry
Gerstner, Louis Vincent, Jr.
Goadby, Arthur McMaster
Goodhue, Francis Abbot
Gormley, John Vincent
Greason, Samuel, Jr.
Green, Harry Thomas Sinclair
Green, Walton Atwater, Sr.
Griswold, John Augustus, Sr.

*Occupations*

**FINANCIERS** (cont'd)

Gross, Andre Eugene
Gruner, Otto Harry, Sr.
Gulick, Ernestus Schenck
Gwynne, Frederick Walker
Gwynne, Walter Lee
Hadden, James E. Smith
Hamill, Robert Lyon, Sr.
Hamilton, Campbell Thorpe
Hamlin, Francis Bacon, Sr.
Hanemann, Edward Lewis
Hard, Anson Wales, Sr.
Harlow, Frank Strobridge
Harper, Joseph Henry, Jr.
Harriman, Edward Henry
Harrison, Milton Strong, Jr.
Hatch, Frederic Horace
Hawke, John Daniel, Jr.
Hazard, William Ayrault, Sr.
Heath, Cuyler
Hendrickson, Charles Le Roy
Herrick, Harold
Herrick, Harold Edward, Sr.
Hewitt, William Wilson, Sr.
Hinckley, Samuel Neilson, Sr.
Hodges, John King
Hodges, Wetmore, Sr.
Hoffman, Horace E.
Hoxie, Isaac Richmond, Sr.
Hubbell, George Loring, Jr.
Hubbell, George Loring, Sr.
Huntington, Ellery Channing, Jr.
Hutchinson, William Furman
Ingraham, Frederick, Sr.
Ingraham, Richard, III
Irwin, Louis Henry
Irwin, Marion Griffin
Ivison, Maynard Cady
Ivison, William Crane
Jewell, John Voorhees, Jr.
Jewell, John Voorhees, Sr.
Jones, Bethune Wellington
Jones, Howard S.
Keating, William J.
Keene, James Robert
Kendall, William Beals
Kendrick, Frederick William
Kennedy, Henry Van Rensselaer
Kimball, Frank Allan
Kip, Ira A., Jr.
Kniffin, Howard Summers, Sr.
Knopf, Samuel
Koehne, Richard Sperry, Sr.
Koons, Franklin Stevenson
Ladd, William Fowle, Jr.
Ladenburg, Adolph
  (aka Moritz Adolph Emil Ladenburg)
La Mont, Herbert Murray
Lamy, Henry Bernard, Jr.
Lancaster, John Edward, Jr.
Lanman, Jonathan Trumbull, Sr.
Larkin, John Adrian, Sr.
Lawrence, Newbold Trotter, Sr.
Lehrenkrauss, Charles Frederick
Leighton, Alexander E.
Leighton, John Langdon
Lewis, Henry Llewellyn Daingerfield, Jr.
Lissberger, Benjamin
Loft, George William
Long, William Henderson, Jr.
Lord, Daniel de Forest, V
Lord, Franklin Butler, Sr.
Lord, George de Forest, Sr.
Lovering, Joseph Swain, II
Low, Ethelbert Ide
Lynch, Edmund Ambrose, Sr.
Lynch, George Philip, Sr.
Mabon, Samuel Clifton
MacDowell, Noah, Jr.
Macy, Carleton
Macy, George Henry
Macy, Valentine Everit, Sr.

*Occupations*

**FINANCIERS** (cont'd)

Maitland, James William
Malcolm, George Ide, Sr.
Mallett, Percy Smith
Mann, Samuel Vernon, Jr.
Marks, Arthur David, Jr.
Marshall, Chauncey, Sr.
Marshall, Levin Rothrock, Sr.
Matthews, John
McCrea, James Alexander, II
McWilliam, Culver B.
Meeker, Samuel Mundy, Jr.
Meissner, William Christen
Merrill, Payson, Sr.
Merritt, Schuyler, II
Miller, John Robinson, Sr.
Mixter, George, Sr.
Moran, Robert G.
Morehouse, David
Morris, McLean Forman, Sr.
Morris, Stuyvesant Fish, Jr.
Moyers, Judith Suzanne Davidson
Mumford, Philip Gurdon
Murphy, William Gordon, Jr.
Myers, Charles
Norris, Alfred Lockwood
Norris, Donald Lee, Sr.
O'Brien, Justin Cameron
Olcott, William Morrow Knox
Olena, Alfred Douglas
Olney, Peter Butler, Jr.
Olney, Peter Butler, Sr.
Olney, Sigourney Butler, Sr.
Orvis, Schuyler Adams, Sr.
Osborne, Lawrence Woodhull
Osborne, Robert Klipfel
Otto, Carl Ludwig, Sr.
Paine, Edward Stetson
Pancake, Carl Oakley
Parker, Henry Seabury, Sr.
Parsons, Argyll Rosse, Sr.

Paterson, Michelle Paige
Peabody, Richard Augustus
Peabody, Rushton, Sr.
Pearce, Arthur Williams, Sr.
Pearsall, Harris Montgomery
Peck, Arthur Knowlton, Sr.
Peck, Arthur Nelson
Peck, Lee Wallace
Pell, Walden, Jr.
Pell, William Watson
Pennington, Harold Douglas
Perkins, Charles Lawrence, Jr.
Peters, Ralph, Jr.
Peters, Ralph, Sr.
Philips, William Frederic
Pidgeon, Ashley E.
Pierce, Walter Bryant, Jr.
Pinkus, Frederick S.
    (aka Solomon Frederick Pinkus;
    Frederick Salo Pinkus)
Polk, Frank Lyon, Sr.
Porter, Henry Hobart, Jr.
Post, Stephen Rushmore
Potter, Lars Sellstedt
Pratt, Frederick Theodore
Pratt, Robert Edward, Sr.
Prescott, William F.
Proctor, William Ross, Jr.
Rasmus, Carl Gerhard
Rawlins, George Foster
Rawlins, Herbert Noel, Jr.
Rawlins, Herbert Noel, Sr.
Raymond, William, Sr.
Remick, Joseph Gould
Rennard, John Townsend
Richard, Auguste
Richards, Junius Alexander, Sr.
Ripley, Joseph Pierce
Ripley, Sidney Dillon, Sr.
Robins, Thomas, IV
Robinson, Beverley Randolph
Roosevelt, Elliott, Sr.

*Occupations*

**FINANCIERS** (cont'd)

Roosevelt, Oliver Wolcott, Sr.
Rose, Reginald Perry
Roth, Arthur Thomas
Ruperti, Justus
Rutter, Nathaniel Edward Caldwell, Sr.
Sage, Russell
St. John, Edward Atkinson
St. John, Frank Lamar, Jr.
Salmon, Hamilton Henry, III
   (aka Hamilton Henry Salmon, Jr.)
Sargent, Charles Sprague, Jr.
Schieffelin, John Jay, Sr.
Schley, Buchanan, Jr.
Schultz, Albert Bigelow, Sr.
Scott, Charles Robert
Scott, Henry Clarkson, Sr.
Scott, John Frederick
Sellar, Norrie, Sr.
Seymour, Origen Storrs, II
Sise, John
Slade, Prescott
Slee, James Noah, Jr.
Sloan, Benson Bennett, Sr.
Sloan, Robert Sage, Sr.
Slocum, Henry Warner, Jr.
Smith, Augustine Jacquelin
Smith, Cyrus Porter, Sr.
Smith, Herbert Ludlam, Sr.
Southgate, Richard
Stanton, Louis Lee, Jr.
Stanton, Louis Lee, Sr.
Steven, Byam Kirby, III
Stevens, Alexander Henry
Stevens, Eben
Stevens, William Dixon
Stevenson, Joseph Hutchinson
Stewart, John Henderson, Jr.
Stewart, Samuel Bradford, Jr.
Stoddard, Caswell Wheeler
Stone, Herman Foster

Stray, Edward James, Sr.
Stricker, Hans Carl
Strong, Edwin Allen
Sturgis, Henry Sprague, Sr.
Sturgis, William James, Sr.
Talmage, Prentice, Sr.
Tarbell, Gage Eli
Taylor, Talbot Jones, Jr.
Taylor, William Reed Kirkland, Sr.
Thomas, Theodore Gaillard, III
Thorpe, Warren Parsons, Sr.
Throop, Enos Thompson, IV
Tilford, Frank
Timpson, James
Tompers, George Urban
Townsend, Edward Nicoll, Jr.
Townsend, Robert Tailer, Sr.
Tucker, St. George Brooke
Tunmore, John Septimus
Tunstall, Harry Gabriel
Tyner, Gerald Kerwin
Underhill, Rawson Kip, Sr.
Vandewater, Benjamin Cornelius
Van Vranken, Garrett Daniel
Van Vranken, John Kellum, Sr.
Varlet, Viscount René Georges
Veeder, Francis Lansing
Vogel, Henry John
Voss, William
Waddell, Wallace MacNab, Sr.
Wainwright, Loudon Snowden, Sr.
Walsh, James William, Jr.
Ward, Rodney Allen
Ward–Smith, Kenneth, Sr.
Warren, Charles Elliott, Sr.
Weed, Leroy Jefferson
Weisselberg, Allen Howard
Welsh, Joseph Wickes, Jr.
White, Thomas Francis, Jr.
Whitlock, Bache McEvers, Jr.
Whitman, Alexander Harvey, Sr.

*Occupations*

**FINANCIERS** (cont'd)

Whitney, Arthur Edward
Whiton, Henry Devereux
Wildermuth, George C.
Williams, Thomas, II
Williams, Thomas Resolved
Wilson, Marshall Orme, Sr.
Winkhaus, John Theodore, Sr.
Wood, Howard Ogden, Jr.
Woodruff, Timothy Lester
Work, James Henry, Jr.
Wright, John B.
Wright, Wilfred La Salles
Wyeth, Leonard Jarvis, IV
Young, Benjamin Swan
Young, Willis Howard, Sr.
Zara, Francesco A.

**INDUSTRIALISTS**

Akin, Albert John, II
Anderson, Roy Bennett, Sr.
Aten, Courtenay Nixon, Sr.
Atwater, Amarah George Cox, Sr.
Atwater, Albert Leonard
    (aka Bert L. Atwater)
Auerbach, Joseph Smith
Baker, Elwood Wilson
Baldwin, William Mood
Ballantine, Herbert Wilgus, Sr.
Ballantine, John Herbert, II
Ballantine, John Holme, II
Banks, Harold Purdy
Bannerman, Perry Elwood
Barnard, John Augustus
Belcher, Edwin Willoughby, Jr.
Belsterling, Charles Starne
Bené, John Raymond
Bentley, Edward Manross
Bierwirth, John Edward
Bigelow, Bushnell
Bishop, Clifford Monroe

Blackwood, Arthur Temple
Blaine, Graham Burt, Sr.
Bloomer, James Ralph
Bond, Walter Huntington
Bossert, John
Bowker, Horace, Sr.
Braman, Chester Alwyn, Jr.
Breed, William Constable, Sr.
Brown, Arthur Alvin, Sr.
Brownback, Garrett A.
Burton, John Howes
Burton, Robert Lewis
Cady, Everett Ware, Sr.
Carl, James Harvey, Jr.
Carter, Russell Steenback
Chapman, Gilbert Whipple, Sr.
Chenault, Kenneth Irvine
Cobb, Boughton, Sr.
Cochran, Alexander Smith
Coe, Elmore Holloway
Cohen, Bennett, R.
Cooper, Leslie Bradford
Cooper, Peter
Crane, Clinton Hoadley
Curtiss, Glenn Hammond, Sr.
Dall, Charles Whitney, Sr.
Dall, Stewart Maurice, Sr.
Davidson, Thomas Charles, Sr.
Davie, Preston, Sr.
de Aguilar, Francis Beauregarde
    (aka Francis Beauregarde Aglar)
Derby, Robert Mason, Sr.
De Saulles Charles Augustus Heckscher, Sr.
Dunstan, James Samuel
Duval, William Hamlyn, III
Dwyer, Martin, Sr.
Edwards, Jesse
Emmons, Walter Reed, Sr.
Enequist, John Theodore, Jr.
Enequist, William Lars
Erhart, William Herman

*Occupations*

**INDUSTRIALISTS** (cont'd)

Feldstein, Martin Stuart
Fogarty, James Francis, Sr.
Fosdick, Clark
Frew, Walter Edwin
Garde, John Franklin, Jr.
Geoghegan, Joseph Gregory
Gerard, Ernest Dudley
Gerard, George Henry
Gerstner, Louis Vincent, Jr.
Gleason, Marshall Wilfred
Gray, James McIlvaine
Greenfield, Jerry
Grew, Henry Sturgis, Jr.
Griffin, Dominic Bodkin, Jr.
Gurney, Thomas Nichols
Halsted, Gilbert Coutant, Jr.
Halsted, Harold Camerden
Hammond, Harry Stevens, Sr.
Handy, Courtlandt Waite
Hard, DeCourcy Lawrence, Sr.
Hart, Alexander Richmond
Hart, Augustin Snow, Sr.
Haughey, William Wallace
Hazard, William Ayrault, Sr.
Herrick, Newbold Lawrence, Sr.
Hinckley, Samuel Parker
Hoag, Charles H.
Hodges, Wetmore, Sr.
Hofheimer, Lester
Horton, Chauncey Todd, Sr.
Hunter, Fenley
  (aka Richard Fenley Hunter)
Huntington, Ellery Channing, Jr.
Hurd, George Frederick
Iger, Robert Allen
Ivison, William Crane
Jackson, Rickard Gilbert
Jacobi, Harold, Sr.
Jacobi, Sanford
Johnson, Lee

Jones, Bethune Wellington
Jones, Howard S.
Jordan, Edward Bailey, Jr.
Kamen, Dean Lawrence
Kane, John Patrick, Jr.
Kip, Ira A., Jr.
Kirkman, Alexander Sampson, Sr.
Knowlton, Eben Joseph
Koehler, Robert Henry
Koehne, John Lawrence, Sr.
La Mont, Herbert Murray
La Montagne, Montaigu
Larkin, John Adrian, Sr.
Lawrence, Clifford Winfield, Jr.
Lawrence, John L., Sr.
Lefferts, Marshall Clifford, Sr.
Leighton, George Bridge
Lewis, Edison
Lissberger, Benjamin
Locke, Campbell, Sr.
Loft, George William
Ludlow, Alden Rodney, Jr.
Macy, Carleton
Macy, George Henry
Mallett, Percy Smith
Marshall, Chauncey, Sr.
McVitty, Edward Quinby, Sr.
Meneely, Charles Dickinson
Merritt, Edward Charles, Sr.
Merritt, Harold Francis, Sr.
Merritt, Schuyler, II
Miller, John Robinson, Sr.
Miller, William Wilson
Minton, Henry Miller
Mixter, George, Sr.
Moller, Hans Eskildsen
Mumford, Philip Gurdon
Murray, Herman Stump
Neilson, Robert Hude
Olcott, William Morrow Knox
Paine, Edward Stetson

*Occupations*

**INDUSTRIALISTS** (cont'd)

Parker, Carleton Allen

Pearce, Arthur Williams, Sr.

Peck, Arthur Knowlton, Sr.

Peterkin, DeWitt, Sr.

Pettit, Townsend Baldwin

Pier, Roy

Pinkus, Frederick S.
   (aka Solomon Friederick Pinkus;
   Frederick Salo Pinkus)

Pittman, Ernest Wetmore

Putnam, Hobart Hayes

Rawlins, Herbert Noel, Jr.

Recht, William, Sr.

Rees, Harold Baxter, Sr.

Reeves, Edward Duer, Sr.

Rhett, William Brisbane, Sr.

Richard, Auguste

Richards, Junius Alexander, Sr.

Ridder, Joseph Edward, Sr.

Ripley, Joseph Pierce

Ripley, Sidney Dillon, Sr.

Roberts, Albert Samuel, Jr.

Robins, Samuel Davis, Sr.

Robins, Thomas, IV

Robinson, Beverley Randolph

Rogers, Edward Sidney

Rolston, Brown, Sr.

Rowe, Reginald Manchester, Sr.

Russell, Frank Henry

Rutter, John Alexandre

Salmon, Hamilton Henry, Jr.

Sanford, George Baylies

Sayer, Murray

Schill, Emil

Scott, Henry Clarkson, Sr.

Searle, John Endicott, Sr.

Seymour, Origen Storrs, II

Slesinger, Laurence Anthony

Sloan, Robert Sage, Sr.

Sloan, Thomas Donaldson, Sr.

Smith, Augustine Jacquelin

Snyder, William Robert

Sperry, Lawrence Burst, Sr.

Spinzia, Peter

Spinzia, Ralph

Stanton, Louis Lee, Sr.

Steinberg, Julius

Stone, Herman Foster

Sturgis, Henry Sprague, Sr.

Sturgis, William, Jr.

Thayer, Benjamin Bowditch, Jr.

Thompson, John Dixwell
   *[See Sampson entry.]*

Tompers, George Urban

Twining, Charles

Tyner, John Hill

Underhill, Enoch William

Veeder, Paul Lansing

Vogel, Henry John

Ward, Rodney Allen

Warren, Charles Elliott, Sr.

Warren, Northam, Sr.

White, Thomas Francis, Jr.

White, Thomas Francis, Sr.

Whiton, Henry Devereux

Wigglesworth, Henry

Wilson, Marshall Orme, Sr.

Woodruff, Timothy Lester

Wright, Wilfred La Salles

Young, Willis Howard, Sr.

Ziegler, Frederick J.

Ziegler, Henry Ludwig W.

**INTELLIGENCE AGENTS**

Atwater, Amarah George Cox, Sr.

Barnard, John Lawrence

Cammann, Marcia de Forest Post

Casey, William Joseph, Jr.

Chambers, Whittaker
   *[See Jay Chambers entry.]*

Huntington, Ellery Channing, Jr.

Huntington, Helen Catherine DuBois

Polk, Frank Lyon, Sr.

605

*Occupations*

**INTELLIGENCE AGENTS** (cont'd)

Rives, Francis Bayard

Woolverton, William Henderson, III

Wright, John B.

**INVENTORS**

Albert, Judith Florence Carman

Buck, Harold Winthrop

Chu, Steven

Cooper, Peter

Curtiss, Glenn Hammond, Sr.

Gleason, Marshall Wilfred

Gurney, Thomas Nichols

Haughey, William Wallace

Hubbell, John Platt, Sr.

Kamen, Dean Lawrence

Kilmer, Dr. Theron Wendell, Sr.
   (aka Theron Sylvester Norton, Jr.)

Massimino, Michael James

Meneely, Charles Dickinson

Recht, William, Sr.

Ridder, Joseph Edward, Sr.

Robins, Samuel Davis, Sr.

Schill, Emil

Sperry, Lawrence Burst, Sr.

Stone, Herman Foster

Van Sickle, Roswell Charles
   *[See Tjaden entry.]*

Wyld, James
   *[See R. H. Wyld entry.]*

Ziegler, Henry Ludwig W.

**JOURNALISTS**

Belmont, Alva Erskine Smith

Bernstein, Lester

Brisbane, Arthur

Cammann, Schuyler Van Rensselaer

Carlin, George Andrew

Crandall, Dr. Floyd Milford

DeMille, Virginia Sindel
   (aka Virginia Maxine Sindel; Ginny Witte)

De Merado, Frank Eliot

d'Utassy, George
   (aka George von d'Utassy)

Farr, John, Jr.

Ferris, Mary Lanman

Ferris, Morris Paterson Douw

Goodwin, Doris Helen Kearns

Goodwin, Richard Naradof

Green, Elsie J. King

Hatch, Alden R.

Hewlett, Roger Sanderson

Holmes, Evelyn Ogden Hatch

Iger, Kristine Carlin Bay
   (aka Willow Bay)

Kobbe, Gustave

Krugman, Paul Robin

Krugman, Robin Wells

McWilliams, Eleanor Arnett Nash

Moyers, Bill

Page, Walter Hines, Sr.

Silvers, Robert Benjamin

Slesinger, Estelle Werner
   (aka Ruth Stuyvesant)

Van Rensselaer, Rose Caroline Tillotson

Vaughan, Donald Cuyler, Sr.

Wickersham, George Woodward

Woodward, William G., Sr.

Youngs, William Jones

**LABOR ORGANIZERS**

Hillman, Bas Sheva Abramowitz

Hillman, Sidney

**MERCHANTS**

Alexandre, Regina Mathilde Saportas

Almy, Frederick, Jr.

Aten, Courtenay Nixon, Sr.

Auchincloss, Samuel Sloan, Sr.

Barnum, Joshua Willets

Barnum, Peter Crosby

Bierwirth, John Edward

Bishop, Clifford Monroe

Blagden, Thomas

*Occupations*

**MERCHANTS** (cont'd)

Blanchard, George Holmes
Brower, Howard Stanley
Cottone, Anthony
Downey, E. Kelly
Durand, Celestin Aloysius, III
d'Utassy, Florence Chapman
Duval, William Hamlyn, III
Ebinger, Walter Dohrmann
Elwell, Ruth Brown
Engs, Russell Larned, Sr.
Finlayson, Margaret Resler Warren
Floyd, Nicoll, III
Forshay, Ralph Hoyt
Grew, Henry Sturgis, Jr.
Gurney, Thomas Nichols
Hoag, Charles H.
Hodgson, Robert John, Jr.
Hofstra, William Sake
Horton, Chauncey Todd
Houghton, Owen Edward, Jr.
Hurry, Renwick Clifton
Hussey, Thomas Jefferson
Ingraham, Frederick, Sr.
Ivison, Sterling Hollingshead, Sr.
Jacobi, Harold, Sr.
Kane, John Patrick, Jr.
Karan, Mark
La Montagne, Montaigue
Lawrence, Alfred Newbold, I
Levy, Isaac D.
Loft, George William
MacDowell, Noah, Jr.
Mallouk, George Elias
Mariani, John Francis, Sr.
Marshall, Charles Alexander
Meany, Margaret Resler Warren
Miller, Frances Tileston Breese
Moore, Rufus Ellis
Morehouse, David
Morgenthau, Julius Caesar, Sr.

Morgenthau, Maximilian, Sr.
Morse, Roy Bertram
Newton, Arthur Ulysses
Orr, Henry Steers
Ossman, John, Jr.
Peacock, Grant Allen, Sr.
Peck, Lee Wallace
Pettit, Townsend Baldwin, Sr.
Pierce, K. Janavince Kerens
Porter, Henry Hobart, Jr.
Quinby, John Gurley, Jr.
Richards, Junius Alexander, Sr.
Sage, Russell
Salmon, Hamilton Henry, Jr.
Sellar, Sybil W. Sherman
Slade, Francis Henry
Southworth, Theodore
Stevens, Alexander Henry
Stewart, Samuel Bradford, Jr.
Tew, Benjamin Taylor
Thorpe, Warren, Sr.
Tilford, Frank
Timpson, Carl William, Sr.
Townsend, Edward Nicoll, Jr.
Tyner, John Hill
Van Rensselaer, Kiliaen Maunsell, II
Vaughan, Donald Cuyler, Sr.
Voge, Harry William
Wallace, Elizabeth Alden
Williams, Ichabod Thomas, II
Williams, Thomas Resolved
Woodward, William G., Sr.
Ziegler, Frederick J.

**MILITARY**

Hammond, John Stevens, Sr.
Palmer, E. T.
Persell, Harry Alexander
Sloan, Robert Sage, Sr.
Sloan, Thomas Donaldson, Sr.
Smith, Clarence Browning

*Occupations*

**MILITARY** (cont'd)
Thomas, Edward Clarke Oertel
Townsend, Robert
Warren, Charles Elliott, Sr.
Wickersham, Cornelius Wendell, Sr.

**NAVAL ARCHITECTS**
Cox, Daniel Hargate
Crane, Clinton Hoadley
Morrell, Robert Whiting

**PHYSICIANS**
Allison, Dr. Benjamin Roy
Anderton, Dr. William Bancroft
Bierwirth, Dr. Julius Carl
Brown, Dr. Frederick Tilden
Chamberlin, Dr. William Taylor
Chenault, Dr. Hortenius
Cox, Dr. Gerard Hutchinson, Sr.
Crandall, Dr. Floyd Milford
De Tienne, Dr. John Antoine
Dooman, Dr. David Stoddard
Fensterer, Dr. Gustave Adolf
Ferris, Dr. Henry Clay, Sr.
Fisher, Dr. Lamont H.
Fisher, Dr. Millie Rhodes
Gesell, Dr. Herbert Ross, Sr.
Harrar, Dr. James Aitken
Jones, Dr. Dunham Carroll
Kelly, Dr. Aquin S.
Kilmer, Dr. Theron Wendell, Sr.
   (aka Theron Sylvester Norton, Jr.)
Lasher, Dr. Frank Hermance
Ludlum, Dr. Charles Henry
Morrow, Dr. Albert Sidney, Sr.
Pardee, Dr. Ensign Bennett
Pardee, Dr. Harold Ensign Bennett
Pardee, Dr. Irving Hotchkiss
Russell, Dr. Thomas Hendrick
Sklar, Dr. Leo
Taylor, Dr. Quintard, Sr.

Thompson, Dr. Benjamin Franklin
Van Vranken, Dr. Garrett Daniel
Weed, Dr. Mabel Scott
Welton, Dr. Thurston Scott

**POLITICIANS**
Belmont, Oliver Hazard Perry
Bloomer, James Ralph
Breed, William Constable, Sr.
Casey, William Joseph, Jr.
Childs, John Lewis
Cooper, Peter
Davie, Eugenie Mary Ladenburg
Edsell, Ralph James, Jr.
Edsell, Ralph James, Sr.
Eustis, James Biddle, Sr.
Gardner, Bertram
Goodwin, Richard Naradof
Greason, Samuel, Jr.
Hillman, Sidney
Hyland, John Francis
Loft, George William
Lowden, Richard
McKinny, Alexander, Sr.
Morris, Alfred Hennen
Moyers, Bill
Olcott, William Morrow Knox
Osterhout, Howard
Parker, Glowacki Redfield
Paterson, Basil Alexander
Paterson, David Alexander
Paterson, Michelle Paige
Pearsall, Harris Montgomery
Persell, Mabel Elizabeth Fornof
Polk, Frank Lyon, Sr.
Robinson, Beverley Randolph
Robinson, Charles M.
Sage, Russell
Schley, Adele Sturges Mason
Schley, Buchanan, Jr.
Shepard, Frederic White

*Occupations*

**POLITICIANS** (cont'd)

Skelos, Dean George

Skelos, Gail M. Bernhardt

Stephan, Albert Ralph

Tew, Benjamin Taylor

Thompson, Dr. Benjamin Franklin

Tucker, St. George Brooke

Vandewater, James Horatio Poole

Weed, Leroy Jefferson

Woodruff, Timothy Lester

Youngs, William Jones

**PUBLIC RELATIONS**

Chu, Lisa Louise Thiebar

DeMille, Sandra Jane Dillingham

DeMille, Virginia Sindel
 (aka Virginia Maxine Sindel; Ginny Witte)

**PUBLISHERS**

Becker, Claude M.

Belmont, Oliver Hazard Perry

Bond, Walter Huntington

Brett, George Platt, Jr.

Brett, Isabella Stevenson Yeomans

Brisbane, Arthur

Bromfield, Percy Butler

Camprubi, Jose Aymar

Childs, Caroline Goldsmith

d'Utassy, George
 (aka George von d'Utassy)

Dwyer, Martin, Sr.

Green, Walton Atwater, Sr.

Harper, Joseph Abner

Harper, Joseph Henry, Sr.

Hart, Alexander Richmond

Howe, Wallis Eastburn, Jr.

Ivison, William Crane

Keene, James Robert

Knopf, Samuel

Leighton, John Langdon

Miller, John Robinson, Jr.

Mills, Edward Shorrey

Moore, Arthur Standish

Moore, Rufus Ellis

Moyers, Bill

O'Brien, Justin Cameron

Page, Walter Hines, Sr.

Parker, Don M., Sr.

Perkins, Charles Lawrence, Jr.

Ridder, Joseph Edward, Sr.

Roever, Charles Sigmund

Townsend, Edward Nicoll, Sr.

Vaughan, Donald Cuyler, Sr.

Weed, Leroy Jefferson

Welton, Dr. Thurston Scott

**REAL ESTATE AGENTS**

Bird, Oliver William, Jr.

Bloomer, James Ralph

Bodine, William Henry Johnson, Jr.

Bowker, Laurence Hewlett

Burr, Laurence Hewlett

Burtis, Devine Franklin, III

Cammann, Herbert Schuyler

Cruikshank, William Morris, Sr.

Deshler, Charles Franklin, Jr.

Elliman, Lawrence Bogert, Sr.

Enequist, William Lars

Gormley, Edna May Yenser

Gulick, Ernestus Schenck

Hubbell, George Loring, Sr.

Hubbell, Sherwood

Kingsland, Mathilde Marie Thieriot

Knapp, Robert Cole

Lawrence, Newbold Trotter, Sr.

Merritt, Virginia Morrill

Ohnewald, George Henry

Parsons, Argyll Rosse, Sr.

Peace, Arthur W.

Pease, Walter Albert, Jr.

Scott, John Frederick

Skelos, Gail M. Bernhardt

Studwell, Joseph Colson Knapp

*Occupations*

**REAL ESTATE AGENTS** (cont'd)

Talmage, John Frelinghusen

Taylor, Talbot Jones, III

Tunstall, Harry Alphonse

Underhill, Rawson Kip, Sr.

Whipple, Dana de Peyster, Sr.

**RESTAURATEUR**

Townsend, Edythe Earle

**SCIENTISTS**

Ayer, Frederick, II

Chu, Jean Holmes

Chu, Lisa Louise Thielbar

Chu, Steven

Nichols, John Treadwell

**SHIPPING**

Addison, Charles Lambert

Alexandre, James Henry, Sr.

Belsterling, Charles Starne

Davie, Preston, Sr.

Dow, Harold Gilman, Sr.

Eldridge, Lewis Angevine, Sr.

Fearey, Morton Lazell, Sr.

Ferris, Morris Douw, Sr.

Goodwin, Robert Henning

Griffin, Dominic Bodkin, Jr.

Harriman, Edward Henry

Leighton, George Bridge

Mooney, Franklin Drake, Sr.

Moran, Robert G.

Olcott, William Morrow Knox

Sage, Russell

Wright, Isaac Merritt, Sr.

**STATESMEN**

Brown, Lewis Dean

Casey, William Joseph, Jr.

Chu, Steven

Goodwin, Richard Naradof

Hawke, John Daniel, Jr.

Keisler, Peter Douglas

Polk, Frank Lyon, Sr.

Townsend, Frances Mary Fragos

Wickersham, George Woodward

Wright, Isaac Merritt, Sr.

**WRITERS**

Arledge, Roone Pinckney, Jr.

Auerbach, Joseph Smith

Ayers, Frederick, II

Belmont, Alva Erskine Smith

Belmont, Eleanor Robson

Belsterling, Charles Starne

Black, Archibald

Brisbane, Arthur

Cammann, Schuyler Van Rensselaer

Casey, William Joseph, Jr.

Childs, Caroline Goldsmith

Chu, Jean Holmes

Chu, Lisa Louise Thiebar

Chu, Steven

Clafin, Dorothea Carroll

Crandall, Dr. Floyd Milford

Crane, Clinton Hoadley

Curtiss, Glenn Hammond, Sr.

DeMille, Nelson Richard
 (aka Jack Cannon, Kurt Ladner,
 and Brad Matthews)

Doolittle, Frederick William, Jr.

Feldstein, Martin Stuart

Ferris, Mary Lanman Douw

Ferris, Morris Patterson

Gerstner, Louis Vincent, Jr.

Gildersleeve, Elena Josefa Mariana de Apezteguia

Glass, Brent David

Gluck, Louise Elizabeth

Goodwin, Doris Helen Kearns

Goodwin, Richard Naradof

Gray, James McIlvaine

Green, Walton Atwater, Sr.

Hanemann, John Theodore, Sr.

*Occupations*

**WRITERS** (cont'd)

- Harper, Joseph Henry, Sr.
- Hatch, Alden R.
- Hatch, Allene Pomeroy Gaty
- Hewlett, Roger Sanderson
- Hinckley, Julian
- Hodges, John King
- Hurd, Patricia E. Kendall
- Jewell, John Voorhees, Sr.
- Jones, Helen McConkey
- Karan, Donna Ivy Faske
- Kilmer, Dr. Theron Wendell, Sr. (aka Theron Sylvester Norton, Jr.)
- Kobbe, Gustave
- Kobbe, Frederick William
- Krugman, Paul Robin
- Krugman, Robin Wells
- Lawrence, Newbold Trotter, Sr.
- Leighton, John Langdon
- Littleton, Martin Wilson, Sr. (aka Martin W. Littleton, Jr.)
- Massimino, Michael James
- McKee, Lanier
- McWilliams, Eleanor Arnett Nash
- Miller, Frances Tileston Breese
- Morrow, Dr. Albert Sidney, Sr.
- Moyers, Bill
- Nichols, John Treadwell
- Page, Walter Hines, Sr.
- Pardee, Dr. Harold Ensign Bennett
- Philbin, Stephen Holladay
- Plunkett, Henry Willoughby (aka Harry Plunkett Grattan)
- Richard, Hetty Lawrence Hemenway
- Robinson, Josephine DeMott
- Roche, The Reverend Spencer Summerfield
- Rogers, Edward Sidney
- Russell, Dr. Thomas Hendrick
- Stevens, Clare Charlton Reynders
- Thompson, Dr. Benjamin Franklin
- Van Tine, Elizabeth Janes Gunn
- Wallace, Edward Secomb
- Welton, Dr. Thurston Scott
- Wickersham, Cornelius Wendell, Sr.

*Josephine DeMott Robinson*
*(Mrs. Charles M. Robinson)*

*Rehabilitative Uses*

## William Sake Hofstra residence, *The Netherlands*

*Rehabilitative Uses*

Non-residential rehabilitative secondary uses of surviving estate houses
listed are current as of 2023. Estates are identified by the original owner.
For subsequent estate owners, see surname entry.

| | |
|---|---|
| COPE Foundation | Harry Alphonse Tunstall carriage house, East Meadow |
| Garden City Jewish Center | Albert Leonard Atwater residence, (aka Bert L. Atwater) Garden City |
| Hofstra University | William Sake Hofstra estate, *The Netherlands*, Hempstead |
| Rock Hall Museum | Josiah Martin residence, *Rock Hall*, Lawrence |
| Seawane Golf Course | Joseph Smith Auerbach estate *Seawane*, Hewlett Harbor |
| Sisters of Saint Joseph Mission Office | Willis Howard Young, Sr. residence, *Willisleigh*, Hempstead |
| Stella K. Abraham High School for Girls | Henry Devereux Whiton residence, Hewlett Bay Park |
| Women's Sports Foundation | Harry Alphonse Tunstall main residence, East Meadow |

*Henry Devereux Whiton estate,
bedroom*

*Statesmen and Diplomats*

*James Biddle Eustis, Sr.*

*Walter Hines Page, Sr.*

*Statesmen and Diplomats*

Listed are only those statesmen and diplomats who resided in the Town of Hempstead.

## Statesmen

**Department of State**

**Acting Secretaries of State –**

    **Polk**, Frank Lyon, Sr. – Wilson administration
        Lawrence and Muttontown

**Under Secretaries, Assistant Secretaries, and Deputy Secretaries of State –**

    **Brown**, Lewis Dean
        – Under Secretary for Management (Nixon and Ford administrations)
        Garden City

    **Polk**, Frank Lyon, Sr.
        – Under Secretary of State (Wilson administration)
        Lawrence and Muttontown

**Department of Justice**

**Attorneys General –**

    **Wickersham**, George Woodward – Taft administration
        *Marshfield*, Lawrence

**Associate, Assistant, and Acting Attorneys General –**

    **Keisler**, Peter Douglas
        – Acting Attorney General (George W. Bush administration)
        – Assistant Attorney General for Civil Division (George W. Bush administration)
        – Associate Attorney General (George W. Bush administration)
        Woodmere

**Department of Energy**

**Secretaries of Energy –**

    **Chu**, Steven – Obama administration
        Garden City

**Department of Defense**

    **Pittman**, Steuart Lansing, II *[See E. W. Pittman entry.]*
        – Assistant Secretary of Defense
            (Kennedy and Lyndon B. Johnson administrations)
        Lawrence and East Hampton

**Department of Treasury**

**Under Secretaries, Assistant Secretaries, and Deputy Secretaries of Treasury –**

    **Hawke**, John Daniel Jr.
        – Under Secretary of Treasury for Domestic Finance
            (Clinton and George W. Bush administrations)
        Rockville Centre

## *Statesmen and Diplomats*

### Diplomats

**Barnard**, John Lawrence
- Consul, Antwerp, Belgium, 1954-1959
- Consul General, Aruba, 1960
- Consul General, Bahamas, 1960-1966

    Lawrence

**Blackwood**, Arthur Temple
- British Vice-Consul in Baltimore during World War II

    Hewlett Neck

**Brown**, Lewis Dean
- Vice-Consul, Leopoldville, Belgian Congo, 1946-1948
- Vice-Consul, Ottawa, Canada, 1948-1952
- Second Secretary-Consul, Paris, France, 1955-1958
- Ambassador to Senegal, 1967-1970*
- Ambassador to Gambia, 1967-1970*
- Ambassador to Jordan, 1970-1973
- Special Envoy to Cyprus, 1974
- Special Envoy to Lebanon, 1975

    Garden City

    *Brown served as Ambassador to Senegal and Gambia simultaneously.

**Eustis**, James Biddle, Sr.
- Ambassador Extraordinary and Plenipotentiary to France, 1893-1897

    Salisbury

**Osterhout**, Howard
- Member United States Peace Commission (Hoover administration)

    Garden City

**Page**, Walter Hines, Sr.
- Ambassador to Court of St. James (Wilson administration)

    Garden City and Bay Shore

**Polk**, Frank Lyon, Sr.
- United States Plenipotentiary to negotiate peace, 1919
- Chairman, United States delegation to Paris Peace Conference, 1919

    Lawrence and Muttontown

**Sayer**, Murray
- Vice-Consul, Stockholm, Sweden, 1917-1919

    Garden City

**Smith**, Clarence Browning
- Delegate (unofficial) to Austrian Reparation Commission after World War I

    Garden City

**Southgate**, Richard
- served in: United States Embassy in Paris, 1917-1918
  - United States Embassy in Rome, 1919-1921
  - United States Legation in Guatemala, 1921-1922
  - United States Embassy in Constantinople, 1922-1923
  - United States Embassy in Havana, 1925-26
- Chief of Protocol and Chief of International Conferences, 1929-1939
- Member, American delegation to Limitation of Armaments Conference, 1921
- Member, London Naval Conference, 1935
- Member, Aviation Conference, 1937
- Chief of Protocol, United States Department of State

    Hewlett

## Statesmen and Diplomats

**diplomats** (cont'd)

**Wickersham**, George Woodward
— Special Commissioner to Cuba, United States War Trade Board during World War I
*Marshfield*, Lawrence

**Wright**, Isaac Merritt, Sr.
— United States Representative to Austro–Hungarian Empire
*The Box*, Hempstead

### Advisors and Personal Secretaries

**Feldstein**, Martin Stuart
— Chairman, President's Council of Economic Advisors (Reagan administration)
— Member, President's Foreign Intelligence Advisory Board (George W. Bush administration)
— Member, President's Economic Recovery Board (Obama administration)
— Consultant, United States Department of Defense
— Member, President's Task Force on Tax Reform (Reagan administration)
Rockville Centre

**Sayer**, Murray
— Secretary to Auditor, Government of Porto Rico, 1906-1907
Garden City

**Townsend**, Frances Mary Fragos
— Member, President's Advisory Board (Reagan administration)
— Deputy Assistant to the President for Homeland Security and Counterterrorism (George W. Bush administration)
— Assistant Commandant for Intelligence, United States Coast Guard
Wantagh

*Francis Mary Fragos Townsend*

*Villages*

## Harold Jacobi, Sr. residence

## Villages

The village references used in this compilation are the current (2023) village or hamlet boundaries and should not be confused with zip code designations. When the owner who contracted for the original construction of the house is known, it is indicated by an asterisk.

### BALDWIN

* \* Baldwin, Francis
  *[See Loft entry.]*
* \* Glover, John Irwin
* Loft, George William, *Lakeview*

### BELLMORE

* Casey, William Joseph, Jr.

### CEDARHURST

* Brown, Frederick Rhinelander
* Browne, Curtis Northrop
* Claflin, Avery
* d'Utassy, George
  (aka George von d'Utassy)
* Edsell, Levi Perin
* Edsell, Ralph James, Sr.
* Elliman, Lawrence Bogert, Sr., *Cluny Lodge*
* La Montagne, Montaigu
* \* Levy, Isaac D., *Roselle Manor*
* Orvis, Schuyler Adams, Sr.
* Pardee, Dr. Harold Ensign Bennett, *The Wild Oat*
* Post, Stephen Rushmore
* Rasmus, Carl Gerhard
* Rawlins, Herbert Noel, Jr.
* Rawlins, Herbert Noel, Sr.
* Schley, Buchanan, Jr.
* Shaw, Munson Gallaudet, Sr.
* Slade, Prescott
* Slocum, Henry Warner, Jr.
* \* Tilford, Frank
* Vandewater, Benjamin Cornelius
* Vandewater, James Horatio Poole
* Vandewater, Neil Horatio

### EAST MEADOW

* Barnum, Joshua Willets, *Meadow Brook Farm*
* Barnum, Peter Crosby, *Meadow Brook Farm*
* \* Belmont, Oliver Hazard Perry, *Brookholt*
* Brisbane, Arthur
* Cochran, Alexander Smith
* Jordan, Edward Bailey, Jr.
* Konta, Geoffrey, *East Meadows*
* Lowden, Richard, *Carman–Lowden Homestead*
* \* Smith, James Clinch
* Terry, Thomas Henry, *Hempstead Farm*
* \* Turnstall, Harry Alphonse
  *[Tunstall owned two houses in East Meadow.]*
* \* Vogel, Henry John

### ELMONT

* \* Manice, de Forest, *Oatlands*

### FLORAL PARK

* \* Childs, John Lewis
* Schwieters, John Francis

### FRANKLIN SQUARE

* Albert, Judith Forence Carman
* Massimino, Michael James

### FREEPORT

* Levy, George Morton, Sr.

### GARDEN CITY

* Ackerman, Raymond Pryor, Sr.
* Adams, John Trevor, Sr.
* \* Addison, James, Jr.
* Anderson, Roy Bennett, Sr.
* Aten, Courtenay Nixon, Sr.
* Atwater, A. G. Cox, Sr.
* Atwater, Bert L.
* Backus, Henry Clinton
* Baker, Elwood Wilson
* Baldwin, William Mood, *Seven Acres*
* Barbatusly, Mark
  *[See Ebinger entry.]*
* Becker, Claude M.
* Beebe, Henry Ward
* Beebe, John Eldridge, Sr.
* Belcher, Edwin Willoughby, Jr.
* \* Bené, John Raymond
* Benkard, Henry Horton
* Berdell, Theodore Van Duzer
* Bishop, Clifford Monroe
* Black, Archibald
* Blanchard, George Holmes
* Bloomer, James Ralph
* Boardman, Andrew H.
* Bodine, William Henry Johnson, Jr.
* Bond, Walter Huntington
* Bossert, John
* Bowman, Archibald
* Breck, Duer du Pont
* Briggs, Albert Martin
* Brown, Arthur Alvin, Sr.
* Brown, Lewis Dean
* \* Brown Lewis Philip
* Brush, Gilbert Palmer
* Burtis, Divine Franklin, III

*Villages*

**GARDEN CITY** (cont'd)

* Carl, James Harvey, Jr.
  Carlin, George Andrew
  Cerriut, Jurge
  *[See H. E. Hoffman entry.]*
  Chalfant, Edward Newton
* Chu, Ju Chin
  Chu, Steven
  Clute, Frank M.
  Coffin, William Haskell, Sr.
    (aka Haskell Coffin)
  Combs, Clinton deRaismes, Sr.
  Corroon, George Aloysius, Sr.
* Cottone, Anthony
* Coupe, Frank J.
  Covert, Charles Edward
  Cowdrey, Loren Montague
  Cruikshank, William Morris, Sr.
  Curtiss, Glenn Hammond, Sr.
  Daingerfield, Algernon Gray
  Davidson, Thomas Charles, Sr.
  Davies, Edward Livingston
  de Aguilar, Francis Paul
  Dean, Howard Brush, Sr.
  De Mercado, Frank Eliot
* DeMille, Nelson Richard
* De Mott, Harry Mead
  Denny, Archibald Marshall, Sr.
  de Saulles, Charles Augustus Heckscher, Sr.
  De Tienne, Dr. John Antoine
  Doolittle, Frederick William, Jr.
* Dooman, Dr. David Stoddard
  Dow, Harold Gilman, Sr.
  Downer, Jesse Halsey, Sr.
  Downey, E. Kelly
  Driggs, Edmund Hope, Jr.
  Dunnell, Frank Lyman, Sr.
  Dunning, Clarence Seymour, Sr.
  Durand, Celestin Aloysious, Jr.
* Durand, Celestin Aloysious, Sr.
  Durand, Celestin Aloysious, III
  Durand, James Francis, Sr.
* Duryea, William H.
  Duval, William Hamlyn, III
  Earnshaw, Geoffrey S.
* Ebinger, Walter Dohrmann
  Egginton, Hersey
  Egly, Henry Harris
  Einhaus, Harry Madison
  Emmons, Walter Reed, Sr.
  Enequist, John Theodore, Jr.
* Enequist, William Lars
  Englis, William Franklin, Sr.
  English, William K.
  Engs, Russell Larned, Sr.
  Fairchild, Willard, Sr.
    (aka Charles Willard Fairchild)
  Fanning, Edward Jerome
  Farquhar, William Joslyn, Sr.
  Fearey, Morton Lazell
* Fensterer, Dr. Gustave Adolf, Sr.

  Ferguson, David, Sr.
  Ferris, Dr. Henry Clay, Sr.
  Ferris, Morris Patterson
  Fletcher, Thomas Clement
  Floyd, Nicoll, Jr.
* Floyd, Nicoll, III
  Forgarty, James Francis, Sr.
* Forman, Harold Baldwin
  Fowler, Rosemary O'Connor
  Fraser, Dougall Charles, Sr.
  Fraser, John W.
  Frew, Walter Edwin
* Fulton, Ralph Whittier
  Gardner, Bertram
  Gaston, George Albert
* Geer, Enos Throop, Sr.
* Geoghegan, Joseph Gregory
  Gerard, Ernest Dudley
  Gerard, George Henry
  Gerard, Henry Dudley
    (aka Dudley Gerard)
  Gesell, Dr. Herbert Ross, Sr.
  Gleason, Marshall Wilfred
  Gormley, John Vincent
* Gray, James McIlvaine
* Greason, Samuel, Jr.
  Griffin, Dominic Bodkin, Sr.
* Gross, Andre Eugene
* Gulick, Ernestus Schenck
* Gurney, Thomas Nichols
  Halsted, Gilbert Coutant, Jr.
* Halsted, Harold Camerden
  Hamilton, Campbell Thorpe
  Hamlin, Francis Bacon, Sr.
  Hammond, Harry Stevens, Sr.
  Hammond, John Stevens, Sr.
  Hanemann, Edward Lewis
  Harryman, Mildred C.
    *[See A. W. B. Wood entry.]*
  Hart, Alexander Richmond
  Hart, Augustin Snow, Sr.
  Hastings, The Reverend A. Abbott
  Haughey, William Wallace
  Heath, Cuyler
* Hendrickson, Charles Le Roy
* Hewitt, Thomas M.
* Hewitt, William Wilson, Sr.
* Hoag, Charles H.
* Hodgson, Robert John, Jr.
* Hoffman, Horace E.
  Hollis, W. C.
    *[See Fogarty entry.]*
  Horton, Chauncey Todd, Sr.
  Houghton, Owen Edward, Jr.
  Howe, Wallis Eastburn, Jr.
  Hubbell, George Loring, Jr.
* Hubbell, George Loring, Sr., *Lonesomehurst*
  Hubbell, John Platt, Sr.
* Hubbell, Ralph Peters, Sr.
* Hubbell, Sherwood

*Villages*

**GARDEN CITY** (cont'd)
   Hunter, Fenley
     (aka Richard Fenley Hunter)
* Huntington, Ellery Channing, Jr.
   Hussey, Robert F.
     *[See W. H. Duryea entry.]*
   Hussey, Thomas Jefferson
   Hutchinson, William Furman
* Irwin, Louis Henry
* Irwin, Marion Griffin
   Ivison, Sterling Hollingshead, Sr.
   Jackson, Rickard Gilbert
   Jewell, John Voohees, Jr.
   Jewell, John Voorhees, Sr.
   Johnson, Lee
   Jones, Bethune Wellington
   Jones, Howard S.
   Keating, William J.
   Kendall, William Beals
   Kimball, Frank Allan
   Kirkman, Alexander Sampson, Sr.
   Knapp, Robert Cole
   Kobbe, Carolyn Wheeler
   Koehler, Robert H.
   Koons, Franklin Stevenson
   Lamy, Henry Bernard, Jr.
   Lannin, Joseph John
   Lasher, Dr. Frank Hermance
* Lawrence, Clifford Winfield, Jr.
* Lehrenkrauss, Charles Frederick
   Littleton, Martin Wilson, Sr.
     (aka Martin W. Littleton, Jr.)
* Mabon, Samuel Clifton
   Mallett, Percy Smith
   Mallouk, George Elias
   Mariani, John Francis, Sr.
   McKinny, Alexander, Jr.
   McKinny, Alexander, Sr.
   McVitty, Edward Quinby, Sr., *Garstead*
* Meeker, Samuel Mundy, Jr.
   Meissner, William Christen
   Mellen, Chase, Sr.
   Meneely, Charles Dickinson
   Merritt, Edward Charles, Sr.
   Merritt, Harold Francis, Sr.
   Miller, John Robinson, Jr.
   Miller, John Robinson, Sr.
   Minton, Henry Miller
   Mooney, Franklin Drake, Sr.
* Moore, Arthur Standish
   Moore, Rufus Ellis
   Moran, Michael Arthur
   Moran, Robert G.
   Morehouse, David
   Morrell, Robert Whiting
   Morrow, Dr. Albert Sidney, Sr.
   Morse, Roy Bertram
* Mortimer, Mrs. Edith
     *[See A. W. B. Wood entry.]*
   Moyers, Bill

   Munson, Lawrence Josiah
     (aka Lauritz Josiah Monsen)
   Murphy, William Gordon, Jr.
   Murray, Francis King
   Naething, Charles Frederick
   Nichols, John Treadwell
* O'Brien, Justin Cameron
   O'Connor, Eugene Franklin, Jr.
   Ohnewald, George Henry
   Olena, Alfred Douglas
* Orr, Henry Steers
   Osborne, Lawrence Woodhull
* Ossman, John, Jr.
   Osterhout, Howard
   Otto, Carl Ludwig, Sr.
   Page, Walter Hines, Sr.
* Pancake, Carl Oakley
   Parker, Don M., Sr.
   Parker, Glowacki Redfield
   Parsons, Argyll Rosse, Sr.
   Peace, Arthur W.
* Peacock, Grant Allen, Sr.
   Pearsall, Harris Montgomery
   Pell, William Watson
   Pennington, Charles Gordon
   Pennington, Harold Douglas
* Persell, Harry Alexander
   Peterkin, DeWitt, Sr.
   Peters, Ralph, Jr.
* Peters, Ralph, Sr., *Wyndymeede*
   Pettit, Townsend Baldwin, Sr.
* Pidgeon, Ashley E.
   Piel, Rudolph Alfred
* Plunkett, Henry Wlloughby
     (aka Harry Plunkett Grattan)
   Pratt, James Edward
   Pratt, James Guy
   Pratt, Robert Edward, Sr.
   Putnam, Hobart Hayes
   Reeves, Edward Duer, Sr.
   Rhett, William Brisbane, Sr.
   Ripley, Joseph Pierce
   Roche, The Reverend Spencer Summerfield
   Roever, Charles Sigmund
   Rose, Reginald Perry
   Rowe, Reginald Manchester, Sr.
   St. John, Edward Atkinson
   St. John, Frank Lamar, Jr.
   Salmon, Hamilton Henry, Jr.
   Salmon, Hamilton Henry, III
     (aka Hamilton Henry, Jr.)
   Sayer, Murray
   Schley, Henry Spaulding, Sr.
   Smith, Clarence Browning
   Smith, Cyrus Porter, Sr.
   Smith, Herbert Ludlam, Sr.
   Snyder, William Robert
* Southworth, Theodore
   Sperry, Lawrence Burst
   Spinzia, Ralph
   Stoddard, Caswell Wheeler

*Villages*

### GARDEN CITY (cont'd)

Stricker, John Fritz
Stuberfield, William Francis
Studwell, Joseph Colson Knapp
Swett, The Reverend Canon Paul Flynn, Sr.
Sylvester, Peter Charles
Tapscott, Ralph Henry
* Tarbell, Gage Eli
Taylor, Dr. Quintard, Sr.
Taylor, Willard Underhill, Sr.
Thomas, Edward Clarke Oertel
Tibbs, Benjamin Hatfield
* Tjaden, Olive Frances
Tompers, George Urban
Townley, The Reverend Frank Maxwell
Townsend, Edward Nicoll, Jr.
Townsend, Edward Nicoll, Sr.
Townsend, Robert
Tunmore, John Septimus
Tunstall, Harry Gabriel
Turnbull, John Gourlay, III
Twining, Charles, *Iris Acre*
Tyner, Gerald Kerwin
Underhill, Rawson Kip, Sr.
* Underhill, Enoch William
Van Vranken, Dr. John Kellum, Sr.
Van Zandt, Federick Neville
Vaughan, Donald Cuyler, Sr.
Veitch, Charles Whitely
Voege, Harry William
* Waddell, Wallace MacNab, Sr.
Ward, Sylvanus Dwight
Ward–Smith, Kenneth, Sr.
Warinner, Asa
  [See W. H. Duryea entry.]
* Warren, Northam, Sr.
Weed, Leroy Jefferson
Welton, Dr. Thurston Scott
Whitney, Arthur Edward
Wigglesworth, Henry
Wildermuth, George C.
Wilson, Marshall Orme, Sr.
Winkhaus, John Theodore, Sr.
* Wood, Arthur William Blake
Wood, Frederick J.
* Woodruff, Timothy Lester
* Woodward, William G., Sr.
* Wyld, Robert Hasbrouck
Young, Benjamin Swan
Youngs, William Jones

### HEMPSTEAD

Addison, Charles Lambert
* Alexandre, James Henry, Sr.
Almirall, Raymond Francis, *Ma Chaumiére*
Amerman, William H. H., Jr.
Anderson, Ellery Oswald, *Waycroft*
* Bannerman, Parry Elwood
Barrett, Gilbert Conklin, Sr.
Belmont, August, II, *Blemton Manor*
Bromfield, Percy Butler
Bromfield, Percy Rushmore
Brown, Albert Winton, Sr.
Cameron, Walter Scott
Carlin, George Andrew
Carroll, Royall Phelps
Chamberlin, Dr. William Taylor
Chenault, Dr. Hortenius
Chenault, Kenneth Irvine
Cooper, Peter
Corwith, Lester F.
Courtenay, Adrian Henry, Sr.
Crandall, Dr. Floyd Milford, *The Pines*
Cruikshank, James
Duncan, Alexander Butler, *The Meadows*
Duryea, Wright, *Shortacre*
Edwards, Jesse
Eldridge, Lewis Angevine, Sr.
Fisher, Dr. Lamont H.
Forshay, Ralph Hoyt
Frost, Newberry Halstead
Hanemann, Edward Lewis
Harlow, Frank Strobridge, *Willisleigh*
Harper, Joseph Abner
Harriman, Edward Henry
* Hofstra, William Sake, *The Netherlands*
Hoppin, Samuel Howland
Hurry, Renwick Clifton
Ingraham, Frederick, Sr.
Ingraham, Richard, III
Jones, Dr. Dunham Carroll, *Bleak House*
Kellum, John
Kendrick, Frederick William, *Boxley*
* Kennedy, Henry Van Rensselaer, *Three Oaks*
* Kernochan, James Lorillard, *The Meadows*
Kilmer, Dr. Theron Wendell, Sr.
  (aka Theron Sylvester Norton, Jr.)
Leighton, Alexander E.
Leighton, George Bridge
Leighton, John Langdon
Ludlum, Dr. Charles Henry
* Lyon, Edmund Burton, *Nearacre*
MacDowell, Noah, Jr.
Mulford, Charles Willian, *Langsyne*
Mulford, Miss Fannie, *Langsyne*
Mulford, Miss Harriet, *Langsyne*
Myers, Charles
Paterson, Basil Alexander
Paterson, David Alexander
Pease, Walter Albert, Jr., *Bethpage*
Pettit, Townsend Baldwin, Sr.
Rawlins, George Foster
Russell, Frank Henry
Stevenson, Maxwell, *The Lodge*
Tew, Benjamin Taylor
Thompson, Dr. Benjamin Franklin
Townsend, Robert Tailer, Sr.
Townsend, Stephen Van Rensselar, Sr.
Vanderveer, Charles, Jr.
Van Vranken, Dr. Garrett Daniel

*Villages*

**HEMPSTEAD** (cont'd)

    Van Vranken, John Kellum, Sr.
    Ward, Rodney Allen
    Weller, Augustus Nobel
    Whipple, Dana de Peyster, Sr.
    Wright, Mary Eliza Bedford, *The Box*
    Wright, Wilfred La Salles
\* Young, Willis Henry, Sr., *Willisleigh*

**HEWLETT**

    Ayer, Frederick, II
    Bertschmann, Jean Jacques
    Blaine, Graham Burt
    Bonner, Douglas Griswold, Sr.
    Cartwright, Henry Rogers, Jr., *Applecot*
    Chambers, William Ely, Sr., *Cornerware*
    Cobb, Henry Ives, Jr.
    Cox, Dr. Gerard Hutchinson, Sr.
    Farr, John, Jr.
    Gruner, Otto Harry, Sr.
    Livingston, Johnston, II, *Homeacre*
      (aka Johnston Livington, Jr.)
\* Macy, Valentine Everit, Sr.
    Malcolm, George Ide, Jr.
    Malcolm, George Ide, Sr.
    Matthews, John
    Miller, Lawrence McKeever, Sr.
    Moller, Hans Eskildsen
    Philbin, Stephen Holladay
    Robins, Thomas, IV
\* Sizer, Theodore
    Southgate, Richard
    Welsh, Joseph Wickes, Jr.
    Whipple, Julian Van Ness, *Rustee Granit*
    Whitlock, Bache McEvers, Jr., *Meadowview*

**HEWLETT BAY PARK**

    Allison, Dr. Benjamin Roy
    Ballantine, Herbert Wilgus, Sr.
    Beadleston, Chauncey Perry
    Bigelow, Bushnell
    Blanchard, Walter Scott, Sr.
    Boulton, Howard, Sr.
    Braman, Chester Alwyn, Jr.
    Brett, George Platt, Jr.
    Buck, Harold Winthrop
\* Cady, Everett Ware, Sr.
\* Carter, Russell Steenback, *The Villa Blue*
    Chambers, William Ely, Sr., *Cornerware*
    Childs, Edwards Herrick
    Cobb, Boughton, Sr., *The Chimney Corner*
    Coe, Elmore Holloway
\* Connable, Arthur W., *Boxwood*
    Crane, Clinton Hoadley
    Davis, William Shippen, Sr.
    Delafield, Lewis Livingston, III
    Deshler, Charles Franklin, Jr.
    Finlayson, Daniel Aylesbury, Jr.

    Fuller, Paul, Jr., *Four Winds*
    Goodhue, Francis Abbot, Jr.
    Goodwin, Robert Henning, *Cedar Corners*
    Green, Harry Thomas Sinclair
    Greenleaf, John Cameron, Sr.
    Griswold, John Augustus, Sr.
    Gwynne, Walter Lee
    Hanemann, John Theodore, Sr., *Aboha Hanta*
    Harper, Joseph Henry, Jr.
    Harrar, Dr. James Aitken
\* Harris, Tracy Hyde, Jr., *Wistaria Lodge*
    Ivison, Maynard Cady
    Jones, Thomas Catesby, Sr., *Green Plains*
    Kane, John Patrick, Jr.
    Kilbreth, James Truesdell, Jr., *Bush Corners*
    King, Hugh Purviance, Sr.
    Kingsland, Harold Nutting
    Kip, Ira A., Jr.
    Lancaster, John Edward, Jr.
    Larkin, John Adrian, Sr.
    Lewis, Henry Llewellyn Daingerfield, Jr.,
      *Merriefield*
    Lovering, Joseph Swain, II, *Sunny Ridge*
\* Macy, Carleton, *Meadowwood*
\* Macy, Carleton, *Wonderwhy*
\* Macy Carroll, *Birch Corners*
    Maitland, James William
    Meany, Shannon Lord, Sr.
    Miller, Danforth, Sr., *Birch Corners*
    Morris, Alfred Hennen
\* Morris, Stuyvesant Fish, Jr.
    Norris, Donald Lee, Sr.
    Olney, Sigourney Butler, Sr.
    Osborne, Robert Klipfel
    Parker, Henry Seabury, Sr., *The Farm*
    Philbin, Ewing Reginald, Sr., *Pine Tree House*
      (aka Erving Reginald Philbin, Sr.)
    Pierce, Walter Bryant, Jr.
    Pratt, Frederick Theodore
    Proctor, William Ross, Jr.
    Ridder, Joseph Edward, Sr.
    Rives, Francis Bayard, *Mapleglades*
    Robins, Samuel Davis, Sr.
    Russell, Dr. Thomas Hendrick, *Channel's End*
    Schultz, Albert Bigelow, Sr.
\* Scott, John Frederick, *Rosebank*
    Slee, James Noah, Jr.
    Slesinger, Laurence Anthony
    Steinberg, Julius
    Stevenson, Joseph Hutchinson, *The Farm*
    Stevenson, Richard Wilson, Jr., *The Farm*
    Strong, Edwin Allen
    Van Rensselaer, Bernard Sanders
    Van Tine, Addison Allen
    Veeder, Paul Lansing, *Meadowwood*
    Voss, William, *Merriefield*
\* Whiton, Henry Devereux
    Wright, John B.
    Zara, Francesco A.

*Villages*

## HEWLETT HARBOR

    Akin, Albert John, II, *Homewood*
    Auerbach, John Hone, Sr., *Seawane*
\* Auerbach, Joseph Smith, *Seawane*
    Dwyer, Martin, Sr.
    Francklyn, Reginald Gebhard
    Kaplan, Louis
        *[See Lissberger entry.]*
    Kingsley, Darwin Pearl, Jr., *High Tide*
    Lissberger, Benjamin, *Twin Gables*
    Loft, George William
        *[See Lissberger entry.]*
    Long, William Henderson, Jr., *Noranda*
\* Marshall, Levin Rothrock, Sr., *Hawkswood*
    Milholland, James Clarke
    Mixter, George, Sr., *Strode*
    Nicoll, De Lancey, Jr., *Three Acres*
    Paine, Edward Stetson
    Peabody, Rushton, Sr., *Cherry Bounce*
\* Pearce, Arthur Williams
    Pier, Roy, *Breezy Way*
    Rolston, Brown, Sr.
    Sellar, Norrie, Sr.
    Thomas, Theodore Gaillard, III
    Thompson, James Walter
    Timpson, Carl William, Sr., *Windy Top*
    Voss, William Hude Neilson

## HEWLETT NECK

    Blackwood, Arthur Temple
    Delafield, Robert Hare, Jr.
\* Dwight, Philip J.
    French, Seth Barton, Sr.
\* Handy, Courtlandt Waite
    Heymsfeld, Ralph
        *[See Handy entry.]*
    Herrick, Harold Edward, Sr.
\* Hewlett, Roger Sanderson
\* Jacobi, Sanford
    Kobbe, Frederick William
    Locke, Campbell, Sr.
    Logan, John Alexander, III
\* Morris, McLean Forman, Sr.
    Robb, Hampton
    Roosevelt, Oliver Wolcott, Sr.
    Searle, John Endicott, Sr.
    Stephan, Albert Ralph
    Steven, William Dixon
    Stewart, Samuel Bradford, Jr.
    Tucker, St. George Brooke
    Van Rensselaer, Kiliaen Maunsell, II
    Van Rensselaer, Maunsell, Jr., *The Haven*
    Varlet, Viscount René Georges
    Veeder, Francis Lansing
    Wallace, Edward Secomb
    Warren, Charles Elliott, Sr., *Still Pond*

## LAWRENCE

    Adams, Charles Closson, Sr., *Oak Lodge*
    Adams, William, Jr.
    Adams, William, III, *Landfall*
    Adams, William Herbert
    Alexandre, Frderick Francis, Sr., *Nieman*
    Almy, Frederick, Jr.
    Anderton, Dr. William Bancroft, *Ye Corners*
    Auchincloss, Joseph Howland, Sr.
    Auchincloss, Samuel Sloan, Sr., *Whale Acres*
\* Ballantine, John Herbert, II
    Barnard, John Augustus, *Tigh-na-Curach*
    Barnard, John Lawrence
    Barnes, Roderic Barbour
    Bateson, Edgar Farrar, Sr.
    Belsterling, Charles Starne
    Benedict, Le Grand Lockwood, Sr., *Nooke*
    Bentley, Edward Manross, *Cherrygarth*
    Bentley, Edward Sailsbury, Sr., *Cherrygarth*
    Bierwirth, John Edward
    Bierwirth, Dr. Julius Carl
    Blagden, Thomas
    Blaine, Graham Burt, Sr.
    Bogert, Henry Lawrence, Jr.
\* Boulton, William Bowen, Sr., *Avila*
    Bowker, Horace, Sr.
    Breed, William Constable, *Whale Acres*
    Brooks, Ernest, Sr., *The Moorings*
    Brown, Mary Crosby Renwick, *Windward*
    Brownback, Garrett A.
    Burr, Robert Page, Sr.
\* Burr, Winthrop, Sr., *Orchard Hall*
    Burton, John Howes, *Albro House*
\* Burton, Robert Lewis, *Albro House*
    Carpenter, Edward Novell
    Chapman, Henry Otis, Jr.
        *[See S. Merritt II entry.]*
    Clark, Samuel Adams, Sr.
\* Crane, Warren Seabury, *East View*
    Dall, Charles Whitney, Sr.
    Dall, Stewart Maurice, Sr.
    Darlington, The Rev. Gilbert Sterling Bancroft
    de Aguilar, Elizabeth Pendleton Slattery
    Delafield, Lewis Livingston, Jr.,
        *Norton Perkins Cottage*
    Derby, Robert Mason, Sr.
    De Veau, George Putnam
    Devereux, Alvin, II
    Dixon, Courtland Palmer, II, *The Causeway*
    Dixon, William Palmer, Jr.
    Du Bois, Arthur Mason
    Dunham, Carroll, III, *Stone Lodge*
    Dunstan, James Samuel, *Brightside*
    Eaton, Walter Bradley, *The Corral*
    Eddy, William Higbie, Sr.
    Edsell, Ralph James, Jr.
    Elwell, Richard Derby, Sr.
\* Erhart, William Herman, *Five Oaks*
    Ferris, Morris Douw, Sr.
    Finch, Stephen Baker, Sr.
\* Forrest, Richard Earp, *Longwood*

## LAWRENCE (cont'd)

Francke, Albert, Sr.
Gamel, Isaac
Garde, John Franklin, Jr.
Geer, William Montague, Jr.
Gildersleeve, Raleigh Colston, *Red House*
Goadby, Arthur McMaster, *Wistaria*
Green, Walton Atwater, Sr.
Greenberg, Henry
    *[See W. Burr, Sr. entry.]*
Greene, Herbert Gouverneur
Grew, Henry Sturgis, Jr.
Hamill, Robert Lyon, Sr.
Hard, Anson Wales, Sr., *Driftwood*
Hard, DeCourcy Lawrence, Sr., *Briarwood*
* Harper, Joseph Henry, Sr., *Brightside*
Harrison, Milton Strong, Jr.
Hatch, Alden R., *Somerleas*
Hatch, Frederic Horace, *Somerleas*
* Hazard, William Ayrault, Sr., *Meadow Hall*
Herrick, Harold, *The Meadows*
Hewlett, George H., *Rock Hall*
* Hewlett, James Monroe
Hinckley, Julian
Hinckley, Samuel Neilson, *Son Ridge*
* Hinckley, Samuel Parker, *Sunset Hall*
Hodges, John King
Holmes, Emlen Williams, II
Hoxie, I. Richmond, Sr.
Hurd, George Frederick
Ivison, William Crane, *Wilcemay Farm*
Keene, James Robert
Kelly, Dr. Aquin S.
* Kniffin, Howard Summers, Sr., *Restleigh*
Knopf, Samuel
Koehne, John Lawrence, Sr.
Koehne, Richard Sperry, Sr.
* Ladd, William Fowle, Jr.
Lanman, Jonathan Trumbull, Sr.,
    *Orchard Hall*
Lawrence, Alfred Newbold, I
Lawrence, John L., Sr., *Moorlands*
Lawrence, Newbold Trotter, Sr., *Homewood*
Lefferts, Franklin Baker
* Lefferts, Marshall Clifford, Sr., *Hedgewood*
Lewis, Edison
Livingston, John Griswold, Sr.
Locke, Campbell, Sr.
* Lord, Daniel de Forest, V, *Sosiego*
Lord, Franklin Butler, Sr.
Ludlow, Alden, Rodney, Jr.
Lynch, Edmund Ambrose, Sr.
Lynch, George Philip, Sr.
Macy, George Henry, *The Bungalow*
Maitland, James William
* Mann, Samuel Vernon, Jr., *Grove Point*
Marmo, Anthony
Marshall, May Louise Bamber
Martin, Thomas Stephen, *Mistletoe Way*
McKee, Lanier, *Recess*
McWilliam, Culver B.

* Merrill, Payson, Sr.
Merritt, Schuyler, II
* Meyerkort, Clara Oakley
Meyerkort, John, Jr.
    (aka Jack Meyerkort, Jr.)
Miller, William Wilson, *Villa Nancy*
Moller, Charles George, Jr., *Wayside*
Moller, Charles George, III
Morrow, Robert
Mumford, Philip Gurdon, *Journey's End*
Newton, Arthur Ulysses
Niles, George Casper
Norris, Alfred Lockwood
Norris, Alfred Oliphant
Olney, Peter Butler, Jr.
Olney, Peter Butler, Sr., *Meadowside*
Palmer, E. T.
Pardee, Dr. Ensign Bennett,
    *Edgewater Cottage*
Pardee, Dr. Irving Hotchkiss,
    *Edgewater Cottage*
Patterson, Edward Liddon, *Rock Hall*
* Peabody, Richard Augustus, *Terrace Hall*
Peck, Arthur Knowlton, Sr.
Peck, Lee Wallace
Pell, Walden, Jr., *Oak Lawn*
* Perkins, Norton, *Whale Acres*
Philbin, Jessie Holladay
* Philips, Frederic Dimon, *Greyhouse*
Philips, William Frederic, *Fairway*
Pinkus, Frederick S.
    (aka Solomon Friederick Pinkus;
    Frederick Solo Pinkus)
Pittman, Ernest Wetmore
Polk, Frank Lyon, Sr.
* Porter, Henry Hobart, Jr., *Lauderdale*
Potter, Lars Sellstedt, Jr.
Pratt, Reginald Tyler
Prescott, William F.
Pritchard, Clarence Franklin
Quinby, John Gurley, Jr.
Raymond, William, Sr.
Rees, Harold Baxter, Sr.
Richard, Auguste, *Tenant Farm*
Richards, Junius Alexander, Sr.
Roberts, Albert Samuel, Jr., *Longwood Hall*
Robinson, Beverley Randolph
* Rogers, Edward Sidney
Ruperti, Justus, *Marigolds*
Rutter, John Alexandre, Sr.
Rutter, Nathaniel Edward, Jr.
Sage, Russell, *Cedarcroft / Cedar Croft*
* Sampson, Sally Phillips Blagden
Sanford, George Baylies, *The Byways*
Sargent, Charles Sprague, Jr.
Seymour, Origen Storrs, II, *Sosiego*
Sherman, Charles E., *The Brae*
* Sklar, Dr. Leo, *Byrnewood*
* Slade, Francis Henry
Sloan, Benson Bennett, Sr., *Ballyracket*
* Sloan, Thomas Donaldson, Sr., *Wilton Gables*

### LAWRENCE (cont'd)

Smith, Augustine Jacquelin, *Sunnyside*
Stanton, Louis Lee, Jr.
Stanton, Louis Lee, Sr.
Stevens, Alexander Henry
* Stevens, Byam Kirby, III
Stevens, Eben, *The Mount*
Stewart, John Henderson, Jr.
Stone, Herman Foster, *The Moorings*
* Strauss, Peter, Sr.
Sturgis, Henry Sprague
Sturgis, William James, Sr.
Talmage, John Frelinghusen
Talmage, Prentice, Sr.
Taylor, Jennie McCombe
  [See A. S. Roberts entry.]
* Taylor, Talbot Jones, Jr., *Talbot House*
Taylor, Talbot Jones, III
Taylor, William Reed Kirkland, Sr.
Thayer, Benjamin Bowditch, Jr.
Thompson, Joseph TodHunter, *Holly Holm*
Thorpe, Warren Parsons, Sr.
Throop, Enos Thompson, IV
Tyner, John Hill
Walsh, James William, Jr.
Walsh, James William, III
Wardwell, Helen R.
  [See F. D. Philips entry.]
Weeks, Herbert Augustus, *Meenahga*
Weeks, Louis Seabury, Sr.
Welsh, Joseph Wickes, Sr.
White, Thomas Francis, Jr.
White, Thomas Francis, Sr.
White, Victor Gerald, Sr.
Whitman, Alexander Harvey, Sr.
Whitman, Eben Esmond, Sr.
Wickersham, Cornelius Wendell, *Briarwood*
* Wickersham, George Woodward, *Marshfield*
Williams, Ichabod Thomas, II
Williams, Thomas, II
Williams, Thomas Resolved, *Windemere*
Wood, Howard Ogden, Jr.
Woolverton, William Henderson, Jr.
Work, James Henry, Jr., *Engleside*
Work, James Henry, Sr., *The Gowans*
Wyeth, Leonard Jarvis, IV

### LIDO BEACH

Bernstein, Lester

### LYNBROOK

Chambers, Jak
  (aka James A. Chambers)
Chambers, Whittaker
  [See Jay Chambers entry.]
Hillman, Sidney

### MERRICK

Arledge, Roone Pinckney, Jr.
Cammann, Herbert Schuyler, *Lindenmere*
* Cammann, Herman Henry, *Lindenmere*
Cammann, Schuyler Van Rensselaer,
  *Lindenmere*
Cohen, Bennett R,
Greenfield, Jerry
Krugman, Paul Robin
Sturgis, William, Jr.

### MINEOLA

Gerstner, Louis Vincent, Jr.

### OCEANSIDE

Iger, Robert Allen

### POINT LOOKOUT

Hillman, Sidney

### ROCKVILLE CENTRE

Feldstein, Martin Stuart
Goodwin, Doris Helen Kearns
Hawke, John Daniel, Jr.
* Hyland, John Francis
Kamen, Dean Lawrence
Roth, Arthur Thomas
Silvers, Robert Benjamin
Skelos, Dean George
* Stray, Edward James, Sr.

### SALISBURY

Davie, Preston, Sr., *The Oasis*
Ellis, Ralph Nicholson, Sr.
Eustis, George Peabody
Eustis, James Biddle, Sr.
* Ladenburg, Adolph, *Heathcote*
  (aka Moritz Adolph Emil Ladenburg)
Lebaudy, Jacques, *Phoenix Lodge*
Olcott, William Morrow Knox, *Phoenix Lodge*
* Roosevelt, Elliott, Sr., *Half Way Nirvana*

### UNIONDALE

Bird, Oliver William, Jr., *Greenhedge*
Hadden, James E. Smith, *Uniondale Farm*
Rennard, John Townsend
* Ripley, Sidney Dillon, Sr., *The Crossways*
Scott, Charles Robert, *The Crossways*

*Villages*

## WANTAGH

Townsend, Frances Mary Fragos
Weisselberg, Allen Howard

## WEST HEMPSTEAD

Brower, Howard Stanley, *Longdrive*
Collins, William
    *[See C. M. Robinson entry.]*
Earle, Alexander Morse, Sr.
Johnson, Samuel E.
    *[See C. M. Robinson entry.]*
\* Parker, Carleton Allen, *Stonehouse*
Robinson, Charles M.

## WOODMERE

Atwell, George Joseph, Sr.
Banks, Harold Purdy
Brett, George Platt, Jr., *Justamere Cottage*
Brown, Dr. Frederick Tilden, *By-the-Way*
Camprubi, Jose Aymar
Candler, Flamen Ball
Chapman, Gilbert Whipple, Sr.
Cooper, Leslie Bradford
Delafield, Maturin Livingston, II
Fosdick, Clark
Furst, Michael
Glass, Brent David
Gluck, Louise Elizabeth
Gruner, Otto Harry, Jr.
Gwynne, Frederick Walker
Hodges, Wetmore, Sr.
\* Hofheimer, Lester
\* Jacobi, Harold, Sr.
Karan, Donna Ivy Faske
Keisler, Peter Douglas
Kingsland, Harold Nutting
La Mont, Herbert Murray
\* Lord, George de Forest, Sr.
Mills, Edward Shorrey
Morgenthau, Julius Caesar, Sr.
Murray, Herman Stump
Neilson, Robert Hude
Nichols, John Dykes, *Nicholyn*
Parkhurst, William Man
\* Perkins, Charles Lawrence, Jr.
Recht, William, Sr.
Remick, Joseph Gould
\* Schieffelin, John Jay, Sr.
\* Schill, Emil
Scott, Henry Clarkson, Sr.
Shepard, Frederick White
Sise, John
Spinzia, Peter

Stricker, Hans Carol, *The Orchard*
Wright, John B.

## WOODSBURGH

Ballantine, John Holme, II, *Homeridge*
Bradford, George Dexter
\* Chapman, Henry Otis, Sr.
Cox, Daniel Hargate
\* Fox, William, *Fox Hall*
Hatch, Frederic Horace
Herrick, Newbold Lawrence, Sr.
Knowlton, Eben Joseph
Low, Ethelbert Ide
\* Marks, Arthur David, Jr.
Marshall, Charles Alexander
Marshall, James Markham, II
\* McCrea, James Alexander, II
\* Morgenthau, Maximilian, Sr.
\* Peck, Arthur Nelson
\* Schlossberg, Arnold, Sr.
Sloan, Robert Sage, Sr., *Chilton Gables*
Stebbins, George Ledyard, Sr.
Timpson, James
Van Siclen, George West
Wainwright, Loudon Snowden, Sr.
Ziegler, Frederick J.
Ziegler, Henry Ludwig W.

*Emily Louise Stevens Ladenburg*
*(Mrs. Adolph Ladenburg)*
*aboard the British tank Britannia in New York City, 1918*

**America's First Age of Fortune:**
**A Selected Bibliography**

Books listed in this section are, in most instances, different from the listings in the section entitled Selected Bibliographic References to Individual Town of Hempstead Estate Owners. Both sections should, therefore, be consulted.

*AIA Architectural Guide to Nassau and Suffolk Counties, Long Island*. New York: Dover Publications, Inc., 1992.
Aldrich, Nelson W., Jr. *Old Money: The Mythology of America's Upper Class*. New York: Alfred A. Knopf, 1988.
Aldrich, Nelson W., IV. "The Upper Class, Up for Grabs." *Wilson Quarterly* 17:3 (Summer 1993).
Allaback, Sarah. *The First American Women Architects*. Urbana, IL: University of Illinois Press, 2008.
Allen, Michael Patrick. *The Founding Fortunes: A New Anatomy of the Super–Rich Families in America*. New York: E. P. Dutton, 1987.
Alsop, Joseph W. *"I've Seen the Best of It: Memoirs."* New York: W. W. Norton & Co., 1992.
Amory, Cleveland. *Celebrity Register: An Irreverent Compendium of American Quotable Notables*. New York: Harper & Row Publishers, 1959. [Published intermittently. Since 1973 it has been edited by Earl Blackwell.]
Amory, Cleveland. *The Last Resorts*. New York: Harper & Brothers, 1952.
Amory, Cleveland. *Who Killed Society?* New York: Harper & Brothers, 1960.
Armour, Lawrence A. *The Young Millionaires*. Chicago: Playboy Press, 1973.
Armstrong, Hamilton Fish. *Those Days*. New York: Harper & Brothers, 1963.
Armstrong, Margaret. *Five Generations*. New York: Harper & Brothers, 1930.
Ashburn, Frank D. *Peabody of Groton*. New York: Coward, McCann & Co., 1944.
Aslet, Clive. *The American Country Home*. New Haven, CT: Yale University Press, 1990.
Aslet, Clive. *The Last Country Houses*. New Haven, CT: Yale University Press, 1982.
Auchincloss, Louis. *The Rector of Justin*. Boston: Houghton, Mifflin & Co., 1964.
Auchincloss, Louis. *The Vanderbilt Era: Profiles of a Gilded Age*. New York: The Macmillan Co., 1989.
Bailey, Paul. *Long Island: A History of Two Counties*. New York: Lewis Historical Publishing Co., 1949.
Baker, John C. *American Country Homes and Their Gardens*. Philadelphia: C. Winston, 1906.
Baker, Paul R. *Richard Morris Hunt*. New York: MIT Press, 1980.
Balmori, Diana, Diana Kostial McGuire, and Eleanor M. McPeck. *Beatrix Farrand's American Landscapes: Her Gardens and Campuses*. Sagaponack, NY: Sagapress, 1985.
Baltzel, E. Digby. *The Protestant Establishment: Aristocracy and Caste in America*. New York: Random House, 1964.
Baltzel, E. Digby. *The Protestant Establishment Revisited*. New Brunswick, NJ: New Jersey Transaction Publishers, 1991.
Baron, Stanley Wade. *Brewed in America*. Boston: Little, Brown & Co., 1962.
Barrett, Richmond. *Good Old Summer Days*. Boston: Houghton, Mifflin & Co., 1952.
Batterberry, Michael and Ariane Batterberry. *Mirror, Mirror*. New York: Holt, Rinehart & Winston, 1977.
Bayles, Richard M. *Bayles' Long Island Handbook*. Babylon, NY: privately printed, 1885.
Beach, Moses Yale. *Wealth and Biography of the Wealthy Citizens of New York City*. New York: The Sun Office, 1845.
Beard, Patricia. *After the Ball: Gilded Age Secrets, Boardroom Betrayals, and the Party That Ignited the Great Wall Street Scandal of 1905*. New York: HarperCollins, 2003.
Beckert, Sven. *The Monied Metropolis: New York City and the Consolidation of the American Bourgeoisie, 1850-1896*. Cambridge, England: Cambridge University Press, 2001.
Bedford, Stephen and Richard Guy Wilson. *The Long Island Country House, 1870–1930*. Southampton, NY: Parrish Art Museum, 1988.
Beebee, Lucius Morris. *The Big Spenders*. Garden City, NY: Doubleday & Co., Inc., 1966.
Beebee, Lucius. *Mansion On Rails: The Folklore of the Private Railway Car*. Berkeley, CA: Howell–North, 1959.
Beer, Thomas. *The Mauve Decade: American Life at the End of the 19th Century*. New York: Alfred A. Knopf, Inc., 1926.
"Behind the Gates of the Last Estates." *Newsday* September 25, 1986.
Bender, Marilyn. *The Beautiful People*. New York: Coward–McCann, Inc., 1967.
Bendix, Reinhard and Seymour Martin Lipset, ed. *Class, Status and Power*. New York: The Free Press, 1966.
Beveridge, Charles and Paul Rocheleau. *Frederick Law Olmsted: Designing the American Landscape*. New York: Rizzoli International Publications, Inc., 1995.
Biddle, Francis. *A Casual Past*. Garden City, NY: Doubleday & Co., Inc., 1961.
Biddle, Francis. *The Llanfear Pattern*. New York: Charles Scribner's Sons, 1927.
Bigelow, Poultney. *Seventy Summers*. 2 vols. New York: Longmans, Green & Co., 1925.
Birmingham, Stephen. *America's Secret Aristocracy*. Boston: Little, Brown & Co., 1987.
Birmingham, Stephen. *The Grandees: America's Sephardic Elite*. New York: Harper & Row Publishers, 1971.
Birmingham, Stephen. *The Grandes Dames*. New York: Simon & Schuster, Inc., 1982.
Birmingham, Stephen. *Our Crowd: The Great Jewish Families of New York*. New York: Harper & Row Publishers, 1967.

## General Bibliography

Birmingham, Stephen. *Real Lace: America's Irish Rich.* New York: Harper & Row Publishers, 1973.
Birmingham, Stephen. *The Right People: A Portrait of the American Social Establishment.* Boston: Little, Brown & Co., 1968.
Birmingham, Stephen. *The Right Places for the Right People.* Boston: Little, Brown & Co., 1973.
Bleyer, Bill. "The Forgotten Roosevelt." *Newsday* October 6, 1985:10-12, 25.
Bloom, Murray Teigh. *Rogues To Riches: The Trouble With Wall Street.* New York: G. P. Putnam's Sons, 1971.
Boegner, Peggie Phipps and Richard Gachot. *Halcyon Days: An American Family Through Three Generations.* New York: Old Westbury Gardens and Harry N. Abrams, Inc., Publishers, 1986.
Bolton, Sarah. *Famous Givers and Their Gifts.* New York: T. Y. Crowell & Co., 1896.
Bradley, Hugh. *Such Was Saratoga.* Garden City, NY: Doubleday, Doran & Co., 1940.
Brandon, Ruth. *The Dollar Princesses: Sagas of Upward Nobility, 1870–1914.* New York: Alfred A. Knopf, 1980.
Bremner, Robert H. *American Philanthropy.* Chicago: The University of Chicago Press, 1960.
Bremner, Robert H. *American Social History Since 1860.* Des Moines, IA: Meredith Corporation, 1971.
*Brooklyn Blue Book.* Brooklyn, NY: Rugby Press, Inc., annual.
*Brooklyn Blue Book and Long Island Society Register.* Brooklyn, NY: Brooklyn Life Publishing Co., annual.
*Brooklyn Blue Book and Long Island Society Register.* Brooklyn, NY: Rugby Press, Inc., annual.
Brooks, John. *Once In Galconda. A True Drama of Wall Street 1920–1938.* New York: Harper & Row Publishers, 1969.
Brooks, John. *Showing Off in America.* Boston: Little, Brown & Co., 1981.
Browder, Clifford. *The Money Game In Old New York: Daniel Drew and His Times.* Lexington, KY: University Press of Kentucky, 1986.
Brown, Jane. *Beatrix: The Gardening Life of Beatrix Jones Farrand 1872–1959.* New York: Viking Penguin Books, 1995.
Browne, Irving. *Our Best Society.* New York: Samuel French, 1875.
Buenker, John D. and Joseph Buenker. *Encyclopedia of the Gilded Age and Progressive Era,* 3 volumes. Armonk, NY: Sharpe Reference, 2005.
Burr, Anna Robeson. *The Portrait of a Banker: James Stillman, 1850–1918.* New York: Duffield & Co., 1927.
Burt, Nathaniel. *First Families.* Boston: Little, Brown & Co., 1970.
Burt, Nathaniel. *The Perennial Philadelphians: The Anatomy of an American Aristocracy.* Boston: Little, Brown & Co., 1963.
Byrnes, Rev. Horace W. *Pictorial Bay Shore and Vicinity: A Souvenir.* Bay Shore, NY: privately printed, 1903.
Cable, Mary. *Top Drawer: American Society from Gilded Age to the Roaring Twenties.* New York: Atheneum, 1984.
Cantacuzene, Princess. *My Life Here and There.* New York: Charles Scribner's Sons, 1921.
Cantor, Jay E. *Winterthur: The Foremost Museum of American Furniture and Decorative Arts.* New York: Harry N. Abrams, Inc., Publishers, 1986.
Capen, Oliver Bronson. *Country Homes of Famous Americans.* Garden City, NY: Doubleday, Page & Co., 1905.
Caro, Robert A. *The Power Broker: Robert Moses and the Fall of New York.* New York: Alfred A. Knopf, 1989.
Carson, Gerald. *The Polite Americans.* New York: William Morrow & Co., 1966.
Cashman, Sean Dennis. *America in the Gilded Age: From the Death of Lincoln to the Rise of Theodore Roosevelt.* New York: New York University Press, 1988.
Catlin, Daniel, Jr. *Good Work Well Done: The Sugar Business Career of Horace Havemeyer, 1903-1956.* privately printed, 1988.
Chanler, Mrs. Winthrop [Margaret]. *Autumn in the Valley.* Boston: Little, Brown & Co., 1936.
Chanler, Mrs. Winthrop [Margaret]. *Roman Spring.* Boston: Little, Brown & Co., 1934.
Chase, Edna Woolman and Ilka Chase. *Always in Vogue.* Garden City, NY: Doubleday & Co., Inc., 1954.
Churchill, Allen. *The Splendor Seekers: An Informal Glimpse of America's Multimillionaire Spenders – Members of the $50,000,000 Club.* New York: Grosset & Dunlop, 1974.
Churchill, Allen. *The Upper Crust: An Informal History of New York's Highest Society.* Englewood Cliffs, NJ: Prentice Hall, 1970.
Clark, Herma. *The Elegant Eighties.* Chicago: A. C. McClurg & Co., 1941.
Clark, Judith Freeman. *America's Gilded Age: An Eyewitness History.* New York: Facts on File, 1992.
Clews, Henry. *Fifty Years in Wall Street.* New York: Irving Publishing Co., 1908.
Close, Leslie Rose. *Portrait of an Era in Landscape Architecture: The Photographs of Mattie Edwards Hewitt.* The Bronx, NY: Wave Hill, 1983.
Cochran, Thomas and William Miller. *The Age of Enterprise: A Social History of Industrial America.* New York: Harper & Row Publishers, 1961.
Cochran, Thomas C. *Railroad Leaders: 1845-1890.* Cambridge, MA: Harvard University Press, 1966.
Conant, Jennet. *Tuxedo Park: A Wall Street Tycoon and the Secret Palace of Science That Changed the Course of World War II.* New York: Simon & Schuster, 2002.
Corry, John A. *1898: Prelude to a Century.* The Bronx, NY: Fordham University Press, 1998.
Craig, Thomas. *Edith Wharton: A House Full of Rooms: Architecture, Interiors, and Gardens.* New York: Moncelli Press, 1996.

## General Bibliography

Craven, Wayne. *Stanford White: Decorator in Opulence and Dealer in Antiquities*. New York: Columbia University Press, 2005.
Crockett, Albert Stevens. *Peacocks On Parade*. New York: Sears Publishing, 1931.
Crofutt, William A. *The Leisure Class in America*. New York: Arno Press, 1975.
Cunningham, Anne S. *Crystal Palaces: Garden Conservatories of the United States*. New York: Princeton Architectural Press, 2000.
Curtis, George W. *Our Best Society*. New York: G. P. Putnam's Sons, 1899.
Curwen, Henry Darcey, ed. *Exeter Remembered*. Exeter, NH: Phillips–Exeter Academy, 1965.
Darby, Edwin. *The Fortune Builders*. Garden City, NY: Doubleday & Co., Inc. 1986.
Dayton, Abram C. *The Last Days of Knickerbocker Life in New York*. New York: G. P. Putnam's Sons, 1897.
Delano & Aldrich. *Portraits of Ten Country Houses*. Garden City, NY: Doubleday, Page & Co., 1924.
Depew, Chauncey M. *My Memories of Eighty Years*. New York: Charles Scribner's Sons, 1924.
*Directory of American Society New York State and the Metropolitan District, 1929*. New York: Town Topics, 1928.
*Directory of Directors in the City of New York and the Tri–State Area*. Southport, CT: Directory of Directors Co., Inc., annual.
Doell, M. Christine Klim. *Gardens of the Gilded Age: Nineteenth-Century Gardens and Homegrounds of New York State*. Syracuse, NY: Syracuse University Press, 1986.
*Domestic Architecture of H. T. Lindeberg*. New York: William Helburn, Inc., 1940.
Domhoff, G. William. *The Bohemian Grove and Other Retreats*. New York: Harper & Row Publishers, 1974.
Domhoff, G. William. *Fat Cats and Democrats*. Englewood, NJ: Prentice–Hall, 1972.
Domhoff, G. William. *The Higher Circles: The Governing Class in America*. New York: Random House, 1970.
Domhoff, G. William. *The Powers That Be: Process of Ruling Class Domination in America*. New York: Random House, 1978.
Downey, Fairfax. *Portrait of an Era*. New York: Charles Scribner's Sons, 1936.
Drexler, Arthur. *The Architecture of the Ecole Des Beaux-Arts*. New York: Museum of Modern Art, 1977.
Drury, Roger W. *Drury and St. Paul's: The Scars of a Schoolmaster*. Boston: Little, Brown & Co., 1964.
Dwyer, Michael M. *Great Houses of the Hudson River*. Boston: Bulfinch Press, 2003.
Eliot, Elizabeth [Lady Elizabeth Kinnaird]. *Heiresses and Coronets*. New York: McDowell, Obolensky, 1959.
Ellet, Elizabeth. *The Queens of American Society*. Philadelphia: Porter & Coates, 1867.
Elliott, Maude Howe. *This Was My Newport*. Cambridge, MA: The Mythology Co., 1944.
Elliott, Maude Howe. *Three Generations*. Boston: Little, Brown & Co., 1923.
Elliott, Osborne. *Men at the Top*. New York: Harper & Brothers, 1959.
"Estates and Their Story." *Newsday* December 1, 1965.
Faucigny–Lucinge, Prince Jean–Louis de. *Legendary Parties 1922–1972*. New York: The Vendome Press, 1987.
Ferree, Barr. *American Estates & Gardens*. New York: Munn & Co., 1904.
Ferrell, Merri McIntyre. "Fox Hunting on Long Island." *The Nassau County Historical Society Journal* 54 (2001):1-10.
Ferry, John William. *A History of the Department Store*. New York: The Macmillan Co., 1960.
Fisher, Kenneth L. *100 Minds That Made the Market*. Woodside, CA: Business Classics, 1993.
Fiske, Stephen. *Offhand Portraits of Prominent New Yorkers*. New York: George Lockwood & Sons, 1884.
Fleming, Nancy. *Money, Manure & Maintenance: Ingredients for Successful Gardens of Marian Coffin, Pioneer Landscape Architect 1876-1957*. Weston, MA: Country Place Books, 1995.
Folsom, Merrill. *Great American Mansions and Their Stories*. Mamaroneck, NY: Hastings House, 1963.
Forbes, Malcolm and Jeffery Block. *What Happened to Their Children?* New York: Simon & Schuster, Inc., 1990.
Fowler, Marian. *In a Gilded Cage: From Heiress to Duchess*. New York: St. Martin's Press, 1993.
Frelinhuysen, Alice Cooning, et al. *Splendid Legacy: The Havemeyer Collection*. New York: The Metropolitan Museum of Art, 1993.
Fuller, Henry B. *The Cliff Dwellers*. New York: Harper & Brothers, 1893.
Garrard, David G. *Stanford White's New York*. Garden City, NY: Doubleday & Co., Inc., 1992.
Gerard, James W. *My First Eighty–Three Years in America*. Garden City, NY: Doubleday & Co., Inc., 1951.
Geus, Averill Dayton. *The Maidstone Club: The Second Fifty Years 1941 to 1991*. East Hampton, NY: Maidstone Club, 1991.
Ginger, Ray. *Age of Excess: The United States from 1877-1914*. New York: The MacMillan Co., 1965.
Gordon, Panmure. *Land of the Almighty Dollar*. London: Frederick Warne & Co., 1892.
Goulden, Joseph, C. *The Money Givers*. New York: Random House Publishers, 1971.
Gouverneur, Marion. *As I Remember: Recollections of American Society During the Nineteenth Century*. New York: D. Appleton & Co., 1911.
Graham, Sheila. *How to Marry Super Rich For Love, Money and the Morning After*. New York: Grosset & Dunlap Publishers, 1974.
Greene, Bert and Philip Stephen Schulz. *Pity the Poor Rich: It's a Losing Battle to Stay on Top But See How They Try*. Chicago: Contemporary Books, 1978.
Gregory, Alexis. *Families of Fortune: Life in the Gilded Age*. New York: Rizzoli International Publications, Inc., 1993.

## General Bibliography

Griswold, Mac K. and Eleanor Weller. *The Golden Age of American Gardens . Proud Owners . Private Estates . 1890–1940.* New York: Harry N. Abrams, Inc., Publishers, 1991.

Gross, Michael. *740 Park: The Story of the World's Richest Apartment Building.* New York: Broadway Books, 2005.

Gunther, Max. *The Very Rich and How They Got That Way.* New York: Playboy Press, 1972.

Halberstam, David. *The Powers That Be.* New York: Alfred A. Knopf, 1979.

Hall, Edward Tuck. *Saint Mark's School: A Centennial History.* Southborough, MA: Saint Mark's Alumni Association, 1967.

Hamm, Margherita Arlina. *Famous Families of New York.* New York: G. P. Putnam's Sons, 1901.

Harmond, Richard and Vincitorio Gaetano. "Working on the Great Estates." *The Long Island Forum* Spring 1988.

Harmond, Richard P. "Lost and Found." *The Long Island Historical Journal* 7 (Fall 1994):125-9.

Harmond, Richard P. "Robert Barnwell Roosevelt and the Early Conservation Movement." *Theodore Roosevelt Association Journal* 14 (2).

Harmond, Richard P. and Donald W. Weinhardt. "Robert Barnwell Roosevelt on the Great South Bay." *The Long Island Forum* 50 (August/September 1987):164-71.

Harriman, E. Roland. *I Reminisce.* Garden City, NY: Doubleday & Co., Inc., 1975.

Harriman, Mrs. J. Borden. *From Pinafores to Politics.* New York: Henry Holt & Co., 1923.

Harriman, Margaret Chase. *The Vicious Circle.* New York: Rinehart & Co., 1951.

Harris, Leon. *Merchant Princes: An Intimate History of Jewish Families Who Built Great Department Stores.* New York: Harper & Row Publishers, 1979.

Harrison, Constance Cary. *Recollections Grave and Gay.* New York: Charles Scribner's Sons, 1911.

Harrison, Constance Cary. *The Well–Bred Girl in Society.* Garden City, NY: Doubleday, Page & Co., 1904.

Havemeyer, Doris Dick. "Memoirs of a Lifetime, 1890-1976." Unpublished manuscript in the possession of the family.

Havemeyer, Harry W. *Along the Great South Bay From Oakdale to Babylon, the Story of a Summer Spa, 1840 to 1940.* Mattituck, NY: Amereon House, 1996.

Havemeyer, Harry W. *East on the Great South Bay: Sayville and Bellport 1860-1960.* Mattituck, NY: Amereon House, 2001.

Havemeyer, Harry W. *Fire Island's Surf Hotel and Other Hostelries on Fire Island Beaches in the Nineteenth Century.* Mattituck, NY: Amereon Ltd., 2006.

Havemeyer, Harry W. *Merchants of Williamsburg: Frederick C. Havemeyer, Jr., William Dick, John Mollenhauer, Henry O. Havemeyer.* New York: privately printed, 1989.

Havemeyer, Harry W., "The Story of Saxton Avenue." *The Long Island Forum* Winter, February 1, 1990, and Spring, May 1, 1990.

Havemeyer, Louisine W. *Sixteen to Sixty: Memoirs of a Collector.* New York: Ursus Press, 1993.

Hefner, Robert J. *East Hampton's Heritage: An Architectural Record.* New York: W. W. Norton & Co., 1982.

Hersh, Burton. *The Old Boys: The American Elite and the Origins of the CIA.* New York: Charles Scribner's Sons, 1992.

Hess, Stephen. *America's Political Dynasties from Adams to Kennedy.* Garden City, NY: Doubleday & Co., Inc., 1966.

Hewitt, Mark Alan. *The Architect & the Country House, 1890–1940.* New Haven, CT: Yale University Press, 1990.

Hoff, Henry B., ed. *Long Island Source Records: From the New York Genealogical and Biographical Record.* Baltimore: Genealogical Publishing, 1987.

Holbrook, Stewart H. *The Age of Moguls.* London: Victor Gollancz, Ltd., 1954.

Holloway, Laura C. *Famous American Fortunes and the Men Who Have Made Them.* New York: J. A. Hill, 1889.

Homberger, Eric. *Mrs. Astor's New York: Money and Social Power in a Gilded Age.* New Haven, CT: Yale University Press, 2002.

Hoogenboom, Ari and Olive Hoogenboom, eds. *The Gilded Age.* Englewood, NJ: Prentice–Hall, 1967.

Hopkins, Alfred. *Modern Farm Buildings.* New York: McBride, Nast & Co., 1913.

Hopkins, Alfred. *Planning for Sunshine and Fresh Air.* New York: Architectural Book Publishing, 1931.

Howath, Susan. *The Rich Are Different.* New York: Simon & Schuster, Inc., 1977.

Howe, Samuel. *American Country Houses of To–Day.* New York: Architectural Book Publishing Co., 1915.

Howell, E. W. *Noted Long Island Homes.* Babylon, NY: E. W. Howell Co., 1933.

Howell, Liz. *Continuity: Biography 1819-1934.* Sister Bay, WI: The Dragonsbreath Press, 1993.

Hungerford, Edward. *Men and Iron: The History of the New York Central.* New York: Thomas Y. Crowell, 1938.

Hunt, Freeman. *Lives of the American Merchants.* New York: Hunts' Merchants' Magazine, 1895.

Hunter, Floyd. *The Big Rich and the Little Rich.* Garden City, NY: Doubleday & Co., Inc., 1965.

Ingham, John. *Biographical Dictionary of American Business Leaders.* New York: Greenwood Press, 1983.

Ingham, John and Lynne B. Feldman. *Contemporary Business Leaders: A Biographical Dictionary.* New York: Greenwood Press, 1990.

*International Celebrity Register.* New York: Celebrity Register Ltd., annual.

Irwin, William Henry, et al. *A History of the Union League Club of New York City.* New York: Dodd, Mead & Co., 1952.

Jaher, Frederic Cople. *The Gilded Elite: American Multimillionaires, 1865 to the Present.* London: Croom Helm, 1980.

Jaher, Frederic Cople, ed. *The Rich, The Wellborn, and The Powerful: Elite and Upper Classes in History.* Secaucus, NJ: Citadel Press, 1975.

*General Bibliography*

Jenkins, Alan. *The Rich Rich: The Story of the Big Spenders.* New York: G. P. Putnam's Sons, 1978.
Jennings, Walter Wilson. *20 Giants of American Business.* New York: Exposition Press, 1953.
Josephson, Matthew. *The Money Lords: The Great Finance Capitalists 1925–1950.* New York: Weybright & Talley Publishers, 1972.
Josephson, Matthew. *The Robber Barons..., 1861–1901.* New York: Harcourt, Brace, Jovanovich, Publishers, 1934.
Kahn, E. J., III. "The Brahmin Mystique." *Boston Magazine* 75 (May 1983):119–161.
Kaiser, Harvey. *Great Camps of the Adirondacks.* Boston: David R. Godine, Publisher, Inc., 1982.
Kamisher, Lawrence, ed. *One Hundred Years of Knickerbocker History.* Port Washington, NY: Knickerbocker Yacht Club, 1974.
Kavaler, Lucy. *The Private World of High Society: Its Rules and Rituals.* New York: David McKay Co., Inc., 1960.
Kent, Joan Gay. *Discovering Sands Point: Its History, Its People, Its Places.* Sands Point, NY: Village of Sands Point, 2000.
Kirstein, George G. *The Rich: Are They Different?* Boston: Houghton Mifflin & Co., 1968.
Klepper, Michael. *The Wealthy 100: From Benjamin Franklin to Bill Gates – A Ranking of the Richest Americans Past and Present.* Secaucus, NJ: The Citadel Press, 1996.
Knapp, Edward Spring, Jr. *We Knapps Thought It Was Nice.* New York: privately printed, 1940.
Knox, Thomas W. "Summer Clubs on the Great South Bay." *Harper's New Monthly Magazine* July 1880.
Konolige, Kit. *The Richest Women in the World.* New York: The Macmillan Co., 1985.
Konolige, Kit and Frederica Konolige. *The Power of Their Glory: America's Ruling Class: The Episcopalians.* New York: Wyden Books, 1978.
Kordes, John Ellis. *A. T. Stewart's Garden City.* Garden City, NY: privately produced film, 1994. [available in VHS and DVD]
Kordes, John Ellis. *Visions of Garden City.* Garden City, NY: privately printed, 2007.
Kouwenhoven, John A. *Partners in Banking: An Historical Portrait of a Great Private Bank, Brown Brothers Harriman & Co., 1818–1968.* Garden City, NY: Doubleday & Co., Inc., 1968.
Kowet, Don. *The Rich Who Own Sports.* New York: Random House, 1977.
Krieg, Joann P., ed. *Long Island Architecture.* Interlaken, NY: Heart of the Lakes Publishing, 1991.
Krieg, Joann P., ed. *Robert Moses: Single–Minded Genius.* Interlaken, NY: Heart of the Lakes Publishing, 1989.
Lamont, Kenneth Church. *The Moneymakers: The Great Big New Rich in America.* Boston: Little, Brown & Co., 1969.
Lampman, Robert J. *The Share of Top Wealth–Holders in National Wealth 1922–1956.* Princeton, NJ: Princeton University Press, 1962.
Landau, Sarah Bradford. *Sources of American Architecture: George B. Post, Architect, Picturesque Designer, and Determined Realist.* New York: The Monacelli Press, 1998.
Lapham, Lewis. *Money and Class in America.* New York: Weidenfeld & Nicolson, 1988.
Lawrance, Gary and Anne Surchin. *The Architecture of Leisure: Houses of the Hamptons, 1880-1930.* New York: Acanthus Press, 2007.
Lee, Henry J., ed. *The Long Island Almanac and Year Book.* New York: Eagle Library Publications, 1931, 1934.
Lehr, Elizabeth Drexel. *"King Lehr" and the Gilded Age.* Philadelphia: J. B. Lippincott Co., 1935.
Lehr, Elizabeth Drexel. *Turn of the World.* Philadelphia: J. B. Lippincott Co., 1937.
Leighton, Ann. *American Gardens of the Nineteenth Century: "For Comfort and Affluence."* Amherst, MA: University of Massachusetts Press, 1987.
Lessard, Suzannah. *The Architect of Desire: Beauty and Danger in the Stanford White Family.* New York: Bantam Doubleday Dell, 1996.
*Lewis & Valentine Nursery.* New York: Lewis & Valentine Co., 1916.
Lewis, Arnold, et al. *The Opulent Interiors of the Golden Age.* New York: Dover Publications, Inc., 1987.
Libby, Valencia. "Marian Cruger Coffin, the Landscape Architect and the Lady." The House and Garden Exhibition Catalog. Roslyn, NY: Nassau County Museum of Fine Art, 1986.
Lindeman, Eduard C. *Wealth and Culture.* New York: Harcourt, Brace & Co., Inc., 1936.
Livingston, Bernard. *Their Turf: America's Horsey Set and Its Princely Dynasties.* New York: Arbor House Publishers, 1973.
Logan, Andy. *The Man Who Robbed the Robber Barons.* New York: W. W. Norton & Co., 1965.
*Long Island Society Register 1929.* Brooklyn, NY: Rugby Press, Inc., 1929.
Lowe, Corinne. *Confessions of a Social Secretary.* New York: Harper & Brothers, 1916.
Lucas, Nora. "The Historic Resource Survey for the Period 1900–1940 of the Unincorporated Sections of the Town of North Hempstead." Preservation Computer Services, 1991.
Lucie–Smith, Edward and Celestine Dars. *How the Rich Lived.* New York: Two Continents Publishing Group, 1976.
Lundberg, Ferdinand. *America's 60 Families.* New York: The Vanguard Press, 1937.
Lundberg, Ferdinand. *The Rich and the Super–Rich: A Study in the Power of Money Today.* New York: Lyle Stuart & Co., 1968.
Lundberg, Ferdinand. *"Who Controls Industry?"* [pamphlet concerning Richard Whitney case], c. 1938.
Lynes, Russell. *The Domesticated Americans.* New York: Harper & Row Publishers, 1963.

MacColl, Gail and Carol McD. Wallace. *To Marry an English Lord.* New York: Workman Publishing, 1989.
Mackay, Robert B., Anthony K. Baker, and Carol A. Traynor. *Long Island Country Houses and Their Architects 1860–1940.* New York: W. W. Norton & Co., 1997.
Maher, James T. *The Twilight of Splendor: Chronicles of the Age of American Palaces.* Boston: Little, Brown & Co., 1975.
Maher, Matthew. "A Study of the Effects of Accelerated Suburbanization [in Nassau–Suffolk] Upon the Social Structure." M. A. thesis, St. John's University, 1982.
Mahoney, Tom and Leonard Stone. *The Great Merchants: America's Foremost Retail Institutions and People Who Made Them Great.* New York: Harper & Row Publishers, 1974.
Marcus, George E. *Lives In Trust: The Fortunes of Dynastic Families in Late Twentieth–Century America.* Boulder, CO: Westview Press, 1992.
Martin, Frederick Townsend. *The Passing of the Idle Rich.* Garden City, NY: Doubleday, Page & Co., 1911.
Martin, Frederick Townsend. *Things I Remember.* New York: John Lane Co., 1913.
Mateyunas, Paul J. *North Shore Long Island Country Houses 1890-1950.* New York: Acanthus Press, 2007.
Maxwell, Elsa. *The Celebrity Circus.* London: Allen, 1964.
Maxwell, Elsa. *R. S. V. P.: Elsa Maxwell's Own Story.* Boston: Little, Brown & Co., 1954.
Mayer, Martin. *The Bankers.* New York: Weybright & Talley Publishers, 1974.
Mazzola, Anthony T. and Frank Zachary, ed. *The Best Families: The Town and Country Social Directory, 1846–1996.* New York: Harry N. Abrams, Inc., Publishers, 1996.
McAlester, Virginia and Lee McAlester. *A Field Guide to American Houses.* New York: Alfred A. Knopf, 1995.
McAlester, Virginia and Lee McAlester. *Great American Houses and Their Architectural Styles.* New York: Abbeville Press, 1994.
McAllister, Ward. *Society As I Have Found It.* New York: Cassell Publishing Co., 1890.
McCash, June Hall. *The Jekyll Island Cottage Colony.* Athens, GA: The University of Georgia Press, 1998.
McCash, William Barton and June Hall McCash. *The Jekyll Island Club: Southern Haven for America's Millionaires.* Athens, GA: The University of Georgia Press, 1989.
McCusker, John J. *How Much Is That in Real Money? A Historical Price Index for Use as a Deflator of Money Values in the Economy of the United States.* Worcester, MA: American Antiquarian Society, 1992.
McKim, Mead & White. *A Monograph of the Work of McKim, Mead & White 1879–1915.* New York: DaCapo Press, 1985.
McVickar, Harry Whitney. *The Greatest Show on Earth: Society.* New York: Harper & Brothers, 1892.
Metcalf, Pauline C. and Valencia Libby. *The House and Garden.* Roslyn, NY: Nassau County Museum of Fine Art, 1986.
Miller, Frances [Breese]. *More About Tanty: A Second Growing Up.* Sag Harbor, NY: Sandbox Press, 1980.
Miller, Frances [Breese]. *Tanty: Encounters With the Past.* Southampton, NY: Sandbox Press, 1979.
Miller, Frances [Breese]. *"Tanty": The Daring Decades.* Sag Harbor, NY: Sandbox Press, 1981.
Mills, C. Wright. *The Power Elite.* New York: Oxford University Press, 1956.
Milne, Gordon. *The Sense of Society.* Cranbury, NJ: Fairleigh Dickinson University Press, 1977.
Minnigerode, Meade. *Certain Rich Men.* New York: G. P. Putnam's Sons, 1927.
"Monograph on Meadow Croft, the Former John E. Roosevelt Estate, Sayville, Long Island." Suffolk County Parks Department, Division of Cultural and Historic Services, 1984. unpublished booklet.
Montgomery, Maureen E. *Gilded Prostitution: Status, Money and Transatlantic Marriage 1870–1914.* London: Routledge Press, 1989.
Moody, John. *The Masters of Capital: A Chronicle of Wall Street.* New Haven, CT: Yale University Press, 1919.
Moody, John. *The Railroad Builders.* New Haven, CT: Yale University Press, 1921.
Morris, Lloyd. *Incredible New York: High Life and Low Life of the Last Hundred Years.* New York: Random House, 1951.
Moses, Robert. *Working For the People.* New York: Harper and Brothers, 1956.
Mountfield, David. *The Railway Barons.* New York: W. W. Norton & Co., 1979.
Myers, Gustavus. *The Ending of Hereditary American Fortunes.* New York: Julian Messner, Inc., 1939.
Myers, Gustavus. *History of the Great American Fortunes.* New York: Random House, 1937.
Newell, Turner and Lockhart Steele. *Hampton Havens: The Best Hampton Cottages and Gardens.* New York: Bulfinch Press, 2005.
Nichols, Charles Wilbur de Lyon. *The Ultra-Fashionable Peerage of America: An Official List of Those People Who Can Be Called Ultra-Fashionable in the United States.* New York: George Harjes, 1904.
Noyes, Dorothy McBurney. *The World Is So Full.* Islip, NY: privately printed, 1953.
Obolensky, Serge. *One Man in His Time: The Memoirs of Serge Obolensky.* New York: privately printed, 1958.
O'Connor, Harvey. *The Empire of Oil.* New York: Monthly Review Press, 1955.
O'Connor, Richard. *The Oil Barons: Men of Greed and Grandeur.* Boston: Little, Brown & Co., 1971.
*Old Oakdale History, Volume I.* Oakdale, NY: William K. Vanderbilt Historical Society of Dowling College, 1983.
*The Old Oakdale History, Volume II: Era of Elegance, Part I.* Oakdale, NY: William K. Vanderbilt Historical Society of Dowling College, 1993.

*General Bibliography*

Ostrander, Susan A. *Women of the Upper Class.* Philadelphia: Temple University Press, 1984.
Packard, Vance. *The Status Seekers.* New York: David McKay Co., Inc., 1959.
Parsons, Schuyler Livingston. *Untold Friendships.* Boston: Houghton Mifflin Co., 1955.
Patterson, Augusta Owen. *American Homes of Today.* New York: The Macmillan Co., 1924.
Patterson, Jerry E. *Fifth Avenue: The Best Addresses.* New York: Rizzoli International Publications, Inc., 1998.
Patterson, Jerry E. *The First Four Hundred: Mrs. Astor's New York in the Gilded Age.* New York: Rizzoli International Publications, Inc., 2000.
Pearson, Hesketh. *The Marrying Americans.* New York: Coward McCann, Inc., 1961.
Pendrell, Nan and Ernest Pendrell. *How the Rich Live and Whom to Tax.* New York: Workers Library Publishers, Inc., May 1939.
Pennoyer, Peter and Anne Walker. *The Architecture of Delano and Aldrich.* New York: W. W. Norton & Co., 2003.
Pennoyer, Peter and Anne Walker. *The Architecture of Grosvenor Atterbury.* New York: W. W. Norton & Co., 2009.
Pennoyer, Peter and Ann Walker. *The Architecture of Warren & Wetmore.* New York: W. W. Norton & Co., 2006.
Persons, Stow. *The Decline of American Gentility.* New York: Columbia University Press, 1973.
Phillips, David. *The Reign of Gilt.* New York: James Pott & Co., 1905.
Pless, Princess Mary. *Better Left Unsaid.* New York: E. P. Dutton & Co., 1931.
Pless, Princess Mary. *What I Left Unsaid.* New York: E. P. Dutton & Co., 1936.
Porzelt, Paul. *The Metropolitan Club of New York.* New York: Rizzoli International Publications, Inc., 1982.
*Prominent Residents of Long Island and Their Clubs.* New York: Edward C. Watson, c. 1916.
Pulitzer, Ralph. *New York Society on Parade.* New York: Harper & Brothers, 1910.
Randall, Monica. *The Mansions of Long Island's Gold Coast.* New York: Rizzoli International Publications, Inc., 1987.
Rattray, Jeannette Edwards. *Fifty Years of the Maidstone Club: 1891–1941.* East Hampton, NY: privately printed, 1941.
Redmond, George F. *Financial Giants of America.* Boston: Stratford, 1922.
*Residences Designed by Bradley Delehanty.* New York: Architectural Catalogue Co., Inc., 1939.
Rodgers, Cleveland. *Robert Moses, Builder of Democracy.* New York: Henry Holt and Co., 1952.
Roosevelt, Felicia Warburg. *Doers and Dowagers.* Garden City, NY: Doubleday & Co., Inc., 1975.
Roosevelt, Robert Barnwell. *Love and Luck: The Story of a Summer's Loitering on the Great South Bay.* New York: Harper, 1886.
Roth, Leland. *Architecture of McKim, Mead, and White, 1870-1920: A Building List.* New York: Harper & Row, 1983.
Roussos, George. *A History and Description of William Bayard Cutting and His Country House, Westbrook, Great River, L. I.* Islip, NY: Board of Trustees of the Bayard Cutting Arboretum, 1984.
Ruther, Frederick. *Long Island Today.* Hicksville, NY: privately printed, 1909.
Sachs, Charles L. *The Blessed Isle: Hal B. Fullerton's Image of Long Island, 1827-1927.* Interlaken, NY: Heart of the Lakes Publishing, 1990.
Salny, Stephen M. *The Country Houses of David Adler.* New York: W. W. Norton & Co., 2001.
Sanger, Martha F. *The Henry Clay Frick Houses.* New York: The Monacelli Press, 2001.
Scheller, William G. *Barons of Business: Their Lives and Lifestyles.* Westport, CT: Hugh Lauter Levin Associates, 2002.
Schlesinger, Arthur M., Jr. *A Life in the 20$^{th}$ Century: Innocent Beginnings, 1917-1950.* Boston: Houghton Mifflin, 2000.
Schlup, Leonard and James Ryan. *Historical Dictionary of the Gilded Age.* Armonk, NY: M. E. Sharpe, 2003.
Schnadelbach, R. Terry. *Ferruccio Vitale: Landscape Architect of the Country Place Era.* New York: Princeton Architectural Press, 2001.
Schrag, Peter. *The Decline of the Wasp.* New York: Simon & Schuster, Inc., 1970.
Sclare, Liisa and Donald Sclare. *Beaux–Arts Estates: A Guide to the Architecture of Long Island.* New York: The Viking Press, 1980.
Sedgwick, Henry Dwight. *In Praise of Gentlemen.* Boston: Little, Brown & Co., 1935.
Sedgwick, John. *Rich Kids.* New York: William Morrow & Co., 1985.
Seebohm, Caroline. *Boca Rococo: How Addison Mizner Invented Florida's Gold Coast.* New York: Clarkson Potter, 2001.
Sheldon, George William. *Artistic Country Seats: Types of Recent American Villa and Cottage Architecture With Instances of Country Club-Houses.* New York: D. Appleton and Co., 1887.
Shelton, Louise. *Beautiful Gardens in America.* New York: Charles Scribner's Sons, 1916.
Shodell, Elly. *In The Service: Workers on the Grand Estates of Long Island 1890s – 1940s.* Port Washington, NY: Port Washington Public Library, 1991.
Shoemaker, Candice A. *Encyclopedia of Gardens: History and Design*, 3 volumes. Chicago: Fitzroy Dearborn, 2001.
Shopsin, William C. and Grania Bolton Marcus. *Saving Large Estates: Conservation, Historic Preservation, Adaptive Re–Use.* Setauket, NY: Society for the Preservation of Long Island Antiquities, 1977.
Shrock, Joel. *The Gilded Age.* Westport, CT: Greenwood Press, 2004.
Silver, Nathan. *Lost New York.* Boston: Houghton Mifflin, 2000.
Simon, Kate. *Fifth Avenue: A Very Social History.* New York: Harcourt, Brace, Jovanovich Publishers, 1978.
Slater, Philip. *Wealth Addiction.* New York: E. P. Dutton & Co., 1980.
Smith, Arthur D. Howden. *Men Who Run America.* New York: Bobbs–Merrill Co., 1936.

*General Bibliography*

Smith, Mildred H. *Garden City, Long Island in Early Photographs 1869-1919*. New York: Dover, 1987.
Smith, Mildred H. *History of Garden City*. Garden City, NY: Garden City Historical Society, 1980.
Smits, Edward J. *Nassau Suburbia, U.S.A.: The First Seventy-Five Years of Nassau County*, New York 1899-1974. Syosset, NY: Friends of the Nassau County Museum, 1974.
Smythe, Ted Curtis. *The Gilded Age Press, 1865-1900*. Westport, CT: Praeger Publishers, 2003.
Soben, Dennis P. *Dynamics of Community Change; the Case of Long Island's Declining "Gold Coast."* Port Washington, NY: Ira J. Friedman, 1968.
*Social Register*. New York: The Social Register Association, annual.
*Social Register New York*. New York: Social Register Association, annual.
*Social Register Summer*. New York: Social Register Association, annual.
Spinzia, Judith Ader. "Artistry In Glass: Louis Comfort Tiffany's Legacy In Nassau County." *The Nassau County Historical Society Journal,* 1991:8-17 and www.spinzialongislandestates.com.
Spinzia, Judith Ader. "Artistry In Glass: The Queens Ecclesiastical Windows of Louis Comfort Tiffany." *Newsletter of the Queens Historical Society,* July/August 1989:8-10.
Spinzia, Judith Ader. "Artistry In Glass: The Undisputed Master, Our Oyster Bay Neighbor." *The Freeholder* 2 (Winter 1998):3-5; and 2 (Spring 1998):3-5, 24 and www.spinzialongislandestates.com.
Spinzia, Judith Ader. "Women of Long Island: Clare Boothe Luce (1903-1987), The Long Island Connection." *The Freeholder* 14 (Summer 2009):3-5; 17-20 and www.spinzialongislandestates.com.
Spinzia, Judith Ader. "Women of Long Island: Cornelia Bryce Pinchot, Feminist, Social-Activist – The Long Islander Who Became First Lady of Pennsylvania." www.spinzialongislandestates.com.
Spinzia, Judith Ader. "Women of Long Island: Mary Elizabeth Jones; Rosalie Gardiner Jones." *The Freeholder* 11 (Spring 2007):2-7 and www.spinzialongislandestates.com.
Spinzia, Judith Ader. "Women of Long Island: Mary Williamson Averell Harriman; her daughter Mary Harriman Rumsey." *The Freeholder,* 12 (Spring 2008):8-9, 16-20 and www.spinzialongislandestates.com.
Spinzia, Raymond E. "Adultery, Drugs, Murder, Untimely Deaths, and Long Island's Prominent Families; A Tangled Web." www.spinzialongislandestates.com.
Spinzia, Raymond E. "Elliott Roosevelt, Sr. – A Spiral Into Darkness." *The Freeholder* 12 (Fall 2007):3-7, 15-17 and www.spinzialongislandestates.com.
Spinzia, Raymond E. "In Her Wake: The Story of Alva Smith Vanderbilt." *The Long Island Historical Journal* 6 (Fall 1993):96-105 and www.spinzialongislandestates.com.
Spinzia, Raymond E. "The Involvement of Long Islanders in the Events Surrounding German Sabotage in the New York Metropolitan Areas 1914-1917." 2019, revised 2022. www.spinzialongislandestates.com.
Spinzia, Raymond E. "Long Island Statesmen and Diplomats." www.spinzialongislandestates.com. revised 2020 and 2022.
Spinzia, Raymond E. "Michael Straight and the Cambridge Spy Ring." *The Freeholder* 5 (Winter 2001):3-5 and www.spinzialongislandestates.com.
Spinzia, Raymond E. "Socialite Spies: The Grandchildren of Henry Baldwin Hyde, Sr." *East Islip Historical Society Newsletter* 16 (March 2008):1, 3 and www.spinzialongislandestates.com. revised 2022.
Spinzia, Raymond E. "Society Chameleons: Long Island's Gentlemen Spies." *The Nassau County Historical Society Journal* 55 (2000):27-38 and www.spinzialongislandestates.com.
Spinzia, Raymond E. "Sumner Welles: Brilliance and Tragedy." *The Freeholder* 9 (Winter 2005):8-9, 22 and www.spinzialongislandestates.com.
Spinzia, Raymond E. "Those Other Roosevelts: The Fortescues." *The Freeholder* 11 (Summer 2006):8-9, 16-22 and www.spinzialongislandestates.com.
Spinzia, Raymond E. "To Look in the Mirror and See Nothing; Long Islanders and the Office of Strategic Services and Its Successor, the Central Intelligence Agency." www.spinzialongislandestates.com. revised December 2017 and 2022.
Spinzia, Raymond E. "Winning the Franchise: Long Island Activists in the Fight for Woman's Suffrage and Their Opponents, Long Island's Anti-Suffragists." www.spinzialongislandestates.com. 2018, revised 2022.
Spinzia, Raymond E. and Judith A. Spinzia. "*Gatsby*: Myths and Realities of Long Island's North Shore Gold Coast." *The Nassau County Historical Society Journal* 52 (1997):16–26 and www.spinzialongislandestates.com.
Spinzia, Raymond E. and Judith A. Spinzia. *Long Island's Prominent Families in the Town of East Hampton: Their Estates and Their Country Homes*. College Station, TX: VirtualBookworm, 2020.
Spinzia, Raymond E. and Judith A. Spinzia. *Long Island's Prominent Families in the Town of Southampton: Their Estates and Their Country Homes*. College Station, TX: VirtualBookworm, 2010.
Spinzia, Raymond E. and Judith A. *Long Island's Prominent North Shore Families: Their Estates and Their Country Homes*, vols. I, II. College Station, TX: VirtualBookworm, 2006, revised 2019.
Spinzia, Raymond E. and Judith A. *Long Island's Prominent South Shore Families: Their Estates and Their Country Homes in the Towns of Babylon and Islip*. College Station, TX: VirtualBookworm, 2007, revised 2021.
Stein, Susan R. *The Architecture of Richard Morris Hunt*. Chicago: University of Chicago, 1986.
Stephens, W. P. *The Seawanhaka Corinthian Yacht Club: Origins and Early History, 1871–1896*. New York: privately printed, 1963.

## General Bibliography

Stern, Robert A. M. *New York 1880: Architecture and Urbanism in the Gilded Age*. New York: The Monacelli Press, 1999.

Summers, Mark W. *The Gilded Age, or, the Hazard of New Functions*. Upper Saddle River, NJ: Prentice Hall, 1997.

Swaine, Robert T. *The Cravath Firm and Its Predecessors, 1819-1948*. vols. 1, 2. New York: Ad Press, Ltd., 1946, 1948.

Talese, Gay. *The Kingdom and the Power*. New York: World Publishers, 1969.

Tankard, Judith B. *The Gardens of Ellen Biddle Shipman*. Sagaponack, NY: Sagapress, Inc., 1996.

Tarbell, Ida. *History of Standard Oil Company*. New York: The Macmillan Co., 1925.

Tauranac, John. *Elegant New York: The Builders and the Buildings 1885-1915*. New York: Abbeville Press, 1985.

Tebbel, John William. *The Inheritors: A Study of America's Great Fortunes and What Happened to Them*. New York: Putnam, 1962.

Teutonico, Jeanne Marie. "Marian Cruger Coffin: The Long Island Estates; a Study of the Early Work of a Pioneering Woman in American Landscape Architecture." M. S. thesis, Columbia University, 1983.

Thompson, Jacqueline. *The Very Rich Book: America's Supermillionaires and Their Money – Where They Got It, How They Spend It*. New York: William Morrow & Co., Inc., 1981.

Thorndike, Joseph J., Jr. *The Very Rich: A History of Wealth*. New York: American Heritage, 1976.

Tishler, William, ed. *American Landscape Architecture: Designers and Places*. Washington, DC: Preservation Press, 1989.

Townsend, Reginald T. *God Pack My Picnic Basket: Reminiscences of the Golden Age of Newport and New York*. New York: Hastings House, 1970.

Townsend, Reginald T. *Mother of Clubs*. New York: Union Club, 1936.

Trachtenberg, Alan. *The Incorporation of America: Culture and Society in the Gilded Age*. New York: Hill and Wang, 1982.

Ulman, Albert. *New Yorkers from Stuyvesant to Roosevelt*. Port Washington, NY: Ira J. Friedman, 1969.

Updike, D. P. *Hunt Clubs and Country Clubs in America*. Cambridge, MA: The Merrymount Press, 1928.

Vanderbilt, Cornelius, Jr. *Farewell to Fifth Avenue*. New York: Simon & Schuster, Inc., 1935.

Vanderbilt, Cornelius, Jr. *Man of the World: My Life on Five Continents*. New York: Crown Publishers, Inc., 1959.

Vanderbilt, Cornelius, Jr. *Palm Beach*. New York: Macaulay, 1931.

Vanderbilt, Cornelius, Jr. *Queen of the Golden Age: The Fabulous Story of Grace Wilson Vanderbilt*. New York: McGraw–Hill Book, Co., Inc., 1956.

Vanderbilt, Cornelius, Jr. *Reno*. New York: Macaulay, 1929.

Van Rensselaer, Mrs. John King. *Newport: Our Social Capital*. Philadelphia: J. B. Lippincott Co., 1905.

Van Rensselaer, Mrs. John King. *New Yorkers of the XIX Century*. New York: F. T. Neely, 1897.

Van Rensselaer, Mrs. John King and Frederic Van De Water. *The Social Ladder*. New York: Henry Holt & Co., 1924.

Van Rensselaer, Philip. *Rich Was Better*. New York: Wynwood Press, 1990.

VanWagner, Judith, et al. *Long Island Estate Gardens*. Greenvale, NY: Hillwood Art Gallery, 1985.

Van Wyck, Frederick. *Recollections of an Old New Yorker*. New York: Liveright, Inc., Publishers, 1932.

Veblen, Thorstein. *The Theory of the Leisure Class: An Economic Study of Institutions*. New York: New Modern Library, 1934.

*Views From the Circle: Seventy–Five Years of Groton School*. Groton, MA: The Trustees of Groton Schools, 1960.

*Village of Lawrence, NY: A Brief History of a Long Island Community*. Lawrence, NY: Village of Lawrence, 1977.

Vollono, Millicent. *Images of America: The Five Towns*. Mount Pleasant, SC: Arcadia Publishing, 2010.

Vollono, Millicent and Lauren W. Drapala. "Designing Suburbia: Olive Tjaden on Long Island." *The Nassau County Historical Journal* 71 (2016): 1-14.

Walker, Stanley. *Mrs. Astor's Horse*. New York: Frederick A. Stokes Co., 1935.

Wall Street Journal, ed. *American Dynasties Today*. Homewood, IL, c. 1980.

Wecter, Dixon. *The Saga of American Society: A Record of Social Aspiration, 1607–1937*. New York: Charles Scribner's Sons, 1937.

Weeks, George L., Jr. *Isle of Shells*. Islip, NY: Buys Brothers Inc., 1965.

Weigold, Marilyn. *The American Mediterranean: An Environmental, Economic, and Social History of Long Island Sound*. Port Washington, NY: Kennikat Press, 1974.

Weitzenhoffer, Frances. *The Havemeyers: Impressionism Comes to America*. New York: Harry N. Abrams, Inc., Publishers, 1986.

Wells, Richard A. *Manners, Culture and Dress of the Best American Society*. Springfield, MA: King Richardson & Co., 1894.

White, Samuel G. *The Houses of McKim, Mead and White*. New York: Rizzoli International Publications, Inc., 1998.

White, Samuel G. and Elizabeth White. *The Houses of McKim, Mead and White*. New York: Rizzoli International Publications, Inc., 1998.

White, Samuel G. and Elizabeth White. *McKim, Mead and White: The Masterworks*. New York: Rizzoli International Publications, Inc., 2003.

White, Samuel G. and Elizabeth White. *Stanford White, Architect*. New York: Rizzoli International Publications, Inc., 2008.

*Who's Who In New York State*. New York: Lewis Historical Publishing Co., annual.

## General Bibliography

Williamson, Ellen. *When We Went First Class.* Garden City, NY: Doubleday & Co., Inc., 1977.
Wilson, Richard Guy. *The Architecture of McKim, Mead & White.* New York: Dover Publications, Inc., 1990.
Wilson, Richard Guy. *Harbor Hill: Portrait of a House.* New York: W. W. Norton & Co., 2008.
Wilson, Richard Guy. *McKim, Mead & White, Architects.* New York: Rizzoli International Publications, Inc., 1983.
Woolson, Abba G. *Woman in American Society.* Cambridge, MA: Roberts Brothers, 1873.
Worden, Helen. *Society Circus: From Ring to Ring With a Large Cast.* New York: Covici, Friede, Publishers, 1936.
Wortman, Marc. *The Millionaire's Unit: The Aristocratic Flyboys Who Fought in the Great War and Invented American Air Power.* New York: Public Affairs, 2006.
Wyllie, Romy. *Bertram Goodhue: His Life and Residential Architecture.* New York: W. W. Norton & Co., 2007.
Zaitzevsky, Cynthia. *Long Island Landscapes and the Women Who Designed Them.* New York: W. W. Norton & Co., 2009.
Zerbe, Jerome. *The Art of Social Climbing.* Garden City, NY: Doubleday & Co., Inc., 1965.

*Dorothy Goddard Ficken Gwynne (Mrs. Frederick Walker Gwynne)*

*the creator of "Sun-ny Jim"*

*her son, the noted actor Fred Gwynne*

*Individual Bibliographical References*

## Selected Bibliographic References to Individual Estate Owners in the Town of Hempstead

This portion of the bibliography contains references not only to the estate owners in the Town of Hempstead, but also to their families and their estates. Since books listed in this section are, in most instances, different from the listings in the general bibliography, America's First Age of Fortune: A Selected Bibliography, both sections should be consulted.

**Adams, William, Jr. – Lawrence**
"William Adams." *Architectural Record* 44 (October 1918):505-25.

**Allison, Ruth Hovey (Mrs. Benjamin Roy Allison) – Hewlett Bay Park**
Department of Historical Records, Connecticut State Library has her papers.

**Arledge, Roone Pinckney, Jr. – Merrick**
Rare Book and Manuscript Library, Columbia University, NYC, has his papers.

**Auchincloss, Samuel Sloan, Sr. – Lawrence –** *Whale Acres*
*Architectural Record* 1918.

**Auerbach, Joseph Smith – Hewlett Harbor –** *Seawane*
Hewlett–Woodmere Public Library has photographs of the house.

**Belmont, Alva Erskine Smith**
**(Mrs. William Kissam Vanderbilt, Sr.; Mrs. Oliver Hazard Perry Belmont) –**
**East Meadow –** *Brookholt*
*Biltmore* Estate, Asheville, NC, has material collected from all Vanderbilt families in their archives.
Dowling College Library, Historical Collection, Oakdale, LI, has photographs of the family.
Melville Library, SUNY Stony Brook, LI, has the National Woman's Party papers on microfilm.
The Nassau County Museum Collection includes photographs of the estate.
Nassau County Museum of Art, Roslyn, LI, has photographs of *Beacon Towers*.
Newport Historical Society, Newport, RI, has material relating to Woman Suffrage events held in Newport by Alva Belmont.
Octagon Museum of American Architectural Foundation, Prints and Drawings Collection, Washington, DC, has photographs and sketches of *Beacon Towers.*
Port Washington Public Library, Port Washington, NY, has local newspaper clippings mentioning Alva Belmont, *Beacon Towers*, and suffrage.
The Preservation Society of Newport County, Newport, RI, has Alva Belmont's personal scrapbook of newspaper clippings about the March 26, 1883, Masque Ball held at 660 Fifth Avenue, New York City.
Queens College Library, Historical Collection, Flushing, NY, has Vanderbilt family records, including 1699 tax rolls and a deposit of 1790–1840 material.
Mrs. Consuelo [Mimi] Russell, Alva Belmont's great-great-granddaughter has a scrapbook about Woman's Suffrage events held July 8–9, 1914, at Marble House, Newport, RI.
Sewall–Belmont House [National Woman's Party Headquarters], Washington, DC, has scrapbooks pertaining to Alva Belmont and photographs of the family.
Suffolk County Vanderbilt Museum and Planetarium archives, Centerport, LI, has photographs of the family and an album of photographs of *Eagles Nest* and *Beacon Towers* taken by Samuel H. Gottscho whose collection is also in the Avery Architectural and Fine Arts Library, Columbia University, NYC, and in the Library of Congress, Washington, DC. The photographs at *Eagles Nest* of *Beacon Towers* show the mansion from all sides. They also have one interior photograph of *Beacon Towers* and an album with Alva Belmont's funeral photographs and newspaper clippings.
    Bedford, Stephen and Richard Guy Wilson. *The Long Island Country House, 1870–1930.* Southampton, NY: The Parrish Art Museum, 1988.
    Belmont, Alva Vanderbilt. "Are Women Really Citizens?" *Good Housekeeping* September 1931.
    Belmont, Alva Vanderbilt. Foreword to article by Christable Pankhurst, "Story of the Woman's War." *Good Housekeeping* November 1913.
    Belmont, Alva Vanderbilt. *Harper's Bazaar* March 1910.
    Belmont, Alva Vanderbilt. "How Can Woman Get the Suffrage?" *The Independent* 31 (March 1910).
    Belmont, Alva. *One Month's Log of the Seminole.* New York: privately printed, 1916.
    Belmont, Alva. "Unpublished 1917 Autobiography of Alva Vanderbilt Belmont." In Wood Collection, Huntington Library, San Marino, California.

*Individual Bibliographic References*

**Belmont, Alva Erskine Smith**
**(Mrs. William Kissam Vanderbilt, Sr.; Mrs. Oliver Hazard Perry Belmont) –**
**East Meadow –** *Brookholt* (cont'd)
>Belmont, Alva. "Unpublished 1933 Autobiography of Alva Vanderbilt Belmont." In Matilda Young Papers, Special Collections Department, William R. Perkins Library, Duke University, Durham, North Carolina.
>Belmont, Alva Vanderbilt. "What the Woman's Party Wants." *Collier's* 23 (December 1922).
>Belmont, Alva Vanderbilt. "Why I Am a Suffragist." *The World To–Day* October 1911.
>Belmont, Alva Vanderbilt. "Woman's Right to Govern Herself." *North American Review* 190 (November 1909).
>Belmont, Alva Vanderbilt. "Woman Suffrage as It Looks To–Day." *The Forum* March 1910.
>Belmont, Alva Vanderbilt. "Women as Dictators." *Ladies Home Journal* September 1922.
>"Belmont to Sell Belcourt." *New York Herald Tribune* December 30, 1908. [Newport estate]
>"Brookholt on the Market." *The New York Times* January 6, 1909:1. [Uniondale estate]
>"Buys Chateau in France: Mrs. O. H. P. Belmont Plans to Live Abroad, Newport Hears." *The New York Times* September 4, 1926:5.
>Geidel, Peter. "Alva E. Belmont: A Forgotten Feminist." Ph.D. dissertation, Columbia University, 1993.
>Keeler, Rebecca T. "Alva Belmont: Exacting Benefactor for Women's Rights." Ph.D. dissertation, University of South Alabama, 1987.
>"Mrs. Belmont's Funeral." *The New York Times* January 27, 1933.
>"Mrs. O. H. P. Belmont Buys a Lighthouse." *The New York Times* February 1, 1924:19.
>"Mrs. O. H. P. Belmont Dies at Paris Home." *The New York Times* January 26, 1933.
>Patterson, Augusta Owen. *American Homes of Today.* New York: The Macmillan Co., 1924.
>Rector, Margaret. *Alva, That Vanderbilt–Belmont Woman: Her Story as She Might Have Told It.* Wickford, RI: The Dutch Island Press, 1992.
>Spinzia, Raymond E. "In Her Wake: The Story of Alva Smith Vanderbilt Belmont." *The Long Island Historical Journal* 6 (Fall 1993):96–105.
>Stasz, Clarice. *The Vanderbilt Women: Dynasty of Wealth, Glamour, and Tragedy.* New York: St. Martin's Press, 1991.
>"To Build Belmont Hospital: Mrs. O. H. P. Belmont the Sponsor for One as a Memorial." *The New York Times* September 17, 1909:1.
>*Town and Country* October 15, 1928.
>"Want Wall Removed: Hempstead Board Denies Mrs. Belmont's Right to Fence Beach." *The New York Times* September 20, 1918:15.
>"What the Woman's Party Wants." *Collier's* December 23, 1922.

**Belmont, August, II – Hempstead –** *Belmton Manor*
Adirondack Museum, Blue Mountain Lake, NY, has Belmont's private railroad car *Oriental* on display.
Shoreline Trolley Museum, East Haven, CT, has Belmont's private railroad car *Mineola*.
>Belmont, Eleanor Robson. *The Fabric of Memory.* New York: Farrar & Straus, & Co., 1957.
>Birmingham, Stephen. *The Grandees Dames.* New York: Simon & Schuster, Inc., 1982.
>Gottheil, Richard James Horatio. *Belmont–Belmonte Family: A Record of Four Hundred Years, Put Together From the Original Documents in the Archives and Libraries of Spain, Portugal, Holland, England and Germany.* 1917.

**Belmont, Eleanor Robson (Mrs. August Belmont II) – Hempstead –** *Belmton Manor*
Avery Architectural and Fine Arts Library, Columbia University, NYC, has Eleanor Robson Belmont's papers.
>Belmont, Eleanor Robson. *The Fabric of Memory.* New York: Farrar & Straus, & Co., 1957.
>Birmingham, Stephen. *The Grandees Dames.* New York: Simon & Schuster, Inc., 1982.
>Gottheil, Richard James Horatio. *Belmont–Belmonte Family: A Record of Four Hundred Years, Put Together From the Original Documents in the Archives and Libraries of Spain, Portugal, Holland, England and Germany.* 1917.
>*Opera News* December 9, 1978.

**Belmont, Oliver Hazard Perry – East Meadow –** *Brookholt*
Hempstead Public Library, Hempstead, NY, has photographs of the estate.
Nassau County Museum Collection includes photographs of the estate.
>*Architectural Annual.* New York: Architectural League of New York, 1912, has interior photographs of the Belmont chapel in Woodlawn Cemetery, The Bronx.
>Black, David. *The King of Fifth Avenue: The Fortune of August Belmont.* New York: The Dial Press, 1981.
>"Brookholt on the Market." *The New York Times*, January 6, 1909:1.
>Gottheil, Richard James Horatio. *Belmont–Belmonte Family: A Record of Four Hundred Years, Put Together From the Original Documents in the Archives and Libraries of Spain, Portugal, Holland, England and Germany.* 1917.

*Individual Bibliographic References*

**Bossert, John – Garden City**
    Howell, Liz. *Continuity: Biography 1819-1934*. Sister Bay, WI: The Dragonsbreath Press, 1993.

**Boulton, William Bowen, Sr. – Lawrence –** *Avila*
    *The Brickbuilder* 1902.

**Breed, William Constable, Sr. – Lawrence –** *Whale Acres*
    *Architectural Record* 1918.

**Brisbane, Arthur – East Meadow**
Special Collections Research Center, Syracuse University Library, Syracuse, NY, has the Brisbane family papers.
    Carlson, Oliver. *Brisbane: A Candid Biography*. New York: Stackpole Sons, 1937.

**Chapman, Elizabeth Fuller (Mrs. Gilbert Whipple Chapman, Sr.) – Woodmere**
Beinecke Rare Book and Manuscript Library, Yale Univerity, New Haven, CT, has her papers.

**Cobb, Boughton, Sr. – Hewlett Bay Park –** *The Chimney Corner*
Nassau County Museum Collection has photographs of the estate.

**Connable, Arthur W. – Hewlett Bay Park –** *Boxwood*
    *Country Life in America* October 1913:2.

**Crane, Warren Seabury – Lawrence –** *East View*
    *Residences Designed by Bradley Delehanty*. New York: Architectural Catalogue Co., Inc., 1939.

**Curtiss, Glenn Hammond, Sr. – Garden City**
Garden City Archives has photographs of the house.
Glenn H. Curtiss Museum, Hammondsport, NY, has material on Curtiss.
National Air and Space Museum, Washington, DC, has the Curtiss family papers.
    Casey, Louis S. *Curtiss: The Hammondsport Era, 1907-1915*. New York: Crown Publishers, 1981.
    Hatch, Alden. *Glenn Curtiss: Pioneer of Aviation*. Guilford, CT: The Lyons Press, 2007.
    House, Kirk W. *Hell-Rider to the King of the Air: Glenn Curtiss's Life of Innovation*. Warrendale, PA: Society of Automotive Engineers International Publishing, 2003.
    Rosebury, C. C. *Glenn Curtiss: Pioneer of Flight*. Garden City: Doubleday & Co., Inc., 1972.
    Shulman, Seth. *Unlocking the Sky: Glenn Hammond Curtiss and the Race to Invent the Airplane*. New York: HarperCollins, 2003.

**Duryea, William H. – Garden City**
Rare Book and Manuscript Collections, Carl A. Kroch Library, Cornell University, Ithaca, NY, has Olive Frances Tjaden's sketches of the house.

**Ebinger Walter Dohrmann – Garden City**
Rare Book and Manuscript Collections, Carl A. Kroch Library, Cornell University, Ithaca, NY, has Olive Frances Tjaden's sketches of the house.

**Eustis, George Peabody (aka George Eustis Corcoran) – Salisbury**
The Louis D. Brandeis School of Law Library, University of Louisville, Louisville, KY, has Eustis' papers.

**Forrest, Richard Earp – Lawrence –** *Longwood*
    *Architectural League of New York* 1908.

**Fox, William – Woodsburgh –** *Fox Hall*
Nassau County Museum Collection has photographs of the estate.

**Gamel, Isaac – Lawrence**
    *Architecture* 1901.

**Glover, John Irwin – Baldwin**
    *American Architect and Building News* 1894.

*Individual Bibliographic References*

**Gulick, Ernestus Schenck – Garden City**
    Embury, Aymar, II. *One Hundred Country Houses: Modern American Examples.* New York: The Century Co., 1909.
    Ruther, Frederick. *Long Island Today.* Hicksville, NY: privately printed, 1909.

**Harper, Joseph Henry, Sr. – Lawrence – *Brightside***
Manuscripts Division, Department of Rare Books and Special Collections, Princeton University Library, Princeton, NJ, has Harper & Brothers Papers, 1909-1960.
    Exman, Eugene. *The Brothers Harper: A Unique Publishing Partnership and Its Impact Upon the Cultural Life of America From 1817-1853.* New York: Harper & Row Publishers, 1965.
    Exman, Eugene. *The House of Harper.* New York: Harper & Row Publishers, 1967.
    Harper, Joseph Henry, Sr. *The House of Harper: A Century of Publishing in Franklin Square.* New York: Harper & Brothers, 1912.

**Hazard, William Ayrault, Sr. – Lawrence – *Meadow Hall***
The New York Public Library, Archives and Manuscripts has the Hazard and Tilden family scrapbooks, 1829-1933.

**Hewitt, Thomas M. – Garden City**
Rare Book and Manuscript Collections, Carl A. Kroch Library, Cornell University, Ithaca, NY, has photographs of the house.

**Hinckley, Samuel Parker – Lawrence – *Sunset Hall***
    Sheldon, George, ed. *Artistic Country Seats: Types of Recent American Villa and Cottage Architecture.* New York: Da Capo Press, 1979. (first published in 1886)

**Hoffman, Horace E. – Garden City**
Rare Book and Manuscript Collections, Carl A. Kroch Library, Cornell University, Ithaca, NY, has Olive Frances Tjaden's sketches of the house.

**Hofstra, William Sake – Hempstead – *The Netherlands***
Special Collections, Hofstra University, Hempstead, NY, has photographs of the estate.

**Hubbell, George Loring, Sr. – Garden City – *Lonesomehurst***
Garden City Historical Society has photographs of the house.
Garden City Public Library has Hubbell's 1893-1900 scrapbook.

**Jacobi, Harold, Sr. – Woodmere**
Center for Jewish History, NYC, has the Jacobi–Schlossberg family papers.
Rare Book and Manuscript Collections, Carl A. Kroch Library, Cornell University, Ithaca, NY, has Olive Frances Tjaden's sketches of the house.

**Jacobi, Sanford – Hewlett Neck**
Rare Book and Manuscript Collections, Carl A. Kroch Library, Cornell University, Ithaca, NY, has photographs of his New Jersey house.

**Jones, Howard S. – Garden City**
    Ruther, Frederick. *Long Island Today.* Hicksville, NY: privately printed, 1909.

**Kellum, John – Hempstead**
    Gardner, Deborah S. *The Architecture of Commercial Capitalism: John Kellum and the Development of New York, 1840-1875.* thesis, Columbia University, 1979.

**Kilmer, Dr. Theron Wendell, Sr. – Hempstead**
Special Collections, Axinn Library, Hofstra University, Hempstead, has his papers.

**Kip, Ira Andruss, Jr. (aka Ira Andrew Kip) – Hewlett Bay Park**
Hewlett–Woodmere Public Library has photographs of the house.
    *Architecture* 1912.

*Individual Bibliographic References*

**Knopf, Samuel – Lawrence**
Nassau County Museum Collection has photographs of the house.
   *Architectural Record* March 1916:197.

**Konta, Geoffrey – East Meadow –** *East Meadows*
Nassau County Museum Collection has twelve uncataloged photographs of the house.

**Lannin / Tunstall House – East Meadow**
Rare Book and Manuscript Collections, Carl A. Kroch Library, Cornell University, Ithaca, NY, has sketches of the house.

**Lawrence, John L., Sr. – Lawrence –** *Moorlands*
Nassau County Museum Collection has eleven uncataloged photographs of the house.

**Lebaudy, Jacques – Salisbury –** *Phoenix Lodge*
   Fuligini, Bruno. *L'Etat C'est Moi: Histore des Monarchies Privees Principautes de Frantaisie et Autres Republiques Pirates.*
   Winsche, Richard A. "Jacques Lebaudy: Nassau County's Emperor of Sahara." *The Nassau County Historical Society Journal* 57 (2000):28-37.

**Lefferts, Marshall Clifford, Sr. – Lawrence –** *Hedgewood*
   *American Architect and Building News* 1905.

**Lewis, Henry Llewellyn Daingerfield, Jr. – Hewlett Bay Park –** *Merriefield*
Hewlett–Woodmere Public Library has photographs of the house.

**Lord, George de Forest, Sr. – Woodmere**
   Howell, E. W. *Noted Long Island Homes*. Babylon, NY: E. W. Howell Co., 1933.

**Macy, Carleton – Hewlett Bay Park –** *Wonderwhy* **and** *Meadowwood*
Hewlett–Woodmere Public Library has photographs of the house.

**Macy, Miss Carroll – Hewlett Bay Park –** *Birch Corners*
Hewlett–Woodmere Public Library has photographs of the house.
   *Architecture* 1912.

**Macy, Valentine Everit, Sr. – Hewlett**
   *Architecture* 1912.

**Manice, de Forest – Elmont –** *Oatlands*
Nassau County Museum Collection has photographs of the estate.

**Mann, Samuel Vernon, Sr. – Lawrence –** *Grove Point*
Hicks Nursery, Jericho, NY, has photographs of the estate.

**Marks, Arthur David, Jr. – Woodsburgh**
Rare Book and Manuscript Collections, Carl A. Kroch Library, Cornell University, Ithaca, NY, has Olive Frances Tjaden's sketches of the house.

**McCrea, James Alexander, II – Woodsburgh**
Hicks Nursery, Jericho, NY, has photographs of the estate.

**Mellen, Chase, Sr. – Garden City**
J. Mitchell Department of Special Collections and Archives, Bowdoin College, Brunswick, ME, has the Mellen family papers.

**Miller, Danforth, Sr. – Hewlett Bay Park –** *Birch Corners*
Hewlett–Woodmere Public Library has photographs of the house.
   *Architecture* 1912.

*Individual Bibliographic References*

**Mooney, Franklin Drake – Garden City**
Nassau County Museum Collection has ten uncataloged photographs of the house.

**Neilson, Robert Hude – Woodmere**
Special Collections and University Archives, Rutgers University, New Brunswick, NJ, has Neilson's papers that pertain to his relationship to the university.

**Newton, Arthur Ulysses – Lawrence**
Archives of American Art, Smithsonian Institution, Washington, DC, has the records of the Arthur U. Newton Galleries.

**Orr, Henry Steers – Garden City**
    Embury, Aymar, II. *One Hundred Country Houses: Modern American Examples.* New York: The Century Co., 1909.

**Otto, Carl Ludwig, Sr. – Garden City**
Nassau County Museum Collection has photographs of the house.

**Pancake, Carl Oakley – Garden City**
Rare Book and Manuscript Collections, Carl A. Kroch Library, Cornell University, Ithaca, NY, has Olive Frances Tjaden's sketches of the house.

**Peabody, Richard Augustus – Lawrence – *Terrace Hall***
    *Architecture* 1901.

**Peck, Arthur Nelson – Woodsburgh**
    *House Beautiful* 1912.

**Perkins, Norton – Lawrence – *Whale Acres***
    *Architectural Record* 1918.

**Peters, Ralph, Sr. – Garden City – *Wyndymeede***
Garden City Public Library has the transcript of Peters' unpublished book *The Long Island Rail Road in the War 1917-1919.*
    Ruther, Frederick. *Long Island Today.* Hicksville, NY: privately printed, 1909.

**Philips, Frederic Dimon – Lawrence – *Greyhouse***
    *Architect and Builders Journal* 1903.

**Porter, Henry Hobart, Jr. – Lawrence – *Lauderdale***
    *The Brickbuilder* 1902.

**Raymond, William, Sr. – Lawrence**
    *Architecture* 1901.

**Recht, William, Sr. – Woodmere**
Rare Book and Manuscript Collections, Carl A. Kroch Library, Cornell University, Ithaca, NY, has Olive Frances Tjaden's sketches of the house.

**Robinson, Beverley Randolph – Lawrence**
New York Historical Society, NYC, has the Robinson family papers.
Oral History Research Office, Columbia University, NYC, has "The Reminiscences of Beverley Randolph Robinson."
The United States Naval Academy has Robinson's collection of naval prints.

**Roosevelt, Elliott, Sr. – Salisbury – *Half Way Nirvana***
Halstead Collection, Franklin Delano Roosevelt Library, Hyde Park, NY, has Elliott and Anna Hall Roosevelt's letters and notebooks.
    *In Loving Memory of Anna Hall Roosevelt.* New York: privately printed, 1892.
    "Representative Society Ladies: Mrs. Elliott Roosevelt." *Leslie's Weekly* November 12, 1889.
    Spinzia, Raymond E. "Elliott Roosevelt, Sr. – A Spiral Into Darkness: The Influences." *The Freeholder* 12 (Fall 2007):3-7, 15-17.

*Individual Bibliographic References*

**Rose, Reginald Perry – Garden City**
Nassau County Museum Collection has photographs of the house.

**Sage, Margaret Olivia Slocum (Mrs. Russell Sage) – Lawrence –** *Cedarcroft / Cedar Croft*
Rockefeller Archive Center, Pocantico Hills, NY, has the Russell Sage Foundation papers.
    *Country Life in America* 37 (1920):18.
    Crocker, Ruth. *Mrs. Russell Sage: Women's Activism and Philanthropy in the Gilded Age and Progressive Era America*. Bloomington, IN: Indiana University Press, 2006.
    McCarthy, Kathleen D. *Women's Culture: American Philanthropy and Art, 1830-1930*. Chicago: The University of Chicago Press, 1991.
    Sarnoff, Paul. *Russell Sage: The Money King*. New York: Ivan Obolensky, 1965.

**Slesinger, Laurence Anthony – Hewlett Bay Park**
Hewlett–Woodmere Public Library has photographs of the house.
    *Architecture* 1912.

**Smith, Augustine Jacquelin – Lawrence –** *Sunnyside*
Hewlett–Woodmere Public Library has photographs of the house.

**Smith, Harold – Garden City**
Rare Book and Manuscript Collections, Carl A. Kroch Library, Cornell University, Ithaca, NY, has Olive Frances Tjaden's sketches of the house.

**Sperry, Lawrence Burst, Sr. – Garden City**
Library of Congress, Washington, DC, has photographs of Sperry in its Digitized Collection.
United States Post Office issued a commemorative stamp featuring Lawrence and Elmer Sperry in its Aviation Pioneers series.
    Davenport, William Wyatt. *Gyro! The Life and Times of Lawrence Sperry*. New York: Charles Scribner's Sons, 1978.
    Hughes, Thomas Parke. *Elmer Sperry: Inventor and Engineer*. Baltimore: The Johns Hopkins Press, 1971.

**Stewart, Alexander Turney – Garden City**
    Cantor, Jay E. "A Monument to Trade: A. T. Stewart and the Rise of the Millionaire's Mansion in New York." *Winterthur Portfolio* 10 (1975):165-194.
    *Catalogue of the A. T. Stewart Collection of Paintings, Sculptures, and Other Objects of Art to be Sold by Auction, Without Reserve, by Order of Henry Hilton . . . and Charles Clinch . . . Executors of the Estate of Mrs. Cornelia M. Stewart, Deceased . . . March Twenty-third, Twenty-Fourth, and Twenty-Fifth . . . Continuing . . . March Twenty-Eighth and Following Days.* 1887. (in NYS library)
    "The Fabled Past: A .T. Stewart." *The North Shore Journal* 13 (November 25, 1982).

**Tarbell, Gage Eli – Garden City**
Garden City Historical Society has photographs of the house.

**Taylor, Talbot Jones, Jr. – Lawrence –** *Talbot House*
    Ferree, Barr. *American Estates and Gardens*. New York: Munn & Co., 1904.
    *The Talbot J. Taylor Collection: Furniture, Wood-Carvings, and Other Branches of the Decorative Arts*. New York: G. P. Putnam's Sons, 1906.

**Thompson, Dr. Benjamin Franklin – Hempstead**
    Klein, Howard. *Three Village Guidebook: The Setaukets, Poquott, Old Field & Stony Brook*. Setauket, NY: Three Village Historical Society, 1986.
    Naylor, Natalie A., introduction. "Benjamin F. Thompson: Long Island in the 1840s." *The Nassau County Historical Journal* 62 (2007):12-21.
    Spinzia, Raymond Edward, Judith Ader Spinzia, and Kathryn Spinzia Rayne. *Long Island: A Guide to New York's Suffolk and Nassau Counties,* third edition. New York: Hippocrene Books, 2009.

**Tilford, Frank – Cedarhurst**
    *Architectural Era* March, 1890:58.

*Individual Bibliographic References*

**Tjaden, Olive Frances (Mrs. Carl Johnson; Mrs. Roswell Charles Van Sickle) – Garden City**
Rare Book and Manuscript Collections, Carl A. Kroch Library, Division of Rare and Manuscript Collections, Cornell University, Ithaca, NY, has Tjaden's papers.
Garden City Public Library has a list of her commissions in Garden City.
    Vollono, Millicent and Lauren W. Drapala. "Suburbia: Olive Tjaden on Long Island." *The Nassau County Historical Journal* 71 (2016):1-14.

**Veeder, Paul Lansing – Hewlett Bay Park –** *Meadwood*
Hewlett–Woodmere Public Library has photographs of the house.

**Voss, William – Hewlett Bay Park –** *Merriefield*
Hewlett–Woodmere Public Library has photographs of the house.

**Ward–Smith, Kenneth (aka Kenneth Ward Smith) – Garden City**
Nassau County Museum Collection has photographs of the house.

**White, Raymond – Garden City**
Rare Book and Manuscript Collections, Carl A. Kroch Library, Cornell University, Ithaca, NY, has Olive Frances Tjaden's sketches of the house.

**Whiton, Henry Devereux – Hewlett Bay Park**
Hewlett–Woodmere Public Library has photographs of the house.

**Wickersham, George Woodward – Lawrence –** *Marshfield*
Harvard Law Library, Harvard University, Cambridge, MA, has the Wickersham Commission papers.
Library of Congress, Washington, DC, has photographs of the estate's Japanese garden in its Francis Benjamin Johnston collection.
Sterling Memorial Library, Yale University, New Haven, CT, has the papers of the firm of Cadwalder, Wickersham, and Taft.
    German, James Clifford. *Taft's Attorney General: George W. Wickersham*. thesis, New York University, 1969.

**Woodruff, Timothy Lester – Garden City**
    Ruther, Frederick. *Long Island Today*. Hicksville, NY: privately printed, 1909.

**Woolverton, William Henderson, Jr. – Lawrence**
Yale University Library, New Haven, CT, has Woolverton's papers.

*Harold Jacobi residence, breakfast room*

***Biographical Sources Consulted***

*Biographical Dictionaries Master Index 1975–1976*. Detroit: Gale Research Co., 1975.

*Biography and Genealogy Master Index 1981–1985*. Detroit: Gale Research Co., 1985.

*Biography and Genealogy Master Index 1986–1990*. Detroit: Gale Research Co., 1990.

*Biography and Genealogy Master Index 1991–1995*. Detroit: Gale Research Co., 1995.

*Brooklyn Daily Eagle* Online 1841-1902, Internet.

*Current Biography Yearbook*. New York: The H. W. Wilson Co. [selected volumes]

Dow Jones News Internet Retrieval.

*The Eagle and Brooklyn: The Record of the Progress of the Brooklyn Daily Eagle*. 2 vols. Brooklyn, NY: The Brooklyn Eagle, 1893.

Levy, Felice, ed. *Obituaries on File*. New York: Facts on File, 1979.

Lexis Nexis Academic Universe, Internet.

Malone, Dumas, ed. *Dictionary of American Biography*. New York: Charles Scribner's Sons, 1935.

*The National Cyclopaedia of American Biography*. Clifton, NJ: James T. White & Co., 1984.

Newsday Internet Retrieval.

*New York State's Prominent and Progressive Men*. 2 vols. New York: New York Tribune, 1900.

*The New York Times Index*. New York: The New York Times. [annual obituaries from 1979–1997]

*The New York Times Obituaries Index, vol. 1, 1858–1968*. New York: The New York Times, 1970.

*The New York Times Obituaries Index, vol. 2, 1969–1978*. New York: The New York Times, 1980.

*Prominent Families of New York*. New York: The Historical Co., 1898.

*Standard and Poor's Register of Corporations, Directors and Executives*. Charlottesville, VA: Standard and Poors, Inc. [selected volumes]

*Who's Who in America*. Chicago: Marquis Who's Who, Inc. [selected volumes]

*Who's Who in Finance and Industry*. Chicago: Marquis Who's Who, Inc. [selected volumes]

*Who's Who in New York*. New York: Lewis Historical Publishing Co. [selected volumes]

*Who's Who in New York City and State*. New York: L. R. Hamersly Co., 1904–1960 [selected volumes]

*Who's Who in the East*. Chicago: Marquis Who's Who, Inc. [selected volumes]

*Who's Who of American Women*. Chicago: Marquis Who's Who, Inc. [selected volumes]

*Who Was Who in America with World Notables*. New Providence, NJ: Marquis Who's Who, Inc. [selected volumes]

# Henry Steers Orr residence

*front facade, 1909*

*living room, 1909*

*Maps Consulted*

*Atlas of Long Island.* New York: F. W. Beers, 1873.

*Atlas of Nassau County, Long Island, N. Y.* Brooklyn: E. Belcher Hyde, Inc., 1906.

*Atlas of Nassau County, Long Island, N. Y.* Brooklyn: E. Belcher Hyde, Inc., 1914.

*Atlas of Queens County, Long Island, N. Y.* New York: Chester Wolverton, 1891.

*Hagstrom's Street, Road and Property Ownership Map of Nassau County, Long Island, New York.* New York: Hagstrom Co., Inc., 1932.

*Hagstrom's Street, Road and Property Ownership Map of Nassau County, Long Island, New York.* New York: Hagstrom Co., Inc., 1946.

*Hagstrom Map of Nassau County.* Maspeth, New York: Hagstrom Map Co., Inc., 2006.

*Real Estate Map of Nassau County, New York.* New York: E. Belcher Hyde, Inc., 1927.

*Bertha Ludington Barnes Smith
(Mrs. James Clinch Smith)*

## Illustration Credits

*American Architect and Architecture,* 267 top, 283, 363

*American Architect and Building News,* 156, 169, 369, 425 top and bottom

*The Architect,* 127 bottom

*Architectural League of New York,* 153 bottom

*Architectural Record,* 2, 15, 32 top and bottom left, 53, 77, 252 bottom, 363 bottom, 418 top and bottom

*Architecture,* 161, 250, 288, 310, 355 bottom, 385 top, 427, 554 top

Ayer, Frederick, II, 18

*The Brickbuilder,* 49, 276

*The Brooklyn Daily Eagle,* 86, 191, 335 top, 336 top, 517

Brooklyn Historical Society, 400

Brown Brothers, 347

Burr, Robert Page, 63, 261

Connecticut State Library, 546

Cornell University, Rare Book and Manuscript Collections, Carl A. Kroch Library, *xvii,* 206 top, 233, 466, 468 all, 469 all, 618 top and bottom, 646

*Country Life in America,* 89

East Meadow Public Library, 280

Embury, Aymar, II. *One Hundred Country Homes,* 139, 181, 648 top

Ferree, Barr. *American Estates and Gardens,* 454, 455 top left

Franklin Delano Roosevelt Library, 401

Garden City Historical Society, 98, 221, 453

Goldberger, Muriel, 445 top

Hedgecoe, John, *The Spirit of the Garden,* 276, 420

Hempstead Public Library, 462

Hewitt, Mattie Edwards, 96

Hewlett Family, 252 top

Hewlett–Woodmere Public Library, 16, 17, 62 bottom, 79, 197 top, 271, 272, 285, 322 bottom, 430, 490, 504, 508, 509 all, 553 top and bottom, 554 bottom, 555 top and bottom, 613

Hicks Nursery, 20, 265, 292 bottom, 301, 357 bottom

Hoeffner, Raymond, Jr., 279

Hofstra University, Special Collections, 612 top and bottom

*House and Garden,* 215

*House Beautiful,* 360 top

Howell, E. W., *Noted Long Island Homes,* 278

*Indoors and Out,* 411

Kuss, Betty, 65

Library of Congress, 521 both, 530 top and bottom, 532, 538, 548, 628

Marccon, 590 right

Multiple Listing Service, 50 bottom, 70 bottom, 71, 88, 137 bottom, 158 top, 179 bottom, 206 bottom, 220, 227, 231 top, 236, 244, 251, 257, 273 top, 326, 362 top and bottom, 364 bottom, 367, 445 bottom, 450, 499, 516, 522

## Illustration Credits

Nassau County Department of Assessment, 1, 3, 6, 7, 10, 12 top and bottom, 19, 22 top and bottom, 27 bottom, 33, 34, 37, 41, 42, 43, 44 top and bottom, 45, 46, 50 top, 56, 58 top and bottom, 61, 62 top, 64 top, 66, 73, 74, 75, 78, 87 bottom, 90 bottom, 91, 92 top and bottom, 93, 94 top, 97, 99, 100, 101, 103, 105, 108, 109, 110 top and bottom, 111, 113, 116, 117 top and bottom, 118, 119, 121, 124, 125, 126 top, 129, 130 top and bottom, 132, 133, 137 top, 138 top and bottom, 142 bottom, 143, 145, 146 top and bottom, 149, 151, 152 bottom, 153 top, 154, 157, 158 bottom, 159, 160, 162, 163 bottom, 164 bottom, 166, 167, 168 top and bottom, 172, 173, 174 top and bottom, 179 top, 182, 185, 187 top and bottom, 188 top, 190, 195, 197 bottom, 198, 200, 202, 203 bottom, 204, 205, 209, 210, 212 bottom, 214 top and bottom, 217, 218 bottom, 219 top and bottom, 222 top, 223, 226, 228, 230 top and bottom, 231 bottom, 232, 239, 241, 243 bottom, 247, 248 top and bottom, 253, 254, 255 top and bottom, 256, 264, 267 bottom, 269, 273 bottom, 274, 281, 282, 284, 290, 291, 292 top, 293, 294, 297, 299, 300, 303, 304, 305, 306, 307, 313, 314, 317, 318, 319 top and bottom, 321, 322 top, 323 top and bottom, 325 top, 327, 328, 333, 335 bottom, 336 bottom, 337 bottom, 338, 340, 342, 343, 344 top, 346, 348, 350, 351 top and bottom, 352, 353, 356, 357 top, 358 top, 360 bottom, 361, 364 top, 365, 368, 370, 371, 374, 377, 378, 379, 380 top, 382, 386, 388, 392, 395, 399 top and bottom, 402, 404 top and bottom, 406, 409 top and bottom, 410, 412, 413 top and bottom, 429, 431, 433, 434, 435 top, 444, 446, 447 top, 451, 452, 460, 464 bottom, 470 top and bottom, 471, 472, 476, 478, 479, 480, 481 top and bottom, 484, 486 top and bottom, 487, 489 top and bottom, 491, 493, 494, 500, 501, 507, 510, 512, 515, 519 bottom, 523

Nassau County Department of Parks, Recreation, and Museums, Photo Archives Center, *viii, xi, xv* top, 84, 85, 90 top, 155 bottom, 245, 325 bottom, 403

New York State Office of Parks, Recreation, and Historic Preservation, 38, 114, 208, 424 top

*The New York Tribune*, 193, 393, 417

Office of the Garden City Historian, Archives, *xii, xiv, xvi*, 262

Ruther, Frederick. *Long Island Today*, 237

Sheldon, George, ed. *Artistic Country Seats*, 212 top

Shelton, Louise. *Beautiful Gardens in America*, 559

Spinzia, Raymond Edward, *ix, x, xv* bottom, *xviii, xix*, 4, 13, 21, 27 top, 28, 29, 32 top right, middle, and bottom right, 52, 60, 64 bottom, 70 top, 72, 80, 81, 87 top, 95, 102, 120, 122, 123, 134, 140, 142 top, 152 top, 155 top, 163 top, 164 top, 165, 171, 178, 188 bottom, 189, 192, 194, 203 top, 207, 216, 218 top, 222 bottom, 234, 235, 243 top, 246, 259, 263, 266, 270, 275, 286 top and bottom, 296 top and bottom, 298, 309, 339, 344 bottom, 345 top and bottom, 354, 355 top, 358 bottom, 359, 366, 380 bottom, 385 bottom, 398, 408, 415, 416, 422, 424 bottom, 435 bottom, 439, 443, 448, 464 top, 467, 477, 485, 488, 495, 502, 505, 511 all, 513, 514, 519 top, 524, 525, 526, 556 top and bottom, 560 top and bottom, 590 left, 611, 614 top and bottom, 617, 638 all, 648 bottom, 650

Suffolk County Historical Society, 94 bottom

*The Tablet*, 337 top

*The Talbot J. Taylor Collection: Furniture, Wood-Carvings, and Other Branches of the Decorative Arts*, *xx*, 455 top and bottom right, middle, and bottom left, 456, 654 top and bottom

Thompson, Benjamin Franklin. *History of Long Island*, 461

*Town and Country*, 47

*View*, 258

Wyoming State Archives, 449

## About the Authors

Judith and Raymond Spinzia are former Long Island residents, now residing in central Pennsylvania. Their first book, *Long Island: A Guide to New York's Suffolk and Nassau Counties* (New York: Hippocrene Books, 1988; 1991 revised; 2008 revised), is a standard reference book which has been used as a textbook for teaching Long Island history and can be found in almost all public libraries and schools on Long Island.

The Spinzias write and speak, jointly and separately, on a variety of Long Island-related subjects including the North and South Shore estates, Tiffany stained-glass windows, and the Vanderbilts of Long Island. On several occasions their lectures have been chosen by the former radio station of *The New York Times*, WQXR, as the cultural event of the day in the New York Metropolitan area. Additionally, they have been featured on local television and radio programs and in articles published by *The New York Times, Newsday*, and other regional newspapers.

The Spinzias served as Long Island history consultants for a local cable television channel that, in an effort to encourage local interest, aired material from their guidebook twice daily. They also were consultants for a Japanese television network for a documentary on Louis Comfort Tiffany and contributed material to the Arts and Entertainment Network's "Biography" series for its presentations on the Vanderbilt and Tiffany families.

Their six-volume documentation of Long Island's estate era presently includes:
*Long Island's Prominent North Shore Families: Their Estates and Their Country Homes.* 2 volumes, 2006, revised 2019.
*Long Island's Prominent South Shore Families: Their Estates and Their Country Homes in the Towns of Babylon and Islip*, 2007, revised 2021.
*Long Island's Prominent Families in the Town of Hempstead: Their Estates and Their Country Homes*, 2010, revised 2023.
*Long Island's Prominent Families in the Town of Southampton: Their Estates and Their Country Homes*, 2010.
*Long Island's Prominent Families in the Town of East Hampton: Their Estates and Their Country Homes*, 2020.

The following articles by the Spinzias can be downloaded at **spinzialongislandestates.com**:

Spinzia, Judith Ader.
"Artistry In Glass: Louis Comfort Tiffany's Legacy In Nassau County." *The Nassau County Historical Society Journal,* 1991:8-17.
"Artistry In Glass: The Undisputed Master, Our Oyster Bay Neighbor." *The Freeholder* 2 (Winter 1998):3-5; and 2 (Spring 1998):3-5, 24.
"Louis Comfort Tiffany: A Bibliography Relevant to the Man, His Work, and His Oyster Bay, Long Island, Home." 2010
"Women of Long Island: Clare Boothe Luce (1903-1987), The Long Island Connection" *The Freeholder* 2 (Summer 2009):3-5; 17-10.
"Women of Long Island: Cornelia Bryce Pinchot, Feminist, Social-Activist – The Long Islander Who Became First Lady of Pennsylvania." 2010
"Women of Long Island: Mary Elizabeth Jones; Rosalie Gardiner Jones." *The Freeholder* 11 (Spring 2007):2-7.
"Women of Long Island: Mary Williamson Averell Harriman; her daughter Mary Harriman Rumsey." *The Freeholder*, 12 (Spring 2008):8-9, 16-20.

Spinzia, Raymond E.
"Adultery, Drugs, Murder, Untimely Deaths, and Long Island's Prominent Families: A Tangled Web." 2011
"Elliott Roosevelt, Sr. – A Spiral Into Darkness" *The Freeholder* 12 (Fall 2007):3-7, 15-17.
"In Her Wake: The Story of Alva Smith Vanderbilt." *The Long Island Historical Journal* 6 (Fall 1993):96-105.
"The Involvement of Long Islanders in the Events Surrounding German Sabotage in the New York Metropolitan Area 1914-1917." 2019, revised 2022
"Long Island Statesmen and Diplomats." revised 2020 and 2022
"Michael Straight and the Cambridge Spy Ring." *The Freeholder* 5 (Winter 2001): 3-5.
"Socialite Spies: The Grandchildren of Henry Baldwin Hyde, Sr." *East Islip Historical Society Newsletter* 16 (March 2008):1, 3. revised 2022
"Society Chameleons: Long Island's Gentlemen Spies." *The Nassau County Historical Society Journal* 55 (2000):27-38.
"Sumner Welles: Brilliance and Tragedy." *The Freeholder* 9 (Winter 2005):8-9, 22.
"Those Other Roosevelts: The Fortescues." *The Freeholder* 11 (Summer 2006):8-9, 16-22.
"To Look in the Mirror and See Nothing: Long Islanders and the Office of Strategic Services and Its Successor, the Central Intelligence Agency." revised December 2017 and 2022
"Winning the Franchise: Long Island Activists in the Fight for Woman's Suffrage and Their Opponents, Long Island's Anti-Suffragists." 2018, revised 2022

Spinzia, Raymond E. and Judith A. Spinzia.
"*Gatsby*: Myths and Realities of Long Island's North Shore Gold Coast." *The Nassau County Historical Society Journal* 52 (1997):16–26.

## Talbot Jones Taylor, Jr. residence, *Talbot House*

*guest bedroom, 1906*

*conservatory, 1906*

www.ingramcontent.com/pod-product-compliance
Lightning Source LLC
Chambersburg PA
CBHW080718300426
44114CB00019B/2410